Perspectives on
GERMAN CINEMA

Perspectives on
FILM

RONALD GOTTESMAN
University of Southern California
and
HARRY M. GEDULD
Indiana University

Series Editors

Perspectives on
GERMAN CINEMA

edited by

TERRI GINSBERG

and

KIRSTEN MOANA THOMPSON

G.K. HALL & CO.
An Imprint of Simon & Schuster Macmillan
New York

Prentice Hall International
London   Mexico City   New Delhi   Singapore   Sydney   Toronto

G.K. Hall & Co.
An Imprint of Simon & Schuster Macmillan
1633 Broadway
New York, NY 10019

Library of Congress Catalog Card Number: 96-23301

Printed in the United States of America

Printing number

1 2 3 4 5 6 7 8 9 10

Library of Congress Cataloging-in-Publication Data

Perspectives on German cinema / edited by Terri Ginsberg and Kirsten Moana Thompson.
    p.   cm.—(Perspectives on film)
   Includes bibliographical references and index.
   ISBN 0-8161-1611-3 (alk. paper)
   1. Motion pictures—Germany. I. Ginsberg, Terri. II. Thompson, Kristen, 1950–
III. Series.
PN1993.5.G3P42   1996
791.43'0943—dc20
                                   96–23301
                                      CIP

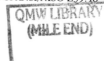

Contents

Series Editors' Note

This series is devoted to supplying comprehensive coverage of several topics: directors, individual films, national film traditions, film genres, and other categories that scholars have devised for organizing the rich history of film as expressive form, cultural force, and industrial and technological enterprise. Each volume essentially brings together two kinds of critical and historical material: first, previously published reviews, interviews, written and pictorial documents, essays, and other forms of commentary and interpretation; and, second, commissioned writings designed to provide fresh perspectives. Each volume is edited by a film scholar and contains substantial introduction that traces and interprets the history of the critical response to the subject and indicates its current status among specialists. As appropriate, volumes will also provide production credits, filmographies, selective annotated bibliographies, indexes, and other reference materials. Titles in this series will thus combine the virtues of an interpretive archive and a reference guide. The success of each volume should be measured against this objective.

It is hard to imagine any collection of essays and articles on German cinema that could more completely validate the title of this series than the present volume. It offers perspectives on every significant aspect of its subject within the context of an innovative and exemplary organization of its contributions. The reader has only to turn to pages 11–12 of the Editors' Introduction to discover the spectrum of key questions that this book confronts and explores authoritatively.

In assembling this paradigmatic text for postmodernist German cinema studies and arranging the various essays and article by leading scholars in the field into meaningful thematic "Constellations," Preofessors Ginsberg and Thompson have brought a welcome coherence to what had hitherto seemed a disorganized and frequently conflicting body of theoretical approaches. In the process they have included not only the finest previously published essays but also such groundbreaking, newly commissioned articles as Tassilo Schneider's provocative study of German cinema and film historiography, John E. Davidson's acute reappraisal of the New German Cinema, Linda Schulte-Sasse's trenchant commentary on Veit Harlan's *Jud Süss*, analyses by Imke Lode and Kent Casper of films by Fassbinder and Herzog, and last, but by no means least, their own introductory overview which must surely stand as a model of its kind.

As the reader samples the extraordinary range and depth of this collection he/she will, we believe, share our conviction that with this volume German cinema studies have at last come of age.

Ronald Gottesman
Harry M. Geduld

Publisher's Note

PRODUCING A VOLUME that contains both newly commissioned and reprinted material presents the publisher with the challenge of balancing the desire to achieve stylistic consistency with the need to preserve the integrity of works first published elsewhere. In the Perspectives series, essays commissioned especially for a particular volume are edited to be consistent with G. K. Hall's house style; reprinted essays appear in the style in which they were first published, with only typographical errors corrected. Consequently, shifts in style from one essay to another are the result of our efforts to be faithful to each text as it was originally published.

Acknowledgments

T HE EDITORS WOULD like to thank Imke Lode, Roy Grundmann, Catherine Sears, and Robin Mendelwager for their intellectual, emotional, and logistical support during the preparation of this project. Thanks go also to Peter Sacks, Alison Harrison, Paula Massood, Noa Steimatsky, David Jacobson, Merrick Wolfe, Harvey Wolfe, Jennifer Clevinger, Patrice Heller, Ulrike Heider, Rick Berg, and Donald Morton; to our colleagues at the NYU Department of Cinema Studies student conference for their comments and critiques during an earlier stage of this project; to the NYU Department of Cinema Studies administrative staff for their helpful assistance; and finally to our series editors, Ronald Gottesmann and Harry Geduld, our editor, Catherine Carter, and our production editor, James Hatch, for their helpful assistance throughout the *longue durée* of this project.

We would also like to express our appreciation to the following authors, journals, and publishing companies for waiving or greatly reducing their permissions fees for essays and articles reprinted in this collection: *New German Critique*, Patrice Petro, Miriam Hansen, Karsten Witte, Gertrud Koch, Eric Santner, Anton Kaes, *Harvard University Press*, Eric Rentschler, Thomas Elsaesser, Timothy Corrigan, *Indiana University Press*, Mas'ud Zavarzadeh, Antonia Lant, *Wide Angle*, Mary Beth Haralovich, Barbara Hyams, Jack Zipes, Roswitha Müller, Patricia White, *Screen*, Christopher Sharrett, *Canadian Journal of Political and Social Theory*, Kaja Silverman, Melanie Magisos, Fredric Jameson, Ben Brewster, Marc Silberman, Stuart Liebman, and, as always . . . Walter Benjamin.

INTRODUCTION

Radical Disorderliness at the
Postnationalist Moment

TERRI GINSBERG and
KIRSTEN MOANA THOMPSON

I N THE WAKE of German reunification and the massive social transformations of the post–Cold War era, the "German" has reemerged as a significant ideological concern on the global stage. During the late 1950s,
beginning with the Benelux countries (Belgium, Netherlands,
Luxembourg) and later including Germany and other Western European
countries, the competing nations of Europe formulated a cooperative economic trading pact—the European Economic Community (EEC)—in an
effort to promote intracontinental economic activity and maintain respective control over national territories. Since that time, this original core of
cooperating countries has tried to form a geopolitical entity—the
European Union (EU)—which, concomitant to the fall of the Soviet Union
and the dismantling of the Warsaw Pact, has had as its aim the reconsolida-
tion of a new, geographically enlarged, economically stimulated Europe
into a global political power bloc touting a single monetary unit ("ecu") to
rival North America and Japan for an equitable share in the global market.
Despite this attempt, which has devolved into the all-but-abandoned
Maastricht Treaty, this would-be power bloc has failed to materialize effectively. Although early EEC moves to lift tariffs and other protectionist trade
barriers did function toward the potential construction of European unity,
the deregulatory turn of the 1980s into renewed laissez-faire practices,
epitomized by the policies of Thatcherism and Reaganomics, have had a
disturbingly disunifying effect. Along with monumental technological
changes brought about by the adoption of the computer in the post–gold
standard marketplace, this turn to deregulation has promoted the influx of
transnational consortiums, the dominance of multinational corporations,
and the formation of a multicultural labor force on the European stage,
and in turn prompted the re-reification of a continental split between the
countries of Europe's former Eastern and Western blocs, this time along
strictly economic rather than ideological-political lines.

While these changes have been advantageous for the upper echelons of
the European economic network, they have exacerbated social inequalities
at other socioeconomic levels, where increased unemployment, social dis-

The authors would like to acknowledge comments made by Ronald Gottesman on an earlier
draft of this essay.

affection, heightened nationalist tensions, and the fracturing of left solidarity have become widespread realities in European everyday life. In the tense social climate produced through these developments, virulent strains of latent, often extreme-right antisemitism, racism, and nationalist xenophobia have erupted as dangerous and erroneous means of explaining the devastating effects of these changes, leading several European countries (England, Belgium, Norway) to express increasing doubt about the benefits of joining or having joined a European (Monetary) Union. Ironically, these doubts have publicly been articulated less in terms of the underlying political economic mechanisms of the EU than in terms of the potential for repeated domination by Germany over the rest of Europe. In Germany, whose critical position as both global leader and intra-European competitor has had the extenuating effect of magnifying the social problematics overdetermining these tensions, the eruption of extreme-right social enmity has been accompanied, as during earlier historical periods, by a renewed focus on the problem of national identity, and a renewed concern to retheorize the ways in which the "German" continues to be mobilized as an emblem of the nationalist phenomenon, both inside and outside Germany proper.[1]

While clearly a pressing concern across the German public sphere, the need to retheorize the "German" has taken on a particular urgency in the Anglo-American scholarly and intellectual arenas, where the conditions prompting the resurgence of European nationalisms have been likened to those prompting some of the darkest moments of German history—National Socialism and the Holocaust—and have subsequently been condemned in relation to more recent global phenomena. These include the bloody breakup of Yugoslavia, with its mass rapes and "ethnic cleansings"; the rise to political prominence of national-populist, far-right, and neo-fascist political parties and leaders in France (Jean-Marie Le Pen), Belgium (Filip Dewinter), Russia (Vladimir Zhirinovsky, Alexandr Prokhanov), the Czech Republic (Miroslav Sladek), Austria (Joerg Haider, Gottfried Küssel), Italy (Silvio Berlusconi, Umberto Bossi), Germany (Karl Lucks, Günter Deckert, Bela Ewald Althans), and the United States (David Duke, Pat Robertson, Pat Buchanan); and the largest outbreak of racist, xenophobic and antisemitic violence in Germany since the Nazi era, now directed against the huge wave of Balkan war refugees (Serbs, Croats, Muslims) as well as other foreign or migrating labor groups long targeted by the German right (the *gastarbeiter* Turks, Hungarians, Armenians, Greeks, Gypsies).[2]

The contemporary global developments in which Germany and the "German" are imbricated have become the crucial structural determinants of a recent wave of Anglo-American scholarship that interrogates the dimensions of German cinematic culture. Spurred by the legitimation of the field of Cinema Studies (itself a relatively recent development), the idea of a "German cinema" has come to signify one of the more politically overdetermined aspects of critical cinematic inquiry, where it comprises the focus of numerous college courses and widely distributed publications.[3] However, while German cinema studies has emerged onto the academic scene ostensively as part of a larger scholarly discipline, its peculiar, even obsessive focus on the logics of its conceptual identity—the "German"—has rendered it distinct from most other areas of cinematic cultural inquiry, themselves more overtly concerned with interrogating the *post*identitarian aspects of global social reality than with rearticulating identities along national-cultural lines.[4] In what follows, we argue that this very tenuous distinction continues to mark German cinema studies' difference from other areas of the cinema studies field and at the same time figures its increasing relevance to the larger, *post*national academy throughout which it is now so forcefully proliferating. Accordingly, we now turn to a brief philosophical investigation into the contemporary cultural politics circumscribing that field—postmodernism—in order to trace the necessary critical connections between cinema studies' implicatedness therein, and the question of the "German" in the ideological and historical study of German film.

Echoing the problematics of Maastricht, the question of what unifies a broad range of competing disciplines and discourses associated loosely with the postmodern is a difficult one; under its aegis, the academy has been marked by a sense of crisis and contestation. From a poststructuralist focus on questions of power and desire as they are situated in the body, to the polysemic slipperiness of the deconstructionist text, to the new philosophical disavowal of the material and turn to the simulacrum, the consequences of the postmodern turn have been profoundly unsettling and disruptive for the verities of the Western canon, with its attendant Eurocentric, humanist, patriarchal, "high" cultural proclivities.[5] Unlike traditional cultural theory, which maps linguistic and discursive developments along a progressive, often linear historical continuum, postmodern theory is characterized by a broad displacement of paradigms previously confined to specific, often discreet fields of scholarly pursuit onto a more general, interdisciplinary spectrum of thickly layered discourses that function in excess of any single teleological line.[6] In the field of Cinema Studies, such discourses range from neoformalism to New Historicism, from psychoanalytic-semiotics to cultural studies, and from cybernetics to performance theory,[7] each arguing in a particular way for a decentered, differential, destabilized subjectivity and textual practice and the subversion and/or dissolution of their institutional and disciplinary boundaries. In its more conservative variations, this postmodern displacement, and the potentially political differences it accesses, are contained, usually under the auspices of ideological concepts such as identity, nation, and rhetorical form, often to the point of recuperating traditional interpellations of these concepts into updated modalities of auteur theory, national cinemas and genre study.[8] At postmodernism's most reactionary, moreover, its praxis of displacement is ironically terminated, the very possibility of difference being disallowed through the suspension of its alterior moments (e.g., nodes of sexual or racial demarcation) into pluralist simulations of ethnicity, class, and culture ("cybersubjectivities") and autonomous states of libidinal excess, virtual flux, permanent undecidability, and essential heterogeneity, what we refer to here as *post-al disorderliness*.[9]

As an ostensively ungrounded state, the condition of post-al disorderliness is unrestricted and deregulated; the subjectivities it interpellates transgress traditional boundaries, hierarchies, and social conventions. One effect of this virtual transgressiveness of special concern to this anthology in its interrogation of German cinema studies through what we articulate below as a *radical* disorderly perspective on German cinema, is its facilitation of a postdisciplinary, postnational sphere of public engagement, somewhat akin to what has recently been termed the "polis of the Internet."[10] While the more firmly entrenched areas of national and auteurist cinema studies have tended more readily to account for, if not embrace, these post-al conditions and ideologies, however,[11] the question of their coherence and applicability remains difficult for German cinema studies, whose deferred entry onto the academic scene and continued association with the problematics of national identity have necessitated only recent engagement with this latest cultural development.

Following World War II, a United States-led program of European economic recovery (the Marshall Plan) promoted the economic incorporation of (West) Germany into the global market. Despite the resulting German Economic Miracle (*Wirtschaftswunder*) of the 1950s, Anglo-American public and scholarly attention to the non-economic aspects of the "German" was, until quite recently, limited to their more ahistorical, apolitical, "high" cultural articulations. Echoing this Anglo-American reluctance to address the complexities of German cultural development, recently emergent German cinema studies has persistently deferred the pressing, potentially progressive question of postmodernism onto the conservative problematics of traditional philosophy, thereby limiting its frame of intellectual reference to metaphysical, often formalist and experientialist modalities,[12] and generally resisting any sustained interrogation of the relation between its overall conceptualization as an academic field and the politics of the postmodern turn. Indeed, most texts of German cinema studies do not explicitly engage postmodern discourse or deploy postmodern terminology or logics, even when their topics are of overtly postmodern concern. Their adoption of traditional frameworks render them more congruent with the Eurocentrism, nationalist certitudes, and social hierarchies of traditional cultural theory than with the newer, disorderly tendencies of the post-al.[13] At the same time, this anti-postmodern tendency, firmly articulated to German cinema studies' difficult emergence at the postmodern moment, has come to symptomize an apparent contradiction: namely, appropriative gestures toward postmodern theory have themselves become emblematic of many of that paradigm's more troubling, even reactionary aspects.

The present anthology is an attempt to intervene into the problematics of this contradiction by calling into question the common theoretical assumptions undergirding and, in turn, sustaining it. Through its particular organizational structure, the anthology fosters an interrogation of the varied, often hesitant ways in which German cinema studies has tried to address, if not incorporate, the post-al. Keeping in mind German film theory's nostalgic moorings in the idealist philosophical tradition, it contends that German cinema studies' hesitancy toward postmodernism has encouraged a decidedly ambiguous interpellation of disorderliness, one whose tenuous participation in the postnational polis of the Internet bespeaks a contemporary Anglo-American crisis in the conceptualization of the "German" and, in turn, of broader understandings of identity, nation, and the social. Put another way, it suggests that German cinema studies, in its persistent deference to philosophical tradition, evinces a neoauthoritarian tact that compels an uncanny (*unheimlich*) replication of discourses linked ideologically to both the problematics of present-day reaction (North American as well as European) as well as to one of the most tremulous upheavals of German history—the fall of Weimar and the rise of the Third Reich. As we illustrate briefly below, this uncanny replication, while pointing to a conservative thematics of hierarchy, convention, even empire, nonetheless finds its rhetorical matrix in the putatively differential, anti-authoritarian legislative institution of democracy and its classical framework of public enactment, the ancient Athenean *polis*.[14]

Centered on the notion of organized assemblies where citizens could debate and vote on issues of common interest, the Athenian *polis* upheld its ruling status by limiting citizenly privileges to property-owning Athenian males, thereby excluding women, slaves, and *metics* (foreign residents who, like the German *gastarbeiter*, for the most part controlled commerce or performed the menial tasks which the citizens of Athens themselves would not perform) from public legitimacy and participation.[15] While thus promulgating a "democratic" ideal, the classical *polis* was marked quite self-consciously, and from the beginning, by fundamental inequalities of class, ethnicity, and gender, a fact recognized and foregrounded by Aristotle himself in his well-known truism, "man is by nature a political animal."[16] Attempts to justify these inequalities through imperatives of birthright and permanent rhetorical equivocation in the citizenly assembly, which Aristotle was the first to advocate, could not—indeed would not—amend the oligarchical basis of what was ostensibly the most "liberal" social structure of the fifth century B.C.E. By figuring its relation to the postmodern turn in the pluralist, often relativizing terms of this classical political logics, recently emergent German cinema studies has by and large propounded the same sorts of exclusivities, inequalities, and contradictions. On the one hand, it substitutes an updated brand of metaphysical formalism for any socially engaged modality; on the other, it cynically elides the political, economic, and ideological contradictions in which it is historically and intellectually situated. And in the space opened up by its dissimulative logics, German cinema studies nostalgically reasserts the notion of an ideal, normative "Germanness" as against any alterative or transformational understanding and theorization of national or social subjectivity.

In the view of many German cinema studies texts, the sorts of social and cultural perspectives which were politically conventionalized in the Greek *polis* have been made utterly banal in today's postmodern arena, their contrasting foci and demands for social change confused and deflected through a dizzying process of conflation, collapse, and projection.[17] To a scholarly field adopting a problematics of "national identity" that has accrued such disturbing resonance over the past century, this banalization and its attendant ideological convolutions appear particularly unsettling, since they enable the discomforting, disidentificatory possibility that the "German" be considered potentially interchangeable with the non-"German," that is, that the "German" veritably "lose" its identity. Rather than explore even the theory of this possibility, however, many texts of German cinema studies have mobilized updated and revised understandings of subjectivity, reformulating old notions of guilt, memory, dreamwork, and imagination, often under the rubric of the new cultural studies, in order to reinscribe traditional identificatory, and thus disciplinary, distinctions. Hence the social positionalities these texts mark out—"class," "gender," "ethnicity," "race," "sexuality"—are figured no less problematically than they were under classical auspices, becoming subject to similar patterns of containment and excess and in turn implicitly aiding the conservative project of reconstructing a putatively dismantled Western canon. As German cinema studies' ambivalence toward its imbrication in postmodern culture has in fact become more strained in proportion to increasing global tensions, moreover, that field's dissimulation of the politics of social subjectivity has devolved into not only a rehabilitation of old social hierarchies but also the granting of privileged status to one of these, "gender," in highly aestheticized terms, at the expense of attending to the likewise politically volatile and destabilizing "class," "ethnicity" or "race." (This is not to mention the pervasive destabilization made available by "sexuality," which German cinema studies has hardly confronted.)[18]

The ramifications of this dissimulation are the *othering*, or conceptual totalizing, not only of gender positionalities but also of class, ethnic, racial, and sexual ones; "woman," "worker," "Jew," "black" and "lesbian" are emptied of political meaning and come to figure merely as gauges of the ideal strength and cohesion of their dominant hegemonic aspects. Their possibilities for eliciting social change are defused and, as in the broader Anglo-American academy, co-opted. In this regard, texts of German cinema studies do not deviate fundamentally from the general post-al strain in academia. While resisting the utter collapse of difference endemic to the disorderliness of much postmodern film theory, the intellectual *polis* of German cinema studies heeds the varied calls of some of the more conservative voices in Anglo-American cultural studies to reform that troubling condition into a tolerable state of unequal coexistence in which "others" may be favorably redeployed toward the consolidation and fortification of a formidable neonationalist disciplinary stronghold within a postnationalist scholarly and intellectual sphere.

As against this co-optive, exploitative cultural politics, our anthology calls for the theorization of a *radical* disorderly German film theory and, in turn, a *radical* disorderly German cinema studies, possibilities that refuse both the experientialist conflations and the (neo)classical "moderations" of identity and difference, "German" and non-"German," East and West, male and female, and so on. In order to register this call, we have organized the anthology into a critical restaging of several key notions that have been theorized in, among other places, the *Passagenwerk* and other critical writings of Walter Benjamin,[19] whose critical, uneasy, and often controversial relationship to German cultural theory, even in its most current articulations, in many ways prefigures our own. This has entailed moulding the trajectory of the anthology into the shape of a double-ended funnel, or hourglass, which at once mimes the chronological passage of time and the breaching of that passage by the conflicts and divisions of the social real vis-à-vis which the anthology is ideologically and historically situated. At one level, this passage figures the trajectory of existential phenomenology, with its mapping of the familiar text-context relation across a linear temporal continuum. At another level, however, it marks a radical disorderly difference from that traditional framework through the peculiar way in which it conceptualizes and organizes its constituent sections—as contestational configurations of political, economic, sociological, historical, philosophical, and cultural discourses which we name, following Benjamin, *constellations*.[20]

Webster's dictionary has defined "constellation" *inter alia* as "a pattern, or arrangement [as in] 'the shifting constellation of power throughout the known world'";[21] and indeed it is with this question of global power that our radical disorderly anthology marks its radical difference from other books of its kind. First, by encompassing a series of essays that mobilize discursive tools from across the disciplines, the constellatory arrangement insists upon the necessity of recognizing, of refusing to deny, the imbricatedness of German cinema studies with non-German cinema studies fields such as political science, economics, history, sociology and philosophy, and thereby acknowledges the centrality of political, economic, historical, sociological, and ideological questions to any discussion of aesthetics and culture. Hence the anthological passage begins, at the outer level of the "hourglass," with two crucial constellations, one on the relation of the global social arena to German cinema studies (embodied by this Introduction), and one on the institutional setting of German cinema studies as regarded from within the Anglo-American academy; moves through the middle of the "hourglass," where it accesses constellations that provide closer readings of particular German films as well as of the academic, sometimes public debates informing them; and winds up at the opposite end of the "hourglass" with its re-turn outward onto broader questions about the contemporary public sphere. Second, by bringing the moments of this arrangement into a multivalenced series of contestations with respect to particular debates in German cinema studies, the anthology invites a likewise multivalenced series of self-conscious recognitions on the part of the reader of the significant ideological absences conditioning both its selection of texts and their organization into discursive blocs. Rather than proffer the discursive layeredness of each constellation as a kind of academic palimpsest, stacked evenly, if antagonistically, with generic themes, tropes and binarisms,[22] however, this organizational pattern is meant to promote a *politically* differential, *materially* grounded, always *ideologically* alert series of interventions into the sociohistorical relations between and among each constellation, each discourse. Aided by the critical questions posed within the short, mini-introductions preceding the constellations, this *radically* differential series of conflicting and coalescing aspects precludes a strictly consumptive, entrepreneurial passage through the anthology, encouraging instead a more collective, committed practice of reading.

Put another way, insofar as the constellatory structure is a differential one, its absences and insufficiencies are as important for comprehending the scope and necessity of German cinema studies as are the texts it actually includes. Hence our decision to exclude certain canonized or widely distributed texts, some of which are frequently reproduced in other anthologies,[23] as well as to question the ideological tendencies of texts, some canonized, some not, that we have in fact included, within the pages of our mini-introductions. In the face of these absences and insufficiencies, the radical disorderly reader is urged to question what discourses predominate and what presumptions are privileged by both the constellatory structure and its contents, a practice requiring a *radically* active reading attuned not only to the empirical "panorama" of German cinema studies but also to the theoretical questions prompted by the studied collision of the discourses between and among each of the anthology's constellatory aspects.

Some of these questions are as follows: What function does German cinema studies serve within the changed historical dimensions of a newly reunified Germany, economically powerful and politically resurgent in the leadership of the EU (Introduction)? Where is German cinema studies situated with respect to this shifting geopolitical scene, and what is its relationship to broader theoretical movements both in cinema studies and the humanities at large (Constellation A)? What ideological connections are traceable between the recently burgeoning area of Holocaust Studies, and German film theory's dual involvement in *Vergangenheitsbewältigung* (working through of the past) and the *Historikerstreit* (the Holocaust historiography debate, including the right-wing "revisionist" tendency)? Do these predominant currents bear any relation to the dissemination of neonationalist discourses (racism, antisemitism/philosemitism, heterosexism) throughout a Central Europe once again fractured by ethnic and racial antagonisms not unconnected with the post-Wall "refugee crisis" and Europe's first major war in fifty years—the internecine violence in the former Yugoslavia (Constellations B and C)? What role is played by the new cultural studies, with its pluralizations and historical specifications of race, nation, gender, and class, in German cinema studies' encounter with these recent shifts and social currents (Constellations D and E)? How are the contours of this encounter affected by queer theory's collapse of long-standing cultural binarisms and linguistic tropes (masculinity/femininity, heterosexuality/homosexuality) (Constellation F)? Despite these new cultural interventions, moreover, what are the implications of the continued dominance of the Frankfurt School, with its stubborn "high-low" hierarchies and its subsequent trivilization of the political significance of the "popular," for a postnationalist German film theory? Does the Frankfurtian tendency to mythologize, even relativize the very notion of the "popular" through psychoanalytic, aestheticist, and ontological discourses disengage it and its "utopian" aspirations from the historical and political dimensions of German culture (Constellation G)? How does this tendency relate to the recent return in German feminist film theory to Weimar and early/silent periods of German filmmaking, where a paradigm shift into existential phenomenology, facilitated by an eerily Christianized appropriation of Benjamin, has come to overdetermine the entire field? What ramifications does this shift now have for German feminist film theory, and what are the connections it portends between feminist examinations of subjectivity and sexuality and the ideology of the family and womanhood in Nazism (Constellation H)? How does it inflect the even more recent historiographic turn in German film theory to the National Socialist era, and how does that turn's crucial attention to the problematical relationship between the Left (SPD, KPD) and the Right (NSDAP) during that era harken back to the *Vergangenheitsbewältigung* of the 1970s New German Cinema (Constellation I)? Finally, what is the relationship between the possible answers to these questions and recent endeavors from within both German cinema studies and the broader academy at theorizing the possibility of a postmodern public sphere (Constellation J)?

We hope that the intersecting, overlapping, differential, generally non-synchronous, but always ideologically contextualized quality of this array of questions will make it apparent that the constellatory structure of this anthology is a political rather than spectacular one, figuring a radical disorderly intervention into the discursive structures and ideological conventions that have helped formulate German film theory at this postnationalist moment. Following Benjamin, we name the reader bound up in this critical process a *stereoscopic* one, insofar as the structure and content of her inquiry are so inextricably related by and to the multidimensional, diachronic, and material enframing of the textual passage that her interpretive navigations through its dense layers become nothing less than catalysts for radical social change.[24]

While not disavowing her own implicatedness in the contradictions of its scholarly contents, the stereoscopic reader of this anthology is one whose awareness of the complexity of those contradictions does not keep her from envisaging their *totality of possible effects*. In recent years, the Anglo-American academy has experienced a boom in the publication of anthologies, most of which organize texts along one of three structural lines: neoclassical obeisance to the master text, in which contradictory elements are aesthetically sutured into a logically resolvable whole; incremental chronology, which at once disavows and attempts complete coverage of a chosen topic; and post-al disorderliness, in which texts are placed into a multivalency often completely detached from any temporal and/or sociohistorical context.[25] While generally well intentioned, the idealist and pragmatic logics undergirding such structures tend to reinforce the politically vacuous, metaphysical notion that all knowledge and all perspectives are ultimately subjective, timeless, inevitable, and often only divinely knowable.

In stark contrast to these predominant anthological modalities, the totality of possible effects envisaged by the stereoscopic reader of this anthology, unlike the democratic/oligarchical structure framing the Athenian/Weimar *polis*, is the mark of a *political allegory*, a discursive structure whose critically foregrounded elisions, exclusions, and structural patternings lead its reader across the systematic, epistemological borders of the larger social framework, to pose the dangerous, unasked questions of German cinema studies, to pressure the contestational organization of each constellation into a vivid *historical* exposure and deconstruction of the political justifications and rationales for those elisions, exclusions, and structural patternings—those "otherings"—in the first place.[26] Informed by the radical disorderly framework circumscribing the anthology, and recalling Benjamin's oft-cited critical dictum that "Progress lodges, not in the continuity of the course of time, but rather in its moments of interference,"[27] the allegorical questions posed by the stereoscopic reader lead her into an act of intellectual "distanciation" (*verfremden*), or ideological resituation of the alienating practices of reification, disavowal, and detachment persisting within the field onto the tremulous terrain of what Benjamin has referred to, perhaps too mystically, as the "lighting flash" of *Jetztzeit*, or "time of the now."[28] Put in more materialist terms, the allegorical structure of the anthology invites the stereoscopic reader to participate in a collective intellectual coup, or global paradigm shift, an unsettling of the conceptual framework currently structuring her perspective on German cinema in the hopes of both dismantling it and, at the same time, preparing it for the possibility of its radical refiguration into a discourse whose historical and intellectual coherence no longer depend upon the systematic and ideological (re)construction of "others."

Organized as the central ideological fulcrum of the anthology's allegorical construction in this regard is the constellation of our "hourglass" which foregrounds more saliently than any of the others the systematic overdetermination of the nexus, German film/German film theory/German social politics, by ideological absences, or "otherings"—"The *Heimat* Debate: Politics of History" (Constellation B). By its very namesake, which signals the idea of the uncanny, unconscious, this-worldly aspect of social discourse, of the ideological delimitation of any cultural or discursive product *prior to* its admission to any public collection or historical archive, "The *Heimat* Debate" emblematizes the crux of the uncertain German cinema studies appropriation of post-al disorderliness which this anthology sets out to critique, prompting urgent questions about the status of the "German" and of "national cinemas" at the postnationalist moment in academic culture. For this reason, we now turn through this crucial passage of the "hourglass" into a closer inspection of its discursive matrix.

As a German response to the American television series, *Holocaust: The Story of the Family Weiss*,[29] the television airing of *Heimat*[30] occasioned much public attention and debate. Reinvoking contemporary social concerns over *Vergangenheitsbewältigung* and the *Historikerstreit*, *Heimat* provoked controversial questions about the national "ownership" of the "right to represent" the Holocaust and the Nazi era, and about the characteristic mobilization of the (non-)"German" as both sign and referent in international culture and cultural criticism.[31] At the same time, *Heimat*'s reinscription of such problematic notions as the universal and the particular, the familial and the familiar, the community and the nation, the mythic and the melodramatic, and the pastoral and the modern framed these questions in nostalgic, politically reactionary terms, terms in fact repeated across the debate included in this anthology as staged in Miriam Hansen, Gertrud Koch, Thomas Elsaesser, and Karsten Witte's "*Heimat* Dossier" as well as later, in Hansen's essay "Benjamin, Cinema and Experience" (also included herein).

For instance, the fictional village of Schabbach, where the film's story is set, resonates with a mythologized nationalism through its conflation of the regionalism and folkloric milieu of the provincial villagers who live far from the urban centers (the particular), and the ethnic idea of the "German" as it embodies a national mythos (the universal). In addition, the film's main focus, the story of the family Simon, is in part a persistent and far from accidental retelling of a classic German (fairy-)tale, its author-ial reconstruction of national identity and character emphasized by the film's subtitle, *Made in Germany*. Alongside these instances are the film's structural elision of the Holocaust, as an event located firmly outside the borders of Schabbach, as well as its related displacement of Nazism and the Nazi Party onto the socially and sexually "decadent" terrain of modern urban space, and its idealist projection of the central Nazi discourses of *Volk* (racial-ethnic community), *Heimat* (homeland) and *Vaterland* (Fatherland) onto the imperialist context of *Lebensraum* (living space), the index of German neonationalist utopia.

Together, these instances figure contradictions restaged in not only Constellations C, D, and G ("The Jewish Question," "The Euroamerican Question," and "Myth and Allegory," respectively), but across the entire anthology. Through their reinvocation of German ethnicity, authority and singularity, they figure the sorts of sociocultural "othering"/normativiza-tion critiqued explicitly by Constellations E, F, and H ("Feminism, Motherhood, Terrorism," "Queer Constructs," "Feminism and Early Weimar," respectively) and implicitly by the other constellations. Thus the classic cultural typologies of the authentic "German" (as emblem of national identity), the wandering "Jew" (as token of economic exchange), the mythical "Woman" (as symbol of fertility and consumption), and the undecidable "Queer" (as barometer of moral decay)—all of which *Heimat* reconstitutes—become, through our specific organization, ideological piv-ots for projecting the reader both forward and backward through the "hourglass," for drawing critical connections between and among the con-stellations and for signaling the global, postnational character of their con-structedness and continued exploitation within German cinema studies.

In view of its ideological disavowals, popular reception and auteurist presumptions, then, *Heimat* symptomatizes much of what triggers the crit-ical project of this anthology, reminding us of the need for a radical politi-cal mediation of the parameters of scholarly dialogue and debate over the significance of a national cinema still resistant to questions of the material, the ideological and the collective, in a world now run along neoliberal, neophenomenological, neonationalist lines. Yet even the most minimal consideration of a radical project can prefigure that project's dismissal from public engagement and its entry into the *silent zone*,[32] an ideational site symptomatizing profound public instability regarding the meaning and import of social praxis. How then can we be sure whether the reader of this anthology will take up our radical disorderly challenge? If, as Benjamin suggests, the labor of radical reading is precisely that of reengaging this "silent zone," of returning it to its historical grounding through a difficult act of radical recollection and deployment,[33] then the reader who continues to elide the political and the concomitant critique of post-al difference may simply find it easier and less taxing to leave this zone of uncanniness untouched. On the other hand, if the reader is conceptually alert to the problematics offered by most contemporary anthologies as these continue to privilege the goals of ideological mastery and immersion in the eclectic, and instead registers the instability and pressurization of its silent zone as her point of intellectual departure, then she will have taken the first step toward refusing to narrate the history of German cinema studies as though she were a "monk fingering the beads of a rosary."[34] Instead grasping "the constellation which [our] own era forms with a definite earlier one," and, as Habermas has suggested, linking "social modernization to other, non-capitalist paths,"[35] she will take our anthology as an opportunity for a spilling out of those beads onto a more ideologically interventionist, socially critical configuration of scholarly inquiry, one whose passionate demand for public engagement with the urgent sociopolitical questions and concerns raised across the ensuing pages calls for a likewise impassioned response across the post-al spectrum. We believe that the elicitation of such a response could well signal the formation of intellectual alliances along lines drawn toward ending (neo)fascism and (neo)nationalism, and toward ending prevailing assumptions that a radical theory of culture is no longer possible.

For if local war and global immiseration have now become the grossest manifestations of nation, race, gender, and class—note the continuing dismemberment of Bosnia/Herzegovina and the sustained decimations of Haiti, Rwanda, and Iraq—then the *polis* of postnational disorderliness has already become the site of a violent and bloody graveyard. In view of this social fact, we conclude our introduction by stressing our belief that a public, political reengagement of these issues by the German cinema studies reader and the postmodern academy is eminently necessary at this time, the fiftieth anniversary of the end of World War II and the liberation of Auschwitz.

—July 1995

Notes

1. For sustained elaborations of this narrative, see: Hans-Georg Betz, "The Two Faces of Radical Right-Wing Populism in Western Europe," *The Review of Politics* 55, no. 4 (1993): 663–85; Chris Bambery, "Euro-fascism: The Lessons of the Past and Current Tasks," *International Socialism* 60 (1993): 3–75; the debate staged across the pages of *Monthly Review*, especially the essay by Dorothy Rosenberg, "The Colonization of East Germany," *Monthly Review* 43, no. 4 (1991): 14–33; also the rebuttal to Rosenberg by Brigitte H. Schulz

and William W. Hansen, "A Response to Rosenberg's Thesis on Colonialism in East Germany," and her subsequent counterpoint, "Rejoinder to Schulz and Hansen," both in *Monthly Review* 44, no. 1 (1992): 51–56, 57–60; Wolfgang Fach and Annette Ringwald, "Curing Germany, Saving Europe," *Telos* 90 (Winter 1991–92): 89–100; and *Telos* nos. 98–99 (Winter 1993–Spring 1994), Special Issue on "The French New Right: New Right, New Left, New Paradigm?"

An interesting addendum to this narrative is the fact that the name of the main far-right organization in Finland, Aryan German Brotherhood, refers not to Finland, as one might expect, but to Germany. This fact is even more striking when considering the diverse cultural and ethnic population of Finland, an observation which illustrates not only the systematic overdetermination of the "German" as an emblem of national(ist) identity, but also the ideological quality of such identity—its function as a spurious means of resolving the crises developing in relation to social difference and antagonism.

2. The condemnations of these phenomena are outlined clearly in the most highly publicized war crimes trial since Nuremberg—the proceedings against the Bosnian Serbs recently undertaken at the Hague. While not denying the verity of Bosnian Serb atrocities perpetrated against Croats and Muslims in the former Yugoslavia, one might critically consider the belated timing of these proceedings, which have taken place at least two years after public knowledge of the Serbian genocidal deeds became widely available.

In regard to right-wing expansion, the April 1995 bombing of the Alfred P. Murrah Federal Building in Oklahoma City allegedly by Timothy McVeigh, who had had connections with the far-right paramilitary Michigan Militia, has highlighted the increasing profile of extreme right-wing violence in the United States, and now raises the question, perhaps for the first time in U.S. history, of the relation between government crackdowns on organized criminality (including international syndicates and cartels) and the rise of antigovernment paramilitary practices. In contrast to its articulation in the European context, where the issue of governments circumventing regular parliamentary channels in order to control leftist terrorism (Irish Republican Army, Red Brigade, Baader-Meinhof gang) has long been the subject of heated public debate, the new U.S. articulation admits an additional, disturbing problem: unlike the left terrorist groups of Europe (and Latin America, for that matter), the American terrorist groups, which share an antigovernment paranoia, are neither unified by a coherent ideological project (consider, for example, the different outlooks and programs of the Identity Christians, the White Aryan Resistance, and the Posse Comitatus) nor associated in any sense with the left, despite implicit suggestions to the contrary by President Bill Clinton in public statements made shortly following the Oklahoma City bombing. For some useful analyses of this left-right conflationism, see *Telos* nos. 98–99 (Winter 1993–Spring 1994), Special Issue on "The French New Right: New Right, New Left; New Paradigm?" President Clinton's association of the left with the contemporary wave of right-wing terrorism recalls the accusations levied by German conservative leader Alfred Dregger against the philosophers of the Frankfurt School, when, in 1977, the left-oriented theory of the latter was deemed the ideological provocation for the wave of far left terrorism that was sweeping West Germany at that time. The subject of the ensuing controversy became the central focus of a collectively directed film, *Germany in Autumn* (dirs. Alf Brustellin, Rainer Werner Fassbinder, Alexander Kluge, Maximiliana Mainka, Edgar Reitz, Katja Ruppe, Volker Schlöndorff, Hans Peter Cloos and Bernhard Sinkel, 1977–78), few if any articles or sustained scholarly essays about which have been published in English. For a critique of the Dregger affair, see Jürgen Habermas, "Apologetic Tendencies," *The New Conservatism: Cultural Criticism and the Historians' Debate*, trans. Shierry Weber Nicholsen (Boston: MIT Press, 1989) pp. 212–228. (This critique is absent from the essay of the same name that we have included in Constellation B. For yet a third translation, see *Yad Vashem Studies* 19 [ed. Aharon Weiss; Jerusalem: Yad Vashem, 1988]: pp. 75–92.)

3. The major instances are: Thomas Elsaesser, *German Cinema: A History* (New Brunswick, NJ: Rutgers University Press, 1989); Anton Kaes, *From Hitler to Heimat: The*

Return of History as Film (Cambridge, MA: Harvard University Press, 1989); Eric Rentschler, ed., *West German Cinema in the Course of Time: Reflections on the Twenty Years Since Oberhausen* (Bedford Hills, NY: Redgrave Publishing Co., 1984); Eric Santner, *Stranded Objects: Mourning, Memory and Film in Postwar Germany* (Ithaca, NY: Cornell University Press, 1990); Timothy Corrigan, *New German Film: The Displaced Image*, 2d ed. (Bloomington and Indianapolis: Indiana University Press, 1994); Julia Knight, *Woman and the New German Cinema* (London: Verso, 1992); Sabine Hake, *The Cinema's Third Machine: Writing on Film in Germany, 1907–1933* (Lincoln: University of Nebraska Press, 1993); Eric Rentschler, ed., *German Film and Literature: Adaptations and Transformations* (New York: Methuen, 1986); Robert Phillip Kolker and Peter Beicken, *The Films of Wim Wenders: Cinema as Vision and Desire* (Cambridge: Cambridge University Press, 1993); Robert C. Reimer and Carol J. Reimer, *Nazi-retro Films: How German Narrative Cinema Remembers the Past* (New York: Twayne Publishers, 1992); Sandra Frieden et al., ed., *Gender and German Cinema: Feminist Interventions*, 2 vols. (Providence, RI and Oxford: Berg Press, 1990); Bruce Murray, *Film and the Left in the Weimar Republic: From Caligari to Kühle Wampe* (Austin: University of Texas Press, 1990); Timothy Corrigan, ed., *The Films of Werner Herzog: Between Mirage and History* (New York and London: Methuen, 1986); Marc Silberman, *German Cinema: Texts in Contexts* (Detroit: Wayne State University Press, 1995); Jane Shattuc, *Television, Tabloids, and Tears: Fassbinder and Popular Culture* (Minneapolis: University of Minnesota Press, 1994); Roswitha Müller, *Valie Export: Fragments of the Imagination* (Bloomington and Indianapolis: Indiana University Press, 1994); Barton Byg, *Landscapes of Resistance: The German Films of Danièle Huillet and Jean-Marie Straub* (Berkeley and Los Angeles: University of California Press, 1995); and Heide Fehrenbach, *Cinema in Democratizing Germany: Reconstructing National Identity After Hitler* (Chapel Hill & London: University of North Carolina Press, 1995). Also significant are the numerous special issues of the journal *New German Critique*, which have taken a particularly anthological approach with topics of interest to the student of German cinema and culture; see, for instance, the recent issues on German film (*New German Critique* no. 60 [1993]) and Rainer Werner Fassbinder (*New German Critique* no. 63 [Fall 1994]). In addition, one should note the scholarly and/or cultural legitimacy bestowed on some of these texts at the moment of German reunification, through the awarding of academic prizes: New York City's Anthology Film Archives (an experimental/avant-garde film and research house) awarded Elsaesser's *German Cinema* the 1990 Cinema Studies Contribution of the Year; also in 1990, *Quarterly Review of Film and Video*, known in the field for its formalist-phenomenological approach, awarded the Elsaesser text the Katherine Singer Kovacs Prize in Film, TV and Video Studies for Best Book, with Kaes's *From Hitler to Heimat* running a close second.

    4. Beginning in cinema studies with Jim Pines and Paul Willeman, ed., *Questions of Third Cinema* (London: BFI, 1989), and continuing through to Pranjali Bandhu, *Black and White of Cinema in India* (Thiravananthapuram: Odyssey, 1992); Fredric Jameson, *The Geopolitical Aesthetic: Cinema and Space in the World System* (Bloomington and Indianapolis: Indiana University Press; and London BFI, 1992); Manthia Diawara, *African Cinema: Politics and Culture* (Bloomington and Indianapolis: University of Indiana Press, 1992); Hamid Naficy, *The Making of Exile Cultures: Iranian Television in Los Angeles* (Minneapolis: University of Minnesota Press, 1993); *The Velvet Light Trap* no. 34 (Fall 1984), Special Issue on "Popular National Cinema"; and the four featured articles in *Screen* 35 no. 3 (1994), which focus on the question of "national cinema." Also note the recent conference, "European Cinemas, European Societies, 1895–1995," hosted at Indiana University in Fall 1995, which boasted a broad inter-European multinationalism, but, strangely, lent scant focus to German cinema.

    5. This characterization is epitomized by the oft-cited notion of the demise of the master narrative of human progress in Jean-François Lyotard, *The Postmodern Condition: A Report on Knowledge*, trans. Geoff Bennington and Brian Massumi, forward by Fredric Jameson (Minneapolis: University of Minnesota Press, 1984). While initially articulated to

texts of socially progressive proclivity (see Michel Foucault regarding the end of reason in "What Is Enlightenment?" trans. Alan Sheridan and others, *Politics, Philosophy, Culture: Interview and Other Writings* [New York: Routledge, 1988]; Roland Barthes regarding the end of the human subject in "The Death of the Author," trans. Stephen Heath [New York: Noonday Press, 1977], pp. 142–48; and Jacques Derrida regarding the deconstruction of philosophy in *Of Grammatology*, trans. Gayatri Chakravorty Spivak [Baltimore and London: Johns Hopkins University Press, 1976]), this Lyotardian move, along with its utter hypostatization in texts of Jean Baudrillard, has reopened space for the reinscription of decidedly conservative, nay, reactionary readings of postmodernism (see Baudrillard, *In the Shadow of the Silent Minorities; Or, The End of the Social, And Other Essays*, trans. Paul Foss, John Johnston, and Paul Patton [New York: Semiotext(e), 1983], for the classic post-al theory of social dissolution; also Heide Ziegler, dir and ed., *The End of Postmodernism: New Directions. Proceedings of the Stuttgart Seminar in Cultural Studies, August 4–18, 1991* [Stuttgart: M & P Verlag für Wissenschaft und Forschung, 1993]). Such readings were first articulated to the Euroamerican power bloc during the 1950s in the domain of journalism as strategies for heralding the destruction of Communism in the Soviet Union and other Eastern European countries which together had formed the Eastern bloc and the Warsaw Pact (e.g., see Daniel Bell regarding the end of ideology in *The End of Ideology* [Glencoe, IL: Free Press, 1960]; and, more recently, Francis Fukuyama regarding the end of history in *The End of History and the Last Man* [New York and Toronto: Free Press; Maxwell Macmillan Canada, 1992]).

6. For an extended theorization of "thick" discourse, see H. Aram Veeser, introduction to *The New Historicism*, ed. Veeser (New York and London: Routledge, 1989), pp. ix–xvi.

7. Respective instances are David Bordwell, *Narration in the Fiction Film* (Madison: University of Wisconsin Press, 1985); Robert Sklar and Charles Musser, ed., *Resisting Images: Essays on Cinema and History* (Philadelphia: Temple University Press, 1990); Jacqueline Rose, *Sexuality in the Field of Vision* (London: Verso, 1986); Ella Shohat and Robert Stam, *Unthinking Eurocentrism: Towards a Multicultural Film Theory* (New York and London: Routledge, 1994); Scott Bukatman, *Terminal Identity: The Virtual Subject in Postmodern Science Fiction* (Durham, SC: Duke University Press, 1993); and Linda Mizejewski, *Divine Decadence: Fascism, Female Spectacle, and the Makings of Sally Bowles* (Princeton, NJ: Princeton University Press, 1992).

8. Perhaps the most recent discursive object of this recuperation, both inside and outside cinema studies, is the paradigm of multiculturalism, whose progressive tendencies toward politicizing, historicizing analysis are slowly being eroded by being subsumed into the politics and power of cultural identity, national difference, and bodily rhetorics. While liberal-to-progressive versions of multicultural discourse have made inroads into the Anglo-American academy, especially in the form of anthologies (see Lawrence Grossberg et al., ed., *Cultural Studies* [New York and London: Routlege, 1992], Andrew Parker et al., ed., *Nationalism and Sexualities* [New York and London: Routledge, 1992]; Constance Penley and Andrew Ross, ed., *Technoculture* [Minneapolis and Oxford: University of Minnesota Press, 1991]; and Sue-Ellen Case, ed., *Performing Feminisms: Feminist Critical Theory and Theatre* [Baltimore and London: Johns Hopkins University Press, 1990]), their effects have often been quickly sensationalized and publically primed for conservative co-optation (as in Dinesh D'Souza, *Illiberal Education: The Politics of Race and Sex on Campus* [New York: Vintage Books, 1992]; and Camille Paglia, *Sexual Personae: Art and Decadence From Nefertiti to Emily Dickinson* [New York: Vintage, 1990]).

9. For instances of this alienated discourse in recent cultural and/or cinematic criticism, see Jean Baudrillard, *The Ecstasy of Communication*, trans. Bernard and Caroline Schutze, ed. Sylvère Lotringer (New York: Semiotext[e], 1987); Gilles Deleuze, *Cinema 1: The Movement-Image*, trans. Hugh Tomlinson and Barbara Habberjam (Minnesota: University of Minnesota Press, 1986) and *Cinema 2: The Time Image*, trans. Hugh Tomlinson and Robert Galeta (Minneapolis: University of Minnesota Press, 1989); Paul Virilio, *War and*

Cinema: The Logics of Perception, trans. Patrick Camiller (London and New York: Verso, 1989); Guy Debord, *Comments on the Society of the Spectacle*, trans. Malcolm Imrie (London and New York: Verso, 1988); Manuel De Landa, *War in the Age of Intelligent Machines* (New York: Zone Books, 1991); and David Kerekes and David Slater, *Killing for Culture: An Illustrated History of Death Film From Mondo to Snuff* (London: Creation Books, 1994).

For general overviews of cybernetic and science fiction film theories, respectively, see Michael Benedikt, ed., *Cyberspace: First Steps* (London and Cambridge: Massachusetts Institute of Technology (MIT) Press, 1991), and Vivian Sobchak, *The American Science Fiction Film* (New York: Frederick Ungar Publishing Co., 1988). For a comprehensive anthological treatment of these topics, see Stanley Aronowitz et al., ed., *Technoscience and Cyberculture* (New York and London: Routledge, 1995). For an example of the insertion of gender and sexuality into the discourse of post-al terminality, see Donna J. Haraway, *Simians, Cyborgs, and Women: The Reinvention of Nature* (New York: Routledge, 1991).

For other, specific articulations of post-al "disorderliness," see Joy Wiltenberg, *Disorderly Women and Female Power in the Street Literature of Early Modern England and Germany* (Charlottesville: University Press of Virginia, 1992); Susan Juster, *Disorderly Women: Sexual Politics and Evangelicism in Revolutionary New England* (Ithaca: Cornell University Press, 1994); Bruce Jackson, *Disorderly Conduct*, forward by William Kunstler (Urbana, IL: University of Illinois Press, 1992); John Dupré, *The Disorder of Things: Metaphysical Foundations and the Disunity of Science* (Cambridge, MA: Harvard University Press, 1993); Rhonda Lieberman, "Shopping Disorders," *The Politics of Everyday Fear*, ed. Brian Massumi (Minneapolis and London: University of Minnesota Press, 1993): 245–65; and R. Robert Russell, "The Disorderly Retreat from Reagonomics," *New York University C. V. Stern Center for Applied Economics Policy Paper 23* (May 1983).

For general critiques of the post-al turn, see Christopher Norris, *What's Wrong With Postmodernism?: Critical Theory and the End of Philosophy* (Baltimore: Johns Hopkins University Press, 1990); Linda Hutcheon, *The Politics of Postmodernism* (London: Routledge, 1989); Jürgen Habermas, *The Philosophical Discourse of Modernity: Twelve Lectures* (Cambridge, MA: MIT Press, 1987); Alex Callinicos, *Against Postmodernism: A Marxist Critique* (Oxford: Polity Press, 1989); and Mas'ud Zavarzadeh and Donald Morton, *Theory, (Post)Modernity, Opposition: An "Other" Introduction to Literary and Cultural Theory* (Washington, DC: Maisonneuve Press, 1991).

For the inaugural use of "post-al" in the politicized sense this anthology wishes to invoke, see *Transformation* 1 (Spring 1995), special issue on "Post-ality."

10. Inaugurated in Alisa Steddom's post-al twist on cultural studies, "Civil Cyborgs: Ethics and Self-Governance in Cyberspace," presented at the New York University Department of Cinema Studies student conference, March 1993. For a more politicized version of this idea, see Paul Hockenos, "Cyberbosnia," *In These Times* 1 May 1995: 8, which describes ZaMir, the German-Bosnian computer network designed to overcome the information blockade spanning the war-torn former Yugoslavia; also Kim Goldberg, "Battling Cyber-Nazis," *The Progressive* May 1995: 13. For a standard exposition of the theory of the "virtual" real, see Michael Heim, *The Metaphysics of Virtual Reality* (New York and Oxford: Oxford University Press, 1993). For a critical anthological treatment, see James Brook and Iaian A. Boal, eds., *Resisting Virtual Life: The Culture and Politics of Information* (San Francisco: City Lights, 1995).

11. For example, Nick Browne, ed., *Cahiers du Cinema 1969–1972: The Politics of Representation* (Cambridge, MA: Harvard University Press, 1990); Mario Cannella, "Ideology and Aesthetic Hypotheses in the Criticism of Italian Neo-Realism," *Screen* 14 no. 4 (1973–74): 5–60; and Randal Johnson and Robert Stam, ed., *Brazilian Cinema* (Austin: University of Texas Press, 1988). While the last of these does not necessarily represent an "entrenched" area of cinematic inquiry, its articulation in Johnson and Stam, as elsewhere, is decidely postnational in outlook and effect.

12. These include the historicism of Hegel, the romanticism of the Jena Circle, the

mythologism of Freud, the intentionalism of Husserl, the onto-theology of Heidegger, the hermeneutics of Gadamer, and the aestheticism of the later Frankfurt School. The key texts here are: G. W. F. Hegel, *The Philosophy of History*, trans. J. Sibree (New York: Dover Publishers, 1956); Friedrich Schlegel, *Philosophical Fragments*, trans. Peter Firchow, introduction by Rodolphe Gasché (Minneapolis: University of Minnesota Press, 1991); Sigmund Freud, *The Interpretation of Dreams*, trans. A. A. Brill (New York: Modern Library, 1950); Edmund Husserl, *Ideas: General Introduction to Pure Phenomenology*, trans. W. R. Boyce Gibson (New York and London: Collier Macmillan, 1962); Martin Heidegger, *The Question Concerning Technology and Other Essays*, trans. W. Lovitt (New York: Harper & Row, 1977); Hans Georg Gadamer, *Truth and Method*, trans. Joel Weinsheimer and Donald G. Marshall (New York: Continuum, 1994); Max Horkheimer, *Critique of Instrumental Reason: Lectures and Essays Since the End of World War II*, trans. Matthew J. O'Connell et al. (New York: Seabury Press, 1974); Theodor W. Adorno, *Aesthetic Theory*, trans. C. Lenhardt, ed. Gretel Adorno and Rolf Tiedemann (London and New York: Routledge, 1986); and Herbert Marcuse, *One-Dimensional Man* (Boston: Beacon Press, 1964).

13. Instances are: Douglas Crimp, "Fassbinder, Franz, Fox, Elvira, Erwin, Armin, and All the Others," *October* 21 (Summer 1982): 63–81; Howard Feinstein, "BRD 1-2-3: Fassbinder's Postwar Trilogy and the Spectacle," *Cinema Journal* 23 no. 1 (1983): 44–56; Gertrud Koch, "Between Two Worlds: von Sternberg's *Blue Angel*," *German Film and Literature*, ed. Rentschler, *op cit.* note 3; Eric Santner, op. cit. note 3; Sabine Hake, op. cit. note 3; Ann Harris, *Taking Time Seriously: Technology, Politics, and Filmmaking Practice*, dissertation, New York University, 1992; Miriam Hansen, introduction to *Public Sphere and Experience: Toward an Analysis of the Bourgeois and Proletarian Public Sphere*, trans. Peter Labanyi, Jamie Owen Daniel, and Asenka Oskiloff (Minneapolis: University of Minnesota Press, 1993); and Wilhelm S. Wurzur, *Filming and Judgment: Between Heidegger and Adorno* (New Jersey and London: Humanities Press, 1990), although this last is quite explicit in its use of the deconstructionist language of Jacques Derrida.

For other Cinema Studies texts emerging out of this *neophenomenological* turn, see Peter Brunette and David Wills, *Screen/Play: Derrida and Film Theory* (Princeton, NJ: Princeton University Press, 1989); P. Adams Sitney, *Modernist Montage: The Obscurity of Vision in Cinema and Literature* (New York: Columbia University Press, 1990); Tom Conley, *Film Hieroglyphs: Ruptures in Classical Cinema* (Minneapolis and Oxford: University of Minnesota Press, 1991); Harold Stadler, *Film as Experience: Phenomenology and the Study of Film Reception*, dissertation, New York University, 1991; Miriam Hansen, *Babel and Babylon: Spectatorship in American Silent Film* (Cambridge, MA and London: Harvard University Press, 1991); Vivian Sobchak, *The Address of the Eye: A Phenomenology of Film Experience* (Princeton, NJ: Princeton University Press, 1992); Allan Casebier, *Film and Phenomenology: Towards a Realist Theory of Cinematic Representation* (Cambridge: Cambridge University Press, 1991); Richard Allen, *Projecting Illusion: Film Spectacle and the Impression of Reality* (New York: Cambridge University Press, 1995); and Frank Tomasulo, "The Text-In-the-Spectator: The Role of Phenomenology in an Eclectic Theoretical Methodology," *Journal of Film and Video* 40 no. 2 (1988): 20–32.

14. Of course, that the matrix of this replication is rooted in the Greek configuration should be of no surprise to anyone even slightly familiar with the history of right-wing reaction and German imperialism. One need only recall the Nazi fetishization of the architecture of Ancient Greece and Rome, instrumentalized by Nazi chief industrialist and Hitler's personal architect, Albert Speer, or consider the critique of such fetishization in Theodor W. Adorno, *The Jargon of Authenticity*, trans. Knut Tarnowski and Frederic Will (Evanston, IL: Northwestern University Press, 1973); Jürgen Habermas, "Modern and Postmodern Architecture,"op. cit. note 2, pp. 3–21; Saul Friedländer, *Reflections of Nazism: An Essay on Kitsch and Death*, trans. Thomas Weyr (New York: Harper and Row, 1984); and more, colloquially, Gillo Dorfles, ed., *Kitsch: The World of Bad Taste*, (New York: Universe

Books, 1975) to realize the connection. For more direct linkage, see Anton Kaes et al., ed., *The Weimar Republic Sourcebook* (Berkeley: University of California Press, 1994). For a broader, more politicized analysis of Nazi cultural practices as "propaganda," particularly in relation to the Nazification of aesthetics (Leni Riefenstahl) and the inscription of the public sphere as total Nazi spectacle, see Martin Chalmers, "Notes on Nazi Propaganda," *Screen Education* 40 (1981–82): 34–47.

15. See Plato, *The Republic*, trans. Desmond Lee (London and New York: Penguin Books, 1987); Aristotle, *The Politics*, trans. Carnes Lord (Chicago and London: University of Chicago Press, 1984); J. M. Roberts, *History of the World* (New York: Oxford University Press, 1993), pp. 155–57; E. M. Wood and N. Wood, *Class Ideology and Ancient Political Theory* (New York: Oxford University Press, 1978); and Peter Murphy, "Romantic Modernism and the Greek Polis," *Thesis Eleven* 34 (1993): 42–66. For a reading of the "polis" as it relates to postmodernism, see Terry Eagleton, "From the *Polis* to the Postmodern," *The Ideology of the Aesthetic* (Oxford and Cambridge, MA: Basil Blackwell, 1990), pp. 366–417.

16. *The Politics*, p. 37 [1:2.2–3]. Importantly, what is meant in this instance by the "political" is not the commonly recognized notion of judicial intrigue and official legislation, but the social and intellectual practice of questioning these practices and the institutions and conventions articulating them, with an aim to their possible alteration or transformation. On this understanding, the possibility of "politics" implies an assumption of the social and theoretical constructedness of any social institution or discursive convention, as well as an arguable sense of those institutions' and structures' imperfections (oppressiveness, exploitativeness, and so on) and need for progressive, if not revolutionary change.

17. For instances of this view in German film theory, please refer to our short, mini-introductions to each section of this anthology. For recent articulations in German cultural theory, see Russell A. Berman, *Cultural Studies of Modern Germany: History, Representation and Nationhood* (Milwaukee: University of Wisconsin Press, 1993); Rob Burns, ed., *German Clutural Studies: An Introduction* (NY: Oxford University Press, 1995); and Michael Kessler and Jürgen Wertheimer, ed, *Multikulturalität: Tendenzen, Probleme, Perspektiven in europäischen und internationalen Horizont* (Tübingen: Stauffenburg Verlag, 1995). See also the proposed 1995 Modern Language Association panel, "Multiculturalism and German Civilization and Literature," to be chaired by Hartmut Heep, perhaps the first of its kind in the field.

On the other hand, see Paul De Man, *Allegories of Reading: Figural Language in Rousseau, Nietzsche, Rilke, and Proust* (New Haven and London: Yale University Press, 1979), for the classic literary theoretical advocation of this banalization in the form of a collapse of the "literal" into/between the "figural" levels of discourse. According to De Man (the recent scandal over whose Nazi collaboration—as with that of Heidegger—cannot be ignored by German cinema studies), the intrinsic metaphoric qualities of rhetorical and figurative language prevent discourse from referring unequivocally to social realities or communicating definitive meanings. While conceding the unstable, differential quality of all discourse and communication, we differ from De Man insofar as we also insist (more along the lines of Benjamin in "The Work of Art" essay, Derrida in *Positions*, and Marx and Engels in *The German Ideology*; see below for citations) upon the political, sociomaterial conditions of any linguistic construction, difference, or reference. For us, that is, the differentiation of language is an ideology-effect of the division of labor before it can even be considered an aesthetic-effect of creative "force" (in Greek, *outis*). See Benjamin, "The Work of Art in the Age of Mechanical Reproduction," *Illuminations*, trans. Hannah Arendt (New York: Schocken Books, 1969); Jacques Derrida, *Positions*, trans. Alan Bass (Chicago: University of Chicago Press, 1981); and Karl Marx and Friedrich Engels, *The German Ideology*, ed. C. J. Arthur (New York: International Publishers, 1989).

18. The reader will note the effects of this phenomenon critically mapped across the pages of this anthology, where texts concerning the question of gender are more

forthcoming (because more available) than are those concerning matters of race, ethnicity, class, or sexuality. This sort of idealized privileging has been registered in several ways. Claudia Koonz's historical analysis of the function and role of the "Aryan Woman" and "Family" in the ideology of the Nazi party provides a more recent scholarly evaluation of the responsibility and effectivity of Woman in the Nazi period. Specifically, the marshalling of sexuality onto the Aryan Woman/Family for the reproduction of the "Master Race" is an example of how Nazi ideology is writ large on the body of Woman. See also Leila J. Rupp, "Mother of the *Volk*: The Image of Women in Nazi Germany," *Signs* (Winter 1977): 362–79. A critique of Koonz is provided by Eve Rosenhaft, "Inside the Third Reich: What Is the Women's Story?" *Radical History Review* 43 (1989): 72–85, who questions the elision of the historical connection of class politics to racism in Koonz' analysis of the role and function of Woman and the Family in the Third Reich. Her call for a more politicized reading of the Nazi feminine ideal, especially as it pertains to the history of the Holocaust, is echoed in Dieter Thöma, "Making Off With an Exile: Heidegger and the Jews," trans. Stephen Cho and Dieter Thöma, *New German Critique* no. 58 (Winter 1993): 79–85, who critiques the idealized privilegings of the "Jew" for representing a "theft" of political and historical difference in the fetishized name of "Germania," the fertile, authentic, salvific German *Heimat* (homeland). Thöma suggests further that such privilegings enable a metaphysical role reversal between German perpetrators and Jewish victims of the Holocaust, whereupon "Heidegger himself becomes the victim *instead of* the Jews" (p. 84). This observation, while cogent and necessary, tends in Thöma's liberal discourse to reinscribe a continued separation of the "German" and the non-"German" in the seemingly innocuous form of a democratic "right to difference." For an essay that raises the question of "German"-"Jewish" interchangeability in terms of public cultural spectacle, see Johannes von Moltke, "Exhibiting Jewish Lifeworlds: Notes on German-Jewish Identity Politics," *Found Object* 3 (Spring 1994): 11–31, which places this question into a decidedly post-al context.

19. Especially "Konvolut N [Theoretics of Knowledge; Theory of Progress]," trans. Leigh Hafrey and Richard Sieburth, *The Philosophical Forum* 15 nos. 1–2 (1983–84): 1–40.

20. Ibid., p. 2 (N 1, 9), p. 7 (N 2a, 3) p. 16 (N 7, 2); and "Doctrine of the Similar (1933)," trans. Jerolf Wikoff, *New German Critique* 17 (1979): 65–69.

21. *Webster's Ninth Collegiate Dictionary* (Springfield, MA: G. & C. Merriam Company, 1988), 281.

22. Recall Hans Günther Pflaum's *Germany on Film: Theme and Content in the Cinema of the Federal Republic of Germany* (trans. Roland Richter and Richard C. Helt [Detroit: Wayne State University Press, 1985]), which although not anthological, stands as the classic German cinema studies example of this sort of facile, New Critical textual arrangement.

23. For instance: B. Ruby Rich, "From Repressive Tolerance to Erotic Liberation: *Mädchen in Uniform*," *Jump Cut* 24–25 (March 1981): 44–50; Bryan Bruce, "Rosa von Praunheim in Theory and Practice," *CineAction!* 9 (Summer 1987): 25–31; Richard Dyer, "Less and More than Women and Men: Lesbian and Gay Cinema in Weimar Germany," *New German Critique* 51 (Fall 1990): 5–60; Jan-Christopher Horak, "Prometheus Film Collective (1925–1932): German Communist *Kinokultur*," *Jump Cut* no. 26 (Dec. 1981): 39–41; Susan Dermody, "Jean-Marie Straub and Danièle Huillet," *Cinema Papers* no. 10 (Sept. 1976): 127–30, 184–85; Sheila Johnston, "The Author as Public Institution: The 'New' Cinema and the Federal Republic of Germany," *Screen Education* 32–33 (1979–80): 67–78; Steve Neale, "*Triumph of the Will*: Notes on Documentary and Spectacle," *Screen* 20 no. 1 (1979): 63–86; Heide Schlüpmann, "'What is Different is Good': Women and Femininity in the Films of Alexander Kluge," trans. Jamie Owen Daniel, *October* 46 (1988): 129–50; Judith Mayne, "Female Narration, Women's Cinema: Helke Sander's *The All-Round Reduced Personality/Redupers, New German Critique* 24–25 (Fall/Winter, 1981–82): 155–71; Thomas Elsaesser, "Lulu and the Meter Man: Louise Brooks, Pabst, and 'Pandora's Box,'" *Screen* 24 no. 4 (1983): 4–36; Patricia Mellencamp, "Oedipus and the Robot in *Metropolis*," *Enclitic* 5 no. 1 (1981): 20–42; E. Ann Kaplan, "Discourses of Feminism, Terrorism and the Family in

von Trotta's *Marianne and Juliane*," *Persistence of Vision* 2 (1983): 65–68; Ellen E. Seiter, "Women's History, Women's Melodrama: *Deutschland, bleiche Mutter*," *The German Quarterly* 59 no. 4 (1986): 569–81; Dominick La Capra, "Representing the Holocaust: Reflections on the Historians' Debate," *Probing the Limits of Representation*, ed. Saul Friedländer (Cambridge, MA: Harvard University Press, 1992), pp. 108–27; Ruth Perlmutter, "German Revisionism: Edgar Reitz's *Heimat*, *Wide Angle* 9, no. 3 (1987): 21–37; Christopher Wickham, "Representation and Mediation in Edgar Reitz's *Heimat*," *The German Quarterly* 61 no. 1 (1991): 35–45; and Gila Walker, "An Analysis of *Der Ewige Jude*: Its Relationship to Nazi Anti-Semitic Ideas and Policies," *Wide Angle* 3 no. 4 (1980): 48–53.

24. This in the spirit of Benjamin's suggestion that "The most significant results . . . achieved by Marx and Engels do not lie in theoretical formulations of the new principle, but in its specific application to a series of questions . . . some of fundamental practical importance, some of extreme theoretical difficulty," "Konvolut N," op. cit., p. 34 (N 17). This notion of "stereoscopic," then, is to be distinguished from its conservative understandings, such as those proffered by Michael Polyani and Harry Prosch (*Meaning* [Chicago: University of Chicago Press, 1975]) in the area of literary studies or Trevor Whittock (*Metaphor in Film* [Cambridge: Cambridge University Press, 1990]) in the area of cinema studies, and for which "stereoscopic" viewing or seeing, *pace* Aristotle, is a matter of tacitly, privately synthesizing (a) focal object(s) through a poetic process of hierarchical "integration" exclusive of explicit, public, politically based understandings of complex perception and cognition.

25. As examples of the neoclassical tendency, see Rentschler, ed., op. cit. note 3; Corrigan, ed., op. cit. note 3; and Frieden et al., ed., op. cit., note 3. Regarding the eclectic turn, see Thomas Elsaesser, ed., *Early Cinema: Space, Frame, Narrative* (London: BFI, 1990); and Simon During, ed., *The Cultural Studies Reader* (London and New York: Routledge, 1993). Following the structuralist turn, this eclectic, incrementalist formation has been termed a *bricolage* or *combinatoire* (see Fredric Jameson, *The Prison-House of Language: A Critical Account of Structuralism and Russian Formalism* [Princeton, NJ: Princeton University Press, 1972]). For instances of the post-al tendency both of critically responding to traditional teleology and at the same time indulging in a rather uncritical discursive practice harkening back to neoclassicism, see Henry Abelove et al., ed., *The Lesbian and Gay Studies Reader* (New York: Routledge, 1993); and Antonio Callari, et al., ed., *Marxism in the Postmodern Age: Confronting the New World Order* (New York: Guilford Press, 1995).

26. See Benjamin, *The Origin of German Tragic Drama*, trans. John Osborne (London: New Left Books, 1977), where allegory is theorized as a radically contestatory replica of the practice of commodification at the level of cultural (re)production. In "Konvolut N" (op. cit., p. 8 [N 3, 1]), Benjamin names one of the forms taken by this political allegory the "dialectical image," which he describes as a "genuinely historical, i.e. not archaic" moment that "bears to the highest degree the stamp of that critical, dangerous impetus that lies at the heart of all reading." For an extended although finally conservative analysis of this concept, see Michael W. Jennings, *Dialectical Images: Walter Benjamin's Theory of Literary Criticism* (Ithaca: Cornell University Press, 1987).

For instances of other anthologies that have structured contestational or agonistic organizations of textual material, see James Knowlton and Truett Cates, *Forever in the Shadow of Hitler?: Original Documents of the Historikerstreit, the Controversy Concerning the Singularity of the Holocaust*, trans. Knowlton and Cates (Atlantic Highlands, NJ: Humanities Press International, 1993); Gina Thomas, ed., *The Unresolved Past: A Debate in German History* (London: Weidenfeld and Nicolson, 1990); Monica Dorenkamp and Richard Henke, ed., *Negotiating Lesbian and Gay Subjects* (New York: Routledge, 1995); Ian Steedman, et al., *The Value Controversy* (London: Verso Editions and New Left Books, 1981); Diane Elson, ed., *Value: The Representation of Labor in Capitalism* (London: CSE Books; Atlantic Highlands, New Jersey: Humanities Press International, 1979); Sakari Hänninen and Leena Paldán, ed., *Rethinking Ideology: A Marxist Debate* (Berlin: Argument-Verlag; New

York and Bagnolet, France: International General/IMMRC, 1983); and Donald Morton and Mas'ud Zavarzadeh, ed., *Theory/Pedagogy/Politics: Texts for Change* (Urbana and Chicago: University of Illinois Press, 1991).

27. "Konvolut N," op. cit., p. 22 [N9a, 7].

28. Ibid., p. 43 [N1, 1], where *Jetztzeit* is qualified as follows: "In the fields with which we are concerned, knowledge (*Erkenntnis*) exists only in lightning flashes. The text is the thunder rolling long afterward"; also "Theses on the Philosophy of History," op. cit., p. 263. In the "Theses," *Jetztzeit* indicates a site not of "homogeneous, empty time, but time filled by the presence of the now . . . the [historical materialist] notion of a present which is not in transition, but in which time stands still . . . [a] notion [that] defines the present in which [the historical materialist] himself is writing history" pp. (261–262). In other words, the Benjaminian *Jetztzeit* is to be distinguished from the misleadingly allegorical "organic instantaneity," "metapolitical presentness" and "permanent traditionality" of such neo-right ideologues as Alain de Benoist and Julius Evola (see the critique in Thomas Sheehan, "Myth and Violence: The Fascism of Julius Evola and Alain de Benoist," *Social Research* no. 48 [Spring 1981]), as well as from the Christian allegorical "divinational intervention" of theosopher Søren Kierkegaard (see his *Fear and Trembling/Repetition*, ed, and trans. Howard V. Hong and Edna H. Hong [Princeton: Princeton University Press, 1983]). For a recent, post-al account of *Jetztzeit* in the field of Cinema Studies, see Anne Friedberg, *Window Shopping: Cinema and the Postmodern* (Berkeley and Los Angeles: University of California Press, 1993).

29. Directed by Martin Chomsky, ABC-TV, 1978.

30. Directed by Edgar Reitz, 1984.

31. One instance of this battle over the "German" that is of particular interest to this anthology is the bureaucratic culture war taking place between the disciplines of language studies and artistic studies in the contemporary academy. In fact, at one university with which we are familiar, the "right to represent" German cinema has been revoked from the Department of Cinema Studies, which is situated in a school of fine arts, and placed into contestation with the Department of German, which is part of the college of arts and sciences. This despite the fact that the persons hired by the Department of German to teach German cinema courses have or are pursuing degrees in (the Department of) Cinema Studies. At present writing, the two departments have reached a temporary compromise, whereby any courses on German Cinema will be cross-listed under both departments in the university course catalog.

32. See Donald Morton, "The Crisis of Narrative in the Postnarratological Era: Paul Goodman's *The Empire City* as (Post)Modern Intervention," *New Literary History* 24 no. 2 (1993): 420.

33. "Konvolut N," op. cit., p. 19 [N 8, 1].

34. "Thesis on the Philosophy of History," op. cit., p. 263.

35. Ibid., "Modernity versus Postmodernity," *New German Critique* 22 (Winter 1981): pp. 3–14.

ARTICLES AND ESSAYS
ON GERMAN CINEMA

CONSTELLATION A
GERMAN CINEMA STUDIES:

POLITICS OF ACADEMIC DISCOURSE

This constellation questions the relationship of the academy to the broader, sociohistorical changes outlined in the Introduction. It also interrogates the relationship of German cinema studies to broader developments in the Anglo-American academy, particularly the humanities. The stereoscopic reader is prompted to ask how the theoretical approaches of these essays mark out and/or transgress ideological borders of contemporary German cinema studies. For instance, why is German film theory still dominated by the Franco-American notion of auteur criticism, which for German cinema is marked by the publication of the Oberhausen Manifesto in 1960? Why, as Tassilo Schneider suggests, does German cinema serve as an exemplar of "high culture" for the U.S. academy, and what role is played in this typology by the dominance in German cinema studies of the aestheticism of the later Frankfurt School? By the same token, how does Schneider's call for a greater scholarly focus on Nazi and post-Nazi German cinemas, which he designates the products of an extreme ontological lapse, ultimately reinscribe the opposite notion, "low culture," toward a likewise problematic aestheticizing of World War II and the Holocaust? Does John Davidson's recommendation of a transnational German cinema studies contest the nationalism implicit in Schneider's argument, or does his support for a multiculturalist understanding of the "German" represent merely the flipside to Schneider's "original heterogeneity"? Where does their ostensive contestation intersect the arrangement of Constellation J ("The Post-al Public Sphere")? On the other hand, how are Schneider and Davidson's differing postmodernisms fielded and contained by Clay Steinman's reception-theoretical recuperation of the Frankfurt School? How does this approach segue into Patrice Petro's neophenomenological revision of the early writings of Siegfried Kracauer, and how are both symptomatic of broader moves into Weimar film historiography in German cinema studies (Constellation H ["Feminism and Early Weimar"])? How does Petro's critique of epistemological difference in Kracauer's oeuvre distinguish her understanding of aesthetic experience from Steinman's privileging of the formal aspect in Critical Theory, and what are the implications of this aesthetic-theoretical difference for Schneider's and Davidson's conflicting postmodern interrogations of German national-cultural identity? Do any of these essays propose a radical disorderly understanding of the postmodern academic arena?

Reading Against the Grain: German Cinema and Film Historiography

TASSILO SCHNEIDER

T HE SCHOOL OF Cinema-Television at the University of Southern California (USC) offers a canon of film studies courses which are designed to provide students with a background in film history, both American and international. Even the most superficial glance at the structure and contents of the syllabuses used in these courses reveals some rather striking differences between the ways the two categories of cinema are treated. Courses in American film history typically screen and discuss films deemed significant in one of two ways: (1) they enjoyed, at the time of their initial release, significant popular success, or were part (and thus, can be regarded as "typical" or "representative") of a particular "tradition," "development," "wave," or genre; or (2) the film in question effected ruptures, changes, or important "events" in institutional history (e.g., changes in censorship codes, introduction of technical innovations, and so forth). In either case, the choices are determined by the films' relation to, or place within, a particular historical context, and American cinema, by and large, continues to be taught—the lasting impact of auteurism notwithstanding—on the basis of the assumption that its history is socially or culturally relevant.

In contrast, the relevance of foreign (particularly European, but also Japanese) films is deemed to be primarily aesthetic or artistic. As a consequence, the screening lists of courses in American film history include some of the biggest box office successes over the decades, while those shown in classes on European cinemas would, with singular exceptions, not be recognized by any European who is not a film scholar. These presumably unproblematic equations (American cinema = popular cinema; European cinema = "art" cinema) are further reinforced by college catalogues that distinguish between "genre courses" (in which American blockbusters rule the syllabi and from which foreign films are virtually absent) and "authorship seminars" (which are generally restricted to a handful of European *auteurs*).[1] The choice of methodologies proceeds accordingly: the theoretical apparatus applied to American cinema tends to be a combination of media sociology, institutional historiography, genre theory, and a cultural studies approach (which approaches dominate

---

This essay was written specifically for this volume, to which it was submitted in its finalized form in 1993, and is published here for the first time by permission of the author.

varies according to the individual academic's critical predilections), while the study of European cinema has, by and large, remained the domain of more or less refined versions of *auteur* criticism.

The historiography of German cinema provides a particularly interesting case in this context, because it is both typical and atypical of the strategies and methodological models outlined above. German film history has been, and continues to be, a privileged site for the analysis of text-society relationships (in ways similar to, yet also radically different from, the treatment of American cinema, as I will illustrate below). At the same time, the construction of that site has been the object of particularly striking forms of the choices and distortions characteristic of the treatment afforded foreign national film histories.

To return briefly to the USC curriculum (which is in no way idiosyncratic, as can be seen not only in any other film studies department across the country, but also in the available scholarly literature on the subject), the typical German Cinema course consists of background information on, and discussion of, the following films: *The Student of Prague* (1913), *The Cabinet of Dr. Caligari* (1920), *Nosferatu* (1921), *Dr. Mabuse, the Gambler* (1922), *Pandora's Box* (1929), *The Blue Angel* (1930), *Aguirre, Wrath of God* (1972), *The Marriage of Maria Braun* (1979), *The German Sisters* (1981), and *Wings of Desire* (1987).[2]

Clearly, the unquestioned 40-year gap in this (and virtually any other available) scenario of German film history is primarily a function of the aforementioned choices of methodological strategies. A film historiography which conceives of European cinema as a cinema of *auteurs* is merely consistent in jumping from, roughly, 1930 to 1970 in the case of Germany because, during the interim period, German cinema is presumably lacking the kinds of films (or *auteurs*) it would need to have in order to be considered part of film history at all.

Of course, the reduction of national film histories to their "significant" or "major" periods (and films) is common practice (although an unthinkable one where the writing of American film history is concerned). In this regard, the writing of German film history might be seen as merely different in degree (if compared to the writing of European film history in general), in that it inadvertently highlights its more absurd implications (that a national cinema can "die," be "reborn," and not exist altogether at particular points in history). What makes the historiography of German cinema different in kind, however (if compared to French and Italian cinema), is that it has, more often than not, taken recourse to the kind of sociological, or psychosocial, modes of analysis generally reserved for the treatment of American genre films.

Thus, discussion of German cinema has always suffered from a rarely acknowledged inherent contradiction: the presupposition that they are dealing with a cinema of singular artistic "masterpieces" (which have been chosen by the critic on the basis of their aesthetic relevance, in fact, their very singularity, or uniqueness) has never prevented writers from using the very same texts as a basis from which to embark on rather ambitious attempts to assess Germany's cultural history, to construct an image of its national identity and self-understanding, and to diagnose the social and psychological condition of its movie-going inhabitants.

Arguably, the writing of German film history has been shaped by the intervention of one particular critic as much as it has been determined by the more general, structural, and methodological constraints outlined above. There is probably no comparable case of a national film history in which the writing and the conceptualization of that history has been determined, in an almost exclusive and monolithic way, by a single overbearing figure the way it has been in the case of Germany. I am, of course, speaking of Siegfried Kracauer and his book *From Caligari to Hitler* (1947).[3] There has arguably been no other film historian (with the possible, albeit debatable, exception of Georges Sadoul) who has exerted such a strong and lasting influence on the way a particular national cinema, its significance for and relation to social, economical, political, and cultural contexts, has been historicized and theorized. While Kracauer's account of German film history is confined to Weimar cinema and its precursors, its structural presuppositions and methodological strategies have continued to exert a determinate influence over the way German cinema, both before and after World War II, has been conceptualized.

To begin with, Kracauer's book (and, thus, its mode of analysis) controlled German cinema as a field of investigation from the time of its publication until the 1970s virtually uncontested. (Lotte Eisner's *The Haunted Screen*, which foregoes Kracauer's psychosociological approach in favor of placing German cinema in a high-cultural/art-historic tradition, is the single notable exception to that claim.[4]) But even once Kracauer's critical monopoly started to crumble, and new and revisionist readings of Weimar cinema began to appear since the late 1970s, *From Caligari to Hitler* has been able to maintain a sort of critical stranglehold even over its most ardent detractors. There has, to my knowledge, yet to appear a treatment of Weimar cinema that is able and willing to bypass *From Caligari to Hitler* and to avoid having the terms of its analysis dictated by Kracauer's perceived merits or shortcomings.

Equally significant—and, to a certain extent, surprising—is the fact that although numerous critics have by now pointed out a variety of problems with Kracauer's analysis, some of its basic presuppositions and parameters still go unchallenged.[5] Although writers have taken issue with

Kracauer's implicit imaginary construction of the German popular audience in the 1920s, and with the problematic "reflection theory" that provides the basis for *From Caligari to Hitler*, they have, on the whole, accepted the book's construction of the very national cinema it is out to analyze. Kracauer's selection of films—a selection rather obviously determined by the need to build toward a comprehensive, homogeneous, and convincing historical narrative—has very rarely been questioned. Thus, only very recently has there been an awareness that German film history hardly began with *The Cabinet of Dr. Caligari*.[6] And only in the last few years has there been some attention to films and genres that were, according to the sparse information available about audience and box office figures in Weimar Germany, among the most popular (like the historical melodrama and the *Bergfilm* [Mountainfilm]) of that period, but which Kracauer's book, despite its mass-sociological claims, treats rather summarily, if at all.[7]

But whatever methodological shortcuts and historical inaccuracies and omissions Kracauer is guilty of, whatever distortions in the concept of German film history the historiography of Weimar cinema has produced—they pale in comparison to those applied in the writing of postwar German film history. After all, the construction, in film criticism and historiography, of that other "great" period of German filmmaking, of the "New German Cinema," has always, at least in part, depended on the assumption that in between (i.e., from *M* [1930] and *The Blue Angel* [1930], to the signing of the "Oberhausen Manifesto" [in 1962]) there happened, precisely, nothing at all.

The standard scenario painted of German film history since 1945 tends to look something like this: after Germany's defeat in World War II and the division of the country into two nations, the West German film industry collapsed and was unable to participate in the country's general economic recovery during the ensuing years, due to a combination of externally imposed and self-inflicted conditions. These conditions included licensing procedures by Allied occupational authorities who were bent on preventing the emergence of another Ufa and, therefore, decentralized domestic production to a crippling extent. The distribution sector was virtually taken over and monopolized by American companies who held exhibitors hostage to Hollywood product; and the little domestic production there was, was so inferior to imports that German audiences preferred American films and, consequentially, relegated the German cinema of the 1950s and early 1960s to enduring insignificance. (All of this was supposedly happening in a country which, in reality, by 1954 had become the world's fifth-largest producer and in which, from 1950 to 1960, domestic productions consistently outscored U.S. imports at the box office.[8])

Thus, world-cinema textbook accounts of the German film between 1945 and 1962 range from one-sentence declarations of its virtual nonexistence, as in John Fell's *History of Films* ("filmmaking was sparse in West Germany for several years"),[9] to a couple of paragraphs that justify the failure to discuss it with its aesthetic and social insignificance, as in David Cook's *History of Narrative Film*.[10]

Of course, plenty is missing from even the most comprehensive of available film histories. After all, many national cinemas do not figure at all in textbooks. What nevertheless distinguishes the image of the postwar German cinema is the fact that it is, at the same time, present in, and absent from, those histories. To put it differently, it is always present as an absence, namely because without that absence the history of the New German Cinema could not have been (and cannot be) written—at least not the way it has been, as even the most casual look at the literature on that body of films (which has been proliferating during the last ten years or so) makes immediately evident.

The writing of the history of the "New German Cinema" (sometimes distinguished from, more often conflated with, that of the "Young German Film") arguably started (in English) as early as 1971, with the publication of Roger Manvell and Heinrich Fraenkel's *The German Cinema*.[11] Even though it was published several years before the appearance of the "New German" directors on the American festival and art-house circuit, in film periodicals and college courses, Manvell and Fraenkel's book framed the image of postwar German film in ways that have never really been challenged since.

Out of *The German Cinema*'s 159 pages, ten are devoted to what the authors call "The Decline."[12] In this chapter, Manvell and Fraenkel introduce most of the critical paradigms which would henceforth be used in conceptualizing the nature of the German cinema before the advent of Herzog, Fassbinder, Wenders and company. It is unfavorably compared with the state of other national cinemas at the time ("the great output of films from West Germany unfortunately represented a cipher in the development of world cinema, which elsewhere was seeing some of the best work," and "the films made represented as a whole the poorest quality of any major country in Europe");[13] it is charged with mindless escapism, if not outright political irresponsibility ("the films of the period were generally sentimentally fatalistic");[14] and it is compared, or implied to be continuous with, the cinema of the Third Reich ("the box office euphoria of the 1950s and early 1960s extinguished the inspiration of the German cinema . . . as Hitler had done in 1933").[15] All of this culminates in a picture dark and dismal enough ("German films sank ever further into a tawdry banality"[16]) to allow the directors of the "Young German Film" to appear on the

scene as figures who finally lit a candle at the end of the tunnel, the phenomenon to which Manvell and Fraenkel's book devotes its final chapter.

Roughly a decade after the publication of the Manvell-Fraenkel book, a
virtual flurry of writings started to appear (in the United States) which, in
one way or another, elaborated on, or expanded, the final chapter of *The
German Cinema*, now in the light of the complete Herzog, Fassbinder,
and Wenders's canons (among those of a few other, less prominent directors) which, in the meantime, had become accessible to English-language
critics. Since 1980 there have appeared at least a dozen book-length treatments of the New German Cinema (besides countless articles in popular
and scholarly periodicals, and several whole issues of journals devoted to
the topic).

Despite often pronounced differences in their theoretical underpin-
nings and applied methodology, most of these books are structured along
the same narrative pattern. An introductory chapter describes the German
situation in the early 1960s as one marked by an accumulation of conditions that not only had turned it into a cultural wasteland but also presented the most formidable obstacles to any attempts at change. At the same
time, the remaining chapters of these books dwell on, precisely, the
impressive and laudable efforts of the "New German" directors to overcome these obstacles and redeem the situation. Occasionally, the book is
structured according to thematic categories. Usually it simply follows a list
of the most prominent directors, further reinforcing the romantic pattern
which conceives of the history of the "New German Cinema" as a narrative
of heroic struggle against the overbearing paralyzing legacy of a past that,
at least as far as the cinema was concerned, continued into the present,
and a narrative of individual achievements in the face of adversary conditions. A brief overview of some of the more prominent representatives of
this literature will illustrate my point.

According to John Sandford, the West German cinema "floundered
through its first decade," "sank without a trace," and, by 1960, was in a
state of "almost total collapse."[17] In James Franklin's account, the German
cinema of the immediate postwar decades was "disastrously moribund";[18]
in Timothy Corrigan's, it was a "Bavarian cottage industry" that proceeded
from a state of "general crisis" to "disaster";[19] and Klaus Phillips describes
"a national cinema that during the first two decades following World War
II [was] probably the worst Europe had to offer."[20] All three authors proceed from their initial diagnosis of the situation in the 1950s and 1960s to
more or less eulogizing descriptions of how the directors of the New
German Cinema "set out on their own road toward . . . new and demanding standards of artistic quality,"[21] "successfully challenged and partially
usurped the postwar hegemony in German cinema"[22] and, finally, were
responsible for the fact that "West Germany is no longer a cinematic
wasteland."[23]

Less auteurist, more thematically oriented treatments of the subject usually paint an identical picture. Thus, Anton Kaes stresses the enormous achievement of the "New German" directors in finding new ways to represent Germany as a cinematic space in the face of the alleged hegemony exerted by "the legacy of the National Socialist film" throughout the 1950s and 1960s ("how were they to find and create images of Germany and German history that deviated from those of the National Socialist film industry?").[24]

A look at Eric Rentschler's work might figure here as an appropriate summary to this brief overview, not only because Rentschler's has been the most thorough and sustained engagement of postwar West German cinema, but also because it exemplifies the most salient characteristics of the American historiography of that cinema. In *West German Film in the Course of Time*, Rentschler contrasts "the past *abuse* of the cinematic medium in Germany" with the achievements of the "New German Cinema."[25] He criticizes "how *insidiously* the powers of the medium had been *debased* and *misused* during the Third Reich *and after 1945*" before a new generation of filmmakers restored it to "integrity" and "sincerity."[26] Rentschler details the lack of recognition by German critics, the sabotaging efforts of distributors, the contradictions of grant-awarding institutions, the hostility of conservative politicians, and the indifference of West German audiences—the effect being that the "New German" directors tend to appear as unjustly unappreciated, yet courageously determined agents of cultural and political renewal: the filmmaker as social hero, misunderstood and self-sacrificing.

Finally, mention needs to be made of one of the most recent (and, possibly, the ultimate) intervention in the historiography of postwar German film, Thomas Elsaesser's *New German Cinema: A History*.[27] Elsaesser's book is, for my own purposes, noteworthy as much for its omissions as for its contributions. It foresakes the image of a heroic struggle by courageous auteurs in favor of a more detailed analysis of the ways in which the New German Cinema's concept of the *Autorenkino* ("cinema of authors") came to perform a variety of ideological functions. And instead of presenting another political or aesthetic indictment of the situation in the 1950s and 1960s, against which the achievements of the young filmmakers could then be measured, Elsaesser contents himself with tracing the economic and institutional history of postwar German film which generated, or at least allowed for, the emergence of the New German Cinema. Thus, even though its contribution to the drawing of a more comprehensive textual map of German film history since 1945 remains limited to the general concession that "some films from the 1950s are due for a revaluation,"[28] Elsaesser's book significantly distinguishes itself from all the narratives of redemption which are marked by the desire to critically support films and filmmakers deemed laudable and, often, a lack of actual familiarity with the products of the German film industry from the 1950s and 1960s.

English-language accounts of the New German cinema abound in presenting hyperbolic claims and contradictory assessments whose paradoxical nature sometimes verges on the absurd. Thus, the German cinema of the 1950s is by the same authors said to be guilty of, at the same time, "idealization" and "romantic wish-fulfillment" and "a paralysis of the imagination."[29] The lack of a stable, economically sound domestic industry (which would be able to withstand the onslaught of American imports) is lamented, while efforts on the part of commercial producers to secure government support for the industry are regarded as a reactionary backlash against the New German Cinema, and the commercial successes of German genre films during the early 1960s become "setbacks" for the signatories of the "Oberhausen Manifesto."[30] The English or American critic can express satisfaction about the fact that the popular German cinema is allegedly inaccessible to the foreign observer (because the films "were, mercifully, confined . . . to the home market") without letting that fact deter him or her from passing judgment on that cinema.[31]

Finally, in the scenario drawn in some of the texts about the New German Cinema, West Germany virtually becomes a country of illiterates unable to appreciate, or even understand, the achievements of its foremost cinematic artists:

> Separated by massive distances between themselves and the literacy level of their audience, the young German producer-directors were in the exasperating position of trying to teach their German audiences a language they didn't know.[32]

It does not come as a surprise, in the light of analyses like this one, if some American critics felt the need to enlist their support in the filmmakers' efforts "to teach" and to enlighten German audiences and critics about the correct understanding and appreciation of some of its directors—a project to which, for example, James Franklin's whole book is ostensibly dedicated:

> Distance . . . offers a desirable objectivity, and objectivity is a quality that has frequently been lacking in the evaluation of West German directors within the Federal Republic itself. . . . May this book and others like it, as evidence of foreign esteem, help convince these filmmakers' skeptical countrymen.[33]

In fact, the alleged neglect and maltreatment of the New German Cinema at home is almost as much of a critical phantom as the cultural vacuum in which it supposedly emerged. While it is true that there have been attacks, particularly in the popular press, on some "New German" directors and their films,[34] the picture of German film history after 1945 that emerges from German film literature is hardly different from the one outlined above. Thus, the film-historical standard text in German, Ulrich Gregor and Enno Patalas's *Geschichte des Films* (*History of Film*), whose coverage extends up to 1962, devotes a whole two pages (out of 556) to what it calls "Film in the Adenauer Era" (*Film in der Ära Adenauer*)—the cursory treatment presumably being justified by the films's "artistic insignificance and antiquated nature"[35]—while the continuing volume, written by Gregor alone, spends 65 pages on the "Young German Film," based on the claim that it had radically changed the German cinema "for the first time since 1933."[36] From Hans Günther Pflaum and Hans Helmut Prinzler's *Film in der Bundesrepublik Deutschland* (*Film in the Federal Republic of Germany*), the encompassing claim of the book's title notwithstanding, one could easily get the impression that before 1965 there were no films produced in Germany at all, were it not for a couple of statistical tables and the laconic claim that "few productions of the Federal Republic in the 1950s deserve to be mentioned."[37]

Even critical projects ostensibly committed to large-scale cultural analysis have steadfastly refused to extend consideration to popular films on the basis that they engage in distorting indoctrination rather than accurate representations of West German "reality." Thus, in his more recent *Deutschland im Film* (*Germany on Film*), which is devoted to an analysis of Germany's "self-image," Pflaum justifies forgoing a consideration of popular films on the basis that he is interested in "representations of Germany" (*Deutschlandbilder*), and not in "misrepresentations" of it (*Deutschland-Trugbilder*)[38]—as if those "misrepresentations" were not part of the German "self-image."

What are the determinants behind these narratizations with all their selectivity, their dramatizations, their omissions, suppressions, and distortions that have marked, and continue to mark, the historiography of German cinema? What are the cultural, institutional, and ideological conditions of which they are a function? As far as German scholarship is concerned, the answer is relatively simple. Cultural criticism and historiography in Germany, until very recently, has been held hostage to the verdicts of the Frankfurt School. Horkheimer and Adorno's notion of the "culture industry" has, among German critics, never been subject to the revisions it experienced in British, American, and French cultural criticism. The effect has been a virtually complete failure on the part of German scholarship to critically engage in an analysis of popular cultural forms that would be willing to forgo simple political condemnation, in favor of a more complex investigation of the relationships between ideological structures and textual production and reception.

Specifically, this failure has traditionally manifested itself in a refusal to acknowledge that neither a text's relationship to its social and political context nor the ideological disposition of its historic audiences are unproblematically retrievable through a mere comparison of fictional characters and narative patterns with historical "reality." The possibility that ideological conflict and contradiction, in their representation (and negotiation) within a textual system, become subject to the specific refigurations and displacements entailed by the conventions of that system (but also by those of specific generic economies of which the particular textual system is a part) has remained unexplored—as has the possibility that an assessment of the films' ideological effects remains problematic as long as the specific historical conditions of their reception, as well as the modes of that reception, remain unaddressed. As a result, German popular culture has virtually remained academic *terra incognita* at home—a subject of silent embarrassment to university professors, an object of ridicule for their students.

In film criticism, the situation has been exacerbated by the determining influence of the writings of Siegfried Kracauer. Kracauer's *Theory of Film* has shaped the face of cinema studies in Germany arguably even more than *From Caligari to Hitler*.[39] Thus, when academic film criticism started to emerge in Germany in the late 1950s, it did so in the shadow of a humanist-realist doctrine, based on simplistic notions of "reflection" and/or "distortion," and restricted, on the whole, to either impressionist aesthetic evaluation or straightforward sociological content analysis. The parameters of German criticism did not markedly change during the following decade, except, ironically, for allowing the former variety to gain a decided advantage over the latter. The "politicizing" of film criticism in the wake of the events of 1968 manifested itself in Germany mainly as a belated discovery of the *politique des auteurs*. It remained uninformed by contemporaneous developments in France and later, England, the result being a continued refusal to pay attention to anything "popular" or "commercial" (unless it had been redeemed by the auteur theory) on the one hand, and a failure to move beyond analyses of character and plot motivation of the most facile kind on the other (an assessment to which the continuity in Ulrich Gregor's work can serve as the most convincing illustration).[40]

The situation has changed somewhat in recent years. There has been, since the mid-1980s, a modest surge of interest in postwar German cinema (which is arguably due in part to the proliferation of commercial broadcasters in Germany, who fill a significant portion of their schedules with old German films and have thus made many of them more easily available). This new interest has generated, besides some nostalgic reminiscing and conservative revisionism, a handful of serious attempts to subject the films and their cultural context to thorough historical and critical analysis.[41] Unfortunately, even the most ambitious of these attempts bear the consequences of German film criticism's prolonged isolation from the theoretical and methodological developments the field has undergone elsewhere over the course of the last twenty years or so. (At German universities, film studies continues to be taught, as an ancillary field of investigation, in theater departments; critical literature from France, England, and the United States is virtually inaccessible due to a lack of translations; and outlets for the publication of academic work in the field are extremely sparse.[42]) Hence, German studies have thus far remained largely uninformed by the tools and insights provided by contemporary film theory and, as a result, are ill-equipped to approach the films in ways that move beyond sociopolitical content analysis.

In English-language criticism, the situation is clearly different, and the reasons for the reduction of German film history to Weimar and "New German" cinema are, I believe, more complex. To begin with, there is the general problem of the accessibility of foreign films. While the claim that the West German production was, until the late 1960s "mercifully confined to the home market" is somewhat of an overstatement, it is true that prints of the films that were, at one point, distributed abroad, have long since disappeared from sight, that only a handful of them have been rereleased on video, and that dubbed or subtitled versions are, in most cases, unavailable (although a few films, particularly some of the German westerns from the mid-1960s, sporadically appear on American cable television). But similar difficulties have, for one reason or another, had less prohibiting effects where the study of equally, if not even more, obscure texts has been concerned (the existing body of literature on the cinema of the Third Reich being an obvious case in point).

Then there are the filmmakers of the New German Cinema themselves who contributed studiously to the representation of the historical conditions out of which they claimed to have emerged. In interview after interview, speech after speech, and article after article, the "New German" directors never tired of rewriting German film history into, as Elsaesser has put it, "a film history conceived as family melodrama."[43] Wim Wenders lamented "the lack of an indigenous tradition"[44] and the fact that, due to a "hole in the film culture of [the] country which lasted thirty or forty years," their films were "new inventions [because] they had to be."[45] Rainer Werner Fassbinder stressed, "we had nothing, and we started with nothing,"[46] and Werner Herzog claimed, "there was no real German film. . . . We, the new generation of film directors, are a generation without fathers. We are orphans."[47] The concern with absent parents, with a desire for "legitimacy," and with the adoption of foreign, primarily American, directors as substitute fathers, became a virtual obsession among the directors of the New German Cinema during the 1970s and early 1980s, and its implications (that there was virtually no West German cinema, that the few films produced after 1945 were nothing but a continuation of the cinema of the Third Reich, and that German popular [film] culture was largely Americanized) came to form the basis of the New German Cinema's mythology—particularly in the United States where they received wide diffusion through popular media.[48]

However, more important facts appear to be the more general dynamics of desire that determine film historiography and that continue to shape not merely our perception of cinema, American and international, but also our understanding of the dynamics of social and cultural history. (It is here where the legacy of *From Caligari to Hitler* might be most readily apparent.) In other words, at issue is not merely the obvious desire, in the case of German film history, to write a meaningful master-scenario in which the emergence, and the existence, of the New German Cinema makes narrative sense (in the way I have described earlier). More significantly, what is at stake is the function of historiography to contain historical heterogeneity through the construction of a meta-narrative which suppresses multiplicity and process—a narrative from which heterogeneous elements have been eliminated and in which, as a result, the remaining parts can find their place without contradiction.

The point, to be sure, is not to preclude the possibility of homogeneity, causality, or continuity altogether. A comparative ideological analysis might in fact find related dynamics at work behind the structures that govern the textual (and generic) economies which negotiate ideological conflict and contradiction in the films of Weimar, Nazi, and German postwar cinema. (An investigation into the development from the *Bergfilm* of the 1920s, to the *Blut-und-Boden* films of the 1930s and 40s, to the *Heimatfilm* of the 1950s, and the complex interrelationships among these genres, could prove illuminating along those lines.) In order to be productive, however, such an analysis would have to call for the abandonment of a position that can conceive of "continuity" only in terms of stylistic, narrative, and/or political (biographical) parallels, in favor of its understanding as a set of differential relations to conflict/contradiction. It would, moreover, have to take into account the extent to which these relations are in turn determined by distinct textual and generic economies whose structuring function cannot unproblematically be collapsed into the effects of personal, institutional, and political history—as historians of German cinema, by and large, have tended to do.

The two paradigms that have been used most frequently to conceptualize West German culture are the notions of "memory" and "forgetting." West Germans, the narrative goes, traumatized by the humiliation of defeat and the disaster of urban destruction and impoverishment in the wake of World War II, but unwilling to come to terms with their own responsibility for sustaining the political regime that had not only unleashed the war but also engineered the largest genocide recorded in history, "chose to forget." Rather than confront, and come to terms with, the catastrophic loss it had inflicted upon itself and upon others, Germany is said to have embarked on a concerted effort to willfully fall victim to collective amnesia—a project allegedly reflected in popular culture, and nowhere more so than in the cinema. Thus, German films of the 1950s and early 1960s, "in their avoidance of all contemporary relevance, let alone political statements or awkward questioning, reflected the mood of the 1950s in West Germany."[49] The films (like their audiences) "were interested in forgetting the present temporarily and the recent past permanently,"[50] and so the West German cinema allegedly embarked on a long "flight from memory," from which it only managed to return with the help of the "New German" directors who "no longer considered German history taboo."[51]

The "memory/forgetting" paradigm has its origin in the work of Alexander and Margarethe Mitscherlich who diagnosed the collective failure on the part of the German people to come to terms with their national identity by means of working through, and "mourning," the loss experienced in the historic collapse of 1945.[52] In fact, *Trauerarbeit* (literally: the work of mourning) has been a central notion in the historiography of postwar German culture—it is the work allegedly avoided by the films of the 1950s and 1960s, and, at the same time, one of the major achievements with which the New German Cinema is generally credited.[53]

The issue of postwar German film's "historical amnesia" is a complex one which warrants close textual analysis of the actual films in question—a necessary project which is beyond the scope of this essay. Suffice it here to point out that the Mitscherlichs apparently didn't go to the movies very often. In the present context, I am more concerned with calling attention to the fact that if short-time memory loss characterizes aspects of the popular German film after 1945, much of the historiography of German cinema is no less a function of it. If film historians can publish whole anthologies whose all-encompassing titles lay claim to the "German Film" or the "German Cinema," without even acknowledging—much less explaining—that twenty years are missing from their "histories," we are obviously dealing with some sort of "forgetting" on their own part.[54]

However, so as not to be suspected of adhering to some sort of conspiracy theory, I hasten to add that the "forgetting" of the popular German postwar cinema is, of course, also the function of more general institutional structures, such as the aforementioned methodological partitions which assign the study of American films to genre theorists and critics of mass culture, and the rest of world cinema to the chroniclers of "high art" and "great men"—partitions that, in turn, are determined by the historiographical desire which turns messy multiplicity and contemporaneity into neat oppositions and linear sequence. Thus, the "memory/forgetting" dichoto-my serves well to impose conceptual order onto the narrative of postwar German cinema (and to rationalize the way that narrative is related by film historians). The selective application of methodological strategies provides for convenient connections (such as the alleged "continuity" between the cinema of the Third Reich and that of the 1950s—a critical construction that, in its intended meaning, will not survive closer textual or genre-theo-retical analysis, although the term could prove useful within a different context, as I have pointed out earlier). Likewise, the more general distinc-tions—with all their gaps and distortions—that categorize the landscape of world cinema ("popular cinema"/"art cinema," for example) have done an efficient job of supplying easy answers to complicated questions. ("Why are there genres in the American cinema? Because Americans are not as sophisticated as Europeans and like, or need, the reassurances of pre-dictability and repetition.")[55]

Even if the reasons for the peculiar dramatizations and conspicuous sup-pressions of film historiography proved eventually elusive, in the case of German film history some of their ideological effects are strikingly appar-ent. One of these effects has been, until very recently, the virtual writing out of women from German film history altogether—on both the institu-tional and the textual level. The career of Leontine Sagan comes to mind, but the most prominent example is clearly Leni Riefenstahl. Turned into a signifier of "fascist aesthetics"—a process strongly determined by Kracauer, although later enthusiastically supported by Susan Sontag[56]—Riefenstahl and her films have become unavailable for any other discourse that might have a stake in claiming them for different purposes (such as feminist film criticism's search for women *auteurs*).[57]

Where women figure at all in histories of German cinema, they often do so in negative capacities, be it as the representatives of an unsophisticated, corruptible mass audience (Kracauer's "little shopgirls"), as politically com-promised careerists (like Riefenstahl, but also Thea von Harbou, Fritz Lang's screenwriting wife to whom critics generally attribute the ideologi-cally more disturbing aspects in Lang's German films),[58] or as "lesser fig-ures" of the New German Cinema (like May Spils or Doris Dörrie who, due to the "popular" or "generic" quality of their films, are either excluded, or criticized, by most American writers).[59] With regard to the latter role, it is also worth noting that while the New German Cinema has clearly been the film movement of postwar Europe to which women, as directors, have made the most significant contribution, one would not necessarily get that impression from most English-language accounts. Sandford's, Corrigan's, and Franklin's director-oriented books more or less ignore women film-makers. Rentschler's *West German Film* repeatedly (and rightly) indicts the discrimination and neglect female directors in Germany are subject to, but itself devotes no space to the discussion of any film directed by a woman.

On the textual level, it is noteworthy that the period of German film history that, as I have pointed out, is the most maligned and ridiculed (if it is not simply ignored), the 1950s and 1960s, is, at the same time, the period whose genres and films arguably afforded German women the most prominent roles and voices. Very possibly, the fact that the "feminine" genres that dominated German theater screens during the immediate postwar decades—the domestic melodrama and the *Heimatfilm*—have thus far failed to attract much critical attention, is not exclusively a function of institutional and methodological constraints.

But the mostly unacknowledged presence of sexual politics at the center of both the German cinema (popular and "New") and its critical representations, has ramifications that go beyond the evaluation of particular films and genres. For example, while there has been an eagerness among critics both to theorize the New German Cinema's engagement of its audience (as opposed to mainstream Hollywood cinema) and to speculate about the films' thematic concerns as representative of those of its spectators (presumably of West Germans as a whole), there has, at the same time, been a relative failure to investigate which spectators are addressed (what gender, what class, and so forth) and whose concerns are represented. Besides the fact that it would seem to be somewhat problematic to engage in mass-psychological speculations on the basis of a body of films that have virtually never had an audience, the refusal to consider German (and European) film beyond the "art cinema" has not merely been an obstacle, in the case of Germany, to a more complex investigation of text-society relationships. In addition, such a refusal has, on a more general level, also largely confined ideological criticism to the evidence provided by American popular culture and, thus, prevented such criticism from becoming informed by more heterogeneous bodies of texts.

Finally, the overall effect of these limitations might well be one that is diametrically opposed to the political concerns of most film critics and historians. Thus, even though American academics might write and teach European (and world) film history with the goal of combating Hollywood's hegemony and to broaden our perception of the medium and its history, they arguably run the danger of achieving rather the opposite by turning the notion of a "national cinema" into a category whose major distinction is its difference from Hollywood. As Stephen Crofts has pointed out in a recent essay, national cinema production is usually defined against Hollywood. This extends to such a point that in Western discussions, Hollywood is hardly ever spoken of as a national cinema, perhaps indicating its transnational reach.[60]

Obviously, American film has in fact dominated the major part of the world market for most of its history. To exempt it, however, from the discourse of "national cinemas" can only contribute to that ideological fiction (eagerly embraced by American producers and distributors) of its "transnational reach." A film historiography that conceives of Hollywood cinema as a "transnational" institution, and of "national" cinemas primarily as different from that "transnational" standard, that tends to discuss, as a result, foreign cinemas primarily in terms of copies of, deviations from, or "subversions" of American standards, and that continues to affirm that America's alone is a popular cinema—such a film historiography does nothing to problematize Hollywood's hegemony (to say nothing of the perpetuation of national stereotypes and cultural essentialism).[61]

To read German film history "against the grain," then, would hold at least the potential to accomplish several goals. Most generally, insisting on the relative arbitrariness of established critical parameters, drawing attention to the fact that European cinema exists beyond the "art film," and showing that foreign national cinemas are not merely different from Hollywood means to throw into question simplistic models based on binary oppositions, historic developments (turned into naturalized evolutions), and ingrained cultural assumptions. It would also mean rethinking the parameters of cultural analysis in the light of new textual evidence, that is, reconsidering the relationships between textual features and generic structures on the one hand, and the historical and ideological context within which they emerge and disseminate on the other. In the case of twentieth century Germany, this constitutes a subject whose particular significance has been well recognized.

Finally, with regard to German cinema, reading the popular films and genres of the 1950s and 1960s back into German film history would mean restoring an original heterogeneity which has been suppressed in its historical reconstruction. It would mean reinscribing into the historical scenario those discourses (of marginalized social groups, of contradictory ideological positions, and so forth) that this historical reconstruction has thus far succeeded in writing out of it.

Notes

1. Admittedly, it is not that uncommon anymore to find authorship seminars on the likes of John Ford, Alfred Hitchcock, Francis Coppola, or Martin Scorsese. I have, however, yet to come across one on European directors of popular films such as, say, Mario Bava, Terence Fisher, George Lautner, or Harald Reinl.

2. The choice of individual films might vary somewhat, but the names of directors never do. The obligatory *Student of Prague*, *Cabinet of Dr, Caligari*, and *Blue Angel* are invariably complimented by one film each of Murnau, Lang, Pabst, Herzog, Fassbinder, and Wenders.

3. Siegfried Kracauer, *From Caligari to Hitler: A Psychological History of the German Film* (Princeton, NJ: Princeton University Press, 1947).

4. Lotte Eisner, *The Haunted Screen*, trans. Roger Greaves (Berkeley: University of California Press, 1969). Of course, Eisner's book performs its own share of collective psychoanalysis and its author is no less confident than Kracauer in diagnosing "the German mind," "the German soul," or "inborn German likings" (see, for example, pp. 9, 17, and 205, respectively).

5. For recent comprehensive critiques of Kracauer in English, see Thomas Elsaesser, "Social Mobility and the Fantastic: German Silent Cinema" in *Wide Angle* 5:2 (1982) 14–25 and "Film History and Visual Pleasure: Weimar Cinema" in *Cinema Histories, Cinema Practices*, ed. Patricia Mellencamp and Philip Rosen (Frederick, MD: University Publications, 1984) 47–84, but also Patrice Petro's *Joyless Streets: Women and Melodramatic Representation in Weimar Germany* (Princeton, NJ: Princeton University Press, 1990).

6. See Paolo Cherchi Usai et al., eds., *Before Caligari: German Cinema, 1895–1920* (Pordenone, Italy: Edizioni Biblioteca dell'imagine, 1990) and, in German, Heide Schlüpmann, *Unheimlichkeit des Blicks: Das Drama des frühen deutschen Kinos* (Basel: Stroemfeld, 1990).

7. On Ernst Lubitsch's historical epics see Sabine Hake's essay "Lubitsch's Period Films as Palimpsest: On *Passion* and *Deception*" in *Framing the Past: The Historiography of German Cinema and Television*, ed. Bruce Murray and Cristopher Wickham (Carbondale and Edwardsville: Southern Illinois University Press, 1992) and her book *Passions and Deceptions: The Early Films of Ernst Lubitsch* (Princeton, NJ: Princeton University Press, 1992). On the *Bergfilm*, see Eric Rentschler, "Mountains and Modernity: Relocating the *Bergfilm*" in *New German Critique* 51 (1990) and the first issue of a new German film journal, *Film + Kritik*, which appeared in the spring of 1992 and which is devoted to Arnold Fanck, the genre's most prolific director.

8. For yearly figures of distribution revenue see Hans Günther Pflaum and Hans Helmut Prinzler, *Film in der Bundesrepublik Deutschland: Der neue deutsche Film. Herkunft/Gegenwärtige Situation* (Munich: Hanser, 1979. In English: *Film in the Federal Republic of Germany* [Bonn: Inter Nationes, 1983]).

9. John Fell, *A History of Films* (New York: Holt, Rinehart and Winston, 1979) 527.

10. David A. Cook, *A History of Narrative Film*, 2d ed. (New York: Norton, 1990).

11. Roger Manvell and Heinrich Fraenkel, *The German Cinema* (New York and Washington, DC: Praeger, 1971).

12. Manvell and Fraenkel, op. cit., 114.

13. Manvell and Fraenkel, op cit., 116, 125.

14. Manvell and Fraenkel, op. cit., 115.

15. Manvell and Fraenkel, op. cit., 113.

16. Manvell and Fraenkel, op. cit., 124.

17. John Sandford, *The New German Cinema* (London: Oswald Wolff, 1980) 6, 10.

18. James Franklin, *New German Cinema: From Oberhausen to Hamburg* (Boston: Twayne, 1983) 26.

19. Timothy Corrigan, *New German Cinema: The Displaced Image* (Austin: University of Texas Press, 1983) 4, 95.

20. Klaus Phillips, "Introduction" in *New German Filmmakers: From Oberhausen through the 1970s* (New York: Frederick Ungar, 1984) ix.

21. Franklin, op. cit., 29.

22. Corrigan, op. cit., 175.

23. Franklin, op. cit., 54.

24. Anton Kaes, *From Hitler to Heimat: The Return of History as Film* (Cambridge, MA: Harvard University Press, 1989) 8.

25. Eric Rentschler, *West German Film in the Course of Time* (Bedford Hills, NY: Redgrave, 1984) 16, emphasis mine.

26. Rentschler 17, emphasis mine.

27. Thomas Elsaesser, *New German Cinema: A History* (New Brunswick, N.J.: Rutgers University Press, 1989).

28. Elsaesser, op. cit., 17.

29. Manvell and Fraenkel, op. cit., 116.

30. Phillips, op. cit., xvi.

31. Sandford, op. cit., 14.

32. Corrigan, op. cit., 5.

33. Franklin, op. cit., 13.

34. Eric Rentschler presents a brief survey of the relationship between German film criticism and the directors of the "New German Cinema," as well as translations of some polemic responses by filmmakers to the treatment of their films in the German press, in the chapter "Filmmakers and Critics" of his anthology *West German Filmmakers on Film: Visions and Voices* (New York: Holmes & Meier, 1988) 152–67.

35. Ulrich Gregor and Enno Patalas, *Geschichte des Films* (Reinbeck at Hamburg: Rowohlt, 1976) 419–21.

36. Ulrich Gregor, *Geschichte des Films: ab 1960* (Munich: C. Bertelsmann, 1978) 123.

37. Pflaum and Prinzler, op. cit., 40.

38. Hans Günther Pflaum, *Deutschland im Film: Themenschwerpunkte des Spielfilms in der Bundesrepublik Deutschland* (Munich: Hueber, 1985) 6–7.

39. Siegfried Kracauer, *Theory of Film: The Redemption of Physical Reality* (New York: Oxford University Press, 1960).

40. Gregor has been occupying, and continues to occupy, a singularly influential position in determining, and representing, the face of film culture in Germany. Not only the (co)author of the only comprehensive film history in German (besides numerous other publications), Gregor is president of the *Freunde der deutschen Kinemathek*, a nonprofit organization dedicated to the promotion of historic and contemporary non-mainstream cinema (it has its own distribution branch, as well as two "alternative" theaters in Berlin), and the organizer of the *Internationales Forum des jungen Films*, the section of the annual Berlin Film Festival devoted to the exhibition of recent nonmainstream, noncommercial productions from Germany and abroad.

41. The epicenter of this recent development is located in Frankfurt, where the sustained efforts of the *Deutsches Filmmuseum* have thus far produced two major retrospectives of German films since 1946, each accompanied by an anthology of critical texts and analyses. See Hilmar Hofmann and Walter Schobert, eds., *Zwischen Gestern und Morgen: Westdeutscher Nachkriegsfilm 1946–1962* (Deutsches Filmmuseum Frankfurt a.M., 1989) and Jürgen Berger, Hans-Peter Reichmann and Rudolf Worschech, eds., *Abschied vom Gestern: Bundesdeutscher Nachkriegsfilm der 60er und 70er Jahre* (Deutsches Filmmuseum Frankfurt a.M., 1991); but also Gerhard Bliersbach, *So grün war die Heide . . .: Der deutsche Nachkriegsfilm in neuer Sicht* (Weinheim and Basel: Beltz, 1985) and Ursula Bessen, ed., *Trümmer und Träume: Nachkriegszeit und fünfziger Jahre auf Zelluloid* (Bochum: Brockmeyer, 1989). For recent examples of the more nostalgic variety, see Manfred Barthel, *So war es wirklich: Der deutsche Nachkriegsfilm* (Munich and Berlin: Herbig, 1986) and Claudius Seidl, *Der deutsche Film der fünfziger Jahre* (Munich: Heyne, 1987).

42. At the moment, the only academic film journals in existence in Germany are the feminist *Frauen und Film* and, since 1992, the aforementioned *Film + Kritik* (the latter being yet another product of the prolific Frankfurt Film Museum).

43. Elsaesser, *New German Cinema* 215.

44. Quoted in Corrigan, op. cit., 3.

45. Wim Wenders, "That's Entertainment: Hitler," *Die Zeit* 5 August 1977 and "Sein Tod ist keine Lösung: Der deutsche Filmregisseur Fritz Lang," *Jahrbuch Film* ed. Hans Günther Pflaum (Munich: Hanser, 1977) 161–65; both articles translated (the latter as "Death

is no Solution: The German Film Director Fritz Lang") and reprinted in Rentschler, *West German Filmmakers on Film* 127–28 and 103, respectively.

46. From a *Time* interview. Quoted in Rentschler, *West German Filmmakers on Film* 97.

47. Werner Herzog, "Die Eisnerin, wer ist das?" *Film-Korrespondenz* 30 March 1982, 1–2, translated as "Tribute to Lotte Eisner" in Rentschler, *West German Filmmakers on Film* 116.

48. See, for example, Andrew Sarris, "The Germans Are Coming! The Germans Are Coming!", *Village Voice* October 27, 1975, 137–38, and Vincent Canby, "The German Renaissance", *New York Times* December 11, 1977, D15.

49. Sandford, op. cit., 11.

50. Phillips, op. cit., xiii.

51. Kaes, op. cit., 9.

52. Alexander and Margarethe Mitscherlich, *The Inability to Mourn* (London: Tavistock, 1975).

53. See, especially, *From Hitler to Heimat*, but also Eric Santner, *Stranded Objects: Mourning, Memory, and Film in Postwar Germany* (Ithaca and London: Cornell University Press, 1990).

54. For a recent example, see Bruce Murray and Christopher Wickham's *Framing the Past: The Historiography of German Cinema and Television* (Carbondale, Ill.: Southern Illinois University Press, 1992). The book claims to cover what it calls the "postwar era" but, in fact, begins its investigation into West German film in 1978.

55. This answer was given as part of a lecture on genre in an introductory college film course I attended.

56. See Susan Sontag, "Fascinating Fascism" in *Movies and Methods* Vol. 1, ed. Bill Nichols (Berkeley: University of California Press, 1976) 31–43.

57. It is not my concern here to enter into a discussion about Riefenstahl's political allegiances, or the ideological implications of her films. I merely want to draw attention to the fact that the only female director generally considered a "great" filmmaker is excluded from the auteurist pantheon due to her appropriation by the discourse about politics and morality. D. W. Griffith's reception provides an illuminating counterexample in this context.

58. See especially Eisner's *The Haunted Screen*, but also her monograph on Lang (*Fritz Lang* [London: Martin Secker & Warburg, 1976]).

59. See, for example, "Beyond Pure Entertainment?" in Phillips, op. cit., 238–49.

60. Stephen Crofts, "Reconceptualizing National Cinema/s" *Quarterly Review of Film and Video* Vol. 14, No. 3 (1993) 49–50.

61. It seems worth pondering for a moment the implications of the fact that it is *German* cinema the understanding of which, as I have argued earlier, has been more profoundly affected by these characteristics of film historiography than that of other national cinemas, while, at the same time, (West) Germany is arguably the country/society most actively and complexly implicated in relation to the United States (cinema) and its "transnational" claims. The most "Americanized" of all non-American societies, in the wake of its own failed "transnational" ambitions, West Germany and its films obviously solicit critical interest in regard to both of these characteristics. But the extent of this interest on the part of (particularly American) critics and, more importantly, its direction (its rather monolithic focus, together with the discursive operations that focus entails—both of which have been the subject of much of this essay) might, in part, well be a function of a more general attempt to come to terms with the more troublesome and threatening aspects of Germany's political, social, and cultural history.

Hegemony and Cinematic Strategy

JOHN E. DAVIDSON

INTRODUCTION

T HIS ESSAY undertakes a reappraisal of the New German Cinema (hereafter NGC), the national cinema brought about over time by the parallel, though hardly unified, efforts of West German politicians, West
German filmmakers, and international, largely U.S. film enthusiasts. I use
the designation NGC to refer to the state-supported, but relatively independent film production of the Federal Republic of Germany (FRG)
between 1962 and 1989, between the Oberhausen Manifesto and the
opening of the Berlin Wall. Though many styles and production strategies
coexisted in NGC, the system itself privileged *Autorenfilme,* essay or feature films by directors who also wrote and produced their material.
Autorenfilme had the most impact on the reception of NGC abroad, and,
as that reception plays an important role in my study, the comments that
follow refer primarily to such films. Given that this broad time frame and
criteria encompass a number of phases and shifts, it is at one level very difficult to speak of a single NGC. Indeed, one often refers to the period
from 1962 to the mid-1970s as the "Young German Film," reserving the
term "New German Cinema" for the period following the mid-1970s, after
these films had gained international recognition. Among others, Thomas
Elsaesser has eloquently argued that the Oberhausen Manifesto had more
to do with the 1950s than with the films of the 1970s, which mark the full
arrival of a new cinema from West Germany on the international cultural
charts.[1] While acknowledging a certain truth in this claim, I want to stress a
continuity between the concerns of the 1950s that led to the declaration at
Oberhausen and the stylistic and thematic elements of the international
"hits" of the 1970s and 1980s. In fact, both appellations—Young German
Film and New German Cinema—bear the mark of that continuity by using
the undifferentiated, only seemingly self-explanatory label of "German."
The purpose of the present essay is to explore the manner in which the
"Germanness" of this cinema has been constructed, to trace the assumptions that lead to its celebration as *the* German cinema and to outline the
implications of a restored German national cinema within an international
context.

This essay was written specifically for this volume and is published here for the first time by
permission of the author.

When placed in an international context, one can best conceive of NGC as constituting something like a film genre replete with institutional imperatives, generic conventions, thematic similarities, auteurist practitioners, and audience expectations centering around "Germanness." I qualify my claim with the indefinite "something like" because the notion of genre in film studies by no means offers a fixed, readily agreed upon concept.[2] The term "genre" is chosen here to maintain or evoke notions that should offer a framework for thinking about NGC's connection to extrafilmic discourses in an international context. First, a genre does not depend simply on the characteristics of the films themselves, but also on the cultural institutions from which they arise, and on the viewer reactions and expectations that accompany them. Second, a genre is a constructed site where societal contradictions get played out, exposed, and/or artificially resolved. As NGC had little or no audience at home, taking account of its audiences's expectations requires an international framework and implicitly posits a multinational viewing public. This study focuses on the American reception, the importance of which cannot be overestimated in the development of NGC. As is the case with traditional film genre such as the western, the sense that we know what we are talking about when referring to a German film springs from the motifs, iconography, conventions, and themes we believe characteristic of them, which should be catalogued. But the important thing is for an analysis to ask not only *what* elements comprise this sense of genre, but also *why* we get that feeling of a genre as a given.[3] What is being negotiated when one "knows" what the label—it's a German film—refers to?

In the first section below, I outline how the parameters of this genre were determined by the disparate, yet interactive desires of the West German state, West German filmmakers, and international audiences. I argue that in the early 1960s the FRG sought to adopt the cultural legacy of "Germany" as its legitimation for the full reintegration back into the dominant economic bloc accomplished by the *Wirtschaftswunder*. The state wanted to revitalize film as an industry for its potential cultural diplomacy within the West, towards the South and against the East, rather than for its direct commodity value. West German filmmakers of the same period sought a protected space within the market economy dominating mainstream film production and distribution, a space from which they could advance aesthetically and politically challenging programs. At the end of the 1960s, after a number of institutions and subsidy regulations had been established or strengthened, films began to emerge from West Germany that did indeed garner attention among international, art-cinema viewers. These viewers and reviewers, particularly those in the United States, retroactively justified the policies and strategies of West German politicians and filmmakers by hailing a new German cinema of young geniuses sprung from what was taken to be West Germany's post–World War II cultural void. Governmental rhetoric, the young geniuses' self-constructions, and viewer expectations of this new national cinema revolved around the notion of German identity as inherently different within the relatively equivalent community of the West.

In the United States, NGC has come to pass for *the* German national cinema despite the fact that it has remained completely marginal at home (with a few notable exceptions). This dual status supports the claim to an oppositional position over there, and attests to the good intentions and effectiveness of those who have worked with this material critically here. On the other hand, this reception also aids in the international dissemination of an image of a particularly "German" cinema (having "aesthetic" and "political" variations) that actually helps reestablish Germany (the FRG) as a "Kulturnation" in a global context, a legitimate member of the Western hegemonic community in the much older narrative of imperialist and neo-colonial capitalism. This cultural redemption of "Germany" from its post–World War II pariah status is enhanced by two different perceptions of NGC: that it marks the return of legitimate German film culture; and, that it evidences an attempt (governmentally sanctioned, though oppositional) to come to grips with Germany's past. Essential to this relegitimation is an often implicit construction of a reverse *Sonderweg*. While the *Sonderweg* found an unavoidable "special path" to National Socialism by reading teleologically back through the nineteenth century, the newer tendency explains Germany's "alterity," its present peculiarity, by reading teleologically from the Nazi period to the present. While German history certainly places particular burdens upon those attempting to negotiate the pitfalls of identity in the FRG, dangers exist in studying this material in such a way as to discursively connect this history to something essential in the German character. This essentialism was, and has remained to a certain extent, a primary assumption in the reception of NGC.

The second section below traces the occurrence of the German's alterity over the course of NGC. I contend that the discourses of German "otherness" correspond to particular cultural needs within the hegemonic formation of "the West" during the period of uncertainty following colonial independence. The economic ascendancy of imperialist capitalism went hand in hand with an ideological construction called "the West." The West, as has often been pointed out, only exists in juxtaposition to the exotic or alien "non-West."[4] Attempting to rethink or redirect such binaries, James Clifford posits the period of colonial independence and neocolonialism as one in which the "exotic" comes ever closer, which disrupts the anthropologists Western/non-Western distinction.[5] Similarly, thinkers such as Homi Bhabha have retroactively questioned the unitary, fixed nature of the subject positions labeled "colonized" and "colonizer."[6] What also must be remembered, however, is that these shifts necessitate a revision of exoticism and colonization that attempts to resolidify the cultural legitimations of the dominant power blocs, be they national, corporate or sociological. The construction of the exotic "within" the West becomes a mode of culturally reasserting control over the breakdown of previous cultural and geopolitical formations. The figuration of German alterity offers a primary example of a "false othering" that helps reanchor the cultural construct that is "the West"; and, while seen in many areas,[7] is particularly pronounced in NGC, a cultural arena based in large part on a discourse of colonization. I will trace this trope of alterity through several films over the course of NGC, films set outside of Germany and "German" history, in order to make clearer the strained pervasiveness of their constructed "Germanness."

I find the construction of German alterity to exist in the institutional roots, the films, and the reception of NGC. While this alterity appears throughout the U.S. reception, one must be careful to distinguish between mainstream and academic responses. The popular press in general centers "the German" around a propensity to fascism; the academic press often defends a "German" culture of philosophy and art victimized or overshadowed by National Socialism. Even the critical academic reception of NGC, which arose as a reaction against just such assumptions, participates in "othering" Germany. While much of the early critical work rightfully stressed a split between progressive (e.g., Kluge and Fassbinder) and conservative (e.g., Herzog) political vision vis-à-vis "Germany" in *Autorenfilme,* this political scale was measured in terms of a "German history" focused around fascism and German subjectivity. This tendency, combined with other institutional biases, had the effect of closing out concerns centered around ethnicity, gender, and sexuality. Already in the 1970s, these exclusions were combated fiercely by those who saw the "alternative" German film industry becoming mainstream by default, and a recognition of these concerns comes much more to the fore in U.S. criticism in the 1980s, a development to be welcomed. In my view, NGC—the institution, the individual films, and their reception—must be considered in light of both such oppositional possibilities and cultural relegitimating functions. Remembering Antonio Gramsci's depiction of the cultural component in hegemonic political formations and of the contradictory role traditional intellectuals play in such formations, NGC can serve as a vital model to explore the complicated workings of international cultural interaction.[8] In this sense, I hope to offer NGC as what Walter Benjamin would have called a dialectical image, showing its contradictory impulses both within and outside of the trajectory of its own history.

I

To begin remapping this history, I return to examine the cultural and political climate in the FRG at the end of the 1950s, reviewing the stories of NGC's prehistory and origins presented by the West German government and West German filmmakers through the 1960s.[9] These groups' positions, despite the struggle they evidence between them, work together to institute a framework of support for a renewal of West German film. They create space in the market for a cultural product that will serve two distinct functions: first, this new cinema should be a site of cultural resistance, both a sanctioned and contained space, yet one in which serious aesthetic and political opposition to dominant policy could be expressed and processed; and second, this new cinema should act as a kind of filmic Olympic team, winning international recognition for individual filmmakers and the nation. At first glance these functions seem incompatible, but over the course of the 1960s and 1970s they evolve as complementary characteristics of NGC.

The 1960 governmental debates on cinema in the FRG center on reclaiming film as a place to reestablish a national identity disrupted earlier in this century, an identity disrupted not merely by the Third Reich but also by the loss of imperial status after World War I. The debates quite clearly evoke the loss of Germany's colonies as both a blessing and a problem to be overcome if the FRG is to return to take its place among other industrialized powers.[10] The advantage of this loss was that West Germany did not have the problem of direct conflict during colonial independence, such as that faced by France in Algeria. But the FRG therefore lacked experience in dealing with the "Third World," which marked again a disadvantage in relation to other Western industrial powers. Film production should be rejuvenated, the argument goes, as a means of constructing a national image and identity to complement the reconstructive work done by the Economic Miracle, restore the FRG's place within the West (as "Germany"), and gain influence among "Third World" nations. While the cultural-diplomatic function of NGC does not come into effect until the mid-1970s, it is already envisioned in the early 1960s.

Colonialism plays a role for the filmmakers responsible for the 1970s breakthrough (primarily Herzog, Syberberg, and Wenders, and to a lesser extent Fassbinder and Schlöndorff), for they structure theirs as an anti-imperialist discourse. They adopt the position of victims resisting practices that have robbed them of an indigenous tradition of film and continue to stifle its reemergence. Thus, the Nazi period becomes constructed as a colonizing agent disrupting "native" traditions, a situation only exacerbated by the post–World War II, cultural imperialism of the occupying powers, particularly the United States. This cultural history directly and indirectly invokes a Year Zero at 1945, which signifies a gap in German culture and history while marking a clean break with the Nazi past. The notion of a clean break in film history had been attacked by the signatories of the Oberhausen Manifesto in 1962, but it returned a decade later to form the basis of a myth proclaiming the rebirth of German cinema out of a cultural void. The aesthetic and/or political opposition of directors such as

Fassbinder, Herzog, and Wenders, then, is intricately bound with its role in cultural legitimation in an international sphere.

Starting in the early 1970s, popular and critical reception of West German films internationally, particularly in the United States, shows that these functions indeed become embodied in NGC, retroactively validating the strategies and directions chosen to recast film as a vital part of the German image abroad. At every turn one finds references to a renewal of the German vision of Weimar film culture by "young geniuses," references that hailed the return of a German national cinema.[11] But no overwhelmingly positive response meets the rise of these newly state-supported cinéastes in the FRG; in fact, insofar as it did win public attention, NGC came under constant fire. Public opinion ignored or opposed these new developments, and the charge of pandering to artists whose production neither corresponded to, nor generated consumer demand in, the FRG can be heard throughout the history of NGC. To be sure, commercial filmmakers, critics, and producers did not bemoan this neglect by the West German audiences. Rather, they objected to the undue attention from abroad paid to films of questionable quality that were not representative of the West German film production as a whole.[12] This lack of enthusiasm at home attests to both the oppositional and international directions of NGC. It also indicates that the German national cinema, as some have suggested, was to a large extent a projection from the U.S. side of the Atlantic. How is it, then, that U.S. reviewers and critics insisted on labeling a selected branch of this film institution as *the* German national cinema? Why demand to know a German national cinema at all?

A description of "what" seems to characterize this cinema in the reception will offer the material on the basis of which we can move to an analysis of this "why." The most basic assumption made in the mainstream. U.S. press is that there is something "essentially" German about these new films arriving in New York. Two sides of that assumption present themselves. First, the constant references to a rebirth of "classical Weimar cinema" and a return of German Romanticism's vision indicate that a stereotyped notion of what constitutes "German" art precedes the arrival of new German films in the early 1970s. These new German geniuses were seen as another wave of Europeans offering alternatives to Hollywood, which were representative of their particular national entities. Far more strongly than the Italian "Neorealism" and the French "New Wave," the NGC was assumed to reflect, and reflect upon, its national origins. The aesthetic value of individual films was perceived to rest as much or more in their theoretical conception as in their technical polish. German cinema was different from the other European art-cinema movements in that it was "philosophical." As Eric Rentschler put it in describing his own initial enthusiasm about NGC, much of the U.S. response was "born of the belief that [NGC] continued the 'other' Germany [of] literature and philosophy."[13] "Other" than what? The answer forms itself involuntarily—"other" than the Germany of National Socialism and the Final Solution. Two Germanies stand opposed in this image: one is characterized by universities, contemplative philosophy, and culture; one is characterized by concentration camps, fanatical dogma, and barbarism.

The second set of assumptions about the "German vision" of these films also rests on these two Germanies, but conflates them. Related both directly and indirectly to this notion of German vision is what Kent Casper and Susan Linville have called the "pervasive cinematic typology of Germans" in American reviews, which takes form "as a search for political parables referring to the Third Reich, or for *mea culpa* gestures, or for an 'exorcising' of Nazi horrors."[14] Noting the role of the U.S. film and television image-industries in promoting the "Nazi metamyth" (251), Casper and Linville rightly argue that through this superficial preoccupation "fascism can be kept at a distance in its otherness, as 'the German burden' or as a species of German exotica" (255). Both these strains of reception— German film as an outcropping of either German romantic vision or German fascism—point to a preconceived notion of "German identity" being expressed (or avoided) in these films. Even progressive academic critics writing later in the 1970s and early 1980s, who were aware of the West German political context out of which the films of Fassbinder, Herzog, Kluge, Schlöndorff, and Syberberg emerged, tended to focus single-mindedly on specifically "German" issues in a way that often seemed to conflate (West) German history and the German psyche. But we should not conclude that these reactions tell us more about US reviewers than about the films, filmmakers and film institutions themselves, for from the very earliest moments in NGC, the assumption of German identity difference saturates their rhetoric and works.

Two arguments need to be made regarding this twofold discursive construction of Germany. First, it should be remembered that these two Germanies of culture and barbarism are neither opposed nor identical, but rather interrelated. One does well here to keep in mind Walter Benjamin's oft-cited comment that there is no document of culture which is not simultaneously a documentation of barbarism. Culture cannot be seen as divorced from historical reality; however, one should not link a "German" cultural text to "German" barbarism in an essentialist fashion. The strength of this opposition in conceiving of "Germany," however artificial it may be, certainly undergirds the U.S. reception of NGC. Academics tend to separate "das Land der Dichter und Denker" from "Das Dritte Reich"; mainstream publications, on the other hand, tend to conflate notions of German Romanticism with a mad genius that goes hand in hand with the "German" propensity to fascism. Neither tendency is completely without basis or usefulness, but neither does justice to the complex relationship between discursive arenas and sociohistorical realities.

Even Rentschler, whose work is the most perceptive engagement with NGC as a large cultural movement, with which the student of West German film can consult, begins with this binary conception of what "Germany" signifies. For many less attuned than Rentschler to contemporaneous political events in the FRG, these two Germanies occupy the entire spectrum of possibility for representations of "German" art.

The second, and I feel more important, implication of my argument lies in demonstrating how these notions about Germany and German identity are played upon continually to be restructured as the internal other of West. The "real" other Germany, the communist German Democratic Republic, is sutured over in this restructuring, as are different marginalized identity positions of class, ethnicity, gender, and sexuality. These exclusions were attacked, though in different ways, by those involved in the journal *Frauen und Film,* and filmmakers such as Helke Sander, Vlado Kristl, Herbert Achternbusch, Rosa von Praunheim, and Sohrab Shahid Saless. These different concerns also came much more to the fore in U.S. criticism in the 1980s, and one can maintain that NGC truly has become a space for many stories rather than just one. Still, the dominant image of this cinema in its production and reception is of German identity difference, a (self-)construction not altogether without precedent, despite all protestations concerning the Germans' unique situation after World War II. The rhetoric that supports the expressive and "deviant" nature of German identity has its roots in the imperialist discourses of the nineteenth century. On the one hand, this rhetoric insists on the German's membership in the European or Western community; on the other hand, it posits the German as a site of essential difference within that community.

NGC's desire for sameness with a difference brings us back to nineteenth-century rhetoric that laid claim to newly industrialized Germany's inherent, European right to empire—"a place in the sun"—within the "friendly" competition between European powers. Cultural legitimations of these more or less openly capitalist and imperialist aspirations needed to differentiate the German within Europe on grounds other than economic, often positing "inherent" characteristics of the German to establish the "difference." This supposed character difference becomes the key to viewing Germany as a *Kulturnation,* the cultural designation that legitimates the domination of the imperialist powers. *Kulturnationen* became the term which posited an internally differentiated but unified collective of those Western nations which were economically and militarily at odds with each other, yet united in imperialism against the "non-West." With this tradition of German "otherness" as a background, the resurgence of rhetoric about the *Kulturnation* and a "colonized" Federal Republic in the 1960s and 1970s takes on a significance within a larger historical trajectory. The assumption of "Germany as other," of inherent German difference within the West, continues a long tradition of discursively figuring Germany as different within Europe.

We find not only a structural parallel to fin-de-siècle rhetoric, but also a confluence of terminology and ideas undergirding the *Kulturpolitik* surrounding the origins of NGC. The influential governmental report on the state of the film industry in 1962 opens: "Die Bundesregierung vertritt die Auffassung, daß die Bundesrepublik—*wie auch die anderen Kulturnationen*—den einheimischen Film erhalten und fördern muß." ("The federal government holds that the Federal Republic [of Germany]—like the other *Kulturnationen*—must preserve and promote domestic [or native] film.")[15] Contrary to much conventional wisdom, we find that the notion of the *Kulturnation* survives the war in West Germany. This reference clearly echoes the imperialist discourses of the turn of the century, which separated European nations from "others" on the basis of cultural evolution measured on a Eurocentric ruler. In the debates around the Film Subsidy Bill (1967–68), one does find an objection by FDP Representative Moersch to the requirement that "the director must be a German citizen or originate from the German cultural tradition" ("aus dem deutschen Kulturbereich stammen") in order to be subsidized.[16] Moersch remarks that this seems to maintain the definition of the *Kulturnation,* but his objection is that it remains too narrow! Such a definition excludes the German filmmakers who emigrated to the United States "back then," but "whom we still should understand as German artists" (201). In other words, the only objection raised to the reintegration of the *Kulturnation* is that it does not do enough to recognize "German" artistic traditions. Neither its nationalistic biases nor its troubling historical resonance seem to raise objections. The return of the *Kulturnation* sheds light on the desired *Mitwirkung* with developing nations which is stressed in many of the film debates. Such "cooperation" should maintain the hierarchy between "developed" and "underdeveloped" lands.[17]

One of the most interesting aspects of the official debates about film in the 1960s is the general agreement on the precedence in this instance of cultural over economic concerns. Ensuring the viability of West German film, the 1960 governmental report asserts, is not so much a question of saving a troubled branch of its industry, as a question of saving a medium that is central to the perception of West German culture at home and abroad:

> Die kulturellen Gründe sind so vorrangig, daß ein Verzicht auf den deutschen Film nicht hingenommen werden kann. . . . Schließlich ist die Erhaltung der Lebensfähigkeit des deutschen Filmes für unsere politische und kulturpolitische Arbeit im Ausland unerläßlich. Die Bundesrepublik braucht den deutschen Film . . . als nationale Repräsentanz. (UFITA 40, p. 76)

The cultural implications are so important that doing without German film cannot be accepted. . . . Ultimately, maintaining the viability of German film is essential to our political and cultural tasks abroad. The Federal Republic needs German film . . . as a national representative.

Film is seen as the most effective national representative, a representation of the nation in the international sphere. Thus, we see that the views presented in the early 1960s by the Government Report under the CDU and by the cultural politicians of the SPD, which came to power later in the decade, did more than merely toe the commercial-film industry's line. The initial push to set up the institutions of NGC takes place within a climate of *Kulturpolitik* recognizing the need to construct an image of "Germany" commensurate with its rejuvenated economic status. This rhetoric establishes the need to reconnect with the cultural traditions disrupted by the Nazi period. This would help relegitimate West Germany as an active member of the *Kulturnationen,* a status Germany in actuality had lost at the end of World War I. These politicians felt film was the medium to reconstruct and project an image of the FRG as "Germany," but one removed from the troubling historical associations with the term. Ironically, these wishes were served best not by the films that painted a positive image of Germany, but rather by those which continually evoked the problems of German identity in German history. Such irony highlights the role of *Kulturarbeit* within the West as the realm in which intellectual struggle against, and identification with, dominant orders are intricately interwoven.

One cannot dispute the aesthetic and/or political opposition of the directors who became "Wunderkinder" in the eyes of the international film community. At the same time one must recognize that the foundation of their opposition was laid upon a relationship to German culture and identity based on loss. Wim Wenders goes so far as to say that the Weimar tradition has been made inaccessible to him. When he saw the films of Fritz Lang for the first time, he found them "very strange. Stranger, at least than the American cinema, or the French, or even the Russian. Because: these films were German films and couldn't get through to me, my head was always full of other images and other enthusiasms. For fathers other than this one."[18] Werner Herzog creates for himself a more active role in reestablishing a tie to the past: he walks from Munich to Paris to save Lotte Eisner, the surviving matron of Weimar film, from death in 1974.[19] The legitimacy of German cinema cannot do without her blessing, he claims. Herzog undertakes the pilgrimage to Eisner much as in "the Middle Ages when someone was crowned as emperor, this was a matter of succession and above all political power, but one had to go to Rome to obtain the necessary legitimacy."[20] Hans-Jürgen Syberberg is another, even more problematic example of a filmmaker who constructs a void in German (film) history out of which he can arise. Germany is a dead and centerless country now, he often writes: "it was above all in the voluntary surrender of its creative irrationality, and perhaps only in this, that Germany really lost the war."[21] Syberberg blames Hitler for destroying the German myths, and it is uncovering those myths from under the rubble of the Third Reich that he takes as his task in his films. In order to enact the "new mythologizing of the soul" he finds it necessary that "Hitler is to be fought . . . with Richard Wagner and Mozart (pp. 8–9)." Because of Germany's past, these filmmakers, and many others, claimed that their language had been violated, their subconscious colonized, their ability to fully develop an identity impaired, and their traditions fragmented.

These notions of loss and colonization rely on the same "year(s) zero" myth evoked by governmental rhetoric on film, despite the different ends these two groups desired. To the FRG state and the filmmakers themselves we must add the U.S. response conceiving of a cinematic void in German film. This American response parallels the desire in the FRG (and other Western countries bent on recouping Germany as a legitimate ally against communism) to distance the atrocities of National Socialism by positing a ground zero at the end of the war. A concentration on underlying "stylistic and formal eccentricities" marked this reception, which immediately takes up the task of describing what made German films different.[22] As we have seen, this difference centered around preconceived connections between German Romanticism and Fascism. The parameters of NGC as a genre are grounded in a sense of German "otherness."

In these stylizations, the West German filmmakers are depicted as colonized subjects engaged in what we might now call a "minor discourse."[23] A "minor discourse" can develop when a subject ostensibly in full control of the dominant discourse (which is, in Deleuze and Guattari's formulation, written language) enacts subtle changes and subversions in it due to traces of a minority status within that culture which cannot be overcome. The similarity of various descriptions of these directors to the elements attributed to a minor discourse are striking if one conceives of the dominant "language" which "minoritizes" them to be that of Western film. The conditions against which the New German Filmmakers rebel are a "product of damage"; the Western eyes viewing this national cinema from without were witnessing a "necessarily collective" expression; indeed, even the struggle with subjectivity is approached as if these directors represent a minority, which "by virtue of [its] very social being, must begin from a position of objective nonidentity" rooted in its "cultural marginalization vis-à-vis the 'West.'"[24] The supposedly self-made "geniuses" who became the focus of the mid-1970s reception of NGC in the (more or less) mainstream, English-language press, all use various articulations of this minor status to promote themselves. The appropriation of a minoritized position by and for these New German cineastes becomes their ticket back into the cultural good graces of the "West."

Certainly, no one could argue seriously that Germany was just like any other European nation in the 1960s and 1970s or that filmmakers there worked under universal conditions. Foreign industrial, legal, and military forces did occupy the country, and the history of German atrocities did occupy the minds of many young German intellectuals trying to effect change. NGC in its international reception—a reception that found German cinema represented best by the "big four" of Fassbinder, Herzog, Syberberg, and Wenders—became an arena in which this minoritized status could be confronted in a variety of ways. My aim here is not to dispute the many progressive elements in West German film, but rather to maintain that NGC has been constructed from within and without as a "minor discourse" in a way that also serves dominant demands. Regardless of intentions, the focus of NGC on the peculiarities of German history in relation to (non-)identity formation repeats and updates a pattern from the end of the last century. Where once the drive toward inclusion in the community of *Kulturnationen* by obtaining an empire was accompanied by a rhetoric of an inherent difference in German character or soul, now the difference lies in the questioning of German identity in the wake of German history. Films offering this reconstruction in its most extreme form erect a straw figure of fascism linked to German culture and inherent in the German personality. Fascism thus becomes reduced to the internal extreme of Western identity formation that is experienced and contained through the representation. Such depictions clearly cannot address the complexities of fascism either as a general political moment within capitalism or as a specific moment in German history. But even films (and their reception) less openly centered on German fascism often use the touchstone of German identity as "other," as uncannily different from within Western identity. The sense of a connection to "German difference" itself persists at every turn, constantly reaffirming German vision as representative of the "inner other" of the West. In the remainder of this essay, I focus on the relationship between the positions of the non-Westerner and the construction of the "German" in the genre of NGC, a relation which both challenges and supports the continuing re-formation of the imagined Western community in the ever-changing configurations of neocolonialism.

II

In exploring my notion of NGC as genre, I have contended that the community for which NGC negotiates contradictions seems to be as much an international as a national one. I refer to this audience as the intellectual strata of "the West," by which I mean not simply the cultural construct created against the "other" or the "exotic," but also the globally hegemonic bloc descended from the late nineteenth-century imperial powers. The structure of German difference within Western sameness that marks the rhetoric around NGC borrows its logic from a contradiction already inherent in Europe at the end of the last century: the struggle of different capitalist powers amongst themselves within the unity of European imperialism's struggle against the non-European world. Furthermore, the post–World War II world of NGC corresponds to the final collapse of European colonialism's formal structures. It may be only coincidental that the rise of NGC parallels colonial independence and the defeat of U.S. aggression in Vietnam, or that the breakthrough year for NGC in the United States (1974) corresponds to the first post–World War II year in which West German exports exceed U.S. exports[25]; however, these are telling coincidences.

These nonfilmic circumstances are elements in the shifts into neocolonialism, a context vital to fully understanding NGC as a cultural event in the broadest sense. This is a period in which the independence and increased mobility of non-Westerners force the "old" power relations of European imperialism and colonialism to enter new stages of crisis and contradiction. It is also an era of intensified intra-Western rivalry marking the beginning of late capitalism.[26] "With neocolonialism comes the idea of a Third World," states Gayatri Chakravorty Spivak in her characteristically pithy manner in an interview with Robert Young.[27] Neocolonialism is economically rather than territorially occupational in nature, hence

> the production of knowledge with neocolonialism seems to have a much subtler role and it's much harder to pin down. It's not just colonialism all over again . . . It's displaced colonialism. . . . This benevolent multiculturalism [centered around identity] is one of the problems of neocolonialist knowlegde-production. . . . Neocolonialism is identity talk (pp. 224, 226, 234).

These final statements indicate that the increasing production of discourses about identity are both enabling and disabling for anti-imperialist and anti-essentialist struggles in marginalized territory. The role of Western intellectuals in these struggles is a contradictory one. Spivak sees present trends in the humanities and social sciences as particularly problematic, for they engage in a kind of "unwitting neocolonialism" as they are very interested in the production of these identity models that will seem like they are coming from other cultural spaces. . . . One of the strongest [functions] of unwitting neocolonialism is the production of models of identity from supposedly the history of other places where the epistemic transformation is rights talk among a certain class. . . . Cultural *ism* in the other Third World is in itself also a class-based thing (pp. 225–26).

Spivak stresses that models of identity from "other cultural spaces" can both combat *and* continue the relations of colonial history.[28]

I find these misgivings about the production of identities from "other" cultural spaces instructive in the case of NGC. The unsystematic, yet sustained construction of Germany (i.e., the FRG) I trace above, when set in a neocolonial framework, shows NGC consistently involved in recreating an "otherized" German identity, which helps resolidify the West in the face of continuing crisis. Such a model of identity from dominant Western cultural spaces that are encoded as "other" would be the counterpart to the kind of neocolonialist identity discourse to which Spivak refers. The continual assertion that German identity springs out of its "other" history ("out of" meaning *from* as well as *away from*) in NGC can then be seen as the home front of a contested neocolonialist knowledge-production. On the one hand, such constructions in NGC offer a space for genuinely oppositional intellectual discourse, both within the FRG, in the United States, and elsewhere. On the other hand, as the parameters of discussion have traditionally remained centered around "German" issues on "German" soil, that space has remained a site for the reproduction of a stereotyped German (non-)identity in crisis.[29] This cultural-identity trouble in an international framework is also a class-based thing, inasmuch as the intellectual re- and deconstruction of German identity maintains an internal, national "other," thus occupying and neutralizing the otherness "infiltrating" and exposing the brittleness of the West.

I do not mean to deny the radical import of much of NGC that has not become mainstream or, for that matter, of many *Autorenfilme*. Rather, I want to stress exactly the contradictory nature of cultural production, particularly "national" cultural production and reception in a world increasingly assumed to be under the sway of internationalism. The multinational corporation dominates the symbolic landscape as *the* vehicle of postmodernization in late capitalism. But this symbolic view, while perhaps allowing one to trace the continued uneven development of global relations, smoothes over the unevenness *of* the development. Nations, nationalisms, and other supposed vestiges of the nineteenth century have not disappeared. As David Harvey contends near the end of *The Condition of Postmodernity*,

> Geopolitics and economic nationalism, localism and the politics of places, are all fighting it out with a new internationalism. . . . Thatcherism still proclaims itself as a distinctive national project resting upon peculiarities of the British (a proposition which both left and right politics tend to accept). International control over finance capital looks inevitable, yet it seems impossible to arrive at that through the collectivity of national interests.[30]

In a manner reminiscent of this description of Thatcherism, NGC has been constructed by both left and right cultural critics as both a unique product and a reflection of German peculiarities. The genre of NGC helps negotiate the precarious balance between the international and national in the identity of the West.

The development of NGC over its first twenty years proves to be dominated by personalities, films, and audiences concerned almost exclusively with German identity difference. Indeed, one finds indications of this already in the films attracting early notice at the 1967 New York Film Festival: Volker Schlöndorff's *Der junge Törleß* and Alexander Kluge's *Abschied von Gestern*. While these two films can usefully be juxtaposed as marking the distance "between a conventional notion of cinematic realism and a more radical one" within NGC,[31] both, to their credit, evidence the beginnings of intense engagement with German history previously absent from post–World War II film. Reviewers' initial reactions to them indicate the tenor of the expectations awaiting these new films. Schlöndorff's film is applauded as an "academic display of the slow, cold tempering of human intellect in a spiritually sterile environment . . . that [has] given us some understanding of the post-Bismarck Teutonic mind."[32] Kluge's attempt to subvert standard viewer identification is disliked because his does not develop the character of Anita G. either as an individual or as an allegory for Germany: he applies "his camera like a clouded microscope, side-stepping simple compassion for bland, clinical detachment" in reference to Anita G..[33] Both the praise for *Törleß* and the dismissal of *Abschied* arise from the expectation that German films not only be "German" in their form, but also about the "German."

No filmmaker shows an awareness of "the German" being the gateway to international audiences' approval as strongly as Werner Herzog. In his *Aguirre, der Zorn Gottes* (1972) we see that the reified preconceptions about German identity in art become the basis of establishing NGC as a genre not only through its reception, but within the films as well. Aguirre is first equated with the alterity of European women and Native South Americans, then he assumes their positions as *the* other at the film's end. This otherness is condensed in a speech invoking the primary taboos of identity formation in Western psychoanalysis and structural anthropology (incest), and in Western sociopolitics (the dynasty of racial purity— National Socialism). The reception of *Aguirre* continually takes the film as an allegory for fascism and (or as) the extreme condition of the human soul. A similar pattern can be located in Herzog's *Fitzcarraldo* (1982), which literally reproduces much of *Aguirre*. These two central figures are marked with the attributes commonly associated with the "German" (protofascist) character: megalomania; unfathomable depth of soul that defies all physical constraint; power to command and control; and mad genius. *Fitzcarraldo*, however, also indicates the generic dilemmas facing

West German filmmakers after the initial successes of the late 1960s and early 1970s, when their films took the New York Film Festival "by storm." One needed to continue playing to expectations by invoking forms and themes considered to be "German," yet change and develop them so that the next project seemed new. The "otherness" of the German remains a necessary, yet shifting response to these expectations throughout NGC.

In arguing for an understanding of NGC as a kind of international film genre, I have maintained the importance of the United States as a site of reception in shaping the expectations of what "German vision" should look like. Indeed, it can be argued that the most important "foreign" setting for West German film after the mid 1960s is "America." To offer further evidence of the importance of the "German" in NGC, I turn to two works from the mid-1980s which engage directly with identity concerns of West German directors in the face of constant U.S. presence. Though they differ radically in tone and style, Wim Wenders's *Paris, Texas* (1984) and Percy Adlon's *Out of Rosenheim* (1987) have much in common: both are narrative films shot on location in the western United States; both were relative box-office successes in this country, despite *Paris, Texas*'s poor reviews in the mainstream press; most interestingly, both mark significant turns in the discursive structuring of the German/American problem which pervades so much of NGC. These films challenge, rework and resituate the stereotypes about "German" identity, which had become the required components expected from a "German" film. We have seen how Herzog's films parallel native South Americans with an explorer marked by "German" characteristics who later usurps their place of "otherness" entirely; Wenders and Adlon parallel the figures of the German and a marginalized woman in such a way as to maintain Germany's "otherness" even while moving toward more equivalent positions in the "western" (German-American) family. They place these women along the circuits of telecommunications, transportation, and attitudes in and about the United States, in and about German film. By mixing elements of the road movie with those of the family (melo-)drama, these films realign the German question in what is represented as the specifically gendered situation of the nuclear family.[34]

I want to situate *Paris, Texas* and *Out of Rosenheim* as important shifts in what may be quickly characterized as typical representations of "America" in NGC: "America" as a kindred, yet troubling identity; "America" as a vast space of opportunity not realized; and "America" as Hollywood. These typical elements may be found not only in the films themselves, but also in American viewers' expectations about "what a German movie about 'America' is." The reception of these pictures in the U.S. press invariably makes specific reference to the role of the German imagination in depicting "America." Reviewers here panned *Paris, Texas* because it failed to adequately live up to those expectations. They depicted Wenders as repeating old projections onto the United States by Germans that once were powerful, but now seem overwrought and symbol-soaked. The film seems motivated by "reasons only French movie critics understand."[35] At the same time, Wenders was condemned for not living up to expectations about what *his* films should be. The national component resonates even more strongly in the "paradox" that "*Stranger than Paradise,* written and directed by Jim Jarmusch, an American born and bred, looks and sounds much more like a Wenders film than *Paris, Texas.*"[36] A switch seems to have taken place, for Americans now make "movies about America [in the style] of an extremely well informed European who resolutely refuses to impose on it any preconceived notions about the country" (Canby). But there is nothing in such reviews to indicate how *Paris, Texas* imposes its preconceptions, or how Wenders's earlier films did not do just that. Adlon, on the other hand, continually received praise for having expanded that German tradition of imagining "America" to make it even more enjoyable. It is precisely his "sentimental vision of America," his "endearingly quirky version of America" that wins him accolades.[37] Thus, the German aestheticizing of America does not in itself explain the different reactions to these films. I would suggest that a key to this discrepancy rests in the position of the "German" *within* these representations. As *Paris, Texas* lacks a specifically German character in the narrative, there is no figure to allow for an obvious self-reflection on the "German" in the film, which would soften the impression of this as a "tourist's home movie." By contrast, Adlon solves the dilemma of seeming to be a tourist with a camera in *Out of Rosenheim* by making the union of a German and an American the core of his story. Adlon shifts his emphasis from the open road to the "home" in which the representatives of Germany and America, ultimately so similar, can come together.

If this presence or absence of "the German" at least partially explains reviewers' reactions, it seems to me they do not do Wenders's film justice. The German/American problem does remain essential to *Paris, Texas,* but it introduces itself at the subnarrative level of casting. Now the "German" questions the "American," rather than the other way around, as was so prevalent in Wenders's work in the 1970s.[38] The West German actor/director Bernard Wicki, playing a drunken doctor, opens the film by asking a lost American man, Travis, about his identity and whereabouts. Serving as the free-floating vehicle of the camera, Travis's journey through the film reestablishes his identity by resolving the story of his marriage to Jane, played by Nastassja Kinski. Jane's role as the partner of Travis's confessional remembering, which solves his riddles and sets him free, makes her vital to the course of the film, despite her minimal time on-screen. Thus, a recognizable German figure has the film's first line and poses the American's identity as problematic, which in turn revolves around a German actress.

The "German" is present, but bracketed beneath the level of narrative.[39] It would seem that Wenders wants to move away from directly thematizing German "otherness," but cannot yet banish it from his films altogether.[40]

Out of Rosenheim responds to new expectations arising out of NGC's previous success, the FRG's economic success, and the shifting "American" moods during the conservative 1980s. Adlon foregrounds this identity problematic by casting Marianne Sägebrecht in the starring role as the German Jasmin Münchgstettner and playing on the notion of Rosenheim as a provincial colony one now must abandon. Several factors must be mentioned which help pave the way for Adlon's marriage of equality between this German and an "other" Westerner, Brenda (played by the African-American actress C. C. H. Pounder). First, the reversals of identity positions in Wenders's *Paris, Texas* are vital, along with its notoriety both at home and abroad.[41] Second, the conservative film policies under Friedrich Zimmermann's *Wende* necessitated a more viewer-friendly approach on the part of filmmakers, which clearly characterizes Adlon's films. Finally, the increasing role of the FRG as the essential economic catalyst at the heart of the West experiencing an illusory stability in the "conservative revolutions" led by Reagan, Thatcher, and Kohl corresponds to the shift in representations of Germans as full partners in the West which *Out of Rosenheim* presents. The move to a relativism of cultural identities that characterizes knowledge production in neocolonialism takes a large step forward in these representations. However, the notion of Germany as "other" remains in place, maintained by the equation of a renewed German woman with Adlon's "representatives" of the U.S.-American underclasses: that is, a black woman, native Americans, and (peripherally) working-class men. Though the family at the Bagdad Café magically works its way up to middle-class prosperity, the false "othering" of the German will continue through to the film's end. The manner in which this marriage of affinity actively displaces problems of race and gender in the U.S. context favors an empty pluralism, which distances the German from "her" past while maintaining a false notion of the German as an "other" which has almost, but not quite, been overcome.

The connection of German identity to circuits of transport and telecommunications in a foreign location essential to *Paris, Texas* and *Out of Rosenheim* reaches a parodic highpoint in Ulrike Ottinger's *Johanna D'Arc of Mongolia* (1989). Ottinger, who uses the suggestive intertextuality of international casting to the full, employs an actress particularly associated with the films and theater of Fassbinder (Irm Hermann) to play a "German cultural traveler" who would be lost without her *Baedeker,* the only German principal in the film. This figure is at the center of a series of discourses about German/Jewish identity and German historical roots, which in turn raise the possibility of a critique of the German film institution itself. *Johanna D'Arc* offers a sensitive and often stunning approach to many of the problems of "false othering" that I have been exploring. In this work, self-reflexive filmic and stylistic techniques intervene in dominant discourses on gender, genre, and sexuality norms, as well as rejecting easy answers to the questions of "German identity" which for so long were the mainstay of *Vergangenheitsbewältigung* ("coming to terms with the past"). In Ottinger's film we can also see a critique of orientalisms based on binaries of East and West, and of the historical tradition of imperial/colonial exploitation. On the other hand, in her production of the "encounter" with the foreign and the nomadic we find troubling repetitions of orientalist discourses from the last century.

The contemporary tendency to privilege the "nomadic" as a trope of resistance underlies *Johanna D'Arc,* in which every possible figure of "otherness" from Western norms appears loaded with the ideological characteristics ascribed to it by fin-de-siècle discourses. Those stereotypes rested, among other things, on a binary of rootedness versus rootlessness; Ottinger's film reverses the nineteenth-century weighting of these terms, privileging the (supposedly) rootless over the rooted. For example, the rootlessness of "Jewish" culture becomes the norm against which the abnormality of a unified and rooted "German" culture falls apart. The nomadic nature of the great melting pots of culture (the United States and the USSR) exposes the notion of "pure national culture" as a farce. *Johanna D'Arc* thus successfully dismantles cultural constructs of otherness, but this strategy of repetition and displacement does not apply to all the oppositions in the film. The triumph of a work like Ottinger's comes from having exposed the fantastic constructions of otherness within the West; its disappointment comes from reinscribing that otherness all too believably onto the Mongolians.

The critiques within *Johanna D'Arc* rest upon accepting cultural stereotypes and playing them up to the point at which their internal contradictions cause them to fall apart. But a danger inheres in this method: it enacts the next stage in the logic of neocolonialist legitimation—the move to complete cultural relativism. The term "cultural relativism" denotes both a recognition of cultural difference and a misrecognition of power relations between cultures. The nineteenth-century Great Chain of Being of the racial sciences, which undergirded so many oppressive social and ethnic hierarchies, denied the status of "culture" to those other than moneyed, European males. This Great Chain of Being corresponded to a material chain of existence also placing the European at the top. Cultural relativism wishes to redress the wrong of denying the worth of other societies, and hence posits that all people have culture that is of equal value. But in assigning this equal value, it often calls upon a relativism whose logic insists on an autonomy for these cultures, which maintains they can only be "understood on their own terms," including material terms. Cultural relativism thus naturalizes the material inequalities to which the previous cultural status (or lack of it) corresponded.

Because of this naturalization of material inequalities, cultural relativism acts as an alibi for neocolonialism. Ottinger's move to the realm of cultural transference aims to enable the imagining of a new type of community, one not bound to nineteenth-century nationalism and national identity. Her brilliant film springs from an acknowledgment of difference and an attempt to appreciate it. But, while revisiting the Silk Road as a "guestbook of cultures" may indeed show how exoticism becomes a function of misunderstanding,[42] it does not necessarily address the question of who can access the book, let alone translate it. Her deconstruction of European orientalisms contains what Rey Chow has called the "double disappearance of domination and othering," which preempts "the insurgency of the confrontation" between the "First" and "Third world."[43] This double disappearance acts to reinforce unequal structures already in place, as this new way of imagining community also corresponds the new phases of late capitalism. The parameters of the "Pacific Rim" offer an example of how new, multicultural communities can be imagined that do not necessarily dispel domination, but rather accommodate real shifts in global economic relations based on more flexible structures of accumulation.[44] The neocolonial slant of this film constructs East-West material relations as a text that has been creatively misread by the dominant cultures of the West. This imaginary construction mirrors the strategies of neocolonial legitimation through cultural relativism. So, while showing up one fallacy of usurping "otherness" from a dominant position, Ottinger advocates a kind of flexible cultural accumulation fully in line with the present phase of neocolonial "othering."

With this very brief examination of key texts, I hope to have indicated how "German identity" has remained a central concern throughout NGC both within individual representations and in their reception. This concern itself causes a double disappearance of domination and othering. While often enabling a vital examination of (West) Germany's past that had been largely absent in films between 1949 and 1962, the tropes of German alterity also served to displace cultural spaces of "otherness" that desperately needed and continue to need attention. Some might question whether the framework I have erected and the type of examination I have undertaken do not compound rather than address this problem. I concede that there is a real danger here and feel one must carefully avoid relegating anything to the status of a "secondary contradiction" or marginal concern. My aim has been to develop the other side of this often progressively intended stress on German history. Seen in the light of neocolonial relations still dominated by the West, the identity of West Germans was not "other." Despite the rhetoric of politicians and filmmakers to the contrary, and despite the American insistence upon finding a national cinema expressing an essentially different nature, their nation and film industry were not colonized in any sense comparable to historical colonization. But it is precisely because of this "false othering" that understanding NGC as a realm of neocolonial knowledge-production is important.

Representations such as Ottinger's 1989 *Johanna D'Arc* indicate that West German film has reached a point at which it can overcome the construction of the "German" that was its mainstay through the early 1980s. What Ottinger's film accomplished in representation, the fall of the Berlin Wall accomplished in geopolitics. The collapse of the GDR signaled the success of the Cold War politics out of which NGC was born. West Germany had adopted the cultural label of "Germany" and had legitimated its reintegration into the West, both economically and culturally. German cinematic production is now making a place for itself in the international market, requiring diminished governmental assistance. This is vital, as the end of the Cold War will give politicians even less incentive to subsidize noncommercial production, though it is still too early to see how they will stand on the cultural ramifications of "free market" initiatives such as the General Agreement on Tariffs and Trade (GATT), which is currently the source of great debate in Europe.[45] More than the death of Fassbinder, the dissolution of the *Autorenkino,* or the conservative *Wende* of the 1980s, the fall of the Berlin Wall has offered a legitimate date to declare an end to NGC. Even though there is much continuity in personnel, themes, and content, film production since 1989 occurs under a completely different set of contingencies. But while the end of the Cold War marks the end of the NGC phase of German film production, it does not mark the end of its concern with German identity formations. In reexamining constructions of German identity in recent film history, we must remain wary of our own assumptions about "the German" in the present and constantly look to see what that configuration, and others like it, excludes from view.

Notes

1. Thomas Elsaesser, *New German Cinema: A History* (New Brunswick, NJ: Rutgers University Press, 1989) 2. For two different, but also relevant periodizations of West German Film, see the introductions to Timothy Corrigan, *New German Film: The Displaced Image* (Austin: University of Texas Press, 1983); and Richard W. McCormick, *Politics of the Self: Feminism and the Postmodern in West German Literature and Film* (Princeton: Princeton University Press, 1991).

2. While we all seem to know what it means to say *Rio Bravo* is a "western," or *Meet Me in St. Louis* is a "musical," these genre designations become very slippery when we try to employ them as critical models. This is not the place for engaging in the debates about genre cinema, nor is a valorization of the term intended here. The shortcomings of most genre studies in film have been exposed time and again, and I list just a few from a particularly insightful article by Alan Williams ("Is a Radical Genre Criticism Possible?," *Quarterly Review of Film Studies* 9.2 [Spring 1984]: 121–25; here 124). Genre criticism appropriates a category of literary production which may not be adequate as a category of film criticism. Genre studies show an excessive reliance on narrative, and often operate with evolutionary assumptions that ignore the subtleties of early films in a particular genre. There is also a methodological circularity of extracting characteristics from an already agreed upon "canon"

to reaffirm it. Finally, genre studies have a nearly exclusive focus on Hollywood as *all* cinema, with a further, ahistorical emphasis on the "classical age" of Hollywood. Williams feels, however, that one might "produce individual genre studies with real historical integrity" by "1) starting with a genre's 'pre-history,' its roots in other media; 2) studying all films, regardless of perceived quality; and 3) going beyond film content to study advertising, the star system, and studio policy. . . . And, crucially [by getting] out of the United States." While the second of these guidelines has not been possible in the scope of the present study, these suggestions inform my approach to NGC as a genre, an approach which I think could contribute to a revision of genre studies.

3. Robin Wood, "Ideology, Genre, Auteur (1977)," *Film Genre Reader*, ed. Barry Keith Grant (Austin: University of Texas Press, 1986) 61.

4. Though many have contributed to making this a common assumption now, two of the most important works have been penned by Edward W. Said: *Orientalism* (New York: Vintage Books, 1978), and *Culture and Imperialism* (New York: Alfred A. Knopf, 1993).

5. James Clifford, *The Predicament of Culture: Twentieth-Century Ethnography, Literature and Art* (Cambridge, MA: Harvard University Press, 1988).

6. For an example based on film analysis, see "The Other Question . . .," *Screen* 24.6 (Nov.–Dec. 1983) 18–31.

7. Historian Michael Geyer has investigated German "otherness" within his discipline in the United States (see his contribution to Michael Geyer, Jeffrey M. Peck, and Frank Trommler, "Germany as the Other: Towards an American Agenda for German Studies. A Colloquium," *GSR* 13.1 [February 1990]: 111–38). While I agree with many of his observations about the writing of German history from this side of the Atlantic, this work seems to confuse constructions of alterity with actual positions of marginality.

8. This view is developed in particular in the sections published as "The Intellectuals" and "The Study of Philosophy" in Antonio Gramsci, *Selections from the Prison Notebooks of Antonio Gramsci*, ed. Quintin Hoare and Geoffrey Nowel Smith. (New York: International Publishers, 1971).

9. The following section summarizes arguments made more fully in my "As Others Put Plays upon the Stage: *Aguirre*, Neocolonialism and the New German Cinema" (*New German Critique* [Summer 1993]).

10. See the essays in *Kultur und Politik im unserer Zeit: Dokumentation des Kongresses der SPD am 28, und 29, Oktober 1960 in Wiesbaden*, Ed. Parteivorstand der SPD (Hannover: J. H. W. Dietz, 1960), particularly Heinz Kühn's "Kulturpolitik im Ausland" (93–102). Sheila Johnston called attention to the pieces in this volume in her "A Star is Born: Fassbinder and the New German Cinema," *New German Critique* 24–25 (Fall/Winter 1981–82): 57–72. In many ways, my work seeks to expand on observations made by Johnston.

11. Many examples are cited in Eric Rentschler, "American Friends and the New German Cinema: Patterns of Reception," *New German Critique* 24–25 (Fall/Winter 1981–82): 7–35.

12. See, for example, *Förderung essen Filme auf: Positionen, Situationen, Materialien.* ed. Gisela Hundertmark and Louis Saul. (Munich: Ölschläger, 1984).

13. Eric Rentschler, *West German Film in the Course of Time: Reflections on the Twenty Years since Oberhausen* (Bedford Hills, NY: Redgrave, 1984) i.

14. Kent Casper, and Susan Linville, "Nazi Reframes: Negative Stereotyping in American Reviews of New German Films," *Literature/Film Quarterly*, 13.4 (1985): 250–57; here 251.

15. "Bericht der Bundesregierung über die Situation der Filmwirtschaft," dated 4.25.62, cited in *Archiv für Urheber-, Film-, Funk-, und Theaterrecht (UFITA)* 40 (1963):76–99; here 76, emphasis added.

16. "Filmförderung in der Bundesrepublik Deutschland," *UFITA* 51 (1968): 201.

17. See, for example, Kühn's "Kulturpolitik im Ausland," 96.

18. "Death is no solution: The German Film Director Fritz Lang" (1976), *West German Filmmakers on Film: Visions and Voices*, ed. Eric Rentschler (New York: Holmes & Meier,

1988) 103. It is also interesting to note that Wenders rediscovers the connection to Lang and the German tradition through a similar intervention in his subconscious: ". . . he's there in *Im Lauf der Zeit*, there's a reference to *Die Nibelungen*, we see two photos of him, one of them from *Le Mépris*. I didn't do all that intentionally. In this film about the consciousness of the cinema in Germany, the father who left us, no, the father we let go, imposed his point of view, slipped in of his own accord" (103–4).

19. See the "journal" of this trip, published in English as *Of Walking in Ice: Munich-Paris 11/24 to 12/14, 1974* (New York: Tanam Press, 1980).

20. "Tribute to Lotte Eisner" (1982) in *West German Filmmakers on Film*, 117.

21. *Hitler: A Film from Germany*. (1978) (New York: Farrar, Straus, Giroux, 1982) citations from pp. 3, 8, and 9 respectively.

22. Eric Rentschler, "American Friends and the New German Cinema," *New German Critique* 24–25 (Fall/Winter 1981–82): 34. Rentschler led a number of progressive critics who in the early 1980s exposed the myth of young geniuses giving birth to a German film again out of a cultural void as an ahistorical fantasy (see particularly the articles by Johnston and Miriam Hansen in the same issue of *New German Critique*). This vital criticism aims to correct false impressions more than to analyze their significance, which I take as my task here.

23. The notion of a minor discourse is developed by Gilles Deleuze and Felix Guattari in *Kafka: Toward a Minor Literature* (1975), (Minneapolis: University of Minnesota Press, 1986). For an attempt to adapt this theory (based originally on the use of language in Kafka) to broader issues of "minority criticism," see Abdul R. JanMohamed, and David Lloyd, "Introduction: Toward a Theory of Minority Discourse: What is to Be Done," *The Nature and Context of Minority Discourse*, ed. Abdul R. JanMohamed and David Lloyd (New York, Oxford: Oxford University Press, 1990) 1–16. For a fuller explication of the notion of NGC as a minor discourse, see John E. Davidson, "'As Others Put Plays upon the Stage': *Aguirre*, Neocolonialism and the New German Cinema."

24. All quotations from JanMohamed and Lloyd, citing or expanding on Deleuze and Guattari's terminology.

25. Ernest Mandel, *The Second Slump: A Marxist Analysis of the Recession in the 1970s* (London: New Left Books, 1977) 47.

26. See Mandel, op. cit. For interesting comments on using "postcolonial" as the adjective and "neocolonialism" as the noun corresponding to global relations today, see Anthony Appiah, "Is the Post- in Postmodernism the Post- in Postcolonial," *Critical Inquiry* 17 (Winter 1991): 336–57.

27. Gayatri Chakravorty Spivak, "Neocolonialism and the Secret Agent of Knowledge," *Oxford Literary Review* 13.1–2 (1991): 220–51; here p. 224.

28. Hence, this suspicion about "other" identity does not mean one must reject identity politics as a meaningful strategy against exclusion or domination; rather, it is the retotalization of "otherness" through pluralistic interest of which one must be wary.

29. This remains the case even as more and more narrative films begin "dealing with" the "Third World." Katie Trumpener demonstrates that the most typical recent representations of West Germany depict it as a "transitional" society with no stable borders of cultural identity ("On the Road: Labor, Ethnicity and the New 'New German Cinema' in the Age of the Multinational," *Public Culture* 2.1 [Fall 1989]: 20–30).

30. David Harvey, *The Condition of Postmodernity: An Enquiry into the Origins of Cultural Change* (Oxford: Basil Blackwell, 1989) 359.

31. Rentschler, *West German Film in the Course of Time*, 58.

32. Bosley Crowther, "The Cruelty of Boys," *New York Times* 25 Sept. 1967: 56.

33. Howard Thompson, "*Yesterday Girl*," *New York Times* 22 Sept. 1967: 22.

34. Despite the centrality of the male-male and female-female "friendships" to these films, they remain heterosexist in both their presentations of sexual desire and resolution of narrative complications. This is not to say that they do not open the space for modes of reception that work against such heterosexism.

35. David Ansen, "Homeless on the Range," *Newsweek* 19 Nov. 1984: 132. Ansen refers to the judges at Cannes, who awarded *Paris, Texas* the Golden Palm earlier that year

36. Vincent Canby, "Directors Evoke Many Americas," *New York Times* 11 Nov 1984: H 30.

37. Respectively from Julie Salamon, "On Film: Magic in the Mojave," *Wall Street Journal* 28 April 1988: 26; and Kevin Thomas, "*Bagdad Café* Serves Endearing and Quirky Version of America," *Los Angeles Times* 4 May 1988: VI. 1.

38. Philip's experiences of the United States in *Alice in den Städten*, Ripley's (Dennis Hopper) role as Jonathan's *Amerikanischer Freund,* and the troubles faced by Bruno and Robert in the shell of the American army post in *Im Lauf der Zeit* all stress the challenge of being German that "America" continually raises.

39. My notion of the effect of this subnarrative "German" presence corresponds neither to the iconic presence of the star in Hollywood films nor to the "essential" figure of Germania Joseph Loewenstein and Lynne Tatlock find every time Marlene Dietrich or Hanna Schygulla appears on screen ("The Marshall Plan at the Movies: Marlene Dietrich and Her Incarnations," *German Quarterly* 65.3–4 [Summer–Fall 1992]: 429–42). The strategic casting of German figures brings with them a kind of "index value" tied to "German identity" as it manifests itself in NGC. The generic presence of German film (i.e., what makes a film from West Germany a "German film" in "our" minds) is evoked by casting Wicki and Kinski in these roles.

40. In a chapter of a work in progress, I offer a reading of *Paris, Texas* that demonstrates the gender politics of the film are inextricably interwoven with the "German" question. Though this is one of Wenders's first and most explicitly gender-conscious films, the interplay of the German and gender questions serves to place this woman (played by a German) in a role either victimized by the reestablishment of the American man's identity or cleansed of past sins (attempting to burn him alive) by it. This happens not merely at the level of narrative, but also inheres in the stylistic and formal connection between the camera and the male protagonist.

41. After winning the Golden Palm at Cannes, the West German release of *Paris, Texas* was delayed until 1985 due to a distribution dispute between Wenders and the *Filmverlag der Autoren*, which he had helped found. Thus, much was written in the FRG about the film, its U.S. and French reception, and the fate of *Autorenfilme* in general before it was ever screened there.

42. See the interview with Roswitha Müller published in the Goethe House brochure which accompanied the Ottinger Retrospective in 1990–91.

43. Rey Chow, "'It's you, and not me': Domination and 'Othering' in Theorizing the 'Third World'," *Coming to Terms: Feminism, Theory, Politics*, ed. Elizabeth Weed, 1989) 159.

44. For an introduction into the notion of flexible accumulation, see Harvey's *The Condition of Postmodernity*.

45. The outcry from independent French and German filmmakers against GATT has been based on a series of arguments about specifically European, national cinematic traditions which need to be maintained. While politicians do not generally pay heed to such arguments, they do recognize the power of this "nationalistic" rhetoric with voters, particularly those who will suffer or derive no direct benefit from more open trade relations.

Reception of Theory: Film/Television Studies and the Frankfurt School

CLAY STEINMAN

A CCORDING TO Tom Bottomore, the "Frankfurt School in its original form, and as a school of Marxism or sociology, is dead" (70). For people in film and television studies in the United States, the Critical Theory of the Frankfurt School has not had much of a chance, even though it offers a valuable way of seeing normally obscured relations of social power in the details of modern capitalist culture. The school's first generation included Theodor W. Adorno, (for a time) Erich Fromm, Max Horkheimer, Leo Lowenthal, Herbert Marcuse, and Walter Benjamin, whose work was so different it deserves separate treatment. Although none of their positions was identical, as a group they were resolutely antagonistic to the culture of domination.[1]

Critical Theory's approach is not easily summarized, but I might be able to clarify a few features by comparing it to an alternative analytic method Patrice Petro recently proposed:

> We may now want to pursue a different reading of mass culture, one which begins from the assumption that mass culture is neither intrinsically "progressive" nor "reactionary," but highly contradictory and historically variable in its form, its meanings, and its effects (5).

As a formula, this seems reasonable enough. For Critical Theory, "mass culture"[2] may indeed be "highly contradictory and historically variable," but invariably it is produced by stratified, industrial societies, and, however contradictorily, it bears their mark. For Critical Theory, most people most of the time encounter culture industry products within a system Marcuse called "one-dimensional," directing energies along paths carved to the measure of the ruling powers, trickling down benefits to others only under pressure. Readings must include this context, or risk reifying their objects. Surely products don't dictate their meanings or effects—how could ideology be intrinsic in that sense?—but just as surely they function within a social system (which includes people's responses) determined by force and interest.

Petro's formula might easily mask the difficulties involved in knowing meanings and, even more, effects. Involved are the virtues and limitations

Reprinted from *Journal of Film and Video* 40 no. 2 (Spring/1988): 4–19.

of empirical research, issues with which Adorno struggled when he reviewed his own work among the empiricists in the United States:

> It is an open question, to be answered only empirically, whether and to what extent the social implications observed in the . . . analysis of music are understood by the listeners themselves, and how they react to them. It would be naive to take for granted an identity between the social implications to be discerned in the stimuli and those embodied in the "responses." It would certainly be no less naive to consider the two things as totally uncorrelated with each other in the absence of conclusive research on the reactions ("Scientific Experiences" 353).

Using a Hegelian term for the movement of society, Adorno argued that "what is regarded by the psychology of perception as a mere 'stimulus' is in fact, qualitatively determined, a matter of 'objective spirit'" ("Scientific Experiences" 343). He opposed "stating and measuring effects" without linking them to the social relations underlying culture industry products "to which consumers in the culture industry . . . react," for "it still had to be determined how far comprehensive social structures, and even society as a whole, came into play" ("Scientific Experiences" 343–344).

If theory alone cannot know effects, and empirical work is mired in problems of defining what it would measure, what can we read when we read "mass culture"? According to Adorno, "hieroglyphs of social significance" ("Scientific Experiences" 342). To accomplish this, Critical Theory insists both on the specificity of each object's forms, of its existence in its details, and on a respect for each object's interconnections with others in the world—in short, on its particularity and on its generality. It insists as well on self-consciousness about the analytical process, itself a social hieroglyph.

But Critical Theory is not just another method one might choose to apply. It sees its criticism as an act of resistance, prefiguring work outside the market system. It assumes the urgency, with no guarantees of political efficacy, of envisioning social life without domination and of criticizing the present society for denying possibilities.

Let's look at one culture industry product from this perspective: reaction shots on network television that feature what Frank Capra called the "reactive character," designed to cue viewers' responses to potentially disruptive ambiguities. Are these shots "inherently reactionary"? No. Response of course would depend upon who is watching and the circumstances of reception, and on their relation to adjoining material. But I think it is safe to say that on network television, looked at from the left, the form generally articulates an historically developed, reactionary social system.

On *Fantasy Island*, for example, the reactive character—Ricardo Montalbán as Mr. Roarke—guides the responses of characters within the diegesis and is designed to serve a similar function for people at home. In a patriarchal culture, in a show aimed at women, it is no accident that this figure is a man, just as it is no accident that in adjacent commercials the narrating voice and reactive character is a man with similar mien, promoting products aimed at the same audience. The effects are likely psychological, ideological (Budd, Craig, and Steinman). But they also move goods and help establish our relations to them; they help the economy reproduce. The shot structure itself is an industrial form that derives from the classical Hollywood cinema, where, in fits and starts, it developed and became standardized as it was found to be commercially practicable. Adorno wrote: "The phenomena with which the sociology of the mass media must be concerned, particularly in America, cannot be separated from standardization" ("Scientific Experiences" 346).

What David Noble says of Thomas Edison's laboratory applies to other standardized inventions of the culture industry: "As in all engineering work, the profit motive did not lie behind the inventive activity but was bound up with it" (8). This is true as well of this form's historical connection to "scientific management": the network and advertisers seek to organize the audience for consumption with the efficiency of managers constructing an assembly line (Braverman; also Ewen). One doesn't have to see the form as "inherently reactionary" to see how, in this example, it is a hieroglyph for a patriarchal market system bent on social control; without these forces, the form would not be standard.

With its focus on textual immanence, Critical Theory can help people in film and television research break through disciplinary limitations that work against combining formal and political-economic analysis. An expert in music, Adorno wrote several detailed studies that suggest how the immanent criticism he argued for might be extended to film and television.[3] Such criticism reads the social within cultural artifacts and, he said,

> takes seriously the principle that it is not ideology itself which is untrue but its pretension to correspond to reality. Immanent criticism . . . names what the consistency or inconsistency of the work itself expresses of the structure of the existent. . . . It pursues the logic of its aporias. . . . In such antinomies criticism perceives those of society ("Cultural Criticism" 32).

In its active readings of structural gaps, immanent criticism resembles French poststructuralism and the British cultural studies of Stuart Hall and others, cited more often than Critical Theory by writers in our field. But there are crucial differences that make Critical Theory worth considering.

Work in cultural studies, for example, tends to follow Louis Althusser in its insistence upon the "relative autonomy" of ideology's cultural forms from economic relations. For Althusser, Hall, and others, this involves raising the mass media to a "central, relatively independent, position in any analysis of the question of the 'politics of signification'" (Hall 83; but see also O'Kane). For Terry Lovell:

> The most striking characteristic of this work is . . . its insistence on the distance which separates the 'relatively autonomous' practices of cultural production from the remaining 'practices' which together constitute the social formation (*Pictures* 2).

A critic of this tendency, she nevertheless rightly considers its contribution "impressive" (*Pictures* 2); over the last 15 years, work under its influence, stressing the complex "specificity" (Hall 83) of mass media practices over their general social roles, has illuminated textual structures and ideological implications previously taken for granted. This is most notable in feminist studies of film.

But there have been costs, and among them has been a devaluation of dialectical strategies such as the Frankfurt School's, which stress not autonomy but interrelation, and which might be used to understand how economic, political, and ideological determinations have worked in specific socio-historical moments and how they must and can be changed. In the cause of this change, Adorno demanded 30 years ago the "right to go from one *genus* to another, to shed light on an object in itself hermetic by casting a glance at society, to present society with the bill the object does not redeem" ("Cultural Criticism" 33). The stress on relative autonomy has discouraged analysis of this kind—moving from one social realm to another, sketching out the dialectical relations of their forms, illuminating what Fredric Jameson has called "historical tropes" and "dialectical puns" (*Marxism* 3–59; "Introduction" 142)— even if it does not preclude it in theory, and film and television studies seems the poorer for it, and less critical. What tends to drop from sight in analyses under the influence of rubrics of relative autonomy is precisely what has made Marxian thought radical: the economic in its most general sense—the social conditions of life's production. As writers of film history and analysis trample each other in a rush to distance themselves from a mechanistic economic determinism, their work becomes less useful for making connections.

In publications devoted to film and television studies, those in our field qualified to take up the Frankfurt School's radical project could read little but denunciations of its general value until recently. This has been everyone's loss, for the first generation of the Frankfurt School lacked three crucial qualifications for producing the critiques we need of culture industry products and their modes of consumption: sensitivity to the power and prevalence of heterosexist subjection, detailed knowledge of the forms of film and television texts, and appreciation of the pleasure bonds of this dystopian Oz.

For more than two decades, United States specialists in Critical Theory have analyzed and extended the work of the first generation and have explored its impact in West Germany and elsewhere, in *New German Critique, Telos*, and other publications. As dissatisfaction with aspects of French theory has grown in the eighties, people in film and television studies have begun looking to other disciplines and theories, and work informed by Critical Theory has appeared with increasing frequency at our conferences and in our journals.[4] Yet this work has yet to have the impact of the attacks on the Frankfurt School published here and in Britain.

It seems useful to consider these attacks, and to try to account for them. The examples I shall discuss are survey articles from three sources that might have attracted the attention of people in film and television studies in the United States: articles by colleagues in the field (Waldman; Boddy); contributions from within and around British cultural studies by Hall and others to one of the most important collections of leftist media theory of the last few years, *Culture, Society and the Media* (Curran, Gurevitch, and Woollacott; Bennett, "Theories"; Hall); and an essay on Marxist theory and criticism in an early issue of *Critical Studies in Mass Communication*, the new Speech Communication Association's interdisciplinary journal that is a potentially important source for analytical *bricolage* (Grossberg). These articles exemplify elements of the prevalent response from the left wing of film and television studies to Critical Theory—dismissing it without a fair hearing. Unfair as they can be in their representations of Critical Theory, these pieces sometimes highlight what it is about the Frankfurt School that has engendered such a benighted reception. But even their most trenchant critiques fail to support their wholesale hostility.

This response has its own political origins and functions, and is related to the sometimes helpful, often debilitating hegemony of alternating currents of French and British thought over most leftist film study in the United States (See Garnham; Lovell, "Marxism"; McDonnell and Robins). Remarkably so, considering its proliferation, this hegemony has usually been caught in the United States like many works of the foreign art cinema—deferentially promoted yet abridged, as long sections of contentious Anglo-European political context are deleted by United States distributors.

I shall concentrate on four claims about Critical Theory that have functioned as strategies of denial: that it failed to envision possibilities for film practice outside the culture industry; that its critique of culture industry products reproduced conservative mass society theories; that it has been too weak conceptually to survive the challenge of empirical communication studies in the United States; and that its notorious pessimism betrays its political irrelevance.

NO ALTERNATIVES

Bitterness gives Critical Theory its strength. Its indictment of control by the few and ruthless impoverishment of the many, its refusal to accept the accommodations our lives demand of us—these are unrelenting. It grounds itself in the emancipatory interests of Marxian theory, and in the Hegelian Marxian emphasis on interconnection and contradiction.

Crucial to emancipatory thought are possibilities of alternatives. If Critical Theory, for example, sees film as essentially realist, then for it there can be no anti-realist film practice, and its value diminishes. Diane Waldman has argued this point in *New German Critique*, which characteristically has been more generous to Critical Theory. While justly attacking caricatures of Critical Theory in the writings of others, including Peter Wollen, she joins Wollen in indicting the "erroneous ontological suppositions and concomitant biases against film articulated by Adorno" (45). She criticizes these suppositions no fewer than eight times without any clear evidence from Adorno's work—with one exception, a comment attributed to Adorno by Wollen:

> That the essence of film lies merely in duplicating and reinforcing what already exists, that it is glaringly superfluous and senseless even in a leisure restricted to infantility, that its duplicative realism is incompatible with its claims to be an aesthetic image—all this can be seen in the film itself, without recourse to dogmatically cited *verités éternelles* (46).[5]

As Wollen provided no source for the quotation, and Waldman could not locate it, she says, "I use it with caution" (46n). Yet she not very cautiously uses the quotation to tie Adorno to André Bazin, who did believe there was something essential about the apparent realism of film (47–9).

Yet it was because Adorno did not have an "ahistorical film ontology" (45)[6] that he was so antagonistic toward products of the motion picture industry: he knew they could be different. There may be no separating Adorno's radical critique from his personal distaste for what he considered unrefined, but neither can it be divorced from the vision that in theory motivated it. Adorno did detest the realist project of culture industry film—so much so that in the essay on which she concentrates, Waldman aptly notes that he and Horkheimer seem to have been insensitive to differences and changes within Hollywood production. But this was a failure of observation, not a theory of film. In his response to Benjamin's "The Work of Art in the Age of Mechanical Reproduction," for example, Adorno questioned whether having a representational quality "really constitutes that *a priori* of the film which you claim it to be," or "whether instead this reproduction precisely belongs to that 'naive realism' whose bourgeois nature we so thoroughly agreed upon" ("Correspondence" 66). Nevertheless, Waldman writes that Adorno did not "distinguish between properties of the medium as they have been exploited under capitalism and these properties as they have or could be utilized under other conditions of production" (49).[7] As Greg Renault and Miriam Hansen have observed, a crucial missing source here is *Composing for the Films*, which Adorno coauthored with Hanns Eisler in the forties but originally did not sign (Renault 257; Hansen, "Introduction" 189n). At times allying itself with aspects of Sergei Eisenstein's radical film theory (65–75), the book advocated forms of production Adorno and Eisler believed were not then possible within the industry: "A discussion of industrialized culture must show the interaction of these two factors: the aesthetic potentialities of mass art in the future, and its ideological character in the present" (xi). This would seem to be the position Waldman wants Adorno to take. The problem here is context. Self-consciously dialectical writings often do not read well as isolated texts. This is even more true of their sentences. The radical potential of Critical Theory, its use value for people teaching and writing critical studies of culture today, lies in the structure of its analysis—its sighting of domination in the very forms that hearken its overthrow—not in the comments of its writers, served up in isolation and, usually, in translation.[8]

MASS SOCIETY

Like others battered by change in the first half of the twentieth century, the Critical Theorists saw competitive capitalism moving toward a system of monopoly administration. As leftists, they analyzed how this movement helped cement the precarious hold of oppressive ruling classes. What was blocking the struggle Marx had predicted against control by the few? Marcuse condemned the administered society as "one-dimensional," repressing, displacing, denying wherever it could the oppositional energies it generated. What was it about this society that made organized rebellion against it so unusual, sometimes unthinkable? How did cultural work reproduce this rebellion—and its uneven containment? Yet despite these radical concerns, over the last decade readers have often associated the Frankfurt School only with its critique of administered life, blind to its vision of liberation—the motivation for Critical Theory in the first place (Horkheimer; Marcuse, "Philosophy").

For example, one reading of Critical Theory has linked it to mass society theory, which in turn has been tied to affection for elite culture and revulsion at advanced market (and socialist) societies' brutalization. As hostile as they tended to be toward culture industry products, Adorno, Horkheimer, and Marcuse wrote much to encourage this view. They also argued for the critical value of a handful of examples of elite art (such as works of Picasso and Schönberg), seeing in them resistance to the culture industry's realm of necessity and praising them for the way, however roughly, they prefigured aesthetic life in the realm of the free. As Waldman says, "one can . . . see how," for example, "Adorno's critique of the culture industry was misunderstood as coming from the same place as that of critics like T. S. Eliot, F. R. Leavis and José Ortega y Gasset" (45).

As Waldman points out, "Unlike these conservative critics, the Frankfurt school refused to defend high culture and tradition as an end in itself" (45). In the early fifties summary of their position, *Aspects of Sociology*, members of the Institute for Social Research in Frankfurt specifically attacked the elitism of Ortega y Gasset and others (75). They were careful to differentiate their critique of the culture industry from a conservative one rooted in an idealist vision of art's unworldliness. The defenders of what Marcuse in 1937 called the "affirmative character of culture" might put it otherwise, but for Critical Theory the conservative insistence that art and culture provide an enclave for the spirit against the world of the mob helps justify existing property relations. "The truth of a higher world, of a higher good than material existence, conceals the truth that a better material existence can be created in which such happiness is realized" ("Affirmative" 121). Defense of the autonomy of the spirit against worldly problems promotes conformism: "It is precisely because the soul dwells beyond the economy that the latter can manage it so easily" ("Affirmative" 126).

Yet Lawrence Grossberg, in an essay dominated by simplistic dismissals of most Marxian work, says of the Frankfurt School on this issue only that Adorno had a "modernist vision of art as a transcendental, autonomous activity which, by projecting utopian possibilities, opens up a space for social critique" (396). He does not say, for example, that Adorno also argued that "all culture shares the guilt of society. It ekes out its existence only by virtue of injustice already perpetrated in the sphere of production, much as does commerce" ("Cultural Criticism" 26).

Unlike others called mass society theorists, Adorno did not find the productions of the culture industry monolithic or without contradictions:

> Since in our society the forces of production are highly developed, and, at the same time, the relations of production fetter those productive forces, it is full of antagonisms. These antagonisms are not limited to the economic sphere where they are universally recognized, but dominate also the cultural sphere where they are less easily recognized ("Social Critique" 211).

Whatever their theories, however, the Critical Theorists have not been known as cultural interventionists—except for Marcuse, who celebrated currents within Afro-American music, literature, and poetry, the "liberating laughter of the Yippies," and the "lyrics and music of Bob Dylan" (*Counterrevolution* 172, 132, 117–18)—and this may have contributed to their reputation as elitists. Also, as Martin Jay reports, they "may have been relentless in their hostility to the capitalist system, but they never abandoned the lifestyle of the *haute bourgeoisie*"; as a result, they have developed—among their detractors, at least—reputations as "mandarins" (*Dialectical* 36). Aside from Marcuse, whose later work shows how Critical Theory might take into account residual and emerging cultural movements (*Essay; Counterrevolution*), the first generation Frankfurt writers showed little interest in ethnic and other expression resistant to corporate administration. Their general disdain of culture industry products affected some of their applications of Critical Theory—most infamously in Adorno's inability to see much critical value in jazz ("Perennial Fashion"). Yet many of the works I cite in this article show that the Frankfurt School has produced some of the most brilliant close analyses ever written revealing the hidden political agenda of cultural products.[9] To dismiss them because of their authors' lifestyles and blind spots is to let star gossip overcome social critique.

Mass society theorists have also been linked to the "magic bullet" or "hypodermic" theory of communication, which ostensibly flourished in the twenties. This theory—more accurately a group of anecdotes centered on the manipulation of the media by the authorities during World War I—argued that the mass media could inject ideas into populations lacking pre-industrial society's allegiances (De Fleur and Ball-Rokeach 156–65). But as Melvin L. De Fleur and Sandra Ball-Rokeach have pointed out, the theory "is not quite as simple as it might appear" (161). Rooted in instinct psychology, it assumed human beings had inherited biological structures, predisposing them toward consistent reponses to certain sorts of stimuli—especially those appealing to irrational emotions (De Fleur and Ball-Rokeach 162–164). But this was hardly the position of the Frankfurt School, for whom psychology was social, conflictive, historical (Adorno, "Sociology"). Accordingly, in *Aspects of Sociology* they argued that there was "no absolutely reliable method for seducing the masses; these vary with the latter's readiness to be seduced" (81).

Still, in *Culture, Society and the Media*, the Frankfurt School is tied to mass society theory in three separate essays and in the introduction (Gurevitch and others 8, 23, 42, 58). In *One-Dimensional Man*, Marcuse is said to have perceived the "media as a stupefying, totally subduing force" (Gurevitch and others 15), even though he says in the book's introduction that there are "large areas within and without" the most highly developed contemporary societies "where the described tendencies do not prevail—I would say: not yet prevail" (Marcuse, *One-Dimensional* xvii).

In another essay, Tony Bennett writes that Horkheimer and Adorno, especially in *Dialectic of Enlightenment*, regarded the "mechanisms and effects" of the United States film and music industries as "virtually wholly narcotic or worse, lobotomic" ("Theories" 44), even though in that book they wrote, "Demand has not yet been replaced by simple obedience" (136). Similarly, in an often useful overview in another anthology, "Loving a Nineteen-Inch Motorola: American Writing on Television," William Boddy claims the Frankfurt School saw the media as "all-powerful manipulators" (4). He offers no evidence in support of the characterization, although evidence against it elsewhere abounds, as I have shown.

Curiously, linking the Frankfurt School to conservative culture critics parallels the strategy of centrist social scientists in the United States in the late fifties and early sixties, who used Daniel Bell's "end of ideology" thesis to club radical intellectuals for their recalcitrance. In Daniel J. Czitrom's observant account, it was Bell himself, along with Leon Bramson, Edward Shils, Raymond Bauer, Alice Bauer, and others, who promulgated the "artificial and spurious construct" of a coherent, monolithic mass society theory supposedly shared by elitists left and right (136). To those in the mainstream, anyone not blinded by ideology would see what democratic social science made plain: despite "a plethora of intriguing titles, speculative generalizations, and an excellent body of laboratory research, there is little evidence of the effect of mass media in American society as a whole" (Czitrom 137).[10] So "mass society theory" was a specious epithet thrown from the center at those who refused to see the media as benign. The Frankfurt School rejected the notion that the media have little or no social effect (Lowenthal, "Popular Culture"; Marcuse, *One-Dimensional* xvii, 144–169)[11], as do most leftist communication researchers working today (Gitlin) and even increasing numbers of scholars closer to the mainstream (Blumler and Gurevitch), yet in Anglo-North American film and television studies, the mass society bugaboo persists.

ACADEMIC LOSERS

For better or worse, the Critical Theorists were by language, politics, and temperament isolated from most mass communication studies in the United States. Considering that, they loom large, strangely, in several critics' thumbnail chronologies. Boddy, for example, folds the work of such Frankfurt School writers as Horkheimer and Lowenthal into the general category of "American culture critics of the 1930s," against which he sets the "postwar emphasis on quantitative communication studies" (4). He further says that the "new generation of communication researchers has modified or refuted the earlier accounts of media influence"—apparently meaning something like the magic bullet theory (5). He says the "model of influence they elaborated, where effects are simple, direct and powerful, was subject to extensive revision at the hands of the researchers who followed them" (4). Besides caricaturing Critical Theory, Boddy has bollixed up his chronology. No wonder he fails to offer any examples of the "earlier accounts of media influence" from the Frankfurt School in the United States in the thirties: Critical Theory did not appear here in English until the forties, and many of its most pointed critiques of the culture industry were not published or translated until the fifties and sixties.

But a more serious problem is the presentation of theoretical conflict as autonomous. Partially because they were ornery, but mostly because of the politics of the work they did, the Critical Theorists were unable to secure reliable funding for their Marxian communication research, as Jay documents in *The Dialectical Imagination*. Lacking an institutional base, worried about money and immigrant status in an anti-Communist climate less than temperate for leftist German Jews, and seeing no United States outlet for publication of non-Communist Marxian criticism until the sixties, they published intermittently and with considerable self-censorship in English while writing radical criticism in German.[12] These are among the reasons the Frankfurt School position had little impact on what there was of United States communication research at the time.

Paul F. Lazarsfeld, a German emigré who was successful as a social scientist in the United States, tried to promote what he saw as the critical dimension of the Frankfurt School to more mainstream audiences. But according to Jennifer Daryl Slack and Martin Allor, Lazarsfeld himself was not clear on Critical Theory's radical project (210–11; for an alternative view, see Kellner). Still, there were intellectuals in the United States who had contact with and absorbed at least elements of the Frankfurt School critique: C. Wright Mills, who worked with Lazarsfeld; David Riesman, who worked with Fromm; and George Gerbner, who worked with Adorno (Kellner). But few social scientists were receptive to Marxism in any form until academics with origins in the New Left began moving into the universities and promoting their critique on the inside. The most cited example of a centrist academic's evaluation of Critical Theory before the late sixties neither takes their arguments seriously nor engages them, instead reviling Adorno, Fromm, Horkheimer, and Lowenthal as foreign Marxists, and un-American (Shils).

None of this seems to have mattered to James Curran, Michael Gurevitch, and Janet Woollacott, however, who disdainfully report in *Culture, Society and the Media* that "To put it bluntly, the work of the Frankfurt School was relatively marginal in developing and generating research in mass communications, in providing a theoretical paradigm within which media studies could proceed" (23)—as if this had been due to the theoretical weakness of Critical Theory, as if there were a market in ideas dividing winners and losers according to their merits. Curran,

Gurevitch, and Woollacott claim that the "clash between the critical theorists' view of mass society and a pluralist-inspired tradition focusing on the effects of the mass media involved a major theoretical confrontation" (23). But *this confrontation never took place*, except in the minds of writers of idealist secondary literature.

ACADEMIC EXCHANGE-VALUE

Whatever the intentions of their authors, the articles I have examined nevertheless seem driven by a similar project—to champion newer theoretical practices at the expense of dispatching Critical Theory to the dustbin without a fair hearing. They and others like them (and, despite my intentions, perhaps this one) provide indices of academic exchange-value within a system, as Russell Jacoby says, whose "commandment of survival and success exactly parallels the capitalist" (144). Belying images of ourselves as independent scholars, we labor within academic institutions, as Steven B. Elworth notes,[13] and our jobs press us to imagine, identify ourselves with, and promote a cutting edge against what becomes designated as out-of-date.

> Marxism not excepted, new schools, innovations, advances, break-throughs, are announced like new brands. Everyone is out to corner a piece of the market. Interlocking directorates, intellectual holding companies and trusts leave tracks in footnotes of gratuitous commendations, dedications and recommendations. The transition from competitive to monopoly capital has brought in its wake intellectual kick-backs, as well as volume sales and cut-rate goods (Jacoby 144).

In this context, it seems useful to emphasize the words in, for example, Waldman's and Boddy's accounts that articulate a discourse of progress. In the academic market, this discourse increases the value of summaries that seem to make it clear, with the sweep and authority of an omniscient narrator, what we need and need not know. Waldman's greatest praise for Adorno is that his writing was the "*first* critique of mass culture from a radical rather than a conservative position," that it, "*anticipates by 25 years* the analysis of such journals as *Cahiers du Cinéma* and *Cinéthique* in France or *Screen* in Britain in the early 1970s" (52). She further recommends "*recent* film criticism and theory" from *Cahiers du Cinéma* and Stephen Heath's writing in *Screen*.

Similarly, near the end of his article, Boddy argues, "If *recent* theorists reject the model of 'administrative research,' there is nevertheless little sense of a *return* to the *earlier* Frankfurt School theories of subjectivity and culture" (10). Boddy doesn't identify the work he advocates with any names or institutions, but he appears to be promoting a combination of critical communication research represented within the *Journal of*

Communication issue, "Ferment in the Field," and Anglo-North American-French poststructuralist, feminist film and television analysis, in the mid-eighties, again associated with *Screen*.

Grossberg, too, writes as if knowledge were progressively obtained, although for him progress is not quite so chronologically bound. He travels through 10 circles of theory, stopping only when he arrives at the one housing the thought of Michel Foucault, who I think would have been astonished to see his work functioning as a *telos*. Grossberg writes as if there were an autonomous intellectual history susceptible to radical distillation. He reduces Critical Theory to the glibly summarized—and, in this form, easily consumed and rejected—work of Adorno. In his concluding summary, he lists Critical Theory under the category "classical approach" in which "culture reflects society; decoding is unproblematic" (417). According to Critical Theory, says Grossberg, "the text imposes forms of consumption which reflect their industrialized modes of production" (417). I cannot imagine anyone wanting to read Critical Theory (or much other socially critical work aside from poststructuralism and Foucault) after reading Grossberg. Given the substantial mainstream audience for *Critical Studies in Mass Communication*, the essay can look forward to a long life in courses with instructors eager to dismiss Marxian work on the basis of Grossberg's "Cliffs Notes." Despite several caveats, the essay never lets on that such a judgment would be irrational considering the complexity of the originals.

PESSIMISM

What seems to bother these writers as much as anything, and seems to push them toward what they see as the new, is what Boddy (4), Curran, Gurevitch, and Woollacott (23), Grossberg (401), Hall (58), and the editors of *Culture, Society and the Media* (8) all identically decry as the "pessimism" of the Critical Theorists. No doubt they were pessimistic. They saw the likelihood recede that classical Marxism's proletariat would liberate humankind. They had experienced Nazism. And aside from Marcuse's optimistic reponses of the late sixties, the first generation Critical Theorists from the late twenties could find no movements capable of taking the proletariat's place. Yet rejection of theory because of its pessimism, because of the unattractive images it constructs of everyday life under late capitalism, smacks precisely of the power of positive thinking Critical Theory eviscerated. In that sense, the rejection of pessimism by so many leftist colleagues only makes me more pessimistic. At stake is not which theory is more correct. As Ana Lopez has argued:

> We must accept the fact that there is no theoretical endeavor which does not also involve politics and interested readings of history, and that it is ultimate-

ly not a question of choosing the better theory, but a question of choosing among different political alternatives (59).

POLITICS AND INTERESTS

There is a pattern here. But what accounts for it? What are the politics? What are the interests? How can so many otherwise thorough academics write so carelessly about one body of theory—and so consistently so?

The two explanations I have already suggested—the advantages of promoting the new and the desire to look on the bright side—are inadequate in themselves since they do not account for the particular drubbing the Frankfurt School receives. Closer analysis of the arguments may; crucial here is pessimism as a matter of politics rather than of temperament.

Clearest on the issues is Bennett, who since at least the late seventies (see his *Formalism and Marxism*) has been a critical enthusiast of the work of Althusser, here the most well-known of the fractious European Communist theorists. In his main contribution to *Culture, Society and the Media*, Bennett makes it plain: the problem of the Frankfurt writers was not so much their theories, which might be used to study the world, as their politics, which seem irrelevant to changing it. *They were not Leninists.*

> In opposition to the Leninist construction of the relationship between theory and practice—that the theory must become practical by gripping the minds and directing the activities of the proletariat through the mediation of an organized political party—the Frankfurt theorists, particularly Adorno, argued that theory must give up the endeavor to change the world by transforming itself into practice. . . . Although they condemned reality in round terms, they had no positive suggestions to make as to how it might be changed (46, 47).

Beginning in at least the early forties, the Critical Theorists opposed Soviet Marxism as a philosophy and practice of domination, although they declined to join the period's anti-Communist celebration. As early as the thirties, they rejected the possibility of using Marxism to develop the revolutionary knowledge Leninists say justifies their leadership. Unlike many of the British Marxists prominent in film and cultural studies, the Critical Theorists severed themselves not only from Stalinism but also from Leninism.

A good place to start for a review of these issues and a sense of their obscure but complex relation to film studies in Britain and North America is Perry Anderson's *Arguments Within English Marxism*. What becomes apparent, and a rereading of Althusser's writings supports this, is that much of the work of the British Leninist Left, which reproduces many of Althusser's formulations, is rooted in a struggle of discourses, of systems of theoretical representation, generated over the last 30 years in the crucible of disputes within the world Communist movement. Writes Anderson:

> The Sino-Soviet dispute . . . is the real political background for the writing of *For Marx* and *Reading Capital*. . . . Althusser's intervention in 1961–1962 was aimed at the Russian line internationally, and nationally at much of the official culture of the [French Communist Party], from a position sympathetic to the Chinese (106, 107).

This was the political context within which Althusser framed the ideas that have had such power in Anglo-North American film and television studies—the attack on socialist humanism and on Hegelian dialectics, the insistence on the autonomy of theoretical work and on the possibility of its break with ideology toward the status of a *science*, the endorsement of the psychoanalysis of Jacques Lacan. Reading Althusser's formulations in the terms Anderson sets out, then reading their reproduction in *Screen*, and then following their course within North America (especially the United States), where Althusser's polemics have been articulated, decontextualized, by people whose circumstances and political views are rarely anything like Althusser's, or Bennett's, breathes life into Lévi-Strauss's argument that people do not think in myths, myths think in people, unaware.

Of course, neither Althusser himself nor his political constellation could determine what people in Anglo-North American film and television studies think and write about. And this is not to say that structuralist and poststructuralist approaches, with their considerable value, would not be abroad in Great Britain or North America if it were not for Althusser. But it is to say that much of their cachet of political radicalism, their polemical thrust, their authoritarian invective is connected to the packaging they received from sections of the French Left and their allies elsewhere.

So it is because the British Marxist-Leninists could not accept Critical Theory politically in any case that they have been quick to write against it without carefully gathering and weighing its arguments. This goes back to Wollen's work of 1968. What are the specifics of this hostility? Leninists tend to believe in the coming crisis of world capitalism and the urgency and usefulness of developing theoretical and organizational forms to precipitate that crisis—fighting the brutal and exploitative operations of hegemony—and to be ready to exert leadership when it comes. Since the Critical Theorists, like non-Leninist leftists generally, did not believe the economic crisis necessarily imminent, or consider it either useful or emancipatory to develop a party on the Leninist model, their work to Leninists seems pessimistic and non-activist, passive indeed. As Bennett puts it: "Theory thus became passive, negative in its function" and in so becoming theory was "deprived of any means whereby it might connect with reality"—a working class in need of a vanguard party—"in order to change it" (46).

It is different for non-Leninist leftists in North America, particularly for those in the largest cities and in university towns. Working within or around collectives and women's and other groups over the last 15 or 20 years, they have seen the viability, difficult and temporary as it might be, of alternative institutions of everyday life. For that reason, they might well find much of Critical Theory, except the later work of Marcuse, out of touch with what they see as possibilities for continued organizing. This may help account for some of the feelings of the United States writers. From a very different starting point than the Leninists, they might similarly find the Frankfurt School too pessimistic. For both, however, the centrist construction and critique of mass society theory makes possible a convenient reading of Critical Theory that seems to situate it historically while belittling its contemporary relevance in an apparently detached way.

Grossberg is right when he says the "point is not so much to choose" between theories (418). It seems irrational to embrace the work of theorists as one might a friend, or a faith, or a political movement, although in a culture lacking in attractive political movements, the appeal of theoretical movements, like that of faith, is sure to grow. This seems particularly true among intellectuals who, as Adorno wrote, "might well be deformed" by the division of labor that isolates them ("Resignation" 165). As the Critical Theorists themselves would argue, the theory given their names cannot be settled. Marked as it is by conservative and radical elements of its historical juncture, it changes, unevenly, in response to social struggles. Critical Theory is, as Lowenthal insists, a "perspective" (Dubiel 145); it cannot dictate political practice.

Bottomore's rejection of the Frankfurt School writers stems in part from their lack of attention to socialist working class movements in Britain and elsewhere (65), which have no recent counterparts in the United States. Again, in words that apply to nearly the entire Frankfurt School, Marcuse made it clear in *One-Dimensional Man* that his "analysis is focused on tendencies in the most highly developed contemporary societies" (xvii). For most of the world, for whom advanced domination uses the stick more than the carrot, different sorts of theories may be more immediately relevant.

In the United States, alternative voices are harder to find every year, even as stratification and public immiserization intensify. This is particularly true for issues of gender, sexual orientation, race and class—and of pleasure, a crucial matter for film and television studies. Pleasure outside the purview of the state and the largest corporations becomes increasingly taboo. Nancy Reagan tells viewers of *The Today Show* that the "sixties were an awful time,"[14] and no one contradicts her on the air. Off the air, people are threatened with mandatory urine and blood tests—How much more deeply could the social order intrude?—and are asked "Are you now or have you ever been?" as if the eighties are to be to the sixties what the fifties were to the thirties, with alternative pleasures and modes of consciousness replacing Communism as the mark of Cain. Government support for education and for critical work in the humanities and the arts diminishes as the language of back to basics fuses with what Marcuse called, after its aspiration, the language of total administration. Marxism—feminist and not—thrives in the universities only to the extent that it becomes disciplined, hermetic, and polite, and keeps its distance from direct confrontation with the ruling powers. Under these conditions, the theory of one-dimensionality, its cultural critique, seems more relevant than ever.

Acknowledgements

*My work on this article has been helped by the generous advice and detailed suggestions of Lynn Appleton, Tom Banks, Chris Berry, Lynn Garrett, Douglas Kellner, Carlos Nelson, Andrea Press, Michael Selig, Janet Staiger, Diane Waldman, and especially Mike Budd and Cathy Schwichtenberg. A different version was presented in New York on June 14, 1985, to members of the Society for Cinema Studies, whose ideas led to substantial revisions.

Notes

1 For historical and theoretical introductions, see Jay, *The Dialectical Imagination*, and Buck-Morss.

2 For Critical Theory in its later formulations, such terms as "mass culture" and "popular culture" mystify the culture industry and its social connections. They risk unreasonably connoting broad participation in the development of the industry's goods, as "folk culture" reasonably does in its realm (Adorno, "Culture Industry Reconsidered" 12).

3 Besides those mentioned elsewhere in the text: "On Popular Music" (written with George Simpson), "On the Fetish-Character in Music and the Regression of Listening," "On the Social Situation of Music," and "The Stars Down to Earth: The *Los Angeles Times* Astrology Column: A Study in Secondary Superstition." For an assessment of Adorno's contemporary relevance as a critic of culture industry music, see Gendron.

4 See, e.g., Allen, Budd, Hansen ("Pleasure"), Levin, Rosen, and *New German Critique* 40 (Winter 1987), a Special Issue on Weimar Film Theory.

5 Waldman here cites Lee Russell (pseud. Peter Wollen), "Cinema—Code and Image," *New Left Review* 49 (May/June 1968): 75.

6 Indeed, Adorno's radically anti-ontological position has drawn serious criticism (Jay, "Adorno").

7 Crediting Waldman, Thomas Andrae echoed this claim in a 1979 article in *Jump Cut*—evidence of the diffusion of Waldman's position, and of Wollen's.

8 The English translations of the Frankfurt School's predominantly German writings have a reputation for unreliability among scholars fluent in both German and English. Although most of Marcuse's major writings were first published in English, translation problems may well have affected reception of the Frankfurt School's German-language texts in English-speaking countries. For an illuminating exchange on the problems involved in translating and publishing one of Adorno's major works (*Aesthetic Theory*), see Hullot-Kentor and Lenhardt.

9   See, e.g., those mentioned in note 3, Horkheimer and Adorno, and Lowenthal, "The Triumph of Mass Idols."

10   Czitrom here is quoting Raymond and Alice Bauer, "America, Mass Society, and Mass Media," *Journal of Social Issues* 16.3 (1960): 22.

11   Marcuse did use the term "mass societies" in *Soviet Marxism: A Critical Analysis* (New York: Vintage-Random, 1961): 72, 78. But his conception was more dialectical than the "mass society theory" label connotes.

12   Compare, for example, Adorno's English-language "How to Look at Television" with his "Cultural Criticism and Society," written for German publication at about the same time.

13   Elworth was citing Staiger.

14   Broadcast on September 19, 1986, on General Electric's National Broadcasting Company.

Works Cited

Adorno, Theodor W. *Aesthetic Theory*. Trans. C. Lenhardt. Eds. Gretel Adorno and Rolf Tiedemann. London: Routledge, Kegan, Paul, 1984.

———. "Correspondence with Benjamin." Trans. Harry Zohn. *New Left Review* 81 (1970): 55–79.

———. "Cultural Criticism and Society." *Prisms*. Trans. Samuel and Shierry Weber. Cambridge, MA: MIT P, 1981. 19–34.

———. "Culture Industry Reconsidered." Trans. Anson G. Rabinbach. *New German Critique* 6 (Fall 1975): 12–19.

———. "How to Look at Television." *Quarterly of Film, Radio, and Television* 3 (1954): 213–35.

———. "On the Fetish Character in Music and the Regression of Listening." *The Essential Frankfurt School Reader*. Eds. Andrew Arato and Eike Gebhardt. New York: Urizen, 1978. 270–99.

———. "On the Social Situation of Music." Trans. Wes Blomster. *Telos* 35 (Spring 1978): 128–64.

———. "Perennial Fashion: Jazz." *Prisms*. 121–32.

———. "Resignation." Trans. Wes Blomster. *Telos* 35 (Spring 1978): 165–8.

———. "Scientific Experiences of a European Scholar in America." Trans. Donald Fleming. *The Intellectual Migration: Europe and America, 1930–1960*. Eds. Donald Fleming and Bernard Bailyn. Cambridge, MA: Belknap-Harvard UP, 1969. 338–70.

———. "A Social Critique of Radio Music." *Kenyon Review* 7.2 (1945): 208–17.

———. "Sociology and Psychology." *New Left Review* 46/47 (1967–68): 67–80, 79–90.

———. "The Stars Down to Earth: The *Los Angeles Times* Astrology Column: A Study in Secondary Superstition." *Telos* 19 (1974): 13–90.

Adorno, Theodor W., with George Simpson. "On Popular Music." *Studies in Philosophy and Social Science* 9 (1941): 17–48.

[Adorno, Theodor W., and] Hanns Eisler. *Composing for the Films*. New York: Oxford UP, 1947.

Allen, Richard. "Critical Theory and the Paradox of Modernist Discourse." *Screen* 28.2 (Spring 1987): 69–85.

Anderson, Perry. *Arguments within English Marxism*. London: NLB, 1980.

Andrae, Thomas. "The Culture Industry Reconsidered: Adorno on Film and Mass Culture." *Jump Cut* 20 (1979): 34–7.

Bennett, Tony. *Formalism and Marxism*. London: New Viewpoints-Methuen, 1979.

———. "Theories of the Media, Theories of Society." Gurevitch, et al. 30–55.

Blumler, Jay G., and Michael Gurevitch. "The Political Effects of Mass Communication." Gurevitch, et al. 236–67.

Boddy, William. "Loving a Nineteen-Inch Motorola: American Writing on Television." *Regarding Television: Critical Approaches—An Anthology*. Ed. E. Ann Kaplan. The American Film Institute Monograph Series 2. Frederick, MD: University Publications of America-American Film Institute, 1983. 1–11.

Bottomore, Thomas. *The Frankfurt School*. Key Sociologists. New York: Ellis-Horwood-Tavistock-Methuen, 1984.

Braverman, Harry. *Labor and Monopoly Capital*. New York: Monthly Review Press, 1974.

Buck-Morss, Susan. *The Origin of Negative Dialectics: Theodor W. Adorno, Walter Benjamin, and the Frankfurt Institute*. New York: Macmillan-Free, 1977.

Budd, Michael, R. Stephen Craig, and Clay Steinman. *"Fantasy Island*: The Dialectic of Narcissism." *Aspects of Fantasy: Selected Essays from the Second International Conference on the Fantastic in Literature and Film*. Ed. William Coyle. Contributions to the Study of Science Fiction and Fantasy 19. Westport, CT: Greenwood, 1986. 87–93.

Budd, Michael. "The National Board of Review and the Early Art Cinema in New York." *Cinema Journal* 26.1 (Fall 1986): 3–18.

Curran, James, Michael Gurevitch, and Janet Woollacott. "The Study of the Media: Theoretical Approaches." Gurevitch, et al. 11–29.

Czitrom, Daniel J. *Media and the American Mind: From Morse to McLuhan*. Chapel Hill: U of North Carolina P, 1982.

DeFleur, Melvin L., and Sandra Ball-Rokeach. *Theories of Mass Communication*. 4th ed. New York: Longman, 1982.

Dubiel, Helmut. "The Origins of Critical Theory: An Interview with Leo Lowenthal." Trans. David Berger. *Telos* 49 (1981): 141–54.

Elworth, Steven B. "Accepting Interpretations: Interpretative Communities of Power." Society for Cinema Studies. New York, June 13, 1985.

Ewen, Stuart. *Captains of Consciousness*. New York: McGraw, 1976.

Frankfurt Institute for Social Research. *Aspects of Sociology*. Trans. John Viertel. Boston: Beacon, 1972.

Garnham, Nicholas. "Film and Media Studies: Reconstructing the Subject." *Film Reader* 5 (1982): 177–83.

Gitlin, Todd. "Media Sociology: The Dominant Paradigm." *Theory and Society* 6 (1978): 205–53.

Gendron, Bernard. "Theodor Adorno Meets the Cadillacs." *Studies in Entertainment: Critical Approaches to Mass Culture*. Ed. Tania Modleski. Theories of Contemporary Culture 7. Bloomington: Midland-Indiana UP, 1986.

Grossberg, Lawrence. "Strategies of Marxist Cultural Interpretation." *Critical Studies in Mass Communication* 1 (1984): 392–419.

Gurevitch, Michael, James Curran, and Janet Woollacott, eds. *Culture, Society and the Media*. London: University Paperbacks-Methuen, 1982.

Hall, Stuart. "The Rediscovery of 'Ideology.'" Gurevitch, et al. 56–90.

Hansen, Miriam B. "Introduction to Adorno: 'Transparencies on Film.'" *New German Critique* 24–25 (1981–82): 186–98.

——. "Pleasure, Ambivalence, Identification: Valentino and Female Spectatorship." *Cinema Journal* 25.4 (Summer 1986): 6–32.

Horkheimer, Max. "Traditional and Critical Theory" and "Postscript." *Critical Theory*. Trans. Matthew J. O'Connell. New York: Continuum-Seabury, 1972. 188–252.

Horkheimer, Max, and Theodor W. Adorno. "The Culture Industry: Enlightenment as Mass Deception." *Dialectic of Enlightenment*. Trans. John Cumming. New York: Continuum-Seabury, 1972. 120–67.

Hullot-Kentor, Robert. "Adorno's Aesthetic Theory: The Translation." *Telos* 65 (Fall 1985): 143–7.

Jacoby, Russell. "A Falling Rate of Intelligence?" *Telos* 27 (1976): 141–6.

Jameson, Fredric. "Introduction to T. W. Adorno." *Salmagundi* 10–11 (1969–70): 140–3.

——. *Marxism and Form: Twentieth-Century Dialectical Theories of Literature*. Princeton: Princeton UP, 1971.

Jay, Martin. "Adorno and Kracauer: Notes on a Troubled Friendship." *Salmagundi* 40 (1978): 42–66.

——. *The Dialectical Imagination: A History of the Frankfurt School and the Institute of Social Research, 1923–1950*. Boston: Little, 1973.

Journal of Communication 33.3 (Summer 1983). Special Issue on "Ferment in the Field."

Kellner, Douglas. *From Fascism to Technocapitalism: Studies in the Critical Theory of Society*, forthcoming, Polity Press, 1988.

Lenhardt, Christian. "Reply to Hullot-Kentor." *Telos* 65 (Fall 1985): 147–52.

Levin, Thomas. "The Acoustic Dimension." *Screen* 25.3 (May–June 1984): 55–68.

Lopez, Ana. "From Photoplays to Texts: Film Theory, Film Studies, and the Future." *Cinema Journal* 24.2 (1985): 56–61.

Lovell, Terry. "Marxism and Cultural Studies." *Film Reader* 5 (1982): 184–91.

——. *Pictures of Reality*. London: BFI, 1980.

Lowenthal, Leo. "Popular Culture in Perspective." *Literature, Popular Culture, and Society*. Palo Alto: Pacific, 1961. 1–13.

——. "The Triumph of Mass Idols." *Literature, Popular Culture, and Society*. 109–36.

Marcuse, Herbert. "The Affirmative Character of Culture." *Negations: Essays in Critical Theory*. Trans. Jeremy J. Shapiro. Boston: Beacon, 1968. 88–133.

——. *Counter-Revolution and Revolt*. Boston: Beacon, 1972.

——. *An Essay on Liberation*. Boston: Beacon, 1969.

————. *One-Dimensional Man: Studies in the Ideology of Advanced Industrial Society*. Boston: Beacon, 1964.

————. "Philosophy and Critical Theory." *Negations*. 134–58.

McDonnell, Kevin, and Kevin Robins. "Marxist Cultural Theory: The Althusserian Smokescreen." Simon Clarke, et al. *One-Dimensional Marxism: Althusser and the Politics of Culture*. London: Allison, 1980. 157–231.

New German Critique 40 (Winter 1987). Special Issue on Weimar Film Theory.

Noble, David F. *America by Design: Science, Technology, and the Rise of Corporate Capitalism*. New York: Galaxy-Oxford UP, 1977.

O'Kane, John. "Althusser, Ideology, and Oppositional Practice." *enclitic* 7.1 (Spring 1983): 104–16.

Petro, Patrice. "Mass Culture and the Feminine: The 'Place' of Television in Film Studies." *Cinema Journal* 25.3 (Spring 1986): 5–21.

Renault, Greg. "Journal Reviews." *Telos* 36 (1978): 257.

Rosen, Philip. "Adorno and Film Music: Theoretical Notes on *Composing for the Films*." *Yale French Studies* 60 (1980): 157–82.

Shils, Edward A. "Daydreams and Nightmares: Reflections on the Criticism of Mass Culture." *Sewanee Review* 65 (Autumn 1957): 587–608.

Slack, Jennifer Daryl, and Martin Allor. "The Political and Epistemological Constituents of Critical Communication Research." *Journal of Communication* 33.3 (1983): 208–18.

Staiger, Janet. "The Politics of Film Canons." *Cinema Journal* 24.3 (Spring 1985): 4–23.

Waldman, Diane. "Critical Theory and Film: Adorno and 'The Culture Industry' Revisited." *New German Critique* 12 (1977): 39–60.

Kracauer's Epistemological Shift

PATRICE PETRO

IT HAS OFTEN been remarked that, until fairly recently, Kracauer's reputation in film theory rested upon the two books he wrote in English: *From Caligari to Hitler* (1947) and *Theory of Film* (1960).[1] These two books, which established Kracauer as a major, if fundamentally flawed, thinker on film, have frequently been compared to the essays and more aphoristic writings of the French film theorist André Bazin, who shared Kracauer's concern for an aesthetics of realism in the cinema.

In standard surveys of film theory, however, the comparison between Kracauer and Bazin is made only to underscore the tendentious and one-dimensional quality of Kracauer's thought. Dudley Andrew, for example, characterizes the difference between Kracauer and Bazin in the following way. He writes:

> Kracauer is the kind of man who decided after forty years of viewing film that he ought to work out and write down his ideas about the medium; so he went straight to the library and locked himself in. There, reading widely, thinking endlessly, and always working alone, always cut off from the buzz of film talk and film production, he slowly and painstakingly gave birth to his theory.[2]

Andrew continues:

> Unlike Kracauer, who spent years alone in a library generating *Theory of Film*, Bazin seems always to have been with people who were making films or discussing them. . . . It has been suggested that the best of his criticism has been lost because it occurred in the form of oral presentations and debates. . . . In any case, Bazin displayed little concern for the future of his ideas. He seemed satisfied that his thoughts could be of service in particular situations.[3]

In this account, Bazin is upheld as the quintessentially French intellectual, collegial in his approach to scholarship and aware of the contingent nature of thought. Kracauer, by contrast, emerges as the stereotypical German pedant, shut off from the world of practical criticism and obsessed with the future of his own ideas. Indeed, what Andrew values most in Bazin is directly related to what he finds most lacking in Kracauer. The local and specific nature of Bazin's theorizing about film—its provi-

Reprinted from *New German Critique* 54 (1991): 127–38.

sional and essayistic quality—is precisely what prevents it, according to Andrew, from becoming the formidable and formidably closed system represented by Kracauer's ponderously Teutonic thought.

This obvious caricature of both Kracauer and Bazin is not merely an expression of an opinion, not simply the reflection of a Francophile sentiment. For while it is that, it is also much more, pointing to the intellectual and historical origins of contemporary film theory. No attentive reader of Anglo-American film theory over the past three decades would fail to miss its distinctly French orientation. From *auteurism* to poststructuralism, French traditions of thought have had the most significant influence on the development of Film Studies as an academic discipline, both in the United States and in Britain. To be sure, German theory has been enlisted along the way to expand the domain of a critical film theory. But it is Freud as read through Lacan, or Marx through Althusser, that has set the terms for the reception of German film theory. Even initial attempts to restore a phenomenological dimension to film study appealed to existential phenomenology rather than to critical theory, Merleau-Ponty and Sartre rather than Kracauer or Benjamin, in order to challenge the analytic and overtly scientific approach of early film structuralism and semiotics.[4]

What this points to, among other things, is the relative ease with which ideas have circulated between French and Anglo-American traditions, and the fundamentally impaired or more limited movement of German theories in the United States and Britain—at least insofar as the recent history of film theory is concerned. The rise of Nazism, which forced some of the most sophisticated theorists of cinema and mass culture into exile, certainly accounts for the loss of texts and traditions that contributed to a vital film culture in Germany during the 1920s. More significant than this, however, was the temporal lag between the translation of important German texts into English and the clearing of an institutional space in the 1970s for serious academic film study.

With no understanding of German theoretical traditions, and with no knowledge of the German language, some of the most prominent film scholars in the seventies had considerable difficulty in seeing any connection between Kracauer's final work on history and Benjamin's *Illuminations*, or, for that matter, any relationship between Kracauer's study of the Weimar cinema and Horkheimer and Adorno's *Dialectic of Enlightenment*. In a thumbnail sketch of Kracauer's career, for example, Andrew mentions only four of his major studies—*From Caligari to Hitler, Theory of Film, History: The Last Things Before the Last*, and *Offenbach and the Paris of His Time*—books originally written in English, or, in the case of the Offenbach study, books readily available in English translation. Had Andrew considered Kracauer's writings for the *Frankfurter Zeitung*, he might have suggested how they share the improvisational character of

Bazin's essays and how they connect to a wider history of German thinking about film.

Unaware of this early work, and failing to appreciate the circumstances
under which *Theory of Film* was actually written, Andrew therefore fails to
assess adequately the reasons for Kracauer's and Bazin's different working
methods. Kracauer, Andrew tells us, "decided after forty years of viewing
film" to write down his ideas about the medium, and "so he went straight
to the library and locked himself in." Bazin, by contrast, is valorized for the
social nature of his criticism, for having always "been with people who
were making films or discussing them." Forced into exile in the early
1930s, Kracauer's solitary mode of scholarship can hardly be compared
with Bazin's, since Bazin was never forced to leave his native France. And
while risking, in the very writing of *Theory of Film*, the possibility of
appearing out of date and overly ambitious, Kracauer also risked what
Edward Said has described in relation to Erich Auerbach as the very real
"possibility of *not* writing and thus falling victim to the concrete dangers
of exile: the loss of texts, traditions, and continuities that make up the very
web of a culture."[5]

Said's discussion of the effects of exile on Auerbach's writing of
Mimesis bears further comparison with Kracauer's *Theory of Film*, not
least of all given the two men's shared affiliation with a formidable tradition of European literature and letters. Said points out that in the epilogue
to *Mimesis*, Auerbach casually mentions his experience of exile in Istanbul,
thereby invoking not merely a place outside of Europe, but also "the ultimate alienation from and opposition to Europe." As Said explains, "For
centuries Turkey and Islam hung over Europe like a gigantic composite
monster, seeming to threaten Europe with destruction. To have been an
exile in Istanbul at the time of fascism in Europe was a deeply resonating
and intense form of exile from Europe."[6]

Said concludes by suggesting how Auerbach's experience of exile in the
Orient ultimately served an enabling purpose, allowing him to convert his
sense of pain and alienation into a work of literary criticism whose insights
derive not simply from the culture it describes but also, and more crucially, from a necessary and agonizing distance from it. The same might be
said of Kracauer's analysis of the Weimar cinema in *From Caligari to
Hitler*, and yet the parallels between Kracauer and Auerbach go further
than this. For instance, Auerbach's own admission of the need to transcend national boundaries ("our philological home is the earth," he writes;
"it can no longer be the nation"[7]) certainly illuminates the final section of
Theory of Film, where Kracauer, drawing directly on *Mimesis*, argues for
an aesthetics of cinema derived from the texture of everyday life. Films
whose composition "varies according to place, people, and time,"
Kracauer writes, "help us not only to appreciate our given material envi-

ronment but to extend it in all directions. They virtually make the world our home."[8]

Even more striking than Auerbach's and Kracauer's shared commitment to a realist aesthetic, however, are the similar effects of their different destinations as refugees from Nazi Europe. If Istanbul was a particularly intense form of exile for a literary critic like Auerbach, so too, was the United States a deeply resonant experience for a film theorist like Kracauer. Since at least the 1920s, Hollywood cinema represented not merely an alternative to European filmmaking but also the very ethos of consumer capitalism that threatened to overtake and subsume other national traditions. Although Kracauer never shared Adorno's antipathy to Hollywood or, indeed, to other forms of commercial filmmaking, he was certainly aware of the dangers of consumerist logic, even if, on the surface, this seems more obvious in his early writings than it does in *Theory of Film*.

In any case, it would be impossible to see Kracauer today as the author solely of *From Caligari to Hitler* or of *Theory of Film*, or to assume that these books contain all of what he had to say about the cinema. The translation of some of Kracauer's most important early writings in the pages of *New German Critique* has gone a long way to ensure a reevaluation of Kracauer's reputation in Film Studies, and has in fact inaugurated a veritable Kracauer renaissance in contemporary film theory. What has emerged from recent discussions is a view of not one but two successive and autonomous theories of the cinema in the corpus of his writings; in other words, one finds a view of "two Kracauers" in contemporary film theory: the early Kracauer of *Das Ornament der Masse* and the later Kracauer of *From Caligari to Hitler* and *Theory of Film*.

The early Kracauer, for instance, is characterized as the practical film critic of the *Frankfurter Zeitung*, the anticapitalist practitioner of a "material dialectics" (if not a dialectical materialism), the phenomenological observer of the local, the ephemeral, the everyday. The later Kracauer, by contrast, is seen to be the massive system-builder and conceptual thinker of *Caligari* and *Theory of Film*, the anticommunist émigré intellectual, the sociological critic turned melancholy realist. While retaining Dudley Andrew's pejorative assessment of Kracauer's American work, this new view also assumes that the inconsistencies in Kracauer's writings constitute overwhelming evidence of a schism or epistemological shift in his thinking about film—a shift that separates the early, improvisational essays of the 1920s from the later, academically imposing, studies of the postwar period.

To be sure, some commentators have suggested that Kracauer's writings exhibit a continuity of concerns, despite apparent inconsistencies in his method or chosen format, be it the exploratory essay or the book-length study. Karsten Witte, for example, maintains that the link between the early and later work "lies in [Kracauer's] intention to decipher social tendencies revealed in ephemeral cultural phenomena."[9] For others, however, Kracauer's work evidences a significant theoretical division, with the later work marking a lapse into a fundamentally flawed or one-dimensional reasoning. Heide Schlüpmann, for example, writes that "in *From Caligari to Hitler* and *Theory of Film*, Kracauer's tendency to generalize, to subsume particulars within conceptual constructs, presents an obstacle to the expression of his ideas." The strength of the early essays, she further contends, "lies in their phenomenological procedure, their taking up of individual manifestations of daily life and dwelling upon them reflectively."[10] Thomas Elsaesser similarly stresses the differences between Kracauer's work written in Germany and in America, claiming that between the 1927 essay "The Mass Ornament" and the 1947 book *From Caligari to Hitler*, Kracauer abandoned the dialectical core of his early criticism in favor of a sociological reductionism and an unredeemed humanism.[11] In Elsaesser's estimation, the early Kracauer's emphasis on the impossibility of separating high art and mass culture distinguishes him as a proto-poststructuralist, whereas the later work places him squarely within the traditions of American sociology and cold war anticommunism. Although the divide between early and later work is therefore variously interpreted, there is little dispute over the fact of a division—a division separating marxist critique from a theory of realist aesthetics, and Weimar Germany from postwar America.

Given the terms of Kracauer's reception in Film Studies, there is some question of whether we must speak of *Kracauer's* epistemological shift, or, rather, of an epistemological shift in Kracauer criticism. Of course, in the context of Film Studies, to speak of an epistemological shift at all is necessarily to invoke David Bordwell's essay on "Eisenstein's Epistemological Shift," which attempts to show how Eisenstein's writings turned from a materialist aesthetic informed by Pavlovian physiology and dialectical materialism to a romantic aesthetic grounded in psychology, organicism, and empiricism.[12] In a surprising reversal of classical film theory's traditional separation of formalist and realist aesthetics, Eisenstein and Kracauer have come to be discussed in remarkably similar ways. In Bordwell's view, Eisenstein's later writings evidence a shift toward political conformity as well as a move from a practical engagement with film to a stance of isolated self-absorption. According to recent commentators like Elsaesser, Kracauer's writings similarly reveal a turn away from dialectical thinking to political conservatism, as well as a shift from practical film criticism to academic film theory. What is at stake, then, in claims for epistemological shifts in the development of film theory are assumptions about intellectual responses to Stalinism and to communism in the cold war era. As one critic has put it (without, however, making any reference to Kracauer): "It is strange to see how the philistinism of the Stalinist regime in the 1930s finds its belated double in the United States of the Cold War two decades later."[13]

Of course, the concept of "epistemological shift" has a wider theoretical lineage, one that can be traced to Louis Althusser's structuralist rereading of Marx, with its claim for a divide separating the young, humanist Marx of the 1844 Manuscripts from the mature, scientific Marx of *Das Kapital*.[14] While clearly an intellectual response to Stalinism and its cult of personality, Althusser's concept of epistemological shift also finds parallels in assessments of other marxist thinkers, notably Lukács, whose work is typically interpreted as split between an early idealism and romantic anticapitalism, and a later orthodox marxism and realist aesthetics.[15] The notion of epistemological shift, however, has even deeper historical resonances in Film Studies, and can be traced to early *auteur* criticism, which stressed the negative impact of American culture on various European directors' careers.[16] Within this tradition, the British Hitchcock was compared to the American Hitchcock, the German Fritz Lang to the American Fritz Lang, and, almost invariably, the American work was found wanting. Recent discussions of Kracauer's epistemological shift would therefore seem to partake of both the marxist critique and the *auteurist* legacy in Film Studies, since his writings are said to split upon both a critical response to Stalinism and an uncritical embrace of American culture.

Kracauer himself would not object in principle to the concept of epistemological shift, since his final study of history provides a compelling analysis of historical time as profoundly fractured and disjunctive.[17] He would, however, insist on seeing his German and American writing as part of a common project, and this, in fact, is one of the main arguments of the *History* book, which attempts to situate his life's work within a continuum of concerns. Although some have suggested that Kracauer manipulated his image for posterity in this final study,[18] it is clear that he was attempting to respond to the critique leveled against him by his longtime friend and former colleague, Theodor Adorno, who argued in a 1965 essay that Kracauer's work became increasingly affirmative in America, that it embraced the possibility of happiness in the world and failed to sustain a critique of the status quo.[19]

The image of Kracauer conveyed by Adorno suggests a familiar story of the émigré intellectual in America: the refugee fleeing from fascist Europe ultimately settles in America where, feeling himself exiled, displaced, and alienated, he writes a scathing critique of his former culture. He then goes on uncritically to accept the English language and is eventually seduced by American culture (not to mention its cinema), finding in it a haven from forced exile and voluntary emigration, thereby mirroring the "end of ideology" criticism fashionable in America in the 1950s. To be sure, Adorno ultimately conceded that the source of Kracauer's conservatism must be sought in the very tensions and pressures of emigration. And yet, by reading Kracauer's career as a mirror reflection of wider historical developments in cold war politics, he failed to consider the range of institutional changes that necessarily separated Kracauer's early and later work.

To begin with, Kracauer confronted very different audiences and institutional arrangements in America than he had known in Weimar Germany. Needless to say, in the United States of the 1940s and 1950s, there was little place in film journalism for a man of Kracauer's training and expertise, even though he was able to find a congenial environment for intellectual work on the margins of academic life. The shift in his writings from practical criticism to academic film theory must therefore take into account the very different sense of place and belonging, as well as the very distinct forms of association and community, entailed in the movement from Europe to America at the time.

Second, it is important to note the changing status of film as a cultural object in the period spanning Kracauer's migration. In the 1920s, Kracauer wrote about the cinema as a marginal sphere of life and about film viewing as an experience that marked the cultural disintegration of absolute values and objective truths. By the 1940s, the cinema could no longer be construed as a marginal phenomenon, since it had clearly emerged as one of the central institutions in modern cultural life. Without an established institutional place for Film Studies in the 1950s and 1960s, however, *Caligari* and *Theory and Film* failed to find a wide or appreciative audience. And when academic film study was formally institutionalized in the 1960s and 1970s, these books became even further marginalized and unreadable, antithetical as they were to the reigning critical orthodoxies of *auteurism*, structuralism, and antirealist film theory.

Today, of course, all this has changed, as some of Kracauer's early writings have been translated into English and interpreted from the perspective of contemporary film theory. No longer is there any doubt of Kracauer's connections to critical theory, and it has become nearly impossible to relegate his materialist aesthetics to a "naive realism" or simple-minded reflectionism. Kracauer's critique of totality and concern for history have also inspired extended comparisons with such poststructuralist thinkers as Baudrillard and Foucault, and it would not be unthinkable to imagine future comparisons between Kracauer's conceptualization of modern culture as a "mass ornament" and the Situationists' description of their own era as "The Society of the Spectacle." That Kracauer's writings have now become readable from the vantage point of poststructuralism is undoubtedly related to the fact that the cinema itself has once again become a marginal sphere, dominated by television and the computer. It is nevertheless ironic that the reevaluation of Kracauer's career has involved elaborate appeals to the authority of French traditions in criticism and theory, and that Kracauer's later work continues to be criticized when it seems most overtly or most resolutely "German."

But it would be too easy to dismiss as ahistorical and disingenuous the recent characterizations of Kracauer as a proto-poststructuralist. And it would also be a mistake to underestimate the role played by what Edward Said has called "borrowed" or "travelling theory." As Said explains:

> Cultural and intellectual life are usually nourished and often sustained by [a] circulation of ideas, and whether it takes the form of acknowledged or unconscious influence, creative borrowing, or wholesale appropriation, the movement of ideas and theories from one place to another is both a fact of life and a usefully enabling condition of intellectual activity. Having said that, however, one should go on to specify the kinds of movements that are possible, in order to ask whether by virtue of having moved from one place and time to another an idea or a theory gains or loses in strength, and whether a theory in one historical period and national culture becomes altogether different in another period or situation.[20]

This concept of "travelling theory" helps to illuminate the reasons for an epistemological shift in recent Kracauer criticism, as well as the shift in Kracauer's own thinking about film. Indeed, what attracts contemporary scholars to Kracauer's early work on cinema, and, moreover, to his final thoughts on history, is precisely his commitment to the feel and texture of experience, his critique of abstraction and totalizing theories of culture, and his investment in questions of the local, the ephemeral, and the everyday. Kracauer's early writings are fascinating for us today because they do not present a theoretically closed or coherent system, but read instead like a phenomenology of everyday life, offering both an analysis of the sensory, perceptual apparatus of film viewing and a critique of its reified institutions. In the wake of the massive system-building of structuralism and semiotics, Kracauer's materialist phenomenology represents a timely alternative to outmoded forms of conceptual thinking and an early historical precedent for what is now called "cultural studies." While the movement of Kracauer's early theory into contemporary Film Studies has necessarily involved processes of representation and institutionalization different from those in Weimar Germany, it has also inaugurated a subtle approach to questions of cultural production and reception from the standpoint of a theory that, one would hope, will one day constitute a history of subjectivity in relation to everyday life.

In this regard, it is important to emphasize that Kracauer's less fashionable American work also merits serious rereading, since it clearly reframes the arguments originally posed in the 1920s and offers a compelling critique of abstraction and conceptual thinking, if often in highly abstract and conceptual terms. *Theory of Film*, for instance, provides a reading of mass culture in relation to the fragmentation and alienation of everyday life and levels a critique against intellectuals for attempting to preserve outmoded aesthetic values under changed cultural conditions. Focusing attention on peculiarly modern forms of subjectivity, *Theory of Film* thus takes up where "The Mass Ornament" left off, analyzing a culture dedicated to the play of surface in and through its representations. Whereas the early essays enlist marxist theory and economic analysis more obviously and more thoroughly, lending equal weight to the manipulative character of mass culture as well as to its emancipatory potential, the later work preserves an interest in dialectical thinking, although it tends to take up either side of the dialectic in individual studies.

In *From Caligari to Hitler*, for example, Kracauer analyzes the cinema as an institution that functioned historically to paralyze social life, reifying it into ornamental patterns, and evacuating the possibility for individual judgment or critical thought. In *Theory of Film*, the reifying process of cinematic representation is interpreted more positively, as a force which energizes the unforeseen and potentially liberating possibilities of a technological medium in an abstract and modern age. This much is suggested by Kracauer when he writes, "We literally redeem this world from its dormant state, its state of virtual nonexistence, by endeavoring to experience it through the camera"; or, again, when he observes that "abstract painting is not so much an anti-realistic movement as a realistic revelation of the prevailing abstraction."[21] Kracauer's final work on *History* then restates the dialectical relationship between critique and possibility in photography and in history, thereby restoring the complicated alternation of ideas that energize the early work.

The corpus of Kracauer's writings therefore suggests the difficulties in viewing his ideas as mere reflections of his time, as Adorno tended to do, for there is, in fact, no linear progression in his thinking about film, and no simple or necessary movement from critique to embrace of mass culture as his theory traveled across time or, indeed, across space. Kracauer's later writings, I would submit, actually reveal less of an epistemological shift than a shift of emphasis in the original theory, resulting in an overstatement and, in places, a simplification of the analysis of mass culture developed in the 1920s.[22] Taken together, *From Caligari to Hitler* and *Theory of Film* constitute a complex dialectical view of the cinema such as one finds theorized in the early writings. When read separately, however, these books tend to suggest a one-dimensional, one-sided, and impoverished account of the relationship between institutional constraints and perceptual possibilities in the cinema and in history. As Adorno might have reminded Kracauer, although here, in a celebrated reply, he is responding directly to Benjamin:

The reification of the great work of art is not just loss, any more than the reification of the cinema is all loss. It would be bourgeois reaction to negate the reification of the cinema in the name of the ego, and it would border on anarchism to revoke the reification of the great work of art in the spirit of immediate use values. Both bear the stigmata of capitalism, both contain elements of change. . . . Both are torn halves of an integral freedom to which, however, they do not add up.[23]

In typical fashion, Kracauer seems to have anticipated this critique in the writing of *Theory of Film* and, as if to defend himself against it, offered a comparison of Marx and Freud that illuminates his own reasons for attempting to extend his theory of film beyond the early writings, precisely by underlining the ways in which the cinema helps us to overcome abstraction and reified thinking through a concrete mode of apprehending and understanding. "Freud probes deeper than Marx into the forces conspiring against the rule of reason," writes Kracauer. "But Marx," he continues, "intent on widening that rule, could not well make use of discouraging profundities." As a kind of afterthought, and in a gesture that speaks both to his experience of exile in America and his own intellectual journey from "The Mass Ornament" to *Theory of Film*, Kracauer adds: "When you want to travel far, your luggage had better be light."[24]

Notes

1. *From Caligari to Hitler: A Psychological History of the German Film* (Princeton: Princeton UP, 1947); *Theory of Film: The Redemption of Physical Reality* (New York and London: Oxford UP, 1960).

2. *The Major Film Theories: An Introduction* (New York and London: Oxford UP, 1976) 107. It should be mentioned here that Andrew borrows his characterization of Kracauer from Peter Harcourt. However, throughout his chapter on Kracauer's film theory, Andrew tends to add Harcourt's description, putting particular emphasis on Kracauer's "incomparable self-confidence and . . . imposing German seriousness."

3. Andrew 135.

4. See, for example, Dudley Andrew, "The Neglected Tradition of Phenomenology in Film Theory," repr. in the second volume of *Movies and Methods*, ed. Bill Nichols (Berkeley and Los Angeles: California UP, 1985) 625–32.

5. *The World, the Text, and the Critic* (Cambridge: Harvard UP, 1983) 6.

6. Said 6.

7. Auerbach, "Philologie der Weltliteratur," qtd. in Said.

8. Kracauer, *Theory of Film* 304.

9. "Introduction to Siegfried Kracauer's 'The Mass Ornament,'" *New German Critique* 5 (Spring 1975): 59.

10. "Phenomenology of Film: On Siegfried Kracauer's Writings of the 1920s," *New German Critique* 40 (Winter 1987): 98.

11. "Cinema—The Irresponsible Signifier, or 'The Gamble with History': Film Theory or Cinema Theory," *New German Critique* 40 (Winter 1987): 85.

12. *Screen* 15.4 (Winter 1974–5): 32–46.

13. Peter Wollen, *Signs and Meanings in the Cinema* (Bloomington: Indiana UP, 1969) 56. After this remark, Wollen adds, "'Realism' has always been the refuge of the conservative in the arts, together with a preference for propaganda of a comforting rather than disturbing kind."

14. *For Marx*, trans. Ben Brewster (London: New Left, 1977).

15. See, for example, Andrew Arato and Paul Breines, *The Young Lukács and the Origins of Western Marxism* (New York: Seabury, 1979).

16. For a historical overview of *auteur* criticism, see John Caughie, *Theories of Authorship* (London: British Film Institute, 1982).

17. *History: The Last Things Before the Last* (New York and London: Oxford UP, 1969). Phil Rosen and David Rodowick have both stressed Kracauer's disjunctive view of historical time. See Phil Rosen, "History, Textuality, Nation: Kracauer, Burch, and Some Problems in the Study of National Cinema," *Iris* 2.2 (1984): 69–84; D. N. Rodowick, "The Last Things Before the Last: Kracauer and History," *New German Critique* 41 (Spring-Summer 1987): 109–39.

18. See, for example, Martin Jay, "The Extraterritorial Life of Siegfried Kracauer," *Salmagundi* 31–32 (Fall 1975–Winter 1976): 49–106.

19. "Der wunderliche Realist. Über Siegfried Kracauer," *Noten zur Literatur* 3 (Frankfurt/Main: Suhrkamp, 1965) 83–108; English version in this issue of *New German Critique*.

20. Said 226.

21. Kracauer, *Theory of Film* 300, 294.

22. And, to complicate things even further, Miriam Hansen has pointed out that Kracauer's early writings also reveal a shift in emphasis, from a concern with metaphysical questions in the early 1920s to a concern with ideology and material practices from 1927 on. See Hansen's, "Decentric Perspectives: Kracauer's Early Writings on Film and Mass Culture," in this issue.

23. Adorno, "Letters to Walter Benjamin," repr. in trans. in *Aesthetics and Politics*, trans. Ronald Taylor (London: New Left, 1977) 123.

24. Kracauer, *Theory of Film* 290.

CONSTELLATION B
THE *HEIMAT* DEBATE: POLITICS OF HISTORY

This constellation, like the inception of German cinema studies itself, marks the interconnected crises of the German academic and public spheres. By highlighting the contrasts and connections between several texts engaging both the film Heimat *and the* Historikerstreit *(the public debate over the historical representation of the Holocaust), the constellation asks how the revisioning of German national history has affected the very notion of that history as a "German" one. As the terms of the published debate facilitated by Miriam Hansen repeat across the array of other texts in the constellation (those by Eric Santner, Anton Kaes, and Jürgen Habermas), the stereoscopic reader is led to ask how and why these terms might repeat or alter in ensuing constellations. For instance, how do concerns in these texts over "history," "memory," and "discourse" differ from those raised by Ingeborg Majer O'Sickey and Annette Van's critique of* Vergangenheitsverdrängung *(denial of the past) in Constellation C ("The Jewish Question")? Why do Santner and Kaes's mutual engagement of these issues deploy the Holocaust as a metaphor for both* Trauerarbeit *(mourning work) and the* unheimlich *(the uncanny), and where do their somewhat varied strategies intersect those of the phenomenological texts in Constellation H ("Feminism and Early Weimar")? What does it mean when Santner, appropriating Habermas, theorizes a "we," or "community," in the face of a contemporary global scene for which the notion of the ideal democratic* polis *is more and more riven with contradiction? How does Kaes's attempt to negotiate French postmodernism (Jacques Derrida, Jean-François Lyotard) with the historicist dimension of the Frankfurt School (Max Horkheimer, Theodor Adorno) qualify the vision of such a "community" through the concept of a* post-histoire? *What are the ideological implications of any of these texts' appropriations of the materialist and/or messianic writings of Walter Benjamin as a means of fielding these questions and concerns, and how does Habermas's own theory of the universalist orientation of democratic values offer a different way of responding to them? Can Habermas's ecumenical moralism, however, adequately address the ideological problem of German and Holocaust "ownership" and of German-Jewish "interchangeability" debated throughout these texts' analyses of the* Historikerstreit *and Holocaust representation, as well as across the anthology? How then is this constellation an allegory for the whole?*

Dossier on Heimat

MIRIAM HANSEN

*H*EIMAT *(HOMELAND)*. 924 mins. Reitz/WDR/SFB; directed by Edgar Reitz; script by Reitz and Peter Steinbach; photographed by Gernot Roll; edited by Heidi Handorf; music by Nikos Mamangakis. Cast: Marita Breuer, Michael Lesch, Dieter Schaad, Karin Kienzler, Eva Maria Bayerwaltes, Rüdiger Weigang, Karin Rasenack, Gertrud Bredel, Kurt Wagner, Gudrun Landgrebe, and many others.

The quotations printed below* are taken from reviews of Edgar Reitz's film *Heimat*, which was released as an eleven-part TV series in the summer of 1984 and subsequently screened in Munich and at film festivals in Venice and London; it reached the United States the following spring. We present these excerpts as contributions to a debate which has yet to take place. The conflicting positions the authors assume have implications beyond this particular film—implications with regard to current political developments in the Federal Republic, especially on the left (or, rather, what used to be considered the left); implications for the discourse on German history; implications for the state of West German film and TV culture; implications for a more general debate in film studies revolving around issues of reception theory, discourse analysis, historical and cultural specificity and a critique of ideology.

Heimat deserves attention, not just as yet another instance of New German Cinema as canonized by international auteurists, not even as yet another film dealing with German history. The most significant aspect of *Heimat* is its reception which includes the overwhelming success of both the TV series and the subsequent theatrical release of the film as well as the conflicting critical responses in part reprinted here. Unlike any other "New" German film, *Heimat* relates to crucial changes in the West German public sphere during the 1980s, ranging from the emergence of the Peace Movement, the Greens, a "new regionalism" and anti-Americanism to the effects of the *"Wende,"*[1] encapsulated in the programmatic shift from Dachau to Bitburg. Whether we define this relationship as one of reflection, intervention or coincidence, the film would certainly not have had the same impact ten years ago; neither *The Journey to Vienna* (1974) nor *The Zero Hour* (1976), two of Reitz's previous films with a similar revisionist approach to German history, made as much as a dent on public con-

---

This dossier is excerpted from the original which appeared in *New German Critique* 36 (Fall 1985): 3–8, 11–16. "From Memory, Home, & Hollywood" was first published in *Monthly Film Bulletin* Feb. 1985, © British Film Institute.

sciousness at the time of their release. (As far as I know, none of these films were ever picked up for distribution in the United States.) While the reception of *Heimat* has to be discussed in the context of the political and cultural discourses surrounding the film, it is also—and I think the Althusserian/Lacanian term is indeed useful here—a question of the kind of "subject effect" the film offers, a question of how the film engages its viewers, through a variety of textual strategies, in a process that imbricates cinematic pleasure with meaning and ideology.

How can a film with the title *Heimat* provoke such positive response on the left or, rather, what does this response tell us about the development of the German left? No doubt the reception of the film feeds upon larger debates on history and popular memory such as they took place during the later 1970s—in France and Britain strongly endebted to Foucault, in Germany to Negt and Kluge.[2] *Heimat* could easily be read in terms of a counter-hegemonic conception of history, as an attempt to reappropriate German history from official commemorations of a collective guilt and its cartoon-like representations on the part of the American media (e.g., the TV series *Holocaust*). Read in that context, Reitz's film would offer an alternative version of history, one that allows people to articulate their experience for themselves, by themselves, and recognize it in others; one that dissolves the closed narrative of History into a multiplicity of stories, stories of everyday life and material culture, told from a local and regional rather than a (necessarily compromised) national perspective; a history of the relationship between people and a place whose aura—"*Heimat*"—is irretrievably lost. Thus, the film would engage its viewers in a work of remembering and mourning, enabling them to confront German history as their own.

Yet, *Heimat* could also be read in the context of what French critics have called "*la mode rétro*," the revisionist fascination with the Nazi period beginning in the mid-1970s, with films like *Lacombe Lucien* and *The Nightporter*.[3] It could be argued that *Heimat* not only romanticizes the notion of popular memory but also participates in what Saul Friedländer describes as a "new discourse about Nazism on the right as well as on the left."[4] But how "new" is this discourse? Considering the film's ambiguous marginalization of the Holocaust and of political violence in general one might wonder if the revisionist gesture does not unwittingly reproduce the unacknowledged continuities of German history; if the evocation of "authentic experience" does not effectively reinscribe the familiar exclusions and distortions, the commonplaces and clichés of the "non-public opinion" (Adorno quoting Franz Böhm) which characterized the inofficial discourse on the Nazi period throughout the 1950s and beyond. The meaning of the phrase "*Aufarbeitung der Vergangenheit*," which Adorno discusses in a 1959 essay well worth rereading today, entails the slippage from coming to terms with the past, in the sense of "working through," to a discourse of denial which strives to restore the damaged collective narcissism by eliminating from consciousness the very events that jeopardized the possibility of national identification in the first place.[5]

Does *Heimat* succeed in untying the double bind of "mourning work" and "rehabilitation," does it overcome, to use Thomas Elsaesser's phrase, "the neat oppositions and conventional polarizations"? How far does the film go "to expose the very logic (or illogic) of the binary construction"?[6] These questions obviously invite a critique of ideology, but they are no less—and perhaps foremost—questions of an aesthetic dimension, of the particular discursive practices without which we cannot speak about ideology. How does the film negotiate the discrepancies of history and narrative?[7] What is the mode of narration, how does it place, or distance, the viewer? What other strategies of identification (e.g., point-of-view editing or lighting techniques) does it use or refrain from? How effective are textual devices that foreground the activity of narration (like the still photographs introduced, by a narrator figure, at the beginning of some installments, or the shifting between color footage and black and white throughout the film), devices that—in tendency at least—would undermine identification in a traditional sense? What kind of awareness does the film display of its intertextual relationships? How does it reflect on the problematic history of the German *Heimatfilm*, including its revisionist turn during the early 1970s? To what degree do the formal strategies of *Heimat* bear out the anti-Hollywood stance asserted in the publicity surrounding the film? How, for instance, does the appeal of Reitz's family-centered narrative differ from that of a commercial TV saga like *Dallas*?

Beyond the case of *Heimat*, questions like these pertain to current debates in film studies concerning concepts of national cinema as well as the scope of formal methods of film analysis (in particular those endebted to semiology and psychoanalysis) in relation to historical and cultural specificity. Recent West German cinema has proved a productive battleground for such debates, as the work of Thomas Elsaesser, Eric Rentschler, Timothy Corrigan, among others, illustrates.[8] The reception of a film like *Heimat* urges these questions upon us with an emotional force which might be, for some of us at least, too close to home—although this would be all the more reason to reconsider the relationship between formalist approaches and a critique of ideology. A critique of ideology which ignores the textual processes that bind cinematic subjectivity within a particular ideology risks stepping into the traps of literalism, historicism and moralism; textual analysis without an awareness of the context of reception (the public sphere, its historical and political dimensions) risks reproducing the same lacunae, distortions, and token acknowledgments that it set out to subvert. Without taking into account the critic's own institutional, ideological, experiential and interpretive affiliations, however, we remain caught in the very binarisms that paralyze the discourse on German history.

Karsten Witte
From: Of the Greatness of the Small People:
The Rehabilitation of a Genre
(*Die Zeit*, September 14, 1984)

When asked, what is *"Heimat,"* some will refer you to the paradox of Ernst Bloch's philosophy of hope; others, to a film with Zarah Leander. More recently, after highly successful screenings in Munich and Venice, one might say that *"Heimat"* is a film by Edgar Reitz which tackles the rather thorny task of thinking Ernst Bloch and Zarah Leander in one, each a scintillating moment of German history, one illuminating the other. This film acknowledges both traditions, rather than blotting out one in favor of the other.

"Heimat" always implies a totalizing grasp, whether directed towards a territory or towards the integration of those who speak a common language. At the same time, *"Heimat"* is conceivable as the locus of a diversity which has succumbed to unification, a non-territorial space which no longer asserts a presence but remains as a trace of the past. *"Heimat"* then would signify an elsewhere, a memory of origin for those who went away. Only the ritualistic Sunday speeches evoke the lost *"Heimat"* as a positive goal and a possibility of restoration. [. . .]

[. . .] A sense of imminent loss may be the strongest effect of the film, *Heimat*, [which was hailed by filmmakers as diverse as Herzog, Kluge, Schlöndorff, von Trotta and Wenders as] "a requiem of the small people." German reviewers are easily carried away by this kind of requiem if it is sung in Italian, be it Bertolucci's *1900*, Olmi's *The Tree of the Wooden Clogs*, or *Padre Padrone* by the Taviani Brothers—as if the Federal Republic had to compensate for the seeming lack of its own history of peasant culture with a nostalgia for that of the neighbors.

The consequences of this lack are not to be underrated. To make a film on the theme of *"Heimat"* in this day and age touches upon a taboo, in particular the fear to produce yet another *Heimatfilm*. Reitz literally had to reinvent that genre, since it was discredited by both the Nazis and their post-war successors in the entertainment industry. The *Heimatfilm* always had the odor of the cheapest fantasies of law and order, the most stupid idealization of rural customs and the meanest exploitation of peasant culture which, in the eyes of urban viewers, could not but appear ridiculous. The genre was beyond repair.

If Reitz has had both the courage and the imagination to give his village and family chronicle the title of *Heimat*, he not only subverted the taboo but also resisted the temptation of re-enchantment. He does not offer an idyl of the provinces. He merely illuminates, with increasing beauty and precision, the breeding-places of German history. His film is a mural of comic despair, a panorama of mourning though not of self-pity. For the peasant culture of the Hunsrück is irrevocably lost. Rather than celebrating this culture, the film honors it with a farewell song—a requiem, an exquisite dirge.

The title of the final section reads: "The Feast of the Living and the Dead." How do these levels go together? Doesn't this kind of temporality explode the chronological sense of a chronicle? Anyone who expected a film about a village to flaunt a crude realism or deft camera movements simulating peasant gestures will be disappointed, definitely at this point. The camera of Gernot Roll, cinematographer of Reitz's *The Zero Hour [Die Stunde Null,* 1976], traces, in an elaborate web, the collective movements of the extended family whose members stumble from Schabbach into the world. The ending assembles all characters and their stories in one space, the morgue, where time is suspended.

Gone are the charm and the bitterness, the cheerful nonsense and the slimy conformism of the villagers. This never-ending farewell feast is not a human affair but a historical one. The nice people of whom we had grown so fond have turned into mummies of memory. The village that appeared so serene and sheltered, spawned nothing but envy and jealousy. This final section thoroughly disturbs any vision of rural harmony that viewers might have subscribed to up until now, as it reveals good and bad energies as inseparably intertwined.

Whoever wants to leave the network of communal concern—which is the promise of any rural life—has to have the strength to become an outsider, to seek his fortune in the cities and to know how to endure it, too. In an endless series of variations, through complicated genealogical ramifications and historical entanglements, *Heimat* tells and retells the story of separations which have to be considered and undertaken. *"Heimat"* is not a place of rest; rather a transit camp for the utopia of social harmony. [. . .]

[The stance of the scriptwriters (Edgar Reitz and Peter Steinbach) towards the characters] is not a sentimental one, but could be described as affection without pity. As a result, the film shows the behavior of exemplary—though not necessarily model—human beings who under no circumstance are given a reprieve from history. Only the section entitled "Hermännchen," an autobiographical portrait of the artist as a young man, appears to me more like an exercise in self-indulgent sentimentality than one of self-criticism.

Heimat divests German History of its claim to greatness, it translates this History into a history of the small people who lead their lives in dignity, albeit without greatness. One has to listen to these memories and see them; only then can one engage in the difficult task of farewell. . . .

Thomas Elsaesser
From: Memory, Home and Hollywood
(*Monthly Film Bulletin*, February 1985)

The American series [*Holocaust*] crossed, inadvertently or not, a certain taboo threshold for the West German media; and Reitz's *Heimat*, begun around March 1979, responds to the challenge by entering into a sort of dialogue not only with *Holocaust*, but with its reception in Germany and the "retro" fashion in general.

Reitz, in fact, had participated in the debate quite directly, with an article he published in the May 1979 issue of *medium*, entitled "Let's work on our memories."[9] It conceives the issues from a partisan aesthetic perspective, as befits a film-political activist and co-signatory of the 1962 Oberhausen Manifesto: "If we are to come to terms with the Third Reich and the crimes committed in our country, it has to be by the same means we use every day to take stock of the world we live in. We suffer from a hopeless lack of meaningfully structured, aesthetically communicated experience (. . .) One should put an end to thinking in categories, even where this terrible part of our history is concerned. As far as possible, we must work on our *memories*. This way, films, literary products, images come into being that enlighten our senses and restore our reflexes."

What stands in the way of this, according to Reitz, is the economic hegemony of Hollywood in the entertainment market, which translates itself directly into a dominance of aesthetic forms. Other national cinemas or individual "film languages" are always at a disadvantage, since their product not only reflects the material difficulties of making films at the margins of the system, they are also judged according to the so-called "international aesthetic criteria" set by the seasonal blockbusters: "The difference between a scene that rings true and a scene written by commercial scriptwriters, as in *Holocaust*, is similar to that between 'experience' and 'opinion.' Opinions about events can be circulated separately, manipulated, pushed across desks, bought and sold. Experiences, on the other hand, are tied to human beings and their faculty of memory, they become false or falsified when living details are replaced in an effort to eliminate subjectivity and uniqueness. (. . .) There are thousands of stories among our people that are worth being filmed, that are based on irritatingly detailed experiences which apparently do not contribute to judging or explaining history, but whose sum total would actually fill this gap (. . .) Authors all over the world are trying to take possession of their history (. . .) but they often find that it is torn out of their hands. The most serious act of expropriation occurs when people are deprived of their history. With *Holocaust*, the Americans have taken away our history." [. . .]

In contrast to simply "replacing" one authority with another, and the "falsifying" of memory and experience by someone like Lucie, most characters in *Heimat* have "irritatingly detailed experiences," giving history a local habitation and a name. But Reitz's engaging plea for a cinema of memory directly communicating individual experience, unprocessed as it were, which would amount collectively to history, does not translate easily into practice, and neither is it his own. It is true that in keeping with many films of the New German Cinema, *Heimat* is poor on plot and suspense, and rich on incident, episode, atmosphere: for a German audience, there must be literally hundreds of details and scores of incidents that feel absolutely right, that spark off personal memories, and allow an audience to recognize themselves in the guise of the other up there on the screen or right there in the living-room. But the strength of the American cinema (and of certain other national cinemas) is precisely that it has established certain gestures, a certain landscape, a certain manner of speaking as unmistakeably, typically American: what audiences recognize and respond to in Hollywood films is the pleasure of always returning to something already seen and experienced. It may not be the authentic, irreducible experience of history Reitz has in mind, but it is experience all the same, and not, as he claims, the pushing back and forth of opinion: Reitz's polemic somewhat over-shoots its target.

Heimat itself is a fairly complexly layered film, full of references to other visual material, other films, current cultural contexts. [. . .] Inadequately translated as "Homeland," the title is an intensely emotional concept, always implying a return to (imaginary or real) origins, roots; it has predominantly rural associations and is therefore close to the land and "soil," to a particular landscape or a region. As such, it has been much abused by German nationalists from the Romantics to this day: every expansionist or annexation policy in German history has been justified by the slogan "Heimat" or, as under Hitler, "heim ins Reich."

In addition, Reitz includes an extract from a very popular 1938 Zarah Leander vehicle called *Heimat* (directed by Carl Froelich). In 1937, Detlef Sierck had made a film called *Die Heimat ruft*, following his 1936 Zarah Leander hit, *Zu neuen Ufern*, a title which itself evokes the symmetrical complement to "Heimat," i.e., "Fernweh." This is in fact the subtitle of the opening episode of *Heimat*, in which Paul returns home, only to be seized by an irrepressible yearning to leave "for new shores." Zarah Leander is a crucial reference point for several characters in *Heimat*, the women who stay home (and dream of Spain, Italy, the "South"), as well as for the men on the Front (who dream of returning home): a movie star becomes the convergence of several (asymmetrically placed) fantasies.

In spite of his diatribe against Hollywood, Reitz is clearly aware that in our century, to talk about memory is to talk about audio-visual representations of events. None of us can escape the force of the images that always already exist, and to build a counter-memory from scratch is as heroic as it is impossible. One might even go so far as to say that Reitz's film is not so much a review of German history as a review of German *film* history, a summa and recapitulation of the German Cinema, its achievements, its themes and images, as well as its battles with critics and producers. This is no criticism of either Reitz's theoretical position or his film: on the contrary, it's a measure of his achievement as a commercial director that he may have founded—building on the work of others and his own previous films—the visual and narrative basis of a "national" film language.

Gertrud Koch

How Much Naiveté Can We Afford? The New *Heimat* Feeling (*Frauen und Film*, 38, May 1985)

In an interview with Heike Hurst in Paris, Edgar Reitz explains why his TV series *Heimat* mentions the annihilation of the Jews only in an extremely marginal way: "The question of the Jews under National Socialism is a theme which has been treated in an infinite number of stories, and if I had included this aspect the whole story would have taken a different turn." Reitz actually puts his finger on the problem, i.e., that in order to tell the myth of "*Heimat*" the trauma of Auschwitz has to be bracketed from German history. Thus Reitz has to revise history—but can one do so in a naive way? Unmistakeably, *Heimat* coincides with a political climate which is distinguished by certain semantic slippages, from Auschwitz over Stalingrad into the Hunsrück, by a shift in paradigms of historical interpretation from "everyday fascism" to "fascist everyday life." Hannah Arendt's metaphor of the family father as the prototype of the 20th-century murderer which thematized the banality of evil collapses in this born-again German nostalgia into a celebration of the purely banal. Semantic slippages, endorsed by Werner Herzog, Alexander Kluge, Volker Schlöndorff, Margarethe von Trotta and Wim Wenders, also characterize the telegram sent by the signatories to the director of the Venice film festival, demanding that *Heimat* should be shown in Venice [in full length]: "'*Heimat*,' the place of birth, is for every human being the center of the world. Of this simple truth Edgar Reitz reminds us in this cosmopolitan age. Sixteen hours are not a minute too long for his European requiem of the small people, a film that encompasses experiences of our whole century of which, as everyone knows, we will have to take leave in no more than sixteen years." This telegram would not deserve any further attention if it had disappeared in the files of the festival bureaucracy. But the text of the telegram was widely circulated, beginning with the Venice festival, and has become part of the publicity material accompanying the new *Heimat*. [. . .] The "simple truth" syntactically refers to the preceding sentence, thus to the categorical assertion that "'*Heimat*,' the place of birth, is for every human being the center of the world." "For every human being"—does this mean that only those human beings are included to whom such a condition applies, does it exclude nomads as well as all those for whom their place of birth has never been, remained or could become a *"Heimat"*? The need to reassert this "truth" is linked to our "cosmopolitan age." "Cosmopolitan" once, in the tradition of Enlightenment, referred to the citizens of the world; in antisemitic propaganda, however, it came to be used as a slogan accusing the Jews of worldwide conspiracy. What do the authors of the telegram mean by this term today? That it's time again to defend the *"Heimat"* against the citizens of the world, or even to maintain a more archaic claim to truth as grounded in the soil? Certainly none of the authors can be suspected of such an intention, no more than Reitz would have wanted us to read it that way. Why then is the awkward phrase allowed to persist and provoke misunderstandings? What is it that makes phrases like these so attractive, in particular their categorical and ceremonious gesture? Not coincidentally, the film is advertised as a "requiem," a mass for the dead—*Requiem for 500,000* is the title of a documentary on the death camps. A semantic slippage, no more, no less, for the so-called "small people" on whose behalf the requiem *Heimat* is celebrated are pretty much alive in Reitz's film; mourning is not exactly one of the dominant moods of the film.

What is being buried in *Heimat* is not the "simple truth" of the "small people" that morality does not thrive on an empty stomach but the precarious consensus that one cannot speak of German history without thinking of Auschwitz. According to Saul Friedländer, this very consensus is at stake in the film: "Since it is a work that claims to rediscover the national past, one has the right to ask if, in its masking of atrocities and shift in emphasis, meaning and values, the film does not participate in the current whitewashing of Nazi terror."[10] The semantic slippages not merely indicate a change of topics but are themselves part of a shift in perspective. This shift is ominous if in its shadow phrases like the following can be written again: "America is the foremost example of the development of this new, this second culture in our world, a culture of emigrants, of those who left home [*der Weggegangenen*]. Their basic principle is individualism, the value of the self. [This creates] a new society of human beings who have no commodity to offer except their selves and thus engage in a life-and-death competition. Whatever these many individuals bring forth in terms of abilities, inventions, products (including agricultural products) becomes the exclusive object of commerce, a commerce which demands ever new, ever more spectacular offers and which relates everything with everything else through the common language of trade. [. . .] Thus arises an internationally communicable culture of emigrants. The Jews, since time immemorial 'people who go away' [*Weggeher*], fit well into this American culture, a culture that only seeks to expand and to compete in all areas, whose very own language is competition."[11] Bad enough that Reitz applies the romantic euphemism of "people who go away" to emigrants from the poor-houses of Europe, to refugees of pogroms and other persecutions, that the language equates the immigration waves from Europe to the United States with current movements of simply bailing out, giving a cold shoulder to the "rural culture of dialect." But why insert "the Jews" at this point? Either Reitz has never read any of the literature of emigrants and is ignorant of the hardships of their fate, or he has internalized the antisemitic stereotype of the "Jewish people of merchants" so well that he is no longer aware of what he is saying.

Such phrases are shocking in that they betray an amazing decline of historical sensibility. The equation of a competitive market economy, of the plague of commercialization, with "the Jews" has been a staple of antisemitic critiques of civilization already in pre-fascist Germany; Chamberlain is just one example among many. Today, the syllogistic line of attack is directed largely against "the Americans" to whom "the Jews" in turn are joined by association. In a polemic against the TV series, *Holocaust*, Reitz goes so far as to assert: "The most fundamental process of expropriation is that which robs human beings of their own history. With Holocaust, the Americans have taken history away from us."[12] Has Reitz forgotten that the Second World War was a *world* war? That Americans, too, died on the battle-fields for the cause of liberation, that Jewish refugees from all over Europe survived in the United States? Does he seriously believe that the world-historical experience of the extermination of millions of human lives has left authentic memory traces only in the soil of the Hunsrück? The false tone in statements like the above derives from the unproblematic use of "we," "us," "our," from the pervasive feeling of community which has to be asserted against external influence. Indeed, at this point in German history, Reitz is not alone; the success he reaped with *Heimat* is evidence of a major concern of the *Zeitgeist* at large: the eloquent celebration of the everyday. . . .

Notes

*All translations from the German are by Miriam Hansen. We are grateful to the authors for permission to reprint.

1. Michael Geisler examines this context in his essay, "*Heimat* and the German Left: The Anamnesis of a Trauma," *New German Critique* 36 (Fall 1985).

2. In *Öffentlichkeit und Erfahrung* (Frankfurt am Main: Suhrkamp, 1972), Negt and Kluge on their part draw on E.P. Thompson, *The Making of the English Working Class* (laundered through Michael Vester's book, *Die Entstehung des Proletariats als Lernprozess*); in *Geschichte und Eigensinn* (Frankfurt am Main: Zweitausendeins, 1981), they offer their own theory of counter-history, derived from a physiological/libidinal/political analysis of human labor power.

3. *Cahiers du cinéma*, 251/2, 268/9, 275, 278 (1974–76), translated in excerpts, including two interviews with Michel Foucault in *Edinburgh Magazine*, 2 (1977); in the same issue see articles by Stephen Heath and Colin McCabe. Also cf. Keith Tribe, "History and the Production of Memories," *Screen*, 18:4 (Winter 1977/78).

4. Friedländer, *Reflections of Nazism: An Essay on Kitsch and Death*, trans. from the French by Thomas Weyr (New York: Harper & Row, 1984; first ed. 1982), p. 13. For a more consistent discussion of the same phenomenon, see Alvin Rosenfeld, *Imagining Hitler* (Bloomington: Indiana University Press, 1985).

5. Adorno, "Was bedeutet: Aufarbeitung der Vergangenheit," *Eingriffe* (Frankfurt am Main: Suhrkamp, 1963), pp. 129, 135f.

6. Elsaesser, "Between Bitburg and Bergen Belsen," *On Film*, 14 (1985), 40.

7. Cf. Hansen, "The Stubborn Discourse: History and Story-Telling in the Films of Alexander Kluge," *Persistence of Vision*, 2 (Fall 1985).

8. Rentschler, *West German Film in the Course of Time* (Pleasantville, N.Y.: Redgrave, 1984); Corrigan, *New German Film: The Displaced Image* (Austin: University of Texas Press, 1983); Elsaesser, "Primary Identification and the Historical Subject: Fassbinder and Germany," *Ciné-tracts*, 11 (Fall 1980); "Fassbinder, Fascism and the Film Industry," *October*, 23 (1983); "Achternbusch and the German Avantgarde," *Discourse*, 6 (1984); also cf. Elsaesser's work on Weimar, e.g., "Film History and Visual Pleasure: Weimar Cinema," in *Cinema Histories, Cinema Practices*, ed. Patricia Mellenkamp and Philip Rosen (AFI Monograph Series, 4) (Frederick, MD: University Publications of America, 1984).

9. [Repr. in: Edgar Reitz, *Liebe zum Kino* (Köln: Verlag Köln 78, 1984). Also cf. the debate on *Holocaust* in *New German Critique*, 19 (Winter 1980).]

10. Friedländer, "Bewältigung—oder nur Verdrängung?" *Die Zeit*, 8 February 1985.

11. [Reitz, *Liebe zum Kino*, p. 145f.]

12. [Ibid., p. 102.]

On the Difficulty of Saying "We": The Historians' Debate and Edgar Reitz's *Heimat*

ERIC L. SANTNER

I

As PRESENTED in 1967 by the Mitscherlichs in their groundbreaking study, *The Inability to Mourn*, the tasks of mourning in postwar German society are double edged and may, more radically, even represent a series of double binds.[1] In order to mourn for the victims of National Socialism, the Mitscherlichs claimed, the population of the new Federal Republic (and it is only for pragmatic reasons that I limit myself to this case) would first have to work through the more primitive narcissistic injury represented by the traumatic shattering of the specular, imaginary relations that had provided the sociopsychological foundations of German fascism. According to the Mitscherlichs, the political religion that was nazism had promised a "utopian" world in which what threatened the self with chastisements of its narcissism—including alterity in its multiple forms and dimensions—could be experienced as a dangerous Semitic supplement that one was free to push to the margins and finally to destroy. This was a utopia, of course, in which a mature self could never really develop. For that complex entity we call the human self constitutes itself precisely by relinquishing its narcissistic position and mournfully, and perhaps even playfully, assuming its place in an order—call it the symbolic— in which I and you, here and there, now and then, signifiers and signifieds, have boundaries, i.e., are discontinuous. It is this passage from a realm of continuity into one of contiguities that signals the advent of the *unheimlich* in human experience. According to the Mitscherlichs, there could be no real mourning for the victims of nazism, no genuine perception of the full magnitude of human suffering caused in the name of the *Volksgemeinschaft*, until this more primitive labor of mourning—the mastery of the capacity to say "we" nonnarcissistically, the integration of the *unheimlich* into the first person plural—had been achieved.

This complex interdependence of the way one says "we" in postwar German society on one hand and the way one positions oneself vis-à-vis the crimes of National Socialism on the other, seems in the last several years only to have become more vexing and complex. In the following I

Reprinted from *History and Memory* 2 no. 2 (1990): 76–96 with the permission of Indiana University Press.

would like to explore two discursive events in which this interdependence has figured in a central way: the Historians' Debate and Edgar Reitz's film *Heimat*.

II

The beginning of this Historians' Debate might be dated with an essay by Jürgen Habermas entitled "A Settling of Damages: Apologetic Tendencies in German Historiography," published 11 July 1986 in the German weekly *Die Zeit*.[2] As the subtitle of that essay indicates, Habermas's concern here is a certain revisionist or "apologetic" tendency in recent German historiography of the fascist period. In the essay Habermas primarily addresses the work of three historians whom he sees as the main exponents of this new historiography: Ernst Nolte, Michael Stürmer, and Andreas Hillgruber.

In an essay published a month earlier in the *Frankfurter Allgemeine Zeitung*, Ernst Nolte had argued for an empathic understanding of the anxieties that ostensibly led Hitler to the admittedly barbaric final solution of the Jewish question.[3] According to Nolte, Hitler had reason to fear that the Russians would subject the Germans to horrific tortures in the event of a westward expansion. Nolte evoked the so-called rat cage, an instrument of torture to which Winston Smith finally succumbs in George Orwell's *1984*, and which, according to anti-Bolshevist literature from the twenties, belonged to the Soviet arsenal, as the recurring nightmare that finally led Hitler to the prophylactic measures of Auschwitz.

> Is it not likely that the Nazis and Hitler committed this "Asiatic" deed because they saw themselves and others like them as potential or real victims of an "Asiatic" deed? Did not the "class genocide" of the Bolshevists logically and factually predate the "racial genocide" of the National Socialists? Doesn't the intelligibility of Hitler's most secret actions owe precisely to the fact that he could *not* forget the "rat cage"? May we not perhaps trace the origins of Auschwitz to a past that wouldn't go away?[4]

The missing link in this causal nexus is, of course, the equation Bolshevist = Jew, an anti-Semitic commonplace from the twenties and thirties.[5] Nolte had elsewhere offered further "evidence" also garnered from fundamentally anti-Semitic nightmare visions of the power of world Jewry, to support this empathic, not to say sympathetic, reading of Hitler's situation. He claims, for example, that Chaim Weizmann's declaration in 1939 that the Jews of the world should ally themselves with England, might justify the thesis "that Hitler was allowed to treat the German Jews as prisoners of war and by this means to intern them."[6]

Other aspects of Nolte's argument involve by now familiar comparisons between the National Socialist genocide and other modern examples of mass murder, from the Turkish slaughter of Armenians to Pol Pot's decimation of the Cambodian population. The thought here is, of course, that the Jewish Holocaust needs to be placed in the context of other cataclysmic events of twentieth-century history all of which may be seen under the general rubric *reactions to modernity*.[7] In defense of such comparisons, Nolte offers yet another familiar analogy, between Auschwitz and the Allied bombing of civilian populations. Nolte's example demonstrates rather clearly that the entire Historians' Debate is in many ways a continuation of the controversies surrounding Ronald Reagan's visit to the cemetery at Bitburg. Each event has, after all, served to challenge many people's understanding of the important differences between the Final Solution and other acts of war and mass murder, between SS-officers and soldiers in the field.

> To be sure, the American President's visit to the military cemetery at Bitburg provoked a very emotional discussion; but the fear of the charge of "settling accounts" [*Aufrechnung*] and a more general fear of making any comparisons at all prevented the consideration of what it would have meant if in 1953 the then chancellor had refused to visit the military cemetery at Arlington, justifying this refusal with the argument that men were buried there who had participated in terroristic attacks against the German civilian population.[8]

For Nolte, what finally distinguishes the Shoah from other cases of genocide in the twentieth century is the technical detail of the use of gas in the extermination of the Jews.[9]

In the end, however, Nolte's argument for a revisionist reading of the place of the Holocaust in modern European history is based on the notion that previous interpretations have been authored by the victors and are thus inherently biased and in need of rewriting from a German national perspective. He offers a curious thought experiment to dramatize his case:

> We need only imagine, for example, what would happen if the Palestine Liberation Organization, assisted by its allies, succeeded in annihilating the state of Israel. Then the historical accounts in the books, lecture halls and schoolrooms of Palestine would doubtless dwell only on the negative traits of Israel; the victory over the racist, oppressive and even fascist Zionism would become a state-supporting myth. For decades and possibly centuries nobody would dare to trace the moving origins of Zionism to the spirit of resistance against European anti-semitism, or to describe its extraordinary civilizing achievements before and after the founding of the state, to show its clear differences from Italian fascism.[10]

Although few professional historians have been guilty of the rhetorical excesses manifest in such prose, Nolte is by no means alone with regard to the general philosophical trajectory of his efforts. In recent writings by

Michael Stürmer we find, for example, an explicit appeal to the historian as that figure in contemporary society who must carry on the work that can no longer be performed by religion, namely the unification and consolidation of the social group. By endowing meaning (*Sinnstiftung*) in the act of historical recollection and interpretation, the historian lays the foundation upon which a national identity may be constituted. Only after achieving such a firm national ego, as it were, may the Federal Republic come to occupy its rightful place as the "central unit in the European defensive arch of the Atlantic system."[11] The task of contemporary German historiography is to allow Germany to find its inner continuity with itself once more, to come home to itself, as it were, so that its Western neighbors may know they have a dependable ally anchored in a firm and unconflicted self-understanding. "For it is here a matter of the German Republic's inner continuity and its calculability in foreign affairs."[12] And like Nolte, Stürmer sees in the performance of this quasi-Homeric task of cultural *Sinnstiftung*—the historian becomes the new bard of the national epos, only now with scientific means—an antidote to the very disorientation that is seen as having given rise to fascism in the first place.

> It is doubtful that the uncertainty first began in 1945. Hitler's rise to power was a function of the crises and catastrophes of a secularized civilization tumbling from rupture to rupture; this was a civilization marked by the loss of orientation and futile searches for security. . . . From 1914 to 1945 the Germans were thrust into the cataracts of modernity to a degree that shattered all traditions, made the unthinkable thinkable, and institutionalized barbarity as political regime. It was for these reasons that Hitler was able to triumph, that he was able to exploit and pervert Prussia and patriotism, the state and the virtues of civil society ["die bürgerlichen Tugenden"].[13]

Finally, what scandalized so many readers of Andreas Hillgruber's study, *Zweierlei Untergang: Die Zerschlagung des Deutschen Reiches und das Ende des europäischen Judentums* (*Two Kinds of Demise: The Shattering of the German Reich and the End of European Jewry*),[14] was Hillgruber's declared identification with the perspective of the defenders of Germany's eastern territories during the period of their collapse, even though these "valiant" efforts to hold back the anticipated reprisals by the Red Army allowed for the machinery of the death camps to continue unabated. Hillgruber distinguishes this "ethics of responsibility" (*verantwortungsethische*) perspective from the "ethics of conviction" (*gesinnungsethische*) perspective of the conspirators of the 20th of July.[15] Perhaps even more distressing in Hillgruber's study is the assimilation of these two "national catastrophes" to a single, overarching narrative of the destruction of the "europäische Mitte" or "European center." As the rather asymmetrical treatment of these two catastrophes indicates—the "shattering of the German Reich" takes up a good two-thirds of the book—in this double plot it is the Germans of the eastern provinces who become the truly tragic protagonists of modern European history.[16]

The gist of Habermas's critique of these trends in the historiography of fascism and the Holocaust is that they attempt to recuperate notions of centrality and modes of national identity no longer feasible in the harrowed cultural matrix of postwar Europe; rather than exploring strategies of coming to terms with a historical experience that changed not just the geopolitical, but also the moral and psychological landscapes of Europe and the West, these historians place historiography in the service of a "national-historical restoration of a conventional identity."[17]

A "conventional identity" signifies in this context a self-structure still rooted in a specular relation to the particular norms, roles, "contents" of a specific social formation such as family, *Volk*, or nation. A more distanced and critical dialogue with the intensely ambivalent cultural legacy of recent German history is thus for Habermas the sign of a cultural self-identity that has begun to work through the radically transformed conditions of identity formation of post-Holocaust and, I would add, postmodern German society. Habermas condenses these determinants of postwar political culture under the sign of what he calls "postconventional identity."

> If among the younger generations national symbols have lost their formative
> powers; if naive identifications with one's origins and lineage have given way
> to a more tentative relationship with history; if discontinuities are felt more
> strongly and continuities no longer celebrated at all costs . . .—to the extent
> that all this is the case, we are witnessing increasing indications of the advent
> of a postconventional identity.[18]

One can no doubt imagine a number of different explanations for the eruption of the Historians' Debate at this particular moment in the history of the Federal Republic. And indeed, as one observer has recently noted, efforts to explain the debate have since generated a minor cottage industry.[19] But there has been a hesitation on the part of commentators to depart from a narrowly drawn framework of political culture in the Federal Republic and attempt to link the Historians' Debate to larger questions concerning the discourses of national identity in postmodern politics and culture more generally.[20] As I have already suggested, Habermas's notion of a "postconventional identity" points us in precisely this direction. And indeed, once we begin to situate Habermas's concept of a postconventional identity within this more broadly drawn postmodern context, the texts of the Historians' Debate quite rapidly become legible as symptoms of a remarkable repetition compulsion; in good postmodern fashion, it is a repetition compulsion that reenacts history in the medium of representations, in this case, historiography.[21]

Where the Jews were once blamed for the traumas of modernity, it would now appear that the Holocaust figures as the irritating signifier of the traumas and disorientations of postmodernity. Now the conditions under which stable cultural identities may be consolidated have indeed *with* and *since* the Holocaust become radically different; the symbolic order to which a German is subjected, i.e., that social space in which he or she first learns to say "ich" and "wir," now contains the traces of a horrific violence.[22] But the conventional sites of identity formation have become destabilized, have become more and more *unheimlich* as it were, for a variety of other reasons that derive more directly from other, more global, social, economic, and political displacements. In the present historical moment, which, perhaps for lack of a better word, we call the postmodern, Orient and Occident, masculine and feminine, guest worker and indigenous host—to name just a few of the binary oppositions that figure in the process of cultural identity formation—would seem no longer to occupy stable positions. The postmodern self is called upon to integrate an awareness of multiple forms of otherness, to tolerate instabilities and complexities of new and rapidly shifting social arrangements, and to be open to more hybrid, more "creole," forms of personal, sexual, and political identity. Furthermore, in the postmodern, the availability of resources of legitimation and orientation in the narratives of European Enlightenment culture—all of which project some form of progressive synthesis of this heterogeneity under a teleological master term—has become highly problematical. The Jews, now no longer available as the signifier of ruptures and disturbances one would like to banish from the inside (of the self, the family, the city, the *Reich*), are being displaced by the event of their own destruction; the Holocaust now figures as the placeholder for the decenteredness and instability experienced as so painfully chronic in contemporary German society, and it is a national historiography to which the task is assigned to reconstitute the center—the "europäische Mitte"— once again, if only in the mode of nostalgic recollection or simulacrum. We are faced here with a refusal to mourn either the particular and deeply traumatic losses to the cultural resources of Germany, i.e., the real and ineluctable fragmentation of the cultural identity that results from Auschwitz or the more "structural" losses that result from a global remapping of political, economic, cultural, sexual, and moral power over the last forty years (I would include the division of Germany and the loss of the eastern provinces within this second series of losses).

In the texts of the neoconservative historians reviewed by Habermas, the subtext of the quest for a renewed and vigorous (virile?) national identity has not just a cold war/NATO component—Germany's unbroken self-identity with regard to the "struggle against Bolshevism"—but a postmodern one as well. A national historiography assumes the task of salvaging, or perhaps more accurately, simulating, sites of identity formation no longer available in a cultural space defined by the double "post-" of the post-Holocaust and the postmodern. If it has become difficult, under the burden of this double post-, to say "wir" in contemporary German society and to know at all times exactly what that little pronoun signifies, i.e., if a certain strangeness, a certain alien presence—call it, with Nolte, the "Asiatic"—has come to haunt the first person plural, splitting it from within, then a new national historiography has busied itself with working out strategies of narrating this *Unheimlichkeit* to the margins, of deporting it as it were. This new historiography thus performs double duty: all the difficulties that have come to complicate the enunciation of the first person plural in contemporary German society are assigned a delimited origin in the Holocaust, which in its turn may then be normalized and marginalized by various techniques of "historicization." Whereas once it was the Jews, it is now the Shoah itself that serves as a screen upon which is projected, as something that intervenes from the outside—from "Asia"—that which ultimately keeps Germans from feeling continuous with themselves.

In this respect we may think of the neoconservative moment in the Historians' Debate as symptomatic of a more general group psychological trajectory of desire toward a respecularization of the terms of German national identity. And in this context one wonders whether the efforts to construct two new museums of national history, the Haus der Geschichte in Bonn and the Deutsches Historisches Museum in Berlin, may not end up with a house of mirrors, an enclosed space in which Germans may go to see themselves reflected and thereby reinstated in an imaginary plenitude and wholeness.[23]

Habermas's interventions in these controversies are directed precisely against this tendency to return to narcissistic patterns of (group) identity formation, patterns that reinscribe, as we have seen, a refusal or inability to mourn. Habermas has of course himself been criticized by just about every postmodern theorist for his refusal to relinquish his commitment to an Enlightenment faith in rationality and the perfectibility of man, and to Western liberal notions of consensus, in short, to the project of modernity. This is not the place to rehearse these debates yet again. I would simply like to suggest that in the context of the Historians' Debate, Habermas's thoughts regarding the pressures placed upon German national identity at the present historical moment invite us to see a more radical potential in his notion of a postconventional identity, a potential that places him much closer to his postmodern critics than we might have imagined possible. For in the context of the Historians' Debate, Habermas has deployed the notion of a postconventional identity as a critique of current tendencies to respecularize the terms of national identity and as an insistence upon the necessity of a continued labor of mourning. Insofar as the "project of modernity" may itself be seen to reinscribe the specular pattern of self-identity, albeit at a very high level of mediation—i.e., if at the completion of this project we all end up looking into the mirror of a white, male, Europe-oriented *Weltbürger*—then the imperatives of a postconventional identity will demand that this project too be worked through—be deconstructed—according to the procedures of the labor of mourning. The following sketches out in a very preliminary fashion the ways in which the displacements and condensations we have seen to be at work in the Historians' Debate also figure in Edgar Reitz's hugely successful film *Heimat*.

<h2 style="text-align:center">III</h2>

Anyone who has seen *Heimat* is familiar with the absence of Jews in the film as well as the film's near total silence on the subject of the Holocaust. The composition of the one scene in which the Final Solution is mentioned is in itself quite revealing. In episode six, "The Home Front," we witness a party at Eduard and Lucie's villa in Rhaunen. In the course of the evening, which takes on a comic undertone through Lucie's exaggerated performance as cultivated hostess, we hear Wilfried whisper news of the extermination camps to two officers: "The Final Solution is being carried out radically and without mercy. I really shouldn't be telling you any of this—between you and me, we know what's what. Up the chimneys, every last one of them." A few seconds later the camera pans across the room and follows Lucie to Eduard who has been sitting alone the entire evening blinking his left eye. When Lucie inquires about this peculiar behavior, Eduard reveals the object of his preoccupation. "I . . . can't . . . stop thinking of little Hans, the basket weaver's boy. That he might still be alive today if only I hadn't taught him that."[24] Eduard, we recall, had tutored Hänschen in the art of sharpshooting, thus helping to begin the boy's short-lived military career. The effect of this sequence, whether consciously intended or not, is the creation of a symmetry: all victims of the war are equal, whether German soldiers killed in battle or Jews murdered in Auschwitz. The symmetry is further underscored by the fact that it was originally through young Hänschen's eyes that we first see a concentration camp earlier in the film. But to speak here of a symmetry may actually be too generous since the Jewish victims remain invisible and Hänschen is a figure we have come to know and for whom we feel quite a bit of affection (one thinks here of the asymmetrical symmetry of Hillgruber's book).[25]

Another quite interesting sequence, in which the fate of the Jews briefly intersects with the various narratives that constitute *Heimat*, comes in the first episode and prefigures, in a certain sense, the scene we have just described. It is 1923; Eduard and Pauline make an afternoon excursion to

Simmern, the next largest town from Schabbach. Pauline wanders off alone and finds herself looking at the window display of the town watchmaker and jeweler. Suddenly a group of young men run up behind her—including Eduard, armed as usual with camera and tripod—and begin throwing rocks at the window of the apartment above the watchmaker's shop where, as we learn, a Jew—in this case also branded as a separatist—resides. They are chased off by police, but the shards of fallen glass have cut Pauline's hand. Robert Kröber, the watchmaker, signals her to come into the shop where he cleans her wound, thereby initiating the love story of Pauline and Robert. (Later on in the film—it is 1933—we hear that the now married Pauline and Robert are buying the Jew's apartment. As Robert remarks, "The house belongs to him and now he wants to sell it. . . . The Jews don't have it so easy anymore"[26]

The importance of this small "Kristallnacht" sequence is that it shows how the shards of the Jew's shattered existence—we never see him in the flesh—are immediately absorbed into a sentimental story of courtship and matrimony, i.e., into experience.[27] Now of course it is the filmmaker who is exposing this mechanism, who is showing us just how experience forms and constructs itself around such blindspots. One wonders, however, whether the filmmaker is not in the end complicitous with such mechanisms, that is, whether he too is not content to absorb the shards of suffering of the other into so many anecdotes of love and family in the provinces.

One way in which this complicity becomes manifest is the remarkable lack of curiosity on the part of just about every character in the film with regard to cases of historical suffering that become visible at various moments in the film. By *historical suffering* I mean precisely the suffering that disrupts, in a radical way, the normal rhythms of the kitchen and the blacksmith's workshop as well as the larger organic rhythms of birth and natural death that are so important to Reitz's vision of village life. The two most striking examples are Lotti's—and everyone else's—total lack of curiosity about her father, Fritz Schirmer, who, as we know, was a Communist and has been taken to a concentration camp. There is actually some confusion in the film regarding Fritz's fate, since there is a scene set in 1943 in which Ursel, Lotti's younger sister, born in 1936, refers to her father as a soldier on the Eastern front. Fritz, as the Schirmer's family tree reveals, died in 1937, in Dachau we may presume. That Lotti has not forgotten her father is suggested by the way she cuts off her sister when she begins to talk about him to Pieritz. And yet we never hear a word from Lotti herself who was, after all, already nine years old when her father was taken. The other, more striking example is the apparent lack of any curiosity concerning the fate of Otto Wohlleben's mother who was, as he himself reveals, a Jew. She is in fact mentioned only in the context of Otto's allusion to his own career difficulties. As a "Mischling" not professing the

Jewish faith—Reitz refers to Otto as "the poor, propertyless half-Jew who could be kept at home and tamed"[28]—Otto was himself in no immediate danger. It is nonetheless quite uncanny—*unheimlich*, we might say—that no one in the film asks about Frau Wohlleben's fate before, during, or after the war. Implicated in this strange sin of omission is also, of course, Frau Wohlleben's (illegitimate) grandson, Hermann. The case of Hermann is especially significant since that figure is, after all, a rather thinly veiled autobiographical portrait of the filmmaker-artist as a young man.[29]

Much more could be said about the occurrences of direct references and allusions to Jews in the film. But in the present context I am more interested in other ways in which the Jews and the Holocaust figure in the narrative and characterological economy of the film (as well as in the conditions and history of its production).

Heimat is, one might say, less about the disappearance of a particular way of life than about the disappearance of a particular relationship to death. In Reitz's view, contemporary society marks the farthest remove from a way of life in which death figured in a central and organic way in individual and communal experience. The postmodern moment (to use a term with which Reitz would perhaps be uncomfortable) is for Reitz not so much the signpost of a heightened sensitivity to difference and marginality as of a world "in which one separates from everything. Where one can separate from parts of one's life and parts of one's soul, one's family, one's experience; wherever we look we find this pattern of seemingly painless separation."[30] What intrigues Reitz about peasant and so-called primitive cultures, is that they still appear to have a deep, existential relationship to death; these cultures still perform formal, ritualized responses not only to mortal loss but more generally to the passing of time as it comes to afflict objects of daily use. These are, as Reitz says in his essay on Chris Marker's film *Sans Soleil*, "ceremonies in which people formally take leave from objects no longer needed, with a dignity that is ever more foreign to us."[31] However, by losing this deep relationship to death and to time, by losing, in other words, the capacity to transform, with the aid of ritual, *chronos* into *kairos*, "consumer society [here Reitz uses the German *Wegwerfgesellschaft*] unconsciously surrounds itself with the ghosts of all these abandoned objects which will one day take revenge on us." The film *Heimat* basically tells the story of the emergence of the postindustrial, consumer society. And indeed, the first great, cataclysmic triumph of the *episteme* governing this society of consumption was, as Reitz has suggested, the Holocaust. Auschwitz is, Reitz has said, "the most extreme manifestation of this throwaway society the world has ever known, a monstrous radicalization of the throwaway society: human beings become waste products."[32]

The semantic field of this term *Wegwerfgesellschaft* includes another word that has proven to be of fundamental importance in Reitz's conception of modernization, that historical dynamic that destroys the idyllic matrix called Schabbach. The word is—and as far as I know it is a neologism of Reitz—*Weggeher* or "one who goes away, one who leaves home." The key *Weggeher* in *Heimat* is Paul Simon who, as Reitz has remarked, eventually becomes a "real American . . . a man without a home, without roots, a sentimental globetrotter."[33] And indeed, America represents for Reitz a land of *Weggeher*—Reitz himself has relatives in Texas who left the Hunsrück in the nineteenth century—a land where the metaphysic of capitalism determines every aspect of human existence.

> America is the foremost example of the development of this new, this second culture in our world, a culture of emigrants, of those who left home. Their basic principle is individualism, the value of the self. [This creates] a new society of human beings who have no commodity to offer except their selves and thus engage in a life-and-death competition. Whatever these many individuals bring forth in terms of abilities, inventions, products . . . becomes the exclusive object of commerce, a commerce which demands ever new, ever more spectacular offers and which relates everything with everything else through the common language of trade.

In the elegiac narrative that Reitz's film relates, it is ultimately the triumph of this language of capitalism—American English as it were—that bears the greatest burden of responsibility for the destruction of the "Heimat."

But then Reitz adds this curious supplementary remark. "The Jews, since time immemorial 'people who go away' [*Weggeher*], fit well into this American culture, a culture that only seeks to expand and to compete in all areas, whose very own language is competition."[34] A remarkable twist is thus added to the story of Schabbach's demise. The Hebrews, whose name means "the ones from the other shore of the river" and who are cited here as the archaic embodiment of the ethic of the *Weggeher*, come to figure as a metonymy for the historical dynamic that rends the fabric of the idyll. As Gertrud Koch has quite aptly noted, this equation of the "plague of commercialization . . . with 'the Jews' [had] been a staple of antisemitic critiques of civilization already in pre-fascist Germany."[35] I have tried to indicate the ways in which the Historians' Debate repeats this ideological gesture in a postmodern, post-Holocaust setting. But the tropological slippages of Reitz's discourse would seem to suggest something more radical still: since Auschwitz is itself only an epiphenomenon of these deep historical processes governing the *Weggeher-/Wegwerfgesellschaft*, the Jews come to signify even further the very forces that lead to their own destruction. The Holocaust thereby becomes in some sense a Jewish dialectic of the Enlightenment.

These two phenomena, the Historians' Debate and *Heimat*, are in large part generated by a political unconscious attempting to undo, by way of various strategies of respecularization, the complexities that make use of the first person plural—that make saying "we"—in post-Holocaust, postmodern Germany such an ambivalent and ambiguous experience. Forgiving the Jews for these difficulties will, of course, not make the experience any easier.

Notes

1. Alexander and Margarete Mitscherlich, *The Inability to Mourn: Principles of Collective Behavior*, trans. Beverley R. Placzek (New York: Grove Press, 1975).

2. Jürgen Habermas, "Eine Art Schadensabwicklung. Die apologetischen Tendenzen in der deutschen Zeitgeschichtsschreibung," *Historiker-Streit: Die Dokumentation der Kontroverse um die Einzigartigkeit der nationalsozialistischen Judenvernichtung* (Munich: Piper, 1987) 62–76. For an English translation, see "A Kind of Settlement of Damages (Apologetic Tendencies)" *New German Critique* 44 (Spring/Summer 1988): 22–39, trans. Jeremy Leaman. Unless otherwise indicated, translations are mine.

3. Ernst Nolte, "Vergangenheit, die nicht vergehen will," ("A past that will not pass away") *FAZ* 6 June 1986, reprinted in *Historiker-Streit* 39–47. The essay was originally intended as a contribution to the Frankfurt Römerberg-Colloquium. For a summary of the events surrounding the publication of Nolte's essay see his letter to *Die Zeit* 1 August 1986, republished in *Historiker-Streit* 93–94, as well as Hilmar Hoffmann's introduction to *Gegen den Versuch, Vergangenheit zu verbiegen: Eine Diskussion um politische Kultur in der Bundesrepublik aus Anlaß der Frankfurter Römerberggespräche 1986* (Frankfurt a.M.: Athenäum, 1987).

4. Ernst Nolte, *Historiker-Streit* 45.

5. Nolte, *Historiker-Streit* 46. A recent effort to historicize the Final Solution by an American historian, Arno Mayer, makes a powerful argument for the importance of the connections between anti-Bolshevism and anti-Semitism in Nazi ideology. Unlike Nolte, however, he does not use the former to displace or absorb the relative autonomy of the latter, nor does he posit the sorts of mechanical causalities that interest Nolte. In Mayer's reading, Nazi anti-Bolshevism is not defensive in the sense in which Nolte presents it but is rather part of an ultimately maniacal crusading ideology. See Arno J. Mayer, *Why Did the Heavens Not Darken? The "Final Solution" in History* (New York: Pantheon, 1988).

6. Ernst Nolte, "Between Myth and Revisionism? The Third Reich in the Perspective of the 1980s," *Aspects of the Third Reich*, ed. H. W. Koch (New York: St. Martin's, 1985) 28.

7. See Nolte, *Historiker-Streit* 33, 46.

8. Nolte, *Historiker-Streit* 42. One might also add to this summary of Nolte's remarkable capacity to equalize distinct historical phenomena the rather bizarre lesson he manages to learn from Claude Lanzmann's film *Shoah*, namely that the film "makes plausible that the SS-staff of the death camps were victims in their own right and that . . . a virulent anti-Semitism was not foreign to the Polish victims of National Socialism" 42.

9. Nolte, *Historiker-Streit* 45.

10. Nolte, "Between Myth and Revisionism" 21. For an insightful analysis of the "pseudo-interrogative mode" of such reflections, see Charles S. Maier's book on the Historians' Debate, *The Unmasterable Past: History, Holocaust, and German National Identity* (Cambridge: Harvard UP, 1988) 83. These sorts of comparisons and analogies are, of course, by no means new, nor are they necessarily clear markers of membership in a particular political or ideological camp. For, as Margarete Mitscherlich, Peter Schneider, and others have pointed out, the German left has deployed such rhetorical strategies quite as much as neoconservative historians and also, one might assume, out of interest in reducing the pressures of the historical burdens weighing upon the postwar generations in Germany.

Commenting upon Helmut Kohl's comparisons of Mikhail Gorbachev's public relations skills with those of Goebbels and the work camps for political prisoners in the GDR with Nazi concentration camps, Peter Schneider points to similar rhetorical moves on the part of the German left. "One has to concede that long before Kohl began formulating his hair-raising comparisons for Goebbels and the death camps, the children of the postwar period had de-historicized the concept of Nazism. After fascism had become a generalized term of opprobrium in Germany, it served hardly at all to refer to the twelve years that gave it its concrete meaning. The term was used mainly to denounce one's political opponents. The rebels of 1968 were as uninterested as today's revisionist historians in the uniqueness of the Nazi crimes. They were seeking comparisons, though for the students, the term of the comparison was capitalist democracy, not Soviet communism. Only now has it become apparent that the leftist misuse of the accusation of fascism is an equally reflexive attempt at relief: for the reduction of the historical profile of nazism to general and transferable characteristics also had, apart from its instructive value, an unburdening function. If National Socialism was the 'conspiracy' of a couple of powerful industrialists, our parents, no matter what they had done, were the victims of the conspiracy." Peter Schneider, *Hitler's Shadow: On Being a Self-Conscious German*, trans. Leigh Hafrey, *Harpers* September 1987: 52. Not surprisingly, one area that has become a key site for this process of political and psychological unburdening on the part of the German left has been Israel and its relations with the Palestinians. See, for example, Margarete Mitscherlich's remarks regarding the vehemence with which the German left has taken up the Palestinian cause, i.e., that of the "victim" against the Jewish, "fascist" oppressor (*Erinnerungsarbeit. Zur Psychoanalyse der Unfähigkeit zu trauern* [Frankfurt a.M.: Fischer, 1987] 102–3). Yet another circumstance in which the boundaries between left and right became somewhat blurred, was the controversy over the attempt to stage Fassbinder's play *Der Müll, die Stadt und der Tod* (Garbage, the City, and Death) at the Schauspielhaus in Frankfurt in the fall of 1985. There it was generally the Left that supported the staging of the play over the protests of the Jewish community which—for good reason—found the play to be full of undigested and unanalysed anti-Semitism, and it was generally from conservative circles, with the *Frankfurter Allgemeine Zeitung* at the forefront, that one heard the strongest public outcry against the staging of the play. These were the very circles that had more or less warned the Jewish community not to interfere with Reagan's visit to the cemetery at Bitburg. The controversy demonstrated, among other things, how the fundamental desire for normalcy in Germany is capable of instrumentalizing a great variety of ideological positions both from the Left and the Right. For an excellent summary of the debates surrounding the Fassbinder play see *New German Critique*'s special issue on the German-Jewish controversy, 38 (Spring/Summer 1986); see also Margarete Mitscherlich's remarks in *Erinnerungsarbeit* 28–30.

    11. Stürmer, *Historiker-Streit* 38.

    12. Stürmer, *Historiker-Streit* 38.

    13. Stürmer, *Historiker-Streit* 36–37. See also Stürmer's *Dissonanzen des Forstschritts* (Munich: Piper, 1986). Martin Broszat, who has at times been associated with the revisionist camp of historians, has noted Stürmer's tendency to overburden historiography with quasi-theological social functions it can never fulfill. Broszat points to parallels with cruder, more explicitly political versions of the same vision of the task of the historian in the remarks of Alfred Dregger, parliamentary leader of the Christian Democratic Union. "We are deeply disturbed by the lack of historical awareness and consideration vis-à-vis one's own nation. Without a fundamental patriotism, which is a given for other peoples, our own people will not be able to survive. Whoever misuses the process of 'coming to terms with the past,' as some have chosen to call it and which no doubt had its place, as a way of foreclosing the future of our people, must face our firm opposition." Quoted in Broszat, "Wo sich die Geister scheiden. Die Beschwörung der Geschichte taugt nicht als nationaler Religionsersatz," *Historiker-Streit* 194.

    14. Berlin: Seidler, 1986.

15. "Looking back at the catastrophe of the winter of 1944/45, the historian is left with only one position, even if it is difficult to assume when it comes to the particulars of the case: he must identify with the concrete fate of the German population in the East and with the desperate efforts of the German forces on land and at sea, suffering casualty upon casualty. These efforts were dedicated to protecting the population of the eastern parts of Germany from the orgies of revenge of the Red Army, the mass rapes, the arbitrary murders and deportations, and to keeping escape routes to the West open in those last moments of the war" 24–25. In the narrative sections of the book this pathos of identification leads to some remarkable passages. "In these events, in which everyone was consumed by the single task of saving what could be saved, the destruction of entire armies stands side by side with the courage and selflessness of individuals; the loss of cities with the protection of river crossings upon which depended the fate of entire treks of refugees. In the catastrophe that was enveloping everyone and everything, many a nameless soldier and citizen found new strength and courage" 36. And further, "Among the National Socialist authorities, there were those who proved themselves in the hour of need . . . while others failed, at times pathetically" 37.

16. As Maier remarks about this asymmetry, "The sufferings of Jews are not evoked: no sealed freight cars, purposeful starvation, flogging, degradation, and final herding to 'the showers' parallels the accounts of the evacuation of East Prussia. If indeed these two experiences are two sorts of destruction, one is presented, so to speak, in technicolor, the other in black, gray, and white." Maier goes on to characterize Hillgruber's elegiac evocation of the lost center as the "geopolitics of nostalgia," *The Unmasterable Past* 23.

17. Habermas, *Historiker-Streit* 73.

18. Habermas, *Historiker-Streit* 75. The notion of a postconventional identity that Habermas has deployed in the Historians' Debate has been a key term in his thinking for some time. See especially his "Können komplexe Gesellschaften eine vernünftige Identität ausbilden?" in Jürgen Habermas, *Zur Rekonstruktion des historischen Materialismus* (Frankfurt a.M.: Suhrkamp, 1976), as well as in the same volume his attempt to use the psychological theories of Jean Piaget and Lawrence Kohlberg to theorize the formation of postconventional identities. See also, "Geschichtsbewußtsein und posttraditionale Identität. Die Westorientierung der Bundesrepublik," in Jürgen Habermas, *Eine Art Schadensabwicklung: Kleine Politische Schriften VI* (Frankfurt a.M.: Suhrkamp, 1987).

19. See Konrad H. Jarausch, "Removing the Nazi Stain? The Quarrel of the German Historians," *German Studies Review* 11 (1988): 293.

20. In the present context, postmodern shall signify a general remapping of political, technological, cultural, economic, and sexual power that has taken place since World War II. These shifts and developments include a redistribution of power and alliances within Europe as well as a general destabilization of European hegemony in the world; the ascendancy of the United States as a world power; the decolonization of the Third World (these three developments were the subject of a lecture by Cornel West entitled "Historicizing the Postmodernism Debate," at Princeton University, 4 December 1988); the women's movement and the emergence of gender issues more generally in the figuration and theorization of otherness; massive migrations of indigenous populations under political and economic pressures; a more international division of labor; the passage into a computer and information-based rather than industrial economy; the availability, with the computer, of vast memory banks allowing for the instant recall of unlimited 'bits' of information; revisions within the sciences of the systems of logic considered to be natural; new forms of image consumption and spectacle; the availability, with nuclear weaponry, of technologies capable of eliminating life on the planet. These developments have put pressures on conventional, i.e., premodern and modern, notions of personal, sexual, and cultural identity that may be insupportable.

21. For a somewhat different reading of this repetition compulsion, see Dan Diner, "The Historians' Controversy—Limits to the Historization of National Socialism," *Tikkun* 2.1 (1987): 74–78.

22. See Habermas, *Historiker-Streit* 247. "Now as before we are faced with the simple fact that those born later also grew up in a form of life [*Lebensform*] in which that was possible. Our own life is not contingently but in its very essence, tied together with that life-context in which Auschwitz was possible. Our form of life is connected with the form of life of our parents and grandparents by way of a tightly woven fabric of familial, geographical, political, and also intellectual traditions that would be most difficult to untangle; we are part of a historical milieu that has made us into the people we are today. No one can escape from this milieu because our identity as individuals as well as Germans is indissolubly tied up with it. That reaches from the level of mimicry and bodily gesture to that of language and into the capillary divarications of one's intellectual habitus." The question that follows is the one we have been addressing all along. "But what are the consequences of this existential imbrication with traditions and forms of life which have become poisoned by unspeakable crimes?" This is, one might say, the central and ultimately suicidal core of Paul Celan's poetry.

23. For an excellent discussion of the debates surrounding the plans for these museums as well as the best evaluation to date of Habermas's interventions here and in the historians' controversy, see once more Maier, *The Unmasterable Past*.

24. Edgar Reitz and Peter Steinbach, *Heimat: Eine deutsche Chronik* (Nördlingen: Greno, 1985) 299.

25. I am very grateful to one of my students, Clare Rogan, for her sensitive discussion of this scene in her seminar paper.

26. Reitz and Steinbach, *Heimat* 148.

27. See Reitz's polemical essay on the American television film *Holocaust* for a discussion of this category so central to the aesthetic of *Heimat* in *Liebe zum Kino: Utopien und Gedanken zum Autorenfilm 1962–1983* (Cologne: *köln* 78, 1984) 99.

28. Reitz, *Liebe zum Kino* 151.

29. Yet a third example that might be included in this series is the curious fact that Anton never seems to have any nightmares about the executions he witnessed on the Eastern front. See J. Hoberman, "Once Upon a Reich Time," *New German Critique* 36 (Fall 1985): 9.

30. Interview with author July 1987.

31. Reitz, *Liebe zum Kino* 128.

32. Interview with author July 1987.

33. Quoted in Michael Geisler, "*Heimat* and the German Left: The Anamnesis of a Trauma," *New German Critique* 36 (Fall 1985): 63.

34. Reitz, *Liebe zum Kino* 145–46, quoted in Gertrud Koch, "How Much Naivete Can We Afford? The New *Heimat* Feeling," *New German Critique* 36 (Fall 1985): 15. Perhaps one should add here that Gypsies (Appolonia) and refugees (Klärchen), i.e., those other people who since time immemorial "go away," would also fit well into this American culture.

35. Koch, "New *Heimat* Feeling" 15.

Holocaust and the End of History: Postmodern Historiography in Cinema

ANTON KAES

I N 1984, in his essay "Of an Apocalyptic Tone Recently Adopted in Philosophy," Jacques Derrida parodied the proliferating discourse that takes it upon itself to proclaim the end, specifically "the end of history, the end of the class struggle, the end of philosophy, the death of God, the end of religions, the end of Christianity and morals, the end of the subject, the end of man, the end of the West, the end of Oedipus, the end of the earth, Apocalypse Now . . . also the end of literature, the end of painting, art as a thing of the past, the end of the past, the end of psychoanalysis, the end of the university, the end of phallocentrism and the phallogocentrism and I don't know what else."[1]

In this amusing inventory of odds and ends, Derrida alludes to a quiescent mood of *post-histoire* that has characterized Western European politics and culture since the 1970s. Following the exhaustion of the utopian impulses and revolutionary energies of the tumultuous sixties, a period of political inertia and *Endzeitstimmung* set in until it was ruptured by the events in Eastern Europe in the late eighties. At the same time, in the United States, Francis Fukuyama, deputy director of the state department's policy planning staff and former analyst at the RAND Corporation, published a much-discussed article entitled "The End of History?" in which he argued that with the demise of communism the ideological struggle between East and West had come to an end and no further evolution of human thought was to be expected.[2] Whatever the merits of such post-Hegelian and pseudo-Hegelian speculations, the very emergence of a new American discourse that predicts (and deplores) a universal posthistorical boredom for lack of ideological conflict should give us pause to think. In West Germany, similar debates about *post-histoire* have a different origin dating back to the apocalyptic finale of the Hitler regime. In 1945, history had indeed ended for more than fifty million victims of World War II, among them six million killed in an industrial genocide. That *something* had come to an end was recognized by calling 1945 *Stunde Null*, as if history could ever begin at point zero. *Post-histoire* in Germany always means history after the apocalypse, in the face of Hitler and Auschwitz.

133

Theodor W. Adorno's often cited remark that no poem can be written in innocence after Auschwitz implies the same *post-histoire* sentiment: "After Auschwitz," he writes in his *Negative Dialectics*, "there is no word . . . not even a theological one, that has any rights unless it underwent a transformation."[3] Following Adorno, Jean-François Lyotard in his book *The Differend* also sees Auschwitz as an endpoint of the historical process as well as of rational reason. Seen from today, he argues, it is as if one sensed that some great disaster had struck, a disaster so massive and at the same time so distant and foreign that no one can adequately articulate it: "Suppose that an earthquake destroys not only lives, buildings, and objects but also the instruments used to measure earthquakes directly and indirectly. The impossibility of quantitatively measuring it does not prohibit, but rather inspires in the minds of the survivors the idea of a very great seismic force. The scholar claims to know nothing about it, but the common person has a complex feeling, the one aroused by the negative presentation of the indeterminate."[4]

The silence, Lyotard continues, that the crime of Auschwitz imposes upon the historian is a *sign* for the common person, indicating "that something . . . cannot be phrased in the accepted idioms."[5] Similarly, in his book *The Writing of the Disaster*, Maurice Blanchot constitutes Auschwitz as an unrepresentable event which has nevertheless left its impressions and traces on every sector of the political and cultural life, reminiscent of the devastations of an earthquake long ago.[6]

The insistence on the impossibility of adequately comprehending and describing the Final Solution has by now become a *topos* of Holocaust research.[7] As Saul Friedlander recently pointed out,[8] how can something that at least on the face of it lacks instrumental rationality find a rational explanation? How can this historical occurrence, which is less understood the more we know about it, be represented in the mass media of today's entertainment industry? We have become rightly skeptical about realistic reconstructions of concentration camp scenes as depicted in the American television mini-series *Holocaust*—one of the most popular and commercially successful Hollywood products, which was sold to fifty countries including West Germany, where its reception nearly caused a mass hysteria in 1978.[9] We also have become perturbed by the unabashed commercial exploitation and trivialization of human suffering as exemplified in such television specials as *Playing for Time* and *War and Remembrance* or in such films as *Sophie's Choice* and *Enemies—A Love Story*, films in which the Holocaust serves more often than not as a mere backdrop to melodramatic private affairs.[10] And, finally, we have come to question films made in the strictly documentary style, such as Joachim C. Fest's highly successful documentary of 1977, *Hitler—A Career*, which, by drawing only on original footage, reproduces precisely those images that the Nazis employed in their skillful manipulation of film as an instrument of propaganda. What is sorely lacking (with few exceptions—Claude Lanzmann's semi-documentary *Shoah* is one of them) are films that deal with Nazism and the Holocaust in ways that challenge the narrowly circumscribed Hollywood conventions of storytelling and not only reflect self-critically on the limits and impasses of film but also utilize its specific potential in the representation of the past.

What Lyotard demands of the historian of Auschwitz, namely to lend an ear "to what is not presentable under the rules of knowledge,"[11] may well be the real domain of the filmmaker; it may, in fact, be expressible only in such a syncretistic medium as film, which makes use of theater, literature, painting, photography, and so on. It is the filmmaker (as visual artist) who can transcend the "rules of knowledge," that is, the documentary evidence, the facts and figures which the Nazis tried to conceal and to destroy. It is the filmmaker who can shed light on the social imagination, perverse as it may be, that underlies these unspeakable deeds. It is the filmmaker who can translate the fears and feelings, the hopes and delusions and suffering of the victims, all unrecorded and undocumented, into pre-verbal images and thereby trigger memories, associations, and emotions that precede the kind of rational reasoning and logical-linear discourse needed in historiographical writing. If it is agreed that the cataclysmic mass destruction that occurred a half-century ago defies not only historical description and quantitative determination but also rational explanation and linguistic articulation, then a new self-reflexive way of encoding history is called for.

I believe that Hans-Jürgen Syberberg's controversial seven-hour film of 1978, self-consciously entitled *Hitler—A Film from Germany*, represents one of the few attempts to come to terms with the Nazi phenomenon in a way that challenges Hollywood story-telling and, above all, utilizes the specific potential of film in the representation of the past. Internationally more acclaimed than other films of the New German Cinema, and more widely discussed abroad than literary works from West Germany, Syberberg's Hitler film has elicited strong reactions for and against its revolutionary postmodernist form as well as its neoconservative ideology. The main objections to the film (particularly among German intellectuals) were its emphasis on the irrational, mythical, and apocalyptic dimension of German history; its Wagnerian excess; its pastiche presentation; and its highly ambivalent exploration of the mesmerizing power of fascism. Syberberg's Hitler film was celebrated by critics in the United States and in France: Susan Sontag praised the symbolist and neosurrealist visual effects and placed Syberberg as avant-garde filmmaker in the tradition of Céline, Proust, and Joyce.[12] French critics hailed the film as an expression of the romantic, torn, irrational—in short, Faustian—German nature; it was even seen in its ambition and scope as a sequel to *Faust:* "Faust, Part III."[13] Scholars such as Philippe Lacoue-Labarthe and Jean-Luc Nancy acknowledge their indebtedness to Syberberg's film in their most recent essay on "The Nazi Myth," which deals with the role of aesthetics in fascist politics.[14]

In the following I will use Syberberg's Hitler film as a vantage point to bring into focus four concerns that seem central for a postmodern historiography on film (the kind of historiography that probes most radically the limits of representation): the rejection of narrativity, the specularization of history, the proliferation of perspectives, and the affirmation of nostalgia.

THE REJECTION OF NARRATIVITY

Highly self-aware of the conditions of the possibility of historical representation on film, Syberberg's Hitler film does not naively attempt to reconstruct the Nazi period or the life and times of Hitler. It has virtually no visual documentary footage, no authentic interviews, no location shots, no sustained linear narrative. The entire film is based on simulation and re-creation: it takes place in a studio on a sound stage, using the artificiality of the setting and the theatricality of the presentation as devices to counter any similarity to the conventionalized images that have come to signify Nazism in popular entertainment films. Syberberg's Hitler film openly acknowledges its own status as a construct, as a performance, as a history horror picture show that has its own aesthetic logic and is independent of any outside referent.

"No human story will be shown," says the master of ceremonies, standing in a circus ring, at the beginning of the Hitler film, "but the history of humanity. No disaster film, but disaster as a film. Apocalypse, flood, and cosmic death" (p. 41).[15] History in this film is "produced" and exhibited in the form of a circus show; it appears as a revue consisting of a large number of self-contained sketches and tableaux. Syberberg is interested less in constructing history as a story with cause and effect (thereby implying a logical development that can be "understood") than in presenting constellations and associations that surprise and shock the audience. His radically contrived and artificial mode of presentation also attacks all those allegedly authentic, in actual fact hopelessly platitudinous reconstructions of the past in which images shot by the Nazis themselves are recycled. Syberberg's film destroys direct referential illusion. What reality, after all, should the film mirror? Past reality is absent and not repeatable; it cannot be visited like a foreign country. A deep gulf separates history as experience from its re-presentation. What is presented can never be identical with the presentation itself.

Syberberg favors a self-reflexive play with images and linguistic signs that *refer to* history in associations that are not bound by time and place. Various temporal layers are interlocked through blatant anachronisms, radically undermining the illusion of continuity and linear development in narrated history. Historical time is stopped and recombined according to principles that derive not from chronology but from the power of association. Visual and aural leitmotifs recur throughout the film, often as only one layer of several on the soundtrack or in the image construction. Syberberg's complex sound-image collages neutralize the linear progress of time and bring history to a standstill. Instead of the "horizontal" development of a story, we have a *vertical* structure in which various levels of meaning and association coexist and resonate on many levels and in many voices.

Everything the camera registers takes place on a studio stage, which is hermetically sealed off from the outer world. Time becomes spatial, a dense web of quotations and references from literature, theater, music, and film. This radical intertextuality also has far-reaching consequences for Syberberg's treatment of historical material. Past events and characters, cut loose from their original contexts, become quotable set pieces in an aesthetic structure that follows its own laws. A closer look at one sequence in the first part of the film may illustrate how Syberberg transforms history into a gigantic sign system.

Against the backdrop of a soundstage cluttered with cardboard figures of the German Expressionist cinema, *Muspilli*, an apocalyptic poem from the ninth century, is read off-screen—"The mountains burn, the trees vanish from the earth, the rivers run dry, the moon falls, and finally the entire earth burns"—and, simultaneously, in original sound, a Hitler speech of 1932 is heard—"We have a goal and we will advocate it fanatically and relentlessly until the grave" (p. 40). The mythical prophecy of the end of the world in the ninth century is associatively related to Hitler's expression of a collective death wish. Such a double coding of old and new, of mythical and documentary, cannot be interpreted in a conventionally hermeneutic sense. These multilayered collages contain no transparent messages, but rather impressions and possibilities; no images of an independent reality, but articulations of autonomous artificial worlds; no straightforward stories, but intricate constellations and meandering paths of associations that do not converge in one point. In a review of the Hitler film the French film critic Christian Zimmer wrote: "No events are incapable of being retold, but there are cases where narration betrays reality and the memory of those who lived through what they themselves called 'unspeakable.' In such cases, the only legitimate and faithful truth is the scream . . . Narrative always involves a little of the hopes of the historian: Is not narrative an explanation and a rationalization of the unthinkable? Is it not a standardization of insanity? Does not narrative always excuse?"[16]

THE SPECULARIZATION OF HISTORY

Syberberg's translation of historical reality into a self-sufficient cosmos of signs, intertexts, quotations, allusions, memories, and associations gives him the freedom to encode German history in a variety of specular forms: as circus spectacle and horror cabinet; as puppet theater, cabaret, and side show; as tribunal; and as allegorical, baroque *theatrum mundi*. The central project of the film is not the representation of Hitler himself but the representation of the various ways in which Hitler has been represented. Syberberg's interest lies in the *possibilities* of presenting a figure which, he feels, "essentially cannot be represented realistically,"[17] not in the least because today the historical subject Hitler has dissolved into a plurality of images. Instead of reducing the phenomenon Hitler to *one* image, Syberberg proliferates images. Thus we are confronted, at the very beginning of the film, with the different roles Hitler plays in the popular imagination: Hitler as Charlie Chaplin in a scene from Chaplin's *The Great Dictator*, as house painter, as raving maniac, and so on, and finally as the compulsive sex killer from Fritz Lang's *M*, who recites his famous defense before invisible judges: "But who will believe me, who, who knows what compels me! I have to, I don't want to, I, I have to, I don't want, I have to, I can't help myself, I can't help myself. I have to, I have to do it, but nobody will believe me. I can't help it, I, I . . ." (p. 61). The monologue, spoken with self-lacerating theatricality by an Austrian actor wearing an SA uniform, is superimposed over a recording from Berlin of 1939, in which masses break out into "Sieg Heil, Sieg Heil" at Hitler's appearance. As the murderer is still whimpering "I can't help it, I, I . . .," we hear the original soundtrack of an SA song.

It is left to the viewer what exactly to make of the connections between the paranoid child murderer from Lang's 1931 film and the Hitler of 1939, between the criminal's blubbering about innocence and the intoxicated masses whose collective madness expresses itself in their enthusiastic "Sieg Heil!" The hysteria of the people and the shocking wretchedness of the captured criminal are related to each other in a montage, but for what purpose? Is Hitler to be exculpated as a victim of his drives? Are we to place the blame on the masses who shouted for a "Führer"? Or is the hysteria of this scene supposed to evoke the atmosphere of the era? Syberberg offers no single interpretation but instead constructs spectacles that allow several readings simultaneously. In one interview he said, "For some Hitler was a god of light, for others a jack-in-the-box and carpet chewer. Both interpretations receive the same weight and are juxtaposed with each other in various forms."[18]

Hitler served the Germans as a screen onto which they could project all their wishes, anxieties, and hopes. He appears as the goal of the Germans' "most secret yearnings," as the object of their suppressed desire for subjugation and the executor of everything they longed for collectively. That is the point of the film's central monologue, spoken by an actor imitating Hitler's voice and gestures, who, in a hallucinatory image, emerges from Richard Wagner's open grave. Hitler, rising from the dead, sits in judgment over the living. To the utter consternation of the audience, Hitler says in his monologue, "After all, there was no one else who would, who could take over my desired role. And so they called upon me . . . I gave them what they put into me, what they wanted to hear, wanted to do, things they were afraid to do. I made and commanded for them, for it was all for them, not for me . . . I was and am the end of your most secret wishes, the legend and reality of your dreams, so we have to get through. Finally. The time of the end? Nightmares? Not by a long shot" (pp. 127–129).

Faced with such a spectacle, the viewer feels helplessly ambivalent, spellbound on the one hand by its visual power and excessive camp eccentricity but shocked on the other hand by the audacity that uses such consciously naive stage magic, in a manner verging on the burlesque and shamelessly mixing the sublime with the ridiculous. And Hitler's politically provocative speech of self-defense, which the spectator instinctively feels challenged to refute, is made unreal by its context, the overly obvious theatrical play. In the staging of such scenes Syberberg does not hesitate to use (in the tradition of Robert Wilson) images of striking simplicity and childlike naiveté, a technique that results, as a critic once put it, in the "paradox of highly reflective infantility."[19]

Transforming the Nazi phenomenon into a gigantic spectacle opens Syberberg up to the criticism of the aestheticization of politics, which for Walter Benjamin was the ultimate strategy of fascism.[20] For example, in a scene such as the one just described, the spectator is most likely too enchanted or bewildered to put up much resistance against the film's seductive pull. All the Brechtian distancing devices that are put in the film as safeguards break down in the face of the genuinely cinematic pleasure of looking. Still, fascism is unthinkable without aesthetics. Hitler and Goebbels, both failed artists, reformulated the political itself as a work of art and had the burning desire to be the creators of a new Germany as a *Gesamtkunstwerk*. Syberberg's film brings the aesthetic dimension of Nazism to the fore and alludes more than once to the underlying affinities between cinema and fascism: both rely on spectacle.

THE PROLIFERATION OF PERSPECTIVES

In order to evoke the "Hitler in us" (one of the subtexts of the film), Syberberg tries to level the distance between ourselves and the historical person; he achieves this by introducing the figure of Karl-Wilhelm Krause, Hitler's conscientious and pedantic servant from 1934 on. Krause's memories, recited drily into the camera for an entire grueling half-hour, give an unusual view of Hitler as private person. The meticulous notation of the course of a day, which to Krause was the same, day in, day out, shows Hitler from a pedestrian perspective that allows the temporal distance between him and the viewer to disappear for moments at a time. For instance, Krause describes the breakfast ritual: "The breakfast always consisted of the same things. Two cups of mouthwarm whole milk, as many as ten pieces of Leibniz zwieback cookies, and then a third to a half of a bar of bittersweet chocolate broken into small pieces . . . For his bath he used pine-needle tablets" (p. 143). In the dull spectacle of our everyday lives, the film seems to suggest, we are all identical. In the cycle of daily routines there is no change from yesterday to today; once again history seems to evaporate in a timeless present. Precisely through his commonplace daily life, his quaint little idiosyncrasies, his ludicrous likes and dislikes—"Isn't it possible for the Führer of the German people to get a pair of decent socks?" Krause reports Hitler to have said one day—and through his dependence on moods and emotions, Hitler becomes "one of us." With an obsessive precision of language and a frighteningly flat voice, the servant also describes Christmas Eve 1937, when he and Hitler wrapped presents and drove incognito in a taxi through the streets of Munich. In the film's pastiche style the private Christmas spirit of the petit bourgeois from Braunau is juxtaposed with the political situation of Christmas 1942: the soundtrack that accompanies the servant's nostalgic description of 1937 features the famous radio broadcast on December 24, 1942, which brought together German soldiers from all fronts across the globe. Sentimentality and expansionism, peaceful Christmas whimsy and imperialist war, *Gemütlichkeit* and terror blend into one.

In the film, the radio broadcast is superimposed over Krause's monologue; he continues speaking, but the radio broadcast ultimately drowns him out. Associative links are suggested between the unbroken loyalty of the servant to his Führer and the fate of millions of German soldiers who died at the front out of loyalty to Germany; also between the administrative tone in which Krause talks about the human and banal side of Hitler and the rational bureaucratic ingenuity that was required to send three hundred thousand soldiers to Stalingrad and transport millions of Jews across Europe to the concentration camps in the east. (Lanzmann's film *Shoah* is similarly concerned with the sheer logistics and technicalities of efficiently murdering thousands of human beings a day.)

"The quality of Syberberg's film," said Michel Foucault in his review of the Hitler film, "consists in its statement that horror is banal, that banality in itself has dimensions of horror, that horror and banality are reversible."[21] Not only the madness and *Rausch* of antisemitic fervor but also the narrow bureaucratic diligence of an ordinary person like Krause was necessary to organize the assembly-line mass murders effectively and in an administratively "correct" way. The end of the scene, however, in Stalingrad, suggests a different, more ambivalent reading. Heavy snow starts falling down, gradually covering Krause, who is quite obviously standing in the middle of a studio. Krause's face finally freezes, an

emblematic embodiment of the trapped and freezing German army outside of Stalingrad. The Germans appear as victims of their high conception
of duty: like Krause, they obey the Führer to the end.

A further layer of associations is added to this scene through a musical
collage that combines march music and motifs from Wagner's *Rienzi*,
Hitler's favorite opera. The vertical structure of this scene is a product of
the layering of various linguistic, musical, and visual codes. Its simultaneous effects can only be approximated in a nonspatial medium like writing
or speaking. Private and political, fictional and authentic, trivial and world-
historical matters are intertwined and evoked at the same time. And the
ensuing scene, added through an abrupt cut, relativizes everything again:
the closeup of the valet's head, covered with ice and snow, and the radio
broadcast from Moscow in February 1943 announcing the defeat at
Stalingrad are followed by a projection (a still) of William Blake's "Shrine
of the Imagination," and André Heller instructing us (in a sudden cut to
another scene) that "Astronomers at the University of California, Berkeley,
have discovered the farthest known galaxy. This tremendous structure of
over a trillion suns is more than eight billion light-years away. The light
now reaching us from there was sent out at a time when our sun and its
planetary system did not even exist" (p. 56). This unexpected shift of perspective from Hitler's private life and German history to the history of the
cosmos seems extremely problematic, for it relativizes everything, suggesting that from the perspective of a billion light-years away *all* world events,
including the Final Solution, seem completely inconsequential and trivial.

Even this (certainly most dubious) "cosmic" model only approximates
what Syberberg calls "the whole." He is obsessed by the insight that
Hitlerism cannot be explained by a single thesis, not by *one* story but by
many. He circumnavigates his theme with a postmodern proliferation of
different voices, actions, recorded memories, quotations from novels,
poems, military reports, autobiographies, speeches, songs, pictures,
melodies: all of them ways of approaching the secret center called Adolf
Hitler, a subject that becomes concrete and comprehensible only in the
distorting mirror of others, a hollow center that is filled to the degree that
we project ourselves into it.

A similarly complex and problematic collage can be found in the representation of the Final Solution in the third part of the film. Heinrich
Himmler, played by the same actor who also impersonates Hitler, is lying
on a massage table and having his muscles loosened by his masseur; he
speaks about his childhood dreams, his recently acquired Buddhist beliefs
in nonviolence, and in the same tone of voice about his higher (and basically unpleasant) "duty" to murder millions of Jews. While he speaks, SS
soldiers and concentration camp guards appear on the back projection
screen to be marching toward the camera, one by one, like phantoms from
another world, while an off-screen voice reads from eyewitness accounts

of unspeakable crimes against women and children committed in the concentration camp as well as from official Nazi propaganda speeches justifying the genocide (p. 163–189). There are also snippets intercut (in original sound) from the speech that a shaken Hitler delivered after the failure of the Staufenberg assassination plot in 1944. Himmler at the same time gushes forth about his plans to introduce a law for the protection of animals as soon as the war is over. "I was extraordinarily interested to hear recently," he muses, "that when the Buddhist monks walk through the town in the evening, they carry a little bell in order to make the forest creatures that they might crush underfoot move aside, so that they may suffer no harm" (p. 175f).

Himmler's infamous speech to the SS in Posen in 1943, which expresses his admiration for those who remained "decent" while facing a mounting heap of corpses, is repeated twice. Only a few still pictures of concentration camp victims are shown as backdrops to the repelling visages of SS soldiers who extol Germanic virtues which for them include the heroic determination to remain unmoved by the suffering caused by the industrial-style mass killing that the Führer has ordered. To have cold-blooded mass murder presented by SS soldiers as a challenging task and a selfless sacrifice surely creates in the spectator a critical distance that exposes in one flash the whole cruel and perverse absurdity of such reasoning.

Still, the construction of such a scene abounds with incongruities, tensions, contradictions, ambivalences, and sudden, troubling shifts of sympathy: Himmler's grotesque concern for the protection of helpless animals is juxtaposed against his ruthless extermination policies vis-à-vis helpless Jews, while he himself, lying half-naked and squirming under the hands of his masseur, is shown as vulnerable. Is the pathologized image of Himmler in this scene meant to humanize him or to demonstrate the utterly schizophrenic project of the Final Solution, in which family fathers were also mass murderers? Are we to associate (as consciously or unconsciously suggested on the soundtrack) the failed plot against Hitler with the stepped-up mass murder in the concentration camps? So many questions suggest an equal number of ways to read a scene like this, which refuses to reduce the contradictions to a single narrative. The film's postmodernist multiple coding and the constantly shifting position of the author/filmmaker as *bricoleur* require an audience ready and willing to enter the slippery realm of textuality (any recourse to statements by the filmmaker that would constrain the potential meaning of the film does injustice to the textual multivalence of the film's collage principle). Not surprisingly, the proliferation, disjunction, and layering of conflicting sounds and images in a *sujet* like Nazism and the Final Solution pose a danger. The sheer number of conflicting angles (including always the angle of the Nazi perpetrator) from which each event is simultaneously viewed leads inexorably to ambivalences that do not preclude readings of the film (such as the

Germans in the role of victims, nostalgia for a *Heimat* and a sense of lost grandeur, and so on) that are clearly revisionist in their implication. The radical (Nietzschean, nihilist?) pluralism of postmodern aesthetics which characterizes this film also embraces conservative, sometimes provocatively reactionary and revisionist motifs and arguments, allusions and references, either expressed in the (often sarcastic) voice-over or evoked by the music of Richard Wagner who, in Syberberg's eyes, had cast a spell over Ludwig II, the romantic Bavarian King, as well as over Hitler. The burden is placed on the spectator to engage in a dialogue with the film and create his or her own version of the Nazi story, which the film lays out in all its daunting complexity.

THE AFFIRMATION OF NOSTALGIA

Syberberg's stylistic strategies of proliferation, juxtaposition, pastiche, contradiction, and intertextuality demonstrate his affinity with a poetics of postmodernism,[22] while his apocalyptic world view, his cultural pessimism, and his static view of history place him in the philosophical tradition of what has become known as *post-histoire*. Postmodernist aesthetics and the tradition of *post-histoire* are related: the ease with which a postmodernist artist like Syberberg uses the past as "material" that can be quoted at will is based on the belief that history and progress have reached their limit and have come to a standstill; the present is itself no more than an assemblage of quotations from the past. In the epoch of the *post-histoire*, originality and innovation mean recycling and pastiche. In this sense postmodernism and *post-histoire* are indeed kindred concepts, with *post-histoire* being the larger term encompassing postmodernist strategies and styles. But while postmodernism has engendered a critical debate that is still growing by leaps and bounds, the term *post-histoire*, coined not accidentally in the restorative Adenauer period and revived in the 1970s, has gone almost unnoticed in this country.

As early as 1952 the German sociologist Arnold Gehlen adopted the expression *post-histoire* from the writings of Paul de Man's uncle, Hendrik de Man, a Belgian socialist thinker who later became a Nazi collaborator. He first used the term to designate an epoch characterized by a state of stability and rigidity, devoid of utopian ideas, change, or development.[23] In 1961, in an article appropriately entitled "Über kulturelle Kristallisation" (On Cultural Crystallization), Gehlen wrote, "I am predicting that the history of ideas has come to an end and that we have arrived at the epoch of *post-histoire*, so that now the advice Gottfried Benn gave the individual, 'Make do with what you have,' is valid for humanity as a whole. In the age in which the earth has become optically and informationally surveyable, when no event of importance can happen unnoticed, there are no more surprises."[24]

Syberberg takes up this motif of crystallization and glacial rigidity in his film about Hitler, and it is no accident that metaphors of coldness, ice, and ossification recur in much of contemporary German literature (most prominently in Enzensberger's long poem *Der Untergang der Titanic*). In the Hitler film the stage itself appears as an emblem of the frozen world. Since, in the philosophy of *post-histoire*, the future has no further prospects and history seems to have come to a halt, there is no longer any existing force that could function like a magnet to pull the fragments of the past into a meaningful (that is, narrative) order. The fragments remain fragments; they lie scattered around on Syberberg's stage, dead and without context. The "spatialization" of time to a confined area in which disconnected fragments from many historical eras are strewn about—the bits and pieces after the catastrophe, as it were—corresponds exactly to the idea of an eternal present expressed by adherents of *post-histoire*. Syberberg's *Hitler* has no forward movement; it evokes instead elegiac memories of past glories, nostalgia, and a sense of waiting for the apocalypse.[25]

This stasis becomes most obvious in the numerous monologues that André Heller carries on in a mock discussion with a puppet that has Hitler's features. At one point the Hitler puppet is addressed with, "You occupied everything and corrupted it with your actions,—everything, honor, loyalty, country life, hard work, movies, dignity, fatherland, pride, faith. You are the executor of Western civilization . . . the plague of our century. The words 'magic' and 'myth' and 'serving' and 'ruling,' 'Führer,' 'authority,' are ruined, are gone, exiled to eternal time. And we are finished. Nothing more will grow here. An entire nation stopped existing" (p. 242).

In this lament, Germany—its myths, its history, and its identity—is irretrievably lost. What remains, according to Syberberg, is a land without a national identity, full of neurotic uncertainties about its own dreams, desires, and myths that define and sustain identity. The act of mourning here turns toward Germany itself as Syberberg vainly attempts to deliver German culture from its fascist past. His film ends with the chorus "Ode to Joy," from Beethoven's Ninth Symphony playing behind a visionary tableau dominated by the black stone from Dürer's famous engraving, "Melancolia," controversially pointing the way from mourning to "salvation" and "healing."

Where no development or change is considered possible, the future vanishes. At the end of history, the artist works in an eternal process of recycling what is at hand. What John Barth argued as early as 1965 in one of the first manifestoes of postmodern literature, *The Literature of Exhaustion*, informs Syberberg's representation of German history: Everything has been said, originality is strictly confined to the recombination of fragments from the past. The entirety of Western culture is now available, a quarry to which one goes to pick out quotations. This is how Syberberg expressed it in 1981: "Now the world is divided up, relinquished to history and the traditions of culture, the source of our works. Huge mines of the old cultures for quotations, which build up by layers to new cultures. Everything we show or speak has been used before, been touched, and only a rearrangement of the systems and fragments produces, if it functions, something new . . . Today's mythologies of the wandering Odysseus are constructed of quotations from the discipline of our history, and the fear of today's Penelope threatens to create chaos on the horizon of our inner landscapes as a foreboding about the future—the end of all history."[26]

The end of Germany is evoked by the pervasive mythologizing of death throughout the film: the original recordings of the National Socialist funeral service for the victims of Hitler's putsch on November 9, 1923, are used regularly as a leitmotif on the soundtrack, and in a film clip from Christmas 1944, Goebbels says, "Forward over graves! The dead are more powerful armies than we on the land, than we on the sea. They stride ahead of us." Syberberg intensifies and totalizes the mysterious collective death wish, characteristic of the National Socialist ideology, into a global longing for the end of the world that can only be grasped through myth. All crimes against humanity, including the extermination of the Indians, which incidentally the film also mentions, and the annihilation of the Jews, are mere symptoms for the fatal disease of the moribund West. Even before the titles appear on the screen, the film announces its position in a voice-over: "Dances of death, dialogues of the dead, conversations in the kingdom of the dead, a hundred years later, a thousand years, millions. Passions, oratorios . . . leftovers of a lost civilization and of a lost life, our Europe before the collapse. Farewell to the West. *Sub specie aeternitatis* and everything on film, our new chance. The story of the death of the old light in which we lived, and of our culture, a remote singing" (p. 32).

The cultural pessimism of such passages allows the concrete guilt of the Germans to dissolve in the general malaise of *post-histoire*. Against the horizon of the apocalypse and of eternity ("sub specie aeternitatis"), "rational" distinctions between perpetrators and victims, between violence and suffering lose their meaning and even their justification. The specificity of the Final Solution is thus conveniently submerged in the problem of universal evil—an evil that for Syberberg is as much associated with the curse of modernity as it is with the Nazi genocide.

Seen from this perspective, Claude Lanzmann's 1985 documentary film *Shoah* offers the necessary corrective to Syberberg's film by drawing a sharp line between Nazi criminals and their victims.[27] Based on interviews with survivors and witnesses, former concentration camp guards and Nazi officials, and bystanders of varying degrees of complicity, the nine-and-one-half-hour documentary on the Final Solution evokes the past not

through an illusionist "authentic" reconstruction but through the survivors' individual memories of the period. Lanzmann does not show any of
the well-known and by now codified documentary concentration camp
footage but focuses instead solely on the power (and failings) of personal
memory and the (admittedly often staged) immediacy of oral history. He is
engaged in *Spurensuche* (search for traces): in detective and reconstructive work undertaken in the hope of recovering and recording the traces
of the distant disaster. It is as if the disaster itself resisted representation; it
is grasped only afterwards by studying, as it were, the aftershocks.

As early as 1979 Lanzmann outlined his project for *Shoah:* "A film
devoted to the Holocaust can only be a counter-myth, that is, an investigation into the presentness of the Holocaust, an investigation into a past
whose wounds are so fresh and so keenly inscribed in consciousness that
they are present in a haunting timelessness."[28] Thus Lanzmann's work
throws Syberberg's project in relief: although both filmmakers believe in
the presence of the past (which explains, on the formal level, their shared
disregard for chronological narratives and their sense of *post-histoire*, of
"timelessness"), ultimately their projects differ radically. Lanzmann sets
out to prove irrefutably and with an enormous array of witnesses the existence of concentration camps; the film focuses almost exclusively on the
annihilation process. Syberberg (not unlike Anselm Kiefer), on the other
hand, stages the myths of the Nazi past—not to glorify them, but to find
some redemptive way back to the spiritual *Heimat* of the Germans, which
he believes has been lost to both fascism and postwar materialism. His
undertaking is completely paradoxical: irrationalism, which the Hitler
movement had appropriated and exploited, is to be wrested away from its
National Socialist associations by means of a film that celebrates irrationalism as the essence of German identity. The attitude necessary for this task
simultaneously constructs and deconstructs, enchants and disillusions,
hypnotizes and alienates: hence the contradictory union of stylistic models
from Brecht and Wagner, and the vacillation between fascination and criticism in the presentation of Hitler and Nazism.

Syberberg places himself in the long tradition of German writers and
artists—Lessing, Goethe, Hölderlin, Nietzsche, Wagner, Tucholsky—who
designed an imaginary, excessively idealized Germany in order to compare
it with the unbearable real Germany which now—after Hitler and
Auschwitz—lives in a period of *post-histoire*, only a shadow of its former
self. It would be worth speculating whether the obsessive preoccupation
with the apocalypse and the imaginary anticipation of the end of the world
in the 1970s and 1980s does not express Germany's subconscious wish to
eradicate its traumatic past once and for all. The longing for the apocalypse and the end of history may be provoked by the utopian hope to
begin once more, to create a pure moment of origin that is not contami-
nated by history.

Notes

1. Jacques Derrida, "Of an Apocalyptic Tone Recently Adopted in Philosophy," *Oxford Literary Review*, 6, no. 2 (1984), 20ff.

2. Francis Fukuyama, "The End of History?" *National Interest*, Summer 1989, pp. 3–18; see also the responses to this article, ibid., pp. 19–35.

3. Theodor W. Adorno, *Negative Dialectics* (New York: Continuum, 1983), p. 367.

4. Jean-François Lyotard, *The Differend: Phrases in Dispute*, trans. Georges Van Den Abbeele (Minneapolis: University of Minnesota Press, 1988), p. 56. See also his "Discussion, or Phrasing 'after Auschwitz,'" reprinted in *The Lyotard Reader*, ed. Andrew Benjamin (Oxford: Basil Blackwell, 1989), pp. 360–392.

5. Ibid., pp. 56ff.

6. Maurice Blanchot, *The Writing of the Disaster*, trans. Ann Smock (Lincoln: University of Nebraska Press, 1986). See also George Steiner, "The Long Life of Metaphor: An Approach to 'the Shoah,'" *Encounter* 68 (February 1987), 55: "It may be that the Auschwitz-universe, for it was that, precisely marks that realm of potential—now realized—human bestiality, or rather, abandonment of the human and regression to bestiality, which both precedes language, as it does in the animal, and comes after language as it does in death. Auschwitz would signify on a collective, historical scale the death of man as a rational, 'forward-dreaming' speech-organism . . . The languages we are now speaking on this polluted and suicidal planet are 'post-human.'"

7. See Saul Friedlander, "The 'Final Solution': On the Unease in Historical Interpretation," *History and Memory* 1, no. 2 (1989), 61–73; Arno Mayer, *Why Did the Heavens Not Darken? The "Final Solution" in History* (New York: Pantheon, 1989), p. xv; Istvan Deak, "The Incomprehensible Holocaust," *New York Review of Books*, 28 September 1989; Judith Miller, *One, by One, by One* (New York: Simon and Schuster, 1990), pp. 9–12.

8. Friedlander, p. 66.

9. On the German reception of *Holocaust*, see Anton Kaes, *From "Hitler" to "Heimat": The Return of History as Film* (Cambridge, Mass.: Harvard University Press, 1989).

10. For an overview and evaluation of films dealing with the Holocaust, see Ilan Avisar, *Screening the Holocaust: Cinema's Images of the Unimaginable* (Bloomington: Indiana University Press, 1988); Judith E. Doneson, *The Holocaust in American Film* (Philadelphia: Jewish Publication Society, 1987); Annette Insdorf, *Indelible Shadows: Film and the Holocaust* (New York: Random House, 1983).

11. Lyotard, *The Differend*, p. 57.

12. Susan Sontag, "The Eye of the Storm," *New York Review of Books*, 21 February 1980.

13. See Jean-Pierre Faye, "Le troisième Faust," Le Monde, 22 July 1987.

14. Philippe Lacoue-Labarthe and Jean-Luc Nancy, "The Nazi Myth," *Critical Inquiry*, 16 (Winter 1990), 291–312; see also Lacoue-Labarthe, "The Aesthetization of Politics," in *Heidegger, Art and Politics: The Fiction of the Political*, trans. Chris Turner (Oxford: Basil Blackwell, 1990), pp. 61–76.

15. The page numbers in parentheses refer to the filmscript. Hans-Jürgen Syberberg, *Hitler, a Film from Germany*, trans. Joachim Neugroschel (New York: Farrar, Straus and Giroux, 1982). A more detailed analysis of Syberberg's cinema can be found in Kaes, *From Hitler to Heimat*, pp. 37–72; Saul Friedlander, *Reflections of Nazism: An Essay on Kitsch and Death* (New York: Harper & Row, 1984); Eric L. Santner, *Stranded Objects: Mourning, Memory, and Film in Postwar Germany* (Ithaca: Cornell University Press, 1990), pp. 103–149.

16. Christian Zimmer, "Our Hitler," *Telos*, 42 (Winter 1979–80), 150.

17. Quoted in Eva-Suzanne Bayer, "Hitler in uns," *Stuttgarter Zeitung*, 15 April 1977.

18. Ibid.

19. Hans Thies Lehmann, "Robert Wilson, Szenograph," *Merkur*, 437 (July 1985), 554.

20. On the politics of aesthetics and the aesthetics of politics under fascism, see Lacoue-Labarthe, *Heidegger, Art and Politics*, pp. 61–76.

21. Michel Foucault, "Les quatre cavaliers de l'Apocalypse et les vermisseaux quotidiens: Entretien avec Michel Foucault," *Cahiers du cinéma* (February 1980), 95ff. Hannah Arendt's account of the Eichmann trial, *Eichmann in Jerusalem* (New York: Viking, 1963) carries the subtitle "A Report on the Banality of Evil." See also Nathan Rotenstreich, "Can Evil Be Banal?" *Philosophical Forum*, 16, nos. 1–2 (1984–85), 50–62.

22. There are many definitions of postmodernism today. I follow here the account of Linda Hutcheon, *A Poetics of Postmodernism: History, Theory, Fiction* (New York: Routledge, 1988); see also Wolfgang Welsch, *Unsere postmoderne Moderne* (Weinheim: VCH, Acta Humaniora, 1988); Hannes Böhringer, "Die Ruine in Posthistoire," *Merkur*, 406 (April 1982): 367–375. See also Christopher Sharrett's interview with Hans-Jürgen Syberberg, "Sustaining Romanticism in a Postmodernist Cinema," *Cinéaste*, 15 (1987) no. 3, 18–20. The interview was held after the New York premiere of Syberberg's new film, *Die Nacht*, a six-hour performance piece with one actress, Edith Clever, dealing with the end of European culture. This film carries on and radicalizes the elegiac tone and antimodernist ideology of his Hitler film.

23. Arnold Gehlen, "Einblicke," in *Gesamtausgabe*, vol. 7 (Frankfurt am Main: Klostermann, 1978), pp. 19, 140. Hendrik de Man, *Vermassung und Kulturverfall: Eine Diagnose unserer Zeit* (Berne: Francke, 1951), pp. 135–136.

24. Arnold Gehlen, über kulturelle Kristallisation," in *Studien zur Anthropologie und Soziologie* (Darmstadt: Luchterhand, 1963), p. 323; reprinted in *Wege aus der Moderne: Schlüsseltexte der Postmoderne-Diskussion*, ed. Wolfgang Welsch (Weinheim: VCH, Acta Humaniora, 1988), pp. 133–143. See also Peter Slöterdijk, "Nach der Geschichte," in *Wege aus der Moderne*, pp. 262–273; Lutz Niethammer, "Afterthoughts on Posthistoire," *History and Memory*, 1 (Spring/Summer 1989), 27–53; Niethammer, *Posthistoire: Ist die Geschichte zu Ende?* (Reinbek: Rowohlt, 1989). Gianni Vattimo begins his essay, "The End of (Hi)story," *Chicago Review* 35 (1987) no. 4, pp. 20–30, with the following sentence: "Probably, one of the most important points on which the descriptions of the postmodern condition agree—no matter how different they are from other points of view—is the consideration of postmodernity in terms of 'the end of history.'" See, further, Henry S. Kariel, "The Endgame of Postmodernism within the Momentum of Modernity," *Futures: The Journal of Forecasting, Planning and Policy*, 22 (January–February 1990), 91–99.

25. On the discourse of the apocalypse, see the essays in *Visions of Apocalypse: End or Rebirth?* ed. Saul Friedlander et al. (New York: Holmes & Meier, 1985). See also Ulrich Horstmann's disturbing desire to have all of mankind eradicated in his semi-literary essay *Das Untier: Konturen einer Philosophie der Menschenflucht* (Berlin: Medusa, 1983).

26. Hans-Jürgen Syberberg, *Die freudlose Gesellschaft* (Munich: Hanser, 1981), p. 83.

27. See the published filmscript, Claude Lanzmann, *Shoah: An Oral History of the Holocaust* (New York: Pantheon, 1985). See also Gertrud Koch, "The Aesthetic Transformation of the Image of the Unimaginable: Notes on Claude Lanzmann's *Shoah*," *October*, 48 (Spring 1989): 15–24; Steven G. Kellman, "Cinema of/as Atrocity: *Shoah*'s Guilty Conscience," *Gettysburg Review*, I (Winter 1988): 22–31; Timothy Garton Ash, "The Life of Death," *New York Review of Books*, 19 December 1985.

28. Claude Lanzmann, "From the Holocaust to the Holocaust," *Telos*, 42 (Winter 1979–80), 143.

A Kind of Settlement of Damages: The Apologetic Tendencies in German History Writing

JÜRGEN HABERMAS

It is a notable shortcoming that the literature about National Socialism does not know or does not want to admit to what degree all the deeds—with the sole exception of the technical process of gassing—that the National Socialists later committed had already been described in the voluminous literature of the 1920s. . . . Did the National Socialists or Hitler perhaps commit an "Asiatic" deed merely because they and their ilk considered themselves to be potential victims of an "Asiatic" deed?

Ernst Nolte, in the *Frankfurter Allgemeine Zeitung*, June 6, 1986

I

THE ERLANGEN historian Michael Stürmer argues for a functional interpretation of historical consciousness: "In a land without history, the future is controlled by those who determine the content of memory, who coin concepts and interpret the past." In keeping with Joachim Ritter's neoconservative image of the world, which was updated by his students in the 1970s, Stürmer envisions the processes of modernization as a kind of unavoidable settlement of damages. This settlement occurs because the individual must be compensated for the inevitable alienation that as a "social molecule" he experiences in material industrial society. In keeping with the molecule metaphor, Stürmer is less interested in the identity of the individual than in the integration of the community. Pluralism in values and interests leads, "when it can no longer find common ground, sooner or later to civil war." What is needed, according to Stürmer, is a "social mechanism for endowing higher meaning, something that, after religion, only nation and patriotism have been capable of." A politically responsible discipline of history will heed the call to activate such a mechanism and produce and disseminate a historical image that can foster a national consensus. The discipline of history is "propelled by collective,

Reprinted from *Forever in the Shadow of Hitler? Original Documents of the* Historikerstreit, *The Controversy Concerning the Singularity of the Holocaust*, translated by James Knowlton and Truett Cates, 1993, pages 34–44. Permission granted by Humanities Press International, Inc., Atlantic Highlands, NJ 07716.

for the most part unconscious, drives toward the inner endowment of higher meaning, but it must"—and this is what Stürmer sees as a real dilemma—"work this out according to scholarly methods." In this view, the discipline sets out to "find the balance between endowing higher meaning and demythologizing."

Let us first observe the Cologne historian Andreas Hillgruber as he walks this tightrope. I feel confident in approaching the most recent study of this renowned historian, even though I have no special competence in the field, since the investigation evidently is addressed to laymen. Hillgruber's study was recently released in a deluxe edition by Siedler Verlag with the title *Zweierlei Untergang* [Twofold Fall]. I will record the observations of a patient subjected to a revisionist operation on his historical consciousness.

In the first part of his study Hillgruber describes the collapse of the German eastern front during the last year of the war, 1944–1945. In the first pages he mentions the "problem of identification." With which side in the conflict should the author identify? Four possible perspectives suggest themselves. He dismisses the position taken by the would-be assassins of Hitler on July 20, 1944, as merely "preferentially ethical" and therefore inferior to the "responsibly ethical" position of the local commanders, state officials, and mayors. This leaves three perspectives for consideration. Hillgruber dismisses Hitler's perspective of perseverance and survival as social Darwinism. Nor does an identification with the victors seem possible; such a perspective of liberation would only be appropriate for the victims of the concentration camps, he claims, and not for the German nation as a whole. The historian has just one choice: "He must identify with the concrete fate of the German population in the East and with the desperate and sacrificial efforts of the German army in the eastern theater and of the German navy in the Baltic. The military forces in the East were trying to protect the German population in the East from the orgies of revenge by the Red Army, the mass rapes, the random murders, and the forced deportation, and . . . to hold open the escape route to the West."

Perplexed, one wonders why a historian in 1986 has to block out a retrospective point of view from the distance of forty years, in other words, his own perspective, a standpoint from which he cannot remove himself anyway. Additionally, his own real-time perspective offers hermeneutical advantages. It sets in relation the selective perceptions of the parties involved; it weighs them against one another and completes them from the perspective of knowledge acquired since then. Hillgruber does not want to write his presentation from this, dare one say "normal" standpoint, because, as he claims, then questions of "morality in wars of annihilation" would come into play. And they are to be ruled out. Here Hillgruber brings to mind the remark by Norbert Blüm. Blüm argued that the actions of annihilation in the camps could in fact continue only as long as the German eastern front held. This fact ought to cast a long shadow on the "picture of horror of raped and murdered women and children" that presented itself to the German soldiers who retook Nemmersdorf, for example. Hillgruber wants to present what happened in eastern Germany from the view of the brave soldiers, the desperate civilian population, also the "tried and true" higher-ups of the Nazi party (NSDAP); he wants to set himself inside the experiences of the fighters of yesteryear, at a point when they are not yet compromised and depreciated by our retrospective knowledge. This intention explains the principle behind his dividing the study into two parts: "Collapse in the East" and "Annihilation of the Jews." These are two processes that Hillgruber precisely does *not*, despite the announcement on the dust jacket, want to show "in their gloomy inter-weaving."

II

After completing this operation in the first part of his study, which evident-ly is the kind of history that Stürmer would call the endowing of higher meaning, Hillgruber does not hesitate in the second part of his study to make use of the knowledge of the latter-day historians in order to prove a different thesis. In the foreword he introduces the notion that the expul-sion of the Germans from the East is in no way to be understood as a "response" by the Allies to the crimes in the concentration camps. By ref-erence to the Allied war aims he argues that "at no point was there ever a prospect, once Germany was defeated, of preserving the greater part of the Prussian-German eastern provinces." He explains the lack of interest on the part of the Western powers in preserving the eastern provinces by referring to a "cliché-image of Prussia" that conditioned the thinking of Allied policymakers. It does not occur to Hillgruber that the structure of power in the Reich could actually have had something to do, as the Allies assumed, with the social structure especially well preserved in Prussia. He makes no use of social-scientific information. Otherwise he could hardly have attributed the transgressions of the Red Army, for example, which occurred not only in Germany but also before that in Poland, Rumania, and Hungary, to the barbaric "notions of war" of the Stalinist period. Be that as it may, the Western powers were blinded by their illusorily per-ceived war aim, the destruction of Prussia. Only too late did they recognize how "all Europe," through the march forward of the Russians, would become "the loser of the catastrophe of 1945."

By setting the stage in this way, then, Hillgruber can push the "struggle" of the German Army of the East into what he sees as the proper light—the "desperate defensive battle for the preservation of the great power status of the German Reich, which, according to the will of the Allies, had to be destroyed. The German Army of the East provided an umbrella of protection for a centuries-old settlement area, the homeland of millions, who . . . lived in the heartland of the German Reich." The dramatic presentation closes then with a wishful interpretation of the surrender on May 8, 1945: Forty years later the question of the "reconstruction of the destroyed European Center (is) . . . as open as it was then. Those living at that time, whether as actors or as victims, became witnesses of the catastrophe of eastern Germany." The moral of the story is obvious (to him): Today at least the alliance of forces is correct.

In the second part, Hillgruber takes twenty-two pages to treat the aspect of the war that he had so-far kept separate from the "tragic" acts of heroism on the eastern front. The subtitle of the book already signals a changed perspective. The "Destruction of the German Reich", something that had been pledged in the rhetoric of the war pamphlets (and that evidently happened only on the eastern front), stands in contrast to the soberly registered "End of the European Jewry." Now, "destruction" requires an aggressive opponent; an "end" seems to some extent to appear on its own. In the first part of the book "the destruction of whole armies" stands "beside the sacrifice of individuals"; in the second part of the book, the topic is "stationary successor organizations" of the *Einsatz-gruppen*. While in the first section "many anonymous people reached beyond themselves in the imminent catastrophe," in the second section the gas chambers are euphemized as a "more effective means" of liquidation. In the first section, we read the unrevised, unpurified clichés of a jargon retained since childhood; in the second section, we experience the frozen language of bureaucracy. However, the historian does not simply switch the perspective of presentation. In the second section he sets out to prove that "the murder of the Jews" was "exclusively a consequence of the radical doctrine of race."

Stürmer was interested in the question, To what extent had it been Hitler's war and to what extent the war of the Germans? Hillgruber poses the analogous question with regard to the annihilation of the Jews. He poses hypothetical considerations about how life would have looked for the Jews if a right-wing coalition like the nationalists and the *Stahlhelmer* [veterans' group] instead of the Nazis had come into power in 1933. The Nuremberg laws would still have been introduced, just as would all other measures up through 1938 that forced on the Jews a "separate consciousness." This would have been so since these measures found "accord with the sensibilities of a large part of the society." Hillgruber doubts, however, that *all* decisionmakers between 1938 and 1941 saw a policy of forced emigration as the best solution to the Jewish question. Still, by that time, two-thirds of the German Jews had "ended up abroad." Finally, regarding the implementation after 1941 of the Final Solution, it was Hitler alone, according to Hillgruber, who had his mind set on it from the beginning. Hitler wanted the physical annihilation of all Jews "because only such a 'racial revolution' could lend permanence to the world-power status of his Reich." Since Hillgruber does not use the verb in the subjunctive, one does not know whether the historian has adopted the perspective of the participants this time too.

At any rate, Hillgruber makes a sharp distinction between the euthanasia programs, to which 100,000 mentally ill fell victim, and the annihilation of the Jews proper. Against the backdrop of the social Darwinism of human genetics, the killing of "life unworthy of living" is supposed to have found support in the populace. However, Hitler in his idea of the Final Solution is supposed to have been isolated even in the narrowest leadership circles, "including Göring, Himmler and Heydrich." After Hitler has been identified as the sole responsible author for the idea and decision, only its execution needs an explanation. But this explanation ignores the frightening fact that the mass of the population—as Hillgruber certainly assumes—was silent throughout all of it.

To be sure, the goal of the difficult neoconservative revision would be endangered if this phenomenon of silence had, after all, to be delivered up to a moral judgment. At this point, therefore, the historian, who has been writing in the narrative mode, switches over to an anthropological-general tone. In his opinion, "the acceptance by the mass of the populace of the gruesome events, events that were at least darkly suspected, points out the historical singularity of the event." Standing firmly in the tradition of the German mandarin, Hillgruber is most deeply appalled by the high proportion of university-trained men who participated—as if there were not a completely plausible explanation for that. In short, the phenomenon that a civilized populace let these horrible things happen is one that Hillgruber removes from the technical competence of the overburdened historian and blithely pushes off into the dimension of the generally human.

III

In the *Historische Zeitschrift* (vol. 242, 1986, pp. 465ff.) Hillgruber's colleague from Bonn, Klaus Hildebrand, commends a work by Ernst Nolte as "showing the way" because the work does the service of removing the "seemingly unique" quality of the history of the Third Reich. As part of the process of historicizing, he categorizes "the destructive capacity of the worldview and of the regime" as part of the global development of totalitarianism. Nolte, who with his book *Faschismus in seiner Epoche* [Fascism in Its Epoch] (1963) had already found wide acclaim, is in fact cut from a different cloth than is Hillgruber.

In his contribution "Zwischen Mythos und Revisionismus" [Between Myth and Revisionism], he based the necessity for a revision on the observation that the history of the Third Reich had predominantly been written by the victors, who then made it into a "negative myth." To illustrate, Nolte invites us to take part in a tasteful thought experiment. He sketches for us the image of Israel that would be held by a victorious PLO after the destruction of Israel: "For decades, perhaps even for a century, no one would venture . . . to attribute the rise of Zionism to its spirit of resistance against European anti-Semitism." Even the theory of totalitarianism, which predominated in German historical scholarship of the 1950s, offered no change in perspective from the negative myth initiated by the historians of the victorious nations; instead, the totalitarianism theory had only led to the Soviet Union also being pulled into the negative image. A concept that lives to that extent off the contrast with the democratic constitutional state is not enough for Nolte; he attributes much to mutual threats of destruction. Long before Auschwitz, Hitler, so he claims, had good grounds to believe that his opponents wanted to destroy him—"annihilate" is the word in the English original. As proof he cites the "declaration of war" that Chaim Weizmann in September 1939 delivered on behalf of the Jewish World Congress and that then was supposed to *justify* Hitler in treating German Jews as prisoners of war—and in deporting them. A few weeks ago one could have read in *Die Zeit* (although without names being named) that Nolte served up this argument to a Jewish dinner guest, his colleague, historian Saul Friedländer of Tel Aviv.

Nolte is the officious-conservative narrator who tackles the "identity problem." He solves Stürmer's dilemma between the endowment of higher meaning and scholarship through an energetic decision and chooses as a point of connection for his presentation the terror of the Pol Pot regime in Cambodia. He reconstructs a background history for mass terror. As it reaches back in time it includes the "Gulag," Stalin's expulsion of the kulaks, and the Bolshevik revolution; he sees antecedents to mass terror in Babeuf, the early socialists, and the agrarian reformers of the early nineteenth century. In all these figures he perceives a line of revolt against cultural and social modernization, a revolt driven by the illusionary and passionate longing for the reestablishment of an understandable, autarchic world. In this context of terror stretching across the globe and over the centuries, the annihilation of the Jews appears as a regrettable, but perfectly understandable, result. It is seen as a reaction by Hitler to what he is assumed to have sensed as a threat of destruction: "The so-called annihilation of the Jews during the Third Reich was a reaction or a distorted copy, but not a first act or an original."

Nolte attempts in another essay to explain the philosophical background of his "trilogy on the history of modern ideologies." This essay will not be discussed here. In what Nolte, the student of Heidegger, calls his "philosophical writing of history," I am interested only in the "philosophical."

In the early 1950s there was a debate in philosophical anthropology about whether human beings were "open to the world" or "captives of the environment." The discussion involved A. Gehlen, H. Plessner, K. Lorenz, and E. Rothacker. Nolte's rather odd use of the Heideggerian concept of "transcendence" reminds me of this discussion. He has been using "transcendence," actually since 1963, to explain the great shift, the historical process of the breakup of a traditional way of life in the transition to modernity; his explanation invokes the timeless category of the anthropological-original. At this depth of abstraction, in which all cats are gray, he pleads for understanding for the anti-modernist impulses. These impulses are directed against an "unconditional affirmation of practical transcendence." By this category of practical transcendence Nolte refers to the putatively ontologically grounded "unity of world economy, technology, science and emancipation." All this fits neatly with attitudes that dominate today—and with the circle dance of Californian worldviews that sprout from it. The leveling of differences required by this abstraction, however, is rather more annoying; from this perspective it makes "Marx and Maurras, Engels and Hitler, despite all the emphasis on their contrasts, nevertheless related figures." Not until Marxism and fascism are acknowledged to be attempts to answer "the frightening realities of modernity" can the true intention of National Socialism be neatly and cleanly separated from its unhappy practice. "The 'atrocity' was not concluded with the final intention, but rather with the ascribing of guilt, a process that directed itself against a human group that itself was already so severely affected by the process of emancipation in liberal society that it declared itself, in the words of some of its prominent representatives, to be mortally endangered."

Now, one could let the scurrilous background philosophy of this prominent, eccentric mind rest on its own merits, if the neoconservative historians did not feel obliged to play the game of revisionism in precisely this way.

As a contribution to this year's Römerberg Talks, a conference that also treated the topic of the "past that will not pass" in presentations by Hans and Wolfgang Mommsen, the culture section of *Frankfurter Allgemeine Zeitung*, June 6, 1986, included a militant article by Ernst Nolte. It was published, by the way, under a hypocritical pretext with the heading "the talk that could not be delivered." (I say this with knowledge of the exchange of letters between the presumably disinvited Nolte and the organizers of the conference.) When the Nolte article was published Stürmer also expressed solidarity. In it Nolte reduces the singularity of the annihilation of the Jews to "the technical process of gassing." He supports his thesis that the Gulag Archipelago is "primary" to Auschwitz with the rather abstruse example of the Russian civil war. The author gets little more from the film *Shoah* by Lanzmann than the idea that "the SS troops in the concentration camps might themselves have been victims of a sort and that among the Polish victims of National Socialism there was virulent anti-

Semitism." These unsavory samples show that Nolte puts someone like Fassbinder in the shade by a wide margin. If the *Frankfurter Allgemeine Zeitung* was justifiably drawn to oppose the planned performance of Fassbinder's play, then why did it choose to publish Nolte's letter?

I can only explain it to myself by thinking that Nolte not only navigates around the conflict between the endowing of higher meaning and scholarship in a more elegant way than others but also has a solution ready for another dilemma. This other dilemma is described by Stürmer with the sentence: "In the reality of a divided Germany, the Germans must find their identity, which is no longer to be grounded in the nation state, but which is also not without nation." The planners of ideology want to create a consensus about the revivification of a national consciousness, and at the same time, they must banish the negative images of the German nation-state from the domain of NATO. Nolte's theory offers a great advantage for this manipulation. He hits two flies with one swat: The Nazi crimes lose their singularity in that they are at least made comprehensible as an answer to the (still extant) Bolshevist threats of annihilation. The magnitude of Auschwitz shrinks to the format of technical innovation and is explained on the basis of the "Asiatic" threat from an enemy that still stands at our door.

IV

If one has a look at the composition of the commissions that have designed the plan for the German Historical Museum in Berlin and the House of the History of the Federal Republic in Bonn, one cannot help but get the impression that the new revisionism is to be realized in these museums in the form of displays and pedagogically effective exhibits. It is true that the expert reports submitted so far have a pluralistic face. But things will be no different with the new museums than they were with the Max Plank Institutes: The programs and memos that regularly precede the founding of a new institution have little to do with what the newly appointed directors actually make of it. That has also dawned on Jürgen Kocka, the token liberal on the Berlin expert commission: "In the end the decisive matter is what person takes charge. . . . Here, too, the devil resides in the details."

No one desires to oppose seriously meant attempts to strengthen the historical consciousness of the population of the Federal Republic. There are also good reasons for a historicizing portrayal that seeks to gain distance from a past that will not pass. Martin Broszat has written convincingly on this. Those complex connections between the criminality and the dubious normality of everyday life under Nazism, between destruction and vital productivity, between a devastating systematic perspective and an intimate, local perspective, could certainly stand being objectified and brought up to date. Then this pedantic co-optation of a short-circuited, moralized past might give way to a more objectified understanding. The careful differentiation between understanding and condemning a shocking past could also help put an end to our hypnotic paralysis. But this kind of historicization would not be guided by impulses such as the ones that provided impulses to the revision recommended by Hildebrand and Stürmer and conducted by Hillgruber or Nolte, who set out to shake off the mortgages of a past now happily made morally neutral. I do not want to impute negative intentions to anyone. There is a simple criterion that distinguishes the people involved in this dispute. The one side assumes that working on a more objectified understanding releases energy for self-reflective remembering and thus expands the space available for autonomously dealing with ambivalent traditions. The other side would like to place revisionist history in the service of a nationalist renovation of conventional identity.

Perhaps this formulation is not unequivocal enough. Those who seek to do more than revivify a sense of identity naively rooted in national consciousness, those who allow themselves to be guided by functional imperatives of predictability, consensus-formation, social integration via endowing meaning, are bound to avoid the enlightening effect of history writing and reject a broad pluralism of historical interpretations. One will hardly misrepresent Michael Stürmer if one is to understand his editorializing in the following way: "When looking at the Germans and their relationship to their history, our neighbors are bound to pose the question: Where is this all leading? . . . The Federal Republic is the centerpiece of European defense within the Atlantic system. But it is becoming evident that each generation living in Germany today has differing, even opposing, views of the past and the future. . . . The search for a lost past is not an abstract striving for culture and education. It is [an undertaking that is] morally legitimate and politically necessary. We are dealing with the inner continuity of the German republic and its predictability in foreign policy terms." In reality, Stürmer is making a plea for a *unified* understanding of history that might replace the increasing privatization of religious values with identity and social integration.

Historical consciousness as vicarious religion—isn't this overtaxing the old dream of historicism? To be sure, German historians can look back on a truly national tradition in their discipline. Hans-Ulrich Wehler recently reminded us of its ideological contribution toward stabilizing the *kleindeutsches Reich* and excluding "enemies of the Reich." Until the late 1950s the discipline had been dominated by an attitude that had been in the process of being shaped ever since the failure of the revolutions of 1848–1849 and the defeat of liberal history writing such as that of Gervinus: "For almost 100 years, liberal, enlightened historians could only be found either isolated or in small fringe groups. The majority in the discipline thought and argued in a way that was conscious and affirmative of nationalism and influenced by the state and the power of the state."

The fact that since 1945, at least among younger historians educated after 1945, not only a new spirit but also a pluralism of modes of understanding [*Lesarten*] and of methodologies has made itself felt is not a mishap that can simply be undone. The old attitude was really just an expression of mandarin consciousness, rampant in the discipline. And this attitude has fortunately not survived the Nazi period. By its impotence against or even complicity with the Nazi regime, the discipline showed itself to be without real substance. The resultant self-reflection by the discipline influenced more than just the ideological premises of German historiography; it also intensified the methodological consciousness of the contextual dependence of *all* history writing.

However, it would be a misunderstanding of this hermeneutic insight if the revisionists of today assume that they can illuminate the present with the spotlights of arbitrarily constructed prehistories and choose from these options a particularly suitable notion of history. The intensified methodological consciousness also means the end of a closed understanding of history and precludes any conception of history that might be prescribed by government historians. The unavoidable pluralism of modes of understanding [*Lesarten*] is a reflection of the structure of open societies. This pluralism provides us with the opportunity to more clearly understand our own identity-forming traditions and their ambivalences. Precisely this is necessary for a critical appropriation of ambivalent traditions and to shape a historical consciousness that is as incompatible with closed and organic images of history as it is with all forms of conventional identity.

What is today being lamented as a "loss of history" is not just an aspect of deliberately repressing and ignoring; it is not only an aspect of being overly focused on an encumbered history that seems to have come to a standstill. If the traditional national symbols have lost their power for younger people, if a naive sense of identification with one's own history has given way to a more tentative way of dealing with history, if the discontinuities are felt more strongly and continuities are not celebrated at every turn, if national pride and a collective sense of self-worth are forced through the filter of a universalist orientation of values—to the degree that these things are true we can speak of evidence for the formation of a postconventional identity. In Allensbach this evidence is described with forecasts of doom. But this evidence seems to reveal one thing: that we have not gambled away the opportunity that the moral catastrophe could also mean for us.

The unconditional opening of the Federal Republic to the political culture of the West is the greatest intellectual achievement of our postwar period; my generation should be especially proud of this. This event cannot and should not be stabilized by a kind of NATO philosophy colored with German nationalism. The opening of the Federal Republic has been achieved precisely by overcoming the ideology of Central Europe that our revisionists are trying to warm up for us with their geopolitical drumbeat about "the old geographically central position of the Germans in Europe" (Stürmer) and "the reconstruction of the destroyed European Center" (Hillgruber). The only patriotism that will not estrange us from the West is a constitutional patriotism. Unfortunately, it took Auschwitz to make possible to the old culture nation of the Germans binding universalist constitutional principles anchored in conviction. Those who want to drive the shame about this fact out of us with phrases such as "obsession with guilt" (Stürmer and Oppenheimer), those who desire to call the Germans back to conventional forms of their national identity, are destroying the only reliable foundation for our ties to the West.

CONSTELLATION C
THE JEWISH QUESTION: POLITICS OF SUBJECTIVITY

This arrangement interrogates the significance of the "other" for a German cinema studies theory of the subject, by asking what it means to reinvoke the centuries-old "Jewish question" (posed in Constellation B ["The Heimat *Debate"] as a "German question") in connection to post-al questions of language, gender, class, and the public sphere. Staging a constellation-wide divergence between Eric Rentschler's articulation of the "Jewish" onto controversial scenes of public ceremony and display, and Ingeborg Majer O'Sickey and Annette Van's later critique of patriarchal discourse in* Europa Europa, *it asks the reader to consider why German cinema studies texts continue to deploy the christological notion of the "Wandering Jew," in its secularized, humanist form, as a site of social disruption signalling national emergency, even and especially when there are so few "real" Jews remaining in post-Nazi Central and Eastern Europe. How does O'Sickey and Van's materialist analysis of* Vergangenheitsbewältigung *either intersect or resist idealist understandings of "mastering the past" or "coming to terms with the past" sustained through Rentschler's more pluralist call for "dialogical exchange" and explicit valorization of the cinematic* auteur *as a means of such historical critique? How does Linda Schulte-Sasse's analysis of* Jud Süss, *as it unpacks the Romanticist elements of Nazi-era anti-Semitism, nonetheless ultimately reaffirm its formal prescription of the "Jewish" as an epistemological necessity in the critical German imaginary? Does her focus on an overtly anti-Semitic film (rather than a more subtly anti-Semitic film, as in Antonia Lant's reading of* Rosa Luxemburg *in Constellation E ["Feminism, Motherhood, Terrorism"]) qualify this critical construction in a way that preserves a christological problematic and consequently formulates an idealizing component continuous with Rentschler's reunderstanding of U.S.–German relations in the wake of Bitburg? How does the problematic invocation of "memory," "wandering," and "economy" already raised by these in relation to the "Wandering Jew" texts segue into Timothy Corrigan's reading of* Kings of the Road *in Constellation D ("The Euroamerican Question") and point ahead to Kent Casper's reading of* La Soufrière *in Constellation G ("Myth and Allegory")? How does Gertrud Koch's experientialist critique of the problematics of anti-Semitism in the public controversy surrounding Fassbinder's theatrical work nonetheless reinscribe a certain philo-Semitic tendency analogous to the christological tendencies evidenced above? Finally, how is O'Sickey and Van's crucial feminist analysis of the structuring of a protean masculinity in* Europa Europa *intrinsicslly dependent upon the discourse of the "Wandering Jew," and how might this potentially jeopardize the radical possibilities of their argument?*

The Use and Abuse of Memory: New German Film and the Discourse of Bitburg

ERIC RENTSCHLER

"From which authority does the president get briefed on World War II history? a) *The Young Lions*; b) *Das Boot*; c) *Hogan's Heroes*. Correct answer: b) *Das Boot*.

Das Boot, featuring a World War II U-boat commander nicknamed Der Alte who refuses to give the Heil Hitler salute, coats a Konrad Adenauer veneer of humanism on fascist soldiers and sailors. This film presents a reassuring image of wartime Germans that our administration believes to be accurate: most were conscripts drafted to carry out the hateful wishes of the Nazis."

Carrie Rickey[1]

"What happened in the past is too monstrous for us to be able to forget it or to domesticate it ridiculously with our Sunday speeches. If wounds would not always open up and bleed anew, as long as we live, how should we live with them? All honour to politicians who help in this direction with an honest heart."

Hans-Jürgen Syberberg[2]

From an AT&T advertisement: "On taking leave of Germany . . . and his teammates. His tour of duty was over. This was his final good-bye. He remembered all the good times, the joking and that special closeness that comes from sharing not only victory, but defeat.

As he shook hands with Willi, Rolf, Dieter and the others, he realized they had become brothers. And that was something he'd never forget."

Time Magazine, 27 May 1985

"'Reagan is emotional,' an anonymous adviser said in recalling why the President did not want to visit a concentration camp. He said, 'Oh God, I know about (the Holocaust), but do I have to see it?'"

quoted in *Los Angeles Times*, 6 May 1985[3]

Reprinted from *New German Critique* 36 (Fall 1985): 67–90.

I

I WANT TO undertake a journey in time, to track a text in a number of contexts, to trace German film history through various epochs, to traverse the
larger field of German history as imaged in a series of different spaces and
settings. What I have in mind is an exercise in intertextuality. This does not
mean, though, a simple play with texts and their recycling, an attempt to
pinpoint certain borrowings and influences, a study of creative and
promiscuous recourse to tradition. This essay has a curious trajectory, one
that will take us from the Nazi Party Congress of 1934 to postwar
Adenauer Germany, from there to a look at returned soldiers from the
World War I trenches on the streets of Berlin, and, stepping back in time a
step further, to a small town's tribute to those who died during the Great
War, before, in conclusion, moving to the present, reliving a celebration
devoted to forty years of peace since 1945. The five examples I will be
using include a documentary by Leni Riefenstahl, a short film by
Straub/Huillet, epic features by Fassbinder and Reitz, and the ABC News
coverage of President Reagan's visit to Bitburg. In each case we will come
upon similar elements: a song, a performance, a spectacle. The song to
which I am referring is "I Once Had a Comrade," a tune from the 19th century commonly used throughout German history during military ceremonies. In essence, then, we will consider five adaptations of the same
song and seek to comprehend how each performance imparts to it different meanings, providing five distinct adaptations of history. These five
examples, so I hope, likewise suggest in miniature something like an
overview of New German Film, starting with the fatal past that spawned it,
the initial critical resolve, subsequent subjective approaches to reclaiming
history, more current lapses into a less acute sensibility, and, finally, the
imposing and continuing challenges to those seeking to capture memory
and preserve a regard for the special terms of German experience today.
The article could well bear the title "From *Triumph of the Will* to Bitburg:
New German Film and the Specter of the Past." But I do not need to be so
shameless; the history I will be recounting is shameless enough.

Any attempt to generalize about national cinema presupposes, as Philip
Rosen suggests, a certain intertextuality to which one attributes a particular "historical weight," a shared nexus of patterned meanings, generic formulas, socio-political impulses and influences, as well as a common
cultural existence.[4] I have previously argued that the most crucial project
of New German Film over the last two plus decades has been a forwarding
of discourse in the face of ready-made history, a battle that has involved a
struggle against the dominant cinema in Germany and its investment in a
bankrupt legacy, a conscious resolve to challenge the establishment media
and their hold over the circulation of fantasy wares and information, and,
finally, a continuing awareness of how American occupation has colonized
and shaped German public images and private dreams.[5] The strength of

New German Film comes from its variety and heterogeneity, the many different ways in which it seeks to engage the past and address the present. In this endeavor these filmmakers have stimulated a regard for the powers of imagination, memory, and subjectivity, all of which function as potential sources of resistance against the mechanisms that stifle human response, vitiate public and private experience, and hinder the open flow of information and ideas.

Eccentric agents of historical memory, New German directors represent a wide spectrum of formal possibilities, ranging from Brechtian concepts of distanciation and epic realism to self-indulgent narratives that frame private obsessions against wider backdrops. One finds markedly documentary attempts at collecting forsaken bits and pieces lest they be consigned to the dustbin of history. Likewise, there remain filmmakers who couch their reclamations of history, however critically minded, in the trappings of straightforward narratives, hoping thereby to engage larger audiences. From Straub/Huillet's minimalism to Kluge's discursive willfulness; from Fassbinder's reconstructions of the past which display a profound awareness of their present significance to Syberberg's desire to exorcize traumas and evoke phantasms in acts of cinematic mourning; or, Sanders-Brahms' very personal account of a shared moment in time with her mother during World War II. One could go on at length: Achternbusch's attempt to atone for the death of six million Jews, Fechner's images of middle-class family life over many decades, Brückner's poignant revisitations of the 1950s and 1960s—among many others. And, to be sure, we might recount some less convincing examples of the same endeavor. And we dare not forget a growing number of commercial filmmakers in West Germany today eager to forego such critical and topical impulses for more accessible and popular generic models, people like Wolfgang Petersen, Hans W. Geissendörfer, as well as the large majority of the younger generation at work today in the Federal Republic.

Before I proceed to my first example, we need to take a look at the Uhland text that will be recycled in five different contexts. Originally bearing the title "Der gute Kamerad" ("The Good Comrade"), the poem was written between the 5th and 14th of September, 1809. Its three verses run as follows:

Ich hatt' einen Kameraden,
Einen besseren findst du nit.
Die Trommel schlug zum Streite,
Er gieng an meiner Seite
In gleichem Schritt und Tritt.

Eine Kugel kam geflogen,
Gilt's mir oder gilt es dir?
Ihn hat es weggerissen,
Er liegt mir vor den Füssen,
Als wär's ein Stück von mir.

> Will mir die Hand noch reichen,
> Derweil ich eben lad'.
> Kann dir die Hand nicht geben,
> Bleib du im ew'gen Leben,
> Mein guter Kamerad!

A literal English translation:

> I had a comrade, you won't find a better one. The drum called us to battle, he walked at my side, in the same step and pace.

> A bullet flew through the air, was it for you or was it for me? It tore him away, he lies at my feet, as if he were a part of me.

> He tries to reach out for my hand just as I am reloading. I can't give you my hand, rest in all eternity, my good comrade!

Only two of the examples I will be working with use the actual lyrics of this text. Nonetheless, each instance retains a sensitivity for the song's emotional connotations and the male bond dramatized in these verses, ones deeply engrained in the collective mind of Germany, lines that have taken on considerable resonance in the course of the song's endless performances at public ceremonies and military demonstrations.

II

This first clip, from Riefenstahl's record of the Nazi Party Congress in Nuremberg of 1934, *Triumph of the Will* (1935), comes from the tenth sequence of twelve. Staged in the Luitpold Arena, it provides a tribute to the war dead, an event whose main participants are Hitler, Himmler of the SS, and Lutze of the SA, plus an all but faceless cast of thousands of soldiers from both organizations. Although homage is paid to those who fell on the fronts of World War I, solemnly and dramatically, the sequence above all circles around other, more recent, casualties, namely the errant SA-members Hitler purged on June 30 shortly before the Congress. Three figures marching down a cleared lane, flanked by the faithful, laying wreaths at a monument for the war dead: an act of mourning, ceremonial in tone, subdued in its choreography, impressive in its grandiosity, straightforward in its presentation. The invocation of the song, "Ich hatt' einen Kameraden," which we hear unclear as to whether it comes from an on- or offscreen source, is not only appropriate, but likewise telling in its suggestiveness. The memory of dead comrades provides a pretext for a double revision of history, an act of rewriting inherent in this seemingly direct performance.

The terms of this directness deserve closer scrutiny. Looking at this spectacle, the viewer gains the impression of witnessing finished events, fixed for all time, complete as they stand, self-enclosed and beyond question. The scene apparently leaves nothing out and demands no search for anything beyond what one sees.[6] *Triumph of the Will* in general and this sequence in particular amount to ready-made reality, a vision arranged in such a way as to deny all challenges and to answer any questions, an approach that disguises a construction as the natural state of affairs. Individual shots provide images of plenitude, yet remain exceedingly uncluttered: the compositional rhythms are marked by geometrical precision and an all-consuming architectonics. Every movement within these frames is controlled, be it the progress of the leaders down the wide lane, be it the deferent attention of the massed soldiers, be it the careful tracking camera seeking to encompass the procession from right to left. The shots, without exception, totalize, alternating between long-shot glimpses of the entire spectacle and closer, more emblematic shots of the *Reichsadler* and the swastika. Not for a second does anything appear uncertain or unexpected. This amounts to a triumph of a *mise-en-scène* both highly stylized and seemingly devoid of frills.

For all of this self-containment and imaginary persuasiveness, the film does not completely succeed in erasing its rhetorical bias, at least for viewers resistant to its intended subject effect, people who refuse to become overwhelmed by these sequenced events. I might add that not only National Socialists have succumbed to this film's allure; over the years, Riefenstahl's epic chronicle has engaged a vast community of cinéastes eager to praise its artistic accomplishment.[7] The *mise-en-scène* of the film in fact represents an attempt to overcome a possible source of discord, to heal some glaring wounds within the New Order. The emotional tenor of the evocation, the tribute to the war dead, by extension places Hitler and his minions alongside these comrades as their legitimate protectors now, ones who have intervened and replaced a moribund leadership who betrayed the front generation's interests at Versailles. Hitler marches as well among the ranks of the living, members of a nation reformed and reshaped by National Socialism, a compact and "united movement." Likewise, though, the scene painstakingly works at demonstrating how Hitler continues to enjoy the trust and fealty of the SA, despite the recent executions of Röhm and his followers. This is the subject of a speech later in the sequence, where Hitler talks of the matter in a roundabout way, as "a black shadow" that has spread over the movement. Interestingly, the sequence images Hitler and Lutze at the memorial in a way causing the former's shadow to envelop the latter's, the two bodies merging, suggesting in two different shots that Hitler and the SA are one, comrades who march in unison amidst a united nation.

Another matter deserves attention and bears consideration in light of the Bitburg ceremony. For all the ostensible control marshalled by the film's director, an artist who had a vast number of cameramen and technicians at her disposal, not to mention nearly unlimited means and access, Riefenstahl complained bitterly about this particular sequence. She had wanted to track Hitler, Himmler, and Lutze from a small vehicle. However, she, as the director put it, "lost one of the most beautiful shots" because the SA would not allow her to enter the lane with her car.[8] She had to move her camera elsewhere; the event admitted only certain perspectives and what she considered a more limited vantage point.

Images of plenitude which in fact reflect a circumscribed perspective, a revision of the past meant to legitimate a present order, a mode of representation aiming to eradicate all discursive traces for the sake of a fixed image of history, a choreographed procession meant to honor the war dead, but more than anything to address the needs of the moment: we have here *in nuce* the basics of Bitburg. This denigration of memory for the sake of contrived history, the white-washing of the past to dress up the present, likewise represents an abuse of the film medium painfully recollected and ardently eschewed by Young German filmmakers of a later generation. The systematic control of images and imagination in Nazi Germany remained an experience of seminal importance to the post-Oberhausen directors. In confronting a burdensome legacy, they needed not only to address German history, but also German film history, in a way that recoded the past in appropriate alternative images.

III

The use of the song "Ich hatt' einen Kameraden" in *Triumph of the Will*, far from merely illustrative, indeed contains interpretive connotations, even if they remain implied, not underlined, an emotional effect of an imposing event. Riefenstahl seeks above all a unification of the various elements at her disposal: composition, editing, sound, and movement. The implied response is determinate, the result of careful orchestration and planning, not intellectual or analytical, but rather affective and tangible, a response that implicates viewers in the diegesis, sweeping them up into the onscreen movement, erasing the distance between spectator and spectacle. Clearly, the strategy employed in Straub/Huillet's *Machorka-Muff* (1963) could not be more different.

The eighteen-minute short film first caused much controversy when it circulated in private screenings at Oberhausen in 1963, having been rejected by the festival selection committee. Based on Heinrich Böll's biting satire, "Hauptstädtisches Journal" ("Bonn Diary"), the oblique and elliptical narrative contains the reflections of a reactivated officer called to the West German capital by the Ministry of Defense. Machorka-Muff receives a warm welcome, word that he has been promoted to a general, and the go-ahead for his plans to establish an Academy for Military Memories, plans that have found official favor in the German parliament. Böll's story appeared originally shortly before the elections of 1956, in which the populace voted on the rearmament of the Federal Republic. Straub, in keeping with the radical and critical resolve of Young German filmmakers who had gathered in Oberhausen to issue a manifesto in 1962,[9] was motivated by the memory of this event as well as its place in a larger history of militarism: "*Machorka-Muff* is the story of a rape, the rape of a country on which an army has been imposed, a country which would have been happier without one. What does it mean to make films in Germany, or rather, to make films against that stupidity, depravity, and that mental laziness which, as Brecht remarked, are so characteristic of that country?"[10] *Machorka-Muff*, in essence, is a film depicting the abuse of memory, at the same time attempting to activate memories in a way engaging them in a historical dialogue.

Making a film in Germany, for Straub/Huillet at least, means confronting the past abuses of image-makers in that country.[11] It means a systematic negation of what movies have done in the past, a thorough-going challenge to the way films tell stories, to how they present history. As Straub is fond of saying: "Ninety percent of the films made are based on contempt for the people who go to see them." Above all, this discursive alternative implicates the spectator in the narrative process, not as a mindless consumer, part of a captive audience, but rather as someone who has room to breathe and a chance to progress with the story, a story presented austerely, minimally, devoid of titillating appeal and cathartic pay-offs. *Machorka-Muff* barely manages to uphold the pretense of a fiction film: its amateur actors are stiff, the dialogue (in a Brechtian fashion) is spoken in monotone, the characters allow for no identification, the camera cuts suddenly and arbitrarily between spaces (e.g., Machorka-Muff leaves the hotel room, he enters Inn's car, and we see him back in bed at the hotel), thus undermining the viewer's sense of participating in an homogeneous and coherent diegetic field. Instead, the film displays a marked aperture, a constant opening up to the world as a polyphony of voices, a multiplicity of texts mirroring a distinct historical context.

Quite literally the film explodes as Machorka-Muff muses at the café overlooking the Rhine. Earlier, in the film's second shot, he gazed at the capital by night and concluded: "There are vital forces waiting to be released." As he celebrates his triumph and peruses the day's papers, the film erupts into a series of articles and headlines from the conservative press, editorials in the *Deutsche Tagespost*, *Frankfurter Allgemeine Zeitung* and *Die Welt*. The camera places the viewer in position of a critical reader, focusing with emphasis on certain key passages, channelling attention through a series of texts which evoke the rearmament of West Germany, official and church apologias for the measure, and in general reflect a public sphere readily beholden to shadowy figures like Machorka-Muff and all he represents. This sequence interrupts the film's already marginal narrative, providing a break in the story's progression, time to pause and reflect about what Straub termed "the rape of a nation" and its legitimators, factors still operative when he and his wife made the film during the final phases of the Adenauer era.

As the General, garbed in his new uniform, dedicates the Academy for Military Memories, a place where historical revisionists find official sponsorship for their activity, the camera stresses Machorka-Muff's act of reading as a process, a labor. The entire ceremony takes on the appearance of a site of meaning construction: we see the band at work playing the obligatory song; we watch the mason carefully lay the cornerstone; we glimpse Machorka-Muff's solemn tap on the structure. The shots here circumscribe the event insofar as they present a close view of single activities orchestrated for a certain purpose. Put in another way: the sequence draws our attention to the fabricated character of this occasion, laying bare its structure in a double sense, both as a contrivance and a travesty.

One crucial image, a shot held for many seconds, essentializes the reflective and reflexive impetus of Straub/Huillet's counter-cinema. As the tune "Ich hatt' einen Kameraden" begins, the onscreen space remains empty, quite literally a *tabula rasa*, the "*Leerstelle*" spoken of by reader-reception theory, a blank space. This gap serves a number of functions. Just as the camera lingered over the General's uniform, studying its buttons and fabric in relation to the speech text in the officer's hand, thereby establishing a connection between a certain role and a certain way of speaking, the empty shot also imparts a dramatic sense for the grain of a text. We become able to see the music,[12] to read its importance in this setting, to reflect on the meaning of this song and the tradition it implies, a tradition the Academy for Military Memories means to restore, a legacy that Straub/Huillet every bit as forcefully want to undermine. If the groundlaying sequence as a whole makes us privy to the enshrinement of those forces seeking to sand off the rough edges of the past, at the same time painstakingly showing this event as a human labor, it in every way crucially involves the spectator in the construction, providing space to see through the historical fiction presented here.

The tribute to the war dead in *Triumph of the Will* amounted to something of a white-washing of history, a cleansing of the past, the eradication of "black shadows." *Machorka-Muff* stands as a film seeking to resist these same forces still at work many decades later. Instead of white-washing history, it washes the image white, pausing for a moment to allow the viewer to grasp the larger continuities at work, the insidious "forces waiting to be released," remnants of a past still very much operative in the film's Adenauer era setting as well as Straub/Huillet's filmmaking present of 1962. *Machorka-Muff* was one of Young German Film's earliest signs of life; it remains to this day a critical work marked by history lessons and formal energies which can only evoke a profound regret for how far New German directors have come since then.

IV

Fassbinder's *Berlin Alexanderplatz* (1980), with its amalgam of identification and distance, also engages an active spectator. Along with Max, the barkeeper, one of the director's surrogate onlookers, we witness the clash between opposing discourses, a conflict foregrounded as a battle between texts and their interpretation. Above all, *Berlin Alexanderplatz* stresses the personal resonance of "Ich hatt' einen Kameraden," subjectivizing the song and the memories it evokes for the singer as well as placing this performance in a wider field of meaning, having it presented before a hostile group at a table and a sympathetic friend onscreen, and at the same time making the offscreen spectator privy to dynamics that go far beyond the single occasion. The altercation takes place in the second episode of the fifteen-and-a-third hour film; Franz has just found employment as a hawker of the *Völkischer Beobachter* in a subway passage. Outfitted with a swastika armband, he speaks with a Jewish merchant about the meaning of his new occupation. He then confronts his old buddies, Dreske and two others, communists with whom he used to run before becoming disillusioned. The scene in the bar, Franz's *Stammkneipe*, continues the discussion, bringing the disagreement to a head between individuals convinced of their cause and a certain vision and a single person surrounded by a world of conflicting voices, cast by material necessity into a role which he, as a basically apolitical soul, does not fully comprehend.

In accordance with the heteroglossia of his textual basis, Döblin's epic novel of 1929, Fassbinder orchestrates his narrative in a way meant to underline the place of his hero in a contradictory, confusing, and compelling world, a historical space bounded by different forces and influences, a pre-formed reality constantly being reshaped and continually providing a multitude of diverse possibilities and positions. Clearly a personal adaptation, Fassbinder's rendering involves one man's attempt to find his way through the streets of Berlin during the late 1920s, to mold a personal discourse in the midst of this clamor, to constitute himself as a subject despite the objective historical and social vicissitudes which stand in the way of this wish. Elsewhere I have discussed how the film dramatizes modernity as something of a vast slaughterhouse, in this way making Franz Biberkopf's life story a very violent one, a tale in which he constantly finds himself and his body threatened by outside forces and moved by uncontrollable urges.[13] Reality and the modern world inscribe themselves on his body, leaving distinct traces of their workings on his person. The sequence at issue here involves Franz in a strategic battle, one in which he employs a series of texts in order to defend himself against possible physical violence. We become inscribed in the event as onlookers, at one level sympathetic like Max, hoping Franz will succeed, and yet at the same time, as an audience with a retrospective awareness of German history, able to discern the social importance of the dialectic here.

The sequencing and positioning of texts within the scene deserve close scrutiny. Dreske and his comrades strike up the "International" in an effort to provoke Franz. They then challenge him to sing along. Franz, hoping to defuse the situation, promises a song, in the meanwhile telling a joke. The short tale about a sandwich which does not allow for easy digestion is told while Franz continues to eat. It suggests in the wider terms of this narrative a body of experience not so easily assimilated, much like Franz's confrontation in the scene with his own past as a progressive. He then goes on to recite a poem, one written by a fellow inmate during his four-year sojourn in Tegel, a space to which the camera flashes back during Franz's recounting. This text as well bears notice. It addresses the various troubles a person has becoming a "male subject" in this world, the challenges posed by a state patriarchy, the vulnerable status of one's frail body. Earlier, Franz was asked repeatedly by a Nazi war invalid whether or not he was "a German man." Fassbinder, as is well known, recycled the large novel as above all a love story between two men.[14] More importantly, though, he shaped Döblin's novel in a way that drew attention to its historical dynamics, as an account of soldiers returned from the World War I front, like Franz and Dreske, trying to find their way through the streets of the postwar city, seeking to understand where the front lies in a 1000-voiced reality. On crucial and repeated occasions we will see how these male subjects do violence to each other—and notably, to women. The story's chronology begins with the beating of Ida; the discourse's end comes in the strangling of Mieze. In the present sequence, Franz's poem provokes comment, lending itself to criticism. Fritz tells him he should take note of what the state does to him, memorizing a few lines does not suffice.

Franz then capitulates to the emphatically repeated call for a song, not reflecting long before he begins to sing "Ich hatt' einen Kameraden." In no way, though, does Fassbinder stage the spectacle in a straightforward manner. First of all, he links the present event with a performance earlier in the film, the moment where a confused and recently released Franz stood in a courtyard and sang "Die Wacht am Rhein," thus establishing a connection between two moments of crisis, ones in which the ex-soldier takes recourse to familiar tunes and the body of experience they connote. The period Franz spent in Tegel, four years, parallels the duration of the First World War. The time behind bars and at the front involves affective relationships with other men, male bonds containing a strong emotional, indeed homosexual, dimension. The song reflects on the power of these attachments just as Fassbinder's rendering of it reflects on the undeniable element of unrequited love in Franz's relationship to his former comrades, people whose resentment appears akin to the jealousy of a jilted lover. Second, by his cuts to the group at the other table and its hostile silence, Fassbinder stresses the loaded atmosphere, unmediated, for the moment at least, by Max's kinder gaze. At the same time, though, Franz's recitation takes on the character of a private recollection linked to a war experience as well as a previous moment of trouble. The relatively long takes show Franz singing almost to himself, framed in a way that doubles his image, suggesting a shadow of the past and how it inheres in the present person. Tegel and World War I have left their marks on Franz and likewise relate to the world Dreske and his chums want to change.

As the situation becomes even more volatile, Franz lets out all stops and taunts the group with the openly chauvinistic "Die Wacht am Rhein," almost provoking the fight he has so studiously sought to avoid. As the sequence comes to a conclusion, the music box in the bar (without apparent cause) starts playing the "Deutschlandslied," yet another instance in which a single text reflects on the larger text of an embattled postwar republic and the general context of a filmmaker's desire to comprehend the special terms of German history in this century and to engage the viewer as an active participant in this exploration of the past. Fassbinder does this, on one level, by constantly shifting between the private and the public, moving back and forth between personal histories and a larger framework, always bearing in mind the retrospective advantage of the spectator in the present. On another level, he irritates the spectator by forcing an identification, at least in part, with a politically incorrect position, aligning our sympathies with a purveyor of the Nazi Party organ, creating a tension between our investment in the story and our knowledge of the larger history from which it is derived. This, of course, is hard to swallow. Like the sandwich described by Franz, the scene does not make for easy digestion; in fact, it keeps on coming up.

A central earmark of Fassbinder's discursive strategy remains the manner in which he shows how texts have a crucial shaping force, providing points of identification and sources of conflict. History for Fassbinder appears as a result of semiosis and amounts to a many-voiced phenomenon; his stories invariably contain a multiplicity of embedded narratives, just as his films, repeatedly and insistently, focus on protagonists desperately seeking to etch out their own story against the challenges posed by 20th-century German history. Out of the bloody spectacle of that past, Fassbinder fashioned texts informed by a discourse endeavoring—albeit in a style quite different from Straub/Huillet, one marked by another mode of address altogether—to lay bare the foundations of West German reality, to provide a relationship to the past which presupposes the standpoint of the present and which commingles both in one larger dialogical exchange.

V

Despite their clearly divergent formal strategies and visual styles, Straub/Huillet and Fassbinder both act as facilitators, engaging the viewer in a dialogue about the German past. In each case, the audience takes part in the construction of meaning, an activity fostered by Straub/Huillet's empty spaces for reflection as well as Fassbinder's dynamic notion of spectatorship, his inscription of multiple viewers both on- and offscreen. *Machorka-Muff* and *Berlin Alexanderplatz* suggest points of access outside of their respective diegesis, an inter- and extratextual space transcending the depicted fiction, an independent realm beyond the films' action and setting, in essence, then, meanings that are not fixed and determinate, but rather bound in a discursive relationship to the spectator and an economy with interests other than only providing pleasure and seeming plenitude. Do we find an equally active notion of spectatorship and historical engagement when we turn to Edgar Reitz's *Heimat*, without a doubt the most celebrated epic account of 20th-century Germany to issue from the 1980s?

Our expectations, of course, are considerable. The film found inordinate resonance when it first played on German television during the fall of 1984, a warm reception both by viewing audiences and media critics,[15] almost (and I stress the word) universal praise for its rendering of German history as "a history of small people who live their lives in dignity,"[16] a reflection of a nation's evolution from the end of World War I to the very present from the perspective of a village in the Hunsrück region. The work came as the culmination of Reitz's own career, the consequential product of a director, who, since the early 1960s and the beginnings of Young German Film, has seen himself as an agent of historical memory. I quote from his programmatic essay of 1979, "The Camera Is Not a Clock: Regarding My Experience Telling Stories from History": "Film has much in common with our ability to remember. It provides not only the possibility to preserve images and events from the march of time, but also the possibility to merge the present and the past in a way which infuses the one with the other."[17] A film directed against what Reitz decried as the international terror of American aesthetics, the forces, for instance, which had coopted German history in the TV-series *Holocaust*,[18] *Heimat* was emphatically billed as an attempt to reclaim one's own past, as a film "made in Germany." A mixture of oral history, evocation to the haptic realities of the everyday and their sensual concreteness, of Reitz's and Peter Steinbach's reworking of more than sixty years of German experience couched in images of a changing landscape, *Heimat* also concern itself with the history of certain technologies, especially photography and radio, i.e., sight and sound, the essentials of cinematic medium. The question remains, though, to what degree the film allows for the reflexivity and retrospective powers Reitz promises.

The sequence of the war memorial comes from the first episode of *Heimat*. It is set in 1922, three years now since Paul Simon has returned from the front. In the midst of a ritual ceremony, the obligatory remembrance of those who fell during World War I and the dedication of a monument in the town square, we confront a disturbance. As the village band plays "Ich hatt' einen Kameraden," we see an old man walking down the lane with a small monument of his own in hand, weeping as he supplies an idiosyncratic rendering of the song, replacing "a bullet flew through the air" with "a bird," making the military tune into a folk song. Paul Simon, who escaped the fate of those being remembered, wonders who this figure is; he is told that it is the baker Böhnke who lost three sons in the war.

This personalization of the text contains elements reminiscent of Fassbinder. The song is linked to the body: the past has imprinted itself on the baker, leaving him with a sorrow etched on his face and the symbolic expression of castration clutched in his hands, the miniature monument that stands for the parts of him lost in the war. The subjective response stands at odds with the public demonstration, suggesting a dissonance between the ritual act of remembrance and the actual fact of human suffering, a disparity between the perspective of a mythic community and that of an estranged individual, an antimony between the organizational structures of public life and the lived realities of single persons. This is an outside perspective, one introduced by the gaze of Paul, an individual who throughout the sequence looks at the village with a growing discontent, and will later leave for America. The baker offers a moment of discord, a resistance to the codified containment of emotion; he, like Paul, has to go "outside" Schabbach to satisfy his sense of lack. A private slant on a public event, an audience engaged by an onscreen spectator, a figure who wears the past on his body like a uniform: in a number of ways, the scene is redolent of *Berlin Alexanderplatz*. Both films use the song as an expression of profound loss which has a jarring effect on its audiences.

The earlier portion of the sequence, prior to the baker's outburst, also seems to duplicate elements found in *Machorka-Muff*. We find before us a construction site, a piece of stone in the middle of Schabbach, as the ex-soldiers Paul and Glasisch Karl look on. The scene foregrounds the dedication as a production and a labor, concentrating on Eduard's choreography and the *mise-en-scène* for the occasion as involving an elaborate unveiling mechanism, the coordination of a speaker, a schoolgirl chorus and a local band. In cutting about the ceremony and tracking around the event, the camera allows for a sense of different responses to the spectacle: the affirmative gesture of a priest, the spontaneous cry of Hänschen Betz, the blank stares of some peasants, the ironic comments of others. As in Straub/Huillet, Reitz's direction provides a certain distance from the goings-on, one marked by humor and analysis as well as insight into the fabricated nature of the moment.

We witness the dynamics of the ceremony and the preparations for the event, at once feeling a certain distance and yet, at the same time, an undeniable bit of suspense: will Eduard's contraption work? Reitz scripts the ceremony so that we gain a realization of its wider connotations: we listen to the chauvinistic speech of an imported speaker, who voices larger social forces at work in the postwar landscape and a spirit of revision eager to rewrite the defeat of World War I as a triumph of heroic spirit, a pathos looking forward to a national revival and a new savior. Reference is made to the proliferation of such events and a virtual memorial industry—with the same ceremonies, the same speeches. Reitz, throughout the sequence, though, remains fixed on the village, embodying these tendencies at large in various denizens of Schabbach, finding individual representatives in each case for wider sociopolitical phenomena, echoes as it were. The microcosm of a small community mirrors the macrocosm of a nation. The passage gains its critical power above all from Reitz's privileging of Paul's gaze, a minority view of the community. The initial part of the ceremony will come to a close and at the same moment the downpour of rain will cease, a sort of ritual catharsis. The introduction of baker Böhnke after this indicates that there remain energies and emotions not so easily cleansed and purged. It is important that Paul relays our gaze to the old man, linking the perspectives of outsiders in a village of insiders.

Heimat concerns itself with the technology of seeing and hearing over the past six decades. It has a discursive narrator who provides an ongoing commentary at the start of various episodes.[19] The film arbitrarily leaps from black-and-white to color in an endeavor to add an epic element to its workings. In its initial episode, *Heimat* aligns its narrative point of view with an individual ill at ease in the small village, critical of its narrowness, a character who looks at the community with skepticism and impatience. Unfortunately this marginal perspective, which works so effectively in the first episode, will be lost when Paul sets off for America. Curiously and tellingly, Reitz will forsake the critical gaze for the entire spectrum of German history from 1928 to 1955, not reinstating the outsider's perspective until episode nine, "Hermännchen."

In the first episode, we also learn of the fate of another outsider living in a community of insiders, the difficulty encountered by Apollonia as a foreigner to Schabbach, her marginal existence in the town. She appears in a dialogue with Maria, the two speaking in a cellar, a subterranean space demonstrating the underworld of Schabbach, as the arrangements for the public ceremony are taken care of above by the town's men. Appolonia—like her only defender, Paul—will depart from the narrative. She will never be heard from once she leaves the Hunsrück. Schabbach and the homeland will, after this initial episode, take on the proportions of a closed system, lacking an outside perspective until much later in the film, displaying a markedly exclusionary propensity, a penchant shared by most of *Heimat*. The film, made by a director who once regretted how the German past had been colonized by American entrepreneurs in *Holocaust*, contains many funerals and acts of mourning. Oddly enough, the film all but ignores the major calamity of 20th-century German history, the genocide of the Jews. Even odder yet, though: a film that has started off so assertive in its distanced perspective, so analytical in its portrayal of the homeland, relinquishes that point of view totally when it approaches the Third Reich, exactly that juncture in German history where such a slant might prove most productive—and necessary.

If we mourn in *Heimat*, it is for members of the small community. The sweeping epic, so concerned with capturing a wide spectrum of human experience, allows much space for certain kinds of emotional demonstration and absolutely none for others. What we have here is a troubling mode of historical discourse, an approach bearing out what Saul Friedländer describes as a general tendency of numerous recent attempts to reflect on the trauma of the German past, namely a spirit of exorcism. I quote from his study, *Reflections of Nazism*, where he characterizes this exorcism and its motivations: "To put the past back into bearable dimensions, superimpose it upon the known and respected progress of human behavior, put it in the identifiable course of things, into the unmysterious march of ordinary history, into the reassuring world of the rules that are the basis of our society—in short, into conformism and conformity."[20] *Heimat* proved to be successful in Germany precisely because it recounted the most disturbing portion of German history in a way that disavowed burdensome aspects of that past, abandoning the critical framework of the film's initial episode, confronting the Third Reich and at the same time evading it, neutralizing and concealing the experience of fascism while simultaneously binding the audience to the narrative by an undeniable appeal to their emotional persons and powers of identification—and definitely not their critical faculties.

The film may have served as a comforting domicile for a nation's TV audience, an experience that allowed people once again to feel at home with a notion that, according to Reitz, has in all epochs of modern German history suggested a "painful mixture of happiness and bitterness."[21] No doubt, Reitz has done considerable sugarcoating here. In the words of Gertrud Koch, a critic expressing a decidedly minority view in the Federal Republic: "What is being buried in *Heimat* is not the 'simple truth' of the 'small people' that morality does not thrive on an empty stomach but the precarious consensus that one cannot speak of German history without thinking of Auschwitz."[22] Hardly the inexorable agent of historical memory, *Heimat*, after a very impressive start, lapses. Ultimately, it served to foster a collective amnesia, dramatizing in a stunning way the forgetfulness that can lie in remembering. And here we are only a few steps away from the discourse of Bitburg.

VI

Bitburg, ostensibly a public ceremony commemorating the 40th anniversary of the end of World War II, was less a matter of remembering than a rewriting of history. Framed from its inception as a media event, President

Reagan's visit to the small cemetery stimulated a wide-ranging controversy about the German past and American investment in it, about the kinds of questions New German filmmakers had so often addressed over the last two decades. In the midst of this gallimaufry of impassioned editorials, official equivocation, and pressure from the German government to go through with the planned agenda, one repeatedly focused on the graves of 49 Waffen-SS soldiers situated among the 1,887 German war dead in the Bitburg cemetery. Concerned spokespersons wondered why, in an ostensible act of mourning for the war dead, so many other war dead were going unremembered, an objection that occasioned Reagan's infamous equation of the dead Nazi soldiers with concentration camp victims. It is curious: as media experts carefully and thoroughly analyzed public response to Bitburg and plotted its potential ramifications, they said very little about the event itself, its staging, its *mise-en-scène*, its terms.

It seems appropriate to speak of the seemingly straightforward ceremony as a dominant fiction,[23] the encoding of history in an all but invisible discourse, one presenting spurious harmonies while repressing all sources of potential disturbance and contradiction. Even the liberal press took things at face value, claiming, as John Corry in the *New York Times*, that "the significance was not in what happened, but what it meant."[24] Quoting from his commentary of May 6: "Bitburg came and went on television yesterday after dominating coverage of President Reagan's trip to Europe all week. On television, the visit to the German military cemetery was brief, wordless and, from the White House point of view, all that could be hoped: a solemn President simply placed a wreath against the base of a stone tower. There were few glimpses of demonstrators, and none at all, apparently, of SS graves." This account ignores a host of considerations, naturalizing a demonstration that was choreographed every bit as carefully as *Triumph of the Will*, a public spectacle that unfolded in self-evident terms, which, nonetheless, if we look carefully, contains numerous signs of painstaking construction.

If Straub/Huillet and Reitz imaged commemoratory ceremonies as both human constructions and human labors, matters bound in a larger nexus of events, the ABC News coverage of the Bitburg visit gives the viewer the impression of being present while matters take their course with a self-understood obviousness. We hear nothing about the Reagan aide Michael Deaver and how he looked over the cemetery beforehand, checking the shooting site for the most advantageous camera angles. No mention is made of the change in plans that came after the public outcry: originally, the *mise-en-scène* was to have included numerous close-ups of the President, casting him in a star role, a role Reagan no longer wanted to assume after the imbroglio.[25] If we see next to no onscreen audience but only players, this clearly reflects official choice, an exclusionary act that made Bitburg into a closed set and sought to eradicate all possible sources of spontaneity and opposition. What we have here is something akin to a scene shot on location for a commercial production: the onscreen actors march down the lane pretending that the camera is not present, taking part in an exhibition whose real audience is not there, just like a fiction film being recorded under controlled circumstances for future popular audiences.[26] Peter Jennings expresses his thanks for pictures "provided by the combined resources of German television," neatly glossing over the state of affairs. The images we see are the same ones screened on German television; they are in fact the *only* moving images captured of the event, the sole perspective allowed on the occasion by the institutional forces that staged it.

The visual style here remains deceptively simple and straightforward, in the main an extended long-shot pan to the left capturing Reagan, Kohl and the two generals as they walk along the north side of the cemetery and progress toward the memorial. A bit of zooming, some cuts that regroup the players, a close-up of a bugler: nothing seems obtrusive, everything appears self-evident. Peter Jennings correctly identifies the song we hear, even providing the original title in a heavily accented German. (Throughout his commentary he manages to botch a series of factual details: Stauffenberg becomes "Schlaufenberg," the attempted assassination of Hitler of July 1944 is described as having taken place in Munich, etc.) It seems obvious: this song goes with this kind of ceremony, things could not be more natural. But they are not. In an event so carefully controlled and constructed, one that left nothing to happenstance, a drama meant as a symbolic demonstration of reconciliation, it seems appropriate to insist on deeper significance in this blend of a song and images. Riefenstahl, as we have seen, used "Ich hatt' einen Kameraden" as a simultaneous appeal to the war dead and the living soldiers, likewise concealing the recent deaths of other comrades and the reasons for the SA-purge. The Bitburg ceremony similarly rewrites the past, making the two heads of state and their generals representatives of forces marching in unison, individuals involved in a common cause. It is as if the spectacle were really celebrating forty years of consequential Cold War, an anti-communism that has united the U.S. and Germany as comrades involved in a struggle against the Soviet Union.[27] Reagan's visit to the grave of the quintessential "*kalter Krieger*," Konrad Adenauer, earlier on the same day seems in this regard only a fitting portion of a larger agenda.

It is crucial that no words are spoken during the Bitburg ceremony, that images are allowed a primacy of solemn persuasiveness. Reagan would go on to talk at the Bitburg Airbase, supplying an interpretation of the demonstration: "Our duty today is to mourn the human wreckage of totalitarianism, and today, in Bitburg cemetery, we commemorated the potential good and humanity that was consumed back then, 40 years ago." Reagan's reading of the Third Reich has much in common with the mystifying popular historiography of the 1950s, attempts to absolve the Germans of war guilt by placing the blame on Hitler and his demonic leadership. I quote Reagan: "The war against one man's totalitarian dictatorship was not like other wars. The evil world of Nazism turned all values upside down. Nevertheless, we can mourn the German war dead as human beings, crushed by a vicious ideology." Reagan is quite conversant with the language of exorcism, forwarding a discourse about evil and suffering which speaks stridently where restraint would be more appropriate, which casts its portrayal of the past in the form of anecdotes and stories lifted from *Reader's Digest*, which only broaches the question of the Holocaust as an afterthought, a response to public outrage.

The Bitburg ceremony signifies strongly in its absences: its exclusion of reference to the Jewish dead, its lack of protesters, its disavowal of those who died in the war against fascism elsewhere, its denial of the SS-graves—the latter being particularly conspicuous in that the TV news camera does not for an instance let us know where these lie in relation to the public figures, in effect literally disclaiming their actual existence by this act of non-representation. Otherwise so image-hungry cameramen did not record the unsettling events that transpired soon after Reagan and Kohl drove off. Two wreaths for the fallen comrades of the SS, hidden during the official ceremony, were placed next to the ones left at the memorial by the President and the Chancellor. Some days later, on May 15, Marvin Kalb published a story in the *International Herald Tribune* containing interviews with bystanders, claims from a young man that Germans and Americans were working well together until the Jews started making trouble, or the comment of an old woman that Reagan only stayed at the cemetery for eight minutes "because of the Jews." The Bitburg cemetery visit was a newsworthy event. It is only in hindsight, though, that we can begin to reconstruct the larger picture.

Some concluding thoughts are in order. The Bitburg ceremony replicated a fatal past, both in terms of its presentation and its abuse of historical memory. It comes as the function of a dominant discourse seeking to eradicate all other possible interpretations, allowing only one set perspective, suggesting that this vantage point contains the definitive version—even to the point of absurdity. (The whole time the viewer has one overriding question: *where* are the SS graves and *why* do we not see them?) At previous junctures in recent West German history, the country's filmmakers have gathered together to reflect on important moments in a way forefronting the continuities between past and present, in a manner allowing alternative points of view. I am thinking here of collective productions like *Germany in Autumn, The Candidate, War and Peace.* Peter Jennings makes a poignant reference to the constant clicking of cameras as the four figures walk through the cemetery. Amidst these photographers were no German filmmakers. They would not have gained access if they had sought it. Beyond that, though, no one seems to have considered making a film about this event. (How easily can one imagine a Kluge-esque exercise about the difficulty of celebration in Germany, replete with documentary footage and expressive historical material.) Even if someone had, they would not have found increasingly conservative film subsidy committees and anxious TV-editors ready to support their undertakings, much less commercial producers.[28]

It is indicative of the devolution of New German Film that its most heralded reconstruction of the past since the death of Fassbinder bears more than passing resemblance to the construction of Bitburg: a similar sort of exclusionary practice, a lack of outside points of view when they are most needed, a predilection for anecdotes and pathos in place of analysis and retrospection, and, above all, a normalization of the past that has a soothing effect on the present. "Some old wounds have been reopened," Reagan said in his speech at Bergen-Belsen, "and this I regret very much because this should be a time of healing." Bitburg, like most of *Heimat*, illustrates a forgetfulness in remembering. The dominant and influential history lesson has not come from reflexive and irreconcilable souls like Straub/Huillet and Fassbinder; instead, as Carrie Rickey points out, one reproduces the popular mythology of *Das Boot*.

One German director, an individual who has gained notoriety for his passionate concern with Hitler and the forces projected into the figure, championed Reagan's performance in rhetoric frighteningly reminiscent of the Third Reich. I quote from Hans-Jürgen Syberberg's article on Bitburg: "The picture of the lonely politician who believes himself to be in the right: how encouraging that would be for democracy, which so often degenerates into the exercise of majority opinions, its politicians to the mere executors of majority transactions."[29] We end then with official history firmly and unshakingly enshrined as the dominant discourse, with few willing or able to continue the critical endeavor that was once the hallmark of New German Film.[30] The present moment is not an encouraging one. With the atrophy of New German Film comes the decline of alternative images about West Germany, different modes of representing an experience marked by fatal contours and a continuing state of emergency. The present situation is one of no experiments, a state of affairs summed up quite well in a phrase uttered by General Machorka-Muff towards the end of Straub/Huillet's film: "Opposition—what's that?"

Notes

*This paper was delivered as a special presentation at MIT on November 12, 1985. I would like to express my thanks to Inez Hedges of Northeastern University and Michael Geisler of MIT for organizing the lecture and encouraging me to present it in that forum. Also, I would like to acknowledge the productive impetus offered in conversation by Miriam Hansen and Gertrud Koch. Finally, I want to credit the UCI Committee on Research whose generous

Faculty Research Fellowship provided the material support that enabled me to write this essay during the fall months of 1985.

1. "Bitburg Briefs: A History Quiz," *LA Weekly*, 10 May 1985, p. 16.

2. "Bitburg," *On Film*, 14 (Spring 1985), 37.

3. George Skelton, "Image of Blundering Fought: Can Eloquence Calm the Furor? Aides to Wait, See," *Los Angeles Times*, 6 May 1985, p. 17.

4. Philip Rosen, "History, Textuality, Nation: Kracauer, Burch, and Some Problems in the Study of National Cinemas," *Iris*, 2: 2 (1984), 69.

5. See *West German Film in the Course of Time* (Bedford Hills, NY: Redgrave, 1984).

6. Cf. Christian Metz, "History/Discourse: Note on two Voyeurisms," trans. Susan Bennett, *Edinburgh '76 Magazine*, p. 21.

7. Cf. Jeffrey Richards, "Leni Riefenstahl: Style and Structure," *The Silent Picture*, 8 (Autumn 1970), 19: "Both in style and in structure, the films of Leni Riefenstahl represent the peak of German film-making, a peak which it has never regained since and perhaps never will." For a survey of literature on Riefenstahl, see Sandra Bernstein and Michael MacMillan, "Leni Riefenstahl: A Selected Annotated Bibliography," *Quarterly Review of Film Studies*, 2 (1977), 439–57.

8. As quoted in Richard Meran Barsam, *Filmguide to Triumph of the Will* (Bloomington/London: Indiana Univ. Press, 1975), p. 54.

9. Straub/Huillet did not sign the document. Nonetheless, they were in touch with many of the signatories and clearly acted as an influential example in the Young German Film's early years.

10. Quoted in Richard Roud, *Straub* (New York: Viking, 1972), p. 29.

11. See *The Cinema of Jean-Marie Straub and Daniele Huillet*, ed. Jonathan Rosenbaum (New York: Film at the Public, 1982), pp. 5–6, particularly the filmmakers' comments regarding German directors and Fritz Lang.

12. Cf. Karsten Witte, in *Herzog/Kluge/Straub*, ed. Peter W. Jansen and Wolfram Schütte (Munich: Hanser, 1976), p. 182. Witte describes the scene similarly, claiming the white passage allows "sound to have space to step into the image."

13. See "Terms of Dismemberment: The Body in/and/of Fassbinder's *Berlin Alexanderplatz* (1980)," *New German Critique*, 34 (Winter 1985), 194–208.

14. See his essay, "Die Städte des Menschen und seine Seele. Alfred Döblin's Roman *Berlin Alexanderplatz*." The article appeared first in *Die Zeit* on 14 March 1980. It was reprinted in Rainer Werner Fassbinder and Harry Baer, *Der Film Berlin Alexanderplatz. Ein Arbeitsjournal* (Frankfurt am Main: Zweitausendeins, 1980), pp. 6–9, and Rainer Werner Fassbinder, *Filme befreien den Kopf*, ed. Michael Töteberg (Frankfurt am Main: Fischer, 1984), pp. 81–90.

15. For an exhaustive collection of media response to *Heimat*, see *Presse-Stimmen*, ed. SFB-Pressestelle und der Abteilung Fernsehspiel des SFB (West Berlin: Sender Freies Berlin, 1984), 2 vols.

16. Karsten Witte, "From: Of the Greatness of the Small People: The Rehabilitation of a Genre," see "Dossier on *Heimat*," *New German Critique* 36 (Fall 1985).

17. *Liebe zum Kino* (Cologne: Verlag KöLN 78, 1984), p. 106.

18. See "Unabhängiger Film nach *Holocaust?*" in *Liebe zum Kino*, pp. 98–105. See also Andree Tournes, "Inquiry on *Holocaust*," trans. Charlotte Vokes-Dudgeon, *Framework*, 12 (1980), 10–11. [See also the special *NGC* issue on *Holocaust*, 19 (Winter 1980). The editors.]

19. Gertrud Koch is mistaken when she attributes to Glasisch Karl a sovereignty he surely does not possess. See her comments in this issue, "'That's Why Our Mothers Were Such Nice Chicks,'" especially her claim that Glasisch Karl's introduction "evokes a rather conventional epic mode, the tradition of the omniscient narrator who peers through windows and into the hidden rooms and tells us how it really happened." From the beginning, Reitz marks Glasisch Karl as a limited intelligence, someone obsessed by a woman he cannot have, an individual scarred by his war experience, a person who stands at the

margins of the events, constantly seeking entrance to the mainstream of Schabbach's history. In this sense he is another example of Reitz's eccentric narrative personas, much like the boy Torsten in *Stunde Null/Zero Hour* (1976), someone who registers rather than passes judgment on what he sees.

20. *Reflections of Nazism: An Essay on Kitsch and Death*, trans. Thomas Weyr (New York: Harper & Row, 1984), pp. 106–7.

21. "The Camera Is Not a Clock," p. 109.

22. "How Much Naivete Can We Afford? The New *Heimat* Feeling," reprinted in "Dossier on *Heimat*," *New German Critique* ibid.

23. I take the phrase from "Jacques Rancière: Interview. The Image of Brotherhood," trans. Kari Hanet, reprinted in *Edinburgh '77 Magazine*, pp. 26–31. Rancière uses the phrase to describe "the privileged mode of representation by which the image of the social consensus is offered to the members of a social formation and within which they are asked to identify themselves" (p. 28).

24. "TV: Search for Meaning at Bitburg," *New York Times*, 6 May 1985.

25. See David Ehrenstein, "Bitburg: A Film by Reagan," *On Film*, 14 (Spring 1985), 36.

26. Cf. Metz, "History/Discourse," p. 23. "During a film-show the public is present to the actor, but the actor is absent to the public, and during the shooting, when the actor was present, it was the public which was absent. So the cinema manages to be both exhibitionist and secretive."

27. Jean-Marie Straub put it aptly in his "Text," *On Film*, 14 (Spring 1985), 37: "The truth is that this old crocodile Reagan had wanted to manifest and celebrate there over dead bodies the solidarity and reconciliation of American capitalism with the capitalism of those who under the direction of Adolph Hitler launched a crusade against what they called bolshevism."

28. For one example, among many current indications, of the depleted state of things in West German film during the mid-1980s, see Helmut H. Diederichs, " 'Filmverlag Autoren' seit der übernahme durch Rudolph Augstein," *epd-Film*, September 1985, pp. 22–26.

29. "Bitburg," p. 37.

30. One notable exception to the rule was Eberhard Rechner's three-part television documentary, *Der Prozess/The Trial* (1984).

Courtier, Vampire, or Vermin?

Jew Süß's Contradictory Effort to Render the "Jew" Other

LINDA SCHULTE-SASSE

Hate implies a kind of love, or at least an inability to rid the mind of obsessions with the hated other. . . . There is no fruit like forbidden fruit; there is
nothing more delicious to enjoy and punish freely than the crimes of sex and
aggression which authoritarian repression has forbidden.

Joel Kovel, *White Racism**

Veit Harlan's *Jew Süß* (1940), which is based on the life of the eighteenth-century financier Joseph Süß Oppenheimer, has been branded
one of the "most vicious . . . motion pictures of all times"[1] appealing to
"the lowest instincts of man."[2] *Jew Süß* owes its notoriety to its singular
production history as a film commissioned to help prepare Germany for
the "final solution," the extermination of European Jews. Consequently,
most studies of the film restrict themselves to a discussion of the film's
subtext, of Goebbels's intervention in the production process, and his
coercion of actors.[3] Unlike other major antisemitic films made in the Third
Reich, however, *Jew Süß* was also a box office success featuring a host of
stars.[4] I want to concentrate on the film text itself, exploring both sides of
the equation: how the film constructs the "Jew" as Nazism's constitutive
social fantasy and how it spoke to ordinary moviegoers.

Like many Nazi historical films, *Jew Süß* fictionalizes history not only by
distorting facts, but also by appropriating a literary paradigm deeply rooted in German culture. The eighteenth-century bourgeois tragedy of writers
like G. E. Lessing and Friedrich Schiller serves as a vehicle helping the film
align its viewers with some narrative positions over others. The first section of my reading focuses on the film's narrative paradigms, beginning
with the recycled bourgeois tragedy, on the film's blending of historical
events with fiction that rewrites "German history" as a bourgeois narrative
in which spectators can pleasurably "recognize" themselves.

From here I explore a narrative slippage specific to *Jew Süß* and necessary to its antisemitism: into the structure of horror. *Jew Süß* modifies the

This essay is published here for the first time by permission of the author. It is part of a larger
study, *Illusions of Wholeness and History: The Case of Nazi Cinema* (Durham, NC: Duke
University Press, 1996); in press. A substantially different version was printed in *German
Quarterly* 61 no. 1 (1988): 22–49.

historical-philosophical presuppositions of the bourgeois tragedy by locating the source of social antagonism in the "Jew" rather than in feudal powers. It thus aims its critique at a "racially" rather than a socially defined group—one presumed to be "outside" of German culture, though spatially located within its boundaries. This structure resembles horror, which imagines an assault upon the social body by something alien that must be destroyed for the social equilibrium to be restored. The Jew's supposed vampiric Otherness is articulated with the help of a specular regime in which he is both possessor of a "castrating" gaze and the object of the gaze.

The second section of the essay charts *Jew Süß*'s incorporation of antisemitic mythology. The "Jew" has an essential function for National Socialism as what Slavoj Žižek calls its social fantasy: he embodies all obstacles to Nazism's harmonious corporatist society, yet, paradoxically, empowers the illusion that this harmony is possible. Since the social antagonism generated by modernity is displaced onto the "Jew" and condensed in him, he is necessary for society to believe in itself, to disavow its internal contradictions.[5] While a film like *Jew Süß* depends on preexisting antisemitic ideas, it also provides the type of fantasy space necessary in order for the fantasmatic "Jew" to exist. Régine Mihal Friedman captures this relationship in the title of her book on antisemitic films, *L'Image et son Juif (The Image and Its Jew)*[6]; namely, the fantasy image itself constructs the "Jew," rather than a preexisting truth being ideologically distorted by antisemitism. Like any other ethnic, religious, or national identity, the "Jew" does not exist apart from his hypostatization by someone, although, as Sander Gilman reminds us, the self-construction of any group is affected by the discourses and images by which others define it.[7]

Jew Süß is a complicated case of identity-construction for the following reason: to say that it is the kind of fantasy vehicle antisemitism needs is not to say that the film's construction of "the Jew" is *identical* to antisemitism's fantasy. The reason is that Nazism's fantasized "Jew" is riddled with contradictions (he is both rich *and* dirty, intellectual *and* vermin, impotent *and* licentious, communist *and* capitalist, etc.), and his essential sexual, mental, moral, and ultimately "racial difference" is imagined and not representable in concrete terms. (Unlike other forms of racism, antisemitism cannot even call upon *reliable* bodily markers.) *Jew Süß*, on the other hand, is *nothing but* a form of representation that follows the imperatives of classical cinema. Its exhaustive catalogue of antisemitic stereotypes has to be forced into this formal framework that, despite a formidable repertoire of villains, is hard-put to demonstrate the "essence" of Jewishness. Often when we say the film *shows* that the Jews are vermin, we are reading our historical knowledge of antisemitism and the Holocaust *into* the film. What the film *shows* are certain codified narrative types found in cinema and that, though identified as "Jewish" by the film's dialogue, have a much more universal application.

My aim is to explore from a variety of perspectives how antisemitic ideas, canonized literary paradigms, and classical cinema come together in this one infamous text attempting to represent Nazism's "Jew." Scholars writing on *Jew Süß* usually take for granted that the film is an effective antisemitic document, which is understandable given the real-life terror in which it is implicated. While both the box office and Security Service reports on viewer response[8] suggest that the film "worked" on some level, this chapter assumes neither that its popular success was a *result* of its antisemitism, nor that the construction of the "Jew" as Other is entirely successful. I will argue that whatever power the film wields is to be found in its cinematic address based on narrative paradigms, onto which antisemitic ideas are "grafted." In other words, the film's (from today's perspective) obvious organization of antisemitic ideas, its logic-of-ideas, is only part of the picture. Moreover, because the film is juggling ideology and a codified cinematic mode of organizing desire, it sometimes entangles itself in contradictions that may even jeopardize its anti-semitic "intention."

The historical Joseph Süß Oppenheimer (1692–1738) was a contro-versial figure during his lifetime, and the subject of documentations and literary works throughout the nineteenth and twentieth centuries.[9] He held the position of financial advisor to Duke Karl Alexander of Württemberg (then an independent duchy) from 1733 to 1737. Württemberg had a dualistic constitution, and the powerful Estates felt undermined by Süß Oppenheimer's efficient and sometimes ruthless service to the sovereign.[10] As Protestants, they were also distrustful of Karl Alexander's Catholicism. The Duke planned a *coup d'état*, of which Süß was not informed, that would increase his power and make Württemberg Catholic. When he died suddenly just before the coup, Süß was arrested for treason and hanged on February 2, 1738 after a trial that "mocked all justice."[11] The film's script by Harlan, Wolfgang Eberhard Möller and Ludwig Metzger, allegedly based on "an exact study of the trial protocol in the Württemberg State Archive,"[12] makes Süß solely responsible for the coup attempt and the rift between Duke and people of Württemberg:

> The film begins in 1733 with Karl Alexander's accession to power as Duke of Württemberg. Lacking enough money to buy a celebratory gift for his wife, the Duke sends his envoy von Remchingen to Joseph Süß Oppenheimer in Frankfurt's Jewish ghetto. Süß ingratiates himself with the Duke by extend-ing him credit on a necklace in exchange for permission to enter the capital city of Stuttgart, which heretofore has been prohibited to Jews. Süß becomes the Duke's financial advisor, and continues to finance the latter's representa-tional excesses (an opera, a ballet, and a retinue) denied by the Estates. To compensate Süß, the Duke grants him control of the roads of Württemberg.

Süß enrages the people by taxing every bridge, gate, and street heavily. He persuades the Duke to lift the ban on Jews entering Stuttgart, as well as to seek absolute power by staging a *coup d'état* with the help of foreign soldiers hired with Jewish money. When Estate-Counselor Sturm rejects Süß's offer to marry his daughter Dorothea, Süß has Sturm arrested as a traitor. In order to evade Süß, Dorothea is hastily married to her lover Karl Faber, who is also arrested for planning a revolt. Dorothea visits Süß in his chamber, begging him to free her husband and father. Süß rapes her, after which she drowns herself. The Duke dies suddenly, whereupon the power of Württemberg falls into the hands of the Estates, who arrest Süß and hang him for having carnal relations with a gentile woman.[13]

I: LITERARY PARADIGMS

THE REPOLITICIZATION OF THE BOURGEOIS TRAGEDY

How does a narrative provide a fantasy space in which a figure like the "Jew" is constructed, or in which an existing cultural fantasy can be enjoyed? It generally does so by writing a story its audience already knows; in the case of *Jew Süß*, this story derives from the eighteenth-century bourgeois tragedy, a genre not only entrenched in the German school curriculum since the nineteenth-century, but familiar as part of a literary canon often performed on the stage. Although, as I will elaborate, *Jew Süß* rewrites the bourgeois tragedy in ways inimical to itself, the film's indebtedness to the genre not only has a crucial connotative value, but preconditions the audience to identify with certain characters and narrative events. By using the bourgeois tragedy as a narrative framework, the film aligns itself with a tradition connoting freedom, virtue, "heart," and a flight from an inhumane modernity. Whatever "conclusions" the narrative invites appear to emerge from the same framework. It is, in other words, its allusions to the bourgeois tragedy that allow *Jew Süß* to be a racist film and yet feel—at least to contemporary audiences not disposed to see movies politically—like an antifeudal invective. In discussing this literary anchorage, I will restrict myself largely to narrative analysis, turning later to its filmic realization.

As one expression of an increasingly self-aware bourgeoisie in the mid-eighteenth century, the bourgeois tragedy attempted to dissolve the absolutist separation of politics from morality. Its stated aim was to "moralize" all citizens, especially the aristocracy, by demonstrating via narrative the tragic consequences ensuing from an absolutist power structure.[14] The genre is organized around two competing value systems: one whose central signifier is (bourgeois) virtue and another centered around an aristocratic notion of power.[15] This essential binarism reverberates in the paradigmatic title of Schiller's 1784 drama *Kabale und Liebe* (Cabal and Love) and might be schematized as follows:

Aristocracy/Court	Bourgeoisie
intrigue/*Kabale*	love, fidelity, honesty/*Liebe*
politics	dedication to community
ambition (power, personal glory)	humanity, sympathy, conscience
materialism	"virtue" above the material
sexual pleasure (*amusement*)	tenderness, love
women as sexual objects	women domestic, virtuous
use of French terms	straightforward language
gallantry, *politesse*	kindness
revenge	forgiveness, trust

Although historically a clear expression of growing bourgeois self-consciousness, the bourgeois tragedy disavows references to social class; it casts the virtue represented by the "bourgeois" world as "human," and not class-specific virtue. Just as reference to class remains covert within the bourgeois tragedy, its political implications are couched in family stories. The Sentimental family serves as a metaphor for the potential harmony of society-at-large; social conflict takes the narrative form of disrupted family harmony. Typically, tragedy results from an aristocrat's attempt to seduce a virtuous bourgeois woman.

This family tragedy is exemplified by G. E. Lessing's drama *Emilia Galotti* (1772), which illustrates particularly well the narrative affinities between the bourgeois tragedy and *Jew Süß*. In Lessing's play, a prince has become infatuated with a bourgeois woman, Emilia Galotti, who is about to be married to the virtuous Count Appiani, an aristocrat of lower rank. The courtier Marinelli persuades the Prince to have Emilia kidnapped on her way to her wedding, so that he may indulge his desire before it is too late. During the kidnapping, Marinelli (unbeknownst to the Prince) murders Appiani. When Emilia becomes a prisoner at court and recognizes the machinations behind the episode, she persuades her father to kill her. While Marinelli is the play's real villain, he is merely a tool of absolutist cabal; the play is more interested in the Prince, whose egotism and libido are the precondition for tragedy. Lessing assails the tyranny of a system in which a master's arbitrary whim can lead to multiple deaths, and juxtaposes it with the autonomous, bourgeois (read: "human") will embodied in a father-daughter alliance.

The characterizations of *Jew Süß*'s males are clearly drawn from the repertoire of dramas like *Emilia*. Germans who did not literally see in the volatile Estate Counselor Sturm bourgeois patriarchs like Emilia's father Odoardo Galotti will have recognized the type. Even Sturm's name suggests the eighteenth-century literary movement *Sturm und Drang* (Storm and Stress). Karl Faber, Sturm's future son-in-law and functional double, recalls the "hot-headed" protagonists of early Schiller Storm and Stress dramas. Moreover, the actor playing Faber, Malte Jaeger, bears a striking resemblance to idealized portraits of the young Friedrich Schiller. Duke Karl Alexander (Heinrich George) echoes *Emilia Galotti's* ambivalent prince. Both *Jew Süß* and *Emilia* critique the infantile narcissism coded as aristocratic, the fact "that princes are human beings" (*daß Fürsten Menschen sind*), to quote the famous closing line of Lessing's play.[16] Although the film portrays the Duke as a vehicle rather than as a source of evil (again parallel to *Emilia*), it hints at his puerility as he revels in watching a young woman being molested in the street procession through town. The syntactic linkage of the molested woman with Dorothea Sturm, who first appears with the next cut, intensifies the Duke's responsibility for social disharmony by anticipating the violation of woman even before the "Jew" enters the narrative. The role of evil is, of course, reserved for the "Jew," whose precarious positioning in this narrative paradigm I will discuss shortly.

Women and the Family Narrative

The film's taxonomy of women corresponds as well to eighteenth-century class coding: male projections of bourgeois female virtue like Dorothea Sturm are juxtaposed with idle aristocratic women (the Duchess, Süß's mistress) who were sexualized by bourgeois discourses in the course of the eighteenth century. The virtuous woman is crucial to the bourgeois tragedy's family narrative, which *Jew Süß* mirrors but also extends. The film tells two stories, a family one and a political one, but the two are clearly parallel, and the nuclear family again stands for social harmony.[17] Patriarch Sturm is at once spokesman for the Estates, whose rights are abused, and father of a daughter who is abused; the rape of Dorothea *is* the rape of Württemberg.[18] In fact, *Jew Süß* mirrors the family metaphor doubly by including a story fragment anticipating the trajectory of the entire film. The bourgeois Fiebelkorn family appears only once, disputing whether daughter Minna should attend a masked ball arranged by Süß in support of the Duke's lascivious desire for "springtime wildflowers." Mother Fiebelkorn is susceptible to the lure of the court while the volatile father correctly anticipates the daughter's sexual violation: "The Jew is arranging a meat market and our daughters are good enough to provide the meat." This constellation, like the Sturms' father-daughter relationship, is typical of the bourgeois tragedy, in which the mother is often either absent or morally compromised. In Lessing's *Emilia Galotti* and Schiller's *Kabale und Liebe*, the social-climbing mother is oblivious to the danger threatening her daughter; in Lessing's *Miß Sara Sampson* and *Nathan the Wise*, the mother is dead (like Dorothea's mother).

The "corruptibility" of *Jew Süß*'s women and their objectification by the camera leads Régine Friedman to assail the film as no less misogynist than antisemitic. Citing Horkheimer and Adorno's equation in *Dialectic of Enlightenment* of Jews and women as objects of similar hatred, Friedman labels *Jew Süß* a "shockingly antifeminine denunciation" whose repudiation of women . . . proves to be no less than that of the Jew."[19] I concur with Friedman's charge of misogyny and its linkage with antisemitism, but prefer to distinguish the film's class-specific "repudiation" of courtly woman from its *functionalization* of bourgeois woman as a metaphor for the social body, which is another extension of an eighteenth-century construction of gender and class. The recurrence of the desirable female in eighteenth-century narrative and her merger with the private sphere was a constitutive element in the assertion of bourgeois power throughout European culture. As Nancy Armstrong has shown with reference to England, the construction of female virtue was part of an attempt to transform a blatantly political struggle into a psychological one, and to evaluate psychological motives according to a set of values in which the bourgeois woman became exalted over the aristocratic woman. It was, above all, the female "on whom depended the outcome of the struggle among competing ideologies."[20] This narrative association of the bourgeois woman with virtue is part of the construction of sexuality Foucault traces in *History of Sexuality*. Contrary to popular belief, Foucault argues, western culture did not repress sexuality, but actually *produced* it as a means of disciplining individual and social bodies. Normative sexuality became crucial to bourgeois identity; the bourgeoisie's sexuality was the "fragile treasure"[21] by which it distinguished itself from the aristocracy, as well as lower classes. Dorothea von Mücke corroborates Foucault's point by demonstrating how a disciplined, bourgeois subjectivity depended on abjection of the female body, at least on a level of representation. Thus, for example, Lessing's *Miss Sara Sampson* (the title character of his first tragedy, 1755) becomes an object of pity, the crucial category of Sentimentality, only after she "has overcome the carnal passions by rejecting the corporeality of the body, female sexuality, and a tyrannical maternal love."[22]

We see in all of the above a historical basis for *Jew Süß*'s strategy of making Dorothea Sturm's body a contested territory that, like the "Jew's" body, is killed off by the narrative. The film adds, however, a "racial" dimension to this threat that is inconsistent with the bourgeois tragedy, which assumes that everyone is amenable to moral improvement. This is a crucial departure from the eighteenth-century genre to which I will return; moreover, I will elaborate how *Jew Süß* strips bourgeois woman of the autonomy her eighteenth-century precursors have, even if this autonomy is viewed through the lens of male projection. We will see how *Jew Süß* most consistently defaces the very woman it pretends to privilege; the rape of Dorothea is "really" a rape of Stuttgart men.

It is significant to note, however, that *Jew Süß*'s xenophobic equation of the virtuous female body with a biologized notion of "race" is not without its foundation in the eighteenth century. Repeated shots in the film showing Dorothea at a harpsichord quote an eighteenth-century iconographic tradition that attests to a similar, if more subtly racist equation of domestic harmony with a "racially" superior community. By analyzing the semiotics of eighteenth and nineteenth-century British colonialist painting, Richard Leppert has demonstrated the significance of the harpsichord throughout Europe as a standard-bearer of Western culture, one that was linked with women.[23] As an instrument that produced harmony, the harpsichord functioned as a subtle legitimator of British colonialist supremacy and complemented the philosophical notions of reason, order, and racial hierarchy. Contemporary conduct literature prescribed the harpsichord as an appropriate instrument for women, and its foregrounding in paintings of domestic life had a special representational status, suggesting the cultural and racial perpetuation of the British. Women grouped around a harpsichord are essential as "the producers of the race" rendering the scene familial as well as musical.[24]

We can see repercussions of the harpsichord's connotative value for early modernity in Nazi films like *Friedrich Schiller, Miss von Barnhelm, Friedemann Bach*, or *Romance in a Minor Key*, which display their female protagonist sitting at a harpsichord or piano. In *Jew Süß*, not only do we first see Dorothea beside a harpsichord, but the film's musical theme, the folk song *All mein Gedanken, die ich hab*, traverses the spheres of public and private intermingled by the film (with its double story of a raped Dorothea and Württemberg). Sung by Dorothea and Faber, the song signals the literal and figurative harmony of the private sphere. Yet it also pervades the film as nondiegetic "background" music, and in moments of pathos shifts into a minor key as if penetrated (like Dorothea) by Eastern sound.

The "Jew" in the Bourgeois Tragedy Narrative

The film's most fascinating maneuver is its location of the "Jew" within a scenario in which neither race nor religion generally play a role.[25] *Jew Süß* both divests the "Jew" of "racial" difference *and* insists vehemently on that difference—depending on whether we examine the semiotics of Süß Oppenheimer for the majority of the film or the structure of the *Jew Süß* narrative. In exploring this paradox, I will begin with semiotics, with the characterization of Süß. If this persona is as familiar as the characters already discussed, it is because this persona is not really "Jewish" (even as constructed by antisemitism), but belongs to courtly *intrigeurs* exemplified by Lessing's villainous Marinelli in *Emilia Galotti*. Like Marinelli, Süß pushes the reticent Duke to indulge his licentious fantasies and to forsake community for self-aggrandizement. Süß's own machinations and sexual

appetite, though again passed off as "Jewish" traits, are thoroughly inscrib-
able in the bourgeois tragedy's sociological coding of "court" as synonymous with an amoral world of debauchery. Süß neither dresses nor talks
"Jewish" throughout most of the film. Whereas antisemitism's "Jew" is, as
Gilman writes, deemed unable to "truly command the national language
of the world in which he/she lives,"[26] Süß masters courtly discourse and is
vastly more elegant and courageous than the Duke himself. The French
vocabulary Süß brandishes (*demoiselle, amusement, par exemple, souper*,
etc.) likewise aligns him verbally with the bourgeois tragedy's courtly figures rather than with German Jews, whose dialect Nazi cinema satirizes in
films like *Robert and Bertram* (1939).[27] From the eighteenth century on,
the use of French, especially on the part of aristocratic literary figures, was
a signifier for an "international" orientation, that is, for those lacking
"heart."[28] France was not only culturally important for the aristocracy, but
exemplified the most successful embodiment of enlightened absolutism.

Of course, the point of the film is to make us believe that Süß's "courtly" self is a mask, a ruse to slip himself into a space where he does not
belong. The film couches in narrative form the warning that is directly spoken in Fritz Hippler's infamous 1940 documentary *The Eternal Jew*: Be
careful! Only the discerning eye can identify an assimilated Jew.
Nonetheless, it is telling that there is so little that is "different" about this
supposedly racially different character; it suggests the contradiction to
which I have alluded. In wanting desperately to make the Jew an "Other,"
to make him fit the fantasy, it has few options outside its own narrative
culture in which to do so. Consequently, it keeps making him act like a
"bad" Aryan, while finding ways to equate this behavior with something
called "Jewishness." It thus unwittingly acknowledges one of Slavoj Žižek's
important insights into antisemitism: "In 'going through the fantasy' we
must in the same move identify with the symptom: we must recognize in
the properties attributed to 'Jew' the necessary product of our very social
system; we must recognize in the 'excesses' attributed to 'Jews' the truth
about ourselves."[29] It is as if the film were revealing its projections onto the
"Jew" to be nothing but projections. I will return to this narrative impasse
and the film's attempts to resolve it in the second section of the chapter.

Jew Süß's narrative structure, combined with a number of cinematic
techniques I will discuss later, tries to remedy the above problem: it
indeed locates the "Jew" as originating from a different space and culture,
and it is here that we run into the limitations of the bourgeois tragedy as a
model for the film. Even though Süß Oppenheimer is coded as a courtly
type, it is not without consequences that the film makes him a Jew and an
Outsider (which are synonymous in antisemitic terms). *Jew Süß*, namely,
forgoes the bourgeois tragedy's binarism in favor of another binarism in
which "Jewish" culture is pitted against "Aryan" culture. To be sure, the
old class opposition of the bourgeois tragedy is present as the precondi-

tion for the Jew's success, and the aristocratic realm remains important as his sphere of operations. Nonetheless, the threat to narrative equilibrium is not the invasion of family by aristocracy (notwithstanding the Duke's dalliances; he is, as I will show, an essentially emasculated figure), but of "Aryan" by "Jewish" culture. What counts, then, in the final analysis, is the "sameness" of aristocrat and bourgeois against an Otherness that we're supposed to believe is "racial." In distinction from the bourgeois tragedy, a diagram of the film's social coding might look as follows:

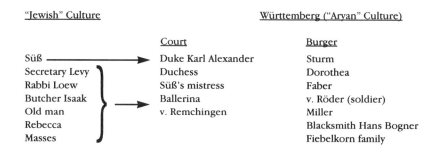

"Jewish" Culture

Württemberg ("Aryan" Culture)

	Court	Burger
Süß	Duke Karl Alexander	Sturm
Secretary Levy	Duchess	Dorothea
Rabbi Loew	Süß's mistress	Faber
Butcher Isaak	Ballerina	v. Röder (soldier)
Old man	v. Remchingen	Miller
Rebecca		Blacksmith Hans Bogner
Masses		Fiebelkorn family

Ultimately, then, *Jew Süß* aligns its audience with the bourgeois tragedy's codified morality only to turn that genre inside out, subtly reversing its "message."[30] We saw how the bourgeois tragedy targets structural flaws within the absolutist system, how *Emilia Galotti* exposes the failure of an autocratic system to account for human fallibility. In replacing the traditional aristocratic villain with a Jew (a transfer historically grounded in the tradition of the "Court Jew" as financial advisor at absolutist courts), *Jew Süß* submerges a challenge to an autocratic social system in a *disavowal* of internal contradictions, which are instead projected onto an outside. In so doing, *Jew Süß* works not toward the depoliticization we associate with kitsch,[31] but toward a *repoliticization* of the bourgeois tragedy: it becomes a racist narrative permitting the "Jew" to function as a social fantasy who makes possible the belief in community. Its framing within the bourgeois tragedy mode allows the film to veil its racism, to legitimate as just punishment the narrative trajectory of eliminating the Jew as a source of social disruption.

At the same time, this fundamental alternation, the desire to locate the source of antagonism "elsewhere," requires *Jew Süß* to take on structural features of a narrative form that, unlike the bourgeois tragedy, is able to accommodate irreducible Otherness: the horror story. Without invoking the supernatural at all, *Jew Süß* repeats the horror narrative's fantasy of a social body penetrated by a monster defined as sexually, biologically different (recall that in many compelling horror genres the monster is assumed *to be* different, but does not *look* different[32]). In its classic forms, the horror narrative drives toward the resolution we find in *Jew Süß*; that the Thing must be "eradicated!"—to use a word ironically spoken by Süß (*Ausrotten!*). This is why the scenes showing torch-bearing crowds frenetically hunting down Süß Oppenheimer so vividly recall horror film classics like *Frankenstein*.

HORROR

It is no coincidence that in *Mein Kampf* Hitler assails the alleged tyranny of Jews as "blood-sucking."[33] The structural similarities between *Jew Süß* and vampire stories, especially Bram Stoker's *Dracula* of 1898, are compelling. Like Dracula, at least in most portrayals since the 1920s,[34] Süß demonstrates a great mobility with respect to his physical appearance. As already discussed, he becomes indistinguishable from nobility, indeed, surpasses in physical appeal the legitimate ruler of Württemberg. Süß also recalls Dracula's spatial mobility, his sexual threat to the male order, his predominant choice of female victims, his contamination of these victims (not explicit in the film but suggested by references to "the blood of our children and children's children"), and, as I elaborate later, his role as an ambiguous figure located somewhere between the self and the Other. Finally, the narratives of *Jew Süß* and Stoker's novel are strikingly similar in trajectory. Both revolve around the transgression of oppositional spaces associated with an alien east ("Jewish" culture and Transylvania, respectively) and a domesticated west (Württemberg/London) with their concomitant cultural associations. Both begin with a figure (the Duke's envoy von Remchingen, Jonathan Harker) traveling from the familiar western space to the space of Otherness. The initial transgression, compromised by the economic grounds by which it was motivated, provides the conditions for the second major journey from east to west, which unleashes evil upon western culture. Finally, both Süß and Dracula are eliminated by a male collective, but not until at least one woman has been sacrificed.

It is obvious that there are also significant differences between *Jew Süß* and *Dracula*: While the Dracula legend harkens back to folklore and superstition, *Jew Süß* is not only a realist narrative but also one that invokes the additional authenticity of history. Second, the alien "eastern" space in *Jew Süß* exists as a microcosm *within* western culture. Süß lives in the Frankfurt Jewish ghetto, a space that, unlike the distant Transylvania, persistently threatens to erupt as a threat to its "host nation." The citizens of Stuttgart do not need to be educated by a "Book of the Jews."

These differences underscore rather than mitigate the importance of structural affinities between *Jew Süß* and the horror story. Namely, the presence of so many vampire motifs in a film calling itself "historical" raises some key questions: What are vampire motifs doing in a historical film? What function do these motifs have in horror, and what might the incorporation of such motifs into a realist narrative tell us about National Socialism? Critical readings of Dracula as a narrative figure in literature and film have concentrated on two general spheres: the narrative negotiation of a real or imagined political threat and of a sexual threat.[35] A political reading of Süß *qua* Dracula sustains what I have already discussed as the film's reconfiguration of the bourgeois tragedy, and lends itself to familiar associations of the "Jew" with money and power.[36] A reading focusing on sexual threat, while by no means excluding the political, opens up perspectives neglected by a study of political implications, which tend to be "rational." Racist obsessions are hardly rational, but, in Joel Kovel's words, "invariably tinged with sexuality: a preoccupation with, a deadly curiosity about, the sexual excesses of the hated group, etched in the imagination by the acid of a harsh moralism."[37] As I hope to illuminate below, a psychoanalytic analysis of Süß as a horror figure offers possibilities of understanding central pathologies underlying National Socialism and how a film like *Jew Süß* attempts to respond to these pathologies.

The connection established by Régine Friedman between women and the "Jew" can be carried further in light of the horror genre, whose gender configurations and organization of looks reverberate in *Jew Süß*. Linda Williams's article "When the Woman Looks" explores why horror film so consistently foregrounds female victims, why the genre seems to punish women for looking at the monster.[38] Williams theorizes a number of affinities between woman and the monster. On the one hand, the woman recognizes in the frightful body of the monster her own difference, her mutilation in the eyes of patriarchy; on the other, both woman and monster pose a potential threat to male power. The connection Williams posits transfers in a number of respects to *Jew Süß*. Although Süß does not have a monstrous appearance, his courtly look is, if we read it with antisemitic logic, only a mask covering up his "real" debased body. Moreover, circumcision renders the Jew visibly mutilated in the eyes of antisemitism—not unlike the woman in Freud's paradigm. Above all, as Theweleit's *Male Fantasies* suggests, the "Jew" represents a threat to male hegemony commensurate only with that posed to the fascist man by devouring women.

Friedman stresses how for the majority of the film Süß controls vision. His possession of the look is inscribed in the film as one of political and economic power, but is also associated with a reduction of others, especially women, to helpless objects of an erotic and humiliating gaze. Indeed, power relations are closely linked with verticality throughout the film, in which power belongs to the figure looking down upon others (cf. the Duke peering over a balcony at ballerinas; the Duke and Süß looking over a balcony at Stuttgart ingenues; the two peering at Minna Fiebelkorn's exposed leg; Süß spying on Württemberger; Süß on a balcony at the execution of Bogner, etc.). Ironically, this principle of verticality will be reversed at Süß's execution, as I will elaborate later.

It is important to stress that, despite the prominence of Süß's abuse of women, not only women are victimized by his look. When estate members invoke Martin Luther in urging the Duke to cast out the Jew, Süß spies on them through a molding in the ceiling. He peers through a mask (literalizing antisemitism's "mask" motif), gaining a god's eye view of subjects who, though perceiving themselves as autonomous, appear to the film viewer, via the Jew's eye, as miniature puppets, as incredible shrinking men. The scene gives narrative form to antisemitism's fundamental paranoia, the conviction that nothing escapes the Jew's eye and ear; he is a malevolent, all-knowing Other whose eye signals his murderous intent.[39] In particular, it suggests that the antisemite feels himself the object of a penetrating gaze, feels himself being "photographed" by an abstract force whose desire cannot be fathomed. Mary Ann Doane argues that paranoia, with its obsessive sense of being watched, is linked with a feminine subject position in that the perception of being on display is equally symptomatic of femininity: "There is a sense . . . in which paranoia is only a hyperbolization of the 'normal' female function of exhibitionism and its attachment to the affect of fear."[40] Doane's analogy transfers smoothly to Süß's destabilizing effect on Württemberg culture. By subjecting males to a powerful and humiliating look, he casts them in a culturally feminized position. The Duke, to be sure, often shares this look, but only when it is orchestrated by Süß.

The Duke's dependency on and simultaneous distrust of Süß likewise recalls a feminine constellation Doane analyzes with respect to the gothic women's film of the forties. In the latter, the (female) protagonist is never sure whether her husband is a murderer. Her subjective vision is foregrounded, but, as in the case of the Duke's delusion of power, it is often proven unreliable (cf. the scene alluding to Schiller's *Wallenstein,* in which the rabbi tricks the Duke into thinking he can control his fate by consulting the stars. Süß controls not only what the Duke looks at, but gives it meaning). The Duke is a feminized figure who must rely on other men to enlighten him (significantly, most important in this respect is the "soldierly" von Roeder); he can never be sure what the "Jew" really wants, and Süß's seduction of his wife signals his effective emasculation.

Even the film's "manly" men are feminized by the Jew's control and panoptic eye, by his appropriation of their women, and his invasion of their "home," the quintessential woman's space. Süß remains what Lacan would call a "stain" in the field of "Aryan" vision that looks back and destabilizes the self. At best the "Aryan" can recognize the stain, as does Faber when he instantly "sees" that Süß is "a Jew." Soon thereafter the camera dollies into a close up of Süß's face, a technique used repeatedly in the film to intensify his threat. In his detailed analysis of shots used in the film, Friedrich Knilli has pointed out that the film devotes a full seven minutes of close-ups to Süß.[41] Indeed, the very first scene in which we see Süß begins and ends with close-ups of him, which in effect frame the scene and elicit the sense of discomfort Westerners feel when someone stands "too" close. This difference is underscored by a hapless attempt to exhibit "racial" physiognomy in two scenes when Süß confronts Sturm and Faber, respectively. In each case "Jew" and gentile appear close-up in profile, highlighting the contrast between supposedly delicate "Aryan" features and more pronounced "Jewish" ones[42] (notwithstanding the fact that the Austrian actor playing Süß, Ferdinand Marian, was not Jewish, but merely a swarthy type not uncommon among Austrians and, especially southern, Germans. I will return to the irony of his casting.).

As suggested by the above, then, Süß is not only the subject, but the object of the look throughout the film. This status does not contradict, but complements his own visual power; he becomes virtually Lacan's gaze *qua object*, the thing that looks threateningly at us. This status relates to another point Linda Williams makes with respect to horror, that the monster displaces woman as the site of spectacle. Despite the film's highlighting of objectified women, Süß's specularization is no less important. In addition to being an obsessive focus of the camera, Süß ornamentalizes himself with opulent clothing, the effect of which is heightened by the contrast between his courtly self and his "original" appearance in caftan and beard.[43] Yet, far from being an object the viewer can master visually, he acts as a threatening voyeur.

The strategy of *Jew Süß* will be to wrestle the look away from the Jew and back into the eyes of the "Aryan" male collective. This restoration of visual power to the film's privileged males is, in effect, its restoration of their potency overall. The film's conclusion, which I will discuss at the end of this essay, turns Süß's own self-specularization against him in an execution in which he becomes a spectacle of a degrading sort, and is himself forced to assume a feminized position. Again in its restoration of male hegemony, *Jew Süß* follows the paradigm of the vampire narrative. From Bram Stoker's *Dracula* on, the trajectory of vampire stories has been to exorcise the threat to the male order usually by means of male authority (especially by Professor van Helsing, standing for the rationality of science). This authority manifests itself in the spectacle of the vampire's execution, which similarly casts him in a feminine position: the pounding of the phallic stake into the vampire's heart.

II: THE PROJECT OF "JEWISH" OTHERNESS

In what follows I specifically examine *Jew Süß* as an antisemitic text, proceeding step by step through the myths with which antisemitism constructs its "Jew." These myths linking Jews with money, abstractness, a distorting rationality, rootlessness, deception, and sexual degeneracy can all be connected to social, economic, and psychological fears of modernity. I will refer back to the preceding analysis, attempting to show how the film's narrative paradigms and cinematic techniques assist or impede its projection of these myths upon Jews.

MONEY AND THE ABSTRACT

Essential to *Jew Süß*, as to antisemitism in general, is its sociohistorical understanding of the history of modernization. The film depicts the development of capitalism, for which absolutism appears as the first step, as a process caused by and to the primary benefit of Jews. A key passage from Hitler's *Mein Kampf* describing the position of the Jew in eighteenth-century Germany anticipates the plot of *Jew Süß*:

> [The Jew] begins slowly to become active in economic life, not as a producer, but exclusively as a middleman. . . . His usurious rates of interest finally arouse resistance; his increasing effrontery, indignation, his wealth, envy. . . . Since he himself never cultivates the soil, but regards it only as a property to be exploited . . . the aversion against him gradually increases to open hatred. His *blood-sucking* tyranny [sic!] becomes so great that excesses against him occur. . . . At times of bitterest distress, fury against him finally breaks out, and the plundered and ruined masses begin to defend themselves against the scourge of God. In the course of a few centuries they have come to know him, and now they feel that the mere fact of his existence is as bad as the plague. . . . Proportionately as the power of the princes begins to mount, he pushes closer and closer to them. He begs for 'patents' and 'privileges,' which the lords, always in financial straits, are glad to give him for suitable payment. . . . And so, his ensnarement of the princes leads to their ruin. . . . The Jew well knows what their end will be and tries to hasten it as much as possible. He himself adds to their eternal financial straits by alienating them more and more from their true tasks, by crawling around them with the vilest flattery, by encouraging them in vices, and thus making himself more and more indispensable to them. With his deftness, or, rather, unscrupulousness, in all money matters he is able to squeeze, yes, to grind, more and more money out of the plundered subjects. . . . Thus every court has its 'Court Jew'—as these *monsters* are called, who in intervals go the way of all flesh (italics mine).[44]

Hitler is referring to the phenomenon of the "Court Jew," with which *Jew Süß* legitimates historically its association of Jews with money and nascent capitalism. It was common practice in eighteenth-century courts to hire Jews as financial and commercial agents in the ruler's service. This service included procuring personal luxury items, as we see in the beginning of *Jew Süß*, or in attending to state policies dealing with currency, provisions, or investments. By gaining control of the Duke, Süß incrementally gains control of the social fabric, taking steps to transform the Württemberg community into a market. In scenes like the following, Jews epitomize the hated "middleman" described by Hitler: a disgruntled miller entering Stuttgart complains to Levy about the increase in road tolls since the Duke has given Süß control of the city streets. Levy attempts to persuade the befuddled miller to be grateful since he is allegedly reaping greater profits from the inflation caused by the higher tolls. As illustrated by the subsequent scene in which Dorothea complains about a sharp rise in food prices, the inflation resulting from Jewish policies will burden the entire community.

In its "anticapitalist" critique, the episode attacks a development that was historically necessary for the transition from a feudal to a capitalist economy: the increasing complexity of systems of product distribution, which required that an ever-greater role be played by "middlemen" not directly involved in production. Large-scale distribution, financing, transportation, and eventually public relations increasingly interfered with what had originally been a one-to-one exchange of commodities. "Late-blooming" nations in this process such as Germany frequently needed centralized controls to accelerate the capitalist process, in order to compete with more advanced countries like England and the Netherlands. The film narrative distorts this process, making it appear as simple exploitation by (Jewish) middlemen, who use verbal acrobatics to disguise this exploitation. The display of such acrobatics is a central diegetic function of secretary Levy, whom one figure calls a "talmudic Jew brain." The Leitmotif of "Jewish reasoning" as a negation of common sense sustains romantic anticapitalism's attack on the abstractness of money and finance capital. It simultaneously contradicts the idea of Jews as subhuman "vermin"; a problem the film tries to explain away by labeling the Jew as "clever, but not smart" (*schlau* vs. *klug*, which connotes a deeper intelligence or wisdom).

Jew Süß's linkage of Jews with modernity also provides one illustration of Nazism's contradictory attitude toward the modernizing process resulting in what Foucault calls "discipline." Whereas in Foucault's analysis, discipline of the body and of society (the social body) are inextricably connected, *Jew Süß* separates these factors in a curious way. Its masses of Jews lack "discipline" in a bodily sense, illustrated by their sloppy dress, unleashed drives, lack of internalized "values," etc. On the other hand, the film links Jews all the more strongly with social "discipline," with a process of structural, financial, temporal, and spatial organization necessary to modernity. As part of Süß's "rape" of Aryan space to be discussed below, he engineers, as in the scene with the miller, a spatial organization of Württemberg that ensures his personal profit. He uses "Jewish" reasoning in another spatial maneuver that destroys tradition in the name of "nature": He demands that blacksmith Hans Bogner pay Süß 80 talers because his house, located where the blacksmith's house "always" was, overlaps with the "natural" line of the street; Süß orders half of the house demolished when Bogner refuses. Bogner is executed after attempting to avenge himself in a physical attack on Süß. The episode sustains the film's anticentralist, anti-disciplinary position, since Bogner's self-defense constitutes an exercise of the "club law" (*Faustrecht*) associated with individualistic late-medieval heroes (epitomized by Goethe's *Götz von Berlichingen*, 1773) who rejected formal legal codes as tyrannical. The "club law" symbolized eighteenth-century critiques of centralists who favored a unified legal code applicable to everyone, which was partially achieved by the Prussian Law Code (*Allgemeines preußisches Landrecht*) of 1794. Codified law was part of the proliferation of writing that, as Foucault stresses, supported the emergence of a "disciplined" world sustained by organized and classified documents. The same association underlies Sturm's remark later that the Jews "twist and *verklausulieren*" everything, or put it in an enigmatic "legalese." His verb *verklausulieren* stems from the word *Klausel* or paragraph, as in a legal code or another contractual document. Sturm can link *verklausulieren* with distortion, because in antidisciplinary ideology they both amount to the same "Jewish" thing.

It is no coincidence that the film juxtaposes a miller and a blacksmith, that is, small businessmen who *produce* essential commodities, with Jews who produce nothing. Moische Postone's analysis of German antisemitism is helpful in understanding why the finance capital of the middleman rather than industrial capital was the target of romantic anticapitalist attacks. Postone explains anticapitalism in terms of the Marxist notion of the fetish, the distinction between what modern capitalism *is* and the way it appears, illustrating the similarity between the characteristics Marx ascribes to the value dimensions of social forms and the characteristics modern antisemitism ascribes to Jews: abstractness, intangibility, mobility, universality. He recalls Marx's notion of commodity form, which shows how the dialectical tension between value and use value requires that their "double character" be materially externalized in value form, appearing "doubled" as money (the manifest form of value) and as the commodity (the manifest form of use-value). Although the commodity is really a social form expressing both value and use value, it appears to contain only the latter, to be only material and "thingly." Money, by contrast, appears to be the sole repository of value, the manifestation of the purely abstract:

> The form of materialized social relations specific to capitalism appears . . . as the opposition between money, as abstract, as the 'root of all evil,' and 'thingly' nature. Capitalist social relations appear to find their expression only in the abstract dimension. . . . One aspect of the fetish, then, is that capitalist social relations do not appear as such, and, moreover, present themselves antinomically, as the opposition of the abstract and concrete.[45]

"Volkish" ideologies understood capital itself only in terms of the manifest form of its abstract dimension: finance and interest capital, which, then, is held responsible for the concrete social and cultural upheaval provoked by the swift development of modern industrial capitalism. Since concrete labor appears to be the opposite of the abstract realm of money, it is not perceived as part of the capitalist process, but rather as the descendent of artisanal labor, which, by contrast to "parasitic finance capital," seems to be "organic" and rooted in nature.[46] This understanding of capitalism as an abstract force is increasingly biologized during the nineteenth century, manifesting itself in theories of race, especially antisemitism, in which the "racial" opposition between Aryans and Jews supplants that of the concrete material and the abstract. Hence Jews do not merely *represent* capital, they come to personify its intangible, pernicious power.[47]

Jew Süß repeatedly affirms this antinomy between the abstract and the "thingly." Although money is crucial to Süß, what the film foregrounds its its value to him as something abstract, power. In contrast, the citizens of Stuttgart attach value to things money buys, albeit a differing value depending on their social status. The film's bourgeois figures even invest money itself with a certain deictic value, as suggested by the implication throughout the film that "Jewish" money is somehow materially different from other money. The same idea underlies Faber's accusation that Süß's money is "blood" money, acquired at the price of our "wives' and daughters'" racial purity. In the same scene, Süß playfully affirms the abstractness of money for him, "money does not stink."

Another example of this contrast is the motif of jewels, the objects through which Süß gains access to the Duke, but which are for him objects of barter. The "magical" (*märchenhaft*) jewels that Süß keeps hidden in a massive chest (a metonymy for hidden Jewish wealth) at once entrance the Duke's envoy Remchingen and become textual metaphors for Jewish power. A tiny jeweled crown topped by a cross that we see enveloped by Süß's hand anticipates Jewish hegemony over Christians. Towering over the seated Remchingen, Süß dangles a string of pearls that Remchingen eagerly grabs; the "reins" by which Süß gains access to and ultimately control over "Aryan" space. Jewelry, especially rings, assume a different, thingly value for bourgeois figures; Dorothea offers Süß her wedding ring to save Sturm and Faber, while the latter refuses to part with his during torture. Süß, by contrast, gives the Duke a ring to "buy" the ballerina, and later taunts Dorothea with an opulent ring.

Of course, Süß's attitude toward money and power fits the paradigm of the corrupt aristocrat and is only "Jewish" if we believe it is Jewish. A scene in the Jewish ghetto preceding the introduction of Süß plays on antisemitism's contradiction between Jews as slobs and as rich, thus imagining a specifically Jewish relation to money. When Remchingen has entered Süß's house, two Jews in the ghetto street discuss in a distinct Jewish dialect the appearance of "such a fine goyish dandy" at "our Oppenheimer's." A kosher butcher or *Schächter*[48] wearing a bloody apron and carrying a large butcher knife, which he wipes off on his apron, explains the nature of the visit to an old man: "[Oppenheimer] will give him a lot, he will, because he's got brains. He *should* give, so we can *take, take, take!*" While the verbal exchange signals the "Jewish" equation of money with power, the slovenly appearance of the men suggests that Jews are too uncouth to even be interested in personal luxury. The *Schächter's* bloody apron evokes the kosher slaughter of animals, conjuring up a similar revulsion to Jewish "cruelty" as do gruesome slaughter scenes in *The Eternal Jew*.

The same scene typifies the film's persistent linkage of money with a free sexuality that, like money, circulates and has the status of an abstract transaction in which the "partner" is merely an interchangeable sign. Next to the old man in the ghetto street is a wanton-looking young woman with long, black hair leaning out of the window, chewing on something resembling a weed. Since she is not involved in the conversation and never appears again, her presence has no function other than to underscore the talk about money with an image of dissolute "Jewish" sexuality, also associated, as both Theweleit and Gilman illustrate, with sickness.[49] The only spoken reference to her, the old man's comment: "Get dressed, Rebecca!" is unrelated to the rest of the dialogue, but merely stresses her exhibitionism.

The film suggests effectively in filmic terms that money is an *abstracting* force, one which strips individuals, particularly women, of their value and renders them commodities. Nowhere is this better illustrated than when Süß throws a purse full of coins onto a table in front of Karl Alexander, which dissolve into the skirts of spinning ballerinas shot from a bird's eye view (signaling that Süß has financed the ballet which the Estates refused the Duke). The dissolve renders visual not only the courtly reduction of art and women to *divertissement*, to a mass ornament, but the link between the Jew and the intangible power of money. Süß uses money to buy the concrete woman for the Duke, but her visual fusion with coins simultaneously renders the woman abstract. Money voids her of content; she is as interchangeable as the coins. Her twirling skirt and circling figure recall the shape and circulation of money itself; her feet in constant movement further link her with the myth of the "wandering" Jew. Consistent with the historical fact that ballet remained a courtly, not a bourgeois, art form, the ballerina represents the ultimate commodified woman in the film's discourse, as I will illustrate with respect to *Friedemann Bach* as well.

The film's linkage of all its courtly women with the Jew likewise voids them, in keeping with the bourgeois tragedy's negative coding of courtly women as heartless. In their homogenized opulent attire and shrill hysteria, the Duchess, who becomes Süß's mistress, and his "official" mistress are barely distinguishable. The nameless mistress laughs with erotic titillation upon seeing a house Süß had ordered half demolished in a metaphoric gesture anticipating his destruction of family and reduction of "men" to puppets: "Such a cute doll's house. . . . You're *so* cruel!" Her enjoyment of the spectacle is one of the film's only "honest" responses, mirroring the pleasure the film audience takes in all its sadistic spectacles.

THE "WANDERING JEW"

As suggested by its analogies to vampire narratives and by the importance of money as a circulating sign, *Jew Süß* is the story of crossed boundaries, of mastered space. The "Jew" seeks to subjugate everything to money or circulation, poisoning "home" (in the double sense of the private and public) as the space that guarantees quality or "self-sameness." The film's opening shot following the credits shows an engraving of Württemberg with Stuttgart encased by a city wall; hereafter we see a variety of Jewish figures entering the city gates. In his first appearance, Süß vows to "open the door" to Württemberg for Jewish domination: "It may be tomorrow, it may be the day after, but it will be!" The two times he literally falls down in the film (when his coach overturns on his way to Stuttgart, and when he is about to rape Dorothea) suggest a revolt of "nature" against the Jew's penetration of "Aryan" space.

The spillover of Jewish culture into Aryan culture even occurs on a formal level, most conspicuously in Harlan's use of the lap dissolve at key moments. After, for example, the film has established the initial harmony between the two dominant "Aryan" milieus of court and bourgeois home, it shifts to a "Jewish" milieu by means of a dissolve. Karl Alexander appears before the people of Stuttgart, standing directly above Württemberg's coat of arms. The camera travels to the coat of arms, which slowly dissolves into a sign with Hebrew writing. On a denotative level the dissolve signals a change from one setting to the next, the Jewish ghetto in Frankfurt. On a connotative level, however, the sign stands for "Jewishness"; it is presumably illegible to the viewer and underscored by ominous music. The scene change could have been achieved with a cut, but the lap dissolve allows the Hebrew letters to "swallow" Württemberg and, by implication, Karl Alexander.[50] The same spillover occurs at times on the level of soundtrack, when sound from one scene at times overlaps briefly with the next. The synagogue scene, for example, concludes with Dorothea's singing voice briefly preceding the cut to her at the harpsichord.

Once this spillover has occurred, "Aryan" spaces are stifled, deprived of *Lebensraum*, suggested by Sturm's act of opening a window and proclaiming "Fresh air!" after an explosive argument with Süß. The film's two brief mass "Jewish" scenes, repeating on a macrolevel what Süß achieved as an individual, have in common a compositional principle of clutter that lends them a claustrophobic quality. They likewise mobilize sound (loud

Hebrew chanting) and (often frenetic) movement to alienate the German spectator the film anticipates. The brief scene in which droves of Jews enter Stuttgart shows a long caravan of chanting Jews appearing dusty and dirty, with their possessions piled high upon wagons. Most shots are composed so that we cannot perceive the beginning or the end of the long line extending diagonally across the frame. The appearance that there is no end to the entering swarm is underscored verbally as a Württemberger cries that the Jews are entering Stuttgart "like locusts."[51] The Sabbath celebration begins with Jews opening a chest and removing a Torah topped by a crown. It thus mirrors on a mass level the early scene in which Süß fondles the jeweled crown (= Christianity); only here the pace of the scene intensifies to an orgiastic mass frenzy.

The claustrophobic effect of mass "Jewish" scenes is intensified by the fact that prior to Süß Oppenheimer's entrance into the narrative, the film is marked by compositional and narrative equilibrium. As we hear, in the opening scene, Karl Alexander's off-screen voice vowing to rule "with fatherly (landesväterlicher) care," we see a massive portrait of the late Duke Eberhard Ludwig, out of which the voice seems to flow. This counterpoint of voice and image suggests continuity in the spirit nurturing Württemberg, or in the terms of Ernst Kantorowicz,[52] though each king's physical body dies, his second, transcendent body lives on in his successors. The camera pans swiftly from the icon of the deceased patriarch to Karl Alexander, again linking them metonymically. Each shot is correspondingly orderly and symmetrical, centered around the patriarch flanked by deferential Estate members; the light emanating from windows high above lends the figures' heads a radiant appearance, as if divinely sanctioned. The first family scene in the Sturm home is composed with similar tableau shots of Dorothea and Faber poised at the harpsichord, likewise illuminated by natural light. As we have seen, the Jew's arrival disrupts such compositional harmony, which will seldom recur until the court scene in which Süß is condemned.

Antisemitism transformed the literary motif of the wandering Jew victimized by modern existence into one burdening the Jew with the blame for modernity. Already by the late nineteenth and twentieth centuries, the motif of the traveler had in part forfeited the positive associations of self-realization accompanying it in the eighteenth and early nineteenth centuries; more precisely, a new motif of the traveler developed alongside the older one of the Bildungsroman. A precondition for the valorized traveler of the latter is the protagonist's possession of a homeland or Heimat to which he or she can return, as in Tieck's Franz Sternbalds Wanderungen. This Heimat is a space of rest guaranteeing that all movement can be arrested and that the traveler will not lose the self in eternal movement. The competing motif of the restless traveler signifies the aimless roaming of an alienated, uprooted subject unable to find its own space in a world dominated by exchange value. Like money, as the embodiment of alien-ation through movement *par excellence*, the traveler without a home is a mere element within an all-present process of circulation characteristic of modern societies. Frequently this motif was merged, as in the case of Kundry in Wagner's *Parsifal*, with the ancient motif of the wandering Jew, which dates back to the Middle Ages but which changed its character sub-stantially during the nineteenth century.[53] In a secular context, this motif often symbolizes the consequences of materialistic attitudes and actions (see, for example, Lienhard's novel *Ahasver am Rhein* of 1903) and the impossibility of redemption as long as materialism determines human actions.

Süß fits smoothly into antisemitism's figure of the wandering Jew turned master of a movement aimed at commodifying space and conquer-ing the abstract realm of circulation and exchange (again like Stoker's Dracula). Hence, his juxtaposition with Dorothea, a nurturing potential mother standing for presence, for *Heimat* as a geographical projection of the need for security. Dorothea and Süß become allegories for stasis and movement, respectively, as they enter Stuttgart together. Dorothea fails to comprehend how Süß can be at home "everywhere": "Don't you have a homeland? . . . But there must be some place you feel the happiest!" Her "natural" movement is strictly confined to the private home, by which she is utterly absorbed (note, for example, her failure to guess in whose honor her father is proposing a toast on the day of the Duke's coronation). At times she appears literally framed by a window, a stance Mary Ann Doane links with the social and symbolic positioning of woman: "the window is the interface between inside and outside, the feminine space of the family and reproduction and the masculine space of production."[54] It is her departures from the walls of her home that imperil her, especially her two autonomous acts, bringing Süß into Stuttgart and visiting him to seek mercy.

"JEWISH" MASQUERADE

The all-pervasive power that antisemitism projects into the Jews is not readily apparent; it lurks behind events, but is not identical with them. Again the film signals "Jewish masquerade" formally through the lap dis-solve in which the bearded Süß of the *Judengasse* emerges as a clean-shaven, wigged courtier en route to Stuttgart. The reverse occurs in a final dissolve at the conclusion of the film, when Süß is arrested and forced to own up to his "true" appearance. Steve Neale has effectively described how bodily marks signify racial order within the film; racial difference needs to be "inscribed and readable, immediately intelligible," which is only possible if racial characteristics are visible.[55] The same semiotic and ideological technique is used to identify the "Jew" as a bodily metaphor for the abstract domination of capital. Complex interdependencies are thus reduced to easily comprehensible bodily constellations. National Socialism masks this reduction by "turning the tables" and implying that the "real" issue is the concealment of bodily indicators by the enemies of society.[56]

Underlying the need for "Jewish" masquerade, of course, is the presupposition that the undisguised Jew is fundamentally and visibly different from gentiles, and simultaneously homogenized with other Jews by his parasitic nature—a presupposition the film tries unsuccessfully, as I'll elaborate shortly, to "prove." Such "proof" would seem to be offered by the scenes depicting a parasitic mass stifling "Aryan" racial health, and by the film's employment of one actor to play all Jewish figures except Süß: Werner Krauss portrays the secretary Levy, Rabbi Loew, the butcher Isaak, and even the old man in the same scene.[57] The collapsing of nearly all Jews into one unclean, coughing, or cackling body tries to efface Jewish humanness, in keeping with Joel Kovel's elucidation of racism as a process of dehumanization via abstraction (e.g., from "body" to "penis" to inanimate "thing") until the group in question reaches the "final point of nothingness."[58] Nazism fantasizes Jews as a kind of void; Jewish identity is posited merely as negativity, existing in transgression and social destabilization.

However, the film endeavors to suggest the subhuman nature of Jews, the bulk of its narrative time and its images are devoted to Süß Oppenheimer—a figure who belies precisely the presupposition the film wants to reinforce. Jürgen Link's theorization of different varieties of "enemy images" in western culture is useful in exploring Süß's precarious status as a figure whom the film refuses to code as identical to its "Aryan" figures, but who also fails to conform to the above description of a Jewish mass. Link posits a distinction between enemies with and without what he calls "subject status."[59] An enemy with subject status, exemplified by Soviet communists as viewed by the postwar West, is perceived as possessing the autonomy and rationality one accords one's own system. Although this enemy may be "evil," he plays by the rules of the metaphoric game, be it poker, chess, or war. The enemy lacking subject status is symbolically coded as chaos; he is located outside the boundaries of a system centered on reason. These enemies, for whom "Muslim fundamentalists" might serve as an example, cannot be conceived as partners or even really as opponents. Their lack of subject status disqualifies them as rationally thinking beings "like us"; they are excluded from the start as co-players in an antagonistic game.

Nazism's metaphoric coding of Jews as rats or vermin is a gesture divesting them of subject status, and this, in turn, is a precondition for engineering consent to their extermination (they don't suffer like we do, etc.). The desire, exemplified by *Jew Süß*, to perpetuate antisemitic thinking via narrative results, however, in the inescapable dilemma to which I have alluded. Namely, in order for Süß to function as the central narrative antagonist, he must be accorded subject status, albeit coded as the devil (cf. the Duke's playful reference to him as *Teufelskerl*). Indeed, central components of antisemitic mythology presume not only subject status, but even a kind of superiority on the part of the Jew (the agility of Jewish reasoning; the persistent ability to dupe the Aryan, etc.). This superiority over others is indeed magnified in the case of Süß, making him a profoundly ambivalent figure—a problem the film tries to resolve by the "other" Jews and the frame device permitting Süß's "true" Jewish essence to emerge.

The selection of the "Aryan" Ferdinand Marian to play Süß only exacerbates the quandary, as the Nazi journal *Der Film* unwittingly admitted in 1940: "Naturally a film like this will encounter casting difficulties in Germany."[60] Although ghetto Jews were used in *The Eternal Jew*, Nazi policies would not have permitted a Jew to star in a feature film; yet without a Jew in the role, it forfeits at least some of its alleged genuineness (invoked elsewhere by, for example, predictable claims of authenticity at the film's beginning). Finally, no "Aryan" male in the film appears as Süß's narrative counterpart; no individual is his equal and only as a group do the citizens of Stuttgart defeat him. Although this narrative configuration encodes Nazi collectivism, it simultaneously enhances Süß's status as a figure essentially unchallenged and unchalleng*eable*.

Another complicating factor is Süß's portrayal as sexy or at least ambivalent. He contradicts the normal coding of the Jewish man in Nazi films as ludicrous and repulsive (cf. Nathan Ipelmeyer in *Robert and Bertram*)—perhaps as a concession to historical legend, which calls for a sexual appeal on the part of Süß Oppenheimer, but more likely to the erotic imperatives of classical cinema. The screen persona of Ferdinand Marian predisposed him to be regarded as an erotic object. Described as a "rather oily matinee idol,"[61] Marian embodied the "characteristics of the attractive, gallant lover intensified by his southern looks, which in the Third Reich were considered foreign and forbidden."[62] According to Veit Harlan's memoirs, Marian received baskets of love letters from fans after appearing in *Jew Süß*. If there is a moment of subversion to be found in the film, it is in the titillation he offers, which Friedman reads as "an instance of rebellion against the denial and sacrifice of the female self demanded of the regime."[63] Although I find Friedman's reading overly optimistic, clearly the prowess and sexuality of the "Jew" that threaten to dislodge the film's "intention" are crucial to its entertainment value. One might say that precisely what makes *Jew Süß* work as *film*, with its codified organization of desire, undermines it as antisemitism.

A further dimension in this casting of an attractive "Aryan" in the role of Süß ties into the film's reliance on horror: its suggestion that the "Jew" be read as an ambiguous figure located in the space between self and other. Süß occupies what Hélène Cixous describes as the space of ghosts: "It is the between that is tainted with strangeness. . . . What is intolerable is that the Ghost erases the limit which exists between two states. . . . It is his coming back which makes the ghost what he is, just as it is the return of the Repressed that inscribes the repression."[64] Just as the ghost, like the vampire, is somewhere in between being alive and dead, Süß resists easy localization: he is somewhere in between Jewish culture and Aryan courtly culture; no longer truly part of the first, and supposedly not integratable in the second. He is also in between as an "Aryan" playing a Jew; as a figure somehow *with* subject status and *without*, he is, above all, in between the me and the not-me. As the figure who is meant to embody this society's own antagonism, he cannot be seen as totally outside, but rather as the repressed that persistently returns.

Freud's reading of paranoia as characterized by an elision of subject-object relations holds for Nazism's paranoid construction of the "Jew" as well. The projection of the society's own antagonisms onto the "Jew" is one attempt to restore that distinction between subject and object, to allow the "Jew" to exist only as Other. This can be, of course, only a strategy that works to a limited degree within narrative; the "Jew" will never be relegated fully to an outside beyond the social totality. As such a creature who is me and not me, and who both embodies for others and pursues for himself forbidden desire, the narrativized "Jew" is a creature of simultaneous repulsion and fascination, and hence a symptom of "the instability of culture, the impossibility of its closure or perfection," the same ambiguity James Donald articulates with respect to monsters: "The dialectic of repulsion and fascination in the monstrous reveals how the apparent certainties of representation are always undermined by the insistent operations of desire and terror. The lurid obsession with archaism and liminality in horror films, and their play on the uncanny ambivalence of *heim* and *unheimlich*, highlight the fragility of any identity that is wrought from abjection."[65]

CONTAGIOUS LUST

Klaus Theweleit uses the term "contagious lust" (*Lustseuche*, literally an "epidemic of lust") to describe antisemitism's projection of "Jewish" sexuality as insatiable and perverse. No spectre was more disturbing to Nazism than that of "parasitic Jews" (*Aussaugejuden*) whom Julius Streicher saw "sitting with blonde German girls in bars and cafes, sapping the sexual and racial strength of their host people and destroying them."[66] The myth of "Jewish" lust again involves an implicit demarcation of boundaries that are transgressed by Jews. *Jew Süß* encodes "contagious lust" most prominently in the rape of Dorothea Sturm that literalizes the rape of Württemberg. The representation of Dorothea's rape is, however, like so many aspects of *Jew Süß*, ambivalent. The film's historical role in antisemitic policies encourages us to read the rape in antisemitic terms, as racial poisoning. Occasional dialogue references to "Jew children" and threatened "blood," as well as the citing of carnal relations with a gentile as grounds for Süß's execution, sustain this interpretation. Viewers familiar with film history, moreover, will be reminded of D. W. Griffith's racist film *The Birth of a Nation* (1915), in which a girl commits suicide to escape being raped by a freed slave. Yet again, from a cinematic or narrative perspective, Süß's sexually exploitative ways are not particularly "Jewish," but fit into a long tradition. To recall my earlier discussion, his sexuality is typically "courtly," as is his lust for revenge, the motivation he articulates for raping Dorothea.[67] My point is not to suggest that Dorothea's violation is not "intended" as a demonstration of "Jewish" racial defilement, but that little in the film text explicitly points to "race." What is definitely clear, whether or not we foreground an antisemitic reading of Süß's sexuality as deviant, is that it threatens male hegemony. Crucial to the portrayal of this threat is the series of spectacles involving not only Süß and women, but other men.

The titillating rape scene, whose mise-en-scène borrows from Sardou's nineteenth-century drama *Tosca* (1887, better known today through Puccini's opera), constitutes Süß's final and definitive opportunity to position another man as feminized spectacle. Dorothea seeks mercy from Süß for the imprisoned Faber, while in a close-by cell the latter is tortured every time Süß displays a white handkerchief outside of his window. Unlike traditional stagings of *Tosca*, where the constraints of the stage only permit the viewer to see Tosca's anguish and eventual murder of her assailant, *Jew Süß* cross-cuts between Süß's bedroom (dominated by his giant bed) and the sight of Faber being tortured. It thus highlights the simultaneity of woman's abuse and man's impotence, and shows on the man's body a violation that conventions of the time do not permit to be shown on the woman's body. Faber's hands, mutilated by thumbscrews, are another bodily mark signaling "Aryan" male inadequacy, his inability to prevent the violation of nature and his "territory."

Significantly, the narrative has persistently disrupted the consummation of Faber's desire; every scene in which he kisses Dorothea is interrupted. Though stylized as a Schillerian hero, he appears throughout as unequal to the Jew or Sturm, even as slightly feminized. During his first appearance at the harpsichord, Dorothea strokes his hair, then walks away and is replaced by Sturm, who repeats her gesture. The replacement of Dorothea by the father anticipates the disruption of the heterosexual couple not only by the Jew, but by the all-pervasive father, whose arrest will even inhibit the couple's union after their marriage. Indeed, Süß's prime opponent in his battle over Dorothea is Sturm, who wields complete control over his daughter's body (another motif left over from the bourgeois tragedy). After proclaiming that Dorothea "will not bring Jew-children into the world," he arranges her marriage to Faber, if not to ensure his own sexual domination over her, then to shield her from the Jew's more potent sexuality.

If we read the film with antisemitic ideology in mind, "Jewish" sexuality is fully consistent with the horror analogy I introduced earlier. Desire, narrative contingency, and editing destine Dorothea and the Jew for each other, as numerous readings of the first Dracula film, Murnau's *Nosferatu* (1922; as well as Werner Herzog's 1979 remake), have claimed for the relationship between Nina (Mina in Stoker's novel) and the vampire. Several times when Dorothea encounters Süß the camera tracks into a close-up of his face, allowing the spectator to share with her the titillating sensation of being the object of his look. As Friedman points out in illustrating women's "corruptibility,"[68] not only does Dorothea first transport Süß to Stuttgart, she veritably runs into Süß's arms. While the naiveté that delivers her to Süß is readable against the background of eighteenth-century codings of innocence, it is also readable as a sublimated desire to be raped, especially in light of her abortive relationship with Faber. The *Illustrierte Film-Kurier*, with which the film was promoted, consistently shows stills of Dorothea and Süß together, or of Dorothea alone dressed as in the rape scene. One montage of production stills in the pamphlet forms a triangle in which Süß and Dorothea face each other, with Faber in the background, as if he, not Süß, were the intruder in the dyadic relationship. The only shot of Faber and Dorothea together shows the latter as a corpse.[69]

Just as *Jew Süß* exerts pressure to eliminate the Jew, Dorothea's rape is, in antisemitic terms, synonymous with her death. Rape by the Jew effects an irreversible contamination of the victim, much like vampirism, as described by Linda Williams: "The vampire's power to make its victim resemble itself is a very real mutation of the once human victim. . . ."[70] Bram Stoker's Mina becomes aware of herself as "unclean" once Dracula has forced her to drink blood from an incision in his chest. The self-disgust she expresses is simultaneously a striking articulation of the threat vampiric sexuality poses to male hegemony: "I must touch him or kiss him [husband Jonathan Harker] no more. Oh, that it should be that it is I who am now his worst enemy, and whom he may have most cause to fear."[71] Stoker's novel explicitly associates vampirism with female sexual arousal. Dracula's first victim, Lucy Westerna, turns from a prim Victorian into a sexualized woman after her attack by Dracula. She receives transfusions by a variety of men, which have been read by numerous critics as a covert metaphor for semen.[72] Antisemitism reverses this symbolization, though to the same effect; here the Jew's semen stands for contamination of woman by Jewish blood, as remarked by Julius Streicher: "During coitus the male semen is fully or partially absorbed into the lining of the female uterus, where it enters the bloodstream. A single act of intercourse between a Jew and an Aryan woman is enough to poison her blood forever."[73]

Again here, however, the film is not explicit—there is no verbal explanation for Dorothea's suicide (except "the Jew has her on his conscience") and cinematically it is only inferred by editing. Unlike in both horror and the bourgeois tragedy, *Jew Süß* also denies any explicit suggestion of sexual pleasure on the part of Dorothea, who seems to have Aryan "blood" but not the "blood" of sensuality of which Lessing's Emilia Galotti speaks. The rape is as much a rape of Faber as it is of her, and although the narrative credits her with the will to die, the film's actual narration does not permit us to see a display of the female will common in the bourgeois tragedy.[74] While we do not see her drown herself (even elliptically), we do see Faber struggling with his wounds. Dorothea is merely stranded between two scenes in which she is *acted upon* by males; the rape and Faber's emergence from a lake bearing her corpse (only a brief clip showing her wandering in a state of derangement and, typically, looking for Faber, separates the two). Dorothea is essentially stripped of her subject status, becoming the thing suggested by actress Kristina Söderbaum's nickname "Reich Water Corpse" (*Reichswasserleiche*).[75]

The cinematic celebration of Dorothea's limp body is at once the height of pathos and the first step in the exorcism of a sexuality imperiling male stability. As her corpse is retrieved from a lake, black night is offset by torches creating a dramatic chiaroscuro effect which recalls the often remarked Nazi love of pyrotechnics, especially in connection with funerals. The camera lingers on the final close-up of Dorothea laid on the ground, her childlike face illuminated, divested of the sexuality that made her the object of "Jewish" lust, and returned to a harmless, de-eroticized state. The dead Dorothea calls to mind Saul Friedländer's analysis of the fusion of "kitsch and death" as typical for National Socialism,[76] but this in turn is indebted to an older tradition of nineteenth-century aestheticism and kitsch motifs like reproductions of the famous "Dead Girl From the Seine."

Dorothea's death seemingly empowers the film's male collective to begin its process of reasserting itself. The scene in which Estate members confer on a punishment for Süß restores the compositional symmetry of the film's beginning, as well as ensuring the final narrative resolution exorcising the Jew. Anecdotal accounts of the film cite Veit Harlan's memoirs, which contend that his original ending showed Süß facing death boldly, hurling a curse on the people of Stuttgart. Goebbels allegedly demanded that the scene be reshot with Süß appearing cowardly—a change in full accord with the film's attempt to restore the look to its destabilized men, and by extension, to the spectators (quasi-literally taking "an eye for an eye," a revenge Sturm insists the Aryans are *not* after).

Süß's execution is a mirror reversal of the earlier execution of blacksmith Bogner, in which the humiliation inflicted *by* Süß is now inflicted *upon* him. The pleasure of seeing Süß made the object of his own staged spectacle is enhanced by the similar cinematography of the two execution scenes. Both are punctuated by the sound and image of drums counting the moments to death; both alternate extreme high and low angle shots reversing the film's vertical coding of power; that is, diegetic and film spectators *look up at* the humiliated and disempowered figure. Süß ultimately becomes the object of a spectacle more humiliating than any he "executed" himself. Several bird's eye shots encompassing the scene invite a feeling of spectator omniscience.

The original version of the scene with Süß cursing would have portrayed Süß as an ethical hero; a Don Giovanni adhering to a Kantian radical evil, an evil so ethical as to remain inexorably resolute even in the face of death. Such an ending would have allowed Süß to retain his narrative ambivalence, ensuring his spectator appeal and permitting him one final assertion of phallic supremacy. Spectators of the execution would have remained his objects. The "Jew," as the stain too close and yet too different from the self, needs not only to be exorcised (in narrative and in life) but to be rendered a thing. Goebbels's alleged revision of the scene complies with this need; it allows male lack felt throughout the narrative to be transferred to Süß. The ultimate feminization of the Jew compensates precisely for his feminizing effect on the Aryan male; consequently it is Faber, rather than Sturm, whom the scene privileges. The actual hanging of Süß is framed by close ups of Faber, the last object of the Jew's humiliating spectacle and now a bold watcher of another spectacle. As Süß is raised in his cage the camera tracks out and up from a shot of Faber, as if from the point of view of Süß himself. This subjective shot adds to Faber's compensation by suggesting that Süß sees Faber watching his death, although in accordance with its aim of dehumanizing Süß, the scene does not permit a reaction shot. Immediately following Süß's death, the camera again tracks into a close-up of Faber, completing the effect that the spectacle was staged primarily for his look. The reassuring effect of this transformation of phallic power at once complements and exceeds the importance of restoring Süß's "true" Jewish appearance.

The final close-up of Süß's body shows his bare feet hanging limp from out of his cage, resembling a slaughtered chicken, a thing lacking subject status. This fragmentation, degradation, and effacing of his body contrasts starkly with the individualizing "death mask" (to borrow Eric Rentschler's phrase) iconography with which Dorothea is celebrated. It represents the film's attempt to cancel out the disquieting appeal of the Jew throughout, and to relegate him to the subhuman being he is supposed to be.[77] Purifying light snow as well as the recurrence of the "Dorothea" song signal the return of narrative harmony. The "Jew" is comfortably restored as Other, as the "You" Lacan maintains is essential to taming the Other. Only Faber's prominently displayed hands hint that the restoration is incomplete; his wounds (i.e., emasculation) loom as a stain reminding of male lack.[78]

OTHERNESS, NARRATIVE, AND CINEMA

Jew Süß's meticulous encoding of antisemitic mythology offers a historical documentation of attempted indoctrination that will remain important for the analysis of ideology. Yet I hope to have demonstrated in this essay that a discursive recounting of ideology in the film does not even begin to grasp it as a totality. This requires a sorting out of the components that make up *Jew Süß*: narrative paradigms with their inherent modes of identification and ideology, the antisemitism woven into these narratives, and their filmic articulation. All of the preceding elements need to be not only de- but reconstructed in a consideration of how they mutually reinforce or work against each other.

The manifold textual components that collaborate to make *Jew Süß* (and I am including here antisemitism and history, which come to us in textual, usually narrative form) are able to work together because of a common narrative delimitation of an "inside," which provides an imaginary fulfillment of the desire for harmony, and an "outside" that threatens harmony. No matter what the narrative form, this dichotomization of "inside" and "outside" is a mere rhetorical strategy, since the inside and outside projected through narration into different, opposite spaces are inextricably related and dependent upon one another. They are each other's Other and cannot exist independently; the "Jew" with his excesses is but the alter ego of those who construct him. The appeal of narrative lies in an imaginary mastery over the "outside" that lives off the certainty that it can never be eradicated, as it is merely the dialectical opposite of the "inside." This illusion of mastery has (and wants) to be renewed— which further suggests that the Other to community cannot be overcome, that the void will never be entirely filled in. The fact that the Nazi *state* did not content itself with trying to eliminate the Other via narrative raises the "what if?" question, whose answer is clear: If Nazism had survived the war and succeeded in exterminating European Jews, it would have deprived itself of its necessary Other. Either that state would have totally reconstituted itself, or would have had the daunting task of generating an Other to replace the Jews.

The inconsistencies that plague *Jew Süß* derive from the different terms in which this outside is defined by its competing narrative paradigms; the moral terms of eighteenth-century literature (making the Other amenable to improvement) clash with the biological and nonrecuperable Otherness of horror and antisemitism. Moreover, cinema, with its reliance on representation and codified paradigms, gives *Jew Süß*'s antisemitic ideology its power yet falls short in trying to represent the essentially "different" Jew who exists only in the imagination. Although there are doubtless perspectives on *Jew Süß* that I have left out, what is clear is that a reading going beyond ideology critique yields a far more complex mode of textual operation than a listing of antisemitic myths in the film would suggest.

The danger in approaching such a notorious film is, I believe, that our knowledge of the terrible events in which it was implicated compel us to use its antisemitism as our starting point and to view everything else about the film as secondary. As long as our focus is the film's *production* history, this approach is indeed appropriate. It becomes more problematic the moment we turn our interest toward how the film worked on an audience. In imagining the response of a paying, movie-going public, I suspect the starting point of analysis should be reversed, proceeding from the experience of cinema and working toward the specific narratives and ideologies that figure into cinematic pleasure. Knowledge that *Jew Süß* was part of an apparatus, ultimately of extermination—while crucially important—should not lead to "automatic" conclusions about what made the film successful and the degree to which its antisemitism translated into real-life antisemitism. Even the most zealous antisemitic ideologue will have responded to Jew Süß *as a movie.* Assumptions of cause and effect impede rather than further understanding of the complex ways in which ideology and practice function.

Notes

* Joel Kovel, *White Racism: A Psychohistory* (New York: Pantheon, 1970) 57.

1. Cited from commentary preceding the film on its video release in the United States by Video City Productions, prepared by David Calvert Smith, and released by the Jewish Media Services JWB. The film is given the subtitle: *The Indoctrination of Racial Hatred.*

2. Helmut Blobner and Herbert Holba, "Jackboot Cinema," *Film and Filming* 8, 3 (1962):16.

3. A wealth of literature exists on the film, though many studies restrict themselves to a discussion of its subtext, of Goebbels's intervention in the production process and his coercion of film personnel. See D. S. Hull, *Film in the Third Reich* (Berkeley: University of California Press, 1969), E. Leiser, *Nazi Cinema* (New York: Macmillan, 1974); P. Cadars/F. Courtade, *Geschichte des Films im dritten Reich* (Munich-Hanser, 1975); J. Wulf, *Theater und Film im dritten Reich* (Reinbek bei Hamburg: Rowohlt, 1966); D. Welch, *Propaganda and the German Cinema. 1933–1945* (Oxford: Clarendon, 1983); D. Hollstein, *"Jud Süß" und die Deutschen* (Frankfurt/Main: Ullstein, 1983); F. Knilli et al., *"Jud Süß" Filmprotokoll, Programmheft und Einzelanalysen* (Berlin: Spiess, 1983).

4. *Jew Süß* was one of the most popular films of 1940, drawing 20.3 million viewers. Its profits were exceeded in 1940 only by *Request Concert;* for the years 1941–1942, it was the sixth most popular film, reaping 6.2 million Reichsmark. See Stephen Lowry, *Pathos und Politik* (Tübingen, Niemeyer, 1989) 269–271. Especially in the late thirties and early forties, many Nazi feature films had strong antisemitic elements, such as *Linen from Ireland* and *Robert and Bertram* (both 1939). Yet few concentrate on the "Jewish question." These include *The Rothschilds* and the "documentary" *The Eternal Jew* (both 1940).

5. See Slavoj Žižek's *The Sublime Object of Ideology* (London and New York: Verso, 1989, especially 87–130). Žižek does not restrict the idea of social fantasy to Nazism, but argues that societies are always marked by ruptures rendering impossible the utopian visions of the ideologies that hold them together. In response to this fundamental rupture or "blockage," societies "invent" social fantasies to mask the impossibility of the ideals by which they identify themselves. Unlike "pure" ideology critique, social fantasy acknowledges the *pleasure* offered by constructs like the "Jew."

6. Friedman, Régine Mihal, *L'Image et son Juif* (Paris: Payot, 1983).

7. *The Jew's Body* (New York and London: Routledge, 1991) 1–9.

8. The SS Security Service filed monthly "Reports from the Reich" that attempted to gauge public reaction, especially to prestigous films. The reports on *Jew Süß* claim that the film indeed generated animosity toward the Jews. See Leiser, op. cit., 152–154. The film was shown to SS units before they were set into action against Jews, to non-Jews in areas from which Jews were to be deported, and to concentration camp guards, some of whom testified at the Nürnberg trials that inmates were subsequently mistreated. Before concluding that the film *necessarily* generated antisemitic sentiments or activities, a number of questions need to be raised: How representative for the general film-going public is a group of, for example, SS men who have clearly been "trained" in antisemitic thought and conditioned to view the film in these terms? When a film like *Jew Süß* has been commissioned by the state, to what extent might expectations and projections have figured in the Security Service reports themselves? Might they, for example, magnify a few antisemitic comments from the audience? (According to the same reports, *The Rothschilds*, which flopped at the box office, was "eagerly anticipated" and created a "flurry of excitement"; see Welch, op. cit., 268.) While *Jew Süß* uses all the tools of classical cinema to involve its spectator emotionally, these are the same tools that can be used to target any individual or group, to generate at least momentary, cathartic feelings. Indeed, even the Security Service reports stress how impressed the public was by the film's performances. Although *Jew Süß* most certainly was a part of a dangerous public discourse, I would be cautious in ascribing too much "political" power to it alone.

9. Besides Harlan's film, the best-known versions are Wilhelm Hauff's novella of 1827, Lion Feuchtwanger's novel of 1925, and a British film, also called *Jew Süß*, by Lothar Mendes of 1934. See also Manfred Zimmermann, *Joseph Süß Oppenheimer. Ein Finanzmann des 18. Jahrhunderts* (Stuttgart: Rieger'sche Verlagsbuchhandlung, 1874), Selma Stern, *Jud Süß: Ein Beitrag zur Deutschen und zur Jüdischen Geschichte* (1929; Munich: Gotthold Müller, 1973).

10. The estates were a national elective assembly representing the social "estates," or orders in a number of European countries from the fourteenth through the eighteenth centuries. Until weakened or abolished by absolutist rulers in the eighteenth century, the estates considerably restricted the powers of provincial rulers. The Württemberg estates were among the most powerful and persistent in Germany; they included almost no nobility and were dominated by Lutheran ministers and burghers. The Württemberg estate constitution, which the Duke vows to respect in the beginning of *Jew Süß*, was in place until 1805.

11. Hollstein, op. cit., 78. For a more detailed summary of Süß's life, see Hollstein, 77–78.

12. *Hamburger Tageblatt*, 18.11. 1939, as quoted in Hollstein, op. cit., 76. Hollstein, who has researched the sources for the film most carefully, concludes that the script virtually ignored both historical and literary versions of the Süß story and produced an "independent version of the . . . topic" (Nollstein, op. cit., 78).

13. The historic Süß Oppenheimer also had a reputation as a womanizer, but was not condemned for the same reason because this would have implicated numerous courtly women involved with him.

14. See, for example, Lessing's debate with his contemporaries about how tragedy affects its reader or viewer: *Briefwechsel über das Trauerspiel: Lessing, Nicolai, Mendelssohn*, ed. Jochen Schulte-Sasse (Munich: Winkler, 1972).

15. The genre does allow for ambiguities that complicate the narratives and allow for convincing characterizations.

16. *Emilia Galotti* V, 8. The prince, unable to see his own culpability, lays the blame on Marinelli: "Is it not enough—to the misfortune of so many—that princes are human beings; must there also be devils disguised as their friends?" "Ist es, zum Unglücke so mancher nicht genug, daß Fürsten Menschen sind; müssen sich auch noch Teufel in ihren Freund verstellen?"

17. This interweaving of private and public reconciles the bourgeois tragedy to

Nazism's "totalization" of the private, to its recasting of divergent individual desires as one collective desire. At the same time, the eighteenth century began to discursively equate the public sphere with family, as suggested by the term *Landesvater*, or father of the country, for the ruler.

18. The film ingeniously preserves the emancipatory "feeling" of the bourgeois tragedy by emulating its anticentralist, antiabsolutist ideology, encoded in Süß's plan to instate Karl Alexander as an absolute, centralist ruler "like the Sun-King in Versailles" (a step that National Socialism codes within a destructive process of modernization). Geraint Parry analyzes the failure of Enlightenment rationality to anchor itself firmly in German cultural life ("Enlightened Government and its Critics in 18th Century Germany, "The *Historical Journal* 2 (1963) 185). Under the influence of Rousseau's reception in Germany, Sentimentality and Storm and Stress (e.g., Lessing, Herder, the early Goethe) reacted against the potential tyranny inherent in an excessively centralized, rational view of society and politics. Increasingly eighteenth-century artists and theoreticians came to focus on the "heart" as a category of humanity, to valorize intuitive knowledge over purely discursive learning. Süß's plan to modify the governance of Württemberg alludes to the historical competition between rulers seeking absolute power and the Estates during the eighteenth century, and typifies centralistic, rationalistic thinking in three ways: (1) it aims at dissolving the Estates, which compromise the sovereign's power; (2) it involves borrowing foreign soldiers to suppress popular revolt—a strategy historically typical of absolutist governments; (3) the idea of replacing the Estates with a ministry emulates the absolutist cameralistic practice of hiring an elite of trained specialists to administer the people's "welfare"—a practice that subordinates community experience to theoretical "expertise." This construction of a political "machine" is also typical of rationalist philosophy, in which the metaphor of the machine is commonly employed to describe the function of politics.

19. Règine Mihal Friedman, "Male Gaze and Female Reaction: Veit Harlan's *Jew Süß* (1940)," in *German Cinema and Gender*, ed. Sandra Frieden et al. (Providence, RI: Berg Publishers, 1993) II: 125–26.

20. Nancy Armstrong, *Desire and Domestic Fiction* (New York and Oxford: Oxford University Press, 1987) 5.

21. Michel Foucault, *History of Sexuality*, Vol. 1, trans. R. Hurley (New York: Random House, 1978) 121.

22. Dorothea von Mücke, *Virtue and the Veil of Illusion: Generic Innovation and the Pedagogical Project in Eighteenth-Century Literature* (Stanford, CA: Stanford University Press, 1991) 113.

23. Richard Leppert, "Music, Domestic Life and Cultural Chauvinism. Images of British Subjects at Home in India," in *Music and Society. The Politics of Composition, Performance and Reception*, ed. Richard Leppert and Susan McClary (Cambridge: Cambridge University Press, 1987) 63–104.

24. Leppert, op. cit., 87. Elsewhere Leppert has analyzed the complementarity of music and violence. Proceeding from the painting of war and hunt scenes on pianos, he argues that musical aesthetics, "marked female, serve as the peaceful product of violence"; the two are linked "answering the cause of mutual justification." Richard Leppert, "Sexual Identity, Death, and the Family Piano in the Nineteenth Century," *The Sight of Sound: Music, Representation, and the History of the Body* (Berkeley and Los Angeles: University of California Press, 1993) 127 and 128. Nazi cinema makes this connection most explicitly in *Das Fräulein von Barnhelm*, where the music Minna plays on the harpsichord becomes a kind of nondiegetic accompaniment in the war-montage sequence that follows.

25. The play that comes to mind when one thinks of the eighteenth century in these terms is Lessing's *Nathan the Wise* (1779), with its famous plea for religious tolerance. While an important step in the development of bourgeois literature, *Nathan* is a "Dramatic Poem" and not a tragedy.

26. Gilman, op. cit., 12.

27. *Robert and Bertram* and *The Rothschilds* also ascribe aristocratic hedonism and egotism to Jews; moreover, both films mock Jews' imitation of an aristocratic lifestyle.

28. Karl Alexander's preference for a "no-nonsense" *(klipp und klar)* discourse contrasts with the embellished and insincere rhetoric of courtly language, and works along with his frequent reference to the people of Württemberg as "my Swabians" to establish him as a fundamentally redeemable character. Military language as well as shared military experiences link him with Colonel von Roeder, whose "soldierly" virtue the film incessantly highlights.

29. Žižek, op. cit., 128.

30. This does not mean we need to assume the bourgeois tragedy was successful in its political agenda, or that it was without its own internal contradictions and misogyny. For a feminist critique of the genre see Dorothea von Mücke or Silvia Bovenschen in *Die imaginerte Weiblichkeit. Exemplarische Untersuchungen zu kulturgeschichtlichen und literarischen Präsentationsformen des Weiblichen* (Frankfurt: Suhrkamp, 1979).

31. Certain characteristics of *Jew Süß* borrowed from nineteenth-century melodrama—like the quotation of *Tosca* in the rape scene or the allusion to the "Dead Girl From the Seine" in the drowned Dorothea—give the film a feeling of kitsch. It is important, however, that the melodrama we think of as "depoliticized" grew historically out of genres like the bourgeois tragedy. Jürgen Link has traced historical connections between popular cultural texts and "high" literary genres like the bourgeois tragedy. Since the nineteenth century, popular narratives have emulated the structure of the bourgeois tragedy, but tended to diminish its articulation of social antagonism by foregrounding the "natural-human" traits (chastity vs. promiscuity, trust vs. calculation, eroticism vs. lack of eroticism, and so forth) that define literary characters while reducing the "social" factors (class, wealth) that define them. Link regards the "black and white" structure of modern popular narratives essential to their affirmative social function; the general devolution of what he calls the social-psychological drama to "kitsch" is not to be sought in either the incompetence of author or public, but in the genre itself and in the society which functionalizes it. J. Link, "Von 'Kabale und Liebe' zur 'Love Story'—Zur Evolutionsgesetzlichkeit eines bürgerlichen Geschichtentyps," *Literarischer Kitsch*, ed. Jochen Schulte-Sasse (Tübingen: Niemeyer, 1979) 121–155.

32. Žižek's analogy of antisemitism's "Jew" and body snatchers rests on the impossibility of distinguishing the latter from "normal" humans, as the unfathomability of the alien's desire; *The Sublime Object of Ideology* 89.

33. Trans. Ralph Manheim (Boston: Houghton-Mifflin, 1943) 309.

34. Dracula first appears in his familiar elegant evening clothes in a drama from the late 1920s by Hamilton Deane and John L. Balderston. The play was set in London, and theatrical conventions of the time prescribed that the villain had to be a person one could believably invite into one's living room. See David Skal, *Hollywood Gothic: The Tangled Web of Dracula from Novel to Stage to Screen* (New York and London: W. W. Norton and Co., 1990) 69–70.

35. See, for example, *Fantasy and the Cinema*, ed. James Donald (London, British Film Institute, 1989) or James Twitchell, *The Living Dead: A Study of the Vampire in Romantic Literature* (Durham, NC: Duke University Press, 1981).

36. Dracula has also been read as a metaphor for fascism itself. Just after World War II, Richard Wasson claimed Dracula was an unconscious parable of Old Central Europe attempting to destroy New Western Europe. For Wasson, Dracula is a fascist besieging western civilization; his first victim is Lucy Westerna (light of the West). See Twitchell, op. cit., 139.

37. Kovel, op. cit., 57.

38. Linda Williams, "When the Woman Looks," in *Re-vision: Essays in Feminist Film Criticism*. ed. Mary Ann Doane et al. (Los Angeles: American Film Institute, 1984) 83–99.

39. Cf. Mary Ann Doane's discussion of the eye as a metonymy for murderous intentions in gothic women's films of the forties, such as *Suspicion* (1941), *Gaslight* (1944),

or *The Spiral Staircase* (1946); *The Desire to Desire* (Bloomington and Indianapolis: Indiana University Press, 1987) 127.

40. Doane, op. cit., 126.

41. Friedrich Knill; "Die Gemeinsamkeit von Faschisten und Antifaschisten gegenüber dem N.S. Film 'Jud Süss'" 66.

42. See Sander Gilman's discussion of the Jewish nose as phallus, 126–27.

43. Kaja Silverman, following C. J. Flugel, has discussed the importance of the eighteenth-century shift in male clothing as a kind of "revisualization of sexual difference," resulting in a despecularization of the male subject and a concomitant hyperspecularization of the female subject. *The Acoustic Mirror* (Bloomington: University of Indiana Press, 1988) 24–27.

44. Hitler, op. cit. 309–311.

45. Moische Postone, "Anti-Semitism and National Socialism: Notes on the German Reaction to 'Holocaust,'" *New German Critique* 11 (1980) 109.

46. Others, of course, have pointed out that "petty-bourgeois anticapitalism" attacks finance capital. See, for example, Daniel Guerin's 1936 study, *Fascism and Big Business:* "Throughout the nineteenth century, the petty-bourgeois theoreticians attacked not *producing* capitalism, but *idle* capitalism—the lender, the banker . . . Fascism, in its turn, concentrates its attacks on 'loan capital', and thereby expresses the aspirations of the middle classes while diverting the working masses from the struggle against capitalism as a whole." (New York: Monad Press, 1973) 82*f.*

47. A certain irony is at work in the film narrative and in Nazi discourse; the abstractness of capitalism is represented by the "Jew," who as I mentioned is a particularly specularized object. This recalls the paradox Kaja Silverman calls attention to with respect to cultural gender coding: "man, with his 'strikingly visible' organ, is defined primarily in terms of abstract and immaterial qualities such as potency, knowledge, and power, whereas woman, whose genitals do not appeal to the gaze, becomes almost synonymous with corporeality and specularity." Silverman, op. cit., 164.

48. *Schächten* (from Yiddish *schechtn*, Hebrew *schachat*) refers to the slaughter of animals and poultry according to a prescribed Jewish ritual, prohibited by the Nazis in 1933. Cf. *Brockhaus Enzyklopädie*, 16: 528 (Wiesbaden: Brockhaus, 1973).

49. See Theweleit, *Male Fantasies*, vol. 2, trans. Erica Carter and Chris Turner (Minneapolis: University of Minnesota Press, 1989) 13, and Gilman, "The Jewish Murderer" 104–27 and "The Jewish Disease," 210–33.

50. Cf. Christian Metz's commentary on the lap dissolve in *The Imaginary Signifier*, trans. C. Britton et al. (Bloomington: Indiana University Press, 1982): "the moment of travel is emphasized and expanded, and this already has the value of a metalinguistic commentary. Moreover, by *hesitating* a little on the threshold of a textual bifurcation, the text makes us attend more closely to the fact that it performs a weaving operation. . . ." (276) "it has a remarkable *capacity to metonymise*" (279).

51. *Jew Süß*'s analogy of Jews to parasites is also central to *The Eternal Jew*, which compares the Jews to rats spreading the plague and juxtaposes scenes of rats to scenes of Jews, who "always remain alien bodies in the organism of their host nation."

52. I am referring to Kantorowicz's well-known analysis of medieval political theory in *The King's Two Bodies. A Study in Mediaeval Political Theology* (Princeton, NJ: Princeton University Press, 1957).

53. Indeed, all of Wagner's protagonists since his first "Wagnerian" opera fit the prototype of a figure who does penance for some original sin by wandering aimlessly, longing fervently for redemption by a woman. Moreover, a number of Dracula renditions code him in a similarly sympathetic way (cf. Herzog's *Nosferatu*, Coppola's *Bram Stoker's Dracula*).

54. Doane, *The Desire to Desire* 138.

55. Steve Neale, "Propaganda," *Screen* 18 (Autumn 1977): 26. Significantly, as Neale

points out, the Aryan character who falls short of the bourgeois moral standard, the Duke, is fat and ugly: "the disorder that is centered on his sexual appetite and which inaugurates Süß's rise to power is marked on his body and reinforced by the contrast between his appearance and that of the other 'Aryan' characters in the film"; Neale, op. cit., 27.

56. Süß's masquerade extends beyond the visual. His adoption of the francophile courtly discourse I discussed earlier serves as another kind of mask, concealing his "real" intentions.

57. According to an interview with Harlan in *Der Film* on January 20, 1940, the choice of one actor for these roles was intended to show the similar roots of Jewry: "It was meant to show how all these different temperaments and characters—the pious patriarch, the wily swindler, the penny-pinching merchant and so on—are ultimately derived from the same roots." Quoted in Welch, op. cit., 287.

58. Kovel, op. cit., 91.

59. Jürgen Link, "Fanatics, Fundamentalists, Lunatics, and Drug Traffickers—The New Southern Enemy Image," trans. Linda Schulte-Sasse, *Cultural Critique* 19 (Fall 1991): 33–53.

60. January 20, 1940; quoted in Leiser, op. cit., 152.

61. Hull, op. cit., 165. Marian's screen personae were often morally compromised, as is Cagliostro in *Münchhausen*, Cecil Rhodes in *Ohm Krüger*, and the lover and husband in *Romance in a Minor Key* and *La Habañera*, respectively.

62. Siegfried Zielinski and Thomas Maurer, "Bausteine des Films 'Jud Süß,'" *"Jud Süß" Filmprotokoll, Programmheft und Einzelanalysen* (Berlin: Spiess, 1983) 32.

63. Friedman, op. cit., 132.

64. "Fiction and Its Phantoms: A Reading of Freud's *'Das Unheimliche'* ('The Uncanny')" *New Literary History* 7 (Spring 1976): 543.

65. James Donald, "The Fantastic, the Sublime and the Popular Or, What's at Stake in Vampire Films?" *Fantasy and the Cinema*, ed. J. Donald (London: British Film Institute, 1989) 247.

66. As quoted in Theweleit, op. cit., 2: 9–10.

67. The film attempts to explain revenge as "Jewish" when Süß refers to the Jewish "God of revenge—an eye for an eye, a tooth for a tooth." It also disavows that revenge is Christian, when it contends he does not seek "retribution, but what is right." An eye for an eye, a tooth for a tooth; that's not our way." Ironically, revenge is precisely what is sadistically and pleasurably carried out in the execution scene that follows Sturm's remark.

68. See also Neale, op. cit., 26.

69. The *Film-Kurier* also highlights Süß's threatening gaze, having on its cover a close-up of him (in his "original" caftan and beard) looking up so as to expose much of the whites of his eyes. Inside is a still (not from the film), in which he looks through magnifying spectacles used to examine jewelry.

70. Williams, op. cit., 89.

71. *Dracula* (New York: Barnes and Noble, 1992) 305.

72. See Twitchell, op. cit., 136–7.

73. Gilbert: *Nürnberger Tagebuch* (Frankfurt, 1962) 119, quoted in Theweleit, op. cit., 2: 12.

74. The filmic articulation of Dorothea's death reveals a shift away from relatively autonomous eighteenth-century women like Emilia. The latter similarly exists as the object of desire and likewise bears a "guilt" (of desiring) which has been the focus of much scholarly discussion. See, for example, Harry Steinhauer, "The Guilt of Emilia Galotti," *Journal of English and Germanic Philology* 48 (1949) 173*ff.* Emilia articulates, however, her own "guilt," which thus becomes linked with her integrity, complexity, and character development. She atones for her guilt by forcing her father to kill her (a fully autonomous act reversing the *Virginia* tradition on which the drama is based, in which the decision to kill the daughter usually rests with the father).

75. Söderbaum was Harlan's wife and one of Nazi cinema's most popular actresses (cf.

Lowry, op. cit., 60–61). Her screen persona was strongly marked by continuity in type and fate, suggesting sadomasochistic elements in her appeal.

76. Friedländer refers to the "frisson" created by this opposition between the harmony of kitsch and the evocation of death and destruction as a "bedrock of Nazi aesthetics." *Reflections of Nazism* (New York: Harper & Row, 1982) 27.

77. Apropos the vampire parallel, in John Badham's film version of *Dracula* (1979), Dracula is "executed" in a strikingly similar, ignominious manner to Süß. Professor van Helsing throws a hook into Dracula's back, by means of which he is hoisted high onto the mast of a ship, where he dangles helplessly until the sun destroys him. The finality of this purgation is called into question, however, like that of *Jew Süß*, as a bat flies into the horizon.

78. Steve Neale has analyzed how the film threatens to rupture its own boundaries at the end, when Sturm exhorts that future generations should uphold the ban on the Jews. The exhortation is spoken to a diegetic audience, but "really" to the film audience, and hence borders on undermining the narrative closure. Sturm's semidirect audience address allows the film to approach a mode of address Neale argues is constitutive of "propaganda": it aligns "the subject as in a position of struggle vis-à-vis certain of the discourses and practices that have been signified within [the text], and signified in such a way as to mark them as existing outside and beyond it." Neale, op. cit., 31.

Torments of the Flesh, Coldness of the Spirit: Jewish Figures in the Films of Rainer Werner Fassbinder

GERTRUD KOCH

T HE POLITICAL discussions and intrigues surrounding Fassbinder's play, *The Garbage, the City, and Death*, have assumed the dimensions of a show trial which, regardless of the jury, pursued only one objective: an unequivocal sentence—guilty of anti-Semitism or not. Whether mud-slinging or whitewashing, the rhetorical fireworks in effect made all distinctions evaporate. Günther Rühle, for instance, performed one such operation during the public discussions in advance of the production, when he poured bleach over the "rich Jew" so as to make him shine above the low life of prostitutes, gays and criminals. Likewise, the masochistic Left in West Germany managed to fade out the last hues of red and to denounce themselves as the black sheep: "even Goebbels started out as a leftist!"

What was lost in all these debates was the possibility to read Fassbinder's fragmentary work for the ways it registers the relationship of those born after World War II toward German history and its Jewish victims. There is little doubt that those "gentlemen with their executive cases in the bar car from Frankfurt to Munich," who, as Jürgen Habermas noted after Bitburg, vent their anti-Semitism with a "new frankness," are the same people who, in public, raise the charge of anti-Semitism against Fassbinder and hope that it will hit the Left—the double standard has a field day. Therefore, it is all the more important that we examine the discursive economy through which these issues are articulated in Fassbinder's work and trace his particular representation of German-Jewish history in the turns of a peculiar history of representation.

Until the mid 1960s, aesthetic debates as to the representability of National Socialism, anti-Semitism, and the Holocaust took place primarily in the area of the theater, where plays of a wide formal variety and different national backgrounds were produced. With *The Investigation* (1965), Peter Weiss offered a dramatization of the Auschwitz Trial which, in its extreme coolness and rigidity, demonstrated the mechanisms of dehumanization. According to a contemporary analysis of the play, Weiss's technique of presentation was tantamount to a renunciation of traditional theater: "It actually ceases to be theater in the traditional sense. If Weiss calls his drama an *oratorio*, that is not only consistent with it being a

Reprinted from *New German Critique* 38 (1986): 28–38.

requiem, but also because the oratorio is defined by a static, *undramatic* quality, a basic lack of action."[1]

A report, which is at the same time an oratorio: that is to say, in terms of content, *The Investigation* reports about a trial and its reconstruction of the reality of the extermination camp at Auschwitz; in formal terms, it recasts the textual material to create an oratorio, a requiem. Peter Weiss' attempt to blend into aesthetic form remembrance and mourning stands under the spell of the historical trial. It is a form which tries to avoid the problem of realistic modes of representation as well as a narrative reduction of the subject matter which focuses on an individual fate, as exemplified by the popular play based on *The Diary of Anne Frank*. The paradox of referring to Auschwitz as a reality, which by definition defies aesthetic representation, a reality which can only be described, and at the same time shaping this very description into the aesthetic form of an oratorio, this paradox delineates the problems more clearly than all of the well-meaning plays, which, in a pedagogical manner, aim at catharsis through identification. These problems are inseparable from the reality of Auschwitz itself: "How does one say it? Auschwitz happened." (Maurice Blanchot) The documentary material of the historical Auschwitz trial as arranged by Weiss offers a resistance to the symbolization of Auschwitz, an opposition to the way in which it is recuperated as an existentially incomprehensible term by tight-lipped official speakers for the purpose of exonerating those who were concretely involved in making it possible. In *The Investigation*, one of the witnesses shows himself to be sensitive in the face of the false tones of pathos, when he says:

"We must drop the lofty view that the camp world is incomprehensible to us. We all know the society that produced a government capable of creating such camps."

Weiss' intention, above all, is to educate the viewer as to the facts of history. At the same time, the form of the oratorio subjects this enlightenment pathos to the remembrance of the dead. The subsequent history of Weiss' *Investigation* has become symptomatic of a new form of repression of the past. Not only was *The Investigation* one of the most-performed plays and now appears as a key work of the time, but it has recently re-emerged, for a second time, in an exemplary position owing to its reception and staging history. After 17 parallel premieres in October 1965, the play was performed on over 30 more stages up until 1967. Thereafter it disappeared from the scene for twelve years. Its revival in 1980 caused a scandal when Schulte-Michels restaged *The Investigation* at the Freie Volksbühne Berlin with a production first presented at the Schlosstheater Moers, but this time for the Berlin stage. Elsbeth Wolffheim described the events in the following way: "To briefly sketch the scandal: extravagantly made-up actors perform in a nightclub atmosphere, walking up and down a catwalk—they laugh, applaud one another, dance to popular music and evoke associations of a Tingel-Tangel show. The intention of the director: First, he wants to unmask the false piety (*Scheinpietät*), which seizes us whenever the subject is concentration camps. Next, he wants to denounce as voyeurism—as a 'gourmet thrill,' as a 'frivolous delight'—the sentimental greed for information already observed in the reception of the 'Holocaust' tv-film. And finally, he thereby intends to assault the repressive mechanisms that sustain the Federal Republic, indeed explode them wherever possible. There is no reason to doubt the sincerity of this intention. However, from the many reactions to this production we may infer that the ensemble and Schulte-Michels sought to realize this intention with unsuitable means. Above all, many audience members and critics rejected the device of having defendants and witnesses be portrayed by the same actors. When it is thus crudely literalized on stage, the interchangeability claimed by the 3rd Witness in *The Investigation* becomes a scandal, a provocation."[2]

With this new production, *The Investigation* had become part of that "reflection of Nazism" which Saul Friedländer has in mind in his study, *Kitsch and Death*.[3] A similar slippage in interpretation can be seen in a comparison of the productions of Sobol's *Ghetto* play by Peter Zadek in Berlin and by the Theater in Haifa. The process of converting fascism and Nazism into myth, which began in the mid 1970s, and which Friedländer describes as a phenomenon observable not only in the FRG, has made its mark even more strongly in West German cinema than in the theater. In his short essay, "What Does That Mean: Working through the Past," Theodor Adorno perceptively pointed out that historical facts themselves could possibly fall prey to repression and denial: "From a socio-psychological point of view, we may infer that the damaged collective narcissism is only lying in wait to be restored and seizes upon everything which allows consciousness to reconcile the past with these narcissistic desires—and that it also, wherever possible, re-models reality in such a way that the damage appears never to have happened."[4]

Part of this re-modelling of reality is the extinguishing of concrete memories of the extermination and expulsion of the Jews, and the displacement of these memories by mythic re-interpretations. That is to say, if Adorno's theory is correct, it could be traced empirically in changed perspectives on Jewish figures since 1945. Noticeable is their exclusion from those films of the 1950s and 1960s which were very much part of the restoration of the film industry. A systematic, empirical analysis would probably show a shift from the anti-Semitic stereotype of the NS films to a philo-Semitic one. Of the roughly 1,000 films which were made in the Federal Republic between 1949 and 1961, it is to be sure an absolute minority which thematizes in any way the history or the present-day existence of the Jews.

In 1961 there was a scandal surrounding Helmut Käutner's film *Schwarzer Kies* (Black Pebbles), a scandal not that dissimilar in structure from the most recent one that surrounded Fassbinder. As I have not seen this film myself, I shall quote Dorothea Hollstein on this conflict: "In April 1961 the General Secretary of the Central Commission of Jews in Germany, Dr. van Dam, brought charges (according to DPA, the German Press Agency) against the film *Schwarzer Kies*, against the director Helmut Käutner, and against the producer Walter Ulbrich, explaining that the film constituted a public defamation of Jews by characterizing a brothel owner as being Jewish."[5] From a contemporary review of the film one learns that in *Schwarzer Kies* the Jewish figure is cursed as a "Jewish pig" (*Judensau*) by an old Nazi,[6] and that it was this sequence which led to the charges. Käutner, who understood his film to be "realistic," had evidently confused realism and reality. Similarly as in the later Fassbinder debates, one finds again and again the attempt to legitimize an aesthetic depiction by direct reference to so-called reality, i.e., the stereotyped argument that, in the final analysis, there *really* were rich Jewish speculators. Above all, the remarkable predilection of West-German cinema for what Alexander Kluge once called "middle-of-the-road realism" (*mittleren Realismus*) is altogether characterized by an incongruity between realistic form and the experientally unfounded stereotyping of people and patterns of action. As a result, a discrepancy arises between a hyper-realistic setting and totally clichéd characters, which lack any psychological conviction.

In an aesthetic configuration such as this, Jewish figures inevitably appear especially stereotyped because, as a rule, the pedantic realism of setting has not been able to develop a code for a Jewish milieu and therefore does not even achieve any appearance of reality. (Among other things, religious artifacts from synagogues are used as decoration in "Jewish" apartments.)

Plausibly enough, a contemporary critic wrote of *Schwarzer Kies*: "Wavering between the documentarist attempt to endeavor to fix a part (a hardly representative part of that) of the realities of the Federal Republic, and the attempt to blend with this a dramaturgical conception of traffic accidents and erotic triangles, the story finally carries off the victory. . . . Accordingly, the time and place (Hunsrück Airbase, October 1960) are convincing only when the action is suspended."[7] A historical analysis of such motifs makes sense in methodological terms only as an analysis of configurations and not as a study of a theme detached from the context in which it appears. Therefore, a serious study of the depiction of Jews in films of the years between 1945 and 1965 would have to concern itself primarily with such concepts of realism.

It would be interesting to study the forms of narrative realism in postwar cinema, to trace their origins in the literary tradition. In a recent analysis of the Jewish figures of Gustav Freytag, Hans Otto Horch[8] has brought attention to the problem of "programmatic realism," based on an "allegorizing conception of figures," which the subsequent reception has been misunderstood as representational realism. Gustav Freytag, especially in his novel *Credit and Debit* (*Soll und Haben* 1855), ranks (contrary to the intentions of the author) as the classical author of anti-Semitic literature, although, in his historical context, he saw himself as an ally of the contemporary Jewish emancipation movement. The debate surrounding Gustav Freytag became topical in the mid 1970s when Fassbinder announced his intention of filming *Soll und Haben*.

In his later films Fassbinder developed a pronounced predilection for forms of allegorizing which challenged the customary representational realism. This stylistic device, however, situated him in a climate in which the boundaries of the critically-intended "programmatic realism" have long since been overstepped by those forms of allegorizing neo-mythologies described by Friedländer. Since Fassbinder is one of the few new German film-makers of consequence who has placed Jewish figures in prominent positions in his work, I will attempt, in the following, to trace the configurations in which these figures stand. It is my belief that Fassbinder, on the one hand, is misunderstood in a similar way as Gustav Freytag, in particular if his allegorical figures are taken for representations, but that, by the same token, he nonetheless conveys anti-Semitic clichés in his allegorizations.

Although a number of thought-provoking, not to say questionable, Jewish figures appear in Fassbinder's films, they are hardly ever discussed by the West German critics. Such omissions reflect the ambivalent construction of the Jewish figures in the films themselves. In the innumerable obituaries the charge of anti-Semitism raised against Fassbinder was occasionally mentioned, but the Jewish figues in his films were never discussed. In the ranks of societal victims, fringe groups, and oppressed people whom Fassbinder emphatically adopted, there is no place for Jews—and there is, I believe, a very good reason for this.

Firstly, for the sake of clarity, we have to differentiate between Fassbinder's explicit statements on society, politics and also his films on the one hand and the textual constructions of his films on the other. As a political figure, Fassbinder was certainly not an anti-Semite, but somebody who related critically to the Federal Republic and German history. Of all his films, this attitude was most present in his contribution to *Germany in Autumn*, in the interview with his mother. Here, as in many of his earlier films, he maintained an analytic coldness in his view of people and the petrified conditions in which they live and under which their emotions start to run amuck.

There are few new German film-makers who are capable of such precise insights into the "marriages of our parents" (as he had called an unrealized film project), into the terrors which the oak-panelled heirlooms of the German bourgeoisie and the scrubbed kitchens of the lower-middle class held for those who had installed them. The early Fassbinder freeze-dried the oppressively claustrophobic atmosphere of Germany and pulverized it; that was his strength. He did not portray Martha's torments in *Martha* as the melodrama of a failed middle-class marriage in a middle-of-the-road realism, but as a horror film of marital power and submission rituals. Not coincidentally, he considered Hitchcock's *Suspicion* to be *the* film about marriage. Films like *Katzelmacher, Why Does Herr R. Run Amok?, Martha, The Merchant of Four Seasons, Love is Colder than Death,* maintain, as it were, a distance from what is being shown. Indeed, they betray a subterranean sadistic delight in the act of staging these rituals. Fassbinder quite mistakenly took himself to task for this distance. He wanted to become what he believed the films of Douglas Sirk to have been: humane and full of sympathy. He admired the one-time star director of Ufa, Detlef Sierck and his lofty melodramas *La Habanera* and *Zu Neuen Ufern* (Life Begins Anew and To New Shores), as well as his American melodramas, to which one could well apply, in my opinion, what Adorno said in his critique of Wagner: "Virtue sentimentally reflects the terrors which it spreads."[9]

It is possible that Fassbinder saw in the person and films of Douglas Sirk a successfully crystallized symbiosis of Ufa and Hollywood aesthetics, with the result that he wanted to build a bridge via Sirk which would free him from the historical heritage of fascist aesthetics, to which Detlef Sierck certainly belonged, and which is still evident in his Hollywood films. When Fassbinder breaks though the floor of his own historical experience into the cellar of German history, he lands in a mythic space which he illuminates according to the Ufa lighting codes of direction and furbishes with sacrificial fantasies, slaughterhouse metaphors and redemption symbolism. Stylistic and thematic motifs can be traced from the drama *The Garbage, the City, and Death*, which was adapted by Daniel Schmidt in his *Shadow of Angels*, through *In a Year with Thirteen Moons*, the Epilogue to *Berlin Alexanderplatz, Lili Marleen* to *Veronika Voss*. In all of these films Jewish figures appear in crucial roles.

In *In a Year with Thirteen Moons* a Jewish brothel owner and real estate speculator, survivor of an extermination camp, is the figure of desire for whom protagonist Elvira undergoes a sex change to become a woman. In a long, impressive sequence set in a slaughter house, Elvira relates the story of her sufferings for passion. The sacrifice of the flesh, which Elvira undertook for love, is however rejected. Gottfried John plays the Jewish character as a cool, superior, manly figure, a man who enjoys women without himself becoming a slave to love. Thus, on a superficial level, the narrative offers a psychological motivation: the name of the extermination camp is a secret code which intervenes even as he makes love. But in the textual economy of the film this remains a rather cynical metaphor, in that it is displaced onto the slaughter house which is iconographically charged with Elvira's sacrifice. In *In a Year with Thirteen Moons* then, a displacement took place which continued to run through the other films: the displacement of the sacrificial fantasies away from the Jews onto those figures who are predestined in Fassbinder's cosmos to experience suffering of the body, to experience the torment of the flesh.

In the first episode of *Berlin Alexanderplatz*, Franz Biberkopf just released from jail, is followed, and finally accosted in the street by Nachum, who is recongizeable as an Eastern European Jew from his appearance (kaftan, hat, beard and ringlets). His background is then confirmed acoustically when we hear his artificial Germanized Yiddish. Nachum takes the confused Biberkopf into the apartment of his brother-in-law, Eliser. Here Biberkopf rolls from the couch onto the carpet, writhes, moans, a suffering lump of flesh, a groaning unhappy body. An inter-title interrupts the scene: "Instruction by example of Zannowich." The rest of the sequence is characterized by the depiction of Biberkopf's body, the whimpering and moaning which forces its way out of his doubled-up body, and Nachum's story of Zannowich, narrated with interruptions. In between, from off-screen, Fassbinder's voice comments, mostly in whispers, on Biberkopf's situation with sentences like "Repent shouldst thou: recognize what has happened; recognize what causes you anguish!" The words of the two speakers scratch into the passive, pained mountain of flesh: the mad, instructive stories of Nachum and the lightly mocking commentary of the narrator. Both dialogue and voice-over are contrapunctual to Biberkopf's groans and moans: He is the one who suffers, the one burdened with pain, while Nachum, on the other hand, may be crazy but has an intellectual relationship to the world, which allows him to interpret it; he does not merely suffer. Here, too, the Jewish figure slips into the privileged position of he who disposes over the interpretation of the world, over language, over the intellect.

Finally, in the Epilogue, which compresses the quintessence of Biberkopf-style life into a collage of operatic elements, with angels and speaking corpses, the slaughter-house metaphor of *In a Year of Thirteen Moons* reappears. The slaughter house is the place of the sacrifice of the body, of torment and failed desire: Women peer out between tiled walls; bodies hang from the ceiling; people in uniform are busy with clusters of bodies. In another scenario Biberkopf is leaning over a torture table ready to be tortured. In all of these scenes of suffering there prevails a sexualized sadomasochistic atmosphere: The body as origin and goal of the somatic perception of pain and desire is the secret theme. The world of images, which feeds on historical extermination, is naturalized, dehistoricized in its projection onto the body. The signs of culture, of the intellect, are derisive symbols of authority: Reinhold, the central love-figure for Biberkopf, wears Christ's crown of thorns; Nachum swings a rosary. As Jewish figures, Nachum and Eliser are not merged into the suffering cosmos; they remain bearers of symbols or distanced observers. Thereby, Fassbinder positions them outside of his sacrificial fantasies, guards them indeed from being falsely bound within the subjective creations of a sado-masochistic projection, but also dismisses them from history. Like most of Fassbinder's Jewish figures, those in *Berlin Alexanderplatz* also are symbols of the cold intellect which looks down upon the enslaved flesh.

A similar constellation governs the relationship between the Jewish concert musician and the Tingeltangel singer in *Lili Marleen*. What begins as physical passion is completely eroded by the course of the film. At the end Willie, the singer, is the victim in the white hell of the sick bed, a destroyed body which sacrificed itself for love. The Jewish lover is betrayed into the hands of the Gestapo, made to listen to her song "Lili Marleen," but never subjected to direct physical torture.

The penultimate sequence of the film carries on a motif from *Berlin Alexanderplatz*. Willie and a decorated Nazi officer, who had supported Willie in her resistance activities on behalf of her lover, are fleeing through the forest—the same forest in which Reinhold murders Biberkopf's girl friend Mieze in the earlier film, and the Nazi officer tells Willie the story of that murder. Thus Fassbinder closes the bracket around his sacrificial fantasy of the body. Shortly thereafter Willie again searches out her lover who has risen to become a celebrated conductor. While he is bathed in ovation by the audience, she leaves him. The Jewish milieu in *Lili Marleen* is presented antipodically: The Mendelssohn family is characterized solely by the abstract medium of exchange and money, according to which the father arranges his son's love life and through which slave-trading is taken to its limit: Cold as the money and the intellect.

Finally, the motif is picked up again in an interlocking fashion in *Veronika Voss*. The drug addict Veronika Voss is a former Ufa star; passive, locked in a sick room, she suffers through the hellish torments of the body consumed by the drug, an exhibit in the horror show of the cold female Doctor Katz, who rules over her and her body. The Jewish doctor possesses all the traits of cold superiority. Then there is the elderly Jewish married couple, who are also dependent on the doctor's drugs. But here, too, Fassbinder elides the dimension of physical suffering: The elderly people show clear signs of an intellectualized aloofness from the world; they determine their own death as if history had placed them in the privileged position of those who have a self-reflected relationship with death and not a physical one. By contrast, we are shown, long drawn-out images of the physical decay, the torments and torture of Veronika Voss.

Fassbinder's creation of Jewish environments and figures which stand at an oblique angle to these sacrificial fantasies has little in common with the image of the *Stürmer* caricature which itself returned as an anti-Semitic cliché during the debate surrounding the play. In Fassbinder's work Jews are not wanton, rich, seductive, power-hungry or amoral. But neither are they included among the tormented victims, oppressed minorities, and suffering creatures like many of Fassbinder's characters. They could be called anti-figures, almost abstract, as in the figure of the "Rich Jew," who presents love negatively in the murder act by not blending it into a romantic *Liebestod*. He preserves love as an abstract idea, not as physical passion. In the film version (*Shadow of Angels*), however, Daniel Schmid's somewhat gentler aesthetic introduces instead a psychological motive, as he unfolds the murder as an act of tender intimacy before the scenery of the city.

Although Fassbinder never makes use of malicious anti-Semitic clichés in his films, there lies at the root of his creation an anti-Semitic motif, which often manifests itself in the form of a philo-Semitic stereotype: the picture of the Jew as the strict patriarch and man of intellect, law-abiding and austere. Latently accompanying Fassbinder's Jewish figures is the repressed anger at those who are seemingly superior, who despite extreme physical suffering still command moral superiority. Fassbinder himself, when asked about his conception of the Jews, refers back to an experience from his childhood when his mother admonished him in whispered tones to be polite and respectful to the neighbours because they "were Jews"—this she whispered behind her hand. In a manner of speaking, Fassbinder's anti-Semitism is a specific product of the mechanisms of repression contained in West German history.

The taboo, the law forbidding contact, the shutting out from the everyday consciousness, can all be located in Fassbinder's Jews: his own coldness and distance is projected onto the Jews as an intrinsic quality. They are the ones who are untouchable, cold, aloof, unattainable, unapproachable, arrogant, taking themselves for something better. At the same time, they function as a screen for the projection of a narcissistic yearning for love as in *In a Year with Thirteen Moons*. The displacement and repression of suffering and sacrifice is absorbed into a cosmos of physical self-mutilation, in which the Jews are allotted the ambivalent role of judges over life and death. This reaches its macabre climax in *Lili Marleen*, with its subliminal suggestion that the Jews had the power to free themselves from the Nazi camps, whereas the oppositional Willie and her helper have to hide in the woods after the liberation so as not to be pursued as Nazi collaborators.

Fassbinder's aesthetic is based upon allegorizing constructions, among which the much-troubled German-Jewish symbiosis assumes a special value. Whether one might share Gershom Scholem's interpretation or not that the German-Jewish symbiosis has never existed and that the idea of such a symbiosis was carried ad absurdum in Auschwitz; its spectre returns on an imaginary level: as a relationship of love or friendship with a fatal outcome. By way of comparison I will conclude with a brief sketch of another film that pertains to the same syndrome. This film contains no manifest or latent anti-Semitic motives but is nevertheless interesting within the context of repressed reactions to German-Jewish history.

In *Last Love* Ingemo Engström stages the German-Jewish symbiosis directly, employing fewer allusions, as a romantic pact of death between lovers. *Last Love* describes the journey of a daughter of Jewish refugees, who travels from Paris to the Rheinland so as to get to know her parent's homeland. The lack of a *Heimat*, (homeland), the motifs of journeying and strangeness provide here also the foil for the longing to dive into a German-Jewish death pact as a double suicide. Visits to a Jewish cemetery anticipate the death motif before the death *wish* is thematized. The young women's romantic involvement with a German teacher ends fatally: In front of a romantic river landscape, the smokestack of an atomic pile appears threateningly through the haze in the background. In Engström's case the diving into a German-Jewish symbiosis takes place as a utopian blending into each other, which is not the case with Fassbinder.

What appears symptomatic in all these films, however, is the coupling of Jewishness with the theme of death. For the survivors and those born after the Holocaust a utopian *longing* for death, the proximity to death meant, and still means little. Rather, it is experienced as an extreme, ever-present threat of survival, of being taken back into the cosmos of destruction.

Translated by Andy Spencer and Miriam Hansen

NOTES

*This is an expanded version of an essay that first appeared in: Elisabeth Kiderlen, ed., *Deutsch-jüdische Normalität: Fassbinders Sprengsätze* (Frankfurt: Pflasterstrand GmbH, 1985).

1. Ernst Schumacher, "*Die Ermittlung* von Peter Weiss," in Volker Canaris, ed., *Über Peter Weiss* (Frankfurt am Main: Suhrkamp, 1970), p. 78.

2. Elsbeth Wolffheim, "Über *Die Ermittlung* von Peter Weiss," in *Spectaculum 33* (Frankfurt am Main: Suhrkamp, 1980), p. 323.

3. Saul Friedländer, *Reflections of Nazism: An Essay on Kitsch and Death* (New York: Harper and Row, 1984).

4. Theodor W. Adorno, "Was bedeutet: Aufarbeitung der Vergangenheit," in *Eingriffe. Neun Kritische Modelle* (Frankfurt am Main: Suhrkamp, 1963), p. 136.

5. Dorothea Hollstein, "*Jud Süss und die Deutschen. Antisemitische Vorurteile im national-sozialistischen Spielfilm*" (Frankfurt am Main: Ullstein, 1983), p. 353.

6. (Marin Ripkens) "Schwarzer Kies," in *Filmkritik*, 5 (1961), p. 248.

7. Op. cit., p. 249.

8. Hans Otto Horch, "Judenbilder in der realistischen Erzählliteratur. Jüdische Figuren bei Gustav Freytag, Fritz Reuter, Berthold Auerbach und Wilhelm Raabe, in Herbert A. Strauss/Christhard Hottmann, *Juden und Judentum in der Literatur* (Munich: DTV, 1985), p. 151.

9. Theodor W. Adorno, "Fragmente über Wagner," in *Zeitschrift für Sozialforschung*, Doppelheft 1/2 (Paris, 1939), p. 4.

Europa Europa: On the Borders of *Vergangenheitsverdrängung* and *Vergangenheitsbewältigung*[1]

INGEBORG MAJER O'SICKEY and ANNETTE VAN

I

SINCE AGNIESZKA Holland's film *Europa Europa* (*Hitlerjunge Salomon*) was released in Germany in summer 1991, it has become one of the most hotly debated films in the recent history of German cinema. Curiously, it was not the general audience's reaction to the story of Salomon Perel's escape from National Socialist persecution that sparked an intensely political debate: the film, which was shown in Berlin and only a few other German cities, received an overall lukewarm response. Instead, discussion about *Europa Europa* in the German press consisted mainly of commentary about the film's supposed aesthetic failures and the German Export Film Union's decision not to nominate *Europa Europa* as Germany's entry for an Academy Award.[2] The union attributed its decision to the film's failure to conform to the U.S. Academy of Motion Picture Arts and Sciences' regulations. On the face of it, adherence to the U.S. Academy of Motion Picture Arts and Sciences' "national content rule" specifically means two things here: first, main artistic contributions should primarily come from German nationals; and second, the film in question should be funded by German monies. Apparently, *Europa Europa*'s multinational production (France and Germany; producers were Artur Brauner for CCC Filmkunst GmbH and Margaret Menegoz for Les Films du Losange) and its Polish director, Holland, violated the U.S. Academy of Motion Picture Arts and Sciences' national content rule.

This official reason for barring *Europa Europa* from the Academy Awards competition was rejected by certain critics, who interpreted the decision as an exclusionary practice motivated by the film's direct confrontation of Germany's Nazi past. "The film," charged Brauner, "doesn't fit into their concept of Germany today. [. . .] We've been censored" (Breslau 1992). Holland stated when she accepted her Golden Globe Award that the rejection of her film betokens Germans' "arrogance and hatred of foreigners," which she saw as having resurfaced in the newly united Germany (Lueken 1992).[3] For months, Germany's leading newspa-

---

This essay was written specifically for this volume and is published here for the first time by permission of the authors.

pers and news magazines became the arena for acrimonious debates on the commission's ruling.[4]

Shortly after the German Export Film Union's public statement of its official reason for barring the film from submission to the Academy, Brauner organized a highly publicized campaign. As reported (Dendler 1992), he brought proof of the film's "pure national origin" from the Ministry of Economy, wrote countless open letters, appeared on talk shows, and took out a one-page advertisement in *Filmecho*, appealing the commission's decision. Well-known film directors, such as Volker Schlöndorf, Wolfgang Peterson, and Michael Verhoeven, joined Brauner's campaign by publicly criticizing the commission's ruling. In one of the many curious twists of this campaign, the film's U.S. distributor (Orion Classics) entered the dispute, firmly supporting Brauner's crusade. It launched a letter campaign to the Oscar Jury and released an official statement that the film was not nominated by the German "Oscar" commission, because the German nominating committee didn't like the film's "political message and content" (Kruttschnitt 1992). In a well-publicized move, *Europa Europa* received the Golden Globe Award for Best Foreign Film in January 1992, an honor that is usually an omen for an Oscar nomination. U.S. coverage of the German Export Film Union's rejection *Europa Europa*'s had a distinct anti-German flavor that was not lost on the German press (Friedman 1992).[5]

What is remarkable about the German Export Film Union's adherence to the Academy Awards national content regulation is that it seems to support the notion that German entries must pass the German "racial purity" test.[6] Censorship thus camouflaged raises the issue of ownership: Who has the authority to tell the story of Nazi Germany? It also implies that national identity confers authority to tell and/or produce *Geschichte* (history) and *Geschichten* (personal stories).[7] If underlying the regulation lurks the peculiar notion that ethnic identity and nationality are related to the authorization to make a film that depicts the persecution of Jews, Holland's credentials more than qualify her. Holland, a Polish woman, whose Jewish father (a Polish Communist) survived World War II only to be apprehended and put to death by the Soviets after the liberation, knows about cultural dislocation; she lived for many years in the Diaspora. In 1981, she escaped from Poland after the military overpowered the Solidarity labor movement.[8] Additionally, her previous cinematic experience on similar subjects (notably, *Angry Harvest*, 1985) would appear to silence those who doubt the ability of an outsider to create a film about Germany during the Third Reich. Likewise, Brauner shares a similarly complex history. Brauner, who escaped from a concentration camp in East Poland shortly before the end of the war, had worked on many projects about the Shoah during his 45-year career.[9] But this essentialist argument misses the point as much as the German Export Film Union's adherence to the Academy's regulation does; basing its argument on an ideology that privileges homogeneity, it ignores the fact that the racialist, expansionist policies during the 12 years of National Socialism's attempt at a Thousand Year Reich transcended nationalities and borders. The notion that cinematic or other modes of representation of this particular part of history belong to Germans is clearly based on nationalist thinking that recalls the ideas of racial purity promoted during the Third Reich.

The failure to adequately distribute the film in German cinemas is as troubling as the politics underlying the national content rule. Since its release in summer 1991, the film was shown with only 30 copies and by March 1992 had been seen by only about 30,000 Germans. Jürgen Wohlrabe, a spokesman for the German distributor, CCC Filmkunst GmbH, justified the film's poor distribution when he said "85 percent of cinema goers are under twenty-six years old, and they are not interested in history" (Kruttschnitt 1992). While Wohlrabe's view that young German audiences are not interested in history is presented in an undifferentiated way, it may have some basis in fact. The film came upon the German scene during a period of intense social turmoil. A growing German neo-Nazi movement and increased nationalist anger, which has manifested itself in racialist attacks directed against both *Gastarbeiter* (foreign "guest workers") and Germans from the "Eastern territories;"[10] xenophobia generated by the runaway costs of unification, including higher taxes to rebuild East Germany, as well as rampant unemployment for the first time in 46 years in East Germany, all factor into reasons explaining the young moviegoers' disinterest in history. Indeed, one could argue that German attitudes toward the Nazi past generally correspond to the political and social events in Germany beginning in 1989 and extending into the 1990s. Consideration should be given to the reality that *Europa Europa*'s release coincided with a period, as after World War II, when some desired and others feared a renegotiation of borders; when constructions of national identity were questioned; when old anxieties about *Lebensraum* ("sufficient land to live on," a term that the Nazis used to justify colonization of other countries) resurfaced in the wake of the migration of a large number of *Volksdeutsche* (Germans who do not live in Germany but have German blood).[11] In fact, it is not outlandish to draw some parallels in terms of both historical moments: 1945 and the present. Arguments in the Adenauer years of Reconstruction during the 1950s, that "this is no time for reflection on the Nazi past," are recycled today. While the focus on rebuilding after World War II was concentrated on West Germany, today the focus has shifted to the construction of a *Wirtschaftswunder* (economic miracle) in the East. The effects of economic and ecological devastation in East Germany demand energies similar to the reconstruction necessary in the West during the 1950s. Moreover, the extent of the damage to East Germany during its experiment with Communism is just beginning to surface. East Germany recent discoveries of the machinations of its Communist regime, especially revelations that their own security forces (the *Stasi*) had compiled 6 million files on 18 million of its citizens, and the discovery that these files were compiled with the cooperation of civilian informers (i.e., their neighbors and family members);[12] the demand for punishment of members of the border death squad (with the indictment of Erich Honecker for murder as its most famed example); the hunt for *Mitläufer* (East Germans who simply went along) and for "politically in/correct" writers (hieroglyphed in the attacks on the East German writer, Christa Wolf), enable many to argue forcefully that it is more urgent to come to terms with events of the last 46 years than with those of the more distant past.

While the opinion that the decision not to nominate *Europa Europa* for the Academy Award was clearly based on the commission's "true motive that once again Germans did not want their working through the past to be disturbed by Jews" (*Der Spiegel*, 30 January 1992) cannot be dismissed as out of hand, the charge should be refracted through the general atmosphere in post-united Germany. Many Germans justifiably feel indignant about one-sided assessments of current manifestations of nationalism in the international press. They point to the numerous counter demonstrations since November 1992, in which hundreds of thousands of Germans of all ages have marched in protest against right-wing extremism in major German cities, that are rarely mentioned by the international press. Nevertheless, whether the fact that this film was made by so-called non-Germans had anything to do with the controversy this film engendered, is a legitimate question.

This would not be the first time that we saw distress about outsiders depicting material related to the Nazi period. The practice was first challenged in 1979 when the American-produced NBC television series *Holocaust* aired in West Germany.[13] At that time, the fact that this series was made by non-Germans made it easier for some West German critics to locate the film's revelations of German participation in racialist policies during National Socialism as being generated from outside of German borders, and it also enabled these critics to position themselves as the victims of an unfair attack by outsiders who "didn't really understand how it actually was." Günter Rohrbach, who was instrumental in bringing the series to Germany, must have anticipated the ownership question when he said that "It would be remarkable if the Germans, whose protagonists proceeded so purposefully in the annihilation of the Jews, were to raise special objections to the treatment of this theme by others" (Kaes 1989, 33). Indeed, this objection was raised, most directly by Edgar Reitz, who conceived his 15 1/2-hour, miniseries *Heimat* (*Homeland*) (1984) as a counterpoint to *Holocaust*, claiming it to be a more even-handed treatment of Germany's past.[14] Reitz accused the Americans of trespassing on German territory: "The most serious act of expropriation occurs when people are deprived of their history. With *Holocaust*, the Americans have taken away our history" (Elsaesser 1989, 272).

There are other similarities between *Europa Europa*'s reception and that of *Holocaust*. The ethicality of presenting stories dealing with the annihilation of more than 6 million Jews in the form of a melodrama and thriller has been raised once again in discussions of *Europa Europa*.[15] Some reviews in the German press denounced *Europa Europa* on similar grounds: the influentially conservative newspaper *Die Welt* called it "annoyingly silly" and "voyeuristic, speculatively sexo-maniacal," echoing one review which faulted the film as a commercially packaged sob-story, whose cardboard figures fail to engage the audience (Bodmer, 1992). Others accused the director and producer of trying to pass an unlikely story as true: Both *Die Weltwoche* and the left-wing newspaper *taz* doubted the veracity of the events portrayed in the film, calling the "story simply unbelievable" (*Der Spiegel*, January 1992). Even the Commission of the German Export Film Union added to the charge of noncompliance with the national content rule the criticism that the film "is embarrassing and does not fit into the atmosphere of luxurious entertainment in Hollywood." One of the Jury members is quoted as having said that "it's just impossible to present the Academy with such garbage" (*Der Spiegel*, January 1992).

It is not surprising, given that most of the films of the "New German Cinema" received more attention in countries outside of Germany,[16] that a central point stressed in many of New German Cinema's *Vergangenheitsbewältigungsfilme*[17] (especially those produced from 1975 to 1985) did not make much of an impression on most Germans. This central point is that the ideology that informed the racialist and sexist policies that characterized the National Socialist regime, was not simply erased. No ideological *tabula rasa*, no so-called *Stunde Null* ("Zero Hour") took place after 1945; on the contrary, certain practices and even desires for authoritarian structures continue from Hitler's Germany to the Federal Republic of Germany and the present unified Germany.

The filmmakers behind the *Hitlerwelle* ("Hitler wave"), as it became known in the West German press, thematized in many of its productions their disillusionment with the course that the new Federal Republic of Germany had taken since 1945. They frequently wove their disagreement with the arbitrary nature of the so-called denazification program, which was shaped and brought to a hasty end by West Germany's recruitment into the Cold War, their objection to West Germany's remilitarization, and their frustration with West Germany's wholesale acceptance of the ideology of the capitalist West into the tales of their films.[18] Feminist filmmakers, such as Helma Sanders-Brahms (*Deutschland, Bleiche Mutter*, 1980), Margarethe von Trotta (*Schwestern*, 1979; and *Bleierne Zeit*, 1981), Jutta

Brückner (*Hungerjahre in einem reichen Land*, 1987), Marianne Rosenbaum (*Peppermint Frieden*, 1983), and Michael Verhoeven (*Nasty Girl*, 1991), went beyond trying to shake West Germany out of its national amnesia from the 12 years of National Socialist rule. Although very different in scope, these films problematize oppressive policies practiced against Jewish men and women, German women, and other marginalized people during the Third Reich by holding these policies up as a mirror to contemporary Germany. While *Europa Europa* does not refract a critique of the present (*Gegenwartskritik*) through its depiction of past events (a failure, which we discuss in Part III), it seems to us that *Europa Europa* can be seen as part of these cultural narratives in that this film also treats themes of hegemonic constructions of national identity and celebrations of nationalism.

II

Indeed, it is clear to us that because the critical response to *Europa Europa* has concentrated on the surface level of commentary about the film's artistic flaws and the debate surrounding the German Export Film Union's ruling, one more layer has been added to Germany's history of *Vergangenheitsverdrängung*. As will be discussed in detail in Part II, *Europa Europa* encourages its audience to recognize that the most dangerous aspects of Nazi ideology lie in its insistence on a unified national subjectivity, in its refusal to accept multicultural and multinational subjects, and in its nationalist, territorialist quest. What follows are an analysis and a critique of *Europa Europa*'s retelling of the story of one individual, Salomon Perel, in terms of its depictions of the negotiation of a multicultural and multinational subject-position. The representation of Perel's irreconcilable status as both German and Jew during the period of National Socialism and, in particular, during World War II, performs a *Vergangenheitsbewältigung* that invites the audience to recognize and acknowledge the dangers of ideologies that privilege homogeneity. *Europa Europa* makes it clear that any individual whose multiple affinities can transgress national borders and jeopardize the integrity of categories of identity, such as race, class, gender, and religion, is always a threat to a political ideology and/or power structure that relies upon the undivided loyalties of its subjects. Salomon Perel's heterogenous identity, as both Jew[19] and German, marks him instantly as a danger to a society that demands absolute and unquestioned obedience. Consequently, he necessarily evokes an intense "border anxiety"[20] within National Socialist ideology. His dual subjecthood cannot be adequately contained within artificially constructed boundaries that function to demarcate both territory and identity. The mere existence of an individual such as Perel (who embodies an irrecuperable difference for

National Socialism) is enough to expose the politics of domination that underlie National Socialist ideology.

Perel is forced first to flee Germany with his family for Poland and then to leave his family behind in order to escape persecution by the Nazis. Throughout the film, the young Perel is depicted as fleeing from environment to environment, each differing widely, in a manner somewhat reminiscent of a picaresque narrative.[21] As Perel moves from the initial security of his family to the Communist boys' orphanage, to the German military unit, then to the prestigious Hitler youth school, the audience is witness to his incredible ability to adapt and assimilate himself. His quick-wittedness and prescience are evidenced numerous times as he must virtually "reinvent" himself on the spot. This ability enables him to traverse, thus call into question the configurations of various national borders. These demarcations of territory function as the nominal bases of national contestations and/or altercations; the manner in which Perel so easily assimilates the hegemonic demands of each particular nation exposes the arbitrariness of those nation's borders. Perel's adaptability challenges essentialist and National Socialist notions of ethnic and racial purity. Each border crossing provides a different challenge to Perel in terms of how he must reinvent his identity in order to disguise himself as being "safe" to the dominant ideology. Significantly, all of the environments in which Perel finds himself are male-identified and/or patriarchal, (e.g., the family, the military, the orphanage, the Hitler youth academy). He usually represents himself as "one of the boys" and in this way successfully reassures those representing the dominant ideology that he poses no threat. The way in which Perel takes advantage of dominant codes of masculinity to ease his movements seems to suggest that the film is challenging the hegemony of those codes. However, while the film does poke fun at his unwitting benefactors, its reluctance to divest Perel of his masculinist hero status belies a certain complicity with upholding those ideals of masculinity.

Within the confines of his family (represented both at the beginning and at the end of the film), Perel's positioning as a Jew remains secure and unquestioned. At the orphanage, he uses his Jewishness to secure safety; he becomes a political refugee of sorts, one who is granted asylum precisely because of his ethnicity. In fact, it is his class affiliation (*bourgeois*) rather than his ethnicity that causes him problems with the Soviets. When he is captured by the Germans, the physical mark of his Jewishness is covered up (his circumcised penis remains hidden), and he quickly reinvents himself as an Aryan. Perel's astonishingly easy assumption of an Aryan identity at this point in the film immediately calls attention to the film's project of exposing the construction of a racial ideal as being tantamount to the creation of a fiction. In an extremely revealing moment, Perel's science teacher at the Hitler youth academy uses Perel to illustrate to the rest of his peers an example of an acceptable Aryan. The teacher measures the dimensions of

Perel's face, takes note of the boy's hair and eye coloring, and then compares them to detailed charts that delineate the characteristics constituting an Aryan. After a few tense moments, the teacher pronounces Perel to be scientifically, indisputably, Aryan (although because of his dark hair and eyes, he is classified as a Baltic German). By first exposing and then interrogating Nazi racialist policies, *Europa Europa* offers its audience an opportunity to understand and critique hegemonic constructions of race, ethnicity, and identity. The irony of this scene plainly exposes National Socialist scientific racism to be far from objective and/or scientific.[22]

The film reveals the institution of the fictitious Aryan as a desired national racial paradigm to be politically motivated. The dominant ideology creates fictions that function to legislate people's desires and behaviors; the National Socialist domestic policy of *Lebensborn* is an excellent example of such an attempt to exert control over a nation's citizens. *Lebensborn* encouraged unmarried German women who most closely resembled the Aryan ideal to mate with and bear the children of German SS men who also closely resembled the Aryan ideal. Hopefully, such a pairing would produce Aryan children. By privileging the male Aryan as the only desirable mate, the German woman's role is valued in relation to her ability to submit to the dictates of *Lebensborn*. Hence her desires become regulated, and her behaviors, such as when Perel's girlfriend Leni decides to bear a child for Hitler, are normalized. Because of his ability to assume multiple identities and ethnicities in accordance with what is required in the particular dominant ideology within which he is operating, Perel escapes many life-threatening situations. Not only is Perel able to disguise his true identity, but he is so talented at acting/hiding and fictionalizing himself that he becomes configured as a person of primary importance in every one of the contexts within which he operates. During his stay at the Russian orphanage, he is shown to be the best (most ideologically correct) orphan. When he is temporarily with the German military unit, he becomes their token of good luck; in fact, he is credited with single-handedly capturing an entire enemy military unit. While at the Hitler youth school, Perel is revered as a "war hero" and is the only boy upon whom the most desired (i.e., most Aryan) girl, Leni, smiles. The audience is quickly made to understand that, to a large extent, Perel is "untouchable"; all events in the narrative conspire to aid him in his efforts to thwart his enemies and/or to allow him to retain his secure position. On at least three occasions, bombs and/or military equipment interrupt dangerous situations in order that Perel may remain unscathed: One bomb destroys the Nazi bureaucratic official who has demanded to see Perel's official papers, and another bomb liberates Perel from the Soviet orphanage; a Nazi jeep runs over the Polish orphan who is attempting to denounce Perel as a Jew; a bomb interrupts an intensely homoerotic moment between Perel and an older homosexual soldier; and so on.

Europa Europa ridicules the gullibility of those who cannot discern Perel's true identity (one that would be abhorrent to them), while they continue to acknowledge his obvious superiority. What, then, empowers Perel to disguise himself so effortlessly, in order that he may move across national borders and through such disparate communities? Early on, it becomes clear that the film configures his mobility as linked to both his ethnicity and his masculinity. The film opens with a scene that depicts Perel as a naked baby being solemnly circumcised in the midst of the father figures of his German-Jewish community. What is being shown here is essentially a celebration of tradition and masculinity. More importantly, this opening scene sets up the film's ongoing preoccupation with Perel's struggles to assert his masculinity (often signified simply by either the penis or the disciplined male body) in an environment that strives to emasculate the Jewish male. In fact, *Europa Europa* spends a great deal of time first establishing and then glorifying the youth's masculinity. This emphasis on rendering Perel's masculinity unimpeachable enacts a complex double effect on the narrative. On the one hand, it combats the National Socialist image of the Jew as feminized and/or bestial; on the other, it reifies patriarchal constructions of masculinity. Thus, the film positions itself on the borders of both *Vergangenheitsverdrängung* and *Vergangenheitsbewältigung* in offering a critique of German constructions of the Jew, even as it ultimately sidesteps issues of gender oppression.

It is important to note the dangers in offering a critique of *Europa Europa* that interrogates Perel's ability to reinvent himself. Such a critique would reinscribe discourses of racial, national, and/or ethnic inauthenticity that have been historically used against Jews. These discourses, which often recall and reproduce the figure of the "Wandering Jew," posit the Jew as intrinsically occupying a nomadic or chameleon-like position. This position departs from the notion of the Wandering Jew engendering multiple possibilities and significations that are unavailable to subjects who remain tied to supposedly stable identities. While this representation of the Jew may be presented under the guise of philo-Semitism, it actually functions to reinscribe anti-Semitic discourses of the Jew as opportunistic.

Indeed, critiques of the film that have circulated prominently in Germany would seem to support the idea that the figure of the Wandering Jew works as an anti-Semitic accusation rather than as anything else. As Stephen Engelberg in his *New York Times* article, "A Life Stranger Than the Movie, *Europa Europa*, Based on It," writes, "the film, which has opened in Berlin, has met with a perplexing response in Germany. *Der Spiegel* called the main character opportunistic and cynical, while a radio reporter questionned his [Perel's] morality during a round-table discussion."

This response becomes somewhat less "perplexing," once we take into account the pervasiveness of Wandering Jew discourse. Rather than reading Perel's ability to occupy multiple positions as either desirable or liberating, the article in *Der Spiegel* and the radio report level a charge of inauthenticity at Perel, raising issues of immorality and morality. Given this tendency for critics of the film to fall into the trap of reproducing the anti-Semitic discourse of the Wandering Jew, it becomes crucial for any treatment of *Europa Europa* to recognize and acknowledge fully the complexities of Perel's subject-position. Hence, when we argue that Perel's ability to negotiate multiple identities quickly is somehow tied to his masculinity, we do not wish to elide the fact that said critique may run the risk of clinging to residual notions of authenticity. In Part III, we argue that the film itself fails to satisfactorily complicate constructs of racial, national, and/or ethnic authenticity. Nevertheless, it seems important that the film's reliance upon and complicity with masculinist ideals be interrogated; an undiluted affirmation of masculinity (while being acted out of specific historical imperatives) would seem to substitute one form of authenticity (gendered) for another, racialized one.

Indeed, the film's reliance upon and complicity with masculinist ideals is apparent from its beginning. The camera immediately marks Perel as beautiful while simultaneously, proclaiming his status as an object of desire. From this point on, Perel's body is signaled as the site upon which the struggles to assert his masculinity (hence, his subjecthood) will occur. Immediately following the scene depicting Perel's circumcision, the audience is presented with the now-teenaged Perel naked in his family home's bathtub. Hearing a disturbance in the street (some young Hitler youths pass by, shout insults, and hurl objects into windows), he rises out of the bathtub, perching his bare feet on either side of the bathtub rim. The camera virtually caresses the back of the boy's naked body as it carefully frames Perel, so that the light from the window can create a halo around the contours of his body.

As the film repeatedly conflates Jewishness with manhood and thus renders the Jewish female invisible, Perel embarks on a quest to make his masculinity eminently visible. However, he is forced to obscure his masculinity in that he cannot participate in the ordinary rites of passage that have traditionally been used to signify a boy's ascent into manhood. Although he is nominally able to lose his virginity through a furtive, in-the-dark quickie with a German Nazi official who fetishises him because he has the same birthday as Hitler, he cannot have sexual relations with his first girlfriend, Leni, because he fears that she would discover his circumcised penis. In fact, this circumstance provides *Europa Europa* with one of its most emotional moments; Perel's anguish at not being able to have sex is plainly manifest. Leni, who wishes to comply with *Lebensborn*, eventually becomes pregnant with another man's child. Despite this setback, Perel's manhood is signaled amply in many other ways: his ability to withstand physical pain, his intelligence, his (hetero)sexual desire, and his physical prowess and endurance all mark him as masculine. Significantly, the retro-spective part of the narrative (of Perel as a young boy) ends as he and his brother stand side by side urinating in public (the literal unveiling of Perel's masculinity).

The first scene then, which shows Perel's circumcision, sets the stage for a masculinist quest narrative depicting the hero's traditional rites of passage into manhood as a political act within an environment hostile to this act. Were it not for the Nazis who divested German Jews of their access to the traditional rites of manhood and masculinity, we might see the narrative of a series of circumstances which function as proof of Perel's manhood as simply a typical, Hollywood coming-of-age story. Perel leaves the confines of paternal authority; he goes to an all-boy boarding school, where he feels the first stirrings of lust; he becomes a war hero; he loses his virginity to an older woman; he falls in love for the first time; reunited with his brother, he once again can display his penis (masculinity) in pub-lic; Perel goes on to participate in the colonization of Palestine, where he assumes the mantle of patriarchal authority that was heretofore only avail-able to him in brief snatches.

It is Perel's beauty, however, that ultimately provides the internal logic of the film. His desirability drives the narrative and explicates Perel's talent for disguising his Jewishness. All characters in the film desire Perel; conse-quently, his passage is, to a large extent, safeguarded. David D'Arcy of *NPR*'s "Morning Edition" remarks upon Perel's power to attract:

> Though his [Perel's] life is constantly threatened, his teen-age hormones push him toward romance, and everyone seems to have romantic designs on him, from a German actor to a matronly Nazi official to a blond, Hitler youth fräulein intent on conceiving a child for the Fuhrer. (*NPR* "Morning Edition" 19 July, 1991, 38)

When people do not have romantic designs on Perel, they covet him in other ways: The German general wants to adopt him; the Polish movie theater manager cannot bear the thought of his leaving; the Communist teacher believes him to be her best student; his German army buddies tout him as a good luck mascot. Rather than proving an obstacle or threat to his various disguises, those who desire Perel actually facilitate his mobility. The German general provides safe passage for Perel away from the front-lines; the German actor functions as a father figure for Perel during his time at the front; and the Communist teacher, an anonymous German, provides the naked Perel with a change of clothes. In contrast with tradi-tional filmic objects of desire (mostly female), who are often represented as passive and ineffective, Perel remains empowered rather than hindered by being marked as an object of desire. In fact, the glorification of Perel's beauty mediates *Europa Europa*'s critique of Nazi racialist policies, in that both entail the privileging of an ideal constructed to serve patriarchal interests.

As in most filmic representations, the hero of this narrative, is configured as male. However, in terms of narrative function, *Europa Europa* departs from the traditional gendering of the object of desire as female. Within what such critics as Teresa De Lauretis have termed the Oedipal narrative, the female usually operates as the bearer of the enigma. She is the key to the hermeneutic code, the mystery that needs to be solved in order to resolve the film. Despite the hermeneutic importance of her role, she is essentially a passive object or vessel (space) upon which the hero's and the viewer's own desires are projected. De Lauretis (1984) explains further:

> But whose desire is it that speaks, and whom does that desire address? The received interpretations of the Oedipus story, Freud's among others, leave no doubt. The desire is Oedipus's, and though its object may be woman (or Truth or knowledge or power), its term of reference and address is man: man as a social being and mythical subject, founder of the social order, and source of mimetic violence. . . . (112)

De Lauretis makes it clear here that the woman as an object functions only in terms of how she facilitates male desire. Consequently, it is only male desire that can confer subjectivity onto the female object of desire. As is evidenced by *Europa Europa*, when the male occupies the position of object of desire, he is not simply a passive object. After all, it is mostly *male* desire that drives the narrative, thus enabling the male character to benefit from his status in a way that is unavailable to the female.

The male as object of desire ultimately upholds the patriarchal system, which is founded on a kind of homosocial desire.[23] This homosocial desire makes sure that women are configured in such a way that they function only to reify male power structures. *Europa Europa* makes this homosocialism explicit but fails ultimately to problematize it. Perel is represented as receiving continued patronage from all who encounter him, and in doing so, his representation valorizes the male-dominated system that ensures his success.

In light of this critique, it is interesting to examine the ways in which the one explicitly homosexual character in the film, the German soldier Robert, functions. The film portrays Robert sympathetically, placing him in a caretaker role towards Perel; in fact, parallels are carefully drawn between their individual positions as outsiders. Robert, as a homosexual, also faces persecution from the National Socialist regime. Because Robert's revelation of his homosexuality is equally dangerous to him as Perel's revelation of his Jewishness is to Perel, the question remains as to why Robert would risk his life by making sexual advances towards Perel. Putting aside the question of credibility as overly facile, it is obvious that the way in which the soldier's sexual desire for the boy leads Robert to risk his own life is consistent with the narrative of the film, in that Perel's desirability works ultimately to his advantage. It is also necessary to point out how the initial characterization of Robert as someone who is unable to control his desires (on pain of death) reproduces homophobic discourses that posit homosexual desire as insatiable and/or dangerous.[24] It appears that Perel's masculine beauty is, once again, upheld at the expense of other constructs of identity.

Once the two discover each other's secret and after Perel has firmly established his heterosexuality, they form a strong friendship that is maintained until Robert's death. The most significant scene in which their friendship is displayed takes place on a snow-covered hillside where Perel shares some of his religious heritage with Robert. It is a highly charged moment, one that simultaneously mimics a domestic scene and reveals the relationship between the two as (homo)erotically charged. Robert and Perel begin wrestling together and tumble down the hillside; the scene cuts abruptly to the noises of artillery fire and bombs falling. The camp value here is obvious to the viewer, but *Europa Europa* itself disavows any such self-consciousness with its investment in the ultraheterosexuality of its hero. Robert's desire to be anything more than a paternal friend is undercut in that Robert's sexual pursuit of Perel turns him into a comic, lascivious figure shown chasing Perel around a barn.

It is crucial for us not to lose sight of the fact that Perel, as a Jew, is persecuted by the genocidal racism of National Socialism; nevertheless, *Europa Europa* reveals that he does benefit from a blatantly patriarchal nation. This uncritical stance towards homosocialism must be recognized as a kind of *Vergangenheitsverdrängung* on the part of the film's overall project, particularly once the problematic representations of the women in the film are taken into consideration.

Europa Europa makes the role of women within the context of National Socialism explicit in terms of their age-old roles as passive reproductive laborers but, here too, the film fails to offer a critique of it. Rather, it reproduces the National Socialist policies of the division of labor as delineated directly through the gendered body—women's work is that of bearing children for the nation (most dramatically enacted in *Lebensborn*), and female desire is represented as being, in fact, desire for the Führer. The Nazi official who accompanies Perel to the Hitler youth academy desires only "der Führer." Leni, Perel's girlfriend, functions simply to reproduce future (hopefully male) citizens for the nation. All the other women in the film are marked by their instantaneous desire for Perel. Leni's mother, who decides to protect Perel's identity once it is revealed to her, lauds Perel for his refusal to sleep with her daughter. (He is, in her eyes, a "gentleman.") However, her decision, even though it involves resistance to National Socialist dictates, is configured as a symptom of her desire for the youth; she tells Perel that he reminds her of her husband. No alternative female configurations are offered: The Jewish women are rendered ineffective, if not invisible; the Polish and Russian women are represented as ventriloquists of, and vessels for, male desire.

In contrast to the reproductive role of the women, the labor of the men in the film is linked explicitly and directly to the virility, strength, and endurance that is signified by the disciplining of their bodies. The national worth of both the German soldiers and the students at the Hitler youth academy is determined by their use value as defenders and upholders of National Socialism; the film makes very clear that their worth is measurable in terms of capital investment: they will provide the requisite number of bodies for the frontlines. The young men at the academy physically exert themselves by engaging in military parades, sports competitions, working in factories, etc. In these ways, they struggle to discipline their bodies in accordance with constructions of the Aryan ideal. Perel, even though his physical beauty already proves his worth, still undergoes a number of episodes that demonstrate his resilience and ability to withstand pain. For example, he is shown to endure a root canal without anesthesia, so that he can avoid the mandatory school physical which would expose his circumcised penis. He is depicted to suffer excruciating physical pain when he attempts to fashion a makeshift foreskin by tying the skin on his penis. Significantly, Perel's project fails and he incurs an infection. Nevertheless, this failure can be read as *proving* his manhood rather than mediating it once issues of Nazi manhood are separated from Jewish manhood (an artificial separation but one that *Europa Europa* attempts to make). Perel's circumcised penis, the mark of his difference and masculinity, becomes constructed as "more than" rather than "lack of" (as National Socialist policies would have it). The primary symbol of his Jewishness cannot be altered or compromised in any way.

By gendering the body in accordance with patriarchal dictates, the film once again can critique racialist policies while both ignoring issues of gender and privileging its constructions of Jewish manhood. In doing this, the film attempts to debunk the Nazi configuration of the Jew as undesirable, feminized, and emasculated. Nevertheless, the problematic effect is that the film also offers its viewers a glorified, God-kissed hero whose exploits can only arouse suspicion concerning the film's project of reviewing National Socialism. Too many vital components of Nazi ideology go uncritiqued and, thus, affirmed. These components include: the positing of woman as a reproductive machine; the glorification of the masculine body and body discipline; and the celebration of the masculinist hero quest.

III

At the end of *Europa Europa*, a split in the film's political agenda and commitment becomes evident. The final frames show the (real) elder Perel, settled in Palestine, standing on top of a hill and singing a song in Hebrew that celebrates his homeland. The song, with its first line of Psalm 133, *Hineh Mah Tov*, meaning "How good and pleasant it is for brothers to live together united," is "also a Zionist song," and "in an unusual omission for a film so subtly (Europeanly) conscious of languages" not translated (Heifetz 1991). An off-camera narrator informs us that Perel has assumed his Jewish identity once again, "barely hesitating" to circumcise his son. This qualification reveals that Perel's memories of the years that he feared discovery that he was circumcised and, hence, Jewish, will always be with him. In the context of the entire sequence at the end of the film, Perel's assumption of the role of Jewish father is shown to be a matter of courage: although he barely escaped death himself for a number of years, he "barely hesitates" to mark his son as his father had marked him. This ending puts us squarely into the middle of a dilemma: How are we to reconcile *Europa Europa*'s celebration of Perel's homeland in this coda with the film's earlier critique of Socialist Nationalist expansionist policies? Does this seamless embrace of a Jewish homeland not obscure, rather than illuminate for criticism, the underlying National Socialist desire of colonization or expanding/redefining national borders that was held up for critique earlier in the film?

It seems to us that such an unquestioning celebration of Perel's unified ethnic and national identity necessarily mediates the examination of Nazi ideology and disables the critique of patriotism, nationalism, and the patriarchal system as a whole. Nevertheless, as Edward Said suggests in his essay "Zionism from the Standpoint of Its Victims," an explicit examination of Zionism in terms of its participation in oppressive ideologies can prove virtually impossible (Said 1990). He explains further:

> Present political and cultural actualities make such an examination extraordinarily difficult, as much because Zionism in the post-industrialist West has acquired for itself an almost unchallenged hegemony in liberal "establishment" discourse, as because in keeping with one of its central ideological characteristics, Zionism has hidden, or caused to disappear, the literal historical ground of its growth, its political cost to the native inhabitants of Palestine, and its militantly oppressive discrimination between Jews and non-Jews. (211)

The creation of a Jewish nation state has, to a large extent, been sanctioned by the West; thus, any criticism of Zionism's ideologies is bound to meet with resistance; this resistance simultaneously reveals the West's *Gegenwartsverdrängung* (denial of the contemporary reality) in regard to the aforementioned border anxiety that informed World War II. This anxiety extends, as discussed in Part I, to the newly unified Germany as well. Parenthetically, this concern about being misunderstood refers to the debate about *Europa Europa* in the German press as outlined in Part I; it may be that some participants in the debate remained stuck in quibblings about form because of the suspicions that a substantive critique would raise. As Said (1990) pointed out: "One must admit, however, that all liberals, and most 'radicals' have been unable to overcome the Zionist habit of equating anti-Zionism with anti-Semitism." (212) It is not a matter of interpretation that Palestinians have been annexed and oppressed since 1948 as a consequence of the Zionist cause and the creation of the state of Israel. Yet, *Europa Europa* is content with enacting a limited kind of *Vergangenheitsbewältigung* on behalf of Germany's role during the Third Reich but is unwilling to extend that examination to include interrogation of Israel's politics (whose effects, along with those of National Socialism, are still felt in the present). In the context of Said's argument that contemporary political and cultural realities make an examination of Zionism extraordinarily difficult, the story that is absent in *Europa Europa* is as telling as that which is present. The history of the colonization of Palestine "is caused to disappear" between the narrative end of the film (Perel and his brother head to Palestine) and the coda (Perel stands, singing on top of a hill looking down on the banks of a river in what is now Israel). While the film asks us to participate in a critique of the institutionalized racialist constructions of national identities during the parts in the film that deal with the Nazi past, it effectively closes off critique of the construction of Perel's Zionist identity. The absence of this historical period of intense conflict reveals the political partiality that informs the film. We are left to wonder whether this segment of world history, one which saw the contestation of numerous borders, is repressed because it would cause a subsequent interrogation of Zionist policies. The unquestioning resumption of a unified ethnic identity after such identities have already been exposed as oppressive and dogmatic rings false.

In addition, it perpetuates the film's tendency to privilege and hold unimpeachable the Jewish *male*. Indeed, it lends credence to our assessment that *Europa Europa* configures the Holocaust primarily as a horrifying historical moment in which Jewish *manhood* was called into question. After all, the moment in the film in which Perel seems to exhibit the most emotional pain occurs when he cannot have sex (normalize his relationship) with Leni. The realization that he cannot conform to normal codes of masculinity causes Perel the most anguish. The coda to the film forces us to read the narrative's privileging of the masculinist quest and assertion of unimpeachable Jewish manhood and compels us to view the war as simply a contestation of masculinities and/or patriarchal cultures. Indeed, the film implicitly suggests that World War II was, in essence, a contestation of masculinity between various patriarchal systems (the National Socialist regime, the Jewish culture, the Stalinist regime, etc.). This contestation is configured, as we have shown, by the film as taking place on the body of Perel. War is evidently about men, between men, and for the benefit of men. Women exist only insofar as they can function as reproductive laborers and as helpmates toward a masculinist, unified subjectivity. The problem with such a presentation is, of course, that the film fails to critique the basis of those contestations.

While it is not our intention to dismiss the film's attempts to depict the impossible negotiation of a multicultural and multinational subject-position in times when those identities are engaged in violent conflict, it is important to stress this recuperative move. While *Europa Europa* convincingly problematizes cultural constructions of homogeneous and/or totalizing national and ethnic identities, it backs off at the last moment when this conflict is too simplistically resolved.

Notes

1. The terms *Vergangenheitsverdrängung* (denial of the past) and *Vergangenheitsbewältigung* (coming to terms with the past) in our title have become popular terms to describe the ways in which Germans have dealt with and still deal with the legacy of the Third Reich. Generally, *Vergangenheitsverdrängung* and *Vergangenheitsbewältigung* are commonly used to describe an either/or situation: Either an individual or a whole group of people deny all of the National Socialist past or they come to terms with all of it. It isn't so simple, of course. The dichotomy established by these terms entails that one is always, to a certain degree, present in the other.

2. Responding to the lack of audience response, the city of Frankfurt arranged a special screening of *Europa Europa* in January 1992. Invited were Michel Friedman, the cultural representative of the Jewish community; Micha Brumlik, a city councilman of the Green Party; the film critic Jürgen Kritz; and Paul Hengge, the original scriptwriter of the film (who later withdrew his name from the film credits). In the discussion following the screening, the audience was not interested in addressing any substantive issues of the film. Instead, the most discussed aspect was the debate in the press about the rejection of the film for the Academy Award competition (*Frankfurter Rundschau* 30 January 1992).

3. Holland's assessment of the political climate in Germany was made months before hundreds of thousands of Germans took to the streets demonstrating against right-wing radicalism in all major cities, beginning on November 9, 1992, in Berlin. Following this demonstration, all major cities quickly organized similar manifestations, such as the candlelight protest march in Munich (January 1993), in which 400,000 Germans protested racially motivated crimes.

4. The press reacted on either side of the divide: *Die Zeit* (31 January 1992) wrote that the the "answer is clear: [the nationality of the producer] decides the national product. [. . .] In the cinema it is money that confers the passport, not art." A long article in the *Frankfurt Allgemeine* (29 January 1992) expressed dismay about the "hypocritical" debate engendered by such "a bad film." Other articles, such as the one in *Rheinischer Merkur* (14 February 1992), argued that the film clearly did not qualify, given its international production. The *Frankfurt Rundschau*'s commentary (30 January 1992) is among the few in the press that challenge the arcane content rule in a time when most European films are indeed coproductions.

5. Clearly, while the fact that *Europa Europa* was widely distributed and successful in the U.S. (where it won excellent reviews, received prestigious prizes, and earned $3 million to date) does not testify to the artistic excellence of the film, it may say something about the American audience's lack of resistance to seeing a representation of the German people's complicity with, and participation in, the perpetration of atrocities during the National Socialist regime. The film distributors obviously perceived that the film would have a more sympathetic American audience, which probably motivated the directo: and producer's vigorous campaign to encourage recognition in the U.S.

6. The Film Union's tacit support of such policies and Artur Brauner's move to convey proof of the film's "pure national origin" brought these adversaries together in a bizarre alliance.

7. That the U.S. Academy of Motion Picture Arts and Sciences still upholds such regulations and that the German Export Film Union accedes to them is remarkable, even if simply for practical reasons. The fact is that the majority of European films are multinational coproductions. In the case of German entries, both institutions' refusal to envision Germany as part of a postnational, postterritorial world, gives us an example of the arcane thinking that must be overcome in the ongoing construction of a United Europe.

8. National Public Radio, "Morning Edition," 19 July 1991.

9. *Der Spiegel,* January 1992.

10. In a recent poll, the question "do applicants for asylum abuse Germany's social system?" was asked. A total thirty percent of Germans polled answered that they agreed completely that foreigners exploit the system; thirty six percent agreed somewhat; twenty three percent said perhaps; and only nine percent said not at all. The nationalities in question were Turks, Jews, Eastern Europeans, and Africans. *Der Spiegel,* April 1992.

11. In 1991, 222,000 *Volksdeutsche* moved to Germany. In the former Soviet Union alone, an additional 500,000 are waiting for entry visas. Cited in *Der Spiegel,* March 1992.

12. *The New York Times Magazine,* 12 April 1992.

13. *Holocaust* was, to date, the most viewed dramatization of National Socialist racialist policies in West Germany. Twenty million people, translating into roughly every other West German, watched at least part of the series. Remarkable, too, is that it provoked unprecedented public discussion during and after its airing in West Germany on January 22, 23, 25, and 26, 1979. The West German filmmaker Edgar Reitz pointed to the impact of the film on Germans: "More than any documentary of any personal account, this fiction film, although of mediocre quality, provoked a truly emotional outburst: after the first telecast [. . .] the ARD staff received more than 5000 frenzied passionate telephone calls, which constituted a veritable event in the history of the relationship between German television and its public" (Elsaesser 1989, 271). We have seen why *Europa Europa* cannot boast such an audience response.

14. Remarkably, even though five of eleven segments of *Heimat* deal with the Third Reich, Reitz's film excludes both thematization and problematization of the Holocaust.

15. Many articles in the West German press criticized *Holocaust* as a melodramatic exploitation with "kitschy music," a sensationalist mining of emotions, and replete with inaccuracies. Again Reitz: The American series, he charged, represents a "glaring example" of "international aesthetics of commercialism" (Kaes 1989, 184). *Der Spiegel* reports Insdorf lambasted the series by charging that "*Holocaust* as docu-drama blurs fact, trivializes events, and neither illuminates nor forces one to think about them" (6).

16. A number of films by New German Cinema filmmakers enjoyed success in the U.S. (especially those films of R. W. Fassbinder, Volker Schlöndorff, Werner Herzog and Wim Wenders) in the 1970s. As a consequence, films made by New German Cinema filmmakers became an export item marketed in U.S. art cinemas and American university courses; the German government (through German embassies, and through the work of the Goethe Institute) supported marketing these films as a commodity that would help counteract prevailing "Hogan's Hero" views of Germans.

17. These are films that explicitly or implicitly critique fascist ideology and deal critically with any aspect of the legacy of the Third Reich, regardless of the period they locate their tale in.

18. R. W. Fassbinder's *FRG Trilogy* ("Trilogy of the Federal Republic of Germany," a project that he began in the mid-1970's, *Die Ehe der Maria Braun, Lola,* and *Die Sehnsucht der Veronika Voss*), Ebbo Deman'ts made-for-TV film *Lagerstrasse Auschwitz* (1979), and the omnibus film *Deutschland im Herbst* (1978) are noteworthy examples of such efforts.

19. The Jewish subject's identity crisis is obviously exacerbated by a growing Zionism movement that is, at this time, already more than 50 years old. Perel's struggle to negotiate and resolve his bicultural heritage becomes even more complex and pressing an issue as the creation of a Jewish nation state appears increasingly imminent. His status begs the question of legal citizenship for the first time.

20. This "border anxiety" can also be said to inform some of the furor that greeted the Film Export's adherence to the Academy's "content rule" that *Europa Europa* generated in the German Press. Furthermore, as discussed in Part I, issues of national ownership of history (i.e., who is authorized to tell the "true" story of National Socialism?) were provoked by the film's multinational production.

21. This similarity becomes even more pronounced through the film's strategic use of humor to punctuate the story. For example, after losing his virginity to a German Nazi official, Perel is shown crouched on top of a train, howling deliriously into the wind. Later on, when finally alone at the Hitler youth academy, Perel does a comical dance in front of a full-length mirror. Nevertheless, the use of humor in *Europa Europa* has not passed without criticism. Nicole David, herself a Holocaust survivor, asks the question "whether turning a survival story into an often humorous adventure might actually trivialize both the terrifying experiences of many who survived and the grim fate of the vast majority of Jews who did not" (*NPR* 1991, 39).

22. Stephen Engelberg's article in *The New York Times* entitled "A Life Stranger Than the Movie, *Europa Europa,* Based on It" relates the revealing story of the real Perel's encounter with a former teacher (the one who quantifies Perel's supposed Aryan qualities in front of the students of the Hitler youth academy) shortly after World War II is ended. The article reads, in part:

> After the war, Mr. Perel said, he met the teacher again, quite by chance, and disclosed his true identity. "'I must say, sir, you made a mistake,' I said to him. 'That's not correct, what you said about me. I'm Jewish.' At first his face turned white, like paper, then the colors returned, like a rainbow. he said: 'Never mind, I knew all along, but I didn't want to make trouble.'" (Engelberg)

The reaction of the teacher reveals his *Verdrängung* concerning his role during the Third Reich, as well as his embarrassment at having been made a fool of by Perel. Perel's revelation that he is not the Aryan that the teacher had paraded him as threatens the integrity of a dominant ideology that, although it has abandoned National Socialist policies, is still engaged in ongoing *Vergangenheitsverdrängung.* The teacher must contend that he "knew all along" in order to repress the shameful exposure of his complicity and compliance with the Nazis.

23. By homosocial, we mean to indicate a patriarchal societal structure that privileges masculinity and male desire. Such a society would be constructed so as to glorify certain kinds of socially acceptable relationships between men. At the same time, heterosexual relationships would function primarily to reify the preeminence of the male subject; male/female relationships become configured as a performance of masculinity enacted for the benefit of other men.

24. The idea that homosexuals are ruled by insatiable sexual drives *tout court* is particularly insistent in homophobic discussions of the AIDS epidemic, in which the disease is judged to be the deserved curse caused by homosexuals' "choice of lifestyle."

250 ❖ INGEBORG MAJER O'SICKEY and ANNETTE VAN

Works Cited

Baecker, Sigurd. "Muß dieser Preis unbedingt her?" *Allgemeine Wochenzeitung der Juden* 30 January 1992.

Beckmann, Gerhard. "Der lange Streit um den 'Hitlerjungen Salomon.'" Rev. of *Europa Europa. Die Welt* 16 January 1992.

Bodmer, Thomas. "Nichts als ein übles Klischee." *Die Weltwoche* 14 May 1992.

Breslau, Karen. "Screening Out the Dark Past." Rev. of *Europa Europa* by Agnieszka Holland. *Newsweek* 3 February 1992: 30.

De Lauretis, Teresa. *Alice Doesn't.* Bloomington: Indiana University Press, 1984.

Dendler, Carolin. "Gold für den verschmähten Salomon." *Die Welt* 20 January 1992.

Elsaesser, Thomas. *New German Cinema: A History.* New Brunswick: Rutgers University Press, 1989.

Friedman, Michel. "Peinlich? Amerika sieht es anders." *Rheinischer Merkur* 14 February 1992.

Heifetz, Hank. "*Europa Europa.*" *Cinéaste.* Vol. 14, No. 4. December 1991: 51–52.

Holland, Agnieszka. *Europa Europa.* Interview. With David D'Arcy. *NPR* "Morning Edition." 19 July 1991: 37–40.

Insdorf, Annette. *Indelible Shadows: Film and the Holocaust,* 2nd ed. Cambridge: Cambridge University Press, 1989.

"Jeder achte Deutsche ein Antisemit." *Der Spiegel* April 1992: 41–50.

Kaes, Anton. *From Hitler to Heimat: The Return of History as Film.* Cambridge: Harvard University Press, 1989.

Kilb, Andreas. "Ohne Oscar." *Die Zeit* 31 January 1992.

Kinzer, Stephen. "East Germans Face their Accusers." *The New York Times Magazine* 12 April 1992.

Koch, Gertrud. Rev. of *Europa Europa* by Agnieszka Holland. *Frankfurter Rundschau* 30 January 1992.

Kruttschnitt, Christine. "Große Schweinerei." *Stern* 30 January 1992.

Lueken, Verena. Rev. of *Europa Europa* by Agnieszka Holland. *Frankfurter Allgemeine Zeitung* 29 January 1992.

"Mehr verdrängt als bewäaltigt." *Der Spiegel* March 1992: 52–66.

Müller, Peter E. Rev. of *Europa Europa* by Agnieszka Holland. *Berliner Morgenpost* 20 January 1992.

Said, Edward, W. "Zionism from the Standpoint of Its Victims." In *Anatomy of Racism,* edited by Devaid Theo Goldberg. Minneapolis: Minnesota University Press, 1990.

Schäfer, Bernd. "Bilder als Beruhigungspille gegen Furcht vor Germany?" *Neue Zeit* 14 February 1992.

"Streitprämie." *Frankfurter Allegemeine Zeitung* 20 January 1992.

"Stur und streng." *Der Spiegel* January 1992: 149.

"Wiederverwertung der Betroffenheit." *Frankfurter Allgemeine Zeitung* 29 January 1992.

Wilmes, Hartmut. "Ein Schaf im Wolfspelz." *Rheinischer Merkur* 14 February 1992.

CONSTELLATION D
THE EUROAMERICAN QUESTION:
POLITICS OF NATION

This constellation takes a stereoscopic look at the ways in which the relationship between the United States and Europe is inscribed across German cinema studies texts and leads to questions regarding the status of such traditional concepts as "nation" and "culture" in the newer, postnational academic arena. How are these concepts revised and updated by Thomas Elsaesser's reading of Lili Marleen, *in which the functioning and effects of the U.S.-funded* Wirtschaftswunder *(Economic Miracle) are explained in terms of sexual desire? Does Eric Rentschler's historicist understanding of the U.S. as Germany's critcal "Imaginary" avoid Elsaesser's psychoanalytic-semiotic collapse of the economic onto the libidinal, or does its placement of European art cinema in a transhistorical, almost mythic, space of symbolic exchange merely encourage an idealist replication of such a move? Where does Rentschler's theory of "displaced" cross-cultural relations intersect Timothy Corrigan's discourse on existential wanderings? In contrast, how does Corrigan's analysis of transnational mobility in Wenders differ from Rentschler's theory by upholding Elsaesser's rather post-al discourse on the internationality of desire? How are the similarities and differences between these texts repeated across Constellations B and G ("The* Heimat *Debate" and "Myth and Allegory"), and how does Mas'ud Zavarzadeh's critique of the politics of family and gender in* Paris, Texas *intervene into that repetition's very ideological structuring? Finally, to what extent is such repetition symptomatic of German cinema studies in general?*

Lili Marleen: Fascism and the Film Industry

THOMAS ELSAESSER

FILMMAKING in West Germany since the late 1960s has a complex background. Its current high productivity follows twenty-five exceptionally arid years, a moribund period for the country's commercial film industry. Hollywood's particularly ruthless exploitation policy as applied to the West German market meant the enforcement by distributors of blockbooking and other near-monopolistic practices. The Germans, unlike the French or British, were unable to protect their own private industry through legislation. Import quotas and the freezing of box-office receipts—the two most frequently applied trade barriers of the 1950s and '60s—proved politically unacceptable in the face of the massive lobbying undertaken by the U.S. State Department on behalf of the Motion Picture Export Association during the Adenauer era. The decline was slow since West Germany did grant subsidies to its ailing industry. A combination of fiscal measures (reduced entertainment tax on films of cultural value) and a levy on all box-office receipts sustained production. The industry remained undercapitalized, however, existing from hand to mouth, from film to film. The general slide into insignificance of other European film industries during the 1960s demonstrated the inadequacy of purely economic incentives. The Hollywood product was superior in almost every respect and the attempt to compete by means of exploitation pictures brought some producers short-term profits but ruined the already volatile market. The loss of the popular audiences was followed by the disaffection of the more serious ones. It was perhaps the very thoroughness with which the Americans "cleaned up" in West Germany that opened the way for a different concept of filmmaking.

How did Europe's most sophisticated and entangled system of government subsidized filmmaking come into existence? It derived partly from the defensive posture of the German industrial establishment in response to the postwar absorption of national industries by American capital and from the European Community regulations protecting trade and exchange between individual member countries. More decisive, however, were the ongoing internal struggles between certain groups of German new wave directors on the one hand, and those organizations representing the old guard commercial film industry, on the other. The manifesto issued at the 1962 Oberhausen Short Film Festival represents a turning point. This

Reprinted from *October* 21 (Summer 1982):114–40 by permission of the MIT Press, Cambridge, Massachusetts, Copyright 1982 for the Institute for Architecture & Urban Studies of the Massachusetts Institute of Technology.

show of strength was premature, as it turned out, but it set in motion a government machinery which culminated in the creation of a production fund for first films (Kuratorium Junger Deutscher Film) in 1965. Two years later, the filmmakers' lobby actually pushed through Parliament the Film Subsidy Law which, since its inception in 1967, has seen no less than three important and hotly debated amendments (1971, 1974, 1979).

With financial aid now becoming available on a relatively extensive scale, the latent conflict between culture and commerce within independent filmmaking began to surface; to this day it continues to be crucial. The Constitution of West Germany provides for the jurisdiction of matters of education and culture by the individual states. Since the Film Subsidy Law created a federal agency, however, its provisions had to be phrased in terms appropriate to an economic aid to industry. Hence the ambiguity in the statutes: "The aim is to improve the quality of the German film on a broad basis, and to ameliorate the structure of the film industry." The "and" in this sentence begs several questions, but the law seems to work in favor of a "cultural" interpretation of filmmaking; at least initially, it relieves the filmmaker of box-office pressure. It also renders the status of the finished film and its relation to an audience increasingly problematic.

One consequence of the German subsidy system has been to impose the identity of an *auteur* upon the filmmaker. Not only are the functions of scriptwriter, director, and producer often united in one person so as to maximize eligibility for aid and cash prizes, the system tends, as well, to reward success and a high international visibility, such as those of Herzog, Wenders, and Fassbinder. Directors tend to turn themselves into superstars, "artists," self-conscious representatives of German "culture," of the new Germany. They become "bankable" within both the subsidy network and the international art market.

By subsidizing and promoting the new German cinema, through its embassies and cultural institutes, the federal government has cut the Gordian knot that ties film to both industry and art. The success of the Subsidy Law confirms that culture has been recognized as a commodity, part of the range of commodities one might call the national heritage, itself a diffuse accumulation of values that demands a distinct marketing strategy. This holds especially for a country such as West Germany, whose prosperity so largely depends upon exports. The mistake in the case of the cinema has been to consider films as material goods, similar to machine tools, BMW or Mercedes cars, and to attempt direct and unsuccessful competition with the U.S. and Hollywood. The French, by contrast, have always been highly successful in retaining the "French" label associated with a variety of material and immaterial products: wine, cheese, Roland Barthes, François Truffaut, and Chanel No. 5, so that "Frenchness" becomes almost an autonomous signifier of value.[1]

Films, compared with other artifacts, are cheap and efficient to transport. Unlike a ballet company or a symphony orchestra, a few cans of film can go by diplomatic bag, if necessary. And unlike literature, films present no insuperable language barriers, and insurance problems pale to insignificance compared with those attendant upon the shipping of paintings or other auratic works of art. If the subsidy system tends to reinforce the status of the filmmaker as a personality, so culture as export detaches the individual film from any historical or aesthetically precise context. It begins to circulate in as many forms as there are occasions for exhibition: as media event, "masterpiece," star vehicle, brand-name product, or as controversial treatment of a sensitive subject. Films are constructed in their coherence, meaning, and value, not at their points of origin or level of intentionality; rather, discernible shape crystallizes around them in the act of consumption. They become objects, but also "texts."

The films of the New German cinema acquire political meaning in ways not always controlled by their makers, and irrespective of their practical, aesthetic, or thematic opposition to West German society and its institutions. The international distribution and consumption of this particular national cinema are such as to make these films opaquely reflecting mirrors in which an audience may find confirmation of its own cultural or psychological identity. They are also official representations, sanctioned and sponsored by a country that has had difficulty in profiling itself either politically or culturally, except through a relatively recent, though intensive preoccupation with its internationally notorious past and its troubled ideological identity as a nation. Hence the special status of this cinema and of Fassbinder's films in the debate on the social function of the artwork today.

The European film director acclaimed at the international festivals is often called upon to make either a European film in Hollywood or international films in his own country. The consequence of even a modest commercial success in filmmaking is a thrust toward capital investments and production values that may structurally modify a nation's cinema as a whole.[2] The new German cinema shows all the symptoms of a success that will force mutations on the very structures that begot it: Wenders's time with Zoetrope, Herzog's years in the wilderness with *Fitzcarraldo*, and the emergence of German "Hollywood" films like *Das Boot* provide instructive case studies about the inadequacy of a precarious balance between television funding and government subsidy. The pressures of an author's cinema caught in changing technologies and changing markets can no longer be regulated by that balance.

Only Fassbinder, with his high rate of productivity, seemed able to meet the relentless demands of productivity imposed on him by success and his role as a symbol of the German cinema. Besides his international art-house films (*Despair, The Marriage of Maria Braun, Lili Marleen*), he revived film genres from Germany's despised 1950s (*Die Grosse Sehnsucht der Veronika Voss*) and filmed his own stage productions (*New York Women*). This productivity made him an important employer. Having silenced and outflanked the remnants of the old film industry lobby, he was able to treat West Germany's largest commercial studio, the Bavaria Atelier in Munich, as his own, virtually private production base.[3] Firmly rooted as he was in Germany, despite his occasional, well-publicized outbursts ("rather a street-sweeper in Mexico than a filmmaker in Germany"), his work, no longer dependent on the subsidy system, offered a constant and intense reflection on the German cinema in transition.

Fassbinder's international reputation was gained by a series of "critical" family melodramas; he thereby appeared to demonstrate his ambition to work in a popular fictional genre, and at least in principle, to aim at a mass audience. It is also evident that very complex theoretical issues of subjectivity and socialization, of spectacle and the relays of power, of meaning and value are addressed in his films. The passion and insistence that sustain these concerns from film to film spring not only from their contemporary or fashionable relevance: they bespeak a personal urgency as well, a strangely earnest conviction that a filmmaker is, in his work, accountable to a public and works within history. Thus, the constant, probing meditation on show business, German fascism, and their relations to the nature of desire.

This essentially bourgeois self-understanding of the artist—and Fassbinder's subversive-provocative variation on it—stems directly from both the specific mode of patronage for West German filmmaking during the last two decades and the acute contradictions encountered, as the ceiling of the subsidy system touched the floor of the fully capitalist international film and television industry.

Fassbinder's films have been made with "real" money, that is, funds that materialize from the dizzyingly complicated profit-and-loss calculations, the write-offs, deferral and refinancing policies, the ceaseless and now wholly self-evident logic of unlimited speculation. This is the most abstract, intangible form of value and exchange known; its manifestations are "everywhere to be felt, but nowhere to be seen"—a phrase that once referred to the creator of the universe.

In films such as *Lili Marleen*, Fassbinder indicates that fascism, forty years on, is neither specifically German nor merely historical as a phenomenon; it is rather the constant shadow cast by the crisis cycle of capitalism and of "world trade." Its crystallization points are the constantly displaced "theaters of war," both local conflagrations and those concentrations of power realized through the mass media and the new technologies; they are promoted and naturalized by the ubiquity of war spectacle and show. In the unmediated, pure presence of "Lili Marleen" on the airwaves during World

War II, "hard" military rule and consolidated corporate interests became "soft" through the relay of the product, the personality, the image, and the sound. Power had channeled, dispersed, and liquified itself, until it became as insubstantial and dematerialized as the air we breathe.

The project of *Lili Marleen* originated in the base proprietary rights of Luggi Waldleitner (West Germany's most industry-oriented producer) to the song and its title. Fassbinder thereby participates in the process by which capitalism strips history to the skeleton of its own truth; to that which survives as bankable assets. One might suggest that he is thus like his heroine, complicit in his exploitation as the figurehead of a particular regime. The vulgarity of nostalgia is the price paid for operating capital in the currently available valid currency of (German-International) show business.

Fassbinder's film is, however, the only film about fascism which constructs its narrative entirely around a paradoxical but historically authenticated montage effect such as the fortuitous encounter of a love song and a world war. The song's former popularity is all that Fassbinder actually takes from history; but it is also all that actually survives. If that "popularity" is indicative of the nature and function of mass culture and the entertainment industry, this is because it designates their products as both objects (commodities) and signs (elements of a discourse). Could Breton have envisaged such a total victory for the *objet trouvé* and its convulsive beauty as the appearance in novelty shops of Taiwan-made ice-cream-cone saltshakers? Did Brecht realize that the aesthetics of the *Messingkauf* (buying a trumpet for its brass value) would be adopted by men such as Luggi Waldleitner, who buy a piece of history for its (song-)title? To talk of commercialization, "exploitation," or commodification is to miss the point. We suffer from overproduction of both commodities and discourses, but we now produce commodities directly *as* discourses (repetition is a form of destruction and recycling). Their consumption is managed, regulated, and assured by periodic de- and revaluations, which is to say, by either adjustment or redefinition of the material support of the signifiers.

The historical montage of Fassbinder's film is a *trompe l'oeil* effect, achieved by suppression and foreshortening of the many specific instances mediating between "Lili Marleen" and a Fascist war. These instances appear as discontinuities, cuts, abrupt transitions, only insofar as they represent different states of power, energizing and reinforcing each other across the gaps of the many media forms, the institutions, the representations, the channels of communication, the circuits of production and consumption. The gaps, modalities, and manifestations of the invisible substance of power also produce "subject-effects," emotions, and intensities. That is the secret of power's hold on desire. Commodities and discourses are, in their "origins," circulation, and destinies, subject to the same disjunctive logic of exchange and transformation that concentrates economic power on one side, while splitting and dividing the subject on the other.

Surrealism, dada, and conceptual art have consciously and unconsciously shadowed this leapfrog logic of monopoly capitalism with their
mimetic or critical discourses. The difference between readings of surrealism as symptomatic or as critical art practice may now, retrospectively,
seem uncomfortably slight. In the cinema, however, it would seem that
the symptomatic *is* the critical discourse, and vice versa. Love stories,
crimes, domestic interiors, disasters, battle scenes, the factory facade, the
city street, the view of Monument Valley are surely in some sense the
equivalents of Duchamp's urinal or bottle-rack or Max Ernst's magazine
illustrations: ready-mades, the material substratum, transformed by cinematographic reproduction and editing into the support of signs.
Preconditions for the discourses of the real and on the real being narrative
découpage, editing, and framing, one might well place Lang, Renoir, Ford,
and Hitchcock in the "avant-garde" beside Richter, Dulac, and Léger,
except that the discursiveness of the latter three lacks an equivalent grasp
of this social materiality of cinema, seen in relation to the act of separation
and disjuncture.

Fassbinder's materials are those of the commercial cinema, the
"industrial products," the commodities and consumer goods, transport-
ed from the hardware stores of show business to the cultural spaces of
the art cinema. For his melodramas have never, in any sense, addressed
the same audience as the Hollywood films of the 1950s that are now so
called. One sometimes wondered where to locate the spectator of the
early films, looking about for the object of the finger pointed in one's
direction. Fassbinder was able to develop forms of textuality in his films
which, while reframing and repositioning the melodrama as a genre, dis-
closed the constant slippage of the economic and the sexual, while
closely adhering to the modes of textuality of the popular cinema;
through pathos and irony the cinematic referent becomes a sign, retaining its materiality. Irony is, however, in many ways a weak kind of textuality, and Fassbinder has increasingly concentrated on narratives which
heighten coincidence, chance, and the apparently unmotivated contiguity of events. His films have become more political and historical in that
they move toward a more explicit "social" textuality. Fassbinder, increasingly concerned with the historical moments of rupture (the inflation
period, World War II, and the early postwar years), has redefined melodrama as a possible deconstruction of the hidden discursiveness in the
realm of the referent, history, material reality, and the psyche, on the
basis of a rigorous and everywhere enforced celebration of the arbitrary.
This regime of invisible division within social life itself is opposed by
Fassbinder in his later films through a textuality which parodies the
social text that is monopoly capitalism and its most flamboyant self-representation: fascism and the war. *Lili Marleen* develops in a series of
gags and jokes which point to the logic, by no means arbitrary, of the

economic and symbolic systems by which our society reproduces its power relations and thus lives its history.

The preoccupation with fascism in the cinema of the last decade is a complex European phenomenon, not satisfactorily explained by references to the appeal of political pornography. For countries without a strong and continuous tradition of filmmaking, international success may depend on an ability to "market" the national history as international spectacle.[4] Common currency, such as the iconography of Nazism, establishes a signifying system no less complete, or replete with antinomies and binarism, i.e., possible narratives, than say, the American West or the Civil War. Has fascism perhaps become Europe's answer to the Hollywood genre cinema? It might be argued that fascism was Europe's last genuinely historical experience, the negative image of unification, against which the troubled emergence of national states within the European Community can be assessed. Or, more accurately, the most violent, spectacular face/phase of capitalist production and of (symbolic) consumption prior to the age of the supermarket and the mass media.

In films such as Visconti's *The Damned*, Cavani's *Night Porter*, Bergman's *The Serpent's Egg*, Losey's *Mr. Klein*, Truffaut's *The Last Metro*, Schlöndorff's *The Tin Drum*, Syberberg's *Hitler—A Film from Germany*, Petersen's *Das Boot*, and Fassbinder's *Lili Marleen*, the Nazi regime and its visual paraphernalia function simultaneously within several other (generic, psychological, authorial, economic) discourses, so that the filmic status of fascism—as signifier, referent, or both—is therefore often extremely difficult to locate. The films of Fassbinder and Syberberg have an advantage in that they foreground those aspects of Nazism which make of it a specific subject of filmmaking in Germany. The establishment of connections between fascism and show business, with a view to a historical and critical placement of their own practice, appears to be the implicit common perspective of *Hitler* and *Lili Marleen*. Both directors have, on the immoderate scale characteristic of the new German cinema, found in the regime's use of radio as technology and as machine of social control a way of locating the present situation of the commercial film industry and state-sponsored German culture; and they have found in it a metaphor for the medium that would in time displace radio as well as the cinema, namely television.

They agree that the cinema can deal with history only when and where history itself has acquired an imaginary dimension, where the disjunction between sign and referent is so radical that history turns on a problem of representation, and fascism emerges as a question of subjectivity within image and discourse (of power, of desire, of fetish objects and commodities), rather than one of causality and determinants for a period, a subject, a nation.

We know that the arts have survived (as commodities for the market, as vehicles of ideology) in the face of all historical evidence of anachronism and subservience by virtue of an intense and sustained self-scrutiny. The cinema is, at this stage in its history, in a similar situation, as though its abandonment as site for ideological work in favor of television had become the necessary condition for a realization of its conceptual dimension. Reflexive films have long existed, but cinema's history is now seen within other histories. In the case of Fassbinder and Syberberg, the mutations and transformations of cinema through the German subsidy system and its marketing abroad as "authentic German culture" (the phrase is actually Herzog's) become the occasion for historical and theoretical reflection. Here, however, similarities end: although both directors are no longer dependent upon direct state funding, Syberberg's quasi-artisanal mode of production contrasts sharply with Fassbinder's essentially industrial form of filmmaking. Syberberg's treatment of profilmic material produces a condensation of image and narrative, reminiscent of certain avant-garde movements of the early twentieth century which attacked pictorial representation and the *romanesque* with the economy of the mechanically reproduced, the collage, and the juxtaposition of heterogeneous verbal and visual material. There is in his work, however, an essayistic discursiveness that owes more to baroque or biblical models of interpretation than to surrealism. Compared to Syberberg's textual system, it is the *romanesque*, with its metaphorical condensation of time into action and argument into character conflict, that appears as the saving reductionism of fictional discourse.

The conceptual dimension of Fassbinder's work derives not from a reduction in the profilmic, the materials of film production, but rather from a certain narrative economy: his grasp of the idioms of popular cinema and the image-work condensed in its narrative stereotypes and dramatic clichés, as well as his understanding of the abstract forces inherent in the rhetoric of mise-en-scène and of editing technique. The devices of illusionistic representation—camera movement, in-depth lighting, point-of-view, and reverse-field cutting—yield, in *Lili Marleen*, a textuality in which the imagined plenitude of filmic representation is opened through ellipsis and disjunctive cross-cutting.

In the classical narrative cinema, a relay of surrogates, a process of substitution, is constantly activated with respect to point-of-view and the delegation of the look. Considered as a system of enunciation, any form of direct address—be it spectacle, "number," or performance—makes the fictional space contract, approximating a kind of zero degree of filmic narration. There are film directors—most notably Sternberg, but also Antonioni (in the films made with Monica Vitti) or Godard in *Pierrot Le Fou*—who use their female stars and their performative presences as a way of literalizing, "representing" the filmic process itself. In Sternberg's

Marlene Dietrich films, spectacle often draws attention to the (absurd, improbable, even tragic) disproportion of means to ends, causes and effects. When, in *The Scarlet Empress*, huge doors are worked by an army of attendants or, in *Shanghai Express*, crowds of extras surround the train with their myriad activities so that Marlene Dietrich can fan herself in statuesque immobility as if to recover from the sight of so much human sweat, do we not have a relation between the cinematic apparatus—camera, crane, technicians, lights, pieces of machinery—invisible to the spectator, and the spectacular display of a mere image, highlighting the narrative insignificance of the action? The ironic and gratified smile of Dietrich on such occasions evokes pleasure (and a measure of self-deprecation) in the immense and absurd labor involved in displaying her image, her effortless entrance, presence, performance. She appears to know that she is watched, not so much by the imaginary or invisible male gazes of diegetically present or inferred audiences, but by the immense business of an elaborate machinery, which is itself a metaphor of (male) sexuality. The psychological motivation provided by the narrative is an expedient disguise for the pleasure that consists in becoming aware of this play, of this discrepancy between the machinations of the apparatus and the phantasmatic nature of the apparition.

In Fassbinder's film, this metaphorical relation of performance, of spectacle to camera and apparatus is disturbed and foregrounded in such a way as to become the condition under which a purely fictive, anecdotal relationship of spectacle to a political or historical referent can be actualized in the cinema. Fassbinder's refusal to construct a "properly" constituted narrative space, the ellipses and elisions of plot information and of image construction and spatial continuity, his very flat, frontal, and symmetrical compositions, juxtaposed with very cluttered, obstructed, wilfully extreme viewpoints, generate a systematic opposition between motivated point-of-view shot and exhibitionist performance which becomes a cinematic signifier in its own right. The spectacle is thus broken down into the imaginary one-to-one relationship between performer and viewer (sign of illusionist immediacy), and the relation seeing/seen comes to signify the agencies that produce the spectacle not behind the scenes, but in front of them. This "in front of" makes possible the entry of the extracinematic referent ("history," fascism) by way of a metaphorical relation to the filmmaking process, for which the action/performance on the screen is the metonymic surrogate. It would therefore be inaccurate to say that the song "Lili Marleen" is a metaphor, or even a representation *en abîme* of Fassbinder's film of that title. But *Lili Marleen*—the fictional narrative and the historical pre-text, the song and its reiterated performance in sound and image, the subject slippage of actress, character, name, and addressee—does create a symbolic field of receding and nested references that places the film both as material object and, in the act of consumption, within the mirror-image of its own subject. To point to an obvious example: Hanna Schygulla plays a woman called Willie, singing a song in which a first-person narrator (a man) addresses an unnamed woman by invoking another woman, named Lili Marleen. Once this song has become popular, because it provides a subject position and a temporality for lonely men in the trenches, Willie autographs pictures of Hanna Schygulla with the name Lili Marleen. Hanna Schygulla is not Willie (in the tautology elaborated over decades by the star system which allows actor or actress to "use up" the fictional character they portray), she is Lili Marleen, because both are identical imaginary objects (or discursive effects) for two historically distinct audiences (soldiers of World War II and cinema spectators now) constructed *en abîme* in relation to each other. Fassbinder, in *Lili Marleen*, isolates something as ephemeral and banal as a popular song, albeit one that, like the cinema, commands its own imaginary and mythological space within history. This space is such that it can be neither metonymically collapsed with history (in the sense that one might be tempted to say that "Lili Marleen" stands for the use of the mass media under fascism) nor metaphorically separated from it (by treating the song as a symbolic representation of the cinema, for instance). It is precisely the complex status of the song as object, irreducible and recalcitrant to the uses it served, and at the same time, product, expression, and signifier of a historical period, which is at issue. The narrative is charged with tying down, anchoring, and articulating these relations and effects in both their metaphorical and metonymic implications.

Lili Marleen is a love story. Love stories such as *Dr. Zhivago* and *Reds*, played out against the background of historical events, advertise themselves as prestige products of the international film industry. Such films, however, represent not only the accumulation of production values and second-unit location work; they represent, as well, a certain textuality in which the narrative organization prescribes roles to the characters that relate them to the events as either embodiments or antagonists of the historical conflicts. As heroes or victims of history, they participate in a rigorously metaphorical discourse. Battles and revolutions, a journey or an exodus, the founding of a nation or the fall of an empire duplicate or counterpoint individual desire or the destiny of a family in a reciprocity of analogies and paradigms. The dramatic and spectacular ingredients of a film epic meet in the contractual coherence of the package deal as a montage of elements which the narrative is called upon to articulate and shape into binarisms and metaphoric equivalences.

Recent novels, as for example, D. M. Thomas's *The White Hotel*, have, with a certain knowing confidence, attempted to employ this popular mode in order to turn it against itself. *Lili Marleen*, like *The White Hotel*, extracts its heroine from narrated history to implicate her in ways that directly challenge the metaphorical construction of classical narrative. Questions of heterogeneity and disjunction in these works are inseparable from questions of sexuality and desire. Fassbinder (dis-)articulates his narrative as a sequence of coincidences, accidents, ruptures, border crossings, and discontinuities: "love" is what always inhabits the spaces in between.

In this respect, a line of development emerges from Fassbinder's career as a filmmaker. The early films could be described as love stories in which the desire of the central character displaces itself ceaselessly in relation to an unattainable object and in which the quest terminates in literal or symbolic death (*The Merchant of Four Seasons, The Bitter Tears of Petra von Kant, Fear Eats the Soul, Fox and His Friends*). In each case the object seems, more or less explicitly, to be the maternal body—a reading which the films, however, attempt, as it were, to block by a rather didactic use of coincidences, underscoring nonpsychological structure. When, for instance, in *The Merchant of Four Seasons*, Hans hires as his assistant the very man whom his wife had taken as her lover, the fact that Hans remains ignorant of the irony is less important than the narrative economy that results from the construction of a dramatic hinge between sexual and economic exchange. Exaggerated coincidences, in films like *Fox and His Friends* or *Fear Eats the Soul*, appear as part of Fassbinder's strategy of redefining melodrama as social parable. In the later films, the structural use of coincidence has if anything increased in importance, especially in the films that deal with fascism; nevertheless, they cannot be read as social parables.

If one looks at *Despair, The Marriage of Maria Braun*, and *Lili Marleen*, one notices that all three films begin with a moment of break, in which an apparently "successful" heterosexual object-choice is disturbed by the more or less violent entry of a completely different referent. In *Despair* it is the Wall Street Crash that seems bound up with the hero's mental dissociation, and in *Maria Braun* an explosion at the Registrar's office anticipates both the violent collapse of the Third Reich and the couple's separation. These political or economic signifieds are casually embedded in the narrative, but the relations of equivalence established between psychological motivation and political issues and events become increasingly precarious. Whereas in *Despair* it is possible to construct an essentially metaphorical discourse which holds the film in place until it deconstructs itself before the spectator's eye as a fiction of filmmaking ("I am a film actor. Don't look at the camera. I am coming out."), the relation between love and war in *Maria Braun* or *Lili Marleen* is the very occasion for a noncongruent, nonmetaphorical discourse. The collisions, divisions, and separations that structure these films when read as metaphorical appear preposterous. It is this which has led many critics to dismiss *Lili Marleen* as just that: a preposterous exercise in bad taste. This judgment is founded on the mistaken assumption (provoked by the manner in which juxtaposition teases the spectator with the promise of a hidden analogy) that the film constructs its coherence on the apparently naive metaphorical relationship between fascism and the song, between a doomed love affair and a war ending in defeat. Yet in *Lili Marleen* both love story and fascism are represented in ways that effectively dismantle the armature of popular romance and historical melodrama.

Maria Braun has generally been interpreted as a further exploration of the critical possibilities inherent in the Hollywood family melodrama. Fassbinder appears to establish a link between emotional privation and economic investment, leaving open the question whether economic activity is a substitute for sexual gratification or sexual activity a displacement of the erotic attraction of power. In this respect, *Maria Braun* does seem to invert the conventions of the melodrama, where the economic is usually the dimension that is repressed and thus gives to the dramatic situation the force of emotional excess. Here, renunciation and emotional coldness underpin a certain puritan work ethic, which provides a meta-psychological explanation for the energy Germans invested in the reconstruction of their national economy. Such a New Left reading of (Sirkian) melodrama by critics (including Fassbinder himself) does not altogether account for the perversity of a film like *Maria Braun* and risks seeing the heroine as an allegorical figure. It is true that in concentrating on the economic repressed of Hollywood melodrama, Fassbinder offers a view of the genre's social function within the historical context of the 1940s and '50s. But Maria Braun mourns her missing husband even after his release, for she engineers situations that send him first to prison and then to Canada where he, too, can make a fortune. The marriage survives because it remains based on separation and is practically unconsummated, except in death, and under circumstances that return to and repeat, in the form of parody and "farce," the historic explosion which opens the film. There is considerable figurative ambiguity about the ending: whether it is an intratextual deferral of the initial violence, thereby constructing the terms of a difference that gives the narrative the circularity of its closure, or the representation of an orgasmic moment that subsumes a psychic and a political referent in a common metaphor, is critically undecidable. It would appear that *Maria Braun* revolves around the heroine's attempt to retain absolute control over the terms of her own libidinal economy within a historical period of rapid and violent economic changes.

Lili Marleen resembles Sirk's *A Time to Love and a Time to Die* in the way it sets love story against the background of historical events. It resembles *Maria Braun* in the way it represents this love as forceful and significant only insofar as it is based on separation, rupture, nonfulfillment. The story about love is doubled (or multiplied perhaps) by a story not, as in *Maria Braun*, about the love object, but about an objectification of this love in a form that both contains it and betrays it, namely the song "Lili

Marleen." But in order to consider the significance of this shift, from the absence of the love object to its displacement by mechanical reproduction in the form of a phonograph record, it is necessary briefly to indicate how *Lili Marleen* actually does refer itself to the codes of filmic melodrama.

The film opens with the lovers in each other's arms. The stereotypical goal of the melodrama is here its point of departure. The subsequent narrative develops out of the interruption of this embrace which ensues when Robert's brother enters the room to remind him of his duty toward his father and the Jewish resistance group operating from Switzerland against the Nazis. The scene sets out all the antinomies that simultaneously structure the conflicts—Jew/Aryan, Nazi/underground, Germany/Switzerland, father/lover—and keep the lovers apart. Since nonfulfillment is not only the driving force but also the goal of the narrative, the conflicting terms are never mediated in a "classical" narrative resolution. Robert's insistent demand to know which side Willie is on never receives an answer. Rather, the condition of their love is that it sustain the territorial and moral divisions that the film sets up. As in *Maria Braun*, object and desire establish a unity in the heroine only across a separating bar which both films represent as, among other things, a geographical border.

At one level, the narrative movement of *Lili Marleen* simply illustrates the pressures that force the lovers to identify themselves with groups opposed to their love—the Jewish resistance on the one side, Nazi show business on the other. Both remake themselves in the image and the terms of the worlds they inhabit, at the same time as they try to use these worlds to realize their love. The world of moral and political obligations which Robert chooses turns out to be dominated in every respect by his father, so that he is defined completely by the oedipal limits of patriarchy. The world of spectacle, show, performance, and self-display which Willie chooses is synonymous with Nazism. The difference between Robert's and Willie's "inscription" into society reproduces the sexual difference which society traditionally sanctions. The Law of the Father allots duty, work, renunciation to him; specularity and objectification to her.

The film also makes a distinction between the vicissitudes of Robert's and Willie's displaced desires. As these are so carefully underscored, *Lili Marleen*, depending on whose destiny one is most concerned with, is actually two films: a melodrama and an antimelodrama. Robert's story follows the lines of the typical German melodrama of the mid–'30s, exemplified, say, by Detlev Sierck's *Schlussakkord* and of "composer" or "great artist" films that Hollywood made popular during the 1930s and '40s. In these films, an impossible love, the lashings of sexual frustration, gives rise to virtuoso performances and master works. This identification, by bourgeois art forms, of art and frustrated love is attributed, in a complexly edited scene near the film's end, to the castration anxiety which empowers the Law of the Father. The face-to-face meeting of Willie and Robert at the

Zurich opera house is mediated by the glances of two women—Robert's mother and his wife. These glances are intercut at several points, however, by an image that cannot be located within the diegetic space of the narrative, but that acts as a kind of master shot for the sequence: this is a frontal mirror shot of Robert's father as a benevolent but threatening spectator of both the triumphant performance onstage and the embarrassing scene backstage. Robert's escape into the world of performance has not liberated him from anxiety as Willie's spectacular resurrection as the mythical Lili Marleen has liberated her by giving her, as she says, "a passport to no longer being afraid."

Willie's story offers a reading that turns the melodrama on its head; it also suggests a kind of psychoanalytic approach to the genre. She, too, sublimates and displaces her unfulfilled desire in music and performance. The substitutive function of "Lili Marleen," when she first sings it in a Munich nightclub, is explicitly established by the phone call she places backstage to Robert in Zurich. Her frank and reiterated declaration of love can be heard, due to a fault in the amplification system, throughout the bar, to the great hilarity of the guests and to the detriment of her performance. The attempt to fix her subjectivity in this way is a disaster, quite literally, insofar as her cabaret number gives rise to a riot in the bar, between a group of young Germans in SA uniforms and some English visitors. The ensuing demolition of the premises is staged and cut in a manner later reserved for the depiction of air attacks and of bomb explosions in German trenches. These shots are themselves intercut with those of bouquets of flowers being tossed on stage in tribute to her smash hit. Here is a good example of Fassbinder's undercutting of the metaphorical use of parallel editing by playing on a pun: "Lily Marleen" is a *Bombenerfolg*, while the bombs are falling; human bodies erupt from the ground like flowers on opening night.

There is another irony at work in Willie's story. Frustration is not sublimated in a symphony, an immortal score, or an unforgettable performance, but in the performance of a popular song on a phonograph record. Fassbinder, however, twice makes the point that no psychological, causal, or intentional relationship exists between the singer and the phonograph record. Frustrated love remains just that: her performance is a flop, and the fact that her Nazi protector insists on recording it merely emphasizes that it is not her desire that speaks, but someone else's desire for her. Even the record would have passed unnoticed, had it not been for the coincidence of the war's breaking out. It takes the additional fortuity of the Belgrade radio operator's finding a stray copy of it among looted spoils for the song to air at all. At the climax of her career, Willie dances around the luxury apartment given to her by the Führer; holding a mirror in front of her, she exclaims, "We've made it, we're above the clouds." Taschner, her pianist and companion, responds as if to complete her sentence, "And the irony is, you have no voice and I'm a lousy pianist." This is the most Sirkian moment in the film, a rapid undercutting of subjective elation with a sobering objectivity. Irony is piled upon irony: Taschner's comment severs, in the most direct and brutal way, any organic or necessary connection that might be thought to exist between singer and song, self-expression and success, talent and recognition, subjectivity and image, authenticity and exhibition value. Which advises us, as spectators, against construing the relationship between love and war as metaphorical—or as merely coincidental.

The all-night recording session in which the song is cut is most revealing of the film's ironies. After several takes, Willie's manager agrees to a short break; it is 6:00 AM. They turn on the radio for the news just in time to hear Hitler announce, "Since 5:45 AM this morning, the German Army is returning fire." The outbreak of the war coincides with the recording of the song. A cliché from the B-picture thriller—the hero on the run turns on the radio to learn that he is wanted by the police—thus serves to introduce a historical referent, a documentary piece of evidence that the cliché clearly cannot contain. Not only has war been declared, but outside in the park, Willie's lover is waiting, having crossed the border illegally and against his father's orders. These three moments of drastically unequal weight and significance are made to coexist within the same narrative space, against all probability, and in breach of every code of verisimilitude (except that which governs the comic book). It is only the artifice of fictional construction, dependent on the viewer's ability to read coincidence as a conceptual montage effect, which unites these events. Otherwise the incongruity between the private, the anecdotal, and the historical remains so radical and unbridgeable as to offend the sophisticated viewer's sense of proportion and even propriety. For having to read the coincidence between the end of a recording session and the start of a world war as significant on the diegetic level—as a moment of symmetry, as an explanation of why the song was so meaningful during the war—amounts to dismissing the film as "not serious."[5] The scene must appear as grotesque, unless one sees the film as pressing narrative coincidence to the point where it deconstructs itself as "gag."

Fassbinder here appropriates, as he had already done in *Satan's Brew* (1976), the logic of film comedy for melodrama—a move that in this case primarily is motivated by his views of fascism and the shortcomings of the melodrama as a socially significant form. The problem with melodrama, as has already been indicated, lies in its particular modes of disjuncture and discontinuity: irony and pathos. Both depend on the spectator's assumption of a secure position of knowledge, which is to say, on a narrative which establishes a strong sense of closure. Depictions of fascism, for example, are ironic, whenever they assume, as they invariably do, the spectator's knowledge of fascism's historical and geographic boundaries. The play of anticipation, rhyme, and echo-effects which this knowledge allows makes the historic referent metaphorical. Fassbinder's problem is precisely how to inhibit this metaphorization, how to stop Nazism from becoming a Hollywood melodrama which is what it becomes in all narrative accounts, since the reader-viewer knows in advance "how it ended." In *Lili Marleen*, May '45 is not the endpoint of the narrative, nor is irony its primary mode. The misconception that fascism has ended, has been contained, that it was just another story is thus disallowed. Instead coincidence is presented as gag and disturbs, with its asymmetry and nonequivalence, the formal closure of popular narrative.

A series like *Holocaust* attempts to contain fascism by translating its effects and making it equivalent to the bourgeois family. What is scandalous to many viewers of *Lili Marleen* is that the relation family/fascism is presented as a structural symmetry onto which the antagonism Jew/Aryan is simply mapped as additional confirmation that the heroine must find her subject position outside either set of value systems or narrative constraints, at the same time as she represents an object—of value, of exchange—for both sides. Her lover's anti-fascism is entirely recuperated within patriarchy. His desires thus become fixed in an object-choice and a mode of "self-expression" that trap him in the melodramatic resolutions of renunciation and sublimation. For Willie, on the other hand, political and subjective value are noncongruent. By resisting all constructions of herself in terms of binary oppositions, she achieves a particular kind of freedom. She becomes a sign without a unique referent. Instead, *several* referents— notably her star image and the phonograph record—are simultaneously attached to her, allowing her desire to exist outside either possession or fulfillment. Neither her show business "personality" nor the song she records and sells represents or expresses her desire, except in the way they permit her to constitute herself outside fascism and outside the family. Spectacle becomes a form of escape. Whereas her lover forcibly unifies himself in a discourse of repression, she lives desire as pure displacement and difference without fetish or object.

Fassbinder becomes aware of the limits of melodrama at precisely the point where the major ideological premise of his earlier work begins to change, namely that "love"—whether given or withheld, whether betrayed or upheld against all odds—is both the supreme source of value and the supreme instrument of inequality and exploitation. In all his early films, emotional, sexual, and economic exploitation are metaphors for each other, substitutable fields that make love "colder than death." Love remains the only currency still valid, but it lends itself to any form of speculation and calculation of gain and loss. Godard links economic and emotional relations under capitalism through the metaphor of prostitution (the ubiquity of exchange-value criticized from a romantic perspective of use-value), so that in his films it is only the active *pursuit* of prostitution

(*My Life to Live, Two or Three Things I Know about Her, Everyman for Himself*) which affords any promise of freedom. Fassbinder, for whom it is above all the way love is traded within the family that provides the condition for perpetuating exploitation elsewhere has, in his recent films, shed any residual romanticism about alienated use-value as the basic source of value in Western societies, and instead begun to analyze what is paradoxical and ideological in the very notions of exploitation and prostitution.

In an obvious, though banal sense, *Lili Marleen* does pose the paradox of the earlier films: is Willie prostituting herself to the Nazis in exchange for fame and wealth, or is she merely being exploited by the regime that launches her on a career? How can she be on the right side (morally) and on the wrong side (physically); how can she work for the resistance and be a figurehead and showcase for the Nazis; how can she love Robert and accept the luxury and glamour with which the Führer himself surrounds her? To think of her as either exploited or as prostituting herself is to hold her to the same binary alternative as her lover does. One sees here a constellation of factors which could structure a much simpler film, a "classical" melodrama where male desire, established and simultaneously divided by the jealousy that results from the oedipal triangulation, salvages itself from its own contradictions through the phantasmatic production of the woman as both victim and villain.

It is through the constant return to periods of economic crisis and collapse in his recent work, the dramatization of an unfulfilled and unfulfillable desire, that Fassbinder represents "exploitation" as a false question, or rather, as merely the partial and particular form of another problem. Recognizing that her desire is unfulfillable—that any desire is unfulfillable—Willie withdraws herself from the sphere of authority and control, from gain and loss. The question becomes no longer one of "exploitation," but of that which underpins and gives currency to exploitation and speculation, namely substitution and substitutability. In short, the realm of metaphor and exchange, where narrative form and the social production of meaning and value converge, is exposed to examination.

At the same time as Willie seemingly consents to lend her voice and body, her image and her performance to the Nazi regime, she also lets herself be used by the other side. Her attempted suicide is seized upon by the Jewish resistance as an occasion for making public to the world press certain facts about the concentration camps. In a countermove, the Nazis revive her in order to bring her back on stage. She is paraded before the same international press, as evidence that the Jewish claims—not about Lili Marleen, but about the concentration camps—are mere propaganda. The "reality" of her performance, of her death, and of the concentration camps, is entirely subsumed by their function as signifiers and shifted from one discourse to another. Her final appearance enacts that blissful version of death which turns the individual into a transparent sign—dematerialized, the human substance which has supported it is used up. Only by turning herself into a site of sign-production, while at the same time insisting on difference, does Willie escape being constructed as an object—of desire and exchange, a commodity.

It is almost entirely within this perspective—which is obviously also the perspective of Fassbinder's own construction as a filmmaker, as a performer in the cultural contexts of sign and commodity production—that fascism becomes specific as well as historical in *Lili Marleen*. Although the well-known iconography of historical spectaculars invades the film, Nazism maintains its metonymic ties with the war, or rather, with several kinds of warfare (the military fronts, the propaganda and media war, and the "secret war" between the Nazis and the Jewish resistance organization). The rigorous and businesslike administration of war destroys existing criteria of value and conventional forms of coherence. War is represented from the point of view of production: it is seen as an acceleration and a unifying force which, by speeding up the productive and reproductive cycles of the economy, intensifies consumption. This is, in the film, the point on which another surreal gag turns. The popularity of the song is confronted with the need of a fascist society to liquidate and destroy surplus material (human and technological) in its attempt to impose the abstract and disguised rationality of war. "Six million"—Willie's face beams as she is told by her Nazi friend how many listeners are tuning in to "Lili Marleen" every night. "Fantastic," she says, trying to hug herself with both arms to confirm that this means her. Turned to the camera in medium close-up, Hanna Schygulla's face reveals the bliss which her definition as a star, by means of sales sheets and rating figures, brings her. Six million— the figure connects her fans, soldiers dying in the trenches, and the Jews dying in concentration camps, as it equates mass consumption and show business with war and organized waste. The coincidence of soldier and fan is turned by Fassbinder into a gag when a pianist-turned-soldier takes his platoon over the hill and straight into the machine gun fire of the Russians whom he mistakes for German troops because they, too, are playing "Lili Marleen."

If this is an example of the way the same becomes different, of the way the song is shown to be nonidentical with itself, the extent to which this is a structural principle of the film as a whole emerges in the sequence in which Willie attempts to prove to her lover that she is on his side. The film documenting the existence of concentration camps in Poland is smuggled out under cover of Willie's Eastern Front entertainment tour; it is given to her during a car ride which is to provide her with an alibi for a meeting with her lover. The Gauleiter's attempt to recover the film (she has hidden it in her bra) is deliberately misinterpreted by her as a sexual advance she rebuffs with the help of her pianist friend, whose assertion of his own sexuality starts off another chain reaction leading directly to his death. During a body search ordered by the Nazi command, he offers to transmit film to the Jewish resistance as a sign of his love for her, even though he knows that for Willie the film is merely a sign of her love for Robert. The film reaches Switzerland at the same time as Robert's father is negotiating the release of his son captured by the Nazis, who demand the film in exchange for Robert's return. The film, which is never actually exhibited, is circulated and exchanged in a number of conflicting deals and "discourses," acquiring from each a different value quite separate from any original meaning or intended use. It is Robert's brother, the "terrorist," who refuses to submit to the logic of these exchanges between sex and politics, cinema and life. He blows up the bridge between Germany and Switzerland, reestablishes their division and distinction, because, as he says, he hates "these dirty deals."

As Willie receives the information about the number of fans who comprise her audience, her face is lit by a lamp, placed conspicuously in the foreground. Her Nazi friend, standing diagonally opposite in the background, idly (and prominently) spins a globe. Glamour lighting of the star image controlled by the global strategies of war, trade, and dominion—or a subjectivity entirely enthralled by itself on one side of the divide, and an objectivity wholly instrumentalized on the other? The fascist war economy and its show business operation appear as a kind of immense and universalized black market where, in the manner of all military dictatorships, the Nazis impose their own rate of exchange—fixed from moment to moment and liable to sudden and surreal reversals—which suspend all moral or referential values other than their own. With this, Fassbinder's view of show business as an instrument that splits sign from referent is doubled by the picture of fascism as a form of crisis management in the economic sphere, called upon to regulate by force the acceleration of production. Seen as eliminating surplus by simple destruction while at the same time developing radio, and organizing through it an elaborate system of transportation and communication, Nazism becomes a particularly flamboyant figuration of capitalism in the sphere of representation—not merely because of its gigantic aspirations or the brutality of its public life, but more because of its power to reorganize a society's ethical, material, and erotic relations in the direction of spectacle or rituals of communal consumption of sounds and images.

The identification, in *Lili Marleen*, of mass coercion (the Nazi regime and the army) with mass consumption (show business and the electronic "global village" of radio and television) interesting is in another respect. The question which Nazism raises today perhaps is less its relation to material production and capitalism, or the monstrous scale and consequence of its demographic planning, than its astounding ability to create a public sphere, a mass audience. The song of Lili Marleen, endlessly repeated as a nightly ritual above and between the sights and sounds of war, is such a fascinating phenomenon, partly because of the discrepancy between the pure presence of the song, hermetically sealed by its technological immediacy from any contact and context, and the ceaselessly destructive and immensely busy machinery of war. Media technology binds, in this case, performer and listener in an imaginary unity. It molds a whole array of social and communicative activities (performance, recording, broadcasting, listening, phoning, and letter-writing) around something which, while still in need of some sort of material support (a phonograph record, a receiver, a broadcasting station), nonetheless has no determinants itself other than a kind of mirror surface for the projection or reflection of desire.

What exactly is this desire? In a sense, "Lili Marleen" voices a protest, a refusal, a critique even: it says no to war, and yes to memory, loss, and love. ("For you and I again to meet/Under the lantern on the street/Like times gone by, Lili/Gone by, Lili Marleen"). One can see why the Nazi leadership felt ambiguous about it, because it gives expression to a death wish at the same time as it disguises and disavows it ("Out of the earthly soil, out of the silent realm/Your loving lips could lift me, as if in a dream/And later, when the fog is rolling in/I'll stand beneath the lamp again/Like times gone by . . .").

This double impulse may well explain the song's popularity during the war; it certainly explains the symptomatic significance which it is granted in the film. As a protest and a refusal, its message would seem to be at odds with its social and political function as a nightly theme song: to boost morale and unite the population—civilian and military—behind the idea of the *Volksgemeinschaft* and the Führer. The stark opposition of love to military discipline in the song, its "politics of subjectivity," is, however, recuperated by the ritual and turned to the advantage of the regime. But the situation is even more complex. Not only is the song repeated nightly (and throughout the film), it is itself entirely built on repetition and refrain ("*wie einst*"—like times gone by). Conjuring up a lost object and a lost moment, both of which the song re-presents and repossesses through the refrain and the overall melodic structure, the song is clearly obsessional and fetishistic.[6]

How is it that mass subjectivity becomes so intricately bound up with this obsessional song? As Robert is tortured by broken snatches of the song, we are given a vivid representation of the hounding persistence of the compulsion to repeat and of the frustration, violence, or aggression it entails. The utterly subjective death-wish expressed in the song stands in symmetrical relation to the historical death to which its listeners are headed. For, by the film's terms, the German popular culture which is massively committed to the articulation and representation of subjectivity and desire works in tandem with an entertainment industry that extends its dominion and economic control more and more firmly into the same area—that of the subject. Here the split, unreconciled in most contemporary theories of culture, between the economic structure of the mass media and the political meaning of subjectivity, is made obvious. As the products of culture reveal their commodity/sign status, which destines them for consumption or the devaluation/revalorization processes of the market, so the subjectivity that articulates itself across these products speaks only of loss and destruction, nostalgia and death. In this respect, the particular "sensibility," the powerfully melancholic, Saturnalian turn of the new German cinema is perhaps nothing other than the precisely perceived demonstration of its political function, the negative truth about its objective condition: the representation of radical subjectivity trapped in commodity form.

The more the song, "Lili Marleen," is repeated, the more it becomes a pure signifier, able to signify any number of different and contradictory signifieds, to enter into any number of conflicting discourses. Caught in a cycle of repetition, it no longer denotes anything, but merely connotes a wholly abstract, generalized structure of absence or loss and reinforces the primary death wish of the subject. Yet the song colludes with fascism only insofar as its repetitive form installs within the subject that same synthesizing force which unites the social system to a fascist politics, unites it, that is, under a single figure, a single image, a single insignium.

The disjunctive though metonymic relations between performer and song on the one hand, and between song and material object/commodity on the other are absolutely fundamental to Fassbinder's conceptualization of the cinema, since they implicate, by way of a series of displaced analogies and *en abîme* constructions, the film object and its author/performer. The song, insofar as it exists prior to and apart from its material shape as record or infinitely repeatable performance, may function as a mode of self-expression, a declaration of love, of morbid protest, of a desire for nostalgic return; it may even, in its circularity, assert a kind of internal closure and coherence, of aesthetic autonomy. Its value as a record of subjective intention, however, contrasts with its exhibition or circulation value, since its intentions become literally immaterial as soon as the work realizes itself in the iterative acts of consumption. It is these acts which establish the commodity as sign, as vehicle (potential or actual) of an infinite number of discourses—the critical discourse being only one among several.

This sign form is, above all, the symbol of the technical and economic power inherent in the mass media, of the power it has to reorganize, from the point of view of consumption, both the production of materials and of meaning. As these totally abstract processes of power emerge in concrete contexts (here, as a song that serves to console soldiers on both sides as they face annihilation; that becomes an instrument of torture, a political weapon in a propaganda war, a means of turning an individual into a star), they assume for their material support not that which is rich, varied, or profound, but that which is bland, banal, devoid of any but the power to circulate. The mass media artifact is thus not the product of a field of combative forces—between the author, for example, and the industry which exploits him or her—but of the site where, through immense technical and logistic effort, all forces are neutralized. The conjunction of Nazism and "Lili Marleen" illustrates the way the logistic-military machinery stages the perfect spectacle as the one from which all external referents are emptied.

Yet there is at work here another, conflicting force. "Lili Marleen" also obliquely, stubbornly opposes itself to all the forces that attempt to appropriate it. When Willie says, "I only sing," she is not as politically naive or powerless as she may appear. Just as her love survives because she withdraws it from all possible objects and objectifications, so her song, through its very circularity, becomes impervious to the powers and structures in which it is implicated. Love and song are both, by the end of the film, empty signs. This is their strength, their saving grace, their redemptive innocence. In this way Fassbinder acknowledges the degree to which his own work is inscribed within a complex system (of production, of dissemination and reception, of devaluation and revaluation) already in place and waiting to be filled by an individual, a locus of intention, energy, and desire. It is this system, after all, that transformed him from the director of this material (Nabokov's, Döblin's, Lale Andersen's) into a personality, a star. Straub and Huillet construct all their films around the notion of the resistance of their materials to the filmic process; Fassbinder, on the other hand, constructs his films around the notion of the inability of materials to resist. It is not through resistance, but through self-cancellation that materials are supposed to achieve any purity in his films.

Fassbinder has written a personal performance for himself into both *Maria Braun* and *Lili Marleen*. In *Lili Marleen* he is the leader of the resistance group who contacts Hanna Schygulla and gives her the film that will document for the "free world" the precise nature of German atrocities. In *Maria Braun* he plays a black-marketeer who gives Hanna Schygulla (again) the evening dress that launches her on a career as the "Mata Hari of the Economic Miracle." He also carries in his black suitcase a bottle of schnaps and the collected works of Heinrich von Kleist. These self-portraits establish the filmmaker as a trader in intoxicants, glamour, culture, and documentary evidence, selling his wares in a world where war and the black market fix the prices.

It is in this light that the direction of Fassbinder's later films, especially *Maria Braun* and *Lili Marleen*, becomes evident. As he deconstructs the irony and pathos of melodrama by highlighting coincidence, turning fortuity into a surreal gag, Fassbinder constructs tighter and tighter narratives. Convoluted and intricate relations of act and motive, of cause and consequence, the manipulative strategies of European history become signifiers of a narrative economy that realizes its objectives through the juxtaposition and equation of noncomparable entities. The logic of the narrative in which move gives rise to counter-move and acts of substitution or parallel editing replace head-on conflict becomes, in a very specific and restricted sense, the textual equivalent of the logic that regulates trade, barter, and exchange and defines value by force, the crossing of borders, and circulation of discourses. The logic which directs Robert's father first to pay for all of Willie's "debts" in order to accumulate enough evidence to obtain an expulsion warrant from the Swiss government, and then to allow Willie to accompany Robert to Munich so that the lovers can be served the warrant and legally separated at the German-Swiss border, is the mirror equivalent of the logic which directs the Nazis to use Willie and Robert as bait for each other and as pawns in the circuit of exchange that results in the release of Robert and the transfer of Jews to Switzerland. The same chiasmic path defines the journeys of the reel of film as it makes its way from Poland via Germany to Switzerland and back and "Lili Marleen" as it circulates between contending forces both within and outside Germany. Robert and Willie's love affair is always masterminded, but it would be inexact to interpret the film's logic—by which the actions and methods of the Jewish resistance and the Nazis parallel each other and seem to hint at some vast conspiracy which locates the lovers (and the spectator) as victims—as paranoid. Each move implies a redefinition of genre (melodrama, thriller, historical epic, musical), a testing of the value of the objects in circulation.

We might say that in this sense *Lili Marleen* reworks and historicizes Fritz Lang's *M* (in which police and organized crime are both in pursuit of the same suspect) and his *Mabuse* films (which are constructed entirely on the exchange and substitution of objects whose values are redefined). Certainly Fassbinder shares with Lang a concern for questions of cinematic enunciation, with the way a film addresses and situates the spectator. The two kinds of discursive practices which confront each other in *Lili Marleen*—the economic one of unlimited exchange-value and the narrative one of metaphor and metonymy—are brought together in a historical reading of a subject position, in a fiction which is not about madness or sexual pathology, but about fascism and the negative desire embodied in a song and a love affair. The theatrical address, the emphasis on performance and spectacle does not work to establish a unified position of knowledge, but to make visible that particular, historical inscription of desire which is controlled by popular fictions. Cinema is indeed a machine that displays desire, but most often this desire is disguised in the endless chains of substitution that make up the narrative. In Fassbinder, it is desire in its disjunctive dimension that displays the machine (the whole institution of film-making, including its part in trade, in film financing). Instead of attempting to arrest the flow of commodities and the marketing of history and its images, Fassbinder has helped to promote their circulation by giving his later films the same complex sign character that social "reality" has under capitalism. He insists, however, by the negativity of his self-consuming narratives and their not-to-be-realized consummations, on the nonreconciliation of sign and desire, of sign and referent. In this way he rescues for the cinema, for spectacle, a dimension of loss and incommensurability that makes desire itself appear a historical force.

Notes

1. See Roland Barthes, *Mythologies*, trans. Annette Lavers, New York, Hill and Wang, 1972, and "Rhetoric of the Image," in *Image-Music-Text*, trans. Stephen Heath, New York, Hill and Wang, 1977, pp. 32–51.

2. If the example of East European filmmakers (Polanski, Skolimowski, Forman, Passer, Jancso, Makaveyev) is politically overdetermined, the careers of Malle, Bertolucci, Wertmüller and of Truffaut, Chabrol, Reisz or Schlesinger have also developed in the 1970s within a field of force such that money from the major companies becomes treacherous, a gamble with a lifetime's work.

3. Two of the most vociferous lobbyists for the old industry, Luggi Waldleitner and Manfred Purzer, acted as producer and scriptwriter respectively on *Lili Marleen*.

4. Britain's BBC television exports and recent trends in the Australian cinema (*Gallipoli, Breaker Morant*) suggest such an assumption.

5. "It is a costly business digging up Germany's recent past. . . . *Lili Marleen* will have to gross over DM 11m at the box office just to recover its production cost. . . . With Fassbinder's favorite actress, Hanna Schygulla, in the title role, the film is a slap in the face of anybody who ever thought Fassbinder an important director: it is pure weepy. . . ." (*The Guardian*, February 6, 1981).

6. The refrain embodies a kind of temporality typical of the ballad form: circular and self-canceling, progressing forward from strophe to strophe while at the same time attempting regressively to rejoin the phantasmatic moment of origin. Presence is signified indirectly, by absence "beneath the street light's glow," "our two shadows," "as if in a dream," and so forth. In this respect "Lili Marleen" functions in a way similar to another famous song in another obsessional and fetishistic film: Marlene Dietrich's "Falling in Love Again" which appears refrainlike at the beginning and end of Sternberg's *Blue Angel*.

How American Is It: The U.S. as Image and Imaginary in German Film

ERIC RENTSCHLER

One might even venture to say that the familiar is reassuring. We more or less know what to expect. What it will be like. It will be familiar. Which may be a good reason why we, every once in a while, wish to get away, to escape from the familiar, to visit some far-off place . . . because we are willing . . . no . . . because we are eager to stretch our imaginations and see something for the first time, something that is not yet entirely familiar. And so, if we are open-minded, we want to introduce to our existence something that is new, something that is different. . . . And then, in no time, we discover that the longer we stay in one place, the longer we sleep in unfamiliar beds, the longer we meet people from other countries, the more familiar it all becomes. How long can something remain unfamiliar? And, perhaps an even more important question is, does the unfamiliar activate and spark our curiosity and interest? Is it a call to us to explore and familiarize ourselves with the unknown?

—Walter Abish, *How German Is It*[1]

I

TAKING STOCK of the American presence in German films, new and old, some remembered moments of one culture's occupation of another: images of Yankees far away from home, Fassbinder's American soldiers for instance, getting drunk in a *Wurstbude*, making passes on a train, or like the debonair Mr. Bill, accepting Maria Braun's invitation to dance and teaching her to speak English. Or one thinks of Wim Wenders' American friends, fictional and real, the cowboy in Hamburg, Tom Ripley, the dying maverick filmmaker, Nicholas Ray. Images, too, of German minds projecting American dreams: Munich low-lifers trying to recreate tough-guy poses gleaned from gangster movies, those back-alley desperadoes in Fassbinder's early exercises in *noir*. "An American in my situation," reflects a troubled Hoffmann in the first shot of Reinhard Hauff's *Messer im Kopf/Knife in the Head* (1978), "would probably shoot blindly out of the window." Images of Germans in Manhattan, matching scenes from above

Reprinted from *German Quarterly* 57 no. 4 (1984): 602–20. Permission to reprint granted by The American Association of Teachers of German.

the Empire State Building some forty years apart: Toni Feuersinger becomes an insignificant dot as he stands on the edifice in Luis Trenker's *Der verlorene Sohn/The Prodigal Son* (1934). Stroszek, Scheitz, and Eva (in Werner Herzog's *Stroszek* [1977]) consider their prospects in the New World from atop the structure before they move on to Railroad Flats, Wisconsin. America also as the refuge for an exiled film culture: Friedrich Munro (a thinly concealed reference to another emigrant director, F. W. Murnau) steps over a remembrance to Fritz Lang on the Hollywood Avenue of Stars in Wenders' *Der Stand der Dinge/The State of Things* (1982). And, not to forget, America as dangerous ground: Bavarians banished from the homeland march to their demise garbed in *Lederhosen* on some Wild West city street in Volker Vogeler's *Verflucht, dies Amerika/Damn This America* (1973). Presentiments, likewise, of America as a plague-bringer: a composition in Wenders' *Summer in the City* (1970) makes an Amoco gas station sign in Berlin read as "Amoc." Postcards and photographs from the U.S. as well: the poor people of Kombach (in Schlöndorff's film) partake eagerly of heartening accounts from peers who have found fortune in Milwaukee. One gazes upon a panorama of Monument Valley in a scorched Berlin during the air lift in Thomas Brasch's *Engel aus Eisen/Angels of Iron* (1980). Scenes of a neon-lit Las Vegas float through the head of an emigrant-to-be on her way to the Munich airport in Uwe Brandner's *halbe-halbe/Fifty-Fifty* (1977).

II

America in the minds of German filmmakers, especially West German ones: a fantasy, a daydream, a nightmare. The persistence of the foreign hold on postwar German imaginations has, to be sure, stimulated much discussion, speculation, and theorizing. Journalists and scholars alike have commented at length about what one critic aptly terms "the familiar cross-cultural fantasy syndrome, that troubled love-hate relationship entertained by Wenders and his peers with things American, expressed in the ubiquitously quoted quote. 'The Americans have colonised our unconscious'"— an approach, as Sheila Johnston goes on to say, "particularly popular with Germanists generally well-versed in identifying *Amerika-bilder* . . . in German literature."[2] The tendency has been to reduce a large complex of influence, borrowing, and interdependence, matters bound in a network of historical and sociopolitical determinants, down to simple variations on single themes. Three explanations dominate previous approaches to this question:

Thesis #1: Kilroy, the Betrayer, or The American Friend Turned Fiend.[3] In this scenario, America poses a threat to a fragile Old World. Cultural imperialism is an object of focus—and criticism, especially for New German filmmakers who grew up under its influence. Replacing the benevolent GIs who brought a shattered nation not only chewing gum and CARE packages, but a new cultural identity as well, American occupiers went on in later years to destroy the trust.[4] Americans have become increasingly ugly, ambassadors of materialism, diminishers of aura, bringers of potential doom. Stressing the virulent rejection of the powerful foreign culture and its diabolical hold on European imaginations, this Manichaean view nonetheless underplays the question of the continuing— and not always unabashedly negative—fascination with and appropriation of things American by young German directors, even after 1968 and Vietnam, and even now.[5]

Thesis #2: The Love-Hatred Syndrome.[6] America also means popular culture and Hollywood, an entertainment industry that galvanized West German imaginations in the postwar era, providing identification figures for a fatherless society. American film has played the role of captivator and liberator, that of a dominant cinema whose patterns limit associations and reproduce the world in codified and ready-made schemes, a procedure harshly taken to task in Horkheimer/Adorno's critique of the culture industry.[7] Film, though, also set free imaginations, presenting an alternative to the drab everyday of a country caught up in the difficult business of reconstruction. American film—and its popular culture in general—filled a very real gap in the fledgling democracy, serving as an ersatz homeland for youths growing up in the fifties, the future young filmmakers.[8]

American film also means a mighty industry, a hegemony over production, distribution, and exhibition which has circumscribed the making and partaking of images throughout the world. New German filmmakers, as Timothy Corrigan observes, are thus caught in a bind, victims of "a history that has been guided and nourished by the splendor of Hollywood and its images and a history that has been painfully aware of the lacks and deceptions at the center of those images."[9] One can even go a step further in this regard. So much of what one speaks of as American cinema came about as the work of emigrant German directors. Hollywood in fact would be unthinkable without the contributions of the Weimar film culture that to a great extent relocated there during the twenties and thirties. A sense of debt and recognition to this relocated film tradition makes the matter even more problematical. For in looking at American cinema, one looks on a simultaneous source of enchantment and disenchantment, a fascinating apparatus and a menacing behemoth. In doing so, though, one regards at the same time traces of one's own lost film history. Witness the often-discussed appropriation of Douglas Sirk by Fassbinder, who gained so much from the director's subversive reshaping of the melodrama in a host of Hollywood studios.[10] Or one recalls the lessons learned by Wenders, a permanent exile "at home on the road," as he considers Fritz Lang's course in time.[11] Numerous Young German filmmakers during the late sixties cast their second-hand gangster fantasies in a *noir* mold.[12] Volker Schlöndorff, upon accepting the Oscar for *Die Blechtrommel/The Tin Drum* (1979) before the Academy Award audience in 1980, acknowledged the connection to this emigrant legacy expressly, taking the prize in the name of "all those who worked here and whose tradition we want to pick up: Fritz Lang, Billy Wilder, Pabst, Murnau, Lubitsch."

Thesis #3: New German Cinema's Historical Amnesia and Escapist Tendencies. Faced with a traumatic heritage of fascism and genocide, Germans growing up in the Adenauer era—as Wenders once pointed out—sought refuge in American popular culture: "In other words, the need to forget 20 years created a hole, and people tried to cover this . . . by assimilating American culture."[13] New German filmmakers, Raymond Durgnat insists, have for this reason wallowed "in a pit of historical amnesia."[14] Unable to come to terms with their parents' past and ill-equipped to confront the social realities of the present, German filmmakers revert to foreign landscapes and other film cultures, anything to take their minds off their own history. This often-posed argument, however, overlooks much. It fails to consider numerous German films that skillfully mediate subjective and historical factors, works one might call (in the Benjaminian sense) "emergency brake films,"[15] works that explore the relation of individual histories to a more encompassing—and for the most part unwritten and repressed—general history. New German Film amounts to a decidedly national cinema, one very much bound up in questions of identity and collective memory, in the trauma of a still unassimilated past which persists in the present as a continuing source of tension and disquiet.

My deliberations focus on films in which German directors look at the United States. In the three examples I will discuss, America no doubt embodies a dream betrayed, a land of disenchantment and social inequity, a place where furious wheeler-dealing produces a vicious circle of materialism. I would like, however, to move beyond the familiar itineraries, the obligatory scenarios found in most popular accounts. America in all three instances—Trenker's *The Prodigal Son*, Herzog's *Stroszek*, and Wenders' *Alice in den Städten/Alice in the Cities* (1973)—does not only appear as a deflowered garden or sinister center of exploitation. More significantly, it functions as a playground for the imagination, as a mirror that reflects and intensifies the preoccupations and imported conflicts of its visitors. The U.S., strangely enough, rarely has an exotic aspect in West German films. Rather, it becomes a catalyst, a foreign terrain one treads while exploring oneself. In this way America figures more as an idea than a reality, more a matter of objects and images and fixations than real people and new experiences: if you will, an imaginary, a site where the subject comes to understand itself through a constant play and identification with reflections of itself as an other.

The motto from Abish's novel, a quote from Jean-Luc Godard, sums up the dynamics at work here: "What is really at stake is one's image of oneself."[16] *How German Is It* (whose subtitle *Wie Deutsch Ist Es* bears out the reflective mechanisms operating in this interaction) employs a strategy central to many West German evocations of America: minds ferment while abroad, but invariably "at the expense of the foreign culture."[17] German directors have made films set in America not so much "in order to 'understand' another culture"; rather, they have used the signs of another country to establish an enriched relationship to their own. Such a procedure "reduces the landscape, everything . . ., to a set of signs, of images and also introduces, not the interpretation itself, but the need for interpretation. . . ."[18] My subsequent remarks present a necessary reinterpretation of how the U.S. functions as a signifying entity in German films of both recent and less recent vintage.

III

Example #1. Luis Trenker, The Prodigal Son *(1934): America as the Dystopian Other or Home Sweet Heimat.* Joseph Goebbels' claim that a film by Trenker could bowl over even non-National Socialists was recently confirmed at a retrospective accorded the now ninety-year-old director at the 1983 Telluride Film Festival.[19] The blood-and-soil fustian, strident pathos, and intense chauvinism of his work seem not to have bothered enthusiastic cinéastes gathered in the Colorado mountain resort. I include the example by Trenker next to ones by Herzog and Wenders not to indulge in a tendentious and all too predictable exercise in ideological criticism—even if such an undertaking would seem to be warranted by the predominantly uncritical treatment the film has received both in print and at places like Telluride. It also does not make sense to attempt to forge spurious connections between two very different epochs in German film history. (Others, to be sure, have tried to do this in the case of Herzog.) What I do want to suggest is how a certain way of presenting America abides in each of these examples. Even in the instance of films made some four decades apart from each other, under very dissimilar conditions, similar ways of presenting America abide—for quite different and time-bound reasons.

The film begins in the Dolomites, with images of cloudy scapes, animals grazing on mountain tops, long shots of pastoral bliss. The first words of dialogue invoke the primeval and timeless sanctity of this realm. Sitting next to Toni Feuersinger, the vigorous ski guide and woodchopper played by Trenker (a German analogue to John Wayne), a village maid sighs: "I'd like to sit here like this forever, Toni." The homeland connotes eternal verities: tradition, tranquility, and communal ties. Toni will return to the village in the film's ecstatic conclusion, following the call of the *Heimat*, to join his father and friends in a *Rauhnacht* celebration, as a player in a ritual act, a carnivalesque festivity half-pagan, half-Christian.

Framed between these sequences, though, is Toni's sojourn in Manhattan. Tracking shots of city streets and store windows capture the empirical facts of life in New York of the thirties: bread lines and lonely crowds. Long shots render Toni a miniature dot amongst frenzied mass spectacles and massive structures. The film historian David Stewart Hull, like most commentators, lauds this passage for its authenticity and realism:

> The scenes of depression New York put similar American efforts to shame. Rarely has the atmosphere of the period been so utterly convincingly conveyed. We see the United States through the eyes of a stranger, and the effect is extraordinary.[20]

Trenker's perspective, no doubt, is that of a stranger. The effect to be certain is extraordinary; but what strikes this viewer above all about the Manhattan passage are the moments when seeming realism gives way to stylization, where representations of the big city turn into reflections of attitudes one has brought over from the homeland.

For all the location shooting, the scenes that capture street life and explore the everyday amidst the shadows of skyscrapers, much of the passage stands out as hardly true-to-life. The sequence features English dialogue (without subtitles), but the accents are decidedly German. We do not hear American voices, much less Big Apple inflections. A landlady who evicts Toni looks more like a Berlin *Wirtin*—just as the shadowy stairwell behind her suggests an Ufa-studio setting. Police are everywhere and they all speak with the same disconcerting Teutonic gruffness. Toni at one point stands in line, hoping to find a job. The man in front of him is a black—or better said, a German actor with a painted face, grinning broadly, trying to sound like a black. New York is every bit as much a found as a staged world in Trenker's film, a curious blend of a strange place and a displaced world, a mix of the foreign and the familiar.

Several other scenes particularly deserve notice because of their apparent incongruity. Unlike mountain scenes that integrate characters into landscapes, the New York sequence displaces Toni. One shot begins with a long camera tilt down the Statue of Liberty to a bench below where the dejected and jobless Toni sits. In the next shot we see him walking along the harbor with his back to the camera, looking out at the water. But in the distance we see Liberty Island: a 180-degree change of angle and location has occurred between shots. What one would expect to have been a continuity cut turns out to be a leap in space across the Hudson River. This is not an unintended error, an "ungrammatical" cut, but rather in keeping with an editing logic that constantly dislocates Toni in the big city, moving him from one borough to another, from downtown to Brooklyn for instance, with no motivation or explanation. Unlike the fluid cutting of the mountain scenes, the overall editing pattern of the Manhattan sequence shows Toni confused and floundering, wandering aimlessly in space—and time, for temporal continuity is lacking as well. At one moment he has a job; suddenly and without cause, he does not. In another scene he stands in a soup line, forlorn and grizzled. In the following scene, though, he appears hale and hearty, gainfully employed as a ringside attendant in Madison Square Garden.

"Father, I couldn't stand it anymore abroad [*in der Fremd'*]," exclaims the prodigal son upon his return. Toni's experience in the U.S. has affirmed the wisdom of a school teacher who once told him, "If you never go away, you never come home." Embodiment of a realm where one lives divorced from landscapes and other people, as a miniscule particle amongst an ungainly mass, divorced from organic forms and emanations of spiritual life,[21] America figures as the foreign incarnate, "die Fremd'," something that exists only for the sake of contrast. Its disjunctive spaces and its lack of communal bonds and shared history provide a reverse image of the homeland Toni leaves and returns to. For all the often-lauded realism of the Manhattan passage, America takes on the status of a cipher in *The Prodigal Son*, an antithesis overcome in the film's overall blood and soil dialectics.

IV

Example #2. Werner Herzog, Stroszek *(1977): America as a Confirmation of What One Already Knew—The World Is a Cage in Which We All Stand Apart.* Herzog over the years has gained a large following (especially in France and America) for his explorations of undiscovered places, bizarre terrains, and exotic venues. Surveyor of the extraordinary and researcher of the undisclosed, he enthralls audiences with his found objects and outlandish characters. In this regard, his visitations of America do pose an exception to the rule—or so it would seem. America takes on a weird countenance in *Stroszek*. As the director once said: "Americans . . . believe that they are normal, that they make sense, and that the *rest* of the world is exotic. They do not seem to understand that they are the *most* exotic people in the world right now."[22] Herzog made *Stroszek*, in the director's words, "to define my position about this country and its culture. . . ."[23] At first glance the film would seem to contradict my thesis, for in *Stroszek* the camera attends to milieux and inhabitants with considerable curiosity. One need only recall some of the oddities encountered during this trek to the U.S.: Railroad Flats with its empty streets, crowded truck stop, run-down gas station, and ugly mobile homes. One's weekend outings involve searching for the still undiscovered victims of a rampant mass murderer. Hostile farmers face off in tractors and wage a war over a slim stretch of soil. People speak strange tongues. CB-radio jargon as well as the whirlwind phrases of auctioneers, a kind of speech where incantation and wheeler-dealing merge surrealistically. A bank official hesitates when offered cash in payment of an outstanding bill he has come to collect: "We usually only accept credit cards and checks." One glimpses an Indian reservation in South Carolina inhabited by Cherokees whose income derives from marketing mementoes from their own depleted culture to tourists.

To dwell on these exotic signifiers, though, brings with it the danger of forgetting their place within a larger pattern of signification. *Stroszek* duplicates a design inherent in all of Herzog's fatalistic films. The camera's attentions to telling details of an out-of-kilter New World *do* offer the basis of a critical approach to America bound in the observation of social conditions. Nonetheless, words uttered by Bruno shortly before his release from an Old World prison serve to invoke a sinister design he will encounter again across the ocean: "Things go around like in circles." The circle is *the* informing structure in Herzog's cinema, the objective correlative to his pessimistic ilk of Romanticism. The circle connotes a trapped life without purpose, a human existence without meaningful activity, merely an eternal repetition of the same, motions that leave us time-bound captives, subject to the whims of inscrutable higher powers. At best one can rebel against this symbolic order and for a moment achieve a purified, ecstatic, and heightened sense of being. Ultimately, though, the typical Herzogian protagonist is overcome by inexorable and mightier elements.

America appears not only as a place full of novel and odd inhabitants; it likewise reflects an intensified version of the tough world Bruno and his chums flee from in Berlin. Before he leaves the mean streets of Kreuzberg, Bruno has a sense of how the world operates. His great hope—and source of his ultimate tragedy—is that things might be different elsewhere. He escapes Berlin only to find the same dynamics at work in the U.S. In fact, *Stroszek* contains a patterned series of reflections mirroring Bruno's experiences at home and abroad. Brutal hoods who break down doors give way to slick bankers who politely knock and apologetically inform their tardy clients that they will have to auction off their home and belongings. A comfortable and idiosyncratically arranged flat with a piano at its center threatened by the outsiders becomes replaced by a mobile home in whose middle stands a TV which is repossessed. Familiar and treasured belongings are transformed into objects packed in plastic and bought on installment. Turkish *Gastarbeiter* living as outcasts in a ghetto mirror an Indian working as a gas station mechanic and disfranchised Cherokees catering to tourists. The spontaneous mynah bird Beo, confiscated by American customs agents, finds New World counterparts among frozen turkeys and frenzied chickens. Life in the harsh confines of Kreuzberg left Bruno ravaged and battered. The fierce verticals of Berlin's cold lanes open up to the horizontal emptiness of the American Midwest, hardly a change in Bruno's life, at best a variation on the same brutal theme. Bruno's trek to the U.S. becomes an extended *Moritat*, a tragic ballad whose conclusion has long since been preordained.

Stroszek begins with a miniature portrait of a world trapped in a glass reflection. As the narrative takes its inevitable course, the reflection grows to a view of a world sinister in design. Herzog's dark Romanticism is at its darkest, where hopes turn out to be vain promises. In the opening sequence, Bruno objects to being asked his name *pro forma* by officials readying to release him. At the conclusion he sits on a ski-lift chair on whose back stands the question: "Is this really me?" The final shots find Bruno seeking to assert himself against the imposing constellations he has encountered at every juncture. He poses the imaginary of a distinct identity against a symbolic order that leaves little room for independence. Caught in a cul-de-sac, he rebels not just against the subtle—and for that reason more insidious—cruelty he comes across in America. Like so many of Herzog's heroes, he strikes out against the world in general. "Things go around like circles," he said to a prison warden in Berlin. His running amok takes the shape of a parody of a world where whirl is king, a mockery of this closed symbolic order. He leaves a stolen tow-truck in flames, the vehicle twisting without a driver around a parking lot. He activates a coin-operated machine in which a dancing chicken gyrates on a spinning platter. Bruno himself goes around and around on a ski lift. We hear an offscreen gun shot, presumably the emigrant's final act of resistance. What kind of land is it that takes Bruno's Beo away from him, he wondered after landing in New York. The narrative as a whole provides an answer: the same country where one later glimpses caged chickens and rabbits, Indians on a reservation reduced to strangers in their own homeland, extensions among many others of a world-wide prison, expressions of the fettered existence Bruno encounters from start to finish of *Stroszek*.

V

Example #3. Wim Wenders, Alice in the Cities *(1973): America as a Semiotic Playground and Dream Landscape.* Throughout his career, Wenders has remained a filmmaker who respects the integrity of the world before him, who denies the temptation to coerce characters, objects, and landscapes into ready-made forms, the patterns of recognition and narrative clichés of dominant cinema.[24] He is more an earnest bystander, a specular presence sensitive to the singularity and vulnerability of the Other. "There's a quotation I have pinned on my wall," he said in his famous conversation with Jan Dawson, "it's one of the few theoretical things about film-making I can accept completely," going on to quote Béla Balázs' claim that the essence and possibility of film art is that everyone and everything looks like it is.[25] This essentializes Wenders' cinema of impartial and gentle gazes. The same feeling inheres in his early writings as well, the celebrations of the direct appeal of rock and roll or the deep regard for the straightforwardness of classical American cinema as embodied in the westerns of John Ford, for instance.[26]

Philip Winter, the journalist travelling through the U.S. in *Alice in the Cities*, awakens from troubled dreams in the Skyway Motel somewhere on the Eastern seaboard. With a start he recognizes John Ford's *Young Mr. Lincoln* (1939) on the TV screen in front of him. Initially bemused, he becomes infuriated when a commercial interrupts the pristine images from out of the past. Winter is afflicted and disoriented; his frantic behavior while riding through America finds an echo in a series of disconnected images, empty compositions, music that begins and ends abruptly, a camera whose random attentions parallel the imagistic desperation of Philip's persistent polaroid shots. Something happens to you when you're on the road in America, he will apologize later when unable to hand in his long-overdue account of the journey to an editor. America is a rich source of images, but his pictures do not capture his experience—in Wenders' terms, they do not show things as they are—nor do they add up to a story. Speaking with an ex-girlfriend in Manhattan, the weary writer tries to explain away his malaise as a function of the foreign country:

> From the moment that you drive out of New York nothing changes anymore, everything looks the same, so that you can't imagine anything else, so that you can't imagine any kind of change. I became a stranger to myself.

America, so he claims, has made him lose all sense of sight and sound; his alienation, so it would seem, is a disease he contracted in the States. But his friend's response to the speech makes it clear that this is old hat. "You don't have to travel through America for that to happen," she insists. "One loses sight and sound when one loses one's sense of self. And you lost that a long time ago." Philip's crisis, in other words, started at home.

The random stimuli and information overload of which Philip partakes while on the East Coast, experiences constantly interrupted or fragmented, only exacerbate a mind wandering through the world without a home base, a fixed horizon. Like other "Road Trilogy"[27] heroes, Philip at first thinks that observing the world will help him to understand it better. But his is a disinterested gaze and specularity alone does not yield insight or a sense of perspective. Memories and impressions remain empty signifiers when unbound in a larger field of signification, a *Zusammenhang*. America aggravates Philip's sense of lack every bit as fiercely as Wilhelm's trip through the Federal Republic (in *Falsche Bewegung/Wrong Move* [1974]) leaves him aware of the distance between him and the world he wants to write about.

Philip's disinterested gazing and imagistic impressionism, however, give way to a sense and regard for the Other when Alice, a lost waif, enters the film. We first see her walking in circles around a revolving door. In joining her in that entrance, Philip walks into a narrative trajectory. Once the unlikely companions return to Europe, a story takes shape, a search for a house on a photograph, the home of Alice's grandmother somewhere in the Ruhr Valley. Images with information, images as well with human substance: after they land in Holland, Alice takes a snapshot of Philip, "So that you at least know what you look like." The picture records not only his face, but also the superimposed features of the picture-taker. Film becomes a record of communication, a medium that represents interaction between people, not just static frames and empty still-lifes.[28] The ugly industrial landscapes in Germany, ones every bit as violated as the commercial strips and busy thoroughfares which sparked Philip's ire abroad, no longer bother him. Returning to Europe means reentering history, gaining a trajectory that will ultimately lead him on his way back to Munich, sitting in a train reading an obituary of John Ford in the *Süddeutsche Zeitung*. The simple directness of the American master may represent for Winter the lost world bemoaned in the article's title, "*Verlorene Welt*." Nonetheless, in his peregrinations Philip has come out of his narcissistic listlessness and uninvolved specularity to gain a world of his own and now looks forward to writing the story that eluded him abroad.

VI

In all three instances, America figures as a way-station for travellers whose manifest destiny lies elsewhere. The U.S. plays the role of an imaginary (in the Lacanian sense), a set of possibilities one contemplates and toys with, or put in another way, as a hall of mirrors one passes through while self-reflecting. Confused, inexperienced, and incomplete human subjects gain wisdom and insight in America. (In Stroszek's case, one finds one's worst presentiments confirmed.) Trenker's and Wenders' heroes put their previous lives into clearer perspective and gain access to the realm of tradition and history, the sphere of articulation and expression—in essence what Lacan terms the symbolic order. Toni comes back to a ritual celebration, receives from his father the mask of the Sun King, and rejoins his bride-to-be. Philip Winter leaves the U.S. to become an ersatz father, in the end finding the assurance to put his insights into words and finish his article. Stroszek's act of rebellion is a demonstration that mocks the very symbolic that fetters him, an outburst that derides a world of vicious circles through its replication.

The entry into the symbolic in these itineraries invariably involves exiting from America. Toni turns his back on a land of spatial and temporal disjunction, a place where the sole communal event we see is a frenzied mass spectacle around a boxing ring. He joins the *Rauhnacht* festivities, assuming his role in an age-old ceremony enacted by a mountain village. *Alice in the Cities* takes on narrative proportions only after Alice and Philip land in the Netherlands. To remain in America, given this cultural coding, means to linger on dangerous ground, to be caught in a dead end, to stand outside of one's own history. Witness the conclusions of Vadim Glowna's *Dies rigorlose Leben/Nothing Left to Lose* (1983). Wenders' *The State of Things*, Werner Schroeter's *Willow Springs* (1973), or Vogeler's *Damn This America*. Unlike films about foreigners in America made by directors from other countries—e.g., Elia Kazan's *America, America* (1963) or Jan Troell's *The Emigrants* (1971)—one finds no recent West German examples more than peripherally concerned with assimilation and the shedding of one's national identity.

America functions as a site of projection, a place where unsure individuals see themselves in sharper focus. In the process America acts as a mirror image, a catalyst for self formation, a reflection against which one can better define oneself. This becomes strikingly manifest in the way German films typically dramatize the passage between inland and America, as if the two countries were doubles. The journey is usually a short one, a fluid movement between the two spaces. In Wenders' films one disappears into an ethereal realm of clouds for a few seconds while characters gaze out of airplane windows or simply fall asleep. Travelling to America seems like entering a dream. (How different this is from the excruciating boat rides in Kazan's and Troell's films.) In *Der amerikanische Freund/The American Friend* (1977), Wenders moves back and forth between Manhattan and Hamburg via rapid cuts, ones that occur so suddenly that the viewer can easily mistake a New York scape for a North German harbor. The final sequence of Walter Bockmayer and Rolf Bührmann's *Flammende Herzen/Flaming Hearts* (1977) shows Peter leaving for the Kennedy Airport in a limousine. We see him several matched cuts later—without any sign of an intervening transatlantic plane ride!—headed for his Bavarian home town on a different local bus. The most dramatic instance of this fluidity, though, comes when Trenker's hero decides to go to America. We see no trip, no means of conveyance. The journey transpires in essentialized terms, as a shot of the Dolomites, rocky crags that dissolve into a perfectly matched image of their *Doppelgänger*, the Manhattan skyscrapers.

In these scenarios, America figures as a crucial stage in a larger process, a process bound in the quest of a national cinema for a sense of cultural identity. The imaginary and ideal representations are not simple ahistorical givens, however; they come as the result of social mediations.[29] The evocation of the U.S. in these films reflects developing images of self and homeland—be it in Nazi Germany or the postwar Federal Republic—ones demanding more careful and context-oriented differentiation.

The dynamics at work in Trenker's *The Prodigal Son* are common to many Third Reich productions as well as to the notorious *Heimatfilme* of the fifties. One distinguishes sharply between *Heimat* and *Fremde*, viewing in the former permanence and stability, in the latter a realm of precariousness and transcience.[30] The fascinating thing about such black-and-white projections, though, is how they sometimes break down to reveal a schism in the minds of the would-be champions of the *Heimat*. Toni's stay in Manhattan amounts to a nightmare indeed, but one with much residue carried over from the homeland, as witnessed by the matching dissolves of Alps and skycrapers, the ubiquitous German accents, not to mention the numerous images of unemployed workers and ever-ready police, factors with direct importance for Germany of 1934. Much of Toni's resistance to the New World stems from his refusal to become a part of a faceless mass, to relinquish his native roots and individuality and be enveloped by an impersonal society.[31] This is of course precisely that which Hitler's state apparatus sought to effect in the Third Reich; in appealing to the mass unconscious and a desire for myth and enchantment, it ultimately wanted to have people assume a place in the large ornament of the Nazi state. (Witness the gigantic geometric patterns made up of marching believers in Leni Riefenstahl's *Triumph des Willen/Triumph of the Will* [1936], a sort of Expressionism imposed on reality.)

For Herzog, America is but one extreme example in a sinisterly designed universe. The U.S. looks something like a large zoo in *Stroszek*, full of exotic creatures and strange caretakers, where people seem to be freer only because they move on longer leashes. Herzog's vision of a fettered humanity, though, a modern-day Romantic fatalism of a decidedly undialectical sort, has equally strikingly been played out in a host of other settings: the Amazon Jungle, the Canary Islands, Biedermeier Germany, and most recently in Australia. He reduces foreign landscapes to metaphors, using them as sites for his inexorable *misère-en-scène*. Other West German filmmakers, the majority in fact, do not share Herzog's problematic brand of ahistorical pessimism. They do, however, share a penchant for making foreign countries into a double for the trouble at home. The coldness of Bavaria segues into the blue-and-white icebergs of Greenland in Herbert Achternbusch's *Servus Bayern/Bye Bye Bavaria* (1977). The mid-life crisis of a journalist erupts in the pyrotechnics of a war-torn Beirut in Schlöndorff's *Die Fälschung/Circle of Deceit* (1981). America, then, is not the only imaginary to which New German directors take recourse, even if it stands as the dominant testing ground. In something akin to a latter-day Expressionism, foreign terrains become intensified reflections of one's situation at home. This works in reverse as well.

Small-town America of the fifties in Douglas Sirk's *All That Heaven Allows* (1955) takes on the appearance of *Kleinbürger* Munich of the early seventies in Fassbinder's *Angst essen Seele auf/Ali: Fear Eats the Soul* (1973). H.W. Geissendörfer, in resetting Patricia Highsmith's *The Glass Cell* in Frankfurt, transformed New York City into Manhattan am Main.[32]

Wenders' constant and continuing recourse to America—his most recent film bears the title *Paris, Texas* (1984)—reflects the quest of a postwar generation for a different history and novel experience, new sights and sounds, other expressions and traditions. But America, as Wenders has come to realize in the course of time, is not simply a source of fresh images and a semiotic playground. If his early films rejoiced in the imaginary of American popular culture, his most recent work increasingly has dealt with the symbolic order constraining the production and circulation of images in the U.S. His latest work (including *Hammett* [1983], *The State of Things*, and the short *Reverse Angle* [1982]) dramatizes, and in its production history embodies, a serious dilemma: the difficulty of making films based on felt emotions and observed details under present conditions. Why must one constantly tell the same stories and replicate the same patterns? "Stories only exist in stories," the director in *The State of Things* tells his cast, "whereas life goes by without the need to turn into story." America figures centrally in this dilemma, both as a reality and a reflection: it is the site of a film industry that lords over the world market with its package deals, tie-ins, and ready-made schemes, its sequels, prequels, and remakes, reruns of the same which are anathema to independent image-shapers. The prohibition of anything but images countenanced by committees and hierarchies harkens back as well to a memory well ingrained in the mind of any German filmmaker, to the prospect of a fettered national cinema and the administration of images from above which once led a legitimate film culture into exile. The evocation of Fritz Lang in *The State of Things* is an admonishment and a reminder, a link between film industries, which regardless of their clearly divergent political constitutions, still vitiate the myths, stories, and images of a nation. Specularity is no easy business in places where fantasy wares are controlled by speculators. Filmmakers like Wenders sought to escape the denigration of living images at home only to find, after an initial period of fascination, a similar dilemma abroad. The closer one looks, the more familiar the foreign experience becomes.

VII

Let us reverse angles for a moment and gaze on American friends of the New German Cinema. One knows well the tale of how foreign admirers brought West German filmmakers recognition and acclaim denied them at home, how domestic observers started taking the *Jungfilmer* seriously after the foreign regard. (Part of the fascination inherent in following this process involves watching Germans watch others watching them. One's self-image very much has to do with the looks of others.)[33] The tendency, though, among American intellectuals who champion the New German Cinema has been to dehistoricize this national cinema, to laud the deconstructed narrative, celebrate directorial eccentricity, and effuse about stylistic and formal singularity. One does this while virtually ignoring or vastly oversimplifying the body of experience which has generated these images—a proclivity that has led to some interesting and surprising misreadings. (An otherwise insightful critic for instance recently identified "the sad-looking old gentleman whose picture appears behind the beginning and end titles of *Lola* [1981] as Josef von Sternberg. For all of Fassbinder's deference to the American *auteur*—something borne out in the film's lighting—the avuncular figure is clearly Konrad Adenauer, not von Sternberg.)[34] It is odd: few American enthusiasts of New German Cinema have paused to consider why they have invested so much interest and energy in this foreign body of films over the last decade.

Just as America has figured as a gap-filler for German filmmakers hungry for other experience, so too has New German Cinema provided American film-goers sustenance less and less to be found at home. It is no coincidence that the films of Fassbinder and his companions began to take on the status of an imaginary for American viewers during the mid-seventies and have become increasingly popular since that time. In a strange way Americans have colonized German fantasies, merchandising the New German Cinema, making it the subject of umpteen journalistic and scholarly examinations, using it regularly in university course offerings, and featuring it as a steady item in campus film series and arthouse retrospectives. New German Cinema became a source of controversy and fascination at a time when individuals were still reeling from post-Vietnam fall-out. It continues to scintillate and galvanize at a moment when the American public seriously confronts the ever-present possibility of doom and destruction. In the nightmare visions of New German Cinema, its gripping tales of angst and disaffection, one finds expressions of a fearful modernity and a world-wide, disenchantment rarely presented by America's either overly sanguine or blatantly cynical dream factory. German nightmares are being redreamed by Americans. *Hitler—ein Film aus Deutschland* (1977) has—in Francis Ford Coppola's telling change of title—become *Our Hitler*. In the words of Hans-Jürgen Syberberg:

> Hitler was proud that no foreigner, not even a sympathetic or a vanquished one, would ever be able to say "Mein Führer." That would remain a privilege of the Germans for all time, like being a citizen of Rome during the age of glory. The Americans are now saying *Our Hitler*. And in talks about this Hitler, who now has become a film, this Hitler suddenly in a quite self-

understood manner becomes "their Hitler." A German coming to America and knowing little or nothing about the strange change of the film's title, which only exists in America, will be surprised or even shocked to hear in discussions and dialogues an American suddenly speaking of this man as "his."[35]

Americans facing potential cataclysm, for some time now, seem strangely drawn to German reenactments of the Third Reich, the Holocaust, the devastation of a nation, journeys into the most unsettling catastrophe in recent Western experience and explorations of its excruciating effects. (This might explain as well the spate of American TV-films like *Holocaust* [1978], *Inside the Third Reich* [1982], or *Playing for Time* [1980].) One revisits past horrors through foreign eyes while rehearsing one's own bleak future.

So what seems to be at hand here is a cross-cultural exchange, a transatlantic give-and-take, in which foreign spectators gaze on another culture's images and constitute them as an imaginary in order to sharpen their focus on themselves. Talking about American friends of the New German Cinema as well as New German filmmakers and their relation to America is like regarding viewers who in looking at the Other simultaneously see reflections of themselves. This singular variation on the mirror stage has produced an interaction exemplified in the snapshot Alice takes of Philip Winter, an image that merges both the person beheld and the beholder: "So that you at least know what you look like."

I return to Abish's quote, with which I began. Does the unfamiliar activate and spark our curiosity and interest? In the case of the interaction I have described, the answer is yes. The unfamiliar provides a distance enabling one to grasp the familiar so often overlooked in accustomed surroundings. Is it a call to explore and familiarize oneself with the unknown? Only to a degree: in the case of both West German filmmakers and their American friends, the seeming unfamiliar helps one above all to fathom the known, to confront the given, to find another approach to one's own national identity and historical situation. Without a doubt this dialogue between Americans and Germans has been a displaced one, a special relationship with very special terms, a sort of meeting—to use two popular and over-worked paradigms—of "the New Subjectivity" and the New Narcissism, where one revels in a foreign culture's images for selfish purposes. "What is really at stake is one's image of oneself."

Notes

1 *How American Is It. Wie Deutsch Ist Es* (New York: New Directions, 1980) 119–20.

2 *Wim Wenders* (London: British Film Institute, 1981) 7. The passage Johnston refers to comes of course from Wenders' *Im Lauf der Zeit/Kings of the Road.*

3 See Karen Jaehne, "The American Fiend," *Sight & Sound*, 47.2 (Spring 1978): 101–103.

4   Cf. Yaak Karsunke's poem, "Kilroy war hier."

5   The spectrum ranges from commercial attempts to replicate the Hollywood film industry in Munich with big-budget bonanzas, international teams, and special effects, like Wolfgang Petersen's *Die unendliche Geschichte/The Never-ending Story* (1984), to critical travelogues such as Hartmut Bitomsky's *Highway 40/West—Reise in Amerika* (1980), as well as features filmed in the U.S. by a host of directors: Hans Noever, Erwin Keusch, Vadim Glowna, and Wim Wenders, among others. Jean-Marie Straub and Danièle Huillet, without a doubt the most subversive and uncompromising filmmakers who have worked within New German Film, completed‛a rendering of Kafka's novel fragment *Amerika* entitled *Klassenverhältnisse/Class Relations* in 1983.

6   The most persuasive expression of this position is to be found in Timothy Corrigan, *New German Film: The Displaced Image* (Austin: Univ. Texas Press, 1983).

7   See the pertinent section in *Dialectic of Enlightenment*, trans. John Cumming (New York: Seabury, 1972).

8   See the discussion, "Kino im Kopf," in *Ästhetik und Kommunikation* 42 (December 1980): 9.

9   "The Realist Gesture in the Films of Wim Wenders: Hollywood and the New German Cinema." *Quarterly Review of Film Studies* 5.2 (Spring 1980): 214–15.

10   The homage originally appeared as "Imitation of Life: Über die Filme von Douglas Sirk," *Fernsehen und Film*, February 1971.

11   Among many instances of Wenders' deep regard for the director, see his obituary, "Sein Tod ist keine Lösung: Der deutsche Filmemacher Fritz Lang," in *Jahrbuch Film 77/78*, ed. Hans Günther Pflaum (Munich: Hanser, 1977): 161–65.

12   The Hollywood *films noirs* reproduced by the young Fassbinder (e.g. *Liebe ist kälter als der Tod/Love Is Colder Than Death* [1969] or *Der amerikanische Soldat/The American Soldier* [1970]) and his peers amounted to a circuitous rediscovery of a German legacy. See Foster Hirsch, *Film Noir: The Dark Side of the Screen* (New York: Da Capo, 1981) 53ff. for a discussion of how "the cinematic origins of *film noir* can be traced to the German Expressionist films of the late 1910s and twenties" (p. 53).

13   Jan Dawson, *Wim Wenders*, trans. Carla Wartenberg (Toronto: Festival of Festivals, 1976) 7.

14   "From Caligari to *Hitler,*" *Film Comment* 16.4 (July-August 1980): 60.

15   See the direct reference made by the filmmaker collective responsible for *Deutschland im Herbst/Germany in Autumn* (1977–78) to this notion of Benjamin's: "In this travelling express train of time we are pulling the emergency brake." Quoted as "*Deutschland im Herbst*: Worin liegt die Partelichkeit des Films?" in *Ästhetik und Kommunikation* 32 (June 1978): 124.

16   *How American Is It*, title page (unnumbered).

17   Taken from a conversation between Abish and Sylvère Lotringer, "*Wie Deutsch Ist Es,*" *Semiotext(e)* 4.2 (1982): 162.

18   Ibid. 163 and 168.

19   Quoted in Erwin Leiser, "*Deutschland erwache!*" *Propaganda im Film des Dritten Reiches*, rev. ed. (Reinbek: Rowohlt, 1978) 16. For a striking example of the spell cast by Trenker's film and of a critic's initial enthusiasms and her later misgivings, see Sheila Benson, "Another View of Trenker's Mountains," *Los Angeles Times*, 25 January 1984: "If ever there was the suspicion that Telluride casts a hallucinatory spell, part attitude, part altitude, proof is seeing the 50-year-old films of little-known Bavarian director/actor Luis Trenker down here at sea level. . . ."

20   *Film in the Third Reich* (New York: Simon and Schuster, 1969) 66.

21   Cf. Siegfried Kracauer, *Das Ornament der Masse*, ed. Karsten Witte (Frankfurt: Suhrkamp, 1977) 51.

22   "*Images at the Horizon*": *A Workshop with Werner Herzog Conducted by Roger Ebert*, ed. Gene Walsh (Chicago Facets Multimedia, 1979) 10.

23   Ibid. 11.

24 Cf. Sheila Johnston, *Wim Wenders* 7.

25 Dawson 23.

26 See "Emotion Pictures (Slowly Rockin' On)," *Filmkritik* (May 1970): 252–55.

27 *Alice in the Cities* is the first leg in the trilogy, whose subsequent stations are *Falsche Bewegung/Wrong Move* and *Im Lauf der Zeit/Kings of the Road*. The heroes in these films seek an escape from nomadic and monadic existences into wider courses in time.

28 Cf. Peter Buchka, *Augen kann man nicht kaufen: Wim Wenders und seine Filme* (Munich: Hanser, 1983) 42.

29 See Kaja Silverman, *The Subject of Semiotics* (New York: Oxford Univ. Press, 1983) 161.

30 See Willi Höfig, *Der deutsche Heimatfilm 1947–1960* (Stuttgart: Enke, 1973) 386. German *Heimatfilme* of the Adenauer era—for all their sentimental whimsy and picture postcard kitsch—supply a stunningly authentic negative image of the Federal Republic during its traumatic epoch of reconstruction, if only one reads everything in reverse, as the fantasy projections of a shattered and shell-shocked nation under occupation.

31 This corresponds to his lesser status in the New World. At home he is a ski champion, an ace mountain climber, and head woodchopper, leading a troop of men. In Manhattan he becomes a day laborer hanging from a vast skyscraper, one dot on the horizon.

32 In the recent film *Ediths Tagebuch/Edith's Diary* (1983), the director took a Highsmith novel set on the East Coast during the McCarthy and Vietnam eras and displaced it to the post-1968 ambience of West Berlin.

33 Cf. Thomas Elsaesser, "Primary Identification and the Historical Subject: Fassbinder and Germany," *Ciné-tracts* 11 (Fall 1980): 52: "The Germans are beginning to love their own cinema because it has been endorsed, confirmed, and benevolently looked at by someone else; for the German cinema to exist, it first had to be seen by non-Germans. It enacts, as a national cinema, now in explicitly economic and cultural terms, yet another form of self-estranged exhibitionism."

34 Richard T. Jameson, "Fassbinder's *Lola*: In the image of Dietrich and Sternberg," *The Weekly* (Seattle), 20 October 1982, 48. For a discussion of the dynamics attending the fate of New German films in the U.S. in general, see my essay, "American Friends and New German Cinema: Patterns of Reception," *New German Critique* 24–25 (Fall-Winter 1981–82): 7–35.

35 *Die freudlose Gesellschaft: Notizen aus den letzten Jahren* (Frankfurt: Ullstein, 1983) 109.

I am grateful to the Alexander von Humboldt-Stiftung for a research fellowship that allowed me the time and leisure to write this article during the summer of 1983.

Wenders's *Kings of the Road:*
The Voyage from Desire to Language

TIMOTHY CORRIGAN

Although it is true that, when either my train or the one next to it starts, first one, then the other may appear to be moving, one should note that the illusion is not arbitrary and that I cannot willfully induce it by the completely intellectual choice of a point of reference. If I am playing cards in my compartment, the other train will start moving; if, on the other hand, I am looking for someone in the adjacent train, then mine will begin to roll. In each instance the one which seems stationary is the one we have chosen as our abode and which, for the time being, is our environment. . . . Perception is not a sort of beginning science, an elementary exercise of the intelligence; we must rediscover a commerce with the world and a presence to the world which is older than intelligence.

Merleau-Ponty, "The Film and the New Psychology"

THE FILMS of Wim Wenders certainly specify and concretize the confrontation with the American film industry and its culture to an extent other German filmmakers often only approximate. While other directors share, willingly or not, Wenders's obsession with the social, artistic, and psychological presence of the American cinema within the German consciousness and theaters, few locate it so effectively and so regularly as the center and persistent background for the argument of their films. Thematically, stylistically, and geographically, Wenders's cinema is dislocated between two cultures, between that of Goethe and Heidegger and that of Ray and Ford; the crisis of identity that the characters experience in his various films is the crisis of the films themselves, as they aim concomitantly to speak, learn, and reinvent a language whose traditional syntax now tends more and more toward insignificance. Like Handke's goalie awaiting the penalty kick, in Wenders's films an unarticulated signified remains unsteadily poised before a foreign—an American—signifier, and in this tension Wenders locates a semantic rift whose origin was a catastrophic attack on the fundamental value of the image, an attack at the very center of the social history of Germany. He explains:

Reprinted from *New German Film: The Displaced Image*, by Timothy Corrigan (Revised ed., 1994), pages 25–41, with the permission of Indiana University Press.

I do not believe that any other people have experienced as great a loss of confidence in their own images, their own stories and myths, as ours. We, the directors of the New Cinema, have felt this loss most acutely in our work. The lack, the absence of an indigenous tradition has made us parentless. . . . There was good reason for this mistrust. Never before and in no other country have images and language been handled as unscrupulously as here, never before and in no other place have they been so debased as vehicles for lies.[1]

Faced with this collapse between an audience and its images, the movements of and in Wenders's films accordingly become figurative and literal journeys back toward the possibility of a communicative significance, hopeful linguistic journeys marked by nostalgia and an anxious need to rediscover a native tongue. Not surprisingly, Robert, the traveler in *Kings of the Road* who, in his words, "specializes in a field somewhere between linguistics and children's therapy," thus describes his patients in a manner that could easily refer to many of Wenders's travelers, themselves dislocated by the course of time. When a child is very young, Robert explains, "the letters and numbers are still an adventure." Later, as the routine of writing sets in ". . . the memory of these fantasies fades away. . . . And only the problems that were brought out by these fantasies remain." For both the characters and the films, in brief, what propels their drive toward the language and images of America (its pinball machines, rock music, etc.) is precisely this nostalgic fascination with the possibility of speech and the contingent hope of fulfilling that possibility with the only language available. That this driving need to tell their stories is, however, repeatedly offset by the failure of the language is of course the crisis of contemporary German cinema: like Philip in *Alice in the Cities*, whose story is derailed by the mass of Polaroid images he collects, Wenders and his voyagers continually confront the fact that the images that recount their stories "never show you what you've actually seen." "In the U.S.," Philip says, "something happens to you, through the pictures you see. . . . I lost my bearings. All I could imagine was things going on and on." This endless and self-perpetuating search for meaning consequently becomes an open voyage through images which often serve only to impede the quest: a quest whose best map is Wenders's extraordinary *Kings of the Road*.

As explicitly as any film ever made, *Kings of the Road* is the story of a journey, an American road film, a film as voyage, and a journey through itself as medium. It announces itself on two levels: (1) the travels of two men, Robert and Bruno, across the plains of Germany and all that involves on a thematic level; and (2) the voyage through the film itself, which involves both the spectator's experience of the film and an analysis of the film mechanism as a means of communication. Like all voyages, the underlying motif for both levels is desire, and the play between desire and the absence of desire becomes the structuring law for the entire film. Like all voyages, that desire implies a goal, and in *Kings of the Road* that goal is described negatively as the desire for what is not there. Yet *Kings of the Road* differs, significantly from its traditional American models: it dramatically turns on the desire that informs it and confronts that desire from an angle of vision that reverses both the direction and possibilities of the cinematic voyage. Positioning itself between the desire that it initiates and a discursive dissection of that desire, *Kings of the Road* thus becomes one of the central and most incisive documents in an understanding of the New German Cinema and the bind of its recent history.

Aptly, the story of Robert and Bruno itself begins not with the desire to be somewhere or the vision of a new direction, but with the desire not to be somewhere and the choice of no direction. After the prefatory material of the film (which I will return to), there are four, very traditional, establishing shots of a VW speeding across the countryside. The camera then cuts to four close-up shots of Robert, the driver, taking out a picture of his handsome, middle-class home and tearing it in two.[2] Shortly afterward, Robert accelerates off the highway and plunges directly into a river. In this rapid and rather cryptic series of shots, a journey is visually established, but at the same time its direction is quickly aborted and transformed into no direction as the VW sinks in the river. The motivation, moreover, becomes rejection, rejection of a past, a home, and, in one sense, of desire itself. The journey that is constructed in one movement is deconstructed in the next.

Directionless, a journey that repeatedly abrogates desire and motivation becomes a sort of contradiction, in fact the central contradiction of the film: from the beginning to the end of *Kings of the Road*, both men find themselves yearning for an undefined, for the suspected but hidden; yet at the very moment that action becomes seated in an object, this object becomes threatening and thus rejected. Desire turns from itself in the very action of being manifested, and thus is formed the film's base figure: the circle, the wheel, and the hole which is the center of both.

Most obviously and regularly, this action is seen in terms of Robert and Bruno's friendship, which starts at degree zero and tentatively forms and unforms itself through the course of the film. At one point, for instance, the two men arrive at a theater and discover that the sound equipment needs to be repaired. While they work behind the screen, their silhouettes are projected and amplified on the screen; they soon get involved in a kind of gigantic, Chaplinesque shadow mime which Wenders depicts by cutting back and forth between the men behind the screen and the audience of children that watches them. They swing on ropes, juggle, and pretend to batter each other with clubs. The game projected on the screen becomes a kind of intimacy, the first intimacy displayed by either of the two introverted men. Yet soon afterward Bruno resentfully berates Robert about the dance-like attention they show each other: "When I was up on that ladder, I got a real shock all of a sudden. I was looking at my shadow, and at the same time I noticed you were watching me. That was it. I wanted to stop then and there. I was furious, and helpless. And then I didn't even know how I got started. And you were fooling around and I didn't have any other choice but to keep it up. That made me even more furious." During this conversation, the two stand before a roadside food-stand which has been remade from an old truck. The conversation is a medium-long shot with the two men standing side by side before the painted-over windows of the truck. When Bruno finishes, Robert responds by saying, "That's how it was with me too"; indignant, the two men spin away in opposite directions. Cutting to a new position at the other end of the truck, the camera is able to capture the circle formed by the men as they walk in different directions around the stand. The segment then closes with a frontal shot of them again side by side in companion windows of a truck. Their mutual attraction and rejection thus creates a literal circle in space; metonymically the two poles of this circle become the ubiquitous image of the two men joined yet separated by the window frames of the truck.

This circuit of desire, as Freud first pointed out, is fundamentally an infantile figure, an image of longing through which the child deals with the loss and return of the mother.[3] Accordingly, the narrative most clearly represents its action when Robert and Bruno return to their childhood homes, temporally dividing from each other before rejoining again later. Robert's return is a reunion with his father that quickly becomes a confrontation when he accuses his father of mistreating his mother. Similarly, Bruno's return is to the summer home where he spent much of his youth: searching out the home in a spirit of playful nostalgia, Bruno quietly explores the darkened, overgrown home, but then suddenly erupts violently, breaking windows and chairs. The visit ends with Bruno refusing to sleep in the house and weeping by himself on the back steps. Driven by a nostalgia for the object lost, desire here becomes a circular return that can only end in bitterness and frustration. Bruno, like Robert, yearns for an undefined something which has been lost, and with the almost cathartic frustration of that yearning, the journey begins again.

Thus the circle of desire becomes at once the emblem of frustration and the emblem of an independent solitude, the action that powerfully moves the characters toward an object from which they powerfully react along an opposite curve. Profoundly private on one level, this desire and its implications are not, however, confined to an interpersonal dimension. For, in *Kings of the Road*, the desire of the individual necessarily becomes involved in a multitude of other experiences, and its force invariably becomes linked to a variety of other voyages, most predominantly the cinematic voyage.

The most direct example of this linkage is the episode in which Bruno meets a young woman, Pauline, who is temporarily managing a cinema. They arrange a rendezvous at the cinema where she works, but the tryst naturally does not follow the Hollywood logic of love and consummation: although sexual expectations are created for the characters and the film's spectators, they are not fulfilled; although Bruno and Pauline spend the night together, it is without any real intimacy. While she works in the cashier's booth, Bruno watches the film; afterward they sit in two balcony boxes, paralleled but separated by the two frames of the boxes; later, when Pauline lies down on a small bed, Bruno retreats to a chair in the theater, where he dozes. When Bruno asks how she lives, Pauline replies, "Alone with my daughter, and it's going to stay that way." Later Bruno echoes her resolution when he tells Robert, "I've never felt anything except loneliness in a woman all the way down to my bones."

Around and intermeshed with this movement of attraction and retraction by Pauline and Bruno is the desire for the cinema itself, the eroticism of the image. Explicitly joining the two, the cinema where Pauline and Bruno meet shows pornographic films which draw a sparse crowd of viewer-voyeurs, indicating that however else the spectator at the cinema and the man on the road may be related, they here share the sexual urge that propels them. The connections pervade the entire episode: Pauline tells of a couple who had to be carried out of the cinema together after the woman suffered a vaginal cramp; when Bruno investigates a blurred spot in the middle of the film's image, he finds the projectionist masturbating; and left alone with Pauline, Bruno splices together footage from the porno film to make a loop film that shows again and again a house that burns and falls, the breasts of a panting woman, and a rape scene. As the culmination of the episode, Bruno's loop film thus unites the figure of the circle with an image of the sexual desire that informs the entire scene. The form of the loop film, as a summation of its content, thus describes the debilitating and redundant predicament of each of the characters.

The conjunction that Wenders makes here is a powerful and complex one, one which Christian Metz has examined closely through his discussion of a psychology of desire and a psychology of cinema in *Le significant imaginaire*. While the applicability of Metz's findings along the total spectrum of films may be suspect, his work does put an acute theoretical light on this central segment and, by extension, on all of *Kings of the Road*, since this crucial segment of the film acts as a kind of discursive, visual deconstruction of the spectatorial desire of the cinema, which Metz has analyzed in terms of its sexual base and its two components of perception and hearing. In Metz's words, "cinema practice is only possible through the perceptual passions: the desire to see (scopic drive, scopophilia, voyeurism), acting alone in the art of the silent film, the desire to hear which has been added to it in the sound cinema. . . . These two sexual drives are distinguished from the others in that they are more dependent on a lack, or at least more dependent on it in a more precise, more unique manner, which marks them from the outset, even more than the others, as on the side of the imaginary."[4] Following Lacan and Freud, Metz's model frequently relies on the Oedipal triangle, which obviously relates to the desire of the two men in the film, who confront fathers and weep over the memory of a mother. But, beyond these anchoring points along the diegetic level, Metz's model is especially valuable for its use of the concepts of lack and scopic desire, the key notions in binding the diegetic voyage and the cinematic voyage, that is, in presenting one as a reflection of the other. Just as the two characters circulate through a voyage bounded by desire and an unattainable object, the cinematic voyager moves between the same two poles, except that his or her journey belongs to the realm of the virtual. The two journeys are strikingly similar, and Metz's description of the desire of the spectator again retrieves the figure of the circle turning forever from itself in the quest for the undiscoverable. Watching the film, the spectator's visual drives

> remain more or less unsatisfied, even when their object has been attained: desire is very quickly reborn after the brief vertigo of its apparent extinction, it is largely sustained by itself as desire, it has its own rhythms, often quite independent of those of the pleasure obtained (which seemed nonetheless its specific aim); the lack is what it wishes to fill, and at the same time what it is always careful to leave gaping, in order to survive as desire. In the end it has no object, at any rate no real object; through real objects which are all substitutes (and all the more multiple and interchangeable for that), it pursues an imaginary object (a "lost object") which is its truest object, an object that has always been lost and desired as such.[5]

A monocular vision that draws the look to an infinite vanishing point is of course a primary factor in this action of scopic desire. But equally important is the nature of the filmic text itself, which is structured on the play of the presence and absence of the signifier. As Metz explains, a film necessarily presents an object whose existence is by definition anterior, an object that is only evanescently present through the medium of a moving text. Thus, the film "represents both the negation of the signifier (an attempt to have it forgotten) and a certain working regime of that signifier, to be quite precise the very regime required to get it forgotten."[6] This play of presence-absence doubly installs the film in the realm of the virtual, where it is first placed through the fiction which is its signified.[7] Through the operation of the film's signifying system itself, the spectator's experience thus approximates the kind of experience into which Robert is plunged as his VW sinks in the river: his desire triggered, he begins a voyage whose course is a somewhat directionless flux and whose central characteristic is the play between presence and absence. Once again, the first images of the film index this play for the characters as well as the viewer, first in presenting an object—notably a photographic object—whose presence is violently annulled and second through the metaphor of the VW as a vehicle which is present one minute and disappears the next into the current of the river.

A river, a film, a circle: all suggest the movement of desire—that of the characters and that of the spectators—as it releases itself on an imaginative level where finally no object can be found to replace the object lost. The spectator of *Kings of the Road* accordingly reflects the predicament of the characters in that the longing to *see* is both excited and frustrated, not only by the material *in* the film but by the material *of* the film. Here the shadow mime episode is perhaps the best metaphor for this fetishistic hiding-revealing power of the Wenders-Müller camera, for in this episode the two men appear only as the shadows of their real presence behind the screen, flickering, momentarily projected, and then disappearing as Wenders cuts from the antics behind the screen to the perspective of the children in the audience awaiting a film. Less metaphorically, shots throughout the film initiate the same action whereby the film teases the audience with the presence of two men and a reality that this audience is drawn toward but can never grasp: the long and unusual silences of this film which echo with so much potential significance, the stark landscapes which are regularly deflected off the mirrors and windshields, and the frontal shot of the truck in which the reflection off the window only allows momentary glimpses of the men in the front seat. The film, in brief, seems aggressively bent on proving the point which Metz specifically makes about framing and camera movement:

> the point is to gamble simultaneously on the excitation of desire and its retention . . . by the infinite variations made possible precisely by the studios' technique of the exact emplacement of the *boundary* that bars the look, that puts an end to the "seen," that inaugurates the more sinister crane-shot (or low-angle shot) toward the unseen, the guessed at. . . . They have an inner affinity with the mechanisms of desire, of its postponements, its new impetus. . . . The way the cinema, with its wandering framings (wandering like the look, like the caress), finds the means to reveal space has something to do with a kind of permanent undressing, a generalized striptease.[8]

In a film in which the movement across the land is so prominent a theme, this last phrase is particularly pertinent, since the movement of the film through the journey of the two characters along the border between East and West Germany is not so much a revelation of the land as a promise of revelation that never comes: the landscape and the towns remain the same throughout; shot mostly through the stationary window frames of the truck, the country passes but does not change.

Despite all of these affinities, though, *Kings of the Road* is significantly more than a duplication or accentuation of a psychoanalytic formula for films in general. Rather, it is an explicit confrontation with that formula and the spectatorial relationship that it implies, not in an attempt to overthrow that formula but in an attempt to assimilate, defract, and readjust it. Necessarily locked within the circle which is the law of all films, *Kings of the Road* nevertheless attempts to create new figures within that circle or at least to disturb the psychological complacency which it inspires in a spectator. In a fundamentally essayistic and metaphoric manner, *Kings of the Road* endeavors to rework and challenge the ideal spectator that Metz describes by introducing, within the figure of the cinematic voyage, other figures which significantly change the nature of that voyage.

Most prominently, Wenders goes to the figurative center of the image with his challenge: he dissects that center, and in that gesture he disrupts the circuit of desire between the moving image and the imaginative spectator who completes the circuit. Metz explains this circuit (circle) this way: "There are two cones in the auditorium: one ending on the screen and starting both in the projection booth and in the spectator's vision insofar as it is introjective (on the retina, a second screen). When I say that 'I see' the film, I mean thereby a unique mixture of two contrary currents: the film is what I receive, and it is also what I release, since it does not preexist my entering the auditorium and I only need close my eyes to suppress it. Releasing it, I am the projector, receiving it, I am the screen; in both these figures together, I am the camera, pointed yet recording."[9] As I have indicated, this double action describes the single figure of the circle (between the screen and the spectator), which Wenders then attempts to disrupt by at least momentarily arresting the desire that creates it. The cinema sequence is again the key illustration of this strategy. Here Bruno notices a blurred spot at the center of the film's image which has remained unnoticed by the apparently entranced audience. He follows the circuit of the image back to the projection booth, where he finds a somewhat elaborate mirror construction which forms a second circle within the booth itself and which catches the image before it leaves the booth in order to project it a second time on the back wall of the booth. With his back to the screen the projectionist is then able to masturbate privately. In addition to retracing the doubly circular route of the cinematic image, this sequence delineates and deconstructs two other elements in a psychoanalytic model of the cinema: namely, the mirror and the phallus. As Metz points out, the mirror is the crucial mechanism of the camera and the machinery of the mind. The psychoanalytic notion of the phallus, however, is more crucial to my argument here, since its disavowal is the foundation for the voyeuristic (fetishistic) desire that initiates and maintains the cinematic voyage. And in this sequence the exposure of the penis as index or metaphor for the phallus becomes a discursive overturning or deconstruction not only of the circular route of the filmic experience but also of the psychoanalytic taboo that upholds that experience (the phallus of the mother). In a partly metaphoric manner (since the penis is not strictly speaking the phallus), Bruno's discovery is that the blurred spot at the center of the image is linked by a series of mirrors to the phallus-penis at the other end of the circuit. Fittingly, under the dissecting eye of Wenders's camera, that original blurred spot on the first screen is paralleled and contrasted by the highlighted image of the penis on the second screen. It is as if the repressive action which Thierry Kuntzel has pointed out as a feature of a film's *défilement* is suddenly stopped and the circuit of desire disrupted.[10] In one and the same shot, this statement is made as the film lies heaped motionless on the floor and the penis lies exposed.

The cinema sequence is doubtless the most self-reflexive mapping out of this strategy of disruption and deconstruction in the film, but this figure of the exposed center is repeated throughout the film in weaker or stronger terms. The sexual dimension is generally underplayed, but the confrontation with scopic desire remains recurrent. There is, for instance, the memorable scene in which Bruno stops the truck so that he can "pee." He in fact defecates; in this medium-long shot against a slope of white sand, the image is aggressively blunt on a number of levels. Besides directly controverting Bruno's own statement, the shot is a frank disclosure of one of the less titillating facts that traditional cinema hides. Just as vomiting substitutes in the film for the character's possibility of speech, the scopic desire of the spectator here confronts excrement at the center of the image.

This figure of a disrupted center is further complemented by yet another figure present in a number of single images and the structure of the whole film. Related to that disrupting center, it can best be described as a swerve, a veering off, or a defraction, and its action is notably opposed to the returning action which creates the figure of the circle. It represents, rather, a "breaking out" of that circle, a defraction from it that forms a tangent pointing nowhere but away from the closed circular form. Imagistically, it is suggested by a large number of shots: for instance, the shot of Robert walking up a diagonal plank that ends in mid-air; his later imitation of a crossless Jesus in its motionless trajectory upward, miniatured and paralleling Robert's own gestures in this low-angle shot; and the sequence in which Bruno defecates, where that act is immediately juxtaposed with Robert leaping out of the frame in the next shot to create the same veering from the logic of the montage. While there is absolutely no narrative logic or explanation for any of these shots, each one, particularly the last, suggests a powerful connection between the disruption of desire—either the character's or the spectator's—and the figure of a trajectory that results and flies off from that movement.

The logic of these three figures—the circle, the disrupted center, and the swerve—or more precisely, the logic whereby the first two generate the third, is what defines the entire film. *Kings of the Road* is finally more accurately described through this figure of a series of swerves or defractions rather than exclusively through the circular model of desire that Metz proposes for the majority of narrative films. Even the characters' voyage is not finally circular (and certainly not linear) but rather a series of loosely connected trajectories and detours which conclude with their two paths veering off from each other. Indeed the voyage of the two men takes the shape of something between a circle and a number of directionless segments, thus paralleling a medium whose circular, unrolling motion is nonetheless a series of separate frames. More importantly, however, the spectator's journey undergoes the same redefinition so that, besides the circular exchange uniting the viewer and the screen, there is the deconstruction of that construction through a forced veering of the trajectory of the spectator's vision—such as Wenders regularly does when he spins the same landscape, once horizontally in the background and again diagonally through the truck's rear-view mirror in the same image.

These variations on the traditional cinematic voyage are the key marks in *Kings of the Road*, since they periodically rupture or buckle the smooth rhythms of the reciprocation of desire that are the foundation of the classical cinema. Through the strategies I have been describing, Wenders attempts to reposition or redirect the spectator along an imaginative channel that leaves him or her standing on the edge of his or her own journey in a position something like the spectacular detour that Robert illustrates when he walks to the end of that rising plank. What this means in terms of the spectator—just as what it means for the two characters—is the radical awareness of a context or field of action outside the route of the voyage. The short-circuiting results in the realization that the voyager is not just a participant in the voyage but a watcher outside and independent of the journey itself. In the film, this realization entails dissatisfaction, isolation, and finally the possibility of action—specifically the action of writing that figures so largely in *Wrong Move* and *Alice in the Cities*. More importantly, for the audience, this realization entails the possibility of a new relationship between the spectator and the screen, one where the enforced spectatorial silence gives way to a reflective, critical language.[11]

In "Histoire/Discours (Note sur deux voyeurismes)" Metz has noted that one of the most important conditions for the filmic voyager-voyeur is that he or she is not regarded and can remain absorbed within the flow of the story, in the anonymity of a voyage where the Me and the Other merge.[12]

This is precisely what Wenders tries to challenge through his acts of deconstruction or, in what is probably the most recurrent shot in the film, by putting the two voyagers—the diegetic ones and the filmic ones—face to face in a situation of forced recognition. Put another way, this means that Wenders turns the spectator in his or her seat; he defracts the line of vision so that the spectator now looks backward into the projection booth where one face of desire meets the other. That Wenders punctuates the film with so many scenes inside the projection booth is only the most obvious effort to locate the viewer's vision at the source of filmic experience and outside the grip of the endlessly metonymic movement of desire. For the entire film moves in its lyrical but relentless manner toward the same awareness, toward the possibility of commentary on desire.[13]

The dynamics of this confrontation are sketched within the story itself when Robert, the man of words and society, joins Bruno, the silent traveler. At first, Robert clearly surrenders to the journey in and of itself. Yet, even in the early stages of the trip, Bruno notices him breaking off and making contact with another level of experience. At one point, Robert returns to his father's newspaper office, and the showdown is aptly a battle of words: "You know, the whole time that I've been gone," Robert says, "whenever I think about or say anything I see it printed immediately. The last time I wanted to talk to you I had to listen the whole damn time. . . . You talk too much." This power of language is intimately bound up with the movement of the mind from the undifferentiated flux of experience to the differentiating consciousness of the individual. And Robert's deviations from the voyage of the truck here and at other points are clearly deviations into language and action, a connection dramatically underlined when Robert takes a newspaper he has found to the end of that striking diagonal platform. This is not to say that the voyage and mental reflection are incompatible, but instead that the voyage remains more or less indecipherable unless marked by the deviation of words. Another more subtle illustration of the same dialectic occurs during one of Robert's wanderings from Bruno: he walks toward a river where some boys are sailing boats made from newspapers. Picking one of the papers, he reads the headlines. The newspaper suddenly pulls Robert back to a different register of experience; the incident marks him and his journey just as the newspaper boat was the single sign to mark the current of the water. The allegory is completed, moreover, at the end of the film, when Robert trades his suitcase for a pad and pencil, and Bruno tears up his itinerary after thanking Robert for helping him "see himself as someone who's put some time behind him." In each of these cases, the unconscious participation in the voyage is assimilated to another register of experience, and this register is explicitly connected with language and the arena of comprehension.

The same change of register, I believe, is literally forced on the spectator of *Kings of the Road* when he or she is brought to the projection booth again and again in the film. Repeatedly, Bruno dismantles projectors and explains their mechanisms, their faulty parts, and their history in numerous scenes usually shot from behind the projector or closely focused on the exposed and sharply lit internal parts: he demystifies the machine whose greatest power is the mystification of the spectator through its hypnotic circuit of desire. At one point he takes a part to the workbench in his truck, where he points to the maltese cross mechanism and explains to the projectionist and the camera that "there wouldn't be a film industry without this little thing." In this way, Bruno turns the spectator, in a sense, from the film: he explains the base of the apparatus so that the viewer becomes a type of comprehending viewer who does not simply experience but is able to identify and differentiate the discrete elements of that experience. The spectator is thus able to "write" a perspective, and the voyage then has the capacity to have landmarks and defining points (such as the one that so loudly marks the river in the film). Before only nostalgic, the voyager is now equipped to analyze, to remember. Within the dream, the voyage, the film, the spectator now has the possibility of changing registers in the manner Robert describes. "Dreaming was writing in a circle," he says, "till I had the idea in the dream to use another kind of ink, the new kind . . . and with the new kind I could suddenly think and see something new . . . and write." The circle of the film, in short, can and should be written on its tangent.

What this change of register involves, and one of the discourses it entails, is clearly indicated by Wenders in the two segments that frame the film. Interviews in a projection booth, these frame sequences pointedly recall the masturbation sequence in a projection booth at the very center of the film (particularly since the frame sequences and the masturbation sequence are both demystifications or deconstructions, one on a psychoanalytic level and the other on a sociohistorical level). The masturbation sequence, as I have indicated, is a deconstruction of the cinematic play of presence/absence and an uncovering of the phallus/penis behind this play. The frame sequences, on the other hand, act as a translation of this central sequence (the exactly central sequence in the film) into another frame of reference, a German historical framework where the absence is just as powerfully present. As told by the two cinema owners, this sociohistorical absence is at once the absence of a home film industry, of good German films, and of a critical audience that might desire German films instead of the pornographic films and American films that it has been weaned on. And in a highly significant fashion, this sociohistorical absence is cryptically indicated within the film when, in an extreme close-up, Robert, without comment, cuts out the face of Fritz Lang from the center of a photograph. This gesture obviously parallels Robert tearing the photograph at the start of the film, Bruno tearing his itinerary at the end of the film, and Bruno figuratively tearing the veil of the projection booth in the masturbation sequence. It, too, becomes an acknowledgment of the absence behind the image, an absence which in this particular shot refers not so much to an object lost as to the loss of a German film audience that Lang had created. Punctuated by nostalgic references to Lang, the frame sequences suggest that there has been no German film industry since UFA and that the hole that has existed in postwar German film history has been covered by an illusion sustained more by the Hollywood industry than by the active participation of spectators.

As Metz has noted, the film industry today has so thoroughly usurped the critical spectator that in the conflux of the desire of the spectator and the feeding of that desire by the industry, the question of a "good" or "bad" film has become nearly irrelevant. Compared to the notion of a "bad" film,

> the "good object" relation is more basic from the standpoint of a sociohistorical critique of the cinema, for it is this relation and by no means the opposite one (which is a local failure of the former) that constitutes the aim of the cinematic institution and that the latter is constantly attempting to maintain or re-establish. . . . The cinematic institution is not just the cinema industry . . . it is also the mental machinery—another industry—which spectators "accustomed" to the cinema have internalized historically and which has adapted them to the consumption of films. The institution is outside us and inside us, indistinctly collective and intimate, sociological and psychoanalytic.[14]

A powerful industry can thus create a situation in which nearly all films are good films in a psychoanalytic sense, in which nearly all films are desirable films. And this is the notion that Wenders forefronts in the frame sequences when the two cinema owners discuss Hollywood's takeover of Germany: as long as desire remains the single controlling principle for the industry and its audience—and it must while the spectator keeps his or her mind solely on the screen—the Hollywood industry in Germany will self-perpetuate with the crucial aid of the indiscriminating metonymic desire of the spectator. The only way out of this bind is for the spectator to move from the mute level of the voyeur to the verbal level of the historian, where to discuss Hollywood's tight hold on scopic drives is to begin a liberation from it or at least the redirection of those drives. To see the absence which motivates the spectator on a psychoanalytic level in terms of the larger content of a historical absence is not the abolition of either. It is, however, the beginning of the possibility of a new filmic spectator and thus new films.

What *Kings of the Road* argues, therefore—particularly by means of the symmetrical positioning of the masturbation sequence and the frame sequences—is that the cinematic voyage is indeed psychoanalytically propelled but, in many important ways, historically conditioned. Both are voyages in their own right, the second being a voyage through the course of historical time. But it is only by demystifying the first that the second can in its turn be properly deconstructed and elucidated. The second level of the voyage is indeed the ultimately important outer context where meaning is written and new questions are proposed. But it is at the first level, in the desire of the individual, that primary and fundamental questions are raised (questions that should inevitably lead back to the second context of the projection booth). What attracts Wenders so profoundly to the American cinema must be, in large part, the knowledge that nearly all modern spectators remain mesmerized in the circle that Hollywood, that great desiring machine, has so competently created. Only by recognizing that circle as a starting point, however, do he and the other German filmmakers have a chance to write themselves out of it. For, like Robert, the spectator and the filmmaker have the option of detours, self-imposed or forced. And like Bruno, they have the possibility of figuratively turning in their seats and of deconstructing their journey. But finally both are first and foremost voyagers, and what the parable of Robert tells us in its simplest form is that one must first be a good voyager if one hopes to be a good writer of history.

Notes

1. *"That's Entertainment: Hitler,* A Polemic against J. C. Fest's Film *Hitler—A Career."*

2. The full text of *Kings of the Road* is available in English in a detailed shot breakdown: Fritz Müller-Scherz and Wim Wenders, *Kings of the Road,* trans. Christopher Doherty (Munich: Zweitausendeins/Filmverlag der Autoren, 1976).

3. See, for example, *Beyond the Pleasure Principle,* pp. 6–26.

4. *Le signifiant imaginaire,* p. 82; and "The Imaginary Signifier," trans. Ben Brewster, *Screen,* vol. 16 (Summer 1975), 59.

5. Ibid., p. 83/p. 60.

6. Ibid., p. 56/p. 45.

7. See ibid., p. 64/p. 48.

8. Ibid., p. 105/p. 74.

9. Ibid., p. 72/p. 53.

10. "Le défilement," in Dominique Noquez (ed.), *Cinéma: Theorie, lectures,* pp. 87–110; or "Le Défilement: A View in Close Up."

11. In his own work, Jauss uses this same circle metaphor and question-answer format (also very prominent in *Kings of the Road*). See "Literary History as a Challenge to Literary Theory," p. 12.

12. *Le signifiant imaginaire,* pp. 113–120.

13. Operating in a political context rather than a psychoanalytic one, Stanley Aronowitz makes a similar point about conventional cinema: "it is only by deconstructing these films that the structure of desire can be revealed and the desiring machine, to borrow a phrase from Deleuze and Guattari, that 'records' and actually creates a mediated reality can be surpassed" ("Film—The Art Form of Late Capitalism," p. 110).

14. Metz, *Le signifiant imaginaire,* pp. 13–14/p. 5. Aronowitz makes a similar point: "film is that art form which requires no ideological justification other than its own production and no legitimation other than its reception" ("Film—The Art Form of Late Capitalism," p. 115).

The Cultural Politics of Intimacy—
Biology and Ideology: The 'Natural'
Family in *Paris, Texas*

MAS'UD ZAVARZADEH

T HE HORIZONS of private life in postmodern culture are set by the discourses of intimacy—the state of plenitude and presence in which
one person, in completeness and without "difference," is accessible to
another. Intimacy, however, like all modes of cultural intelligibility, is a
social construct and produced in response to the needs for the particular
modes of subjectivities necessary for reproducing the dominant relations
of production. Through naming and thus recognizing certain kinds of
relating to others as *intimacy* and by implication designating other modes
of relating as *indifference* or *hostility*, the reigning ideology organizes the
historically available relationships along socially necessary lines. In doing
so it privileges a specific set of values that then becomes part of the complex ensemble of social strategies of intelligibility used to construct and
circulate what it regards to be "the real."

Intimacy, contrary to this commanding common sense, is the effect of the
intricate political operations involved in interpellating subjects, and modes
of intimacy vary not only from culture to culture but quite significantly within the same culture from one class to another. Intimacy is therefore neither
universal nor "natural." Discourses of ideology, however, represent intimacy
as inevitably "natural" and thus as private, asocial, personal, and, most
important, transdiscursive—they mark it as situated outside the cultural
series. This ideological representation of intimacy is politically critical
because if intimacy can be represented as outside the reach of history and
culture then, it follows, those who are intimate with each other derive their
relationship not from a given historical and social situation but by virtue of
their own panhistorical individuality. They are, in other words, free subjects
whose freedom is "given" and not implicated in the discourses of culture or
in social and political modalities. Intimacy is thus the ultimate sign of their
sovereignty as individuals; it signals their freedom. In fact intimacy is made
to appear so private in order for it to be taken as "natural" as the personal
seems to be: I am what I am (a "natural" and transhistorical fact) and,
because of what I am, I have certain types of relations and particular forms
of intimacy (which are also "natural" and transhistorical).

Excerpted from *Seeing Films Politically*, copyright 1991 SUNY Press, Albany, pages 113–116,
136–151.

These forms of intimacy, however, are always already limited by the historical situation in which the subject is located and thus by the subject positions available. One "chooses" one's intimates not "freely" but in an overdetermined way from within the constraints of class, sex, race, and religion, to mention only the most significant ones. However, to acknowledge these constraints is to see the operation of economic, political, and ideological practices in the production of intimacy. Furthermore, it is to become aware that intimacy in late capitalist societies is far from being a mark of individuality and freedom, rather it is one of the most apersonal and socially overdetermined modes of subjectivity in postmodern life. Intimacy is one of the social apparatuses of intelligibility necessary for the operation of the existing social arrangements. It produces "free" individuals who are then recruited by the dominant economic order, which is maintained by such notions as "free enterprise," "entrepreneurship," "originality," and, most important, "competition."

The limits of the "freedom" of the individual, however, immediately become clear as soon as she enters the domain of the social, and discovers the extent of her embeddedness in the social "collectivity." Such a sense of social solidarity works against the fundamental notions of "free enterprise" and its accompanying "free market" based on "competition." To background this social solidarity, the discourses of ideology designate the social as secondary and privilege "intimacy" as the site for manifesting true and authentic selfhood. What, of course, makes the dismissal of the social as the site of difference, absence and lack—secondariness—so commonsensically possible in postmodern culture is the ideological organization of the social in late capitalism. The social is represented as the space of the "role" not the "self," the site of "division" not "unity" where, in short, one is not a "true" person but is involved, as in the (false) fictions of the theatre, in playing a game. Such a representation of the social as essentially and universally nonpersonal, false, and thus a form of "absence" erases the historical specificity of the social in contemporary society and gives intimacy its particular features.

Postmodern intimacy is (historically) specified above all as the "other" of the social: it is the moment of "unitariness," "presence," "noncompetition," and contrary to the social, noninterrogatory, and "supportive." It is basically emotional and affirmative instead of analytical and inquiring. Under such terms of familiarity, one does not "know," rather one "feels" the other. Such a relationship prohibits any form of critical reflexivity about the relationship and forbids any investigative attitude toward it. In contemporary intimacy, supportive relationships prevail—whether in the appreciation of art in the aesthetic domain, the worship of God in the religious space of culture, or parent and child interactions in the realm of the family. In each the emotional is privileged while the analytical and interrogatory are suppressed. This denial of the interrogatory is necessary for the security of the dominant ideology and the view of reality it propagates: the ideological and its common sense survive only in the sphere of the emotional out of reach of social interrogation. An interrogative attitude in a relationship is thus represented as a form of aggression, a mode of hostility: the hostile, it is understood, is not suitable for intimacy and its user will be relegated to (punished by) "loneliness."

The assumption underlying such a view of intimacy is that closeness is a moment of plenitude, presence, and pellucidity: an instant in which intimates are free from the mediating forces of culture and society and directly present to each other's consciousness, feelings, and perhaps bodies. An interrogative intimacy (almost a paradox in postmodern culture) is represented in the dominant discourses as aggressive and hostile, but it actually seeks to reground relationships by exposing the political presuppositions and assumptions about intimacy and demystifying the expectations and frames of intelligibility each intimate brings to the association. It points out that private intimacy, which is postulated by dominant culture as the embodiment of similarity, transparency, closeness, and plenitude, is but an exemplary instance of difference, opacity, distance, scarcity, and gaps. It is not the "other" of the social in capitalism but in fact its mirror image. It reveals that opacity and gaps are inevitably inscribed in any relationship in culture, which is a set of conflicting discourses attempting to "explain" its social contradictions. People in contemporary culture are not only incomprehensible to one another but also to themselves. Clarity and transparency are only ideological constructs projected onto intimacy to hide the unavoidable opacity of people produced by the contradictory practices and discourses of a consumer society. A truly interrogative intimacy inquires into the production of codes and the way these codes form and shape intimacy. It is a form of political knowledge of the situatedness and historicity of the relationship as well as of the people involved and regards intimacy as a mode of social collectivity and thus an effect of the social. Through interrogation, intimates locate the politics of intimacy, and instead of forming atomistic relationships, they achieve what Sartre calls the "fused group" (*Critique of Dialectical Reason*).

The privatization of intimacy—whether in the domain of "friendship," "love," or "family," to take three main instances in postmodern culture—is ideologically, politically, and economically necessary. Through such privatization of intimacy, the subjectivities needed by the prevailing organization of the social are produced and maintained. In this space of emotional transcendence the individual who is "exhausted" in the daily competition of the marketplace is "repaired" and restored as part of a viable labor force. Intimacy, in other words, is itself a mode of production: not the production of "things" but the production of that force which produces things—the all-important labor force that is competent, competitive, and consenting to the social relations required for the reproduction of the pre-vailing economic order. . . .

The historical functions of many of the institutions of contemporary life such as family, friendship, marriage, and parenting (in other words, the various modes of intimacy) are put in question by the cultural contradic-tions of postmodern society. However the prevailing ideologies of contem-porary culture that support and legitimate the dominant social order are produced and circulated through these institutions. It is therefore politi-cally necessary for the continuation of the existing socioeconomic rela-tions to preserve and prolong these institutions and the values they foster. One of the most ideologically effective moves to prolong the life of these institutions of intimacy has been to deny that they have been historically formed in response to certain socioeconomic demands that, judging by the crisis these institutions are now facing, may no longer obtain.

By denying the historicity of intimacy, these institutions are represented as "natural," universal phenomena beyond the constraints of any particu-lar historical moment and thus "eternal." Presenting "family" or "mar-riage," for instance, as "natural" provides the commonsense logic of culture with a way of explaining away the crisis that faces these institutions at the present moment. If the institutions of intimacy can be proven to be natural and thus universal and transdiscursive, then the ills that have befallen them in postmodern culture are easily demonstrated to be mat-ters of "accident" and not of the "essence" of the institutions themselves. By naturalizing social organizations such as family and separating their "essence" from the circumstantial "accidents" (namely history) affecting them, the dominant ideology privatizes the problems of intimacy repre-sented in marriage, family, and parenthood as the failures of individuals. In doing so it demonstrates that these institutions of middle-class life are in good shape and far from breaking down, saving them from the pres-sures of a sustained interrogation and enabling the continued mystifica-tion of their practices in contemporary thought.

Wim Wenders's film *Paris, Texas* is an exemplary instance of such mys-tification of the postmodern bourgeois family. The film's ideological pur-pose is to provide a post of intelligibility from which the spectator produces a tale in which the seeming crisis that has affected the family and problematized all kinship ties is narrated as being engendered by individu-als and their private problems, whereas the family as an institution is seen as not only remaining intact but continuing to provide the ultimate grounds for living. Wenders's project is carried out in terms of a close study of the families of two brothers (Walt and Travis) whose five mem-bers are portrayed in a home movie within the film. The home movie is shown at a strategic point when the first "quest" of the film—retrieving Travis from the wilderness—is completed and before, as Wenders himself puts it, "the movie turns and starts walking on a new territory"

(Dieckmann, 1984–85, 4). The "new territory" is, of course, the film's second "quest," in which Travis's wife Jane is retrieved from the Keyhole Club, a peepshow palace in Houston. It is true that the home movie within *Paris, Texas* echoes Wenders interest in metafilm and in the question of filmic reflexivity in general, but the home movie (the film within the film), like all modes of postmodern reflexivity, has a specific political function beyond its aesthetic specularity. Its function is to record in an honest and truthful manner the life of the two families together before crisis hits one of them. As a "home movie" it is honest in that it is unmade, unadorned, and above all silent, which is to say it is, like Travis, "mute" and, in Wenders's vocabulary, signals "authenticity" and the "veracity" of experience. As a film within a film, it has the authority of truth that a reflexive text obtains by turning itself into its own subject of inquiry, thus acquiring a solid, incontestable basis for its terms of intelligibility. Its veracity results from its awareness of itself as a filmic production—by admitting that it is a film it puts its "honesty" above question. The home movie is a "document" of connection, human togetherness, and above all family happiness. This sense of family happiness as recorded in the home movie becomes the implicit standard of human happiness and self-reflexive presence against which all human experiences in the film are measured.

The home movie portrays Walt and his wife, Anne, who is French, and Travis and his wife, Jane, and their son, Hunter. It is shot during a vacation and is the only vivid sign that Hunter has of his mother, who has since abandoned him. The happiness recorded in the home movie ended when Travis suddenly disappeared and Jane left Hunter with Walt and Anne who have raised him as their own child. Travis's mysterious disappearance is the ostensible cause of the breakdown of his family, but later in the film, it is explained in terms of his own private emotional problems. He is unable to deal with the complexities of life, including living with another person, Jane. For him Jane is the site of otherness: he neither understands her nor is able to accept his lack of understanding of her utter difference as part of the problematics of human communication. To feel related to Jane he must turn her otherness into his own sameness and to achieve this goal he resorts to emotional and physical violence. The spectator inscribed in the dominant ideology makes sense of the disintegration of their marriage by regarding it as the effect of Travis's pathological desires and not as the outcome of marriage itself—marriage as a private mode of intimacy. All Travis does is take the idea of private intimacy to its logical conclusion and unknowingly reveal the contradictions of the ideology of intimacy as a private mode of connecting: love as owning the other and thus a naturalization of the code of private property.

During the early stages of his marriage to Jane he is happy. But he becomes more and more dependent on her, and although he describes this dependency as the sign of their utmost happiness together—they cannot leave each other even for a short period of time—the film constructs his dependency as a mark of his deep-rooted troubles. He becomes so in need of Jane for his emotional sustenance that he gives up his job so that he can stay at home with her all day. After a while, to support her, he has to go back to work again, but this time while he is at work all day his mind is on Jane wondering whether she is spending her day with another man. Coming home he is angry and unleashes his violence on her. Travis lives with the constant fear that Jane may run away; it is this fear that makes him tie a bell around her ankle so that if she tries to leave in the night, he will hear the bell. The entire sequence of Travis's actions involving Jane has echoes of psychopathologic behavior, and his account of this period of his life with Jane ends with an engulfing fire that almost kills him. One night he gets up to find Jane, who always dreamed of running away, has left with Hunter and flames of fire are consuming his clothes. He manages to escape the fire, but once outside his house, he does not stop to look back. He continues to walk for several days, and this unbroken walk begins his journey that ends, after four years, in the parched Texas desert—the opening scene of the film. The breakup of his family is thus directly linked to Travis's emotional problems and mental state. He is produced in the film as jealous, sexually insecure, and intellectually incapable of dealing with such complexities as the opacity of another human being. He is possessive (the other side of his sexual insecurity and jealousy), sentimental (the underside of what he calls his love for Jane), and lacks the rigor and toughness of a grown man—which allows the film to represent him largely as a "child," a child who for most of the film has to rely on his own child to orient himself in the world of adults. Thus Travis—and not the marriage-as-private-intimacy—is responsible for the disaster that befalls them.

The psychomythical dimension of childhood and its effects on the adult (a loosely Freudian model of the "family romance") is elaborated in the film; in fact it forms one of the ideological strategies of the film for asserting the personal causes of family crisis. It claims that the person involved precipitates the crisis because of his or her own childhood traumas. Travis, the film implies, has had a childhood of unsettled emotions. His father and his part-Spanish mother (another marker of otherness in the film) were never really visible to each other. The problems in Travis's family, in other words, are referred-deferred to his father's family and thus protected from a political and social understanding. His mother was a "plain" woman but his father (who like Travis was a complex of troubled dreams and visions) refused to see her as such. He saw her as a fancy woman from Paris, which turns out to be Paris, Texas, but his father, in introducing her or talking about her always drops his voice and eliminates Texas so that it is often misconstrued as Paris, France. Travis has heard from his father that his parents conceived him in Paris, Texas, and as a way of finding a connection with his origins and holding on to a tangible link with his parents,

Travis purchases a vacant lot in Paris, Texas, which is little more than sand and tumbleweed. The ideological position in which the spectator is located foregrounds Travis's attachment to his past, making his troubles intelligible only in terms of the dark, inaccessible recesses of his unconscious. History here means "going back"; it is a mere chronology and not the social, economic, and ideological practices of culture that interpellate the individual as the subject of private intimacy. By such emphasis on his private troubles, the film undermines the social side of the family crisis that Travis-Jane-Hunter are facing and accents Travis's own role as the troubled source of the crisis.

The film stresses this personalization of difficulties by, among other things, representing them in Travis's physique: from the opening shot of *Paris, Texas*, he is seen as "different." Wandering in the Texas desert he wears a white shirt and tie, a faded double-breasted jacket, a baseball cap, and shoes so worn out nothing is left of them. It is not only the confused ensemble of his garments that places him in a different space from the norm. His face has the vacancy of the mentally lost: the lines of his face reflect the agonies of sleepless nights, and his eyes are those of someone intimate with alien realities.

Travis is not only responsible for the breakup of his family, but also for the plight of Jane. After he left, Jane also disappeared, ending up in a peepshow palace called the Keyhole Club in Houston, where lonely men talk to the women of their desires for a fee. The connection between the club's male patrons (one of whom is Travis) and the women is through a one-way mirror and a telephone, that is by means of words: a narcissistic relationship that was, the film implies, all Travis had with Jane at the beginning of their marriage and is now all he has with her at the end of his contact with her. Narcissism is inscribed in bourgeois intimacy but is concealed in the folds of its contradictory discourses. Although Jane, like Travis, has left her son (Hunter), unlike Travis, she has not forsaken him; every month out of her meager income she has sent some money for Hunter. Whereas the neurotic Travis is self-mesmerized and can think only in terms of himself, Jane is constantly worried about their child. Although she finds any knowledge of him too painful to bear, there is an unbreakable *blood relationship* between her and Hunter.

It is exactly this lack of blood relationship that marks the otherwise completely comfortable and almost luxurious life Hunter is living with Anne and Walt. Not only do they love him, but, as a mark of their love, they provide him with the entire range of contemporary "kid culture" so that he is part of the contemporary languages of his culture. He owns not only an impressive array of electronic gadgets, but, most important, he is fully immersed in the discourses of his culture. He speaks a language that is a tissue of references to space technology, astronomy, and science fiction. Although Travis is a complete alien to this culture, Walt is quite comfortable with it. In fact Walt owns a company that erects billboards all over Los Angeles to make the discourse of consumer culture available to everyone. Hunter has no visible problem communicating with Walt, and Anne is the embodiment of an unconditional love for Hunter. She is so close to Hunter and so attuned to his emotions that she cannot imagine a life without him. When Travis is found in the Texas desert and brought home by Walt, Anne senses that the end of her "motherhood" is close at hand and realizes that the arrival of Travis signals the termination of her own "family." First she tries to discourage Walt from the "business" of pushing Hunter and Travis together. When Walt violently objects, reminding her that they *are* already together by virtue of their blood relationship, Anne resorts to the last device left to her. She reveals to Travis that Jane sends a nominal sum of money for Hunter every month and that she had the money traced to a bank in Houston. She hopes Travis will go in search of Jane and leave Hunter alone. Travis does leave to find Jane but takes Hunter with him.

After his arrival, Travis attempts to open direct communication with his son but fails at first. There is a sharp conflict of discourses here. For instance, he does not own a car ("nobody walks anymore," Hunter tells Anne in response to her urging him to walk home from school with Travis); he is not dressed "properly" (that is in the attire of a successful professional); and he does not speak the contemporary language of a consumer culture. In fact the first day that Travis appears at the school to walk home with Hunter, Hunter is so embarrassed that he hides and rides home in a neighbor's car. Later that evening Walt finds Hunter in the garage sitting behind the wheel of his car "driving"—thus signaling his utter discursive difference from his "natural" father. The second time— after Travis has familiarized himself with the discourse of fatherhood by wearing a three-piece suit picked out with the help of Walt and Anne's Spanish maid, who symbolically becomes his "nanny," helping him to grow up into the codes of culture—Hunter walks home with him, but allegorically for two-thirds of the way home, they walk on opposite sides of the street. The third time Travis appears at the school, he is more at home with the discourses of paternity and the culture; he is even driving an old battered pickup truck. Thus, when he informs Hunter that he is about to leave in search of Jane, Hunter decides to go with him. The three meetings between father and son show the decreasing emotional distance between them, but the discursive gap remains more or less the same. They rarely talk to each other directly, and it is interesting to note that, when they are driving in the pickup truck, we often see Hunter sitting in the open back talking through a walkie-talkie to his father who remains inside the cab.

Hunter's decision to leave his life with Anne and Walt and go with Travis, with whom he cannot communicate most of the time, is "explained" in the (ideo)logic of the film as a mark of his instinctual pull toward his "real" (i.e., biological) parents. Although Hunter has grown up with Walt and Anne and has spent four out of eight years of his life with them and despite the fact that the discourses of the culture he is familiar with are utterly alien to his father, the spectator (from the viewing place offered by the framing ideology) produces a tale in which Hunter is seen as "knowing" that he should be with him. This assertion of the priority of blood relationships over discursive relationships in the film is of primary significance and offers a set of subjectivities that have profound social and political implications for naturalizing the dominant social arrangements. The film sets up two kinds of families: the natural family based on blood ties; and what might be called a *discursive family*, whose members do not have biological ties but share in the common codes of culture. The film privileges the biological family and thus reifies the traditional bourgeois family as the very grounds of a person's existence. Through such privileging *Paris, Texas* reconfirms the "values" that bourgeois culture derives from the family: the idea of the "individual" as a unitary person whose wholeness and totality is provided through the cohesion created by uncontested connections with the family. The most significant idea extracted from the reification of the traditional family is the notion of authority. The biological family implies that it is "natural" for the father to be the dominant figure and for the mother and children, in varying degrees, to be subjects (of his desire and command): within the (patriarchal) family, the father acts as what Althusser called the "unique and central other Subject," in whose name members of the family are interpellated as subjects. In other words, the "natural" authority of the father authorizes the subjectivities of the family members—those subjectivities required for continuing the relations of social exchange, which in turn confirm and legitimate the organization of the patriarchal family. In the same way that one cannot break a (natural) family tie, one cannot avoid its dictates, which are all based on the notion of the authority of the father. The natural family then is an ideological space in which the underlying abstract hierarchy of a patriarchal society is translated into everyday practices. It is a closed entity placed outside history and in the realm of nature. The "discursive family," on the other hand, is not "eternally" bound, and as such it is a free congregation of people who are joined together by a set of codes; if those codes change, their relationship will change. Such an open space is inherently unstable and threatening because it constantly reorganizes itself through its codes; and codes, unlike genes, are transformable and changing.

Paris, Texas then has Hunter leave his discursive family as emotionally unsatisfactory—as somehow lacking the natural qualities of a family—and join his natural father. By doing so it reinstates the codes of patriarchy that were bracketed for Hunter while Travis was away. In rejecting the "artificial" discursive family, here represented by Walt and Anne, the film implicitly rejects all family organization based on shared social codes rather than genes (natural codes), and Wenders's target of attack is ultimately the socialist idea of family. The socialist model of the family, which like Anne-Walt-Hunter is based on a set of shared (and thus changeable) social codes and political practices, is the most frightening challenge to the bourgeois sense of selfhood, parenthood, authority, and of course private property, which is transmitted through true natural heirs. To emphasize the alienness of such a concept of parenthood, the film represents the "mother" of the discursive family in the film (Anne) as an "alien," a Frenchwoman who cannot even speak English without an accent. The fact that Hunter confesses that he has no clear and vivid image of Jane except the one seen in the home movie, however, reveals, despite the film's purpose, that "distance," "otherness," and "alienness" are conditions of possibility of the natural family as much as they are, supposedly, the enabling conditions of the discursive and artificial family.

Enroute to Texas in search of Jane, father and son have a grand time together: they are engaged in an incessant set of games, and the trip becomes a timeless blot in which the two recapture the innocence of childhood. Hunter is away from the "surveillance" (unnatural suppression) of Anne, the school, and other social agencies and Travis in his truck has a domain of his own. Father and son (members of the biological family) are immediately available to each other—the two know each other although they do not fully understand each other, and the notion of "parenthood" as a mode of plenitude, presence, and transcendental knowing is strongly developed by the film.

After locating Jane in the peepshow palace, Travis cannot talk to her at first. Looking at her through a one-way mirror, he breaks down and leaves his booth abruptly. In his second visit to the place, Travis manages to tell Jane, again through the telephone and one-way mirror, the allegory of his life: the loving but self-destructive husband whose emotional knots break up his family. Travis's project in finding Jane is, of course, to bring Hunter and Jane together because the relationship between mother and child—natural intimacy—according to him is the most authentic form of connection. The subject position enabling the spectator to make this intelligible is based on the ideological assumption that such a bond is so "obvious" that even someone so pathologically narcissistic as Travis cannot avoid acknowledging it. The spectator, in other words, is reassured of the founding notion of the natural family. The child comes from the body of the mother and as such the connection between the two is the most "natural" and unconstrained by the codes of affection that culture imposes upon other modes of relating. Through privileging the body-blood relationship between mother and child, Travis justifies his own action in taking Hunter from his discursive mother and reuniting him with his biological mother. It is also his belief in the body connection that finally explains not just the title of the film but also Travis's almost mystical act of purchasing a piece of land in Paris, Texas. It is to own the place of his conception, to go beyond the ritual of parenting to the locus of the act of begetting himself that Travis buys the land. There is, obviously, a close connection between Travis's view of the body (the site of genuine affection) and the land itself because the land—especially the wide open desert spaces of Texas not yet tamed by culture—like the body is truthful; it lies beyond and under all the surface changes (of culture) and remains literally the final ground of all modes of living. The conjuncture between body and land in *Paris, Texas,* is what gives meaning to the obscure picture of the vacant lot he always carries with him. The significance of the picture is not clear to others: Walt almost ridicules him for buying a vacant lot, and Hunter teases Travis about his dream place because going to Paris, Texas, can only mean "living on dirt" to the sophisticated boy raised by Anne and Walt.

Travis's act of reuniting Jane and Hunter is a symbolic reinscription of patriarchy in culture—the natural family is back together, and the values of family life are reaffirmed. Fullness is returned to family life in the same manner that Travis achieves wholeness of self by purchasing the lot in Paris, Texas. This completeness of self is "expressed" through the language of silence—silence being the mark of the authentic subject in the film. Thus, when leaving Hunter, Travis says his farewells in a tape-recorded message since he cannot use the language of direct communication between father and son. The taped message is once more a sign of his cultural inability; it is a form of muteness and thus conveys the veracity of his emotions. His "muteness" in this section of the film draws upon the ideological investments made in the sign of "muteness" in the first part of the film. In a sense the entire film is framed by these two moments of "nontalking": between his waking up, after a heat stroke, in a clinic in the Texas desert and his leaving the hotel after having made a taped message for Hunter. The "talking" that takes place between these two moments of muteness and silence is nothing more than cultural bubble—talk of the mundane and the quotidian.

Critics, who have regarded the film as a split between a "hugely portentous opening" of mythic dimensions with "desert, vultures, dogged muteness and an attempt to flee back to the desert," and a rather disappointing and empty second part that is hardly more than a "tiny domestic drama" that no television producer would accept, miss the typological nature of the film's structure. Elements of the second part of the film assume their significance only by reference to points established in the first part: the first part of the film is not a literal "exposition" and "preparation" for the second part but a matrix of signifiers that are the enabling conditions of the "meanings" of the signifieds of the second part. The taped message that Travis leaves for Hunter is clear enough on its own terms only if one is interested in the "informational" content of the message. But without locating the taping of the message in the general set of signifiers of "muteness" that are elaborated and developed in the first part, the ideological investments of the film remain unclear. The film is a statement about the "natural" status of the family and represents the "natural" as a state of existence that is understandable without any mediation of language, culture, or other forms of textuality. It is as available, real, concrete, and obvious as the desert in which Travis was found wandering. "Muteness" is part of the transgression of cultural boundaries and their linguistic codes, and it is seminal to the reinscription of the natural in the general ideological climate of the film.

In fact the entire film is made, according to Wim Wenders, as an act of asserting the "natural" and the uncontested real that lies beyond all modes of cultural textualities and political mediation. In the *Film Quarterly* interview, he elaborates his views on the subject of the "real" as it relates to the act of film making, and since what he says about the art of film making is directly related to the ideological pressures in *Paris, Texas*, it is necessary to quote him at some length:

> I've made quite a number of films that were more concerned with reflecting themselves than reflecting anything that exists apart from movies. And you can call that life, or truth, or whatever. Reality. Doesn't matter. I mean, all those forbidden words. And I see lots of movies and was getting frustrated not only by my own work and the reflexiveness of it but with other movies, too, because it seemed there was no more way out. Whatever film you went to see, it had its nourishment or its life or its food, its roots, in other movies. In movies. I didn't see anything anymore that was really trying to redefine a relation between life and images made from life. Whatever you go to see these days, you sit there and after some time you realize that you're involved again in something that was born and has been recapitulating an experience that comes from other movies. And I think that's a really serious dead end for something that I love very much, which is movies. And I did my share of that. *Paris, Texas* was—I wouldn't say desperate, because I wasn't so desperate while I was making it—but at the end of *The State of Things*, there was no other choice than to redefine, or find again, or rediscover what this is: to film something that exists, and film something that exists quite apart from movies. (Dieckmann, 6)

"Muteness" in Wenders's new cinematography is the sign of this possibility of breaking through the intervening systems of signification—stopping the language whose signifiers constantly refer to other signifiers rather than a "real" located uncontestably beyond them—and reaching the state of the real, the natural. Talk is unnatural; it is the work of culture. Muteness is natural; it is an antilanguage that blankets the bubble of culture and attains the purity of plenitude and self-presence.

In fact, in absolute "muteness" Jane and Hunter first encounter each other in the hotel. Their natural intimacy finds expression only in the natural language of nontalk, silence, and muteness—the ultimate mode of forceful "presence." There is nothing *said* between them except the caresses and spinning embrace Jane gives Hunter. While the bodily relationship (mother and son) is resurrected, Travis, who is looking up at the hotel room from the parking lot, leaves once again to disappear into the muteness of the lands that lie beyond the skyscrapers of Houston.

Travis's self-effacement in bringing mother and son together, like his muteness, is typologically anticipated in the first part of the film. In that section of the film, Walt selflessly goes to Texas to bring his brother back in spite of all the difficulties he encounters (Travis's silence, his refusal to leave the ground and fly to L.A., his attempts to return to the desert). Walt's devotion to the idea of family—recovering his "natural" brother and reuniting him with his "natural" son, Hunter—as the basis of human connection is reasserted in the ending. The film's ideological move to "prove" that family is the uncontested "natural" ground of community and living comes to a rest with Travis's bringing together mother and son—something that, the film implies, he himself never had and whose lack is behind his failure as a father. His leaving the scene eliminates the element of crisis that the family has been facing, and his absence thus assures the continuation of the natural course of living in the family. Travis along with Flap and Emma are all individuals who have failed in establishing private intimacy; thus they disappear so that the sphere of the family as the site of free subjectivities cultivated through the call of intimacy remains intact.

Works Cited

Diekmann, Katherine. "Interview with Wim Wenders," *Film Quarterly* 38 no. 2 (1984–85): 2–8.

CONSTELLATION E
FEMINISM, MOTHERHOOD, TERRORISM:
POLITICS OF GENDER

What are the effects of experientialist discourses that privilege subjectivities and practices disengaged from history? This constellation interrogates the ways in which the question of gender is constructed in German feminist filmmaking and German feminist film theory from the New German Cinema period to the present. As films directed by Margarethe von Trotta, Helma Sanders-Brahms, Jutte Brückner, and others sought to account for the historical experience of German women, especially during the Nazi period, the psychoanalytic and phenomenological discourses deployed to explain them both in these films and their feminist readings have tended to dehistoricize those experiences in the names of "motherhood" and the "body," in turn depoliticizing them through a continued separation of the private and public spheres. In view of this, and harkening back to Ingeborg Majer O'Sickey and Annette Van in Constellation C ("The Jewish Question"), we ask what sort of politics are continually wrought by the historical conflation of "family," "motherhood," and the "German," even in texts like those of Susan E. Linville or Barbara Hyams which ostensibly critique that conflation. How, for instance, do Linville's basic affirmation of Hunger Years's *allegory of consumption, and Hyams's philo-Semitic criticism of* Germany, Pale Mother *disavow historical and critical responsibility for both "consumer culture" and the Holocaust? Likewise, how does Antonia Lant's necessary critique of the idealized and mythologized representational practices in* Rosa Luxemburg *on one hand point to the occlusion of crucial aspects of the historical Luxemburg's Jewishness and Leninism while on the other hand fail to contextualize the larger theoretical implications of this occlusion as it symptomatizes German feminism's problematic efforts to "come to terms with the past"? By contrast, which questions are enabled, and which disallowed, by Mary Beth Haralovich's materialist feminist reading of sexuality, age, political allegiance and class in* The Marriage of Maria Braun? *How does this reading, along with that of Linville, connect the question of gender to the political and economic questions raised by Mas'ud Zavarzadeh in Constellation D ("The Euroamerican Question")? How does such a reading relate to questions posed by Lisa DiCaprio and Jack Zipes concerning the re-privatization of gender in* Marianne and Juliane *and* The Lost Honor of Katarina Blum? *What are the connections between Jack Zipes's analysis of* Blum's *critique of the Springer Press and the question of the intellectual public sphere raised in Constellation J ("The Post-al Public Sphere")? How does DiCaprio's analysis bring a feminist perspective to that problematic that enables a more politicized approach to Vergangenheitsbewältigung than either that of Koch or Habermas in Constellation B ("The* Heimat *Debate")? How do these texts call for a left response to these questions and concerns in the face of German state suppression of left-wing "terrorism" (Baader-Meinhof) and, indeed, the Left? How does this call differ from responses to state terrorism offered by Imke Lode in Constellation F ("Queer Constructs") and Kaja Silverman in Constellation G ("Myth and Allegory")? Finally, to what degree are any of these feminist reconfigurations of the relation between private and public discourse implicated in a disengagement of gender from the politics of history?*

Self-Consuming Images:
The Identity Politics of Jutta Brückner's
Hunger Years

BY SUSAN E. LINVILLE

In the universe of consumerism, there is an object more beautiful, more precious, more striking than any other—heavier with connotations than even the automobile; it is the body.[1]

Jean Baudrillard

I need the cinema in order to reconstruct my physical person. Women's physical persons have been destroyed by history. Thus, for us, we need the cinema in an urgent fashion.[2]

Jutta Brückner

JUTTA BRÜCKNER describes her 1979, autobiographical film *Hunger Years in a Land of Plenty* (*Hungerjahre—in einem reichen Land*) as "very, very German." Set in the formative years of the West German *Wirtschaftswunder*, this stark black-and-white film maps the complex cultural landscape of Brückner's youth: the nation's division into East and West, its denial of the Nazi past, the Cold War, anticommunism, sexual repression, and bulimic consumerism (bulimia, from the Greek: great hunger). Well-received by both critics and the public in Germany, *Hunger Years* surprised its director by the strength of its appeal to female audiences internationally. Even Egyptian women, with their markedly different cultural context, found that the film spoke to them.[3] Yet scholars have paid *Hunger Years* disappointingly little attention here. Robert and Carol Reimer's *Nazi-Retro Film: How German Narrative Cinema Remembers the Past*, for example, fails even to mention the film, despite its protagonist's efforts to comprehend her country's fascist history, and notwithstanding the film's unsparing critique of the mother and grandmother—a critique that, perhaps more than any other in film, dovetails with Claudia Koonz's analysis of socially conformist, apolitical women's roles in abetting fascism.[4] Nor until recently have feminist scholars in the United States considered Brückner's work, despite her filmic ruminations on key feminist

This essay was written specifically for this volume and is published here for the first time by permission of the author. The author wishes to thank Richard McCormick, Catherine Wiley, Kent Casper, and the editors, Kirsten Thompson and Terri Ginsberg, for their incisive questions and valuable comments on earlier versions of this essay.

tropes and topics: the masquerade, the veil, the gendered gaze, the woman at the keyhole (eating as she observes the primal scene, no less), the consumer and the consumed.[5]

My aim is not to attempt to account for the film's reception or neglect. Instead I want to examine the innovative, powerful ways that *Hunger Years* represents the relationship between disordered consumption—whether of food, goods, or images—and German political identities. Split along conceptual polarities of public/private, West/East, Right/Left, abundance/dearth, male/female, present/past, 1950s West German identity constructs depended on the social and psychological devaluation of the second term in each pair.[6] Brückner's film deconstructs these dualisms while simultaneously showing their cultural operations and consequences. The central identity which the film explores is, on one level, her own, but undigested histories, private and public, emerge as interdependent; neither is graspable in isolation from the other. Thus the conventional, proper, self-displaying and displacing identity construct which the protagonist seeks to assume creates two effects: first, a reification of the female body as the ultimate consumerist image, and second, a neurotic splitting between the female self as subject and as object, and between the culture and the past it evades through rampant consumerism.

In terms of the film's personal discourse, its central dilemma is an adolescent girl's version of the problem set forth in Joan Rivière's "Womanliness as Masquerade" and by Riviere's own life: What does it mean to be intellectual and female?[7] To be sure, the women's circumstances are historically discrete. The two contradictory—and internally conflicted—identities that split and block Ursula, the film's protagonist (and Brückner's surrogate), consist of a failed German citizenship ideal, foundering on repression of the Nazi past, and a self-destructive notion of femininity forged in a decade that inflated the female body's iconic status as consumer commodity to parodic proportions, yet enforced female prudery and bodily shame. In contrast to the amoral Maria Braun, Fassbinder's allegorical "Mata Hari of the Economic Miracle," Ursula seeks to satisfy both the nation's need for moral reflection on its Nazi legacy, and the culture's contradictory requirements for feminine "modesty" and for self-specularization. The film exposes the latter as a self-consuming narcissism in which alienation, in the sense of "sale" or "transfer of property to another" (as in "inalienable rights"), subtends feminine self-representation.

Even though, as Anne McClintock observes, women have been "subsumed only symbolically into the national body politic,"[8] a situation that has inhibited their power to direct national policy, effect change, or act publicly to address issues of collective guilt, the protagonist's desire that these issues be addressed is central to her sense of self. Her need persists even as the repressive politics of patriarchally conditioned, maternally

enforced female self-surveillance augment *unhealthy* self-shame and radically curtail her capacity to act. In fact, the disproportion between the
girl's experiences of a lack of agency and her profound sense of the necessity for responsible action motivated by appropriate shame, by the national
body politic, is probably *Hunger Years's* most harrowing dilemma. In this
context, the film offers an unflinching critique not only of patriarchy but
also of the mother, who binds the daughter to the same patriarchal contractual terms that she was forced to accept. Far more than Sanders-
Brahms's *Germany, Pale Mother* or von Trotta's films, *Hunger Years*
articulates a stark assessment of a maternal legacy marked by passive complicity with the status quo, both under Hitler and after.[9]

Hunger Years remembers both the repressed and the mechanisms of
repression—that is, systems of substitution and commerce on which familial and state repression under patriarchy depend. *Hunger Years* foregrounds and explores the apparati of exchange, bodily discipline, and
control as they are enmeshed in the nexus of consumerism, consumption
and consummation—that is, buying/spending, eating, and enacting a sexual identity.[10] These are obviously key issues shaping the fantasies and iden-
tity-formation of adolescent girls, whose heightened narcissism intensifies
the equation of self with body.[11] Moreover, like Ulrike Ottinger's
Countdown (1990), a documentary on the dismantling of the Wall,
Hunger Years exposes consumerism as a substitute for and evasion from
all kinds of vital but missed connections at a pivotal historical moment. In
Ottinger's film, the transition to German unification is filled up, in terms
of activity and awareness, with goods—buying food, clothes, souvenir
pieces of the Wall, military hats and uniforms—activities that divert attention from the "walls" of poverty, xenophobia, and homophobia that
remain. In the *Wirtschaftswunderwelt* being formed in *Hunger Years*,
consumer goods, including food and sexual spectacle, impede personal,
familial, social, and historical awareness, and in particular, the *Aus-
einandersetzung* (articulation), *Verarbeitung* (working through), and
Verdauung (digestion) of the horrific Nazi legacy. The consumerist dynamic laid bare in *Hunger Years*, then, is not just a process of creating artificial
needs rather than addressing natural ones, as consumerism is theorized by
the Frankfurt school; nor is it only a question of social climbing and differentiation, according to the Baudrillard model.[12] Brückner's memory
reveals that it is also a *Verdauungsstörung*—a blockage of the process of
coming to terms with the past, an obstruction in which reifying representations of women are made to play a crucial role. Commodity fetishism is
thus the urge to accumulate goods in a futile effort to satisfy needs and
eliminate feelings of deprivation unconnected with the products consumed: consumerism is a lure away from addressing psychological needs
produced by history—the needs for remembrance, acknowledgement of
affective ties with the Third Reich, and consequent guilt, shame, and

mourning; the need to experience *Mitleiden* for the Jewish victims of the Holocaust. Indeed, rather than face the monstrous criminality of their history, West Germans broke affective bridges with that history. Describing the situation in the 1950s and early 1960s, Alexander and Margarete Mitscherlich assert, "a great number if not a majority of the citizens of democratic West Germany have been unable to identify themselves with anything beyond its economic system."[13] Inevitably, commodifying the female body enforced the diversion and disavowal, especially for the woman or girl. The reified female body constituted a special price paid for evading history. Thus my contention is that *Hunger Years* not only corroborates the Mitscherlichs's findings, but also exceeds them to elaborate important feminist and filmic ramifications of West German identification with its economic and consumerist systems.

Illuminating in this context is a 1981 interview with Patricia Harbord in which Brückner theorizes the connection between women's film spectatorship and consumerism. The filmmaker discusses how women's constricted means of appropriating the visible world have made them especially susceptible to consumerist cinematic spectatorship. She points out that the most frequent cinemagoers during the heyday of the Hollywood "woman's film" were women.[14] Putting the situation in a wide cultural perspective, Brückner asserts, "because women couldn't conquer the outside world with their look the way men could, their look became voyeuristic, of necessity. So that, quite literally, for instance, they peeped through keyholes like Ursula watching her parents make love."[15] What this situation means for women as cinema-goers, in Brückner's view, is that

> women are particularly willing to submit themselves to this mechanism of identification which forms the basis of film—much more willing than men. The classic Hollywood film played on this [willingness] for a whole decade, by supplying women with films in which their daydreams came true—and the poverty of their situation revealed itself, because, for instance, their daydreams were never something radically different, but only . . . [b]eing married to an especially rich or loving husband, being especially beautiful and wearing especially wonderful clothes—never anything different! Always just "richer" or "better."[16]

To be sure, Brückner's use of "voyeurism" and her account of the woman's film differ from Mary Ann Doane's important theorizations in this area. Doane genders voyeurism male and associates it with a distanciated epistemological drive; she labels the kind of spectatorship activated by the woman's film nonvoyeuristic and identifies it with affect and spatial proximity.[17] Conversely, Brückner ascribes voyeurism to women and describes it as primarily a sociohistorical effect rather than in strictly psychoanalytic or cinematic terms.[18] Brückner's perception seems to be that a female scopic drive which is at least partly epistemological and power-driven, becomes channeled through the woman's film into the kind of affective, overidentified, repetitive structures theorized by psychoanalysis. Her own aesthetics, both in theory and praxis, depend upon a well-conceived balance of identification and distanciation, affect and intellect, and an acknowledgement of the contradictory social positioning of women. Her feminist politics clearly entail dilating the female gaze and the world it surveys.

At the same time, Brückner's analysis of the impact of Hollywood woman's melodrama by no means contradicts Doane's, insofar as both accentuate the genre's role in reconciling women to the existing social order; both, then, enable us to see an irony in America's belief that Hollywood cinema, along with other U.S. products, would promote denazification in Germany in the postwar years, when American movies inundated West German theaters.[19] In direct reaction against the Hollywood woman's film, *Hunger Years* shifts the identificatory capacity of women away from a neurotically repetitive, socially conformist commodity-orientation and toward a more authentic identification—"with the forgotten areas of their selves, with the repressed stories of their past," as Brückner explains.[20] Through *Hunger Years*, Brückner denounces the Hollywood woman's film's equation of femininity with aestheticization as a form of violence and redirects women's gazes toward moral and political engagement.[21]

Further, her goals in *Hunger Years* match the objective that Doane has designated for feminist films which retrieve history: "The task must be not that of remembering women, remembering real women, immediately accessible—but of producing remembering women. Women with memories and hence histories."[22] In *Hunger Years* that task is realized through the film's thirty-something voice-over, spoken by Brückner herself. "I had tried to forget for years," she asserts at the film's beginning. "I could remember towns, houses, places, other people, but had managed to suppress myself out of my memories." The voice-over then details the hysterical symptoms that led her to make this film—a cinematic version of the "talking cure," to use the phrase for therapy coined by Josef Breuer's patient Anna O. The film, however, contrasts with the familiar Hollywood formula in which the woman's recollection is induced and enforced by the patriarchal medical or legal apparatus, as in, for example, Robert Siodmak's *Dark Mirror* (1946). It also contradicts Freud's assertion that for a woman of 30, "there are no paths open to further development."[23] The woman in *Hunger Years* speaks for herself—precisely as the path to further development.

Because the film is not well known here, and because much of its power depends on its particulars, I will describe and discuss how *Hunger Years* unfolds in detail. The film has a three-part structure and covers the years 1953, 1955, and 1956, when the protagonist is thirteen, fifteen, and sixteen, respectively. Each of the film's three segments begins with a shot of a waterside restaurant, a setting whose importance to plot emerges late in the film. And each segment emphasizes claustrophobic interiors shot in low-key lighting, the customary mise-en-scène of domestic melodrama rendered in its most elementary, imprisoning, least accommodating form.

Hunger Years's first section introduces the West German lower-middle class Scheuner family: Ursula (played brilliantly by Britta Pohland), her highly repressed, ambitious, socially conformist mother Gerda (Sylvia Ulrich), and the passive father Georg (Claus Jurichs), whose long-term socialist sympathies led him to limited acts of resistance to Nazism during the war, efforts which Gerda insisted he give up. Significantly, the first question young Ursula asks in the film is, "Papa, what is a veil?"—a query that enables the film to gesture toward both the film's general theme of repression and the difficulty of existing concepts of femininity within patriarchal society. (Later, she will also ask, "What is freedom?") Though Herr Scheuner offers no response to his daughter's question, plenty of other "papas" have, Nietzsche, Lacan, and Derrida not the least among them. Their answer, very generally: the veil is the mask the woman wears in her culturally assigned, eroticized function as fetish, figure, or trope, as the representation of a range of contradictory things she can signify but not understand, see, or possess—truth, untruth, lack, and the phallus.[24] Largely absent from these men's analyses of veils and masks is any consideration of their sociopolitical implications or their connections to relations of power and resistance as these shape the historical and economic circumstances of nonfigural female lives. This is to say that, implicit in much recent patriarchal philosophy, but untheorized, is the reduction of the female to a token of exchange in the marketplace of ideas.

Polyphonic interior monologue in voice-over from the three family members conveys their private dreams, their isolation, and noncommunication. Dialogue between Ursula and her parents also reveals communicative disorders. Neglectful of ego boundaries, Gerda disqualifies what her daughter says and projects her own desires onto Ursula, in a pattern typical of families with anorexic daughters.[25] For example, early in the film Ursula looks longingly out the window of the family's new apartment—a highly gendered activity she often repeats—and asks her mother, "Do you think I'll find a new friend here?" Instead of responding, Gerda announces to Georg that Ursula wants an accordion for Christmas, a wish Ursula never expresses. Family exchanges, including those with the grandmothers, often hinge on this kind of displacement of authentic needs and pleasures through the discourse of consumable goods. In the first section and throughout the film, scenes of eating and drinking, offering, and taking food as compensation, substitution, apology, or evasion, abound. When Gerda secures a job, it is to augment her consumer capacity in order to overcome past deprivations: she stocks the family larder, and the family proudly affords a used car. Johannes Schmölling's mocking Brechtian-style score provides ironic musical commentary on the new acquisition.

Editing juxtaposes public and private, visible and more hidden forms of oppression, subverting the hierarchies that privilege the former. For example, editing connects the adolescent girl's quest for autonomy with East German workers' demonstrations for their rights, and the teenager's psychological and intellectual famine with the workers' physical hunger. Thus, a sequence early in section one graphically depicts Ursula's ménarche—an event no one has informed her about—and includes what may be cinema's first close-up of a sanitary napkin. After masking Ursula's menstruation from her father by pretending that overeating made Ursula sick, Gerda warns her daughter that the fear of pregnancy now necessitates severe restrictions on her behavior. Ursula energetically questions and resists these limits. At one point, she gazes at couples outside her window and announces her intention to take a bicycle tour of Europe. Gerda abruptly shuts the window on her daughter's pleasurable spectatorship, rejects such trips as impossibilities, and decries the folly of girls who get pregnant. Counterposed with scenes dramatizing the girl's hunger for freedom and knowledge is footage of the East Berlin uprising of June 17, 1953, a workers's revolt prompted by the bad state of the economy, unemployment, and food shortages. Newsreels expose brutal repression of the workers; two radio broadcasts, one from the East and one from Adenauer, construct conflicting discourses on the uprising. Hearing the events reported on the radio, Ursula demands, "Why don't they give the people freedom?" and "What is freedom?" "When things are going well for us, and we don't have to be afraid," is her mother's wholly privatized, visibly self-absorbed response, a reaction conditioned by her selective war memories. In fact, Gerda's timid misdefinition recalls the *fear* of freedom shown by German women with authoritarian yearnings in the years prior to the Nazi rise to power.[26] Moreover, Gerda's earlier identification of womanhood with illness and apprehension means that her sense of female identity is incompatible even with liberty as she defines it. From the more progressive Georg, Ursula soon learns that people play fast and loose with the word "freedom"—a term the West German government applies to the release of a concentration camp *Kommandant* from prison. Through these sequences and exchanges, then, the film promotes a deconstructive reading of the discourses differentiating the "free" West from the East, public history from private experience, and current events from past atrocities. Brückner's aim is not to equate the terms of these binarisms, but to expose and explore what has had to be repressed, left out, and marginalized to form each binary pair.

The complexities of repressive sexual politics are further developed when the father's leftist, antifascist positions, which have earned Ursula's admiration, are undercut by his marital infidelity and conformity with the sexual double standard. Feeling betrayed, Ursula angrily declines, then secretly devours the sweet roll Georg offers her as a token of apology. Not knowing the source of Ursula's sadness, her mother offers her chocolate to cheer her up. Ursula and Gerda both become alienated from Georg, cling to each other, and in what Brückner calls "the most horrible moment" in the film,[27] imagine an exclusive, fundamentally unchanging mother-daughter dyad into futurity, an arrested preoedipal bond like the one that traps Gerda's celibate sister and, to a slightly lesser degree, Gerda herself, with their own intensely narcissistic mother. Section one of the film ends with Gerda's attempt to win Georg back. Reluctantly following her mother's patriarchal marital advice, Gerda has sex with Georg. Ursula peers through the keyhole to her parents's bedroom and witnesses the scene, chewing on some food as she watches. Then refusing the oedipal situation, the girl runs to the bathroom and flushes the toilet to drown out her father's noisy, orgasmic moaning. This is the film's most concrete rendering of the primal scene; at other points, *Hunger Years* is haunted by Ursula's mindscreen images of her mother's naked body lying in the grass, a man's shadow ominously cast across it. I will return to these images.

The film's second section is dated 1955. In this middle segment, fifteen-year-old Ursula's fantasies turn to heterosexual romance through day-dreams revealed at various moments in voice-over. Ironically paired with these fantasies are scenes of sexual harrassment and extradiegetic documentary footage of a Miss World beauty contest, footage which shows an audience of gazing males judging contestants in swimsuits. Just as the new family car serves as a symbol of prosperity in the beginning of section one, the beauty contestants function as parallel signs of wealth at the beginning of section two. And just as music mocks the car's symbolism, a surreal, disembodied laugh-track, coupled with popular song lyrics about onanism, provides distanciating, sardonic counterpoint to the pageant, revealing the degrading underside of objectification. Thus the female body's coding and function, like the car's, are exposed as a public symbol of men's success and control, and as a means of solipsistic escape from past traumas and deprivations.

The key organizing concepts of the 1955 section are lost youth and passive complicity with the status quo. Isolated and alienated, the girl yearns for popularity, admiration for her poetry, and the love of a boy, while the mother insists that Ursula stay away from boys, remain "innocent," and concentrate exclusively on her grades. That the mother is passing on a legacy of loss wherein the daughter, like the mother, becomes her own jailer, emerges clearly when Gerda recollects her own total lack of youthful independence through voice-over. She remembers being made to move directly from her mother's to her husband's guardianship, never experiencing independence or going to the theater, cinema, or dancing until age 23. Little wonder she failed to support her husband's attempts to resist fascism, let alone mount any political stance of her own. Her continued inability to question her own or Ursula's diminished positions within patriarchy perpetuates the maternal legacy of loss. An old photograph of Gerda and her mother concludes this scene.

First Georg, and later Ursula's teacher, continue the pattern of reminiscence and sorrow over forfeited youth. Their recollections in each case are brought to a close by a series of historical photographs. The father's voice-over recounts with sadness and anger, years of unemployment, war, and political disaffection. A poignant scene of the grown man, alone, kicking a soccer ball accompanies his narrative. During a physical education class, Ursula's teacher reflects on the past, first recalling the pleasure of participating in the Bund deutscher Mädel BDM (the girl's Hitler youth) and later the pain and extreme bitterness for leaders who deceived young people and betrayed their youthful trust and idealism.

As in the film's first section, personal experience and public life are tessellated rather than reduced to hierarchic binarisms. The scene with the schoolteacher reveals that the history class never gets around to studying the atrocities of the Hitler era. The teacher's reminiscences are contextualized in relation to the ominous 1956 government plan to reintroduce compulsory military service and the government ban on the communist party. In a characteristically deconstructive gesture, the film uses photographs and documentary footage from 1956 of police aggression and mass arrests in order to give the lie to the announcements we hear from Secretary Schröder that moderation will be used in enforcing the interdiction against communism. The scene typifies how the film text works to redefine political identity by disclosing historical contradictions that other forms of narrative often repress; that is, the film exposes incoherencies within the dichotomous identity constructs of nationhood; disjunctions that counterpoint the narrator's increasing personal fragmentation as she tries to forge an impossible synthesis among the imperatives of the given sexual, intellectual, and moral identity constructs.

The two sequences that conclude *Hunger Years*'s second section starkly dramatize the fissures within and between the intellectual and sexual worlds Ursula tries to inhabit and her powerlessness in these contexts. The first sequence contains Ursula's confrontation during an outdoor luncheon with Georg about his past failure to resist the Nazis more forcefully. As Ursula points out, Georg's comrade lost part of his arm while an inmate at Dachau. A warden hacked it off with a spade. Why has Georg no bodily proof of *his* antifascist stance? Similarly, she criticizes her father's current lack of active opposition to rearmament and to the ban on communism. She prays forlornly that everything will be made all right. The final sequence, played out in a lush, natural waterside setting, made vaguely ominous by a leftward-panning long shot, presents Ursula boasting to a young male companion about her (fictitious but much desired) sexual independence. The film then shows Ursula in medium shot, as the boy forces alcohol down her throat during what seems an interminable take. The sounds of raucous, disembodied male voices and dissonant music replace birds' singing; the frame freezes, then fades to black. The pastoral setting and Ursula's earlier dreams of romance devolve into a brutal scene of violation and oblivion.

In part three, mother and daughter argue about Ursula's compulsive eating habits, which now take the form of a serious disorder that includes use of diet pills and cigarettes. Rebellious, but also increasingly isolated and depressed, Ursula regresses to mutism. In one haunting shot indicative of her need for rebirth, she lies in bed in a fetal position sucking sweetened condensed milk from a tube. The voice-over—spoken by Brückner—switches among fragmented identities and encompasses the retrospective reflections of the thirty-something narrator, as well as a whispering, destructive voice identified with her younger, sixteen-year-old self. The remembering persona explains, "I didn't feel at home anywhere," and describes her experience of herself as superfluous and "like a machine racing around out of control." Documentary footage showing simulated nuclear explosions and their impact on test mannequins follows these ruminations. The images work both as oblique mirrors of Ursula's highly disturbed, apocalyptic mental state, produced by her wish to regress from an impossible sexual identity within patriarchy, and as reminders of the palpable threat of nuclear war—an especially real danger for Germany, which was the first likely battleground between the superpowers. The images of devastation thus suggest an enmeshed political dynamics, matching personal neurosis with the international insanity that passed for normalcy.[28]

The film cuts to a scene at a public park. In the background of the shot is a fountain; in the foreground Ursula lies prostrate, parallel to the picture plane, as a grandmotherly figure with a walker slowly passes "over" her in middle ground and stares at her disapprovingly. Parallel to Herzog's *Kasper Hauser*, shown in a similar shot horizontal under the "weight" of the black-cloaked father figure who initiates him into culture, Ursula is depicted as burdened by the weight of the maternal figure. But while Kasper undergoes a terrible "fall" into language, Ursula's has been a regression into mutism—a highly gendered fall *out* of language and a "fall out," the editing insists, as inseparable from the global threat of nuclear "fall out" as it is from Germany's cataclysmic past.

The girl then sets the lap of her skirt on fire while playing with matches, an "accident" that signals a confused mix of sexual desire and self-destructiveness. She runs to the fountain, where a black Algerian comes to her aid, douses the fire, and befriends her. A revolutionary, he tells her about the new face of war as it exists in his country and ironically describes how

"The stupid colored Algerians are chasing the French, who have been so good to them, out of the country." Her Eurocentrism prevents her from immediately grasping his meaning—for her war is World War II. Sensitive to her unhappiness, he offers her rare moments of emotional connection in a strikingly photographed lake-side setting made lushly surreal by the heightened sounds of birds. But pressuring her by claiming that girls of her age are already married mothers in his culture, he tries to seduce her then forces himself on her. Over her protests, he masturbates between her legs, as she, ultimately resigned, stares off into space.

The scene raises vexing questions of response for the spectator, whose desire for clear moral intelligibility is frustrated. The scene is perhaps best understood if we contextualize it in relationship to the film's earlier juxtaposition of a clandestine protest against the prohibition of the communist party with Gerda's bodily entrapment under her oblivious husband, deep in post-coital slumber, and her wish that she could tear her ovaries out so as not to fear pregnancy. So contextualized, the scene with the Algerian seems an assertion that revolutionary movements, whether based in anticolonialist, antiracist ideologies or in First World feminisms, must acknowledge each other and look to each other as contexts. Accordingly, Brückner privileges neither gender nor race as primary to a determinant reading of the sequence. She neither vilifies nor excuses the Algerian for taking obvious advantage of the girl's vulnerability. While he seems practiced in this sort of seduction, the contrast between him and the boy who forces alcohol on Ursula works to counterbalance negative racial stereotyping. Further, Brückner represents Ursula's passivity to her victimization as a consequence of her lack of access to her own desire (be it desire to abstain or to be sexually intimate), an acculturation that parallels her mother's.

After spending the night outdoors, Ursula and the Algerian go to the waterside restaurant which appears in the shots that partition the film. To Ursula's surprise and profound dismay, the man tells her he is leaving Germany to return to his own country. She then returns home and faces her mother, whose angry, punishing gaze here epitomizes the mechanism of maternal control in patriarchy's service. Contemptuously washing her hands of the girl, Gerda leaves for work, while Ursula, desperately alone, looks out the window. In an exchange evocative of *Rear Window*, a woman with binoculars returns Ursula's gaze from the opposite apartment window and in the process mirrors her voyeurism and domestic confinement. The exchange differs from a Foucauldian panoptic regime, because in *Hunger Years*, the warden-spectators are simultaneously the wards of their micropolitical prisons. As Brückner asserts, the moment is "at once real and surreal."[29] After closing the window and curtains, Ursula resolves to "bake a cake." Consuming pills, sweets, and whisky, she engages in a voracious suicidal ritual, or so it seems. Then a photograph—a close up—

of Ursula's face appears, creating an edit that recalls and repeats a pattern from the "lost youth" segments in the film's central section. That is, the photograph offers the same kind of visual punctuation for the film as a whole that photographs do for earlier sequences. The mother's voice-over asks why the daughter never said anything, and insists that the daughter had everything, didn't she? As a flame eats across the photograph, the autobiographical voice-over asserts, "Wer etwas ausrichten will, muss etwas hinrichten—sich selbst"———Whoever would achieve something must destroy something—oneself. Brückner, in an interview, has interpreted this sequence—Ursula "does not kill herself physically, but kills the images, the false representations that we carry inside ourselves and that choke us."[30] Indeed, the "thing" destroyed is the alienated image-object, the mode of being for the other, that has been confused with and substituted for an authentic identity. More broadly and metaphorically, this incendiary gesture violently protests against cinema as a technology of image consumption for women, according to the usual commercial terms—in which alienation, as transfer or sale of property, paradoxically tends to underlie the representation of the female and her too proximate (nonalienated) position as spectator. From the point of view of both film structuration and national history, what the ending overcomes is the compulsion to repeat, to collapse the past onto the present, at personal and collective levels.

The way that this gesture at film's end "answers" two related, reflexive moments from part one—a mirror scene and the primal scene—deserves special attention. The first of these entails a brilliantly conceived, richly suggestive shot of Ursula practicing a feminine masquerade: sitting in front of two mirrors, her body reflected in one on the right, her head framed by a smaller, higher mirror on the left, she hikes her skirt up, crosses her legs, pulls her socks down, and poses with a cigarette, contemplating her reflections. Her posing is interrupted when the doorbell rings, and the film cuts to a shot of Ursula's face juxtaposed with the comic mask that hangs by the door in a dramatic pair.

By demonstrating how Ursula "practices" femininity and works to become, in effect, a self-consuming artifact, the scene exposes what commodity fetishism conceals—the labor and the alienated laborer behind the manufactured "feminine" image, an image which is also fetishized according to the psychoanalytic paradigm, to please the male gaze. Implicitly, commodity fetishism feeds into feminine masquerade—a woman makes a fetish of the commodities that adorn her in order to become a more desirable commodity fetish herself. Her objectified "identity" is as lacking in subjectivity as "the goods" are lacking in power to address their (her) own fundamental social needs. By depicting Ursula's self-surveillance and divided consciousness, the shot reveals the splitting which, according to John Berger, inheres in classical, alienated feminine consciousness of self: "The surveyor of woman in herself is male: the surveyed female. Thus she turns into an object—and most particularly an object of vision: a sight."[31] Or, as Doane puts it, "the increasing appeal in the twentieth century to the woman's role as perfect consumer (of commodities as well as images) is indissociable from her positioning *as* a commodity and results in the blurring of the subject/object dichotomy."[32] Accordingly, Ursula constructs the reflections and yet literally mistakes the images for herself. In order to expose this perceptual blurring, the scene simultaneously figures self-production and consumption, masquerade and narcissism, self-alienation (or distance) and spatial proximity to the image. It thereby both reveals woman's contradictory positioning under patriarchy and generates an engaged yet critical viewing point for its female audience. In other words, female spectatorship within the filmic diegesis comments on extradiegetic spectatorship and promotes active, critical reflection on and identification with the contraditions and fragmentation in Ursula's position.

The decapitation that the mirror images create also signals the intrinsic violence of the male gaze that Ursula interiorizes, and the violence of the filmic close-up, a shot that the smaller mirror image effectively frames. Analyzing the relationships among the close-up, narcissism, and the commodification of women, Doane explains, "The face, more than any other body part, is *for* the other. . . . And this being-for-the-gaze-of-the-other is, of course, most adequate as a description of the female subject, locked within the mirror of narcissism."[33] Doane's conclusions about filmic uses of women's faces illuminate *Hunger Years*'s final image—a still close-up in flames—in relation to consumerist dynamics: "It is not at all surprising that the generalized social exchange of women should manifest itself in the cinematic institution as a proliferation of close-ups of the woman."[34] The film's closing image refuses the terms symbolized by the earlier decapitation scene, in which "the goods" (i.e., Ursula) are violently self-divided.[35]

The mirrored reflections that arrest Ursula's gaze also recall Freud's well-known reading of the Medusa's decapitated head as a symbol of the mother's castration. Looking at her body in transvestite terms—as male-spectator and as feminine masquerade—Ursula is in no position to see what Cixous calls the laugh of the Medusa, a perception that would find all of her body beautiful and deem the idea of woman's castration/decapitation laughable. Instead, she sacrifices her own desire in the name of "the acceptance of 'castration,' the humility, the admiration of men" that defines "the conception of womanliness as mask."[36] To be sure, as noted before, Ursula's face is aligned with a comic mask present in the mise-en-scène, a positioning that evokes the Lacanian view of sexual masquerade as comic.[37] Ursula's posing is partly humorous, as is her later peer through the keyhole when her parents have sex. But the violence implicit in the mirror/decapitation scene—suffering more aligned with the tragic mask that Ursula's face covers—recalls Rivière's theorization of feminine masquerade as psychically painful. Indeed, the scene fits the larger dynamics of the film in being neither tragic nor comic but more precisely ironic melodrama, the genre that subtends *Hunger Years* and is critiqued by it.

Not surprisingly, the kind of self-alienation plus overidentification with the body shown in this reflexive dual-mirror scene has been implicated in studies of both female eating disorders and hysteria. Noelle Caskey observes, "It is the literal-mindedness of anorexia to take 'the body' as a synonym for 'the self,' and to try to live in the world through a manipulation of 'the body,' particularly as it is reflected to the anorexic by the perceived wishes of others. Anorexia is the cultivation of a specific image *as an image*—it is a purely artificial creation and that is why it is admired."[38] In contrast, the male subject's image—at least as created by cinema—has been theorized as a mirror of control, uniting body and identity as the basis of discursive authority.[39] What *Hunger Years* reveals is that, for the female, mistaking the body for identity is precisely the problem, an incapacitating dilemma that conventional cinema exacerbates.

Moreover Ursula's disorderly eating, like that described by Caskey,[40] and by popular author Kim Chernin,[41] is grounded in confusion about sexual identity and fear of sexual maturity. The daughter sees the mother as the embodiment of female maturity and associates her with limitation rather than agency; for Ursula, the mother is also associated with timorous complicity and callous self-absorption during the fascist regime. The contemporary socioeconomic context of Ursula's "years of hunger" is widespread West German identification with *Wirtschaftswunder*-consumerism.[42] On the face of it, a marginal figure in this context, Ursula is pulled to the center by this deconstructive film, her impossible position under patriarchy symptomatizing those contradictions that arrest the nation's potential for change, genuine growth, and mature accountability for its history.

At the same time, Ursula's refusal to take meals with her family, on their terms, suggests an unconscious political act of resistance. Indeed, her eating behavior calls to mind Chernin's assertion that "an eating disorder is a profoundly political act,"[43] and, to a lesser extent, Valie Export's position on the politics of anorexia.[44] Export terms this behavioral disorder one of "the great feminine forms of rebellion" because it refuses the feminine body and patriarchal images of that body.[45] Unlike Export, however, Brückner asserts, "I need the cinema in order to reconstruct my physical person. Women's physical persons have been destroyed by history. Thus, for us, we need the cinema in an urgent fashion."[46] In the film, Gerda's intense antipathy toward her own body is presented as a primary instance of the problem to be solved.

As for Ursula's hysteria, her experience conforms with Howard Wolowitz's description of the hysteric as someone caught up in a process that "leads further and further away from the self becoming the basis for

gratification and experience into a sense of emptiness, experiential deficiency and a wish to regress back into the dependency of early childhood
as a haven."[47] Ursula's behavior in the final segment of the film provides
vivid images of this kind of regressive retreat, including her curling up in a
fetal position to suck sweetened milk from a tube. And like Anna O.,
whose hysterical symptoms included disruptive polylingualism, Ursula
experiences speech disruption. In Ursula's case, the symptoms include
mutism and, at one point, feeling more "at home" speaking French when
she buys sugar for herself. The film positions us to read her verbal masquerade and mutism as politically significant.

Analyzing Anna O.'s verbal symptoms, Dianne Hunter has argued that
they "may reflect a refusal of the cultural identity inscribed in the order of
(coherent) German discourse and an unconscious desire, become conscious in certain contemporary feminist writers, to explode linguistic convention."[48] Ursula's speech disorder signals a similar kind of refusal, in this
case, an unconscious rejection of a 1950s German identity that demands
of her a "feminine" mindlessness—a "good girl's" ignorance—about the
fascist past. At the level of cinematic utterance, Brückner's film in effect
transforms her earlier speech pathology into conscious, strategic disruptions and interventions. Brückner's deconstructive method of including
newsreels and photographs, her deliteralizing of the film's final image, and
more broadly what Jacqueline Aubenas terms *Hunger Years*'s "primitive"
style—all exemplify such strategic disruption.[49] The film exposes contradictory public discourses by foregrounding how East and West Germany generate politicized and highly contradictory media reports on strikes and
civic unrest, and it repeatedly underscores the public school's hypocritical
duplicity about the Holocaust. Thus the girl's hysterical symptoms are
metamorphosed into the woman's feminist exposé. Brückner *unveils* and
criticizes divisive and duplicitous public discourses, revealing them to be
sites of unresolved conflict, methods of management and containment,
and, in effect, hysterical symptoms produced by repression and denial.[50]

The other reflexive scene already mentioned—a primal one from the
film's first section—presents Ursula eating and peering through the keyhole at her parents's intercourse. The scene not only evokes Freud's
mythical originary moment in which hunger and sexuality are united, but
also the "primitive" or "primal" root fantasy of the maternal melodrama,
as Linda Williams theorizes this genre.[51] Like many feminist films—
Sanders-Brahms's *Germany, Pale Mother*, von Trotta's *Marianne and
Juliane*, Potter's *The Gold Diggers*, and Akerman's *Jeanne Dielman*
among them—*Hunger Years* works within and against the conventions of
the maternal melodrama. By contextualizing the shared psychic roots of
melodrama and consumerism in relation to a specific cultural moment,
the scene dialogizes psychoanalytic, historicist, and filmic issues in innovative feminist terms. This dialogization militates against our taking any of

its constituent parts as a totalizing discourse. Thus, the scene allows for a differentiated understanding of the historical dynamics and conditions of female spectatorship.[52]

The reflexive keyhole image also recalls Metz's theory linking cinema spectatorship in general with the primal scene and the founding moment of oedipal identity. The stark dynamics of the adolescent daughter's gaze, however, reveal important psychic and cinematic differences from Metz's rather nostalgic theorization of voyeurism and the primal scene. Unlike Metz's theory, Brückner's image takes sexual, maturational, and cultural differences into account, including the experience that oedipal issues reemerge with full force during adolescence. The daughter's eating as she peers suggests an oral sexuality linked with preoedipal fantasy, including oral rage. The scene follows dramatizations of the daughter's bisexual wavering—typical for her age—about the relative importance of father and mother and of the positioning each represents. This oscillation complicates our sense of the daughter's response to the drama she witnesses.[53] Her identification, moreover, would seem to entail a perception of the mother's position as victim, the father's as callous and perhaps sadistic—not a misperception given the state of the parents's sexual relations. In a provocative essay on Freud's Dora, Maria Ramas argues that by and large children's interpretation of the fantasy of the "primal scene" as sado-masochistic is accurate: "The fantasy, quite simply, expresses erotically the essential meaning of sexual difference in patriarchal culture"; thus Ramas counters the usual view that the child misinterprets the scene "due to the influence of a specific libidinal phase—the anal-sadistic stage."[54] If we accept Ramas's view, then Georg's leftist sympathies with underdogs in public politics and Gerda's indifference to the plight of subordinates and victims in the same realm, stand in fundamental contradiction to the sexual politics that they enact. These dissociative paradoxes further complicate and frustrate Ursula's identificatory positioning.

Moreover, in contrast to the situation described in Metz's theory of voyeurism, proximity to a concrete event, rather than safe distance, defines Ursula's look. Closeness here is decidedly not just a consequence of Ursula's "feminine" relation to representation. Nor is this nearness simply or predominantly a psychological consequence of what Thomas Elsaesser sees as Ursula's desire to identify with her mother, though identification with the mother's body figures in the dynamics of the scene. Oddly, Elsaesser argues that *Hunger Years* on the whole contradicts Brückner's statement that she makes films in order to identify with herself: "the self with which the heroine of *Hunger Years* tries to identify is the mother," he asserts.[55] Quite the contrary, throughout the film, it is the mother who demands that her daughter be someone with whom *she* can identify, a narcissistic mirror of the kind that Gerda and her sister continue to be for their mother; hence, Ursula's desparate attempts to escape the confinement of this "good girl's" looking-glass trap.[56] Ursula must escape it in order to claim for herself a tenable position both as a German, with all the complex cultural weight that that identity carries, *and* as a sexual being. She must break free from her incarceration within the mother's home and patriarchally conditioned, somatophobic relationship to the female body.[57]

Indeed, as the film presents it, Ursula's proximity to what she witnesses, her spectatorial closeness, is largely a sociological effect—a consequence of having a place in the world denied her. Her space is narrowly domestic, and her gaze, diminished by social strictures, includes the required substitution of extreme self-surveillance for a look that desires and learns. She can be a woman at a keyhole, a window, or a mirror, apprehending life naively, indirectly, and vicariously. And what the mirror reflects back to her is her image reduced to the scope of the close-up, in film, a shot less tied than others to the spatiality and implicit agency of perspectival realism. Thus encased inside a privatized sphere, Ursula cannot satisfy her hunger to appropriate her own experience or her need for *Vergangenheitsbewältigung*—coming to terms with the past. Indeed, as the film reveals, Ursula's relational world becomes regressively smaller, rather than expanding, as the teenager moves toward physical maturity and womanhood.[58] *Hunger Years* as a whole is a remarkable attempt to historicize, expose, and transform the terms of the female gaze on which it reflects. Its incendiary ending aims radically to subvert the established aesthetic, social, and economic functions of cinema, so that film may contribute to the construction of an identity politics that serves related German and feminist needs.

Notes

1. Jean Baudrillard, *La Société de consummation* (Paris: Gallimard, 1970), 196, as quoted in Maureen Turim, "Gentlemen Consume Blondes," in *Issues in Feminist Film Criticism*, ed. Patricia Erens (Bloomington: Indiana University Press, 1990), 106.

2. Jutta Brückner, "Entretien," with Jacqueline Buet and Françoise Collin, in *Jutta Brückner, Cinéma Regard Violence*, ed. Françoise Collin (Brussels: Les Cahiers du Grif, 1982), 44 (my translation here and in subsequent references).

3. In an interview with Patricia Harbord, Brückner expresses wonder that her film has struck strong resonant chords with "so many women—not just women from other countries, but from totally different societies," and with different generations of women. She explains *Hunger Years*'s wide appeal on the basis of its success in revealing "collective gestures," for example, "certain types of inhibition" (*Screen Education* 40 [Autumn/Winter 1981–82]:51–52). In Europe, the film garnered the following awards: Audience Prize, Sceaux (1980) and Brussels (1981); International Film Critics's Award, Berlin (1980); and The German Film Critics's Award (1981).

4. Claudia Koonz, *Mothers in the Fatherland: Women, the Family and Nazi Politics* (New York: St. Martin's Press, 1987).

5. Gabriele Weinberger speculates, "Many reasons could be named for [*Hunger Years'*] rather reserved—although generally positive—reception [in the United States],

among them probably the film's expressionistic aesthetic, its negative portrayal of motherhood, its special kind of sexual explicitness, ending in a suicide attempt and the interspersed violent visual clusters of German political memory which have neither denotational nor connotational meaning for the American audience" (*Nazi Germany and its Aftermath in Women Directors' Autobiographical Films of the Late 1970s* [San Francisco: Mellen Research University Press, 1992], 166). Weinberger is among those feminist scholars who have begun to give *Hunger Years* the kind of attention it deserves. For other recent feminist perspectives on Brückner, see Sandra Frieden, "'For Heaven's Sake, Anything But That!' Jutta Brückner's *Hungerjahre*," *Schatzkammer* 14.2 (1988):80–86; Renate Fischetti, *Das Neue Kino: Acht Porträts von deutschen Regisseurinnen* (Frankfurt: Tende, 1992), 175–210; Julia Knight, *Women and the New German Cinema* (New York: Verso, 1992); and especially Barbara Kosta, "Representing Female Sexuality: On Jutta Brückner's Film *Years of Hunger*," in Sandra Frieden et al., eds., *Gender and German Cinema*, vol. 2 (1993), 241–52. In contrast to *Hunger Years*, both Margarethe von Trotta's *Marianna and Juliane* and Helma Sanders-Brahms's *Germany, Pale Mother* have found advocates who see them as the most powerful films of their era to take up the question of *Vergangenheitsbewältigung*. On *Marianne and Juliane*, see Paul Coates, *The Gorgon's Gaze: German Cinema, Expressionism, and the Image of Horror* (Cambridge: Cambridge University Press, 1991), 222; and on *Germany, Pale Mother*, see the Reimers, *Nazi-Retro Film: How German Narrative Cinema Remembers the Past* (New York: Twayne, 1992), 203–204.

6. Hélène Cixous denounces all patriarchal binary thought of this kind, with its underlying opposition man/woman, and terms it: "A universal battlefield. Each time, a war is let loose. Death is always at work." That is, death results from the equation of the feminine either with passivity or nonbeing: "Either woman is passive or she does not exist" (*The Newly Born Woman*, with Catherine Clément, trans. Betsy Wing [Minneapolis: University of Minnesota Press, 1988]), 64.

7. For a related discussion of this issue, see Renate Möring, "Jutta Brückner," in *Jutta Brückner, Cinéma Regard Violence*, 9–16; reprinted from *Die Frau mit der Kamera* (Munich-Vienna: Carl Hanser Verlag, 1980).

8. Anne McClintock, "'No Longer a Future Heaven': Women and Nationalism in South Africa," *Transition* 51 (1991): 105.

9. What made this critique of her mother possible, Brückner asserts, was first filming *Do Right and Fear Nobody*, which charts the mother's experiences as a subject of sociohistorical forces. Brückner explains, "I could never have made [*Hunger Years*] without making the film about my mother first. After my first film I felt I could really begin to 'settle accounts' with my past—now that I had explained how my mother had become how she was, now I'd justified her, I could start to criticise her." Brückner also notes "how my mother broke out of this mould—very late, through a private catastrophe . . . and she tried to become a completely different person, someone strong and brave who speaks her mind" (Harbord, op. cit., 50, 51). For an important discussion of the difficult position of motherhood in feminist discourse, see Marianne Hirsch, *The Mother/Daughter Plot: Narrative, Psychoanalysis, Feminism* (Bloomington: Indiana University Press, 1989), esp. 169.

10. This nexus comes across effectively in the French *consommer* and *le consummation*, which apply to commodities, to marriage, and to meals. (The word "sumptuary," signifying dress and food expenditures, is related.) For a relevant discussion of the reciprocal relationship between eating disorders (specifically gorging) and shopping, see Ira Mintz, "Self-Destructive Behavior in Anorexia and Bulimia," in *Bulimia: Psychoanalytic Treatment and Theory*, ed. Harvey J. Schwartz (Madison, WI: International University Press, 1988), 160–61.

11. In psychoanalytic terms, the genesis of this consumerist knot might be traced to what Jean Laplanche and Jean-Bertrand Pontalis call Freud's "Mythical moment at which hunger and sexuality meet in a common origin," the "mythical moment" of disjunction "between the object that satisfies and the sign which describes both the object and its

absence" ("Fantasy and the Origins of Sexuality," in *Formations of Fantasy*, ed. Victor Burgin et al. [New York: Methuen, 1986], 25).

12. For a valuable summary of these theories, see Douglas Kellner, *Jean Baudrillard: From Marxism to Postmodernism and Beyond* (Stanford: Stanford University Press, 1989), 14.

13. Alexander and Margarete Mitscherlisch, *The Inability to Mourn: Principles of Collective Behavior*, trans. Beverly R. Placzek (New York: Grove Press, 1975), 27.

14. Patricia Harbord, op. cit., 57–58.

15. Ibid., 56.

16. Ibid., 57.

17. See Mary Ann Doane's entry on "The Spectatrix," *Camera Obscura* 20–21 (May–Sept. 1989): 144–145, and her *The Desire to Desire: The Woman's Film of the 1940s* (Bloomington: Indiana University Press, 1987), 12–13.

18. For a relevant discussion of female voyeurism and fetishism with a difference, see Linda Williams, "Something Else Besides a Mother: *Stella Dallas* and the Maternal Melodrama," in *Issues in Feminist Film Criticism*, ed. Patricia Erens (Bloomington: Indiana University Press, 1990), esp. 154–158, where Williams asserts the need for "examining the contributions that animate women's very active and fragmented ways of seeing" (157).

19. John Sanford observes, "It was an axiom of the American 're-education' programme that if Germany were flooded with the products of American culture, the Germans would, by some mysterious process of osmosis, be transformed into shining exemplars of Truth, Justice, and The American Way. Hollywood was delighted: here was a vast market, potentially the biggest in Europe, that had been closed to them throughout the war years. A great backlog of films that had already paid their way elsewhere could now be rereleased at prices that would undercut any competition. The Germans, not unnaturally, were pleased too, and flocked to see the films they had been denied access to by the Nazis (*The New German Cinema* [Totowa, NJ: Barnes & Noble, 1980], 9).

20. Patricia Harbord, op. cit., 57.

21. While Fassbinder's *Marriage of Maria Braun* deals with the same era and some of the same economic and political issues as *Hunger Years*, his cinema in general is characterized by a pronounced aestheticization of women, of violence against women, and of women's suffering, which militates against a positive feminist reading of his work. For further discussion, see Thomas Elsaesser, "*Berlin Alexanderplatz*: Franz Biberkopf'/S/Exchanges," *Wide Angle* 12 (1990): 40.

22. Mary Ann Doane, *Femme Fatales: Feminism, Film Theory, Psychoanalysis* (New York: Routledge, 1991), 93.

23. Sigmund Freud, "Femininity," in *The Standard Edition of the Complete Psychological Works of Sigmund Freud*, ed. and trans. James Strachey (London: Hogarth Press, 1953–74), 22: 135.

24. For a summary of the theories of Nietzsche, Lacan, and Derrida in this context, see Stephen Heath, "Joan Rivière and the Masquerade," *Formations of Fantasy*, 45–61, and Mary Ann Doane's excellent "Veiling Over Desire: Close-ups of the Woman" (*Femmes Fatales* 44–75). Lacanian Eugénie Lemoine-Luccioni's answer to Ursula's question would be, "The veil is constitutive of the feminine libidinal structure" (quoted in Heath, op. cit., 52). Heath asserts, "the strongest commentator on and respondent to the masquerade is no doubt Nietzsche, troubled with woman and truth and masks and veils and feminism" (50).

25. See Noelle Caskey, "Interpreting Anorexia Nervosa," in *The Female Body in Western Culture: Contemporary Perspectives*, ed. Susan Rubin Suleiman (Cambridge, MA: Harvard University Press, 1986), 178.

26. Koonz explains, "such an inchoate longing [for authoritarianism] did not necessarily impel women to vote for the Nazi Party before 1933, but it did prepare them to welcome the Nazi state," (op. cit., 12–13).

27. Jutta Brückner, "Entretien," in *Jutta Brückner, Cinéma Regard Violence*, 108.

28. The sequence calls to mind Julia Kristeva's assertion that, "On close inspection, all literature is probably a version of the apocalypse that seems to me rooted, no matter what its socio-historical conditions might be, on the fragile border (borderline cases) where identities (subject/object, etc.) do not exist or only barely so—double, fuzzy, heterogenous, animal, metamorphosed, altered, abject" (*Powers of Horror: An Essay on Abjection* [New York: Columbia University Press, 1982], 207).

29. Jutta Brückner, "Entretien," in *Jutta Brückner, Cinéma Regard Violence*, 27.

30. Ibid., 109.

31. John Berger, *Ways of Seeing* (New York: The Viking Press, 1973), 47.

32. Mary Ann Doane, *The Desire to Desire*, 13.

33. Mary Ann Doane, *Femmes Fatales*, 47.

34. Ibid., 48.

35. In other words, the ending points toward a time in which "the goods get together," to borrow Luce Irigaray's phrase ("Des marchandises entre elles" [When the goods get together], trans. Virginia Hules, *New French Feminisms*, eds. Elaine Marks and Isabelle de Courtivron [New York: Schocken, 1980], 107–10).

36. Joan Rivière, "Womanliness as Masquerade," *Formations of Fantasy*, 43.

37. For a discussion of Lacan's ideas, see Mary Ann Doane, *Femmes Fatales*, 37–38.

38. Noelle Caskey, "Interpreting Anorexia Nervosa," op. cit., 184.

39. See Mary Ann Doane, *The Desire to Desire*, 19.

40. Noelle Caskey, op. cit., 187.

41. Kim Chernin, *The Hungry Self: Women, Eating, and Identity* (New York: Harper & Row, 1985), 42.

42. To be sure, it was not only in West Germany but also throughout much of the West, that a consumer dynamic became definitive in the 1950s, as the consumer society that had been delayed by the Depression and World War II was no longer impeded. This period saw the incidence of anorexia among daughters of middle-class families sharply increase (Noelle Caskey, op. cit., 177).

43. Ibid., 92.

44. Valie Export, "The Real and Its Double: The Body," *Discourse* 11.1 (Fall-Winter 1988–89): 25.

45. Ibid., 22.

46. Jutta Brückner, "Entretien," *Cinéma Regard Violence*, 44.

47. Howard Wolowitz, "Hysterical Character and Feminine Identity," in *Readings on the Psychology of Women*, ed. Judith M. Bardwick (New York: Harper & Row, 1972), 313.

48. See Charles Bernheimer and Claire Kahane, eds., *In Dora's Case: Freud–Hysteria–Feminism*, 2nd ed. (New York: Columbia University Press, 1990), 9.

49. Jacqueline Aubenas, "Le Cinéma brut ou la brutalité de la biographie," in *Jutta Brückner, Cinéma Regard Violence*, 57.

50. For related perspectives on hysteria as a form of revolt against partriarchy, see Hélène Cixous and Catherine Clément, *The Newly Born Woman*, 147–60. Clément's discussion of the connections among cinema, hysteria, and the exchange of money also merits attention. See esp. p. 13.

51. Linda Williams, "Film Bodies: Gender, Genre, and Excess," *Film Quarterly* 44.4 (Summer 1991): 10.

52. As a theorist, Brückner has dedicated considerable energy to the topic of the female spectator. For a bibliography of Brückner's critical work, see Renate Fischetti, op. cit., 306.

53. In theory, when the daughter sees the primal scene and the mother's subordination to the father's power, the girl gives up attachment to the mother as love object and switches to the father (Freud) or adds the father without relinquishing the mother as love object (Chodorow)—assuming a heterosexual development.

54. Maria Ramas, "Freud's Dora, Dora's Hysteria," in *In Dora's Case*, 157.

55. Thomas Elsaesser, *New German Cinema: A History* (New Brunswick, N.J.: Rutgers University Press, 1989), 195.

56. As Nancy Chodorow observes, a daughter "does not receive the same kind of love from her mother as a boy does, i.e., a mother, rather than confirming her daughter's oppositeness and specialness, experiences her as one with herself; her relationship to her daughter is more 'narcissistic,' that to her son more 'anaclitic'" (*Feminism and Psychoanalytic Theory* [New Haven: Yale University Press, 1989], 72). The film shows Ursula's need precisely to have her "oppositeness and specialness" affirmed. For further discussion of Chodorow's relevance to *Hunger Years*, see Jan Mouton, "The Absent Mother Makes an Appearance in the Films of West German Directors," *Women in German Yearbook*, vol. 4, Jeanette Clausen (New York: University Press of America, 1988), 72–74.

57. The feeling of entrapment within the body and sense of imprisonment within domestic spaces are visually linked by the striped pullover Ursula habitually wears and the striped wallpaper in the home.

58. For important discussions of the attendant difficulties of this process for adolescent American girls in the 1980s, see Carol Gilligan et al., eds., *Making Connections: The Relational World of Adolescent Girls at Emma Willard School* (Cambridge, MA: Harvard University Press, 1990).

Is the Apolitical Woman at Peace?:

A Reading of the Fairy Tale in *Germany, Pale Mother*

BARBARA HYAMS

Becoming guilty, although one simply obeyed the law, carried out orders from above, and sought happiness where the Bible promises it: in wedlock, with child. Faithfulness is an age-old virtue, but what has this faithfulness brought?

—Helma Sanders-Brahms[1]

A line of peace might appear if we restructured the sentence our lives are making, revoked its reaffirmation of profit and power, questioned our needs, allowed long pauses. . . .

—Denise Levertov[2]

THROUGHOUT HELMA Sanders-Brahms's career as a filmmaker, her work has suffered from discrepancies between intellectual premises and final products.[3] *Germany, Pale Mother* (1979) is no exception. It tries to do too much, and the result is a film that is neither clearly feminist nor politically quite focused. It uses "woman" as (a traditional) allegory for "the people" in an era that is highly conscious of feminist calls for the destruction of circumscribed gender roles. Yet it is also autobiographical and at the same time an attempt to portray a generation of (gentile) women that experienced its young adulthood under National Socialism.

The historical setting for *Germany, Pale Mother* is the late 1930s to 1950s, from the war years through the Economic Miracle. Some of the minor characters in the film shift their allegiance from fascism to the new social democracy with a chameleon-like ease that is reminiscent of Kurt Hoffmann's portrayal of the former Nazi turned West German industrialist in *The Prodigies* (1958). Sanders-Brahms's fictionalized parents are not of this ilk, but also not as comfortingly innocent as their predecessors in many German films of the early 1950s. Her "mother," Lene, is a passive, apolitical young woman who learns, of necessity, to make her way in the world without the physical or emotional support of men. She takes care of her daughter, but is hardened to the fate of those around her. Her husband, Hans, is a passive, apolitical young man who is among the first to be sent off to fight, precisely because he hasn't declared his allegiance to the Nazi Party. After the war, he is not as adept as his ex-Nazi friend at climb-

Reprinted from *Wide Angle* 10.3 (1988): 40–51.

ing the career ladder. Meanwhile, his military experience has cut him off from emotional intimacy with women and children, so that after the external war is over, the "internal war" begins: there is no common ground, except for the proverbial roof over their heads, in which Lene and Hans can still meet.

Sanders-Brahms's mother, to whom the film is partly dedicated, was a young bride when World War II began. Her daughter (the *auteur* and narrator of the film) was born during the war, her granddaughter (the third generation, to whom the film is also dedicated) in the Federal Republic of the 1970s. Through this matriarchal line, the film presents a "woman's view" of German history. While I would not go so far as to call it an apology for many Germans' passive relationship to authority, I do see it as a fascinating analysis of the phenomenon, an analysis that runs the distinct danger of appearing to defend what it portrays.

Germany, Pale Mother uses the cliché of "woman as victim" to problematize, through allegory, the popular conception that "little people" (i.e., *male or female*) are always the victims of all political systems. Believing that they have no control over historical events, they try to build their lives around whatever seems personally within their grasp. In her version of *Vergangenheitsbewältigung* (coming-to-grips-with-the-past) Sanders-Brahms tries to find the similarities between her generation and that of her parents, rather than the differences. Pathos outweighs blame, and this is usually pointed to as the film's major shortcoming. The perspective of the younger generation, at any rate, provides an interesting twist on the type of postwar films made in the early 1950s which John Sandford describes in his introduction to *The New German Cinema*:

> The hero of the early postwar films was the "little man": the problem was that he was all too conveniently and comfortingly innocent. The "little man" (and presumably most audiences found no difficulty in identifying with him) was the victim of history; the Nazis were "the others," the villains, demonized or satirized into a safe distance. Nazism was all too often presented as Evil Incarnate, a malevolent Fate whose dark mysteries were not worth probing: the horrible fact that it had descended on the "little man" was material enough for an archetypal struggle of good and evil.[4]

Through Lene, we are meant to see the effect of "total war" on the ("Aryan") "everywoman," but Sanders-Brahms has not been quite successful in the eyes of most critics in imbuing her mother's personal story with universal significance. The director strives to show that private survival becomes a heroic effort as food and shelter can no longer be guaranteed by husbands who are fighting and, in many cases, perishing on the battlefield. Contingency forces her mother to become more independent, more courageous, more versatile in her approach to life. The "private" realm of women merges with the "public" as women take on jobs and roles originally meant for men.[5] Immediately upon the end of the war, women begin to build out of the rubble, to conduct trade on the black market. Now that the ideologically separate realms of the public and private have been openly ruptured, Lene reacts to postwar society's attempt to reestablish the illusion of their mutual exclusivity. Her reaction manifests itself physically as a horrible facial paralysis and ultimately as a desire to die.

Bourgeois women function well as an allegory for the German people because of their traditionally dependent social status. Their ambivalence towards men arises from a double-edged dependence and deep mistrust. They have been simultaneously sheltered and banished from the realm of public decision-making. And yet, as the film shows all too clearly, the seemingly neat division between public and private realms is operative only as an ideology that some men and women try to perpetuate.

My thesis is that the film conveys two major attitudes toward women/Germans. One is their status as passive victims; the other involves the issue of responsibility for the crime of silence. Without the latter, the film would be truly reactionary. Feminist critics have read "silence" in the film in terms of the female voice, but no one has suggested that Sanders-Brahms is exploring the connections between bourgeois women's values and their social responsibility. I believe that the film makes connections between them, but is marred by an extensive use of pathos.

The consensus among recent critics of the film is that it is an interesting experiment but only a partial success, because it foregrounds an autobiographical mother/daughter experience while stumbling over the allegory of German(y)-as-mother-figure during and after the Third Reich. Angelika Bammer, E. Ann Kaplan, and Ellen E. Seiter,[6] reading Sanders-Brahms's memories in terms of recent feminist theories (e.g., Gilligan, Irigaray, Cixous, Kristeva) of the psychology of the mother/daughter relationship, have provided us with many valuable insights into the psychology and political implications of this relationship and its representation in melodrama. Kaplan, for example, finds Sanders-Brahms's decision not to marry enigmatic and perhaps indicative of an inability to separate from the mother.[7] Angelika Bammer's main objection to this primal portrayal of matrilineal heritage is that it paves the way for a reactionary revision of German history.

> For the inseparability of mother and daughter, which effectively denies both of them autonomy, also, by implication, denies both of them responsibility: those who refuse to claim their autonomy as historical subjects also cannot own their responsibility as agents of history.[8]

While I can see how this type of revisionism could be construed in the film, I read the film as the daughter's self-reflective admonition against an automatic feeling of superiority when evaluating the behavior of past generations. It tries to show that many people, both women and men, perceive historical events as a kind of backdrop to their own lives, while they are simultaneously (and quite probably on account of these very perceptions) both the victims of history and the silent accomplices to a myriad of crimes against their fellow human beings. What I would like to add to the discussion of this film, then, is another interpretation of its political implications, based on a close reading of the centrally important fairy tale sequence.

THE FAIRY TALE: VICTIM OF A LEGAL SYSTEM

In an interview with Renate Möhrmann, Sanders-Brahms said that the dialogue in the film was not in the least bit improvised. The only unsettled matter in the script was the story that Lene would tell her young daughter Anna on their trek through the forest. The refrain of "The Robber Bridegroom" from Grimm's *Fairy Tales* occurred to her during filming: "Turn back, turn back, thou bonnie bride,/Nor in this house of death abide."[9] The fairy tale, Sanders-Brahms told Möhrmann, represents "the primal psychic fears that women have of men. . . . But, at the same time, this fairy tale also describes German history."[10]

Bammer finds the fairy tale sequence potentially the most reactionary part of the film. She argues that the film "sets out to deconstruct the ideological structure of allegory" but destroys its own purpose in its presentation of the fairy tale. "For instead of sustaining a critique of the politics of mythical discourse, Sanders-Brahms ends up reconstituting woman as a once again mythical, and thus mystified figure."[11] Kaplan, too, sees the fairy tale as a means to isolate Lene and Anna in a fantasy world of their own:

> No better than robbers, the Nazis dismember citizens' bodies as in the fairy tale. But mother and daughter are able to withstand the horror of the outside world as long as they remain alone in their fantasy—a dreamlike realm made possible by the abnormal conditions of war.[12]

And Seiter:

> The rape metaphor is the logical result of the association at the beginning of the film in the poem by Bertolt Brecht between the maternal body and Germany. But whether the mother is used as an image of sanctitude, as in Nazi ideology, or of defilement, as in the Brecht poem, the usage robs women of their own social and political history and mystifies their oppression.[13]

As I see it, the fairy tale sequence mystifies "woman's" closeness to nature and equates human law with rape, but not, as others have suggested, by cutting itself off from recognizable coordinates of time and space.[14] It is immediately preceded by documentary footage of Adolf Hitler's burning bunker and a radio announcement that the *Führer* "died fighting until his last breath in Germany's war against Bolshevism" [DbM, p. 92]. The "male dream" personified by Hitler was "victory or annihilation" and the image of fire represents male defeat. The documentary soundtrack continues with a message from Dönitz, while there is a cut to a closeup of Lene singing a "May Song" to a ladybug on her finger. The time of year, if we don't already recognize it by historical events, is Spring, the season of rebirth. Lene's face is framed by a soft green, soft focus ring of leaves. There is a brief closeup of Anna. Then three newsreel documentary shots of, respectively, a crashed airplane with its nose on fire, the bloody head of a dead German soldier, and the soldier's red, partially-closed hand, accompany the Dönitz speech before the film moves completely into the world of the fairy tale. In this way, Sanders-Brahms introduces a severe polarization of images of life and death which will reappear in the fairy tale sequence itself. Women (and by extension, the German people) are associated with life and nature, while men (as politicians uttering phrases like "victory or annihilation") bring unnatural, premature death to those over whom they have power. At this juncture, it seems appropriate to review the tale itself in some detail.

A miller has a beautiful daughter of marriageable age. An apparently wealthy suitor comes along, and the miller gives his consent to an engagement. The daughter, however, feels an inexplicable horror toward her betrothed. One day, he comes to her and invites her to visit his home in the forest. The girl protests that she doesn't know the way, but the bridegroom offers to scatter ashes along the path to guide her. On the appointed day, she fills her pockets with lentils and peas and ventures into the forest, marking her trail behind her. When she reaches the house, it is dark and deserted. She goes inside, and a bird in a cage cries, "Turn back, turn back, thou bonnie bride,/Nor in this house of death abide." The girl looks in all the rooms. In the cellar, she meets an old woman who takes pity on her. The old woman reveals that she is in a den of robbers who kill beautiful young girls and eat their flesh. She hides the girl behind a hogshead. When the robbers return, they bring a young maiden with them. Under protest, she drinks three glasses of wine: one of white, one of red, and one of yellow. After the third glass, her heart bursts in two, and the robbers hack up her body and sprinkle it with salt. One of the robbers sees a gold ring on her finger, and when it won't come off readily, he chops off her finger, which flies across the room and into the breast of the girl hiding behind the great hogshead. When he begins to look for it, the old woman convinces him to have dinner and to continue his search in the morning. She gives the men a sleeping potion and escapes from the house with the miller's daughter. The wind has blown away the ashes scattered by the bridegroom, but the peas have sprouted, so they are able to find their way out of the forest by moonlight. Upon her return home, the girl tells her father everything. Soon thereafter, the miller invites the robber bridegroom to dinner, along with all of the miller's friends and relations. Everyone at the table is invited to tell a story. When her turn arrives, the miller's daughter tells her betrothed about a "dream" she's had, exactly relating the actual events of her journey into the forest, but with the refrain, "This was only a dream, my love." However, when she comes to the point at which the finger flies into her breast, the miller's daughter shows the finger to the assembled company. The robber bridegroom's complexion, meanwhile, has turned "as pale as ashes." He tries to escape, but is held fast. The rest of the gang is then captured and executed for its crimes.

The fairy tale sequence occurs in the second half of the shortened version of the film and lasts for approximately 15 minutes. It includes non-diegetic cutaways to, for example, an aerial traveling shot of bombed-out Berlin, a shot of a veteran playing a legless piano, and a brief but horrifying scene in which Lene is raped. The latter consists of the approach of American soldiers,[15] sounds of the rape while the camera focuses on Anna, a detail shot of Anna's feet moving down the stone steps to her mother, and Lene's remark to Anna, "That's the victor's right, little girl. He takes things and women."[16] The duration of this scene is one minute. Lene then recites the end of the fairy tale in four minutes as she and Anna ride along on the back of a train.

The film's musical theme accompanies most of Lene's account of the fairy tale. Sound elements are particularly important in this sequence: for example, when Lene hears a bird singing, she looks up, and the camera travels up the length of a factory smokestack. The bird itself shortly appears in the fairy tale itself with its cry of warning. Meanwhile, the violent domination and murder of Jews is evoked by the image of the smokestack: Germany itself becomes the house of death. As the camera lingers for a moment on the top of the smokestack, Lene recites, "and then she was overtaken by a great fear."

True to Grimm's fairy tale, Lene tells the story of the girl's trip to her prospective bridegroom's house twice: once as straight narrative, once as narrative within a narrative, i.e., relating a dream. The disavowal of reality by the miller's daughter as the mere ramblings of her own unconscious is an ironic device. But she must produce tangible evidence (the severed finger of the maiden) in order to expose the bridegroom as a killer and fraud. The film produces "evidence," too, by cutting away to documentary aerial footage of Berlin just after the war. A seemingly endless traveling shot speeds along on a slight diagonal plane as the piano melody is almost destroyed by the use of growling, dissonant, bass-heavy chords. This is the evidence that Sanders-Brahms provides of Germany's submission to Hitler's war machine.

Lene's telling of the tale is broken off during the second cycle with the words, "This was only a dream, my love!" After the traveling shots of Berlin and the legless piano, we see the deserted factory again. Two drunken American soldiers enter the frame from the extreme right. The scene is shot with available lighting; therefore, it is relatively dark in the factory, and the soldiers become ghoulish silhouettes when they see Lene and Anna and begin to run towards them. Their running takes on a joyous, bounding quality. The camera moves laterally on a right-to-left pattern as the soldiers pursue Lene, whereas Lene's journey through the forest has been filmed from left to right. The conflicting patterns of movement, coupled with the cinematic convention that movement from left to right is more comfortable to the western eye, forebodes trouble. The Americans offer wine (another fairy tale image) to Lene, then quickly turn to violence when she snubs them.

On the surface, the fairy tale does not challenge the legality of women as male property, for it upholds a belief that the legal system will arrest and try those men who abuse it. On a deeper level, however, the fairy tale reveals a profound female ambivalence toward men, as is particularly evident in its polarized juxtaposition of feminized images of life and rebirth against masculinized images of death and destruction: the bridegroom offers to strew ashes along the path to his house in the forest (and his face turns ashen when he is exposed), but the girl scatters peas and lentils which will later sprout and guide her back to her father's house. In this tale, marriage is unmistakably linked with a woman's death and destruction (consider also Lene's accusatory declaration to her husband Hans after the war, "You have destroyed everything for me."). Allegorically, it shows Germany's fatal engagement with National Socialism and also alludes to its occupied status since World War II.

Ironically, in light of the end of the fairy tale ("But the guests seized him and handed him over to justice. And he and all his band were executed for their crimes."), the Americans have put a stop to Hitler's control over the German masses, and the Nuremberg Trials will prosecute German war criminals for their atrocities. The sociopsychological ambivalence of women in connection with patriarchal models corresponds to the German people's relationship to its *Führer* and subsequently, to the "imperialist" Allies. Sanders-Brahms's decision in shooting the film to cut most of the "farmyard" sequence from the script and to use the fairy tale sequence instead of Lene's rape by Russian soldiers and subsequent abortion by a Russian doctor [DbM, 72–80] has the effect of evading discussion of differences between the superpowers. Seiter is troubled by the sympathy with fascism that seems to be conveyed by the rape metaphor:

> By intercutting Lene's story with documentary footage of bombed-out buildings, Sanders-Brahms connects Lene's rape with the "rape" of Germany by the Allies. This is a very disturbing metaphor, with its association of the humilia-

tion of rape and the military defeat of fascism, especially in a film which has failed to examine the Nazi manipulation of and ideology about women.[17]

I understand the metaphor somewhat differently. The documentary footage indicts Hitler's "total war" policy and does not lament the fall of fascism at all; yet it definitely fails to examine Nazi ideology and maintains the attitude of the passive victim by vilifying America, the new master of post-war West Germany, through the metaphor of the American soldiers who rape Lene. The atmosphere of outward "peace" in the 1950s eventually triggers Lene's facial paralysis and, eventually, her attempted suicide. The stabilization of West Germany under American supervision, the reinstitution of family life under Hans's supervision—these parallel impositions of order function as an ongoing assault on Lene's emotional life.

The Germans in this film are implicitly as brutalized by American-imposed denazification as they were by Nazi totalitarianism. This is possible only as long as women/Germans perceive themselves as passive victims of men/governments. As victims, their only line of recourse is suicide, the final bastion of dignity or despair. The ambiguous valuation of suicide in the face of domination by others extends back to the 18th-century bourgeois heroine in Lessing's *Emilia Galotti*. Lene's attempted suicide is thus, as allegory, a portrait either of staunch German dignity in the face of the Cold War that superseded World War II, or of despairing self-hatred.

BRECHT'S "GERMANY": THE CRIME OF SILENCE

The Brecht poem[18] from which the film takes its title makes the association between women (specifically, mothers) and Germans in order to show the responsibility of the Germans for their crimes. They were not simply "raped" by Hitler. He, and the National Socialists with him, were also engendered by the country. Consequently, the various images of woman as wife/property, rape victim, and mother of a violent brood complicate, if not confuse, the political allegory.

Brecht's poem allegorizes Germans as victims of each other. Sons have harmed their own brothers and implicated their (ideal) mother,[19] who is also responsible on some level for the grotesque violence in her household, in their crimes. She is both laughingstock and terror among the nations, for her sons—without question, the Nazi Party—are both ridiculed and feared by the rest of the world. In the poem, Germany inspires wariness among the community of nations: "But whoever sees you grips his knife/As on seeing a murderess." In the original German, "a murderess" is literally "a female robber" (*Räuberin*). This image bridges the gap between the poem, the fairy tale, and the film as a whole.

In the fairy tale, there are three images of women: the old woman who cooks for the robbers, the maiden who is killed, and the miller's daughter.

Female survival turns on the old woman's decision to rescue one maiden, as the other is already consigned to the fate of many before her. We don't know anything about this old woman except that she, too, is held prisoner in the robber's den and has been waiting for an opportunity to escape. Like many prisoners, she is forced to participate in the murder of her own kind. Yet she is part of the robbers' band insofar as she possesses a sleeping potion but hasn't attempted an escape until now. It is also not inconceivable that such factors as envy of youth and beauty have influenced her complicity with the robbers. The most casual acquaintance with fairy tales, which are often structured around basic (and not always pleasant) human emotions, confirms this possibility.[20] It would seem that the old woman has chosen to help this particular maiden because she has something to offer in return: a marked path through the forest.

In the film, Germany is indicted for its internal, domestic brutality. The following lines of Brecht's poem similarly implicate Germany in her sons' crimes: "The exploited/Point their fingers at you, but/The exploiters laud the system/Devised in your house." In the lines of the ensuing stanza, the German mother is seen in the act of hiding the blood on the hem of her skirt. While I believe that the fairy tale also incriminates some women in acts of murder, many critics argue that it is a dangerous vindication of women's fears of men, and that Lene and her daughter exist apart from, or perhaps in spite of, the crimes of men. As Bammer and Seiter clearly warn, Sanders-Brahms's mystification of the differences between men and women's lives in a patriarchal society appears to exonerate women from historical responsibility. Bammer writes:" . . . [A]s women we cannot claim allegiance only to an as yet only imaginary nation of women. For we are, inescapably, also part of the collective people of our nation, our culture, our race and our class."[21] And Seiter concludes: "What the sons have done to the mother is to place her outside history. Her daughters cannot afford to do the same."[22] If a so-called feminist film does argue that women exist apart from history, it's a reactionary message. However, the key to Sanders-Brahms's attempt to locate her mother's (and by extension, the German people's) responsibility to history lies in her allusions to the Holocaust.

Since the Jews figure all too prominently among the groups of "sons" who were to be persecuted by their brothers, we will look at three scenes in the film in which Lene does not persecute Jews herself, but does nothing to prevent their persecution. In this way she functions as a co-conspirator, although it is also apparent that she is bullied by an oppressive regime. The film does not, as Bammer suggests, "plead Lene's essential innocence" or "beg the essential questions of guilt and responsibility."[23] These scenes demonstrate, if anything, the veracity of Hannah Arendt's accounts of the "banality of evil."

In a very brief scene early in the film, the as yet unmarried Lene crawls into bed to comfort her lovesick sister, Hanne. They hear a window breaking nearby and look outside to see what's happening. Hanne's schoolmate, Rahel Bernstein, is being taken away, and Hanne is upset.

Hanne: That's the Bernstein's window. There's Rahel. Rahel! What is it?

Helene: C'mon, be quiet.

Hanne: That's Rahel. She's in my class.

Helene: I thought you were a Party member.

Hanne: Yes, but that's Rahel.

Helene: C'mon, let's get into bed. We'll think about Ulrich.

Hanne: You can be so hard-hearted. [DbM, p. 32]

Lene sees Jews being taken away, but through her silence she allows it to continue. Lene herself is not a party member and is attracted to Hans because he isn't either; however, this passive form of resistance, or "inner emigration," does not help anyone else.

Another brief but important scene which precedes the fairy tale sequence casts female solidarity (*including the narrator's relationship to her mother*) in a critical light. Lene is a young married woman anticipating Hans's return on leave from Poland. She is embroidering a dress for the occasion, but runs out of red thread.

Helene: I'm out of red, I have to go to the Ducksteins' and get some more.

Hanne: They're gone. They were Jews, you know.

Helene: Them . . . Jews? But they were ancient.

Hanne: It doesn't change anything that they were Jews.

Helene: But I need the red. You can't get it anywhere else. [DbM, p. 43]

Both this scene and the one before it show how integral Jews were to the everyday fabric of German life as well as the ways in which fellow Germans rationalized their disappearance. Lene implies that *old* Jews shouldn't have to be rounded up by the authorities, while Hanne offers a meek defense of their value as human beings. The roles that Lene and Hanne play in this discussion have not essentially changed since the incident with Rahel Bernstein. Lene is "hard-hearted" (*hart*) and persists solely in acquiring the thread. When she arrives at the store, she finds it boarded up. A large yellow Star of David is painted on the boards, and someone has added a swastika in chalk. Lene pleads with a neighbor woman to let her inside the store, which has already been ransacked by others since the Ducksteins were taken away. She is fixated on red thread, but there is none left, so the old woman convinces her to take blue instead.

> *Frau:* But hurry up. If someone sees, I'm done for. And all because of embroidery thread.
>
> *Lene:* I won't be able to finish the dress otherwise.
>
> *The woman heaves a sigh.* [DbM, p. 44]

The old woman knows that she is profiting from the Jews' disaster, more-over at the severe risk of enraging the Nazis. Unlike the old woman in the fairy tale, however, she definitely bears guilt for her actions. And Lene, as we can see, survives through tenacity and denial. She won't let herself care about Jews who have disappeared, but only about "her realm," i.e., the task of making herself beautiful for her husband. The film shows us once again that her silence *is* a political action, an action just as political as that of any man in the "public" realm who looks the other way for the sake of personal survival in a despotic power structure. Thus, it is not sufficient for women to help one another as an end in itself, for the choices involved always have ethical and political implications.

The third reference to the fate of the Jews combines, as described earli-er, the cinematic elements of sound (both the bird's song and Lene's voice narrating the fairy tale) and the movement of the camera up the length of a factory smokestack. Has Lene, who has lost her home and carried her small daughter through the wintry countryside, changed at all by this point in the film? She is unquestionably more self-sufficient, but the reference to the smokestack is an insight belonging to the director and the viewer, not to Lene. Development of self-sufficiency and personal strength has no *nec-essary* connection to political activism.[24]

In Sanders-Brahms's "Preface" to the published script of the film, she stresses what is generally thought of as the "feminist" aspect of the film: her mother's unsuspected strength during the war:

> . . . She had experienced how far her strength could go, that she only need-ed herself and a hope, this child or this man, and now, when this hope was fulfilled, but her strength was no longer needed, she lost her face. [DbM, p. 10]

The original goal for so many women like Sanders-Brahms's mother (and for many men as well), according to the "Preface," was "the simple life," which is for her a constant, a universal, that she, as a member of the next generation, also wants. She sees the passivity in her parents' behavior, but claims that her generation is essentially no different:

> It is true, and I believe them, that they did not want any of it to happen. But they did not prevent it. We accuse them but what right have we?
> How are we better, except that we have the advantage of being born later?
> Our self-righteousness is that of he who laughs into the mouth of a tiger: the lion won't eat me. . . .
> I don't live differently than my parents, just at a different time. [DbM, p. 11]

The words "being born later" (*die Nachgeborenen*) evokes another Brecht poem, "To Those Born Later." But Brecht writes as a protestor, as one in exile, a thoroughly political person who confronts the crime of silence directly in the first part of the poem: "A talk about trees is almost a crime/Because it implies silence about so many horrors. . . ."[25] Although Brecht's choice of "trees" suggests nature poetry, we might nonetheless substitute "Ulrich" or "red thread" when thinking about the poem in relation to the film. In the "Preface" itself, however, Sanders-Brahms only addresses an aspect of "To Those Born Later" that begins its third part, a memory of that dark episode in history "Which you have escaped." Indeed, the crux of the matter in *Germany, Pale Mother* is remembrance of dark times, with empathy and understanding for those caught in them, but also with a universal view of human beings (allegorized through bourgeois women) as desiring a quiet, private life untouched by the demands, problems and conflicts of the world. Brecht's "Germany" is a bullied, perhaps even battered woman who commits the horrible crime of keeping silent. As long as she submits to her battered existence, she cannot speak. Speaking up exposes her to new dangers but gives her a new sense of self, a new dignity which releases her from the two previous identities of "a mockery or a threat."

I read the narrator/*auteur*'s decision not to marry as an ideological break with the institution of marriage, motivated by the narrator's childhood experiences but conditioned by later intellectual and social influences that are not presented directly in the narrative structure. Both her life and her film function simultaneously as acknowledgment of family ties and declaration of a separate voice. The filmmaker is in a position parallel to that of the miller's daughter, who exposes the crimes of the robbers but is still enmeshed in the system that has only apparently brought the previous system to justice.

As filmmaker, Sanders-Brahms has broken the chain of silence, yet she discounts the liberating potential of speech by calling herself and her own generation *scheinheilig* ("holier than thou") in so many words. She claims that people live no differently than they did in her parents' youth, yet we see that she no longer believes in marriage. She expresses herself through the highly public medium of film in order to uncover the contradictions in that ideal and, moreover, the ideal of a totally private life. But that, in itself, is not enough. In order to benefit from the cinematic "evidence" she has compiled, her audience must understand that hindsight makes it easy to fault the behavior of past generations without truly illuminating the problems of the present. One system may bring another to trial without effectively promoting freedom.[26] Speaking out as a woman per se ("mother tongue") is not a *guaranteed* solution, for it may lead to self-delusion or to dissolution through the forces of cultural hegemony in the Federal Republic of Germany. The film ends with an aborted suicide and, with it, a precarious (and unsatisfying) hold on the possibility of peaceful change in the present and future Nuclear Age.

I began this essay with two quotes, one from Sanders-Brahms and the other from Denise Levertov, an American poet whose work distinguishes her as an outspoken opponent of militarism and other forms of human destructiveness. Sanders-Brahms empathizes with the guilt that women (Germans) suffer for obeying the laws and seeking happiness through loyalty to their families (governments), although her film underlines her ambivalence toward obedience and loyalty. Levertov's poem calls for restructuring our lives, and part of this restructuring involves questioning the needs that are apparently private but are ultimately also public. Sanders-Brahms also breaks her mother's silence (she has a child without a marriage, she makes a public statement by creating a film that problematizes silence during the Third Reich), and like Levertov, but much more (indeed, perhaps too) circuitously, compels her audience to question the profit and power that those laws may serve. Whereas Sanders-Brahms's film evokes a generation that either supported a fascist regime or was deathly silent about it, breaks the silence with her voice but chastises her own generation for being "holier than thou," Levertov allows for another kind of silence, a silence born of reflection—"long pauses"—before it is ultimately too late to stop "business as usual." The work of art, in this instance the poem, cannot function as a prescription for making peace, but as a model for the kind of thinking that could make it a reality. Sanders-Brahms's model is less positive than Levertov's and politically less focused, but it certainly must be counted as a contribution, however flawed, to the New German Film's insistence ". . . on producing works that leave room for audience participation, on making films whose meaning presupposes spectator investment."[27]

Notes

I would like to thank Anton Kaes and the German Academic Exchange Service for an interdisciplinary summer seminar on "Images of Postwar Germany in the New German Cinema," as well as numerous members of the Coalition of Women in German, for helpful comments on this article along the way.

1   Helma Sanders-Brahms, "Exposé mit Vorrede" ("Preface") in *Deutschland, bleiche Mutter: Film-Erzählung* (Reinbek: Rowohlt, 1980), p. 11. Quotations from this work are hereafter cited in the text as [DbM, p. . . .]. The translation of the "Preface" was provided by the film's German distributor, Basis-Film Verleih GmbH, but I have made a few minor changes. Translations of the film script are entirely my own.

2   Denise Levertov, "Making Peace," in *Breathing the Water* (New York: New Directions, 1987). Reprinted by permission of the publisher.

3   Renate Möhrmann, *Die Frau mit der Kamera: Filmemacherinnen in der Bundesrepublik Deutschland: Situation, Perspektiven. Zehn examplarische Lebensläufe* (Munich: Hanser, 1980), pp. 141–60.

4   John Sandford, *The New German Cinema* (London: Wolff, 1980), p. 10.

5   The Third Reich raised women's status as childbearers to a national contribution and sentimentalized their lives at home, but the reality of everyday life was that women were increasingly drafted into armaments factories and low-level political organizations that monitored their sentiments toward the Reich. Late in the war effort, young girls were also drafted to fight when the supply of men gave out. Vojtech Jasny's film adaptation (1976) of Heinrich Böll's *The Clown,* for example, presents its protagonist's poignant longing for his dead sister and Böll's biting critique of the blindly patriotic mother who sacrificed her daughter to a doomed war effort.

6   Angelika Bammer, "Through a Daughter's Eyes: Helma Sanders-Brahms's *Germany, Pale Mother,*" *New German Critique* 36 (Fall 1985), pp. 91–109; E. Ann Kaplan, "The Search for the Mother/Land in Sanders-Brahms's *Germany, Pale Mother,*" in Eric Rentschler (ed.), *German Film and Literature: Adaptations and Transformations* (New York: Methuen, 1986), pp. 289–304; and and Ellen E. Seiter, "Women's History, Women's Melodrama: *Deutschland, bleiche Mutter,*" *German Quarterly* 59:4 (Fall 1986), pp. 569–81.

7   Kaplan, p. 295.

8   Bammer, p. 105:
. . . *[W]e see (and, on a primal level, once again experience) the terrifying power of the mother from whom the daughter/child is always separate, yet never completely able to separate. . . . [D]enial of women's autonomy, and, by implication, the refusal to acknowledge the fact of their responsibility, has serious consequences, especially in the context of current discussions of the role of women under fascism, of women's participation in the construction of a fascist state.*

9   Translations and summary of the fairy tale are based on the following edition: The Brothers Grimm, *Fairy Tales,* trans. E. V. Lucas, Lucy Crane, and Marian Edwardes (New York: Grosset and Dunlap, 1935), pp. 255–58.

10   Möhrmann, p. 155.

11   Bammer, pp. 106–07.

12   Kaplan, p. 299.

13   Seiter, p. 580.

14   Cf. Bammer, pp. 107–08:
Rather than being in history and of it, they seem merely to be passing through, wandering through a time and space at once deeply familiar and utterly foreign to them. Appropriately, therefore, throughout the entire Märchen *scene the coordinates of Lene's and Anna's reality are deliberately left unmarked. (Historical) time and (geographical) space have become irrelevant categories of measurement. For Lene and Anna are, as it were, living in a world of their own.*

15   Cf. Sanders-Brahms's thoughts on the setting for the fairy tale sequence:
But the fairy tale achieves a great deal—it describes rather precisely Lene's story and German history in a very transparent metaphor. . . . The ruins are those from the old freight station (Anhalter Güterbahnhof) *here in Berlin. . . . Also, no condemned buildings, like in the other rubble scenes. These condemned buildings. Kreuzberg. Wedding. Moabit. The English, the French, the Americans, in short the Occupying Powers, conduct war games*

in them before they are completely torn down. Film companies and maneuvers take turns, before they're completely gone. It's like a story by Andersen: house, with workers, Zille's milieu, then the war, then yet another war, the second one, coal thefts and such things, then the Turks, then demolition, and once more the film and the as-if-war. Practicing for war. Also constantly here in the forests around the lumber clearing. On the paths one sometimes runs into green jeeps with Americans in them who are playing "the enemy." [DbM, p. 116]
The work of art "plays" with a ruin quite differently than do war manuevers. Sanders-Brahms may well fear that the military's form of play will prove apocryphal before the film has any effect on its viewers' consciousness.

16   This is the same line that Lene was to say after being raped by Russian soldiers. [DbM, p. 79]

17   Seiter, p. 580.

18   Bertolt Brecht, *Poems 1913–1956,* ed. John Willet, Ralph Manheim, and Erich Fried (New York: Methuen, 1976), pp. 218–20. Reprinted by permission of the publisher.

19   See Kaplan's analysis of the trope of the ideal mother(land), pp. 290–92.

20   Cf. Bruno Bettelheim, *The Uses of Enchantment: The Meaning and Importance of Fairy Tales* (New York: Random House, 1975).

21   Bammer, p. 109.

22   Seiter, p. 580.

23   Bammer, p. 108.

24   The original "farmyard" complex, which was largely replaced by the fairy tale sequence, also contains a third allusion to the Holocaust: Lene smells something burning while she is learning to milk a cow, and the Polish woman who's teaching her says, "People. Dead people." [DbM, 75] There can be no doubt that the question of what the people knew vs. what they *wanted* to know is an important thematic aspect of the film.

25   Brecht, pp. 318–19.

26   I am suggesting that Adorno and Horkheimer's critique of progress (*Dialectic of Enlightenment*) is implicitly part of the film's intellectual framework.

27   Eric Rentschler, *West German Film in the Course of Time: Reflections on the Twenty Years since Oberhausen* (Bedford Hills, N.Y.: Redgrave, 1984), p. 13.

Barbara Hyams is an assistant professor of German at Boston University, where she teaches New German film, literature, and language. She has published and presented papers on Robert Musil, Austrian literary history, New German Film, and feminist criticism.

Incarcerated Space: The Repression of History in Von Trotta's *Rosa Luxemburg*

ANTONIA LANT

Postwar Germany has been irrevocably sundered from its prewar history. The aftershocks of World War II have recontoured the social and political landscape of the preceding era, leaving visible only partial and disjunct strata. This reshaping of the past has produced in the present a troubled cultural condition which even the nation's most articulate contemporary Brahmins cannot help but perpetuate. They strive to answer difficult questions about their own history, but in the process stage complicated acts of historical repression which distort and splinter the pre-Nazi period. Their efforts to confront Nazism paradoxically reinforce its segregation from the adjacent pre- and post-Nazi eras that are themselves defined by Nazism's quarantine. On a visual level, the surreal circumstances of West Berlin itself provide a perfect figure for such an intellectual divide. This unique satellite city is embedded deep inside the Communist bloc and yet is preserved by the West as an outpost of capitalism and liberty: its major streets radiate from a walled-off architectural heart but are kept artificially alive through the financial transfusions with which the West German government attempts to stave off massive depopulation. The Kaiser Wilhelm Church is emblematic of this repression; disfigured by patches of white concrete covering over bomb-blasted crevices, it remains deliberately unrestored as a reminder to those who have stayed.

Margarethe von Trotta has already established her importance as a filmmaker concerned with feminist issues of postwar Germany: *The Second Awakening of Christa Klages, Marianne and Juliane,* and *Sheer Madness* all deal with sexual difference and personal politics.[1] However, when she seeks to represent a pre-Nazi social structure, the cultural schism of contemporary Germany forces her to romanticize and sentimentalize the past. The result is that in her film *Rosa Luxemburg* a vital revolutionary woman is transformed into an unnecessarily mythic and nostalgic character. Von Trotta's apparent simplification of Luxemburg's life has been described by critics as an unexpected lapse in the director's otherwise challenging output.[2] However, this film should be understood not merely as a trivializing instance in one individual's work but as a vivid example of precisely how committed contemporary German culture is to representing itself in either pre-Nazi or post-Nazi terms in order to elide the literal fact of Nazi

Reprinted from *Yale Journal of Criticism* 1.2 (1988):107–24.

Germany. It is not enough to describe the film as an incomprehensibly censored vision of Rosa Luxemburg: von Trotta's work provides a subtle and crucial instance of the dilemma faced by contemporary German intellectuals when representing their own past.

Rosa Luxemburg is bound by a particular history and particular discourses which determine the space within which the director can speak. In this it exemplifies Julia Kristeva's conception of film practice as a fulcrum, as "the locus of contradiction" between "the subject . . . and its exterior, or, if you will, its *negative*."[3] *Rosa Luxemburg* inevitably registers von Trotta's position within the "negative" of contemporary German culture as shaped by World War II. As a feminist she recognizes a genealogical link between herself and Luxemburg, but this link is almost impossible to represent because Luxemburg belongs to the romanticized, prelapsarian past. The earnest desire of von Trotta's generation to come to terms with the atrocities of the Nazi era denies the historical "thickness" of the period which precedes it; even representations of its mundane political or domestic work have been sentimentalized. The intervening war has barred any sense of cultural continuity with this past, and von Trotta's film is the ground on which the historical evidence of a revolutionary woman and the need to idealize a lost era collide. What emerges is both an envy and a mockery of Luxemburg, who can have no notion of the impending campaign of national genocide. She is a precursor whom von Trotta must honor *and* malform: von Trotta represents her emblematically as a woman and as a feminist but is compelled by her own position in contemporary Germany to misread her.

Von Trotta's work has been labeled feminist because, in her rare position as a woman who commands feature-film budgets, she has dramatized such issues as the need for child-care facilities (*The Second Awakening of Christa Klages*), feminist magazine publishing and abortion rights (*Marianne and Juliane*), the problems of single parenthood and the bonds of sisterhood (all her films). She has challenged the conventions of narrative filmmaking primarily through her subject matter but has also taken an avant-garde stance in her choice of actors and in her use of complex, multiple narrative temporalities, *Marianne and Juliane* being the most obvious example. However, when she turns to Rosa Luxemburg, this thoughtful, avant-garde intellectual creates a formally conservative film which represses many aspects of Luxemburg's life that were clearly important to Luxemburg herself and that might have been expected to engage von Trotta. Ironically von Trotta drains away crucial details of Luxemburg's existence and whitewashes the contradictions she lived: she has reinvented Luxemburg as a pacifist who didn't know Lenin and as a non-Jewish woman whose daily routine is dominated by patient imprisonment rather than political activism. Von Trotta makes nothing either of the specific relevance of Luxemburg's work for recent feminist debates or of the paradox that Luxemburg herself had little time for suffragism. This is ostensibly because her film is aimed at a large popular audience, presumably unreceptive to Luxemburg's politics. But further, and more decisively, the very strength of von Trotta's "ancestor" forces her to overlook Luxemburg's pertinence to contemporary political life. As a consequence, von Trotta sentimentalizes Luxemburg by accentuating her oneness with nature, renders her naive by exploiting her necessary ignorance of Nazi history, censors her erotic life, and allows half an hour of screen time to elapse before giving any hint of Luxemburg's legendary power as an orator. The dehistoricization is so thorough that von Trotta even overlooks the origin of her own medium, film—in contrast to Luxemburg herself, who recognized in this newly emergent medium a powerful metaphor for celerity: "Clara Zetkin was here, but only cinematographically—I saw her speeding by."[4]

The process of denaturing in von Trotta's film is implemented through her emphasis on scenes of imprisonment. Figurative or literal prisons unite all her films; this multivalent, negative "space" signifies everything from the relation of women to history and the relation of one history to another to the postwar state of West Berlin. *Christa Klages* opens as Christa's voice-over says, "I had to create my own jail before I realized what had happened to me"; through a misguided bank robbery she has been literally shut out of motherhood. In *Sheer Madness* Ruth's mental instability makes her a social outcast; when she finally "frees" herself by killing her unbearable husband, the state locks her away. In *Sisters* the younger one, Anna, who is rarely filmed outside the confines of her modern apartment, complains that she is "boxed in" by fear; she eventually commits suicide, leaving her elder sister and roommate Maria to live "both their lives."[5] Marianne of *Marianne and Juliane* is an imprisoned Baader-Meinhof terrorist who also commits suicide, according to the official story; and in von Trotta's latest film Luxemburg is imprisoned nine times, as the script explicitly states (fig. 1).

Although imprisonment clearly fascinates von Trotta, she does not focus on the tales of productivity in asylum, exile, or captivity that belong to Genet, Courbet, van Gogh, Gramsci, and even Luxemburg herself. Instead she uses the space of female imprisonment to represent the patience, sheer endurance, political ineffectiveness, and coercion that she believes all German women have experienced, revolutionaries or not.[6] It is not surprising then that the original production title of *Rosa Luxemburg* was "Die Geduld der Rosa Luxemburg" (The Patience of Rosa Luxemburg). In this film incarceration serves a crucial additional purpose: through this space von Trotta's turn-of-the-century heroine enters the arena of contemporary German feminism. Imprisonment spans the Nazi period, bringing this pre-Nazi woman forward to show analogies between her life and Marianne's in *Marianne and Juliane,* and even von Trotta's. The same actress, Barbara Sukowa, plays both Marianne and Luxemburg, wearing an identical, plain inmate's tunic in both films. Thus the costume of a great revolutionary who died in 1919 corresponds exactly to that of a contemporary terrorist (figs. 2, 3). The radically reduced mise-en-scène of the prison compounds the temporal rapprochement; the absence of distinctive period costuming and furnishings makes the prison space both transhistorical and ahistorical. When the Karl Liebknecht character visits Sukowa/Luxemburg in prison she surreptitiously slips him a letter; on discovering it he asks how she managed it and she replies, with a double entendre, "I've had a lot of practice." Such gestures of assimilation allow von Trotta to articulate the contemporary German predicament through images of the past: Luxemburg's imprisonment mirrors von Trotta's own experience.

The meshing of the carceral figure with its particular audience is most helpfully illuminated by Stephen Heath's theoretical work on spectator-positioning. Heath has described the relation of narrative to space in the cinema as one of a dynamic interaction that constantly provides room for the spectator's vision: the subject's look is continuously being mobilized and reframed through perspective systems, camera movement, and the development of the narrative—all contained by the incarcerating camera eye. The practice of making coherent filmic worlds is therefore intricate and ideological, necessitating the foreclosure not of the film's production—which is "often signified as such from genre instances down to this or that 'impossible' shot—but [of] the terms of the unity of that production . . ., the other scene of its vision of the subject, the outside—heterogeneity, contradiction, history—of its coherent address."[7] Von Trotta's film provides an especially compelling example of this foreclosure because the terms of its particular unity are so fractured and because the omissions of its historical context are so visible. The narrative space of incarceration expedites an ostensibly simple—and sometimes literal—stripping down of this powerful political figure, while it simultaneously facilitates her removal from her own cultural, economic, and political matrix and repositions her in the milieu of the contemporary German spectator who is offered multiple positions of identification through the film, ranging from the distant, controlling vantage points of silent prison guards to masochistic alignment with the image of Luxemburg. In the process, the Nazi period virtually falls away, displaced by the melding of pre- and post-Nazi images.

To elide, gloss over, or bypass awkward historical differences and identifications is the major function of ideology, and, as W. J. T. Mitchell has recently reminded us, Marx used the metaphor of a camera obscura—a darkened room of distorted or inverted images—to describe the process.[8] The same trope is uncannily replicated in von Trotta's films, for it is in metaphorical and literal prisons that her narratives are built and that her characters' lives are ordered. In *Rosa Luxemburg* the carceral is yet another darkened room in which Luxemburg's position vis-à-vis her own history is distorted, becoming at once a metaphor for and an instance of the historical acts of repression of postwar Germany. In her attempt to film Luxemburg's imprisonment, von Trotta has effectively repeated it, and in doing so exemplifies Kristeva's formulation that "there is no object which is not already given in a practice . . .; but neither is there a subject which is not refounded, modified, by practice, within the object as its negative."[9] The negative relation of women to history has been reinforced in the necessary failure attached to von Trotta's goal of honoring an individual who was murdered precisely because of her efforts to effect historical change.

This evidence of dehistoricization is interestingly at odds with von Trotta's own professed intention of recreating an authentic, rich historical ambiance for her dramatis personae. The incorporation of many peripheral historical "characters"—Clara and Kostia Zetkin, Sonja and Karl Liebknecht, Luise and Karl Kautsky, to name a few—and the use of temporal oscillations and multiple languages (Polish, German, and French), lead to that fracturing of the main narrative which has come to signify the "historical" film. British feature films made under the extreme conditions of World War II, such as *The Bells Go Down, The Gentle Sex*, and *A Canterbury Tale*, exemplify this trait by representing the domestic Front through narratives in which there is no single main character or couple with whom to identify, but instead a range of types and their respective narrative strands. This proliferation of characters thematizes the frangible bonds that form at times of political upheaval and the fragmentary nature of human memory, that most arbitrary aspect of historical formation. In *Rosa Luxemburg* the eponymous heroine clearly anchors the narrative, and, in contrast to the British films, her trajectory is interwoven with a general "texture" of the past carried through low lighting, chintz curtains, Victorian dress, and a convoluted, at times inverted, chronology. Period costume is a central, if ambiguous, signifier of history ruled out of play in those wartime films which attempt to represent the present.

Von Trotta's film omits any reference to Luxemburg's contemporary—and the leader of a successful revolution—Lenin. When challenged on this point she replied that "any film with Lenin in it looks horribly fake."[10] Her remark recapitulates *New Lef*'s repulsion at Eisenstein's *October*, commissioned to celebrate the tenth anniversary of the Russian Revolution. Osip Brik insisted that instead of using an actor to play Lenin (an actor who incidentally made a fortune over many years as a Lenin look-alike), existing footage of Lenin be exhumed and incorporated; he ranted at the "absurd falsification which could only carry conviction for someone devoid of any respect or feeling for historical truth."[11] It is through a peculiar logic then that Barbara Sukowa playing Rosa Luxemburg can be less fake than any actor playing Lenin. Von Trotta persists in the legend that Lenin is representationally inimitable and yet is able to cast a non-Jewish, blue-eyed woman as Luxemburg and even insert, toward the end of her film, among other contemporary footage fragments, a few seconds of what seems to be the real Rosa shaking hands with officials on a podium. Von Trotta's double standard, which permits the "real" and "fake" Rosas but excludes a "fake" Lenin, exists entirely within the terms of a narrative cinema renowned for its capacity to patch over differences of temporality, of actor, of location, and so on, because of its compelling ability to make an "impression of reality."[12] The standards of fakeness and realism to which von Trotta adheres seem curiously bound then to sexual difference. Pierre Francastel perhaps inadvertently sheds light on this when he writes, "It is men who create the space in which they move and express themselves. Spaces are born and die like societies; they live, they have a history."[13] In ideological terms it is *men* who own and make the space of history, while women belong to its absence—to fiction. Lenin is omitted by von Trotta not because he would be fake per se but because he cannot be made to shed his history as readily as his female equivalent; his presence would pull von Trotta too far away from German issues, into the history of Russia. Luxemburg, on the other hand, less legendary and iconic, and female, can be recast as sentimental and emotional, shorn of her publications and her intellectual sparring partner, on the grounds that the interested spectator will learn the "other" side of her life.

It is indeed a problem that the most important aspects of Luxemburg's legacy are, by their nature, essentially noncinematic; it begs the question of how well one can present political tracts, political differences, and political encounters through cinema. Revolutionaries rarely appear on the feature screen, and there are few filmic precursors for *Rosa Luxemburg*: perhaps *Julia* (USA 1977); *Reds* (USA 1981), in which Emma Goldman is a marginal figure; or, most directly, von Trotta's own *Marianne*. The limited iconography provided by this diminutive genre includes bold pronouncements on the irrelevance of marriage, an explicitly suppressed desire for motherhood, and the classic scene of male comrade tossing on the couch while female comrade sleeps soundly in bed. *Rosa Luxemburg* borrows more than a little from this limited cache; indeed, in emphasizing Luxemburg's personal life, von Trotta joins those epics that cente "great" love stories in the political turmoil of revolution, particularly the Russian Revolution, and that diverge from the model of dominant cinema at least in terms of their extreme lengths: *Gone with the Wind* (USA 1939), *Reds*, and *Dr. Zhivago* (USA 1965).

Rosa Luxemburg shares the "invisible" manufacture—the realism—of these films, and because of this, critics have measured it almost entirely against the protagonist's life, refraining from questioning esthetic and temporal strategies, and how these inflect this particular story. What needs to be discussed, through specific instances in the film, is the construction of the narrative through frequent shifts in chronology; the question of Luxemburg's lost ethnic identity; the issues of authenticity, ahistoricism, nostalgia, and sentimentality; and von Trotta's preoccupation with the space of imprisonment. An examination of the film—its choice of fin-de-siècle costumes and interiors, of flashbacks and forwards, of a protagonist's voice-over, of rampant wildlife, its elision of Luxemburg's male companions, and its lack of explicit reflection on the processes of history and filmmaking—suggests why, despite the difficulties, the figure of Luxemburg so attracted von Trotta that, as she has herself admitted, a crucial lack of distance from her subject took over; Rosa Luxemburg haunted her throughout production.[14] Von Trotta's identification with this woman seeps in from the first moments as the handheld camera, which under any circumstances emphasizes the human gait, emerges as a formal parallel to Luxemburg's leg disability: as the shot lurches along the prison boundary and later down a prison corridor, it replicates the limp of Sukowa's Rosa-walk.

The film opens with a bleak, extremely low-angle shot of a high perimeter wall at dawn; the wind howls and a solemn, orchestral score intensifies the atmosphere of barrenness. A silhouetted guard with rifle and helmet strides into right-frame, and as the camera pans unevenly leftward, a second military figure appears pacing toward the first through the sparse, winterkilled grass tufts above the wall. When the two men meet and turn to retrace their steps, the camera tilts down to eye level, "sinking" past a barred prison window and below several feet of old brickwork which are now revealed to have been supporting the guards. At this lower level a middle-aged woman dressed in black hobbles slightly as she walks rightward through the prison moat. She is accompanied by a similarly waddling raven and a prison warden close behind. The subsequent high-angle shot makes explicit the depths this woman inhabits, but this second view is half obscured for the spectator by several horizontal metal bars that mark the foreground of the frame. This combination of shots and camera movements suggests an old fort as much as a prison, with its counterscarp, dike, earth ramp, and military uniforms, and already the film's narrative is placed behind a boundary wall.

A female voice-over coincides with the woman's appearance: "Sonjuscha, you are bitter over my long imprisonment and ask: how is it that people have the right to determine the lives of other people? . . . This has deep roots in the material conditions of existence . . . [but] consolation, knowledge and patience can be derived from observing nature, where the question 'what for?' is irrelevant. To what purpose are there blue titmice?" The shot cuts to several (oversized) blue titmice pecking on a windowsill, but these are also behind bars, for by now the camera has moved inside to inhabit the woman's interior—her prison cell. As she steps away from the window to her desk, which is cluttered with biological specimens and mementos, including a photograph of a cat, she ends the recitation and signs and dates a letter. In a closing camera zoom we see, and hear, "Ihre Rosa. Wronke, den 7. 12. 1916." being set down on the page, tethering the historical facts.

Character identification is now reinforced by the credits, which advertise "Barbara Sukowa" in "Rosa Luxemburg" and list the film's dedication to its costume designer, Monike Hasse, long-time coworker of von Trotta's who died during production. The opening sequence is rounded off with a return to the exterior, this time in a high-angle shot of a patrolling guard who walks between the prison buildings at ground level through the snow. When the music finally dies out the image blackens and the time of the diegesis shifts ten years to another prison cell in Warsaw (the date 1906 is given only in an English subtitle), where Rosa awaits an earlier decision about her fate. In sum, the film opens in a prison and flashes back to a prison while the "spoken" letter states, "You are bitter over my long imprisonment."

The original German version of the film contains only two explicit references to dates—Rosa's opening letter, and "1900" arranged in flowers, which comes into the final shot of a New Year's fancy dress scene. The costume ball marks the historical transition from one century to the next—"their" century to "ours." The year must also be spelled out to counteract the multitude of different costumes which confuses the chronology. The spectator customarily relies on costume, especially that of women, to identify a particular historical era: costumes function as a kind of shortcut to history. The relative lack of literal dating in *Rosa Luxemburg* encourages the spectator to adopt this habit, but on occasion the film uses costume to slide away into ambiguous historical and class marking: boating on the Gardasee, the wealthy Luise Kautsky and the indebted Rosa Luxemburg wear, and discuss, identical frilly hats. Costume camouflages the divisions of the period as much as it emphasizes them, suggesting a deeper significance to the film's dedication than just the memory of its costume designer.

Although the English print contains many more references to dates than the German one, there is no print that is entirely without subtitles, for the film's characters speak Polish and French as well as German, and varying combinations of these languages are translated for different audiences. Sukowa deliberately learned Polish for the part and so prevented any possibility of a "pure," unsubtitled version for a "pure" German viewer. Instead the illuminated letters inscribe a link between the film's diverse cosmopolitan audience and Luxemburg herself: they are a hieroglyph for the contemporary European intellectual. This esthetic differs from the nightmarish difficulty of subtitling a film like Godard's *Two or Three Things I Know About Her*, whose multiple and simultaneous levels of signification—billboards, diegetic speech, and voice-over—at least occur in one language.

On the surface it might seem that supplementary dates and place-names meet an English-speaking audience's need for more historical guidance, but the fact that the film relishes costume while undercutting its reliability and switches between multiple temporalities, returning to Wronke three more times before finally "passing" that year and moving chronologically on to Luxemburg's death in 1919, makes the historical sequence of events hard even for the German viewer to follow.[15] All these qualities contribute to a weak but general sense of the historical past which does not specify Luxemburg's precise political activities or their intersection with momentous historical events. This "atmosphere" is enhanced by a color-bleaching laboratory process which converts noisy modern colors into turn-of-the-century pastels, coding the film as one (de)composed of the faded relics of history—remains which have deteriorated in the intervening years, as much through memory loss as through aging. (In its chromatic techniques the film parallels other recent "historical" pictures such as *The Return of Martin Guerre* and *The Name of the Rose* in which technology stimulates otherworldliness, in this instance facilitating nostalgia for the pre-Nazi era.)

Von Trotta represents only two recognizable architectural sites in her film, both landmarks of this lost age. One shot shows Luxemburg in front of the original Berlin Reichstag, later burned in Hitler's ultimately successful election campaign of 1933 and subject of the sensational trial. The other building is Berlin's Brandenburg Gate, incorporated in one of the film's six fragments of surviving contemporary footage. In the shot, crowds riot during the revolutionary uprising of 1918. Such archival material is distinct from Franz Rath's fresh footage in being monotone, silent, shot at slower speed (that is, appearing faster), very grainy, and without identifiable characters. It is carefully inserted, overlaid with gunshots on the sound track, and some eyeline matches, especially in the barricade scene at *Vorwarts*, where original images of dead street-fighters are intercut with Luxemburg's impassioned tirade against those not ready for revolution. It is significant that the documentary footage is included only when the film reaches Wronke for the fifth and final time, and then leaves it to move directly to the end of World War I. It occurs *after* the temporal richocheting because it is used as "real" evidence of the violent Germany that gave birth to later Nazi atrocities, making the newer footage indeed read as relatively "fake" or utopian. These fragments are used once Luxemburg's campaign is virtually over, when a hint of Nazi Germany emphasizes the contemporary German feminist's loss in Luxemburg's death.

The personal aspects of Luxemburg's fascinating and tragic existence are known to us through some two thousand letters as well as memoirs, photographs, and newspaper reports. Correspondence sent from Wronke and Breslau prisons during World War I are most revealing of her private life, and it is these which form the basis of von Trotta's script. The texts of the opening voice-over and of the film's half-dozen other voice-overs are taken from letters which reminisce to Sonja Liebknecht, Luise Kautsky, and Hans Diefenbach of earlier experiences of freedom.[16] Since it is frequently only through these transcribed memories that the intimate details of Luxemburg's life are known, it is appropriate that von Trotta originates her narrative in the same place that Luxemburg did—at Wronke in 1916. However, the opening voice-over does more than merely initiate and situate the film in prison; it is tied through the image track to the body of Sukowa/Luxemburg and suggests her deep and continuing interest in history, in class struggle, in Marx, and in the natural world. But the cumulative effect of the prison scenes is to stress Luxemburg's social and political isolation rather than her political engagement. In the film her prison is connected to the outside world only through what she calls her "botanizing." She is always shown with animals and plants—a raven, blue titmice, a molehill, buffalo, a horse chestnut leaf, and a cat photograph—while in fact her surviving letters from prison are as full of references to authors, artists, musicians, and poets as they are to nature: she quotes or mentions Goethe, Mörike, Marx, Mehring, Mignet's *History of the French Revolution*, Beethoven, Hugo Wolf, Jean François Millet and the Venus de Milo. Furthermore, von Trotta omits the fact that, while in prison, Luxemburg wrote *The Anti-Critique*, a response to critics of *The Accumulation of Capital*.

The references to the natural world that are indeed present in Luxemburg's letters are usually measured against some human need or event, which in many instances has been strained out of the film entirely. The most telling example of this kind of omission is the so-called "buffalo" incident, in which a letter written to Sonja Liebknecht from Breslau in December 1917 is carefully edited. Rosa is seen walking along the prison perimeter through the winter snow, as usual followed at a distance by the guard; she comes upon a pair of buffalo pulling a cart, one of which has been wounded by the driver. Sukowa's voice-over intones, quoting the letter: "Tears were running down my face—they were *his* [the buffalo's] tears. I quivered in my impotence at his silent suffering. Oh my poor buffalo! My poor beloved brother!"[17] The film omits the historical significance of both the buffalo and their load, which Luxemburg carefully introduces in her letter. These were "military wagons [which] often arrive, packed full with sacks, or old uniforms and shirts often spotted with blood. . . . They are unloaded here, passed out in the cells, mended, then reloaded, and delivered to the military. The other day, such a wagon came by drawn by water buffalo rather than horses. This was the first time I saw these animals up close. . . . They come from Rumania, they are trophies of war. . . . The soldiers who drive the wagon say that it was a very hard job to catch these wild animals and even more difficult to use them, who were so used to freedom, as beasts of burden."[18] Her pain is intensified by the parallel between the situation of the buffalo and the inevitable involvement of female inmates in the war—as seamstresses—despite their ostensible removal from it through imprisonment. This example of shrewd censorship illustrates Luxemburg's conversion into a sentimental and emotional woman who weeps at the sight of wounded animals in a reaction cut off from its political sources: the deaths, imprisonments, injuries, and injustices of World War I.

Four scenes prior to the buffalo sighting, another peculiar ellipsis occurs which distorts Luxemburg further by normalizing her erotic life: the dramatization of the "death" of Kostia Zetkin. During the first third of the film, Leo Jogiches has been established as her lover through two bedroom scenes and through an oblique reference to an abortion when Rosa smashes a mirror, seeming to crack the screen in one of Heath's "impossible" shots which foregrounds production. After many temporal switches, the film comes to rest temporarily in 1907, and Leo, who has fled Poland where he has been living underground, arrives in Berlin to live with Rosa. Suspicious, she forces him to admit that he has been unfaithful to her with a party comrade, and she asks him to leave her apartment forever. They are estranged throughout the rest of the film, although some physical reconciliation is suggested in the closing scenes when they meet after Rosa's release from prison. The pair are again filmed through distorting glass—this time the entry doors to Leo's apartment—and Leo kisses Rosa tenderly as she leaves for another, "safer" hideout with Karl Liebknecht in January 1919.

The film—following Hannah Arendt and J. P. Nettl—puts the whole weight of the break with Jogiches on his betrayal rather than on the general deterioration of the relationship or on Luxemburg's gradually developing attachment to Kostia Zetkin during Leo's absence in Poland.[19] More important, the film implies that Rosa was in love with Kostia from 1907 until his death (in the film) in 1917 by showing them together in her apartment in 1914, just before he leaves for war, and by a curiously ambiguous prison sequence set in 1917. A black-edged letter arrives at Breslau for Rosa; she opens the death announcement and after reading it holds it away from her toward the framed desk photograph of Kostia that now replaces Mimi the cat. The camera lens zooms in toward her pained face but she never looks across to the photograph: instead the shot cuts to a close-up of Kostia's picture. The trained spectator would not doubt the link between Luxemburg's grief and her young lover, but in fact this manipulation of cinematic convention censors knowledge of her more numerous male companions. According to letters and memoirs, Luxemburg's relationship with Kostia deteriorated in 1909, and they finally broke off their friendship in 1912; Kostia lived on into the 1930s. Von

Trotta's version is not entirely misleading, however, in that Luxemburg's close friend Hans Diefenbach, with whom she corresponded at length during her imprisonments, *was* killed in action in October 1917. Her letters to Luise Kautsky make it clear that she was deeply distressed by his death. In the film, when Luise visits her friend in prison shortly after the bad news, she says "I can't believe it. First your Mimi and now . . .," but at this moment Luxemburg interrupts her, saying, "Don't talk about it." The viewer is spared hearing a new name, Diefenbach, associated with her sorrow.

The point here is not to chastise the film for giving a distorted version of Rosa Luxemburg's life, although for that matter it entirely omits the political fact that Luxemburg married Gustav Lübeck in 1898 in order to exchange her Russian nationality for German citizenship and so be able to enter Germany. What *is* significant is that, by conflating Zetkin and Diefenbach, von Trotta presents an oversimplified, even purifying view of Luxemburg's sexuality, implying that she was loyal for two long periods of time to two men and that her first lover's unfaithfulness was the primary cause of her transition to the second relationship. In addition, completely lost in this representation, which repeatedly emphasizes Luxemburg's private at the expense of her professional life, is the care she took to keep her private life private.[20]

A second aspect of Luxemburg's sexuality is repressed by the film, in this instance one that could be expected to be particularly significant to a feminist director. Von Trotta recounts in her book that during preproduction she gained access to one of Luxemburg's personal prison journals and was fascinated to notice a red cross had been marked at monthly intervals on the calendar; apparently Luxemburg had used her menses to chart the course of her imprisonment.[21] The account offers no explanation for the subsequent omission of any reference to Luxemburg's period in the film, but it would appear that the inclusion of this intimate biological detail, which intersected both Luxemburg's emotional and political life, would have made her too mortal, too modern, and would have been too unromantic, impeding the sentimentalization of the narrative. The exclusion of Luxemburg's voluntary use of her period for exercising a degree of control over her prison term contrasts strongly with the film's inclusion of a humiliating anal examination to which she is subjected when entering the Berlin jail. While the biological omission suggests Luxemburg's ability to endure—and her anticipation of the future—the inclusion emphasizes her victimization at the hands of others.

The foregrounding of Luxemburg's love life serves to veil and divert attention from her great historical interventions as an orator and as a writer. This distraction is supported by formal devices of the film text such as the zoom-in followed by a close-up of Zetkin's portrait and the establishment of fluctuating and ambiguous impressions of temporality. These strategies also obviate the need to examine other contradictions of Rosa

Luxemburg's life: her desire for children and domestic stability versus her choice of unrewarding lovers and her enthusiasm for a demanding political itinerary; her insistence on fidelity versus the secrecy with which she conducted all her relationships; her love of bourgeois luxuries versus her identification with the working class; her glibness over women's issues—she described herself and Clara Zetkin as "The last two real men [sic] of the Social Democratic Party"—even though she suffered abuse on account of her sex; and her dismissal of anti-Semitism as an irrelevant issue while she herself was a Jew. This last exclusion is one of the most prominent acts of censorship in the film. At a New York Goethe House screening von Trotta described it as a "sensitive decision for a German director," implying that disposing of Luxemburg's Jewishness spared any audience guilt that might be triggered through its association with Nazism and the Lebensraum policy. On a more telling level, however, to have represented Luxemburg's ethnic identity would have made her life's work seem futile: had she not died in 1919, she would have died in a concentration camp during World War II. Through the elision of her Jewishness, Luxemburg can be immortalized. The film's concurrence with Luxemburg's "refusals"—the contradictions she lived—is yet another layer of repression in its formal and figural structure, yet another instance of its negative imprisonment.

Toward the end of three of her earlier films, von Trotta includes an "exotic" escape location which contrasts strongly with the grim, repressive German society her protagonists usually inhabit: Cairo in *Sheer Madness*, Portugal in *The Second Awakening of Christa Klages*, and Mount Etna in *Marianne and Juliane*. All the key characters have language difficulties in these strange lands, but their voyages facilitate fundamental personal revelations or other massive switches in the plot. One could imagine a similar experience at the Finnish fjords with Lenin for Luxemburg, but von Trotta seems to have had no need for this other world in *Rosa Luxemburg*. The tonalities of the film, its morass of temporalities, its mixture of Polish, French, and German, its insistence on an authentic mise-en-scène, but most importantly its "freedom" from the events of World War II make it distinct enough from contemporary experience. This is consistent with von Trotta's overall desire to offer her audience, after four films about contemporary German women's problems, a pre-Nazi German whose world held a chance for change and revolution, for history to take a different course. But this utopian vision is ultimately controverted by the space of incarceration through which she links that remote era to the present. If *Rosa Luxemburg* functions as sequel to *Marianne and Juliane*, a historical analogy representative of a period of broader political options, all optimism is lost in the last black scene of the film when the only space left for the spectator is an interminably long blank screen and the sound of Luxemburg's murderers' truck receding into the historical distance.

Rosa Luxemburg and *Marianne and Juliane* share the same director, screenwriter, producer, assistant director, cinematographer, editor, musical director, and costume designer. Over the years von Trotta has built up a regular team of assistants who sometimes move through very different roles: Margit Czenki, the real-life Christa Klages, had a small part as well as the job of continuity for *Marianne and Juliane* and was an assistant director for *Rosa Luxemburg*; Christiane Ensslin, the real-life Juliane, coauthored *Rosa Luxemburg: Das Buch zum Film*, assembling the chronology and participating in a three-way interview about it. It is clear at the very least from this book that Ensslin and von Trotta saw parallels between the lives of Gudrun Ensslin, Christiane's sister, and Rosa Luxemburg, especially in their revolutionary fervor and long imprisonments. Gudrun was a member of the Baader-Meinhof terrorist trio found dead in Stammheim Prison in 1977; Christiane, believing her sibling had been murdered, researched furiously to prove her suspicions, and her story formed the basis of von Trotta's script, which renames Gudrun Marianne and Christiane Juliane.

By looking back nearly a hundred years von Trotta finds a story parallel to Gudrun Ensslin's, but whereas Marianne is acerbic, silent, and angry, Luxemburg is made pitiable in her suffering. Through flashbacks Marianne is presented as the more law-abiding sister in childhood, but in adult life she adopts diametric tactics to achieve her political goals that she describes as "Mein Kampf." Interpretations of the Marianne character have been hotly debated, but there is no such ambivalence for *Rosa Luxemburg*'s audience.[22] Identification is reinforced through pathos by the abrupt juxtaposition of scenes such as Rosa's youthful fascination with roses in 1877 and her prison interrogation of 1906, or her quite domestic Christmas with Mimi in 1914 and her subsequent, brutal police arrest. Through her frequently incorrect statements, Luxemburg becomes a naïf, an unreliable narrator, who can pronounce to the prison governor when he questions the feasibility of her politics, "History will prove you wrong." History never did prove him wrong, for there never was a full revolution in Germany after 1919, and in fact the Freikorps who killed Luxemburg were a key breeding ground for future Nazis. The film transforms Luxemburg into a more perfect and peace-loving precursor of Marianne, paradoxically less powerful, untainted by Nazism, and indeed murdered by them: she is a purer female revolutionary and a better role-model for the contemporary German spectator, whom von Trotta chastises in several uncomplimentary remarks of her script. Rosa comments to Luise Kautsky, "You are the only German with whom I can be so free," and when asked by the same prison governor whether she loves or hates the Germans Luxemburg answers, "The German people are children who have never appreciated freedom."

Von Trotta has described Luxemburg's murder as the first crime of the Nazi party, suggesting that her film ends where Nazism begins—that Nazism enters in that black final shot. I argue instead that Nazism lurks in the film's margins—pressed to the edges—from the very opening moment, precisely because the pre-Nazi period is molded by Nazism. The two soldiers who patrol the beginning sequence wear rounded, "horse-shoe crab" helmets which familiarly signify World War II Germany.[23] By contrast, Kostia's unit and the soldiers exercising in the snow wear *pickelhaubes*—spiked-helmets associated with German troops of an earlier era. When the camera tilts down below the initial pair of guards it literally sinks into history, dropping through the archeological layers of mud, bricks, and mortar, past the barred window of Nazism to the body and voice of a woman who can bear witness to conditions in pre-Nazi Germany. This history is built backward from the present, filtered through the experience of World War II, that blockage in the memory of von Trotta's generation. The space between pre- and post-Nazi remains in the film in the guise of these peripheral guards and soldiers who mark off the lateral limits or illusory depths of the frame. They patrol the film's borders until the narrative arrives simultaneously at the birth of the Nazi party and Luxemburg's demise. They then descend to take up roles as the most unsympathetic characters of the film, the vicious and brutal members of the Freikorps.

The structure of the film, then, entraps Luxemburg within the events of World War II, even though they are precisely what von Trotta attempts to leave out of her narrative. The film accentuates Luxemburg's pacifism, through devices such as the wounded buffalo, because of the brutality of Nazism, even though in her life she supported all strategies to keep the masses conscious and fighting for their rights. The emphasis on imprisonment and suffering renders Luxemburg blameless, helpless, and innocent of the terrible history that was to come, and in the process also severs Luxemburg from her own history and her link with the one successful revolution of her era. Her imprisonment through the camera's eye is a synecdoche for the imprisonment of contemporary Germans by World War II.

In its imprisonment of the past, therefore, von Trotta's film recapitulates the political anomaly best represented by the divided geography of modern Berlin. This severed city too is framed by myriad layers of imprisonment: wide concrete swathes, blockades, tank traps, and sentry boxes, all manned by armed guards and officials, mark its limits. At the western entry point, a massive T-34 tank rises above the skyline on a concrete plinth, its gun angling across the split capital. Under its caterpillar tracks, Communism is celebrated in letters which read, "To the glory of the Russian Army." Even inside these barriers the traces of the war remain, just as they do in *Rosa Luxemburg*. The marginal soldiers of the film are here, but below ground, glimpsed on the closed platforms of the East German

S-Bahn as the West's U-Bahn rushes by. Just as the city remains incarcerated in the daily reexperience of its wartime legacies, so von Trotta's representation of Rosa Luxemburg entraps her in the cultural schizophrenia of contemporary Germany.

Notes

I would like to thank Sara Suleri, the other editors of *YJC*, and Jennifer Wicke for their comments and encouragement in the writing of this essay. Andrew Brower, Leslie Camhi, and Thomas Lant provided additional information.

1 The German titles of these films are *Das Zweite Erwachen der Christa Klages* (1977), *Die Bleierne Zeit* (1981), and *Heller Wahn* (1982).

2 The film won Barbara Sukowa the Best Actress Award at Cannes in 1986, but it opened in New York to mixed reviews, just as it had in Germany. Critics were persuaded by Sukowa's powerful acting and by von Trotta's attempt at such an intrinsically interesting subject, but, despite their overall consensus that it would be impossible to contain the complexity of Luxemburg within a single film, they repeatedly pointed to the film's omissions—Luxemburg's Jewish background, her avoidance of work for women's suffrage, the Lenin connection, and so on. Reviews described the film as von Trotta's "most balanced film to date" but "a two-hour talk marathon" (*Variety*); "intensely human and dramatically memorable" (*Gannett News Service*), but a "side-dish" to her other works (*Films and Filming*); "a first-rate introduction to an extremely complicated personality" (*New York Times*), but in the end "rather a stodgy disappointment" (*Sight and Sound*). Reviews and notes on *Rosa Luxemburg* appeared in *Art Forum* November 1985 by Wolfram Schutte; *Films and Filming* August 1986 by Derek Elley; *Film Journal* May 1987 by David Bartholemew; *The Nation* 25 April 1987 by Daniel Egger; *The New Republic* 8 May 1987 by Stanley Kauffmann; *New York Magazine* 1 June 1987 by David Denby; *The New York Times* 1 May 1987 by Vincent Canby; *La Revue du Cinema* October 1986 by Jacques Chevallier; *Sight and Sound* 55, no. 3 (Summer 1986) by Penelope Houston; *Variety* 2 April 1986 and 28 January 1987; *Village Voice* by J. Hoberman, 12 May 1987.

3 Julia Kristeva, "Cinéma: Practique analytique, practique revolutionnaire." *Cinéthique*, no. 9/10, p. 73.

4 Letter from Rosa Luxemburg to Luise Kautsky, written in Friedenau-Berlin, mid-August 1911. *The Letters of Rosa Luxemburg*, Stephen Bronner, ed. (Boulder, Col.: Westview Press, 1978), 144.

5 The German title of *Sisters, or the Balance of Fortune* is *Schwestern, oder Die Balance des Glücks* (1979).

6 In doing so she presents a kind of inversion of Foucault's panopticism: she describes the "other," negative space, the one controlled by the gaze of the prison guard or camera.

7 Stephen Heath, "Narrative Space," in *Questions of Cinema* (Bloomington: Indiana University Press, 1981), 54.

8 W. J. T. Mitchell, "The Rhetoric of Iconoclasm: Marxism, Ideology, and Fetishism," in *Iconology: Image, Text, Ideology* (Chicago: University of Chicago Press, 1986), 160–208. See also *Camera Obscura* 1, no. i (Fall 1976), pp. 8–9.

9 Kristeva, "Cinéma: Practique analytique, practique revolutionnaire," 73.

10 Quoted in *The Nation*, 25 April 1987, p. 549.

11 *New Lef*, no. 4 (1928), reprinted in *Screen Reader*, no. 1 (1977):317.

12 As Christian Metz has written, "There seems to be an optimal point, film, on either side of which the impression of reality produced by the fiction tends to decrease. On the one side there is theater, whose too real vehicle puts fiction to flight; on the other, photography and representational painting, whose means are too poor in their degree of reality to sustain

a diegetic universe." Christian Metz, "On the Impression of Reality in the Cinema," in *Film Language: A Semiotics of the Cinema*, trans. by Michael Taylor (New York: Oxford University Press, 1974), 13.

13 Pierre Francastel, *Etudes de Sociologie de l'Art* (Paris: Denoel, 1970), 136–37. Cited in Heath, *Questions of Cinema*, 29.

14 See for instance the discussion among von Trotta, Ensslin, and Sukowa in *Rosa Luxemburg: Das Buch zum Film* (Nördlingen: Greno Publishers, 1986), 109–19.

15 The complete list of temporal shifts is enough to boggle any spectator's mind: from Wronke in 1916 back to Warsaw 1906, then back to Warsaw 1877, forward to Warsaw 1906, back to earlier in 1906, back to 1899, including the 1900 New Year scene, forward to Wronke in 1916, back to 1906, back to 1899, forward to 1906 into 1907, forward to Wronke in 1916, back to Berlin in 1907, moving chronologically up through 1910, Frankfurt in 1913, and 1914, forward to Wronke in 1916, back to Berlin in 1914 to 1915, back to Warsaw in 1877, forward to Berlin in 1915, and from then on chronologically to the end, incorporating six sections of surviving documentary footage in this last section.

16 The use of a woman's voice-over is found in both Hollywood films and in more recent films made by women which attempt to inscribe female subjectivity. Von Trotta has used this technique in *Marianne and Juliane* and *The Second Awakening of Christa Klages*, but it is also present in *Julia, Darling*, and many other utterly apolitical films such as *Mildred Pierce, Brief Encounter*, and *Letter from an Unknown Woman*. In these last three the voice-over is tied to a confused temporal web which develops into an insidious esthetic form for the "otherness" of the female mind; there is a danger that this code intersects with von Trotta's *Rosa Luxemburg*.

17 Quoted from the film's English subtitles.

18 Bronner, *The Letters of Rosa Luxemburg*, 241. The buffalo was presumably a European wisent, or bison.

19 Hannah Arendt, *Men in Dark Times* (New York: Harcourt Brace Jovanovich, 1968). This contains a review of J. P. Nettl, *Rosa Luxemburg*, 2 vols. (London: Oxford University Press, 1966). See additional evidence in Elzbieta Ettinger, *Rosa Luxemburg: A Life* (Boston: Beacon Press, 1986), 146–47.

20 The "Polish connection," for example, including the letters to Jogiches, was unearthed by biographer J. P. Nettl in his researches in the 1960s.

21 Ensslin and von Trotta, *Rosa Luxemburg: Das Buch zum Film*, 111.

22 E. Ann Kaplan has suggested that *Marianne and Juliane* examines two widely diverging choices of action for German women (terrorist violence or feminist article-writing); Charlotte Delorme argues that this choice is presented unevenly and that in fact the Marianne character is painted very negatively as a bad mother and ruthless human being who causes her own mother and sister great sadness. Delorme criticizes the film's "over-emphasis on sexual relationships, on introspection, [and] on this deep-seated willingness to suffer which the film praises." See E. Ann Kaplan, "Discourses of Terrorism, Feminism and the Family in von Trotta's *Marianne and Juliane*," *Persistence of Vision*, no. 2 (1985):61–86, and Charlotte Delorme, "On the Film *Marianne and Juliane* by Margarethe von Trotta," *Journal of Film and Video* (Spring 1985), trans. Ellen Seiter from *Frauen und Film* 31 (1982):47–51. Quotation from p. 51.

23 The helmets worn by the German army toward the end of World War I were actually slightly different from the World War II version: they lacked the "stepped" profile.

The Sexual Politics of *The Marriage of Maria Braun*

MARY BETH HARALOVICH

THE APPROPRIATION of Marxist social theory in the films of Rainer Werner Fassbinder has been criticized by Richard Dyer as "left-wing melancholy." In his summary of the sexual politics of Fassbinder's films, Dyer acknowledges that the films explore "the specifically (historically determinant) capitalist source and character of misery." Yet he finds them melancholy because of their pessimism and despair about the possibilities for social change. The films' stress on victimization does not allow for working class solidarity or collective action. Because their characters are held within the tight boundaries of capitalist social relations, the films cannot provide room for resistance or subversion. Unlike other political filmmakers, Fassbinder's analysis of social relations does not explicitly elicit a call to action. Yet Dyer also recognizes that because of the difficulty of interpreting them, "Fassbinder's films often provoke better discussion of sexual political issues" than other "more ideologically acceptable films." And, as Thomas Elsaesser once argued, "the fact that such a cinema continues to exist is Fassbinder's real achievement, and the implicit challenge that makes his work political."[1]

One widely recognized source for both the "left-wing melancholy" and the political challenge of Fassbinder's films is the way they integrate Hollywoodian entertainment with political cinema.[2] The films fit comfortably in neither mode. The political effectivity of *The Marriage of Maria Braun* has been appraised in ways which emphasize the political and deconstructive assumptions at the basis of the film. Formal analysis of sound and mise-en-scène shows how the film blurs the boundaries between personal history and public history, integrating characters with the capitalist economic miracle of postwar Germany and suggesting alignments between Germany's past and present. Through its adaptation of melodrama (coincidence, the independent woman, the "happy ending"), political engagement is possible because the conventions of melodrama, of entertainment cinema and of bourgeois social relations are called into question.

Anton Kaes, Joyce Rheuban and Howard Feinstein have all shown how *The Marriage of Maria Braun* is structured not only by the specific history of postwar Germany but also by larger ideological forces. Kaes discusses

Reprinted from *Wide Angle* 12.1 (1990): 6–16.

how the film participates in critical historiography. Through its "subtle signs of directorial intervention" and its presentation of "the past in its multi-layered and heterogeneous complexity," Kaes finds that the film "activates the spectator's search for the most persuasive reading" of history. Rheuban situates the film within what she describes as Fassbinder's "doubled-edged purpose . . . to make it easier for the audience to see the latent meanings that the prevailing ideology needs to hide." She finds that Fassbinder's films provide social criticism in forms which can also engage an audience. In his discussion of the intersection of melodrama and history in Fassbinder's post-war trilogy, Howard Feinstein argues that "Fassbinder's presentation of history is aleatory and dialectical." Because the films "extend the social relationships imbedded within the narrative into a larger and *continuous* historical process," the conventions of melodrama are subverted, "creating a critical distance on the part of the spectator" (emphasis in original).[3]

The following analysis of the film will expand, in some detail, on Feinstein's materialist approach to the role economics plays in the narrative of the film. Feinstein concentrates on the large structure of the film to illustrate how Maria Braun's progression through the narrative parallels the development of the German postwar economy within "free market capitalism."[4] A closer analysis of the narrative shows how Maria's relationship to the economy is informed by two fundamental and primary conditions of capitalist life: (1) the essential role of economic exchange in organizing human life and maintaining existence, and (2) the impact of economic exchange on woman's sexual identity. This interpretation may not "retrieve" *The Marriage of Maria Braun* from the pessimism of "left-wing melancholy." Such a retrieval may never be possible. But I hope to demonstrate how the film articulates multiple and complex relationships between sexual identity and economics. *The Marriage of Maria Braun* thus requires an interpretive strategy which recognizes that gendered identities are informed by economic relations.

About the importance of exchange for organizing social life, Ben Fine writes that exchange is "the most immediate economic relationship" and one in which all people participate. The effects of social organization through relations of exchange extend beyond the exchange of, for example, commodities for money or labor for wages. Three of these greater aspects of exchange have special implications for *The Marriage of Maria Braun*. First, sexuality is a commodity which can be exchanged. Second, in order for something (or someone) to have exchange value, it (or she) must be made to exist "in a form in which it can be exchanged." And third, "the influence of exchange extends beyond economic relations . . . [it] causes relations between [individuals] to be governed by relations of private property . . . [and carries] over into social relations in general."[5]

The Marriage of Maria Braun can be divided into four large sections which chart Maria's progression through these social relations of exchange. She cultivates a nostalgia for an enduring romantic marriage to which she will retreat after the seemingly temporary need to maintain her exchange value in the marketplace. Until the explosive ending, Maria is convinced that she understands how the sexual economy works, that she can make it work for her, and that she can keep her various social identities (wife, lover, worker) separated from each other. However, in each section of the film, Maria becomes progressively more governed by the social relations of exchange, eventually becoming alienated as her exchange value (as worker, as wife, as lover) comes to dominate her and turns against her. At the end of the film, Maria recognizes her own alienation, the fact that her existence is contained within relations of exchange in which she does not freely operate.

In his discussion of the concept of alienation in Marxist theory, Gajo Petrovic quotes A. O. Ogurtsov. Alienation is "the objective trans[s]formation of the activity of man and of its results into an independent force, dominating him and inimical to him, and also the corresponding transformation of man from an active subject to an object of social process."[6] As Maria increases her participation in relations of exchange, her activities of exchange (worker, wife, lover) become a force independent of her. Further, while Maria thinks that she is in control of these relations of work and sexuality, she is actually governed by exchange in two ways: through the contract between Oswald and Hermann (whereby Hermann agrees not to return until Oswald is dead, and Oswald agrees to leave the bulk of his estate to Maria and Hermann) and through her increasing separation from everything but work. Her growing hostility toward other people is more than a character trait born of frustration. It is also evidence that Maria has been subsumed within the activities of exchange.

In this process of alienation. Maria is transformed from an "active subject" into an "object of social process." When she enters the black market or Oswald's textiles business, she is seemingly an "active subject," aware of the relations of exchange and confident of her ability to control the exchange value of her sexual identity. In her affair with Oswald, she is determined to separate her personal value as a woman from her business value as a worker. But at the end of the film, she becomes aware of her alienation, that she was an "object" of exchange between Hermann and Oswald, an "object of social process" rather than an active subject. This "capitalist (narrative) logic" places "exchange," "alienation" and a type of consciousness" (if you will) in a causal narrative relationship.[7] Maria's "realization" of the degree to which the social relations of exchange organize life occurs just prior to the explosion at the end of the film. In a way, this "capitalist (narrative) logic" cannot continue after consciousness is raised. Through the closing portraits, the only "resolution" suggested is a recognition of the continuity of capitalist social relations through today. Any "happy ending" would have to deny the strength of the logic of exchange.

1. MARIA ENTERS THE RELATIONS OF EXCHANGE

The first exchange in *The Marriage of Maria Braun* occurs after the opening credits sequence which clearly situates the marriage of Maria and Hermann within the specific historical context of World War II in Germany. In this first section, Maria enters the relations of exchange. While she is motivated by the need for subsistence in the wartime economy, this section also integrates sexual politics with the marketplace and positions the emotions associated with character "change" and development as a consequence of market relations. Marx wrote that satisfying the needs of life (food, clothing, shelter) is the "first presumption of all human existence, and therefore of all history." No act is without consequences in this process of exchange because "the action of satisfying and the instrument which has achieved this satisfaction leads to new needs."[8]

In the family's apartment, Maria's mother eats dried bread softened with water while standing by a photograph of the absent Hermann in civilian attire. Maria arrives with some firewood, bread, and potatoes. Taken together, these comprise the exchange value of her wedding dress. As this first exchange demonstrates, the role of bride has little currency in a wartime economy. However, in selling her wedding dress, Maria exchanges one womanly identity—wife—for basic needs. The absence of men as husbands gives Hermann's shaving mug no exchange value at all. Maria cries when she catches a glimpse of the picture of Hermann. In the next section, this process of exchange continues as Maria learns what aspects of feminine and masculine identity are worth something and what the larger economic system which encompasses these sexual politics is. Maria herself becomes an object with exchange value, redesigning herself as "currency" within the available economy. Yet, throughout the film, she retains a nostalgia for an idealized and impossible wifely role. This identity as wife is not something Maria lost or never had (in the sense of "Rosebud"). Instead, as *The Marriage of Maria Braun* shows at its conclusion, "wife" as a social identity separate from an economy of exchange does not exist.

2. MARIA REDESIGNS HERSELF

In the second section of the film, Maria initiates a series of exchanges in order to redesign herself as a bargirl. She uses the "instrument" of exchange in order to become a commodity form with exchange value. In the opening scene at the train station, three systems of exchange important to the film's structure intersect: marriages disrupted because soldiers offer their lives for their country; the value of the cigarette, a foreign-made commodity available through the American economy of occupation; and Maria's awareness of her exchange value for American soldiers. This intersection also establishes two terms which will continue the relations of exchange in the next section of the film: one is Maria's incorrect assumption that she can control her identity in systems of exchange; the other is an international economy dominated by American money.

At the train station, the widowed nurse tells Maria about the exchange value of her sailor husband's life. For her husband's life, the widow received a plaque. On it was a painting of a wreath floating on water. The ribbon read: "they died that Germany might live."[9] The women's conversation is punctuated two times by soldiers noisily diving for cigarette butts tossed to the floor. The excess of these instances marks the cigarettes as significant and highlights the intensity of their exchange value. German men are absent in the service of the nation during World War II. The resultant economy circulates around American men and the value of American commodities.

Maria recognizes the exchange value of her sexuality after her retort to the American soldier's sexual remark. In apology but also in response to her self-assertion, the soldier gives Maria two packs of cigarettes. Maria laughs, thus beginning to understand herself as a material force which can enter into market relations. The exchange value of cigarettes within the economy of the American military is the first link in a chain of exchanges through which Maria develops as a commodity. In this process, the intense value of the cigarettes is transferred to the commodities which the cigarettes purchase. Maria exchanges two packs of cigarettes for her mother's brooch. Their value is reiterated as Maria's mother replicates the soldier's dive for cigarettes. Maria exchanges the brooch for a rare commodity, a black dress in her size, and liquor.

Unlike her wedding dress, the black dress invests Maria with an exchange value so high that she can promise the bar owner that he won't need anyone else if he hires her. The contradictions and complexity of sexual politics come forward in Maria's conversations with other women: her mother, her sister Betti, and Vevi (another bargirl at the off-limits club). As the four women participate in the process of transforming Maria into an object with exchange value for the international marketplace, they talk about the relationship between woman's sexuality and economics.

As Maria's mother hems the black dress, she drinks to compensate for her complicity in her daughter's objectification. Yet she also comments that Maria's legs are pretty and that she "should show them off." In this scene, the display of woman's body is acknowledged and then adjusted for the new erotic market. While Maria's mother does not approve of what Maria is about to do, she also works to enhance Maria's "materiality." The mother's encouragement that Maria "at least" obtain a pair of stockings suggests how Maria's entry into the market will mobilize the display of her body. The value of Maria's legs will help her attain the stockings which will, in turn, help her to increase the value of her legs.

Betti also helps Maria to recreate herself within the terms of the market economy. As they fix Maria's hair, the women acknowledge how the context of international capital and the wartime absence of husbands informs social relations and sexual politics. At the mirror, the women sing a popular song whose words signify the shift in Maria's identity from monogamous wife to bar girl: "Don't cry baby. There's more than one man on earth." Betti has swept Maria's hair up into "the latest thing," a curly poodle. As she did at the train station when she received the cigarettes, Maria laughs with her knowledge of the economy: "I'll bet the Americans are crazy about poodles." The sisters disassociate gender relations from monogamous love and place them in the context of international market forces. With her curly hair and black dress, Maria is poised for a new synthesis as a bar girl.

At the off-limits club, Vevi dismisses Maria's nostalgia for "love" and articulates the economic relationship between sex and hunger. The atomized emblem of these sexual politics, Vevi restates the fact of economic relations: that filling basic needs (sex, hunger) is the first step to organizing human social relations. To obtain what she needs, Maria has redesigned her sexual identity according to the needs of the market. "I want to look great right now," she comments as she goes to Bill, the American soldier. Maria's relationship with Bill will continue her trajectory in exchange by moving her to the valuable intersection of sexuality and the English language.

At Maria's trial for Bill's murder, the American military court tries to mask the social relations of capital which the American economy initiated and maintained. The judge assaults Maria's moral character by accusing her of the venal exchange of sexuality for "chocolates and silk stockings." The club, for American soldiers, was off-limits to Germans "except for the girls who worked there." The American court attempts to efface the role of economics in organizing sexual identities. By blaming Maria for her fall from wifely grace, the court refuses to recognize the complicity of American currency in making German women available to American soldiers in the off-limits club.

Undaunted, Maria counters these accusations about her morality by distinguishing between two kinds of affection: "I was fond of Bill and I love my husband." This articulation of two modes of sexual identity is something the American ideology can neither tolerate nor even translate correctly. The court interpreter tells the judge: "She loved Bill and she loves her husband." Yet Maria's statement has implications beyond the way in which it complicates the American court's attempt to naturalize woman's social place as wife. It also points to Maria's confidence in her ability to separate her participation in exchange from her role as Hermann's wife. This belief in the separation of personal and work relations informs the next development in Maria's play with the economy, the beginning of her alienation.

The second section concludes with Maria visiting Hermann at the prison where he is incarcerated for Bill's murder. The film offers no specific motivation for Hermann's confession and is emphatic in its refusal to clarify his action. In Rheuban's analysis, Hermann's imprisonment allows Maria to meet Oswald and is also congruent with Hermann's "image of himself as women's protector. . . . Similarly, his long separation from Maria after prison is a consequence of his belief in an ideal of male self-sufficiency."[10] Indeed, at Maria's trial, Hermann's reaction to her statement "I love my husband" is intensely physical.

That Hermann goes to prison for Maria indicates, at least, that he accepts their relationship. At the prison, in a conversation clouded by an excess of noisy sound, Hermann also appears to easily accept Maria's plan that they raise her child by Bill as their child. And at the end of the prison scene, Maria and Hermann are both laughing as if this were a happy ending: "Our life will start again when we're together again." In the meantime, Maria will attempt to keep her personal life separate from her working life, and her marriage separate from her exchange value. And Maria and Hermann will have many discussions about the use value of Maria's labor for Hermann.

3. MARIA REDEFINES HER EXCHANGE VALUE

In the third section, with Hermann in prison for Bill's murder, Maria redefines her exchange value for the post-war international economy. She attempts to separate her sexual identity as Oswald's mistress from her work identity as Oswald's employee. However, the social relations of exchange are shown to be greater than Maria in two ways. First, she fails to control the exchange value of her sexuality. Unknown to Maria, Oswald and Hermann enter into a contract in which she is exchanged between them as if they owned her as private property. Second, Maria becomes alienated, so grounded in exchange that what she produces (a bank account for her future with Hermann, a sexual identity as Oswald's lover) become independent forces turned against her.

The third section of the film parallels the first in many ways: Maria enters a market defined by the intersection of American money and the exchange value of sexuality. With her facility in English learned "in bed," Maria is confident about her ability to play this market to her advantage. In her knowledge of this sexual economy, Maria has become cold and calculating. While in the first section of the film she was motivated by subsistence, in this third section Maria articulates the "new needs" which Marx predicted would result from exchange. Confronted with the differences between first and second class train travel, Maria seeks the quiet and comfort of a higher class. In this section, as in the first, Maria recreates herself to enter the relations of exchange. But now, unlike before, her transformation into a commodity is quick and sure. A cramped train bathroom replaces the soft contemplation before the mirror with Betti.

As in the first section, Maria is rewarded for asserting herself against sexual remarks by an American soldier. But the terms of the market and the dialogue have changed. The American military economy gives way to an international civilian economy. Maria's target is Oswald, the French owner of a German textile factory. Now Maria's retort is in vulgar English. Like the soldier in the first section, Oswald does not understand the words Maria speaks. But he rewards her self-assertion after she explains that she learned English in bed. Oswald hires Maria as his "personal advisor" and for access to American investment. Senkenberg, the accountant, cautions Maria to "never forget that it all has to do with money." And, as with the American military economy, women are central to the international marketplace, as Maria advises Oswald Textiles in its negotiations for American machines to make stockings for German women.

Aware of these larger economic forces, Maria actively positions herself within the social relations of exchange. Further, she is determined to retain control over her own exchange value as a worker and as a lover, and to keep her fondness for Oswald separate from her love for Hermann. This impossible split between private and work lives is developed in this section of the film. A discourse on the complex and necessary intersection of sexual politics and economic relations is worked through three couples: the marriage of Maria and Hermann, the work and personal relationship of Maria and Oswald, and the marriage of Willi and Betti.

In each of Maria's four visits to Hermann in prison, Hermann becomes progressively more disturbed by the way Maria inverts the gender and economic relations of marriage. In the first visit, Hermann is merely uncomfortable at the idea of Maria working "to make a home for us." A "man's foot" is what Hermann calls "somebody you let work for you." During her second visit, Hermann is disturbed by the information that Maria is sleeping with Oswald. Maria reiterates the difference between Hermann and Oswald and explains why she initiated the affair: in order to be "in control" of "at least" their personal relationship because in their economic relationship "he is my employer and I am dependent on him." In Maria's third visit, Hermann walks away, refusing her offer to give everything to him so he "can feel independent": "It's your money and your life, Maria. I live my life and I won't let anybody give me theirs." On the fourth and last visit Hermann has left Maria a note explaining why he has gone away: "We'll live together when I have become a man, and not until then." For

Hermann, in the sexual politics of exchange, it is the man who gives his economic life to the woman.

With Oswald, Maria claims to want clear terms for their relationship: the separation of private and business lives, of the exchange values of labor and sex. However, even Maria crosses these lines. At the office, reserved for work relations, Maria insists upon a salary based on her work, not her self. Then she fondly kisses Oswald. In a reverse of her relationship with Hermann, Maria is unable to keep the personal from informing the economic with Oswald. Oswald and Hermann enter into the contract in which the men share knowledge withheld from Maria. They arrange for Hermann to leave Maria in order to "become a man," and not return until Oswald is dead, and for the dying Oswald to leave the bulk of his estate to both Maria and Hermann. The revelation that Oswald and Hermann subverted Maria's determined efforts to keep her value as a woman separate from her value as a worker stuns Maria in the last section of the film.

Willi, the socialist labor negotiator, admires and respects Maria for her success in the modern economy and for her apparent liberation from the oppressive social relations of marriage. However, while Willi recognizes the exploitation of labor, he does not apply his proletarian consciousness to the economic conditions of Maria's corporate rise, nor is he able to acknowledge the patriarchal relations of gender. In Maria's economic exchange value, Willi sees an independent woman who is man's "equal." But Maria's nostalgia for an idealized wifely role is complicated by Betti's unhappiness and Willi's boredom with his wife.

Instead of a representative of management and capital, Willi sees in Maria a woman who has "made it" and against whom he measures his wife, Betti: "I need somebody I can talk to, and I've got somebody that cooks for me . . . she never learned what's important . . . she's not happy all the time." Betti freely admits her unhappiness and her husband's boredom. But Betti seemingly cannot situate her own happiness outside of herself as Maria claims to be doing for Hermann. Maria is happy because "a man can't be happy about an unhappy wife."

Like the exploited textile workers, Maria is rowing someone else's boat and living a contradiction: an independent woman who has designed her life for someone else. Economic "independence" does not free women— or men—from the oppression of sexual politics.

The exploration of these various attempts to subvert or deny the integration of economic and social relations concludes with Hermann's release from prison. Two times, when she is informed of Hermann's release and when she learns that Hermann has left her, Maria responds by burying herself in her adding machine, punching the buttons repeatedly like an automaton. Whether working on a job to earn money or calculating her wealth, the intensity of these actions exhibits the stress of alienation which will build in the last section of the film. This acute computation is associated both with Hermann's release from prison and with his departure for Canada. In the first instance, Hermann rejects both Maria's identity as a wife and the exchange of labor through which she produced a bank account. With Hermann's release, the deteriorated marriage, topsy-turvey in its gendered economic responsibilities, must be faced. After Hermann leaves, Maria buries herself deeper in the relations of exchange in which she is already so well grounded. In the fourth and final section of the film, relations of private property take over relationships between people.

4. MARIA'S ALIENATION

Maria begins the third section of the film by attempting to control her position within an economy of exchange. By its end, she seeks refuge by repeatedly punching the buttons of an adding machine. In the fourth section of the film, Maria becomes progressively more alienated, a condition partially exhibited through her increasing emotional stress and hostility to other workers. Oswald dies, Hermann returns, Maria is stunned to learn of the contract between Oswald and Hermann and accidentally (or not) blows up her house. Both Kaes and Rheuban have explored the significance of these narrative events by situating them within Maria's realization that she has been an object of exchange. In Kaes' analysis, Maria learns that "she had never been in command of her story at all" and was "far from being an agent of her own fate." For Rheuban, this is evidence of a "male-dominated culture" which "secretly governs the lives of others," both Maria and the women of Germany. Feinstein enlarges the context of these events by observing that "emotional and spiritual decline, however, parallel commercial success."[11] It is this relationship between materialism and consciousness that I would like to pursue.

Maria is the first in her family to obtain what Marx has called "the consequence of alienated labor," private property. The last section begins with Maria moving into her new house and overtly exhibiting her alienation through her treatment of the mover and her attitude toward labor. Maria has reified money, making it the object of work and the means of communication between people. Marx has written that "the nature of money is . . . that the *mediating activity* of *human* social action . . . is *alienated*. . . . When man exteriorizes this mediating activity he is active only as an exiled and dehumanized being" (emphasis in original).[12] When her mother reproaches her for abusing the mover, Maria snaps: "The man is being paid for his work. The least you can expect is that he does it properly." To the worker as he stands waiting for a tip: "Why didn't you just say so? You have to demand what's due you." And, "I'd rather pay than still have to thank somebody."

Maria's hostility and demands for service extend to her work and personal relationships. She rudely demands sexual attention from Oswald and viciously terrorizes her secretary. Maria is alienated because she has lost herself within the system of exchange which she initially thought she could control and which has turned back on her. About alienation, Marx wrote: "Finally, the alienated character of work for the worker appears in the fact that . . . in work he does not belong to himself but to another person . . . the activity of the worker is not his spontaneous activity. It is another's activity, and a loss of his own spontaneity."[13] The life that Maria thought she was producing was actually producing her. Maria's emotional turmoil and distractedness stem from her inability to any longer reconcile her life within the social relations of capital. She worked for a life with Hermann who then left her until he could reestablish or regain his manhood through his own economic endeavors.

What can rescue Maria from this alienation? The return of Hermann and the romance of her marriage. Ruth McCormick describes Hermann's return as "the 'big moment' [when Maria] might fall ecstatically into Hermann's arms and move on to a happy, new life." And this is what Maria assumes when Hermann arrives. But, as Rheuban observes, "the 'reunion' of the 'lovers' does not resolve the various lines of tension."[14] Their reunion does underscore the way sexual politics and economic relations are bound together. Having made his fortune, Hermann has regained his manhood. Having regained his manhood, Hermann no longer needs money. Hermann refuses Maria's offer of everything she has and gives Maria everything he has: "Because I became your husband today and don't need anything anymore." In order to retrieve his masculine identity from Maria's economic power, Hermann had to attain his own, separate economic prowess.

Like Maria, Hermann based his actions on the assumption that sexual identity and economic identity are equivalent. However, while Maria resisted the interrelationship of those identities, Hermann could not untangle "a life" from "a checkbook." As long as he owed Maria his life, ("somebody you have to give back his life to") he could not love his wife. Maria and Hermann were motivated in the same ways. Maria worked and Hermann left "for us," in order to establish their life together. For Maria, their life together would begin with Hermann free from prison. But Hermann could not owe Maria "a life" and also love her as a husband. The exchange value of "a life" was greater than Hermann could afford to give.

At first glance, this reunion moves toward a "happy ending" in which Maria and Hermann are realigned in a relationship where one partner has "everything" (money, property) and the other has his masculinity. But this potential resolution to the intersection of sexual politics and economic relations is disturbed by the reading of Oswald's will. In revealing the contract Hermann and Oswald entered into while Hermann was in prison, the will affirms the relative independence of men and the contribution their arrangement made to Maria's stressful existence. The contract also requires that Maria confront her alienation, that she was an "object" of exchange and not an active subject. Feinstein has argued that in Fassbinder's postwar trilogy "an exploitative and misunderstood love relationship . . . functions in microcosm as an indicator of the generally unperceived economic and historical forces which determine each relationship."[15] The marriage in *The Marriage of Maria Braun* is "misunderstood" by Maria because she mistakenly holds it outside of the social relations of exchange.

Maria is stunned by this new consciousness. After the reading of the will, Hermann reminds Maria that he has given her everything: "All the money. I don't care about it." Maria reminds Hermann that "I gave you everything, too. My whole life." For the first time, Maria admits that she exchanged her life for her marriage with Hermann.

For the first time, the money Maria earned does not compensate for her life. When confronted with the knowledge of her own alienation, Maria blows up the house. Whether coincidental, accidental, or intentional, the explosion is also the final logical resolution of the narrative. Any "happy ending" for *The Marriage of Maria Braun* would necessarily have to deny the capitalist (narrative) logic which moved it forward. It would have to deny the role of historical-materialist forces in structuring the film and replace them with a forced happy ending: an ending which walks hand in hand with a nostalgia for the bourgeois marriage; an ending which masks the oppression of social relations under capital and disavows the logic of materialism. As Feinstein wryly observes, "the priority of the material necessarily results in apocalypse."[16]

In his analysis of the conventions of historical-materialist narration, David Bordwell discusses how an "interrogative cinema" of the 1960s and 1970s "preserve[d] basic tenets of the Soviet model" while refusing "the fixed doctrine and clearly didactic purpose that had informed the Soviet approach. . . . The characters and/or the narration pose questions about political theory and practice—including the practice of cinematic representation." Because of its Hollywoodian tendencies, *The Marriage of Maria Braun* does not easily fit into these available categories of political cinema. However, Richard Dyer concedes that "Fassbinder's work has been *effective* in stimulating debate and thought. . . . That political effectivity—limited though it is—may be far more important than the film's own political despair" (emphasis in original).[17]

As Dyer has observed about other Fassbinder films, *The Marriage of Maria Braun* does not explicitly articulate the relationship between class and sexual politics.[18] Except where it is buried amid the contradictions of Willi's socialism and feminism, political consciousness is not a liberating force in the diegesis of the film. However, the film does explore the many ways in which woman's sexual and social identity is caught within economics—as wife, as bargirl, as independent woman, as man's "equal," as worker. In doing this, *The Marriage of Maria Braun* calls for a recognition not only of the specific history of Germany but also of the larger processes of capitalist social relations which link gendered identities with economics.

Notes

1   Richard Dyer, "Reading Fassbinder's Sexual Politics," *Fassbinder*, Tony Rayns, ed., third revised edition (London: British Film Institute, 1980), pp. 54–64; Thomas Elsaesser, "A Cinema of Vicious Circles," *Fassbinder*, Rayns, ed., p. 36.

2   See Judith Mayne's discussion of how *Ali: Fear Eats the Soul* integrates melodrama and political cinema. Judith Mayne, "Fassbinder and Spectatorship," *New German Critique* 12 (1977), pp. 61–74. More recently, Kaja Silverman has explored how Fassbinder's cinema places identity itself "at risk." Kaja Silverman, "Fassbinder and Lacan: A Reconsideration of Gaze, Look and Image," *Camera Obscura* 19 (January 1989), pp. 54–85.

3   Anton Kaes, "History, fiction, memory: Fassbinder's *The Marriage of Maria Braun* (1979)," *German Film and Literature*, Eric Rentschler, ed. (New York: Methuen, 1986), pp. 279 and 286; Joyce Rheuban, "*The Marriage of Maria Braun*: History, Melodrama, Ideology," *The Marriage of Maria Braun*, Joyce Rheuban, ed. (New Brunswick, New Jersey: Rutgers University Press, 1986), pp. 5 and 18; Howard Feinstein, "BRD 1-2-3: Fassbinder's Postwar Trilogy and the Spectacle," *Cinema Journal* 23. 1 (Fall 1983), p. 45.

4   Feinstein, p. 48. Tom Bottomore has explained that the concept of materialism in Marxist social theory "is employed simply to designate the fundamental, primary conditions of human existence," that is, the relationship of individuals to the production of their material life. Tom Bottomore, *Karl Marx: Selected Writings in Sociology and Social Philosophy* (New York: McGraw Hill, 1964), p. 21.

5   Ben Fine, "Exchange," *A Dictionary of Marxist Thought*, Tom Bottomore, *et. al.*, eds. (Cambridge, Massachusetts: Harvard University Press, 1983), p. 155.

6   Gajo Petrovic, "Alienation," *A Dictionary of Marxist Thought*, p. 13.

7   Thomas Elsaesser uses the term "vicious circle of capitalist logic" to describe Fassbinder's abundant production of films. Elsaesser, p. 36.

8   Karl Marx, in Bottomore, p. 60.

9   All direct quotations from the film are taken from "The Continuity Script," Joyce Rheuban, ed., *The Marriage of Maria Braun*.

10   Rheuban, pp. 14–5.

11   Kaes, pp. 283 and 285; Rheuban, p. 16; Feinstein, p. 48.

12   Marx, in Bottomore, pp. 168 and 171.

13   Marx, in Bottomore, p. 170.

14   Ruth McCormick, review of *The Marriage of Maria Braun*, *The Marriage of Maria Braun*, Joyce Rheuban, ed., p. 226. Originally published in *Cineaste* 2 (Spring 1980), pp. 34–6; Rheuban, p. 15.

15   Feinstein, p. 46.

16   Feinstein, p. 48.

17   David Bordwell, *Narration in the Fiction Film* (Madison, Wisconsin: The University of Wisconsin Press, 1985), pp. 271–2; Dyer, p. 63.

18   Dyer, *passim*.

I would like to thank Eileen Meehan and Peter Treistman (Department of Media Arts, University of Arizona) for their discussions of Marxist social theory.

Marianne and Juliane/The German Sisters
Baader-Meinhof Fictionalized
LISA DICAPRIO

O N OCTOBER 18 1972, three members of the Baader-Meinhof gang, condemned to life imprisonment in the high-security Stammheim prison, were found dead in their cells. Andreas Baader and Jan-Karl Raspe had been shot through the neck; Gudrun Ensslin was discovered hanged. Prison officials maintained that the prisoners had committed suicide. Although it went to great lengths to substantiate this claim, the German state could never explain how handguns had found their way into the isolation cells of Baader and Raspe. Many members of the Left, not only in Germany, but in Italy and France as well, challenged that official explanation. Among those who refused to concede to the State version of the deaths was Gudrun Ensslin's sister Christiane. Christiane's experience forms the subject matter of *The German Sisters*, and to her Von Trotta has dedicated the film.

The German Sisters[1] is the latest in a series of films by actress-turned director, Margarethe von Trotta which deal with political themes as they touch on the lives of women. She has said that this film, the German title of which is *Die Bleirne Zeit*, or "heavy, leaden years," concerns "the continuing weight of the past on the present." In fact, she depicts two "pasts"—one, of Nazi Germany, which has laid a heavy moral burden on von Trotta's own generation, and the other, of the Baader-Meinhof gang itself.

At the height of Baader-Meinhof activity, from about 1969 to 1977, the German state engaged in massive wiretapping, intimidation, and harassment of radicals. Over 300,000 members of the Left were interrogated. Many among those who refused to collaborate were persecuted for activities with which they had profound disagreement. Most of those whose lives were touched by the Baader-Meinhof group were never the same again. One life so influenced was that of Christiane Ensslin. Von Trotta has chosen to dramatize the tremendous strain of this period of state intimidation—and its "continuing weight" today—by examining the lives of the two Ensslin sisters.

The German Sisters roughly covers the period shortly before Ensslin's capture in June of 1972 (after three years of underground life) and her death in Stammheim prison in 1977.[2] Although in many ways the film parallels the real lives of the sisters, von Trotta does not offer a narrative that

---

Reprinted with permission from *Jump Cut* 29 (1984): 28–32

renders the history of their lives exact, but dramatized the conflict between the two sisters. While the character representing Gudrun Ensslin, played by Barbara Sukowa as "Marianne" has chosen to become a member of the Baader-Meinhof group, the character based on Christiane Ensslin, played by Jutta Lampe as "Juliane," actively works in the women's movement and writes for a feminist magazine. In the film, the sisters share a common moral outrage at Germany's past and present, but their conception of how to act on this outrage pulls them in opposite direction.

The intense political conflict between Marianne and Juliane provides the vehicle for von Trotta to deal with a multiplicity of themes in her film: von Trotta's own life and her generation; the two Ensslin sisters' political evolution; the Baader-Meinhof group's history; the conflict between feminists and women who remained within the male-dominated Left; and the Holocaust.

When the State captures and imprisons Gudrun (Marianne), Juliane suddenly must deal with the State's repression of the Baader-Meinhof group while attempting to maintain her feminist perspective. Following Marianne's murder, Juliane becomes obsessed with uncovering the reasons for her sister's death. Her personal and political activities become entirely reordered as all of Juliane's activities become focused on exposing this state political crime.

A "labor of mourning," according to von Trotta, "can be related to a person, but also to a country." Juliane's obsession symbolizes von Trotta's generation's efforts to come to terms with the Holocaust. Von Trotta has said, "We were quick to push aside guilt and responsibility. The tendency in public life not to admit feelings of guilt at all, or at least to forget them as quickly as possible, still exists."[3]

As recently as 1978, 24% of German respondents to a survey agreed to a statement that "National Socialism" was a good idea badly carried out.[4] One year after this survey was conducted, the US television series *Holocaust* was broadcast in Germany. According to *Variety*, more than 15 million West Germans saw *Holocaust* and responded favorably.[5] Nevertheless, more that 50 years after the fact, the subject of Nazism, initiated public debate. Prior to the series' showing, several groups of demonstrators protested *Holocaust* as anti-German, and some stations which showed another related program, *The Final Solution*, were bombed.

To broadcast *Holocaust* represented a significant political decision on the part of German media because this TV series exposed millions to images and issues from the Nazi period which mainstream German television rarely has dealt with. In his article, "German Filmmakers Seldom Focus on the Legacy of Nazism," *New York Times* critic Tony Pipolo writes:

> For all their seriousness and their willingness to be critical, few German
> filmmakers working in the commercial mainstream of the industry have

openly confronted the most troubling subject of all: the World War II period and its twin evils, Nazism and the Holocaust. There are signs that this is
now changing, and that some filmmakers are beginning to approach this
difficult historical legacy head on and to make links between the past and
the present. But for the most part, these ghosts from the past have been
either avoided or indirectly hinted at, as the dark specter that haunts the
lives of characters and may be at the root of the undefined malaise within
contemporary Germany.[6]

Among those confronting the Holocaust are directors of the New German
Cinema, such as von Trotta. In fact she belongs to the same generation as
Gudrun Ensslin, born in 1942—only two years after Gudrun. Von Trotta,
too, experienced the bombing raids of World War II; she, too, deeply
experienced the Holocaust's legacy as a child.

Through a series of flashbacks in *The German Sisters*, von Trotta firmly
establishes her characters—the two sisters'—sense of guilt for the past,
and she describes how each formed a social consciousness, which serves
to bind them together throughout the ordeal of Marianne's imprisonment.
The film indicates both sisters were raised in a heavily religious background. In real life, Gudrun's and Christiane Ensslin's father served as a
pastor of the "German Evangelical Church". This church was formed in
1945, the year of Hitler's defeat, and claimed its origin in the "Confessing
Church" formed in opposition to the Hitler *Reichskirche*—the unification
of 29 German Protestant churches; as part of its ritual, it stressed examination of conscience. The Ensslin children were educated to be against rearmament and for reunification, to concern themselves with social
problems, especially those of the Third World.

As we see this process of coming to social awareness in the film,
Juliane's and Marianne's first exposure to the crimes of the Hitler era
comes from viewing a newsreel made at the time of the liberation of the
concentration camps.[7] They and we see depictions of corpses—thousands
being turned over, lifted up, and buried in huge graves with bulldozers.
Survivors barely skeletons, stand and lie in their familiar striped camp uniform. The film-within-a-film presents the Nuremberg trials, where everyone claims innocence. As the documentary's narrator states the national
problem: "I'm not to blame," says the Kapo. "I'm not to blame," says the
officer. Then who is to blame?

From these common roots, however, von Trotta's two sisters evolve in
opposite political directions. Why? Von Trotta implies that Juliane's feminism comes as a natural outgrowth of her early rebellion. Flashbacks show
us Juliane as the nonconformist. She acts the role of the real rebel, while
Marianne stays safely on the sidelines. Called on to recite a poem by Rilke
in school, Juliane refuses saying, "I prefer the 'Ballad of the Jewish
Whore.'" She gets thrown out of class, while Marianne remains and does

not protest. Juliane is also always being reprimanded for her choice of clothes, which she wears as an emblem of non-conformity. In contrast, Marianne attempts to mediate family conflicts by playing father's favorite, a tactic that Juliane very much resents. Here the Ensslin father is depicted as a typical German patriarch, symbolizing the traditionally authoritarian character of German society.

The German Sisters, then, does not provide an objective treatment of the two sisters, but very much gives a partisan defense of Juliane. No real reference is made in the process of Gudrun Ensslin's real-life transformation from student anti-war activist into terrorist. We know from the film's flashbacks to childhood that the character Marianne felt compelled by a sense of moral urgency. But why take the specific route of joining the Baader-Meinhof group? From a psychological perspective it appears that Marianne is drawn to the rigidity of Baader-Meinhof lifestyle, where critical thinking was often suspended in the name of preserving strict discipline. Thus the film offers a partial explanation of how some left activists have turned to terrorism. Von Trotta even implies that Marianne's conversion resulted from a relationship with the man for whom she left her husband, rather than as an independent decision.[8]

If von Trotta has very clearly weighted the scales in Juliane's favor, the character Juliane provides a vehicle for von Trotta to express her own search for moral identity. Von Trotta's own priorities are feminist: yet she realizes the parameters history imposes on one's free will. From the film's beginning, von Trotta establishes the two sisters' interdependency, despite their political disagreements. Marianne's life (and then her death) constantly intrudes on her sister's, just as the Holocaust haunts all aspects of German politics today. Juliane attempts to maintain a safe distance between herself and Marianne, but she cannot.

In the film's opening sequence, Marianne's husband, Werner, attempts to persuade Juliane to assume responsibility for the son Felix. (When Ensslin went underground, she left behind her husband, Bernard Vesper, and an 11 month-old son Felix Robert.) Werner, a writer, has been offered a position outside Germany. Juliane, rejects his suggestion, saying that she will not let her own life be ruined while "Marianne is attempting to save humanity." Felix then figures prominently throughout *The German Sisters*. As a child in need of care, he provides a connection to Marianne that Juliane cannot sever. Felix represents an extension of Marianne, a responsibility progressively makes its weight felt on Juliane's life despite her will.

The film's next sequence shows Juliane speaking at a women's demonstration demanding the repeal of Paragraph 210, the German abortion law which has remained virtually intact since Bismark first unified Prussian Germany. Juliane denounces the hypocrisy of those who oppose abortion. She cites statistics about German women's oppression—30,000 cases of abortions a year, 20,000 children put up for adoption, 3,000,000 women forced to live in temporary housing. This scene establishes Juliane's identification with the average German woman, for whom Marianne will only exhibit contempt.

In the first two sequences, then, we gain an appreciation for Juliane as an intelligent, sensitive woman committed to pursuing her career and political work. We sense that Juliane has carefully laid out the course of her life, almost with "German precision," as she meets her personal and political responsibilities with an ordered discipline. Although the feminist issues Juliane raises have revolutionary potential, she always operates within the legal boundaries of capitalism. She faces minimal risks to her personal safety. And her political activity is related to her paid work on a feminist journal; Juliane's life, however, soon becomes disrupted. Marianne emerges from underground and immediately confronts the legitimacy of Juliane's personal and political priorities. In marked contrast to her sister, Marianne lives an entirely unpredictable day-to-day life. Her whole existence is a secret one, as she must live in fear of arrest, with no dependable source of income or housing.

Marianne first makes her presence felt while Juliane is at a meeting at work. Juliane receives a call and then announces that she must leave, with the abrupt, "I've been looking for her for two years." Julianne and Marianne meet secretly in a cemetery statuary warehouse, prefiguring Marianne's death. Marianne appears disguised in a wig and wearing stark clothing. Her features are tensely drawn. She waves aside Juliane's concern for her safety.

As they sit down to drink coffee, Marianne confronts her feminist sister with the self-righteous tone that will characterize all her future discussions, "Are you *still* working for the magazine? Do you really think it is important, *absolutely* essential work?" Nothing that Juliane can do will win Marianne's respect or appreciation. Similarly, when Juliane informs Marianne that Marianne's husband has committed suicide, Marianne responds impassively, "He had a penchant for death—a neurotic intellectual." Marianne moves on to her practical concerns—asking that Julianne care for the son. Again Juliane refuses, "You are always trying to cast me in the role you don't want anymore."

Marianne ends this, her first discussion with Julianne in two years, with the statement, "Ideas are not acts. Older women cannot wage the class war." Who is the "older woman," since the distinction in age between the two sisters is not that dramatic? Probably Marianne means women tied to job or family responsibilities. Since she narrowly defines "class war" as confined to terrorism, Marianne negates both women's oppression and women's ability to participate in significant political activity.

Unconvinced by Marianne's harsh criticism, Juliane returns to her world of "ideas" and political organizing. We see Juliane assembling an exhibit about Hitler's policies towards women. Hitler said, "Giving birth enobles women It is women's sacrifice for the survival of the nation." In Nazi Germany, not having children was considered subversive. Juliane's work gets interrupted as Marianne is arrested.

Despite their intense conflicts, Juliane immediately drives out to the prison to visit Marianne. Juliane must submit to the humiliation of stripping and then is made to wait in an empty visiting room. While waiting, she flashes back to their childhood. Scenes of the two girls competing against each other in a running match are superimposed on the brick prison structure. Their competition has continued through adulthood, alternating with their deep sense of mutual dependence. Juliane is awakened by the matron with the words, "Your sister won't see you." The matron gives no reason. Deeply hurt, Juliane is consoled by her boyfriend who suggests as an explanation, "That lifestyle (of the Baader-Meinhof group) makes people numb." He suggests that she write a letter asking how to help. Finally, the two sisters do meet in prison. While psychiatrists look on and take detailed notes, the two characters shout at each other. Juliane screams, "Your bombs ruined it all, all of our work." To Marianne, of course, Juliane's "work" is worthless—perhaps evidence of selling out to the system.

An earlier scene had dramatized Marianne's contempt for ordinary people's lives and daily routine. At 3.00 a.m., Marianne and her male comrades burst into Juliane's apartment. Marianne makes herself at home. She insists that she have coffee over Juliane's objection that the grinder will wake up the whole building. The two sisters do not converse. Finally, as she is leaving, Marianne runs to Juliane's room and begins systematically to go through Juliane's clothes, rejecting each piece of clothing, and throwing it on the floor, with undisguised contempt: "There is nothing here I can use."

Juliane experiences this as a double affront. Not only has Marianne invaded her privacy, assuming that what belongs to her sister must also rightfully be hers; but in expressing distaste for the clothes Juliane needs for work, Marianne again condemns Juliane's life-choice of political activity. Later, when in prison, Marianne explains her actions, "We gave you your last chance to join us." Juliane responds, "If I had done that, if I *had* joined you, I couldn't be here to help you."

Marianne's prison demands are many and we see Juliane preparing several packages. Juliane's boyfriend reprimands, "You are wrecking your life for her." Juliane answers, "I will never agree that nothing can be done." Juliane's ability to act, however, often gets restricted by Marianne's own purism. At one point, in the prison, the two sisters quickly exchange sweaters. Inside Marianne's sweater, Juliane finds the note: "Get your liberal friends to do something." Juliane is persuaded by her own magazine staff to write an article on her sister. Then Marianne attacks the article with a vengeance, screaming, "Are you writing for the Springer press now?" (Axel Springer maintains a virtual monopoly on the Berlin press and is notorious for his yellow journalism.)[9] Again, Juliane attempts to help her sister, but faces rejection.

Despite our alienation from Marianne's self-centered rigidity, we share Juliane's horror at the German state's increasing brutality. We begin to see, in very vivid terms, the process of Marianne's destruction. Ironically, she becomes more human for us as she begins to lose her self-confidence. At the hands of her jailers, Marianne must suddenly confront reality; as a result, she becomes less the stereotype of a political robot. In one particularly memorable scene, which begins with the two sisters' usual outbursts of political disagreement, Juliane asks, "If you consider yourself an elite, why are you asking for ordinary treatment?" Marianne is on the 25th day of a hunger strike to protest treatment of the Baader-Meinhof group members in prison. One member, Holger Meins, would die on November 9, 1974. Marianne has already lost 10 pounds. Juliane asks, "Why are you destroying yourself?" Marianne shouts back with eyes flaring,

> "Do you know what they are doing to us? I am in a cell by myself. They keep the lights on all day and night so I can't sleep. I pound on the cells next to me. There is no one there. The cells are empty. There is no one to talk to. I listen to my breath entering my mouth and leaving through my nostrils. They want to kill us."

After, we see Juliane attempting to simulate force-feeding through a tube so she can experience for herself the treatment Marianne is undergoing at the hands of the prison "doctors."

During what is to be their last prison visit, a new sense of understanding emerges between the two sisters. In the dehumanizing conditions of prison, Marianne's features become transformed; they seem softer and more relaxed. Now Juliane and Marianne must speak via microphones through glass. They can no longer touch each other. Juliane says, "I dreamed that I set you free." As the visiting time draws to an end, Marianne's face begins to fade away as she asks with urgency when Juliane will return. Marianne is visibly disturbed to hear that Juliane will not be back for two or three weeks for, with some reluctance and at her boyfriend's suggestion, Juliane has decided to take a vacation and plans to return in time for the trial.

Outside Germany, Juliane cannot relax but is constantly thinking of Marianne. We see Juliane and her boyfriend in Sicily looking down into the rim of Mount Etna, an active volcano that symbolically represents their situation. Her "explosion" occurs while the couple are in a restaurant, and Juliane's boyfriend sees Marianne's face for a brief moment on the television screen. Neither can understand or speak Italian to understand what has taken place. Juliane rushes to a telephone, calls home, and discovers that Marianne has been found hanged in her cell.

Next, the film flashes to the prison where Marianne's body has been laid out. We see the body from a distance as if it had been properly embalmed with all traces of the death Marianne encountered erased. Slowly, the camera accompanies Juliane to confront the corpse's distorted face, Marianne's eyes wide open, as at the moment of death. In the final invasion of her privacy, the final humiliation and vengeance by prison officials, the German state has its last word laying out Marianne's body to "rest" in the most grotesque form, denying the sanctity of human life. (This scene reflects the difficulty the Ensslin family had in real life finding a cemetery willing to bury the dead members of the Baader-Meinhof group. That real-life burial was shown with actual footage in the film *Germany in Autumn*. Many Leftists attended the ceremony with red scarves covering the lower part of their face so as not to be identified by the German police. Later, visitors to the graves of the Baader-Meinhof members were required to produce identification cards.)

Confronted with Marianne's unexpected death, Juliane prepare a case to prove that the hanging was not suicide, as claimed by prison officials, but murder. This preparation will take many years. (In real life, Christiane Ensslin did carry out such an exhaustive study which will soon be published in German.) Juliane studies medical reports, simulates the hanging, and enlists the help of a lover. At one point, her boyfriend shouts at her,

> "Nobody will believe you. We have a lifetime ahead of us. A lifetime with a corpse between us. You're destroying yourself and you want me to watch. You are ruining ten years of our lives."

Juliane's boyfriend's words seem to represent a realistic position in terms of the issue of exposing Marianne's murder. In many ways, Juliane's relationship with her boyfriend is presented as a positive one in which each lover respects the other's career and shares in household tasks. However, he mainly fears jeopardizing the security of their shared existence for a political cause. He initially feels sympathetic towards what Juliane is attempting to accomplish, but rapidly replaces that with resentment towards Marianne.

Viewed within the framework of von Trotta's overall theme of moral responsibility, this young man's "realism" has a negative connotation. He is a "good" person who commits no evil acts, but whose resignation in the face of adversity is a form of complicity with evil. It was, for example, on the suggestion of her boyfriend that she re-direct her energies in a "positive" direction, that Juliane left Germany on a vacation, thus being absent at the very time of Marianne's murder. His pessimistic statement, "Nobody will believe you," can also be seen as meaning "Nobody can grasp the Holocaust."

Hitler, after all, did depend on the very monstrosity of his crimes for protection. One can easily grasps a regime's selectively executing its political opponents, but the wholesale extermination of millions based on arbitrary considerations of ethnic background and sexual preference—this almost surpasses human imagination. Several decades later, in 1977, the average German would have difficulty believing the assertion of the German Left that prison officials would murder members of the Baader-Meinhof gang (shortly before they were to go to trial) and then make their deaths appear to be the result of suicide. In terms of the scale of human life involved, of course, we can make no comparison, between the Holocaust and the murder of Baader-Meinhof members. But von Trotta demonstrates for us that the *lacunae* involved in both historical instances is the same.

Her boyfriend's challenge to Juliane, "Do you really think you can accomplish anything?" thus stands for the fundamental question, "Could fascism's rule of terror have been successfully resisted?" No definitive answer to this question can be given. We know that Hitler's most active opponents were rounded up in the first hours of the Third Reich. Yet the complacency of many "good" Germans was essential for the Nazis to successfully carry out their aims. Juliane's boyfriend may offer an accurate appraisal of the task Juliane has set for herself, but it is with Juliane's determined effort that von Trotta would have us identify. In subtle ways, von Trotta poses the question, "If no effective opposition is organized against this crime (the murder of the Baader-Meinhof members), who will be the state's next victims?"

As *The German Sisters* approaches its conclusion, we see how Juliane has become as relentless searching for the truth as Marianne had become in her commitment to the Baader-Meinhof group. Yet, when Juliane calls the press, she is informed, "Nobody cares anymore. Your sister, the movement—that was the 70s. Now people are interested in the energy crisis, the Third World." When Juliane pleads, "But my sister was trying to draw attention to the Third World," the man responds, "You know the rules of journalism. If it is not current, it is useless—it can only be used in book form as an historical subject."

In the final sequence, we see Juliane with Marianne's son Felix. Earlier we had seen Juliane and a woman doctor visiting Felix in the hospital, where he was covered with bandages from burns, unable to move or speak. While he was in a cave where he often played, someone threw in gasoline and lit it. Felix was set on fire because his mother threw bombs. After this incident, which occurred to Gudrun Ensslin's son in real life, Juliane must finally assume responsibility for Felix's care. Traumatized by his near death, Felix exhibits tremendous anger at both Juliane and his mother. He expresses outrage at Marianne by ripping up a poster of her, shredding it into small pieces and throwing it out with satisfaction. Juliane watches with understanding, knowing the source of his anger. She responds quietly, without reproach, but with firmness, "Your mother was a fine person. Someday I will explain it all to you." With the same determination that informed his mother whom he now hates, Felix commands, "Begin now!" This shout ("Fang an!") not only means: "Preserve Marianne's memory," but on proper reflection, it can be interpreted as a general moral command: "Tell my generation everything!" Thus, the child's command is the basic imperative of von Trotta's work.

Finally, *The German Sisters* poses these two questions: How are we to view the political legacy of the Baader-Meinhof group? and what is the responsibility of the German Left to the Baader-Meinhof group? For the first question, von Trotta passes an obviously negative judgment on the political value of Baader-Meinhof activities. The Baader-Meinhof group, which arose in 1970, was Germany's first urban guerrilla group—a desperate response to the lethargy of the German proletariat, presumably bought off with an abundance of consumer goods.[10] All that the terrorists have accomplished is to perhaps relieve their guilt for living in an imperialist nation. Thus, when Marianne is displayed in her coffin, there is a marked contrast between her contorted physical frame and the soaring, religious organ music in the background. Marianne, in death, is finally at rest in her soul and spirit. She—and the film—have renounced the "new Germany" which attempts to forget its menacing past through the pursuit of materialistic aims. As Gunter Grass, who knew the real Gudrun Ensslin in Berlin, said, "She was idealistic with an inborn loathing of any compromise. She had a yearning for the absolute, for the perfect solution."

While we are left with a very definite impression of Marianne's character as a terrorist, *The German Sisters* leaves open to interpretation how to view Juliane. Von Trotta contrasts Felix's decisive demand for truth with the negative results obtained by Juliane when she finally presents proof of Marianne's murder to the press. In the end, the film does not show whether or not Juliane will pursue her investigation and continue her attempt to get her findings published. Juliane has destroyed her ten year relationship with a sensitive man, and we may presume that she has lost her job at the magazine. In exchange for giving up her personal happiness and abandoning her feminist work, Juliane has seemingly run up against a dead end. How are we to judge her? Von Trotta herself spoke about such issues earlier in 1980, and her words delineate the political boundaries of her concerns:

> "Hope arises from the realization that you have to find the way back to yourself. This is less of a rallying call than a pessimistic statement. Personally I see very few chances of exploding the power complex established by the alliance between economics and science, and above all, I see no movement on the

present political horizon capable of achieving this. I believe we still have a very naive approach to this terrifying power complex. Naturally I fight against it despite my skepticism, for it is certain that those who do not offer resistance are already defeated. To propose new ideas is the duty of art. Just the same I doubt whether it is possible to put these utopian ideas into effect. But because I am alive I fight."

The German Sisters thus expresses the strengths and weakness that also characterize the works of von Trotta's two well-known contemporaries in the New German Cinema: her ex-husband Volker Schlöndorff and the late Rainer Werner Fassbinder. The films of all three directors are unsurpassed for their incisive critique of the moral corruption of German society and for relating the past to the present. However the collective weaknesses of these directors lies in their deep cynicism about the potential for any significant social change. *The German Sisters* has a strong emotional impact on the viewer and challenges us, but it does not point to any political direction by which we can collectively meet this challenge.

Notes

1 *The German Sisters* was the original title of the film when it premiered in Chicago during the November 1982 International Film Festival. The film was released commercially in New York as *Marianne and Juliane*. Its German title was *Die Bleirne Zeit*.

2 A German audience would know about the Baader-Meinhof group. For U.S. viewers, information needs to be supplied for a full appreciation of *The German Sisters*. Gudrun Ensslin was involved for some years as a student activist at the University of Tübingen and the Berlin Free University. In 1967, Gudrun rejected open political work and began to engage in terrorist activities. In October 1968, Ensslin and three other Baader-Meinhof members were found guilty of bombing and setting fire to a department store and sentenced to three years imprisonment. In June 1969, they gained release from jail pending an appeal to be heard in November 1969. The Supreme Court rejected the appeal. Ensslin and two members went underground. After a brief stay outside Germany, Ensslin returned to Berlin in early 1970. She was re-arrested on June 7, 1972. Ensslin was tried at Stammheim for murder, bank robberies, forming criminal associations, etc., and sentenced to life imprisonment.

3 Tony Pipolo, "German Filmmakers Seldom Focus on the Legacy of Nazism," Sunday *New York Times*

4 This survey is analyzed in an article, "The Imperfectly Mastered Past: Anti-Semitism in West Germnay Since The Holocaust" by Frederick Weil, *New German Critique* (Spring/Summer 1980).

5 According to Weil, the impact of the TV series *Holocaust* as far as altering existing public opinion in Germany seems varied, depending on the specific question posed to those surveyed. For example, in polls conducted shortly before the showing of the U.S. program in Germany, 19% of those surveyed thought that all adult Germans in the Third Reich were guilty to some degree. After the series, this figure rose only six percentage points to 22%. Similarly, prior to *Holocaust*, 45% of those interviewed believed that Germany had a moral obligation to make reparations to Holocaust victims. After the series, an additional 10% held this opinion. According to Weil (who was in Germany at the time *Holocaust* was broadcast), the only issue on which *Holocaust* had any discernible effect was about the war crimes statute of limitations. After *Holocaust*, those who favored enforcing such a statute diminished

from 62% to 50%. Weil writes, "Since the Parliament voted several months later to lift the statute of limitations and permit war criminals to continue to be brought to trial, the film's effect on this issue may have been very great indeed, even if it only encouraged an already existing public opinion."

Such a positive finding, however, must be placed in the overall context of German public opinion to the Nazi period. Analyzing *Holocaust* within a historical framework, Weil concludes, "A quarter or a third of the population still refuses to find the historical Nazi regime all bad, although there is a long term trend towards rejection."

6 Pipolo, op. cit.

7 According to the information presented in Pipolo's article, it is unlikely that the Ensslin sisters would actually have seen such newsreels. Only in 1962 did the Ministers of Education formulate standards for teaching the history of the Third Reich, thereby allowing for such subjects as the Nazi's goals, anti-Semitism, and the Holocaust to be introduced into the German school curriculum.

8 In reality, Ensslin brought her lover, Andreas Baader, into organized political activity. The turning point in Gudrun's decision to reject mass political organizing appears to have been the killing of a young student protester, Benno Ohnesorg, at a protest against the Shah of Iran's visit to Berlin in 1967. The demonstrators lined up in front of the German Opera House. Police began to disperse them using water cannons. A group was trapped in a courtyard. A policeman shot Ohnesorg in the back of the head, claiming self-defense, although Ohnesorg was actually running away in the opposite direction. Gunter Grass called the killing, "the first political murder in the Federal Republic." On June 8, 8000 turned out to hear the funeral orations.

At an SDS meeting during this period, Gudrun seemed at the point of hysteria. She shouted that "the fascist state" is out to "kill us all" and argued that "violence must be met with violence". She emphasized, "It is the Auschwitz generation. You can't argue with them." The policeman responsible for Ohnesorg's murder was merely charged with "careless manslaughter" and found not guilty—a scenario of police brutality which finds similar expression in the U.S.

9 In an earlier film, *The Lost Honor of Katharina Blum*, von Trotta deals with the destructive effects of the sensationalist Springer press. The film is based on the novel (with the same title) by Heinrich Böll. Böll himself was held up to ridicule by the Springer press for denouncing the "trial by press" of Baader-Meinhof member Ulrike Meinhof. In his novel Böll creates the fictional character Katharina Blum. She becomes involved with a man who, unknown to her, is a political fugitive from the law. Blum refuses to cooperate with the police, steadily maintaining that she knows nothing concerning the fugitive. She is taken to task by the Springer press which pursues her case with such a vengeance that first her reputation and then her life are entirely ruined.

10 The bombing and arson charges for which Gudrun first served time in 1968 show the extent to which she had become almost pathologically alienated from the German people. The Frankfurt department store bombing in which Gudrun participated was inspired by an earlier department store burning at À L'innovation store in Brussels. At least 300 people perished in this fire which the terrorists immediately declared a success because "it brought Vietnam home to Brussels," and showed ordinary complacent consumers what it was like to be bombed in Vietnam. A leaflet circulated May 24 at the Berlin Free University where Gudrun attended classes had the caption, "When will the Berlin stores burn?" It ended with the exhortation, "Burn, warehouse, burn." Gudrun and others took up the call. In court, she claimed responsibility for herself and Andreas Baader explaining, "We did it out of protest against the indifference toward the war in Vietnam."

I wish to give special thanks to Ramona Curry, program director of the Goethe Institute in Chicago, without whose valuable assistance and expertise this review could not have been written.

The Political Dimensions of *The Lost Honor of Katharina Blum*

JACK ZIPES

IN THE CASE of novels and films which are explicitly political, the necessity to begin with a specific social reality as the basis for comprehending the narrative techniques and thematic conceptions developed in the works is obvious. Two good examples are Heinrich Böll's novel *The Lost Honor of Katharina Blum* and Volker Schlöndorff's film adaptation of this novel. A comparison of the two works might open up interesting questions concerning narrative techniques and media representations of reality. But what is more significant at present, given the highly problematic reality of political repression in the Bundesrepublik, is the different ways in which Böll and Schlöndorff appropriate and explore the political dimensions of this reality. The ideological and political struggle of the 1970s sets the dimensions for both works of art, and these dimensions are questioned in the novel and film and in turn make these works questionable. But, before we can understand how Böll and Schlöndorff immerse themselves in different artistic processes to question and criticize a similar reality, we must first ask what exactly is this Bundesrepublik reality of 1972–75 which figures in these works of art?

On one level the entire history of the student movement or extra-parliamentary opposition (APO) provides the subject matter of the novel and film. That is, the socio-political attitudes and conditions which are depicted in these works result from the conflicts of the late 1960s and early 1970s. It is important here to be aware of the fact that the SPD government which had at first been open to reforms has yielded to a conservative backlash that has its irrational and brutal side. Whereas political reform characterized the period from 1966 to 1971, it is now political repression which marks the spirit of the 1970s. In part—and only in part—this is due to the fact that some militant terrorists organized as the Baader-Meinhof Group (or the RAF) have played into the hands of the more conservative forces in the government. Due to violent actions of the RAF, the state and mass media have made it appear that the entire Left in the Bundesrepublik and even progressive reformers are ruthless, destructive, brutal, irrational, etc. Thus, an atmosphere of fear and hysteria has been created at times causing the average citizen practically to identify radicalism (i.e., socialism, Marxism) with terrorism. Capitalizing on the mistakes made by the Left

Reprinted from *New German Critique* 12 (1977): 75–84.

which has become divided and sectarian since 1969, the state has persecuted radicals and socialists with a rigorous systematization that smacks of fascist methods.[1] In 1971, a decree was issued against radicals in the civil service which has come to be known as *Berufsverbot* (professional proscription).[2] This decree has legitimated the state's McCarthy-like witchhunt of progressives and reformers in the civil service or those who are applying for civil service jobs. Since 1971, over 800,000 people have been investigated and interrogated by a special police force which has expanded its authority and powers during this period. The increase in police surveillance and intrusion has been justified by the state which plays up various kidnappings, bank robberies and bombings allegedly executed by terrorists. The political repression engendering fear is intended mainly to *prevent* the possibility of organizing a democratic, autonomous public sphere counter to the state and big business. Indeed, the reaction of the state and its police force has been out of proportion to the real threat by terrorists who are small in number and distrusted by the Left itself. The Bundesrepublik has remained very much a land of law and order, and the population very much law-abiding. The danger of a *coup d'état* from the Left or from consistent terrorist attacks is minimal. Nevertheless, political prisoners have been subjected to harsh solitary confinement and maltreatment. Their lawyers have been deprived of their rights as citizens and have experienced an arbitrary curtailment of their legal activities. Many have even been imprisoned, publicly defamed, or have had their homes ransacked. In addition to these attacks by the state on political activists, police control at all borders and public transportation facilities has been augmented. Even citizens have been mobilized to act like police and to be on the constant lookout for "enemies of the state."[3]

The pernicious atmosphere of distrust created by the state to maintain its bureaucratic authoritarian rule and to safeguard the interests of corporate capitalism has been helped by the institutions of mass media where radicals and reformers have either been dismissed or intimidated so that the policy of the state receives little criticism. Indeed, it is difficult to read or obtain sober accounts of political repression or acts of violence in the better known newspapers, magazines, books and TV and radio broadcasts. In particular, the Springer Press, which exercises great control over the popular newspapers, has led a vicious campaign against progressives and radicals and has been joined by other newspapers and mass media organizations which seek to distort the purpose of the reform movements in West Germany. Oskar Negt and Alexander Kluge have described the situation as follows: "In the systems of the monopoly of the press, the mass media and the illusory public sphere, the actual social relations of power are reproduced. Thereby, cause and consequences are reversed. Since this power has an effect upon the relations of power which have already been socially produced and internalized in individuals, an illusion arises as to who the perpetrator is, as to who is individually responsible for a crime. Therefore, it is not by chance that demented people and social outsiders appear as the perpetrators of violent actions. Their acts are prepared by a social production process which itself disappears in the act of violence."[4] In other words, the establishment's perspective will always be *imposed* upon the populace through legal institutions and the mass media which it controls. This in itself is a violation of the rights of citizens to create their own methods and means to perceive and come to terms with social conditions. The violence of the state goes unnoticed since the law and social order legitimate such violence as "government" for the people's interests.

The origins of violence and the violation of human rights through totalitarian methods and institutions have been a major concern in Heinrich Böll's writings from the beginning of his career. This concern has become more intense and political as conditions in the Bundesrepublik have led to a resurgence of police brutality and conservatism. In the winter of 1971 the atmosphere in the Bundesrepublik became hysterical during the manhunt for the Baader-Meinhof Group. Professor Peter Brückner, Director of the Psychological Institute at the Technische Hochschule Hannover, was a victim of this panic created by the state and mass media. Falsely accused of hiding members of the Baader-Meinhof Group, he was smeared by newspapers, magazines, radio and TV and was suspended from the university.[5] Soon thereafter, the same thing happened to Böll, who wrote an article in *Spiegel* requesting pardon for Ulrike Meinhof.[6] Not only was Böll subjected to a vicious defamatory campaign by the Springer Press, but he was privately harassed and his house was raided by the police. From 1972 until the publication of *The Lost Honor of Katharina Blum* Böll consistently defended the democratic rights of political prisoners and has opposed the unwarranted political repression of the state. Moreover, as a novelist and journalist he has voiced his concern about the demagoguery of the mass media and has urged a reform of the press, radio and TV. The act of writing his novel *Katharina Blum* must be seen then as social and artistic engagement with the political reality of the Bundesrepublik.

The subtitle of *Katharina Blum* explains the purpose of Böll's undertaking: *How Violence Can Develop and Where It Can Lead*. His fictive narrative is a case study of violence, and the fiction is to shed more light on reality than the supposed non-fiction reports which are carried by the mass media. Both the narrative style and the subject matter form a counter model to the objective conditions of Bundesrepublik reality. First of all, we have a narrator who is scrupulous in assembling facts, reports, data, etc. His purpose is to provide his readers with a complete, sober account of how an act of violence originated and what the consequences mean. Secondly, the heroine of the novel, what one might call an average petty bourgeois citizen of the Bundesrepublik, resists the political repression and slander of the state and mass media. The independent actions of both the narrator and the heroine are untypical of present-day Bundesbürger, who comply with the laws of the state and tend to be unquestioningly obedient, and yet, in their untypicality they demonstrate ways of uncovering the reasons for the existence of violence in their society.

This is not to argue that Böll has created the perfect model for explaining the socio-political dynamics of violence in the Bundesrepublik. On the contrary, Böll's case study is limited, and in its limitations can be found its effectiveness. Rainer Nägele has already pointed to this: "The political dimension of this narrative is limited. It is precisely for this reason that one should not unnecessarily generalize about it so that it loses its real connections. The political dimension finds its strongest expression thematically and formally in the language."[7] Both the narrator and Katharina Blum are extremely cautious in their use of words, for it is in such use that they express their attitudes toward other people. The socio-linguistic level of the novel serves as the basis for Böll's critique of both the state and mass media. Whereas the inspector Beizmenne and the reporter Werner Tötges fling words around indiscriminately, causing traumatic experiences for other people under the illusion of truth, the narrator and Katharina Blum weigh each word in a painstaking manner to create genuine communication and to share experiences. Their efforts are made to foster comprehension and more humane social behavior. The entire second chapter of the novel is worth citing as an example of the socio-linguistic mode which Böll sets up as exemplary. "If this report—since there is such frequent mention of sources—should at times be felt to be 'fluid,' we beg the reader's forgiveness: it has been unavoidable. To speak of 'sources' and 'fluidity' is to preclude all possibility of composition, so perhaps we should instead introduce the concept of 'bringing together,' of 'conduction,' a concept that should be clear to anyone who as a child (or even as an adult) has ever played in, beside, or *with* puddles, draining them, linking them by channels, emptying, diverting, and rerouting them until the entire available puddlewater-potential is *brought together* in a collective channel to be diverted onto a different level or perhaps even duly rerouted in orderly fashion into the gutter or drain provided by the local authorities. The sole objective here, therefore, is to effect a kind of drainage. Clearly a due process of order! So whenever this account appears to be in a fluid state in which differences in and adjustment to level play a part, we ask the reader's indulgence, since there will always be stoppages, blockages, siltings, unsuccessful attempts at conduction, and sources 'that can never come together,' not to mention subterranean streams, and so on, and so on."[8] Böll's narrator, somewhat pedantic, somewhat ironic, but nevertheless straightforward, reveals great integrity as researcher in this passage. His scruple about finding the right word to describe the process for putting together his data and his admission that he might not be able to bring everything together are signs of openness which allow us as readers to share in his discoveries with a critical eye. As described by the narrator, his work of 58 small chapters is a *process* of piecing together material in which the reader participates. This is in contrast to the police and the mass media which hit the reader over the head, confront the audience not with truth but the power of their positions. Interesting is that Böll's narrator describes his narrative process as a kind of drainage, and certainly the draining of his anger is partially behind Böll's purpose of writing. But the draining is also intended to clear up blockages and allow for communication on all levels—the public and the private.

The narrator's struggle for open communication is public and contains a critique of the mass media. Katharina's life history as it is presented to us shows the private side of the same public struggle. Her childhood, marriage, working relationships and friendships depict a woman struggling to define herself and establish contact with people whom she can trust. The intrusion of the public sphere with its system of power relations is immanent in her life, and her self-clarification process must take form in opposition to the public sphere. That the power relations are so one-sided, i.e., the fact that she has virtually little power to determine her life and self-expression, leads ultimately to her act of violence. However, unlike the newspaper, radio and TV reports, Böll's narrative reverses power relations and sets new political dimensions so that her act of violence can be judged as an act of integrity.

Yet, the reversal of power relations and the new set of political dimensions do not completely shed light "on how violence can develop" in West Germany. The major weakness of Böll's novel lies in its strength—the moralist focus on an exceptional case of political resistance. In other words, we are presented with a phenomenon that apparently has no connections to the manifold cases of political repression and the widespread political controls used by the state to prevent democratic self-organization and open dissent in the 1970s. The maltreatment of Katharina could indeed be considered a "blunder," just as there have been so-called "blunders" by the FBI and the CIA in the United States. One could argue that the police are merely overzealous in tracking down a wanted criminal, and that in the process a muckraking journalist tries to make this a sensational story about sex and intrigue. Certainly we gain no sense of the wholesale nature of political repression in the Bundesrepublik as in Peter Schneider's . . . *Schon bist du ein Verfassungsfeind*. There are no allusions to numerous other cases and examples, and Katharina remains untypical in a negative and positive sense. This is not to argue according to Engels' dictum of "typicality" that Böll's novel fails to capture the political totality of the Bundesrepublik, but to point to the limitation of his moralist and individualistic approach. Ultimately, the power of his narrative is derived from his concentration on language and a singular incident and also from his countering the systematic deprivation of human freedoms with idealis-

tic models embodied in the narrator and Katharina Blum. From this perspective which informs the style and characterization of the novel, the
individual heroic stance for humanitarian behavior becomes the focus of
reality. On the other hand, the origins of violence become too personalized for us to gain a clear picture of the power relationships of the political reality in the Bundesrepublik.

It was with the hope of making the network of power relationships in
the *Bundesrepublik* reality more clear that Volker Schlöndorff along with
Margarethe von Trotta decided to adapt *Katharina Blum* for the screen.
His choice of *Katharina Blum* indicates his relationship to mass communication and the Bundesrepublik reality. After his first films appeared—incidentally he has done screen adaptations of Robert Musil's *Die Ver-
wirrungen des Zöglings Törless* (1967) and Heinrich von Kleist's *Michael
Kohlhaas* (1968/69)—Schlöndorff took an active part in organizing an
alternative film distribution company which sought to provide an outlet
for political filmmakers who would also control the reception of their
products. In commenting on this project he has stated: "Now I see that the
few people who make films are not only able to bring a child into this
world but must also look after its growth. Filmmaking today also includes
the responsibility of production and distribution, and because of this,
almost two-thirds of the attention is being focused on these other fields."[9]
While assisting in the establishment of Hallelujah Film GmbH in 1969,
Schlöndorff began opposing the power relations in the public sphere
especially where the mass media was used to cover up the manipulation of
truth and the political acts of violence perpetrated by the state. Since the
early 1970s he has been somewhat disappointed by the fact that the left
movement which was in the process of creating a counter public sphere in
the late 1960s has abandoned many of these significant organizational
attempts to channel and make protest more effective. As he puts it, "one
cannot militate with film in a society where there is no militant activity at
all."[10]

It is due to the lack of a cohesive left movement that Schlöndorff utilizes established corporations and institutions to point to the necessity to
oppose political repression. Given his concern for collective opposition to
such repression, it is perhaps contradictory that he would choose
Katharina Blum as his subject matter to make a comment on the present
state of things. When asked whether he believed that the *individual* act of
violence by Katharina Blum was the sole response possible to political
manipulation in the Bundesrepublik, he answered: "I don't believe at all
that this is the sole response, nor is it the best. But I say that it exists. Our
task is not to discuss that it exists but rather to confirm its existence. This
is, by the way, the situation that produced the Baader-Meinhof Group and
immediately produced in turn that complementary disproportionate
response which has spread throughout Europe, for example the anti-

terrorist convention which is an instrument that one will make use of in ten years to eliminate the opposition movements in France or Italy."[11]

The purpose in making *Katharina Blum* then was to reach a wide audience through an American distributor and to raise the consciousness of this audience so that it would become more critical of political repression. In other words, Schlöndorff saw in the material of Böll's novel a vehicle to delineate the political reality of the Bundesrepublik more clearly for a popular audience which might be moved to think more critically about its situation *vis-à-vis* violence and repression. His starting point was the political reality and the problem of spreading word about this reality more efficaciously—a problem of production and distribution.

Schlöndorff focuses on the power relations in the case of Katharina Blum in order to facilitate the viewer's comprehension of how the police and mass media conspire to victimize private citizens. Yet, in his attempt to reduce the complex problem of police machinations, mass media manipulation and individual violence to intelligible terms and to capture this in images for a mass audience, Schlöndorff becomes too simplistic. Everything is told in black and white. Stereotypes abound. Melodrama is used to move our emotions but not our critical understanding. As Schlöndorff himself has stated, his film about Katharina Blum has allowed him more opportunities to work with TV and other film distributors because the film was fortunately "not too political."[12] The viewers wanted to see a human story of passion. Schlöndorff wanted to make a human story of passion to bring out the intrusive politics of the mass media and state but failed. This is not to say that his film is a total failure. Indeed, it successfully plays upon the emotions of the audience by shifting the narrative perspective from that of the objective reporter in Böll's novel to the point of view of the victimized. The audience is moved through cinematic techniques of close-ups and positioning to identify and suffer with the maltreated and eventually to seek justice. Ironically, however, it is just this kind of manipulation process that Schlöndorff wanted to criticize.

The very beginning of the film sets the audience's visual perspective which almost immediately obliges us to take sides. We watch the police watching and following Ludwig Götten the deserter. Though we are not certain whether Götten is a criminal, the behavior of the police is slanted in such a way that we hope for his escape. He is the silent hero, the oppressed. The cops are sinister plotters. The slanted perspective reaches its heights when the police prepare for the daybreak invasion of Katharina's apartment. Armed to the teeth, the police look like soldiers from outer space. The intricate military preparations are of a scale similar to those for clandestine operations in a foreign country. Their actions border on the preposterous, and we are clearly on Katharina's and Götten's side after the daybreak raid. Schlöndorff's use of such visual and narrative perspective is self-defeating since we are not provided information or background to understand why the police have gone to such preposterous lengths to catch Götten or put Katharina to shame. Like the very political manipulation the film wishes to condemn, we are hit over the head with black and white figures and actions which tell us how to feel and think. All techniques and devices of melodrama are employed to play upon our moral and humanitarian sentiments which is not necessarily bad. As Thomas Elsaesser has argued "melodrama, at its most accomplished, seems capable of reproducing more directly than other genres the patterns of domination and exploitation existing in a given society, especially the relation between psychology, morality, and class consciousness, by emphasizing so clearly an emotional dynamic whose social correlative is a network of external forces directed oppressingly inward, and with which the characters themselves unwittingly collide to become their agents."[13] But here the melodrama actually reproduces the patterns of domination and struggle and conditions of a market commodity where monopoly rules. The viewer *cannot* make up his or her mind about the narrative sequence of events. There are bad cops and good cops, sleazy reporters and good friends, curious gullible people and morally incensed people, hypocrites and trusting souls.

The cinematic account builds one scene of humiliation and degradation upon the next which are clearly caused by the detective Beizmenne's callous attitude toward other human beings and the reporter Tötges' ambition to make money by writing sensational stories. At different points Schlöndorff shows how these two conspire together to attain their ends, secretly exchanging information, patting shoulders and padding pockets. But the reasons for their "villainous" behavior never become clear. Why does Beizmenne pursue Katharina and Ludwig with a vengeance? Why does Tötges have such a low opinion of people? All we see is persecution, systematic slander and victimization. Katharina's act of violence follows logically from the straightforward, melodramatic portrayal. As if this isn't enough, Schlöndorff tries to make us incensed by ending with "an unctuous graveside eulogy by the reporter's boss, who acclaims the democratic virtues of freedom of the press in phrases so dripping with complacent hypocrisy that they might be taken as provocation for a general smashing of the city's newspaper plants."[14]

But, as Schlöndorff knows only too well, movie-goers rarely get up and rush to smash the establishment. Yet, they do and can rethink their positions about social reality, prompted by cinematic technique which seeks to alter perspective. This does not occur in this film because the melodramatic devices prevent the disclosure of how the relations of power intrude not only into the victims' but also the victimizers' lives. The network of relations which cause violence and violation of human rights remains impenetrable because evil is personalized. The workings of the institutions and the effect on the social relations in the Bundesrepublik reality remain a vague backdrop for the film. It is almost like the American TV cops and robbers films—there are good cops and bad cops, and we've got to have *faith* that justice will triumph in the end.

Both Böll and Schlöndorff ultimately fail to lay bare the manner in which West Germans internalize the power structure of their state and become legislators of their own fear. Schlöndorff's film is particularly weak since he melodramatizes Böll's narrative in an attempt to provide more causal links. In doing this, he binds the spectator to a narrative thread which is much more intricate in Böll's novel and in reality. The oppression depicted and criticized in the film is ironically maintained by the cinematic technique. Böll manages to break this somewhat by creating a fictional model for scrupulous reporting while Schlöndorff relies too much on melodrama to convey oppositional views about state power and the abuse of the mass media to a mass audience. The melodramatic portrayal only reaffirms what most people think about the establishment and police officers. Böll at least shows us how language can be used more carefully and considerately for grasping social and political relationships. The language and narrative technique provide us with a basis for approaching similar cases and channeling protest. Obviously, the Bundesrepublik political reality does not receive adequate portrayal, but the tools to deal with that reality are developed. In Schlöndorff's film, there is an implicit critique of Böll in that the filmmaker does try to trace the conspiratorial nature in the behavior of members of the state and mass media. Yet, in trying to make the implicit in Böll more explicit, he does not develop a cinematic technique which could free the viewer from traditional Manichean patterns.

The weaknesses in the art works of Böll and Schlöndorff as political works ironically tell us more about the political reality of the BRD than their actual messages. The potential for art works to be politically efficacious, to take hold of problems and make them meaningful in our everyday lives depends upon the quality of the political action in a given period. The artistic engagement with the reality of the BRD is bound to be limited by the political dimensions set by the struggle over power in the public sphere. Just as the act of violence by Katharina Blum is an act of frustration, so, too, the artistic acts of Böll and Schlöndorff result from a breakdown in communication and a frustrated struggle to break the stranglehold of repression that maims expression.

Notes

1. Cf. the statement by the former Vice-President of the Free University of West Berlin, Uwe Wesel, "Zur gegenwärtigen Offensive des Staatsapparats," *alternative*, 95–96 (April–June, 1974), 50–51.

2. There are now volumes of literature on this subject. For the best and most recent anthology of essays, see Wolf-Dieter Narr, ed., *Wir Bürger als Sicherheitsrisiko* (Reinbek bei Hamburg). See also, Hans-Jochen Brauns & David Kramer, "Political Repression in West

Germany," *New German Critique*, 7 (1976), 105–121; Wolf-Dieter Narr, "Threats to Constitutional Freedom in West Germany," *New Critique*, 8 (1976), 20–42; Martin Oppenheimer, "The New German Repression," *Nation* (September 11, 1976), 201–02.

3. See Sebastian Cobler, *Die Gefahr geht von den Menschen aus* (Berlin, 1976) and Jürgen Seifert, "Defining the Enemy of the State," *New German Critique*, 8 (1976), 42–53.

4. *Öffentlichkeit und Erfahrung* (Frankfurt am Main, 1972), p. 140.

5. Hanno Beth discusses the importance of Brückner's situation for Böll in "Rufmord und Mord: die publizistische Dimension der Gewalt," in *Heinrich Böll*, ed. Hanno Beth (Kronberg/Ts, 1975), pp. 59–61.

6. See Frank Grützbach, ed., *Heinrich Böll: Freies Geleit für Ulrike Meinhof* (Cologne, 1972).

7. *Heinrich Böll: Einführung in das Werk und in die Forschung* (Frankfurt am Main, 1976), pp. 164–65.

8. *The Lost Honor of Katharina Blum*, tr. Leila Vennewitz (New York, 1975), pp. 8–9.

9. Barbara Bronnen & Corinna Brocker, eds., *Die Filmemacher. Der neue deutsche Film nach Oberhausen 1962* (Düsseldorf, 1973), p. 86.

10. "Cinema et consensus social: un entretien avec Volker Schlöndorff," *Politique Aujourd'hui*, 1–2 (1977), 125.

11. Ibid., p. 127.

12. Ibid., p. 125.

13. "Tales of Sound and Fury: Observations of the Family Melodrama," *Monogram*, no. 4 (1972), 14.

CONSTELLATION F
QUEER CONSTRUCTS: POLITICS OF DESIRE

How is it that the incursions made by Queer studies into the contemporary academy have had such scant theoretical impact in the field of German cinema studies? While texts of the new cultural studies are largely dominated by progressive configurations of phenomenology, aesthetics, and empiricism, texts of German cinema studies have persisted in proffering rather conservative equations between queerness, seen as sexual "perversion" or "deviance," and Nazism, seen as the epitome of ethico-moral decay. Note, for instance, Imke Lode's analysis of the state-terrorism relation in psychoanalytic terms of sadomasochism, which while staging a necessary and socially engaged critique of the facile anarchical deployment of "homosexuality" as a flagship for the break-up of entrenched social forms, reinscribes a pre-Queer studies tendency to normalize sexual identifications through a process of dynamical conflation and collapse. Or consider that, with the exceptions of B. Ruby Rich's widely disseminated, nay canonized, essay on the classic lesbian film, Mädchen in Uniform, *and Patricia White's textual analysis of the experimental lesbian cult-favorite,* Madame X, *the dominant theoretical tendency regarding queerness in German cinema studies has been the* auteur-*oriented reading of Fassbinder (i.e., gay male) films. Because this constellation marks the beginning of the second half of the anthology, we ask the stereoscopic reader to consider how the exceptional theoretical dearth its topic signifies for German cinema studies ironically counterposes, and therefore subtly continues, both the Anglo-American academic construction of the "German" as a site of overdetermined absence, and the German national-public dissimulation of that concept as the problematical "Heimat." While Patricia White's close reading of* Madame X *demands critical attention to the elisions that have traditionally marked feminist film theory, following from its failure to account for the lesbian spectator, for instance, does it avoid more traditional tendencies toward sexual normalization and auteurism? How does its formalist mapping of* Madame X's *modernist strategies, which include the practice of criminal violence, contrast post-al rearticulations of such strategies in Roswitha Müller's and Christopher Sharrett's readings of* Dorian Grey *and* Querelle, *respectively? Do either Müller or Sharrett, with their inscriptions of queer imagery and/or desire onto such inchoate notions as "gender-fuck" and the post-al "simulacrum," enable a politicized reading of queerness at the postnationalist moment, or do their invocations of post-al sex/gender heterogeneity imply that the theorization of a radical disorderly sexual subject is, practically speaking, impossible?*

413

Terrorism, Sadomasochism, and Utopia in Fassbinder's *The Third Generation*

IMKE LODE

To Hector Rodriguez

"THAT'S WHY *The Third Generation* (1978–79) is a comedy, because the terrorists behave like politicians. They actually work for the system in order to confirm the existing order and to make it final."[1] Rainer Werner Fassbinder's description of terrorism exemplifies one of the director's fundamental strategies in this film: to establish a rigid opposition between two contradictory terms (between the state and terrorism), and then to subvert that opposition by revealing that the two elements secretly mirror one another.

It is my thesis that the filmmaker undermines the distinction between the Law and violent political subversion through his insistence that the two practices engage in a similar form of rationally organized and callously executed violence. The first task of this paper, then, will be to illuminate the nature of this oxymoronic double-bind: the terrorists take part in the same social order they are trying to fight. As I will demonstrate, Fassbinder aesthetically inscribes a utopian dimension with the possibility of social change into the dynamics of his film's relation of violence between state and terrorists. It is a dynamic relation insofar as violence is executed and power is distributed and attained on continually unstable and shifting grounds. Thus, personal and political relations can be perceived as constantly shifting bonds of domination and submission within the network of power. This flux of positions creates the possibility for a continuous reinvention of identity and relatedness between and beyond fixed boundaries, articulated through what I will call a "sadomasochistic aesthetics." The second task of this paper will therefore be to illuminate this cinematic strategy as well as the social utopia—the capacity to imagine a better world—it generates. Although my approach does not claim to exhaust the multiple thematic and formal layers of the film, I hope this analytic framework will be fruitful for the study of Fassbinder's work as a whole and *The Third Generation* in particular.

The film tells the story of a group of terrorists who plot a break-in into the public office of registration, plan a bank robbery, and conspire to kidnap the industrialist P. J. Lurz—all supposedly "in the name of the

---

This essay was written specifically for this volume and is published here for the first time by permission of the author

people and for the sake of the same." Spoken dead seriously by the terrorists, this original German expression, "im Namen des Volkes und zum Wohle desselben" ironically evokes—much more than its English translation—its usual application by representatives of the Law (courts, police). Thus, state and organized subversion are rendered interchangeable: not only their violent methods, but their asserted motivations and goals also appear identical because both use the same rhetoric and linguistic tools to express them.

The film's title, *The Third Generation* illuminates this point further. By referring to the terrorists as the "third generation," Fassbinder places them in a lineage of political subversion, while emphasizing the differences between these latest terrorists and their predecessors: the first generation, that of 1968, was motivated by an idealism which the second generation, the Baader-Meinhof Group or Red Army Faction, inherited and took one step further into illegal armed struggle. In contrast, the third generation in Fassbinder's film lacks any motivating idealism or ideology, and in the director's own words "doesn't [even] know what it is doing."[2] It is a group of people that acts exclusively for its own sake, trying to live "the last adventure of humanity," shaping their thoughtless actions after terrorist models, "denn das macht man eben so" ("because that's the way one's supposed to do it"). As Fassbinder stresses in his preproduction essay on the film, this last generation distinguishes itself from the previous two because it has "less in common with its predecessors than with this society and the violence it perpetrates, to whoever's benefit."[3]

This similarity, this mirroring effect between society and terrorists, can be understood in terms of sadomasochistic power relations that both state-supported *and* subversive violence engage in and perpetuate. Fassbinder's cinematic strategy seems, thereby, to echo one of Herbert Marcuse's main arguments in *Eros and Civilization*:

> [F]ormerly autonomous and identifiable psychical processes are being absorbed by the function of the individual in the state—by his public existence. Psychological problems therefore turn into political problems: private disorder reflects more directly than before the disorder of the whole, and the cure of personal disorder depends more directly than before on the cure of the general disorder. The era tends to be totalitarian even where it has not produced totalitarian states.[4]

Fassbinder insists on the interrelationship between seemingly personal psychological structures and social practices and institutions, showing how libidinal relations shape, and are in turn dialectically determined by, the dominant social order. Processes of domination and submission recur throughout the political and sexual spheres, undermining the distinction between the two. The characters' relations in *The Third Generation* demonstrate this interwoven structure in their transgressive sexual, generational, socioeconomical, and psychological interconnectedness with each other.

The film thus undermines any clear protagonist-antagonist opposition, and refuses to provide any one hero or heroine, thereby simultaneously inviting and frustrating a viewer's desire to identify with any single character in the group of terrorists. Of course, to speak of a generic spectator is always problematic. But Fassbinder's desire to address a broad audience, to create a large public sphere for social change, is of particular political concern to him in this film. Against the backdrop of the kidnapping and killing of Hans-Martin Schleyer by the Red Army Faction and the violent state response—the liberation of the kidnapped Lufthansa airplane "*Landshut*" in Mogadishu by a special military unit—, the filmmaker intended *The Third Generation* to redefine "cinema a[s a] center of communication"[5] in response to these immediate events of 1977–78. The entire West German democratic system was questioned in its national and political identity, in its relationship to terrorism, in its citizens' partaking in and perpetuation of a network of violent power relations. Accordingly, the group of terrorist protagonists in *The Third Generation* exhibits this dialectic relation: they are also their own antagonists due to their sadomasochistic entwinements with each other and the state.

The character of Susanne Gast (Hanna Schygulla) exemplifies this scenario: as the devoted secretary of computer magnate Peter J. Lurz (Eddie Constantine), she promotes his business and thus her own socioeconomic dependence on him. At the same time, however, she uses her professional situation to aid her terrorist friends in kidnapping him. This attempt to undermine Lurz's position serves, ironically, its opposite end: the increase of terrorist activity enables the industrialist to sell even more of his security devices to the state and others for protection against precisely such subversive attacks. Police chief Gerhard Gast (Hark Bohm) summarizes this grotesque paradox when telling Lurz about a dream he had: "I had a dream the other day, in which capitalism has invented terrorism in order to force the state to protect it better. It's very funny, isn't it?"

Besides this interdependent socioeconomic relation with Lurz, Susanne's untenable situation "between all stools" becomes further complicated: she is sexually involved with her father-in-law, Gerhard Gast, in whose house she lives with his wife, her husband and child. He is the same police chief who is in charge of protecting Lurz from terrorism and of leading the brutal campaign against the terrorists.

Consequently, Susanne's circumstances demonstrate a no-win situation in which her own attempts to refute and escape from the violence of the patriarchal, Oedipal, and capitalist order only lead her right back into the father's house—just through a different entrance. Her position is inescapable due to the penetration of violence and a submission-dominance pattern running through all spheres of her life: be they political or psychological, economical or sexual.

Consciously or not, Susanne turns her awareness, sadness, disgust, and anger against herself, that is, when she assists in the kidnapping of Lurz, thereby eliminating her own job and exposing herself to be killed by her father-in-law and lover Gerhard Gast. On the other hand, her own physical and verbal violence against, for example, Lurz, Gast, and her co-terrorist husband Edgar (Udo Kier) deploys her sadistic libido in a narrative of desperate activity and (terrorist) action. At the same time, Fassbinder emphasizes how much her behavior is grounded in a desire to escape her sadomasochistic entanglements which have become devoid of any pleasure.

In the scene portraying her last sexual encounter with Gast in a hotel, Susanne recognizes her self-destructiveness with a seriousness which borders on pathos, laying bare her self-reflexive feelings below the melodramatic cover of her incestuous relationship. The dark hotel room is primarily illuminated by a vertical line of flashing red neon letters outside the window that visually splits the room into two sides, each occupied by one of the characters. The frontal medium close-up of Susanne's face, in alternation either covered by the light of the red neon letters or enveloped in complete darkness, seems to double her experience of a divided Self: both impotent and capable of effective agency, both lost in helpless submission and recovered in painful self-assertion. She calmly explains to Gast that their hatred for one another is far less important to her than her own self-hate. In response to Gast's hysterical laughter at her admitted self-disgust, she asserts: "This isn't funny, not funny at all. On the contrary, Gerhard, because I really despise myself. And that hurts to despise oneself." This sequence can be read in terms of Thomas Elsaesser's notion of a "self-estranged exhibitionism:"[6]

> [T]he individual's most satisfying experience of subjectivity may be paradoxically as an exhibitionist, a conformist, in the experience of the self as object, not for anyone in particular but under the gaze of the Other—be it history, destiny, the moral imperative, the community, peer groups: anyone who can be imagined as a spectator.[7]

Susanne's self-display of vulnerability is not, however, positively affirmed: at first, Gast's gaze is held on-screen, and instead, replaced by his reaction in the form of an off-screen histrionic laughter. When he is finally displayed, Gast's continuous, sadistically ridiculing laughter is grotesquely encaged in a high-angle extreme close-up that distorts his face into a clownish grimace, eerily side-lit by a night table lamp. This visual strategy seems to obviate the possibility of spectatorial identification with him.

The viewer's emotional investment in the dramatic scenario is further complicated by an insistent deployment of distancing devices: during most of Susanne's self-revealing monologue, the camera does not show her but rather the red neon letters outside the window. During a long take, the flashing neon sign is displayed by the camera in a slow downward tilt from Susanne's point-of-view while simultaneously detracting from her as the center of dramatic interest. By emphasizing such alienating visual effects, Fassbinder opens up the possibility that the viewer might adopt a sadistic attitude toward Susanne's self-hatred, coldly enjoying her exhibitionistic suffering.

These cinematic strategies testify to the complexity with which Fassbinder undermines any one-sided articulation of spectatorial desire and identificatory positions along sadistic or masochistic lines. While Fassbinder's use of certain cinematic modes (e.g., shot–reverse shot sequences, melodramatic point-of-view shots, Oedipal narratives) have been associated with the influence of classic Hollywood melodrama in the tradition of Douglas Sirk, the filmmaker also distances his cinematic characters via frequent mirror shots and several layers of diegetic framing (doorways, arches, windows, hallways, artificial spaces/frames created through various light sources). In reference to *Despair*, Elsaesser has elaborated on how Fassbinder has used such a notion of complexity and ambiguity in his visual compositions with the effect of mobilizing cinematic self-reflexivity. The red flashing light, for example, has been associated with a film projector, thus stressing Fassbinder's cinematic self-reflexivity (cf. Peter Ruppert, "Fassbinder, Spectatorship, and Utopian Desire," *Cinema Journal* 28.2 [Winter 1989], p. 40). Elsaesser's analysis also holds true for *The Third Generation*:

> Rather than define characters by the degree to which they participate in or act upon events, what counts is their relationship to the screen, how they figure in the constantly created and rearranged field that fixes positions for characters, audience and camera.[8]

Along the same line, Fassbinder's cinematic self-reflexivity extends to the soundtrack in which the ambiguity of the audience's sadomasochistic positioning is reiterated: through the constant sound-bombardment with diegetic and off-screen television news, multiple layers of music and dialogues, the film terrorizes the viewer in the most literal sense. The spectator is forced to constantly struggle with either masochistically submitting to the aggressive flow of sound or with trying to overcome the soundtrack's dominance by focussing consciously on the visual elements of the film.[9]

The violence of the spectatorial experience thereby mirrors the themes of psychic and political, individual and social, sadomasochistic relations of aggression and power on a third level—the cinematic screen. At the level of sound, plot, characterization, camera placement, and spectatorial position, Fassbinder insists on the impossibility of a clear separation between perpetrator and victim, and, consequently, of any easy alignment with a leftist political agenda of representing the underdog sympathetically, and of suggesting any tangible alternatives for sociopolitical change. Among others, Richard Dyer and Thomas Elsaesser have criticized this absence, especially in terms of the filmmaker's refusal to politically empower the working class or address homosexual identity as a "positive alternative" to the bourgeois, Oedipally structured society.[10] These criticisms seem to be partly justified, yet they reveal, perhaps, more about their authors' desires to find a leftist politics in Fassbinder's films than about the filmmaker's openly contradictory cinematic strategies which defy any "positive-negative" categorization, any clear bipolar alternatives. They deny the temptation of masochism which can be part of the traditionally leftist privileging of oppressed groups, by revealing *all* of them as partaking in sadomasochistic power relations.[11]

I do not, however, argue that, in Fassbinder's eyes, a leftist politics should neither privilege victimized minorities nor provide locales of personal and political resistance—quite the contrary. Yet, whenever domination is perceived as a rigid victim-victimizer dichotomy,[12] any radical identification with the oppressed runs the risk of becoming trapped within a masochist position. By desiring his or her own submission, the masochist also partakes in and perpetuates a network of power relations. A cinematic (and [thus] political) masochist locale seems therefore limited and limiting in its capacity to contribute to political change.

Thomas Elsaesser actually characterizes one of the evolutions of Fassbinder's thematics as a "replace[ment] of the oppressor/ oppressed model [of his early films] by the sadomasochistic double-bind."[13] In the course of his argument, though, Elsaesser abandons its sadistic dimension. He deciphers the mechanisms which, in his eyes, Fassbinder tries to lay bare as only "livable 'from within' the vicious circle," thus positing "masochism to the point of self-abandonment . . . [as] the gesture of freedom that alone restores identity."[14] In Elsaesser's view, then, Fassbinder revokes the political dimension of melodrama's challenge to the "bourgeois split and separation between public and private,"[15] since the filmmaker seems to arrest the possibility for social change at the spectatorial and diegetic site of self-pitying pessimism[16] and of individual narcissism and paranoia in the psychological and political realm of (self-assigned) exile and submission to fate and futility.[17]

Kaja Silverman equally locates a masochistic aesthetic in Fassbinder's films, but, in contrast to Elsaesser, she sees in it a subversive potential to create "a certain kind of homosexual man as 'a woman's soul enclosed in a man's body.' "[18] She describes the Freudian male masochist in these terms:

> And although he seems to subordinate himself to the law of the father, that is only because he knows how to transform punishment into pleasure, and severity into bliss. This male masochist deploys the diversionary tactics of demonstration, suspense, and impersonation against the phallic "truth" or "right," substituting perversion for the *père-version* of exemplary male subjectivity.[19]

Appropriating this idea for her reading of Fassbinder's films *In a Year of Thirteen Moons* and *Berlin Alexanderplatz*, Silverman concludes that these films "are committed to the utter ruination of masculinity. At the same time, they make the process of experiencing and observing that ruination conducive of a pleasure bordering on ecstasy."[20] Fassbinder's pursuit of a "ruination" pushed to its limits indeed targets a potential turn into its opposite of "delirious joy." *Jouissance* in *The Third Generation* does not, however, seem connected to a celebration of terrorism and violence per se but to the joy of playful forms of human identity and relatedness. Silverman's celebration of masochistic bliss remains limited in accounting for the multiplicity of Fassbinder's various forms of gendered/sexualized spectatorial pleasure. Her exclusively masochistic reading runs as much along Oedipal lines as a possible understanding of Fassbinder's narratives in merely sadistic terms.

As the active counterpart to masochism, sadism may be inherent in the libidinal urge to shape the world in accordance with desire. It can be viewed as the very movement that seeks to conquer and master the world in pursuit of pleasurable fulfillment. It is this moment of action which the character of Susanne Gast tries to envision and engage in without becoming trapped in its reverse implications and circular masochistic inversions. Laura Mulvey, in her well-known essay "Visual Pleasure and Narrative Cinema" (1975), has pointed out that sadism and narrative are profoundly connected: "Sadism demands a story, depends on making something happen, forcing a change in another person, a battle of will and strength, victory/defeat, all occurring in a linear time with a beginning and an end."[21] Mulvey, however, argues that sadism follows an Oedipal logic; but, once again, Fassbinder's film shows sadism (*and* masochism) to be present even in those interpersonal relations and stories that do not follow a clear heterosexual Oedipal pattern. Homosexual and bisexual characters, who resist stable patriarchically constructed gender-identities, may nonetheless engage in patterns of domination and submission.

In *The Third Generation*, the professionally trained assassin Paul (Raul Gimenez) is both the target of August's (Volker Spengler) homosexual attraction and of Hilde's (Bulle Ogier), Susanne's, and Petra's (Margit Carstensen) combined voyeuristic heterosexual stares upon his introduction to the group. Furthermore, he is also the rapist of Hilde, whose "Reich" without a "Führer" he invades in a fascist move to sadistically conquer a new, "foreign" territory. The accompanying sound track's playing of the German national anthem at a sporting event underscores and doubles this fascist subtext.

Consequently, even the very labels "homosexual," "heterosexual," and "bisexual" are inadequate to express the excessive mobility of a sadomasochistic, preoedipal desire that cuts across and undermines any clear gender categorization or fixed sexual identity. The sadomasochistic scenario is a dynamic one in which the victim can easily exchange this position for that of the perpetrator. In this dynamic lies the power that overflows the narrative confines of the Oedipal drama, pointing toward the utopian dimension of those relations that retain the polymorphous perversity of the preoedipal child.[22] The primacy of the Oedipal scenario with regard to violence, submission-dominance structures, and the formation of sexual orientation and gender is called into question.

Both Elsaesser and Silverman, however, remain faithful to analyses that focus on the Oedipal triangle. Diverging from the Freudian notion that masochism develops in the context of the Oedipal child "witnessing" the primal scene, Gaylyn Studlar appropriates Gilles Deleuze's concept of masochism in her theory of a cinematic masochistic pleasure rooted in the infant's oral stage and its relation to the presymbolic mother. In its masochistic desire to submit to the phallic mother, the infant tries to disavow its separation from the stage of symbiosis with the mother. This previous symbiotic relationship had enabled the child to (incestuously) identify with its mother's procreational powers and to preserve a polymorphous/polysexual identity. Thus, Studlar concludes that the infant, the masochist, and the film spectator engage, not in a sadistic look yearning to master the woman of the Oedipal scenario, but rather in a pleasurable gaze of submission to the female as "maternal imago."[23]

Studlar (and Deleuze) insist on the separation of sadism and masochism as two very distinct perversions with two very different "languages" and aesthetics.[24] Yet they overlook the seeming differences in the aesthetics of Sacher-Masoch and Sade (upon whose literary works they exclusively rely to establish their theories of sadism and masochism) that might be more circumstantial, that is, individually psychosocial and historical, rather than necessarily prescriptive for the definition of two very different perversions. Louise J. Kaplan, in fact, points out:

> [W]e come much closer to an understanding of the perverse strategy when we do not think of perversions as separate, neatly defined clinical entities but rather as performances that are designed to bring about different elements or facets of the same overall perverse strategy.[25]

Psychoanalytic clinicians and theorists like Janine Chasseguet-Smirgel[26] and Kaplan have argued that perversions develop as an intertwined continuity of preoedipal and Oedipal traumas. Kaplan writes:

> Perverse scenarios are attempts at rectification of the early infantile abuses and deprivations, but they are also dedicated to creating primal scenes in which a once betrayed and humiliated child defeats and humiliates the betraying parents.[27]
>
> [T]he fetishist brings to his misperception of anatomical differences [in the primal scene] the themes of *absence* and *presence* that belong to early infancy. A little boy who has not been able to make emotional sense of the mysterious absences and presences of his mother will bring his anxieties about abandonment and separation to the later time when he begins to reckon with the differences between the sexes. As an adult, he will reduce a genital difference to a dichotomy—an absence of something or a presence of something.[28]

As both Kaplan and Chasseguet-Smirgel point out, the perverse scenario attempts to disavow the differences between the sexes and the generations, all differences in fact, in order to reconstitute the polymorphously perverse scenario of the preoedipal stage. The desire to retrieve both the lost polysexual identification and the limitless pleasure-principle of the presymbolic phase is itself historical: it depends upon the degree of surplus repression perpetuated by the social gender stereotypes and bourgeois values in any Western society. I am using here Marcuse's notion of "surplus repression" which he defines as follows: "Within the total structure of the repressed personality, surplus-repression is that portion which is the result of specific societal conditions sustained in the specific interest of domination."[29]

Fassbinder illustrates this effect of surplus-repression in his use of a collection of quotes with which he introduces the six parts of his film comedy: they are anonymous graffiti from men's public toilets, oscillating between sexual and social implications. This graffiti demonstrates the meshing of public and private instances of historical German traumas, that is, in particular the Nazi period and the Holocaust. For example, the fourth superimposed intertitle of a continued graffiti dialogue reads as follows, with each line/group of lines written by another person:

> All turks are pigs.
>
> They stink and only think of fucking.
>
> Exactly.
>
> Turks out.
>
> Germany again for the Germans. And everyone, without any exception, everyone will be sent back.

Right! Send them back, the pigs!

Why actually send them back? Just gas them. One ought to exterminate them, the best way is to gas them. Exterminate and gas them—
that's what one should do.

But not the Jews.

You are all pitiable idiots.

Nazipigs.

Dirty Communist.

And one day, it will also be your turn, so help me God.

(this author's translation, adapted from the screen's original, superimposed text and the subtitles)

This graffiti is contextualized as part of a capitalist discourse due to its
locale of origin, the men's toilet in one of the biggest department
stores in Germany, the KaDeWe in Berlin. But, more importantly, it
depicts a movement from xenophobia via sexuality and neo-Nazi slo-
gans to assaults directed both to left- and right-wing political positions.
This underlines the meshing and confusion of highly problematic
issues of Germany's Nazi past with which, as Fassbinder seems to suggest, Germans have not successfully dealt. Psychic and sexual conflicts
related to the formation of individual German identities are indeed difficult to untangle and, thus, cannot be successfully unraveled here, and
perhaps nowhere, completely. Yet, the apparent finger-pointing at the
next postulated enemy in this graffiti dialogue seems to reveal a desire
of these speakers for an unambiguous moral clarity (*Klarheit*) and
racial, ethnic, and sexual purity (*Reinheit*). Fassbinder highlights this
subtext by means of the contrast between, on the one hand, the desire
for a "clean" *Reinheit* and, on the other, the graffiti's location in a public toilet, the site of a literal display of uncleanliness and anality. The
filmmaker stresses the contemporary urgency and reality of these
protofascist themes by providing the precise dates and locations when
and where the graffiti were found during the few weeks of his film
shooting.

Another film-sequence also addresses the current problem of Germans'
relationship to their historical heritage, particularly the intertwinement of
bourgeois values within the Nazi/Holocaust era. During Hilde Krieger's
history lesson on the revolution of 1848, a student indicates this continuity by asking the high school teacher: "Didn't the same bourgeois values,
'Bewahrung des Besitzstandes, Ruhe und Ordnung im Lande, Treue der
Obrigkeit gegenüber, Zuverlässigkeit und Strebsamkeit' [the protection of
property, law and order, loyalty to the authorities, trustworthiness and
ambition] lead to the Third Reich, and up to today?" But Hilde, history

teacher and terrorist—a warrior as her last name "Krieger" suggests—refuses to discuss this question. She stubbornly insists that this question on the development of the Third Reich does not belong in this present lesson on 1848. The student's question posits, however, that the historical past is not something absolutely other, totally cut off from the present. Fassbinder insists that the past is, rather, the *prehistory* of the present, connected to our time by profound continuities.

It is the interaction between social conditions and individual psychic development which can create traumas and, subsequently, perversions of any kind. I would propose that Fassbinder is attracted to perverse narratives because he sees in them a liberating potential. Liberation does not, however, result from perversion as such, but from the recognition, inherent in the mobility and position shifts of perverse subjectivity, that libidinal and social organizations can be changed. At the same time, perversion is not *simply* liberating. By celebrating perverse pleasure itself as a utopian moment, Studlar and Silverman alike run the danger of ignoring the traumatic subtext that is insinuated below the surface of the screen's display of the perverse scenario (e.g., through fetishistic narratives, character constellations, props). The unambiguous defense of a perverse subjectivity can ultimately only affirm that repressive social order that contributes to causing perversions. Perversion in Fassbinder's films represents both a symptom of social domination and a harbinger of liberation.

What seems to be restaged in Fassbinder's cinematic work, then, is not only Marcuse's aforementioned argument about the intertwinement of psychic and political spheres but also his concept of utopia in the realm of fantasy and, subsequently, art. Following Sigmund Freud's theoretical model of the pleasure principle, Marcuse locates the latter's survival, even after the reorganization of the ego through the reality principle, in the realm of fantasy: "[P]hantasy (imagination) retains the structure and the tendencies of the psyche prior to its organization by the reality, prior to its becoming an 'individual' set off against other individuals."[30] Christian Braad Thomsen, in his essay "Der doppelte Mensch" ("The Double Human Being", 1989), very lucidly locates Fassbinder's bisexuality and personal double-bind of being always simultaneously both lover and child, in precisely that polymorphous-perverse condition prior to the advent of individuality.[31] This is a condition that spills over into Fassbinder's films, "his children", as the filmmaker called them during his last press-conference in Berlin.[32] Braad Thomsen diagnoses the challenge these "cinematic children" pose to the audience: "[O]ur children resist us constantly, their demands we call impossible, their fantasy wild, from their honesty we hide, their anarchy we try to discipline and to protect ourselves against."[33] The preoedipal libido tries to burst the Oedipal walls of family and society, thus embodying a utopian moment of resistance against the fields of patriarchy and capitalism.

Fassbinder does not, as emphasized beforehand, celebrate the "reality" of bisexual or homosexual relationships, insofar as he sees them as equally penetrated by a sadomasochistic power game as heterosexual ones. Rather, the utopian moment seems to lie in the tension of shifting between masochism and sadism, which permits a memory of the polymorphous-perverse promises and, simultaneously, expresses a utopian desire for "the historical possibility of a non-repressive society".[34]

It is the ideal of a nonrepressive society in Fassbinder's films that Peter Ruppert has called a "repressed social desire, that is, the desire for overcoming alienation and fragmentation, or the desire for community and more meaningful social relationships" rather than any "repressed private (sexual) desire—exhibitionism, sadism, masochism."[35] On the one hand, I disagree with Ruppert's separation between social and sexual desires, because I view them as inherently intertwined, continuously interacting with one another (see also Marcuse's concept of entwined psychic and political spheres; Kaplan's and Chasseguet-Smirgel's notion of both pre-oedipal and social influences in the creation of perversion). On the other hand, however, Ruppert directs our attention toward the utopia embedded in Fassbinder's construction of a dialectical relationship between screen and spectator which generates a "search for meaning outside the boundaries of the text."[36] Ruppert states:

> [I]n Fassbinder's films, the display of utopian desire and its wish-fulfilling projections are not a way of turning away from reality—a way of smoothing out social problems with false and illusory solutions—but a way of mediating the viewer's relationship to social reality. Thus, the utopian dimension of Fassbinder's melodramas supports and implies a political practice—a practice in which the possibilities of utopian desire are directed not toward a reality to which desire must adapt, but toward a reality apprehended as something to be changed.[37]

It might have been precisely in order to institute a multifaceted "counter-utopia" that Fassbinder shaped *The Third Generation* by adapting the tradition of the genres of the grotesque and fantastic. In an interview, Fassbinder was asked how to categorize *The Third Generation*, and he used the introductory motto of the film:

> [It is] a comedy, or, rather a parlor game on the topic of terrorism. . . . Biting and mocking, with emotions and suspense, polemics and caricature, brutality and stupidity, in an atmosphere like a dream, a fairy tale. Like the fairy tales you tell children so they're better equipped to bear their lives as people buried alive.[38]

The obviously stylized unreality implicit in Fassbinder's appeal to comedy, dream, and the fairy tale actually works toward its opposite end: to bring "reality" closer to the viewer, since, in Fassbinder's eyes, "the truer things become, the more they become like a fairy tale."[39] The filmmaker uses aesthetic methods, which, in a Brechtian tradition of the *Verfremdungseffekt*, work contrary to a realistic or documentary effect. The playful mode of the fairy-tale produces a shock of recognition which underscores the violence of the present, the memory of a lost past, and the roots of any viable future in the "working through" of the historical heritage *(Vergangenheitsbewältigung)*. The *Verfremdungseffekt* effaces *Entfremdung* (alienation): the shock of recognition eradicates the gap between the supernatural world of the fairy tale and the sociohistorical world of the audience's present.

Toward the same end, the comic elements of *The Third Generation* can be read in terms of a Bakhtinian notion of the Rabelaisian world of laughter which facilitates a disclosure and recognition of power relations and the surmounting of existential fears.[40] As Fassbinder elaborates in an interview with Wolfgang Limmer and Fritz Rummler, he uses laughter as a predecessor to the viewer's shock of recognition:

> And, naturally, I hope that then, beyond the laughter, a kind of shock happens to the viewer. Because this is basically not funny.[41]

Shock and laughter create violent immediacy which produces a space for a possible redefinition of power relations in the utopian realm of the grotesque and the fantastic. As Fassbinder reiterates Susanne's sincerity about her self-contempt, Gerhard Gast's laughter strikes us as the helpless gesture of the grotesque, pointing toward the vastness of her despair, as the sudden void in this otherwise seemingly closed sadomasochistic scenario.

What I call the utopian forms of subjectivity generated by a shifting between masochistic and sadistic positions can be understood as an extension of Peter Ruppert's model in which a third, utopian entity is created outside of the film, through the dialectic relationship between screen and spectator. This third dimension can also be described as an excess that stages unstable identities and narratives with the intention of insinuating an underlying "wish to love." Fassbinder's "wish to love" shines through the veils of the violent sadomasochistic and exploitative relations of the patriarchal and capitalist system he depicts in his films. It expresses the filmmaker's dream of the one ideal state of a nonabusive, radically authentic, and vulnerable humanness, of the libidinally unconstricted polymorphously perverse psychic state of the preoedipal child. Fassbinder states in one of his last interviews:

> Well, I believe . . . that this system we live in is no system in which you can really love. This system is suitable to also exploit love because it is in general

a system of exploitation. And, in fact, no matter how love occurs and in whichever circumstances. This is something quite terrifying. On the one hand, of course, and also in my wishful imagination, there's something you can, sort of, call love. On the other hand, I know quite well that I cannot simply recommend to love. *I can recommend the wish to love, but not to love. But you should always allow the wish to become larger and larger, and clearer and clearer—then perhaps something will happen.* (Emphasis added, this author's translation)[42]

Since Fassbinder locates his entire belief in social change in a radical, anarchist humanness, he focuses strongly on the cinematic spectator since he or she is the crucial site for change—the site where sexual, psychological, and economic processes dialectically entwine. As mentioned in the beginning, Fassbinder's desire to create a public sphere for social change was especially urgent in *The Third Generation*. Fassbinder has himself suggested that *The Third Generation* is his radical answer to those German films which he describes as "very skillfully avoid[ing] the risk that the viewer might be reminded of his own reality".[43] The filmmaker envisions his film as the site where perhaps that can happen which, in his eyes, has neither been performed by the population nor the representatives of the German state: to come to terms with the contemporary problem of terrorism and terrorists, whether practically or even just mentally, that is, ideologically.[44]

His project sounds chillingly urgent for the contemporary, united Federal Republic of Germany where violent neonazism and xenophobia are indeed still prevalent, where guilt and responsibility are easily assigned in ambivalent efforts to distinguish between victims and perpetrators.[45] Yet, ironically and unfortunately, Fassbinder's *The Third Generation* is one of his least screened, least discussed films, and is not even available on videocassette—in the United States or in Germany. His invitation to thoroughly deal with terrorism and violence is perhaps all too frightening, since it ultimately addresses the entire sadomasochistic double-bind that pervades German identity on the personal and social/national level. In this sense, Fassbinder's film offers a therapeutic invitation that has not been accepted: it asks the spectator to sit still, to endure his or her sadomasochistic partaking in the cinematic event and narrative, in the pain, in the mourning process, and in the opportunity to discover a utopia beyond the dynamics of the sadomasochistic scenario.[46] It is an enlightening process that *seeks* to circumvent the traps of enlightenment.

Notes

Special thanks go to Hector Rodriguez whose continuing supportive friendship, patience, critical insight, and editorial talent have been crucial in my intellectual growth, and to whom I, thus, dedicate this paper. Our exchanges on Marcuse, masochism, and cinematic identity-construction (or, rather its pitfalls) have greatly influenced this essay. For their contribution of insightful discussions, critical readings, significant material, and persistent support, I want to thank Roy Grundmann, Ann Harris, Anton Kaes, Emma Marciano, Mary McCabe, Catrina Neiman, Julian Onderdonk, Andreas Timmer, and the editors. I am grateful to my colleague Noah Isenberg for retrieving the original Fassbinder-interview in *Filmfaust*.

1. Rainer Werner Fassbinder, interview, "'Alles Vernünftige interessiert mich nicht.' Gespräch mit Rainer Werner Fassbinder," *Rainer Werner Fassbinder, Filmemacher*, Wolfgang Limmer (Reinbek bei Hamburg: Rowohlt, 1981), p. 58, this author's translation.

2. Rainer Werner Fassbinder, "The Third Generation" (December 1978), in *The Anarchy of the Imagination. Interviews, Essays, Notes*, ed. Michael Töteberg and Leo A. Lensing, trans. Krishna Winston (Baltimore and London: John Hopkins University Press, 1992), p. 132.

3. Ibid.

4. Herbert Marcuse, *Eros and Civilization. A Philosophical Inquiry into Freud* (1955; Boston: Beacon Press, 1966), p. xxvii.

5. Fassbinder, "Third Generation," p. 130.

6. Thomas Elsaesser, "Primary Identification and the Historical Subject: Fassbinder and Germany" (1980), in *Narrative, Apparatus, Ideology*, ed. Philip Rosen (New York: Columbia University Press, 1986), p. 549.

7. Ibid., p. 546.

8. Thomas Elsaesser, "Afterword. Murder, Merger, Suicide: The Politics of *Despair*," in *Fassbinder*, ed. Tony Rayns (London: British Film Institute, rev. and exp. ed., 1980), p. 40.

9. Anton Kaes also notes the aggressive character of the soundtrack. He concludes, however, that, in conjunction with the film's disorienting cuts, its ultimate effect is a frustration of the viewer and, furthermore: "Utopia no longer appears as even a vague possibility" ("The Presence of the Past. Rainer Werner Fassbinder's *The Marriage of Maria Braun*," in *From Hitler to Heimat*, ed. Anton Kaes [Cambridge MA: Harvard University Press, 1989], p. 101). This interpretation seems justified as long as a positive utopia is expected to be displayed *in* the film instead of in the margins of its absence, to be invented by the viewer *outside* of the film.

10. Cf. Richard Dyer, "Reading Fassbinder's Sexual Politics," in *Fassbinder*, Tony Rayns (London: British Film Institute, 1980), pp. 54–56, and Thomas Elsaesser, "Afterword," pp. 39–40, 53.

11. Another critic, Richard Linnett, evaluates *The Third Generation* as "pseudo-critique" due to Fassbinder's refusal to discern the ideals and values which "are in power at any given moment, and in any given place." Linnett's view is a revealing example of a "left" request from the filmmaker to "elaborate on the multitude of social ironies" so that the feature does not become "uninformative and muddled" ("The Third Generation," review, *Cineaste* 11.1 [Winter 1980–81], p. 42). It is precisely the condition of a "muddled", a meshed sadomasochistic structure, though, that Fassbinder tries to establish as the reality against which a utopia shall be invented. Thus, he envisions an audience which is rather capable and creative in its response and responsibility than in need of being spoon fed enlightening "information" for revolutionary change.

12. Compare here in contrast Michel Foucault, *History of Sexuality. Vol. 1: An Introduction*, trans. Robert Hurley (New York: Vintage Books, 1980), pp. 95–96.

13. Thomas Elsaesser, *New German Cinema. A History* (New Brunswick, NJ: Rutgers University Press, 1989), p. 228.

14. Ibid.

15. Cf. Elsaesser, "Afterword," p. 39.

16. Cf. Thomas Elsaesser, "A Cinema of Vicious Circles," in *Fassbinder,* ed. Tony Rayns (London: British Film Institute, 1976), pp. 27–28.

17. Cf. Thomas Elsaesser, "Afterword," p. 44.

18. Cf. Kaja Silverman, *Male Subjectivity at the Margins* (New York and London: Routledge, 1992), back cover.

19. Ibid., p. 213.

20. Ibid.

21. Laura Mulvey, "Visual Pleasure and Narrative Cinema" (1975), in *Visual and Other Pleasures* (Bloomington, IN: Indiana University Press, 1989), p. 22.

22. Achim Haag also understands Fassbinder's work, and particularily *Berlin Alexanderplatz,* in sadomasochistic terms, yet he follows Freud in his notion of sadomasochism as reconstruction of the Oedipal father-son constellation ("'Er hat immer diese Sehnsucht nach Liebe gehabt.' Franz Biberkopf und Reinhold: Die Kontrahenten der Seelenkämpfe R. W. Fassbinders," *Text + Kritik: Rainer Werner Fassbinder,* Heinz Ludwig Arnold, ed. [July 1989], no. 103, p. 40). Haag ignores, however, the preoedipal dimension of the perverse scenario. Miriam Hansen discerns the reenactment of a sadomasochistic ritual in Valentino films which, consequently, dissolves subject/object dichotomies and thus renders the possibility of a female spectatorial position of erotic reciprocity ("Pleasure, Ambivalence, Identification: Valentino and Female Spectatorship," *Cinema Journal* [Summer 1986], vol. 25, no. 4, pp. 6–32). This is precisely the spectatorial effect of Fassbinder's *The Third Generation.* I would add, nevertheless, that Fassbinder's sadomasochistic aesthetic rests less on one character than it penetrates all elements of his cinematic representation (characters, narrative, camera movement, and so forth).

23. Gaylyn Studlar, *In the Realm of Pleasure: Von Sternberg, Dietrich and the Masochistic Aesthetic* (Urbana: University of Illinois Press, 1988), pp. 15–16, 27–30.

24. Studlar, ibid., pp. 10, 14, 18–26. Gilles Deleuze, "Coldness and Cruelty," *Masochism* (New York: Zone Books, 1991), pp. 12–13, 15–46.

25. Louise J. Kaplan, *Female Perversions. The Temptations of Emma Bovary* (New York: Anchor Books, 1991), p. 21.

26. Janine Chasseguet-Smirgel, *Creativity and Perversion* (New York and London: W. W. Norton, 1984).

27. Kaplan, p. 72.

28. Ibid., p. 73.

29. Marcuse, pp. 87–88.

30. Marcuse, p. 142.

31. Christian Braad Thomson, "Der doppelte Mensch," *Text + Kritik,* Arnold, ed., p. 9.

32. Ibid.

33. Ibid., this author's translation.

34. Marcuse, p. 5.

35. Ruppert, "Fassbinder, Spectatorship, and Utopian Desire," *Cinema Journal* 28.2 (Winter 1989), p. 39.

36. Ibid., p. 46.

37. Ibid., p. 45.

38. Rainer Werner Fassbinder, interview, "'Madness and terrorism': Conversations with Gian Luigi Rondi about *Despair* and *The Third Generation,*" *Anarchy,* Töteberg/Lensing, eds., p. 126.

39. Rainer Werner Fassbinder, "Interview I," with Wilfried Wiegand, *Rainer Werner Fassbinder,* Peter W. Jansen and Wolfgang Schütte, eds. (Munich: Carl Hanser, 1983, 4th ed.), p. 89, this author's translation.

40. Michail M. Bachtin, *Literatur und Karneval. Zur Romantheorie und Lachkultur,* trans. into German Alexander Kaempfe, (Frankfurt/Main: Fischer, 1990), pp. 34–35.

41. Limmer, p. 58, this author's translation.

42. My translation slightly differs from the one by Jytte Jensen and Scott de Francisco. See first the original German response by Fassbinder:

> Also ich glaube ja . . . , daß dieses System, in welchem wir leben, kein System ist, in dem man wirklich lieben kann. Dieses System ist dazu geeignet, weil es überhaupt ein System der Ausbeutung ist, die Liebe auch auszubeuten. Und zwar egal, wie sie passiert und in jedem Fall. Das ist etwas ziemlich Entsetzliches. Auf der einen Seite gibt es natürlich, auch in meiner Wunschvorstellung, irgendetwas, was man so Liebe nennen kann. Auf der anderen Seite weiß ich ganz direkt, daß ich so simpel nicht empfehlen kann zu lieben. Ich kann den Wunsch zu lieben empfehlen, aber nicht zu lieben. Man sollte aber schon den Wunsch immer größer werden lassen, immer klarer werden lassen—und dann passiert vielleicht irgendetwas.
>
> (Bion Steinborn, Rüdiger v. Maso, "Ein Gespräch mit Rainer Werner Fassbinder. 'Ich bin das Glück dieser Erde, ach wär' das schön, wenn's so wäre,'" [Berlin, March 16, 1982, 11 p.m.–3 a.m.] *Filmfaust* 27 [April/May 1982], p. 8).

The differences between the Jensen/de Francisco translation and this author's ~~one~~ lie primarily in the last two sentences. See the former translators' version:

> I can recommend the wish to love, but not love itself. The *wish* to love should always be emphasized, always made clearer—then perhaps something will happen.
>
> (Bion Steinborn, Rüdiger v. Maso, "An Interview with Rainer Werner Fassbinder," trans. Jytte Jensen, Scott de Francisco, *Wedge* 2 [Fall 1982], p. 23.)

Two issues seem important: (1) Fassbinder emphasizes the activity of loving, "to love," not "love" as a noun, an object or a fixed entity. (2) The last sentence entails a recommendation to let the wish grow but does not imply that any other person is making it grow or helping to clarify it. This distinction is crucial since it illuminates Fassbinder's cinematic theme that any true social change starts with emotional and social growth within an individual, not with influences and transformations induced by the outside.

43. Fassbinder, "Third Generation", p. 129.

44. Ibid., p. 131

45. See in this context the recent debate around the sculpture by Käthe Kollwitz of a "grieving mother holding her son," which chancellor Helmut Kohl decided to place in the *Neue Wache* (former East Berlin, street of Unter den Linden) with the inscription "To the Victims of War and Tyranny." When, on November 14, 1993, this national monument was dedicated "to honor victims of past conflicts," the celebration was disturbed by angry protestors and boycotts. While Kohl considered the monument an important symbol of a reunited Germany, its democratic system, and constitutional rights, his opponents had several concerns, as Stephen Kinzer summarizes:

> The protestors disapprove of the site, which has been a prison and was a monument during the Nazi era, and the statue, which they say fails to portray the

horror Germans inflicted on their own citizens and on citizens of foreign lands. But they are most strongly opposed to the inscription, which they say fails to differentiate between victims and perpetrators . . . "German murderers are not victims!" they shouted as police arrested them.

("The War Memorial: To Embrace the Guilty, Too?" *New York Times* [November 15, 1993], p. A4.)

The problem of how far Nazis could also have been victims, and if so, what this assumption would imply for *Vergangenheitsbewältigung,* what the consequences would entail for contemporary Germans, stirs up a very intense debate—a discussion which is unlikely to ever be finished.

46. Ruth McCormick pointedly describes Fassbinder's therapeutic project as follows: "He [Fassbinder] has said that he would like to make psychoanalysis available to those who can't afford it, and, like a good analyst, he uses a sometimes-painful Socratic method. It is as if he were trying to blast away the preconditioning of his audience by showing them themselves (and himself in the bargain) through the mirror of cinema" ("Fassbinder's Reality: An Imitation of Life," *Fassbinder,* Ruth McCormick, ed. [New York: Tanam Press, 1981], p. 91).

Bibliography

Bachtin, Michail M. *Literatur und Karneval. Zur Romantheorie und Lachkultur,* trans. Alexander Kaempfe. Frankfurt/Main: Fischer, 1990.

Chasseguet-Smirgel, Janine. *Creativity and Perversion.* New York; London: W. W. Norton & Co., 1984.

Deleuze, Gilles. "Coldness and Cruelty." In *Masochism.* Deleuze, Gilles and Leopold von Sacher-Masoch. New York: Zone Books, 1991, pp. 9–138.

Dyer, Richard. "Reading Fassbinder's Sexual Politics." In *Fassbinder,* ed. Tony Rayns. London: British Film Institute, revised and expanded ed., 1980. pp, 54–64.

Dreyfus, Hubert L. and Paul Rabinow. *Michel Foucault. Beyond Structuralism and Hermeneutics.* Chicago, IL: University of Chicago Press, 1983, 2nd ed.

Elsaesser, Thomas. "Afterword. Murder, Merger, Suicide: The Politics of *Despair."* In *Fassbinder,* ed. Tony Rayns. London: British Film Institute, rev. and exp. ed., 1980, pp. 37–53.

———. "A Cinema of Vicious Circles." *Fassbinder,* ed. Tony Rayns. London: British Film Institute, 1976, pp. 24–36.

———. *New German Cinema. A History.* New Brunswick, NJ: Rutgers University Press, 1989.

———. "Primary Identification and the Historical Subject: Fassbinder and Germany." (1980) In *Narrative, Apparatus, Ideology.* ed. Philip Rosen. New York: Columbia University Press, 1986. pp. 535–549.

Fassbinder, Rainer Werner. "'Madness and Terrorism': Conversations with Gian Luigi Rondi about *Despair* and *The Third Generation.*" (1978/79) In *The Anarchy of the Imagination,* ed. Michael Töteberg and Leo A. Lensing, trans. Krishna Winston. Baltimore and London: John Hopkins University, 1992, pp. 124–127.

————. "The Third Generation." In *The Anarchy of the Imagination*, ed. Michael Töteberg and Leo A. Lensing, trans. Krishna Winston. Baltimore and London: John Hopkins University Press, 1992, pp. 128–133.

Foucault, Michel. *The History of Sexuality. Vol. 1: An Introduction*, trans. Robert Hurley. New York: Vintage Books, 1980.

Haag, Achim. "'Er hat immer diese Sehnsucht gehabt.' Franz Biberkopf und Reinhold; Die Kontrahenten der Seelenkämpfe R.W. Fassbinders," Heinz-Ludwig Arnold *Text + Kritik: Rainer Werner Fassbinder*, 103 (July 1982): pp. 35–50.

Hansen, Miriam. "Pleasure, Ambivalence, Identification: Valentino and Female Spectatorship." *Cinema Journal* 25:4 (Summer 1986): pp. 6–32.

Kaes, Anton. "The Presence of the Past. Rainer Werner Fassbinder's *The Marriage of Maria Braun*." In *From Hitler to Heimat*, ed. Anton Kaes. Cambridge; MA: Harvard University Press, 1989, pp. 73–103.

Kaplan, Louise J. *Female Perversions. The Temptations of Emma Bovary*. New York: Anchor Books, 1991.

Kinzer, Stephen. "The War Memorial: To Embrace the Guilty, Too?" *New York Times*, November 15, 1993, p. A4.

Limmer, Wolfgang. *Rainer Werner Fassbinder, Filmemacher*. Reinbek bei Hamburg: Rowohlt, 1981.

Linnett, Richard. Review of "The Third Generation." *Cinéaste* 11:1 (Winter 1980–81): pp. 39–42.

Marcuse, Herbert. *Eros and Civilization. A Philosophical Inquiry into Freud* (1955), Boston: Beacon Press, 1966.

McCormick, Ruth. "Fassbinder's Reality: An Imitation of Life." In *Fassbinder*, ed. Ruth McCormick. New York: Tanam Press, 1981, pp. 85–97.

Mulvey, Laura. "Visual Pleasure and Narrative Cinema," (1975) in *Visual and Other Pleasures*. Bloomington: Indiana University Press, 1989, pp. 14–26.

Rayns, Tony, ed. *Fassbinder*. London: British Film Institute, 1976 and 1980, rev. and expanded ed.

Ruppert, Peter. "Fassbinder, Spectatorship, and Utopian Desire." *Cinema Journal* 28:2 (Winter 1989): pp. 28–47.

Silverman, Kaja. *Male Subjectivity at the Margins*. New York and London: Routledge, 1992.

Steinborn, Bio and Rüdiger v. Maso. "Ein Gespräch mit Rainer Werner Fassbinder. 'Ich bin das Glück dieser Erde, ach wär' das schön wenn's so wäre.'" *Filmfaust* 27 (April/May 1982): pp. 2–16.

————. "An Interview with Rainer Werner Fassbinder," trans. Jytte Jensen and Scott de Francesco. *Wedge* 2 (Fall 1982): pp. 18–29.

Studlar, Gaylyn. *In the Realm of Pleasure: Von Sternberg, Dietrich and the Masochistic Aesthetic*. Urbana: University of Illinois Press, 1988.

Thomson, Christian Braad. "Der doppelte Mensch." In *Text + Kritik: Rainer Werner Fassbinder*, ed. Heinz-Ludwig, Arnold, 103 (July 1982): pp. 3–9.

Töteberg, Michael and Leo A. Lensing, ed. *The Anarchy of the Imagination,* trans. Krishna Winston. Baltimore and London: John Hopkins University Press, 1992.

Wiegand, Wilfried. "Interview I" with Rainer Werner Fassbinder. In *Rainer Werner Fassbinder.* (Reihe Film 2), ed. Peter W. Jansen and Wolfgang Schütte. Munich: Carl Hanser, 1983, 4th ed., pp. 75–94.

Madame X of the China Seas

PATRICIA WHITE

Madame X, a harsh, pitiless beauty, the cruel, uncrowned ruler of the China Seas, launched an appeal to all women willing to exchange an everyday existence of almost unbearable boredom, though safe and easy, for a world of uncertainty and danger, but also full of love and adventure.

THESE ARE the first words of Ulrike Ottinger's lesbian pirate film, *Madame X: An Absolute Ruler*, before the credits, spoken over the exquisite image of the junk *Orlando*'s figurehead, exact replica of the pirate queen (both played by coproducer and costume designer Tabea Blumenschein), shot against a deep-blue sky. The promise sounds much like that of cinema itself—the guarantee of pleasure is the beautiful, cruel woman. Here, however, that woman speaks this contradictory, gender-specific appeal. Feminism's promise to transform our everyday existence, too, is contradictory; it does not engage "all women" in the same way or with the same agenda. Ottinger's film, in taking up the appeals of both cinema and feminism, both "collective fantasies," both "public spheres," addresses the spectator not only as *female* (a claim Teresa de Lauretis makes for women's films such as *Born in Flames* and *Jeanne Dielman*),[1] but also, I will try to demonstrate, as *marginal*.

Such a spectator might be willing to agree with one of the film's characters: "This is something—this is *extreme*—the *Outlaw*—the *Misfits*—This is what I was looking for!" exclaims Betty Brillo.[2] The excess encapsulated by her remark is not foreign to Ottinger's cinema, is indeed its defining characteristic. Her films feature elaborate costumes, painterly shot composition, antirealist performances, and eclectic and abundant musical and sound quotations. Ottinger manipulates a visual and aural collage technique drawing on sources from the Shangri-La's to Yma Sumac, Gustave Moreau to Man Ray, Oscar Wilde to Virginia Woolf, to produce a feminist surrealism, or what might be called queer cinema. However, I wish to go beyond the notion that Ottinger's style appeals to a marginal audience through some subcultural sensibility or gay aesthetics. Rather, Madame X's invocation to her crew and the test of the fool Belcampo's gender identity function to foreground the *construction* of the film's address.

Teresa de Lauretis has recommended that we "re-think women's cinema and aesthetic forms . . . in terms of address—who is making films for whom, who is looking and speaking, how, where, and to whom," in the

---

Reprinted from *Screen* 28.4 (1987) 80–95.

context of her claim that "feminism has not only invented new strategies or created new texts, but more importantly it has conceived a new social subject, women: as speakers, readers, spectators, users and makers of cultural forms, shapers of cultural processes."[3] *Madame X: An Absolute Ruler* was produced within and in reference to the current wave of feminism. It dramatizes the relation of women as social subjects to woman as supported and produced by the cinematic apparatus. As yet another remake of the Hollywood *Madame X*, it acknowledges a long history of female spectatorship. The pirate genre provides the context for a feminist adventure in which social gender roles are transformed by role-playing and inversion, thematized as both sexual inversion and carnival. Ottinger's citations and disruptions of classical cinematic codes take women's visual pleasure, even fetishism, for granted, displacing the presumably masculine spectator. And, as I shall attempt to demonstrate through an analysis of the love scene, the film also reworks the relation of woman as image to the apparatus. Lesbianism foregrounds the difference of women from woman, insisting on spectatorial desire as well as identification. My final brief discussion of feminist film theory suggests that the impasse regarding female spectatorship is related to the blind spot of lesbianism.

The China Seas upon which the junk *Orlando* sails is a thinly disguised Lake Constance, where Ottinger shot the film in 1977. It was funded by ZDF, German television, and the low budget is at least partially responsible for the innovative sound mixing. Ottinger continued to use post-sync sound, however, on her next, better-funded feature, *Bildnis einer Trinkerin (Ticket of No Return*, 1979). Many of the actresses in *Madame X* worked with Ottinger in later films, and filmmakers Cynthia Beatt and Yvonne Rainer appear in the film. Criticized or ignored upon its release, Ottinger's first feature has a cult following and is beginning to be critically reevaluated.[4]

The film's first movement is the collection of a motley crew of women from "various nations and all walks of life" who join Madame X (mistress of "satanic sea art") and her faithful servant Hoi-Sin on board the *Orlando*. The voice-over introduces each exemplary character, who receives the following message, delivered in German or English, often via an actual communication system (newspaper, analysis session, car telephone): 'Chinese Orlando—stop—to all women—stop—offer world—stop—full of gold—stop—love—stop—adventure at sea—stop—call Chinese Orlando—call Chinese Orlando—stop."[5] The telegram stops insist on the danger of the proposition, the prohibition of the wish. Yet each character "makes her decision and her judgment in a flash" and sets off for the ship. The community (of women) is constructed by the look of astonishment on the face of each woman when she reaches the ship. We are refused the reverse shot; the first image of the next woman in the chain stands in its place. The crew are summoned by a call "to all women," but their consent implies something like Monique Wittig's definition of homosexuality: "the desire for something else that is not connoted. This desire is resistance to the norm."[6]

Each character is representative, overdetermined by costumes, names, activities, props, and music. Flora Tannenbaum, German forestry expert and Goethe admirer, is seen breakfasting outdoors dressed in hunter's green. A dachshund delivers the *Frankfurter Allgemeine* in which she reads Madame X's message; she shoulders her rifle and marches off to military music. Blow-up, an Italian cover girl, instructs her chauffeur to change direction as Satie's *La Diva de l'empire* plays on the sound track. Betty Brillo is disenchanted by "all that American Hausfrauen-dream" and Noa-Noa, a native of Tai-Pi, has been rejected by her husband for infringing a taboo. Australian bush pilot Omega Centauri would rather be an astronaut; Josephine de Collage, international artist on roller skates, is "bored to death by the academic cultural round"; and psychology graduate Carla Freud-Goldmund arrives at the ship in a rickshaw pulled by her Chinese analysand, as a heart beats on the sound track.

So the characters are not realistic. Nor are they allegorical. They serve as so many figures in a mise-en-scène of female bodies which work through specific possibilities and scenarios of desire within the background fantasy of the pirate ship, the women's movement, lesbian utopia. Seduction, jealousy, and mutiny culminate in the successive deaths of all but one, the "primitive" Noa-Noa. Madame X herself survives, as does Belcampo, the hermaphroditic manicurist whom the crew rescue en route.

The classical fool aboard the Ship of Fools, Belcampo is subjected to a personality test, the object of which is the determination of his/her gender. "The decision—a man—would doubtless have meant being thrown overboard." But Belcampo passes the test by jamming the apparatus. (To Carla Freud-Goldmund's questions Belcampo replies with flash-forwards, flashbacks, and false fragments of the film. The sequence ends with aggression against the analyst, to the crew's cheers.) Then the women direct their course to the pleasure yacht *Holliday*, at the hands of whose unsubtle crew Belcampo had suffered exactly that threatened fate. The women "massacre" Lady Divine and the other pleasure-seekers on board the yacht to the sound track of a B horror flick and divide the spoils.

In the film's final sequence, the crew of the *Orlando* is reassembled onshore not by an explicit invocation but by the ritual of carnival. The women are resurrected, via costume change, as new versions of their former personae. The sadistic Carla Freud-Goldmund returns as a bike dyke in leather; Hoi-Sin, who had finally committed ritual suicide, comes back as the femme, *Leader of the Pack* on the sound track. The imperialist Flora Tannenbaum now wears blackface and jailbird stripes and sweeps the sidewalks. "All the discontent within them was unified into one overriding power and they set sail one day with a favorable wind behind."

The staging of regeneration is, on one level, resonant of Woolf's *Orlando*, in which the eponymous hero/ine is both transsexual and transhistorical. A flashback presents the director herself as Madame X's lost lover Orlando, narcissistically reading Woolf's novel—the inscription of the author as "Wunschbild der Vergangenheit" ("ideal of the past," to use Ottinger's term). On another level, the film's ending points to an indefinite number of possible re-visions. Put another way, *Madame X* recommends not the "destruction of pleasure as a radical weapon" as Laura Mulvey proposed in 1975,[7] but the radical reconstruction of a number of possible cinematic pleasures for women. Teresa de Lauretis suggests:

> Cinema could be made to re-present the play of contradictory percepts and meanings usually elided in representation, and so to enact the contradictions of women as social subjects, to perform the terms of the specific division of the female subject in language, in imaging, in the social.[8]

It is within such a problematic that I would like to situate Ottinger's film as an exemplary remake. For not only does it simultaneously embrace and reject the terms of the cinematic production of femininity, it does so in reference to a specific Hollywood text—or rather set of texts, for *Madame X*, the melodrama of the unknown mother, was filmed in six Hollywood versions, spanning from the silent screen to the made-for-TV movie. She was played by Dorothy Donnelly (1916), Pauline Frederick (1920), Ruth Chatterton (1929), Gladys George (1937), Lana Turner (1966), and Tuesday Weld (1981). Feminist film theory has rhetorically proclaimed the historical absence of "woman *as* woman" from Hollywood cinema (and even from cinema audiences). "Madame X" can be seen as a synecdoche for the critical proposition of woman's absence from history, while insisting on her (almost uncanny) return. Ottinger articulates the contradictions of this representation within the social field of feminism, and "meanings usually elided in representation" are central to this lesbian remake of what must already be considered a fetish text.

But it is not so much the maternal melodrama as the frame of the pirate film which allows Ottinger's *Madame X* to rewrite gender within genre. The film is not merely an *inversion* of a dominant genre (although inversion may be its theme), for it enacts not "women on top"[9] but a homosocial world (including male homosexuality, represented by Belcampo and the Russian sailor he rescues). Women's exile is both utopian premise and cause for rebellion. From real Chinese women pirates pictured in the screenplay, to *Anne of the Indies* and *La Fiancée du pirate*, two key texts in early feminist film culture;[10] from classical camp like *The Pirate* and *China Seas* to gay films such as Anger's *Fireworks*, Fassbinder's *Querelle*, Shroeter's *Weisse Reise*, and Ottinger's own short *Infatuation of the Blue*

Sailors, the implication of ships and sexual identity has a connotatively rich cultural and cinematic lineage.

The freaks on board the *Orlando* (Ottinger takes up the theme in her 1981 feature *Freak Orlando*), whose photos are snapped by Lady Divine aboard her spectator-ship the *Holliday*, have affinities with the Ship of Fools as well as with Hollywood. Ottinger sums up her method: "I use traditional cinema's clichés for my own purposes."[11] The pirate captain's prosthesis becomes the remarkable studded leather glove through which Madame X "speaks." Her dismembered right hand functions as a joke on castration, circulates in Belcampo's antics and is reembodied later in the film. The conventional parrot appears here as a character, although a mute one.

The film cites Hollywood conventions, yet ignores the construction of narrative space by dialogue and classical editing. This selective appropriation extends to the choice of genre. Critics have seen the strong generic expectations attached to certain films as enabling ideological rupture. Ottinger goes this critical claim one better, actually bringing to life signifiers of femininity repressed in the classical tradition (notably the ship's figurehead) with re-sounding implications for narrativity, closure, and identification. The refusal of dialogue emphasizes women's oppression, while the film incorporates quotations from Hollywood films, by synchronizing snatches of music and sound effects with characters' gestures and with larger fragments of the film.

Discussing *Madame X's* reception, Ottinger commented: "Some women have accused me of sexism and leather fetishism. I do not see it this way. I do not think women should now turn into grey mice."[12] The question of what women *should* turn into touches on the theme of metamorphosis in the film as well as on de Lauretis's assertion that "women's cinema has been engaged in the transformation of vision."[13] Laura Mulvey's claim that "women . . . cannot view the decline of the traditional film form with anything much more than sentimental regret"[14] is the only gaze specifically allocated to women in her classic essay. Drawing on classical cinema, Ottinger's *Madame X* exploits the radical potential of this sentimental regret, thereby taking up Claire Johnston's challenge: "in order to counter our objectification in the cinema, our collective fantasies must be released: women's cinema must embody the working through of desire: such an objective demands the use of the entertainment film."[15]

Character positions within the film are used to establish not only the geography of the junk, but also narrative space itself. Madame X's point of view is established as a high-angle shot. Hoi-Sin is depicted in the background to the side of her mistress; in close-up she looks left. The figurehead is shot in low-angle profile. Noa-Noa takes up the figurehead's position twice, gesturing and pointing towards Belcampo's raft and later towards the yacht. Her identification with the figurehead is one indication of how "woman" as guarantor of cinema is distributed across a number of positions in this film, with its plethora of female characters, each connoting, in her own way, to-be-looked-at-ness.

Taking up these already established character positions, the film's love scene makes use of conventional filmic construction to represent the unrepresentable. The following analysis will help to demonstrate how the cinematic apparatus is made strange in order to "embody the working through of desire."

The women find Madame X's gaze intolerable and draw lots to determine who will attempt to appease her. Noa-Noa loses (wins?). Here is the shot breakdown of the seduction:

1 Madame X, wearing a huge hat decorated with mirrors, in low-angle, medium close-up (the same as an earlier shot which denotes her unapproachability); a lion on sound track.

2 Noa-Noa in high-angle, long shot, wearing "ritual headdress"; arranges and dances within a circle of leeks; drum music.

3 Madame X as in shot 1, glove drawn back defensively silent.

4 Noa-Noa as in shot 2; drums beat faster.

5 Jump cut to Noa-Noa, long shot, bearing tray of "exotic fruits" climbs steps towards camera; plucked strings and percussion instruments.

6 Hoi-Sin in close-up, shielded behind mast; looks left; percussion continues.

7 Noa-Noa creeps up to Madame X's feet in medium shot; camera reframes to include Madame X's face; she thrusts her glove several times at Noa-Noa, who cowers but timidly persists, standing to offer Madame X a cauliflower; the movements of the glove are accompanied by roars, grunts and growls; no music.

8 Hoi-Sin as in shot 6; raises her eyebrows as growls become more frequent, softer.

9 Madame X and Noa-Noa as in shot 7; Madame X accepts a bunch of bananas from Noa-Noa and sits at her side; camera reframes as Noa-Noa makes more offerings; silent until end of shot, Polynesian music fades in.

10 Hoi-Sin as in shot 8; narrows eyes, pinches lips, does an exaggerated double take; music continues.

11 Madame X's extended silver-heeled foot, medium shot; camera tilts up her leg; she pulls Noa-Noa toward her by her shell necklace; camera reframes to include their faces; they caress each other tentatively; camera tilts down to Noa-Noa's hand on Madame X's leg; music continues.

12 Hoi-Sin as in shot 10; blinks, rolls eyes, and looks away; music continues.

13 Madame X and Noa-Noa as in shot 11; Madame X runs her studded glove through Noa-Noa's hair, they continue to caress each other awkwardly; loud purring, music continues.

14 Hoi-Sin as in shot 12; looks down sadly; music continues.

15 Madame X and Noa-Noa as in shot 13, camera moves to frame Madame X's pump and Noa-Noa's bare feet as Noa-Noa runs her hand down Madame X's leg; music fades, loud purring.

16 Madame X framed against sky as in shot 1, claps once; no music.

With the exception of the jump cut in shot 5, the editing is classical. And although the mast logically obstructs Hoi-Sin's gaze at the lovers, the point of view construction is naturalistic in effect. The scene takes place in pantomime; the decisive action occurs on the sound track as the roars and growls dubbed to Madame X's thrusts and parries are tamed to the purring of a kitten. The mixing of musical themes in Hollywood romance is parodied. Noa-Noa's charms are associated here and, during her subsequent flirtation with Blow-up, with Polynesian music; and purring returns as the couple's theme. Exaggerated makeup and mugging, absurd fetishes (the long, thin chains Noa-Noa wears from her waist to her wrists, vegetables, and purring), contrasts between hat and headdress, leather and grass skirt, and replacement of explicitness by the eroticism of texture and sound combine as hilarious musical comedy, reworked to suit a love triangle among women. The humor of the offscreen growls which pique our curiosity as we watch the watcher, as well as adherence to the one-foot-on-the-ground rule, suggest the pleasurable effects of Hollywood censorship. The refusal of the kiss (denied Belcampo and the sailor as well) simulates suspense, yet goes further to indicate the ultimate incompatibility of the apparatus with the representation of homosexuality.

The crew, said to represent women from all walks of life, are actually highly coded cinematic stereotypes. A consideration of Noa-Noa as "woman of color," or of the exoticism of Hoi-Sin, Madame X, and the venture itself, must attend to this insistence on the stereotype. Noa-Noa is the object of desire in this love story. She is presented as spectacle differently from the others. Her breasts are bare and her dance is performed for Madame X's gaze. Her primitivism is emphasized by her interest in the pirate queen's metallic ornaments and by her selection of a huge tortoise in the division of the booty from the *Holliday*. She expresses herself entirely through pantomime.

Structurally, too, Noa-Noa is set off from the other women; drawing last in the otherwise silent lottery scene, her timid approach is accompanied by music. She is the last to join the crew, approaching the ship alone in her canoe. Like Belcampo, she comes from the sea. Most importantly, she survives the journey, and with Madame X and Belcampo assembles the resurrected crew at the end. Her privileged position is assumed at the expense of Hoi-Sin, who was "in place" at the beginning of the journey. It is suggested that the women encoded as non-white survive one cycle of the Ship of Fools' passage as Madame X's servant/lover. Hoi-Sin is an ordinary crew member in the next round. Perhaps next time the character in blackface will take Noa-Noa's place?

Thus relations of domination are explicitly thematized and erotically invested. Madame X as "oriental despot" is more powerful than Hoi-Sin as Chinese cook. Ottinger's orientalism is at the same time Germanic, an appropriation of the (generally male homosexual) traditions of aestheticism and decadence for lesbian representation, and a provocative masquerade. She allows the feminine, the ornate, and the East to be aligned, impenetrable, and parodic, yet pleasurably textured. The "primitive" represented by Noa-Noa deploys a different set of imperialist codes. Her specificity, in contrast to the relative interchangeability of the other women, can also be understood in terms of the production of difference within other, more conventionally narrative, lesbian texts.[16] Noa-Noa is the film's major concession to narrativity itself. With the exception of the victimized Russian sailor whose similar position as object of desire should not be overlooked, the entire cast is coded feminine. Noa-Noa, however, is the "girl."

Because Blow-up is presented as a spectacle of Hollywood femininity, coded "cultural" in contrast to Noa-Noa as "natural" beauty, the romance between the blond, glamorous diva and the "exotic" is in some sense transgressive. Blow-up will later direct her third attempt at mutiny against the ship's figurehead, displacing the struggle with the terms of her imaging from the heroine to the image-making machine, reciprocally made in woman's image. Blow-up trips a mechanism and is strangled by the *imago;* her body is taken up in the arms of Omega Centauri who, quite literally, longs for the stars. In turn, Omega is killed for having discovered the switch that animates the figurehead, exposing the apparatus.

Madame X's identification with this animated figurehead puts cinema on the side of women's self-presentation; the apparatus does not merely secure an image of woman as not-man. An exact replica of Madame X, the figurehead fits the image, produces the illusion perfectly. The image (woman) animates the mechanized, or enchanted, leather-clad female body which stands in for the apparatus (the title of the film appears across the first image of the figurehead). For the figurehead itself is given an image of woman "made to speak," reciting "Gold, Liebe, Abenteuer" when Madame X wishes to give "convincing proof of her absolute power and authority." It is both the pirate queen's narcissistic projection (the double à la Dorian Gray, a figure Ottinger later returned to in *The Image of Dorian Gray in the Yellow Press*, 1984), and a fantasmatic representation of her omnipotence which crushes Blow-up's rebellion.

Yet the fact that the figurehead in turn produces Madame X in its own image prevents any simple reading of women's reappropriation of the means of representing woman. Madame X's robotic movements and mechanical sounds indicate that she is not altogether human: her severed hand is restored like a spare part. The synchronization of sound effects associates her body with the register of sound mixing. One in particular refers unmistakably to the MGM lion, whose roar authorized the unfolding of decades of Hollywood stories. Finally, Madame X's gaze is one of the major organizing principles of the film.

The figurehead is the conventional female emblem of piracy, and of sailing in general, gendering the ship itself. It is significant to *Madame X's* narrative structure that the translation from male genre to female utopia maintains this marking of the journey. On the one hand the film's moral can be read off, as Ottinger suggests in interviews, as the inability of the women's movement to do away with figureheads of power: on the other, power itself is granted the various affirmative connotations it has within contemporary lesbian feminism. As an antidote to "Mister X," the anonymous yet coherent "invisible guest" of classical cinema, Madame X herself is split between the conditions of production of her femininity. The pirate queen is caught between her projected image (the figurehead) and the film which takes her name. She is no more than a *figurehead* of absolute authority, for Madame brings the X into an uneasy relation with patriarchal naming.

> In saying that a film whose visual and symbolic space is organized in this manner *addresses its spectator as a woman*, regardless of the gender of its viewers, I mean that the film defines all points of identification (with character, image, camera) as female, feminine or feminist. However, this is not as simple or self-evident a notion as the established film-theoretical view of cinematic identification, namely, that identification with the look is masculine and identification with the image is feminine. It is not self-evident precisely because such a view . . . is now accepted: that the camera (technology), the look (voyeurism), and the scopic drive itself partake of the phallic and thus somehow are entities or figures of a masculine nature.[17]

What might indeed be self-evident in this context is that any elaboration of *lesbian* spectatorship must displace the "established film-theoretical view." Ottinger's text allows us to do this in the direction of de Lauretis's revision.

The figure of Belcampo offers a condensation of the film's address to the marginal subject. For if the crew respond "naturally" *as women* to

Madame X's call (recognizing themselves in the address and their desire in the promise), the interpellation of Belcampo, as unnatural "woman," is more problematic. Classically, the fool's discourse frustrates sexual identification. In the personality test sequence, two discursive models are opposed: psychoanalysis and its imposition of order (represented by Carla Freud-Goldmund, who administers the test), and carnival as ritualized disorder. Psychoanalysis's negotiation of sexual difference is staged, and Belcampo negotiates for his/her life on the stakes of femininity itself. It is important to realize, however, that Belcampo's sexual indeterminacy is not posited as some postgendered answer to patriarchal oppression. Belcampo is accepted as a "woman" by the onlooking crew at the end of the sequence; moreover, the question of his/her suitability to the enterprise is resolved by their approval. Belcampo's case attempts to make sense of the non-sense of gender. S/he makes explicit the film's trope of female impersonation that might be considered germane to lesbian identity. Finally, "his" romance with the Russian sailor, whom "he" rescues and attempts to shield from Madame X's wrath, introduces yet another "invert" trajectory to the lesbian narrative, hinting at the alliance between gay men and lesbians which Ottinger's representational strategies reflect.

The test sequence opposes a "realistic" mise-en-scène, in which Carla quizzes Belcampo and times his/her answers with a stopwatch, to extradiegetic images and sounds which Belcampo enunciates. A third space is represented by the reaction shots of the other characters which dominate the end of the sequence.

Belcampo's first answer, given as flashback, is in response to the question: "Are you an important personality?" We see the exact *reverse* of the shot immediately preceding Belcampo's rescue, where the women were represented as "eating" a meal prepared by Hoi-Sin with a close-up of a large fish violently attacked by chopsticks, as seagulls screeched on the sound track. This time the fish is reconstituted. The jangle of a tambourine marks the beginning of this shot, which is followed by a detail of Carla clicking her stopwatch. Belcampo's carnival defies the linear unfolding of the film and the logic of question and answer, fleshing out the film's fantasy of regeneration as enacted in the final scene. The trick shot foregrounds the apparatus. Attempting inversion among the inverts, Belcampo draws Madame X herself into his/her discourse, breaking down the established hierarchy, if only momentarily. Carla asks if Belcampo feels strongly attracted to members of his/her own sex: s/he is literally unable to comprehend the question. Carla repeats it and we see, instead of Belcampo, Madame X throwing back her head with a resounding lip-synched laugh. Our understanding of the question coincides with hers in the only appropriate answer—defiant but affirmative laughter. As Blow-up and Betty Brillo caress each other in the following shot, gazing seductively at the camera, Carla asks in voice-over: "Have you always wanted to be a woman?" Although her question seems to decide the very issue the test is designed to resolve, assuming the you addressed is not already a woman, the connoted desire for "resistance to the norm" (implying both the advantages of being a woman and the option of refusing to become woman) is unmistakable here as in the film as a whole.

Three questions bear directly on spectatorship. Carla asks Belcampo, "Do you see around you things, or creatures of fable, that others do not see?" The response is an image of Madame X, as if standing in for the film, a fabulous hallucination. Later in the sequence Belcampo is asked whether s/he enjoys adventure stories. This prompts Belcampo to transgress the spatial boundary set up even in this transgressive sequence. S/he leaves the analytic space for the outside world (the diegetic spectators' realm) and takes Omega Centauri's water pistol, returning to squirt the analyst. We are reminded of Mulvey's description: "In contrast to woman as icon, the active male figure . . . demands a three-dimensional space. . . . He is a figure in a landscape."[18] The conventions of spectatorship again inform Carla's last question: "Do you like to see love scenes at the movies?" At this point both Carla and Belcampo lose discursive agency (Carla's mouth is taped shut) and we see a rapid montage of the crew participating in general disorder. On the sound track Betty Brillo sings the words from her opening speech as the film's romantic theme: "Jesus, Babyfolks! This is extreme. . . ." The preferred response to Carla's question is "*this* is what I was looking for!"

Mary Russo, in her article on carnival (of) theory, cautions: "In liminal states . . . temporary loss of boundaries tends to redefine social frames, and such topsy-turvy or time-out is inevitably set right and on course."[19] Within the social frame of Madame X's absolute authority, however, setting right and on course means continuing the women's journey with the figurehead in the bow. Having rescued the damsel in distress, the women direct the junk "south-south-west" (the figurehead mouths the words) to revenge "her" injustice. Carnival is recovered for the marginal. Belcampo's sexual difference is not a simple critique of the rigidity of gender, but serves to shift the terms of its elaboration within the course of the lesbian adventure tale.

Here is the film's invocation once more:

Madame X, a harsh, pitiless beauty, the cruel uncrowned ruler of the China Seas, launched an appeal to all women willing to exchange an everyday existence of almost unbearable boredom, though safe and easy, for a world of uncertainty and danger, but also full of love and adventure.

To what degree does *Madame X* the film offer to spectators the booty promised by Madame X to all willing women? Isn't there a contradiction in the fact that a film which purports to call on all women is excessively long, "boring," has no synchronous dialogue, too many heroines and a hero in drag? One can certainly refuse to take part in what Ottinger has described as the film's initiation stories; one might regard "a comedy about the women's movement" as unfunny.[20] As an all-too-willing spectator, I believe I have struck gold.

Feminist film theory has argued that if "cinematic codes create a gaze, a world, and an object, thereby producing an illusion cut to the measure of desire,"[21] female spectators pledge themselves at their own risk, for very uncertain pleasures. *Madame X*, which posits a female gaze ("Madame X's gaze was so fearsome that the women trembled"), a female world (of playfully evoked erotic domination and submission), and a female object (like mainstream cinema, Ottinger's film attaches desire to women's gaze at woman), is a dangerous enterprise. Love is certainly on offer at the movies, is even considered a specific (albeit masochistic) appeal to the women in the audience. Yet love is tied into a very precise ideological project concerned with endlessly reproducing the heterosexual couple. Women enjoy adventure films surreptitiously, wearing, to quote another of Mulvey's tailor-made metaphors, "borrowed transvestite clothes."[22] Both assumptions—the impossibility of the female spectator's desire on the one hand; her trans-sex identification on the other, have left lesbians in the dark.

In her 1981 "Afterthoughts" Laura Mulvey returned to "Visual Pleasure and Narrative Cinema" to face up to the female spectator. Narrative cinema was reevaluated in the light of the author's "own love of Hollywood melodrama,"[23] but visual pleasure remained unaddressed. Mary Ann Doane would write that same year: "One assumption behind the positing of a female spectator (that is, one who does not assume a masculine position with respect to the reflected image of her own body) is that it is no longer necessary to invest the look with desire in quite the same way."[24] Assuming that it is necessary to posit the female spectator differently, I would like to redress this disavowal of female fetishism through a brief discussion of the implications of the figure of the transvestite.[25]

Mulvey describes her earlier position: "at the time, I was interested in the . . . 'masculinization' of the spectator position regardless of the actual sex (or possible deviance) of any real live moviegoer."[26] Lesbianism, although nowhere mentioned explicitly, would seem to coincide so exactly with "masculinization" in these arguments as to constitute an *impossible* deviance. In any case, it is *not* deviance but actual sex to which Mulvey returns in the figure of the transvestite. She writes: "as desire is given cultural materiality in a text, for women (from childhood onwards) transsex identification is a *habit* that very easily becomes *second Nature*. However, this Nature does not sit easily and shifts restlessly in its borrowed transvestite clothes."[27] This nature, secondary or not (as indeed the little girl's heterosexuality can be said to be *second* nature in the Freudian account upon which Mulvey draws), sounds suspiciously essentialist. For why must *transvestite* clothes be borrowed? This process would be more accurately described as masquerade, a metaphor Doane opposes to transvestism in her essay "Film and the Masquerade."[28] It is the question of desire which leaves her restless with Mulvey's use of the term.

Doane argues that "the transvestite wears clothes which signify a different sexuality, a sexuality which, for the woman, allows a mastery over the image and the very possibility of attaching the gaze to desire."[29] Yet the different sexuality in question is evidently not homosexuality. In fact, the very possibility of *any* desire of one's own is eradicated by the next sentence: "Clothes make the man, as they say." Doane dismisses this supposedly facile "masculinization": "sexual mobility would seem to be a distinguishing feature of femininity in its cultural construction. Hence, transvestism would be fully recuperable." Lesbians must take issue with this assumption of mobility which, if true at all, has only been made possible by feminist mobilization. Transvestism, unlike the masquerade, is not a psychoanalytic concept. Nor does this use of the term imply the social practice of transvestism, which clearly does not make the man. The "metaphor" seems to be a thinly veiled reference to an impossible, reprehensible, or at best recuperable deviance on the part of the female spectator. Masquerade is to be considered as less "recuperable [than] transvestism precisely because it constitutes an acknowledgment that it is femininity itself which is constructed as mask—as the decorative layer which conceals a non-identity."[30] But the false opposition between masquerade and transvestism impoverishes even the "straight" story, discovering a new essential femininity in the non-identity behind the mask, defined as nothing more than a screen for male desire.

Masquerade (as "hyperbolization of the accoutrements of femininity"[31]) and symptomatic transvestism are of course not irrelevant to the consideration of women and cinema. Nor to Ottinger's film, which draws on the genre loosely termed spectacle, for example, de Mille's *Madam Satan*, in which a costume party aboard a blimp ends in disaster. These figures for spectatorship beg the question of the real live moviegoer and her visual pleasure. As Ottinger's characters "lay aside their petticoats to try their luck at new trouser roles,"[32] they become figures of spectatorial desire. And if Belcampo (who is of course not an hermaphrodite, but a male transvestite) permits transsex identification in "his" adventure story, deviance is made explicit.

Doane writes, "It is quite tempting to foreclose entirely the possibility of female spectatorship. . . ."[33] I would suggest that we succumb to other temptations. We can continue to gaze with sentimental regret at the classical Hollywood construction of femininity without becoming grey mice. My reading of *Madame X: An Absolute Ruler* argues that the film's address displaces two assumptions—that feminism finds its audience "naturally," and that the female spectator is destined to miss the boat. Gold, love, and adventure lie just beyond the horizon.

Notes

1. See Teresa de Lauretis, "Aesthetic and Feminist Theory: Rethinking Women's Cinema," *New German Critique* 34 (Winter, 1985) pp. 154–175.
2. Ulrike Ottinger's screenplay, *Madame X: Eine Absolute Herrscherin* (Basel/Frankfurt: Stroemfeld/Roter Stern, 1979) contains not only narration of this kind, but a mass of material, both written and visual, relating to the film.
3. Teresa de Lauretis, p. 163.
4. Marc Silberman, "Surreal Images: Interview with Ulrike Ottinger," *Jump Cut* 29 (1984) p. 56. See also, Miriam Hansen, "Visual Pleasure, Fetishism and the Problem of Feminine/Feminist Discourse: Ulrike Ottinger's *Ticket of No Return*," *New German Critique* 31 (Winter, 1984) pp. 95–108.
5. The voice-over remains unidentified; the call is delivered by Yvonne Rainer. Due to lack of space, I am unable to discuss the number and kinds of relationships the film posits between the woman's body and the woman's voice, without, however, granting her speech. See Kaja Silverman, "Dis-Embodying the Female Voice," in Mary Ann Doane et al., eds., *Revision: Essays in Feminist Film Criticism*, American Film Institute Monograph Series 3 (Frederick, MD: University Publications of America, 1984) pp. 131–149.
6. Monique Wittig, "Paradigm," in George Stambolian and Elaine Marks, eds., *Homosexualities and French Literature* (Ithaca: Cornell University Press, 1979) p. 114.
7. Laura Mulvey, "Visual Pleasure and Narrative Cinema," *Screen*, vol. 16, no. 3, (Autumn, 1975) p. 7.
8. Teresa de Lauretis, *Alice Doesn't: Feminism, Semiotics, Cinema* (Bloomington: Indiana University Press, 1984) p. 69.
9. See Natalie Zemon-Davis, "Women on Top," in her *Society and Culture in Early Modern France* (Stanford: Stanford University Press, 1986) pp. 124–152.
10. See Claire Johnston, "Femininity and the Masquerade: *Anne of the Indies*," in Claire Johnston and Paul Willemen, eds., *Jacques Tourneur* (London: British Film Institute, 1975) pp. 36–44. "It is hardly surprising that [Tourneur] should have chosen a pirate film aimed at children's audiences to represent such an extraordinary masquerade, for children's literature is rich in bisexual phantasy," pp. 37–8.
11. Marc Silberman, p. 56.
12. Roswitha Müller, "Interview with Ulrike Ottinger," *Discourse* 4 (Winter, 1981/1982) p. 120. Ottinger's sentiments are shared by Kaja Silverman, who suggests that "the sartorial reticence of North American feminism . . . is the symptom of what might almost be called 'The Great Feminine Renunciation'" in "Fragments of a Fashionable Discourse," in Tania Modleski, ed., *Studies in Entertainment* (Bloomington: Indiana University Press, 1987) p. 149.
13. Teresa de Lauretis, "Aesthetic and Feminist Theory," p. 159.
14. Laura Mulvey, p. 18.
15. Claire Johnston, "Women's Cinema as Counter Cinema," in Claire Johnston, ed., *Notes on Women's Cinema* (London: SEFT, 1975) p. 28.
16. Butch/femme or marked differences in age and experience structure lesbian films from *Daughters of Darkness* to *The Bitter Tears of Petra von Kant*. Jackie Stacey's "Desperately Seeking Difference," *Screen* (Winter, 1987) vol. 28 no. 1, pp. 48—61, discusses the narrative implications of one woman's identification with and desire for another in *All About Eve* and *Desperately Seeking Susan*.
17. Teresa de Lauretis, "Aesthetic and Feminist Theory," p. 161.
18. Laura Mulvey, pp. 12–13.

19. Mary Russo, "Female Grotesques: Carnival and Theory," in Teresa de Lauretis, ed., *Feminist Studies/Critical Studies* (Bloomington: Indiana University Press, 1986) p. 215.

20. Roswitha Müller, "Interview with Ulrike Ottinger," p. 121. "This, if you wish, is also my feminist point of view, the freedom for women to go out and experience on their own. This freedom, of course, also includes the possibility to fail. These ideas are contained in the notion of adventure, the freedom to try out things, and the freedom to fail."

21. Laura Mulvey, pp. 12–13.

22. Laura Mulvey, "Afterthoughts on 'Visual Pleasure and Narrative Cinema' Inspired by *Duel in the Sun*." *Framework* 15/16/17 (1981) p. 15.

23. Ibid., p. 12.

24. Mary Ann Doane, "*Caught* and *Rebecca*: The Inscription of Femininity as Absence," *Enclitic*, vol. 5 no. 2/vol. 6 no. 1 (Fall, 1981/Spring, 1982) p. 76.

25. Miriam Hansen has also discussed this choice of metaphor; see her "Pleasure, Ambivalence, Identification: Valentino and Female Spectatorship," *Cinema Journal*, vol. 25 no. 4 (Summer, 1986) p. 8. Jackie Stacey, op. cit., addresses a similar omission in feminist film theory: "While this issue [of the woman spectator's pleasure] has hardly been addressed, the specifically homosexual pleasures of female spectatorship have been ignored completely," p. 48.

26. Laura Mulvey, "Afterthoughts," p. 12.

27. Ibid., p. 13.

28. Mary Ann Doane, "Film and the Masquerade: Theorizing the Female Spectator," *Screen* (September-October, 1982) vol. 23 no. 3–4, pp. 74–87.

29. Ibid., p. 81.

30. Ibid., p. 82.

31. Ibid.

32. *Hosenrollen*. See Ulrike Ottinger, *Madame X: Eine Absolute Herrscherin*, p. 4.

33. Mary Ann Doane, "Film and the Masquerade," p. 87.

The Mirror and the Vamp

ROSWITHA MÜLLER

O SCAR WILDE'S novel *The Picture of Dorian Gray* conjures the narcissistic fantasy of eternal youth and beauty against the background of
a story of seduction, initiation and failed social responsibility. The device
of visualizing the moral turpitude of Dorian in the form of an ever
increasing ugliness in his portrait addresses not only the romantic theme
of the double, it also invokes a peculiarly modern preoccupation: questions of identity no longer conceived of in terms of some "inner" substance, but, in the face of the enormous proliferation of images, as a
problem of appearance. Little less than half a century later, the story of
Dorian Gray acquired a new sinister bend, namely the possibility of
manipulating lives through the manipulation of images. As Fritz Lang's
worst apprehensions—crystallized in the figure of Dr. Mabuse—were surpassed by political realities shortly after, the wave of euphoric expectations about the emancipatory potential of the mechanical reproduction of
sound and image subsided throughout Europe. Ulrike Ottinger's new film
The Image of Dorian Gray in the Yellow Press (Dorian Gray im Spiegel
der Boulevard Presse) which premiered at the Berlin Film Festival in 1984
(ominous year and title for another grim future fantasy of the misuse of
the media), gives little cause for optimistic speculations about impending
changes for the better in this area.

Like all of Ottinger's films *The Image of Dorian Gray in the Yellow
Press* is built around a narrative, a story line so slender and simple that it
threatens to be swallowed up by the sumptuous way of its execution. It
could be summarized by quoting the program of the powerful media
tycoon by the familiar name of Mabuse, a lady (Delphine Seyrig), whose
charm and beauty stand contrapuntally to the evilness of her designs. She
proposes to invent and create events, scandals and personalities instead of
chasing after them. Her guinea pig and choice victim, the inexperienced,
naive, narcissistic Dorian Gray, is to be seduced/introduced into life's pleasures and excesses, only to be destroyed in the end—all for the benefit of
a busy swarm of spies and reporters and an increase in circulation. The
sub-plot constructed as a story within the story is a colonial opera about
the conquest of the Canary Islands by Don Luis de la Cerda, Infante of
Spain. This closely researched historical instant of power and subjugation
acts as a mirror to the machinations of the unscrupulous Dr. Mabuse. The
conquest of the Canary Islands was colonial Spain's rehearsal for the con-

Reprinted from *New German Critique* 34 (1985): 176–93.

quest of the Americas. The naive young Infante, played by the same actress who plays Dorian (Veruschka von Lehndorff) is at first drawn in by Andamana, the matriarchal ruler of the islands and lives quite contentedly among the native people, adjusting to their life-style rather than imposing Spain's rule upon them. It is not until the arrival of the Grand Inquisitor/Mabuse (Delphine Seyrig), who coerces the Prince to exploit the island's riches, that the dynamics of domination take effect.

While reducing the film in this manner to its story content is admittedly an abstraction, yet, taken as such, a set of propositions can be extrapolated which point to their own contingency: events, "stories" are not independent of the manner and condition of their presentation by the apparatus, the press, radio and television, but the latter are the presupposition upon which events are dependent for their existence. Mabuse's deliberate intervention and creation of a person is hardly an exaggeration of the practices of the average scandal sheet and at the same time it thematizes the production of events[1] by the media in general. Dorian's ordeal at the hands of Mabuse is the quintessential human interest story which permeates ever larger sectors of the media, television in particular. The refrain of the press ball song: "Politics is taboo, X equals U," summarizes and underlines the string of absurdities, the twisted and inverted patterns of causal logic, which characterize the stylistic oddities of much cheap journalism.

EPISODES AND STORY

Parody and irony are the most obvious means this film employs to subvert straight-forward narrative meaning. Yet, for an analysis of the function of narrative in Ottinger's films, the relation between the storyline, i.e., chronological series of events and autonomous episodes, is of far greater importance. The press ball episode is a good example for such an investigation. Among the seventy-five episodes the film comprises, it stands out as one of the longest and most self-contained. It is a single take of eight minutes duration. Measured against the length of the entire episode, the story-related material is negligible. Dorian is introduced into the social circles where he is most likely to meet his new love Andamana. Less than one tenth of the duration of the entire event is devoted to this forwarding of the action. For the rest, the press ball episode lavishly elaborates on the situation for its own sake. From the newspaper-covered ballroom as background to the black and white costumes, the sparse outer-space music/muzak, the slow moving gestures (not slow motion but slow acting) to the fragmented dialogues directed at nobody, every detail is composed to achieve an effect within the episode rather than the entire film. Nevertheless, the autonomy of the episode is relative. The mood created by the precise composition of images and sound, a mood of isolation and alienation in the midst of a social gathering, comments on the sphere of power in which Mabuse is about to involve Dorian. And, as an example of a more direct linkage, the two songs interrupting the eight-minute shot add both a satirical and parodic take on the workings of the media tycoon.

The Image of Dorian Gray in the Yellow Press is the third in a trilogy of films which includes *Ticket of No Return* (Bildnis einer Trinkerin) and *Freak Orlando*. All three films are structured episodically; yet, in each one there is a difference in the way chronological story and episodes relate. In *Ticket of No Return*, the episodes as such develop (arbitrarily) along the lines of the initial voice-over announcement that we are witnessing a woman's determination to drink herself to death and to arrange the setting for this event as a kind of sight-seeing tour. The sight-seeing tour motif recurs frequently in Ottinger's films—it appears again as the "horror tour by night" in *The Image of Dorian Gray*. Without doubt this is partly attributable to the episodic structure which is built into the sight-seeing tour. The order of the different episodes in *Ticket of No Return* is for the most part interchangeable. However, the mise-en-scène and, in particular, the color composition are carefully worked out to mark a progression that ends in isolation and dissolution. The color scheme in the costumes of the drinker, for example, works its way from an initial flaming red to the icy shades of blue and silver which predominate at the end.

Freak Orlando, on the contrary, hinges on a story which coalesces with history. It attempts to show the fate of outsiders and social misfits through the ages. The episodes proceed in orderly fashion from mythological times to the present. Yet, here, the resistance to a totally diachronic narrative lies in the costumes, the dialogues and the settings. While the autonomy of the episodes in *Ticket of No Return* is safeguarded by their relative interchangeability, in *Freak Orlando* the independence from linear narrative progression is expressed in some of the aspects of the mise-en-scène. The importance of the choice of location, background, sets and costumes in Ottinger's films derives precisely from their function as equal partners in the total composition, with the power either to establish narrative continuity or to detract from it. In *Freak Orlando* these elements counteract the historical progression from episode to episode by introducing cases of simultaneity. When myths are on sale in a modern department store and a medieval cathedral turns out to be an old cooling tower of the Berlin gas works, or when a group of men, dressed like members of the Inquisition, is suddenly transformed before our eyes into goose-stepping blackshirts with gasmasks over their faces, resembling a more recent death squadron with clear fascist connotations, the self-referentiality and relative independence of each episode from the linear-historical narrative is maintained.

However different their methods, both films achieve a balance between the linear telling of a story and the inclusion of heterogeneous, synchronic elements that tell stories and histories of their own, complementing, commenting, and sometimes plainly contradicting the main story. The same is true of the last film in the trilogy. However, in *The Image of Dorian Gray*, the tension between diachronic and synchronic elements is much greater. One reason for this increase in tension lies in the film's more intricate connections between episodes, which present a greater challenge to episodic autonomy. Neither the more or less arbitrary sequence of episodes in *Ticket of No Return* nor the historical pageantry of outcasts in *Freak Orlando* are, with respect to the story, causally related. *The Image of Dorian Gray*, on the other hand, displays enough plot-related causal interdependence to suggest the author's ironic imitation of Fritz Lang's tightly organized plot structure, a fitting device to launch as provocative a figure as a female Dr. Mabuse. Thus a mock thriller develops around the negative of a picture taken of Mabuse as she pays a large sum of money for the pleasure/horror tour she has organized for Dorian. Possession of the negative proves fatal. Anyone holding this piece of evidence of Mabuse's machinations dies in obviously orchestrated accidents. First, the only resisting journalist of the media concern, disparagingly called the "Little Doctor," who gave the negative to Dorian as a birthday present, is pronounced dead as a result of jumping from his apartment window in "a fit of depression." The second victim is the actress Andamana, whose loyalty to Mabuse becomes divided in the process of complying with her strategy to involve Dorian in a love affair. Andamana's stage death turns into reality when the trick knife is "accidentally" exchanged for a real one. Finally, it is Dorian's turn to die. He is coerced into taking poison and receives a most magnificent burial, for one last headline-making event.

To the degree that the mock plot develops, and causal connections are established, the episodic structure weakens. Stronger measures are now necessary to counteract the emphasis on story line. The device used for this purpose is a double ending that poses rather than resolves the question of power, manipulation and victimization. The difficulty of representing simultaneity is overcome by alternating the sequences from two different scenarios: after Dorian has taken the poison, he receives the negative of Mabuse through the mail as a last token of Andamana's love. The ensuing sequence, rather than showing Dorian's death, shows Dorian finding his way into Mabuse's inner sanctuary, the conference room, where he wreaks vengeance on her and the entire retinue of journalists. And, in an instant repetition of these alternating sequences of Dorian's and Mabuse's death, Dorian is carried to his grave in a funeral procession, replete with dromedary and monkey and accompanied by Mabuse and the journalists. Again, this sequence is interrupted when Dorian reappears in his red racing car, mowing down the attendant crowd. Within the terms of linear-logic causality, the reappearance of Mabuse and Dorian after their explicit deaths could only be considered some sort of dream which would allow for such states of simultaneity. The film, however, makes no effort to integrate this ending as a dream or fantasy sequence within the plot, providing clear marks of transition from one state to another. On the contrary, simultaneous narration coexists on an equal footing with linear narration, without any attempt to subordinate one to the other.

If linear narrative re-enacts, as Roland Barthes has argued, the Oedipal drama—the passage from misrecognition to knowledge and the identification with the father who has the power of castration, Ottinger's films can be seen as seeking a confrontation with patriarchal discourse, not only because of the mockingly playful imitations of a linear plot construction, but also in the countervailing narrative-temporal tendencies such as simultaneity, circularity and repetition. In her article in *Women's Time*, Julia Kristeva has characterized these temporal modalities as pertaining to female subjectivity: "As for time, female subjectivity would seem to provide a specific measure that essentially retains repetition and eternity from among the multiple modalities of time known through the history of civilization."[2] In Ottinger's film, the linear-logic and dialogic story is embedded in and coupled with another mode of relating. This mode does not so much contradict the story as point to the site of its contradiction, the unspoken terrain surrounding the story: *mater*iality, surface, plurality, process, aspects which, like non-linear temporalities have been coded as feminine in our culture. They are characteristic of the realm which Kristeva calls the semiotic, the space before the Oedipal prohibition interferes with the closeness to the mother's (female) body, before language and the symbolic. Woman's special relationship to this realm is characterized by the "impossibility of ever completely establishing herself as Other than the mother—even if that is what patriarchal culture has told her she must do if she wants to write."[3] Society's relegation of the female child to the semiotic space with her mother, whose body she duplicates, on the one hand, and exhortation to leave that realm, in order to participate in the symbolic puts women in a double bind. In order to express themselves artistically women must deal with a very high degree of tension between the semiotic and symbolic spaces.

Ottinger's strategy is to maintain this tension both by inscribing the feminine into patriarchal discourse and by disrupting the semiotic *locus amoenus* by introducing linear elements. In *The Image of Dorian Gray*, the inscription of the feminine occurs alongside and in constant counterpoint to classical and patriarchal discourse not just on the level of narrative structure, but on other levels as well: composition, mise-en-scène, motifs and roles, to mention just a few. Such an inscription set off as it is against a patriarchal discourse, which is in itself placed at an ironic distance, makes apparent the cultural contingency of sexual difference and affords the pleasure which results from playful indeterminacy and equivocation.

REPETITION

Structurally, repetition is located in the episodic excess of the narrative. The recurring images of groups of three women, for example, function both decoratively and symbolically, but do not participate in plot-related action. Mabuse's three female aids—Susy, Passat and Golem—are the stylish backdrop to the tycoon's actions and at the same time represent the whole host of techno- and bureaucrats that uphold the enormous media concern. The corresponding trio in the opera section are the three goddesses of fate, played by the same actresses. They help Dorian with the difficult process of memory, a process which takes him through the "sea of stones" until, at the furthest recess of this journey, he happens upon a scene of taboo-breaking: a kosher butcher is handing to the child Dorian the skinned head of a pig. The force of this transgression of the Law catapults Dorian into two awakenings. First, the child Dorian wakes up to the adult Dorian still holding the rope and the pig's head. (The image also brings full circle the departure scene of the prince/Dorian in the opera, where he sets out onto the "sea of stones," his vision obstructed by a cloth tied over his eyes and equipped with a guide: a pig tethered to a rope.) And, second, the adult Dorian wakes up from his opium dream to the world of Dr. Mabuse.

The divergent function this repeated constellation of three serves suggests that repetition is not employed here to stabilize the subject-ego, providing cohesiveness in the narrative,[4] but rather to abolish this unity by drawing attention simply to the autonomous existence and transformation of this constellation. The parodic use of triad—three naked old men (Independence, Non-Partisanship, Objectivity) embodying the virtues of journalism in Mabuse's archive—should emphasize this point even further. The same applies to the many double and twin configurations in the film, a couple of Bavarian spies, Siamese twins, twin children by the name of Right and Left, and so on. These recurring pairs do not act to bind the spectators into the plot; they are symbols, if anything, of the opposite narrative concern: plurality and diversity. Yet, in keeping with the mock plot, there is also the kind of repetition which lends itself to a narrative strategy interested in maintaining the illusion of continuity and unity. Naturally, these repetitive narrative patterns are handled with a good deal of irony and humor, befitting their mock status. The woman in gold, who knows the "open sesame" and whose excessive size metonymically refers to her function as Mabuse's foil by virtue of her sheer irrepressibility, turns out to be the key to the "enigma" of Mabuse's stronghold. A more confusing series of clues was never invented. The woman in gold appears at the beginning of the "story" thwarting one of Mabuse's spies from communicating an apparently urgent message. She does this by blithely occupying the only telephone booth in sight for the sole purpose of correcting her make-up. Next we see her riding a boat on a body of water, which, as an extended camera shot reveals, borders directly on the "sea of stones" which we have seen traversed by Dorian's aimless wanderings. As she is treading the boat, she is singing sovereignly conducting her own song, while behind her in tow are the Siamese twins swaying gracefully in the breeze. Her voice is drowned out by the concerted efforts of a great number of fog horns, which reinforce the romantic lure and promise of this comical Siren. The absence of her voice is all the more effective, as it finally proves to be the instrument which opens Dorian's passage into Mabuse's underground realm. At the end of this series of narrative clues, the irony that this figure, representing irrepressible and uncontrollable forces, should provide cohesiveness to the story becomes apparent. Structurally ordering while representing chaos, she serves narrative unity while aiding in the destruction of the creator of stories, Dr. Mabuse. This "both and" attitude again testifies to the film's capacity to support the contradiction between linear traditional narration and modernist autonomy of the fragment and repetition for its own sake.

The same attitude is strongly embedded in the compositional principles as well as in the point-of-view structure of the film. As an example of the former, Mabuse's conference table provides a good focus for discussion. Because of its great length, this table acts as a line, which divides the image into two equal parts. The symmetry of this centrally composed view is further emphasized by the enormous circular vats placed on either side of the divide. The vats also furnish the frame with additional depth of field already established by the vanishing point of the table's outline. This balanced and contained view positions the spectator-subject in an identification with the camera, affording him/her clarity and coherence of vision that central perspective has come to mean since the Renaissance.[5] Camera movements and movements by the characters in the frame are slight enough (not) to upset the spectator's sense of mastery over the spectacle. Yet, at the head of the conference table, the strongest point in this composition, stands the villainous, powerful Dr. Mabuse as if the whole tableau had been created just for her—charming, to be sure, but hardly an object of display for the master-spectator. She is master herself and contemptuously throws back the look, so forcefully that the camera actually begins to recede, very slowly revealing one after another the obliging journalists for whom she has nothing but scorn. And slowly, very slowly, the spectator, instead of being in control, feels pushed to the side, cringing because the one final oppositional voice at the other end of the table proves so pitifully weak and ineffectual. The sense of power usually granted the spectator in classical examples of central perspective is undermined through a switch in the gender of the object of secondary identification. Yet, the reversal is not quite as simple. The phallic woman, upholding and representing male order, succumbs to a discourse of an entirely different kind.

NARCISSISM—REFLECTION

Somewhere along the way in Mabuse's attempt to turn Dorian into her creature, she grows fond of him. A likeness emerges and the constellation persecutor-victim is all but reversed at the end of the film. After Dorian gains access to the conference room the table is literally turned. Mabuse occupies for the most part the camera end of the table, i.e., her look is identified with the look of the camera watching Dorian's slow approach. Through the alignment of looks of the spectator, the camera and Mabuse, Dorian's stabbing of Mabuse spells his revenge not only on the person of the media tycoon but on the medium and the audience as well. Harking back to Oscar Wilde's novel, the stabbing of Mabuse can of course also be seen as the annihilation of his own image, both of the media image created by Mabuse and the reflection of his own character in Mabuse. A good deal of Mabuse's fondness for Dorian has to do with the fact that he is her best student. She was assured of that from the beginning, relying as she did on his "narcissism and inexperience." Between the feeling of omnipotence afforded Dorian by his Chinese nurse-servant by the name of Hollywood, who treats Dorian like a diva and suffocates him with attention, and the actual power wielded by Mabuse, lies a difference in degree only.

In the opera segments, Mabuse and Dorian are the only visible specta-tors (in glaring contrast to the sound track, which is that of a large audi-ence). Perched high up in a rocky niche draped to look like a theatre box, they are watching themselves through binoculars. The same constellation of brute power and narcissistic egotism in all its seductiveness is held up to them. But divided as it is into spectator and spectacle, the mirroring goes a step beyond merely drawing a historical parable. It characterizes the spectacle/spectator relationship precisely in terms of narcissism and power and the equivocation of the two. Dorian, the spectator, immediately identifies with his reflection, Don Luis, on stage and, absorbed by the spectacle, utters his wish for a happy end. Mabuse's harsh laughter and commentary informs Dorian that the powerful never compromise or renounce their claims. She explains the spectacle to him just as she pro-poses to "explain and interpret the world" on their "horror tour by night," which consists of a string of spectacles directed and orchestrated by Mabuse for Dorian's amusement. This association places Mabuse on the side of the spectacle, if that is not already well established through her position as the boss of a media concern and the reference to the illustrious hypnotist, her namesake. Their interdependence, not to say symbiosis, now becomes clearer. Both rely upon each other for the gratification of their narcissism. Dorian's spectatorial narcissism allows him to see his own reflection in everything and to continue to feel at the center of the uni-verse, while Mabuse, the director, enjoys the thought of re-creating the universe in her own image. I would like to take the reflections and equivocations surrounding the pair Dorian-Mabuse one step further: there seems to be a refusal, especially towards the end when Dorian is surpassing his master in business-like know-how, to draw absolute lines of separation between the oppositional poles of spectator-spectacle, oppressor-oppressed. The interdependence of roles creates a threshold between subject and object allowing for a constant transformation from one position to the other, and in this sense a unity of the two. The impression of playfulness created by this operation has been criticized as "gratuitous"[6] or even trivial. Yet, the extremes of triviality and complexity are treated as if they were the same by classical systems of logic, since they both lead to incomprehensibility in traditional terms.[7]

Possibilities for expanding our tolerance for what is comprehensible could be described in terms of the strategies emerging in some of the recent "postmodernism" debate: "It is precisely at the legislative frontier between what can be represented and what cannot that the postmodernist operation is being staged."[8] In fact, most of the aspects discussed so far concerning Ottinger's latest film are vital issues in these debates: the loss of the spectator's mastering position vis-à-vis the spectacle, the equilibrium between episodic and linear narration and a plurality of discourses allowing for heterogeneity and an inclusion of the one *and* the other.

From this perspective, it is important to take up once again the oppositional pair Dorian-Mabuse and to emphasize that the reflection and transformation of one into the other does not deny difference or reduce opposites to sameness; rather, it questions the fixity of oppositions and of sexual opposition in particular. In fact, instead of talking about opposition, Ottinger's films invite discussion in terms of position. The position of the young dandy—traditionally a male figure—is physically assumed by the female actress and the social position of power, normally in the hands of men, is represented by a woman. Not only do the women function as classical distancing device (by filling the traditional male position, they defamiliarize these positions), questioning power as well as narcissistic dandyism, they also weaken the field of the biological determination of sexual difference. It might be objected, of course, that masquerade and assuming a man's position are traditional devices women have used to speak and to represent themselves. Yet, against the background of a general dissolution of sexual roles, as is suggested by the interchangeability of characters and gender positions in Ottinger's films, these devices function like bold propositions rather than meek excuses for change-ability.

Another aspect of non-oppositionality or rather non-polarization in the midst of diversification is the collage technique which is so pervasive in, if not the very basis of, Ottinger's films. While the use of collage in her early films (especially *The Seduction of the Blue Sailors*) relies mainly on the associations established between short fragments, ready-mades, quotes, etc., bearing a definite affinity with the classical modernist principles of

Dada and Surrealism, the most recent development of that technique could best be described as the layering of discourses in image and sound, running separately-parallel from each other but also intersecting and linking up with new meanings. There is, for instance, the discourse of the travelogue in *The Image of Dorian Gray*, the picture postcard aspect of Berlin and of the Canaries, where the opera segment was shot. Dorian is associated most distinctly with this discourse, which also comments on his parasitic voyeurism. The discourse of the avant-garde is mainly expressed in costumes, architecture and decor. Most worthy of mention are: the fin-de-siècle frame of the opera, with motifs by Gustave Moreau, the Mendelsohn house, one of the perfectly intact examples of Bauhaus architecture in Berlin, as a choice for Dorian's residence (here Ottinger's loving care for detail is particularly striking in the selection of furniture and interior decor down to the indirect lighting prescribed by Mendelsohn), the costumes of Mabuse's aide inspired by Dali, and Dorian's scooter outfit, a reference to Mayakovski. There is the colonialism/imperialism discourse, which in the opera has sub-plot status but reverberates throughout the film, particularly in the image of the "Sarotti-Mohr" sent by Mabuse with the deadly dose of poison for Dorian. The turbaned Moor has appeared as emblem on every bar of Sarotti German chocolate for many decades. In the figure of the Chinese servant "Hollywood," the colonial discourse intersects with the discourse on the movie industry. As Hollywood begins to tell the story of the death of Dorian's parents at the hands of a monkey practicing what he had seen at an uprising in China, the hand-held camera slowly flickers from image to image of glamourous Hollywood couples from the 1930s and 1940s. Such linkages leave their traces and comment upon each other in a constant process of associations which would require many studies to unravel.

What comes across immediately is the brilliance of surfaces in the film. Ottinger embraces the notion of surface in much the same sense as the fin-de-siècle artists did, or Rilke, for example, who, in his studies of Rodin's sculptures, identified *Oberfläche* (surface) to be the point where the external and the internal meet. This again demonstrates an avoidance of polarization. For Ottinger, calling attention to the material is as important as her concern with composition. Her surfaces are radiant to the point of liquidity. From the brilliant quality of the film stock itself to the shiny and sometimes translucent costumes, glossy make-up and mirror-like surfaces of decor, the whole film is a celebration of materiality. This concern with materiality and surface is the one stylistic feature which lends cohesion and a semblance of unity to the film's otherwise heterogeneous and eclectic elements—a semblance of unity only, because the various elements remain distinct and to some extent discrete.

Both the playful juxtaposition of disparate elements and the emphasis on materiality as surface, at times referred to as simulacrum, have however raised questions from some quarters of the postmodernism debate. In fact, in Fredric Jameson's extensive article on "Postmodernism or the Cultural Logic of Late Capitalism," the two aspects are seen in relation to each other. The "play at random stylistic allusion"[9] is here seen as pastiche or, one might call it, parody without bite because, as Jameson elaborates, in the absence of one determining style (a consequence of the disappearance of the bourgeois subject), the sarcastic or otherwise ridiculing dimension of parody falls flat. This mode of pastiche is then linked with "the appetite for a world transformed into sheer images of itself and pseudo-events," the condition of simulacrum whose "new spatial logic" effaces what used to be historical time. Jameson's attempt to define a cultural dominant at the same time as he offers a periodizing hypothesis has the effect of a rather global non-differentiation, or rather a distinction on the basis of just a handful of more or less formal criteria which are then related at various points to the economic base. One is tempted to think of Lukács' treatment of Expressionism in the 1930s and plead, as did Brecht, for greater independence for individual texts from the notion of a cultural dominant, while, at the same time paying closer attention to their function. In other words, rather than concentrating on a mere description of stylistic features, an examination of the conditions of production of texts within a historical period is in order and might throw more light on the use of certain formal strategies.

Ottinger's new film is a point in case in this argument. On one level *The Image of Dorian Gray in the Yellow Press* is a discourse on its own conditions of production. How does a woman succeed in making films today in West Berlin? The hurdles and obstacles to be taken before the various Mabuses of the consolidated media world are side-stepped to arrive at this goal are of truly Herculean proportions.[10] Is it necessary, therefore, to conjure up the image of the casual consumer when talking about the elimination of a unifying style? Is it not equally justified to consider the juxtaposition of disparate elements and styles as indicating a desire for inclusion? Here, it seems that the concerns of postmodernism and of feminism intersect both formally and theoretically. In Ottinger's films the mixing of styles, of quotidian gestures and lofty symbols, of "high" art and kitsch and the juxtaposition and interweaving of discourse is done with great care to achieve specific effects. The opera is an excellent example of this. The highly artificial acting style, reminiscent of the exaggerated gestures of expressionist film, clashes with the natural scenery, with the actual ocean, beach and rocks of the Canary Islands where the historical landing of the Spaniards took place. This clash of styles, held together, moreover, by the fin-de-siècle frame of the opera relates in its own way the impact of the Spanish conquerors on the indigenous culture of the Islands. Under the rule of Andamana, the exchange and "swapping" of customs and costumes produces a motley, slightly chaotic but peaceful group of people, whereas the demands of the Grand Inquisitor to homogenize, to "convert" everything to the logic of the "One"—one standard, one style—results in violence and death.

Notes

1. Pierre Nora, "Monster Events," *Discourse*, 5 (Spring 1983), 5–20.

2. Julia Kristeva, "Women's Time," *Signs*, 7:1, 23.

3. Alice Jardine, "Pre-Texts for the Transatlantic Feminist," *Yale French Studies*, 62 (1981), 229.

4. Timothy Corrigan, "On the Edge of History"; paper delivered at film conference on German avantgarde film of the 1970s at Milwaukee, 1982.

5. Stephen Heath, *Questions of Cinema* (Bloomington: Indiana, 1981), pp. 27–33.

6. Claire Barwell, "Letter from Sceaux," *Framework*, 25 (1984), 110.

7. Eva Meyer, *Zählen und Erzählen* (Vienna-Berlin, 1983), p. 31.

8. Craig Owens, "The Discourse of Others: Feminists and Post-Modernism," in *The Anti-Aesthetic*, ed. Hal Foster (Port Townsend: Washington, 1983), p. 59.

9. Fredric Jameson, "Postmodernism or the Cultural Logic of Late Capitalism," *New Left Review*, 146 (1984), 66.

10. Miriam Hansen, "Visual Pleasure, Fetishism and the Problem of Feminine/Feminist Discourse," *New German Critique*, 31 (Winter 1984), 96.

The Last Stranger: *Querelle* and Cultural Simulation

CHRISTOPHER SHARRETT

When the real is no longer what it used to be, nostalgia assumes its full meaning. There is a proliferation of myths of origin and signs of reality; of second-hand truth, objectivity, and authenticity.

Jean Baudrillard

For Fassbinder's story is a history of a sellout, a sellout of the new style life. The man who once, in his early work, had rejected the customary shot/countershots, tracks, and zooms became in the end a master of a style he had himself discredited, the practitioner of a banal craft. In this way he became the bootlicking mirror image of the German establishment, the showpiece, in the guise of an outsider, of a corrupt and disaster-stricken Germany into whose favorite and most syrupy cliches he breathed new life, without any of the irony or the checks you would expect from a detached or objective mind. It was a pact forged by the outsider with the old oligarchs of the film industry, to turn the overworked formulas of "*Heimatfilm*" into those of the faggot film.

Hans-Jürgen Syberberg on Fassbinder's death

SYBERBERG'S BLAST should be seen not simply as a condemnation, an anti-eulogy for his colleague, but as a criticism of the schizophrenia which has developed into the dominant mode of consciousness of post-modernism.[1] For Syberberg, Fassbinder's work represents the stalemate of Western society, caught between mythic and ideological readings of history, but inevitably opting for the comfort of mythic (patriarchal) structures. Although the West has found the traditional mythic narratives supporting capital to be increasingly ludicrous in the wake of Nazism and imperialist ventures of the postwar years, it currently finds genuine ideological consciousness distasteful, naive, and insupportable after May '68 and the failures of numerous radical or bourgeois democratic movements of the sixties. (The situation in the U.S. describes the problem ideally: rather than recognize the historical lesson of Vietnam and Watergate, the populace has turned to the myth of regeneration through violence, pretending that the crises of the past twenty years were aberrations).

"The Last Stranger: *Querelle* and Cultural Simulation" was first published in *Canadian Journal of Political Social Theory* 8.1–2 (1989): 115–28.

Rainer Werner Fassbinder's career is an acute representation of this predicament, although Syberberg misses the true resolution to Fassbinder's aesthetic and ideological positions. While Fassbinder, an artist of consciousness, attacked representation and illusionism, he was nevertheless a product (like most of the New German directors) of a "neo-colonial" political and economic system. Raised on American popular culture,[2] he remained enamored of Sirk and Fuller, of genre cinema, of narrativity, and dreamed of a "German Hollywood" at the same time that he decried the postwar ravaging of Germany by multinational corporate interests. Nonetheless, Fassbinder attempted to undermine the centrality of the American imperialist culture with cynicism and a Brechtian distance in his artistic practice. Still, Syberberg accuses Fassbinder of refusing to confront directly the objects of Western fascination (including the gaze itself) within the text of a work, as in Syberberg's own *Our Hitler* and *Parsifal.* Syberberg has never suggested that his work has successfully parted company with the hero myth or the dream of Utopia embodied in the narratives of journey and recovery. Rather, he holds that his Brecht/Wagner conjunction has demonstrated the need for a critical apparatus within the artwork itself, as the audience of postmodernism remains in limbo between representation and presentation, between patriarchal myth and historical analysis.

Syberberg's assault on Fassbinder's work, especially his critique of Fassbinder's "Syberbergian" last reel of *Berlin Alexanderplatz*—with its pastiche apocalypse-cum-puppet show—is based on the notion that Fassbinder appropriated an effect, a style, without removing it from the province of illusionism and without either incorporating it within or distancing it from what is essentially a melodrama. Fassbinder's problem then, according to Syberberg, is common to the cultural inversion of postmodernism.[3] Syberberg's tirade is ironic in that the real subject for investigation, Fassbinder's last film, is nowhere in evidence. *Querelle*, the film utilizing the greatest "Syberberg-effect," and demonstrating the lesson Syberberg has to teach, is Fassbinder's most important achievement as a work representative of the postmodern temperament.

Querelle de Brest, Genet's 1947 novel, has been analyzed chiefly in terms of its Dostoyevskian themes of degradation, penance, and redemption, and for concerns usually associated with Genet.[4] It is remarkable and fortuitous that his project should have been taken on at a point just before the filmmaker's death. It has been suggested that *Querelle* is a transitional work rather than a "final testament"; it is important that the audience is forced to confront this work as a text on which is inscribed a significant transition in cultural history.

What is foregrounded in *Querelle* is an exploration of the mediated environment of postmodernism that has unwittingly bankrupted subjects of fascination in capitalist production and the Western narrative tradition.

Querelle de Brest has the distinction of being an ideal model for intertextual discourse, exemplifying the need to reevaluate the subtexts of works within changing historical circumstances. In the hands of Fassbinder, *Querelle* becomes a device for the examination of a depleted signifying practice.

The "death of the hero," or the collapse of hero mythologies central to Western narrative art, is the subject of increased scholarly and popular discourse,[5] particularly as the patriarchal ideology underneath this master narrative becomes temporarily appealing in the reactionary climate of the 1980s. Not ironically, *The Saturday Evening Post* has published an article outlining the transmutation of the hero myth that is relevant to an understanding of *Querelle*'s exegesis.[6] With the anxiety associated with that "Silent Majority" publication, the *Post* describes the transferance of the public's collective fascination from figures of historical relevance (MacArthur, Lindbergh) to entertainers whose presence, although heavily mediated, affected cultural transformation and, as signifiers, had some foundation in the Real (Elvis Presley, James Dean, Marilyn Monroe). The situation is now quite troublesome. The historical dimension is inscribed with the names of "Dynasty" and "Dallas" characters—and Reagan as well—all as free-floating signifiers divorced from the referential, thus reinforcing delusions of the Imaginary. What the *Post* has informally described is the precession/procession of simulacra outline by Baudrillard:

it [the image] is the reflection of a basic reality

it masks and perverts a basic reality

it marks the absence of a basic reality

it bears no relation to any reality whatsoever: it is its own pure simulacrum[7]

The relevance of Baudrillard's precession formula to the hero myth is the rupture of the myth from its signifying practice and historical role. *Querelle*, in its positioning the star/hero, has a unique place in this discourse. In *Querelle*, we do not have Dean/Presley/Brando incarnating within the field of the postwar spectacle Orphic/Dionysian myths, but Brad Davis—with a peculiarly characteristic slouch, cigarette centered in the mouth, eyes wary—simulating Dean/Presley/Brando. The film's sexual politics, i.e., its representation of homosexuality, must be approached exclusively through the exploration of the bankrupt signifying practice it undertakes. *Querelle* can be understood only as "pure cinema," wherein the signifier (sexual and otherwise) is no longer adversarial but decorative, necessitating a discussion of the co-optation of sexual politics previously seen as adversarial by the dominant culture. The film's discourse is also a representation of the purely superstructural rebellion undertaken by adversarial sexuality, a rebellion now dissolved in the media. Questions about the disappearance of "love"[8] in the film and *Querelle*'s static text become obviated by this form of address.

Like much of the allusive art of postmodernism,[9] *Querelle* contains an array of references to the implosion of meaning[10] in narration to the point that its ostensible subject (criminality/sexual alienation) is actually erased. Fassbinder has constructed a Black Mass (with dolorous liturgical soundtrack) for the earlier cinematic communion centered on the sexual charisma of the movie star, or, rather, for the cult of male eros which has substituted for the chivalric romances and the sagas of the epic enablers. The simulacra have taken predominance as the hero no longer has an association with the political or the historical. It is not coincidental that Lt. Seblon—the repressed homosexual who idealizes Querelle—should function in the film not as the authorial *raissoneur* of Genet's novel, but as a figure for the mediation of desire with which the audience can identify. Seblon refers also to Aschenbach in *Death in Venice*, the invert who represents a cultural and ideological dilemma, viz., the torpor of the bourgeois *fin de siècle* (now become *fin-de-millenium*) temperament, driven into masochism and apocalypse out of an exaggerated self-image and expectation.[11] The Romantic idealization of Tadzio in *Death in Venice*, particularly when considered within the epic scope of Visconti's film version, reminds bourgeois society of its tacit contract in this enterprise, a pathological fixation located first in the bourgeois ideology of High Modernism, then in the particular scopophilia of postmodern culture. Fassbinder's *Querelle* pursues the crisis of Mann's novella and Visconti's film but in a reflexive manner, viewing the crisis at its end-point. The aspiration of Lt. Seblon must be contexted in its specific cinematic configuration. Seblon is, after all, Franco Nero and necessarily becomes a simulacrum, more so than Dirk Bogarde in *Death in Venice*, whose referential is a certain literary and historical reality. The beefcake hero of *Camelot* and *A Professional Gun* and numerous American and European grade-B genre films, Nero throws the cognoscenti back onto a contemplation of cinema's nurturing of the cult of male beauty.[12] Could the casting of Franco Nero be a joke? We attend also to the fact that Martin Sheen, a James Dean simulacrum, was an alternative to Brad Davis at an early stage of the film's production.[13] The gaze itself, as it is focused on the simulacra of Hollywood "Homeros"[14] is given its requiem in *Querelle*, along with some of the ideological assumptions underneath that phase of aesthetic production.

The term "simulacrum" may seem overextended or inaccurate in this discussion, particularly when applied to someone like Martin Sheen (really an elder statesman of the cinema already reproduced in teen-idol simulations), who could more easily be termed an "imitation" or an actor "influenced" by another. The concept of the simulacrum, as used by Baudrillard, refers to the copy for which no original exists, the philosophical contention from antiquity which finds its concrete example in computer-generated imagery. The basis for the concept is the divorce of the image from representation, not just of a figurative sort, but in terms of the image's foundation in history and a mode of production. The Hollywood star was always in a precarious position in the representation process, but the increased cloning of stars, advancing rapidly with the voraciousness of the spectacle, has thrown the star into the category of the simulacrum. The undifferentiated chaos in which the star/hero is located is at the crux of Querelle's parody. Brad Davis and Martin Sheen become simulacra as we perceive their separation, in the current environment, from the radical assumptions that made a James Dean part of an adversarial cultural tendency.

It would be erroneous to periodize the destruction of male eros/divine enabler within the time frame increasingly associated with postmodernism (the past twenty-five years or so). Both the erasure of Dean/Presley/Brando as adversarial signifiers and the recycling of such figures as "trash archetypes" (fully enunciated myths produced in the mediascape as kitschy posters and associated souvenir art) are part of a long-term Enlightenment project, one that returns the concepts of sacrifice and hierarchy to Christianity. In his painstaking study of the representation of Christ's sexuality in Renaissance art and its erasure by the Enlightenment mind, Leo Steinberg notes that the depiction of Christ's genitals in Renaissance iconography affirmed the concept of God's alliance with the human condition.[15] The puritan ideology constituting the "modern oblivion" to which Christ's sexuality was consigned effectively destroyed the humanization of the divine, the merger of the sacred and the profane. The tendency to appropriate the most progressive aspects of Christianity, and to re-define them in terms that will validate hierarchical systems and prevent class consciousness, have been controlling aspects of image production in the West. The setting of a progressive myth representing a transitional historical moment within a production system which can co-opt and overwhelm it is, of course, a feature of bourgeois ideology evidenced continually in the history of representation.

The signifying practice of the cinema inadvertently accomplished much in halting the desacralization process by the incarnation of its various pagan messiahs: the rough trade, hustlers, bums, and cultural rebels who proliferated in popular art at mid-century. The sensibility underneath this practice was represented very well by the work of Tennessee Williams, already perceived as a "Southern Gothic version of Jean Genet for his mixing of sex, death, and salvation in beguiling contradiction."[16]

The sensibility of Williams (indeed shared by Genet) demonstrates the relevance of the homosexual experience to the mythic impulses of the narrative tradition; the influence is of such a magnitude as to necessarily cause it to be moved into a range of cultural and ideological discourse beyond the parochial limits both of conservative critics and Williams' and Genet's protectors within the gay intelligentsia. The myth of the dying and reviving god, the hero who brings fertility to the land, is absolutely central to Williams' plays and to their filmic renderings—in particular *Orpheus Descending, Sweet Bird of Youth, Suddenly Last Summer*, and *Night of the Iguana*. The myth of the fertility god, a conservative emblem in the hands of T.S Eliot, became for Williams representative of an important moment of radical culture flux. The charismatic stranger who is "the influence of evil, disruption, or destruction"[17] and threatens the established order becomes a concept of enormous relevance, perhaps for the last time, in the upheaval which began in the 1950s and culminated in the activity of the 60s. Recent evidence[18] that Williams may have rewritten *Battle of Angels* (later *Orpheus Descending*) so that the central figure, Val Xavier, becomes a wandering guitar player allegorizing the rise of Elvis Presley, suggests Williams' prescience and the preeminence of the myth in question. Although the mid-50s rebel hero became a representation of an assault on sexual and racial assumptions and a force disturbing to Eisenhower America, the figure was also circumscribed not only by the problematical hero myth and its attendant cult of individualism, but also by the desire generated by the gaze, by the culture industry that turned even vital, activist individuals (Brando lived up to his image) into effigies.

The commodification process implicit in the gaze becomes the death knell to this final manifestation of the hero myth, a manifestation wanting in credibility at its outset due to its production circumstance. The language "consensus" inscribed in the cinema's myth of the hero, in this phase of modernism and of image production, is exposed in *Querelle* as a fraud. Notwithstanding the audience-industry relationship, the myth in question is seen by Fassbinder's project as fraudulent because of its superficiality and circumscription by the narcissistic gaze. The stasis and staginess of *Querelle* which so upset critics is Fassbinder's Syberbergian maneuver: Genet's criminal becomes a conceit for exposing both the Hollywood narrative (upon which Fassbinder was always dependent) and audience positioning in this narrative tradition.

The parodic element to *Querelle* is immediately available. The theme of the journeying, revivifying hero was already there, explicit in Genet's novel,[19] except that Genet, unlike Williams, turns it on its ear. While Val Xavier in *Orpheus Descending* becomes a symbol of sexual liberation and racial harmony for the women of Two River County, Querelle brings alienation and inversion to the city of Brest. The notion of the stranger causing a *disruptive* as well as redemptive process is essential to the hero myth and the messianic impulse; the revolutionizing of society necessarily brings a phase of upheaval, an element visible in the narrative of the New Testament and the epic romances. In Fassbinder, the emphasis on the disruptive function is meant to precipitate a reevaluation of the premises of the myth itself. *Querelle* demonstrates that as the population remains fixed on the gaze,[20] unable to apprehend the myth as collective *projection*, the disruptive function becomes predominant. The tendency of the bourgeoisie as audience, with its association of the hero with the primacy of individualism, is to project the figure solely as ideal ego rather than as an image signifying a transitional historical moment. Examples of the relationship between the gaze and the hero as metaphorical figure are rife in the international cinema.

Films such as *The Fugitive Kind (Orpheus Descending)* propose the hero as an awakened radical potential in the population.[21] Other, more mainstream films of Hollywood narrative demonstrate how easily co-opted this archetypal myth is (particularly when it is understood precisely as "archetypal" and metaphysical rather than created by a language system, as Levi Strauss would approach the topic), and how it is ultimately inadequate in providing metaphors of revolutionary change. Joshua Logan's *Picnic* (based on Inge's play—a watered-down variation of a theme developed by Williams) suggests that not only can bourgeois society be easily recuperated after the stranger's passing, but that the stranger's principal function is as object of the gaze. This problem is represented in Hal Carter (William Holden), both through narrative strategy and in the film's famous ad campaign (Kim Novak kneeling behind Holden as he demurely covers/brandishes his nude torso, a device borrowed from Brando in *A Streetcar Named Desire*). Such narratives, at best, merely reverse (temporarily) the scopophilic construct in which the female is usually the object. In *Picnic* (and in the far more conservative *Shane*) the changes posited are relatively superficial and never address class relations or the politics of the intimate. At the same time that *Picnic* offers a challenge to upwardly mobile capital (Hal Carter's betrayal by Benson and Madge's rejection of Benson in favour of Carter) and to sexual mores of Middle America, the film waxes nostalgic in its Norman Rockwell depiction of 50s culture. More important, the only narrative that could "follow" *Picnic* would be a tempestuous romance between Madge and Hal. The sense of disruption figured in such films has more to do with a "shaking up" of society only to permit its recuperation. Narrative closure becomes complete, along with concepts of bourgeois normality.

Pasolini's *Teorema* is the most radical challenge to the messianic (patriarchal) impulse underneath the hero myth prior to *Querelle*. The film occupies a kind of middle ground in its thesis on the hero, since the Stranger (Terence Stamp) unleashes a number of disruptive forces within a bourgeois family—signifying the overturning of society—while at the same time being delineated by Pasolini as projection. The distinction between this film and, say *Picnic* is the parodic attitude toward the heroic figure. In one important sequence, the Stranger poses in the manner of a Bernini saint as the daughter takes snapshots, suggesting a sardonic self-consciousness on the part of the object of fascination—self-consciousness missing from the populace. The film occupies "middle ground" since the parody is limited, as well as the film's revolutionary faith. While the notion of the hero and the primacy of individualism are sent up, the disruptive forces unleashed suggest no specific revolutionary program beyond anarchy and the attack on bourgeois sexuality and religiosity. *Teorema* is certainly the inverse of *Shane* (with which it is often compared),[22] but the heroic process is kept relatively intact not only through the heavy mediation by this myth but because of a traditional Marxist perspective toward the social. More problematic is the Stranger's radicalizing function being reducible to a kind of "atomic individualism,"[23] with its key images alluding as much to Christian iconography as to the literal and figurative wasteland of postwar industrial society.[24]

Querelle is a more "advanced" film not in a revolutionary sense but in its situation within the culture of simulation and its total refusal of the idea of the social which provided consensus to the heroic narrative. The forces Querelle unleashes are *merely* disruptive: they are in no way efficacious from the standpoints of recuperation or transformation. Fassbinder establishes this quickly in a voice over passage by the Narrator, reworked from Genet, as we gaze at Brad Davis:

> Gradually we have come to recognize how Querelle, already part of our flesh and blood, grows larger inside ourselves, how he germinates within our souls and feeds from the best we have in us. Now that we acknowledge that Querelle is part of us, we want him to become a hero even to those who would deny him. When we follow his growth within us, we can see how perfect he is as a hero and how he will be fulfilled in his ending, an ending that is to be both his destiny and desire. The drama we wish to relate is the transposition of the familiar Event, and Querelle is its revelation. We can further say of this event that it is comparable to the Annunciation to the Virgin Mary by the Archangel Gabriel.[25]

Fassbinder's "belief" in Querelle is manifestly less than Genet's. The entirety of the preceding narration is a metatheatrical gesture. The "gradual" process of Querelle's adoration by Seblon/the audience is involved wholly in projection; that is, in the construction of Querelle as ego ideal through the gaze. The audience does not study the process of the hero's "growth within us" in a self-conscious manner, which would deny the myth through its articulation. Fassbinder suggests that projection as such must remain intact for the hero to be accepted "even by those who would deny him" (read: by those who would see this figure as merely part of an historical process). The insight of this passage is in the notion of the individual becoming a transcendent subject at the moment that the projection of the bourgeois collectivity is complete. Querelle becomes a hero only insofar as he is desired, and as individuals recognize this desire saturating the community. Seblon's personal inadequacy (his scopophilia and inversion signified both by his fixation on Querelle and his attraction to imagery such as his art books in general) recapitulates the Aschenbach/Tadzio construct alluded to earlier. Such Romantic self deprecation is transmuted into the media simulacrum of Seblon.

The operation of the Imaginary necessary to sustain this form of narrative is assaulted, however, with Querelle as subject performing at odds with the projection of his perceivers. Querelle represents a reified alienation traditional to Genet which in the cinematic context takes on the messianic configuration associated with the star/hero. The aggrandizement of alienation is made clear by the presence of Franco Nero as interlocutor, as signifier of this manifestation of projection in pop culture. A constant sense of irony informs Fassbinder's delineation of the hero myth; Querelle's "blood sacrifice" (the killing of Vic) has no relationship to the "humiliation" envisaged by Seblon, who sees Querelle as a messiah out of his exaggerated self image, his feeling that he "lacks the charm to subjugate someone else."[26] Seblon's role as a Naval officer does not represent him as a "closet case" (although he admits to this), nor is his position as voyeur distinguished merely by his class security and Romantic longing for ideal beauty (as in *Death in Venice*). His scopophilia is wholly of a bourgeois cast, with its ego projection built on associations of sexual charisma with power. But Seblon's projections, which form the text of his life, dissolve as the projection/fantasy of this mediated figure dissolves in the narrative. The figures of the gay counterculture threatening to bourgeois society, including Theo, Mario (in his "hot cop" phase), Nono, and Querelle himself, are so heavily mediated by pop culture (the Village People, etc.) as to be innocuous as figures of ideological change.

A great virtue of Fassbinder's rendering of the novel is his adherence to Genet's sense of theatre, or, rather, to performance as essential to interaction in bourgeois society. As it is developed in the cinema, Genet's theatricality exposes projection as a byproduct of the experience of the gaze, making the incorporation of the means of the oppressor one element of Genet's theme of identification clearer in film than it is in novelistic or dramatic presentation. Although unconscious of the phenomenon operating transpsychically among them, the characters of the film lose their fascination for Querelle as the Self/Other demarcation dissolves and as Querelle is made human. The process of humanization in this case, in contrast to the myth underneath the projection of Seblon/the narrator, actually "desanctifies" Querelle. While the messianic figures of the Christian tradition dispel alienation, Querelle, as signifier of the total alienation of the simulated environment (mediated society), represents the individual's viability only as image. Thus, it is very difficult to see Genet's work as other than parodic in Fassbinder's hands. The exaggerated desire centered on

Querelle explodes gradually, first with Querelle's attempt to "give in" to Seblon on the docks of Brest, then with the final alienation of Lysianne, keeper of the brothel/inn theatre.

Until about midway into the narrative, when Querelle becomes involved fully in the affairs of the world (the Gil episode), Querelle is the quintessential subject of idealization central to the Romantic style and the scopophilic drive advanced by bourgeois ideology. Relationships as projection continue in the choreographed duel (itself a parody of male bonding rituals) between Querelle and his brother, a confrontation based on the notion of Querelle as ideal (or "evil") Other in a parody of the good/bad brother construct. At this point a mock procession to Calvary interrupts the action of the narrative itself, exploring the operation of myth in the most presentational manner. Then, with the attempted reciprocation by Querelle with his admirer (Seblon), and with the exposure of Querelle as merely flesh (a criminal), Querelle is abandoned. Querelle is a hero only when static, not when fully involved in the narrative (history). The emblematic stills of the film are of Brad Davis leaning against a lamppost (quoting numerous images of the 50s rebels), or Davis covered with soot from the *Vengeur*'s boiler room (Dean in *Giant*).[27] At the film's conclusion, these images are returned to us, as Querelle is offered as transcendent subject even as alienation within society is complete (represented by the pathetic situation of Lysianne). There is no irony here, since the "Angel of the Apocalypse" has proceeded into the range of the simulacra: the social has ceased to exist.

Querelle's apotheosis occurs at the moment he enters "the lofty region where mirror images converge and are united."[28] Yet while the narrative suggests the myth's final reification, the narrative ends up running in two separate directions; the audience is hyperconscious by now of Fassbinder's presentation of Querelle as myth, and the very presentational ending underscores the beginning of Querelle's failure, the disintegration of his credibility as myth for the characters in the narrative. None of this signifies, however, that the dimension of the historical has been entered into and the mythical left behind. Even as Querelle begins to collapse under the projection of the collectivity and the myth that has been constructed around him, his receding does not prevent the recuperation of the idealization process. The political lesson of the film, and Fassbinder's most incisive remark on postmodernism (irrespective of Syberberg), is the bolstering of the commodity status of the image. The film, very fittingly, ends up as a "beautiful" coffee table book, each still of which recalls Hollywood and the cinematic history which "masked" the fact that the image, in constantly repeating the myth, has destroyed the bourgeois narrative/history which has depended on mythic consciousness for its survival. We are left with the frozen moment of the still, the image as pure exchange value. The audience is made complicit in a situation which

Genet could not have intuited at a time before the triumph of the spectacle and "technotronic"[29] society. The myth of the hero which Hollywood tried to recuperate but bankrupted is chronicled and eulogized in *Querelle*. The historical situation (and fate) of the spectator within the climate of postmodernism becomes aligned to the degree of recognition that

> narcissism, sadomasochism, a hyperactive will and imagination combined with unusual passivity in practical matters, a compulsive attraction to ritual, and a tendency to take the sign for the substance . . . are qualities that belong to . . . Genet's heroes, and to the Genet who reveals himself in his style.[30]

This extends as well to the transpsychical crisis which has incorporated the spectator into this style.

Notes

1. The definitive discussion of schizophrenia as emblem of post-modernism is in Fredric Jameson, "Postmodernism and Consumer Society," in *The Anti-Aesthetic: Essays on Postmodern Culture*, Hal Foster, ed. (Port Townsend, Washington: Bay Press, 1983), pp. 111–126. A more developed version of this essay is in Jameson's "Postmodernism, or the Cultural Logic of Late Capitalism," in *New Left Review* 146 (July–August 1984), pp. 53–94.

2. This is discussed in John Sandford, *The New German Cinema* (New York: Da Capo Press, Inc., 1980), pp. 63–103.

3. See the cited discussions of postmodernism by Jameson.

4. Representative works are Richard N. Coe, *The Vision of Jean Genet: A Study of His Poems, Plays and Novels* (New York: Grove Press, 1968), pp. 170–213; Bettina Knapp, *Jean Genet* (New York: St. Martins Press, 1968), pp. 70–87; Philip Thody, *Jean Genet: A Critical Appraisal* (New York: Stein & Day, 1970), pp. 119–141.

5. The range of (ideologically divergent) discourse can be seen in, for example, the special issue of the arts journal *ZG*, No. 8 (the "Heroes" number), and in the various publications of the Popular Culture Association, including Ray Browne and Marshall W. Fishbank, eds., *The Hero in Transition* (Bowling Green, OH: Bowling Green University Popular Press, 1983).

6. Jay Stuller, "Legends that Will Not Die," *The Saturday Evening Post*, July/August, 1985, pp. 42–54.

7. See Jean Baudrillard, *Simulations*, trans Paul Foss, Paul Patton and Philip Beitchman (New York: Semiotext[e], 1983), p. 11.

8. Paul Taylor and Adrian Martin, "Where is Love? Describing Querelle," *ZG*, No. 12, Fall, 1984, p. 19. A discussion of Querelle's sexual politics is in James Roy MacBean, "Between Kitsch and Fascism: Notes on Fassbinder, Pasolini, (Homo)sexual Politics, the Exotic, the Erotic and Other Consuming Passions," *Cinéaste*, Vol. XIII, No. 4, 1984, pp. 12–30.

9. See Noel Carroll, "The Future of Allusion: Hollywood in the Seventies (and Beyond)," *October* 20, pp. 51–83.

10. This concept is derived from Baudrillard's piece "The Implosion of Meaning in the Media," in *In the Shadow of the Silent Majorities . . . or the End of the Social*, trans. Paul Foss, Paul Patton and John Johnston (New York: Semiotext[e], 1983), pp. 95–113.

11. I refer here to the notion of desire developed in René Girard, *Deceit, Desire and the Novel: Self and Other in Literary Structures*, trans. Yvonne Freccero (Baltimore: The Johns Hopkins University Press, 1965).

12. See for example, Donald Spoto, *Camerado: Hollywood and the American Man* (New York: Plume/New American Library, 1978), and also Michael Malone, *Heroes of Eros: Male Sexuality in the Movies* (New York: Dutton, 1979).

13. Described in Dieter Schidor's foreword to Rainer Werner Fassbinder, *Querelle: The Film Book,* trans. Arthur S. Wensinger and Richard H. Wood (New York & Munich: Schirmer/Mosel-Grove Press, 1983), p. 7.

14. See Parker Tyler, *Screening the Sexes: Homosexuality in the Movies* (New York: Holt, Reinhart and Winston, 1972), p. 17, passim. Also relevant to this discussion is Tyler's *Sex, Psyche, Etcetera in the Cinema* (New York: Penguin Books, 1971), pp. 73–78.

15. Leo Steinberg, *The Sexuality of Christ in Renaissance Art and in Modern Oblivion* (New York: Pantheon/October Books, 1983), p. 11.

16. Foster Hirsch, *A Portrait of the Artist: The Plays of Tennessee Williams* (Port Washington, NY: Kennikat Press, 1979), p. 14.

17. John Howlett, *James Dean: A Biography* (New York: Simon and Schuster, 1975), p. 128.

18. Elaine Dundy, *Elvis and Gladys* (New York: Macmillan, 1985), pp. 298–300.

19. See Tom F. Driver, *Jean Genet* (New York: Columbia University Press, 1966), p. 22.

20. Probably the most incisive discussion of the gaze and the cinematic experience is Laura Mulvey, "Visual Pleasure and Narrative Cinema," reprinted in Brian Wallis, ed., *Art After Modernism: Rethinking Representation* (Boston: Godine, 1985), pp. 361–375. I might suggest that also relevant to my comments on spectator relationship to the star/hero is Parker Tyler's description of Brando portrayed "with a maximum of artifice" in *One-Eyed Jacks*. See Tyler's *Sex, Psyche, Etcetera in the Cinema*, p. 76.

21. An intelligent comment on the changing cultural perception of the heroic enabler is in John E. Mack's remarkable biography of T.E. Lawrence, *A Prince of Our Disorder* (New York: Little Brown, 1976), pp. 198–242. A transitional figure in the bourgeois conception of heroic individualism, mention of Lawrence is appropriate to this discussion. The work of Herman Melville now seems an especially important prelude to *Querelle*. See Robert K. Martin, *Hero, Captain, Stranger: Male Friendship, Social Critique, and Literary Form in the Sea Novels of Herman Melville* (Chapel Hill: Univ. of North Carolina Press, 1986).

22. Raymond Durgnat, *Sexual Alienation in the Cinema: The Dynamics of Sexual Freedom* (London: Studio Vista, 1972), p. 211.

23. Ibid, p. 219.

24. Ibid, pp. 212–220.

25. *Querelle: The Film Book*, p. 81.

26. Ibid., p. 132.

27. The movement of these figures into simulations (and the periodizing and trivialization of revolt in the postwar years) is seen in, for example, David Dalton and Ron Cayen, *James Dean: American Icon* (New York: St. Martins Press, 1984) and Jerry Tillotson, "James Dean: End of the Cult Gods?" in *Hollywood Studio Magazine*, May, 1984, pp. 8–11.

28. *Querelle: The Film Book*, p. 174.

29. This is the "end of ideology" concept of the rightist strategist of postindustrialism, Zbigniew Brzezinski. See *Between Two Ages: America's Role in the Technotronic Era* (New York: Penguin Books, 1970).

30. Tom F. Driver, p. 22.

CONSTELLATION G
MYTH AND ALLEGORY: POLITICS OF UTOPIA

If texts in the preceding constellation attempted to inscribe a theory of desire not reduced or limited to heterocentric authority and binarity, the following texts take quite a different direction en route to a theory of difference and possibility. While ostensibly arguing for social change, and notably compelled by utopian aspirations, these texts take the question of will, or desire, to the problematical plane of mythical and allegorical idealism. In Kaja Silverman's analysis of Helke Sander, for example, a call to vitalist action (voluntarism) against the hegemonic, state-enforced discourse of sexual difference reinvokes an essentialism of the female body both reminiscent of texts in Constellation E ("Feminism, Motherhood, Terrorism") and prefigurative of others in Constellation H ("Feminism and Early Weimar"). How does this reinvocation of essentialism compare to Melanie Magisos's formalist analysis of modernism in Not Reconciled? *Is the Brechtian "destruction of narrative pleasure" to which she refers necessarily incommensurate with the putatively oppositional deployment of desire affirmed by Silverman? That is to say, does Magisos theorize "narrative pleasure" against the common notion of female bodily actionism or simply reinvoke it as somehow implicitly revolutionary? Don't both Magisos's and Silverman's understandings of desire function mutually toward the reconstitution of an ideal (nostalgic or mythic) future, or do their respective appropriations of Brechtian distanciation (*verfremden*), as these point forward to Constellation I ("The Return to History"), instead signal more divergent, differential aims? How do either of these aims resonate across Fredric Jameson's psychoanalytic reading of conservative allegory in Syberberg, and how are the conclusions drawn by Jameson in the face of Syberberg's construction of a certain proto-fascist and ahistorical mythos countered by Anton Kaes in Constellation B ("The* Heimat *Debate") and Eric L. Santner in Constellation I ("The Return to History")? What are the consequences of such reading for a theory of radical proximity? of radical pleasure? Do any of these texts' investigations of rhetorical play and/or friction enable a materialist analytics of the possible? How does Kent Casper's materialist analysis of apocalypticism, eschatology, and evacuated temporality in* La Soufrière *contest such investigations? Finally, where does his critique of the film's use of the Holocaust as a Christian allegory of messianic futurity counterpose Walter Benjamin's critique of German fascism in Constellation J ("The Post-al Public Sphere")?*

Helke Sander and the Will to Change

KAJA SILVERMAN

THE FILMS of Helke Sander manifest so intense a preoccupation with and resistance to boundaries that they can perhaps best be read as border-crossings. *Redupers* (1977), for instance, is as much the story of things which flow through the Berlin wall (TV and radio waves, germs, the writings of Christa Wolf) as it is of Edda Chiemnyjewski, photojournalist. Indeed, the two stories are closely intertwined since Edda judges the success of many of her photographs by the degree to which they deny the difference between East and West.

Thus Edda produces a photo montage of the two Berlins, emphasizing their quotidian similarities rather than their ideological divergences. She also hangs photo posters of the wall itself, suggesting that what separates East from West is less the referent than the sign. Finally, she and a group of women build a curtained platform from which to look into East Berlin, and invite West Berlin to the unveiling.

All three projects are motivated by the desire to tear down the wall, or at least to prevent it from functioning as the dividing line between two irreducible opposites. The photo montage, photo posters, and curtained platform are all attempts to deterritorialize Berlin, to blur the border rendered so absolute by the wall that—as Blanchot remarks—"to cross over it [means] to pass not from one country to another, nor from one language to another, but within the same country and language from 'truth' to 'error,' from ['good'] to ['evil'], from 'life' to 'death'"[1]

Redupers makes the wall a signifier for psychic as well as ideological, political, and geographical boundaries. It functions there as a metaphor for sexual difference, for the subjective limits articulated by the existing symbolic order both in East and West. The wall thus designates the discursive boundaries which separate residents not only of the same country and language, but of the same partitioned space.

Sander's second feature, *The Subjective Factor* (1980) focuses even more insistently on sexual borders, and on the means by which they are established and maintained. It provides a very sophisticated critique of certain discursive mechanisms for effecting closure and exclusion, mechanisms which are complexly imbricated with sexual difference. It also demonstrates a number of formal strategies for resisting closure and exclusion, projecting in the process a revolutionary aesthetic.

Reprinted from *Discourse* 6 (1983): 10–30, copyright Kaja Silverman.

The Subjective Factor deals with a leftist commune started in Berlin in 1967. The commune serves as a synecdoche for the West German student movement, but one which affords a rather different view of that movement than that provided by existing histories[2]—different because Sander's close-up of its domestic economy foregrounds relations which are not recognized by orthodox chronicles. (This is not to say that we are given a truer or less mediated access to the events of the late sixties, or that those events are presented as having an extra-discursive status. On the contrary, the film stresses at all times the "subjective factor" in any perception, recollection, or account. It also shows that factor to be an effect of discourse. Sander's film refracts a particular construction of history—an SDS construction—through the discourses of feminism and communal life,[3] noting their multiple points of divergence and non-equivalence.)

The commune portrayed by *The Subjective Factor* houses assorted male leftists, ranging from SDS members to a terrorist, as well as a reformed juvenile delinquent, a black American, a small boy, and three women. Not surprisingly, the three women find themselves burdened with traditional responsibilities—housework, child-care, typing—and excluded from political discussions. On one occasion Anni, the central character, is simply relegated to the kitchen during a planning session. On another, more public occasion, she and the other women sit underneath the platform on which the male leaders of the SDS make their speeches.

The female members of the commune are not only silenced, but denied political representation. They attempt repeatedly to introduce into the larger movement such issues as day-care, the domestication of women, and the sexually differentiating role played by the media. However, their male colleagues decline to address any problem specific to woman within the present social order, objecting that such problems fall outside a classic socialist critique. Laughter greets Anni's suggestion that women are a class, and ridicule her attempt to outline a history of the female gender (Uwe, her lover, characterizes her observation that the oppression of women can be traced back to Neanderthal man as "unscientific").

Through the dramatization of these and a number of other similar confrontations between the student left and an emerging women's movement, *The Subjective Factor* isolates three discursive mechanisms for limiting the field of knowledge and the area open to transformation: the establishment of discursive fellowships, the insistence on orthodox usage, and the pretension to objectivity or scientific accuracy. A discursive fellowship creates the conditions under which a given discourse can be employed, and makes certain that only those who have been initiated—who have undergone the necessary apprenticeship, and who meet all other requisite criteria—are permitted to occupy the speaking position of that discourse.[4] All currently dominant discourses, right or left—all, that is, which are congruent with an existing social order—make sexual difference an implicit deciding factor for admittance to their fellowships. Women enter these fellowships only under exceptional conditions, and are permitted to remain there only so long as they conform with absolute precision to house rules.

Discursive fellowships are closed not only to "outsiders," but to competing discourses. They insist, that is, on orthodox usage. To use a discourse in orthodox ways is to maintain it in its current condition—to safeguard it against change, preserve its integrity. Orthodox usage also implies keeping power where it has already been consolidated, and leaving unaltered the status of both the speaking and spoken subjects.[5]

Employing a discourse in traditional ways will only seem imperative so long as that discourse is believed to have truth-value, to offer its practitioners an objective or scientifically accurate view of some aspect of reality. Since any modification would presumably interrupt that privileged access, a very high premium is placed upon the already-heard and the already-written.

A discourse always projects the objects appropriate to its exercise. To the degree that it successfully imposes its "will to truth"—its claim accurately to reflect or account for the real—only those objects will seem genuinely important and worthy of discussion.[6] All others will be dismissed as subjective and illusory. Together these three mechanisms—discursive fellowships, insistence upon orthodox usage, and pretension to truthfulness—perform a castrating function, insisting on certain users, norms, and objects to the exclusion of all others. So strenuously do they resist incursions from the "outside" that the transition to a competing discourse becomes a journey from "'truth' to 'error,' from ['good'] to ['evil'], from 'life' to 'death.'"

The Subjective Factor challenges all three mechanisms for effecting closure and exclusion. It insists on crossing discursive borders as freely as any others, denying the binary logic of orthodox usage and "initiates." On its premises there are no rules either as to who may employ a given discourse, or in what way. Indeed, *The Subjective Factor* goes so far as to privilege non-orthodox over orthodox usage, since only through the violation of existing norms can anything new be said.

Not only does *The Subjective Factor* ignore the boundaries between discourses, and employ the latter in highly irregular ways, it also generates productive syntheses. Sander's second film is a model of discursive adaptability, a testament to the saving grace of knowing how to shift the center and expand the limits of one discourse by combining it with others. These combinations make available a number of new aesthetic possibilities, and point the way toward an alternative political praxis.

DISCURSIVE ADAPTATIONS

The organization of *The Subjective Factor* can best be described as communal—as capable of accommodating private as well as public events, everyday life as well as history, the poetic as well as the didactic, dissonance as well as melody. It utilizes such diverse editing strategies as the long take, the shot/reverse shot formation, montage and brief autonomous shots; such diverse musical modes as classical opera, revolutionary songs, and jazz improvisation; and such diverse sound/image relationships as synchronized dialogue, voice-off, voice-over, and noise overlap. However, the most remarkable alliance is the one it forges between the documentary and the fiction film.

In an early interview Sander noted her preference for what might be called "generic bricolage"—for the collapsing of cinematic categories:

> Truthfully speaking, the distinction between genres means nothing to me. I don't believe in settled or finished things. [In *Redupers*] there is a juxtaposition of the most diverse problems which neutralize each other, mutually influence each other, and overflow onto each other.[7]

The film practice described by Sander is one in which seemingly incompatible discourses are forced into a creative cohabitation, are adapted to each other and to the desires of the authorial subject. As a consequence of this collective living experience, many elements of those discourses undergo a radical metamorphosis and come to signify in altogether different ways.

There can scarcely be a wider discursive spread than that between the documentary and the fiction film. The former stakes its right to exist on the historicity of the profilmic event, whereas the latter measures its success by how well it has been constructed, and how fully it has engaged the desires of its audience. The documentary has traditionally aspired to objectivity and facticity, subordinating its sounds and images to the real. The fiction film, on the other hand, has aligned itself with the fantasmatic, concerning itself much more centrally with the signifier than the referent, and more with the viewing subject than with the profilmic object.

The Subjective Factor does not so much deny as rearticulate the differences between the documentary and the fiction film. The defining characteristics of the former cease to be objectivity and historical authenticity, and become instead the traces which it bears of a certain authorial subjectivity, and the particular real that it projects. Similarly, the fiction footage is no longer relegated to an exclusively fantasmatic register, but is openly shown to adjoin the social field.

However, the two are never collapsed into one (as in Hollywood's docu-drama). Because both are presented as discourse, and because both are understood to participate in the (re)construction of a particular social real, boundaries can be crossed which are normally kept closed. At the same time we are given a much clearer understanding than usual of the differences which have traditionally separated the documentary from the fiction film—of the discursive operations and the social real specific to each. *The Subjective Factor* often exploits these differences for dialectical purposes.

The most obvious documentary element upon which Sander draws is newsreel footage; *The Subjective Factor* cuts frequently from dramatized footage to stock images of riots, demonstrations, and political rallies from Berlin in the late sixties. This footage is generally tinted in some way, as if to draw attention to the discursive filter through which we regard events. This de-naturalizing device is supplemented from time to time by others—slow motion, musical accompaniment, startling shot juxtapositions. Other documentary elements are less evident, since they have been incorporated into the dramatized portions of the film and have been transformed in the process. One such element is the hand-held camera, and another the third-person voice-over.

The dramatized or fiction footage, which constitutes the major part of the film, is shot almost entirely in hand-held camera. This is of course a camera style we associate with newsreel footage exposed under stressful conditions. It has consequently come to connote "history" and "facticity." Here, however, it seems to be the visual correlative of Anni's journey through an uncharted territory (early in the film the voice-over speaks of Anni discovering "totally new experiences at thirty—new ideas, new words, new books"); it shares her tentative, exploratory attitude, her point of view. Since, moreover, the film's reliance upon hand-held camera dispenses with the usual code of camera movement (with the pan, the tracking shot, the zoom) the image track can only be described as one long series of subjective shots—of shots which cannot be tabulated according to any "objective" or commonly held criteria. Hand-held camera thus comes to signify the opposite of what it signifies in the documentary; instead of functioning as the impinging trace of an external world, it functions as the scopic signature of a given subjectivity.

The third-person voice-over undergoes a similar transformation. A regular feature of the documentary, it is conventionally male, anonymous, and omniscient—the phallic voice of the Law. It occupies a space outside the diegesis, and seemingly outside subjectivity. The third-person voice-over has also traditionally spoken without seeming to address anyone in particular—to emanate from "on high."[8]

The third-person voice in *The Subjective Factor*, on the other hand, is female, and closely identified with the point of view which structures the image track—i.e., with Anni. Although its grammatical form is "impersonal," it contrives somehow to be intimate and conversational. Not only is this voice humorous, reminiscent, contemplative (in short, the antithesis of the "objective" chronicler), but it indicates both its discursive vantage and its point of address.

At the beginning of the film, Andres, Anni's grown son, pays her a visit, bringing with him two books of photographs from the late sixties. The year is 1980. As he and Anni begin to look through the books, the image track cuts to demonstration footage contemporary with the photographs.

Anni's voice-off says to Andres, apparently in response to a documentary image of herself, "That's me there in the car—your mother." The film then shifts to the late sixties, where it largely remains. Anni continues to provide occasional commentary, but now in the form of a third-person voice-over.

Anni's voice is at a considerable temporal remove from the events to which it refers. It also has recourse to what Benveniste would call the "historical" construction, one which usually serves to conceal all traces of enunciation.[9] Here, however, we never lose sight either of the speaking subject or the object to whom the utterances are directed. Above all, we are never permitted to forget that we are being discursively engaged.

Although *The Subjective Factor*'s third-person voice speaks "over" the images and sounds of an earlier period, it is not extra-diegetic. Not only does it speak from within the same narrative (albeit at a later moment than the events upon which it comments), but from the same discursive position: the position of a feminism struggling to achieve an alliance with Marxism.

Finally, the third-person voice-over in Sander's second film moves back and forth between domestic and romantic concerns on the one hand, and issues connected with work, books, and politics on the other—between the traditionally female and the traditionally male. The duality of its preoccupations (public as well as private) represents yet another of the many ways in which *The Subjective Factor* refuses to recognize borders.[10]

In addition to effecting a series of cross-overs between the documentary and the fiction film, *The Subjective Factor* engages the two genres in a number of dialectical exchanges—exchanges that are disruptive of existing power-relations and that bring about startling shifts of perspective. The most confrontational of these generic encounters occurs on the occasion of an SDS rally, and is a study in systematic opposition.

This sequence alternates between black and white documentary footage and dramatized color footage, cross-cutting between the two. The documentary images are devoted to the male participants, while the dramatized images focus instead on the female audience. These contrasts are reinforced by a number of others: whereas the men sit on a platform, rising amid much applause to address the crowd, the women huddle in a segregated area, apparently under the platform. The former are thus identified with the public sphere—with discourse and political power—while the latter are relegated to the private sphere, excluded both from speech and action. The two groups are even vertically differentiated, since the male members of the SDS are situated above their female counterparts. Finally, the deployment of documentary footage to represent the male participants, as well as the conspicuous presence within the footage of Rudi Dutschke, associates them with history, whereas the use of dramatized footage and actresses to represent the female listeners associates them with the fantasmatic register.

The Subjective Factor reveals through this complex antithesis the sexual differences at the center of Marxism. It also indicates what happens to those differences when the women de-activate their subjectivity within the discourse of Marxism, and take up residence instead within the discourse of feminism. This displacement is negotiated through a dramatic alteration in the relationship between the two sets of sounds and images.

As the film moves back and forth between the male speakers and the female listeners, the sounds of the former spill over onto the space in which the latter sit. At first this sound/image relationship is a hierarchical one, the men's voices dominating even when our visual attention is concentrated on the women. However, at a certain point—the point when a male voice speaks of the city as a means of production which belongs in the hands of the producers, and of the necessity of co-determination—authority shifts to the side of the female image. A revolutionary discourse can only define itself in opposition to established power and privilege; when it becomes the agency of oppression, articulating itself across the surface of prone and subjugated bodies whose desires it in no way addresses, it ceases to be a revolutionary discourse. And when the cinematic apparatus allies itself with those prone and subjugated bodies, offering us a viewing position in contradiction to the sound track, we are permitted to see what would otherwise escape our line of vision—the phallocentricity of Marxism's discursive fellowship.

It is of course through a parallel alienation that Anni and her friends come to understand that they are as excluded from the category of "producers" as they are from the platform and the agenda. Finally one of them says: "We can't maintain a condition of permanent revolution if this division of labor continues." They decide to hold their own, simultaneous meeting—to draw up a list of what they call "*our*" events. For the remainder of this sequence the women are no longer listeners but speakers; their voices compete with, and indeed largely drown out, those of Dutschke and the other men.

Montage by association provides the vehicle for a much less schematic juxtaposition of the documentary and the fiction film—one which does not so much invert traditional power relations as totally transform our way of looking at a piece of stock footage. This brief sequence begins with a rose-colored newsreel shot of the Shah of Iran arriving at the Berlin Opera House on June 2, 1967, with his second wife, Farah Dibah. The value of this footage within an historical analysis of West Germany in the late sixties would be its evocation of the student riots that greeted the Shah's visit, and the brutal police retaliation that resulted in the death of Benno Ohnesorg. *The Subjective Factor* does not deny this signified; indeed, it later shows footage of the police and students battling. However, it adds another *point de capiton*, ties down the signifying chain at a second, very different juncture: as the journalist's exploratory camera comes to rest on

Dibah's hair, arranged in an elegant upsweep, Sander freezes for several frames and then cuts.

The next shot offers a full-color view of a poorly-dressed woman hurrying down the street. Her hair has also been arranged in an upsweep, but quite unsuccessfully. Suddenly the false bun that provides the upsweep with its necessary support falls to the ground. The woman registers its loss, but is both too rushed and too embarrassed to stop. Andres is playing outside, and observes the incident (the second shot, although fictional, is presumably contemporary with the first, since Andres is still a child). He calls out to Anni, on the balcony of the commune, "She lost her bun." Anni, who has also witnessed the moment of social unmasking, smiles good-naturedly.

The first shot displaces attention away from the Shah to Dibah—from the male to the female subject. It also shifts the focus from the historically significant (West Germany's support for an Iranian dictator, the emergence of the student movement) to the historically insignificant (changing hair styles), seeming in the process to equate woman with the epiphenomenal. However, the second shot suggests that the epiphenomenal rides the waves of history—that West Germany's support for the Shah may be "read" in the widespread vogue generated by Dibah for the upsweep.[11] It thus challenges the division of the public from the private.

At the same time, the montage sequence indicates that transactions between the two areas are complexly and indirectly negotiated. Since the women who adopted the upsweep in the late sixties did not necessarily approve of the Shah, or even know of his existence, we are obliged to look elsewhere than to politics for the mediating element between Dibah and the German public—to look, in short, for the subjective factor. We are assisted in this search by the sound track.

The opera performed on the night of the Shah's 1967 visit to Berlin was *The Magic Flute*, a work upon which *The Subjective Factor* frequently draws for purposes of ironic counterpoint. *The Magic Flute* is characterized by an unusually blunt misogyny; indeed, it would be difficult to find a more absolute sequestration of the "male" from the "female"—a map on which the divisions between "truth" and "falsehood," "good" and "evil," or "life" and "death" are more firmly etched, or more sexually coded. The opera's plot is organized around the conflict between the Queen of the Night, representative of an unspecified evil, and Sarrastro, representative of a goodness that is finally synonymous with fraternal loyalty. The chief site of their struggle is Pamina, the Queen's daughter, who is ultimately obliged to renounce her mother. Pamina's lover, Tamino, wins her hand by becoming a member of Sarrastro's discursive fellowship. Not only is the constituency of that fellowship exclusively male, but it seems to be governed by only two (anti-feminist) rules—never trust a woman, and never speak to one inside the sacred meeting place. Significantly, the attribute most consistently associated with woman is discursive unreliability.[12]

The first shot of the montage sequence is accompanied by the aria in which the Queen of the Night, robbed of Pamina and thwarted in her attempts to make good that loss, demands the death of Sarrastro. Representing as it does one of the opera's climaxes, the aria functions as a shorthand inscription of the binary oppositions determinative of male and female subjectivity within phallocentric culture. It stands for what might be called the "symbolic logic" of sexual differentiation.

The mirror relationship of the two shots in the montage sequence draws our attention to a second subjective factor, one much more concerned with establishing similarities than differences. Through the juxtaposition of Dibah and a working class woman who aspires to look like her, Sander emphasizes the imaginary bases of subjectivity—the part played there by identification and imitation. She also suggests that imaginary operations, like symbolic ones, find their locus in gender, since despite the economic and social gulf which separates the two, Dibah functions as a prototype for the other woman. This sequence speaks to the cultural imperative for the female subject to conform to a seemingly universal ideal—an imperative to which she is singularly vulnerable as a result of the castrations and exclusions inflicted upon her by sexual difference.

When the false bun falls out of the working woman's hair, the ideal represented by Dibah is literally deconstructed. The material conditions (time, money) which make that ideal possible are exposed through their absence, rendering uncomfortably palpable the distance between the two terms in the imaginary dyad. Not only do these usually unwanted signifiers of class and capital obtrude, but the German woman ceases to be an appropriate object for the (bourgeois) male gaze, which is coded to the "eternal feminine."

Curiously, the values of illusionism and visual pleasure are entirely located on the side of the documentary image in this montage sequence, while the fictional image is associated instead with distantiation and what might be called "visual humor." Not only is the dramatized shot much more fully inflected than its documentary equivalent by questions of class, economics, and sexual difference, but it articulates an altogether different scopic field. Whereas the first shot places a fourth wall between Dibah-as-spectacle and the viewing subject, thereby encouraging the most complete identification, the second shot locates us—along with Anni and Andres—inside what is recognizably a discursive space, and invites our metacritical participation.

Not only do these discursive adaptations subject the documentary and the fiction film to a number of startling transformations and creative combinations, but they work toward corresponding changes in the social field.

They represent strategies for breaking down sexual barriers as well as generic ones—for collapsing the divisions between "male" and "female" as well as those between the historical and the fantasmatic.

KÜCHE, KINDER

The zoning laws against which *The Subjective Factor* most energetically struggles are those separating work from home. As Annette Kuhn points out, that division is a product of capitalism, and it rests upon the distinction between paid and unpaid labor:

> The sexual division of labor takes on specifically capitalist social relations in being overdetermined by the separation of work and home. Indeed the very formulation "work and home" only becomes possible in capitalism, signifying as it does a qualitatively new kind of distinction between the production of use values (by domestic labour) and the production of exchange values (through wage labour). The latter comes to be exclusively defined as work, partly because of the exchange values of the commodities produced, but crucially and specifically in capitalism because that work is performed in exchange for a wage. Labour in the household—domestic labour—remains the province of women, of wives, although at the same time the women of the proletarian class are drawn also into commodity production. The terms of their entry into the capitalist economy are, however, given by their pre-existing relation to domestic labour in such a way that they take on some of the characteristics of an industrial reserve army. . . . [13]

Although large numbers of women work outside the home, they are defined by the unpaid labor which they continue to perform within the home, labor which is defined in terms of personal needs rather than the demands of capital. The definition of women in terms of unpaid labor produces female subjects who can be paid less than their male counterparts when they do assume outside jobs (who are, indeed, often paid beneath the cost of their own reproduction), and who can be easily reabsorbed back into the home when their labor is no longer wanted. It is also the particular form which patriarchy assumes within capitalism, and it implies not only an economic, but an architectural, political, and discursive exclusion. As a consequence of the separation of work from home the female subject is isolated from wages, the factory, political representation, and the exercise of discursive power.

The Subjective Factor suggests that the student movement of the late sixties failed to re-negotiate the relationship between work and home, and as a result in no way altered the position of woman; as in capitalism and classic Marxism, the female subject found herself once again the victim of a complex exclusion. The continuity between the discourse of capitalism and the student left on the question of woman is most painfully evident on the occasion when Anni attempts to introduce into a political discussion a number of issues related to sexual difference and representation, and is sent to the kitchen to talk over these problems with Anne-Marie, another female member of the commune. As Anni leaves the meeting room we hear the now disembodied voices of the men speaking about the importance of encouraging "spontaneous action by the masses," and of being open to new ideas from them. There can be no doubt as to the gender of these masses.

Anni opens the door onto what looks like a reception area. Anne-Marie sits directly across the room, with a large poster of Che Guevara on the wall above her, draped in black. A number of shot/reverse shots follow, registering the non-verbal but by no means non-rational communication between the two women. A piano and violin perform a dissonant extra-diegetic duet during this visual exchange. Finally Anni looks to the viewer's right, and the camera moves with her gaze, scanning stacks of pamphlets and books before finally coming to rest on Anne-Marie's face. One more shot/reverse shot follows, pregnant with the unsaid—with what is in effect unspeakable within the discourse of classic Marxism. As the camera returns to Anne-Marie, she smiles faintly; the joint train of thought seems to have reached some sort of resolution.

This interior sequence is interrupted by a long, exterior take of the apartment building in which the meeting is taking place. Two windows, one above the other, are illuminated, and people seem to be moving about behind them. Anni's voice-off asks: "Why shouldn't we take the phrase 'her weakness is her strength' seriously? Maybe we're not less intelligent, helpless, deficient; maybe we're just different. . . . Maybe there are many kitchens with people just like us—what incredible energy! Maybe we're strong." While she speaks the light goes on and then off again in two adjacent windows, which seem to frame a stairway. The light in the other windows remains constant, lending credence to Anni's assertion of strength.

The camera resumes its interior position, but it now focuses on the area to the left rather than to the right of the table. A man comes in, chucks Anne-Marie under the chin, takes some food out of the refrigerator, and joins the two women at the table. His manner is almost willfully casual. Suddenly the room assumes a domesticated quality, becomes a place where food is cooked and eaten—becomes, in short, a kitchen.

In this sequence a space which has always been characterized by consistency reveals its hidden heterogeneity; the private is shown not only to open onto the broadly social, but to *contain* it. The table at which Anni and Anne-Marie sit in the final shot is simultaneously a desk and an eating area; they are surrounded by books as well as by dishes, revolutionary posters as well as refrigerators and stoves. The "moral" is clear: political inquiry not only coexists comfortably with domestic labor, but is a necessary extension of it.

The male members of the SDS send Anni into the kitchen in the hope of reasserting the traditional division between home and factory, the personal and the political. The behavior of the man who comes into the room to eat and relax serves a similar purpose; it seems calculated to return the kitchen to its univocal status. However, the double valence of that room denies all such distinctions, challenging the closed door of discursive fellowships and orthodox usage, and dramatizing the advantages of a collaboration between Marxism and feminism.

The subjective implications of such a discursive collaboration are explored in a closely adjacent sequence, one organized around perhaps the most important of the many posters that layer the film's image track. That sequence shows Anni speaking on her bedroom telephone to a male friend who has taken a sleeping pill, and who is using the conversation as a supplementary soporific. She seems bored and impatient.

The telephone caller wonders why he never sees Anni anymore, remarking that they used to be "so close." When Anni disputes this, the man asks irritably, "You know something better?" She transfers her gaze to a poster on the wall as she answers "yes." The camera follows her look, holding for a moment on the image of a North Vietnamese woman holding a baby in one arm and a gun in the other, as the male voice complains: "What about me? I have my own thoughts and desires, too."

At this point Anni puts down the phone, picks up a stuffed toy and a duster and, deploying those articles as surrogate child and gun, imitates the pose of the female guerilla fighter. The inclusiveness of that pose—its affirmation for woman both of motherhood and political struggle, the private and the public—contrasts markedly with the arrogant assertion of male desire, and the repressive binarism of the home/work division.

The mirror relationship which Anni establishes with the poster of the Vietnamese woman suggests that imaginary prototypes play as central a role within revolutionary subjectivity as they do within classic models. However, imaginary transactions cannot be separated from the symbolic matrix within which they occur, and which confers meaning and value upon them. Two shots inserted at a later juncture of *The Subjective Factor* indicate that the scopic exchange between Anni and her beloved poster lacks any symbolic support, and hence remains at the level of a purely utopian projection.

In the first shot, Achim, one of Anni's lovers, sits possessively at the desk in her bedroom. The poster of the female guerilla fighter leans against the far wall, turned upside down. In the next shot the poster remains in its deprivileged position, but Achim is gone, and Anni has returned to her desk. Her voice-over says: "The most permanent thing is work; living together posed some problems." Anni's attempts to bridge the division between the public and the private have obviously resulted in failure. She has been obliged, much against her will, to align herself with one to the exclusion of the other.

The juxtaposition of Achim with the inverted poster functions as yet another reminder that Marxism's speaking subject, like its capitalist counterpart, is male. Indeed, as the film progresses it becomes increasingly difficult to distinguish between the two discourses on any "domestic" issue. Marxism's and capitalism's discursive fellowships seem almost to converge in a profoundly pessimistic collage/montage sequence toward the end of *The Subjective Factor.*

That sequence begins with a long take around the walls of a room filled with posters, most of which feature male revolutionaries (the only exceptions are two cinematic "fictions"—Godard's *La Chinoise* and Malle's *Viva Maria.)*[14] It continues with shots of newspaper clippings, which become more and more contemporary. The clippings show heads of state (Carter, Schmidt, Giscard D'Estaing, Brezhnev, Honecker) embracing and posing together. The only woman in any of these photographs is Thatcher, whose internal and external policies hardly situate her on the side of feminism. The equation of power and male subjectivity becomes increasingly insistent.

The collage/montage concludes with three sharply delineated images: first, a military plane with rows of guns lined up in front in a v-formation; then a room full of Jewish skulls; and finally the head and shoulders of Andres, wearing the clothes he has on when he visits Anni at the beginning of the film. The dissonant and urgent jazz saxophone which overlays these images—a saxophone which dwells, moreover, upon several bars from the Queen of the Night aria—adds a further apocalyptic dimension, seeming to urge the conflation of male subjectivity not merely with power, but fascism. Andres's Nordic blond looks seem perfectly congruent with that vision, particularly in so far as it finds its locus in German culture.

However, the film resists that easy conflation, largely because it refuses to align Andres exclusively with classic male values. Andres makes regular appearances as a youthful member of the commune, but only three as an independent adult. One of those three appearances occurs at the beginning of *The Subjective Factor,* when he visits Anni with the book of photographs from the late sixties. Another takes the mediated form of the black and white photograph that ends the collage/montage sequence. The other (earlier) appearance of the adult Andres is even more oblique, consisting as it does of a reflection on the wall of a doll-house. This last inscription suggests that Andres somehow transcends the existing field of sexual relations—that he has internalized Anni's point of view, and made her concerns his own.

Andres makes the most utopian of his adult appearances in the context of a three-shot sequence, each component of which takes in an increasingly broad field of vision. The first shot is an extreme close-up of a cockroach behind glass. The second shot shows the same cockroach, but from a greater distance; it can now be seen to be crawling inside a glass-bottomed sauce-pan resting on its side on top of a stove. A tea-kettle and a wall-plaque are also visible, the latter framing a German proverb about the advantages of having one's own kitchen. Andres's adult face is reflected on the wall behind the stove, preternaturally large. As Anni's voice-off asks "Do you know we were already here thirteen years ago?" a recording of the Rolling Stones singing "Time is on My Side" cuts in, very loudly, and then dies out as abruptly. The third shot reveals the kitchen in its entirety. An enormous tomato sits on the table, dwarfing everything but the overgrown cockroaches crawling over the stove and floor. The reflected faces and upper bodies of Anni and a very young Andres fill the right half of the wall. Once again the faces are out of proportion with the room. Suddenly it becomes clear that we are looking at a doll-house, whose miniature dimensions are responsible for the spatial disequivalence between the room and its furnishings on the one hand, and the tomato, cockroaches, and human images on the other.

These three shots effect a number of dislocations, constantly shifting the terms of the relationship between spectacle and viewing subject. Not only does the sudden intrusion of the Rolling Stones open a sensory door onto the late sixties even as we seem to be situated with Anni and an adult Andres in 1980, but we participate in a thirteen-year regression between shots two and three; we move, that is, from the time of Andres's visit to his mother to the beginning of the story she shares with him—from the level of the (diegetic) enunciation to that of the narrative proper. In addition, our gaze shifts with that of the protagonists from the left to the right side of the miniature kitchen, and our perception of that room undergoes a dramatic transformation as we grasp its size. The distance which separates the camera from the kitchen, and the degree of magnification to which it has recourse, also change markedly from shot to shot.

A number of subjective factors further defamiliarize and destabilize the kitchen, the conventional locus of the familiar and the stable. Indeed, most of the perceptual dislocations have a subjective basis. Our shift from 1980 to 1967, like that from the left to the right side of the kitchen, is motivated by Anni and Andres's return to an earlier scene in their own subjectivity, one within which the mother/child dyad was still strongly privileged. (The final shot in the sequence provides a classic articulation of the mirror stage; not only does the child's image look back at him, but the imaginary transaction finds maternal support.) The inscription of the gaze in the last two shots—the reflection, that is, of the characters whose vision mediates our own—also makes clear the degree to which the epistemological vantage structures (indeed produces) its object.

The selection of a doll-house as the target of this highly subjective scrutiny is not accidental, nor is the fact that the camera never leaves the kitchen. *The Subjective Factor* is, after all, the story of a commune—of a living arrangement which, like a doll-house, functions as a small-scale model of a projected future. The latter thus serves as a metaphor for the former; Anni and Andres look into the commune through the doll-house. And since their mnemonic excursion is motivated by the desire to understand the failure of the commune (as well as that of the larger movement it represents), they focus on the room which was both its unacknowledged center and the site of its most rigorous sexual differentiations.

The constant spatial and temporal dislocations in the doll-house sequence encourage us to look again at the kitchen—suggest that it is not what it seems at first (or second) glance. The placement of a real tomato on a miniature table, like the juxtaposition of a life-sized cockroach with a toy kettle, serves a similar function; those alignments imply that things were strangely out of proportion in the communal experiments of the sixties—that the capitalist division of labor has no place within a socialist collective.

The Stones' song speaks to another, more optimistic level of meaning in this three-shot sequence—to a future at odds with the past. It attests, that is, to the psychic structuration of Andres in ways which belie the division of work from home, public from private, male from female. The lyrics of that song encourage us to see that despite the failure of the student movement, time really is on the side of feminism, particularly insofar as it intersects with the praxis of motherhood. Not only does Andres's most striking moment of childhood self-recognition occur within the kitchen, but as an adult he still embarks upon imaginary expeditions in Anni's company. Although her face is not reflected alongside his in the second shot, as it is in the third, her voice (rather than that of a real or symbolic father) organizes what he sees, just as it provides him with access to the past. Andres seems somehow to have incorporated Anni's point of view, to have adopted her discursive position. His willingness to enter into her narrative and to look with her into the miniature kitchen holds out the possibility that no subjectivity is for all time—that sexual borders can be not only crossed, but erased.

THE TERRORIST CONNECTION

A surprising number of recent films (*Journeys from Berlin, Empty Suitcases, Splits, Germany in Autumn, Leaden Times*) posit a link between feminism and terrorism—suggest that women are so fully excluded from the exercise of traditional political power that they are obliged to turn instead to organized violence. *The Subjective Factor* also glances in the direction of terrorism, but finds it to be an even more formidable adversary than Marxism. The former is shown to be more dangerous than the latter because of its seeming receptivity to other alienated discourses—a receptivity which foretells recuperation. *The Subjective Factor* suggests that terrorism functions through a misappropriation of what I have termed "discursive adaptability."

Apart from Andres, the only male character in the film who seems interested in straying beyond traditional subjective categories is Till, Anne-Marie's student lover. He is a member of the commune only for a short time, but while there he enters almost passionately into domestic matters, participating in cooking, childcare, and the division of labor. He seems not merely indifferent, but openly antagonistic to the other men; indeed, he comes into sharp conflict with at least one (Jorn). Till appears as uncomfortable with the existing field of sexual relations as do Anni and Anne-Marie, and as fully estranged from the SDS fellowship. Eventually he leaves the commune, taking Anne-Marie with him.

After his departure, Till makes only three brief appearances, one in order to recover a cooking pot he left behind, and another which is a chance encounter with Anni in a bar. On the second of these occasions we learn that he has left the university, despite doing well on his exams, and that he has moved out of another commune. Anni tells him with considerable vehemence that he's "on the wrong track." Anni obviously has in mind more than his abandoned university career, but her meaning remains unclear. Till continues to sip his drink and pursue his solitary game of pinball, wearing an attitude of hostile indifference.

The last sequence in Anni's story also marks Till's final appearance. That sequence takes place shortly after several major crises have occurred in the commune, leaving something of a power vacuum. Anni sits at the desk in her bedroom, nervously tidying papers and packing a handbag as the camera focuses on her hands. A male voice-off says: "When the doorbell rings I want you to go to the kitchen. Is that clear?" Anni agrees, and the camera cuts to Till, source of the command. He waits for his unspecified visitor with an exposed revolver, a docile Anne-Marie at his side. It is now apparent that the "wrong track" to which Anni earlier referred is Till's involvement with terrorism.

Till's relegation of Anni to the kitchen indicates that feminism has no more to gain from terrorism than from orthodox Marxism. However, Anne-Marie's bowed head suggests that it has a good deal more to lose. Because of its radical dissatisfaction with all existing cultures, and because it adopts a welcoming attitude toward other exiles from the dominant discursive field, terrorism seems open to alliances to which the established left is often closed—alliances with feminism, for instance. At the same time, as Baudrillard points out, terrorism remains complicitous with the very order it opposes, offering up its signifiers to a constant reappropriation:

Everything in terrorism is ambivalent and reversible: death, the media, violence, victory. Who plays into the other's hands? Death itself is undefinable: the death of the terrorists is equivalent to that of the hostages; they are substitutable. In spite of all the efforts to set them into radical opposition, fascination allows no distinction to be made, and rightly so, for power finally does not make any either, but settles its accounts with everyone, and buries Baader and Schleyer together at Stuttgart in its incapacity to unravel the deaths and discover the fine dividing line, the distinctive and valid oppositions which are the secret of law and order.[15]

The Subjective Factor attests to this reversibility—to the difficulty of maintaining the distinction between terrorism and the state—not only through a demonstration of the way in which the former restates the latter's sexual differences, but through an extraordinary juxtaposition of the film's two diegetic levels. That juxtaposition occurs over the boundary separating the time of the story from the time of its recollection, bringing together an image from the past with one from the present. We are offered in relatively quick succession[16] the shot of Till with gun in hand, emblem of left-wing anarchism, and a photographic memorial to Dutschke, who died in 1980 of injuries suffered as a result of a right-wing assassination attempt in 1968—an attempt which was largely inspired by the Springer press.[17] The dominant signifiers generated by these two shots are "victimizer" and "victim," signifiers which obscure the "fine dividing line" between legality and illegality, order and disorder. In other words, a certain equivalence is established between Till and Josef Bachman (Dutschke's assailant) on the one hand, and the visitor for whom Till waits and Dutschke, on the other. These equivalences make it increasingly difficult to distinguish the state from terrorism, or terrorism from the state.

The Subjective Factor carefully differentiates the semiotic confusion promoted by terrorism from its own border-crossings. Far from generating new social possibilities, terrorism is shown only to reaffirm existing ones—to return women to the kitchen, and power to the state. Like all classically oppositional discourses, it is ultimately an extension of what it purports to negate. However, terrorism makes that intimate relationship much more explicit than usual, collapsing the retaining wall between itself and the state. The resulting chaos is always beneficial to the status quo, since it arouses in the socius a nostalgia for a strong and clearly-articulated state. That nostalgia justifies the establishment of more repressive laws, and the extension of surveillance into ever new areas.

The Subjective Factor, on the contrary, is dedicated to productive syntheses. It refuses to adopt a classically oppositional relation to other discourses, knowing full well the complicity and homage such a relation implies. Instead, it raids the existing discursive field, carrying away what it can use and abandoning the rest. The result is a *"combined formation,* constructed from bits and pieces, various intermingled codes and flux, partial elements and derivatives."[18] Since, moreover, Sander's second feature film transforms the elements it appropriates, it renders recuperation virtually impossible.

Despite its seeming irreverence for tradition, terrorism also relies heavily upon the mechanism of closure and exclusion discussed earlier in this essay. Although it recruits fellows from other discourses, it puts them through a rigorous initiation, severs their ties with those other discourses, and insists upon the scrupulous observance of its own rules. Thus Till not only removes Anne-Marie from the commune, but ultimately wrests her away from the discourse of feminism; she sits unhappily but quietly as he relegates Anni (the non-believer) to the kitchen. Finally, terrorism's mortal opposition to the "falsehoods" of other discourses reveals a powerful will to truth. That imperative finds blunt expression through the gun Till holds as he awaits his mysterious visitor.

The Subjective Factor, as we have seen, refuses the safety of discursive fellowships, opting instead for mixed company and communal relations. It not only critiques orthodox usage, but practices a creatively non-orthodox discursivity. Last, but by no means least, it replaces the will to truth with what can only be called the "will to change"—with an affirmation of the desire and the capacity for transformation.

As Anni stands looking at the memorial photograph of Dutschke at the end of the film, a female friend comes up behind her and says: "You know, Mae West is dead now, too. Do you remember what she used to say? 'When I'm good I'm good, but when I'm bad I'm better.'" The quotation from West displaces Anni's (and consequently the viewer's) attention away from a male to a female icon. It also effects a witty neutralization of the moral boundaries dividing good from evil, removing the wall which separates one "country" from the other. Most importantly, it points to the profound interdependency of non-orthodox usage and the will to change. *The Subjective Factor* reminds us through West that discursive orthodoxy always leads to repetition, to a return of the same, but that a violation of the rules may very well produce something not only different, but better.

Notes

1. Maurice Blanchot, "The Word Berlin," trans. James Cascaito. *Semiotext(e),* IV, No. 2 (1982), p. 63. Whenever "good" and "evil" are in brackets, this indicates a reversal of the order in which these terms appear in the original translation.

2. The standard left account of those years available in English, for instance, F.C. Hunnius, *Student Revolts: The New Left in West Germany* (London: War Resisters' International, 1968) deals exclusively with "public" events—with confrontations between students and the police, university reform, the attacks on the Springer press. A more wide-ranging discussion of the West German student movement, Lawrence Baron, Gad Ben-Ami, Katherine Goodman, Asta Heller, Otto Koester, and Anthony Niesz, "Der 'anarchische' Utopismus der Westdeutschen Studentenbewegung," in *Deutsches Utopisches Denken in 20 Jahrhundert,* eds. Reinhold Grimm and Jost Hermand (Stuttgart: Kohlhammer, 1974),

touches briefly on the formation of day-care centers, and the two most famous communal experiments, but makes no mention of the women's movement, or of its conflicts with the SDS.

3. Although *The Subjective Factor* offers a very different version of the student movement from that found in "orthodox" histories, it is quite compatible with that offered by Hilke Schlaeger, "The West German Women's Movement," trans. Vicki Williams Hill and Carol Poore, *New German Critique,* 13 (1978), pp. 59–68, an essay which occupies a similar discursive space.

4. This is a concept I have appropriated from Michel Foucault, who speaks in "The Discourse on Language" of "'fellowships of discourse,' whose function is to preserve or to reproduce discourse, but in order that it should circulate within a closed community, according to strict regulations, without those in possession being dispossessed by this very distribution" (See *The Archaeology of Knowledge,* trans. A.M. Sheridan Smith [Harper & Row: New York, 1972]), p. 225.

5. The distinction between the speaking subject and the subject of the speech belongs to Emile Benveniste, who uses it to account for the relation between a user of discourse and the discursive component through which he or she is defined as subject. In the case of an English speaker, this discursive component would in all likelihood be the pronoun "I." Benveniste writes in *Problems of General Linguistics,* trans. Mary Elizabeth Meek (Coral Gables: Univ. of Miami Press, 1971), p. 220: "It is by identifying himself as a unique person pronouncing *I* that each speaker sets himself up in turn as the 'subject'". In *The Subject of Semiotics* (New York: Oxford Univ. Press, 1983), I suggest that the cinematic text obliges us to add a third category to the two proposed by Benveniste since that text promotes the construction of a subject other than its speaker—the construction that is, of the viewing subject. I call this third category the "spoken subject."

6. For a fuller discussion of the will to truth, see "The Discourse on Language," pp. 217–220.

7. "Interview with Helke Sander," trans. Elizabeth Lyon, *Camera Obscura,* Nos. 3/4 (1979), p. 227.

8. For a more extended treatment of the voice-over, see Pascal Bonitzer, *Le regard et la voix* (Union Générale d'Editions (10/18): Paris, 1976), pp. 9–24; Mary Ann Doane, "The Voice in Cinema: The Articulation of Body and Space," *Yale French Studies,* No. 60 (1980), pp. 33–50; and Kaja Silverman, "Dis-Embodying the Female Voice," in *Woman, Language and the Look: Essays on Women and Film,* eds. Mary Ann Doane, Patricia Mellencamp, and Linda Williams (forthcoming from A.F.I.).

9. *Problems in General Linguistics,* pp. 206–207. Christian Metz elaborates the significance for film of the distinction between historical and discursive constructions in "Story/Discourse (A Note on Two Kinds of Voyeurism)," in *The Imaginary Signifier,* trans. Celia Britton, Annwyl Williams, Ben Brewster, and Alfred Guzzetti (Bloomington: Indiana Univ. Press, 1982), pp. 91–97.

10. Sander also employs a third-person female voice-over in *Redupers,* although it remains extra-diegetic throughout, is less intimately identified with the central character, and lacks a specific point of address. Experimentation with the female voice is a regular occurrence in recent films by women, taking particularly complex and resonant forms in the work of Marguérite Duras and Yvonne Rainer.

11. Miriam Hansen assures me that this vogue was indeed extensive.

12. The priests who safeguard Sarrastro's discursive fellowship warn Tamino that "Women do little and talk much," and that their words are "empty" and full of "treachery."

13. "Patriarchy and the Relations of Production," in *Feminism and Materialism,* eds. Annette Kuhn and Ann Marie Wolpe (London: Routledge and Kegan Paul, 1978), p. 30.

14. Hunnius indicates the way in which the Malle film was appropriated by the left, and stripped in the process of any feminist meaning: apparently the SDS theoretician Bernd Rabehl based his argument for the possibility of a peaceful coexistence of Marxism and

anarchy on the relationship between the Jeanne Moreau and Brigitte Bardot characters in *Viva Maria*, concluding triumphantly, "The scientific and anarchist components of Marxism are joined for the first time since Lenin's *State and Revolution* of 1917. Maria and Maria have come together again, *Viva Maria*" (*Student Revolts,* pp. 37–38). The citation in the collage/montage sequence of the poster advertising the Malle film obviously serves an ironic function.

15. Jean Baudrillard, "Our Theater of Cruelty," trans. John Jonston, *Semiotext(e)* IV, No. 2 (1982), p. 109.

16. The only intervening sequence is one in which Anni looks in a two-way mirror at a scar on her forehead.

17. Indeed, Fritz Teufel indicates that the SDS held the Springer papers responsible for the assassination attempt; as he puts it, "It was a very clear to us that Springer's agitation had hit one of us" ("On Rudi Dutschke's Death," trans. Barbara Kosta, *Semiotex(e)* IV, No. 2 [1982]), p. 117. It thus becomes, for all intents and purposes, an act of state violence.

18. Gilles Deleuze and Félix Guattari, *Anti-Oedipus: Capitalism and Schizophrenia,* trans. Robert Hurley, Mark Seem, and Helen R. Lane (New York: Viking, 1977), p. 117.

Not Reconciled

The Destruction of Narrative Pleasure

MELANIE MAGISOS

J EAN-MARIE STRAUB'S second film, *Not Reconciled* (1965), establishes a set of problems for the viewer by violating nearly every convention of Hollywood narrative filmmaking. He makes the viewer aware of the film as a construct, forces him/her to participate in the production of meaning, rather than allowing the viewer to identify easily with the characters and narrative. *Not Reconciled* denies the viewer certain pleasures offered by traditional cinema. And this is Straub's intention—to *destroy the narrative as something which can be instantly and pleasurably consumed*. It demands hard work on the part of the viewer to reach any sort of understanding.

Straub's use of narrative structure, acting style, screen space and the combination of fiction and documentary footage create difficulties. His refusal to bow to the traditions of eyeline matches and cutting on action to establish continuity between shots and scenes furthers these problems. It is nearly impossible to grasp the narrative without knowledge of the plot obtained from the novel on which *Not Reconciled* is based, Heinrich Böll's *Billiards at Half-Past Nine*. At times it is even a struggle to identify the main characters.

However, Straub does offer several ways of beginning to understand the film and, in the final analysis, the form of *Not Reconciled* shapes the content and the filmmaker's thematic concerns. This paper attempts to identify the specific elements Straub uses to destroy viewer pleasure, how his use of these elements differs from that of Hollywood directors and how they relate to the thematic concerns of the work.

Straub constructed the narrative around a complex series of flashbacks in which little if any differentiation is made between past and present events. Because of this, a chronological summary is in order. The story contained in *Not Reconciled* spans fifty years, from the time Heinrich Fähmel makes his home and career in Cologne in 1910 to the day of his eightieth birthday.

Fähmel, a young architect, is successful in having his design for the building of St. Anthony's Abbey chosen over those of the city's most well-known architects. Always conscious of the image he presents to the world, he eats a strange breakfast of "paprika-cheese" at a cafe each day and decides to marry Johanna Kilb, the daughter of one of Cologne's oldest

Reprinted from *Wide Angle* 3.4 (1980): 35–41.

and wealthiest families. They have a daughter and three sons. The daughter and the first son, Heinrich, die at a young age. During World War I Johanna is declared harmlessly insane by a military tribunal to save the family from disgrace after she commits the political indiscretion of calling the Kaiser a fool. In 1933 the third child, Robert, becomes involved in an anti-Nazi group, is implicated in a bombing plot and is forced to flee the country with Schrella, a friend and supposed accomplice. After two years his mother is able to get him readmitted to Germany under the conditions that he not involve himself in politics and that he go directly into the army after his graduation from school. He returns to marry Edith, Schrella's sister, with whom he has a son and daughter, Joseph and Ruth, and to find that his brother has joined the Nazi cause. Robert joins the army and becomes a demolitions expert. During the last days of World War II he needlessly blows up his father's masterwork, the Abbey at St. Anthony. His brother Otto is killed at Kiev; Edith dies in the bombing of Cologne and Johanna goes mad again and has to be put in an asylum. Robert's son also studies to be an architect and has a chance to rebuild the Abbey, but decides against it when he learns the well-kept secret that his father is responsible for its destruction. On the eldest Fähmel's birthday, the day of the film's main actions, Schrella returns to Germany after years of exile; Johanna shoots a politician during a parade and Robert decides to adopt Hugo, the bell boy at the hotel where he plays billiards each day, because he has the smile of the dead Edith.

All of this narrative information is included in Straub's film. However it is made unreadable by the form. The narrative is presented through a series of unexplained flashbacks via the memories of various characters. One problem encountered by the viewer is that there is "too much" narrative for the film's fifty-three minutes. Straub removed every bit of the Fähmel family's story from the novel that he felt was unneeded information, as well as the aspects of conventional film language which indicate the passage of time and transitions into flashbacks. Straub explains his method:

> I deliberately discarded everything in Böll's novel that could be qualified as picturesque or anecdotal, psychological or even satirical: my aim was to create through the story of a middle-class German family from 1910 to our times a pure cinematographic, moral, and political reflection on the past fifty years of German life, a kind of film-oratorio. . . . I have been careful to eliminate as much as possible any historical aura in both costumes and sets, thus giving the images a kind of atonal character.[1]

The result is confusion for the viewer.

The first post-credit shot is of Robert Fähmel playing billiards. He glances off-screen and says, "Tell what, boy?" The second is a long shot of two teams of school boys playing rounders; voice-over narration explains the situation: Nettlinger, a teammate of Robert's, had risked their chances of winning by throwing the ball to an opponent so he could hit Schrella with it. There is a straight cut between the two shots, no indication that this is a flashback to Robert's sixteenth year except for the narrator's description of the scene in the past tense. The Hollywood convention is to cut from a character's off-screen glance to what he/she is looking at. Straub breaks this rule in the transition between the first and second shots of the film. From the beginning the viewer is confused.

Later, Hugo stands at the hotel bar where he has gone to get Robert a cognac. The bartender says, "At least seventeen women, young and old, are searching for you. Clear off quick, here comes another." Hugo begins to leave the frame and Straub dissolves to a two-shot of an old woman playing cards while Hugo sits beside her. The next cut is to Hugo looking out a window. These shots go by much too quickly, the dialogue is too sketchy and ambiguous for the viewer to grasp the narrative. The film is filled with these unexplained jumps in time.

The absence of explanation of events and character motivation and the confusion they cause in the viewer lead to a frustrating lack of narrative tension in the usual sense. One cannot understand enough of the story to want to know what happens next. A traditional Hollywood film sometimes allows the viewer to be confused about time or place but always attempts to drive the viewer on, to make him/her want to know what happens at the end of the story. The confusion tantalizes the viewer and eventually all the questions asked in the narrative are answered. In *Not Reconciled* not enough information is given to cause the viewer to ask the usual narratively motivated questions.

Even the climax of the film, the shooting scene, is deadened by Straub's minimalizing of the narrative. The entire scene, which takes place on the balcony of a room in the Prince Heinrich Hotel, is presented in one shot from behind Johanna, the would-be assassin. The camera tracks back to a medium long shot as she raises the gun and fires a quiet and unexciting sounding bullet (because of Straub's use of direct sound) at a place and victim the viewer cannot see. It is doubtful that most viewers can even guess the identity of the victim; he is named by Heinrich only as "your grandson's murderer." After the shot is fired, Straub cuts to another scene. His paring down of narrative events to the point of incomprehensibility and the lack of explanation of jumps in time are two ways Straub destroys the pleasure/satisfaction derived from a traditional narrative.

Within an already confusing narrative, Straub makes the characters difficult to identify. The Hollywood tradition is to focus on one or more dominant characters and their progress through the narrative. A part of this tradition is to use the same actor to represent one character at each stage of his/her life except perhaps for scenes of the character as a young child.

An example of this is *Letter from an Unknown Woman* in which Max Ophüls used Joan Fontaine to portray a character from age thirteen to mid-thirties. There is never any difficulty identifying the Joan Fontaine character; this is comfortable for the viewer because of the continuity it provides. Straub does focus on the present and pasts of three characters, Heinrich, Johanna and Robert Fähmel, but he uses different actors to represent them at different times in their lives. Also, Straub uses the same actor to play two parts: the same blond actor plays the roles of Hugo and Ferdi Progulske, a friend of Robert's who is beheaded for throwing a tiny bomb at Vaccano, the school sports master. Straub forces the viewer to be careful in naming the characters, a rather frustrating position when compared with how carefully identified the characters are in traditional narratives.

The pre-credit Brecht quote, "Instead of wanting to create the impression that he is improvising, the actor should rather show what the truth is: he is quoting," gives an indication of the style of acting in the film. Richard Roud points out that audience reaction to *Not Reconciled* was violently negative when it was first screened at the Berlin Film Festival and suggests that one reason for this was the dialogue delivery.[2] The actors in *Not Reconciled* do indeed appear to be quoting from someone else's text rather than living the event as actors do in traditional Hollywood films; there is no attempt to trick the viewer into believing that the situations are reality. Dialogue is delivered in monotone; it is chanted by the actors almost like a litany. The characters go through their actions slowly and with no emotion, like machines. Facial expressions are neutral even in what should be climactic moments such as the restaurant scene between Nettlinger and Schrella when, in what could be a passionate outburst, Schrella stands up in the middle of the meal and says, "Would you rather I killed you? I can't stand it any more." This is consistent with Straub's desire to destroy narrative tension.

All of the actors are non-professionals and in the case of the woman who plays the present day Johanna, Straub gave her lines to recite shortly before shooting; it was only later she learned that the Johanna character was insane. Her long monologue in the hospital is one of the most difficult in the film. Not only does she speak of several different years in a stream-of-consciousness style, but she speaks like a person under hypnosis. The viewer must struggle to pay attention.

The acting style adds to one's frustration because of its radical difference from what is usually seen in narrative films. It is derived from Brechtian distanciation: art should never be escapist, should never allow one through identification to slip into the world of the work. The viewer must constantly be aware that what he/she is watching is a construct, the product of the labor of an artist.

The term "Brechtian" has recently been used to describe a wide variety of film techniques and styles.[3] Stephen Heath has pointed out the problem of applying Brecht's theories too loosely to cinema. It is not enough for a film merely to draw attention to itself as a film—many bourgeois films do this without disturbing the viewer in any way and thus possibly bringing about any significant political reflection. An example of this is the films of Mel Brooks, but as Heath points out, the same is essentially true of Lindsay Anderson's *O Lucky Man*, which on the surface may seem to be a serious candidate for the term "Brechtian."[4] The real issue involves a disturbing of the positionality of the viewer:

> The aim is no longer to fix the spectator apart as a receiver of a representation but to pull the audience into an activity of reading; far from separating the spectator, this is a step towards his inclusion in a process . . .[5]

Not Reconciled is a film which creates precisely this type of Brechtian effect.

In addition to the problem for the viewer created by forcing him/her to guess at the emotional content of characters' interactions, Straub does not show enough of many actions to allow the viewer understanding. He frequently cuts to an action just as it is completed or away from a shot as an action is begun. An example of his cutting to a completed action is the scene in which Mrs. Trischler bandages Robert's back after he has been brutally beaten with a barbed whip. Straub cuts to the shot as she takes her hands away from his bandages. More often, he cuts away from an action as it is begun; the viewer rarely sees a completed action. Perhaps the best instance of this is the scene between Johanna and Robert in the hospital. Johanna stands by the door speaking about her past/present and her son Otto who is a Nazi. "Perhaps there's only one way to set him free," she says while raising her hand as if to fire a gun. Straub cuts to a shot of Robert just as she raises her hand. In another scene Robert is tied to a barred window. The camera pans down to a barbed whip leaning against the wall as a hand comes into the frame and begins to raise the whip. Straub cuts to the next scene—Trischler's row boat pulling up to the shore. He gives the viewer only a suggestion of most of the film's important events.

Because of its sexual content one of the most interesting shots Straub prematurely cuts away from (according to convention) is the kiss between Robert and Edith. It is a closeup of their faces, framed in a totally conventional manner with Edith's face more towards the camera than Robert's, hence the center of the viewer's attention. Robert leans closer to kiss her and Straub fades out, thus doing away with the erotic and voyeuristic pleasure the viewer could have received from vicarious participation in the kiss. In fact, there are no shots in *Not Reconciled* in which the female body is used as either spectacle or fetishized object.

In contrast with many of the film's main actions not being seen fully, Straub often continues a shot after the characters exit the frame. Richard

Roud claims that because of his use of direct sound, Straub insists on holding a shot until the sound exists the frame as well as the actors.[6] His example is the scene in which old Fähmel speaks to the secretary in Robert's office. They exit the frame to the right and the shot holds until one hears them go out two doors, until they've completely left the building. However, it seems that sound is not always Straub's reason for holding on an empty frame because there are just as many instances where he holds on an empty frame with no off-screen sound. After Schrella shows Robert the whip marks on his back, they exit the frame down a stairway. The frame is empty and one hears nothing. Another example of this is when Fähmel is told by his commanding officer that he will not be allowed to join the fighting during WWI. They leave the frame down a stairway and again, the camera holds on an empty frame with no off-screen sound.

In general, Straub values the feeling of absence generated by the empty frame. Besides the instances when the frame is emptied of characters, there is one point when the viewer is subjected to what can be called the ultimate empty frame—total image absence. Straub fades to a black screen accompanied by Robert's voice-over narration. Later, in a variation, Heinrich visits Johanna at the asylum. He enters the room through a door, greets Johanna and they both exit to the right, closing the door behind them. Straub holds on the closed door, total whiteness, while Johanna speaks to her husband off-screen. Actions in *Not Reconciled* are suggested, non-action and empty frames are explored.

Eyeline matches in a traditional film are used to create a filmic space and to help the viewer understand to whom a character is speaking. Straub rarely follows these laws of convention; rather, he sets out to destroy the logic of shot/reverse-shot editing. Characters speaking to someone off-screen almost never face the direction the viewer expects, nor does Straub place them in the usual position in the frame. In a two-shot sequence between Fähmel and the priest in charge of the Abbey project, Straub cuts from a shot of the priest on the left side of the frame looking off-screen to the left as he asks Fähmel a question, to Fähmel as he gives his reply from the right side of the frame looking off-screen frame right. They are speaking to each other but the viewer's expectations (determined by traditional film language) are destroyed. The characters seem to be facing away from each other.

Another example of Straub's destruction of eyeline match rules is the conversation between the hotel desk clerk and Nettlinger. The expected shot/reverse-shot sequence is not used. The desk clerk speaks facing off-screen right; the reverse shot of Nettlinger is from an impossible angle—it is too high to be the desk clerk's point of view and his shoulder is not included in the corner of the frame as it would be in a traditional shot/reverse shot sequence. Nettlinger also looks off-screen to the right. According to the logic of traditional editing, the two men could not be looking at each other. This shot of Nettlinger also contains an interesting example of Straub's minimalizing of the narrative: Nettlinger pushes money across the desk towards the clerk in an attempt to bribe him. The shot is framed so that Nettlinger's hand holding the money is in the extreme lower right corner of the frame. It is almost impossible for the viewer to grasp the total situation. The effect is to disorient the viewer, to force him/her to examine the conventions of film editing rather than allowing him/her to slip into the fictional discussions between characters. The lack of eyeline matches does not allow the viewer to establish spatial boundaries in the film. One encounters difficulty both in determining where characters are in a room and exactly what the room looks like.

Straub's characters rarely look at one another within the frame. There is almost no eye contact between the characters in *Not Reconciled*, which gives the film a feeling of extreme alienation. Twice old Fähmel puts his head in Johanna's lap. Neither time do their eyes meet. In one scene, in which Nettlinger drives Schrella to lunch, the camera is positioned in the back seat of the car. The viewer sees only the backs of their heads. The men never so much as glance at each other; their eyes never meet. Again, the viewer is an outsider, never allowed to feel placed securely within the narrative space.

As Heinrich Fähmel tells Leonore about the destruction of the Abbey during WWII, Straub cuts to newsreel footage of bombed buildings, the Kaiser's mobilization proclamation and troops preparing for war both from WWI and WWII. These shots are confusing to the viewer both because of the mixture of shots from both World Wars and because of the mixture of newsreel and fiction footage. In addition to these things Straub includes one shot of a priest and Fähmel in front of an obvious rear projection of what is presumably the bombed Abbey. We often see obvious rear projections in Hollywood films, usually the result of poor special effects, but Straub's use is purposeful. The conversation between the priest and Fähmel supposedly took place at the end of the war, but the characters look exactly the same as they do in the present day scenes. This calls attention to the film as a constructed sequence and makes the viewer work to produce meaning.

Straub does give the viewer some graphic continuity and visual links between the characters that suggest character relationships. Graphically he creates many shots dominated by a diagonal line. Characters are linked by repeating certain compositions and shooting the family members by windows.

Straub often composes shots to include a strong diagonal line within the frame. Either camera position in relation to subject placement of actors or objects within the frame is used to obtain this line. An example is the shot of Johanna leaving the hospital in search of a gun. The camera is positioned far away and to the left of the sidewalk leading to the door. The sidewalk and hospital steps create a diagonal line from the upper left to the lower right corners of the frame.[7] Another example of a diagonal line being formed is found in the shot of young Heinrich lying on the floor reading. His body divides the frame almost perfectly in two halves from corner to corner. Still another way Straub creates a diagonal line is by arrangement of objects in the frame. After Mrs. Trischler bandages his back, Robert lies on his stomach in the bed. His hand, head and the objects on a table, half a glass of milk and an apple, form a perfect diagonal from opposite corners. Straub's shots, for the most part, are so still, so devoid of actions and events that these compositions provide the frame with visual tension as well as providing the film with graphic continuity.

Frontal shots of buildings or objects in rooms are rare; however, when he does compose frontal shots, they are almost perfectly symmetrical. The first shot of the rounders scene illustrates this. The camera is set up at the end of the field with the goal post in the middle of the frame. This shot provides an interesting contrast with Straub's use of the diagonal.

Since the narrative in *Not Reconciled* is virtually unreadable by a viewer unfamiliar with Heinrich Böll's novel, it raises questions about a film's relationship to its source material. The Hollywood tradition is to create an "adaptation" which appears totally complete and separate from the novel upon which it is based; the narrative and themes can be understood just by viewing the film, although the viewer's appreciation may be enriched by knowledge of the novel source. For example, no one who sees *Gone With the Wind* needs to read the novel to understand the film. But as J. L. Anderson points out, the Hollywood tradition of adaptation is not always followed in other cultures. "In Japanese culture a film can be seen as an extension of, a commentary on, a novel. The quality of art commenting on art is a characteristic of Japanese art (including film) . . ."[8] This idea can be applied to the relationship between *Not Reconciled* and *Billiards at Half-Past Nine*: the film not only makes references to the novel but the narrative is incomplete without a viewer familiar with the story. Böll's novel was extremely well-known in Germany, almost to the point of being common cultural knowledge. Many had read the novel; those who hadn't probably knew of it. This knowledge of the novel makes it possible to recognise elements of the narrative and identify themes which are otherwise unreadable. It also allows the viewer to make connections between form and content.

Straub gives the viewer some visual links between the characters. One example of this is the way he uses the repeated composition of Fähmel lying his head in Johanna's lap both in the hospital and in the scene from WWI. The actors playing the characters in these two scenes are different, but the repeated action helps the viewer to understand that the characters are the same.

Also, most of the family members are linked by compositions involving windows. Heinrich Fähmel is first introduced by the back of his head as he looks out a window. He gazes out of windows in several flashbacks such as the shot in which we hear his son reciting poetry off-screen. Hugo, the newest member of the family, stands by a window as he asks Robert about his past. Robert and Edith are shot facing each other in front of a window while Robert's voice-over explains, "I had sworn to a young girl called Edith, sworn to her face, never to taste of the Buffalo Sacrament." And, finally, during her rambling monologue to Robert, Johanna stands gazing out a window. These compositions provide at least one source of continuity, provide the viewer with a way to link the characters.

Besides the blood ties between the family members, they share a spiritual bond. They question their personal pasts, their crimes, as well as those of the nation. On a metaphorical level, the Fähmels look out of their "prison" windows for a way to absolve themselves of their guilt. The film's climax takes place on a balcony outside of windowed doors. Johanna steps on to the balcony as she takes a step towards providing herself with one possible solution: she shoots the Minister M., the future murderer of her grandson. In the background of this shot is the Cologne Cathedral, the greatest symbol of German unity as well as the center of Church resistance to Nazism. Against this background Johanna's act is one of resistance to the present political forces.

After destroying much of the pleasure usually associated with the narrative form in film, Straub allows form and content to shape each other. On the most basic level, the characters in *Not Reconciled* are alienated from themselves and their environment to the point of not being able to look each other in the eyes. They are so absorbed in the past that they cannot act in the present. Johanna, the "insane" mother, makes little distinction between past, present and future. This reflects the major theme of the film: Nazism, the fascist outlook, have been everpresent in German society. Johanna cannot tell the difference between the past and present because there is no real difference.

The character of Nettlinger illustrates this. In the Thirties when he was a Nazi, he helped arrange and carry out beatings, arrests and disappearances. Today, presumably after being de-Nazified, he is a "democrat by conviction." At one point he is framed against the background of a rug which reminds one of swastikas. He may be only half a fascist, like the carpet design is only half swastikas, but as Schrella says, "The roles you played then and play today are the same." Nettlinger calls Vaccano "incorrigible" but Nettlinger has only changed on the surface. The name is changed but fascism survives.

Another way the theme of Nazism's cyclical nature is reflected is in the structure of the family. The male members of three Fähmel generations are all architects. Heinrich built, Robert destroyed and Joseph is supposed to rebuild. Like his father, Joseph attempts to break with the past by refusing to rebuild the Abbey but, again like his father, he is only reacting against it. Robert destroyed the Abbey because his nation was responsible for so much destruction, but his action added to that destruction. No matter whether Joseph takes the opportunity to rebuild the Abbey or not, someone will accept the task. The past is inescapable; it always returns. This is reflected in the flashback structure of the narrative. The viewer has difficulty distinguishing between past and present. Thematically, it is all the same.

The overall tone of *Not Reconciled* is one of entrapment—in rooms and in history. The characters want change but are unable to take action toward any goal. Straub, rather than allowing the viewer to empathize with the characters, to vicariously experience their frustration, constructed a film which creates those feelings in the viewer. One cannot fully separate the past from present and one never gets a full picture of the truth. The form of the film makes the viewer experience the discomfort and alienation of the characters rather than empathize with their situation.

The problem in *Not Reconciled* is the inability to either accept one's past or make any change. None of the characters can break away except for Johanna whose insanity, the inability or refusal to root herself in the present, allows her to see solutions clearly as well as cushioning her from the repercussions of her actions. She shoots the Minister M. knowing that she can plead "paragraph 51," the insanity clause, in her defense. Insanity allows her to be the sanest of the characters.

Her decision to act leads her husband to participate in that action. Earlier, when Heinrich recalls WWI and the first time Johanna was tried for political crimes, he says, "I did not say what I ought to have said, that I agreed with my wife." This time Johanna plans to shoot Vaccano, then Nettlinger, but Heinrich directs her attention away from the moral criminals of the past to the criminal of the present and future, the politician who only participates in the fighters' parade because it may win him more votes.

Straub is saying, through his arrangement of events and the physical form of the film, that Germany in the Sixties suffers from the same political problems it has for the last century. The tension for the characters comes from the desire to act contrasted with their inability to do so. The tension for the viewer stems from expecting a traditional narrative and not getting one.

Notes

1. Richrd Roud, *Jean-Marie Straub* (New York, 1972), p. 40.
2. Roud, p. 44.
3. This paragraph is taken from Peter Lehman's unpublished discussion of "Allegory and Alienation in the New German Cinema," by Brigitte Peucker presented at The Twenty-First Midwest Modern Language Association, November 9, 1979, Indianapolis.
4. Stephen Heath, "Lessons from Brecht," *Screen*, Vol. 15, No. 2 (Summer 1974), p. 112.

5. Heath, p. 111.

6. Roud, p. 52.

7. The camera position leads the viewer to expect Johanna to walk straight out the door past the camera. But Straub never gives the expected. Johanna steps out the door, around to the side of the building and disappears into the shadows. Straub holds the shot for several seconds after she disappears.

8. J. L. Anderson, "The Spaces in Between: American Criticism of Japanese Films," *Wide Angle*, Vol. 1, No. 4 (1977), p. 4.

"In the Destructive Element Immerse": Hans-Jürgen Syberberg and Cultural Revolution

FREDRIC JAMESON

HAD SYBERBERG not existed, he would have to have been invented. Perhaps he was. So that "Syberberg" may really be the last of those puppets of mythical German heroes who people his films. Consider this, which has all the predictability of the improbable: during the war a certain stereotype of the German cultural tradition ("teutonic" philosophy; music, especially Wagner) was used by both sides as ammunition in the accompanying ideological conflict; it was also offered as evidence of a German national "character." After the war it became clear that: 1) the history of high culture was not a very reliable guide to German social history generally; 2) the canon of this stereotype excluded much that may be more relevant for us today (e.g., expressionism, Weimar, Brecht); and 3) the Germany of the economic miracle, NATO, and social democracy is a very different place from rural or urban central Europe in the period before Hitler. So people stopped blaming Wagner for Nazism and began a more difficult process of collective self-analysis which culminated in the anti-authoritarian movements of the 1960s and early 1970s. It also generated a renewal of German cultural production, particularly in the area of film.

The space was therefore cleared for a rather perverse counter-position on all these points: on the one hand, the affirmation that Wagner and the other stereotypes of German cultural history are valid representations of Germany after all; and, on the other, that the contemporary criticism of cultural "irrationality" and authoritarianism—itself a shallow, rationalistic, "Enlightenment" enterprise—by repressing the demons of the German psyche, reinforces rather than exorcizes them. The Left is thus blamed for the survival of the fascist temptation, while Wagner, as the very culmination of German irrationalism, is contested by methods which can only be described as Wagnerian.

As Syberberg undertakes in his films a program for cultural revolution, he shares some of the values and aims of his enemies on the Left; his aesthetic is a synthesis of Brecht and Wagner (yet another logical permutation which remained to be invented). The Wagnerian persona is indeed uncomfortably, improbably strong in Syberberg; witness the manifestos which affirm film as the true and ultimate form of the Wagnerian ideal of the "music of the future" and of *Gesamtkunstwerk*; poses of heroic isola-

Reprinted, with permission, from Fredric Jameson, *Signatures of the Visible* (New York and London: Routledge, 1990): 63–81.

tion from which he lashes out at philistine fellow artists and critics who misunderstand his work (but who are, for him, generally associated with the Left); satiric denunciations in the best tradition of Heine, Marx, and Nietzsche of the anti-cultural *Spiessbürgers* of the Federal Republic today, complete with a *sottisier* of the most idiotic reviews of his films.[1]

Meanwhile, Syberberg is both predictable and improbable in yet another sense: in a high-technology medium, ever more specialized and self-conscious, in which the most advanced criticism has become forbiddingly technical, he suddenly reinvests the role of the naif or "primitive" artist, organizing his vision of the filmic art of the future not around the virtuoso use of the most advanced techniques (as Coppola or Godard do, though in very different ways), but rather around something like a return to home movies. What he produces is the low-budget look of amateur actors, staged tableaux, and vaudeville-type numbers, essentially static and simply strung together—all of which must initially stun the viewer in search of the vanguard of "experimental" novelties.

Though at first astonishing, however, Syberberg's strategy is quite defensible. As in the other arts, the stance of the amateur, the apologia for the homemade which characterized the handicraft ethos, is often a wholesome form of de-reification, a rebuke to the *esprit de sérieux* of an aesthetic or cultural technocracy; it need not be merely machine-wrecking and regressive. Nor is his seemingly anachronistic position regarding the German cultural past without theoretical justification: in the work of Freud, first of all, and the distinction between repression and sublimation which we have come to understand and accept in other areas;[2] in an orthodox criticism of dialectical reversals by which a binary or polar opposite (rationalistic Enlightenment forms of demystification) is grasped as merely the mirror replication of what it claims to discredit (German irrationalism), locked within the same *problematic*; in a perfectly proper reading of German history which defines imprisonment in essentially Jacobin, pre-1848 (*Vormärz*) forms of bourgeois ideology critique (for which Marx, Marxism, and the dialectic itself still remained to be invented) as the price which oppositional movements have traditionally had to pay for German political underdevelopment; in a new conception of cultural revolution, finally, which, drawing its inspiration from Ernst Bloch's aesthetics and his "principle of Hope," his impulse towards a utopian future, is not merely unfamiliar outside of Germany, but has also—under Syberberg's own work—been untested as an aesthetic program for a new art language.

If the films were not worth bothering about, of course, it would be idle to debate these questions. But what would it mean to employ traditional judgments of value for something like the seven-hour *Hitler, A Film from Germany* (1977, titled here *Our Hitler*)? With what would we emerge except formulations such as the "not good but important" of a German newspaper critic ("Kein 'guter' Film, dafür ein wichtiger")? The Wagnerian length involves a process in which one must be willing or unwilling to immerse oneself rather than an object whose structure one can judge, appreciate, or deplore. My own reaction is that, after some three or four hours, it might as well have lasted forever (but that the first hour was simply terrible from all points of view). Perhaps the most honest appraisal is the low-level one which chooses the episodes one likes, complains about what bores or exasperates. The dominant aesthetic of this film, which works to produce an "improvisation effect," seems, at any rate, to block all others.

This improvisation effect is clearly derived from the interview format of cinéma-vérité. Against the composed and representational scenarios of fiction film, ciné-vérité was read as a breakthrough to the freshness and immediacy of daily experience. In the hands of filmmakers such as Syberberg or Godard, however, the illusion of spontaneity is exposed as a construct of preexisting forms. In Godard's films the interview is the moment in which the fictional characters are tormented and put to the ultimate test: full-face, head and shoulders against a dazzling monochrome wall, they reply with hesitant assent or inarticulate half-phrases to the demand that they formulate their experiences, their truth, in words. The truth of the interview, however, lies not in what is said or betrayed, but in the silence, in the fragility of insufficiency of the stammered response, in the massive and overwhelming power of the visual image, and in the lack of neutrality of the badgering, off-screen interviewer. It is in Godard's recent television series, *France/Tour/Détour/Deux/Enfants* (1978), that the tyrannical and manipulative power of this investigative position is most clearly exposed. There the still Maoist interviewer questions school children whose interests, obviously, are radically different from his own. At one point he asks a little girl if she knows what revolution is (she does not). If there is something obscene about exhibiting something—class struggle—to a child who will find out about it in her own time, there is, no doubt, something equally obscene about the Syberberg child (his daughter) who wanders through the seven hours of *Our Hitler* carrying dolls of the Nazi leaders and other playthings of the German past. These children can, however, no longer be figures of innocence. Rather they mark the future and the possible limits of the political project of these filmmakers, each of whom inscribes his work within a particular conception of cultural revolution. In Syberberg, then, a mythic posterity, some exorcised future Germany, its bloody past reduced to the playroom or the toybox; in Godard, the vanishing "subject of history," the once politicized public that will no longer reply.

Syberberg's documentary and interview techniques are developed in a whole complex preparatory practice which precedes his major films, from an early documentary on Brecht's training methods, through interviews with Fritz Kortner and Romy Schneider (and an imaginary one with Ludwig II's cook, Theodor Hierneis), to a five-hour "study" of Winifred Wagner. The background of a Syberberg interview, characteristically unlike the nonplace of the Godardian wall (with its properly utopian colors, as Stanley Cavell has noted[3]), is generally a house or mansion whose monumental and tiered traces of the past gradually absorb the camera work in such a way that what began as an interview turns into a "guided tour." This unexpected formal emergence is a stunning solution to the dilemma of the essentially narrative apparatus of film as it confronts the absences of the past and the task of "working through" what is already over and done with. So in the Wagner documentary,

> you come to see how the bourgeois utopia of private life turns into idyll, how the whole system breaks down without that music which the master was still able to bully out of himself and life. Without the music of Wagner, Wahnfried [the family estate] was doomed to decline and fall.[4]

The very primacy of the great house, as well as the form of the guided tour, is dictated by Syberberg's material and by the weight of the essentially bourgeois past of German cultural history as he conceives of it—from the nineteenth-century palaces of Ludwig II, or of Wagner, or Karl May's Villa Shatterhand, all the way to Hitler's Reichskanzlei, that is to say, the ultimate destruction of those buildings and the emergence of the misty placelessness (better still, the scenic space) of *Our Hitler.* It is not easy to imagine anything further from the Parisian outer belt of Godard's films, with their shoddy high-rises, noise, and traffic; nor can one imagine Godard filming a documentary on Versailles, say, or the houses of Monet or Cézanne. Yet this effort of imagination, as we shall see, is the task which Syberberg has set himself, the form of his "estrangement effect": imagine Godard listening to Wagner![5] Or, to turn things around, imagine Syberberg confronting middle-class prostitution, the commodification of sexuality.

Similarly striking is the contrast between Godard's deliberate revelation of his interviewer's manipulations and Syberberg's sense of the *tendresse* and the self-denial demanded of the maker of documentaries and interviews:

> The maker of such films must serve in the archaic, virtually monastic, sense; with all his heightened attention and his superior knowledge of the motifs and the intersections or lateral relationships of what has already been said and what is yet to come, he must remain completely in the background during the process, he must be able to become transparent. . . . You come to understand the grand masters of the medieval *unio mystica* . . . and maybe that is why we get involved in such a suicidal business. It costs sweat and effort, often more than the kind of excitement one feels in realizing the fantasies of fiction film. You're completely washed out in bed at night, still trem-

bling all over from having had to listen, comprehend, and direct the camera. You are directing from the score of another composer, but in your own rhythm.[6]

Yet it is perhaps this very conception of the self-effacing mission of the documentary artist which underscores the complacencies of *Our Hitler*, the lengthy indulgences which it allows itself. Such complacency is the consequence of a self-serving glorification of the artist in modern, or more specifically, capitalist society. Artists working in a social system which makes an institutional place for cultural production (the role of the bard or tribal storyteller, the icon-painter or producer of ecclesiastical images, even the roles foreseen by aristocratic or court patronage) were thereby freed from the necessity of justifying their works through excessive reflection on the artistic process itself. As the position of the artist becomes jeopardized, reflexivity increases, becomes an indispensable precondition for artistic production, particularly in vanguard or high-cultural works.

The thematics of the artist novel, of art about art, and poetry about poetry, is by now so familiar and, one is tempted to say, so old-fashioned (the generation of fifties aesthetes was perhaps the last to entertain aggressively the notion of a privileged role for the poet) that its operation in mass culture and in other seemingly non-aesthetic discourses passes, oftentimes, unobserved. Yet one of the forms taken by a crisis in a discourse like that of professional philosophy is precisely the overproduction of fantasy images of the role and necessity of the professional philosopher himself (Althusserianism was only the latest philosophical movement to have felt the need to justify its work in this way, while the Wittgensteinian reduction of philosophical speculation marks a painful and therapeutic awareness of its loss of a social vocation). It was thus predictable that the emergence of that new type of discourse called theory would be accompanied by a number of overweening celebrations of the primacy of this kind of writing. Yet the "alienation" of intellectuals, their "free-floating" lack of social function, is not redeemed by such wish-fulfilling reflexivity. Political commitment, for example the support of working-class parties, is a more concrete and realistic response to this dilemma, which is the result of the dynamics and priorities of the market system itself, its refusal of institutional legitimation to any form of intellectual activity which is not at least mediately involved in the social reproduction of the profit system.

In mass culture, popular music, through its content and its glorification of the musician, provides a most striking example of the workings of this thematics of crisis. The rapidity with which the role of the musician has become mythicized is particularly evident in the instance of rock music: first as a balladeer (Bob Dylan, for example), and then as a Christ figure, through the fantasy of university redemption or individual martyrdom (as in Ken Russell's *Tommy* [1975] or many David Bowie cycles). My objection to the overdetermined content of such works (which, it should be understood, have social and psychic resonance of their own, quite distinct from the supplementary fantasies about their own production) is a reaction to the tiresomeness of their continued and outmoded appeal. Surely the "hero with a thousand faces," let alone the Christ figure, excites no one any longer, is imaginatively irrelevant to the problems of consumer society, and is a sign of intellectual as well as aesthetic bankruptcy.

Yet this is precisely the solution to which Syberberg rather anachronistically returns in *Our Hitler,* spreading a panoply of mythic images before us. His conception of the mythic derives, it is true, more from Wagner than from Joyce, Campbell, or Frye, but it is no less exasperating for all that (even Syberberg's philosophical mentor, Ernst Bloch, has suggested that it would be desirable to substitute a fairy-tale, that is to say a peasant, Wagner for the official epic-aristocratic one). Initially, however, the complacent and auto-referential developments in Syberberg seem to derive from the anti-Wagnerian tradition of Brecht, with whom he also entertains a "mythic" identification: the circus barker of the opening of *Our Hitler* surely has more in common with the streetsinger of *The Threepenny Opera* than with the nineteenth-century religion of art. Yet very rapidly the apologia of film as the Wagnerian "music of the future" and the *Gesamtkunstwerk* of our time, the loftiest form of artistic vocation, emerges from the populist framework. A miniature replica of the first movie studio, the little wooden shack which Thomas Edison called the Black Maria and in which he experimented with the "kinetoscope," the ancestor of the movie camera, becomes the Holy Grail. And the quest, then, becomes the yearning for a well-nigh Lukácsian "totality," the impulse towards a Hegelian Absolute Spirit, the self-consciousness of this historical world and the place from which, if anywhere, it might hope to grasp itself through the medium of aesthetic representation.

The problem of totalization is surely a crucial one in a world in which our sense of the unity of capitalism as a global system is structurally blocked by the reification of daily life, as well as by class, racial, national, and cultural differences and by the distinct temporalities by which they are all defined. But the film goes beyond this crucial concern to make an outrageous proposal: we are not merely to accept the filmmaker as supreme prophet and guardian of the Grail, but Hitler as well.

The conjunction of Hitler and film, the interest which he had in the medium is, of course, historically documented. Syberberg provides some of the most interesting specifics: He liked Fred Astaire and John Wayne movies particularly; Goebbels would not let him see Chaplin's *The Great Dictator,* but screened *Gone with the Wind* for him as compensation— which he thoroughly enjoyed; after the first reverses in the East, he began to restrict himself to the viewing of newsreels and documentary footage from the front—to which he occasionally offered editorial suggestions. But by 1944 he had even stopped watching these and reverted to his old Franz Lehar records.

Syberberg, however, proposes that we see Hitler not merely as a film buff, nor even as a film critic, but as a filmmaker in his own right, indeed, the greatest of the twentieth century, the *auteur* of the most spectacular film of all time: World War II. Although interpretations of Hitler as a failed artist have been proposed in the past (and renewed by the memoirs of Albert Speer, himself the prophet of an unrealized architectural "music of the future"), they have generally been diagnostic and debunking, rejoining a whole tradition of analysis of political visionaries, especially revolutionary leaders, as failed intellectuals and bearers of *ressentiment* (thus, even Michelet described the more radical Jacobins as so many *artistes manqués*). There is, indeed, a striking science-fiction idea (not so strikingly realized in its novel form, *The Iron Dream,* by Norman Spinrad) in which, in an alternate world, a sidewalk artist and bohemian named Adolf Hitler emigrates to the U.S. in 1919 and becomes a writer of science fiction. He incorporates his bloodiest fantasies in his masterpiece, *Lord of the Swastika,* which is reproduced as the text of Spinrad's own novel: "Hitler died in 1953, but the stories and novels he left behind remain as a legacy to all science-fiction enthusiasts."

Syberberg's purpose is, however, a good deal more complicated and sophisticated than this and aims at no less than a Blochian cultural revolution, a psychoanalysis and exorcism of the collective unconscious of Germany. It is this ambition with which we must now come to terms. Bloch's own "method," if we may call it that, consists in detecting the positive impulses at work within the negative ones, in appropriating the motor force of such destructive but collective passions as reactionary religion, nationalism, fascism, and even consumerism.[7] For Bloch, all passions, nihilistic as well as constructive, embody a fundamental drive towards a transfigured future. This Blochian doctrine of hope does not moralize; rather it warns that the first moment of collective consciousness is not a benign phenomenon, that it defines itself, affirms its unity, with incalculable violence against the faceless, threatening mass of Others which surround it. The rhetoric of liberal capitalism has traditionally confronted this violence with the ideal of the "civilizing" power of commerce and of a retreat from the collective (above all, from the dynamics of social class) into the security of private life. Bloch's gamble—and it is the only conceivable solution for a Left whose own revolutions (China, Vietnam, Cambodia) have generated a dismaying nationalist violence in their turn—is that a recuperation of the utopian impulse within these dark powers is possible. His is not a doctrine of self-consciousness of the type with which so many people, grown impatient with its inability to effect any concrete praxis or change, have become dissatisfied. Rather, it urges the program so dramatically expressed by Conrad's character, Stein (in *Lord Jim*): "in the destructive element immerse!" Pass all the way through nihilism so completely that we emerge in the light at its far side. A disturbing program, clearly, as the historical defections from the Left to various forms of fascism and nationalism in modern times must testify.

In accordance with this doctrine, the vision of history which emerges in Syberberg's trilogy[8] is not simply one of the "roads not taken," not simply a Lukácsian project to rescue and reinvent an alternate tradition of German culture. Syberberg's fascination with Wagner's royal patron, Ludwig II of Bavaria, results not from the identification of a moment of cultural choice, a historical turning point which might have changed everything. Although it is that too, of course, and he represents Ludwig as a form of artistic patronage and cultural development which he systematically juxtaposes with the commercialism of the arts and cultural illiteracy of the middle-class in Germany today. (Indeed, in one of his most interesting proposals, especially in the light of the neglect of his own films within the Federal Republic, Syberberg imagines a "Bayreuth" for the modern film where special state theaters for avant-garde filmmaking would be supported by the various provincial governments.) Even more significant, however, is his representation of Ludwig II as the anti-Bismarck: the tormented and dilettantish unheroic, and often ridiculous symbol of a non-Prussian Germany, of the possibility of a German federation under the leadership of Bavaria rather than the unified state under Brandenburg and the Junkers. Yet Syberberg's treatment of the "virgin king" in Ludwig— *Requiem for a Virgin King* (1972) is no less deliberately ambivalent than his treatment of Hitler, as we shall see.

It is the second film in the trilogy—*Karl May—In Search of Paradise Lost* (1974)—which most faithfully sets out on the Blochian quest for an earthly paradise, the search for utopian impulses within the contingent forms and activities of a fallen social life. The film takes as its theme the popular writer Karl May, who, as a kind of late nineteenth-century German combination of Jules Verne and Nick Carter, made the Western over into an authentically German form that was read by generations of German adolescents, including Hitler himself. The juxtaposition of Wagner's patron and this immensely successful writer of best-sellers is the strategic isolation of a moment of crisis in modern culture, the moment at which culture and emergent mass culture began to split apart from one another and to develop seemingly autonomous structures and languages. This dramatic moment in the development of culture marks a break, a dialectical leap and transformation in capital, just as surely as, on the level of the infrastructure and of institutions, the coming into being of the monopoly form. Syberberg has, it is true, expressed this emergent opposition in what are still essentially unified class terms, for the villa of Karl May and the palaces of Ludwig can still be seen as two variants of a culture of the upper bourgeoisie, or, perhaps, of the high bourgeoisie and the aristocracy, but only on the condition that Ludwig's "residential" aristocratic style is viewed as already infected with the kitsch of nineteenth-century middle-class taste.

Clearly the film's diagnosis transcends the individual writer and can be extended to all the national variants of the popular literature of nascent imperialism, of the mystery of these last "dark places of the earth" (Conrad) which suddenly become perceptible at the moment of their penetration and abolition—as in the novels of Verne or, in another way, of Rider Haggard (and even of Conrad himself), in which the closing of capitalism's global frontier resonates through the form as its condition of possibility and its outside limit.

> Through its monologue form, the film presents the inner world of "the last great German mystic in the last moment of the decline of the fairy tale," and presents it as a monstrous kind of closet drama, developing according to the laws of some three-hour-long chamber music: "The soul is a vast landscape into which we flee." One can thus seek one's paradise, as the historic Karl May did, in so many trips and voyages to the real sites of his fantasies, thereby knowing ultimate failure as May himself did in his breakdown. . . . Karl May transposed all his problems and his enemies into the figures of his adventures in the wild West and in an Orient that extended all the way to China. [In the film] we return them to their origins and see his filmic life as the projected worlds of the inner monologue. A man in search of paradise lost in the typically German misdirection, restlessly seeking his own salvation in an inferno of his own making. Job and Faust, combined, with a Saxon accent, his fanatical longing dramatized in a national hero for poor and rich alike, a hero both for Hitler and for Bloch, and acted out with all the familiar faces and voices of the *UFA* [the major German film company up to 1945], with Stalingrad music at the end which swells relentlessly out of history itself. It may be that other nations can rest at peace in their misery (perhaps also it is not so great as our own), but here we can see it percolating and seeking its own liberation as well as that of others.[9]

Nowhere, then, is the utopian impulse towards the reappropriation of energies so visible as in this attempt to rewrite the fantasies of a nascent mass culture in their authentic form as the unconscious longing of a whole collectivity.

Ludwig, however, presents a more complex and difficult vision, as we may judge from its delirious final image:

> After his resurrection from the scaffold of history. Ludwig throws off his kingly robes and in a Wagnerian finale yodels at the Alps or Himalaya landscape from the roof of the royal palace. . . . Even the bearded child-Ludwig from Erda's grotto is included, with his requiem-smile through the mist. The curse

and salvation of the legendary life of the child-king spreads out our own existential dream- and wish-landscape before us in amicable-utopian fashion.[10]

The bliss or *promesse de bonheur* of this kitsch sublime, as glorious as it
is, is deeply marked, both in its affect and in its structure as an image, by
its unreality as the self-consciously "imaginary resolution of a real contradiction."

Yet such a moment will perhaps afford us a surer insight into the
dynamics of Syberberg's aesthetic, and of his "salvational critique," than
the narrative analysis we have hitherto associated with the "method" of
Bloch (and in which the very shape of the story or tale, or the narrative
form, expresses the movement towards the future). Since Syberberg's are
not in that sense storytelling films (although they are films *about* stories of
all kinds), a narrative or diachronic analysis does them less justice than the
synchronic focus to which we now turn, and by which the movement of
filmic images in time is grasped as the "process of production" of relatively
static tableaux similar to this one of the Ludwig apotheosis. Such
moments, so characteristic of Syberberg's films, can become emblems of
the films themselves—as in the widely reproduced logo of *Our Hitler* in
which Hitler in a toga is seen rising from the grave of Wagner. Such quintessential images, which share, certainly, in the traditions of symbolism
and surrealism, are, as Susan Sontag has pointed out, more accurately
understood according to Walter Benjamin's conception of the allegorical
emblem.

Yet the originality of Syberberg's images, related as they are to his political project, his attempt at a psychoanalysis and exorcism of the German
unconscious, advances beyond these historical references. The surrealist
image—"the forcible yoking of two realities as distant and as unrelated as
possible"—and the Benjaminian allegory—a discontinuous montage of
dead relics—each in its own way underscores the heterogeneity of the
Syberberg tableau without accounting for its therapeutic function, since
the surrealistic aesthetic aimed at an immediate and apocalyptic liberation
from an impoverished and rationalized daily life, and the Benjaminian
emblem, while it displayed the remains and traces of "mourning and
melancholia," was not an active working through of such material; it was
perceived as a symptom or an icon rather than, as in Syberberg, a "spiritual method."

Such a "method" may be characterized as *dereification*: a forcible short-
circuiting of all the wires in the political unconscious, an attempt to purge
the sedimented contents of collective fantasy and ideological representation by reconnecting its symbolic counters so outrageously that they dereify themselves. The force of ideological representations (and what we
call culture or tradition is little more than an immense and stagnant

swamp of such representations) derives from their enforced separation within our minds, their compartmentalization, which, more than any mere double standard, authorizes the multiple standards and diverse operations of that complex and collective Sartrean *mauvaise foi* called ideology, whose essential function is to prevent totalization.

We have, in American literature, a signal and programmatic enactment of this short-circuiting in Gertrude Stein's neglected *Four in America,* in which Ulysses S. Grant is imagined as a religious leader, the Wright Brothers as painters, Henry James as a general, and George Washington as a novelist.[11] There is but a step from this "exercise" of a reified collective imagination to Syberberg's presentation of Hitler as the greatest filmmaker of the twentieth century. The force of his therapy depends on the truth of his presupposition that the zones of high culture (Wagner, Ludwig's castles), popular and adolescent reading (Karl May), and petty-bourgeois political values and impulses (Hitler, Nazism) are so carefully separated in the collective mind that their conceptual interference, their rewiring in the heterogeneity of the collage, will blow the entire system sky-high. It is according to this therapeutic strategy that those moments in Syberberg which seem closest to a traditional form of debunking, or of an unmasking of false consciousness (as in the reports of Hitler's bourgeois private life) must be read. The point is not to allow one of the poles of the image to settle into the truth of the other which it unmasks (as when our sense of the horror of Nazi violence "demystifies" Hitler's courteous behavior with his staff), but rather to hold them apart as equal and autonomous so that energies can pass back and forth between them. This is the strategy at work in the seemingly banal monologue in which the Hitler puppet answers his accusers and suggests that Auschwitz is not to be judged quite so harshly after Vietnam, Idi Amin, the torture establishments of the Shah and the Latin American dictatorships, Cambodia, and Chile. To imagine Hitler as Nixon and vice versa is not merely to underscore the personal peculiarities they share (odd mannerisms, awkwardness in personal relations, etc.), but also to bring out dramatically the banality, not of evil, but of conservatism and reaction in general, and of their stereotypical ideas of social law and order, which can as easily result in genocide as in Watergate.

It is important at this point to return to the comparison between the different "cultural revolutions" of Syberberg and Godard. Both filmmakers are involved, as we have noted, in attempts to dereify cultural representations. The essential difference between them, however, is in their relationship to what is called the "truth content" of art, its claim to possess some truth or epistemological value. This is, indeed, the essential difference between post- and classical modernism (as well as Lukács's conception of realism): the latter still lays claim to the place and function vacated by religion, still draws its resonance from a conviction that through the work of art some authentic vision of the work is immanently expressed. Syberberg's films are modernist in this classical, and what may now seem archaic, sense.[12] Godard's are, however, resolutely postmodernist in that they conceive of themselves as sheer text, as a process of production of representations that have no truth content, are, in this sense, sheer surface or superficiality. It is this conviction which accounts for the reflexivity of the Godard film, its resolution to use representation against itself to destroy the binding or absolute status of any representation.

If classical modernism is understood as a secular substitute for religion, it is no longer surprising that its formulation of the problem of representation can borrow from a religious terminology which defines representation as "figuration," a dialectic of the letter and the spirit, a "picture-language" (*Vorstellung*) which embodies, expresses, and transmits other inexpressible truths.[13] For the theological tradition to which this terminology belongs, the problem is one of the "proper" use of figuration and of the danger of its becoming fixed, objectified into an externality where the inner spirit is forgotten or historically lost. The great moments of iconoclasm in Judaism and Islam, as well as in a certain Protestantism, have resulted from the fear that the figures, images, and sacred object of their once vital religious traditions have become mere idols and that they must be destroyed in order that there may be a reinvigoration by and return to the authentic spirit of religious experience. Iconoclasm is, therefore, an early version (in a different mode of production) of the present-day critiques of representation (and as in the latter, the destruction of the dead letter or of the idol is, almost at once, associated with a critique of the institutions—whether the Pharisees and Saducees, the hierarchy of the Roman Catholic Church, or the "whore of Babylon," or modern-day ideological state apparatuses such as the university system—which perpetuate that idolatry for the purposes of domination).

Unlike Hegel—whose conception of the "end of art," that is, the ultimate bankruptcy and transcendence of an immanent and figural language, foresees a final replacement of art by the nonfigural language of philosophy in which truth dispenses with picture-making and becomes transparent to itself—religion and modernism replace dead or false images (systems of representation) with others more lively and authentic. This description of classical modernism as a "religion of art" is justified, in turn, by the aesthetic reception and experience of works themselves. At its most vital, the experience of modernism was not one of a single historical movement or process, but of a "shock of discovery," a commitment and an adherence to its individual forms through a series of "religious conversions." One did not simply read D. H. Lawrence or Rilke, see Jean Renoir or Hitchcock, or listen to Stravinsky, as a distinct manifestations of what we now term modernism. Rather one read all the works of a particular writer, learned a style and a phenomenological world. D. H. Lawrence became an absolute, a complete and systematic world view, to which one converted. This meant, however, that the experience of one form of modernism was incompatible with another, so that one entered one world only at the price of abandoning another (when we tired of Pound, for example, we converted to Faulkner, or when Thomas Mann became predictable, we turned to Proust). The crisis of modernism as such came, then, when suddenly it became clear that "D. H. Lawrence" was not an absolute after all, not the final achieved figuration of the truth of the world, but only one art-language among others, only one shelf of works in a whole dizzying library. Hence the shame and guilt of cultural intellectuals, the renewed appeal of the Hegelian goal, the "end of art," and the abandonment of culture altogether for immediate political activity. Hence, also the appeal of the nonfictive, the cult of the experiential, as the Devil explains to Adrian in a climactic moment of Mann's *Doctor Faustus*:

> The work of art, time, and aesthetic experience [*Schein*] are one, and now fall prey to the critical impulse. The latter no longer tolerates aesthetic play or appearance, fiction, the self-glorifications of a form which censures passions and human suffering, transforms them into so many roles, translates them into images. Only the non-fictive remains valid today, only what is neither played nor played out [*der nicht verspielte*], only the undistorted and unembellished expression of pain in its moment of experience.[14]

In much the same spirit, Sartre remarked that *Nausea* was worthless against the fact of the suffering or death of a single child. Yet pain is a text. The death or suffering of children comes to us only through texts (although the images of network news, for example). The crisis of modernist absolutes results not from the juxtaposition of these fictive works with nonfigurative experiences of pain or suffering, but from their relativization by one another. Bayreuth would have to be built far from everything else, far from the secular babel of the cities with their multiple art languages and forms of post-religious "reterritorialization" or "recording" (Deleuze). Only Wagner could be heard there in order to forestall the disastrous realization that he was "just" a composer and the works "just" operas, in order, in other words, for the Wagnerian sign system or aesthetic language to appear absolute, to impose itself, like a religion, as the dominant code, the hegemonic system of symbols, on an entire collectivity. That this is not a solution for a pluralistic and secular capitalism is proved by the fate of Bayreuth itself, yet directs our attention to the political and social mediations which are present in the aesthetic dilemma. The modernist aesthetic demands an organic community which it cannot, however, bring into being by itself but can only express. Ludwig II is, then the name for that fleeting mirage, that optical illusion of a concrete historical possibility. He is the philosopher-king who, by virtue of a political power that resulted from a unique and unstable social and political situation, holds out, for a moment, the promise of an organic community. Later, Nazism will make this same promise. Of Ludwig II also, then, it may be said that had he not existed, he would have to have been invented. For he is the socio-political demiurge, a structural necessity of the modernist aesthetic which projects him as an image of its foundation.

What happens, then, when the modernisms begin to look at one another and to experience their relativity and their cultural guilt, their own aesthetic nakedness? From this moment of shame and crisis there comes into being a new, second-degree solution which Barthes describes in a splendid page so often quoted by me that I may be excused for doing so again:

> The greatest modernist works linger as long as possible, in a sort of miraculous stasis, on the threshold of Literature itself, in an anticipatory situation in which the density of life is given and developed without yet being destroyed by their consecration as an [institutionalized] sign system.[15]

Here, in this contemporary reflection on the dialectic of figuration and iconoclasm, the ultimate reification of the figural system is taken to be inevitable. Yet that very inevitability at least holds out the promise of a transitional moment between the destruction of the older systems of figuration (so many dead letters, empty icons, or old-fashioned art languages) and the freezing over and institutionalization of the new one. A rather different Wagnerian solution may be taken simultaneously as the prototype and the object lesson for this possibility of an aesthetic authenticity in the provisory. Bayreuth was the imaginary projection of a social solution to the modernist dilemma: the Wagnerian leitmotif may now be seen as a far more concrete, internal response to this dilemma. For the leitmotif is intended, in principle, to destroy everything that is reifiable in the older musical tradition, most notably the quotable and excerptable "melodies" of romantic music, which as Adorno noted, are so readily fetishized by the contemporary culture industry ("the twenty loveliest melodies of the great symphonies on a single long-playing record"). The leitmotif is designed, on the one hand, *not* to be singable or fetishizable in that way and, on the other, to prevent the musical text from becoming an object by ceaselessly redissolving it into an endless process of recombination with other leitmotifs. The failure of the attempt, the reconsecration as an institutional sign system, then comes when we hum Wagner after all, when the leitmotifs are themselves reified into so many properly Wagnerian "melodies," of which, as familiar known quantities, one can make a complete list, and which now stand out from the musical flow like so many foreign bodies.

It is not to be thought that a postmodernist aesthetic can escape this particular dilemma either. Even in Godard, the relentless anatomy and dissolution of the reified image does not prevent the latter's ultimate triumph over the aesthetic of the film as sheer process. Godard's structural analysis—by which text demonstration of the structural heterogeneity of such Barthesian "mythologies"—demands in some sense that the film destroy itself in the process, that it use itself up without residue, that it be disposable. Yet the object of this corrosive dissolution is not the image as such, but individual images, mere examples of the general dynamic of the image in media and consumer society, in the society of the spectacle. These examples—represented as impermanent, not only in themselves, but also by virtue of the fact that they could have been substituted by others—then develop an inertia of their own, and, vehicles for the critique of representation, turn into so many representations "characteristic" of the films of Godard. Far from abolishing themselves, the films persist, in film series and film studies programs, as a reified sequence of familiar images which can be screened again and again: the spirit triumphs over the letter, no doubt, but it is the dead letter that remains behind.

Syberberg's "cultural revolution" seems to face quite different problems, for the objects of his critique—the weight of figures like Karl May, Ludwig, or Hitler himself as figures in the collective unconscious—are historical realities and thus no longer mere examples of an abstract process. Late capitalism has elsewhere provided its own method for exorcizing the dead weight of the past: historical amnesia, the waning of historicity, the effortless media-exhaustion of even the immediate past. The France of the consumer society scarcely needs to exorcize De Gaulle when it can simply allow the heroic Gaullist moment of its construction to recede into oblivion at the appropriately dizzying rate. In this respect, it is instructive to juxtapose Syberberg's *Our Hitler* with that other recent New York sensation, Abel Gance's 1927 *Napoléon* (restored by Kevin Brownlow in 1980 and, in the United States, slightly shortened and presented by Francis Coppola's Zoetrope Studios.) Even if we leave aside the proposed critique of Napoleonic politics in the unfilmed sequels, this representational reappropriation of the past is only too evidently ideological: the idealization of Napoleonic puritanism and law and order after the excesses of the Revolution and the Directory (read: the great war and the twenties), the projection of a Napoleonic unification of Europe (this will come to sound Hitlerian in the 1930s and early 1940s, liberal once more with the foundation of NATO and the Common Market). These are surely not attempts to settle accounts with the past and with its sedimented collective representations, but only to use its standard images for manipulative purposes.

Syberberg's aesthetic strategy presupposes some fundamental social difference between the Federal Republic of the Restoration and the *Wirtschaftswunder,* of the *Berufsverbot* and the hard currency of the *Deutschmark,* and the other nation states of advanced capitalism with their media dynamics, their culture industries, and their historical amnesia. Whether Germany today is really any different in this respect is what is euphemistically called an empirical question. Syberberg's idea is that the German *misère* is somehow distinct and historically unique and can be defended by an account of the peculiar combination of political underdevelopment and leap-frogging "modernization" that characterizes recent German history. Still, there is some nagging doubt as to whether, even in the still relatively conservative class cohesiveness of the *Spiessbürger* which dominates West Germany today, the secret of the past may not be that there is no secret any longer, and that the collective representations of Wagner, Karl May, even of Hitler, may not simply be constructions of the media (perpetuated and reinvented by Hans-Jürgen Syberberg, among others).

But this must now be reformulated in terms of Syberberg's filmic system and of what we have described as his political project, his cultural revolution, or collective psychoanalysis. In order for his method to work, these films must somehow continue to "take" on the real world, and his Hitler puppets and other Nazi motifs must somehow remain "referential," must preserve their links as allusions and designations of the historically real. This is the ultimate guarantee of the truth content to which films such as this lay claim. The psychodrama will have no effect if it relaxes back into sheer play and absolute fictionality; it must be understood as therapeutic play with material that resists, that is, with one or the other forms of the real (it being understood that a collective representation of Hitler is as real and has as many practical consequences as the biographical one). Clearly the nonfictional nature of the subject matter is no guarantee in this respect; nor is this only a reflection of the "textual" nature of history in general, whose facts are never actually present but constructed in historiography, written archives. Aesthetic distance, the very "set" towards fictionality itself, that "suspension of disbelief" which involves an equal suspension of belief, these and other characteristics of aesthetic experience as they have been theorized since Kant also operate very powerfully to turn Hitler into "Hitler," a character in a fiction film, and thus removed from the historical reality which we hope to affect. In the same way, it is notorious that within the work of art in general, the most reprehensible ideologies—Céline's anti-Semitism, for instance—are momentarily rewritten into a thematic system, become a pretext for sheer aesthetic play and are no more offensive than, say, Pynchon's "theme" of paranoia.

Yet this is not simply to be taken as the result of some eternal essence of the work of art and of aesthetic experience: it is a dilemma which must be historicized, as it might be were we to imagine a Lukácsian defense of the proposition that, in their own time, Sir Walter Scott's historical romances were more resonantly referential and come to terms with history more concretely than do these equally historical films of Syberberg. For the imperceptible dissociation, in the modern world, of the public from the private, the privatization of experience, the monadization and the relativization of the individual subject, affect the filmmaker as well, and enforce the almost instantaneous eclipse of that unstable situation, that "miraculous suspension," which Barthes saw as the necessary condition for an even fleeting modernist authenticity. From this perspective, the problem is in understanding Syberberg as the designation of a particular modernist language, a distinctive modernist sign system: to read these films properly is, as I have said, a matter of conversion, a matter of learning the Syberberg world, the themes and obsessions that characterize it, the recurrent symbols and motifs that constitute it as a figural language. The trouble is that at that point, the realities with which Syberberg attempts to grapple, realities marked by the names of such real historical actors as Wagner, Himmler, Hitler, Bismarck, and the like, are at once transformed into so many personal signs in a private language, which becomes public, when the artist is successful, only as an institutionalized sign system.

This is not Syberberg's fault, clearly, but the result of the peculiar status of culture in our world. Nor would I want to be understood as saying that Syberberg's cultural revolution is impossible, and that the unique tension between the referential and aesthetic play which his psychodramas demand can never be maintained. On the contrary. But when it is, when these films suddenly begin to "mean it" in Erik Erikson's sense,[16] when something fundamental begins to happen to history itself, then the question remains as to which played the more decisive role in the process, the subject or the object, the viewer or the film. Ultimately, it would seem, it is the viewing subject who enjoys the freedom to take such works as political art or as art *tout court*. It is on the viewing subject that the choice falls as to whether these films have a meaning in the strong sense, an authentic resonance, or are perceived simply as texts, as a play of signifiers. It will be observed that we can say the same about all political art, about Brecht himself (who has, in a similar way, become "Brecht," another classic in the canon). Yet Brecht's ideal theater public held out the promise of some collective and collaborative response which seems less possible in the privatized viewing of the movie theater, even in the local Bayreuths for avant-garde film which Syberberg fantasized.

As for the "destructive element," the Anglo-American world has been immersed in it long before Syberberg was ever heard from: beginning with Shirer's book and Trevor-Roper's account of the bunker all the way to Albert Speer, with sales of innumerable Nazi uniforms and souvenirs worn by everybody from youth gangs and punk rock groups to extreme right-wing parties. If it were not so long and so talky, Syberberg's *Our Hitler*—a veritable summa of all these motifs—might well have become a cult film for such enthusiasts, a sad and ambiguous fate for a "redemptive critique." Perhaps, indeed, this is an Imaginary which can be healed only by the desperate attempt to keep the referential alive.

Notes

1. See in particular Syberberg's two books *Hitler, ein Film aus Deutschland* (Hamburg: Rowohlt, 1978); and *Syberbergs Filmbuch* (Frankfurt: Fischer, 1979).

2. "Syberberg repeatedly says his film is addressed to the German 'inability to mourn,' that it undertakes the 'work of mourning' (*Trauerarbeit*). These phrases recall the famous essay Freud wrote during World War I, 'Mourning and Melancholia,' which connects melancholy and the inability to work through grief; and the application of this formula in an influential psychoanalytic study of postwar Germany by Alexander and Margarete Mitscherlich, *The Inability to Mourn*, published in Germany in 1967, which diagnoses the Germans as afflicted by mass melancholia, the result of the continuing denial of their collective responsibility for the Nazi past and their persistent refusal to mourn" (Susan Sontag, "Eye of the Storm," *The New York Review of Books*, XXVII, 2 [Feb. 21, 1980], 40). The trauma of loss does not, however, seem a very apt way to characterize present-day Germany's relationship to Hitler; Syberberg's operative analogy here is rather with the requiem as an art form, in which grief is redemptively transmuted into jubilation.

3. In Stanley Cavell, *The World Viewed: Reflections on the Ontology of Film* (New York: Viking, 1971).

4. Syberberg, *Filmbuch*, pp. 81–82.

5. We do not, in fact, have to imagine Godard listening to other kinds of "classical music," since this last is omnipresent in his recent films. "Music is my Antigone," he declares in the extraordinary *Scénario du film "Passion"* (1982), a videotext not merely of great interest on what is surely his finest later film to date (*Passion*, 1982), but which may stand as an apotheosis of the visionary and prophetic vocation of the artist equal to anything in Syberberg (and rather tending to confirm J.-F. Lyotard's idea that the "modern"—in this case a more traditional glorification of the aesthetic—comes *after* the "postmodern"—or in other words the Godard of the 1960s and early 1970s).

6. Syberberg, *Filmbuch*, pp. 85–86.

7. See the chapter on Bloch in my *Marxism and Form* (Princeton: Princeton University Press, 1970). In a seminal essay, whose diffusion in Germany was surely not without effect either on Syberberg's own aesthetic or on the reception of his films, Jürgen Habermas attributes a similar method to Walter Benjamin; see "Consciousness-Raising or Redemptive Criticism—The Contemporaneity of Walter Benjamin," *New German Critique*, no. 17 (Spring 1979), 30–59.

8. The trilogy consists of: *Ludwig—Requiem for a Virgin King* (1972), *Karl May—In Search of Paradise Lost* (1974), and *Hitler, A Film from Germany/Our Hitler* (1977).

9. Syberberg, *Filmbuch*, pp. 39, 45–46.

10. Ibid., p. 90.

11. Gertrude Stein, *Four in America* (New Haven: Yale University Press, 1947).

12. This is, I take it, what Sontag means to stress in her characterization of Syberberg's essentially symbolist aesthetic.

13. See the chapter on religion in Hegel's *Phenomenology of Spirit*; Rudolf Bultmann's work is the most influential modern treatment of the problem of figuration in theology.

14. Thomas Mann, *Doktor Faustus* (Frankfurt: Fischer, 1951), p. 361.

15. Roland Barthes, *Writing Degree Zero* (London: Cape, 1967), p. 39.

16. Erik Erikson, *Young Man Luther* (New York: Norton, 1958).

Herzog's Apocalypse as Eternal Return: The Circularity of *La Soufrière*

KENT CASPER

"**H**ERZOG'S EXPERIENCE of time," observes Thomas Elsaesser, "is that of an apocalypse that never arrives, of transitional states, of boredom and degradation. The situation of *La Soufrière* corresponds perfectly to the basic condition of all his films: 'an inevitable catastrophe that did not happen.'"[1] Elsaesser's insight is accurate and provocative. Eschatological tropes and themes have long been a Herzogian preoccupation, from *Signs of Life* (1967) through *Lessons of Darkness* (1992). In documentaries as well as fiction films (an always slippery distinction in his work), Herzog demonstrates a kind of postlapsarian obsession with the fallen world, its decay, homogenization and commercialization. This preoccupation is often expressed through a profusion of "sublime" and hypnagogic doomsday images (as in *Fata Morgana*, *Heart of Glass*, and *Lessons of Darkness*) deployed within overarching "mythical" structures that resonate with the discursive traditions of Christian millenarianism. (*Fata Morgana* is divided into the narrative units "Creation," "Paradise," and "The Golden Age." *Lessons of Darkness* contains thirteen mythically titled sequences that portray the burning oil fields in Kuwait in the aftermath of the Gulf War, as a Johanine landscape of end-time conflagration, complete with Herzog's voice-over recitations from Revelations.) Concomitant with the recurring scenarios and tropes of apocalypse is Herzog's existentialist idealism that attempts to privilege prediscursive, spontaneous, "natural existence"—usually, and revealingly, projected in terms of non-Western cultures—that fetishizes individual experience at the physical extremes, and that has long been engaged in a desparate and despairing search for what he calls "new images." The "new images" constitute for Herzog, a form of aesthetic redemption of the world, but one that attempts to circumvent, get behind or beyond, coded reality—an obsession Terry Eagleton calls "the romantic pursuit of the irreducibly lived."[2] The impossibility of realizing this desire to capture unmediated reality is directly related to Herzog's sense of time as the "apocalypse that never arrives": the always-deferred catastrophe functions as a nostalgically longed-for epiphany that can be (pre)figured only in discursive formations, as a diverse series of signifiers in search of an elusive signified. This aesthetic position gives rise, to be sure, to a certain kind of (modernist) ironic

---

This essay was written specifically for this volume and is published here for the first time by permission of the author.

reflexivity, but one that is resolutely ahistorical. Strikingly absent from Herzog's films are any historical representations that are not subsumed into his mythical-cyclical patterns or usurped by the material presence of his images.[3]

In this essay I examine *La Soufrière* through a discussion of conflicting critical discourses that conceptualize the modern idea of apocalpyse. One such that would appear to have an ideological congruence with Herzog's sensibility is the literary-critical discourse on modern "apocalyptic" narratives employed by Frank Kermode in *The Sense of an Ending*.[4] Kermode's biblically based argument points to a long tradition of apocalyptic narratives, beginning with the Revelations of St. John, that derive their structures and strategies from an endlessly deferred end, from an "imminent" catastrophe/theophany, signaled by an accretion of end-time warning markers that accumulate in the "transition" before the "final event."[5] When this pattern is transposed into the modernist narrative of a James Joyce (or the filmic discourse of Herzog), its figurations describe an immanent more than imminent condition, in which a virtual state of devastation/illumination is actualized in various flashpoints as epiphanies of crisis, but simultaneously aesthetically "redeemed" through the formal-mythical structuring of the writer. Thus, for Kermode, *Kairos*—the revelation of significance in time, charged with meaning because of its relation to both origin and end and thus exhibiting a "concordant" temporality—intervenes periodically in chronos—the sheer passing of time, the state of "reality," by virtue of the creative interventions of the writer. Even Beckett, that "perverse theologian of nihilism," cannot escape this kind of aesthetic theodicy.[6] (Overtones of early Nietzsche here: "it is only as an aesthetic phenomenon that life is justified.") However, in Kermode's view, it is the acute self-consciousness of the modern writer that saves one from becoming enmeshed in the irrationalism of myth; reflexivity, conveyed through the rhetorical strategies of the text, keeps one aware of the fictiveness of the fiction. Otherwise, there is always the danger, exemplified by Yeats, Pound, Lewis, Benn, and Jünger, of confusing one's apocalyptic fictions with a mythical reality, the ideological expression of which is fascism. That same reflexivity, however, also keeps the awareness alive that fictive arrangements, however revelatory of meaning, are finally an imposition upon experience, "impoverished in the face of being itself."[7]

Constituted in this dualistic-idealist way, the aestheticized, ahistorical, autonomous, reflexive subject is caught in a vicious, solipsistic circle: the ontological privileging of temporal, brutal reality means that the maker of intervening fictions will always be driven to self-ironic critique of the process of representation, and then back to the chaos of nihilistic reality, back to "the horror." The aestheticized self-consciousness, in Frank Lentricchia's words, "does not urge the uncovering and bringing to bear of alternative perspectives which in dialectical interplay might offer constraints to the excesses and blindness of single-minded ideology."[8] Rather, it urges paralysis and despair—or, as in the case of Herzog, the impossible search for aesthetic representation of a reality that lies "before" or "outside of" discursive codes, the attempt at "redeeming the signified."[9] When that reality is figured as catastrophe or apocalypse, it amounts to an aesthetisizing of horror—for a modern German "after Auschwitz," a highly charged and problematic undertaking that can hardly avoid complicity with fascistic ideology. Indeed, the Holocaust is the embedded but unacknowledged referent that haunts Herzog's apocalyptic figurations, all-too-present precisely because of its conspicuous absence.

Walter Benjamin's reformulation of Jewish messianism, especially in its "materialist" conceptualization, constitutes a discourse of apocalypse that counters and critiques the idealist constructs of existential humanism/modernism. For Benjamin, the "fallen" character of human history, ironically codified in the bourgeois notion of "progress" and the avant-garde notion of the "new," is a product of the commodity culture's repression and forgetting of the past. The modern coalesces with prehistory, that is, with mythical repetition in the guise of the "eternal recurrence" of commodity exchange, in which "the self-identical perpetually presents itself as the new."[10] Bourgeois culture is thus characterized by the compulsive repetitions of the frozen world of myth, a fetishized realm. "Progress as catastrophe" is therefore "the sign under which the ruins of bourgeois civilization present themselves for decipherment" and "catastrophe" is what is "given at any given moment."[11] The key to "redemption" or the messianic era is inscribed in crucial past moments of history which, when wrenched into relationship with the political present, create the shock of a dialectical image that has the potential power of "blasting apart" the "naturalness" of the reified social condition. These punctual moments of *Jetztzeit* "shot through with messianic splinters," function to help shape a new image-sphere in which the contours of freedom—that is, of a future egalitarian society—are prefigured. The heightened moments of "profane illumination" involve a form of reflexivity that is materialist and historical: self-consciousness, "illumined" in this way, is always consciousness of the self in its social-historical relations.[12]

Throughout his filmic work, Herzog has shown a predeliction for portraying, in almost surrealistic fashion, the debris of modern civilization, ruined artefacts of technology, towns struck by catastrophe and emptied of life (the ghostly abandoned factories in *Fata Morgana*, blocks of board-ed-up, abandoned shops in Brooklyn in *Huie's Sermon*, the plague-devastated town of Wismar in *Nosferatu*, miles of burned-out military vehicles in *Lessons of Darkness*). Such images of immanent apocalypse are often situated in Third World landscapes that have been subject to colonization and Western commercial exploitation, but that are strangely devoid of vital native life—or at least of that life in its communal patterns (*Herdsmen of the Sun* is an exception). Herzog claims to have an anthropologist's curiosity about non-Western cultures, an assertion that on the surface seems to be supported by his fondness for documentaries in Africa and Latin America. Yet his choice of characters and of interviewees in the documentaries reveals an idiosyncratic and recurrent privileging of individual survivors, often filmed in the isolation of the landscape of ruin. Their images and voices are, for Herzog, existential witnesses of quotidian catastrophe—or, frequently, it is the *loss* of voice in the face of horror, the refusal to speak, that is the more "eloquent" testimony to the devastation of the human spirit. Again, this gesture is consonant with the existential humanism of conservative modernism: articulation remains, finally, impotent in the face of the "unspeakable" or the "ineffable."

In August 1976, Herzog heard the news that the volcano La Soufrière on the island of Guadeloupe was about to explode, and that the threatened town of Basse Terre had been evacuated except for a couple of peasants who refused to leave. Just two months earlier, he had completed the filming of *Heart of Glass*, his strange, controversial meditation on "apocalypse" in the context of an eighteenth-century German village. In that film, the final catastrophe predicted by the seer Hias is prefigured by the loss of the "ruby glass" secret, a mythical loss that sends the community spinning into disintegration and self-destruction. In many ways, *Heart of Glass* set the stage for the *La Soufrière* project. Both films revolve around a central lack—the formula for ruby glass, the missing volcanic explosion—that betrays a longing for mythically charged ontological certainty, and both films subsume the economic plight of the poor into existentialist typologies.

Herzog flew into Guadeloupe with cameramen Ed Lachmann and Jörg Schmidt-Reitwein, filmed the deserted town, interviewed three peasants who had remained, took various shots of the volcano and environs, then returned to Germany and pieced together a documentary on the experience that includes a photo narration of an earlier (1902) volcanic eruption on the neighboring island of Martinique. The result is a film that incorporates, in "postmodern" fashion, a mix of documentary's historical styles, all of which are placed, as it were, in quotation marks. Herzog draws on the Griersonian tradition of the off-camera authoritative direct address, but infuses his voice-over with irony and self-deprecation, undermining the subject position it creates. He presents what seem to be purely observational passages—the sequences involving the volcano—but renders them parodic by the missing climax and, consequently, by the incongruously dramatic music of Wagner and Rachmaninoff.[13] The interviews with the peasants seem at first to capture a piece of unaffected reality. They involve a minimum of intervention and seem to suggest social critique, yet retroactive reading reveals these to be shaped and staged, aesthetically appropriated. The sequence involving the empty town of Basse Terre records a site that has been hastily evacuated, the hand-held camera conveying a sense of raw actuality, but montage and voice-over combine to produce a familiar sci-fi genre pattern. A photo-reportage segment with Herzog's voice-over narration tells the story of the 1902 volcano tragedy on Martinique, appealing to historical actuality; yet simultaneously and explicitly the narrative is constructed in dramatic units as a (Christian) parable of doomsday. This eclectic mosaic of documentary styles and narrative constructs is manipulated by a "voice" (to use Bill Nichol's term for the organizing intelligence of a documentary) that insistently evokes the existential absurdity of the dramatic nonhappening, assimilates the unusual into the quotidian, and calls attention to the filmmaker as an active fabricator of meaning.[14]

The ironic reflexivity of the film stems in part from the constructs of catastrophe that, within a "documentary," are recognizably drawn from the literary/cinematic archive. The Basse Terre sequence, for example, is shaped as a variation on a 1950s sci-fi movie featuring a town ominously emptied by an alien force, leaving behind pathetic artefacts of the human community (redundantly we are told, at the end of this sequence, that the scene was "as spooky as a sci-fi locale.") Then, in one of Herzog's most arresting gestures, the Basse Terre scenario of lifelessness is juxtaposed with a photo-reportage of the Martinique volcanic catastrophe of 1902. This is legendary material: a wave of flaming gases utterly destroyed the town of St. Pierre and its 30,000 inhabitants within minutes. In this segment, Herzog films a series of old sepia photographs that are linked together to form a successive narrative; coupled with Herzog's verbal commentary, it has the impact of a morality tale. First, we are shown photos of the thriving town of St. Pierre shortly before the devastation, then a shore-side picture of residents gathering restlessly on the day before the explosion. Herzog informs us that the town authorities had made the decision not to evacuate until after an important municipal election had taken place. Finally, we see a bizarre, fuzzy-focus picture of the harbor of St. Pierre after it had been hit by the volcano blast, a hellish, Bosch-like scene of grotesque animal carcasses adrift and a large-winged vulture swooping down against the background of the shattered town. Farther out in the harbor, a rescue ship, half-sunk, founders, its passengers all perished.

Herzog stresses that this scene of the final cataclysm is a photograph, not a painting, thus appealing to an implied historical authenticity through the mimetic verisimilitude of photographic reportage. Yet the effect is not the immediacy of "reality," but rather the distancing of art, the sense that the apocalyptic event can only be alluded to, legendized or figured through the diffusion and mediation of images. Catastrophe is situated in spectator awareness as an aesthetic construct, as a moving picture of still photos, the editing necessarily foregrounded as technique and technology, the narration as dramatic eschatological parable.

The Basse Terre and St. Pierre sequences circulate in this film as variations on the deserted-town and doomsday typologies of Herzog's other films, recouping images from his past repertoire and anticipating future repetitions. This closed loop of Herzogian intertexts encompasses documentary and fiction films, "found" images and character constructs. The St. Pierre narration contains, for example, an arch-Herzogian figure: the sole survivor of the volcanic conflagration was the young thief Ciparis, so irredeemable that he had been kept in underground solitary confinement. Consequently, when the explosion came, he was burnt badly but still survived. Later, Herzog says, he was taken to America and exhibited as a freak in a travelling circus side-show. This bit of information places Ciparis in the company of Kaspar Hauser, Hombrecito, the king of Punt, and "young Mozart" (in the circus sequence of *Kaspar Hauser*), and of the dwarves and misfits that inhabit his other films. Their commonality, what makes them "freaks" for bourgeois eyes, is (in Herzog's view) that they are representatives of "absurd" experience at the margins or extremes of society, unassimilable into the homogenizing structures of mainstream culture. But they are, of course, assimilated into the circulating commodity of Herzog's filmic universe.

Herzog's interviews with the three peasants who refused to be evacuated are also artfully constructed so as to place them within the intertextual loop. They are curiously indifferent to the impending disaster, the first two placing themselves in God's hands because "we all must die sometime," "we are all sitting on a powder keg," and in any case, they have nowhere to go. "Death, like life, is forever," says the first peasant, uttering a (coached?) phrase that succinctly captures the paradox of the Herzogian discourse. "Death," for Herzog, is an existential virtuality to all moments and actions, a Bergsonian *durée*, the quotidian apocalypse that is dispersed into present time and has "already happened," yet "never arrives."

Similarly, the second poor peasant declares "there is not a thing you can do," a sentiment that resonates with the situation of most of Herzog's characters. For Strozsek, Aguirre, Woyzeck, Harker, and Bruno, "action" is illusory in the sense of some teleology or linear movement, and is invariably revealed to be futile, circular, a downward spiral. The anti-action scenario is then further illustrated by the composition of shots during the interview of the third man. He is filmed standing in the middle of a street intersection in Basse Terre, indicating by words and gestures that he could either leave or stay, go this way or that. The camera leaves him in the same shoulder-shrugging position. All three interviewees convey an attitude of calm indifference. They are not heroic, fatalistic, or even resigned. Rather, they are presented so as to emphasize that the present catastrophic situation is no different from daily life—which is to say that they inhabit narratives completely congruent with Herzog's fictions.

At the end of the film, Herzog claims that it is not the volcano that remains in his memory, but rather the "neglect and oblivion in which those black people lived." The statement is not so much one of social conscience as it is one of aesthetic appropriation (he uses the words "neglect and oblivion," not "poverty and misery"). Herzog has here carried out one of his repeated "rescue operations," into film, of poor and marginalized persons who otherwise, under "normal" circumstances, would be invisible and faceless. A similar gesture is evident during an aerial panorama track of the town, when Herzog's hushed voice-over says that he felt he was filming the last images anyone would ever see of Basse Terre. The salvaging of disappearing worlds into images has, of course, long been a part of the visual documentarist's project, in particular Herzog's.[15] But, as we have seen, Herzog tends to "save" them by incorporating them into heavily coded intertextual constructs that are, finally, Eurocentric and ahistorical.

At the ideological heart of Herzog's pervasive images of "circles of futility" is a romantic-existentialist sensibility which, while ever roaming the world in search of forms and images of "pure" experience, finds itself consigned to recycle the prepackaged. This form of repetitiousness constitutes, precisely, Benjamin's frozen world of myth, in which the "new" circulates as always-the-same commodity. In Herzog's case, the commodity repetition can also be understood as the self-reproducing of "Herzog the death-defying visionary auteur" within the system of distribution. La Soufrière emphasizes, albeit somewhat whimsically, the imminent threat to the lives of the "mad" Herzog and his crew, adding another dimension to the stories, scandals, and profilmic excesses that surround the making of a Herzog film and that promote his image of eccentricity.[16]

One result of this recycling of the same under the guise of the new, is that anywhere, anytime, anyone can be made to figure as an instantiation of Herzog's abstract mythical scheme of alienation or "daily apocalypse": if an impending volcanic eruption on Guadeloupe in 1976 can be made meaningful through its typological alliance with Herzogian intertexts and Christian apocalyptic discourse, the same can be done for burning oil fields in Kuwait in 1992. The film's signifying units are thus drained of specificity and historical context; they become loosely allegorical, formal, operating within an idealist framework. Lessons of Darkness is a prime example of dense, sensuous imagery in the service of a universalizing discourse that places the Gulf War and its aftermath in an apolitical no-man's-land, where fiery spires of oil take on the "naturalness" of a volcanic eruption and the only humans to be seen are mytholigized firefighters and interviewees who have been struck mute or inarticulate as a result of the war's brutality. This is, of course, familiar stuff from the Herzogian repertoire, and it illustrates "once more" how his representation of apocalyptic end-time functions within what is essentially the empty, homogeneous time of eternal repetition.

Notes

1. Thomas Elsaesser, "An Anthropologist's Eye: *Where the Green Ants Dream*," in Timothy Corrigan, ed., *The Films of Werner Herzog* (New York: Methuen, 1986), 142.

2. Terry Eagleton, *The Ideology of the Aesthetic* (Oxford and Cambridge: Basil Blackwell, 1990), 319.

3. See Timothy Corrigan, *The Films of Werner Herzog*, 15.

4. Frank Kermode, *The Sense of an Ending* (London and New York: Oxford University Press, 1966).

5. Ibid., 18.

6. Ibid., 115.

7. See Frank Lentricchia, *After the New Criticism* (Chicago: University of Chicago Press, 1980), 35.

8. Ibid., 56.

9. Thomas Elsaesser, "An Anthropologist's Eye," 145.

10. See Richard Wolin, *Walter Benjamin: An Aesthetic of Redemption* (New York: Columbia University Press, 1980), 129.

11. Ibid., 130

12. Ibid., 132–135.

13. See William Van Wert, "Last Words: Observations on a New Language," in *The Films of Werner Herzog*, 68.

14. Bill Nichols, "The Voice of Documentary," in Alan Rosenthal, ed., *New Challenges for Documentary* (Berkeley and Los Angeles: University of California Press, 1988), 48.

15. See Susan Sontag, *On Photography* (New York: Delta, 1978), 75–82.

16. For a discussion of Herzog's promotion of the drama of his filmmaking, see Eric Rentschler, "The Politics of Vision: Herzog's *Heart of Glass*," in *The Films of Werner Herzog*, 159–178.

CONSTELLATION H
FEMINISM AND EARLY WEIMAR: POLITICS OF DISTRACTION

What does it mean when spectatorship theory appropriates the writings of Siegfried Kracauer and Walter Benjamin in ways that comprehend postmodern changes in history and subjectivity through aestheticist and phenomenological lenses? The very recent turn in German cinema studies to the films of the Weimar period has been characterized by the adoption of Benjamin and the early Kracauer, especially by feminist theorists (recall Patrice Petro in Constellation A ["German Cinema Studies"]), for investigating the functions of gender, sexuality, and class in the construction of the postmodern, or "distracted," spectator. The problematics of aestheticism and phenomenology traversing these investigations raises a number of questions that are mobilized by this constellation and the texts it includes. What are the ideology-effects of Thomas Elsaesser's equivocal negotiation of the Kracauerian "mass ornament" and the Benjaminian "arcades" into a post-al theory of film reception, and how are his ambivalent distinctions between "theory" and "history," "aesthetics" and "culture" symptomatic of these effects? Where does his position on the role of theory in Cinema Studies intersect that of Tassilo Schneider in Constellation A? How does Miriam Hansen's mysticist reading of Benjamin in regard to the issues of language and the Jewish sublime aestheticize, even Christianize, her feminist consideration of them? Don't her invocations of romantic anticapitalism and a gendered spectatorial imaginary reinscribe the sorts of mythologizing and "othering" associated with the conservative wing of the Holocaust debate (Constellations B and C ["The Heimat *Debate"; "The Jewish Question"])? To what degree does her rejection of the Frankfurt School, whose Critical Theory is otherwise recognized and appropriated by Clay Steinman in Constellation A ("German Cinema Studies"), contribute to these conservative tendencies? How does Patrice Petro's important feminist response to such tendencies nonetheless reconstitute them at the level of (hetero)sexual difference, thus recalling debates on normalization, authority, and alterity figured in Constellation F ("Queer Constructs")? How is this reconstitution facilitated by the suspension of "otherness" she accomplishes via a somewhat facile reconciliation of Benjamin, Heidegger, and Kracauer? Are Petro's and Hansen's phenomenological theories of perception at odds with Andreas Huyssen's psychoanalytic reading of the male gaze in* Metropolis? *Or doesn't Huyssen's class-conscious critique of the patriarchal transcription of "technology" onto "femininity" return him to their, as well as to Elsaesser's, fetishism of cultural and discursive form?*

535

Cinema—The Irresponsible Signifier or "The Gamble with History": Film Theory or Cinema Theory

THOMAS ELSAESSER

ILM THEORY has attained the degree of self-reflexivity appropriate to a cognitive endeavour by constantly rearticulating a seemingly ineluctable dualism: that between realist tendencies of the cinema and formalist ones. For nearly a hundred years the opposition Lumière vs. Méliès, long take vs. montage, mimetic vs. discursive, ontology of the image vs. linguistic theory of signification, phenomenology vs. semiology, perceptual vs. enunciative theories have dominated the debates.[1] Crucial in each set of terms is the importance given to the basic discontinuity of the filmic process when set against the perceptual continuity of the viewing process, i.e., whether priority is accorded to film as a specific form of production (aesthetic, technological, semiological) or a specific form of experience (perceptual, psychic, cognitive).

These antinomical tendencies name polarities that are intertwined and inseparable, and their common ground over the past two decades have been psychoanalytical theories of spectatorship and ideological theories about spectatorial effects.[2] On the other hand, specific historical or sociological considerations have rarely informed the arguments to any significant degree. The discontinuity of the filmic process, for instance, has not been historicized other than in terms of the heroic modernism which inspired constructivist theories of art.[3] The continuity-effect of the viewing process, while giving rise to acute analyses of the "basic ideological effects of the cinematic apparatus"[4] (as well as critical theories of realism and anti-illusionism) has not been seen in the context of specific social, demographic or economic changes: they have been the province of film history as it began turning itself into cinema history.[5] The question is therefore whether film theory can remain film theory or whether it, too, ought to move towards a historicizing self-reflexivity which would mark the transition from classical film theory to cinema theory. At present, film theory and theories of the cinema are not the same thing, and they continue to stand in a certain unresolved tension to each other.

German theory—the writings of Béla Balázs, Rudolf Arnheim, Siegfried Kracauer—generally seems to be film theory as opposed to cinema theory, and falls uneasily between the formalist and the realist tendencies,

Reprinted from *New German Critique* 40 (1987): 65–89.

between the film-as-art debate and arguments from ontology. German theory as *film* theory has not had the continuing influence of either Bazin's thinking on realism, or Eisenstein's importance for both theory and practice of cinematic language. By contrast, German *cultural* theory, in the form of Frankfurt School critical sociology, has tended to marginalize the cinema, depriving it of any historically significant specificity within the overall context of the mass-media and the culture industry.[6] Thus, neglect of these traditions in recent discussions of the cinema seemed to some extent justified. However, both sides of German theory might yet prove productive, especially if, as will be the case in what follows, the perspective taken intersects with aspects of the postmodernist debate.[7]

In the light of recent shifts in film theory, towards considerations of subjectivity and signification, visual fascination and gender-specific forms of spectatorship, German *film* theory can be re-centered and opened up for reinspection: firstly, in recalling, as Miriam Hansen and Gertrud Koch[8] have done in previous issues of *New German Critique*, the crucial interest in spectatorship and visual pleasure among early writers on the cinema; and secondly, in the way that writers in the tradition of Western Marxism, such as Lukács and Benjamin, can be read as offering a theory of the cinema (again, in contrast to film theory) which makes the discontinuity of the filmic process and its subject-effects central to aesthetic as well as historical considerations, thereby sketching a cinema theory rather than a film theory.

German *cinema* theory is part of a social theory about the emergence of a new form of culture—the "*Angestelltenkultur*" (White Collar culture) and the transformations of subjectivity entailed by it; its key concept is that of "distraction," a historically specific form of spectatorship and perception, but also of social behavior generally. Originally a negative attribute (opposed to contemplative concentration), the term underwent a number of mutations during the 1920s which sought to anchor it in a proletarian (or at least non-bourgeois) mode of visual and sensorial experience, and to isolate what might be the progressive elements in the emergent mass-media. Such an evaluation of "distraction" led Benjamin to arguments favoring montage as the basis of film form, while Kracauer used it to support what appears to be a realist form of filmmaking: both attempted to disengage the notion of temporality from that of narrative, and visual pleasure from that of voyeuristic-narcissist spectacle.[9]

This makes the concept useful both for a materialist grounding of avant-garde practices and for an investigation of gender-specific spectatorship. For insofar as German cinema theory is also a film theory, it is a theory of the image (of the analogy with photography), as opposed to a theory of narrative (crucial in semiological accounts of the syntagmatic relations between images). Thus, its main theoretical thrust today is in the direction not of textual analysis, but in illuminating the historical conditions of spectatorship and identification, both within and outside Freudian terms in which these questions are usually posed.

"EPHEMERAL PHENOMENA" AND THE "ALL-OUT GAMBLE OF HISTORY"

Kracauer is generally considered a specialist in the field of film sociology: there are few writers theorizing the relation of cinema to social history who have not relied on *From Caligari to Hitler*[10] to clarify their method or used it as a critical sounding board. For a number of reasons, not the least the postwar ideological suspicion which fell on emigré intellectuals in the United States, Kracauer himself was at pains to play down the antecedents to this remarkable book: his extensive writings on sociology, on aspects of mass-culture other than the cinema. These were written mainly during the last years of the Weimar Republic and indicated an acute awareness of the impact that industrialization and urban life were to exert on aesthetic production, by transforming the experience of subjectivity and thus the context of reception.

Only in 1963, three years before his death in New York, did Kracauer's German writings find a new generation of readers. On the recommendation of T. W. Adorno, Suhrkamp published a collection made up of articles that had originally appeared between 1922 and 1933. The title, *Das Ornament der Masse (The Mass Ornament)*[11] is taken from one of the central essays and makes it clear that Kracauer's fascination with the film medium remained embedded in a critical and more general interest in what he called "ephemeral phenomena." Karsten Witte, Kracauer's German editor, draws attention to the implication:

> If (Kracauer's essays from the 1920s) were to be re-examined in a new and productive manner, they could well lead to a different assessment of Critical Theory's formative period. Most important about Kracauer's early work is that his critical gaze looked to the marginal areas of high culture, and to (. . .) popular culture: film, the streets, sports, operetta, revues, advertisements and the circus. The link between his early and late work, such as *From Caligari to Hitler*, lies in his intention to decipher social tendencies revealed in ephemeral cultural phenomena.[12]

What gave Kracauer's work its contemporary radicalism was that he conducted his cultural analyses very much in the spirit of Freud's *Psychopathology of Everyday Life*, as a reading of signs and symptoms:

> An analysis of the simple surface manifestations of an epoch can contribute more to determining its place in the historical process than judgements of the epoch about itself (. . .) (Their) very unconscious nature allows for direct access to the underlying meaning of existing conditions.[13]

Das Ornament der Masse, dedicated to Adorno, is indeed a revelation. It contains twenty-four essays, divided into six sections, with titles like "Natural Geometry," "Constructions," "Perspectives" and "Vanishing Point." The subjects range from topical glosses on the Paris street map, on boredom, hotel lobbies, on best-sellers and biographies, to extensive essays on photography, dance, musical revues, the picture palaces, white collar office workers and changing trends in film-making. Other articles are on Georg Simmel, Walter Benjamin, Franz Kafka. The titles have a casual air, in the typical feuilleton manner of the highbrow *Frankfurter Zeitung* for which most of the pieces were written. But any impression that these are a former journalist's improvisations now gathered in a late attempt to redeem a life's work that never quite fulfilled its initial promise would be misleading: the mathematical severity of the section headings in the book alerts the reader to the intellectual tension between the parts and the articulated whole. An inner logic and a theoretical perspective hold them together despite the juggling with first publication dates. In this sense, *Das Ornament der Masse* is a worthy companion to Bloch's *Erbschaft dieser Zeit (Heritage of Our Times)*, Horkheimer and Adorno's *Dialectic of Enlightenment* and Benjamin's *Illuminations*, and might have been as much a key text in the rediscovery of Critical Theory as these proved to be, had there been commentaries (and a translation) in English to do it justice. In West Germany, the influence of early Kracauer (the "sensibilist" of *Das Ornament der Masse*, in contrast to the sociologist of *From Caligari to Hitler*) is clearly in evidence among filmmakers and critics of the New German Cinema.

Das Ornament der Masse is also an excellent introduction to Kracauer's other unknown works: his sociological reportage *Die Angestellten* (1930), his phemenological study *Der Detektivroman* (1971), his autobiographical novels *Ginster* (1928) and *Georg* (1973), and his political history disguised as a musicological treatise, *Jacques Offenbach und das Paris seiner Zeit (Jacques Offenbach and the Paris of his Time)* (1937). All of them bear rereading today: they make Kracauer a very contemporary writer indeed, more so, perhaps, than Adorno, whose mentor he once was, but whose Hegelian Marxism he did not share; consequently, Kracauer's own immanent thinking tends to be more responsive to the feel and texture of experience than Adorno's often rather formalist dialectical machinery.

It is important to recall the historical and conceptual context in which the cinema became an issue: against the prevailing tendency of trying to define an ontology (is cinema an art? what is its specificity? does it have a language?), Kracauer and others insisted on the materialist social and economic base. Against those who saw in films mainly the work of financiers and speculators, he elaborated the ideas of "mass-ornament" and "distraction," and thus a theory of entertainment which recognized the much more subtle (and potentially subversive) dynamic at work in the mass media between subjectivity and social experience. While the surrealists in their writings on the cinema had tried to explore the effects of mechanically produced discontinuity for a poetry of the material imagination, Kracauer refused such aestheticization: even where the subtitle to *Theory of Film*[14] speaks of "the redemption of physical reality," the object of analysis is the historical process itself, as it affects the relation between reality and its mimetic doubling, rather than a theory of either poetic or social realism. Kracauer's historical perspective was a broad one, and not free of metaphysical pessimism: "Weltzerfall," the disintegration of life, the homelessness of the individual in the modern world are his hermeneutic vantage points. But as in the case of Georg Lukács, whose *Theory of the Novel* made a lasting impression on Kracauer, anchoring an argument in metaphysics need not preclude insights into the history and sociology of aesthetic forms.

A return to Kracauer's own project, as it can be discerned in *Das Ornament der Masse*, might bring one close to the specific postmodern stance on the impossibility of separating high culture from mass-culture, and even help to bridge the gap between phenomenology and semiology, in that Kracauer's method implies reading surface phenomena as texts. Furthermore, these insights themselves would assume a place within a historical perspective, if only insofar as Kracauer's lack of trust in the ability of 'history' to set limits to the play of signifiers and surface effects strikes a distinctly 'post-historical' note. More importantly, Kracauer's *Ornament der Masse* indicates the extent to which he saw the cinema in wider social (the rise of a specific class in competition with others) and demographic contexts (the cinema as a specific entertainment space among others), without sacrificing—as some of the new film history seems in danger of doing—a consideration of the ideological function of the films themselves. Kracauer's cinema theory is most relevant where it conceived of film as part of a new mode of representation (spectacle and spectacular display), recognizing the momentous political significance which a new experience of (gendered) subjectivity plays in the general field of a social semiotics.

A certain detour through Kracauer's sociology is thus in order, touching on his theory of entertainment as a spatialization of time, and his concept of the mass-ornament as a form of mythical thinking. Only then do Kracauer's views on photography, history, temporality and memory (discussed elsewhere in this issue) begin to make sense in the context of speculations which lead Kracauer to this most Baudrillardian formulation: that the "turn to photography" in general, and the cinema in particular, is the "all-out gamble of history."[15] In the often tortuous dialectic between photography and history which Kracauer was at pains to tease out all through his life, the cinema is given a redefinition which, it seems to me, is neither strictly ontological nor epistemological, and yet allocates it a place in a fundamental development of the Western mind: the systematic translation of the experience of time into spatial categories, as a necessary precondition for an instrumental control over reality, but with its equally necessary corollary, namely a narcissistic or melancholy bind of the subject to that reality as *image*, itself envisaged in the psychologically coherent but ideologically ambivalent form of loss and nostalgia, fragment and fetish.

THE "ANGESTELLTENKULTUR"

Kracauer's dialectical bent was not Hegelian. His early thinking about modernity was indebted to Dilthey's *Lebensphilosophie*, to Max Weber and above all to Georg Simmel's phenomenological sociology. But he brought to this tradition a specificity of observation and an apparent narrowing of focus which paradoxically traces a much more dynamic historical perspective. Benjamin recognized this well when, in a review of *Die Angestellten*, he described Kracauer's method:

> Not as an orthodox Marxist, and even less as a practical agitator does he penetrate dialectically into the conditions of the white collar workers. (. . .) However, his project leads him to the heart of the Marxist edifice precisely to the degree that the ideology of the white collar workers constitutes a unique superimposition of the memory-images and wish-fulfilling fantasies inherited from the bourgeoisie onto their existing economic reality, which is very close to that of the proletariat.[16]

By piecing together, through their own words, samples of false consciousness, *Die Angestellten* reconstructs the "life-world" of a class which did not consider itself as one, the male and female office workers of Berlin in the late 1920s. What Ernst Bloch's *Erbschaft dieser Zeit* attempted to do for an entire national culture—to argue the coexistence and interpenetration of non-synchronous layers of consciousness at a given historical moment— Kracauer undertook on behalf of the most symptomatic social group to have emerged as a direct consequence of technical and administrative rationalization: the urban employees. The condition for German industry to modernize itself was that it successfully modernize its social basis. This it did by helping to create a new kind of culture. Whereas Bloch concentrated on the "materialist" kernel contained in (romantic and post-romantic) popular and highbrow culture, in a bid to redeem irrationalism for progressive and utopian social action, Kracauer focused on rootlessness, physical isolation, emotional insecurity and psychological stress as the material conditions which necessitated a new life-style: one increasingly dedicated to what we would now call consumption and conspicuous leisure, and which Kracauer was the first to recognize as a historically new phenomenon. No longer did those who made up this class demand from art and entertainment that it represent them in idealized form, nor that it should show their lives as individually meaningful or heroized in the attitude of struggle, as was typical of a bourgeois form such as the novel: but simply that it should be able to aestheticize, turn into play what was experienced as the primary reality of urban life: depersonalization, violence, the drill and routine of the working day. If modern mass-culture was a form of compensation, it was one where pleasure was derived from artifice and show, from the more or less imaginary but in any case brilliant imitation of life:

> Nothing is more typical of this life (. . .) than the manner in which it conceives of the higher things. They are not aimed at a content, but at glamour. (. . .) A typist given to ruminations expressed herself to me (as follows): "The girls here usually come from simple backgrounds and are attracted by glamour." She then gave a curious explanation as to why they generally avoided serious discussions (ernste Unterhaltungen): "seriousness is merely a distraction from what is happening and stops one from having fun." When a serious conversation is deemed to be a distraction, then the pursuit of distraction is indeed serious business.[17]

Paradigmatic spaces of this new culture—apart from movie theaters— were the Berlin cafes and dancehalls with their exotic decor, their sentimental but also cynical reproduction of regional and national stereotypes; above all, Kracauer highlights the role of popular music as the index of unfulfillable desires in an unredeemable life. What he finds is not Bloch's uneven development, but an acceptance of the self as façade, and a preference for effects and illusions over substance and realism:

> At the same time as the offices are being rationalized, the big cafes rationalize the pleasure of the office-workers' armies. (. . .) The ambiance is especially opulent at Haus Vaterland, which is the perfect prototype for the style also aimed at in movie palaces and the establishments frequented by the lower middle classes. Its core is a kind of giant lobby, over whose carpets the guests of Hotel Adlon might stride without feeling humiliated. The lobby exaggerates the decor of the *Neue Sachlichkeit*, for only the latest fad is good enough for the masses. Nothing could reveal more strikingly the secret of the New Objectivity: behind the pseudo-severity of the lobby architecture there leers the spirit of Grinzing. Down the stairs and one is surrounded by the rankest sentimentality. A characteristic of the New Objectivity is to present a façade which hides nothing, which does not emerge from a depth but merely simulates one. (The Vienna room, the Bavaria room, the Negro-Cowboy-Jazz Band room, the Spanish room of Haus Vaterland) do not show

the world as it is, but as it appears in pop songs (Schlager). The geography of such refuges for the homeless is born from the pop song, and even though as a rule the songs possess only vague local knowledge, the panoramas are painted with painstaking care (. . .). Floodlights and neon strips as used in the department store complete the composition (. . .) with color effects which the sinking sun could not hope to rival. Lighting is such an integral part that one cannot but think these places have no existence during the day. Every evening they are created anew. Yet the true power of light is its presence. It estranges the flesh on the bodies, throws a costume over that which it transforms. The light's secret powers give substance to glamour, and distraction becomes intoxication. But when the waiter eventually works the switch, the nine-to-five day stares back at you.[18]

Kracauer, perhaps more attracted to the "left melancholy" of *Neue Sachlichkeit* than he is here prepared to admit, described a form of entertainment and a life style that has survived the destruction of places like Haus Vaterland, the Adlon or the Residenzkasino because the conditions that necessitated them and made them profitable have survived. Glamour as a value enjoyed for its own sake ("der Similiglanz der gesellschaftlichen Scheinhöhen"[19]) and estrangement as a form of disguise allow the fantasy self to experience itself as the true self: this is the social basis also for the cinematic imaginary.

What is striking in the chapter on popular entertainment in *Die Angestellten* ("Asyl für Obdachlose") is Kracauer's premise that the content of the fantasy scenarios is interchangeable, and only at one remove a representation of desires for social mobility: a theme commonly identified with Kracauer's work and more strongly present in essays like "Shopgirls at the Movies" (1927). While jokingly noting the symbolic value of escalators in the dance casinos ("presumably to demonstrate the ease with which one can rise to the higher echelons"[20]) he sees the meaning of Haus Vaterland less in its promise of a better life than in the function that certain social spaces (the luxury picture palace, the sports palace, the hotel lobby) assume as catalysts, by translating questions of power and status at the place of work—"everyone wants to give himself the appearance of being more than he is," as one of his interviewees put it[21]—into occasions for spectacle and self-display.

The same goes for the illustrated magazines and the cinema: images have became icons whose function is not to give a window onto the world, but to block the view:

(. . .) through always repeated visual motifs, (they) (. . .) intend to plunge into image-less forgetfulness those contents which are not encompassed by the construction of our social existence, but actually bracket it. The flight into images is the flight from Revolution and from death.[22]

What gives Haus Vaterland prototypical value is the emphasis on spectacular effects, on self-display and the 'architectural' as well as high-tech/special effects in the creation of distance and transport through time and space. The mimetic element is not the Spanish decor or the Vienna waltz music *per se*, but the structure of the experience: the organization, division, compartmentalization of geography and history into discrete scenic spaces. The views and vistas reproduced merely have the function of signifiers, referring to other signs, the total effect deriving from the montage, the contiguity and coexistence of the heterogeneous: this gives both an experience of power and control, but also mimics the objective reality of a commodity-producing society.

REPORTAGE OR MONTAGE: WRITING MASS-CULTURE

The sign character of spectacle and the image also poses a challenge for the analyst of culture: does he merely report what he sees or shape the particles by an act of intervention and conscious de-montage?

> Writers know no higher ambition than to report: reproducing observations is trumps. A hunger for immediacy which no doubt is a consequence of the malnutrition caused by German idealism. The abstractness of idealist thinking is counterpointed in the reportage by the self-advertisement of lived existence. But life is not fixed by having it at best duplicated (. . .). A hundred reports from a factory cannot be added to make up its reality but remain forever hundred different aspects. Reality is a construction.[23]

These lines echo Benjamin's quotation from Brecht in respect of photography: that reality has slipped into the functional and is no longer to be seized by representations. The essays contained in *Das Ornament der Masse*, too, bear out the tension between "reality" and "construction" but, unlike Brecht's, Kracauer's object of knowledge is precisely a culture dedicated to surface, which has to be seized as surface, in and through its representations.

Kracauer's method is materialist and dialectical less in its concepts and vocabulary, than in the significance it attributes to its own form. The structure of *Das Ornament der Masse* is the key to its argument: from what Kracauer calls "Natural Geometry" (the arena of a bull-fight in Aix-en-Provence; the Paris street map as the condensation of a social history and the figuration of space as text) to the social geometry of photography and advertising, mass-spectacles, rush-hour crowds and best-sellers. Motivated by a movement from myth and the archaic to technology and the modern, the essays describe a historical development in the guise of a journey, and the ever greater penetration of matter by conceptual categories, which is

Kracauer's philosophical theme, gives rise to a style at once mimetic and analytical.

The metaphor that predominates is that of travel, the traversal of space in the medium of time, to which corresponds—quite ambiguously—the role of the subject as observer, flaneur, tourist, since for Kracauer, time and temporal extension are always at crucial moments frozen into the snapshot, the vista, and thus are most intensely experienced as space. Kracauer is well aware that this is itself the subjective correlative of a history rather than a topography: the history and victory of capital, making time and space variables of money and labor in the form of rationalization, to which correspond the increasingly available apparatuses of mechanical reproduction. For his reason, the reflections on the film world appear rather late in the book's internal organization, since the cinema is in this sense the endpoint of a development, but also its apotheosis and synthesis; perhaps—as the end of "the historical"—even its radical transformation. The articles headed "Kino" close the volume, except that they are followed by two brief essays, one a meditation on the Lindenpassage, a Berlin arcade in the process of being demolished, described by Kracauer very much in the manner of Benjamin's *Passagenwerk*: sketching a conceptual passage from one era to the next; the other one is on boredom: a pessimistic coda, intimating that the new era (of history as spectacle) will be under the sign of a powerful negativity.

Read diachronically, *Das Ornament der Masse* is a history of visual fascination from bull fights to cinematic spectacle whose "vanishing point" as Kracauer calls his final section, is the ambivalence between boredom ("self-forgetting in the act of looking, and the large, dark hole filled with the semblance of life which belongs to nobody and uses up everybody"[24]) and nostalgia (here typified by the surrealism of commodities displayed among fake Renaissance pillars and ornamental ironwork). Read synchronically, the book weaves a dialectic between spaces which try to resist the revolutionary onslaught of capitalism (by remaining invisible) and those that transform the energy of rationalism into aesthetic pleasure.

Hence the importance, but also the irony of the term "geometry" in the course of *Das Ornament der Masse*: metaphor for an instrumental control and mastery of the real through projection and measurement, it alludes to the violence done to reality in the process of representation. Kracauer's equivocal use of an architectural vocabulary points self-consciously to the effort of interpreting modernity and its shaping forces without either having recourse to wholly conceptual categories, or merely rendering the appearance things give to the eye of reportage, but in the terms in which change and process manifest themselves on the face of things themselves, as apprehended by an almost tactile intelligence in the act of seizing the ephemeral. Making visible, arranging in spatial formation, and offering the world to a cold eye emerge as the telos of modernity, and Kracauer's project, namely to analyze his culture's "spatio-temporal passions,"[25] includes the realization that the critic is in some sense obliged to mimic the very processes he is analyzing. In structure and progression the book is a simulacrum of its subject. Thus, the deliberately constructivist gesture, the spirit of *Neue Sachlichkeit* which becomes apparent behind the ordering of the collection, is indicative of the irony pervading the work: *how* Kracauer discusses the new culture of distraction and immediacy mirrors *what* he sees as its underlying historical tendency. The combined powers of geometry and rationality produce a different kind of investment in surface, in the fragment, the local and the ephemeral.

THE MASS ORNAMENT

Kracauer's own style of theorizing is thus an attempt to remain faithful to this new immanence without depth or transcendence. Its manifestations in cultural life, however, were spectacles, as the typical entertainment forms of an urban population. Unlike more recent theories of specular seduction, it led him not to a notion of individualized voyeurism or gender-specific perception, but to a coinage which wanted to preserve the collective nature and de-personalizing force of modern visual pleasure: the concept of the mass ornament, an idea first introduced in an essay in 1927. By mass ornament, Kracauer initially characterized female revue numbers like the Tiller Girls, but he also had in mind the growing popularity of gymnasts in formation at athletic events or in a stadium. More generally, Kracauer anticipated the importance which highly ornamentalized and decorative patterns at parades or in the visual representation of crowds or armies would assume when displayed to a detached or distant eye, what we would now call "media-events" or "monster events" existing only in order to be perceived by a camera (or television) eye.[26]

What Kracauer diagnosed in virtually all modern manifestations of mass-entertainment, including the cinema, was not only the collective form of reception but a fundamentally different manner of self-representation and identification. This he saw as one of the many signs of the ambiguous status of abstract rationality under capitalism and, in particular, its relation to mythic thinking. According to Kracauer, the opposition between myth and reason in modern, industrialized societies is only apparent, since they are the two sides of the same coin: the drive for abstraction at all levels of social as well as economic existence.

> Abstraction in modern thought is two-faced. Viewed against mythical thought, in which nature naively triumphs, the processes of abstraction as practiced by the natural sciences are an advance, a gain in rationality which breaks the hold of nature. Viewed from the perspective of reason, however, the same principle of abstraction appears as itself a remnant of nature: it

loses itself in an empty formalism, under whose cover nature has free reign, because formalism deflects reason from seizing the natural in the human. Thus, the dominant abstractness indicates that the process of demythologization is arrested half-way, it has not been completed. The more this abstractness consolidates itself, the less human beings will come to a rational understanding of themselves.[27]

The mass ornament allows this absence of rational understanding to become invested with pleasure. By representing the relation of self to body in terms of vision and self display, as for instance in the crowds at sports events or public occasions, the mass ornament created a powerful social space for the articulation of subjectivity (as violence, or masquerade), but one where the real world of the individual has become what Kracauer calls "desubstantiated."[28] This is the historical prerequisite for the public sphere of populist political movements on the one hand, and the concept of a leisure culture on the other. In the mass ornament, visual display is not representational but an elaborate configuration of easily identifiable cultural icons and emblems in a space devoid of any signified other than confirming the spectators' own presence: in Kracauer's terms, spectacle becomes "the functional but empty form of ritual."[29] Social space, the external environment is transformed into the site of figural play; extending Kracauer's notion of the mass ornament, we would have to include the kind of blank page which a cityscape is today for billboard advertising, or for architects designing corporate skyscrapers, but also the violence of football fans, or the elaborate dressing up and masquerade at homecomings, Royal Weddings or the nightly Disneyland parade, with its hypnotizing music.

These views about the mass ornament, about myth and rationality are to some extent extrapolated from Max Weber's theses on rationalization entailing the progressive "disenchantment of the world" through bureaucracy administering the social world, and the principle of measurability or calculability taking over not only in the natural sciences but the humanities as well. The originality of Kracauer's analysis (and also its debatable premise) is that he tries to make explicit how a phenomenon like the Tiller girls or spectator-sports can stand in a structural homology to capitalism and its specific mode of production. In an affirmative, quasi-utopian reversal of values, the revues and sporting contests parody the reality of the Taylorized assembly-line factory system, by celebrating a happily reified consciousness:

> The legs of the Tiller Girls correspond to the hands on the machines in the factory. But beyond the manual aspect, emotional dispositions are also tested for their psycho-technical aptitude. The mass ornament is the aesthetic reflex of the rationality to which our economic system aspires.[30]

Kracauer discerned in high culture as well as in popular entertainment, in the religious spiritualism, the youth movements and body cults of the 1920s, but also in philosophy, in cultural criticism and serious literature the same return of mythical thought, not so much in reaction to capitalism, as some had argued, but as its inevitable complement, its dominant cultural form and an expression of part of its historical character. The mass ornament, rather than heralding a triumph of rationality, was actually a sign of the return of myth:

> There is a view of capitalism which accuses its rationalism of raping mankind; those who hold it long for the advent of a community which will protect the so-called human substance better than capitalism does. But this misunderstands the core of capitalism: it doesn't rationalize too much, but too little. The thinking to which it gives rise stops short of completing the move towards reason as it speaks in human beings.[31]

The mass ornament, in other words, arrests the progress of reason, even though its abstract sign character partakes in it. Myth and rationality, dialectically conceived by Kracauer, are in the cultural forms typical of capitalism, held in a state of suspended animation, or rather, caught in a double reflection. This is presumably what makes the mass ornament pleasurable: the degree to which a workaday reality appears in it transfigured and transcended in the very act of being mirrored and reproduced.

KRACAUER'S THEORY OF DISTRACTION AND SUBJECTIVITY

What is particularly useful in Kracauer's early analysis is the connection he makes between the mass ornament, understood as a form of "institutionalized spectacle" whose sign/image character is the mirror of capitalist production, and the mass ornament as a mode of collectively experiencing subjectivity. For rather than simply seeing in its pervasive presence the superstructural consequence of a given form of production, in the manner of orthodox Marxist ideological criticism, Kracauer credits it initially with a progressive role in training a different form of perception and attention, socially useful for mastering an increasingly complex visual environment: a form of perception that Benjamin called distracted attention, alertness under conditions of discontinuity, and as such echoing the observations of the early Lukács as well as the aesthetic precepts of Brecht.[32]

Kracauer's theory of distraction is only today being reassessed as to its full implications for a history of the cinema. One of its central features I take to be the analysis of certain processes which the cinema shares with other industrial modes of production: precisely its fundamental discontinuity at the level of the primary material—but also a heterogeneity of the basic apparatus (optical, mechanical, chemical). Both entail the combination of discrete components and parts in such a way as to create the impression of a unified commodity, the "surface."[33] The manifest importance of external appearance, of visual impact in modern culture as the plane of consciousness on which both difference and value define themselves, cannot, as Kracauer well realized, be seized analytically in a supposed dialectic of appearance and essence, illusion and reality. Instead, it lead him to focus, following Simmel and Lukács, on the peculiar form of attentiveness required from participants in a consumer-culture and solicited by mass media spectacles. With visual spectacle becoming the dominant mode of entertainment (and even of sociability), surface flow and disconnected sensory stimuli gradually typify the conditions of reception of all modern art, regardless of its intentionality as either high art or mass-product.

In particular, "The Cult of Distraction" (1926) has been seen to offer a new departure point, not only because this essay is genuinely dialectical in the way it assigns the audience an active role in the reception process, but also because in this attempt to develop a theory of pure surface, Kracauer identifies as one of the preconditions for understanding cinematic fascination the play of discontinuity and symmetry, and thus seems to offer an alternative to aligning visual pleasure with psychoanalytically interpreted scoptophilia and fetishism:

> Audiences act more in their own deeper interest, if they increasingly avoid high-culture events and instead prefer the superficial glamor of stars, films, revues and expensive production numbers. Here, in pure externality, they encounter themselves: in the rapid succession of disconnected sensory stimuli they see revealed their own reality.[34]

Heide Schlüpmann rightly sees in Kracauer's analyses the rather problematic attempt to come to terms with, and to control his own fascination with the cinema, by way of mass sociology and a theory of compensatory wish fulfillment, projected mainly onto women. Yet what I take to be one of Kracauer's crucial points is that apart from the sociological significance of this form of spectatorship—the mechanisms of miscognition and disavowal affecting a whole class—Kracauer recognizes the pleasures of the cinema to be the pleasures of depersonalization, nostalgia and loss: pleasures of the narcissistic self, regardless of sex, and existing in their purest form in films whose narratives do not impose social parables on their material, such as those which preoccupy Kracauer in *From Caligari to Hitler*. In this perspective, the essay entitled "Shopgirls at the Movies," sometimes cited as Kracauer's most serious early draft of a theoretically coherent analysis of the cinema's ideological function,[35] obscures rather than clarifies his overall project and his own involvement, because it falsifies the concern with the cinema as a marginal sphere of life and its fascination as an experience of surface effects.

Kracauer, for instance, agrees that distraction is, for a modern urban population, a legitimate mode of aesthetic experience, more truthful to their historical situation than the objects or experiences put in circulation as *"Kultur."*

> When large parts of reality (*"grosse Wirklichkeitsgehalte"*) have become withdrawn from visibility, then art has to manage with what is left, for aesthetic representation is the more real the less it cuts itself off from the reality outside it. However small one estimates the value of the mass ornament to be, its degree of reality is higher than those aesthetic products which recultivate the cast-off finer sensibility in outdated forms.[36]

The mode of perception and attention appropriate to modernity would thus be present in an exemplary form in the cinema, where technology and the conditions of production permeate the content and penetrate the representational material even prior to any ideological construction of narrative and the image. Accordingly, the mass ornament becomes the enabling condition of aesthetics under capitalism, but also the implied social matrix and norm by which all possible referents are articulated: nothing passes as real or representable lest it can assume the form of spectacle. The abstraction which this process implies is a sign of its historical truth, when measured against attempts to preserve a cognitive status for the art-object and a contemplative stance for the mode of reception.

This exactly parallels Bloch's contention in *Erbschaft dieser Zeit*, where he examines the decline of the serious newspaper and the social class which it represented:

> Those seeking distraction run away from real life, but those who used to find themselves only in belles-lettres were no closer to it. What today is still peddled in public lectures or on the radio as culture (*Bildung*), in the ready-made form of a commodity merely reifies twice over. A mind, educated to raise his sights above the everyday, is worse than [that desire for] distraction, which, when it turns from the everyday in order to escape from it, acknowledges the emptiness it seeks to fill.[37]

Thus, the aesthetic speculations of Kracauer, Benjamin or Bloch were directed towards understanding the role the art-world would assume once aesthetic value could no longer be defined independently of social function. Benjamin, for instance, categorically declared that:

> as far as the traditional art work is concerned, in relation to its exhibition value, the functions usually defined as the aesthetic ones may already have become quite secondary.[38]

Kracauer and Benjamin were interested in the cinema insofar as the priority of "exhibition value" was the condition of its existence, its *raison d'être*, and the designation of a film as "art" constituted not a value judgment, but a mark of differentiation in respect of a market. For Kracauer, as for other thinkers, the question was essentially whether distraction and the mass ornament would establish themselves as the "norm" of popular entertainment and spectacle, and thus retain a measure of symptomatic historical truth-value, or whether its power of disjuncture, surface effect, immediacy and pure presence would, on the contrary, be harnessed and organized into an illusion of coherence, taken in charge by "art," and turned into an instrument of ideological manipulation.

It was the reinjected cultural cachet, the new psychologism and inwardness, what Kracauer called the "re-synthesis of elements offered up as organic creations"[39] which effectively recuperated the cinema as a technologically based mass medium and made it into an essentially bourgeois art form:

> Externality has honesty on its side. Truth is not in jeopardy because of it, rather, it is threatened by the naive affirmation of cultural values that have become illusory, by the unscrupulous abuse of terms such as personality, feeling, tragedy, etc.: words designating no doubt noble ideas, but social change has stripped them of a good deal of their credibility and basis in reality, so that in most cases, they now have acquired a bad taste, because they unduly divert attention from the objective ills of society and personalize the issues.[40]

Kracauer's later work is nothing if not consistent in this respect. If, for instance, one were to replace "Hitler" as the constantly implied referent of the argument in *From Caligari to Hitler*, one would find a very incisive analysis of bourgeois conceptions of narrative and subject-positions. This, I think, is one of the main reasons why the book has remained so convincing and almost unanswerable despite the manifest inadequacy if not absurdity of its apparent central thesis. Kracauer's antipathy to Weimar films was ultimately due more to their gentrification of the cinema than to any anticipation of the course of history in narrative and fictional form. His distrust of the bourgeois arts, revamped and adapted for the screen, is one of the reasons, for example, why he argues so persistently against the *Großfilm* (the international prestige film), in favor of sentimentality, low-brow forms, and even honest kitsch—material without high-culture pretensions. There may have been elements of reverse snobbery and nostalgia involved in Kracauer's retrospective construction of a popular art, more authentically respecting subjective needs, but there is little evidence of wishing for a more high-brow "art cinema."

MANIPULATION AND THE MASS ORNAMENT

This distinction, between the mass ornament as the representation of reified social relations in the form of mythic yet technological spectacles and the mass ornament as support for historical or existential mythologies in the service of bourgeois good taste, might account for the fact that between the 1927 essay, "The Mass Ornament" and the 1947 *From Caligari to Hitler*, Kracauer seemed to have abandoned the dialectical core of his concept in favor of a more simple assertion of "the human." Discussing the mass ornament in *Die Nibelungen* he writes:

> it is amazing that despite their too pronounced beauty and their somewhat outmoded taste—a taste already outmoded in 1924—these pictures are still effective. The constructional austerity they breathe may account for it. Lang knew why, instead of resorting to Wagner's picturesque opera style or to some kind of psychological pantomime, he relied upon the spell of such decorative compositions: they symbolize fate. The compulsion Fate exerts is aesthetically mirrored by the rigorous incorporation of all structural elements into a framework of lucid forms. [. . .] It is the complete triumph of the ornamental over the human. Absolute authority asserts itself by arranging people under its domination in pleasing designs. This can also be seen in the Nazi regime, which manifests strong ornamental inclinations in organizing masses. [. . .] *Triumph of the Will* [. . .] proves that in shaping their mass ornaments the Nazi decorators drew inspiration from *Die Nibelungen*. Siegfried's theatrical trumpeteers, showy steps and authoritarian human patterns reappear, extremely magnified, in the modern Nuremberg pageant.[41]

Similarly ambivalent are his comments about *Metropolis*, where in spite of having acknowledged that Lang's conception of character and plot is rigorously anti-psychological, he is nonetheless moved to observe:

> In *Metropolis*, the decorative not only appears as an end in itself, but even belies certain points made by the plot. It makes sense that, on their way to and from the machines, the workers form ornamental groups; but it is nonsensical to force them into such groups while they are listening to a comforting speech from the girl Maria during their leisure time. In his exclusive concern with ornamentation, Lang goes so far as to compose decorative patterns from the masses who are desperately trying to escape the inundation of the lower city. Cinematically an incomparable achievement, this inundation sequence is humanly a shocking failure.[42]

The difference between the original concept of the mass ornament and its later application to Lang and fascism allows one to draw an important conclusion. What in the 1920s had been seen as the ambiguous figuration of the political and social spaces created by capitalism, had from the vantage point of the end of the war become symptomatic of proto-fascism and fascist iconography. The bridge, but also the gap between the two tests by Kracauer is the analysis of fascism made by members of the Frankfurt School, and in particular by Walter Benjamin's 1935 Artwork essay, where one discovers Benjamin to have been a close reader of Kracauer:

The increasing proletarianization of mankind today and the increasing formation of masses are two sides of the same process. Fascism tries to organize
the newly emerging proletarian masses, without touching the property relations, whose elimination the masses' very existence press for. Fascism sees
its salvation in granting the masses self-expression and self-representation as
opposed to granting them their rights.[43]

And in a footnote Benjamin added:

Here, especially with regards to the newsreels whose propaganda value cannot be overestimated, a technical factor is of importance. Mass reproduction
is particularly congenial to the reproduction of people as mass. In the large
festivals, the monster congresses, the mass-assemblies, at sporting events or
in war, which are all occasions directly brought before the photographic or
radio apparatus, the masses can look themselves in the face. This process
whose historic significance needs no special emphasis, is intimately connected with the development of the reproduction and recording techniques.
Mass movements in general are more clearly visible to the camera than to the
eye. Formations of a hundred thousand are best seen from a bird's eye perspective. And even if this perspective is as attainable to the human eye as it is
to the camera, the image which the naked eye can take away does not permit
the kind of enlargement which film or photography is subject to. This means
that mass movements, including war, represent for the camera a particularly
congenial form of human behavior.[44]

Benjamin, clearly indebted to Kracauer's analysis of the mass ornament
from the late 1920s, is both sharper and more farsighted in 1935 than
Kracauer's reprise of his own argument in 1947. Linking fascism with capitalism, and capitalism with the technologies of representation, especially
the apparatus of cinema and of radio, Benjamin is able to sketch both the
counter-revolutionary function and the sources of pleasure associated with
the new visual and aural media. In *From Caligari to Hitler*, Kracauer takes
from Benjamin the direct identification of the mass ornament with fascism,
without however adopting either Benjamin's anticapitalist stance or his
analysis of technological reproducibility. The result is a flawed reasoning.
If Benjamin might be faulted for defining fascism too exclusively in terms
of the technologies of reproduction and narcissistic self-representation,
and thus as an aesthetic and psychological phenomenon, Kracauer pays far
too little attention to technological mediation. Otherwise he might not
have singled out Fritz Lang, who if anything forestalls the kind of self-representation of the masses as participating spectators which Benjamin has
in mind. Instead, all his films—including *Metropolis*—draw attention to
the fact that modern technologies of communication present a false sense
of immediacy and give rise to mere illusions of self-expression and authentic being.

Benjamin frequently returned to the reality-effects of the cinema (the "equipment-free aspect of reality") as involving a new and politically ambivalent experience of immediacy and presence. Like Kracauer, he anticipated the idea of the cinema (amongst other forms of reproduction and representation in the technological age) as an organized pseudo-physis (in Baudrillard's words: a "simulacrum"[45]) of subject-effects.

SEMIOLOGY, OR IRRESPONSIBILITY TOWARDS THE REFERENT

For Lukács, on the other hand, the cinema as pseudo-physis was the false resolution (and therefore the collapse) of the traditional philosophical problem of the relation between forms (whether defined Platonically or in Kantian terms) and life (whether defined phenomenologically or in terms of dialectical materialism). By its very existence, the cinema had made a certain philosophical constellation redundant: the question of the mediation between the abstract and the concrete, for instance, had to be drastically redefined. What Adorno called the "reconciliation between the general and the particular" had taken place, but in appearance only, because it was a false synthesis: film had become the instrument of a pleasurable and illusory reconciliation of the spectator to his or her own reification, by the uncanny, comic or emotionally moving anthropomorphisms which the camera could lend to things, humanizing the world, giving it beauty and a "soul," by endowing inanimate objects and mere shadows of people on the screen with feelings and life. The cinema seemed to have filled the gap between reality and its penetration by man's transforming labor: it anticipated the revolution, betraying it by turning it into spectacle. The cinema

> is a life without measure or order, without being or value, a life without soul, mere surface. . . the individual moments, whose temporal sequence brings about the filmed scenes, are only joined with each other insofar as they follow each other without transition and mediation. There is no causality which could join them, or more precisely, its causality is free from and unimpeded by any notion of content. "Everything is possible": this is the credo of the cinema, and because its technique expresses at every moment the absolute (even if only empirical) reality of this moment, "virtuality" no longer functions as a category opposed to "reality": both categories become equivalent, identical. Everything is true and real, everything is equally true and real; this is what a sequence of images in the cinema teaches us.[46]

These thoughts (again, startlingly close to certain postmodernist positions) deeply disturbed Lukács and they run like a secret thread through his early work, from *The Soul and its Forms* and *Theory of the Novel* to *History and Class Consciousness*. To the extent that Lukács and Kracauer shared a similar concern, namely that film and photography are not bound to the referent by a necessary connection, and that filmic or photographic representations are, despite their mimetic promise, arbitrary, or rather, in more moralizing terms, irresponsible *vis-à-vis* the referent, their speculations find their most exact demonstrations precisely in the films of Lang, only superficially concerned with the ironic reversibility of reality and illusion, and much more centrally with the simulacrum, the fascination of the false, as a source of both power and pleasure.

What united the theoretical efforts of Lukács, Kracauer, Balázs, Benjamin and others with respect to cinema, but also what gives Kracauer a certain exceptional status within this tradition, was the recognition that the cinema could endow the ephemeral with the illusion of substance and presence: at the price of turning reality into arbitrarily manipulable fragments connoting subject-effects ("soul," "expression") which through their very partiality could give the impression of a totality (as signs where the part stands for the whole). Depending on the political and philosophical position these theorists took regarding the question of immediacy or mediation, expression or trace, revolutionary moment or duration and process, they evaluated the emancipatory potential of the cinema differently, and also its cognitive status. Each, however, constantly returned to the realization that the cinema rendered pleasurable a specifically modern form of self-estrangement, which signalled not only the end of bourgeois notions of the individual, but also of its critiques in the name of the authentic self.

Notes

1. Cf. Dudley Andrew, *The Major Film Theories* (New York: Oxford University Press, 1976) or Brian Henderson, *A Critique of Film Theory* (New York: E.P. Dutton, 1980).

2. Cf. the essays brought together in *Narrative, Apparatus, Ideology*, ed. Philip Rosen (New York: Columbia University Press, 1986).

3. Cf. among others, the chapter on Eisenstein in Peter Wollen, *Signs and Meaning in the Cinema* (Bloomington: Indiana University Press, 1969).

4. Jean-Louis Baudry, "Ideological Effects of the Basic Cinematic Apparatus," repr. in *Narrative, Apparatus, Ideology*.

5. Cf. *Cinema Histories, Cinema Practices*, ed. Patricia Mellencamp and Philip Rosen (Frederick, MD: The American Film Institute Monograph Series, IV, 1984).

6. For an exception, cf. T.W. Adorno, "Transparencies on Film 1966," *New German Critique* 24/25 (Fall-Winter 1981–1982).

7. Cf. *Postmoderne: Zeichen eines kulturellen Wandels*, ed. Andreas Huyssen and Klaus Scherpe (Reinbek bei Hamburg: Rowohlt, 1986).

8. Cf. Miriam Hansen, "Early Silent Cinema: Whose Public Sphere?," *New German Critique* 29 (Spring/Summer 1983), and Gertrud Koch, "Re-Visioning Feminist Film Theory," *New German Critique* 34 (Winter 1985).

9. Cf. Walter Benjamin, "The Work of Art in the Age of Mechanical Reproduction," *Illuminations*, tr. Harry Zohn (New York: Schocken Books, 1968).

10. *From Caligari to Hitler* (Princeton, 1947).

11. *Das Ornament der Masse* (Frankfurt a.M.: Suhrkamp, 1977).

12. "Introduction to Siegfried Kracauer's 'The Mass Ornament,'" tr. Barbara Correll and Jack Zipes, *New German Critique* 5 (Spring 19764), 59.

13. "The Mass Ornament," *New German Critique* 5 (Spring 1975), 67.

14. *Theory of Film* (New York: Oxford University Press, 1960).

15. "Über Photographie," *Das Ornament der Masse*, p. 137.

16. "Politisierung der Intelligenz," *Angelus Novus* (Frankfurt: Suhrkamp, 1966), p. 423. (Unless otherwise indicated, the translations are my own.)

17. Siegfried Kracauer, *Schriften 1*, ed. Karsten Witte (Frankfurt a.M.: Suhrkamp, 1971), p. 282–3.

18. Ibid., p. 286–7.

19. Ibid., p. 289.

20. Ibid., p. 288.

21. Ibid., p. 284.

22. Ibid., p. 289.

23. Ibid., p. 216.

24. *Das Ornament der Masse*, p. 322.

25. Ibid., p. 42.

26. Cf. Pierre Nora, "Monster Event," *Discourse* 5 (Spring 1983), or Daniel Dayan and Elihu Katz, "Electronic Ceremonies," *On Signs*, ed. Marshall Blonsky (New York: Oxford University Press, 1985).

27. *Das Ornament der Masse*, 58, and *New German Critique* 5, 73.

28. Ibid., p. 59, and *New German Critique*, 74.

29. Ibid., p. 61 and *New German Critique*, 75.

30. Ibid., p. 54 and *New German Critique*, 70.

31. Ibid., p. 57 and *New German Critique*, 72.

32. Cf. Walter Benjamin, *The Author as Producer* (London: NLB, 1976).

33. Cf. "Dada/Cinema?" *Dada and Surrealist Film*, ed. Rudolf Kuenzli (New York: 1987).

34. "Kult der Zerstreuung," *Das Ornament der Masse*, p. 314–15.

35. Cf. Witte, "Nachwort," loc. cit. p. 338; Martin Jay, "The Extraterritorial Life of Siegfried Kracauer," *Salmagundi*, 31–32 (Fall 1975/Winter 1976), 55; cf. also T.W. Adorno, "Der wunderliche Realist," *Noten zur Literatur III* (Frankfurt: Suhrkamp, 1965).

36. *Das Ornament der Masse*, p. 54–55 and *New German Critique*, 70.

37. *Erbschaft dieser Zeit* (Frankfurt a.M.: Suhrkamp, 1962), p. 39–40.

38. *Illuminationen* (Frankfurt a.M.: Suhrkamp, 1961), p. 157.

39. *Das Ornament der Masse*, p. 316.

40. Ibid., p. 314.

41. *From Caligari to Hitler*, p. 93–95.

42. Ibid., p. 149–50.

43. *Illuminations*, p. 174–5.

44. Ibid., p. 184.

45. Jean Baudrillard, *Simulations* (New York: 1983).

46. "Gedanken zu einer Ästhetik des Kinos," (1913) *Kino-Debatte*, ed. Anton Kaes (Tübingen: Niemeyer, 1978), p. 114.

Benjamin, Cinema and Experience: "The Blue Flower in the Land of Technology"

MIRIAM HANSEN

In the representation of human beings through the apparatus, human self-alienation has found a most productive realization. ["The Artwork in the Age of Its Technical Reproducibility" (first version, 1935)]

Concerning the *mémoire involontaire*: not only do its images not come when we try to call them up; rather, they are images which we have never seen before we remember them. This is most clearly the case in those images in which—like in some dreams—we see ourselves. We stand in front of ourselves, the way we might have stood somewhere in a prehistoric past, but never before our waking gaze. Yet these images, developed in the darkroom of the lived moment, are the most important we will ever see. One might say that our most profound moments have been equipped—like those cigarette packs—with a little image, a photograph of ourselves. And that "whole life" which, as they say, passes through people's minds when they are dying or in mortal danger is composed of such little images. They flash by in as rapid a sequence as the booklets of our childhood, precursors of the cinema, in which we admired a boxer, a swimmer or a tennis player. ["A Short Speech on Proust," delivered by Benjamin on his fortieth birthday, 1932]

B<small>ENJAMIN'S REPUTATION</small> in contemporary film theory and criticism rests to a large extent upon his 1935/36 essay, "The Work of Art in the Age of Mechanical Reproduction," probably the single most often cited text by Benjamin or any other German writer on film.[1] That the essay was written under the influence of Brecht facilitated its assimilation to debates on Brechtian cinema as they took place during the 1970s, for instance, in the British journal *Screen*. The particular blend of Marxism and modernism that determined the reception of Benjamin's work, however, tended to obscure the more incongruous and ambivalent features of the Artwork Essay, not to mention its problematic status in relation to Benjamin's other writings. Such a reading was no doubt encouraged by the programmatic tenor of the essay itself, the construction of its argument through a sequence of theses. Yet the one-sided and reductive gesture that may have secured the essay a place in college textbooks cannot be taken at face

Reprinted from *New German Critique* 40 (1987): 179–224.

value; it is just as bound up with the political constellation in which the essay was written as are the contradictions that it so desperately tried to resolve.

In the following, I will elaborate on some of the incongruities of the Artwork Essay and situate them in relation to a theory of experience as it emerges from some of Benjamin's middle as well as later texts. Brushed against the grain of its programmatic message, the essay still speaks to a number of questions arising at the boundaries between film history, film theory and film criticism. More specifically, Benjamin's remarks on film touch upon an area for which Tom Gunning, borrowing from Eisenstein, has proposed the productively ambiguous term "cinema of attractions." This term offers a historical concept of film spectatorship which takes its cue from modes of fascination prevalent in early cinema, feeding on attractions such as the magical and illusionist power of filmic representation, its kinetic and temporal manipulations (not yet subordinated to character movement and the chronological momentum of linear narrative) and, above all, an openly exhibitionist tendency epitomized by the recurring look of actors at the camera. With the standardization of the narrative film (in the U.S. around 1906–07), such "primitive" attractions were systematically suppressed—if not pressed into service—by narrative strategies of viewer absorption and identification. Rather than disappear, Gunning contends, the cinema of attraction continued "underground," both in certain avant-garde film practices and as a component of particular genres (e.g. the musical) and, I would add, in the erotic appeal of particular stars.[2] Although the historical phenomenon in question can be traced most distinctly through the process of its elimination and appropriation, it nonetheless preserves, in its underground existence, an alternative vision of cinema—a range of film/spectator relations that differ from the alienated and alienating organization of classical Hollywood cinema.

The dual focus of this argument is itself indebted to a historical discourse on the cinema. It resumes a perspective articulated among Western European avant-garde artists and intellectuals during the 1920s which was marked by an enthusiasm for the possibilities of the new medium and a simultaneous critique of its actual development, in particular its opportunistic recourse to traditional literary and theatrical conventions. In this spirit, Dadaists and Surrealists celebrated the cinema's primitive heritage, especially slapstick comedy with its anarchic physicality or trick films in the style of Méliès. Likewise, many writers on the left seized upon contemporary Soviet film as an alternative to mainstream cinema, as a model of realizing—and reconciling—the cinema's aesthetic and political potential (cf. the German reception of *Potemkin*).

A decade later, when Benjamin wrote his Artwork Essay, the "all-out gamble of the historical process" (Kracauer) in which film and photography were to play a decisive role[3] seemed all but lost; instead of advancing a revolutionary culture, the media of "technical reproduction" were lend-ing themselves to oppressive social and political forces—first and foremost in the fascist restoration of myth through mass spectacles and newsreels, but also in the liberal-capitalist marketplace and in Stalinist cultural poli-tics. Nonetheless, Benjamin's concern with the photographic media still participates in the avant-garde perspective of the 1920s (unlike Adorno's work on mass culture which clearly belongs to another period). The belat-ed moment of the Artwork Essay only enhances the utopian modality of its statements, shifting the emphasis from a definition of what film *is* to its failed opportunities and unrealized promises. Thus, the cinema becomes an object—as well as a medium—of "redemptive criticism," the same effort of critical preservation that inspired Benjamin's work on Baudelaire and the Paris Arcades, the *Passagen-Werk*.[4]

Benjamin actually conceived of the Artwork Essay as a heuristic con-struction, a "telescope" which would help him look through "the bloody fog" at the "phantasmagoria of the nineteenth century" so as to delineate in it the features of a future, liberated world.[5] The "bloody fog" of 1935 made him deploy, in a strategic confrontation, the transformation of expe-rience in industrial society (of which the cinema was both symptom and agent) against traditional notions of art, in particular a belated cult of *l'art pour l'art*. He had been pursuing a critique of the latter for quite a while, specifically in his polemics against the George circle. Now, with the grow-ing threat of fascism—not only in Italy and Germany but other European countries as well—he perceived a complicity of aesthetic ideology (and individual intellectual exponents like Ernst Jünger and F.T. Marinetti) with the fascist aestheticization of politics and war.[6]

From this perspective, reproduction technology figures as an uninten-tional ally, as it were, prior to any revolutionary possibilities (*I*, 231). To repeat the familiar argument: the technical reproducibility of existing works of art and, what is more, its constitutive role in the aesthetics of photography and film have created a historical standard which affects the status of art in its core. With the elimination of qualities that accrued to the artwork as a unique object—its presence, authenticity and authority, its "aura"—the standard of universal reproducibility shatters the cultural tradition that draws legitimacy from the experience of art, thus baring the entanglement of art and social privilege. At the same time, technical repro-duction assumes a crucial role in view of the crisis and reorganization of the urban masses. In this constellation, technical reproduction converges, as an objective development, with self-critical tendencies within the insti-tution of art itself, forced into the open by avant-garde movements such as Dada and Surrealism (*I*, 237–38, 249–50).

Having established the terms "aura" and "masses" as opposite poles of the political field of force, Benjamin proceeds to assert a functional affinity between masses and the media of technical reproduction by way of what might be called a phenomenological syllogism. If the aura is defined as "the unique phenomenon of a distance, however close it may be," the contemporary masses are characterized by an antithetical intention, "the desire [. . .] to bring things 'closer' spatially and humanly, which is just as ardent as their bent toward overcoming the uniqueness of every reality by accepting its reproduction."

> Every day the urge grows stronger [*unabweisbarer*, i.e. less refutable] to get hold of an object at very close range by way of its image [*Bild*] or, rather, its copy [*Abbild*], its reproduction. Unmistakably, reproduction as offered by illustrated magazines and newsreels differs from the image. Uniqueness and permanence are as closely linked in the latter as are transitoriness and reproducibility in the former. To pry an object from its shell, to destroy its aura, is the mark of a perception whose "sense for the universal equality of things [*Sinn für das Gleichartige in der Welt*]" has increased to such a degree that it extracts it even from a unique object by means of its reproduction. Thus is manifested in the field of perception what in the theoretical sphere is noticeable in the growing importance of statistics.[7]

Mounted as an argument about large-scale historical shifts in the collective organization of human perception, this passage distinguishes between two, perhaps three, interdependent aspects of such a change: its manifestation along spatial and temporal registers (distance/proximity, permanence/transitoriness), and the modality of an object in relation to others, defined by the register of singularity vs. multiplication, similarity or likeness. These aspects may overlap in illustrating the decay of the aura, yet they give rise to diverging lines of argument when Benjamin tries to establish a functional affinity between media and masses.

The spatio-temporal line of argument links film and photography to social change through the concept of "shock," which Benjamin was to elaborate in his 1939 essay on Baudelaire ("Some Motifs in Baudelaire") and which he already assumed in the Artwork Essay, especially the early versions. The adaptation of human perception to industrial modes of production and transportation, especially the radical restructuring of spatial and temporal relations, has an aesthetic counterpart in the formal procedures of the photographic media—the arbitrary moment of exposure in photography and the fragmenting grip of framing and editing in film. With its dialectic of continuity and discontinuity, with the rapid succession and tactile thrust of its sounds and images, film rehearses in the realm of reception what the conveyor belt imposes upon human beings in the realm of production.[8] Resuming Kracauer's concept of "distraction," Benjamin cites this grim parallel for its cultural negativity, because it alledgedly subverts the bourgeois cult of art and a mode of reception predicated on individual contemplation and illusionist absorption.[9] In its emphasis on formal discontinuity and disruption, film's rehearsal of the shock effect would thus coincide with the tenets of political modernism, i.e. the Brechtian elements of a "cinema of attraction." (Yet, as I will argue later, the psychoanalytic premises of Benjamin's concept of shock certainly point beyond this affiliation).

While the spatio-temporal reorganization of experience is traced primarily in the realm of cinematic reception, the line of argument that stresses likeness and multiplicity seems to rely, to a greater extent, on the peculiarity of cinematic representation, the iconic relationship between film and referent. Following an interesting discussion of screen acting,[10] Benjamin establishes the masses as the pre-eminent subject matter of a liberated cinema which he sees prefigured in certain Russian films (e.g. Vertov): "Any man today can lay claim to being filmed" (*I*, 231). To be sure, this phrase also concerns changes in the relations of reception, in particular, the democratization of expertise which upsets the traditional hierarchy between author and reader/viewer. But modelling his notion of expertise on the fluctuating boundary between commentator and participant in popular discourse on sports events (e.g. newspaper boys discussing the outcome of a bicycle race), Benjamin draws a problematic analogy between live events and a medium of spatio-temporal displacement—an analogy that assumes an unproblematic relationship between film and reality. Relying thus upon the iconic self-evidence of photographic reproduction, he suggestively conflates semiotic and political senses of representation, making the latter vouch for the revolutionary potential of the former.

Moreover, by illustrating this revolutionary potential with references to statistics and polytechnical education, he clearly places the cinema on the side of the "experimental poverty" (*Erfahrungsarmut*), a term that marks a problematic slippage, in Benjamin's writings of that period, between a historical phenomenology tracing the decline of experience and the political endorsement of such a decline for the sake of what he calls a "new, positive concept of barbarism."[11] In light of this agenda, the distinction between "*Bild*" (image) and "*Abbild*" (image in the sense of copy, reflection, reproduction) congeals into a binary opposition; reduced to one side of that opposition, a politically progressive cinema would have to become a training ground for an enlightened barbarism. With the denigration of the auratic image in favor of reproduction, Benjamin implicitly denies the masses the possibility of aesthetic experience, in whatever form (and thus, like the Communist Party during the 1920s, risks leaving aesthetic needs to be exploited by the enemy). More important yet, he cuts himself off from a crucial impulse of his own thought—crucial at least to a theory of experience in the age of its declining communicability. Since Benjamin's contribution to current debates in film studies rests upon an elaboration of the place of cinema in conjunction with this very theory, I will take a detour through some aspects of his concept of *"Erfahrung,"* a term which "experience" approximates only in the vaguest and most preliminary sense.

The self-denigrating slant of the Artwork Essay comes into focus only when compared with other writings of his middle and later period in which Benjamin actually tries to redeem an auratic mode of experience for a historical and materialist practice. Relevant here are above all his essays on Surrealism, on photography and on the "mimetic capability"; his work on Proust, Kafka, Leskov and Baudelaire; his epistemological remarks on the "dialectical image" in the *Passagenwerk*; and, finally, his first-hand account of the effects of hashish. Whether concerned with aesthetic, psychological or historical questions, all these texts contribute to a theory of experience in which the phenomenon Benjamin calls "aura" plays a precarious yet indispensable part.

Benjamin's attitude towards the decline of the aura is profoundly ambivalent, just as the concept of aura itself displays an "irritating ambiguity."[12] In his 1931 essay on photography, he ventures a first definition of the phenomenon ("a peculiar web of space and time"[13]) which he resumes, with slight modifications, in the Artwork Essay.

> We define [the aura] as the unique appearance [*Erscheinung*] of a distance, however close it may be. Resting on a summer afternoon and letting one's gaze follow a mountain range on the horizon or a branch which casts its shadow on one—that means breathing the aura of those mountains, that branch. [*I, 222–23*]

With this image of an impersonalized subjectivity, Benjamin defines the aura as a mode of perception experienced in relation to natural objects; yet the definition is offered by way of illustrating a historical development—the withering of the aura in the traditional work of art. If the perception of the aura thus refers to a particular appearance of nature in potentially all objects, it is also conceptualized, from the start, as dependent upon the social conditions of perception, as contingent upon historical change.

What then is the particular quality of auratic perception, what makes it indispensable to experience (*Erfahrung*) in the emphatic sense of the word? Significantly—and, perhaps, at first sight paradoxically—the perception of the aura in natural objects rests upon "a projection of a social experience among human beings onto nature."[14] That experience, as Benjamin elaborates in his later essay on Baudelaire, is the anticipated reciprocity of the gaze: "The person we look at, or who feels he is being looked at, looks at us in return. To experience the aura of a phenomenon means to invest [*belebnen*] it with the capability of returning the gaze. This experience corresponds to the data of the *mémoire involontaire*" (*I*, 188).

While Benjamin alludes to a phenomenological concept of the gaze, he above all invokes the romantic metaphor of nature opening its eyes (*Augenaufschlagen der Natur*) which already occurs, in a kabbalistic guise, in his 1916 essay on language.[15] The notion of "*Belehnung*" implies both a particular kind of attentiveness or receptivity (the human capability of responding to another's gaze, whether visual or intentional) and the actualization of this intersubjective experience in the relationship with non-human nature. Hence the experience of the aura in natural objects is neither immediate nor "natural" (in the sense of mythical) but involves a sudden moment of transference, a metaphoric activity.[16]

The gaze that nature appears to be returning, however, does not mirror the subject in its present, conscious identity, but confronts us with another self, never before seen in a waking state. Undeniably, this kind of vision is not wholly unrelated to the sphere of the daemonic, in particular Freud's notion of the "uncanny" to which I will return in conjunction with the sexual and gender-specific implications of auratic experience. The Freudian connotation, like the reference to the *mémoire involontaire* and Benjamin's glossing of Proust as an expert in matters of the aura, suggests what commentators have pointed out: that the "unique appearance of a *distance*" which manifests itself in the perception of spatially present objects is of a *temporal* dimension, marking the fleeting moment in which the trace of an unconscious, "prehistoric" past is actualized in a cognitive image.[17]

Indeed, an important aspect of Benjamin's notion of the aura is its complex temporality—which inscribes his theory of experience with the twofold and antagonistic registers of memory and history. First of all, Benjamin leaves no doubt that, being contingent upon the social conditions of perception, the experience of the aura is irrevocably in decline, precipitated by the effects of industrial modes of production, information, transportation and urbanization, especially an alienating division of labor and the proliferation of shock sensations. Yet only in the process of disintegration can the aura be recognized, can it be registered as a qualitative component of (past) experience. The first impact of that decline in turn marks a particular historical experience, which is what Benjamin reads, as a "hidden figure," in the work of Baudelaire.

The traumatic reorganization of perception that masquerades as modernity manifests itself most obviously in spatial terms, as an uprooting of the subject from a human range of perception which Mary Ann Doane describes as a "despatialization of subjectivity."[18] Since for Benjamin, however, space is conceptually inseperable from time, this shift is ultimately and more crucially a matter of detemporalization. The images of loss that he evokes in his essay on Leskov, "The Storyteller" (1936), drift from the erosion of spatial relations crucial to the epic tradition—the proximity of the collective of listeners, the mystery of faraway places—to that of the temporal conditions of experience, the dissociation of collective memory and individual recollection, the latter surviving only in the privatized subjectivity of novel writing and reading. The reification of time not only has eroded the capability and communicability of experience—experience as memory, as awareness of temporality and mortality—but the very possibility of remembering, that is imagining, a different world. "The decay of the aura and the atrophy of the vision [*Phantasievorstellung*] of a better nature (owing to the defensive position of class struggle) are one and the same."[19]

Superimposed upon the historical-materialist trajectory of decline is a less linear—though no less pessimistic—sense of belatedness, indebted to the temporality of Jewish Messianism. The affinity of the concept of aura with Benjamin's early speculations on language (see note 15, above) suggests another concept of history, defined by the trajectory of Fall and Redemption. The tension of destructive and utopian impulses characteristic of radical Jewish Messianism[20] could actually be seen as a matrix for Benjamin's ambivalence towards the aura, even before that ambivalence was enforced by revolutionary intentions and political despair. Thus, because the aura as the necessary veil of beautiful appearance (*schöner Schein*) pretends to a premature, merely private reconciliation with a fallen world, it requires the destructive, "masculine," demystifying gesture of allegory, the mortifying grasp of knowledge, of critical reading. For only in a fragmentary state, as "quotation," can the utopian sediment of experience be preserved, can it be wrested from the empty continuum of history which, for Benjamin, is synonymous with catastrophe.[21]

The possibility of transforming an auratic mode of experience, of redeeming it from the dead-end of cult and social privilege, turns on a particular moment in the development of the productive forces—which Benjamin designates as the "dialectical, Copernican turn of recollection." This moment is the anticipated awakening of the "dreaming collective," a key metaphor in the sections of the *Passagen-Werk* written before 1935, and the dream refers to the historical nightmare of capitalism. "Capitalism is a natural phenomenon with which a new dream-sleep came over Europe, and in it, a reactivation of mythic powers."[22] With this theoretical trope, Benjamin added a decisive—and, to critics like Adorno, dangerous—twist to the philosophical concept of "*Naturgeschichte*," according to which both terms, "nature" and "history," are dialectically mediated rather than antithetical. Thus, while man's historical subjection of (both inner and outer) nature left nothing in nature that was not historical (and hence alienated), history itself had assumed the appearance of nature, masking its social and economic relations as mythical fate.[23] Taking this concept one step further, Benjamin decided to treat the 19th century, with its unprecedented proliferation of ever new commodities, consumer goods and fashions, as "an original form of prehistory [*Urgeschichte*]" (N3a,2) so as to get at the layer of dreams that both sustained and exceeded the historical order of production. As mythical images, the phantasmagorias of modernity were by definition ambiguous, promising a classless society while perpetuating the very opposite; yet as dream images they could be read and transformed into historical images, into strategies of waking up. To quote Susan Buck-Morss,

> The nightmarish, infernal aspects of industrialism were veiled in the modern city by a vast arrangement of things which at the same time gave corporeal form to the wishes and desires of humanity. Because they were "natural" phenomena in the sense of concrete matter, they give the illusion of being the realization of those wishes rather than merely their reified, symbolic expression. [. . .] It was as "dream-images of the collective"—both distorting illusion and redeemable wish-image—that they took on political meaning.[24]

Benjamin found this perspective prefigured in the Surrealists, especially their explorations of "the most dream-like object in the world of things": the city of Paris. In Aragon's *Paysan de Paris* and Breton's *Nadja,* he recognized his own fascination with an urban landscape cluttered with objects that had lost their value as commodities, the most recent casualties of the cult of the New. Surrealism "was the first to perceive the revolutionary energies that appear in the 'obsolescent,' in the first iron constructions, the first factory buildings, the earliest photos, the objects that have begun to be extinct, grand pianos, the dresses of five years ago, fashionable restaurants when the vogue has begun to ebb from them."[25] To be sure, such energies are revolutionary primarily in their negativity; the misery revealed in the afterlife of interiors, of enslaved and enslaving objects, translates into politics as a "revolutionary nihilism." Yet, as "everything forgotten mingles with what has been forgotten of the prehistoric world," the outdated displays of the Paris arcades present an "ideal panorama of a primeval time barely gone by [*einer kaum verflossenen Urzeit*]," "a world of secret affinities."[26] Thus, the unruly assimilation of the modern to the archaic not only challenges history's claim to progress; it also offers a chance of redeeming auratic experience as a cognitive mode, transformed by the historical demolition of the aura under the impact of shock. As Habermas observes: "The experience released from the ruptured shell of the aura was, however, already contained in the experience of the aura itself: the metamorphosis of the object into a counterpart [*Gegenüber*]. Thereby a whole field of surprising correspondences between animate and inanimate nature is opened up, wherein even *things* encounter us in the structures or trail intersubjectivity."[27]

To Benjamin, the Surrealists signalled the possibility of such a redemptive turn by their efforts to overcome the esoteric, isolating aspect of inspiration, to give the auratic promise of happiness a public and secular meaning—to make it a "profane illumination." Whether in their collective anamnesis of dreams, their experiments in automatic writing or pursuits of erotic passion, they defined the sphere of political action in terms of the sphere of their physical and psychic existence and vice versa, projecting an integral "sphere of images [*Bildraum*]" that might be up to the experiential needs of a "collective physis." Clearly, Benjamin was not interested in Surrealism as a literary movement (nor in its occult and neo-romantic tendencies) but, rather, in the anti-aesthetic impulse of its manifestos, collages and performances—in the radical crossing of the artificial flowering of images of second nature with a mode of experience traditionally reserved for those of an ostensibly more primary nature. "We penetrate the mystery only to the degree that we recognize it in the everyday world, by virtue of a dialectical optics that perceives the everyday as impenetrable and the impenetrable as everyday."[28]

The possibility of experience in a disenchanted world, indeed the very possibility of conceptualizing experience in its temporal and historical dynamic, also implies a crossing in another sense, the charting of a historical and epistemological transition, a veritable "work of passage." A figure probably closer to Benjamin's intellectual persona than the Surrealists is that of the flaneur, a key figure in both the *Passagen-Werk* and the essays on Baudelaire. Already in 1929, the year he wrote the essays on Surrealism and on Proust, Benjamin sketched out his theory of experience in a review of a contemporary book on Berlin, "The Return of the Flaneur."[29] This review illuminates the connection between Benjamin's notion of the aura and a secularized, profane mode of experience in a number of ways, anticipating the most important aspects of his theory of experience. The journey of the writer as flaneur (in this case Franz Hessel) is diametrically opposed to that of the tourist who seeks out the monuments and exotic attractions of foreign sites; rather, it is a purposeless purposeful drifting into the past which turns the city into a "mnemotechnic device." The muse of memory takes the flaneur, invariably, on an itinerary which leads, "if not down to the Mothers [of Goethe's *Faust*], so into a past which is all the more fascinating since it evokes more than the author's merely individual, private [. . .] childhood or youth, more even than the city's own history." As the detective/priest of the "genius loci," the flaneur reads this "more" in the phenomenology of the minute and inconspicuous, the "scent of a particular threshold or the touch of a particular tile." Since such images "inhabit" the city as a collective space, the literal "wooden threshold" turns into a "metaphoric" one, and the "penates" or "threshold goddesses"—like those that fascinated Benjamin at the entrance of the Paris arcades—become spatial allegories of a temporal crossing or historical change ("*Zeitenwende*"). For anybody who can read its signs, who can make the "stony eyes" of these pagan deities "look back at us," this crossing harbors a density of meanings, at once habitual and disjunctive, intersecting past and future, history and myth, loss and desire, individual recollection and collective unconscious.

It is this mode of reading which Benjamin tried to theorize, from an anthropological-historical perspective, in his speculations on the "mimetic faculty." Like Kracauer's earlier and Adorno's later concepts of "mimesis," Benjamin's too has to be distinguished, absolutely, from the traditional, Platonic concept of mimesis as well as from contemporary Marxist theories of reflection (*Widerspiegelung*); it was actually in explicit opposition to the latter—as much as in observance of the Biblical taboo on representation—that the writers of the Frankfurt School endorsed and redefined the idea of mimesis. Moreover, the concept of mimesis complements the philosophical analysis of *Naturgeschichte,* in that it envisions a relationship with nature that is alternative to the dominant forms of mastery and exploitation, one that would dissolve the contours of the subject/object dichotomy into reciprocity and the possibility of reconciliation.[30]

Benjamin himself referred to the first version of the essay, "The Doctrine of Similarity" (written 1933), as a "theory of language" and explicitly linked it to his 1916 essay, "On Language as Such and on the Language of Man." Two years later, after finishing the second version of the essay, "On the Mimetic Faculty" (1935), he thanked Gretel Adorno for sending him Freud's essay on "Psychoanalysis and Telepathy," emphasizing its affinity with his own reflections on the mimetic residue of language.[31] Considering these two points of reference, it seems safe not to expect anything resembling a realistic concept of representation. In semiotic terms (following Peirce), mimesis is not concerned with an iconic relationship, a perceptual likeness between sign and reality. If the correspondences actualized by the mimetic faculty pertain to any aspect of signification, then it is to the realm of the indexical, which involves a relationship of material contiguity hinging upon a particular moment in time and thus brings into play the disjunctive temporality of all reading.[32]

The mimetic faculty in human beings reponds to patterns of similarity or correspondence in nature; it is the capacity to recognize and produce such correspondences in return. Benjamin traces this capacity back to phylogenetic and ontogenetic modes of imitating nature, the former a necessary conforming to nature's superior force, the latter still present, without obvious purpose, in the games of children. "A child not only plays at being a grocer or a teacher, but also at being a windmill or a train."[33] As both examples suggest, the mimetic faculty, like the analogical patterns that stimulate it, is subject to historical change. Thus, our capacity of perceiving similarity has definitely diminished; but the similarities we perceive consciously (e.g. in faces) relate to the "countless similarities perceived unconsciously or not at all" like "the tip of the iceberg" to its submarine volume. "The question is whether we are concerned with the decay of this faculty or with its transformation." Obviously, this question overlaps with the question of the aura as a medium of mimetic (re)cognition, and the rephrasing of the question, as we shall see, opens up an important dimension in Benjamin's theory of experience.

A key term for understanding the transformation of the mimetic faculty is the notion of "non-sensuous similarity" ("*unsinnliche Ähnlichkeit*") which Benjamin illustrates, in a characteristic detour, with reference to astrology (a paradigm he himself relates, in a preliminary note, to the question of the aura; *GS* II.3: 958; 956). In an archaic past, he insists, there was a mimetic correspondence between a person's moment of birth and the constellation of the stars; more important yet, it was perceived by the ancients and passed on to the new-born as the gift of mimetic knowledge. The perception of this correspondence, however, was bound to a moment in time, a fleeting instant (the moment of birth, the particular constellation of the stars) and depended upon the presence of a reader, individual or collective, for an interpretation. Astrology is merely a belated—and rather "crooked"—theory in relation to this early practice, reinterpreting— and often misinterpreting—the latter's dates which by now have lost any sensuous and experiential basis of similarity.

Benjamin might as well have used the example of psychoanalysis: the Freudian theory of repression similarly relies on the assumption that there is meaning in everything and that everything truly significant has already happened in the past; the repressed moments of infancy return in our adult lives as alien, distorted (and distorting), unreadable signs. But Benjamin leaves the child playing at being a windmill or a train and instead turns from astrology to another "canon of non-sensuous similarities"—language. It need hardly be repeated here that Benjamin's theory of language is diametrically opposed to a Saussurean view of language as a system of arbitrary and conventional signs. This does not necessarily mean that he subscribes to an onomatopoetic view of the origin of language.[34] Rather, he shifts, via the problem of translation—the impossible desire to get words of different languages to denote an identical meaning—to an area central to the tradition of linguistic mysticism: written language, the graphic image of words and letters. "The most important of these connections may well be the one . . . between written and spoken language," governed by a similarity of a highly abstract, non-sensuous degree.

At this juncture, psychoanalysis enters through the backdoor of graphology which "has taught us to recognize images, or more precisely picture puzzles [*Vexierbilder*], in handwriting" as a hidden trace of the writer's unconscious.[35] The mimetic faculty expressed in individual writing, Benjamin suggests, must have played an even more important part in the archaic history of written language: "Thus, along with language, writing has become an archive"—and, he adds later, our "most complete archive"—"of non-sensuous similarities or non-sensuous correspondences." This "magic" aspect of language, however, is inseparable from its semiotic aspect and the meaning of each manifests itself only through the material basis of the other. Hence, the perception of similarity is bound up with the temporality of reading, the momentary and ephemeral configurations of meaning, their "flashing" into a constellation. Yet the growing speed of writing and reading also enhances "the fusion of the semiotic and the mimetic in the sphere of language," to a point where (and here the 1935 version departs from the earlier one) the transformed "powers of mimetic production and comprehension [. . .] have liquidated those of magic."[36]

Rather than a theory of language as such, Benjamin's reflections on the mimetic faculty imply a theory of writing and reading. The mimetic dimension of reading responds to a level of meaning which Roland Barthes, *faute de mieux,* has termed the "third" or "obtuse" meaning.[37] For Benjamin, the semiotic aspect of language encompasses both Barthes's "informational" and "symbolic" levels of meaning, whether in abstract philosophical, political, psychoanalytic or narrative discourses, while the mimetic aspect would correspond to the level of physiognomic excess. As the reference to Barthes implies, Benjamin's notion of reading was not confined to written material, but ranged from the ancient reading of constellations on the surface of the sky—"to read what was never written" (Hofmannsthal)—to a critical reading of the "natural" phenomena of nineteenth-century capitalism. The medium of such critical reading is language, to be sure, but the "temporal abyss," the cognitive disjunction which propels such reading, is more than a metaphor of the aporetic nature of all language.[38] While language and experience in Benjamin are intimately interlocking terms, they can neither be identified with, nor hierarchically subsumed by, each other.

What is at stake for Benjamin is the possibility of a different *use* of language, one that could mobilize the mimetic power historically concentrated in language against the "'Once upon a time' of classical historical narrative" (*PW,* N3,4). Defining the "pedagogic side" of the Arcades Project, he quotes Rudolf Borchardt: "To train our image-making faculty to look stereoscopically and dimensionally into the depths of the shadows of history" (N1,8). This heuristic gaze should produce, not hermeneutical images (in which past and present mutually illuminate each other as a continuum), but "dialectical images"—images "in which the past and the now flash into a constellation." The dialectical optics of the historical gaze arrests the movement of ("natural," archaic, mythical, dreamlike) images in the moment of their "coming into legibility"; it gives them a "shock," that is, it allegorizes them into quotability. But only "at a standstill" can they become genuinely historical images, monads that resist the catastrophic continuity of time.[39] "The first stage in this voyage will be to carry the montage principle over into history" (N2,6).

Before I resume the question of film by way of what might seem like a surreptitious analogy, i.e., via the concept of montage, I will briefly return to the notion of "non-sensuous similarity" and the implied distinction between similarity (or resemblance) and sameness, between affinity and identity—which is at least as crucial to Benjamin's vision of the cinema as the principle of montage. As we could see from his genealogy of the mimetic faculty, the category of similarity itself has undergone a change of meaning. It has withdrawn into non-sensuous, i.e. figurative, correspondences, not only because the subjective and intersubjective capability of perceiving similarity has declined, but because, for related reasons, the status of sensuous, i.e. obvious and literal, correspondence is irrevocably compromised by the effects of universal commodity production and a concomitant standardization of social identity and subjectivity. Indeed, experience in the emphatic sense confronts these reified forms of similarity with a different kind of similarity—which Benjamin unfolds in his "Image of Proust" (1929): "The similarity of one thing to another which we are used to, which occupies us in a wakeful state, reflects only vaguely the deeper resemblance of the dream world in which everything that happens appears not in identical but in similar guise, opaquely similar one to another" (I, 204).

In Proust, the logic of unconscious association that distinguishes similarity from identity is that of the *mémoire involontaire*, the involuntary recollection (*Eingedenken*) which interweaves remembrance and forgetting into a textual counterpart or, rather, inversion of "Penelope's work," yet like hers a work that stems itself against the linear course of time. Remembrance, in the Proustian as well as Freudian sense, is incompatible with conscious remembering (*Erinnerung*) which tends to historicize, to fixate the image of memory in an already interpreted narrative event (*Erlebnis*); not self-reflection, but an integral "actuality," a "bodily," to some degree absent-minded "presence of mind," is its prerequisite.[40] Proust turned day into night and remembering into an unceasing, interminable textual process, driven by a "blind, senseless, obsessive [. . .] will to happiness," which nearly made Benjamin's own heartbeat stop in affinity. The "elegiac" direction of Proust's quest, after all, was Benjamin's own, just as the writer's solitary endeavor to recapture, "synthetically," a formerly collective mode of experience remained a daemonic shadow for the critic's career, inseparable from his political itinerary and historiographic project. Moreover, the compulsion to transfigure a distorted existence into a "prehistoric" world of correspondences marks a decisive ambiguity, in the idea of "eternal recurrence," between the mythical reproduction of catastrophic sameness and the utopian craving of "the yet once again" which characterizes the movement of desire, the inexhaustible structure of the wish:

Children know a symbol of this world: the stocking which has the structure of this dream world when, rolled up in the drawer, it is a "bag" and a "present" at the same time. And just as children do not tire of quickly changing the bag and its contents into a third thing—namely, a stocking—Proust could not get his fill of emptying the dummy, his self [*die Attrappe, das Ich*], at one stroke in order to keep garnering that third thing, the image which satisfied his curiosity or, more precisely, assuaged his homesickness [. . .] homesickness for the world distorted in the state of resemblance, a world in which the true surrealist face of existence breaks through. [*I*, 204–5]

The distortion, as Irving Wohlfarth points out in an excellent reading of this passage, "lies in the eye of the beholder *qua* identical subject." If the "true face of existence" is "surrealist," the only adequate mode of representation is one of mimetic transformation, figuration or disfigurement—the "distortion of distortion."[41]

It is no coincidence that the distinction between similarity and sameness again comes into play, a few years later, in Benjamin's "Hashish in Marseilles" (1932). A physiognomic experiment *par excellence,* the drug had evoked in him "a deeply submerged feeling of happiness" which was more difficult to analyze than any other sensation he experienced in that state. Groping for a description, he recalls a phrase from Johannes V. Jensen's *Exotic Novellas* (1919): "'Richard was a young man with a sense for everything in the world that was the same [*Sinn für alles Gleichartige in der Welt*].' This sentence had pleased me very much. It enabled me now to confront the political and rational sense it had had for me earlier with the individual, magical meaning of my experience yesterday" (*R*, 142–43). If before he had taken Jensen's phrase to underscore the significance of nuances in an age of unprecedented standardization, it acquired a different meaning in conjunction with his artificially distorted perception: "For I saw only nuances, yet these were the same." Benjamin attributes this blurring of similarity and sameness to a sudden "ravenous hunger to taste what is the same in all places and countries," but he introduces this hunger by way of a metaphoric operation, a double troping of the Marseillean cobblestones (which might as well have been in Paris) as the bread (loaves) of his imagination. Towards the end of the passage, Benjamin recalls a train of thought beginning with, "All men are brothers," whose last and—he assures us—"less trivial link" might have involved "images of animals." In other words, in the sensual experience of egalitarian effect, similarity and sameness converge.

When, soon after, under the impact of the deepening political crisis, Benjamin reaches the conclusion that intellectuals on the left cannot but actively promote the demolition of the aura, he finally seems to abandon the distinction between similarity and sameness altogether, collapsing the mimetic faculty into the manifest, "obvious" iconicity of photographic representation. The quotation from Jensen returns in the Artwork

Essay in a slightly modified form, as a general mode of perception whose growing "sense for things in the world that are the same [*Sinn für das Gleichartige in der Welt*]" has seized even the unique object by means of technical reproduction—and young Richard is elided in favor of the "contemporary masses" as the collective exponent of that sense.[42] Incurring Adorno's charge of romanticizing the proletariat, Benjamin splits off the element of similarity from his concept of mimesis and attaches it, as "sense of sameness," to the masses; he further positivizes it by placing it in diametrical opposition to the aura. Thus, he not only surrenders the ground of his theory of experience, the motivating tension of difference and affinity; he also makes the discontinuities of memory and history congeal into the linear presence of polytechnical education, popular expertise and a pseudo-scientific notion of "testing" which cannot be dissociated from its industrial-capitalist origin. If anything in Benjamin, it is this lapse into presence which would have to be considered nostalgic, especially in light of his later writings (the second Baudelaire essay and the "Theses on the Philosophy of History") which restore the dimensions of dialectical temporality to his thought, at a time when the political—and with it his personal—situation had darkened beyond recall.

Even in the Artwork Essay, however, there are glimpses of mimetic cognition and figuration, suggesting that the cinema's role in relation to experiential impoverishment could go beyond merely promoting and consummating the historical process. Undeniably, the medium of film, like photography, participates in that process. As a technology of reproduction, it expands, to an unprecedented scope, the archive of "voluntary, discursive memory" and thereby inevitably reduces the play of involuntary recollection. Likewise, film's mechanical procedures intervene in temporal and spatial relations, disregarding "natural" distances, and thus compound the proliferation of shock sensations that seal human consciousness in a permanent state of psychical defense. And, finally, the cinema epitomizes, in the very structure of the apparatus, the decline of the human capability to return the gaze, a historical experience Benjamin found registered in Baudelaire's description of eyes that could be said to "have lost the ability to look" (*I*, 189). But precisely because of its contemporaneity and complicity with the industrial transformation of human perception, film could also fulfill a cognitive task: "Film is the first art form capable of showing how matter interferes with people's lives. Hence, film can be an excellent means of materialist representation" (*I*, 247). Chaplin's exercises in fragmentation are a case in point: by chopping up expressive body movement into a sequence of minute mechanical impulses, he renders the law of the apparatus visible in its impact on human movement—"he interprets himself allegorically" (GS I.3: 1040; 1047).

Besides allowing for an allegorical analysis of the shock effect, the mimetic capability of film also extends to specific techniques designed to make technology itself disappear. The complex and highly artificial manner in which film creates an illusion of reality, Benjamin argues, gives it a particular status in the technical mediation of contemporary life. As if by a logic of double negation, film grants us "an aspect of reality which is free of all equipment," which is what human beings are "entitled to expect from a work of art" (I, 234).

> The shooting of a film, especially of a sound film, [. . .] presents a process in which it is impossible to assign to a spectator a viewpoint which would exclude from the scene being enacted such extraneous accessories as camera equipment, lighting machinery, crew, etc.—unless the position of his eye were identical with that of the lens. [. . .] In the theater one is well aware of the place from which the events on stage cannot immediately be detected as illusionary. There is no such place for the movie scene that is being shot. Its illusionary nature is a nature of the second degree, the result of editing. That is to say, *in the studio the mechanical equipment has penetrated so deeply into reality that its pure aspect, freed from the foreign substance of equipment, is the result of a special procedure, namely, shooting from a particular camera set-up and linking the shot with other similar ones.* The equipment-free aspect of reality here has become the height of artifice; the sight of immediate reality has become the "blue flower" in the land of technology. [I, 232f.]

This passage is one of the most puzzling in the essay and it is not exactly illuminated by Zohn's translating of the proverbial "blue flower" of German Romanticism, Novalis' "blaue Blume," into an "orchid." What does Benjamin mean by the "equipment-free aspect of reality"? How, one might ask somewhat bluntly, does it differ from the reality effect, the masking of technique and production which film theorists of the 1970s were to pinpoint as the ideological basis of classical Hollywood cinema?[43] First of all, the reality conveyed by the cinematic apparatus is no more and no less phantasmagoric than the "natural" phenomena of the commodity world it endlessly replicates; and Benjamin knew all too well that the primary objective of capitalist film practice was to perpetuate that mythical chain of mirrors. Therefore, if film were to have a critical, cognitive function, it had to disrupt that chain and assume the task of all politicized art, as Buck-Morss paraphrases the argument of the Artwork Essay: "not to duplicate the illusion as real, but to interpret reality as itself illusion."[44]

Still, why did Benjamin choose, not without a shade of irony, the highly auratic metaphor of the Blue Flower—the unattainable object of the romantic quest, the incarnation of desire?[45] I perceive in the above passage an echo of the "distortion of distortion" that Benjamin traces in the work of Proust, of which the "dialectical optics" of the Surrealists is just a more contemporary, collectivized (and perhaps less memorable) version. Accordingly, "the equipment-free aspect of reality" that even generations who have learned to live with a declining aura and its false resurrections are "entitled to expect from a work of art" seems to me linked, in whatever alienated and refracted manner, to that "homesickness for the world distorted in the state of resemblance" which Proust's writing pursued to the point of asphyxiation. Such film practice, however, would have to desist from submerging the contradictions of second nature in mythical images of the first, itself long domesticated and enslaved, and instead lend its mimetic capability to "a world in which the true surrealist face of existence breaks through."

Benjamin himself may not have made that connection explicit (and might not have approved of it), yet several lines of his argument suggest a position from which the cinema could be redeemed—for film history, film theory as well as film practice—as a medium of experience. To develop these lines, I will double back on the question of human self-representation which I had mentioned earlier, in conjunction with Benjamin's short-circuiting of the iconic aspect of cinematic representation with the political rights of the masses. In the first version of the Artwork Essay, Benjamin elaborates in greater detail on the relationship between human beings and technology which, instead of liberating them from myth, confronts them as a force of second nature just as overwhelming as the forces of a more elementary nature in archaic times. This confrontation is rehearsed, in the field of art, whenever an actor plays before a camera instead of the physically present, virtually absent theater audience: "To act in the stream of klieglights [*Jupiterlampen*] and simultaneously meet the requirements of sound recording is a highly demanding test. Passing this test means to maintain one's humanity in the face of the apparatus." The screen actor has to muster a total and bodily presence of mind while foregoing the aura that emanates from the here and now, the presence of the stage actor. At the same time, he or she knows, when confronting the inhuman gaze of the camera, that it substitutes for another gaze, physically absent yet intentionally present—that of a mass audience. The latter's interest in the actor's performance preexists the individual film, story or character portrayed: the actor becomes a stand-in, a representative of their own daily battle with an alienating technology.

For it is likewise an apparatus [*Apparatur*] that supervises the process by which, every day, the overwhelming majority of people living in cities and working in offices and factories are expropriated of their humanity. In the evening, the same masses flock to the movie theaters to watch an actor take revenge in their place, not only by asserting *his* humanity (or whatever may appear to them as such) in the face of the apparatus but by making that very apparatus serve his own triumph. [*GS* I.2: 450]

In the later version of the essay, Benjamin comes close to reversing his argument, now emphasizing the audience's placement on the side of the camera and admitting identification with the actor only insofar as the viewer identifies with the testing, critical, impersonal attitude of the apparatus (*I*, 228)—i.e. trimming it to a Brechtian concept of distanciation. Bracketing the obvious idealization at work in the earlier (though just as much in the later) version, I still consider the unrevised passage significant because it recognizes historical and collective dimensions even in a more naïve form of spectatorial involvement, aspects of fascination and identification that are not necessarily exhausted by the textual interplay of scopic and narrative registers.[46] Granted, Benjamin had every reason to mistrust the masses' interest in the screen actor, whether it fuelled the pseudoauratic cult of the star or redefined standards of success in the arena of politics (*I*, 247)—an observation even more to the point in the 1980s than in the 1930s. If he appears to be taking a more positive view in the passage quoted above, he does so on no less political grounds. For the rhetoric of New Objectivity and proletarian culture notwithstanding, the triumph of the actor's "humanity" is, after all, a Pyrrhic victory; its power to move an audience is due to the negative reality it temporarily eclipses, the social and historical experience of alienation. Hence the alternative to the cinema's mirroring and administering of reified forms of identity is not simply a positive representation of the masses but, rather, a film practice that would give aesthetic expression to the scars of human self-alienation (Marx's term *Selbstentfremdung*).

The mimetic transformation of such scars is not confined to the human body; it extends to the relationship between human beings and their environment—indeed, to invoke the more recent (and perhaps unique) example of Claude Lanzmann's *Shoah*, the most radical sight/site of human self-alienation might be that of an environment evacuated of human life. This possibility is adumbrated in Benjamin's "Short History of Photography" (1931), an essay which anticipates (along with a first definition of the aura) another strand of the Artwork Essay: the metaphor of the "optical unconscious." In his genealogy of photographic representation, Benjamin traces a dialectical movement from early images of the human countenance, the last refuge of auratic intimations of desire and mortality; through late 19th-century portrait photography, with its masquerade of social identity against the backdrop of bourgeois interiors; to Atget's photographs of deserted Paris streets, courtyards and shopwindows (shot "like scenes of crime") in which the human form has been displaced with serial formations of everyday objects (rows of bootlasts, hand-trucks, uncleared tables). Having thus initiated "the emancipation of the object" from a deteriorated auratic context, Atget inspired the more programmatic efforts of Surrealist photography to promote a "therapeutic alienation between environment and human beings"—therapeutic again in the sense of a "distortion of distortion," the dialectics of defamiliarization and similarity. Only a break with the personality-centered, commercial tradition of representation, Benjamin concludes, will restore a physiognomic sensibility towards both the human body and the world of things. This is demonstrated by "the best of Russian films" which teach us that, like the faces of people who have no investment in photographic immortality, "even milieu and landscape will reveal themselves only to those photographers who can read the nameless appearance [*namenlose Erscheinung*] inscribed in their countenance."[47]

The "nameless appearance" of things and faces in film and photography is merely a more mystical designation of the phenomenon for which Benjamin coined the shorthand of the "optical unconscious," "*[das] Optisch-Unbewusste*." In the 1931 essay, he elaborates on a mimetic affinity of photographic technique (especially the possibilities of enlargement and split-second exposure) with the physiognomic aspects of its material, with "image worlds [*Bildwelten*] that inhabit the smallest things, readable though covert enough to have found shelter in daydreams" (*GS* II.1: 371). As he will repeat in the Artwork Essay, "it is evidently a different nature that speaks to the camera than that which speaks to the naked eye; different above all because it substitutes, for a space interwoven with human consciousness, another space, an unconsciously permeated space" (*I*, 236f.).

The attribution of psychic, physiognomic, even psychoanalytic faculties to the camera is a topos of early 1920s film theory, notably in Jean Epstein and Béla Balázs.[48] Benjamin's conceptualization of the "optical unconscious" in the context of photography, however, points to a more specific source, Kracauer's great essay of 1927. Prefiguring the superimposition of modernity and prehistory that Benjamin was to advance in his essay on Surrealism and the *Passagen-Werk*, Kracauer's reflections on photography locate the radical function of the medium (intercut with an analysis of its ideological, mythological function) in the arbitrary moment of exposure, the moment of chance that might capture an aspect of nature at once alienated and released from the tyranny of human intention—the "dregs of history."[49] In that tradition and, like Kracauer, indebted to Jewish mysticism, Benjamin develops the notion of an "optical unconscious" from the observation that the temporality of some early photographs, despite all preparation and artistry on the part of both model and photographer, compel the beholder to seek the "tiny spark of accident," the "here and now" by which the image is branded with reality, and thus to find the "inconspicuous spot" which might yield, in the quality of that minute long past, a "moment of futurity responding to the retrospective gaze" (*GS* II.1: 371).

Such a belated form of "magic" is unavailable to the medium of film, given the compulsory temporality of the code of movement, not to mention narrative. This may be one answer to the question Benjamin poses in his notes to the Artwork Essay: "If the aura is in early photographs, why not in film?" (*GS* I.3: 1048). When he resumes the metaphor of the "optical unconscious" with reference to film, he complicates and to some extent revises that question, though again evading any explicit differentiation between the two media. While the Photography Essay illustrated the "optical unconscious" with examples from biophysics and botany, the Artwork Essay draws on the imagery of a social and mechanized world, the discourse of alienated experience. Significantly, Benjamin introduces the "optical unconscious" in the Artwork Essay (later version) with a reference to Freud's *Psychopathology of Everyday Life*, noting the historical impact of this work on the perception of conversational parapraxes ("*Fehlleistungen im Gespräch*"). As Freud has altered our awareness of language, he argues, cinematic techniques such as close-up, time lapse and slow motion photography and, above all, montage have changed our perception of the visual world:

> Our taverns and city streets, our offices and furnished rooms, our train stations and factories appeared to have us locked up beyond hope. Then came film and exploded this prison-world with the dynamite of one-tenth seconds, so that now, in the midst of its far-flung ruins and debris, we calmly embark on adventurous travels. [*I,* 236].

In this context, Benjamin emphasizes the fragmenting, destructive, allegorizing effect of cinematic devices, their tendency to cut through the tissue of reality like a surgical instrument (*I,* 233). Revealing the "natural" appearance of the capitalist everyday as an allegorical landscape, the camera's exploration of an "unconsciously permeated space" thus overlaps with the area of investigation pursued, in different ways, by the flaneur, the Surrealist, the dialectical historian. Not surprisingly, Benjamin envisioned an "impassioned" film on the archeology of Paris in the *Passagen-Werk* (C1,9)—and we might add examples from a whole tradition of city films ranging from Vigo and Vertov through Godard, Kluge, Sander and Ottinger.

If the mimetic capabilities of film were put to such use, it would not only fulfill a critical function but also a redemptive one, registering sediments of experience that are no longer or not yet claimed by social and economic rationality, making them readable as emblems of a "forgotten future." In other words, although film as a medium enhances the historical demolition of the aura, its particular form of indexical mediation enables it to lend a physiognomic expression to objects, to make second nature return the look, similar to auratic experience in phenomena of the first. Such film practice, however, would not only have to reject the misguided ambition to adapt and prolong the bourgeois cult of art; it would also have to abandon classical standards of continuity and verisimilitude and, instead, focus its mimetic devices on a non-sensuous similarity, on hidden correspondences in which even the dreamworld of commodities may "encounter us in the structures of frail intersubjectivity." Such a return of the gaze, in the emphatic sense, would always involve a transgressive, unsettling moment; it is certainly not, as Benjamin observes regarding commercial conventions of direct address, "a question of the photographed animals, people or babies 'looking at *you*' which implicates the customer in such an unsavory manner."[50]

Like his remarks on film throughout the Artwork Essay, Benjamin's elaboration of the "optical unconscious" oscillates between a description of technical innovations and their emancipative possibilities, between historical analysis and a utopian discourse of redemption. Rather than merely a case of methodological confusion, this sliding is motivated by a dialectical movement within certain key concepts (e.g. "nature," "history," "aura") and theoretical tropes (e.g. "eternal recurrence," "dreaming collective") whose meaning depends upon the particular constellation in which they are deployed. Thus, the recuperation of the cinema as a medium of experience brings into play a constitutive ambiguity in Benjamin's concept of "shock," an ambiguity crucial to his endorsement of a "distracted" mode of reception.

In the historical etiology emphasized earlier, shock figures as the stigma of modern life, synonymous with the defensive shield it provokes and thus with the impoverishment of experience. But the term is also used to describe the moment of sexual recognition (as in Baudelaire's sonnet "À une passante," *I*, 169) which, while linked to a particular historical experience (the alienation inflicted upon love by urban life), an experience of loss, exemplifies the catastrophic and dislocating impact of auratic experience in general.[51] In this dialectical ambiguity, however, shock may assume a strategic significance—as an artificial means of propelling the human body into moments of recognition. Introducing a "tactile" element into the field of "optical reception" (*GS* I.2: 466), allegorical devices like framing and montage would thus have a therapeutic function similar to other procedures—the planned rituals of extraordinary physical and mental states, like drug experiments, flaneurist walking, Surrealist seances or psychoanalytic sessions—procedures designed to activate layers of unconscious memory buried in the reified structures of subjectivity. "From this perspective, film and photography could be considered as staged events [*Veranstaltungen*] for reclaiming collective and species-historical [*menschheitsgeschichtliche*] experiences which become 'quotable' as such only at the point when their actual, historically perverted substance disintegrates."[52]

It is the possibility of such critical reinscription, finally, which makes the cinema indispensible to a new epic culture (in the Brechtian sense), as Benjamin suggests in his 1930 review of Döblin's *Berlin Alexanderplatz*. The cinema's promise of collectivity resides less in the miraculous conversion of economically motivated quantity into political quality suggested in the Artwork Essay (*I*, 244), than in the shock-like configuration, or re-figuration, of social documents—images, sounds, textual fragments of an alienated yet common experience. The revolutionary potential of montage thus hinges not only upon the formal rehearsal of the shock-effect but also, and perhaps primarily, upon the mimetic power of its elements, the "complicity of film technique with the milieu." Since the unconsciously permeated space revealed at this historical juncture can only be a collective one, the cinema becomes a place in which traditional class structures collapse, allowing the bourgeois intellectual to cross over, a possibility—and no doubt an autobiographical need—which Benjamin had already spelled out in his defense of Eisenstein's *Potemkin*: "The proletariat is the hero of those spaces whose adventures make the bourgeois abandon himself with a throbbing heart in the movie theater, because he must relish the 'beautiful' even and especially where it speaks to him of the annihilation of his own class."[53]

The discontinuous return of an auratic mode of experience through the backdoor of the "optical unconscious" allows us to reconsider the concept of aura itself and perhaps to demystify some of its implications. The physiognomic quality that the Surrealists—and before them Proust—sought in the most ordinary objects may invite Marxist terms of analysis but ultimately eludes theories of commodity fetishism and reification. When Adorno proposed a clarification of the notion of aura along those lines, suggesting that the trace of the "forgotten human residue in things [*des vergessenen Menschlichen am Ding*]" was that of reified human labor, Benjamin insisted that this was not necessarily the object of forgetting and remembering he had in mind in the Baudelaire essay. "The tree and the bush that we endow [with an answering gaze] were not created by human hand. Hence, there must be a human element in objects which is *not* the result of labor."[54] That forgotten human element, as Marleen Stoessel argues in her ingenious commentary, is nothing but the material origin—and finality—that human beings share with non-human nature, the physical aspect of creation which Benjamin himself had conspicuously eclipsed from his reading of Genesis in the 1916 essay on language. The dialectic of forgetting and remembering which constitutes his theory of experience therefore has more to do with a different kind of fetishism: the curious economy of knowledge and belief that occupied Freud.[55]

The pull of the past that maintains the auratic wish as unsatisfiable may be veiled in metaphors of prehistory—Baudelaire's *vie antérieure*—but it has a psychic source which is, quite literally, too close to home. The desire that beckons Benjamin from Goethe's line, *"Ach, du warst in abgelebten Zeiten meine Schwester* oder *meine Frau"* ("Oh you were in bygone times my sister *or* my wife")[56] is clearly transgressive. And Benjamin's autobiographical revelation (in the letter to Adorno quoted above) as to the "root of [his] 'theory of experience'" leads us straight to what we might have suspected all along. Remembering childhood summer vacations with his family, he recalls his brother saying, after obligatory walks through idyllic landscapes, *"Da wären wir nun gewesen"* ("there we would now have been"). The curious temporality of auratic memory—the utopian glimpse of a prehistoric past at once familiar and disturbingly strange—not coincidentally resembles certain dreams that Freud describes in his essay on "The Uncanny" (1919), relating them to a male perception of the female genitalia as something uncanny (*unheimlich*):

This *unheimlich* place, however, is the entrance to the former *Heimat* [home] of all human beings, to the place where everyone dwelt once upon a time and in the beginning. There is a humorous saying: "Love is home-sickness"; and whenever a person dreams of a place or a landscape thinking, still in the dream, "this place is familiar to me. I have been there before," we may interpret the place as being the mother's genitals or her body. In this case, too, the *unheimlich* is what was once *heimisch*, home-like familiar; the prefix "*un*" is the mark of repression.[57]

The pre-Oedipal wish can only survive as repressed, as displaced and transformed by fetishistic denial which for Freud, in any case, is a defense against the threat of castration. Benjamin's writing seems driven by a desire at once to reverse and to rehearse that displacement, to destroy the fetishistic illusion while preserving the promise of happiness that it allowed to sustain. His theory of experience hovers over and around the body of the mother—as a memory of an intensity that becomes the measure of all cognition, of critical thought. As he announces in one of the earliest sections of the *Passagen-Werk*: "What the child (and, weakly remembering, the man) finds in the old folds of the mother's skirt that he held on to—that's what these pages should contain" (K2,2). Yet even this rare reference to the mother's body succumbs to fetishistic mediation—memory resides in the fabric of the cloth—and thus refers us to the section on fashion (*Konvolut* B); here fetishism is explicitly linked to death, the "sex appeal of the inorganic" which guides the senses through the "landscape of the [female] body" (B3,8; B9,1). The image of the mother's body, as disturbing to Benjamin as to patriarchal discourse in general, shortcircuits desire and mortality—of which castration is perhaps the most powerful metaphor.

More often, therefore, the source of anxiety and fetishistic displacement remains textually unacknowledged (or ironically distanced): threat and promise of the pre-Oedipal wish are in a sense re-fetishized, held in a semi-repressive abeyance which allows him to garner the reflections of its psychic, aesthetic and experiential intensity. This complex strategy of allusion and evasion is nowhere as evident as in Benjamin's concept of the gaze, pitched between auratic vision and the historical reorganization of subjectivity. In a note to his essay on the mimetic faculty (1935), Benjamin speculates on the connection between the aura and astrology: "Are not the stars with their distant gaze the *Urphänomen* of the aura? Can we conclude that the gaze was the first mentor of the mimetic faculty?" (*GS* II.3: 958) Again, a prehistoric, phylogenetic perspective is offered instead of a more obvious one, namely, the constitution of the gaze in the relationship between mother and child. The memory of what is all too close has to be projected into a stellar distance; yet this metaphoric defense allows Benjamin to conceptualize a dimension of reciprocity which defies the social and historical organization of looking, with its ceaseless reproduction of the subject in terms of mirror identity, unity, presence and mastery.

Benjamin comes closest to naming the absent mentor of the gaze in the second Baudelaire essay, when he cites Proust as implicitly touching upon a theory of the aura: "'Some people who are fond of secrets flatter themselves that objects retain a trace of the looks that once rested upon them.' (What else but the ability of returning the gaze.)" (*I,* 188). The prototype of a look that leaves a residue, that lingers beyond its actualization in space and time, is the paternal look that children (of both sexes) know upon themselves even as they are separating, and which actually enables them to separate.[58] Assimilated to an Oedipal economy, the memory of this imagined glance is likely to succumb to repression—and hence bound to return as distant and strange. Elucidating Proust's "evasive" remarks, Benjamin shifts to Valéry's characterization of perception in dreams ("The things I see, see me just as much as I see them") to arrive at Baudelaire's lines, "*L'homme y passe à travers des forêts de symboles / Qui l'observent avec des regards familiers.*"[59] The "gaze heavy with distance" that Benjamin reads in Baudelaire's "*regard familier*" turns on the same axis that, according to Freud, links "*unheimlich*" to "*heimlich,*" a psychic ambivalence which challenges the narcissistic complacency of the gaze: "The deeper the absence of the counterpart which a gaze had to overcome, the stronger its spell. In eyes that merely mirror the other, this absence remains undiminished" (*I,* 189–90).

Benjamin undeniably participates in a patriarchal discourse on vision insofar as the auratic gaze depends upon a veil of forgetting, that is, a reflective yet unacknowledged form of fetishism which reinscribes the female body as source of both fascination and threat. In his almost obsessive and experimental undoing of that remystifying defense, however, he seems to be seeking a position in relation to vision, to the image and the eye, which has traditionally been assigned to women, as a group historically excluded from scopic mastery. Insofar as the social organization of vision is predicated on sexual difference, it is epitomized in the conventions of classical cinema which center the viewer in a position of voyeuristic separation and fetishistic distance. Given the centrality of the female image to a voyeuristically and fetishistically defined spectatorial pleasure, the woman's look occupies a precarious (if not impossible) place, because it remains too close to the body, narcissistically over-identified with the image.[60] The distance that appears in the auratic gaze is not exactly the same thing as the fetishistic distance that affords the male subject pleasure without anxiety (nor is the "absence" that the gaze has overcome to be equated with a Lacanian "lack").[61] On the contrary, the pre-Oedipal wish that propels, albeit in a semi-repressed mode, Benjamin's concept of the gaze potentially upsets the fetishistic balance of knowledge and belief, calling into question the binary opposition of distance and proximity that governs 'normal' vision, along with its alignment of sexual difference, subjectivity and identity. If anything, the auratic gaze seeks to unravel the compromise that sustains "the dummy, the self" so as to conjure up the memory of a different world, a "world distorted in the state of resemblance." By definition, such a mode of vision destabilizes the identical subject: "I have experience," Benjamin quotes from Kafka, "and I am not joking when I say that it is a seasickness on dry land" (*I*, 130).

To recapitulate: the register of distance and proximity in Benjamin's concept of the gaze—and theory of experience—exceeds spatial parameters, just as the gaze itself comprises both the visual sense and that of a phenomenological intentionality. Not only are distance and proximity entwined in a single metaphor of psychic ambivalence, but their political significance is bound up with the question of temporality, referring at once to the mnemonic slant of experience and to the historical conditions of its possibility; indeed, the congealing of the temporal dialectic of experience into spatial categories (the negative distance of reified labor or aesthetic contemplation, the illusory closeness of the commodified image) is itself a sign of the times. With the "optical unconscious," Benjamin readmits dimensions of temporality and historicity into his vision of the cinema, against his own endorsement of it as the medium of presence and tracelessness. The material fissure between a consciously and an "unconsciously permeated space" opens up a temporal gap for the viewer, a disjunction that may trigger recollection, and with it promises of reciprocity and intersubjectivity.[62] That these promises remain largely unrealized, given the imbrication of vision, narrative and subjectivity in classical cinema, does not diminish the critical force of the argument. Rather, it reminds us that the privatized, isolating and one-sided voyeurism that defines spectatorship in classical cinema represents a particular historical formation—and not necessarily an ontological function of the apparatus as theorized, for instance, by Metz and Baudry.

Moreover, the notion of the optical unconscious offers a perspective on marginalized forms of spectatorship, historically associated not only with early cinema (the "cinema of attractions") but also with the precarious position of female audiences in relation to classical modes of narration and address. Whether defensively stereotyped by male commentators or articulated in women's own analysis of their *Kinosucht* (addiction to the cinema), female spectatorship was often perceived as a mode of reception at once excessive and compensatory, as seeking a distance in the gaze which was increasingly denied by social reality—and, for that matter, by dominant film practice.[63] In her 1914 study of motion picture audiences, Emilie Altenloh found women—across class boundaries—generally responding more strongly than male moviegoers to the synaesthetic and kinetic aspects of film, besides expressing a greater interest in social dramas, especially if they featured female protagonists; and even though they were likely to have forgotten plot or title of a particular film, the women interviewed vividly remembered sentimental situations, as well as images of waterfalls, ocean waves or drifting ice-floes. In the over-identification with such images, in the failure to maintain a narratively stabilized distance, is there not an element of Benjamin's "daydreaming surrender to faraway things" (*I,* 191)? What is more, this different economy of distance and proximity also recalls a different organization of public and private spheres, a time when looking was not yet reduced to voyeuristic isolation. To quote Horkheimer and Adorno's notorious statement: "In spite of the films which are intended to enhance her integration, the housewife finds in the darkness of the movie theater a place of refuge where she can sit for a few hours free of obligations [*unkontrolliert*], just as she used to gaze out of the window, when there were still homes and the hour after a day's work [*Feierabend*]."[64] Such a mode of absorption may be regressive, to be sure, just as the identification—to the point of tears—with sentimental situations may not be wholly unrelated to masochism, yet it also has a cognitive function, in Adorno's words, in giving "temporary release [. . .] to the awareness that one has missed fulfillment."[65]

The affinity with a disposition attributed to female spectatorship crucially distinguishes Benjamin's notion of "distraction" from a Brechtian concept of distanciation (*Verfremdung*). Certainly, the political valorization of a distracted mode of reception (as first elaborated by Kracauer) converges with the intentions of epic theater in its negation of the bourgeois cult of culture, in its radical critique of fetishistic illusionism and corresponding attitudes of individual contemplation and catharsis. Likewise, we can see how Benjamin, in his search for contemporary aesthetic models, might have assimilated Brecht's strategy of demonstrating patterns of alienation (*Entfremdung*) through devices of estrangement (*Verfremdung*) to his own notion of a dialectical optics, the mimetic displacement he traced in Proust and the Surrealists. Yet the temporal gap that opens up with the optical unconscious, the surrender of spatial orientation to the gravity of the gaze, the memory image that seizes the beholder rather than vice versa—these aspects of Benjamin's theory of experience belie his endorsement of entertainment as critical expertise. If anything, distraction still contains the possibility of losing oneself, albeit intermittently, of abandoning one's waking self to the dreamlike, discontinuous sequence of sense impressions that Benjamin sought in his own experiments with hashish or drifting through the Paris Arcades.

The psychoanalytic undercurrent of Benjamin's quest for experience, finally, links the Marxian analysis of alienation to the frontier between psyche and body, the realm which Freud troped as the bodily ego. The notion of human self-alienation implies the historical exchange with nature as *Naturgeschichte,* just as the idea of a reconciliation with nature crucially entails accepting the memory of those aspects of human nature which are sacrificed, from generation to generation, for the sake of the social domination of non-human nature. While Benjamin knew well enough that ideology and class interest were most effective on the level of the unconscious, especially if propped onto Oedipal necessity, he nevertheless—like Adorno and, for that matter, Marcuse—took eros to be a source of resistance against social forms of identity, a defiance of fate.[66] Invariably, however, the subject's relationship to the body is governed by the same dialectic of forgetting and remembering as the auratic gaze and, like the latter, can be traced only through tropes of psychic ambivalence—distance and proximity, strangeness and familiarity. Thus Benjamin speaks in his essay on Kafka of the body, "one's own body," as "that most forgotten alien land [*Fremde*]" (*I,* 132; 126), a territory as strange and familiar as the frontier creatures that populate Kafka's tales.

Forgetting may be the prerequisite of auratic experience; but there is an aspect to forgetting which does not necessarily reach the reflective level of fetishism. Whether or not it plays a part in fetishism, the most purposeful form of forgetting is repression, and the price of repression is distortion, "the form that things assume in oblivion" (*I,* 133). The projection of a "mysterious guilt" that Benjamin observes in Kafka's figures of distortion (or in Tieck's "Fair Eckbert"[67]) takes us back once again into the domain of the uncanny. For the self which auratic vision calls up from a prehistoric past, unsolicited and unexpected, is a daemonic double, more likely an antagonist than a narcissistic ego-ideal.[68] Although he would not have concurred with the Freudian reading of this double, Gershom Scholem elucidates the importance of this figure in his speculations on "Benjamin's Angel," as a condensation of utopian, satanic and melancholy strands in his friend's troubled genius. Benjamin himself often enough associated auratic vision with a moment of danger, even the confrontation of death, as in the speech on Proust he delivered on his fortieth birthday (see epigraph). According to Scholem, this was the date of his intended—though at the time not executed—suicide.[69]

By the same token, the gap of human self-alienation that opens itself to the technically mediated gaze by virtue of the optical unconscious is not exactly of an idyllic, harmless, let alone nostalgic quality. Benjamin's recourse to psychoanalysis, especially in connection with the cinema, takes on its full significance only against the backdrop of the particular social and political constellation. In the first version of the Artwork Essay, the reference to Freud's *Psychopathology of Everyday Life* is missing; instead, the section on the "optical unconscious" is entitled "Mickey Mouse" and continues, past the ending of the section in the second version, with a speculation on its eponymic hero. With its techniques of mimetic figuration, Benjamin suggests, film can visualize a whole range of experiential modes outside so-called normal perception—deformations, displacements, catastrophes, forms of psychosis, hallucinations, dreams and nightmares—a process which involves translating individual experience into a collective form: "Film has launched an attack against the old Heraclitean truth, that in waking we share a world while sleeping we are each in separate worlds." This is evident, according to Benjamin, not so much in cinematic renderings of the dream world, but in "the creation of figures of the collective dream such as the earth-encircling Mickey Mouse" (*GS* I.2: 462).

The collective dream is as much subject to historical change as individual dreams, and just as he attempted to put a phenomenology of dreaming and waking at the service of historical materialism, Benjamin also insisted on the historicity of dreams themselves: "The statistical analysis of dreams would push beyond the serenity of anecdotal landscapes into the waste land of battle fields. Dreams have decreed wars, and wars since the beginning of time have settled right and wrong and have defined the limits of dreams."[70] Adorno, as is well known, had severe objections to Benjamin's notion of the "collective dream," not only because he suspected shades of Jung but because in his view any existing collectivity could only be false.[71] Right as he may have been in questioning Benjamin's political illusions concerning the self-organization of the proletariat, he underrated his friend's insights into mass psychology. The bourgeois taboo on sexuality, as Benjamin argues in another context, has imposed particular forms of repression upon the masses, thereby fostering the development of sadistic and masochistic complexes which could in turn be used for purposes of domination.[72] Thus, while references to Disney in the *Passagen-Werk* stress the utopian content, albeit weakened and repressed, of the collective fantasy, the Artwork Essay reads the figure of Mickey Mouse more specifically in terms of the political constellation of the 1930s. Given the technologically enhanced danger of mass psychosis, certain films may function as a kind of psychic vaccination: hyperbolizing sadistic phantasies and masochistic paranoia, they allow their viewers a premature and therapeutic acting out through collective laughter. In this historical constellation, Mickey Mouse joins the tradition of the American slapstick film, up to and including Chaplin, and as with the latter Benjamin never forgets that "the laughter [these films] provoke hovers over an abyss of horror."[73]

Benjamin's reflections on Mickey Mouse, cut from the final version on Adorno's advice, are remarkable especially in comparison with Horkheimer and Adorno's indictment of Donald Duck in their chapter on the "Culture Industry" in *Dialectic of Enlightenment* (1944). Much as the Disney films themselves may have changed in the intervening years, Horkheimer and Adorno's analysis of the sadomasochistic mechanisms operating in "the iron bath of fun" reveals a relatively reductive, behaviorist model of spectatorship: "Donald Duck in the cartoons, like the unfortunate in real life, gets a beating so that the viewers can get used to the same treatment."[74] Benjamin's conception of spectatorship is in the end more complex, because he is less interested in a critique of ideology than in redeeming the reified images of mass culture and modernity for a theory and politics of experience.

Granting film dimensions of figurative difference and mimetic experience that Horkheimer and Adorno reserved only for works of high art, Benjamin could envision a cinema that would be more than a medium of illusionist presence, a cinema that would release its archaic dream into a practice of profane illumination. To be sure, this vision has to be grounded in a critical analysis of the culture industry or, to use Hans Magnus Enzensberger's term, the "consciousness industry"—all the more since Horkheimer and Adorno's pessimistic assessment has not only been vindicated in retrospect but is daily being surpassed by political reality. Benjamin's concept of experience, however, with its emphasis on memory, historicity and intersubjectivity, remains a crucial ingredient in theories concerned with an alternative organization of the media, in particular Oskar Negt and Alexander Kluge's study, *Public Sphere and Experience* (1972). Adorno himself, especially in some of his later essays, resumed Benjamin's perspective, to some extent revising his earlier objections surrounding the issue of collectivity and reception.[75] I conclude with a quotation from Adorno's "Prologue to Television" (1953) which asserts the utopian promise of auratic distance in the very technology that appropriates and reproduces the viewer's desire as that of a consumer.

> It is impossible to prophesy what will become of television; its current state has nothing to do with the invention itself, not even the particular forms of its commercial exploitation, but with the social totality in and by which the

miracle is harnessed. The cliché which claims that modern technology has fulfilled the fantasies of the fairy tales only ceases to be a cliché if one adds to it the fairy tale wisdom that the fulfillment of wishes rarely benefits those who make them. The right way of wishing is the most difficult art of all, and we are taught to unlearn it from childhood on. Just as the man whom the fairy has granted three wishes spends them on wishing a sausage on his wife's nose and then wishing it away again, the contemporary whom the genius of human domination of nature allows to see into the distance perceives there nothing but the usual, embellished by the lie that it is different, which lends a cloak of false meaning to his existence. His dream of omnipotence is consummated as impotence. To this day, Utopias have been realized only to disabuse human beings of any utopian desire and commit them all the more thoroughly to the status quo, to fate. For television [*Fernsehen*, literally: seeing for] to realize the promise that still resonates in its name, it would have to emancipate itself from everything that revokes its innermost principle, the most daring sense of wish fulfillment, by betraying the idea of Great Happiness to the department store of the small comforts [*die Idee des Großen Glücks verrät ans Warenhaus fürs kleine*].[76]

Notes

1. "Das Kunstwerk im Zeitalter seiner technischen Reproduzierbarkeit" ("The Artwork in the Age of Its Technical Reproducibility"), *Gesammelte Schriften* (=*GS*), I.2, ed. Rolf Tiedemann and Hermann Schweppenhäuser (Frankfurt: Suhrkamp, 1974): 471–508; French version trans. Pierre Klossowski, pp. 709–739. The English version is included in *Illuminations*, trans. Harry Zohn, ed. Hannah Arendt (New York: Schocken Books, 1969): 217–51, in the following footnotes cited as *I*, translation in most cases modified. The *Illuminations* essay is reprinted in one of the most widely disseminated college textbooks in the field, Gerald Mast and Marchall Cohen's *Film Theory and Criticism: Introductory Readings*, third edition (New York: Oxford University Press, 1985): 675–694; this edition omits Benjamin's footnotes which contain large chunks from the handwritten and second (1974) versions. [Editors' Note: The first complete typed version of Bejamin's Artwork essay was published in *Gessamelte Schriften*, 7 (Frankfurt: Suhrkamp, 1989): 350–84; it was based on an earlier handwritten version of Benjamin's manuscript (pp. 431–469) upon which Hansen's 1987 essay is also based.

2. Tom Gunning, "The Cinema of Attraction: Early Film, Its Spectator and the Avant-Garde," *Wide Angle* 8.3/4 (1986): 63–70. The question of the difference or alterity of early cinema has been debated by a number of film scholars—among them Robert Allen, Charles Musser, Noël Burch, David Bordwell and Kristin Thompson. On the transgressive potential of eroticism in the star cult see my article, "Pleasure, Ambivalence, Identification: Valentino and Female Spectatorship," *Cinema Journal* 25.4 (Summer 1986): 6–32. Thomas Elsaesser examines similar questions with regard to the historical specificity of Weimar Cinema; see "Film History and Visual Pleasure: Weimar Cinema," in *Cinema Histories, Cinema Practices*, ed. Patricia Mellenkamp and Philip Rosen (Frederick, MD: University Publications of America, 1984), 47–84.

3. Siegfried Kracauer, "Die Photographie" (1927), in *Das Ornament der Masse* (Frankfurt: Suhrkamp, 1963; 1977), 38–39.

4. Jürgen Habermas, "Consciousness-Raising or Redemptive Criticism: The Contemporaneity of Walter Benjamin" (1972), *New German Critique* 17 (Spring 1979): 30–59; Habermas in fact includes the Soviet film of the twenties among the objects of Benjamin's redemptive criticism, a claim that is borne out by a comparison of the status of

Soviet film in the Artwork Essay with Benjamin's earlier, somewhat more distanced and critical report on "The Situation of Russian Film Art" (1927), *GS* II.2: 747–751, and his defense of *Battleship Potemkin* in his response to Oskar Schmitz, ibid., 751–55. The first to emphasize the redemptive thread running through Benjamin's work, connecting philosophy of history, aesthetic theory and the phenomenology of everyday life, was of course Siegfried Kracauer whose own work of the 1920s testifies to a deep affinity with such intentions, likewise rooted in Jewish mysticism: "Zu den Schriften Walter Benjamins" (1928), *Ornament der Masse*, 249–255. Also see Richard Wolin, *Walter Benjamin: An Aesthetic of Redemption* (New York: Columbia University Press, 1982).

    5. *Das Passagen-Werk* (=*PW*), ed. Rolf Tiedemann (Frankfurt: Suhrkamp, 1983), II: 1151. An important section of the *Passagen-Werk*, Konvolut N ("Epistemology, Theory of Progress"), trans. Leigh Hafrey & Richard Sieburth, is included in *The Philosophical Forum* 15.1–2 (Fall-Winter 1983–84): 1–40. On the relationship between the Artwork Essay and the *Passagen-Werk*, see Susan Buck-Morss, "Benjamin's *Passagen-Werk*: Redeeming Mass-Culture for the Revolution," *New German Critique* 29 (Spring/Summer 1983): 212.

    6. Epilogue to the Artwork Essay, *I*, 241–42; "Pariser Brief " (1936), *GS* III: 482–95; "Theories of German Fascism," *New German Critique* 17 (Spring 1979): 120–128. On the political context of Benjamin's rejection of the German aesthetic tradition, see Burkhardt Lindner, "Technische Reproduzierbarkeit und Kulturindustrie: Benjamins 'Positives Barbarentum' im Kontext," in: Lindner, ed., *"Links hatte noch alles sich zu enträtseln . . .": Walter Benjamin im Kontext* (Frankfurt: Syndikat, 1978), 180–223.

    7. *I*, 223, translation modified. Zohn's translation obliterates the crucial distinction between *Bild* and *Abbild*, obviously related terms which have acquired an anti-thetical meaning at this particular historical juncture: "Every day the urge grows stronger to get hold of an object at very close range by way of its likeness, its reproduction." Likeness, reproduction—same difference. At a loss for an antithetical term in what follows, Zohn instead constructs an opposition between "reproduction" on the one hand and "image seen by the unarmed eye" on the other, a free-style addition to Benjamin's text.

    8. Draft notes relating to the Artwork Essay, *GS* 1. 3: 1040; also see "Baudelaire," *I*, 175.

    9. Cf. Kracauer, "Cult of Distraction" (1926), *Ornament der Masse*, translation in *New German Critique* 40 (1987).

    10. The question of screen acting is treated at much greater length in the first two versions of the essay (*GS* 1.2: 449–455) where it furnishes an important link between Benjamin's notion of shock and the political function of the cinema, a point to which I will return later.

    11. "Erfahrung und Armut" (1933), *GS* II.1: 213–219. Other essays in which Benjamin tips the scales in this direction include "The Author as Producer" and some of his commentaries on Brecht (*Understanding Brecht* [London: NLB, 1973]) as well as the short piece, "The Destructive Character," *Reflections* (=*R*), ed. Peter Demetz, trans. Edmund Jephcott (New York: Harcourt Brace Jovanovich, 1978), 301–303. For a contextualizing defense of Benjamin's plea for a "positive barbarism," see Lindner (note 6, above).

    12. Marleen Stoessel, *Aura, das vergessene Menschliche: Zu Sprache und Erfahrung bei Walter Benjamin* (Munich: Hanser, 1983), 25. The following remarks to some extent retrace Stoessel's argument. Also see Habermas, 44–47.

    13. "Eine klein Geschichte der Photographie" ("A Short History of Photography"). *GS* II.1:378. There are several translations of this essay: one by Stanley Mitchell in *Screen* 13.1 (Spring 1972): 5–26; another in *One-Way Street and Other Writings*, trans. Edmund Jephcott and Kingsley Shorter (London: NLB, 1979); and a third—and probably least reliable—by Phil Patton in *Artforum* 15.6(February 1977): 46–61.

    14. "Central Park," *GS* I.2:670; *New German Critique* 34 (Winter 1985: 41; "On Some Motifs in Baudelaire," *GS* I.2: 646–47; *I*, 188.

    15. "On Language as Such and the Language of Man," *R*, 314–32; 325ff. In the kabbalistic framework of this essay, the motif of endowing nature with an answering gaze is

prefigured, in an acoustic and metaphysical dimension, in the problem of translation, in the disjunction between the mute language of nature and the multiplicity of human languages, and the fragmentary relationship of either to a paradisical language of names. Also see "The Task of the Translator" (1923), *I*, 69–82.

16. Perhaps deliberately understating the connection, Benjamin explains in a footnote that the endowment of nature with an answering gaze is "a source of poetry" and adds that "words, too, can have an aura," illustrating this remark with one of his favorite quotations from Karl Kraus: "The closer you look at a word, the greater the distance from which it looks back" (*I*, 200).

17. Stoessel, 45. Also see Benjamin's comments on Baudelaire's "correspondances" which are not simultaneous, as those of the Symbolistes, but are "data of remembrance," conveying the "murmur" of a prehistoric past (*I*, 182 and note 13, 198–99). The emphasis on the momentary, epiphantic character of auratic experience is linked to a Messianic concept of time, in particular the notion of *Jetztzeit*, the time of the Now.

18. Mary Ann Doane, "'When the Direction of the Force Acting on the Body Is Changed': The Moving Image," *Wide Angle* 7.1&2 (1985): 44. Doane's argument invokes both the Artwork Essay and Wolfgang Schivelbusch's Benjaminian study, *The Railway Journey: Trains and Travel in the 19th Century*, trans. Anselm Hollo (New York: Urizen, 1979).

19. *PW*, J76, 1. It is significant that this sentence is preceded by a description of auratic experience in the reciprocity of the erotic gaze, linking individual sexual desire to the Utopian longings of the human species, and followed by a somewhat laconic equation of the decay of the aura with the decay of potency. While the issue here is impotence in Baudelaire, along with the historical dissociation of sexus and eros (J72a, 2), Benjamin places it in a political context of the bourgeoisie's ceasing to concern itself with the future of the productive forces unleashed in its service, the decline of the Utopian imagination (J63a, 1; J75, 2). The connection between libidinal and political imagination is resumed in the second of Benjamin's "Theses on the Philosophy of History," *I*, 253–54 (even more explicit in the restored German edition, *GS* I.2: 693–94), where the redemptive promise of erotic happiness is established as the basis of that "weak Messianic power" which links every generation to the preceding ones and by which the past "is referred to redemption." In this context, also see Christine Buci-Glucksmann, *Walter Benjamin und die Utopie des Weiblichen* (Hamburg: VSA, 1984), 34–35.

20. Anson Rabinbach, "Between Enlightenment and Apocalypse: Benjamin, Bloch and Modern German Jewish Messianism," *New German Critique* 34 (Winter 1985): 78–124. Also see Gershom Scholem, *The Messianic Idea in Judaism* (New York: Schocken Books, 1971), 1–36. Rabinbach shows convincingly that Benjamin's theology of language cannot be separated from particular political configurations concerning the position of German Jews towards World War I, just as Benjamin scholars like Buck-Morss, Wohlfarth and Wolin have argued for a complex, if problematic, interdependence of his theological thought with his later Marxism. See Rolf Tiedemann, "Historical Materialism or Political Messianism?," *Philosophical Forum* 15.1–2 (Fall-Winter 1983–84): 71–104; Irving Wohlfarth, "On the Messianic Structure of Benjamin's Last Reflections," *Glyph* 3 (1978): 148–212.

21. The trajectory between allegorical destruction and redemption links Benjamin's earlier work, in particular *The Origin of German Tragic Drama* (1925) and his major essay on Goethe's *Elective Affinities* (1922), to his writings of the final years, especially section N of the *Passagen-Werk* and his "Theses on the Philosophy of History" (1940). Also see his "Central Park," 46: "The image of 'redemption' entails the firm, seemingly brutal grasp [*Zugriff*]."

22. *PW*, section K; K1, 1; K1a,8. Buck-Morss, "Passagen-Werk," 214ff.; Rudolf Tiedemann, Editor's Introduction, *PW*, 26ff.

23. Susan Buck-Morss, *The Origin of Negative Dialectics* (New York: The Free Press, 1977), 52–57 ("Natural History and Historical Nature"); Wolin, 166f.; Burkhardt Lindner, "'Natur-Geschichte': Geschichtsphilosophie und Welterfahrung in Benjamin's Schriften," *Text*

+ *Kritik* 31/32 (1971): 41–58. In his programmatic speech of 1932, "Die Idee der Naturgeschichte," Adorno resumed a crucial theme of Benjamin's study of the Baroque Trauerspiel and joined it with the Hegelian concept of "second nature" as elaborated by Lukács, in *History and Class Consciousness* (1923), in terms of Marx's analysis of commodity fetishism. Poststructuralist attempts to conflate Benjamin's concept of nature with a Barthesian notion of "myth" not only reduce the historical dialectic within the term but also occlude the utopian perspective of a "reconciliation with nature."

24. Buck-Morss, "*Passagen-Werk*," 213–14.

25. "Surrealism: The Last Snapshot of the European Intelligentsia" (February 1929), R, 181 (trans. modified). In a letter to Scholem of 1929, Benjamin refers to the Surrealism Essay as "an opaque paravent before the Arcades project" (*PW*, 1090). For an earlier statement on Surrealism see his "Traumkitsch" (1927), GS II.2: 620–22.

26. "Franz Kafka" (1934), *I*, 131; *Passagen-Werk* II: 1045.

27. Habermas, "Consciousness-Raising or Redemptive Criticism," 45–46.

28. "Surrealism," R, 192, 190; GS II. 1: 309f., 307. The political implications of this program are fleshed out more clearly in Adorno's commentary on Benjamin's recourse to the discourse of dreams: "The absurd is presented as if it were self-evident, in order to strip the self-evident of its power." *Über Walter Benjamin* (Frankfurt: Suhrkamp, 1970), 54. It should also be remembered that Benjamin saw Surrealism as a practical critique of official Marxism, the tradition of "metaphysical materialism" which has consistently neglected the unconscious and libidinal side of human experience and failed "to win the energies of intoxication for the revolution." Also see Benjamin's draft notes, GS II.3: 1021–41.

29. "Die Wiederkehr des Flaneurs" (review of Franz Hessel, *Spazieren in Berlin*, 1929), GS III: 194–99. One might as well substitute Benjamin's own writings on Berlin, "Berliner Kindheit um Neunzehnhundert" (1932; an earlier version of which is "A Berlin Chronicle," R, 3–60), as well as the fragments of *Einbahnstrasse* (1928) and the series entitled "Denkbilder," GS IV.1: 305–438. The "Denkbild" (thought image) is the medium of Benjamin's peculiar mode of theorizing which attempts to resolve the opposition between a philosophical (Kantian) concept of experience and the historical (and thus temporally disjunctive) texture of the lived moment. In this context, the importance of childhood memory for Benjamin's work cannot be emphasized often enough, in particular his insistence on the historicity of the childhood experience of each generation; see Buck-Morss, "*Passagen-Werk*," 217ff.

30. On "mimesis" in Adorno and Benjamin, see Buck-Morss, *Origin*, 87f. The concept is central, not only to the Frankfurt School's philosophy of history, most notably Horkheimer and Adorno's *Dialectic of Enlightenment* (1944), but also to Adorno's posthumously published *Aesthetic Theory* (1970).

31. Editors' commentary, GS II.3: 950–58; another source Benjamin himself suggests in a letter to Scholem is the kabbalistic book of Zohar.

32. Philip Rosen has recently drawn attention to the connection between indexicality and temporality in the film theory of André Bazin ("History of Image, Image of History: Subject and Ontology in Bazin," *Wide Angle*, forthcoming 1987). On the basis of Rosen's redemptive critique of Bazin, there are indeed some interesting parallels between Bazin and Benjamin, although their concepts of history are worlds apart, owing not only to the latter's commitment to historical materialism but likewise to a different religious and theological background.

33. GS II.1: 205, 210. The second version of the essay is translated in *Reflections*, 333–36; the first version, translated by Knut Tarnowski, with an introduction by Anson Rabinbach, in *New German Critique* 17 (Spring 1979): 65–69. In the following I rely on the first, longer version unless otherwise indicated.

34. "On Language as Such and on the Language of Man" (1916), R, 314–332; "The Task of the Translator" (1923), *I*, 69–82; 74; "Probleme der Sprachsoziologie: Ein Sammelreferat" (1935), GS III, 452–480; also see Rabinbach, "Introduction," 63.

35. On different directions in graphology, among which he singles out a more recent psychoanalytic approach against earlier positions, in particular Klages, see Benjamin, "Alte und neue Graphologie" (1930), *GS* IV.1,2: 596–98.

36. *R*, 336. It is no coincidence that, in a note relating to the mimetic faculty, the name of Brecht appears as an example of "a language purified of all magic elements" (GS II.3: 956).

37. Roland Barthes, "The Third Meaning: Research Notes on Some Eisenstein Stills" (1970), *Image-Music-Text*, ed. & trans. Stephen Heath (New York: Hill and Wang, 1977).

38. The most brilliant attempt to claim Benjamin for the tradition of linguistic skepticism is the late Paul de Man's reading of "The Task of the Translator," *Yale French Studies* 69 (1985): 25–46. "Now it is this motion, this errancy of language which never reaches the mark, which is always displaced in relation to what it meant to reach, it is this errancy of language, this illusion of a life that is only an afterlife, that Benjamin calls history. As such, history is not human, because it pertains strictly to the order of language; it is not natural, for the same reason; it is not phenomenal, in the sense that no cognition, no knowledge about man, can be derived from a history which as such is purely a linguistic complication; and it is not really temporal either, because the structure that animates it is not a temporal structure. Those disjunctions in language do get expressed by temporal metaphors, but they are only metaphors" (44). For an early response to deconstructionist readings of Benjamin, see Irving Wohlfarth, "Walter Benjamin's Image of Interpretation," *New German Critique* 17 (Spring 1979): 70–98.

39. *PW*, N2a,5; N3,1. "Theses on the Philosophy of History," *GS* I.2: 702–03, *I*, 262–64.

40. *GS* II.1: 311; *I*, 202; "On Some Motifs in Baudelaire," sections II and III; "Madame Ariane," *R*, 89.

41. Wohlfarth, "Image of Interpretation," 80.

42. The first version of the Artwork Essay still includes a reference to Jensen (*GS* I.2:440). Zohn's translation of the phrase as "sense of the universal equality of things" (*I*, 223) substitutes political pathos for physiognomic perception, exaggerating Benjamin's own tendency in the Essay.

43. Christian Metz, *The Imaginary Signifier* (Bloomington: Indiana University Press, 1982); and Jean-Louis Baudry, "Ideological Effects of the Basic Cinematic Apparatus," repr. in Philip Rosen, ed., *Narrative, Apparatus, Ideology* (New York: Columbia University Press, 1986), part 3.

44. Buck-Morss, "*Passagen-Werk*," 214.

45. Also see Benjamin's review of Aragon, "Traumkitsch" (1927), which begins with a reference to Novalis' *Heinrich von Ofterdingen*: "It is not so easy any more to dream of the Blue Flower"—instead of opening up a blue distance, the dream world has turned gray with dust (*GS* II.2: 620).

46. Laura Mulvey, "Visual Pleasure and Narrative Space"; Stephen Heath, "Narrative Space," both reprinted in Rosen, ed. Narrative, Apparatus, Ideology; Mary Ann Doane, "Miscognition and Identity," *Ciné-Tracts* 3.3 (Fall 1980): 25–32; Teresa de Lauretis, *Alice Doesn't* (Bloomington: Indiana University Press, 1984), esp. ch. 5.

47. *GS* II.1: 380; 379. The auratic connotation, inseparable from Benjamin's political assessment of photography, obviously gets lost when "*namenlose Erscheinung*" is translated as "anonymity" (*Screen* 13.1: 21); for a link between Benjamin's kabbalistic notion of the "name"—as in the paradisical language of names—and his concept of mimesis, of similarity as the organon of experience, see *PW*, 1038; also Buck-Morss, *Origin*, 88–90.

48. Epstein, *Bonjour Cinéma*, especially the essays "Grossissement" ("Magnification," *October* 3 [1977]: 9–15) and "Le Ciné-Mystique" (*Millennium Film Journal* 10–11 [Fall-Winter 1982–83]: 191–93), both translated by Stuart Liebman whom I thank for drawing my attention to Epstein's review of Herbier's *El Dorado* in *L'Ésprit Nouveau* 14 (Oct./Nov. 1921): 1969–70. On the psychoanalytic undercurrent in Balázs's film theory, see Gertrud Koch, "Béla Balázs: The Physiognomy of Things," *New German Critique* 40 (1987). Also see Balázs's amazing essay, "Physiognomie" (1923), which anticipates not only the notion of an optical

unconscious but also key aspects of Benjamin's theory of mimetic reading, including a similar concept of "distance," *Schriften zum Film* I, ed. Helmut H. Diederichs (Munich: Hanser, 1982), 205–8.

49. Kracauer, "Die Photographie" (note 3, above), 24–25, 28, 32, 37–39; also see Heide Schlüpmann, "Phenomenology of Film: On Siegfried Kracauer's Writings of the 1920s," *New German Critique* 40 (1987).

50. "Short History of Photography," *GS* II.1: 371; *Screen* 13.1: 8. Also see Benjamin's remarks on the complementary relationship between star cult and the "cult of the public" in the Artwork Essay, first version (*GS* I.2: 452; 456) which anticipate an important point of Horkheimer and Adorno's critique of the Culture Industry. On the question of the "fourth look"—the look of the character at the spectator which breaks the voyeuristic fiction—see Paul Willemen, "Letter to John," *Screen* 21.2 (Summer 1980): 53–65, 56; Peter Lehman, "Looking at Ivy Looking at Us Looking at Her: The Camera and the Garter," *Wide Angle* 5.3 (1983): 59–63.

51. Cf. For conflicting interpretations of Benjamin's notion of "shock," see Karl Heinz Bohrer, *Die Ästhetik des Schreckens: Die pessimistische Romantik und Ernst Jüngers Frühwerk* (Munich: Hanser, 1978), part III, and Ansgar Hillach, "Erfahrungsverlust und 'chockförmige Wahrnehmung': Benjamins Ortsbestimmung der Wahrnehmung im Zeitalter des Hochkapitalismus," *Alternative* 132/33 (1980): 110–118; also see Stoessel, 238f.

52. Stoessel, 161.

53. "Erwiderung an Oscar A.H. Schmitz" (1927), *GS* II.2: 753. The review of *Berlin Alexanderplatz* is entitled "The Crisis of the Novel," *GS* III: 230–36; on montage, 232f. The function of film, as of Döblin's novel, is similar to that Benjamin ascribed to the flaneur as "epic narrator"—a sharpening of the "sense of reality, a sense for chronicle, document, detail" (III: 194).

54. Letter from Adorno to Benjamin, 29 February 1940; Benjamin's response, 7 May, 1940, repr. *GS* I.3: 1130–35; 1132.

55. Stoessel, 61f., 72–77, and ch. 5, especially 130ff. Adorno, in his letter to Benjamin, had proposed a distinction between two kinds of forgetting that come into play in Benjamin's theory of experience, an "epic" and a "reflectory" ["*reflektorisches*"] forgetting (*GS* I.3: 1131). It would be interesting to consider this distinction in light of the ambiguity that riddles Freud's own interpretation of fetishism, as to whether the fetishist's inconsistency is located in processes of repression (i.e. in the unconscious) and a compromise-formation ("Fetishism" [1927]) or whether it actually entails a splitting on the same level, as in his later text, "Splitting of the Ego in the Process of Defense" (1938); J. Laplanche & J.-B. Pontalis, *The Language of Psychoanalysis*, trans. D. Nicholson-Smith (New York: W.W.Norton, 1973), 119.

56. *I*, 187; my emphasis.

57. Freud, *On Creativity and the Unconscious* (New York: Harper & Row, 1958), 152–53; trans. modified.

58. Jessica Benjamin, "A Desire of One's Own: Psychoanalytic Feminism and Intersubjective Space," Center for Twentieth Century Studies, Milwaukee, *Working Papers* 2 (Fall 1985), 9ff.

59. "Man wends his way through forests of symbols / Which look at him with their familiar glances" (*I*, 181–82; 189).

60. Mary Ann Doane, "Film and the Masquerade: Theorizing the Female Spectator," *Screen* 23.3–4 (Sept.–Oct. 1982): 74–87; 78–80.

61. Terry Eagleton attempts to read Benjamin's concept of the gaze through Lacan ("Of the Gaze as *Object Petit a*") in *Walter Benjamin or Towards a Revolutionary Criticism* (London: Verso, 1981), 38f.; this attempt—as most of the book—bears out the metaphor of cannibalism which culminates in the author's poem, "Homage to Walter Benjamin" (184). Undoubtedly, there are a number of contiguities between Benjamin and Lacan's concept of the gaze (perhaps owing to a common phenomenological undercurrent), but there are also

crucial differences: Benjamin, like Freud, was obsessed with questions of temporality and memory; Lacan's concepts, as far as I can tell, fundamentally rely upon spatial models, which may account for their often criticized lack of historicity.

62. This temporal gap that opens up in the world of things has nothing to do with the time-lag between seeing and knowing that assures the male child a cognitive superiority with regard to the regime of castration (Doane, "Masquerade," 79f.). Rather, it is structurally closer to the effect of "*trompe l'oeil*" which Doane describes in her essay on "The Moving Image" (note 18, above), 45–49, as an undoing of a psychical defense by staggering and thereby breaking down into its elements the compromise of knowledge and belief that constitutes fetishism.

63. Patrice Petro, "Perceptions of Difference: Contours of a Discourse on Sexuality in Early German Film Theory," *New German Critique* 40 (1987): 115–146; Heide Schlüpmann, "Kinosucht," *Frauen und Film* 33 (Oct. 1982): 45–52; Hansen, "Early Silent Cinema: Whose Public Sphere," *New German Critique* 29 (Spring/Summer 1983): 147–84; 173ff. The term "Kinosucht" is used in Emilie Altenloh's dissertation, *Zur Soziologie des Kino* (Leipzig: Spamersche Buchdruckerei, 1914), 65. Benjamin himself, in the first version of the Artwork Essay, singles out women as a particularly susceptible target for the capitalist film industry's strategies of illusory mass participation (*GS* I.1: 456). On the other hand, he motivates his "philosophical" interest in fashion by referring to "the extraordinary scent [*Witterung*] which the female collective has for things awaiting us in the future" *PW*, B1a, 1).

64. Max Horkheimer and Theodor W. Adorno, *Dialectic of Enlightenment* (1944; 1947), trans. John Cumming (New York: Seabury Press, 1969), 139.

65. Adorno, "On Popular Music," *Studies in Philosophy and Social Science* 9.1 (1941): 41–42.

66. See *PW*, O1,1, where he links sexual libido to the kabbalistic concept of the "name": "The name itself is the cry of naked lust." Also see "Eduard Fuchs, Collector and Historian" (1937), trans. Knut Tarnowski, *New German Critique* 5 (Spring 1975); 27–58; 50–54. The idea of a reconciliation with nature in the end turns on this libidinal materialism, just as the notion of a "complicity of nature with the liberated human being" which children know from fairy tales is associated with the rare experience of erotic bliss (*Glück*) (,I 102).

67. Stoessel points out that the repressed which returns in Tieck's story as uncanny is the "forgotten" knowledge that the hero's deceased wife was actually his half-sister (*Aura*, 138f.). Though Benjamin invokes this story again in his exchange with Adorno concerning the question of forgetting, he carefully avoids any reference to the incestuous nature of the "mysterious guilt."

68. Freud discusses the phenomenon of the daemonic double in his essay on the uncanny (*On Creativity and the Unconscious*, 140–143). At a later point in the essay, he reports two incidents—one autobiographical and one involving the physicist Ernst Mach— illustrating the shock of seeing oneself or, rather, mistaking one's own image for someone else's, in Mach's case a "shabby-looking school-master" and in his personal case an unpleasant looking elderly gentleman (156). Doane elaborates on this effect (which in both cases is linked to movement) as an instance of the *trompe l'oeil* ("When the Direction . . .," 44ff.).

69. Scholem, "Walter Benjamin and His Angel" (1972), in *On Jews and Judaism in Crisis* (New York: Schocken Books, 1976), 198–236; 236. Also see Scholem's *Walter Benjamin: The Story of a Friendship*, trans. Harry Zohn (Philadelphia: Jewish Publication Society of America, 1981), 186ff.

70. "Traumkitsch," *GS* II.2: 620.

71. Adorno, "On the Fetish Character in Music and the Regression of Listening" (1938), repr. in *The Essential Frankfurt School Reader*, ed. Andrew Arato & Eike Gebhardt (New York: Urizen, 1978), 270–99; this essay was intended as a response to the Artwork Essay. Also see letters to Benjamin, tr. H. Zohn, in *Aesthetics and Politics* (London: NLB, 1977), 113, 118f., 123f.

72. "Eduard Fuchs," 51.

73. *GS* I.2: 462; II.2: 753. In Benjamin's radically anti-auratic essay, "Experience and Poverty" (1933), Mickey Mouse appears in a somewhat ambiguous role as the dream hero of those who are fed up with the accumulated experiences of culture and humanity (*GS* II.1: 218f.). In the material accompanying the Artwork Essay, however, we find the fragmentary note: "The availability of Disney's method for fascism" (*GS* I.3: 1045).

74. *Dialectic of Enlightenment*, 138 (trans. modified).

75. See especially his essay, "Transparencies on Film" (1966), trans. Thomas Y. Levin, *New German Critique* 24–25 (Fall/Winter 1981–82): 199–205; further references in my introduction to this essay, 186–198.

76. Adorno, *Eingriffe* (Frankfurt: Suhrkamp, 1963), 80.

Modernity and Mass Culture in Weimar: Contours of a Discourse on Sexuality in Early Theories of Perception and Representation

PATRICE PETRO

"BERLIN," WRITES one historian, "aroused powerful emotions in every-one. It delighted most, terrified some, but left no one indifferent, and it induced, by its vitality, a certain inclination to exaggerate what one saw."[1] The pertinence of these remarks for an analysis of representation and theories of perception in Weimar cannot be underestimated. Indeed, for journalists, artists and intellectuals in Germany of the 1920s, Berlin served not only as a convenient short-hand for a number of technological innovations thought to profoundly alter perception and experience (trains, automobiles, and telephones as well as photography, photojournalism, and film); even more crucially, Berlin also served as the decisive metaphor for modernity, and modernity was almost invariably represented as a woman.

There are, of course, historical grounds for associating Berlin of the 1920s with modernity: as the capital of the Reich and the most populated and industrialized of all German cities, Berlin was also the center for mass cultural entertainment, a fact which is hardly remarkable given that large scale urbanization was the precondition for the expansion and differentiation of the mass cultural audience in Germany.[2] What *is* remarkable, however, is that contemporary observers repeatedly imagined the city to take a female form. For example, in a 1929 issue of *Der Querschnitt*, an Ullstein magazine for intellectuals, Harold Nicholson describes the particular charm of Berlin by invoking the figure of woman as metaphor for the enigmatic and, hence, desirable "otherness" of the city:

> What on earth gives this city its charm! Movement in the first place. There is no city in the world so restless as Berlin. Everything moves. The traffic lights change restlessly from red to gold and then to green. The lighted advertisements flash with the pathetic iteration of coastal lighthouses . . . Second to movement comes frankness. London is an old lady in black lace and diamonds who guards her secrets with dignity and to whom one would not tell those secrets of which one was ashamed. Paris is a woman in the prime of life to whom one would only tell those secrets which one desires to be repeated. But Berlin is a girl in a pullover, not much powder on her face, Hölderlin in her pocket, thighs like those of Atalanta, an undigested educa-

Reprinted from *New German Critique* 40 (1987): 115–146.

tion, a heart which is almost too ready to sympathize, and a breadth of view
which charms one's repressions . . . The maximum irritant for the nerves corrected by the maximum sedative. Berlin stimulates like arsenic, and then
when one's nerves are all ajingle, she comes with her hot milk of human
kindness; and in the end, for an hour and a half, one is able, gratefully, to go
to sleep.[3]

Where Nicholson calls upon the image of the female adolescent (the
"girl in a pullover, not much powder on her face") to describe the curious
mixture of old and new in the city, playwright Carl Zuckmayer invokes a far
more sexualized and, indeed, far more demonic female figure to describe
what he sees as Berlin's peculiar mixture of seduction and cruelty:

This city devoured talents and human energies with a ravenous appetite,
grinding them small, digesting them, or rapidly spitting them out again. It
sucked into itself with hurricane force all the ambitions in Germany, the true
and the false . . . and, after it had swallowed them, ignored them. People discussed Berlin . . . as if Berlin were a highly desirable woman, whose coldness
and capriciousness were widely known: the less chance anyone had to win
her, the more they decried her. We called her proud, snobbish, *nouveau
riche*, uncultured, crude. But secretly everyone looked upon her as the goal
of their desires. Some saw her as hefty, full-breasted, in lace underwear, others as a mere wisp of a thing, with boyish legs in black silk stockings. The
daring saw both aspects, and her very capacity for cruelty made them the
more aggressive. All wanted to have her, she enticed all . . . To conquer
Berlin was to conquer the world. The only thing was—and this was the ever-
lasting spur—that you had to take all the hurdles again and again, had to
break through the goal again and again in order to maintain your position.[4]

Berlin, it is obvious, inspired powerful emotions in everyone and
induced a tendency to exaggerate what one saw. Yet it is equally obvious
that this tendency to exaggerate in representing Berlin as a woman reveals
less about women in Weimar than it does about a male desire that simultaneously elevates and represses woman as object of allure and as harbinger
of danger. While it would seem that Zuckmayer's claim that "to conquer
Berlin was to conquer the world" defines the particular contours of this
male desire, it is, in fact, his admission that "you had to take all the hurdles again and again . . . to maintain your position" which reveals its fundamental paradox: the paradox of a male fascination with femininity which
threatens to subvert masculine identity, and which therefore requires the
constant work of repression and projection so as to keep the fears and
anxieties provoked by woman at a safe and measured distance.

The passages I have cited from Nicholson and Zuckmayer are far from
anomalous. One need only look at the images of the city made famous in
the paintings of Georg Grosz and Otto Dix, or read the city poems of
Bertolt Brecht, Erich Kästner and Walter Mehring, to realize how numer-

ous artists and writers responded to modernity by imaginatively re-constructing Berlin as demonic, as alienating, and as female. Even an apparently abstract film like Walter Ruttmann's *Berlin: Symfonie einer Grossstadt* (1927) builds its investigation of spatial and visual fragmenta-tion around the spectacle of woman—a spectacle barely hidden at the (narrative) center of the film. Yet if there thus exists a wealth of evidence to read responses to modernity in Weimar as constructed upon male subjectivity and desire—where woman is absent as subject and yet over-present as object—I would nevertheless like to raise the following ques-tions: What kind of historical response to modernity does the textual and artistic inscription of woman in Weimar conceal? And can we discern in this historical response another way of talking about subjectivity, per-ception and sexual difference in Germany of the 1920s? In other words, is there a way to reread early discussions of modernity in Weimar so as to situate woman as an inhabitant of the city she so frequently serves to represent?

To begin to answer these questions, we need to recall that the Weimar years were not only marked by multiple political, economic and social crises, but also that these crises were often experienced as contributing to the loss of (male) cultural authority.[5] That responses to the loss of this authority inevitably involved woman should hardly come as a surprise, especially when we reflect on the fact that it was only in the early twenti-eth century that the woman's movement gained a contending voice in German political and cultural life.[6] In this regard, it is all the more signifi-cant that artists and intellectuals construed modernity as feminine, and as effecting an almost complete transformation of the cultural and perceptu-al field. While mass culture in general was frequently associated with modernity (and hence, as several theorists have pointed out, with woman),[7] it was the cinema in particular which seemed to crystallize the relationships between modern life, modes of perception and male per-ceptions of gender.

Art critic and theorist Egon Friedell, for example, expressed the widely held belief that perception and representation had been transformed under the impact of industrialization when he remarked in 1912: "the film is short, quick, somewhat fractured, and it stops at nothing. It has some-thing curtailed, something precise, something military about it. This fits in well with the modern era, which is an era of extracts. For today we are less concerned with the idyllic relaxation or epic repose with objects that was considered poetic in the past."[8] While the loss of a poetic repose with objects concerned a theorist like Friedell, other critics, particularly those on the political left, celebrated the loss of this repose in the cinema for dispensing with outmoded aesthetic values and for inaugurating an address to a mass industrial audience. Significantly, however, even critics on the left warned against the tendency of the cinematic image to immobi-

lize the spectator, to induce a passive response characteristic of technological modes of production more generally. As Spartacist poet, Bruno
Schönlank, describes in his poem "Kino";

> . . . Factory workers, tired
> from the drudgery of the day.
> Salesgirls, seamstresses, spinning
> golden fairy tales of luck and the wages of true love
> Beautiful girls follow the pictures
> and swallow in the lies.
> They gladly let themselves be led astray
> by that which enchants their souls.
> Drunk with the glitter they return home
> and in the dark room see yet another light,
> which breaks through their dreams as bright as the sun
> till grey everyday life puts it out again.[9]

This description of cinematic spectatorship suggests how discussions
about representation and perception in Weimar were often divided along
sexual lines. According to Schönlank, the appeal of the cinema derives
from its illusory plenitude ("golden fairy tales of luck and the wages of
true love") which draws one closer; and, in his view, it is the female spectator—and not her male counterpart (represented by the poet himself)—
who proves most susceptible to the cinematic illusion, who is unable to
achieve a critical distance from it.[10] Far from being understood as a spectator who assumes an "epic repose" (a repose considered poetic in the
past), the female viewer is understood as that spectator not only willingly
duped by the image, but also most easily deceived by its lies.

While early assessments of perception and spectatorship in Germany
hardly promote a neutral understanding of spectatorship and sexual difference, it would be a mistake to assume that current discussions of spectatorship have somehow moved beyond the implicit premises of these early
debates. Indeed, notions about modernity that circulated in turn-of-the-
century Germany—where woman is both equated with the image and, at
the same time, situated as that spectator unable to separate from it—continue to inform even the most sophisticated analyses of perception and
subjectivity in current film theory. Most strikingly, contemporary film theorists retain the assumption that film technology so profoundly alters perception and experience that it completely reorganizes the spectator's
relationship to space, vision and structures of desire.

In his essays on psychoanalysis and the cinema, for instance, Christian
Metz invokes the metaphor of the cinema as an "apparatus"—a technological, institutional, and psychical "machine"—so as to suggest how the film
spectator internalizes certain historically constituted and socially regulated

modes of psychical functioning.[11] According to Metz, the cinema is more perceptual than other arts, since it mobilizes a larger number of axes of perception: analogical image, graphic image, sound, speech, dialogue. But, as Metz points out, if the film is thus more perceptually present than other art forms, that which it depicts is manifestly absent. Metz therefore concludes that the cinema involves the spectator in the Imaginary, where the absence of the objects seen provokes a realignment of spectatorial knowledge and desire. As Metz explains:

> How can one say that the visual and auditory drives have a stronger or more special relationship with the absence of their object, with the infinite pursuit of the Imaginary? Because, as opposed to other sexual drives, the 'perceiving drive' . . . concretely represents the absence of its object in the distance at which it maintains it and which is part of its very definition: distance of the look, distance of listening . . . To fill in this distance would threaten to overwhelm the subject, to lead him to consume the object (the object which is now too close so that he cannot see it anymore) . . .[12]

Since cinematic representation entails the absence of the object seen, and since all desire depends on the infinite pursuit of an absent object, Metz maintains that film spectatorship can only be delineated in terms of voyeurism or fetishism—as precisely a pleasure in looking at a distance. Although Metz does not concern himself with questions of gendered spectatorship, his description of the relationship between film technology and perception nevertheless raises fundamental issues about the function of gender in spectatorial response. Most obviously, are we to assume that the woman's relationship to the image is the same as a man's, and that she, too, partakes of a (male) voyeuristic or fetishistic pleasure in looking?

In an attempt to respond to this question, Mary Ann Doane has proposed that "both the theory of the image and its apparatus, the cinema, produce a position for the female spectator . . . which is ultimately untenable because it lacks the attributes of distance so necessary for an adequate reading of the image."[13] As Doane goes on to explain, the female spectator's infamous inability to distance herself from the image—her tendency to "over-identify" with events on the screen—suggests that the woman is constituted differently than the man in relation to the image and to structures of looking. "For the female spectator," Doane writes, "there is a certain over-presence of the image—she *is* the image. Given the closeness of this relationship, the female spectator's desire can be described only in terms of narcissism—the female look demands a becoming. It thus appears to negate the very distance or gap specified by Metz . . . as the essential precondition of voyeurism."[14]

Although Doane takes pains to modify the Metzian model by theorizing a kind of fetishism available to the female viewer (what Doane calls the "masquerade"), her discussion of female spectatorship significantly rests upon notions of perception and sexual difference that tend to corrobo-rate—rather than challenge—certain time-honored assumptions about see-ing and knowing in the cinema. In line with Metz, for example, Doane attributes knowledge and pleasure in the cinema to a necessary distance from the image. As she proposes, the mode of looking developed by the cinema depends on an image of woman which is fixed and held for the pleasure and reassurance of the male viewer. While this image automati-cally produces voyeuristic or fetishistic separation in the male spectator, she explains, it also threatens to overwhelm and consume the female spec-tator for whom that image is too close, too present, too recognizable. For this reason, Doane surmises that when the female spectator fails to dis-tance herself from the image of woman, she necessarily merges with that image and, consequently, loses herself. In thus equating cinematic percep-tion with a male epistemology, Doane winds up affirming the theory of spectatorship she initially sets out to expose: conflating vision with intel-lection, Doane maintains that the female spectator can only "see" (and thus assume a position of knowledge) in the cinema by manufacturing a distance from the image and taking up the position of fetishist. In a formu-lation of the problem that is remarkably close to Metz's own, she writes; "A machine for the production of images and sounds, the cinema generates and guarantees pleasure by a corroboration of the spectator's identity. Because that identity is bound up with that of the voyeur and the fetishist . . . it is not accessible to the female spectator, who, in buying her ticket, must deny her sex."[15]

Unlike early German film theorists, Metz and Doane ground their analy-ses of perception and spectatorship in rigorous psychoanalytic concepts. Yet behind these psychoanalytic concepts lies an historical argument about modernity and perceptual response that also locates gendered spec-tatorship within the terms of a phallocentric discourse. Indeed, Freudian psychoanalysis is itself premised upon a far from impartial reading of his-tory: Freud, like several theorists after him, identifies the transition from a matriarchal to a patriarchal society in the simultaneous promotion of sens-es at a distance (i.e. sight and hearing) and devaluation of senses of con-tact (i.e. touch, taste and smell).[16] The perceptual distance thought to provide a privileged means of access to knowledge and pleasure in psy-choanalytic accounts of film spectatorship thus derives its force from a his-torical argument which gives sight a quite specific meaning; to borrow from Doane, it is not sight in general, but the sight of the female body which provokes the defensive, and thus more mediated visual response of the film voyeur and fetishist.[17]

I believe there is sufficient cause to challenge psychoanalytic descrip-tions of perception and subjectivity with respect to gendered spectator-ship; and, indeed, the most useful feminist reappraisals of psychoanalytic theory have been those which have taken concepts of voyeurism, fetishism and narcissism on their own terms and demonstrated how each elides questions of female subjectivity so as to confirm male modes of knowing in patriarchy. But I also believe that we need to challenge the historical argument underpinning discussions of perceptual and visual response in psychoanalytic film theory, and to work back through the clichés about gendered spectatorship so as to recognize how they conceal a fairly complex history rooted in responses to modernity and male perceptions of sexual difference. It will be my concern in the following pages to offer such a challenge, and to trace concepts relating to perception and spectatorship back to philosophical and theoretical debates over mass culture and modernity as they were waged in Germany of the 1920s.

I will focus on the writings of Martin Heidegger, Walter Benjamin, and Siegfried Kracauer, since each of these theorists aims to underline the historical nature of subjectivity and identity, and thus to situate perceptual changes within a profoundly historical understanding of modernity. To be sure, there are several other important theorists who wrote about spectatorship and perception during the Weimar years; notably, Béla Balázs, Rudolf Arnheim and Bertolt Brecht. For several reasons, however, I believe the work of Heidegger, Benjamin and Kracauer is most useful for reconsidering the relationship between mass culture, perception and modern experience, and for discerning the contours of a discourse on sexuality that continues to shape our understanding of cinematic representation and spectatorship.

Without a doubt, each of these theorists exerts considerable influence on the ways in which contemporary scholars approach questions of representation and subjectivity as they relate to the problem of modernity.[18] Beyond the current interest in the work of these theorists, however, I believe that a reexamination of their writings from a feminist perspective will allow us to pursue issues of gendered spectatorship in a far more precise manner than has hitherto been the case. Rather than appeal to the operative binarisms familiar to contemporary film theory (active/passive, absence/presence, distance/proximity), Heidegger, Benjamin and Kracauer define the impact of technology on perception in a much more differentiated and subtle manner. The notions of "contemplation" and "distraction," for instance, enable these theorists to describe the difference between artistic and mass cultural reception, and yet to conceptualize the simultaneous response of passivity and activity, proximity and distance in the spectator's relation to the image. This is not to say that Heidegger, Benjamin or Kracauer completely agreed on the historical meaning of changes in perceptual response. Indeed, not only do all three theorists take different approaches to questions of modernity, but they also exhibit markedly distinct attitudes towards the social and political function of mass cultural spectatorship—attitudes ranging from contempt to ambivalence to celebration.

Most importantly, however, the writings of Heidegger, Benjamin and Kracauer disclose a historical dimension to modernity which allows us to take up questions of gender and spectatorship as they exist, as it were, between the lines of the debate over mass culture. For all three theorists, it is male spectatorship which remains the (unspoken) subject of theoretical exploration. Nevertheless, because they stress the historicity of experience, their writings unwittingly reveal how the coincidence of cinematic technology with the crisis of perception (where the subject becomes an object) is inseparable from the crisis of male authority and the emergence of women's demands for an equal share in German culture. For this reason, the writings of Heidegger, Benjamin and Kracauer provide us with a way of contesting traditional notions of perceptual response and gendered spectatorship, and thus with a way of recognizing in the metaphors of modernity both the city and the cinema in Weimar which were, undeniably, inhabited by women.

PERCEPTION, MASS CULTURE AND DISTRACTION: THE
PHENOMENOLOGY OF MARTIN HEIDEGGER

Everything is going on as if reading Heidegger had nothing to do with sexual difference, and nothing to do with man himself, or, said in another way, as if it had nothing to do with woman, nothing to interrogate or suspect . . . Perhaps one could even speak of [Heidegger's] silence as uppity, precisely arrogant, provocative, in a century where sexuality is common to all the small talk and also a currency of philosophical and scientific knowledge, the inevitable *Kampfplatz* of ethics and politics . . . And yet, the matter seems to be understood so little or so badly that Heidegger had immediately to account for it. He had to do it in the margins of *Being and Time* . . .[19]

Jacques Derrida

There are certainly a number of reasons for the continual appeal to Heideggerian phenomenology in contemporary theories of culture and representation. Most obviously, contemporary theorists are drawn to Heidegger's attempt to think more primordially about modern existence—his effort to transcend the division between subject and object by subordinating epistemology to ontology so that critical understanding ceases to be a simple "knowing" in order to become a way of "being." Part of the appeal of this primordial thinking, however, undoubtedly derives from Heidegger's effort to get beyond questions of sexual difference and thus to transcend that inevitable *Kampfplatz* where the sexual is political and vice versa.

And yet, as Derrida himself insists, Heidegger only appears to be silent on questions of sexuality and sexual difference, for in both his early writings on experience and his later writings on language, Heidegger had quite specific things to say about gender (even if he did relegate these remarks to the margins of his philosophy). To fully understand Heidegger's views on gender, it is necessary to outline his position on modernity; indeed, as we shall see, Heidegger's approach to the question of sexual duality in experience was fundamentally linked to his exploration of modernity and mass culture.

In his *magnum opus* on modernity and experience, *Being and Time* (*Sein und Zeit*, 1927), Heidegger railed against the technological thinking of the modern age, and thus communicated something of the sense of urgency that pervaded German culture in the wake of World War I. As one historian explains, "Heidegger's life—his isolation, his peasant-like appearance, his deliberate provincialism, his hatred of the city—seemed to confirm his philosophy, which was a disdainful rejection of modern urban rationalist civilization."[20] Or, in the words of Hans Georg Gadamer, who refers less to the man himself than to the reception of his writing: "The contemporary reader of Heidegger's first systematic work was seized by the vehemence of its passionate protest against . . . the levelling effects of all individual forms of life by industrial society, with its ever stronger uniformities and its techniques of communication and public relations that manipulated everything."[21]

Heidegger's critique of modernity and technological forms of communication cannot be separated from his critique of epistemology for its holding vision to be a superior means of access to certainty and truth. In *Being and Time*, for example, he refers to a modern obsession with the visual over other sensory faculties and describes this as a privileging of seeing (*sehen*) over understanding (*verstehen*) which contributes to the impoverishment of the senses and a fundamental "distraction" (*Zerstreuung*). In contrast to "concern," or a mode of perception guided by circumspection and contemplation, "distraction" lends itself to what Heidegger calls a "restless" and "curious" gaze. He writes:

> When curiosity has become free . . . it concerns itself with seeing, not in order to understand what is seen . . . but just in order to see. Consequently, it does not seek the leisure of tarrying observantly, but rather seeks restlessness and the excitement of continual novelty and changing encounters. In not tarrying, curiosity is concerned with the constant possibility of distraction . . . Both this not tarrying in the environment and this distraction by new possibilities are constitutive items for curiosity; and, upon these are founded the third essential characteristic of this phenomenon, which we will call the character of never-dwelling-anywhere (*Aufenthaltlosigkeit*).[22]

As Heidegger suggests, the character of "never-dwelling-anywhere" points to the relationship between the "curious" and the "distracted" gaze, for both succumb to the restlessness and banality of the merely novel ("what one 'must' have read or seen"). In his later writings on poetry and language, Heidegger specifically links the most "distracted" cultural activities to the "everyday" phenomena of mass culture—the cinema, the illustrated press, and television.[23] Rehearsing a mode of perception which Heidegger calls "amazed to the point of not understanding," these mass cultural practices produce the world as image, as picture, as purely subjective experience. As he explains in his 1938 essay, "The Age of the World Picture":

> The fundamental event of the modern age is the conquest of the world as picture. The word "picture" [*Bild*] now means the structured image [*Gebild*] that is the creature of man's producing which represents and sets before. In such producing, man contends for the position in which he can be that particular being who gives the measure and draws up the guidelines for everything that is.[24]

Heidegger's assessment of mass culture would seem to anticipate the feminist critique of representation for securing the male viewer in a position of mastery over the visual field. But where the feminist critique insists on the manner in which the *woman* is made into an object for the pleasure of the male gaze, Heidegger's analysis suggests how it is *man* himself who experiences becoming and then being an image, who is made to yield his existence for another's use. In an early section of *Being and Time*, for example, Heidegger writes:

> *Dasein's* everyday possibilities of Being are for the Others to dispose of as they please. These Others, moreover, are not *definite* Others. On the contrary, any Other can represent them . . . In this inconspicuousness and unascertainability, the real dictatorship of the "they" is unfolded. We take pleasure and enjoy ourselves as *they* take pleasure; we read, see, and judge about literature and art as *they* see and judge; likewise, we shrink back from the 'great mass' as *they* shrink back; we find 'shocking' what *they* find shocking . . . Overnight, everything that is primordial gets glossed over as something that has long been well known. Everything gained by a struggle becomes just something to be manipulated. Every secret loses its force.[25]

According to Heidegger, the modern subject must learn to distance himself from the tyranny of the "they"—from that seductive force of "distraction" which remains the preserve of Others. And in his view, only painting and poetry afford such distancing, since both artistic forms demand a leisurely "contemplation" that not only provokes reflection but also allows for a repossession of self [*Eigentlichkeit*]. If Heidegger clearly refuses the kind of mastery he associates with a mass-produced visual culture, he nevertheless preserves the hope of recovering mastery on a more profound level; in other words, contemplation becomes a means of compensating for power-lessness, a way of overcoming the radical alterity of the self in a more detached and, hence, more intellectually mediated aesthetic experience.

This brief analysis suggests how Heidegger retains the familiar distinctions between art and mass culture and the structures of contemplation and distraction associated with each. Significantly, however, "distraction" comes to figure in Heidegger's writings both as a perceptual response to mass culture and as the originary structure of experience—the splitting and division of the subject in language. In view of this apparently paradoxical "double meaning" of distraction, it is crucial to raise the following questions: What is the relationship between the "alienation" of mass culture and the "dissociation" of the subject in language? Does this alienation or dissociation have something to do with sexual difference?

As Derrida has recently suggested, Heidegger employed the concept of "distraction" in order to address the role of sexual duality in the constitution of modern experience.[26] This is not to say that Heidegger recognized sexual duality as constitutive of different experiences in the modern world; on the contrary, he saw duality as concealing a neutrality and even a certain asexuality in our experience of being-in-the-world (our experience of being-there as marked by the term *Da-sein*). Through close analysis of a series of lectures Heidegger delivered at the University of Marburg in 1928, Derrida details and defends Heidegger's attempt to "neutralize" the issue of sexual duality since, in Derrida's view, it was only by neutralizing questions of sexuality and experience that Heidegger avoided the binary logic inherent in anthropology, biology and psychology.

Derrida points out that Heidegger was quite careful in his Marburg lectures to pass from the masculine to the neutral term when defining the theme of his analysis: "For the being which constitutes the theme of this analysis," Heidegger writes, "we have not chosen the heading 'man' (*der Mensch*) but the neutral heading '*das Dasein*'."[27] Heidegger's neutralization of the question of being (or the subject of the inquiry), Derrida further remarks, also carries over to his postulation of a certain neutrality or asexuality of experience (*das Dasein*). Again, as Heidegger writes: "the neutrality signifies also that the *Dasein* is neither one of the two sexes."[28] Now, for both Heidegger and Derrida, the neutrality of *Dasein* or our experience of being-in-the-world does not mark a negativity, but instead marks a positivity or powerfulness (*Mächtigkeit*). As Derrida puts it, "neutrality does not de-sexualize, rather to the contrary: it does not use ontological negativity with regard to sexuality itself (which it would instead liberate), but with regard to the mark of difference and, more strictly, to sexual duality."[29]

For Derrida, as for Heidegger, sexual difference is not a property of biology or something that originally exists in human beings. Nevertheless, because the question of "sexuality itself" comes to displace questions of experience in the writings of both theorists, the historical and social construction of gender is effectively elided. Heidegger, for example, denies sexual difference a determining role in his analysis of experience because sexual duality marks a fundamental negativity (woman as non-man). At the same time, however, sexuality itself is said to retain a "neutral" signification (woman as the same as man) since it allows sexuality to emerge as multiplication, dissemination, even liberation. The subject whose sexuality is, in fact, liberated in the passage from the masculine (*der Mensch*) to the neutral (*das Dasein*) is revealed in the interpretative gesture which must repress the feminine term in order to achieve "neutrality." If, in this way, Heidegger's ontology avoids binary logic, it also effaces the feminine as a term within language and as a social position for women that is symbolically constructed and historically lived.

This is not to imply, however, that femininity as it relates to *male* identity is completely effaced in Heidegger's ontology. It should be recalled that Heidegger's description of mass cultural dissociation (where the "I" is forced to yield his existence to the "they") leads him to argue for a repossession of self in contemplation—a repossession that will alone restore mastery under the conditions of pervasive powerlessness. If it is fairly obvious that Heidegger's ontology represents a response to modernity and to the loss of cultural mastery, it is also clear that something quite specific seems to have precipitated this loss: namely, the emergence of a mass cultural audience and the presence of Others previously excluded from mass cultural reception. In this regard, it is highly symptomatic that Heidegger sees division as both constitutive of subjectivity and as debasing to cultural experience. Indeed, his plea for a "neutralization" of sexuality and experience is undeniably a plea to get beyond the difficulties of gender more generally: to dissolve the Other which inhabits the self and, equally, to repress the Other which contends for access to culture in the modern age. Referring to the appropriation of Heideggerian phenomenology in recent postmodernist and psychoanalytic theory, Alice Jardine writes, "Could it be that the new philosophically valorized 'neuter anonymity' of text or world—a valorization of singularities beyond sexual difference—is but a new attempt to escape the rising voices of women?"[30]

PERCEPTION, MASS CULTURE AND DISTRACTION: THE CRITICAL THEORY OF WALTER BENJAMIN AND SIEGFRIED KRACAUER

Benjamin recalled his sexual awakening when, en route to the synagogue on the Jewish New Year's Day, he became lost on the city streets . . . [He writes:] "While I was wandering thus, I was suddenly and simultaneously overcome, on the one hand, by the thought 'Too late, time was up long ago, you'll never get there'—and, on the other, by a sense of the insignificance of all this, of the benefits of letting things take what course they would; and these two streams of consciousness converged irresistibly in an immense pleasure that filled me with blasphemous indifference toward the service, but exalted the street in which I stood as if it had already intimated to me the services of procurement it was later to render to my awakened drive."[31]

Susan Buck-Morss, on Benjamin's "A Berlin Chronicle"

Few theorists have addressed Benjamin's fascination with the city and the street as it reveals assumptions about sexuality and sexual difference[32] Indeed, it is not sexual politics but politics in general which remain the central topic of debate in Benjamin criticism. As one commentator puts it, "The Left has been . . . concerned to defend [Benjamin's] legacy from mystical appropriations of it, the Right to establish its distance from any orthodox canon of historical materialism."[33]

If we are to believe those theorists who claim to position themselves on neither the Left nor the Right of this debate, Benjamin's writings owe less to Marxism and to mysticism than they do to ontological phenomenology. In his introductory essay to *Reflections*, for example, Peter Demetz argues that Benjamin's "hermeneutical urge" to read cities and social institutions as if they were sacred texts reveals his allegiance to Heideggerian philosophy or that "turn to language which alone communicates what we can philosophically know."[34] In much the same manner, Hannah Arendt maintains that Benjamin was as keenly aware as Heidegger of "the break in tradition and loss of authority which occurred in his lifetime," and that both theorists discovered strikingly similar ways of responding to the past and the present. Benjamin's remarkable sense for language and for history, she continues, actually confirms that he had more in common with ontological thought than "he did with the dialectical subtleties of his Marxist friends."[35]

Without a doubt, Benjamin's reflection on language and history reveals the profoundly phenomenological dimension to his thinking (and it is to Arendt's and Demetz's credit to have pointed this out). Nevertheless, this phenomenological dimension should not be confused with Heideggerian philosophy, for it was Benjamin's attempt to combine phenomenology with social theory that established his strongest intellectual affinities: not with Heidegger or ontological phenomenology, but with Siegfried Kracauer and critical theory.

As colleagues and collaborators, Benjamin and Kracauer were among the first intellectuals in Weimar to think seriously about the perceptual and political effects of mass produced art on subjectivity and experience. In contrast to Heidegger, who tended to dismiss mass culture as thoroughly vacuous and degraded, Benjamin and Kracauer insisted on the perceptual possibilities of photography and film and went so far as to claim that mass culture alone responds to the changed reality of technological and industrial society. Drawing upon the phenomenology of Georg Simmel,[36] Benjamin and Kracauer analyzed the entire urban panorama—moving from photography to film to the city and the street—in an effort to discern how all aspects of modernity register the historical process in which an absorbed or concentrated gaze has been replaced by a more distracted mode of looking. While claiming to describe psychic and economic changes as they reveal structures of a general historical nature, Benjamin and Kracauer at the same time elaborate a theory of subjectivity which assumes a very specific theory of sexuality and sexual difference.

In his essay, "Some Motifs in Baudelaire" (1939), for example, Benjamin argues that the "experience of shock" has transformed the spatio-temporal register of distant and proximic sense perception. As he explains, modern modes of production and technology have submitted the human sensorium to a "complex kind of training": in order to cope with the rapid succession of ever-increasing stimuli, tactile senses have been trained in abruptness and optic senses have been trained to deal with distraction. Benjamin writes:

> The invention of the match around the middle of the nineteenth century brought forth a number of innovations which have one thing in common: one abrupt movement of the hand triggers a process of many steps . . . One case in point is the telephone, where the lifting of a receiver has taken the place of a steady movement that used to be required to crank the older models . . . Tactile experiences of this kind were joined by optic ones, such as are supplied by advertising pages of a newspaper or the traffic of a big city. Moving through this traffic involves the individual in a series of shocks and collisions . . . Whereas Poe's passers-by cast glances in all directions which still appeared to be aimless, today's pedestrians are obliged to do so in order to orient themselves to traffic signals.[37]

It is well-known that Benjamin's response to these changing perceptual relations remains fundamentally ambivalent. In some instances, he argues that the modern experience of distraction and shock revealed in techniques of photography and film provide for a deepening of perception, extending the range of "unconscious optics."[38] In other instances, however, he maintains that shock experience reduces the play of the imagination, inducing a fragmented perception that drains memory of its content.[39] Benjamin's ambivalence towards mass cultural distraction is perhaps most strikingly articulated in his essay on Baudelaire. Furthermore, the manner in which he expresses his ambivalence reveals how he often projected his own fear of and fascination with mass culture on to the figure of woman (in particular, the prostitute), and on to Baudelaire's description of the big-city crowd.

"As regards Baudelaire," Benjamin writes, "the masses were anything but external to him; indeed, it is easy to trace in his work a defensive reaction to their attraction and allure."[40] Benjamin defends his preference for Baudelaire's poetry by stressing that, in contrast to such conservative philosophers as Bergson, Baudelaire did not consider the poet to have privileged access to structures of experience and memory. Instead, like Benjamin himself, Baudelaire understood the need to direct attention to the metropolitan masses, for they alone came to experience modernity in the form of shock perception. As Benjamin makes clear, if the metropolitan masses had a privileged relationship to modern experience, the spectacle of the masses also inspired fear and dread among the most sympathetic of observers. Poe and Engels, as Benjamin documents, found the big-city crowds "barbaric," a vortex of confusion inspiring fear, revulsion, even horror. And when Benjamin explains that it was precisely this image of the big-city crowd that became decisive for Baudelaire, he unwittingly reveals how his own reaction to the spectacle of mass culture involves elements of attraction and dread, fascination and horror.

In Baudelaire's sonnet, "A une passante," for example, Benjamin detects Baudelaire's attraction to a "figure that fascinates," an unknown woman mysteriously carried along by the crowd who comes to represent "the object of love which only a city dweller experiences."[41] That this figure becomes an object, however, anticipates the crowd's equally menacing aspect. The "distracted" gaze that has lost the ability to look in return—a crucial aspect of what Benjamin calls the "aura"—serves to describe the gaze of the prostitute which inspires as much fear as fascination in the poet. Benjamin writes:

> The deeper the remoteness which a glance has to overcome, the stronger will be the spell that is apt to emanate from the gaze. In eyes that look at us with mirrorlike blankness, the remoteness remains complete . . . When such eyes come alive, it is with self-protective wariness of a wild animal hunting for prey. (Thus the eye of the whore scrutinizing passers-by is at the same time on its guard against the police. Baudelaire found the physiognomic type bred by this kind of life delineated in Constantin Guy's numerous drawings of prostitutes. "Her eyes, like those of a wild animal, are fixed on the distant horizon; they have the restlessness of a wild animal . . . but also the animal's sudden tense vigilance.")[42]

To cope with the experience of shock, and thus to guard against a profoundly sexualized threat, Baudelaire, Benjamin explains, adopted one of two strategies: either he would assume an "attitude of combat" and battle the crowd or he would adopt the posture of the old women he describes in the cycle, "Les Petites vieilles," who stand apart from the crowd, "unable to keep its pace, no longer participating with their thoughts in the present."[43] Interestingly enough, Benjamin thus assigns to the figure of woman in Baudelaire's poetry both the threatening character of distraction as well as the contained repose of distance. Nevertheless, at the conclusion of his essay, Benjamin recalls how Baudelaire imagined himself to be betrayed by the old women and suggests how this left him with only one option. Benjamin explains:

> To impress the crowd's meanness upon himself, [Baudelaire] envisaged the day on which even the lost women, the outcasts, would be ready to advocate a well-ordered life, condemn libertinism, and reject everything except money. Having been betrayed by these last allies of his, Baudelaire battled the crowd—with the impotent rage of someone fighting the rain or wind. This is the nature of something lived through (*Erlebnis*) to which Baudelaire has given the weight of an experience (*Erfahrung*). He indicated the price for which the sensation of the modern age might be had: the destruction of aura in the experience of shock.[44]

When read from the perspective of Benjamin's own critical ambivalence towards mass culture, these remarks concerning the "price" Baudelaire paid for his battle with the crowd acquire a special meaning. Benjamin, too, could not stand apart from the spectacle of mass culture but was determined to struggle with its contradictory meanings and effects. However compelling Benjamin's ambivalent relation to mass culture remains, it is important to recognize how this ambivalence came to be expressed through reference to the metaphorical figure of woman (a figure that stands as much for modernity as it does for the continually renewed search for a lost plenitude). Benjamin's essay on Baudelaire certainly provides us with enough clues for discerning an ambivalence towards woman and mass culture, but it is his essay on Karl Kraus which gives these clues the status of an explanation.

Referring to the "demon" of ambiguity and ambivalence, Benjamin explains that "all men of letters" find themselves at some time in the position of the prostitute: "the life of letters is existence under the aegis of mere mind, [just] as prostitution is existence under the aegis of mere sexuality."[45] Yet it is not simply the intellectual's identification with the prostitute that provokes his ambivalence; instead, as Benjamin proposes, ambiguity is itself the "demon" of the intellectual's existence and, not surprisingly, this demon is also a woman. Benjamin writes: "Surrounded by feminine mirages, 'such as the bitter earth does not harbor,' the possession of demonic sexuality belongs to the ego that enjoys itself."[46] I believe we can take Benjamin at his word here, for the "feminine mirages" in his own writings in fact reveal less about women in Weimar than they do about the ambivalence of male desire and that imaginary "demon" of male subjectivity. Indeed, it is for this reason that Benjamin's analyses of modernity remain profoundly historical and at the same time highly personal, less the product of a preconceived idea about mass culture than, to use

Benjamin's own words, "more a convergence in memory of accumulated and frequently unconscious data."[47]

In his essays on the cinema and mass culture which he wrote in the 1920s, Kracauer not only anticipated Benjamin's analysis of modernity by several years, but he also elaborated a similar theory of historical changes in structures of perception and experience. In his 1927 essay, "Cult of Distraction" (*Kult der Zerstreuung*), for example, Kracauer maintains that distraction in the cinema models itself upon the rationalization of labor more generally, and thus reveals how processes of abstraction have come to permeate forms of perception, representation, and experience. For this reason, Kracauer argues against those artists and intellectuals who condemn the cinema as vacuous or superficial "distraction," explaining that such condemnation fails to understand that distraction involves a complete restructuring and a different logic in social reality. Kracauer writes:

> One says the Berliners are addicted to distraction (zerstreuungssüchtig); this accusation is petit-bourgeois. Certainly the addiction is stronger here than in the provinces, but stronger and more apparent here is also the tension of the working masses, a basically formal tension that fills the day without fulfilling the person . . . The alienation [revealed in cinematic distraction] has an inherent honesty. Through it, truth is not jeopardized. Truth is only jeopardized through the naive affirmation of cultural values . . . which, because of social changes, have lost all basis in reality.[48]

Kracauer's insistence that cinematic distraction reveals an "inherent honesty" about modern social reality was not a simple endorsement of alienation in cinematic reception or industrial modes of labor. In fact, even though Kracauer criticizes artists and intellectuals for attempting to preserve outmoded aesthetic values, he also explains that distraction in the cinema carries with it a contradictory "double meaning." On the one hand, Kracauer argues that cinematic distraction is progressive, since it translates modes of industrial labor into a sensory, perceptual discourse which allows spectators to recognize the loss of individual mastery and the need for collective action under the changed conditions of modern social reality: "In the pure externality of the cinema, the public meets itself, and the discontinuous sequence of splendid sense impressions reveals to them their own daily reality. Would it be concealed to them, it couldn't be attacked or changed."[49] On the other hand, Kracauer insists that cinematic distraction contains reactionary tendencies, since it rationalizes perception to such an extent that spectators fail to recognize forms of exploitation and therefore lose the ability to act: "The production and mindless consumption of abstract, ornamental patterns distract from the necessity to change the present order. Reason is impeded when the masses into which it should penetrate yield to emotions provided by the godless, mythological cult."[50]

Significantly, however, when Kracauer discerns the most reactionary tendencies of mass cultural reception, he refers less to an emotional involvement that impedes reason and more to a rationalized response that impedes involvement. In his 1931 essay, "Girls and Crisis," for example, Kracauer suggests how mass culture has adopted the capitalist goals of streamlining and administration in order to mask contradiction and promote uncritical consumption. Choosing the American dance troupe, The Tiller Girls, to represent this trend, Kracauer writes:

> In that postwar era, in which prosperity appeared limitless and which could scarcely conceive of unemployment, the Girls were artificially manufactured in the USA and exported to Europe by the dozens. Not only were they American products; at the same time they demonstrated the greatness of American production . . . When they formed an undulating snake, they radiantly illustrated the virtues of the conveyor belt; when they tapped their feet in fast tempo, it sounded like *business, business*; when they kicked their legs with mathematic precision, they joyously affirmed the progress of rationalization; and when they kept repeating the same movements without ever interrupting their routine, one envisioned an uninterrupted chain of autos gliding from the factories into the world, and believed that the blessings of prosperity had no end.[51]

Kracauer's description of the abstraction and fragmentation of the female body in the service of capitalist expansion certainly attests to his awareness of the construction of woman in mass culture as spectacle, as object of desire and endless exchange. Yet it is clear that Kracauer is less interested in the cultural construction of woman than he is in the effects of rationalization on the mass cultural spectator. Kracauer implies, for example, that the structures of seeing which the mass ornament develops in order to insure its readability depend on images of artificially manufactured women. And while these images serve to reassure the mass cultural spectator, they also function to "distract" or divert attention away from the irrationality at the basis of a capitalist social order. Kracauer thus suggests a relationship between the untrustworthiness of the image and the vulnerability of the mass cultural spectator, both of which run the risks he associates with femininity—the risks of passivity, uniformity, and uncritical consumption.

A somewhat different reading of mass culture and spectatorship emerges from Kracauer's series of essays, "The Little Shopgirls Go to the Movies" (1927).[52] Although Kracauer continues to associate the most dubious aspects of mass culture with passivity and femininity (as, for example, when he refers to the vacuity of the *Tippmamsells* or the "stupid little hearts" of the shopgirls), his analysis also reveals that modes of spectatorship and representation in Weimar were not always based on rationalized models. In the eighth essay in the series, for example, Kracauer begins his analysis of film melodrama by describing a symptomatic narrative: A young woman, left in poverty by her father's suicide, is subsequently abandoned by her fiancé who is concerned with promoting his career as a lieutenant and avoiding any hint of poverty or indecency. In order to support herself, the young woman takes a job under an assumed name as a dancer on the stage. After many years, the lieutenant and the woman meet again, only now the lieutenant wants to put things right and suggests marriage. But, as Kracauer explains, "the unselfish dancer poisons herself in order to force her lover, through her death, to think only of his career."[53] Following this narrative description, Kracauer offers a critique of the sentimentality in film melodrama in which he implies a correspondence between the figure of woman in melodrama and the female spectator. He writes: "There are many people who sacrifice themselves nobly, because they are too lazy to rebel. Many tears are shed because to cry is sometimes easier than to think. The stronger the position of power in society, the more tragically act the weak and stupid . . . ."[54] At the conclusion of this critique, Kracauer remarks, somewhat enigmatically, "Clandestinely the little shopgirls wipe their eyes and powder their noses before the lights come up."[55]

In spite of its patronizing tone, Kracauer's analysis clearly contests the view that all cinematic practices require a rationalized or distracted attention; indeed, the little shopgirls may be distracted from everyday life, but they are clearly in a state of absorption and concentration at the movies. In fact, it is Kracauer's *own* gaze that is distracted by the presence of female spectators—spectators whose emotional response cannot be easily reconciled with the allegedly reactionary aspects of mass cultural reception. It should be recalled that Kracauer holds distraction in the cinema to be reactionary only when spectators passively consume abstract, ornamental patterns and fail to recognize the loss of individual mastery under the changed conditions of modern social reality. While the little shopgirls's emotional response may reveal an acknowledgment of a loss of mastery (or, more precisely, an acknowledgment of a mastery that was never their own), their absorbed gaze is neither entirely passive nor distracted. In an effort to resolve this apparent paradox, Kracauer concludes that when spectators acknowledge their loss of mastery, they often lose the ability to act.

While Kracauer does not consider that women may have a different relationship to mastery and loss (and thus to melodramatic narrative and cinematic representation), his discussion of female spectatorship allows us to challenge the view of the cinema and perceptual response in Weimar as thoroughly streamlined, rationalized and distracted. In other words, even though Kracauer refers to female spectatorship and film melodrama in a disparaging manner, his analysis nonetheless suggests the existence of a mode of spectatorship and form of representation that failed to keep pace with rationalized models in the realm of leisure. Following from

Kracauer's observations, we may draw the conclusion that women's relationship to modernity in the 1920s was entirely different from what was
commonly projected on to the figure of woman during the Weimar period.
Indeed, we may suspect that women's relationship to modernity and mass
culture has all too frequently been confused with male desire, and with
male perceptions of gender.

WOMEN IN WEIMAR: AT WORK AND AT THE MOVIES

It is certainly one thing to claim that modernity has transformed experience. But it is clearly quite another to conclude that various phenomena
of modernity, such as film, photography, or mass culture in general, have
transformed experience so profoundly that they admit only one form of
perception or one kind of experience; that constitutive of the male spectator or subject.

However, it would be difficult to deny the similarities between early
assessments of perception and representation in Weimar and contemporary theories of the cinema and spectatorship. Indeed, the writings of
Heidegger, Benjamin and Kracauer serve in many ways to corroborate
what Christian Metz has analyzed as the inherently masculine economy of
film technology and spectatorship, where the cinema exists as a male prerogative and vision remains a masculine privilege. More precisely, the
emphasis on male identity in early theories of perception would seem to
confirm Mary Ann Doane's argument about the non-identity of woman in
theories of representation and spectatorship: the over-presence of woman
as object or metaphor and her non-existence as subject within a phallocentric discourse.

But unless we want to dispense with questions of female spectatorship
altogether, it is crucial to challenge the assumption that vision is inherently masculine or that the cinema and mass culture are merely synonymous
with the further repression and exclusion of women. As I have suggested,
the almost obsessive attempt of artists and intellectuals in Weimar to delay
the loss of male authority reveals a simultaneous attempt to distance a
mass cultural audience perceived as threatening, as Other, and as female.
While this response certainly attests to the tenacity of male desire, it also
points to a threat that was neither purely imaginary nor metaphorical. In
other words, mass culture and the cinema in Weimar cannot be aligned
with the complete exclusion of women, since both were in many ways
responsive to women's demands for a greater share in German cultural
and economic life.

The growing visibility of *women* in Weimar in fact goes a long way to
explain the defensive reaction towards *woman* in the discourses of artists
and intellectuals: their attempt to distance and thereby master the threat
perceived as too close, too present, too overwhelming. While this defensive

reaction can be explained in psychic terms (the threat of castration, the trauma inspired by the female body), it can be explained in historical and economic terms as well. For example, German law prohibited women from attending public meetings or joining political organizations until 1908.[56] And even after women were granted the right to assemble, the very act of a woman attending a public gathering was considered scandalous, even immoral. Nevertheless, the cultural sanction against women's right to assemble was not heeded by the promoters of mass cultural entertainment, who sought to capitalize on changes in women's legal status and thus to profit from the economic potential of female audiences. The cinema, in particular, became one of the few places in German cultural life that afforded women a prominent position and a privileged access, and the growing visibility of women at the movies did not go unnoticed by those who held mass culture responsible for exacerbating the decay of standards brought about by industrialization and modernity more generally.

Of course, it was not only the presence of women at the movies but also their visibility in traditionally male spheres of labor that provoked resentment and contributed to the perception that women had made enormous strides towards reaching economic parity with men during the Weimar years. (This latter perception may indeed account for the attempt by media institutions to cater to female audiences, since women were now considered to have a disposable income of their own.) The intensive rationalization of industry after 1925, for instance, made the hiring of cheap, unskilled labor possible—and women were an available source. While women never came close to replacing men in industry (and never achieved anything like economic parity in the workplace), the very fact of an industrial female labor force was nevertheless considered a powerful challenge to traditional divisions of male and female labor. As historian Renate Bridenthal explains, "the picture of women streaming into assembly-line jobs while men were pounding the pavement looking for work [gives] a superficially persuasive but fundamentally misleading impression. Contrary to the commonly held assumption, loudly voiced during the Depression, women were not displacing men. Rather, they were themselves displaced, moving out of agriculture and home industry into factories where they were more visible as a workforce and thus more likely to provoke resentment."[57]

Quite obviously, the presence of women in places they had never been before (most notably, in industry and in the cinema) explains the perceived threat of woman registered in various discourses during the Weimar years. And while it would be a mistake to assume that either the workplace or the cinema was entirely liberating for women, it would also be wrong to confuse male perceptions of woman with women's perceptions of themselves, for to do so would be to mistake male desire for female subjectivity.

To theorize female subjectivity in Weimar therefore requires that we revise notions about perception and spectatorship in the cinema and explore the ways in which modernity was experienced differently by women during the 1920s. The female spectator's absorbed attention in the cinema, for example, suggests that women were indeed constituted differently than men in relation to the image and to structures of looking. In psychic terms alone, we may say that women in Weimar did not share the male fear of the female body or retain the same investment in aesthetic detachment. Although the female spectator's particular passion for perceiving was commonly disparaged and set against the male spectator's more objective, detached, and hence more mediated gaze, it is obvious that women's closeness to the image can only be conceived as a "deficiency" within a masculine epistemology. In other words, women's absorption in the image can only be considered regressive or dangerous if representation itself is assumed to be so thoroughly masculine that it admits only one kind of vision or perceptual response. The threat of losing oneself to mass culture, it should be recalled, was central to Heidegger's claim that the loss of self is inseparable from the specter of losing oneself to Others. Since it would be difficult to equate this sense of self with female spectatorship, it becomes crucial to discern the psychic and historical determinants of women's experience in Weimar—their experience of mass culture and of everyday life as well.

It is here that the writings of Benjamin, Kracauer and (to a lesser extent) Heidegger prove useful for revising notions about spectatorship and perception in Weimar. In spite of their almost exclusive attention to male spectatorship and identity, each of these theorists aims to suggest how sense perception is neither natural nor biological but the result of a long process of differentiation within human history. Benjamin's analysis of changes in perception, for example, clearly underscores the ways in which technology and capitalism have transformed vision and experience. Furthermore, Benjamin focuses his attention on the metropolitan masses since, in his view, the masses alone have a privileged relation to industrial modes of labor and thus to changes in perception and experience. While Benjamin insists on the historical nature of subjectivity and experience, he elides any discussion of female subjectivity when he proposes that all forms of perception are modelled upon industrial modes of labor and reveal the process in which an absorbed or concentrated gaze has been replaced by a distracted and defensive way of looking. (That Benjamin's description of "shock" experience in modern life refers solely to the male subject becomes strikingly apparent when we consider how he attributes this "shock" to the remoteness of a female gaze that fails to return the male look.) Benjamin's approach to questions of perception and experience can still be appropriated for an analysis of female subjectivity in Weimar, for women's absorbed attention in the cinema reveals as much about a perceptual response to modernity as it does about a social experience: that is to say, about an experience of cultural and economic change that was not accompanied by changes in the cultural definition of female labor.

The years between 1916 and 1929 were in fact years of intensive and rapid transition in the employment patterns of German women. Historian Tim Mason explains that "older types of work, many of them of a pre-industrial kind, persisted alongside a proliferation of new opportunities in commerce, administration and industry, and in the 1920s, women had a remarkably wide range of roles in the economy."[58] But, as Mason goes on to point out, this apparently remarkable range of roles served merely to reflect in an accentuated form the unequal development of German capitalism as a whole: the tensions within a social and economic structure in which technically advanced industrial monopolies existed side-by-side with peasant farms and economically precarious corner-shops. For women seeking employment outside the home, this usually meant that job possibilities were limited to the least modern sectors of the economy: shops, bars, cafes, or the workshops of husbands, fathers, or other male relatives. The vast majority of women in Weimar, moreover, lived either from unearned income, or from pensions, or from the earnings of children or husbands: in other words, the majority of women in Weimar did not work outside the home at all.[59]

The economic crises in Germany of the 1920s merely exacerbated the precarious definition of women's work in both industrial and domestic spheres. Women who worked in industry, for instance, typically suffered cutbacks in unemployment insurance, received lower compensation due to an original wage differential, and in many cases were more likely to find employment in uninsured home industry or temporary jobs.[60] After 1925, when the demand for unskilled, underpaid female labor actually increased, women's household tasks similarly increased. As historian Atina Grossmann points out, inflation and depression particularly affected lower-middle and working-class women who not only fell victim to unemployment but who also endured physical and emotional stress since most of them had two additional jobs: housework and childcare. "On a material level," Grossmann explains, "social reproduction such as health care and food production was reprivatized into individual households" as a result of governmental cutbacks in social welfare. Furthermore, on an emotional level, "women were called upon to stabilize the family in a turbulent time, to soothe the tensions of unemployment, and to mediate the conflicts supposedly caused by increased competition for jobs between men and women."[61] Given the multiple demands placed on female labor during the 1920s, it is hardly surprising that women often experienced modernity as merely intensifying traditionally defined gender roles and responsibilities.

The positioning of women's work between modernity and tradition may also account for what Kracauer recognized as the female spectator's very different attention in the cinema. The sensory deprivation of household labor, where women were called upon to manage an ever more precarious family existence, may indeed explain women's particular passion for the cinema: their desire to escape the monotony of routine in the heightened sensory experience of filmviewing. Furthermore, it is obvious from Kracauer's analysis that a number of films in Weimar actually gave expression to women's experiences by organizing a contemplative rather than a distracted aesthetic.[62] As Kracauer implies, the film melodrama seemed to speak to women's experiences of modernity, at least in part because it elicited a kind of attention that failed to keep pace with industrialized models in the realm of leisure.

To associate Weimar melodrama with a contemplative aesthetic does not necessarily entail the distinction between art and mass culture that Heidegger makes in his use of contemplation as a perceptual category. Indeed, where Heidegger assumes mass culture to be thoroughly rationalized and degraded, I have suggested that mass culture in Weimar actually negotiated artistic conventions in popular forms. Furthermore, although Heidegger links contemplation to perceptual distance and intellectual detachment it is possible that contemplation also accounts for the female viewer's intensely concentrated gaze. In other words, if Weimar melodrama appealed to both male intellectuals and female audiences, it nevertheless afforded different kinds of contemplative experience: for male intellectual audiences, the film melodrama may have in fact inspired disinterestedness and detachment; but for female audiences, the film melodrama almost certainly provoked an intensely interested and emotional involvement, particularly since melodramatic representation often gave heightened expression to women's experiences of everyday life.

Once we understand the appeal of contemplation in this way, it becomes possible to appropriate certain tenets of Heideggerian phenomenology for a more precise conceptualization of female spectatorship. Heidegger's critique of epistemology for holding vision alone to confirm knowledge and subjectivity, for example, is especially useful for revising clichés about gendered spectatorship. As I have suggested, the female spectator's concentrated attention in the cinema cannot be understood in terms of vision alone, since modes of looking—even contemplative modes of looking—only become meaningful when we attend to the historical determinants of subjectivity and experience. Male or female spectatorship, in other words, cannot be theorized apart from questions of gender and experience, for perceptual response is constructed as much in history as it is by the positioning and address within individual films.

Notes

1. Peter Gay, *Weimar Culture: The Outsider as Insider* (New York: Harper and Row, 1928), 129.

2. For an extremely illuminating discussion of modernity and film culture in Weimar, see Anton Kaes, "Introduction," *Kino-Debatte: Texte zum Verhältnis von Literatur und Film, 1909–1929* (Tübingen: Max Niemeyer Verlag, 1978).

3. Harold Nicholson, "The Charm of Berlin," *Der Querschnitt.* (Mai 1929); (originally in English) reprinted in *Der Querschnitt: Das Magazin der aktuellen Ewigkeitswerte, 1924–1933* (Berlin: Ullstein Verlag, 1980), 261–63.

4. Carl Zuckmayer, *Als Wär's ein Stück von mir* (1966), 311–14; reprinted in translation as *A Part of Myself*, trans. Richard and Clara Winston (New York: Harcourt, Brace and Jovanovich, 1970), 217.

5. This argument is developed more fully in the study from which this article is drawn. See my "Joyless Streets: Film, Photojournalism, and the Female Spectator in Weimar Germany," (University of Iowa, dissertation, 1986).

6. On the feminist movement in turn-of-the-century Germany, see Richard J. Evans, *The Feminist Movement in Germany 1894–1933* (London: Sage Studies in Twentieth Century History, vol. 6), 1976; Werner Thönnenssen, *The Emancipation of Women: The Rise and Fall of the Women's Movement in German Social Democracy 1863–1933* (London), 1973.

7. See, for example, Miriam Hansen, "Early Silent Cinema: Whose Public Sphere?," *New German Critique*, 29 (Spring-Summer 1983), 147–84; Tania Modleski, "Femininity as Mas(s)querade: A Feminist Approach to Mass Culture," *High Theory/Low Culture*, ed. Colin MacCabe (Manchester University Press, 1986), 37–52; Andreas Huyssen, "Mass Culture as Woman: Modernism's Other," forthcoming in *Theories of Contemporary Culture*, ed. Tania Modleski, (Indiana University Press, 1987); and my own, "Mass Culture and the Feminine: The 'Place' of Television in Film Studies," *Cinema Journal*, 25:3 (Spring 1986), 5–21.

8. Egon Friedell, "Prolog vor dem Film," in *Blätter des deutschen Theaters, 2* (1912); reprinted in *Kino-Debatte*, 43. All translations that follow are mine unless otherwise indicated.

9. Bruno Schönlank, "Kino," in Gunter Heintz, ed. *Deutsche Arbeiterdichtung 1910–1933* (Stuttgart, 1974), 293–94.

10. Here, I am drawing upon Mary Ann Doane's useful analysis of gender and perception in her essay, "When the Direction of the Force Acting on the Body is Changed: The Moving Image," *Wide Angle*, 7:1–2 (1985), 42–57.

11. Christian Metz, *Psychoanalysis and Cinema: The Imaginary Signifier*, trans. Celia Britton, Annwyl Williams, Ben Brewster and Alfred Guzzetti (London: The MacMillan Press), 1982.

12. Christian Metz, "The Passion for Perceiving," in *Psychoanalysis and Cinema*, 59–60.

13. Mary Ann Doane, "Film and the Masquerade: Theorizing the Female Spectator," *Screen*, 23:24 (September–October 1982), 87.

14. "Film and the Masquerade: Theorizing the Female Spectator," 78.

15. Mary Ann Doane, "Woman's Stake: Filming the Female Body," *October*, 17 (Summer 1981), 23.

16. Sigmund Freud, *Civilization and Its Discontents*, trans. James Strachey (New York: Norton, 1962), 46–47.

17. See Mary Anne Doane, "When the Direction of the Force Acting on the Body is Changed: The Moving Image," cited above.

18. The impact of Heidegger's and Benjamin's writings on postmodernist philosophy is certainly a case in point, but even Kracauer's early writings have recently gained the attention of theorists interested in defining a resolutely historical approach to questions of cinematic

perception and spectatorship. The renewed interest in Kracauer's work has been obvious in recent conferences (the Society for Cinema Studies held in New York in 1985, for example), in scholarly journals, and in plans for publication of Kracauer's previously unavailable and untranslated early writings.

19. Jacques Derrida, "Geschlecht: différence sexuelle, différence ontologique," *L'Herne* (September 1983), 419–420. I am indebted to Natasa Durovicova for her astute translation of this essay.

20. Gay, *Weimar Culture*, 82.

21. Hans George Gadamer, "Heidegger's Later Philosophy," in *Essays in Philosophical Hermeneutics*, trans. David E. Linge (Berkeley and Los Angeles: University of California Press, 1976), 214–15.

22. Martin Heidegger, *Being and Time*, trans. John MacQuarrie and Edward Robinson (New York: Harper and Row, 1962), 216–17.

23. See, for example, Heidegger's series of essays collected in *Poetry, Language, Thought*, trans. Alfred Hofstader (New York: Harper and Row, 1972). Heidegger was perhaps most explicit in his condemnation of mass culture in his 1955 lecture entitled "Memorial Address." This address in available in translation in *Discourse on Thinking*, trans. John M. Anderson and E. Hans Freund (New York: Harper and Row, 1966), 43–47.

24. Martin Heidegger, "The Age of the World Picture," in *The Question Concerning Technology*, trans. William Lovitt (New York: Harper and Row, 1974), 134. "Die Zeit des Weltbildes" was first given as a lecture at Freiburg University in June 1938.

25. *Being and Time*, 164–65.

26. Jacques Derrida, "Geschlecht: différence sexuelle, différence ontologique," cited above.

27. Quoted in "Geschlecht," 421.

28. Quoted in "Geschlecht," 422.

29. "Geschlecht," 423.

30. Alice Jardine, *Gynesis: Configurations of Woman and Modernity* (Ithaca and London: Cornell University Press, 1985), 177.

31. Susan Buck-Morss, "Benjamin's *Passagen-Werk*: Redeeming Mass Culture for the Revolution," *New German Critique*, 29 (Spring-Summer 1983), 223, fn. 27.

32. Notable exceptions, however, are Heide Schlüpmann's discussion of early German film theory in her essay, "Kinosucht," *frauen und film*, 33 (October 1982), 45–52; and Christine Buci-Gluckmann's essay on Benjamin and allegory, "Catastrophic Utopia: The Feminine as Allegory of the Modern," *Representations*, 14 (Spring 1986), 220–229.

33. Ronald Taylor, *Aesthetics and Politics: Ernst Bloch, Georg Lukács, Bertolt Brecht, Walter Benjamin, Theodor Adorno*, ed. Ronald Taylor (New York: Schocken Books, 1977), 200.

34. Peter Demetz, "Introduction," to *Reflections: Essays, Aphorisms, Autobiographical Writings*, trans. Edmund Jephcott (New York and London: Harcourt, Brace, Jovanovich, 1978), xxi.

35. Hannah Arendt, "Introduction," to *Illuminations*, trans. Harry Zohn (New York: Schocken Books, 1969), 46.

36. A founding text of critical theory is indeed Georg Simmel's "Die Grosstadt und das Geistesleben," (Dresden, 1903), reprinted in translation as "The Metropolis and Mental Life," in Kurt H. Wolff, ed., *The Sociology of Georg Simmel* (New York: The Free Press, 1950).

37. Walter Benjamin, "Some Motifs in Baudelaire," trans. Harry Zohn, in *Charles Baudelaire: A Lyric Poet in the Era of High Capitalism* (London: New Left Books, 1973), 131–34.

38. As Benjamin suggests through Baudelaire's example, "In his 'Salon de 1859,' Baudelaire lets the landscape pass in review, concluding with this admission: 'I long for the return of the dioramas whose enormous, crude magic subjects me to the spell of a useful

illusion. I prefer looking at the backdrop paintings of the stage where I find my favorite dreams treated with consummate skill and tragic concision. Those things, so completely false, are for that reason much closer to the truth, whereas the majority of our landscape painters are liars precisely because they fail to lie.'" "Some Motifs in Baudelaire," 151. See also, Benjamin's "The Work of Art in the Age of Mechanical Reproduction." *Illuminations*, 217–251.

39. "Some Motifs in Baudelaire," 146.

40. "Some Motifs in Baudelaire," 122.

41. "Some Motifs in Baudelaire," 125.

42. "Some Motifs in Baudelaire," 150–51.

43. "Some Motifs in Baudelaire," 123.

44. "Some Motifs in Baudelaire," 154.

45. Walter Benjamin, "Karl Kraus," *Reflections*, 258.

46. "Karl Kraus," 255. Translation modified.

47. "Some Motifs in Baudelaire," 110.

48. Siegfried Kracauer, "Kult der Zerstreuung," in *Das Ornament der Masse* (Frankfurt: Suhrkamp, 1977), 313–14.

49. "Kult der Zerstreuung," 315.

50. Siegfried Kracauer, "Das Ornament der Masse," in *Das Ornament der Masse*; reprinted in translation as "The Mass Ornament," *New German Critique*, trans. Barbara Correll and Jack Zipes (Spring 1975), 75.

51. Siegfried Kracauer, "Girls und Krise," *Frankfurter Zeitung*, 27 (Mai 1931); quoted in Karsten Witte, "Introduction to Siegfried Kracauer's 'The Mass Ornament,'" *New German Critique*, 5 (Spring 1975), 63–64.

52. Siegfried Kracauer, "Die kleinen Ladenmädchen gehen ins Kino," in *Das Ornament der Masse*, 279–94. It should also be noted that Kracauer was concerned, in both his early and later writings, to redeem cinematic practices which rejected abstraction as well as outmoded artistic values by attending to the contradictions of modern experience. This, in fact, may explain his fascination with the little shopgirls' absorbed and emotional response.

53. "Die kleinen Ladenmädchen gehen ins Kino," 291–92.

54. "Die kleinen Ladenmädchen gehen ins Kino," 292.

55. "Die kleinen Ladenmädchen gehen ins Kino," 292–93.

56. For a discussion of the legal status of women in turn-of-the-century Germany, see Hal Draper and Anne G. Lipow, "Marxist Women Versus Bourgeois Feminism," in *The Socialist Register 1976*, ed. Ralph Miliband and John Saville (London: The Merlin Press, 1976), 179–216.

57. Renate Bridenthal, "Beyond *Kinder, Küche, Kirche*: Weimar Women at Work," *Central Eurupoean History* 6:2 (June 1973), 158. This essay has also been reprinted, with additions from another author. See Renate Bridenthal and Claudia Koonz, "Beyond *Kinder, Küche, Kirche*: Weimar Women in Politics and Work," in *Liberating Women's History: Theoretical and Critical Essays*, ed. Berenice A. Carroll (Urbana, Chicago and London: University of Illinois Press, 1976), 301–329.

58. Tim Mason, "Women in Germany, 1925–1940: Family, Welfare and Work: Part I," *History Workshop—A Journal of Socialist Historians*, 1 (Spring 1976), 78.

59. Tim Mason, "Women in Germany, 1925–1940," 78.

60. See Atina Grossmann's excellent essay, "Abortion and Economic Crisis: The 1931 Campaign Against Paragraph 218 in Germany," *New German Critique*, 14 (Spring 1978), 119–38.

61. Atina Grossmann,"The New Woman and the Rationalization of Sexuality in Weimar Germany," in *Powers of Desire: The Politics of Sexuality*, eds. Ann Snitow, Christine Stansell and Sharon Thompson (New York: Monthly Review Press, 1983), 157.

62. In associating a contemplative aesthetic with female spectatorship, I aim to challenge the assumption that "contemplation" is the sole prerogative of (male) intellectual

audiences in Weimar. Indeed, although several theorists persist in arguing that the female spectator's absorption in the cinema has nothing to do with contemplation (i.e. the female spectator is merely "swept away" by the image and lacks the capacity to reflect on its meaning), I have suggested that a contemplative aesthetic goes a long way to account for women's emotional and highly concentrated gaze. This attempt to redeem a contemplative aesthetic for female spectatorship in Weimar, moreover, is the topic of another chapter in the study from which this essay is drawn (see note 5, above).

The Vamp and the Machine:
Fritz Lang's *Metropolis*

ANDREAS HUYSSEN

F RITZ LANG'S famous and infamous extravaganza *Metropolis* has never had a good press. While its visual qualities have been praised,[1] its content, more often than not, has been condemned as simplistic, ill-conceived, or plain reactionary. When the film was first released in the United States in 1927, Randolph Bartlett, the *New York Times* critic, reproached the director for his "lack of interest in dramatic verity" and for his "ineptitude" in providing plot motivation, thus justifying the heavy re-editing of the film for American audiences.[2] In Germany, critic Axel Eggebrecht condemned *Metropolis* as a mystifying distortion of the "unshakeable dialectic of the class struggle" and as a monumental panegyric to Stresemann's Germany.[3] Eggebrecht's critique, focusing as it does on the emphatic reconciliation of capital and labor at the end of the film, has been reiterated untold times by critics on the left. And indeed, if we take class and power relations in a modern technological society to be the only theme of the film, then we have to concur with these critics. We would also have to agree with Siegfried Kracauer's observation concerning the affinity that exists between the film's ideological punch line, "The heart mediates between hand and brain," and the fascist "art" of propaganda which, in Goebbels' words, was geared "to win the heart of a people and to keep it."[4] Kracauer pointedly concluded his comments on *Metropolis* with Lang's own words describing a meeting of the filmmaker with Goebbels that took place shortly after Hitler's rise to power: "'He (i.e., Goebbels) told me that, many years before, he and the Führer had seen my picture *Metropolis* in a small town, and Hitler had said at that time that he wanted me to make the Nazi pictures.'"[5]

One problem with such ideology critiques based on notions of class and political economy is that they tend to blur the political differences between the Weimar Republic and the Third Reich by suggesting that social-democratic reformism inexorably contributed to Hitler's rise to power. The more important problem with this approach is that it remains blind to other aspects which are at least as important to the film's social imaginary, especially since they are clearly foregrounded in the narrative. While the traditional ideology critique is not false, its blind spots lock us into a one-dimensional reading of the film which fails to come to terms

Reprinted from Andreas Huyssen, *After the Great Divide; Modernism, Mass Culture, Postmodernism* (Bloomington: Indiana University Press, 1986): 65–81.

with the fascination *Metropolis* has always exerted on audiences. This fascination, I would argue, has to do precisely with those elements of the narrative which critics have consistently shrugged aside. Thus the love story between Freder, son of the Master of Metropolis, and Maria, the woman of the depths who preaches peace and social harmony to the workers, has been dismissed as sentimental and childish (Eisner, Jensen); the elaborate recreation of Maria as a machine-vamp in Rotwang's laboratory has been called counterproductive to the flow of events (Kracauer); certain actions of the mechanical vamp such as the belly dance have been called extraneous and inexplicable (Jensen); and the medieval religious-alchemical symbolism of the film has been criticized as inadequate for the portrayal of a future—or, for that matter, present—urban life (Eggebrecht). I am suggesting, however, that it is precisely the doubling of Maria, the use of religious symbolism, the embodiment of technology in a woman-robot and Freder's complex relationship to women and machines, sexuality and technology, which give us a key to the film's social and ideological imaginary. Even though Kracauer's concrete analysis of *Metropolis* remained blind to this constitutive mesh of technology and sexuality in the film, he was essentially correct when he wrote in *From Caligari to Hitler: "Metropolis* was rich in subterranean content that, like contraband, had crossed the borders of consciousness without being questioned."[6] The problem is how to define this subterranean content, a task which Kracauer does not even begin to tackle in his analysis of the film.

Of course the critics' attention has always been drawn to the film's powerful sequences involving images of technology, which, to a large degree, control the flow of the narrative.

—The film begins with a series of shots of the great machines of Metropolis moving and turning in inexorable rhythms.

—The machine room where Freder witnesses the violent explosion and has his vision of technology as Moloch devouring its victims, and the sun-like spinning disk of the central power-house present technology as an autonomous deified force demanding worship, surrender, and ritual sacrifice.

—The imagery of the tower of Babel (the machine center of Metropolis is actually called the New Tower of Babel) relates technology to myth and legend. The biblical myth is used to construct the ideological message about the division of labor into the hands that build and the brains that plan and conceive, a division which, as the film suggests, must be overcome.

—The capital/labor conflict is present in the sequences showing the Master of Metropolis in his control and communications center and the workers in the machine room, with the machines being subservient to the master but enslaving the workers.

—Finally, and perhaps most importantly, technology is embodied in a female robot, a machine-vamp who leads the workers on a rampage and is subsequently burned at the stake.

Eggebrecht and Kracauer were certainly correct in relating Lang's representation of technology to the machine-cult of the 1920s which is also manifest in the literature and the art of *Neue Sachlichkeit*.[7] In my view, however, it is not enough to locate the film within the parameters of *Neue Sachlichkeit* only. The simple fact that stylistically *Metropolis* has usually and mainly been regarded as an expressionist film may give us a clue. And indeed, if one calls expressionism's attitude toward technology to mind, one begins to see that the film actually vacillates between two opposing views of modern technology which were both part of Weimar culture. The expressionist view emphasizes technology's oppressive and destructive potential and is clearly rooted in the experiences and irrepressible memories of the mechanized battlefields of World War I. During the 1920s and especially during the stabilization phase of the Weimar Republic this expressionist view was slowly replaced by the technology cult of the *Neue Sachlichkeit* and its unbridled confidence in technical progress and social engineering. Both these views inform the film. Thus on the one hand, *Metropolis* is strongly indebted to Georg Kaiser's expressionist play about technology, *Gas*. In both works the primary technology is energy, gas and electricity respectively, and the industrial accident sequence in *Metropolis* is remarkably similar to the explosion of the gas works in Act I of Kaiser's play. But, on the other hand, the shots of the city Metropolis, with its canyon-like walls rising far above street level and with its bridges and elevated roads thrown between towering factories and office buildings are reminiscent of Hannah Höch's dadaist photomontages and of scores of industrial and urban landscape paintings of the *Neue Sachlichkeit* (Karl Grossberg, Georg Scholz, Oskar Nerlinger).

Historically and stylistically then Lang's *Metropolis*, which was conceived in 1924 during a visit to the United States (including New York) and released in January 1927, is a syncretist mixture of expressionism and *Neue Sachlichkeit*, and, more significantly, a syncretist mixture of the two diametrically opposed views of technology we can ascribe to these two movements. More precisely, the film works through this conflict and tries to resolve it. Ultimately the film, even though it pretends to hold on to the humanitarian anti-technological ethos of expressionism, comes down on the side of *Neue Sachlichkeit*, and the machine vamp plays the crucial role in resolving a seemingly irreconcilable contradiction. For his indictment of modern technology as oppressive and destructive, which prevails in most of the narrative, Lang ironically relies on one of the most novel cinematic techniques. Schüfftan's *Spiegeltechnik*, a technique which by using a camera with two lenses, focuses two separate images, those of models and actors, onto a single strip of film. As I shall argue later, doubling, mirroring and projecting not only constitute the technological make-up of this film, but they lie at the very core of the psychic and visual processes that underlie its narrative.

THE MACHINE-WOMAN: A HISTORICAL DIGRESSION

To my knowledge, the motif of the machine-woman in *Metropolis* has never been analyzed in any depth. In his recent reinterpretation of *Metropolis*, Stephen Jenkins has taken an important step by pushing the question of the significance of the female presence in Lang's films to the forefront.[8] Although many of Jenkins' observations about Maria and Freder are correct, his analysis is deficient in three areas: his reading remains too narrowly Oedipal, moving as it does from Maria's initial threat to the Law of the Father to her and Freder's reintegration into Metropolis' system of domination; secondly, Jenkins never problematizes Lang's representations of technology and thus remains oblivious to that central political and ideological debate of the 1920s; and thirdly, he never explores the question how or why male fantasies about women and sexuality are interlaced with visions of technology in the film. It is my contention that only by focusing on the mechanical vamp can we fully comprehend the cohesion of meanings which the film transports.

Why indeed does the robot, the *Maschinenmensch* created by the inventor-magician Rotwang and intended to replace the human workers, appear with the body features of a woman? After all, the world of technology has always been the world of men while woman has been considered to be outside of technology, a part of nature, as it were. It is too simple, to suggest, as Jenkins does, that the vamp's main function is to represent the threat of castration to Freder; that purpose could have been achieved by other narrative means, and it also leaves unanswered the question of what technology may have to do with female sexuality and castration anxiety. Precisely the fact that Fritz Lang does not feel the need to explain the female features of Rotwang's robot shows that a pattern, a long standing tradition is being recycled here, a tradition which is not at all hard to detect, and in which the *Maschinenmensch,* more often than not, is presented as woman.

A historical digression is in order.[9] In 1748 the French doctor Julien Offray de la Mettrie, in a book entitled *L'Homme machine*, described the human being as a machine composed of a series of distinct, mechanically moving parts, and he concluded that the body is nothing but a clock, subject as all other matter to the laws of mechanics. This extreme materialist view with its denial of emotion and subjectivity served politically in the 18th century to attack the legitimacy claims of feudal clericalism and the absolutist state. It was hoped that once the metaphysical instances, to which church and state resorted as devices of legitimizing their power, were revealed as fraud, they would become obsolete. At the same time, however, and despite their revolutionary implications, such materialist theories ultimately led to the notion of a blindly functioning world machine, a gigantic automatton, the origins and meaning of which were beyond human understanding. Consciousness and subjectivity were degraded to mere functions of a global mechanism. The determination of social life by metaphysical legitimations of power was replaced by its determination through the laws of nature. The age of modern technology and its legitimatory apparatuses had begun.

It is no coincidence that in the same age literally hundreds of mechanics attempted to construct human automata who could walk and dance, draw and sing, play the flute or the piano, and whose performances became a major attraction in the courts and cities of 18th-century Europe. Androids and robots such as Vaucanson's flutist or Jacquet-Droz's organ player captured the imagination of the times and seemed to embody the realization of an age-old human dream. With the subsequent systematic introduction of laboring machines, which propelled the industrial revolution, the culture of androids declined. But it is precisely at that time, at the turn of the 18th to the 19th century, that literature appropriates the subject matter transforming it significantly. The android is no longer seen as testimony to the genius of mechanical invention; it rather becomes a nightmare, a threat to human life. In the machine-man writers begin to discover horrifying traits which resemble those of real people. Their theme is not so much the mechanically constructed automaton itself, but rather the threat it poses to live human beings. It is not hard to see that this literary phenomenon reflects the increasing technologization of human nature and the human body which reached a new stage in the early 19th century.

While the android builders of the 18th century did not seem to have an overriding preference for either sex (the number of male and female androids seems to be more or less balanced), it is striking to see how the later literature prefers machine-women to machine-men.[10] Historically, then, we can conclude that as soon as the machine came to be perceived as a demonic, inexplicable threat and as harbinger of chaos and destruction—a view which typically characterizes many 19th-century reactions to the railroad to give but one major example[11]—writers began to imagine the *Maschinenmensch* as woman. There are grounds to suspect that we are facing here a complex process of projection and displacement. The fears and perceptual anxieties emanating from ever more powerful machines are recast and reconstructed in terms of the male fear of female sexuality, reflecting, in the Freudian account, the male's castration anxiety. This projection was relatively easy to make; although woman had traditionally been seen as standing in a closer relationship to nature than man, nature itself, since the 18th century, had come to be interpreted as a gigantic machine. Woman, nature, machine had become a mesh of significations which all had one thing in common: otherness; by their very existence they raised fears and threatened male authority and control.

THE ULTIMATE TECHNOLOGICAL FANTASY: CREATION WITHOUT MOTHER

With that hypothesis in mind let us return to *Metropolis*. As I indicated before, the film does not provide an answer to the question of why the robot is a woman; it takes the machine-woman for granted and presents her as quasi-natural. Thea von Harbou's novel, however, on which the film is based, is quite explicit. In the novel, Rotwang explains why he created a female robot rather than the machine *men* Frederson had ordered as replacements of living labor. Rotwang says: "Every man-creator makes himself a woman. I do not believe that humbug about the first human being a man. If a male god created the world . . . then he certainly created woman first."[12] This passage does not seem to fit my hypothesis that the machine-woman typically reflects the double male fear of technology and of woman. On the contrary, the passage rather suggests that the machine-woman results from the more or less sublimated sexual desires of her male creator. We are reminded of the Pygmalion myth in which the woman, far from threatening the man, remains passive and subordinated. But this contradiction is easily resolved if we see male control as the common denominator in both instances. After all, Rotwang creates the android as an artifact, as an initially lifeless object which he can then control and dominate.

Clearly the issue here is not just the male's sexual desire for woman. It is the much deeper libidinal desire to create that other, woman, thus depriving it of its otherness. It is the desire to perform this ultimate task which has always eluded technological man. In the drive toward ever greater technological domination of nature, Metropolis' master-engineer must attempt to create woman, a being which, according to the male's view, resists technologization by its very "nature." Simply by virtue of natural biological reproduction, woman had maintained a qualitative distance to the realm of technical production which only produces lifeless goods. By creating a female android, Rotwang fulfills the male phantasm of a creation without mother; but more than that, he produces not just any natural life, but woman herself, the epitome of nature. The nature/culture split seems healed. The most complete technologization of nature appears as re-naturalization, as a progress back to nature. Man is at long last alone and at one with himself.

Of course it is an imaginary solution. And it is a solution that does violence to a real woman. The real Maria has to be subdued and exploited so that the robot, by way of male magic, can be instilled with life, a motif, which is fairly symptomatic of the whole tradition. The context of the film makes it clear that in every respect, it is male domination and control which are at stake: control of the real Maria who, in ways still to be discussed, represents a threat to the world of high technology and its system of psychic and sexual repression; domination of the woman-robot by Rotwang who orders his creature to perform certain tasks; control of the labor process by the Master of Metropolis who plans to replace inherently uncontrollable living labor by robots; and, finally, control of the workers' actions through Frederson's cunning use of the machine-woman, the false Maria.

On this plane, then, the film suggests a simple and deeply problematic homology between woman and technology, a homology which results from male projections: Just as man invents and constructs technological artifacts which are to serve him and fulfill his desires, so woman, as she has been socially invented and constructed by man, is expected to reflect man's needs and to serve her master. Furthermore, just as the technological artifact is considered to be the quasi-natural extension of man's natural abilities (the lever replacing muscle power, the computer expanding brain power), so woman, in male perspective, is considered to be the natural vessel of man's reproductive capacity, a mere bodily extension of the male's procreative powers. But neither technology nor woman can ever be seen as solely a natural extension of man's abilities. They are always also qualitatively different and thus threatening in their otherness. It is this threat of otherness which causes male anxiety and reinforces the urge to control and dominate that which is other.

VIRGIN AND VAMP: DISPLACING THE DOUBLE THREAT

The otherness of woman is represented in the film in two traditional images of femininity—the virgin and the vamp, images which are both focused on sexuality. Although both the virgin and the vamp are imaginary constructions, male-imagined "ideal types" belonging to the realm Silvia Bovenschen has described as *"Imaginierte Weiblichkeit,"*[13] they are built up from a real core of social, physiological, and psychological traits specific to women and should not be dismissed simply as yet another form of false consciousness. What is most interesting about *Metropolis* is the fact that in both forms, femininity, imagined as it is from the male perspective, poses a threat to the male world of high technology, efficiency, and instrumental rationality. Although the film does everything in terms of plot development and ideological substance to neutralize this threat and to reestablish male control in Metropolis, the threat can clearly be perceived as such throughout the film. First, there is the challenge that the real Maria poses to Frederson, the Master of Metropolis. She prophesies the reign of the heart, i.e., of affection, emotion, and nurturing. Significantly, she is first introduced leading a group of ragged workers' children into the pleasure gardens of Metropolis' *jeunesse dorée*, suggesting both childbearing ability and motherly nurturing. But she also alienates Freder from his father by introducing him to the misery of working-class life. While at the end of the film Maria has become a pawn of the system, at the beginning she clearly represents a threat to the Master of Metropolis. This is shown in the sequence in which Frederson, led by Rotwang, secretly observes Maria preaching to the workers in the catacombs. The very fact that Frederson did not know of the existence of the catacombs deep underneath the city proves that there is something here which escapes his control. Looking through an aperture in a wall high above the assembly at the bottom of the cavern, Frederson listens to Maria preaching peace and acquiescence to the workers, not revolt. Prophesying the eventual reconciliation between the masters and the slaves she states: "Between the brain that plans and the hands that build, there must be a mediator." And: "It is the heart that must bring about an understanding between them." Rather than perceiving this notion as a welcome ideological veil to cover up the conflict between labor and capital, masters and slaves (that is certainly the way Hitler and Goebbels read the film), Frederson backs away from the aperture and, with a stern face and his fists plunged into his pockets, he orders Rotwang to make his robot in the likeness of Maria. Then he clenches one fist in the air and continues: "Hide the girl in your house, I will send the robot down to the workers, to sow discord among them and destroy their confidence in Maria." In social and ideological terms this reaction is inexplicable, since Maria, similar to Brecht's *Saint Joan of the Stockyards*, preaches social peace. But in psychological terms Frederson's wish to disrupt Maria's influence on the workers makes perfect sense. The threat that he perceives has nothing to do with the potential of organized workers' resistance. It has, however, a lot to do with his fear of emotion, of affection, of nurturing, i.e., of all that which is said to be embodied in woman, and which is indeed embodied in Maria.

The result of Frederson's fear of femininity, of emotion and nurturing, is the male fantasy of the machine-woman who, in the film, embodies two age old patriarchal images of women which, again, are hooked up with two homologous views of technology. In the machine-woman, technology and woman appear as creations and/or cult objects of the male imagination. The myth of the dualistic nature of woman as either asexual virgin-mother or prostitute-vamp is projected onto technology which appears as either neutral and obedient or as inherently threatening and out-of-control. On the one hand, there is the image of the docile, sexually passive woman, the woman who is subservient to man's needs and who reflects the image which the master projects of her. The perfect embodiment of this stereotype in the film is the machine-woman of the earlier sequences when she obeys her master's wishes and follows his commands. Technology seems completely under male control and functions as intended as an extension of man's desires. But even here control is tenuous. We understand that Rotwang has lost a hand constructing his machine. And when the robot advances toward Frederson, who stands with his back to the camera, and extends her hand to greet him Frederson is taken aback, and recoils in alarm, a direct parallel to his first spontaneous physical reaction to Maria. Later Rotwang transforms the obedient asexual robot into Maria's living double, and Frederson sends her down to the workers as an *agent provocateur*. She now appears as the prostitute-vamp, the harbinger of chaos, embodying that threatening female sexuality which was absent (or under control) in the robot. Of course, the potent sexuality of the vamp is as much a male fantasy as the asexuality of the virgin-mother. And, indeed, the mechanical vamp is at first as dependent on and obedient to Frederson as the faceless robot was to Rotwang. But there is a significant ambiguity here. Although the vamp acts as an agent of Frederson's manipulation of the workers, she also calls forth libidinal forces which end up threatening Frederson's rule and the whole social fabric of Metropolis and which therefore have to be purged before order and control can be reestablished. This view of the vamp's sexuality posing a threat to male rule and control, which is inscribed in the film, corresponds precisely to the notion of technology running out-of-control and unleashing its destructive potential on humanity. After all, the vamp of the film *is* a technological artifact upon which a specifically male view of destructive female sexuality has been projected.

THE MALE GAZE AND THE DIALECTIC OF DISCIPLINE
AND DESIRE

It is in this context of technology and female sexuality that certain sequences of the film, which have often been called extraneous, assume their full meaning. The mechanical vamp, made to look exactly like Maria, the virgin-mother-lover figure is presented to an all male gathering in a spectacular *mise-en-scène* which Rotwang has arranged in order to prove that nobody will be able to tell the machine from a human being. In steam and light the false Maria emerges from a huge ornamental urn and then performs a seductive strip-tease attracting the lustful gaze of the assembled male guests. This gaze is effectively filmed as an agitated montage of their eyes staring into the camera. Cinematically, this is one of the film's most interesting sequences, and it casts a significant light on earlier sequences involving appearances of Maria and the robot. The montage of male eyes staring at the false Maria when she emerges from her cauldron and begins to cast off her clothes illustrates how the male gaze actually constitutes the female body on the screen. It is as if we were witnessing the second, public creation of the robot, her flesh, skin, and body not only being revealed, but constituted by the desire of male vision. Looking back now on earlier sequences it becomes clear how the eye of the camera always places the spectator in a position occupied by the men in the film: the workers looking spell-bound at Maria preaching from her candle-lit altar; Frederson, his back to the camera, staring at Rotwang's robot; Rotwang's flashlight pinning Maria down in the caverns, and symbolically raping her; and, finally, the transference of Maria's bodily features onto the metallic robot under the controlling surveillance of Rotwang's gaze. Woman appears as a projection of the male gaze, and this male gaze is ultimately that of the camera, of another machine. In the mentioned sequences, vision is identified as male vision. In Lang's narrative, the male eye, which is always simultaneously the mechanical eye of the camera, constructs its female object as a technological artifact (i.e., as a robot) and then makes it come to life through multiple instances of male vision inscribed into the narrative. This gaze is an ambiguous mesh of desires: desire to control, desire to rape, and ultimately desire to kill, which finds *its* gratification in the burning of the robot.

It is also significant that the artificial woman is constructed from the inside out. First Rotwang constructs the mechanical "inner" woman; external features such as flesh, skin, and hair are added on in a second stage when the body features of the real Maria are transferred to or projected onto the robot in an elaborate chemical and electric spectacle. This technical process in which woman is divided and fragmented into inner and outer nature is later mirrored in the subsequent stages of the vamp's destruction: the outer features of the vamp burn away on the stake until only the mechanical insides are left and we again see the metallic robot of the earlier scenes. My point here is not only that construction and destruction of the female body are intimately linked in *Metropolis*. Beyond that, it is male vision which puts together and disassembles woman's body, thus denying woman her identity and making her into an object of projection and manipulation. What is interesting about Lang's *Metropolis* is not so much that Lang uses the male gaze in the described way. Practically all traditional narrative cinema treats woman's body as a projection of male vision. What is interesting, however, is that by thematizing male gaze and vision in the described way the film lays open a fundamental filmic convention usually covered up by narrative cinema.

But there is more to it than that. Lang's film may lead us to speculate whether the dominance of vision *per se* in our culture may not be a fundamental problem rather than a positive contribution to the advance of civilization, as Norbert Elias would have it in his study of the civilizing process.[14] Actually Elias' sources themselves are open to alternative interpretations. He quotes for example from an 18th-century etiquette manual, La Salle's *Civilité* (1774): "Children like to touch clothes and other things that please them with their hands. This urge must be corrected, and they must be taught to touch all they see only with their eyes." And then Elias concludes as follows: "It has been shown elsewhere how the use of the sense of smell, the tendency to sniff at food or other things, comes to be restricted as something animal-like. Here we see one of the interconnections through which a different sense organ, the eye, takes on a very specific significance in civilized society. In a similar way to the ear, and perhaps even more so, it becomes a mediator of pleasure, precisely because the direct satisfaction of the desire for pleasure has been hemmed in by a multitude of barriers and prohibitions."[15] The language both in the source and in Elias' text is revealing. Corrections, barriers, prohibition—the terms indicate that there is more at stake here than the satisfaction of desire or the progress of civilization. It is, of course, Michel Foucault who, in his analysis of modernization processes, has shown in *Discipline and Punish* how vision and the gaze have increasingly become means of control and discipline. While Elias and Foucault differ in their evaluation of the observed phenomena, their micrological research on vision corroborates Adorno and Horkheimer's macrological thesis that the domination of outer nature via science and technology in capitalist society is dialectically and inexorably linked with the domination of inner nature, one's own as well as that of others.[16]

I would argue that it is precisely this dialectic which is the subterranean context of Lang's *Metropolis*. Vision as pleasure and desire has to be subdued and manipulated so that vision as technical and social control can emerge triumphant. On this level, the film pits the loving, nurturing gaze of Maria against the steely, controlled and controlling gaze of the Master of Metropolis. In the beginning Maria eludes his control since the catacombs are the only place in Metropolis remaining outside of the panoptic control system of the Tower; if only for that she must be punished and subdued. Beyond that, her "inner nature" is replaced by the machine. Ironically, however, the attempt to replace the real woman by the machine-woman fails, and Rotwang and Frederson have to face the return of the repressed. Once Maria has become a machine or, which is the other side of the process, the machine has appropriated Maria's external appearance, she again begins to elude her master's control. It seems that in whatever form woman cannot be controlled. True, the robot Maria does perform the task she has been programmed to do. In an inflammatory speech supported by sensual body language she seduces the male workers and leads them to the rampage in the machine rooms. In these sequences, the expressionist fear of a threatening technology which oppresses workers is displaced and reconstructed as the threat female sexuality poses to men and, ironically, to technology. Thus the machine-woman, who is no longer recognized as a machine, makes all men lose control: both the upperclass men who lust after her at the belly-dance party, and who, later, run deliriously with her through the streets of Metropolis shouting "Let's watch the world going to the devil," and the workers in the catacombs whom she turns into a raging machine-destroying mob. Significantly the riot is joined by the workers' wives who are shown for the first time in the film—in a state of hysteria and frenzy. The mob scenes thus take on connotations of a raging femininity which represents *the* major threat not only to the great machines, but to male domination in general. The threat of technology has successfully been replaced by the threat of woman. But while the machines only threatened the men who worked them, the unleashed force of female sexuality, represented by the vamp and the working-class women,[17] endangers the whole system of Metropolis, uptown and downtown, masters and slaves, and especially the workers' children who were abandoned underground to the floods unleashed by the destruction of the central powerhouse.

THE FEMALE MINOTAUR AS TECHNOLOGY-OUT-OF-CONTROL

Cliché has had it that sexually women are passive by nature and that the sexually active woman is abnormal, if not dangerous and destructive. The machine vamp in *Metropolis* of course embodies the unity of an active and destructive female sexuality and the destructive potential of technology. This pairing of the woman with the machine is in no way unique to Lang's film. Apart from the literary examples I cited earlier, it can be found in numerous 19th-century allegorical representations of technology and industry as woman.[18] More interesting for my purposes here, however, is Jean Veber's early 20th-century painting entitled "Allégorie sur la machine dévoreuse des hommes."[19] In the right half of the painting we see a gigantic flywheel which throws up and devours dozens of dwarf-like men. A large rod connected with the flywheel moves to and fro into a metal box on which a giant woman is sitting naked, with parted legs and smiling demonically. Clearly the painting is an allegory of sexual intercourse, of a destructive female sexuality unleashed upon men. It suggests that the woman has appropriated the phallic power and activity of the machine and that she now turns this power violently against men. It is easy to see that the allegory is indicative of male sexual anxieties, of the fear of an uncontrolled female potency, of the *vagina dentata*, of castration by woman. Whereas in this painting woman and machine are not identical, but stand in a relationship allegorizing a specific kind of female sexuality as imagined and feared by men, woman and machine are collapsed into one in the machine-vamp of *Metropolis*. Since the painting is sexually more explicit, it can help us unearth another major aspect of the film's subterranean content. What Eduard Fuchs, the famous art collector and art critic, said about Veber's allegorical painting in 1906, he could have said as well, with even more justification, of the machine-vamp in *Metropolis*: "Woman is the symbol of the terrifying, secret power of the machine which rolls over anything that comes under its wheels, smashes that which gets caught in its cranks, shafts, and belts, and destroys those who attempt to halt the turning of its wheels. And, vice versa, the machine, which coldly, cruelly and relentlessly sacrifices hecatombs of men as if they were nothing, is the symbol of the man-strangling Minotaur-like nature of woman."[20] A perfect summary of male mystifications of female sexuality as technology-out-of-control!

EXORCISM OF THE WITCH MACHINE

In light of Veber's painting and Fuchs' interpretation even earlier sequences of the film assume a different meaning. In her first appearance Maria, accompanied by the workers' children, seems to represent only the stereotypical innocent virgin-mother figure, devoid of sexuality. Such an interpretation is certainly in character, but it is nevertheless only one side of the story. It is significant, I think, that Freder's first gaze at Maria is heavily loaded with sexual connotations. Just before their encounter, Freder is playfully chasing a young woman back and forth around a fountain splashing water at her. Finally they collide in front of the fountain. Freder takes her in his arms, bends over her, and is about to kiss her when the doors open and Maria enters with the children. Freder releases the woman in his arms and in point of view shot stares raptured at Maria. This context of Maria's appearance as well as the hazed iris effect surrounding Maria as Freder gazes at her clearly indicate that Maria has instantaneously become an object of desire. To be sure, the passions she arouses in Freder are different from the playful sexuality suggested by the preceding sequence, but they are anything but asexual. The use of water imagery can give us another cue here. Just as the floods of the later sequences allegorize female frenzy (the proletarian women) and threatening female sexuality (the vamp), the fountain assumes sexual meaning as well. Except that here the water imagery suggests a controlled, channelled and non-threatening sexuality, the playful kind that is permitted in Metropolis. Similarly, the choreography of body movements in the fountain scene emphasizes geometry, symmetry and control, aspects which also inform the preceding track race sequence in the Masterman Stadium which was later cut from the film. Both athletics and the sexual games of the Eternal Gardens are presented as carefree, but controlled diversions of Metropolis' gilded youth. These scenes show us the upper-class equivalent of Lang's ornamental treatment of the workers in geometric, mechanically moving columns.[21] Already here Maria clearly disrupts the status quo. In response to her appearance Freder's body movements and gestures assume a new quality. From this point he becomes all impulse and desire, charges blindly from place to place, and seems unable to keep his body under control. Even more importantly, it is in pursuit of Maria that Freder descends underground and ends up in the vast machine halls of Metropolis. Whether she has "led" him there or not, the narrative links Freder's first exposure to the great machines with his sexual desire, a link which becomes even more manifest in the explosion sequence. For all of the subsequent events in the machine room actually mirror Freder's internal situation. The temperature rises relentlessly above the danger point and the machines run out of human control. Several blasts throw workers off the scaffoldings. Steam whirls and bodies fly through the air. Then comes a sequence in which Freder, in a total state of shock, begins to hallucinate. In his vision, the aperture high up in the belly of the great machine, in which we can see revolving cranks, changes into a grotesque mask-like face with a gaping mouth equipped with two rows of teeth. A column of half-naked workers moves up the pyramid-like steps, and two priests standing on either side of the fiery and blinding abyss supervise several muscular slaves who hurl worker after worker against the gleaming cranks which keep rising and falling amid clouds of smoke and steam. Of course, the meaning of Freder's nightmarish hallucination is quite clear: technology as Moloch demands the sacrifice of human lives. But that is not all. If we assume that Freder in pursuit of Maria is still sexually aroused, and if we remember that his second hallucination in the film deals explicitly with sexuality (that of the machine-vamp Maria), we may want to see the imagery in this sequence as a first indication of the *vagina dentata* theme, of castration anxiety, of the male fear of uncontrolled female potency displaced to technology.

Such an interpretation has implications for the way in which we perceive the real Maria. Rather than keeping the "good," asexual virgin Maria categorically apart from the "evil" sexual vamp,[22] we become aware of the dialectical relationship of these two stereotypes. On the level of sexual politics, the point of the film is precisely to subdue and to control this threatening and explosive female sexuality which is inherently and potentially there in any woman, even the virgin. It is in this context that the elaborate sequence portraying the laboratory creation of the machine-vamp is—contrary to Kracauer's claims—absolutely essential for a full understanding of the technology/sexuality link in the film. After Rotwang has brought Maria under his control, he proceeds to take her apart, to disassemble and to deconstruct her. In a complicated chemical and electrical process he filters her sexuality out of her and projects it onto the lifeless robot who then comes alive as the vamp Maria. The sexuality of the vamp is thus the sexuality of the real woman Maria transformed by a process of male projections onto the machine. After this draining experience, the real Maria is no longer the active enterprising woman of before, but assumes the role of a helpless mother figure who is totally dependent on male support. Thus in the flood sequences she seems paralyzed and has to wait for Freder to save the children, and in the end again she has to be saved from Rotwang's hands.

Just as Maria, under the male gaze, has been disassembled and doubly reconstructed as a docile sexless mother figure and as a potent destructive vamp who is then burnt at the stake, so Freder's desires have to be disentangled and controlled, and the sexual element purged. This happens mainly in the sequences following Freder's encounter with the false Maria in his father's arms. Freder suffers a physical and mental breakdown. During recovery in bed he hallucinates with terrified wide open eyes precisely that *mise-en-scène* of the vamp which Rotwang had set up on that same evening. Although this sequence can be read according to the Freudian account of the primal scene, the castration threat of the father, and the Oedipal conflict,[23] such a reading remains too limited. The goal of the narrative here is not just to bring Freder back under the Law of the Father by resolving the Oedipal conflict; it is rather to associate all male sexual desire for women with the threat of castration. This becomes amply clear as Freder's hallucination ends with a vision of the cathedral sculptures of the Seven Deadly Sins. As the central figure of Death moves toward Freder/the camera/the spectator swinging his scythe, Freder screams in horror and sinks back into his pillows.

The fact that Freder has learned his lesson and has been healed from sexual desire shows when he reappears in the catacombs and attempts to expose the false Maria and to keep her from seducing the workers. Separating the false, sexual Maria from the real Maria in his mind suggests that he is now working actively against his own sexual desires. This point is allegorically emphasized by his successful struggle against the floods inundating the workers' quarters where he saves Maria and the children. By the end of the film, Maria is no longer an object of sexual desire for Freder. Sexuality is back under control just as technology has been purged of its destructive, evil, i.e., "sexual," element through the burning of the witch machine.

It is, then, as if the expressionist fear of technology and male perceptions of a threatening female sexuality had been both exorcised and reaffirmed by this metaphoric witch-burning, which, as all witch burnings, guarantees the return of the repressed. It is as if the destructive potential of modern technology, which the expressionists rightfully feared, had to be displaced and projected onto the machine-woman so that it could be metaphorically purged. After the dangers of a mystified technology have been translated into the dangers an equally mystified female sexuality poses to men, the witch could be burnt at the stake and, by implication, technology could be purged of its threatening aspects. What remains is the serene view of technology as a harbinger of social progress. The transition from expressionism to the *Neue Sachlichkeit* is complete. The conflict of labor and capital—such was the belief of the *Neue Sachlichkeit* and such is the implicit message of the film—would be solved through technological progress. The notion that the heart has to mediate between the hands and the brain is nothing but a lingering residue of expressionism, an ideological veil which covers up the persisting domination of labor by capital and high technology, the persisting domination of woman by the male gaze and the reestablished repression of female and male sexuality. The final shots of the film with their visual separation of the workers from their masters and with the resumed ornamental treatment of human bodies in motion show that the hands and the brain are as separate as ever. Henry Ford's infamous categorization of humankind into the many hands and the few brains, as it was laid out in his immensely popular autobiography, reigns supreme. It is well-known how German fascism reconciled the hands and the brain, labor and capital. By then, Fritz Lang was already in exile.

Notes

1. Cf. Paul M. Jensen, "Metropolis: The Film and the Book," in Fritz Lang, *Metropolis* (New York: Simon & Schuster, 1973), p. 13; Lotte Eisner, *The Haunted Screen* (Berkeley and Los Angeles: University of California Press, 1969), pp. 223 ff.

2. Randolph Bartlett, "German Film Revision Upheld as Needed Here," *The New York Times* (March 13, 1927).

3. Stresemann was one of the leading "reformist" politicians of the stabilization phase of the Weimar Republic after 1923.—Axel Eggebrecht, "Metropolis," *Die Welt am Abend* (January 12, 1927).

4. Goebbels at the Nuremburg Party Convention of 1934.

5. Siegfried Kracauer, *From Caligari to Hitler* (Princeton, New Jersey: Princeton University Press, 1947), p. 165.

6. Ibid., p. 164.

7. On the *Neue Sachlichkeit* see John Willett, *Art and Politics in the Weimar Period: The New Sobriety, 1917–1933* (New York: Pantheon Books, 1978). On the machine-cult of the 1920s see Helmut Lethen, *Neue Sachlichkeit 1924–1932* (Stuttgart: Metzler, 1970) and Teresa de Lauretis et al. (eds.), *The Technological Imagination* (Madison, Wisconsin: Coda Press, 1980), especially the section "Machines, Myths, and Marxism."

8. Stephen Jenkins, "Lang: Fear and Desire," in S. J. (ed.), *Fritz Lang: The Image and the Look* (London: British Film Institute, 1981), pp. 38–124, esp. pp. 82–87.

9. In the following I am indebted to Peter Gendolla, *Die lebenden Maschinen: Zur Geschichte der Maschinenmenschen bei Jean Paul, E. T. A. Hoffmann und Villiers de l'Isle Adam* (Marburg: Guttandin und Hoppe, 1980).

10. Examples would be Jean Paul's *Ehefrau als bloßem Holze (1789)*, Achim von Arnim's Bella in *Isabella von Ägypten* (1800), E. T. A. Hoffmann's Olympia in *Der Sandmann* (1815), and Villiers de l'Isle Adam's Hadaly in *L'Eve future* (1886), a novel which strongly influenced Thea von Harbou in the writing of *Metropolis*. More recent examples would be Stanislav Lem's *The Mask* (1974), the puppet mistress in Fellini's *Casanova* (1976/77), and a number of works in the Franco-German art exhibit *Les machines célibataires* (1975).

11. The disruptions which the early railroads inflicted upon the human perceptions of time and space have been magnificently analyzed by Wolfgang Schivelbusch in his book *Geschichte der Eisenbahnreise: Zur Industrialisierung von Raum und Zeit* (Munich: Hanser, 1977); an English translation was published by Urizen in 1979. Cf. also Leo Marx, *The Machine in the Garden: Technology and the Pastoral Ideal in America* (New York: Oxford University Press, 1964).

12. Thea von Harbou, *Metropolis* (New York: Ace Books, 1963), p. 54.

13. Silvia Bovenschen, *Die imaginierte Weiblichkeit: Exemplarische Untersuchungen zu kulturgeschichtlichen und literarischen Präsentationsformen des Weiblichen* (Frankfurt am Main: Suhrkamp, 1979).

14. Norbert Elias, *The Civilizing Process: The Development of Manners* (New York: Urizen Books, 1978).

15. Ibid., p. 203.

16. See Max Horkheimer, *Eclipse of Reason* (New York: Oxford University Press, 1947) and Theodor W. Adorno/Max Horkheimer, *Dialectic of Enlightenment*, trans. John Cumming (New York: Herder & Herder, 1972).

17. In his thorough analysis of the Freikorps literature of the early Weimar Republic Klaus Theweleit has shown how in the presentation of proletarian women the themes of revolution and threatening sexuality are consistently interwoven. The way in which Lang places the working-class women in his film corroborates Theweleit's findings. Klaus Theweleit, *Männerphantasien: Frauen, Fluten, Körper, Geschichte*, vol. 1 (Frankfurt am Main: Verlag Roter Stern, 1977), esp. pp. 217 ff. English translation forthcoming from University of Minnesota Press.

18. See Cäcilia Rentmeister, "Berufsverbot für Musen," *Ästhetik und Kommunikation*, 25 (September 1976), 92–112.

19. "Allegory of the men-devouring machine." Veber's painting is discussed in Rentmeister's essay (see note 18) in relation to Georg Scholz' painting "Fleisch und Eisen" of 1923, a painting that can be attributed to *Neue Sachlichkeit*; it is also discussed in Theweleit, p. 454.

20. Eduard Fuchs, *Die Frau in der Karikatur* (Munich, 1906), p. 262.

21. On the cultural and political implications of Lang's ornamental style in *Metropolis*, cf. Siegfried Kracauer, "The Mass Ornament," *New German Critique*, 5 (Spring 1975), 67–76.

22. See Robert A. Armour, *Fritz Lang* (Boston: Twayne Publishers, 1977), p. 29.

23. That is the way Jenkins reads the sequence, "Lang: Fear and Desire," p. 86.

CONSTELLATION I
RETURN TO HISTORY: FASCISM, SOCIALISM, COMMUNISM

In contrast to the tendency of texts in the preceding constellation to mystify spectatorial practice and film form, the essays in this cluster take a more historical stance, foregrounding both the impact of particular ideological shifts in German history and concomitant disseminations of their cultural effects. These ideological shifts are irremedeably associated with the development and dissolution of two different and oppositional political systems, communism and fascism, whose impact on the German peasantry, working class and petit bourgeoisie has (with the exception of Ben Brewster's essay on Brecht in exile) only recently become a topic of scholarly focus within German cinema studies, despite long years of scrutiny in the disciplines of Sociology and Political Science. From a sociological perspective that recalls Patrice Petro's use of Kracauer in Constellation A ("German Cinema Studies") and Miriam Hansen's naturalization of a gendered imaginary in Constellation H ("Feminism and Early Weimar"), Lynn Abrams provides an empirical justification for associating early German cinema with the pre-Nazi fragmentation of the German working class. While her critique of the ways in which mass-marketed cinema contributed to the commercialization of leisure time opens space for a new theorization of urban cultural resistance to constructed "time off," its stereotypical assumptions of working-class lustfulness and the automatic functioning of capitalism evade the more complex explanations of the failure of left politics and culture in pre-Hitlerian Germany. Answering to such simplifications is the essay by Ben Brewster, whose historical inspection of the political economic relationship between Marxist Bertolt Brecht and the German and American commercial film industries raises questions about copyright ownership and intellectual property that resonate back toward problematics of Holocaust cultural ownership inscribed across Constellation B ("The Heimat *Debate") and toward the issue of German post-nationalist theory and cinema raised by both Tassilo Schneider in Constellation A ("German Cinema Studies") and Katie Trumpener in Constellation J ("The Post-al Public Sphere"). How does David Welch's historiographic investigation of proletarian cinema and socialist realism contrast both Abrams' sociological approach to working-class culture and Brewster's political economic understanding of film production? Where does Welch's cognitive mapping of the relationship between the Left and the Right in German culture and society intersect Marc Silberman's multiculturalist positioning of that relationship (Constellation J)? How do the new historicist notions of specificity and localization in Eric Rentschler's reading of the 1920s* Bergfilme *and Eric L. Santner's theory of a German fascist aesthetics actually qualify such cognitivist positionings by together occluding broader, less empiricist, more political (including political allegorical) approaches to the question of cultural politics? Do either Rentschler or Santner nonetheless rapproche Jameson's post-Marxist, allegorical reading of Syberberg (Constellation G ["Myth and Utopia"]), and if so, what does this say about the "difference" between right and left theories of cultural resistance in mainstream German cinema studies?*

From Control to Commercialization: the Triumph of Mass Entertainment in Germany 1900–25?

LYNN ABRAMS

I

Pubs, clubs, *Tingel-Tangels*, dance-halls, and parish fairs (*Kirmes*) were the staple diet of the urban working class in their leisure time until the turn of the century in Germany. Neighbourhood amusements based around residual cultural loyalties—religion and nationality—and further subdivided by occupation, sex, and age, filled the limited non-work time of the majority of working-class people. The first decade of the twentieth century, however, signalled a turning point in people's perception and experience of leisure and entertainment in Germany. In the immediate pre-war years, urban leisure activities began to embrace a more dynamic, exciting dimension. The cinema spearheaded this entertainment explosion which was characterized by large-scale mass amusements appealing to broader sections of the urban population. At first sight this development appears rather incongruous against a backdrop of the moral disapprobation and 'rational recreation' philosophy popular in the 1880s and 1890s, when the working classes were encouraged to partake of leisure activities that were uplifting and morally beyond reproach: strolling in public parks, reading books borrowed from public libraries, and attending 'public entertainment evenings' laid on by well-meaning local voluntary organizations. In reality, however, the 'new' entertainments on offer were both a continuation of more established popular recreations, revamped and publicized by astute entrepreneurs, and an extension of the increasingly public amusements enjoyed by the middle classes. It was the urban bourgeoisie who, while decrying the drinking and dancing of the lower classes, began to take their own recreations into the public arena: they visited theatres, played sport, strolled in the parks and zoological gardens, and commandeered trains to transport them out of the cities. Simultaneously, municipal councils and the larger employers began to legitimize leisure for the working class by providing new facilities expressly for non-work pleasures. While the vast majority of the working class never accepted the organization of leisure on middle-class terms, they never entirely rejected the con-

Reprinted from *German History* 8.3 (1990): 278–93.

cept of public leisure either. Although the public entertainment evenings were not wildly popular, the provision of open spaces in crowded, dirty cities was appreciated, football pitches were well used, and libraries gradually found working-class support, especially when located in working-class residential areas. Ironically, the rational recreation efforts of bourgeois reformers gave an impetus to the leisure industry by identifying a market and breaking down some of the initial barriers which had hitherto 'ghettoized' working-class leisure activities and hindered the emergence of a broad-based, mass, public leisure industry. The cinema is, of course, the most celebrated example of the mass entertainment phenomenon, but moving pictures were just one element of a much larger trend towards the provision of entertainment designed to appeal to the wider fee-paying audience.

The suggestion that a mass commercial leisure market emerged in the 1900s would seem to presuppose the undermining of the class-, gender-, ethnic-, and religion-specific cultures of the Kaiserreich centered on the neighbourhood public house, the church, and local sports and social clubs, not to mention party-political activities organized by local Social Democrat activists.[1] I have argued elsewhere that, in the leisure sphere at least, an explanation of the Imperial social system, at least in the towns of the industrial Rhine-Ruhr, cannot be explained solely in rigid class/party political terms. Certainly in the industrial towns in the region, residual cultural allegiances were crucial, resulting in a vast network of pubs, clubs, and entertainment establishments catering for one group or another. Labour-movement cultural activities were just one element of a multifaceted recreational scene. It is one of the aims of this article to examine the extent to which residual expressions of working-class culture were eroded and replaced by a homogeneous leisure culture based on mass consumption of national values peddled by the State and transcultural agencies. Did mass commercial entertainment displace the sectional cultures which had hitherto characterized working-class life, and were 'sharp cultural class barriers' swept away by the new means of mass communication?

II

The preconditions for the development of a mass entertainment and leisure industry were all present in Germany from the end of the 1890s.[2] The presence of large and concentrated centres of urban population provided the necessary supply of 'punters'. The rise in real income of a large proportion of the working class was a further prerequisite of the emergence of a mass leisure industry. Spending power on non-necessary items increased as real wages steadily rose on average between 1871 and 1914. From the 1890s on, a more rapid increase was experienced than previously—around 13 per cent between 1900 and 1913.[3] The amount of leisure time available to the industrial labour force also slowly increased. Although the decisive breakthrough in this respect, the eight-hour day, was not achieved until 1918, the daily average declined gradually from twelve to thirteen hours in the 1870s to between ten and eleven before the First World War. The construction of an efficient local urban transport system was a further impetus for the emerging commercial leisure sector. It made it possible for people to travel out of their neighbourhood for their entertainment and facilitated the reduction in time and energy taken by workers to travel to and from work. Formerly, extensive travel on foot meant that workers were too tired and disinclined to venture far in the evenings. It also enabled entertainment acts to reach more towns, thereby creating national and international stars. Finally, technological innovation as applied to the entertainment industry reached Germany from Britain and the United States. The motion-picture camera and kinetoscope had the most obvious impact on the early development of the leisure sector, but later the gramophone and the radio were also to transform people's leisure time. So too, in less dramatic ways, did the invention of the pneumatic tyre and the application of rubber to sport (for the bladder inside leather footballs, for example). Even the humble *Bierkneipe* was transformed by technological innovation with the introduction of electronic pianos and gramophones.

As the old entertainment establishments responded to demand by updating their decor and introducing modern attractions, new facilities were built on a large scale. Public halls were gradually provided in the town centres to house all manner of amusements and increasingly purpose-built premises, able to accommodate hundreds and sometimes thousands of spectators, dominated the entertainment profile of a town. By the outbreak of war, it is estimated that there were around 2,500 cinemas in Germany with an average capacity of 200 seats.[4] The larger theatres were able to house up to 1,000 people at once. Düsseldorf's Apollo was attended by over 600,000 people in 1922–3 and about two million people were said to visit the cinema every day by this date.[5] Sporting events began to attract similar numbers of participants and spectators. At the end of 1905 the German Football Association had 433 affiliated clubs with 24,462 members. By 1920 membership had reached a million, a trend reflected at the local level. The famous Gelsenkirchen club, FC Schalke 04, consisted of a mere 16 members at its foundation in 1904. Ten years later this figure had increased to around 90, and after the war and the expansion of the club to include boxing, athletics, and handball sections as well as football, over 1,000 people belonged to it.[6] Spectator sports such as cycle-racing and boxing gained in popularity, aided by the construction of huge arenas and commercial marketing strategies. Düsseldorf's new multi-purpose sports stadium erected after the war seated 40,000 spectators around the main arena and another 20,000 around the cycling track, catering for the hordes of cycling fans, many of whom belonged to clubs. By 1924 the combined membership of the Workers' Cycling Associations, *Solidarität* and *Freiheit*, totalled 304,500.[7] Crowds of people converged on transport networks, particularly at holiday times. As early as 1905 it was estimated that over 100,000 people used the trams to reach the Düsseldorf fair in July, and Bochum's tram and railway stations were frequently crowded, especially at Easter and Whitsuntide, with people heading for the countryside.[8]

III

Mass commercial entertainment, meaning the provision of a product or a service by a commercial organization for widespread, even nationwide, public consumption, was not a sudden invention of the 1900s. A similar strategy had been pioneered by the pamphlet-fiction publishers and distributors of the 1870s and 1880s. Their product was cheap, accessible, cleverly marketed, and widely distributed. It succeeded in reaching millions of readers. Their success lay in an astute interpretation of the market and an ability to adapt to and meet its demands and vicissitudes.[9] Reading remained the most frequent everyday leisure activity well into the Weimar Republic, particularly amongst young people who were to become the most important market for the new recreational products. Immediately before the outbreak of war the cinema emerged as a dynamic accompaniment (not a rival) to this already well-developed and ingrained popular leisure culture. 'In many ways', wrote an early historian of the film industry, 'cinema was simply a filming of those pulp-fiction pamphlets, a pictorial recitation of their contents, but one that was far more effective because the actions and adventures were actually portrayed visually.'[10] Indeed, many regarded this new medium as little more than trash literature in living pictures.[11]

The comparisons between these two successful manifestations of commercial culture are numerous. The roots of popular fiction were to be found in the popular culture peddled by the army of itinerants earlier in the century. Similarly, moving pictures were first popularized by travelling entertainers eager to outdo their competitors by introducing a new attraction. The late 1890s was the age of the travelling cinema or *Wanderkino* which accompanied the mechanical gimmicks and amusements which turned up at fairs, in public houses, and at variety shows all over the country. Just as entertainers had been forced to go on the road with their acts, continually in search of new audiences, the early cinemas also had to be itinerant; films were expensive to purchase and could not be shown too often in the same place. Only when film companies began to lease films for hire were the first static cinemas established around 1904–5.[12] Initially these were fairly humble affairs: an empty shop hired for the purpose or the back room of a pub, the windows blacked out with paper and adorned with a few posters and handwritten programmes.[13] In some of the smallest 'cinemas', or *Kintopps* as they were known, the screen was set up in the middle of the room, so those seated behind the screen saw the film back-to-front. By 1912 there were around 1,500 of these early cinemas in Germany, mostly in densely populated industrial areas and ports which could furnish a regular audience. Düsseldorf possessed ten cinemas by this date; some of the first films were shown at the Apollo theatre as early as 1900. The first cinema erected specifically for the purpose of showing films opened in 1906. For its size, however, Düsseldorf was not particularly well provided with cinemas: in 1910 Essen had no fewer than 21, while Hamburg possessed 40, and Berlin residents could visit any one of 139 cinemas.[14] In some places the demand for cinemas was such that venues previously used for other forms of entertainment, such as classical theatres and the circus, were converted into cinemas. By 1914, entrepreneurs in the entertainment business had recognized the full potential of moving pictures and were willing to invest considerable sums in the new venture. This investment provided almost two and a half thousand cinemas by 1914, with a further thousand being opened between 1914 and 1920. The highpoint was not reached until 1925, when almost one and a half million seats were available in 3,878 cinemas around the country.[15] By then, moving pictures were big business. Cinema owners organized themselves into the *Verein Deutscher Kinematographentheaterbesitzer* (Association of German Cinema Owners) to protect their interests against what they saw as the insidious entertainment tax (*Lustbarkeitssteuer*) exacted from receipts by municipal authorities and the volatile policies of government. The major German film company, *Universum Film Aktien gesellschaft* (UFA), had been formed in 1917. A number of journals devoted to films and the cinema, such as *Der Kinematograph*, were published. And probably the most obvious sign that the cinema had become a mass recreational pursuit was the negative reaction it elicited from moral watchdogs and the implementation of censorship.

The cinema certainly emerged as the most popular form of entertainment in the urban centres. It was even said to rival the public house in the affection of the working class, threatening the existence of many drinking places as well as the variety theatres and circuses. A visit to the cinema was a relatively cheap form of entertainment: between 10 and 30 Pfennigs gained entry to the early silent films, cheaper than standing room in the theatre. When purpose-built cinemas were erected, seating even became quite comfortable. And cinema owners often adopted an open-all-hours policy, running film reels continually so people could just call in when they had some spare time.

But there was also an element of fascination with the living pictures that attracted so many sections of the population to the cinema. The novelty value of the silver screen caused great excitement, particularly amongst young people and members of the working class who seem to have formed the vast majority of cinema audiences at least until the 1920s, when movie-going became more respectable. Within the ranks of the working class, women and children were particularly keen cinema-goers. Women found the local cinema the ideal place to spend their infrequent leisure time. Working-class women might call in during the day, often with children in tow, while working girls visited the cinema after work. But it was the youth of Germany, both girls and boys, more than any other group, who were the most enthusiastic supporters of the cinema. The group who had wholeheartedly adopted the commercial cultural and leisure pursuits of the pre-war years, pulp-fiction and dance halls in particular, universally accepted the cinema with little sexual or class demarcation. In spite of the numerous alternatives on offer, by the end of the Weimar Republic the majority of young people were attending the cinema: 50 per cent of boys and 62 per cent of girls at some time or another.[16] For some, the chance to pursue a leisure activity in the company of friends rather than family (most went with friends of their own sex), to escape parental supervision, or to pursue a relationship in the relative privacy of the darkened cinema was just as much an attraction as the films were.[17] Briggs' statement that 'the cinema did not so much divert an older audience from other kinds of entertainment as create an enormous new one' rings as true for Germany as it does for Britain.[18]

Yet, in spite of the convenience of the cinema as a leisure venue for numerous groups, in the final analysis it was the films themselves that drew people to the 'movies'. The quest for excitement and the desire for sensation on the part of the masses was satisfied by the content of the most popular types of films, the so-called 'dramas'. In Düsseldorf the police commented upon the 'desire for sensation by the masses . . . which the multiple murder, suicide, adultery, and other crimes [provide] at present in increasingly crass forms'.[19] This alleged need for excitement was neither new nor restricted to the cinema, however. In theatres variety acts were becoming increasingly dare-devil and suggestive, and popular reading material reflected the same trend. Neither was this sensationalism a mere gimmick invented by the film industry. Film-makers seemed to be responding to a real demand from the punters.

Critics were correct in equating these films with popular commercial fiction; cinema was said to 'bring the sensational pictures to life'. But they stood on shakier ground when positing a link between trash literature, sensational films, and urban crime, especially juvenile crime. Films portraying criminal acts were said to encourage imitation. Loose morals allegedly held by young people were partially blamed on the erotic content of popular dramas. Youth and working-class people alike were credited with few powers of distinction between fiction and reality. Any critical analysis was thought to be suppressed by the emotions engendered by the films. Censorship was thus deemed to be the most effective method of sanitizing film content.

Cinema censorship was first introduced in Berlin in 1906, after considerable lobbying by pressure-groups such as the *Kinoreformbewegung* (Cinema Reform Movement), which later became the *Kinematographische Reformpartei* (Cinema Reform Party). By 1910, the police in the Düsseldorf administrative district were applying their own censorship code to all films shown, although not equally, one may add.[20] Censorship was more severe in industrial towns such as Essen, where the cinemas were said to be frequented by the 'uneducated' members of the working class, 'given to brutality and violence'. It was less harsh in towns such as Düsseldorf whose cinema-goers consisted of a larger proportion of supposedly more discriminating, better-educated inhabitants.[21] In 1912 the Düsseldorf police announced that they would censor all 'films with immoral content', all those containing 'frightening scenes' which might strain the nerves of the audience or harm young people, all those which contained 'crimes, particularly murder, attempted murder, robbery, theft, forgery, fraud, prostitution, suicide, torture of animals', and all those in which the establishment, people in authority, and those wearing uniform were ridiculed. There were also a number of extra provisions for children's films.[22]

During the war special censorship measures were introduced, banning the trashy, sensationalist films that were regarded as incompatible with the gravity of the situation, as well as all foreign films.[23] This action seriously diminished the quantity of films released for public screening, since between 80 and 90 per cent of all films shown before the war had been produced abroad.[24] At the same time it was a fillip to the domestic film industry, especially the newly formed newsreel companies.[25] After the war, however, for a brief period before the implementation of the Weimar constitution, a wave of films was produced of the sexual enlightenment genre, the so-called *Aufklärungsfilme*, for example, *Hyenas of Lust, From Brothel to Marriage*, and *Vows of Chastity*. The latter, incidentally, caused an anti-semitic street riot by the generally orderly bourgeois cinema-goers of Düsseldorf.[26] While the Weimar constitution did include a commitment to freedom of art and expression, a compromise between the Social Democrats, the Liberals, and the Centre Party produced a qualifying clause which reserved the right to introduce censorship in certain conditions and specific circumstances. Such a provision within the constitution was partly a reflection of conservative policy towards youth and the control of popular culture, but it also suited the Social Democrats to retain the right to suppress manifestations of a culture they regarded as neither worthy nor genuine.[27] On the same note the so-called *Schund- und Schmutzkampf*, which began in the Kaiserreich as a war against pornographic literature, was taken up again in the 1920s, purportedly to protect young people but quite clearly also as an element of a political ideology.[28] The 1920 *Reichslichtspielgesetz* ruled that a film could be banned if it threatened public order, was blasphemous in any way, or damaged national security, with the rider that permission was 'not to be refused for political, social, religious, ethical, or ideological reasons as such'.[29] Only ninety films failed to gain the censor's approval between 1924 and 1929, just over 1 per cent of all films reviewed, and the same number as before 1920.[30]

The key point here is not the number of films stopped by the censor but the extent of interference in and control over the production and consumption of a popular cultural form. In her seminal paper on mass entertainment, Asa Briggs rightly highlights 'the way in which massive market interests have come to dominate an area of life which until recently was dominated by individuals themselves with the intermittent help of showmen and the more regular help of . . . innkeepers and bookmakers'. 'The massiveness of the control', he continues, 'is certainly more revealing than the often dubious statements made by the controllers about the character of the "masses" whose wants they claim they are satisfying.'[31] Certainly Social Democrats regarded the commercial cinema as an agent of bourgeois propaganda, controlled from above, targeted to render the working class totally passive on receipt. A contributor to the leading socialist journal, *Die Neue Zeit*, wrote of the hypnotic effect of the events on the screen on working-class audiences who were too tired after a day's work to examine the contents critically.[32] Few on the left credited the cinema with any positive influence. Emilie Altenloh was an exception. In 1914 she wrote; 'rest from work should not place any new demands on the individual . . . the average person needs something which is effortless', citing the cinema as a good example.[33] For the majority of SPD leaders, however, effortless meant dangerous; cinema had replaced religion as the opiate of the masses. Its popularity implied the anonymity of a mass culture which had the ability to undermine the workers' culture painstakingly shaped by the Party, a danger which became more imminent in the Weimar Republic. To what extent did the new commercial mass culture undermine and then supersede the specific proletarian culture(s) of the Kaiserreich? How far were residual expressions of working-class culture eroded and replaced by a homogeneous Weimar leisure culture based on the mass consumption of national precepts?

IV

While the cinema and other new forms of amusement were certainly attracting vast numbers of people, it would not be wise to extrapolate from this that local, residual cultural values were being eroded. However, a number of related factors conspired to create, in appearance at least, a more universal, homogeneous leisure culture in urban centres. The transformation of urban leisure culture, while appearing to accelerate from the turn of the century on, has to be judged against a history of several decades of attempts by the state to superimpose a national culture on the German people and break down the local, religious, and ethnic cultural divisions which were seen as threatening the stability of the new Germany. Thus, attempts were made to repress local and regional customs and traditions such as the parish fair (*Kirmes*), and particular religious and ethnic cultural forms, such as the Polish associational movement, were encouraged to integrate into a fictional all-embracing German culture. Simultaneously, cultural forms were imposed from above, such as the Sedan Day celebrations and events revering the monarchy.

Yet, independent of this movement inspired and guided from above, the production of popular culture gradually receded from local control. The disintegration of the close-knit community was often the cause of the disappearance of community-based recreations such as animal-baiting, and the acquisition of former common land by local authorities signalled the demise of some neighbourhood festivals. As urban populations increased and the demand for entertainment grew from the 1890s on, local entertainment entrepreneurs, notably the publicans-turned-concert-or-dance-hall-proprietors, failed to keep pace with the changes. Leisure and entertainment moved into the hands of big business: the owners of large theatres, halls, and cinemas operated on a far larger scale with greater profit margins. They no longer relied on special occasions to boost their incomes in order to break even. 'Time is money' was their motto—and they stayed open all hours to attract enough custom to maximize their profits.

Moreover, most of the large entertainment establishments in which the newest films were shown, the most famous variety acts appeared, and the most exciting sporting events took place, were located in the city centres. This drew people away from the comparatively less exciting and more familiar entertainment on offer in their own neighbourhoods. So leisure and entertainment not only became concentrated in the hands of relatively few wealthy entrepreneurs, but also became geographically centralized. This had the effect of squeezing local entertainment provision at both ends. Centrally located entertainment also benefited from the demand for more sophisticated amusements from rural inhabitants. While they already received watered down versions of the new commercial culture on their doorsteps, such as the popular press, serialized and pamphlet fiction, and travelling cinemas, the advent of cheap transport enabled them to swell the ranks of urban revellers. For it was often easier for countryfolk to reach the town centre than the suburbs. Previous forms of entertainment had not only confirmed and perpetuated the rural-urban divide but had also emphasized religious, gender, ethnic, and occupational divisions within the working class. Pubs usually had a clientele drawn from the immediate neighbourhood, voluntary associations were often deliberately organized along ethnic or religious lines, and most leisure pursuits had been dominated by men. Some of the new amusements, while not eliminating these divisions, certainly papered over the cracks. In purely practical terms such differences were no longer recognized or important in the huge, anonymous auditoria and stadia and darkened cinemas. Even the seating allowed the mingling of different groups who could avoid any real social contact with one another.

The key to success in this highly competitive era was not necessarily innovation as it had been in the past. Competition within the industry was conducted along the lines of excellence, fame, and an ability to read the market whilst maintaining the broadest popular appeal. National and international artistes of the highest calibre were preferred to local amateurs, films were imported from abroad, mainly from the United States, and even sporting events drew the largest crowds when nationally or internationally famous sportsmen were involved. In 1911 a film of a world championship boxing match between the Americans Jeffries and Johnson drew enormous crowds in Germany wherever it was shown, although, or perhaps, because it had already gained notoriety by sparking-off race riots in the United States.[34]

Localism, regionalism, and the representation of religious, ethnic, or other interests did not fill seats in huge cinemas, auditoria, and stadia. Universal values with an appeal to all groups did. The producers of commercial culture tried to avoid any reflection of 'real life' which would have meant tackling social divisions and antagonisms. One of the prime, indeed defining characteristics of mass commercial entertainment was its homogeneity. The silent films were the forerunners of this trend. They were easily accessible and understood by Germans and non-Germans, literate and illiterate alike. In terms of content, in spite of their sensationalist nature, films remained fairly neutral. 'There can be little arguing', writes Paul Monaco, 'that feature films only rarely addressed [themselves] directly to contemporary social problems. Instead, movies find their relationship to society in oblique symbolism. . . . One of the most striking characteristics of film is its kinship to the dream.'[35] And of course the more foreign films were imported to be shown to German audiences, the less likely they were to relate directly to their viewers' experience.

Homogeneity or universalism was to be found on the sports field too. Although teams built up considerable local followings, they began to compete against one another in regional, national, and international competitions, necessitating formal, uniform rules, organization, and discipline, eventually promoting a wider identification with one's country on the part of both players and supporters. The Olympic Games were revived in 1896, and by the 1920s national and international sports displays and competitions organized by the Workers' Sport Movement were regular events: they too held their alternative Workers' Olympiad.[36] In non-socialist sport, the game (and preferably success) became the focus of interest of most players and supporters. The players of one of the most famous football teams in the Ruhr, FC Schalke 04, were typical when they said: 'We want to play football. We want nothing to do with anything else. . . . Politics and religion have no role to play in our association.'[37]

Universal values were fostered and promoted in a far more sophisticated, direct, and far-reaching way than ever before, by means of the mass media. Film and, later, radio did far more than simply advertise what was on offer. They contributed to the emergence of a mass culture by transmitting the same message to readers, viewers, and listeners belonging to all classes, nationalities, religions, and regions. The press, film, and radio were able to create a mass market for products and services by dictating taste and fashion in areas such as music, dancing, and clothing.

Young people were particularly important as receivers and transmitters of the new cultural values. They were avid cinema-goers and easily influenced by the associated fashions, music, and stars, just as young people are today.[38] Young men were also prominent in the sports movement, although greater sexual freedom and modern fashions permitted young women to take part in more active recreational pursuits too. By 1926 there existed seventy-six national youth associations in Germany, with almost four and a half million members under the age of 21. In fact, 43 per cent of 14- to 21-year-olds belonged to one or more youth organizations, the majority in sports clubs (46.8 per cent of boys and 17.7 per cent of girls).[39] The inclination of young people towards sectionally biased organizations, such as religious youth associations or the youth branches of the labour movement, was less remarkable than the growing membership of non-affiliated groups. At the same time, however, a trend towards membership of youth groups expressing nationalist sentiments was also noticeable. Increasingly, young single people, male and female, came to represent a new force in consumer demand, moving away from their parents' loyalties and embracing the new commercial, mass leisure culture instead.

The gradual encroachment of a commercial entertainment culture into the hitherto sectional cultures that existed in urban working-class communities could never have gained such a hold in the 1920s without tapping a new consumerist ideology amongst a working class that was undergoing change in terms of its structure, geographical distribution, level of integration and political loyalty. The religious, ethnic, and other loyalties which continued to divide the working class in towns such as Bochum and Düsseldorf until the outbreak of war were nevertheless losing their sharpness. This was the result of secular trends, the 'Germanization' of foreign immigrants, and more general improvements in housing and education which contributed to the alleviation of the physical and psychological ghettoization of the working class as a whole and groups within it. It also resulted from the greater spending power of all groups, the growing ability to make choices about how to spend one's leisure time, and exposure to cultural influences which were not obvious attempts at 'social control', compared with, say, the rational recreation initiative of the 1890s.[40] All of this caused the Social Democrats much frustration. As they saw it, the working class was stuck on the first step of the evolutionary relationship to bourgeois culture. 'They are proud of the fact that they can imitate everything bourgeois,' complained one SPD functionary; 'for the most part, they have petit-bourgeois ideals: drinking, trashy literature, jazz, boxing, and so forth.'[41]

The early years of the Weimar Republic are famous as the heyday of the socialist cultural initiative expressed via a dense network of educational, recreational, and sporting associations affiliated to the SPD and the KPD, transcending residual divisions within the working class and bringing about vast improvements in the conditions for the implementation of this policy. In Germany as a whole, by 1914 the SPD possessed almost 500 trade union hostels and meeting rooms, 77 trade-union houses, 581 libraries and 98 reading rooms, 429 education committees, and 451 youth commissions.[42] On the other hand, success in this department was tempered by a failure to come to terms with, and successfully compete against, the commercial leisure industry. The problem lay in the SPD's refusal to accept cultural forms which they regarded as the 'poison of civilization'; alcohol, the pub, the cinema, and trashy literature were regarded as the antitheses of educational improvement.[43] Of course, this rejection of proletarian culture, the culture of everyday life, had been a constant feature of socialist cultural policy throughout the Kaiserreich but only now did this attitude threaten the internal strength of the labour movement. Possibly comforted or even protected by the apparent increase in membership of the party and its associated clubs and organizations—the workers' sports associations alone boasted over a million members by the late 1920s—the SPD refused to acknowledge the sheer scale of the working-class embrace of commercial pleasures.

The cinema was an obvious medium for the labour movement to use, both for propaganda and education, a fact acknowledged by a few in the movement as early as 1914. Writing in *Die Neue Zeit*, Franz Förster commented that 'the cinema has become a strength to be reckoned with by publicists, politicians, legislators, and, particularly, the Social Democratic education initiative'. Förster recommended that the SPD purchase its own equipment and establish its own cinemas, making use of the numerous trade union premises, and employ travelling cinemas to reach smaller towns. He also proposed the publication of film reviews and critiques in the party press.[44] Although practical impediments to these suggestions (mainly the high cost of equipment and the need to adhere to official fire

regulations) hindered any large-scale exploitation of the cinema, one cannot escape the conclusion that an absence of political will within the party
leadership was equally to blame for the SPD's failure to tap this important
market. By contrast, in 1925 a propaganda film was shown in all cinemas
promoting the candidacy of Hindenburg in the forthcoming presidential
elections.[45] The cinema had been a popular means of entertainment and
communication at least since the end of the war, but it was not until the
late 1920s that the SPD took full advantage of its benefits. Even then, the
labour movement always had difficulty in raising the finance to produce its
own films—the cost could be upwards of 300,000 Marks—and it had limited success in founding its own cinemas.[46] The KPD overcame the financial
hurdle by buying in films from the Soviet Union, such as Eisenstein's
Battleship Potemkin, and eventually both parties restricted themselves to
propaganda films. Neither ever discarded its distaste for the medium
which they both described as 'the most important capitalist means for controlling people'.[47]

The split in the labour movement after 1919 intensified a problem that
was bound to affect it anyway. The growing working-class ability to partake
of a leisure culture previously beyond its grasp ran up against a socialist
leadership intent on sticking to its definition and practice of culture. When
added to improved living and working conditions, this could only widen
the gap that already existed between the everyday experiences of the
working class and the horizons of political culture. '"Workers' culture" as
labour movement culture and the everyday popular culture of the lower
classes were [still] mutually exclusive.'[48]

V

None of the new mass commercial leisure forms was the sole province of
the working class in general or any group within it. The cinemas, sports
arenas, and fun-fairs became spaces where the classes, religions, ethnic
groups, and sexes could mix. Thus some degree of social harmony in
leisure was achieved, a dream which had existed only as a utopian vision
in the minds of liberal reformers several decades earlier. Indeed, the transcendent nature of commercial leisure was its strength, coupled with its
ability to communicate to all groups, irrespective of individual loyalties.
Some historians have interpreted this as the democratization of leisure,
and even culture. 'Cultural goods [Bildungsgüter], which had hitherto
been status symbols of a narrow upper class, were made available to the
broadest groups in the population via records, film, radio, and paper-
backs,' writes Heinrich August Winkler. 'On the other hand, popular entertainment products from jazz and the pop-song to the comedy film,
penetrated the higher milieu.'[49] It is this degree of widespread acceptance
of products of the commercial leisure sector (and note the waning of criti-

cism of the cinema in particular after the war), and the extent to which goods and services filtrated both upwards and downwards, that distinguished leisure in the 1920s from that of the pre-war period. To quote Winkler once again: '"mass culture" . . . was distinguishable not only from traditional workers' culture, but also from conventional bourgeois culture', forming what he calls a 'type of bourgeois-proletarian mixture'.[50]

However, the triumph of commercial leisure did not necessarily signal the disappearance of older, 'traditional' forms and expressions of working-class culture. Most, if not all, of the leisure activities enjoyed by the working class—festivals, drinking, dancing, and associational life—persisted into the 1920s, some less vibrant or reformed, others revitalized or adapted to changing circumstances. Similarly, the middle classes, while enjoying the cinema, and later, in the privacy of their own homes, the radio and gramophone, continued to patronize the classical theatre, opera, cafés, and restaurants and formed the vanguard of modernism in Weimar Germany.[51] Commercial culture, then, was an arena where the two groups could meet on neutral ground while not excluding the simultaneous enjoyment of some more class-bound activities. The working class began to lose its marginal position in urban society, becoming more integrated into the mainstream, and the mainstream shifted so that it was no longer the creation and provenance of the bourgeoisie.

In the Weimar Republic, cultural socialism lost its sense of direction in the public, commercial leisure sphere although, as Dieter Langewiesche has rightly pointed out, it did have successes in education and influenced other aspects of everyday life such as child-rearing, family life, even housing and furniture design.[52] Moreover, it should not be forgotten that it was only after 1918 that the labour-movement club culture really flourished. However, one institution retained its place and importance in the political culture of the working class—the tavern. Ethnic, occupational, and religious differences which had fostered an intense localism around tavern life gave way, particularly in the cities, to political affiliations. This process is vividly illustrated by Anthony McElligott's study of political street violence in Hamburg in the early 1930s, a phenomenon which centered upon taverns dominated by the SPD, the KPD, and the National Socialists.[53]

Those involved in overt political activity, such as the 1918–19 revolution and the battles on the streets at the end of the Republic, were doubtless a minority. Was political passivity the consequence of the masses' embrace of the commercial sector? Mass entertainment was certainly escapist and diversionary, and the dominant values transmitted by this culture, while not overtly bourgeois and conventional, were not alternative or oppositional either. Did audiences transfer their hopes and dreams onto the stars of stage, screen, and football field? Did the new consumerist ideology, the ability of many to buy 'luxuries', cushion the later effects of economic stagnation and depression? The later success of the National

Socialists in tapping the mass media would suggest that commercialization had succeeded in creating an individualist mentality and diverted energy from seeking fundamental change. There is little evidence to support the alternative hypothesis, that working-class exposure to mass commercial culture created a feeling of frustration at not being able to achieve what they saw on the screen.

By the 1920s commercialization had virtually imposed a national culture on the masses, a process which had little to do with control from above. Several decades of government attempts to impose a homogeneous national culture came to nothing. Rather, it was the result of a supply-and-demand curve determined by a new group of consumers and entrepreneurs. The working class now regarded leisure as a right, not a luxury, and it was its consumer power which stimulated the production of new forms of entertainment to transport it away from reality to a world dominated by excitement, sensation, and collective fervour. It has been suggested that the 1930s witnessed the 'democratization' of leisure, when leisure was regarded as a right for everyone of any age, sex, and occupation, and when the benefits of sufficient leisure time were finally acknowledged. Although the Nazis' *Kraft durch Freude* policy corrupted this tendency, the floodgates were already open for all to spend their leisure time in ways both beneficial and enjoyable.

Notes

1 For a more detailed discussion of this subject see my 'Aspects of Popular Culture, Leisure and Recreation in Imperial Germany: with particular reference to Bochum and Düsseldorf' (PhD. University of East Anglia, 1988). On the fragmentation of working-class culture in the Ruhr see Stephen Hickey, *Workers in Imperial Germany: The Miners of the Ruhr* (Oxford, 1985).

2 See Asa Briggs, *Mass Entertainment: The Origins of a Modern Industry* (Adelaide, 1960).

3 Gerhard Bry, *Wages in Germany*, 1871–1945 (Princeton, 1960), p. 54.

4 F. von Zglinicki, *Der Weg des Films* (Hildesheim, 1979).

5 D. Langewiesche, 'Working-Class Culture and Working-Class Politics in the Weimar Republic', in R. Fletcher (ed.), *Bernstein to Brandt* (London, 1987), p. 110.

6 *Statistisches Jahrbuch für das Deutsche Reich*, 28 (1907); R. A. Woeltz, 'Sport, Culture and Society in Late Imperial and Weimar Germany: Some Suggestions for Future Research', *British Journal of Sports History*, 4 (1977), 304–5. For information on FC Schalke 04, see Siegfried Gehrmann, 'Fußball in einer Industrieregion. Das Beispiel FC Schalke 04', in J. Reulecke and W. Weber (eds.), *Fabrik, Familie, Feierabend* (Wuppertal, 1978), pp. 377–98, here p. 385.

7 Heinz Haeffs, 'Sport und Turnen', in H. A. Lux (ed.), *Düsseldorf* (Düsseldorf, 1925), pp. 301–3; *Statistisches Jahrbuch für das Deutsche Reich*, 1926.

8 *Düsseldorfer Volkszeitung*, 25 July 1905; *Märkischer Sprecher*, 5 June 1900.

9 See R. Fullerton, 'Toward a Commercial Popular Culture in Germany: the Development of Pamphlet Fiction, 1871–1914', *Journal of Social History*, 12 (1979), 489–512.

10 Walter Panofsky, *Die Geburt des Films* (1944), cited by Gary Stark, 'Cinema, Society

and the State: Policing the Film Industry in Imperial Germany', in G. Stark and B. K. Lackner (eds.). *Essays on Culture and Society in Modern Germany* (Texas, 1982), pp. 122–66, here p. 130 (n. 24).

11   Bernhard Zeller (ed.), *Hätte ich das Kino* (Stuttgart, 1976), p. 67.

12   On the development of the early cinema in Germany see Zglinicki, *Der Weg*, and Stark, 'Cinema, Society and the State'.

13   Zeller, *Hätte ich das Kino*, p. 57.

14   Zglinicki, *Der Weg*, p. 319.

15   Ibid.

16   D. Peukert, *Jugend zwischen Krieg und Krise. Lebenswelten von Arbeiterjungen in der Weimarer Republik* (Cologne, 1987), p. 218.

17   In 1933, 53.1% of boys went to the cinema with another male, 20.2% with a girl; 42.8% of girls went with a girlfriend and 26.5% with a boyfriend (ibid.).

18   Briggs, *Mass Entertainment*, p. 18. See also Dietrich Mühlberg, 'Kulturgeschichte der Arbeiterklasse und Kino—Ueberlegungen zu einem möglichen Forschungsansatz', *Filmwissenschaftliche Beiträge*, 2 (1981), 13–14.

19   Hauptstaatsarchiv Düsseldorf (HStAD), Regierung Düsseldorf (RD) 9004: Düsseldorf Polizei-Verwaltung, Erlass einer Polizeiverordnung über die Kino-Zensur, 24 Jan. 1910.

20   See Stark, 'Cinema, Society and the State', for a comprehensive account of censorship of the film industry in Germany.

21   HStAD, RD 46077: Filmzensure, Essen, 26 Sept. 1915.

22   HStAD, RD 46077: Conference of Düsseldorf police inspectors on the censorship of public cinema performances, 17 Jan. 1912.

23   See Stark, 'Cinema, Society and the State', on censorship policy during the war.

24   See Thomas J. Saunders, 'Comedy as Redemption: American Slapstick in Weimar Culture?' *Journal of European Studies*, 17 (1987), 253–77, here p. 254.

25   On the development of the German film and newsreel industry during the war, see David Welch, 'Cinema and Society in Imperial Germany, 1905–1918', *German History* 8 (1990), pp. 28–45.

26   On the so-called 'Aufklärungsfilme', see P. Monaco, *Cinema and Society. France and Germany during the Twenties* (New York, 1976), pp. 52–3.

27   D. Peukert, *Grenzen der Sozialdisziplinierung: Aufstieg und Krise der Deutschen Jugendfürsorge 1878 bis 1932* (Cologne, 1986), pp. 181–4.

28   D. Peukert, 'Der Schund- und Schmutzkampf als "Sozialpolitik der Seele"—eine Skizze' (unpublished paper, Essen, 1982).

29   Reichslichtspielgesetz, 12 May 1920.

30   Monaco, *Cinema and Society*, p. 56.

31   Briggs, *Mass Entertainment*, pp. 28–9.

32   S. Drucker, 'Das Kinoproblem und unsere politischen Gegner', *Die Neue Zeit* 32 (1914), p. 868.

33   Emilie Altenloh, *Zur Soziologie des Kino* (Jena, 1914).

34   HStAD, RD 46077: newspaper cutting from Gelsenkirchen (unidentified), 18 Mar. 1911.

35   Monaco, *Cinema and Society*, p. 7.

36   See Robert Wheeler, 'Organised Sport and Organised Labour: The Workers' Sport Movement', *Journal of Contemporary History*, 13 (1978), 191–210.

37   Gehrmann, 'Fußball in einer Industrieregion', p. 398. This contrasts somewhat with the situation in England and Scotland where the confessional allegiances of Liverpool and Everton and Celtic and Rangers are legendary.

38   Peukert, *Jugend*, p. 219.

39   Ibid. 220–1.

40   For general details regarding the working class's spending power, leisure time, and social and geographical mobility in the Weimar Republic, see H. A. Winkler, *Der Schein der*

Normalität, Arbeiter und Arbeiterbewegung in der Weimarer Republik 1924 bis 1930 (Berlin/Bonn, 1985), especially ch. 1, pp. 13–176.

41   Kurt Heilbut, cited in Wilfried van der Will and Rob Burns, *Arbeiterkulturbewegung in der Weimarer Republik* (Frankfurt am Main, 1982), p. 187.

42   H. Groschopp, *Zwischen Bierabend und Bildungsverein. Zur Kulturarbeit in der Deutschen Arbeiterbewegung vor 1914* (Berlin, 1985), p. 115.

43   For the labour movement's attitude not only to the cinema but to other forms of proletarian amusement, see Mühlberg, 'Kulturgeschichte der Arbeiterklasse und Kino'.

44   Franz Förster, 'Das Kinoproblem und die Arbeiter', *Die Neue Zeit*, 32 (1914), 483–7.

45   Frank Heidenreich, *Arbeiterbildung und Kulturpolitik* (Berlin, 1983), p. 93.

46   On the response of the SPD to the rise of cinema, see Langewiesche, 'Working-Class Culture and Working-Class Politics', pp. 110–15.

47   Ibid. 113.

48   Peukert, *Grenzen der Sozialdisziplinierung*, p. 188.

49   Winkler, *Der Schein der Normalität*, p. 145.

50   Ibid. 144–5.

51   Modris Eksteins, *The Rites of Spring: the Great War of the Twentieth Century* (London, 1989).

52   Langewiesche, 'Working-Class Culture and Working-Class Politics', p. 109. On proletarian lifestyle and *Wohnkultur*, see also W. L. Guttsman, 'German Labour Movement Culture and German Working-Class Culture during the period of the Weimar Republic: a case of cohesiveness or a case of confrontation' (unpublished paper presented to European History Research Seminar, University of East Anglia, 1986).

53   Anthony McElligott, 'Street Politics in Hamburg 1932–3', *History Workshop*, 16 (1983), 83–90.

Brecht and the Film Industry
(on *The Threepenny Opera* film and *Hangmen Also Die*)

BEN BREWSTER

I N 1930, Brecht's publisher signed a contract with Nero-Film AG for the latter to make a film adaptation of Brecht and Weill's stage success, *The Threepenny Opera*. Despite clauses in the contract guaranteeing Brecht and Weill's right to collaborate in the adaptation and a subsequent agreement between Brecht and the film company on the detailed arrangements for this collaboration, joint work soon broke down, Nero went ahead (with Tobis and Warner Brothers), and Brecht and Weill sued. The case was heard in November of that year. Brecht lost his action (though Weill won his) and then settled out of court with the film company rather than appeal. The film of *The Threepenny Opera*, directed by Pabst, was premiered in February of 1931.

In 1941 Brecht arrived in California and settled in Los Angeles, deriving most of his income until he left the USA in 1947 from work as an independent scriptwriter for the film industry. Early in 1942, he and the American, formerly German, director Fritz Lang conceived a film story based on the recent assassination of Heydrich, the *Reichsprotektor* of German-occupied Czechoslovakia. When they had roughed out a treatment, Lang offered the story to Arnold Pressburger, who raised the money to make it into a film. A German-speaking American scriptwriter, John Wexley, was assigned to work out a shooting-script with Brecht, in consultation with Lang. Disappointed by Lang's advice as to the requirements of a Hollywood script, Brecht began to draft a second, so-called 'ideal' script with Wexley, which was never completed and has subsequently disappeared. Relations between Brecht and Wexley subsequently deteriorated. The final version of the script, totalling some 280 pages, was only just ready when Pressburger told Lang shooting must start within a week; Lang then independently cut the script to 190 pages and shot the film, which, despite these cuts, is, at 140 minutes, a long film by contemporary Hollywood standards. When the film was ready, Wexley demanded the full script credit, and was granted it after a hearing of the case before the American Screenwriters' Guild, so Brecht is only given a joint credit (with Lang) for

Reprinted from *Screen* 16.4 (1975–76): 16–29. This essay was origianlly delivered as a conference paper in 1975 and was followed by a public discussion whose published version has not been included here. The essay should be read with this context in mind.

the story. Hence it is not true, as has sometimes been claimed, that Brecht publicly dissociated himself from the film; on the contrary he was extremely indignant at Wexley's attempt to obtain full script credit and fought it as hard as he could. However, he says himself in his diary that this was mainly for career reasons—the better credit he obtained the more jobs would be available to him in the industry. Thus his struggle does not represent an endorsement of the film. The *Arbeitsjournal* Brecht kept in Hollywood in the 1940s shows that despite a certain amount of enthusiasm about the project during the early stages of drafting the script with Wexley, Brecht was deeply disappointed by the final 280-page script and by what he saw of the shooting. Even the title *Hangmen Also Die* he disliked—it was adopted because there were copyright problems with the original title *No Surrender* (which he preferred), and his own favourite title, *Trust the People*, was never seriously considered.

So, in both cases, in Germany and America, we have a familiar story: the story of the poet and the industry, of the incompatibility of art and commerce. Tempted by money and the hope to try his talents in the new medium, the writer travels to Neubabelsberg or Hollywood, only to have his work confiscated and distorted beyond recognition. Finally embittered, he takes his tormentors to court and loses. Would that he had resisted the blandishments of the market place! Or, alternatively, would that those in charge of the industry were culturally qualified to recognise and respect the artist's true worth! Perhaps this presentation is slightly caricatural, but such arguments certainly occur, and particularly in the way the story of *Hangmen Also Die* is given by left-wing writers, especially in Eastern Europe: its supposed incompatibility with the capitalist industry legitimizes the notion of the creative genius and his masterpieces. But the hero of this story is Bertolt Brecht, who fought throughout his life in literary work and theory against the elevated notion of art and artist embodied in such velleities. And in both clashes, Brecht left behind documents which show that in his relations with the film industry he rejected the conventional writer's position, was indeed concerned to reveal its nullity. Whether for all that he fully escaped it, is a question I shall consider later. In 1931, he published in the series of his works collected under the title *Versuche* (Experiments) a long polemic, *Der Dreigroschenprozess* (The Threepenny Lawsuit) on the lawsuit and its press reception. In 1942, he recorded his work on *Hangmen Also Die* in his *Arbeitsjournal*, a record of his work, not simply a personal diary, compiled, if not for future publication, at least for future reference.

In undertaking the lawsuit in 1931, Brecht and Weill knew that they were taking up a contradictory position. As Brecht says:

> Our position in this lawsuit revealed great contradictions from the very beginning: before a court that, even as we appealed to it, we had no wish to

recognise as a place of right, we were forced to seek our rights; and these were only available to us as rights to private property. Moreover, we saw straight away that even in this form we should not obtain those rights.

They conceived the lawsuit as a social experiment designed to expose the illusions surrounding artistic production maintained and sustained in three domains: first, amongst the intelligentsia, the notion that the work of art is only authentic as the expression of an individual creative personality; second, in the domain of the courts, the support given this notion by making it the basis for the law guaranteeing the immaterial property of the individual artist (while in practice this law is interpreted so that it cannot hinder the capitalist production of artistic commodities); and third, in the film industry itself, the toleration of this old notion of art to an extent that, while not preventing the production of saleable artistic commodities, does encourage its 'stupidities' in film-making and hinder the development of the quite different notion of art and quite different collective organisation of 'artistic' production present in germ in the capitalist cinema.

Brecht's contract with Nero gave him the right to collaborate in the preparation of the shooting script and to have final approval of the finished version before shooting. He arranged with the company to prepare an outline with Dudow and Neher and pass it on to the scriptwriters appointed by the company, Vaida and Lania, eventually joined by Balázs. Brecht, Dudow and Neher wrote their outline (*Die Beule* or 'The Welt') and Brecht communicated the first part of it to Lania orally. The scriptwriters wrote up these scenes. Brecht then gave them the rest of the outline, which deviated much more from the stage version. The company then broke off the writing and offered to buy Brecht out of his right to collaborate. He refused, the company went ahead with its own script, and Brecht sued. The court rejected Brecht's suit essentially on three grounds: that transferring a play to the film medium requires radical adaptation, and the writer must accept the firm's expert advice on how this is to be done; that the firm had contracted to make a film of a stage success and justifiably wanted to make the film in time to cash in on that success, so even Brecht's quite short running over deadlines (only a few days in one case) constituted a serious breach of contract on his part; that the changes Brecht wanted to introduce constituted the outline as a different work from the stage success, and hence also encroached on assumed terms in the original contract which would have enabled the firm to exploit the success of the stage version—ie in signing the contract the firm was guaranteed a script recognisably close to the original opera.

Brecht argues that this judgement shows that the courts in a capitalist society, as a superstructure of a capitalist-dominated economy, have to interpret the law in such a way as to ensure the ability of capital to make a profit: that is, they cannot operate in such a way as to interfere vitally with the production of commodities. On the other hand, they must carry out this interpretation within a legal tradition dominated by the notion of private property, in artistic matters defined by the property rights of an individual author over his personal creation, his immaterial property rights. The potential contradictions between these two factors can usually be easily resolved: the author's rights are alienable, like all property rights, and can therefore simply be bought by capital. Brecht cites the case of the architect who sued a hotel owner for changing the facade of the hotel the architect has designed for him; he won the action, that is, the right, not to restore the original facade, but to damages for the affront to his immaterial rights, his creative personality.

In the end, this was the solution reached in the Threepenny Lawsuit, though, as Brecht says, the firm settled financially rather than fighting the case through the higher courts not so much because it feared that the first judgement would be overthrown, but because it wanted to go ahead as fast as possible with the production of the film but was reluctant to do so with a lawsuit still hanging over its head. However, Brecht and Weill pushed the court into something close to an admission that the production of films is itself a collective activity and hence incompatible with a system of law based on notions of individual creativity.

So far, the analysis might be acceptable to those who argue that art and commerce are incompatible; as Nero Film's lawyer said at the trial: 'All honour to the writer who refuses to allow his work to be filmed.' Brecht, however, argued on the contrary that in a capitalist society all art of any consequence, including literature, is produced as commodities and only obtains an audience via the market, and that the new apparatuses, radio and film, collective in production as well as distribution, open up possibilities of 'artistic' production of a new type, a type present in germ in the capitalist industry, but held in check so long as the new medium is maintained as a medium of reproduction, conveying individual art works of the old type in a new way. In this perspective, the Threepenny Lawsuit judgement, by insisting on the independent creative activity of the adaptation process as distinct from that of the individual writer whose work has been adapted, represents a progressive position compared to that of those writers who insist on individual creativity as the definition of art and hence its incompatibility with mass reproduction.

What is this new conception of 'art' present in germ in the capitalist film? First, it is an art which is *useful,* and to specific social groups with specific tastes and interests:

> Now within a determinate class . . . taste is perfectly capable of being productive, insofar as it creates something like a 'life-style'. Immediately after the bourgeois revolution of 1918, tendencies in this direction could be

detected in film. Broad strata of white-collar workers who saw in the inflation the possibility of an ascent into the ruling class learnt from Bruno
Kastner and so on a remarkably stylised manner that could be studied in
every coffee-house.

This is the theme of the *model* present in a great deal of Brecht's work: art
is something that is useful because it provides models of behaviour.
Second, this new 'art' is one that is external, anti-introspective, demonstrative, an art of the scientific instrument:

> In reality, the film requires externalisation and nothing introspectively psy-
> chological. And in this tendency capitalism has quite plainly a revolutionary
> effect, insofar as it provokes, organises and automatises determinate needs
> on a mass scale. It destroys wide stretches of ideology when, concentrating
> only on the 'external' action, dissolving everything into processes, renounc-
> ing the hero as a medium, man as the measure, it demolishes the introspec-
> tive psychology of the bourgeois novel.

On the other hand the effect of the old conception of art is directorial stupidity and naturalism:

> The ordinary director, concerned to work as true to nature as possible, mean-
> ing by nature what he has seen on the stage, ie. concerned to provide as indis-
> tinguishable an imitation of a work of art as possible, attempts to conceal all
> the failings of his apparatus in giving this true-to-nature reflection. . . . He is
> miles away from any inkling that precisely these failings of his apparatus
> might be advantages, for this would imply a refunctionalisation (*Umfunktion-
> ierung*) of the film.

Thus, according to Brecht, the dominance of this type of art in the cinema is the effect of an outdated ideology necessary to the superstructure of
the capitalist social formation in the era of imperialism, but already in
direct conflict with the process of production on which the extraction of
surplus value in the film sector depends. 'Capitalism is consistent in practice because it has to be. But if it is consistent in practice, it is inconsistent
in ideology.'

It is worth stopping to analyse this argument a little more closely.
Brecht bases it not only on the Threepenny Lawsuit, but also on a remarkable German appeal court judgement of 1923, overturning a previous
judgement that a film production company which signs a contract for a
film script from a writer is then obliged to make a film from that script, as
would be the case with a publisher and an author, or with a theatre and a
playwright. The appeal court ruled: 'It is not possible to say, as is said in
the judgement in dispute, that there are no visible grounds to treat the
film writer any differently from, or worse than, the theatrical writer or the

author of a book.' It offered two arguments in support of this. First, the greater risk taken by the film production company.

> The film entrepreneur . . . is the manufacturer of a mass-produced commodity which is to go all over the world. Because of this, and the concomitant economic risk, he has to bear a greater financial burden; hence the financial contributions have to be judged differently. . . . Moreover, he has to work on payments made in advance and is far more dependent on the changing times, public taste, the actuality of the subject-matter, competition in the world market, etc, than the theatrical director in his town. . . . Hence a rational adjustment of interests—the starting-point of a sound economic life—between the film writer and the film manufacturer cannot be conceived in the same way as that between writer and publisher or playwright and theatre director.

Second, the fact that filming a written script is not just a process of duplication, as printing is supposed to be the duplication of the author's manuscript, but a creative process in its own right:

> The film has its own laws, which are not just of an optical kind [ie, of a purely mechanically reproductive kind], but affect and determine the essence and content of what is represented. The essence is the dissolution of the dramatic process into individual images, as is clear from the disappearance of the word and the concentration on short individual pictorial scenes. Their concatenation and combination, arrangement and endowment with verisimilitude are only contained in germ in the original film script. They follow determinate principles which are different from those of verbal drama and also contrast with those of pure theatrical mime. To transpose all these requirements as it were into reality, not just to give them a stage form, is the concern of the film director. He is not just the agent of the film writer, but at least his collaborator.

Brecht's interpretation: 'The defence of the author's immaterial rights has disappeared, since "a greater financial burden" falls on the manufacturer. . . . The whole is . . . a document of the most decisive materialism.' Significantly, he concentrates on the first reason, ie the fact that the firm takes a greater financial risk, and pays much less attention to the second, ie the attribution of creativity to the director in the film-making process itself.

In German, what the English and Americans call copyright is called *Urheberrecht*, in French *droit d'auteur*, in Italian *diritto di autore*, all of which mean 'author's rights'. The English term is more pragmatic and more naked. What is at stake in this domain of the law is not the defence of the immaterial property of the individual author or artist so much as the security of the publisher, the mass producer of copies. He ensures himself against plagiarism by buying the exclusive reproduction rights from the author, and the author's claim to those rights depends on his individual 'creative contribution' to the work in question. The distribution of works of art as commodities is based on the attribution of alienable immaterial rights in those works to those designated as their authors, since authors, unlike copiers, are supposed to make a creative contribution to them. The history of copyright in the photographic arts is essentially a history of the extension of the legal definition of what constitutes a creative contribution; initially both photograph and film were regarded as reproductions of the pro-filmic object or event, or the text which these themselves reproduced, and hence were vested with no immaterial rights in themselves. Brecht's 1923 judgement is a fairly early example of immaterial rights being vested in the film as such as itself a 'product of creation'. In bourgeois law, this creation is always individual—works of art must be the expressions of an individual personality, or of several individual personalities. The 1923 judgement, with its Kuleshovian definition of filmic creativity, plainly singles out the director as another creative individual in this sense. In Brecht's day, immaterial property in the cinema still essentially resided in written texts—the film script or the book adapted, and the films themselves merely reproduced the text, but subsequently the notion of creativity has become so extended that almost any *prise de vues* is legally recognised as a creative product.

Thus though Brecht is correct to assert that the 1923 judgement and the verdict in the Threepenny Lawsuit represent the courts guaranteeing capital's appropriation of immaterial rights in its products, the immaterial rights of the author or individual artist are not in general an outdated obstacle to a capitalism he sees as no longer bothered about contracts ('Are there contracts in nature? Does nature need contracts? The great economic interests unfold with the force of nature'), they are precisely the instrument whereby capital carries out that appropriation. The immaterial rights of individual artists have if anything grown in importance with the rise of finance capitalism, and the film industry, rather than more and more proletarianising its brain workers, has maintained more and more of them in the state Brecht calls 'proletaroid' in the *Notes to Mahagonny*: 'co-earners or sharers in the profits—hence co-rulers economically speaking, but socially already proletaroids'—a formulation which, though written in 1928, more or less describes his own position in Hollywood, with royalties or fees in lieu of royalties as the form of his payment, but working as an independent, not on contract or as an employee of one of the film companies. Concomitantly, rather than recognising any degree of collective creativity, or finding individual creativity a bar to artistic production, capital has attributed more and more individual creativity to its more specifically cinematic workers. Brecht has not fully escaped an immediate reflection of his immediate class position: as a writer living off royalties earned on works sold as commodities. He has inverted his values, seeing this position not as a nobler realm of old liberties increasingly encroached on by the marketplace, but as an outdated one, a bar to the advance of social productivity and the establishment of a new social order bringing with it a new place for the artistic worker and artistic production. This enables him to see much more clearly than even the left wing of his colleagues, and more, to cause much of this to be seen in the sociological experiment of the Threepenny Lawsuit. But I think it is undeniable that the real movement of capitalism has just escaped him, and the general tendency of production in the capitalist film industry has been not the one he foresaw of an increasing proletarianisation and an increasing necessity to recognise the direct creativity of the film apparatus as a whole; on the contrary, it has been far more in the other direction towards the increasing recognition of a wider and wider variety of individual creative contributions.

The same insight, and some of the same blindspots, can be seen in the Hollywood experience. Here, too, Brecht tried to engage with the film industry, hoping to get some results, if only in the form of an experiment, from the collaboration. (Here the form the experiment takes is not the public one it took in Germany in 1931, with a trial and texts accompanying it, but the form of the archive record which he kept of his work.) His main intellectual enemies, as revealed by the *Arbeitsjournal*, are the same traditional intellectuals (of right and left) he attacked in the *Threepenny Lawsuit*—the defenders of the freedom of the creative individual against the encroachments of the market economy (from which they derived their incomes): most specifically in California the exiled members of the Frankfurt School (Horkheimer, Adorno, Pollock) whom he labelled *tuis* (from an earlier 'Sinification' of 'intellectual') and about whom he invented or embroidered scurrilous stories with Hanns Eisler, who of the people he knew in America at that time was probably closest to him in formation, position and understanding. However, the position was as contradictory as that in the Threepenny Lawsuit. The *tuis* were his neighbours and social friends—he ate at their houses and vice versa. His circle consisted of émigré intellectuals, writers and actors, and Brecht shared their social position and, spontaneously, much of their hostility to American life. It is striking that in the *Arbeitsjournal* there is none of the liking for America, even at the level of landscape, that is expressed, for example, by Douglas Sirk in his interviews. Brecht had to some degree shared in the 1920's German Americanism, but it is clear that America was a major disappointment to him, both the East coast, which he had visited in 1935 for the New York production of *The Mother*, and the West Coast where he lived during the War. Brecht's sense of his position is clearly expressed in a note on an argument against Pollock at a meeting of the Frankfurt School members: 'Eisler and I lost patience and put ourselves in the wrong, for want of anywhere better to put ourselves.' His relations with Lang, however, show the same tendency to see himself as the writer, indeed the creative individual, though consciously he would not have allowed himself that status, facing

Lang, the director as representative of the film industry. Thus, except for one occasion when he went behind Lang's back to get more money, Brecht seems never to have dealt with Pressburger directly, but always through Lang. But at this time, Lang was no longer on contract, he was, as he says, 'free-lancing'. Hence his legal relation to the film industry was the same as Brecht's, however much more secure he may have been in that position as a well-known director with some successful American films behind him. But Brecht's image of his own part in the deal with Pressburger and Arnold Productions is not just that of a less experienced and less prestigious partner of Lang's, but rather that of a creative writer leaving the business side of the deal entirely to Lang:

> 'While I dictate the story, Lang is upstairs in the studio negotiating with the money men. As in a propaganda film, figures and mortal shrieks come down to us: "$30,000"—"8 per cent"—"I can't do it". I got out into the garden with the secretary. The thunder of guns from the sea. . . .'

Hence also, to Lang's present indignation, he tends to be cast as the villain in the *Arbeitsjournal* when Brecht's real dispute is with Pressburger or Wexley. The script collaboration with Wexley broke down completely, through no fault of Lang's, who, unlike Pressburger, spoke for Brecht at the ASG hearing over the script credit. From both Lang's and Brecht's accounts it seems that Brecht used the *Arbeitsjournal* to vent objections to Lang's advice on what was or was not possible in Hollywood that he did not at the time put to Lang. On the other hand, it is also clear that there was no realisation of Brecht's conception of a genuine collective work on the film, that is the kind of work which was established in the case of *Kuhle Wampe*, and exactly the words he applies to the *Threepenny Opera* film are true of *Hangmen Also Die*: 'At no time during the work . . . did the participants have the same conception of the subject-matter, of the aims of the film, of the audience, of the apparatus, and so on.'

Let me close by examining the two films that we saw yesterday in the light of this discussion. In *The Threepenny Lawsuit*, Brecht himself more or less refuses to talk about the film Nero, Tobis and Warner Brothers eventually made; he dismissed it as an unfortunate byproduct of a valuable sociological experiment:

> 'There are progressive tendencies which lead to results signifying regressions in themselves. One of the reasons for this is the fact that such tendencies can have several results at the same time (in our case, for example, other results than, precisely, the film).'

In Germany the lawsuit, its effects in the press and the resultant text; in Hollywood the record that went into the archive, and more important the money, are the valuable results; the films in both cases are unfortunate and reactionary by-products. His final word on *Hangmen Also Die* was 'The Lang film (now called *Hangmen Also Die*) has given me the breathing space for three plays'.

Brecht's outline for *The Threepenny Opera* film introduced a wholly new element, precisely the 'welt' of the title. One of Peachum's beggars interferes with MacHeath's theft of a grandfather clock for his wedding and denounces his gang to the police. The gang retaliate by robbing Peachum's safe and beating up the beggar—hence the welt. Peachum exploits the welt as a sign of the decline of law and order rather than the coronation procession to blackmail Tiger Brown. While MacHeath is in gaol, Jenny takes over a bank by legal means in his name, and the banking community demand the release of their new colleague. Tiger Brown realises the power of the organised poor through a nightmare and finally decides to sacrifice his friend Mackie, while Peachum similarly sees the danger of unleashing this power in his campaign for the man with the welt. The two meet and agree to gaol the man with the welt as an agitator instead. Meanwhile mounted messengers (in a limousine flanked by police motorcycles) arrive with MacHeath's release.

The shooting-script, which differs markedly from the film finally released, starts by following the outline fairly closely—the wedding sequence is put before the presentation of Peachum's headquarters, and the incidents of the beggar's denunciation of the clock robbers and the theft from Peachum's safe are added, but the second half of the script, presumably the section written after collaboration with Brecht broke down, returns to the original opera, simply stressing the legal control of a bank acquired by the gang under Jenny, and ending with Peachum defeated, Mackie and Tiger Brown united in the bank, MacHeath's bail money serving as the latter's contribution to the bank's capital. The mounted messenger is more or less suppressed.

The film, on the other hand, makes a number of significant changes in relation to the script, mostly bringing it closer to the opera. For a start, it suppresses all elements in the shooting script relating to the welt, the incident with the grandfather clock now being given a new motivation by MacHeath's message to Tiger Brown. It retains the reversed order of the first two acts and the emphasis on the bank, and has a finale closer to that in *The Welt*, all three main male characters uniting in the bank, and a few other details from *The Welt* are added—for example, the scene where Polly and Mrs. Peachum stand in front of the shop-window admiring the wedding dress as MacHeath's reflection appears beside it. But despite sticking closer to the opera than either the outline or the shooting script, the approach represents a radical deviation from its intentions. Firstly, all songs are suppressed that have no diegetic motivation (save the Cannon Song at the end, which is sung in the manner of a musical with the

assumption that characters can simply break into song, and the later introductions of the *Moritat*, diegetically introduced in the first sequence but
thereafter addressed directly to the audience as a punctuating device
roughly corresponding to the breakdown into acts of the stage version),
and there is none of the opera's emphasis on the difference between the
acting and singing expressed both in the stage direction calling for a different lighting for songs and action in the opera, and in the annotation that
singing style and acting style should be kept as far apart as possible.
Secondly, the songs suppressed include all Brecht's adaptations from Villon
(some still remain in the shooting script). In the lawsuit, Nero's lawyers resurrected the charge of plagiarism that had been made against Brecht himself for incorporating lines from Ammer's translations of Villon in his own
versions, and hence Nero had more or less admitted Ammer's copyright,
which is one reason these songs may be missing. On the other hand, this
suppression is again one of heterogeneity: something which has been taken
from outside and represents quite another world than that of the action of
the opera has been removed from the film, reinforcing the overall homogeneity of atmosphere and representation. Thirdly, Andreiev's sets and
Pabst's direction concentrate on creating the atmosphere of an imaginary
turn-of-the-century or even Dickensian London. This is most obviously
marked by the change of the setting of the wedding from the Duke of
Somerset's stables where it is set in opera, outline and script, to a warehouse which gives Andreiev the chance to construct a dockland set with
brick vaults, hanging ropes, stairways and drums drawing on the tradition
of romantic illustration from Piranesi on. Finally, the actual, rather than
dreamed presentation of the beggar's procession, defeated by police, banks
and business, establishes the film within a tradition which Benjamin called
left-wing melancholy, embodying a defeatist belief in the inevitability of successful counter-revolution, leaving only nostalgia for the good old days
when gangsters were gangsters, not bank directors. The last lines of the version of the *Moritat* written by Brecht for *The Welt*—

> For some are in the darkness
> the others in the light
> and one sees those in the light
> those in darkness one does not see

—are sung in the film against shots of the demonstrating beggars disappearing into the darkness. Brecht's point in the song, and indeed in the
whole opera, is that its action remains totally within a bourgeois world
which depends on the labour of the proletariat and is going to be overthrown by it but in which the proletariat can never appear in person, only,
precisely, as a nightmare; the nonappearance of the real proletariat is thus
a reprieve for this bourgeoisie in the outline, whereas in the film it is the
real proletariat that disappears back into the darkness, leaving behind the
victorious alliance of finance and industrial capital and the state. The fate

of the mounted messenger is symptomatic here: whereas for Brecht he is a *deus ex machina*, saving bourgeois characters and bourgeois operatic forms simultaneously—which is why, as Brecht insisted, he should arrive on a horse, because he appears from outside the world of the play and gives a resolution which does not exist in capitalism itself (as a comparison Brecht suggested that the journalist who arrives at the last minute with the vital evidence clearing the hero in a court-room drama should be drawn on to the stage in a swan); in the film, however, the dignified old bank messenger, a subordinate character within the action and a typical representative of the German bureaucracy, arrives to save the ruling class.

In *Hangmen Also Die*, Brecht clearly hoped to save certain elements of the demonstrative cinema he had proposed in *The Threepenny Lawsuit* from the peripeteia of the intrigues Lang insisted were necessary for a Hollywood film. He hoped to be able to include certain scenes from the script in the *Versuche*, if and when this series was continued:

> If I could go on with the *Versuche*,. . . I should print in them some scenes from the script of *Trust the People*. The first scene, say, in which, before the assassination, Heydrich shows Czech industrialists the leaflets with the slow-down tortoises that have been found in the munition works. This is an intelligent description of a modern tyrant: terror is imposed because the Czech workers sabotage production for Hitler's war. German terror is thereby given the same impersonality as the Czech assassination.—Then there are some of the hostage scenes, showing class distinctions in the concentration camp. Five minutes before the Nazis take hostages to their execution, there are anti-semitic outbursts among them, etc.

Lang implies that he wanted these scenes separable from the film in the same way:

> Brecht put forward the proposal to work up the scenes with the hostages . . . so that later, when the Hitler régime in Germany had been overthrown, it might be possible to show them in Germany apart from the original film as a separate, quasi-documentary film. I was quite in accord with the idea.

Once again, this is Brecht's notion of the model: the scenes representing typical actions or gests, even if anti-social, could be taken out of the film and used to demonstrate the nature of the Nazi régime to the German people themselves after the War. However, nearly all the hostage scenes were cut by Lang from the final version of the script, leaving of the scenes Brecht mentions only the first scene on the Hradschin. Significantly, as Brecht noted during the shooting, the demonstrative character could only be given to the Nazi scenes:

> When Lang rehearses a fist-fight between the Gestapo commissar and the heroine's fiancé something almost like art emerges, the work has worth, the respectability of handicrafts. It is not uninteresting artistically how precisely

and elegantly a prostrate man is kicked in the chest and then in the ribs! Of course, this fist-fight is arranged here and not on the supposedly nobler occasion when the kitchen staff of a restaurant prevent the capture by the Gestapo of an underground cell.

And it is notable how different these two scenes of violence are in the film, Gruber's efficiency and the demonstrative quality of the presentation is missing in the restaurant, where strikingly composed photography captures a mess of defenceless people incompetently trying to save the members of the underground. Whereas repetition is used as a distanciation device in the first sequence (Heydrich's German speeches are translated for us by an interpreter, a device used again in the scene of Professor Novotny's arrest), in the scene (which Lang says 'could only have come from Brecht') where Professor Novotny dictates a letter for his son to his daughter Anna in the camp shortly before he is shot, her repetitions of what he says are made utterly perfunctory: Anna repeats only very few of her father's words, so his speech becomes 'the truth' of the action spoken to us—he does more or less directly address the camera—and we are never given the distance we should have if he was genuinely dictating a letter to be learnt and Anna was genuinely learning the letter. The 'Brechtianism' of some of the scenes (and I would particularly stress the interrogation scenes, where Rheinhold Schünzel gives a far better performance as Inspektor Ritter than he did as Tiger Brown in *The Threepenny Opera*), is completely subordinated to a dramaturgy of empathy whenever it is the heroes, the representatives of the people, or the people themselves who appear. Thus whatever judgement is made of the film released as a whole, little is left in it to enable us to assess Brecht's intervention and how successful his intentions could have been.

Notes

Quotations, information and concepts in this paper are drawn from the following sources:

Bertolt Brecht: *Gesammelte Werke in 20 Bänden*, Frankfurt-am-Main 1967, especially 'Der Dreigroschenprozess' in Vol 18, pp 139–209.

Bertolt Brecht: *Texte für Filme II Exposés, Szenarien*, Frankfurt-am-Main 1969, especially 'Die Beule', pp 329–45.

Bertolt Brecht: *Arbeitsjournal* 1938–55 (two vols), Frankfurt-am-Main 1973.

The shooting script of *The Threepenny Opera* film in *Masterworks of the German Cinema*, introduced by Roger Manvell, London 1973, pp 179–276 (German text in BFI Library).

Bernard Edelman: *Le Droit saisi par la photographie (Eléments pour une théorie marxiste du droit)*, Paris 1973.

Filmkritik n 223, July 1975 (special issue on *Hangmen Also Die* containing Lang's response to Brecht's account in the *Arbeitsjournal*).

The Proletarian Cinema and the Weimar Republic

DAVID WELCH

The Germans are odd people, all the same! What with their profound thoughts and ideas they are forever pursuing and introducing all over the place, they really do make life hard for themselves.

Goethe

SIEGFRIED KRACAUER viewed the German cinema in the period immediately after the First World War as a 'unique inner monologue' of a very revealing nature.[1] Certainly these were strange years for Germany. Lotte Eisner claims that 'the German mind had difficulty adjusting itself to the collapse of the imperial dream'.[2] Not surprisingly, the most obvious characteristic of the films of this post-war period is disharmony. The tortured characters of the German silent screen are part of an alien, malevolent world, permeated by fate (*The Cabinet of Dr Caligari, The Golem, Nosferatu, Destiny, Dr Mabuse, The Gambler, Waxworks*). Later on, with the advent of sound and the apparent stability of Weimar democracy crumbling, there emerged a wave of escapist films based on operettas (*Two Hearts in Waltz Time, War of the Waltzes, Congress Dances*). Yet despite the subject matter, the overall thematic cluster is most easily associated with the political right; it is either imbued with a deep pessimism reflecting fears that had haunted German culture for many years, or, in an era so economically unstable, it consciously discards political and social reality for a grandiose world of laughter and fantasy. For writers like Kracauer and Eisner it appeared that during these convulsive years the German people were unable (or unwilling) to realise that there were a great many different types of society between anarchy and dictatorship.

While it is true that the German cinema, almost from its inception, became a conservative weapon in the class war, it is, nonetheless, an unwarranted simplification to equate the content of *all* films of this period to a conservative ideology. In fact both the Socialist and the Communist parties would endeavour to construct, quite separately, an independent proletarian cinema that would capture the restlessness in the community and portray the social conditions of the working class. Yet the initial enthusiasm that would inspire these ventures was to remain largely unful-

---

Reprinted from *Historical Journal of Film, Radio and Television* 1.1 (1981): 3–18.

filled. However, it would be misleading to assert, as Richard Taylor has rightly pointed out, that there was an unbridgeable gap between the proletarian and commercial cinema in Weimar Germany.[3] Particularly after the advent of sound, a number of commercial films contained strong elements of social realism (*The Testament of Dr Mabuse*, *The Joyless Street*, *West Front 1918* and *Comradeship*).

The following analysis of films made by the German Social Democratic Party (SPD) and the Communist Party (KPD) reveals the practical influence of Soviet film-makers on both parties, although neither would enter into the aesthetic debates on socialist realism that characterised Soviet film-making in this period. The KPD did, however, distribute Soviet films on a regular basis, as well as receiving financial and technical assistance in the production of their own films. But both the SPD and the KPD would fail ultimately to create a distinctive cinematic style of their own and as such to provide a radical alternative to the commercial film organisations in Germany. However, to trace the proletarian cinema in the Weimar Republic is of interest not only because of the extraordinary lack of documentation on the subject,[4] but also for the revealing light it sheds on the attitude of government authorities towards left-wing productions and the repressive legislation invoked in the cultural life in general.

The working class became aware of the importance of the medium of film relatively late, and significantly only after right-wing elements had already secured the cinema for their own interests and the imperial state had used it as a means of propaganda in the Great War.[5] The First World War gave the German cinema its great opportunity. Not only did the box office turnover increase but the status of the cinema also improved; the middle class who had previously disregarded the cinema now began to attend to see the First World War newsreels. For the working class the cinemas were also a source of shelter and warmth when both food and fuel were in short supply. Thus between 1914 and 1917 the number of German cinemas increased from 2446 to 3130.[6] Only gradually however did the German government begin to appreciate the possibilities of the cinema for influencing morale and public opinion. In the early years of the war, film propaganda had been the responsibility of a number of separate agencies whose films were subject to censorship by the military. However, with the entry of America into the war and a sudden flood of anti-German films it became of paramount importance to make an impact on public opinion in neutral countries. Thus in January 1917 the Supreme Command not only introduced censorship of films for export in an attempt to control the image of Germany abroad, but it also established its own organisation, the Photographic and Film Office (*Bild- und Filmamt*), or Bufa.[7]

Bufa's role was clearly political and extended beyond making purely military propaganda films. Although its statute described it as a 'military institution',[8] its real task was to co-ordinate the activities of the whole film industry in an attempt to counter the growing infiltration of enemy propaganda. Even General Ludendorff called for the centralisation of the German film industry. In a celebrated letter to the War Ministry on 4 July 1917, he outlined the importance of film as a medium of propaganda:[9]

> The war has shown the overwhelming force of pictures and films as a medium for educating and influencing the masses. Unfortunately our enemies have used the advantage they have over us in this field so completely that we have suffered considerable damage. . . . For this reason it is desirable, if the war is to be brought to a successful conclusion, to ensure that film is used to make the deepest possible impression wherever German influence is still possible.

As a direct result of Ludendorff's 'suggestions' a new combine *Universum-Film-Aktiengesellschaft*, or Ufa was founded on 18 December 1917. Its capital was RM 25 million of which RM 8 million was supplied by the state and the rest by private industry.[10] This was the beginning of the economic and subsequently ideological alliance of the German film industry with powerful militarist and capitalist groups which was to prove fatal for the development of any artistic cinematography depicting conditions of the working class during the Weimar Republic.

Following the Armistice and with Germany in a state of turmoil, the government's involvement in Ufa was revealed in a fierce debate in the National Assembly where it was strongly criticised. It was even suggested during the debate that Ufa had been responsible for prolonging the war by deliberately concealing the facts about Germany's military position.[11] This led one speaker to demand that the film industry be nationalised. He declared that film should be a means of helping and educating the masses, of creating experiences that could be shared by the mass of the population as opposed to manipulating them in the interest of the existing order.[12] However despite the fact that the state was eventually forced to sell its holdings in Ufa (to the Deutsche Bank!), any suggestion of outright nationalisation of the film industry was out of the question.[13] One reason was that with the desire for escapist entertainment the post-war German film industry began to enjoy an unprecedented boom. The success of Ufa encouraged other smaller investors to enter into the industry; the number of production companies rose from 28 in 1913 to 245 by the end of 1919.[14]

The radical mood of 1918–1919 also retained sufficient force to affect the content of films. Initially, the commercial film companies responded to what they believed were the demands of the working class by producing a number of short 'revolutionary' films with titles such as *Sons of the People, Liberty Equality Freedom, August Bebel, Lay Down Your Arms*. However, they soon discovered that there was a demand for films dealing with sexual themes. Under the guise of 'sexual enlightenment' these companies swamped the market with pornographic excursions into the dangers of syphilis (*Let There Be Light*), sexual freedom (*Hyenas of Lust*) and homosexuality (*Different From Others*).[15]

In retrospect it would appear that these films simply reflected the moral and political ferment of the time. But the ramifications of such films on the long term development of a working class cinema would prove extremely damaging. Immediately after the war the Council of People's Representatives abolished all censorship, a measure that was to be short lived as a result of the commercial speculation in sex films. Conservative opinion had always favoured film censorship and the Democrats and Socialists, who initially opposed it, changed their minds when it seemed that Germany was being flooded with pornographic films. The drafting of the State's Film Law (*Reichslichtspielgesetz*) is a confusing affair. A form of film censorship was envisaged in the fourth draft of the new German Constitution (18 June 1919), though the three previous drafts had rejected any form of censorship. Indeed, Article 117 of the Constitution (11 August 1919) confirmed freedom of expression but specifically exempted films.[16] However, after consultation with representatives of the film industry a comprehensive film law was drawn up and became law on 12 May 1920.[17] The examination of films was delegated to two Censorship Offices (*Prüfstellen*) in Berlin and Munich. Each Office had two chairmen who examined films with the aid of four assessors drawn from the teaching and legal professions and the film industry itself. Decisions were arrived at by means of a majority vote and in the case of a film being banned the producer could appeal to the Supreme Censorship Office (*Oberprüfstelle*) in Berlin. Censorship regulations forbade films to contain anything that would harm German prestige abroad or in any way disturb public order at home. Clearly such legislation was intended to maintain the existing political and economic order and would be interpreted thus throughout the life of the Republic. The censor would prove a constant hurdle for all left-of-centre productions, whether they were socialist or Communist films.

The origins of an organised proletarian cinema can be traced to an organisation known as the International Workers Aid (IWA) which was founded in 1921 by Willi Münzenberg with the original intention of providing relief for a famine-stricken Soviet Russia.[18] Münzenberg established the *Aufbau, Industrie- und Handels-AG* (Construction Company) which allowed him to distribute in Germany (and the rest of the world) a number of Soviet-made documentaries on themes such as *Famine in Soviet Russia, The Third Congress of the Communist International, Children's Homes and Education in Soviet Russia* and *The Death of Lenin*. This umbrella organisation enabled Münzenberg not only to provide aid for Soviet Russia but also to create support for the class war in Germany. *Aufbau* would eventually set up its own publishing house as well as an illustrated magazine for the working class (*Workers' Illustrated*) and would be instrumental in establishing a cinematic link between the Communist parties in Germany and the Soviet Union.

But before discussing the work of the KPD, it should be noted that the first tentative attempts at producing and distributing indigenous working class films were undertaken by the SPD in conjunction with socialist trade unions. In 1922, they founded the 'People's Cinema' (*Volksfilmbühne*) and began to show short documentaries about various Party activities, like workers' sports festivals, at their political meetings. Shortly afterwards, two feature films *The Forge (Schmiede)* and *Free People (Freies Volk)* were directed by the young socialist film-maker, Martin Berger. They were distributed on a nation-wide network in 1924 and 1925 respectively. However, they met with very little financial or critical success.[19] The reasons for their failure are extremely interesting because they highlight the ambivalent intentions of their makers—the SPD. Both films can be summarised briefly:

The Forge is about confrontation within a workshop between two groups of workers; those who are on strike and those who are not. The strikers are protesting for higher pay and improved working conditions. These workers are depicted as the more enlightened section of the workforce although they do not appear to have any obvious leader or to be well organised. Their actions undoubtedly create tensions within the workforce as they are seen by their fellow workmates as subversive and disloyal. Eventually the owners promise the strikers better working conditions if they end their dispute. They refuse, but when the factory is threatened by a 'freak' storm they forget their differences and save the company. The moral of the story is that in the final analysis it is not the workers' demands but the factory which is the most important consideration.

In *Free People*, Berger follows a similar format. He shows on one side a feudal family of the old world, and on the other side a young village teacher whose modern social-democratic ideas inspire the landowner's daughter. Capitalist speculation directly leads to war . . . but the workers' solidarity ends the aggression in the form of a world strike. The film's final shots are of an international demonstration for peace with the couple (the intellectual and the landowner's daughter) at the head.

These 'proletarian superproductions', for this is how they were described, attempted to show the need for concerted action in the class struggle and for this reason alone Berger's films possess a certain political message. But their ideological leanings were directed not towards the inequalities in German society but rather class reconciliation (the rebellious teacher with the capitalist's daughter turned workers' leader). In *Free People* one also detects, apart from its innate political naiveté (a world strike), an elitist allocation of positions within the classes (the intellectual at the head of the workers' demonstration). The predominant feature, therefore, of these early SPD films is their fundamentally reformist tendencies; but their failure to attract box office or critical acclaim is linked to wider events and the ambiguous nature of the political situation in Germany at this time.

In accepting the status quo, the SPD were content to work within its given limitations. Indeed, the vast majority of films produced in the early twenties, whether by the SPD or, more naturally, the commercial film-makers, consciously ignored the manifestly obvious connection between the living conditions of individuals and the phenomenon of the proletarian mass. They avoided class analysis for the simple reason that it would exacerbate class tensions in an era so politically and economically unstable. Publicly, companies like Ufa held little truck with contemporary psychological studies relating to the ills of society; instead they tried to promote a healthy world with very, very 'German' characters. These characters took on increasingly authoritarian tendencies. Indicative of this trait is *Fridericus Rex* (1922), a Ufa production, and a piece of pure propaganda for the restoration of the monarchy.

There is some evidence to suggest that organised working class groups were initially prepared to use force to prevent such films from being shown. In 1923 workers armed with pistols entered Berlin cinemas to prevent *Fridericus Rex* from being shown, and in Leipzig cinema apparatus was wrecked and copies of the anti-Soviet film *Dance of Death (Todesreigen)* destroyed. Invariably such extreme measures were isolated incidents and certainly not effective enough to disrupt the commercial cinema's production and distribution network. The events concerning *Fridericus Rex* are particularly interesting, for they illustrate the ambiguous nature of the political situation at this time. The thinly disguised pro-monarchist and anti-democratic propaganda in Ufa's many treatments of the life of Frederick the Great were offensive to both Liberals and Socialists. When the film was premiered in January 1922 *Vorwärts* and the Communist *Freiheit* called for the masses to boycott the film and the *Berliner Tageblatt* demanded police intervention.[20] The Reichswehr is even said to have loaned a machine gun to the Ufa-Palast theatre to ward off an enraged 'Bolshevik' mob. If this was so it was unnecessary as the film was generally popular in working class areas and attracted full houses.[21] Indeed a local Communist news-letter the *Kammerspiele Ilmenau* invited its readers to visit *Fridericus*—"a great artistic historical film . . . the permission of the Communist Party of Ilmenau". Granted, no conclusions should be drawn from these incidents, but as Alfred Kerr, who was *Oberprüfstelle* assessor at the time noted: "sometimes it seemed that the national instinct, and the worship of force for its own sake, had deeper roots in the average German than any question of political outlook or even party feelings. Otherwise the transition from Communism and Socialism to Nazism would not have been so easy for Germany's workers as it unfortunately proved to be".[22] These were ominous portents; later under the National Socialists the German film industry would use the concept of Völkisch unity as the simplistic solution to internal political conflicts.[23]

Whereas the SPD were prepared to work within the capitalist system, the German Communist Party (KPD), since the establishment of *Aufbau*, had attempted to construct a self-financing Communist production-distribution industry based largely on imported Soviet films. In 1925 they published a discussion pamphlet which outlined the difficulties they had been encountering and the magnitude of the task ahead. It observed: "The production of anti-capitalist and anti-bourgeois films in Germany is becoming increasingly difficult, if not impossible. The production of films which reveal the situation of the proletariat and give a revolutionary solution . . . will only be possible if the working class wield power, as in Soviet Russia".[24] To this end in February 1926 the *International Workers' Aid* acting through *Aufbau* and a small private company *Deka-Schatz-Kompanie*, founded *Prometheus-Film GmbH*. *Prometheus* remained the key commercial distributor of Russian and German Communist films until its liquidation in 1932.[25]

Prometheus now held exclusive rights for the distribution of Soviet films and its chief of propaganda, Willi Münzenberg, decided to start the company's activities by concentrating on the struggle to screen the Russian revolutionary film *Battleship Potemkin*. This powerful and brilliantly produced film (by Sergei Eisenstein), dealt with a mutiny in the Russian Black Sea Fleet after the defeat of the Czarist Empire in the Russo-Japanese War. It was a struggle that was to last seven months and end with the German Censor cutting over three hundred feet of film (about four minutes); the famous perambulator sequence had gone, and so had virtually all the dramatic close-ups. The permission for showing the film, which had been given in April 1926, was withdrawn in July of the same year. *Potemkin* was an immense success with both the critics and the general public before the inevitable prohibition was issued on the grounds that it was "calculated to undermine authority in the army, navy and civil service". In August 1926 the film was released again, but this time in its castrated form. As H. H. Wollenberg noted, "It is an important point that the *military* aspect and no other had decided the politics of the German censor".[26] Even when the ban was lifted and the film was exhibited in its severely censored version, the German armed forces were still forbidden to go and see it![27]

The problem for *Prometheus*, and for all left-wing companies in general, was that not only did they have to compete with an increasingly reactionary censor but they were also competing with the commercial companies, such as Ufa, for scarce resources like film studios, film personnel and equipment as well as the artists themselves. To complicate matters even further they also had to produce what were called *Kontingentfilme*. These were very cheap films with little artistic or political interest, made solely to enable their producers to import Soviet films. In September 1920 a 'Quota Law' (*Kontingentgesetz*) was passed which limited the number of foreign films in Germany to 15%. When it proved impossible to maintain this figure the system was altered: for every feature film imported into Germany a German film had to be produced. By the mid-1920s there were numerous ways of evading this law, most notably by means of co-productions. Thus from 1926 onward, *Prometheus* embarked upon a series of co-productions with the Soviet branch of the International Workers' Aid, *Mezhrabpom* (an acronym of the Russian words for the IAH). The first product of this collaboration was *Superfluous People* (*Überflüssige Menschen*), made in 1926 from a Chekhov short story. The film was directed by the Russian Alexander Rasumny and starred Wilhelm Diegelmann, Heinrich George, Eugen Kloper, Werner Kraus and Fritz Rasp, all of whom were later to appear in Nazi propaganda films. The quota laws would eventually prove to be a strong incentive to *Prometheus* to go into production in its own right. From less than 1,000 metres of film material in 1924, production would eventually rise to over 15,000 m in 1928.[28]

In 1927, another KPD organisation, *Weltfilm* was founded. It was to become the most important centre for its non-commercial production and distribution of films to the Communist party and its ancillary organisations. These 'agitational' films and documentaries were designed to complement the more artistic and conventional feature films of *Prometheus*, although both organisations were producing short documentaries intended to strengthen the workers' sense of class solidarity with the cause (*Reunion of the Red Front at Magdeburg, The Red Front Marches Against the Danger of War and Fascism, Children's Tragedy*). Invariably these films would be opposed or restricted by the censor, but workers always found ways of showing completed versions—or even forbidden films, at their meetings.[29] Indeed, by 1927 most of the political parties in Germany had begun to make use of film for party propaganda. These usually took the form of a simple reportage of the party congresses, although as a means of election propaganda, they also produced a sort of animated lecture which juxtaposed prominent figures with the party's slogan and election list number. It was at this stage that Alfred Hugenberg absorbed Ufa into his giant publishing empire, the *Scherl Konzern*, and started to use newsreels (*Ufa-Tonwoche*) as a bulwark against 'Bolshevik' films and as propaganda for his own party, the right-wing German National People's Party (DNVP).[30]

It was largely due to the efforts of *Weltfilm* that the Communist (*Agitprop*) groups could produce their own material and develop a type of 'worker-cameraman'—similar in fact to the 'Kino-Eye' experiments being carried out in Russia by Dziga Vertov. This was how, in 1929, at the great demonstration in the Wedding Quarter of Berlin, cameras hidden in the roofs and passing cars filmed fascinating material which Piel Jutzi used for the montage sequence in his film *Bloody May* (*Blut Mai*). It was in a similar fashion that material was collected for the party newsreel, *Welt der Arbeit* released for the first time in 1930 as counter information to Hugenberg's Ufa newsreels. These new *Agitprop* films were a new departure in that they contained elements of realistic film art similar, both in terms of subject matter and theme, to those discovered at this time by the great Soviet directors, Eisenstein and Pudovkin. Professional actors were now abandoned in favour of 'adequate types from the street', and wherever possible directors left the studios and shot the genuine milieu instead. However, although this new style exerted considerable influence on progressive artists in Germany, it was still limited to observing and recording events rather than actually bestowing them with an interpretation; little attempt was made to constitute specifically Marxist aesthetics of the cinema. Moreover, this aesthetic conservatism was a feature of the KPD's film criticism. With regard to the Soviet cinema, for example, the party press wholeheartedly praised the work of 'safe' directors like Dovzhénko, while remaining openly ambivalent towards the more radical films of Eisenstein and Vertov. Therefore despite building up a talented group of film-makers and as well as establishing the foundations for a self-financing production-distribution base, KPD activity in the cinematic field lacked both artistic innovation and an ideological commitment to Marxist aesthetics. The one exception is *Kuhle Wampe*, the last feature film to be produced by *Prometheus* before its liquidation in 1932. The film will be discussed in some detail later on.

The importation of Soviet films and particularly the 'succès de scandale' created by *Battleship Potemkin* had considerable effect on the activities of the SPD. After the failure of their initial experiences with *The Forge* and *Free People*, and since the KPD had apparently found viable ways of organising and distributing films both for commercial and non-commercial sectors, the SPD decided to intensify its own cinematographic activities. On the one hand the SPD was extremely careful not to be associated with the Communists; films like *The Forge* and *Free People* had already been classified as 'bolshevik' in both right wing and liberal press,[31] and yet the SPD was determined to establish a proletarian cinema. Therefore in 1928, The Popular Association for Film Art (*Volksverband für Filmkunst*) was founded to "fight reactionary trash on the one hand, and on the other, to develop artistically progressive films". Its mission was to "collect together those masses of cinema goers and educate them in critical perception".[32] Sponsored by G. W. Pabst, Karl Freund, Erwin Piscator, Heinrich Mann and others, this association of social democrats and Communists (although they went to great lengths to point out that their ranks "consisted of three times more non-communists than Communists")—organised groups on a nation-wide scale to fight against what they believed was the falsification of reality which marked most of the films then produced.

Members of the Association were able to visit their own specially erected cinemas at least ten times a year, and by maintaining a fixed monthly subscription of not more than 50 pfennig they were able to regulate entrance prices strictly according to the cost of films. Eventually a parallel organisation, The Film and Picture Service (*Film und Lichtbilddienst*) was formed to procure and distribute all types of films to local party and trade union organisations. This type of cinema show was in great demand in the rural areas where cinemas were scarce and it thus served to introduce the SPD to a section of the electorate (under the guise of 'entertainment') that was largely excluded from the main political campaigns waged in the cities and towns. One of the *Volksverband's* first performances which produced a scandal is recounted by Béla Balázs:

> It arranged film shows and would have shown newsreels of its own, but the censorship banned them. So they bought old Ufa newsreels, which had long finished their run and had been approved by the censorship in their time. From these we cut new reels (with a few discreet new titles). . . . Skating rinks and guests on the terrace of a luxury hotel. 'This, too, is St Moritz': a melancholy procession of ragged, hungry snow-shovellers and rink sweepers (cut from an earlier place in the reel, before its original audience could note the contrast). A 'Brilliant Military Parade' was followed by disabled ex-servicemen begging in the streets. . . . The police were itching to ban these newsreels, but could not do so, as they were all respectable Ufa newsreels, everyone of them approved by the censorship. Only the order of the showing had been altered a little.[33]

Balázs maintained that "this red-tinged film stirred Berlin audiences to clamorous demonstrations". There is little evidence of this, however; the censor soon prohibited further performances and the surface radicalism of this short-lived *Volksverband* soon gave way to an easy conformism, or else when a radical experiment was undertaken it was frustrated by an ever-vigilant censor. For the SPD in particular, these were to prove insoluble obstacles: *Free Trip* (*Freie Fahrt*, 1928), for example, was intended to be a work of political propaganda for the Social Democrats. It started with a retrospective look at the conditions of workers under the Kaiser and ended with the current activities of the party and the areas in which they had succeeded in changing such conditions. In fact it proved to be nothing more than a pictorial manifesto which, if anything, highlighted their failings. Such films are a clear reflection of the party's failings and inhibitions, yet in 1930 they were still urging that better use should be made of film:

> A party with almost a million members has the means for such an undertaking (ie. the production of proletarian films). Equally, it would have to possess the will—for even the unlikely fear of financial failure should not deter it from this task. Let us recall the degree to which Soviet films have used pro-

letarian festivals and assemblies, when the occasions were suitable. We too have made use of such opportunities and are prepared to in the future to release considerable financial sums for propaganda films which achieve these aims.[34]

Despite such aspirations, only two films emerged from all those made by the SPD and its affiliated trade unions that proved to have any lasting political or cinematographic value, *Wages Clerk, Kremke* (*Lohnbuchhalter Kremke*, 1930) directed by Marie Harder and especially *Brothers* (*Brüder*, 1929) by Werner Hochbaum. In *Wages Clerk, Kremke*, Marie Harder describes the fate of an old man who loses his job as a wages clerk when his company decide to invest in an adding-machine. Although everything he believes in collapses, he still retains the values of a society perpetuated by a caste system. However, when he loses his daughter to a lorry driver, who he believes is below their social rank, he sees no point in living and drowns himself. The film ends with a mass demonstration outside the Reichstag by the unemployed people of Germany who demand that they be given work. For the socialist press, it was a film "of great significance for the proletarian mass . . . a realisation of our own efforts concerning a socialist production". For the KPD press it was a film containing "the despicable petit-bourgeois ideology . . . the plea by those who have been expelled from the capitalist production to the Reichstag is a farce, since the State itself is the exploiter". Despite such ideological differences, all shades of opinion appreciated the realism of the film which can undoubtedly be compared to the proletarian productions of the KPD.

However, it is with *Brothers* that the SPD came closest to fulfilling its own aspirations regarding the fictional presentation of a proletarian feature film. It tells the story of the Hamburg dockers' strike of 1896 (this reconstruction of an historical event is a radical departure in itself) when workers revolted against the practice of working a thirty-six hour shift. Hochbaum describes incidents in the life of one of the dockers who called for the strike. The film recounts the poverty, the deplorable conditions and wages and the tightly regimented atmosphere of the port. An isolated incident precipitates the strike; an old man collapses under the load of a container much too heavy for him. A friend comes to his aid but is driven back by the foreman. Resisting the urge to attack the official, the friend persuades his fellow workers to join him in asking for a rise in wages and more humane working conditions. As the management send him away with an excuse about the high cost of new investments, he decides that the only possible recourse is a mass strike.

The strike, of course, only increases their misery. Moreover, the strike-leader's wife is very ill and has no money to buy the necessary medicines. It is Christmas and, mid-way through their meal of herring tails and boiled potatoes, the police arrive and arrest him for being the strike leader. When the strikers hear of this they attempt to overrun the station and in the process, a worker is killed. At the police station the workers' leader meets his brother, a policeman with whom he had previously broken contact (Hochbaum's psychological study of this relationship is extremely interesting in its anticipation of neo-realism). In a flash of conscience the brother perceives the injustice of the situation, sets free the accused man and decides to leave the police force, just one incident in the essentially anti-authoritarian stance of the film.[35] The strikers' leader returns to his home where he discovers his friends waiting to protect him from the pursuing police. But he has learnt an important lesson from these events—"We are mistaken to fight in such isolation. Stay faithful to the cause, take strength from the community, then time and solidarity will destroy the system and the future will be ours". He is arrested and taken to prison. After eleven weeks his prophecy is put to the test when the strike ends in disillusioned defeat for the workers. The final shot is of a bitter, but still determined leader clenching his fists behind bars juxtaposed with a quotation from Karl Liebknecht: "In spite of everything".

Brothers was made with non-professional actors but despite its unmistakably political tendencies it is by no means an unequivocally 'revolutionary' film. Its agitational aggressiveness (although defeated after the strike, the workers are still waving the party flag) and its political message are counter-balanced by humanist tendencies which reduce its radicalism; or else the director, in his anxiety to make a political statement, succumbs to what can only be termed the use of crude imagery. In the final scenes, for example, the leader is arrested and in the process is forced against a wall where a nail pierces his hand in what is an explicit image of crucifixion. The film was not made with the German censor in mind, as Werner Hochbaum produced it for the party organisations and not for the general public. Thus although *Brother* corresponds to a very real political situation, it is portrayed by means of ambivalent pronouncements typical of the heroically defeatist attitude which characterised the SPD throughout the 1920s.

In the winter of 1929–30 the German economy experienced its first serious setback since the end of inflation. Unemployment rose and the political temperature rose with it. Curiously the artistic impulses behind German film-making, which had languished during the 'stabilised' period, now began to tackle controversial subjects with a realism of presentation that was eventually to be enhanced by the use of sound. 1929 was an important year for the proletarian cinema in the Weimar Republic; there was *Brothers* for the SPD and *Mother Krausen's Journey to Happiness (Mutter Krausens Fahrt ins Glück)* for the KPD. The Communists produced a number of interesting films in this period. Among them is *Salamander* (1929), one of *Prometheus'* co-productions with *Mezhrabpom*. Directed by Grigori Rochal and Vera Stroieva the screenplay was written by the Soviet People's Commissar for Enlightenment, Anatoli Lunacharsky together with George Grebner. The film was specifically aimed at intellectuals and was intended to illustrate materialistic science through the use of genetics. A professor who is conducting experiments with salamanders on the relationship between heredity and the environment is attacked by representatives of the establishment who feel threatened by such disclosures. The point being made is that throughout history the genetic inheritance of a small minority of the population had determined who would govern the country. It was rather a confused and superficial film but the censor banned it as an "anti-German agitation film", because it contributed to "lowering the reputation of German spiritual life" due to the fact that "the content and leanings of the film threatened national unity". Considering the Comintern left-turn in 1928, *Salamander* is of particular interest today as the only proletarian film aimed at intellectuals. It corresponds to the KPD's continued attempts at this time to cultivate the left-wing intelligentsia in Germany, culminating in the short-lived *League of Film Clubs* which encouraged the participation of such notables as Heinrich Mann.

But perhaps the most important *Prometheus* film of the 1920s was Piel Jutzi's *Mother Krausen's Journey to Happiness*. It is a proletarian story with something of the slow, humble intensity of Käthe Kollwitz's portraits of workers and their wives. The bitter social truths of this film are mainly about unemployment and the appalling housing conditions as experienced by a Berlin family. To augment her small income as a newspaper seller, Mother Krausen has let one room to a wastrel lodger and his prostitute girl-friend, while she and her grown-up children Paul and Erna are virtually forced to live in the kitchen. Jutzi shows how politically naive these people are in their lack of class solidarity. The son, Paul, has spent all the money his mother has earned selling newspapers on alcohol and is so demoralised by being one of the 'six and a half million unemployed', that he turns to crime and ends up in prison. Piel Jutzi demonstrates that the cause for so much suffering lies unequivocally with the authorities who are remote and indifferent to the plight of these people. When a warrant arrives evicting the Krausens, the camera focuses on the Prussian seal, then moves to the daunting profile of the German eagle surmounting Mother Krausen's clock. In desperation Erna tries to prostitute herself in order to find the money for her rent. Her fiancé, Max, who has a picture of Marx pinned on his wall, does not understand her action and threatens to leave her. However, his friend shows him the need to free himself of such petit-bourgeois feelings towards such sexual matters. He points out that it is not Erna, but her environment that is to blame: "One can destroy a person as easily with wretched housing as with an axe".

When Paul, her son, is arrested by the police, Mother Krausen does not want to live any longer; she knows nothing of the social conditions that have determined her miserable life. In her death she takes with her a frail child whom nobody cares about, wishing only to spare it the misery and degradation that she has experienced. However, while her ignorance is itself a criticism of the social relations of her time, there is an alternative in the form of the two lovers, Erna and Max. The young generation still have the opportunity of choosing another road to happiness, free from the constraints of 'petit-bourgeois' respectability. The film ends with a Red Front demonstration and the two lovers reunited and determined to change their living conditions. *Rote Fahne*, the central organ of the KPD, commented: "What unfolds here is not a film just about misery or a description of poor people, but rather a class conscious film of the revolutionary proletariat".[36] Indeed, many screenings of the film were sabotaged by right-wing groups (particularly the Nazis), who recognised exactly what distinguished 'Mutter Krausen' from other films of this genre, namely its call for those who were suffering to march in the streets. Certainly, the film belongs to a small group of left-wing films which not only depict the suffering of the working class, but also the possibilities open to them. However, the didactic ending was overshadowed by the sad fate of old Mother Krausen, who totally dominated the film at the expense of the other, more 'revolutionary' characters. It is the underlying sadness which pervades the film and inevitably this diminishes its radical implications. Siegfried Kracauer observed that this sadness, which at times borders on sentimentality, is the product of minds not too seriously concerned with emancipation; "It is as if these minds were ready at any moment to retreat from their vanguard positions into uncommitted neutrality".[37] Only nine months after the premier of *Mother Krausen's Journey to Happiness* these radical ideas were to be overshadowed by a romanticized Völkisch unity which transcended both politics and class differences. When the Brüning administration, ruling without the backing of a coalition and parliamentary majority, failed to master the unemployment crisis, the mood of the people became increasingly one of despair. This disaffection was mirrored in the results of the Reichstag elections on 14 September 1930, in which the National Socialists captured no less than 107 seats.

The growing radicalisation of left-wing productions together with an increasing political and social instability were to turn film censorship once again into an issue of political controversy. On December 5 1930, Nazi demonstrations skilfully organised by Joseph Goebbels succeeded in preventing a performance at the Marmorhaus in Berlin of the American anti-war film *All Quiet on the Western Front* (*Im Western nichts Neues*), which as a novel had already antagonised the right by its claim that the German Army, far from having been stabbed in the back at home, had lost the Great War at the front. Subsequent attempts to screen the film led to repeated riots. Three days later the censor viewed the film taking the unusual step of removing the press, and banned it as "likely to endanger

Germany's reputation abroad". It was obvious, however, that the ban arose solely on account of the Nazi demonstrations. These were clear indications that the forces of reaction were even stronger than in 1920 when the original film law was drafted.

The film immediately became a 'cause célèbre'. The events surrounding *All Quiet on the Western Front* caused a storm in the newspapers; all the Scherl papers, controlled by Alfred Hugenberg, supported the demonstrations and the subsequent banning. Finally, an important debate took place in the Reichstag with opinion split along party lines. Hugenberg's DNVP demanded that the film be removed;[38] the KPD called for the abolition of all censorship;[39] the SPD on the other hand asked the *Oberprüfstelle* to state their reasons for banning the film.[40] They rightly pointed out to the censors that the ban alone had caused more harm to Germany's reputation than any film could possibly have done. A few days later Berlin cinemas were to be the scene of further demonstrations, only this time they were organised by the Communists and directed against Ufa's first sound addition to the saga of Frederick the Great, *Flute Concert at Sans Souci (Flötenkonzert von Sanssouci)*. The police responded by making 14 arrests and the censors ignored the incident![41]

The SPD was finally forced into action when the censor refused to pass an SPD propaganda cartoon *Into the Third Reich (Ins Dritte Reich)*, which was specifically aimed at the Nazis. They introduced an amendment to the Film Law which allowed films banned from exhibition to the public to be shown to restricted audiences.[42] Demands for tighter censorship continued and they were met by a new clause which gave the censor power to ban any film if it was "liable to endanger vital state interests". Such a measure undoubtedly anticipated the attitude of the Third Reich towards film censorship, and could only serve to inhibit film-makers from tackling controversial issues. One exception, however, occurred in the summer of 1932. A KPD sponsored film, *Kuhle Wampe*, was banned by the censor (who invoked the new clause) but was subsequently passed with cuts, after a well-organised protest campaign.[43] The *Kuhle Wampe* was controversial because, for once, a proletarian revolutionary film really did have a revolutionary message.

Kuhle Wampe was subtitled *Whose World Is It?* and was directed by a young Bulgarian, Slaton Dudow. Bertolt Brecht wrote both the script and lyrics. What is also interesting about this film is that in 1932 Prometheus (who produced it) had virtually collapsed under pressure from its opponents; the banks refused credit terms because its films "endangered state interests" and as a direct result of their "Bolshevik provocation" the film consortiums forbade Prometheus to use their studio facilities. Yet in spite of this, the most important proletarian film was finally made by Prometheus during its liquidation. The title of the film is the name given to the colony of the unemployed who lived in tents outside Berlin at that time. The first part of the film reveals the misery and suffering of the unemployed workers, while the final part is more optimistic, and deals with a workers' sports festival. For Siegfried Kracauer, this was the first and last film which overtly expressed a Communist viewpoint".[44] Certainly it is one of the few proletarian feature films (*Brüder* is another) where the proletariat, 4,000 workers from various leftist organisations—effectively participated. It is also the only film which clearly departs from the traditional aesthetic structure of the current Weimar screen. Brecht's depiction of unemployment and its consequences squarely sets out the social and political problems involved and calls for action rather than melodramatic solutions; the stock answer for so many left-wing productions in both the Communist and socialist camps.

Kuhle Wampe opens with a montage of the existing milieu; empty factories are juxtaposed with men on bicycles chasing vainly after work in a headlong race. The director, Slaton Dudow, then concentrates on one particular disillusioned working-class family in which only the daughter, Anni, has a job. The father resorts to drink, and the son to suicide. Evicted from their lodgings, the family is forced to move out to the community settlement, Kuhle Wampe. Anni is pregnant but rejects her lover (Fritz) when he is reluctant to marry her and urges her to have an abortion. Later Fritz changes his mind, and the engagement is celebrated with a party. The older people get very drunk and the young couple observe their decadent behavior with disgust. Some critics have argued that in this sequence Dudow and Brecht are playing Communists against Social Democrats and youth against middle age. There is a good deal of evidence in the film to support particularly the latter suggestion, for the young couple decide to leave the 'reactionary' world their parents represent and join a left-wing workers' sports organisation where the old and ugly are excluded. The fundamental weakness of the film is that it implies that only the young are capable of showing solidarity and a desire to change their environment. This is apparent in the famous S-Bahn scene, when the youngsters enter into a discussion with other passengers about the burning of the coffee harvest in Brazil. A young Communist scornfully attacks his elders for their political apathy and when one of the 'bourgeoisie' retorts by asking who will change the world, a girl quickly replies: "Those who don't like it!" The film ends with the young radicals marching into Berlin singing their 'Solidarity Song':

> Don't be resigned,
> Be determined to alter and improve the world.
> Forward, not forgetting our street and our field.
> Forward, not forgetting
> Whose street is the street,
> Whose world is the world?

Kuhle Wampe is interesting as a document portraying the various splits within the broad left of German politics as well as a symptom of its illusions. Politically, its gravest mistake is its spiteful attack on the 'petty-bourgeois' old workers, intended of course to stigmatize the apathy of social democratic behaviour. At a time when the Republic appeared to be tottering and National Socialism was making itself felt throughout Germany, it is indicative of the general weakness and confusion of the KPD that in making a film about workers' solidarity they should end up alienating a large section of them. Nevertheless, with *Kuhle Wampe* the proletarian cinema came full circle. The first films of both the SPD and KPD concentrated on social conditions (*Free People*). These productions depicted a suffering proletariat as either a passive and immobile class (*Wages Clerk, Kremke, Mother Krausen's Journey to Happiness*), or they dwelt on their failure to organise themselves *(The Forge* and even *Brüder)*. In each case (with the possible exception of *Brüder*) their radicalism went no further than a critical examination of society. The exploitation of the picturesqueness of poverty was a typical German approach to theme, and married many sincere attempts at 'socialist realism'. *Kuhle Wampe* broke these conventions not only in its radical plot construction (the son kills himself at the beginning—a new departure for the German film) but also by making a direct, explicit appeal for political action. The closing song together with the scene of nude group bathing proved too dangerous for the censor. In March 1932 the censor banned the film on the grounds that: *"Kuhle Wampe* gives the spectator the impression that the state is unwilling and unable to lead the mass of the population out of their misery and suffering. . . ."[45]

It is perhaps ironic that the cinema should have been first used as a propaganda weapon by left-wing forces in Germany. No doubt influenced by the Soviet example, both the KPD and the SPD were able to build up a talented team of cameramen, designers and directors. Yet despite increasing their film production throughout the 1920s, neither party was successful in constructing their own separate self-financing production-distribution networks to challenge Ufa and the commercial cinema in general. Moreover, the cinema presented the Left with problems in both theory and practice. Not only did it prove more difficult to dissuade proletarians from visiting the commercial cinema than it did to keep them away from the church or subscribe to the bourgeois press, but the aesthetic conservatism which characterised all left-wing productions was largely due to the use of censorship, which had a vested interest in the preservation of the existing political and economic order. We have seen that the idea of film censorship in the Weimar Republic was initially a democratic one:

The permission for films to be shown may not be withheld out of political, social, religious, ethical, or ideological tendencies. But the intervention of censorship was permitted when a film endangers public order and safety . . . or endangers the German image or the country's relationship with foreign states.

However, because films of the Right were less concerned with contemporary social and political problems, and expressed the thoughts and conventions of the middle-classes, they found no great obstacles in such a law. Consequently, the scope given to the German cinema in the years before 1933 was both temporary and conditional. 'Realism', which contrasted both the old fantasies and the new escapism, emerged in a society where officially proclaimed and actual liberties did not correspond. In many cases the same laws applied in different ways to different groups. It is within the framework of this relationship between law and state, with an anti-Left tendency partly encouraged by the state, that the National Socialist film could advance unhindered by such restrictions, while the proletarian cinema was doomed from its beginning.

Notes and References

1. Kracauer, S., *From Caligari to Hitler* (Princeton, 1947), 3–11.

2. Eisner, L., *The Haunted Screen* (London, 1973), 9.

3. Taylor, R., *Film Propaganda* (London, 1979), 148.

4. Kühn, G., Tümmler, K., Wimmer, W. (eds) *Film und revolutionäre Arbeiterbewegung in Deutschland 1918–1932* (Berlin, GDR, 1975), 2 vols.

5. By 1911 a number of groups, collectively referred to as the *Kino reformbewegung*, were campaigning for the production of more cultural and educational films. In contrast to the state which saw film as a propaganda weapon, they viewed films as a means of bringing 'higher culture' to the masses.

6. Zglinicki von, F., *Der Weg des Films. Die Geschichte der Kinematographie und ihrer Vorläufer* (Berlin, 1956), 328.

7. Vogel, W., *Die Organisation der amtlichen Presse- und Propagandapolitik des deutschen Reiches von den Anfangen unter Bismarck bis zum Beginn des Jahres 1933* (Berlin, 1941), 30–31.

8. Ibid., 31. See also, Traub, H., *Die Ufa* (Berlin, 1943), 137.

9. The full text of the letter is reproduced in both Zglinicki, *op. cit.*, 394–395, and Traub, op. cit., 138–139.

10. Ibid., 10.

11. *Verhandlungen der Verfassunggebenden Deutschen Nationalversammlung*, Band 328, 1593, *Stenographischer Bericht der 58 Sitzung, 16.7.1919* (Berlin, 1920).

12. The speaker was the Social-Democrat, Harry Sussman.

13. However, the government's involvement in Ufa was criticised in the National Assembly, *Verhandlungen der . . . Nationalversammlung*, Band 328, 1953.

14. Jason, A., 'Zahlen sehen uns an . . .', in *25 Fahre Kinematograph* (Berlin 1943?), 67.

15. Cf. Kracauer, op. cit., 43–45.

16. I am indebted to Marcus Phillips for drawing attention to this point.

17. The text of the law is reproduced in Albrecht, G., *Nationalsozialistische Filmpolitik* (Stuttgart, 1969), 510–521. The author conveniently compares it to the 1934 revised version.

18. Munzenberg's role in the IWA is discussed in: Fischer, R., *Stalin and German Communism* (Cambridge, Mass., 1948), 610–615; cf. Gross, B., *Willi Münzenberg. Eine politische Biographie* (Stuttgart, 1967), and Münzenberg, W., *Die dritte Front* (Berlin, 1930).

19. Both films were referred to as 'Bolshevik' by the right wing press. *Vorwarts* analyses the reaction to *The Forge* on 21 November 1924. For a review of the press reaction to *Free People*, see Kühn *et al.*, *Film und revolutionäre Arbeiterbewegung*, vol. 2, 431–442.

20. Kalbus, O., *Vom Werden deutscher Filmkunst. Teil II: Der stumme Film* (Altona-Behrenfeld, 1935), 55.

21. Ibid., 55.

22. Kerr, A., *The Influence of German Nationalism and Militarism upon the Theatre and Film in the Weimar Republic* (London, 1945), 10–11.

23. For a detailed discussion of the use made of Völkisch themes in Nazi film propaganda see: Welch, D., *Propaganda and the German Cinema, 1933–1945* (Doctoral thesis, London, 1979: to be published by Oxford University Press 1981).

24. Münzenberg, W., *'Erobert den Film! Winke aus der Praxis für die proletarische Filmpropaganda'* (Berlin, 1925).

25. Kühn, op. cit., vol. 2, 9.

26. Wollenberg, H. H., *Fifty Years of German Film* (London, 1948), 33. At the same time, the editor of the *Süddeutsche Arbeiterzeitung*, Fritz Rauh, was sentenced to nine months imprisonment for his review of the Russian film about Lenin, *His Warning Cry* (1926).

27. Kühn, op. cit., vol. 1, 323–332.

28. Ibid., vol. 2, 12.

29. Taylor argues that in this respect, KPD propaganda in the Weimar Republic may be compared with that of the Bolsheviks in Russia before the October Revolution. Taylor, op. cit., 150.

30. Traub, op. cit., 65–69.

31. See above, note 19.

32. Schwartzkopf, R. (Director of the Volksverband), reprinted in *Close-Up*, May, 1928, 21.

33. Balázs, B., *Theory of the Film* (London, 1952), 165–166.

34. *Das freie Wort*, No. 4, 1930.

35. Despite making the anti-Nazi propaganda film, *Zwei Welten* (1929), Hochbaum went on to work for the Nazis on such officially approved films like *Drei Unteroffiziere* (1939).

36. Quoted in Schumann, P.B., *Ecran*, No. 20, December (Paris, 1973), 41.

37. Kracauer, op. cit., 198; cf. Kreimeier, K., 'Das als Ideologiefabrik', in *Kinemathek*, No. 45, November (West Berlin, 1971), 29–33.

38. *Verhandlungen des Reichstages, V Wahlperiode*, Band 449, *Antrag 507: Spahn und Genossen*, 10 December 1930.

39. Ibid., *Antrag 576: Stöcker und Genossen*, 12 December 1930.

40. Ibid., *Antrag 596: Breitscheid und Genossen*, 12 December 1930.

41. *Licht-Bild-Bühne*, 8.12.1930. Interestingly enough, the film was also attacked in left-wing circles as an expurgation of the original novel by Remarque.

42. The amendment, known as *Lex Remarque* was passed on 31 March 1931.

43. Kühn, et al., op. cit., vol. 2, 159–183; cf. Brecht, B., 'Kuhle Wampe' in Gersch, W. and Hecht, W. (eds), *Protokoll des Films und Materialien* (Frankfurt-am-Main, 1969), 101–139.

44. Kracauer, op. cit., 243.

45. Quoted in Kühn, et al., op. cit., vol. 2, 137, and Gersch and Hecht, *op. cit.*, 112–113.

Filmography

The following list contains the films cited in the text; abbreviations used are as follows: p: Producer: d: Director: Lp: Leading Players: C: Censor (forbidden to be shown): L: length of film: sc: Screenplay: Ph: Photography: m: Music

1924
Schmiede (The Forge)
  p: ? (Probably Veritas Film GmbH, Berlin) d: Martin Berger, L: 1815m.

1925
Freies Volk (Free People)
  p: Veritas Film GmbH, Berlin, d: Martin Berger: First distributed on 18 November 1925.

1926
Überflüssige Menschen (Superfluous People)
  p: Prometheus, d: A. Rasumny, Ph: O. Kanturek, K. Attenberger, m: E. Meisel, L: 2693m.

1927
Kindertragödie (Children's Tragedy)
  p: Prometheus, d: P. Jutz, sc: S. Lutz, L: 1989m
Die Rote Front marschiert gegen Kriegsgefahr und Fascismus (The Red Front Marches Against the Danger of War and Fascism)
  p: Prometheus, d: (Montage) P. Jutzi, L: 1719m.

1928
Salamander
  p: Prometheus/Mezhrabpom, d: G. Rochal and V. Stroieva, sc: A Lunacharsky and G. Grebner, Ph: Louis Forestier L: 2370m, C: 17 January 1929 (forbidden).

1929
Blutmai (Bloody May)
  p: Weltfilm, Edited by P. Jutzi, Ph: Proletarian Cameramen, L: 335m.
Brüder (Brothers)
  p: Werner Hochbaum Filmproduktion GmbH, Hamburg, d: W. Hochbaum, Ph: G. Berger, Lp: non-professional actors.
Mutter Krausens Fahrt ins Glück (Mother Krausen's Journey to Happiness)
  p: Prometheus, d: P. Jutzi, Ph: P. Jutzi, sc: Dr Willy Döll, Jan Fethke and the Prometheus Collective, L: 3297m, Lp: Alexandra Schmidt, Ilse Trautschold, Gerhard Bienert, Vera Sacharowa.

1930
Lohnbuchhalter Kremke (Wages Clerk, Kremke)
  p: Naturfilm Hubert Schonger, Berlin, d: M. Harder, Ph: Franz Koch, Robert Baberske, L: 1878m.

1931/2
Kuhle Wampe.
  p: Präsens Film GmbH (assumed responsibility for the film after Prometheus went into liquidation), d: S. Dudow, sc: B. Brecht, S. Dudow, Ernst Ottwalt, Ph: G. Krampf, m: H. Eisler, C: 1) 31 March 1932, 2) 9 April 1932, 3) 21 April 1932, Released on 30 May 1932, L: 2017m, Lp: Hertha Thiele, Ernst Busch, Martha Wolter, Adolf Fischer, Lilli Schönborn. 4,000 workers, members of the 'Red Mouthpiece', the Uthmann Choir. Helen Weigel and Ernst Busch sang the ballads of Bertolt Brecht.

Mountains and Modernity:
Relocating the *Bergfilm*

ERIC RENTSCHLER

Fanck films for our weary and distraught contemporaries. For the veterans of war, for warriors who need a rest. Fanck films for everyone.

—Hans Feld, "Der Fanck-Film der Aafa," *Film-Kurier* 3 February 1931

Ach, Lenichen—that's exactly what's so nice about you, what I like so much, that people don't need to take you the least bit seriously.

—Arnold Fanck speaking to Leni Riefenstahl at the reception following the premiere of *Olympia*

(Although I don't want to equate 'special effects' with 'woman,' it is interesting to note the many instances in which 'woman' is a man-made concoction in the classical cinema.)

—Patricia Mellencamp, "Oedipus and the Robot in *Metropolis*"

I DISCURSIVE SPACES

A Topography of the Mountain Film

A COMBINATION OF auratic landscapes, breathtaking atmospherics, and high-pitched emotions, the mountain film (*Bergfilm*) is a prominent Weimar genre often spoken of as a precursor of National Socialism. These narratives, claim commentators, glorify submission to inexorable destiny and elemental might, anticipating fascist surrender to irrationalism and brute force. Regressive parables, they play a central role in Siegfried Kracauer's *From Caligari to Hitler*: in his teleology, the stunning cloud displays of *Avalanche* (*Stürme über dem Montblanc*, 1930) segue into the celestial prologue of *Triumph of the Will* (*Triumph des Willens*, 1935).[1] Even if Kracauer's "psychological history" of Weimar cinema has its many detractors, his criteria still govern how we approach much of classical German film—and this is particularly the case with the *Bergfilm*.[2]

As a genre, the mountain film receives mention as a preview of coming attractions, an "anthology of proto-Nazi sentiments,"[3] reactionary fantasies

---

Reprinted from *New German Critique* 51 (1990): 137–161.

which fed on and fueled anti-modern persuasions, stirring documentaries whose allure above all was one of images rather than characters and stories. Kracauer and others in his wake thereby overemphasize how the mountain film points ahead to the Third Reich and underestimate how it functions within the Weimar Republic. The status of the mountain film seems all but cast in stone. Kracauer's harsh verdict has had the effect of stifling further discussion; respondents either accept or reject his conclusions, but have little else to say. In the midst of much reevaluation of Weimar cinema, we take pause here to reexamine this genre and to question its critics, to comb the archives and to take a fresh look at rarely screened films. We want to know more about the reception accorded these films upon their initial release and to reconsider, with care and all due skepticism, eyewitness accounts and memoirs of their creators. Wider perspectives will, let us hope, enhance our focus, allowing us to discern with more precision the place of the *Bergfilm* within Weimar culture and classical German cinema.

Rescanning the treatment of the genre in *From Caligari to Hitler*, we encounter several peculiar lapses, a sudden change of tone and a glaring blind spot, both of which urge us to reopen a seemingly closed case. In his overarching tale of a German collective soul oscillating between images of tyranny and chaos after World War I, Kracauer analyzes various endeavors by the cinema to offer a way out of impasse, to provide sanctuary for homeless spirits. Read symptomatically, the mountain film manifests a desire to take flight from the troubled streets of modernity, from anomie and inflation, to escape into a pristine world of snow-covered peaks and overpowering elements. With much enthusiasm, Kracauer lauds the genre for its eschewal of studio settings and its explorations of "the silent world of high altitudes." Recollections of mountain films give rise to an uncharacteristic moment of lyrical effusion, an indication just how profoundly these images resonated in the mind of the German exile many years later:

> Whoever saw them will remember the glittering white of glaciers against a sky dark in contrast, the magnificent play of clouds forming mountains above the mountains, the ice stalactites hanging down from roofs and windowsills of some small chalet, and, inside crevasses, weird ice structures awakened to iridescent life by the torchlights of a nocturnal rescue party (111).

Nonetheless, Kracauer immediately ceases his flight of exuberance, insisting that these rousing documentary images do not offer firm spiritual footing in uncertain times; rather, they reflect the rarefied sensibilities of students and academics who would venture into the Alps of Southern Germany on weekend pilgrimages.

The cultish credo of these mountain climbers—popularized in the films' overwrought scenarios—was one of anti-rationalism, a belief in the laws of a mighty and inscrutable nature, a disdain for the statutes of civi-

lization and the denizens of the city.[4] Indeed, one such student, the young
Joseph Goebbels, rejoiced during a winter outing, finding spiritual renewal in a communion with the elements:

> That was my yearning: for all the divine solitude and calm of the mountains,
> for white, virginal snow.
> I was weary of the big city.
> I am at home again in the mountains. I spend many hours in their white
> unspoiledness and find myself again.[5]

The narratives of the mountain films, claims Kracauer, culminate in acts of
heroism which involve abandon and self-sacrifice, rehearsing "a mentality
kindred to Nazi spirit. Immaturity and mountain enthusiasm were one"
(112). At center stage in these Alpine dramas stands "the perpetual adolescent" (258), the confused male subject under scrutiny in the author's psy-
cho-historical treatment of Weimar Germany.[6] Curiously, throughout his
entire exegesis, the analyst has precious little to say about matters of sexual difference. He reduces women to secondary factors in his terse and frequently ironic plot descriptions and desists from any sustained comment
about their constant and conspicuous appearance in these films.[7]

These two instances of disturbance provide a challenge and a point of
departure. Why does Kracauer so vehemently disavow his initial fascination for the mountain film? At what cost does his ideological analysis
repress female presence in the *Bergfilm*?

Renegotiating a Popular Space

Almost universally, commentators praise the mountain film's images and
scoff at its scenarios. Assailants of the genre's histrionics and plot contrivances still acknowledge its sterling photography and picturesque vistas,
recalling enemies of early narrative production in Germany who nonetheless support films displaying "the landscapes of the German fatherland,
the characteristic beauty of the homeland."[8] The *Bergfilm*'s celebrations of
Alpine scenery echo the enthusiasms of 18th-century nature aesthetics and
share the emphases of German romantic landscape painting. The genre
would become a major force in German film history: continuities of casts,
crews, sources, and titles link the *Bergfilm* with the blood-and-soil productions of the Third Reich as well as the homeland films of the Adenauer era.
Arnold Fanck stands out as the great pioneer of the mountain film, a figure
who influenced virtually all subsequent efforts in this vein. He trained
both Luis Trenker and Leni Riefenstahl, initiating a host of important cameramen whose craft would make indelible marks on German cinematography through the 1950s, including Sepp Allgeier, Hans Schneeberger,
Albert Benitz, and Richard Angst. With a relish for authentic locations, athletic daring, and technical resourcefulness, Fanck gained renown as a
director of film crews, snowscapes, and seas of clouds.

Career descriptions suggestively proclaim a heroic impetus shaped Fanck's self-understanding, thereby linking his wartime experience, scientific research, and textbook writing with his activities as a mountain climber, explorer, still photographer, and filmmaker.[9] He prided himself as an artist whose popular productions brought modern times renewed reverence for nature's incomprehensible majesty.[10] An adversary of Hollywood's linearity and "tempo," a filmmaker whose aesthetics accorded preeminence to "contemplation and meditation," Fanck recognized the inevitability of narrative concessions were his films to reach larger audiences and thus ensure him a steady and continuing basis of production beyond the confined format and limited impact of travelogues and *Kulturfilme*.[11] After initial efforts of a purely documentary cast, his mountain epics assumed narrative contours and a fixed ensemble: high altitude locations, a collective of male comrades, climbers, and guides—plus an obligatory female presence.

The mountain film evolved into a precarious balance between the expressive shapes of nature and the romantic triangles of melodrama. For Kracauer this amounted to an ill-begotten pastiche, something "half-monumental, half-sentimental" (257), an infelicitous mix of "precipices and passions, inaccessible steeps and insoluble human conflicts" (110). For all their masterful imagistic immediacy, these films are seriously inept—and misguided—in their negotiation of narrative terrain. Kracauer's topography, however, is not the most reliable guide either. It affords only a partial and somewhat cloudy view, leaving crucial points half-sighted or uncharted, obscuring how the *Bergfilm* inhabits dialectical fields of force and a much wider discursive territory in the Weimar Republic.

First, reviewing the effective history of the mountain film, we cannot help being struck by the wide acclaim the genre received, from one end of the political spectrum to the other.[12] Not only venerated by reactionary and nationalistic sectors, the *Bergfilm* engaged a host of supporters on the Left, indeed finding some of its most ardent partisans there. The reviewer for the Social Democratic *Vorwärts* lauded *The Holy Mountain* (*Der heilige Berg*) and recommended Fanck: "He imparts to millions, both in Germany and throughout the entire world, visual delight [*Freude am Schauen*] and a heightened feeling for nature's vast and demonic powers."[13] The Communist Party organ *Die Rote Fahne* celebrated *The White Hell of Pitz Palü* (*Die weiße Hölle von Piz Palü*) as "undoubtedly one of the best German films ever," praising the film's visual effects ("outstanding achievements of inordinate beauty and gripping suspense") and its realistic physicality.[14] The same newspaper also spoke highly of *Avalanche*: "The director was able to visualize the power of nature (without any idyllic razzle-dazzle in its treatment of nature) in constantly changing, stirring images."[15] These accolades echo the jubilation we encounter across the board, be it in trade journals like *Der Film-Kurier, Lichtbild-*

Bühne, Kinematograph or in dailies like the *Berlin Börsen-Courier,
Berliner Tageblatt*, and the Nazi *Völkischer Beobachter*.[16]

The most eloquent and ardent advocate of the *Bergfilm* was the leftist
Béla Balázs, who also wrote the script for Leni Riefenstahl's *The Blue Light
(Das blaue Licht)*.[17] In his article, "Der Fall Dr. Fanck," Balázs extols Fanck
for his redemption of nature's countenance in an age of instrumentality.[18]
Fanck sensitizes mass audiences to the physiognomy of the organic world,
granting mountains a subjective vibrancy, making them players in his dramas: "Natural elements become dramatic elements, living companions."[19]
Balázs goes on to attack those souls who would impugn Fanck's sentimental narratives, characterizing these responses as a function of an effete and
complacent *Sachlichkeit*.[20] Balázs's apologia expresses a desire to commune with a less functionalized reality, a non-synchronous sentiment on
which the Right surely had no monopoly. It bears much in common with
Ernst Bloch's 1930 essay, "Alps without Photography" ("Alpen ohne
Photographie"), a recollection of a monumental world both tangible and
inspiring, an epiphany that grants towering peaks mystery and majesty, an
uncanny, unsettling, and therefore all the more invigorating effect. Bloch
challenges the reader to imagine an *unmediated* access to the sublime, to
contemplate Alpine spaces untamed and uncontaminated by modern perspectives. (Imagine today how might we stand before the Matterhorn,
never having seen a tourist bureau poster of it—or never having been to
Disneyland.) Bloch's "untimely observations" eschew sterile genre paintings and picture postcards which reduce nature to a miniature form and
kitsch object, diminishing and thereby domesticating its demonic and transcendent aspect.[21]

In sum, the mountain films enthralled both Right and Left; they engaged
and even involved progressive spirits, indicating common needs and shared
desires that crossed party lines. No matter how radically Kracauer and
Balázs differed in their assessment of the mountain film, both believed that
cinema's calling lay in fostering a more direct experience of reality and a
revitalized interaction with the physical world. "What we want," Kracauer
would later say, "is to touch reality not only with our fingertips but to seize
it and shake hands with it."[22] This fiercely held conviction may well explain
why Kracauer—for all his ideological misgivings—could not fully deny the
haptic frisson of the mountain film. These dynamics, at any rate, suggest
that Kracauer's one-way street from the cult of the mountains to the cult of
the Führer leaves out some crucial attractions.

Second, the genre does not simply emanate a virulent anti-modernity
nor does it only retreat to a sublime sphere beyond time.[23] Initial reviewers registered keen awareness of the numerous temporal markers in the
Bergfilm. Besides snowy scapes, billowing clouds, and unpeopled expans-
es, the films show us tourists, resort hotels, automobiles, airplanes, obser-
vatories, and weather stations. Weimar contemporaries frequently hail the

ability of Fanck's camera at once to hallow and to penetrate nature, to sanctify its secrets and still disclose its uncanny properties. The pristine world of the mountains and a surveying cinematic apparatus do not conflict; rather, as the contemporary critic Fritz Walter remarked in his notice on *The White Hell of Pitz Palü*, the two entities merge to offer scenes "in which the object and its filmic representation blend together in a remarkable, moving unity, in which the authentic, documentary, and real in fact take on stirring, sublime, and beautiful attributes."[24] Walter eulogizes a synthesis of mountains and machines, of natural force and technological power, of bodily energy and spiritual endeavor, all of which stand as complementary elements in a filmic hybrid, a merger between the physical world and the sophisticated scientific devices which measure and elaborate it.

Fanck revered technology as much as he did nature and constantly carried the most advanced machinery available with him on location.[25] Modern tools not only produce the sublime; they assume natural qualities: a reviewer of *The White Hell of Pitz Palü* describes war hero Ernst Udet's airplane in the same sentence both as a "miraculous machine" and a "bird."[26] Fanck claimed nature remains mute and unexpressive unless captured by a camera. This is a striking variation on a theme of romantic transcendentalism, a modern restatement of Schelling's belief that man's awareness of himself and the world around him brings "the unconscious life in nature to conscious expression."[27] In this way, mediated effects become natural presence, formal will imparts to raw material its true identity, man's machines render the real authentic.[28] The gaze of an optical instrument, in short, grants life and motility to otherwise inert nature.

Finally, the customary dichotomies between art film and genre cinema, between avant-garde endeavor and mass culture, collapse when we speak of the mountain film. Besides their expressive visual patterns, these films display well-known romantic constellations, demonstrating an indebtedness to 19th-century landscape painting, modernist formalism, and melodramatic convention. Fanck was perceived both as a cinematic pioneer and a crowd pleaser, as an appreciation of *Avalanche* in *Lichtbild-Bühne* makes clear:

> An exiting evening. Surmounting the peaks of Europe . . . the peaks of cinematic art. Only an exhilaration which takes people to the outer limits of human capacity can manage to stir our entire being in such a manner.[29]

The visual impact of the mountain films rested in an overwhelming mix of aura and abstraction. Fanck's images drew heavily on the iconography of romantic painters, evoking the impetus of artists like Caspar David Friedrich, Philipp Otto Runge, and Joseph Anton Koch to imbue landscapes with transcendent and mystical powers. Mechanically reproduced images aim to rekindle in a contemporary mass (and vastly urban) public the "pleasant stirrings" Kant once described as the mark of the beautiful and the sublime.[30] The cinematic medium becomes a vehicle to simulate unmediated experience, a modern means of restoring pre-modern wonder and enchantment.

The human body acts as the sole point of comparison in Fanck's mise-en-scène of clouds and mountains; he leaves out anything which might relativize their ineffable proportions and diminish their monumental mass.[31] Nighttime torch processions across snowy scapes mesmerize with the *Stimmung* of haunted screen chiaroscuro. Many of Fanck's works (particularly the early ski-films) manipulate screen space and dynamize the frame with their ornamental flourishes, silhouette outlines, and expressive blocking. The camera glides and scrambles in his films with athletic dexterity and daring.[32] Scenes of downhill racers and enthusiastic onlookers reflect on the enthralling power of spectacle in a manner characteristic of many other Weimar films. On occasion, the montage of competition scenes gives way to a formal play of angle, movement, and line, akin to the emphases of Oskar Fischinger and Walter Ruttmann.[33] Figures moving in nature assume geometric shapes and approach the realm of nonrepresentation. Fanck's images defy narrow cubbyholing: they defer to the painting of a previous century as well as to cinematic modernism, recasting nature in a dynamic array of expressive patterns.

Critics readily assented to the coexistence of mountain magic and modern machinery. They could not, however, accept Fanck's narrative constructions, consistently complaining that his romantic plots diminish otherwise heroic endeavors. In particular, the melodramatic scenes were seen as anathema to the stunning visuals. The reviewer of the *Berliner Tageblatt* uses biblical language to articulate his high regard for *S.O.S Eisberg*, going on to lament:

> In virulent contrast to this divine work of nature, the film's tacked-on plot becomes here, quite frankly, a prime example of the human intellect's capacity for presumptuousness.[34]

In his review of *The Holy Mountain* from 1927, Kracauer likewise lauds the film's visual effects, but has only sarcasm for its plot: "In some of the images," he remarks, "the malevolent spirit of the story [*der Ungeist der Handlung*] has taken over."[35]

Recent scholars focus with enthusiasm on Weimar film's strained relationship between story and discourse, concentrating on its unstable, elided, and ambiguous narratives, valorizing it as a significant deviation from the dominant cinema.[36] Oedipal constellations may well dominate the epoch's films, regardless of intended impact or audience appeal; nonetheless, they systematically avoid classical transparency and linear logic. In mountain films, plot contents regularly take a back seat to pictorial interests. Domestic conflicts and triangulated desire provide at best a loose semblance of organization, binding a variety of non-narrative foci to a basic scenario, be they protracted spectacles (competitions, races, torch-light processions), visual displays framed by advanced tools of seeing (microscopes, telescopes, binoculars, airplanes), or elaborate demonstra-tions of the modern media (particularly radios and telecommunication). For this reason, the *Bergfilm* abides as a blend of striking images and insidious stories. Fanciful, but not terribly complex, the mountain film seems to represent a somehow less intriguing byproduct of Weimar cine-ma.

Generic Crossings

There is an undeniable discrepancy between the Weimar cinema we find in contemporary trade papers and the one we encounter in recent film historiography. Looking through the pages of *Film-Kurier* and *Lichtbild-Bühne*, we read about a heterogeneous film culture with a wide range of genres and formats, about matinee idols and mass audiences, about a national cinema that produced 200—and at times many more—feature films annually.[37] The view is much different in Thomas Elsaesser's influen-tial metahistorical essay. Weimar cinema, seen from the perspective of 1984, revolved

> around the very existence of a strong author's cinema, and the economic as well as ideological conditions that made it possible for Germany to develop a film industry which, for a certain period, included a prestigious thriving sec-tor not primarily or exclusively oriented towards a mass audience.

In Elsaesser's estimation, "The Weimar cinema has never been a particular-ly popular cinema. It has always been something of a filmmakers' or a film scholars' cinema."[38] This approach pares down a vast and unwieldy phe-nomenon, referring to a very small number of titles and directors, under-cutting the wide variety of possibility represented even in extant holdings from the period, leaving us with a rarified art cinema in which personal style, avant-garde praxis, and formative experimentation dominate the scene.[39] What once was a film culture's vigorous heteroglossia now becomes a theorist's select gathering of authorial voices.

The *Bergfilm* eludes Elsaesser (who does not deal with it), for here we find a cinematic praxis quite self-conscious of its double status as an artis-tic and a popular endeavor. Its appeal lay in primal nature explored with advanced technology, in pre-modern longings mediated by modern machines. This is a genre where visceral and visual pleasure meet, where the haptic and the optic are of a piece. It reflects all of the romantic motifs, specular obsessions, and narrative peculiarities which Elsaesser views as singular to Weimar film. And yet, it transcends any apparent dichotomy between art cinema and mass spectacle, operating as a genre with its spe-cial emphases in tandem with a host of contemporaneous possibilities. It is hardly a surprise that we encounter numerous points of convergence and shared discursive space. To comprehend the *Bergfilm*, we must view it in the context of other Weimar fantasies that unreeled before audiences in the same movie houses.

Contemporary reviewers insistently describe the *Bergfilm* in language virtually identical to that reserved for the film of the fantastic. Mountain films impart to natural forces an uncanny, threatening, and monstrous potential, rendering Alpine spaces in a gripping and a frequently frenzied manner. The *Frankfurter Zeitung* notice (not by Kracauer) on *The White Hell of Pitz Palü* speaks of a nocturnal procession of torches as "uncanny, truly ghostly"; the clouds, likewise, "glide swiftly through the sky like brightly contoured ships of death." Fanck, claims the critic, captured

> . . . the seductive force and mysterious power which the mountains exude and which force people into an inescapable dependence. The mountain rages and demands sacrifices.[40]

Writing in *Film-Kurier* about the same film, Hans Feld depicts the mountain as an endangered behemoth (the formulation recalls the dragon facing Siegfried), a beast fighting for its life in a mythical showdown.[41] In many phrasings, mountains take on the proportions of Nosferatu or destiny incarnate, an essence that is formidable, inscrutable, and inexorable. Inherent in the sublime experience of Alpine reaches rests a simultaneity of beauty and terror, of fascination and horror, of solace and peril.[42] In this way, a consonance exists between the expressionist impulse and mountain film narcissism; in both instances, the external world becomes a projection of inner forces and the embodiment of human propensity.[43] In *The Holy Mountain*, Diotima talks to the climber Robert who has just returned from an Alpine excursion:

> It must be beautiful up there.
> Beautiful—severe [hart]—dangerous.
> And what does one look for up there—in nature?
> One's self!

Bergfilme, in any event, share with films of the fantastic an affective dynamic: mountains and monsters come alive as functions of human projection.

There is likewise a structured, indeed logical opposition between the seemingly dissimilar likes of the street film (*Straßenfilm*) and the *Bergfilm*, both of which figure crucially in Kracauer's teleology. Streets, roving males, and femmes fatales in the former correspond to the mountains, Alpine wanderers, and female intruders in the latter. The phantasmagoria of the big city—as marked for instance in the protagonist's opening vision in Karl Grune's *The Street* (*Die Straße*, 1923)—finds its generic counterpart in high-altitude epiphanies. The city, like the mountains, is a perplexing locus of fascination and peril. In its more fearful countenance, the metropolis becomes associated with female eroticism just as the threatening aspect of nature relates to energies coextensive with female sexuality. This parallels the special relationship we find between monsters and women in the films of the fantastic (e.g. *The Cabinet of Dr. Caligari/Das Kabinett des Dr. Caligari, Destiny/Der müde Tod,* and *Nosferatu*).[44] No single instance essentializes the inherent bonds between the two genres more strikingly than Luis Trenker's *Bergfilm* of 1934, *The Prodigal Son (Der verlorene Sohn)*: a hero from the mountains languishes in a big city after allowing himself to be lured abroad by a vampish foreign woman; in the end, he will return to the homeland and take his place in a local community as a dutiful son and husband. A single shot, a matched dissolve between the Dolomites and Manhattan skyscrapers, illustrates how Alpine reaches and urban edifices are mirror images. The *Bergfilm*, in short, is the *Straßenfilm*'s double.

In her provocative recent discussion of women and melodramatic representation in Weimar Germany, Patrice Petro privileges the melodrama—especially the chamber play film (*Kammerspielfilm*) and the *Straßenfilm*—as an expressive form concerned with everyday experience, questions of gender, and above all, female identity. Curiously, she excludes the mountain film from her inventory of melodramatic possibility, asserting that it reveals "different narrative emphases and visual preoccupations."[45] Weimar contemporaries, as we have seen, were quick to recognize melodramatic elements in the *Bergfilm*, viewing the romantic plot and heroine as irritations and disturbances. Taken as a corpus, the press reviews localize the mountain film's appeal in its masculine authenticity, onscreen heroism that reflects behind-the-scenes feats of strength, the collective product of a male community of athletic actors, daring assistants, and feckless technicians. Wolfgang Ertel-Breithaupt's review of *S.O.S Eisberg* in the *Berliner Tageblatt* extols fearless outdoorsmen and their unflagging spirit of sacrifice while bitterly deploring how the actress Leni Riefenstahl undermines the film's monumental impact, diminishing documentary verisimilitude by dint of her fictional presence: "In the midst of a horizontal setting larger than life, this romantic silliness struck one as unbearable kitsch."[46] If there is a primary disruptive agency, it in fact emanates from woman.

Although Kracauer ridicules the *Bergfilm*'s plot contrivances and "inflated sentiments" (111), as we have noted, he strangely overlooks its ultimate source of melodramatic initiative.[47] Female players figure keenly in the generic economy of the mountain film; above all, they represent and embody a spirit potentially inimical to male images, be they Fanck's imposing vistas or the inner landscapes of his heroes. We turn now to woman and her special effect on three exemplary mountain films, focusing on her relationship to nature and the cinematic apparatus, scrutinizing the place of gender in this genre.

II THE GENERIC ECONOMY OF MALE FANTASY

A Female Cesare out of the Cabinet of Dr. Fanck

The opening sequence of Arnold Fanck's 1926 film, *The Holy Mountain*, his initial collaboration with Leni Riefenstahl, rehearses the affective energies of the mountain film. The first title informs viewers that the film's physical stunts are authentic—not photographic sleight of hand. Our point of departure, as the credits point out, is a contradictory location, a scenario without spatial and temporal designation ("ort- und zeitlos"), which, nonetheless has its roots in Fanck's Alpine experiences over two decades. The initial image, which follows the film's title, provides a glimpse of rocky peaks over a stretch of ocean. Later we will learn that this is an imaginary tableau, separate entities brought together in a special effect, discreet natural images whose blend produces an artificial (indeed: fantasy) landscape. The next title bears the ex-soldier Fanck's dedication to "my friend who was killed in the war, the mountain climber, Dr. Hans Rohde." A personal loss and a battlefield casualty thus offer an additional point of departure.

Following the title sequence, the film opens on an extreme close-up of a woman's face seen straight on. Her eyes are shut; we seem to be looking at a death mask. The introduction activates and animates her as an essence whose home is the ocean. The initially unnamed woman reappears, first as a silhouette, then as a special effect, a phantom image that arises out of coastal cliffs to assume corporeal substance. The central part of the prologue bears a title and gives the performer a name, proclaiming "Diotima's Dance to the Sea." Diotima is both a natural force and an energy harnessed by an apparatus: her free ballet by the shore unreels in slow-motion; her gestures parallel rhythmic cross-cuts of breaking waves. At the conclusion of her tribute, she looks out to the water and, in a reverse shot, we glimpse what she sees, a reprise of the film's opening shot—but with a difference. An Alpine peak slowly superimposes itself over the image of the ocean.

The film's master shot, the result of a special effect, becomes reproduced and reprojected as a female fantasy. Somehow, a deeper relationship abides between Fanck's camera and his female player's gaze; she, too, reappears as a superimposition. The artificial image that introduces the film becomes her mental creation, a merging of the fluid space by the sea (her homeland) with the mountain landscape, a topography at once allegorical and sexual. The reiterated image dissolves into a further imaginary landscape, a phallic male outline seen from a low angle, a silhouette figure on top of a rock with cloud and sky behind him, a function of the dancer's intoxicated yearning.[48]

Diotima's fantasy catalyzes the film's story, a story revolving around the energies her image and presence arouse in two men. Her evening performance in the Alpine Grand Hotel overcomes Robert (the climber in her dream image) and enchants Vigo, his young comrade. Distraught by the powerful feelings the dancer unleashes in him, Robert retreats into the mountains, as an intertitle puts it, "to gain control over the overwhelming impression." He will later come undone after witnessing another traumatic spectacle, the image of Diotima embracing another man, whom he will learn is his best friend Vigo. Robert's reaction is one of horror; he shuts his eyes and falls back, stunned and petrified. A close-up renders his face a death mask (cf. our first glimpse of Diotima), cutting to a mental image of a mountain landscape that explodes with the force of his inner turmoil. The climactic pilgrimage into the stormy mountains with Vigo will lead to perdition for the unwitting romantic rivals who expire in the cold. In the end, Diotima stands by the ocean, alone with her recollections of dead lovers.

If any logic sustains the narrative, it is the drive to tame, harness, and neutralize the inordinate power exercised by a woman. In a film introduced by male loss (the evocation of a fallen comrade) and in a narrative governed by Diotima's disruptive effect on two friends, we find an obsessive and recurring attempt to counter the stirring effect of a female image and body. The film begins with a death mask and ends with living death, Diotima languishing in sorrow, bearing only the thought of her deceased lovers. *The Holy Mountain* is a male fantasy, a dream about a woman whose sole occupation becomes dreaming about men. It is a film that confronts the fearful dynamics that ensue when men dream too ardently about a woman: her image alone gives rise to powerful reactions; her gaze likewise transmits a remarkably arresting force. In this way, Diotima commands and distracts her male audiences, compelling them to react strongly. Robert sets out with Vigo on a suicidal climb, pushing his friend over a cliff when it becomes clear that the youth also loves the dancer. As Robert regains his senses, he grasps the cord on which Vigo's body dangles, refusing to let go. The male bond persists as the two surrender in the stormy cold. The conclusion turns on Diotima in a ritualistic act of exorcism. Fanck transforms his female player from an agency who has a special effect over narrative to the special effect of a film, a zombie-like being characterized in the scenario's closing lines as "a dark, diminished countenance."[49]

"All She Thinks about is Skiing and Science!"

Mountain films in many ways reiterate scenes and images documented in Klaus Theweleits' well-known study of Freikorps subjectivity, *Männerphantasien*. Fanck's films, however, do not simply relegate women to the margins nor do they always succeed in reducing them to silence. Clearly, *Bergfilme* render exterior nature and female bodies as spaces of exploration and sanctuary, mountains and women representing unpredictable and autonomous natural forces that attract and overwhelm. The opening sequence of *The White Hell of Pitz Palü* (1929) simultaneously seeks to tame both: impressive shots of mountain peaks and snowscapes lead us to the supine figure of a woman (Maria, played by Riefenstahl) over whose body we see the shadow of a man. The panoramic arrest of sublime landscapes goes hand-in-hand with a desire to shape and subdue female presence. In this sense, both mountains and women are objects of a projective anxiety, a formative will, an instrumental zeal, properties men revel in and at the same time fear, essences that arrest gazes and threaten lives, elements therefore that one tries to contain and control with the modern means at man's disposal—with mixed success.

Among all of Fanck's mountain films, no other title displays the coexistence of natural forces and modern technology as strikingly as *Avalanche* (1930). Here advanced tools permeate the text conspicuously, emphasizing a desire to measure and negotiate physical space with wind gauges, telescopes, radios, and airplanes, all of which play important roles in this narrative. The film has at its center the obligatory romantic triangle: Hella (the female lead played by Riefenstahl) comes between two comrades, a meteorologist and a musician, causing the former to despair and forsake the world when he learns that his friend has also fallen in love with her.

Hella enters the film as a disembodied hand, which in a series of close-ups engages the massive machinery of an observatory. A cut to a fuller view shows the woman (only now can we specify gender) in a laboratory uniform gazing through a gigantic telescope. Later, she ascends to the weather station atop Mont Blanc with her father and we witness a scene where two men wash dishes in the background while Hella commands our attention as she peers through a microscope. She only cares about skiing and science, claims her father: "Oh well, girls nowadays. They're not good for anything." A subsequent passage intimates a causality between Hella's desiring gaze at the meteorologist and the catastrophic death of her father, as if her sexuality, somehow in harmony with the treacherous terrain, provokes the calamity. (The last thing the father sees is his smitten daughter walking with the meteorologist, a scene that causes him to look downward with a troubled countenance.) The narrative closes with a female hand in control of the situation, Hella lighting a fire while her admirer stands by paralyzed, incapacitated by the cold, a shot that reverses the film's initial image of male limbs warming themselves over a stove.

In *Avalanche*, a woman controls elements and instruments in a way that prompted vehement critical demurs upon the film's release, impassioned outcries that Hella's heroic rescue mission was utterly "improbable."[50] Precisely those factors—a woman masters the mountains in a storm and commands the narrative in its closing moments—render *Avalanche* not only an improbable film, but also a symptomatic text. Hella is, as befits a fantastic entity, many things at once, a bundle of contradictory properties: modern scientist and nature girl, sexless being and erotic projection, disembodied hand and nurturing presence. A figure introduced as an anonymous appendage, an individual who confounds fixed notions of gender, whose hands ultimately replace the male limbs which occupy the opening image, Hella represents the controlling interest of *Avalanche*, a film that suggests a connection between men's battle with external elements and their troubled relationship to the opposite sex.[51]

The Seductive Power of Radical Distortion

Leni Riefenstahl, in conceptualizing *The Blue Light*, wanted to create a *Bergfilm* in which a woman played a more prominent role than the mountains.[52] In so doing, she clearly recognized their paradigmatic equivalence in the generic economy. The result was, we recall, a cooperative production with the progressive Béla Balázs, who gave shape to the script and apparently played a considerable role in the direction.[53] Framed in a contemporary setting of tourism and automobiles, *The Blue Light* recounts a village tale for a modern audience, revealing the mechanisms behind the making of a myth and disclosing the psychosocial function of that text in the present. The story dramatizes the plundering of nature and the undoing of a woman, Junta (Riefenstahl starring in her directorial debut), stylizing the double violation in the form of a chronicle.

Much like Fanck's films, but even more emphatically, *The Blue Light* crosses borders and defies fixities. It involved a director who would become Hitler's premier hagiographer and a scriptwriter who was a respected leftist; it blends anti-modern sentiment and a rational solution;[54] it combines romantic iconography, sophisticated technical innovation, and a generic framework. Riefenstahl's film mines the romantic legacy with the tools of modernity, merging nature worship and instrumental reason, a preindustrialized world and the ways and means of the present.[55] The film portrays a female outsider as a source of intense and dangerous fascination. A blue light (a quirk of nature caused by crystals illuminated by a full moon) issues from Junta's mountain sanctuary. The enchanting glow becomes virtually indistinguishable from her erotic attraction: boys from the village, gripped by an uncontrollable urge, risk peril and find death in their attempts to penetrate the space that harbors the mysterious woman and the seductive beam. The film displays Junta as an (albeit unwitting) source of fatal temptation, above all to the community's young males.

Junta's transformation into an icon comes in the film's concluding moments. A sublime property—both threatening and alluring—becomes an image and a commodity, a kitsch object hawked by children to tourists, a face framed by crystals which also adorns the cover of the written version of the popular village tale. Just as the townspeople mine her mountain retreat, they also recycle Junta, a metamorphosis that shapes disruptive forces—a fluke of nature and a strange woman—into more manageable forms. As a painter from Vienna stands over the expired Junta in the morning light, Riefenstahl's camera (in a matched dissolve) changes the once vibrant character played by Riefenstahl into a stylized still image, the onscreen artist's gaze coalescing with that of the cinematic apparatus. A male look commanded by a female director processes Junta's countenance and body, transmuting the dead woman into a living legend.

The reconstitution of Junta in *The Blue Light* recalls that of Maria in Fritz Lang's *Metropolis*.[56] As Andreas Huyssen points out, Lang's film demonstrates how woman can at once embody threatening nature and an out-of-control technology: the real Maria stirs the workers; the machine Maria runs amuck. In Patricia Mellencamp's account, *Metropolis* amounts to a frenzied series of projections:

> There are actually four Marias: machine, virgin, mother, and whore. The crisis in the film is one of identifying the 'real' or *proper* Maria, of setting up the *proper* deployment of sexuality.[57]

In *Metropolis*, woman becomes a special effect of a man-made desire machine, a site of attraction and a source of disturbance, the bearer of a compelling gaze and the bringer of intense confusion. Whether essentialized as maternal nature or projected as an infernal machine, she poses a threat. The controlling presence in the *Bergfilm* as well, woman exerts a force equivalent to both mountains and film. Like the former, she possesses for modern men an irresistible primal fascination, bearing powers that impassion onscreen beholders and lead them to self-surrender and perdition. Like film, she exercises the captivating potential of a influential apparatus, acting as a medium of the story and desire, indeed, *"der Ungeist der Handlung."*

Let us, in conclusion, reconsider these three examples and ponder the generic economy of the mountain film. *The Holy Mountain* articulates a wish, namely that woman be recreated in the service of man. Diotima becomes a mourning machine, a "dark, diminished figure" devoid of any arresting potential or personal volition. *Avalanche* expresses the corresponding fear motivating that wish, the fear of emotional and erotic dissolution. The film ends with a woman's hand in control of the scene and the situation, an incapacitated and frozen admirer looking on as Hella stands in and takes over. *The Blue Light* radicalizes the fantasy, enacting it not only in a filmic legend, but extending it beyond the realm of fiction, making the wish, as it were, come true. A woman stars in and directs her own fantasy of self-destruction, creating a film about the fateful sacrifice of a woman for the sake of a community, a martyr role cast in accordance with the painter's look that transmogrifies Junta into a mythical essence. Leni Riefenstahl far exceeds her fictional calling as Diotima and Hella and becomes the consummate crafter of male fantasies, a person Hitler, with some justification, would later call the Third Reich's "ideal German woman." In *The Blue Light*, she is no longer just an actress who incarnates Fanck's distortions, but a filmmaker who engenders, indeed enshrines them. With a gaze as intuitive and unconscious as it is radical, she fashions ineffably beautiful images of female abandon made to the measure of male desire.[58]

My comments on the *Bergfilm* are part of an ongoing project, a larger investigation of how Weimar Germany's complex interplay between modern and anti-modern sensibilities found cinematic expression. In the mountain film, we confront a spirit of surrender and heroic fustian which, without a doubt, anticipates Nazi irrationalism. (Here Kracauer was correct—to a fault.) At the same time, it also reflects nonsynchronous energies active across the political and aesthetic spectrum in post-World War I Germany. This initial exploration has shown how the genre forged a singular alliance between pre-modern yearning and advanced technology. Mountain films addressed the needs and gained the affections of mass audiences. It would seem that the *Bergfilm* became a popular genre both because of and in spite of its melodramatic contents. To gain increased accessibility, Fanck moved from pure documentaries to semi-features. In the process, woman became a narrative medium, the source of conflict and disturbance, virtually competing with the mountains for men's affections and attentions. To comprehend the mountain film we need to fathom the genre's inherently gendered quality. Like other Weimar productions, but perhaps with more insistence, it enacts the male fantasies of a shattered and distraught postwar nation, casting woman in an ever shifting phantasmagoric role, making her at times a force of nature, at others a modern medium, and on occasion both. At any rate, she stands out—in the films themselves and in critical responses to them—as a problematic force, the locus of ambivalent, contradictory, and, as we have seen, quite volatile projections.

Notes

1. Siegfried Kracauer, *From Caligari to Hitler: A Psychological History of the German Film* (Princeton: Princeton UP, 1947) 257–8. Subsequent citations from this source will be referred to in the text by page number.

2. See, for instance, David A. Cook, *A History of Narrative Film*, 2nd ed. (New York/London: Norton, 1990) 129–30n. The author describes the genre as "an exclusively national phenomenon . . . which exploited the Germanic predilection for heroic scenery and winter sports. . . . These were all fiction films, stunningly photographed on location . . . which relied heavily upon spurious sentiment and inflated plots for their dramatic effect. Nevertheless, they enjoyed quite a cult among the German audience, and according to Kracauer, their popularity was a harbinger of the heroic and irrational appeal of Nazism." For similar accounts that rely on Kracauer, see Eric Rhode, *A History of the Cinema: From Its Origins to 1970* (New York: Hill and Wang, 1976) 197–8; and Ulrich Gregor and Enno Patalas, *Geschichte des Films 1895–1939* (Reinbek: Rowohlt, 1976) 61–2. For comparative perspectives regarding the genre and its presence in other national cinemas, see Pierre

Leprohon, *Le Cinéma et la Montagne* (Paris: Susse, 1943). It must not be forgotten that numerous mountain films also came out of Austria and Switzerland during the 1920s.

3. Susan Sontag, "Fascinating Fascism," in *Under the Sign of Saturn* (New York: Random House, 1981) 76.

4. Kracauer described the genre's intended audience more harshly in his notice, *"Der Heilige Berg," Frankfurter Zeitung* 4 March 1927, reprinted in *Von Caligari zu Hitler*, ed. Karsten Witte (Frankfurt/Main: Suhrkamp, 1979) 400: "There may be here and there in Germany small youth groups which attempt to counter everything that they call mechanization by means of an overrun nature worship, i.e. by means of a panic-stricken flight into the foggy brew of vague sentimentality. As an expression of their particular manner of not existing, the film is a masterpiece" (Trans. by Thomas Y. Levin). The mountain films reviewed by Kracauer in the *Frankfurter Zeitung* include Arnold Fanck's *Das Wunder des Schneeschuhs (The Miracle of the Snow Shoe)*, 16 June 1921; William Karfiol's *Firnenrausch (Glacier Fever)*, 30 March 1924; Max Frankl's *Die Gefahren der Berge (The Dangers of the Mountains)*, 15 November 1924; Fanck's *Der Berg des Schicksals (The Mountain of Destiny)*, 9 April 1925; Johannes Meyer's *Der Wilderer (The Poacher)*, 20 March 1926; and Mario Bonnard's *Die heiligen drei Brunnen/Symphonie der Berge (The Holy Three Fountains/Symphony of the Mountains)*, 20 April 1930.

5. Joseph Goebbels, *Michael*, trans. Joachim Neugroschel (New York: Amok, 1987) 70. The autobiographical novel was apparently written in 1923 but not published until 1929.

6. For discussions of the master narrative at work in *From Caligari to Hitler*, see Thomas Elsaesser, "Film History and Visual Pleasure: Weimar Cinema," in *Cinema Histories, Cinema Practices*, ed. Patricia Mellencamp and Philip Rosen (Frederick, MD: University Publications of America, 1984) esp. 59–70; Philip Rosen, "History, Textuality, Nation: Kracauer, Burch, and Some Problems in the Study of National Cinemas," *Iris* 2.2 (1984): 71–5; Patrice Petro, *Joyless Streets: Women and Melodramatic Representation in Weimar Germany* (Princeton: Princeton UP, 1989) 9–17. For recent German contributions to long-standing debates in the Federal Republic about Kracauer's theoretical and methodological assumptions, see *Siegfried Kracauer: Neue Interpretationen*, ed. Michael Kessler and Thomas Y. Levin (Stuttgart: Stauffenburg, 1990). Among numerous recent East German discussions of Kracauer (and Weimar film theory in general), see Jörg Schweinitz, "Die Grundlagen des filmtheoretischen Denkens Siegfried Kracauers," *Beiträge zur Film- und Fernsehwissenschaft* 34 (1988): 111–26; and Peter Wuss, "Kult der Zerstreuung: Kracauers Filmkritik als Gesellschaftskritik," *Film und Fernsehen* 18 (1/1990): 45–7.

7. Kracauer's discussion of *The Blue Light* would seem to pose an exception; its protagonist, after all, is a woman. Still, he overlooks Junta's erotic attraction and the sexual frenzy she catalyzes in the community's young males. (We see, for instance, the innkeeper's son lie in wait for Junta like a beast of prey and attempt to rape her.) Instead, Kracauer explains the villagers' active hostility toward her as a result of superstition alone: because this woman, "a sort of gypsy girl [sic]," seems to enjoy sole access to the blue light, people consider her a witch (*From Caligari to Hitler 258*).

8. Wilhelm Spickernagel, "Der Kinematograph im Dienst der Heimatkunst," *Hannoverland* 6 (1912): 234; quoted in Willi Höfig, *Der deutsche Heimatfilm 1947–1960* (Stuttgart: Enke, 1973) 153.

9. See Fanck's letter of 24 April 1972 in *Fanck—Trenker—Riefenstahl: Der deutsche Bergfilm und seine Folgen*, ed. Klaus Kreimeier (West Berlin: Stiftung Deutsche Kinemathek, 1972) 4: "I admit without reservation—even today at the age of 83—to my heroic conception of the world and in this respect I share the good company of almost every great German mind from centuries before Hitler." Among Fanck's many film books, see his autobiography (whose title derives from a formulation by Béla Balázs), *Er führte Regie mit Gletschern, Stürmen und Lawinen. Ein Filmpionier erzählt* (Munich: Nymphenburger, 1973). See as well the Fanck career interview and homage in *Filmhefte* 2 (Summer 1976). A recent West

German television film provided a sympathetic biographical account in conjunction with a Fanck retrospective: Hans-Jürgen Panitz, *Wer war Arnold Fanck?* (NDR/BR/Omega Film, 1989).

10. Fanck employs an insistent rhetoric of quantification to elucidate his popular appeal in the letter to Kreimeier quoted above, stressing the "millions" of enthusiastic viewers who have applauded his films, the "many thousands" of otherwise hardnosed critics who have praised his work.

11. Arnold Fanck, "Der Kultur-Spielfilm," *Nationalsozialistische Monatshefte* 147 (June 1942) 361 ff. See also the unsigned Fanck portrait, "Der Mensch in der Natur. Die Filmarbeit Arnold Fancks," *Der Deutsche Film* 3.1 (July 1938): 3–5. Even the most beautiful images of nature, he would lament in his autobiography, do not seem capable of entertaining and captivating a popular audience for longer than twenty minutes (*Er führte Regie mit Gletschern* 131).

12. This is not to say, however, that it met with universal accolades; on the contrary, it had quite a few detractors. Béla Balázs's apologia, "Der Fall Dr. Fanck," systematically addresses elements of the *Bergfilm* ridiculed by critics, making it clear that there were numerous deriders of the genre. The essay originally appeared as the foreword to Fanck's film book, *Stürme über dem Montblanc* (Basel: Concordia, 1931) V–X. It is reprinted in the second volume of Balázs's *Schriften zum Film*, ed. Wolfgang Gersch (Munich: Hanser, 1984) 287–291. All citations are taken from this latter source.

13. Notice from 19 December 1926, quoted in Arnold Fanck, *Das Echo vom Heiligen Berg* (Berlin, 1926) 7.

14. W. S., *Die Rote Fahne* 19 November 1929.

15. *Die Rote Fahne* 5 February 1931. Quoted in *Fanck—Riefenstahl—Trenker* E8.

16. See Fanck's own documentations of the press response to *Der heilige Berg* (quoted above in note 13), *Die weiße Hölle vom Piz Palü* (Berlin, 1929), and *Die Tochter des Samurai* (Berlin, 1938) as well as the materials assembled in *Fanck—Riefenstahl—Trenker*. The director's obsessive collecting of approving words as well as his hypersensitivity towards detractors remind one of Hans Jürgen Syberberg.

17. For details regarding Balázs's work with Riefenstahl, see Joseph Zsuffa, *Béla Balázs: The Man and the Artist* (Berkeley: U of California P, 1987) 217–30; and John Ralmon, Béla Balázs in German Exile," *Film Quarterly* 30.3 (Spring 1977): 12–19. Balázs was not the only prominent leftist active in the production of mountain films. The dramatist Friedrich Wolf, working under a pseudonym, co-scripted Fanck's *S.O.S. Eisberg*. See Wolf's account, reprinted in "Friedrich Wolf und der Film: Aufsätze und Briefe 1920–1953," ed. Ruth Herlinghaus, *Beiträge zur Film- und Fernsehwissenschaft* 33 (1988): 50. Paul Dessau, likewise, collaborated on the music for *Stürme über dem Montblanc*, *Der weiße Rausch*, *Abenteuer im Engadin*, *S.O.S. Eisberg*, and *Nordpol-ahoi!*, before emigrating to Paris.

18. See note 12. After World War II, Fanck would repeatedly call on Balázs as a character witness, using the leftist and Jew to debunk ideological critics and their attacks on his films. Consider Fanck's vehement comments about Siegfried Kracauer in his letter to Klaus Kreimeier of 24 April 1972, cited in *Fanck—Trenker—Riefenstahl*: "Because 'Kracauer' is a pure Jewish name [*ein rein jüdischer Name*], I would like to let him in on something which he surely does not yet know: that the vast majority of my films were in fact financed by Jews and produced by Jewish companies; that all of those involved did not even have the foggiest notion that they were helping to lead the masses into the arms of Hitlerism."

19. "Der Fall Dr. Fanck" 288. For a similar formulation, see the unsigned review, *"The White Hell of Pitz Palü,"* *Close Up* 5.6 (December 1929): "Other mountain films we have had, but we have never had *mountains*—almost personifiable, things of wild and free moods, forever changing."

20. "Der Fall Dr. Fanck" 290.

21. Ernst Bloch, "Alpen ohne Photographie (1930)," in *Literarische Aufsätze*

(Frankfurt/Main: Suhrkamp, 1965) 498. Also see Georg Simmel, "Die Alpen," in *Philosophische Kultur*, 2nd rev. ed. (Leipzig: Kröner, 1919) 134–41. Simmel exercised a crucial intellectual influence on both Balázs and Kracauer.

22. Kracauer, *Theory of Film: The Redemption of Physical Reality* (London/Oxford/New York, 1960) 297.

23. Cf. Ulrich Gregor and Enno Patalas, *Geschichte des Films* 61; also, Rainer Ruther, "Le Heimatfilm un genre typiquement teutonique," *Cahiers de la Cinémathèque* 32 (Spring 1981): 131. The influential Nazi film critic, Oskar Kalbus, also characterizes Fanck (albeit positively) as an anti-modern and anti-urban spirit, in *Vom Werden deutscher Filmkunst: Der Tonfilm* (Altona-Bahrenfeld: Cigaretten-Bilderdienst, 1935) 37.

24. Fritz Walter, "Im Ufa-Palast am Zoo läuft *Die weiße Hölle von Pitz Palü,*" *Berliner Börsen-Courier* 16 November 1929.

25. See Thomas Brandlmeier, "Arnold Fanck," in *Cinegraph*, ed. Hans-Michael Bock (Munich: edition text + kritik, 1984ff.). Fanck, for instance, was the fifth person to buy the newly available Arriflex camera in 1938 (E4).

26. Lucy von Jacobi, *"Die weiße Hölle von Pitz Palü,"* *Tempo* 16 November 1929. The critic even goes so far as to grant the mechanical apparatus a supernatural status: "A remarkable miracle of our times, this camera, a divine extension of our weak human eyes." In a review of *Stürme über dem Montblanc*, *Lichtbild-Bühne* 3 February 1931, the critic praises both Fanck's monumental nature scenes and his impressive images of an observatory, as if the two were of the same cast. Reprinted in *Fanck—Riefenstahl—Trenker* E4. One might add there is an unquestionable relationship between the mountain film and later Nazi films about flying. *The Wonder of Flying (Das Wunder des Fliegens*, 1935), for instance, features the star flyer Udet reflecting on his past exploits while we see clips from Fanck films of the twenties and early thirties. The final sequence involves yet another rescue mission by Udet in the mountains.

27. William Vaughan, *German Romantic Painting* (New Haven/London: Yale UP, 1980) 66.

28. Cf. Hans Feld, "Der Fanck-Film der Aafa," *Film-Kurier* 3 February 1931. Reprinted in *Fanck—Trenker—Riefenstahl* E6; see also the cinematographer Sepp Allgeier's account, *Die Jagd nach dem Bild*, 2nd rev. ed. (Stuttgart: Engelhorns, 1931), esp. his description of location shooting on *The Holy Mountain:* "Sometimes we had to lend a bit of a helping hand when nature did not provide us with camera-ready footage" (62). Compare this to Joachim Kroll, "Die filmische Landschaft," *Der Deutsche Film* 3.6 (December 1938): 148. For Kroll, landscapes maintain a photographic interest only to the degree to which they reflect human presence.

29. Review in *Lichtbild-Bühne* 3 February 1931. In *Fanck—Trenker—Riefenstahl* E3.

30. Immanuel Kant, *Observations of the Feeling of the Beautiful and Sublime*, trans. John T. Goldthwait (Berkeley: U of California Press, 1965) 47.

31. Cf. Simmel, "Die Alpen" 140. Brandlmeier observes that Fanck's compositions frequently lack a middle ground (E2).

32. Fanck, Trenker, and Riefenstahl all stress the athletic element in their film work. In this regard their career reflections frequently echo Werner Herzog's descriptions of the physical hardship, on-location vicissitude, and heroic struggle which ensue in one's endeavors as a director. Herzog's work shows a clear indebtedness to mountain film iconography. See, for instance, *The Great Ecstasy of the Sculptor Steiner (Die große Ekstase des Bildschnitzers Steiner*, 1974), *Heart of Glass (Herz aus Glas*, 1976), and *The Dark Glow of the Mountains (Gasherbrum—Der leuchtende Berg*, 1984).

33. Fanck called his documentary film of 1921 *Battle with the Mountain (Kampf mit dem Berge)*, a "symphony of the Alps." Brandlmeier claims Fanck is at his best when engaging in formal and abstract experimentation, proceeding to note that the director's use of authentic locations and photographic realism also anticipate the *Neue Sachlichkeit* (E3). For

a similar discussion that considers Fanck and Ruttmann in the same breath, see Hanno Möbius and Guntram Vogt, *Drehort Stadt: Das Thema "Großstadt" im deutschen Film* (Marburg: Hitzeroth, 1990) 42.

34. Wolfgang Ertel-Breithaupt, *Berliner Tageblatt* 31 August 1933; reprinted in *Fanck—Trenker—Riefenstahl* E23.

35. Kracauer, *"Der Heilige Berg,"* reprinted in *Von Caligari zu Hitler* 400.

36. See, for instance, Noël Burch and Jorge Dana, "Propositions," *Afterimage* 5 (Spring 1974): 43–6; and Thomas Elsaesser, 70ff.

37. For annual production figures, see "Chronik 1895–1930," in Ilona Brennicke and Joe Hembus, *Klassiker des deutschen Stummfilms 1910–1930* (Munich: Goldmann, 1983) 236ff. The inordinate vitality of the era's film culture inheres as well in the large amount of media attention devoted to it. A 1930 survey by Erwin Ackerknecht lists over 160 film periodicals (including three daily trade papers) that had appeared in German-speaking countries. See Heinz B. Heller, "Massenkultur und ästhetische Urteilskraft: Zur Geschichte und Funktion der deutschen Filmkritik vor 1933," in *Die Macht der Filmkritik: Positionen und Kontroversen*, ed. Norbert Grob and Karl Prümm (Munich: edition text + kritik, 1990) 37.

38. Elsaesser 75, 81.

39. In general, Elsaesser's emphasis on Weimar's film artists and his relative neglect of its popular audiences blur the fact that works by even the most renowned auteurs like Lang, Murnau, and Pabst regularly occasioned elaborate publicity campaigns, extensive media coverage, and gala premieres. We need, I think, to question the tendency to privilege a few art films alone and to set them apart from popular culture. How are we otherwise to explain, for instance, that the two biggest German box office hits for the 1929–1930 season were Fritz Lang's *Woman in the Moon* (*Frau im Mond*) and Fanck and G. W. Pabst's *The White Hell of Pitz Palü?*

40. f. t. g., "Gletscher-Märchen, " *Frankfurter Zeitung* 15 November 1929.

41. Hans Feld, *Film-Kurier* 16 November 1929.

42. Cf. Carsten Zelle, *Angenehmes Grauen: Literaturhistorische Beiträge zur Ästhetik des Schrecklichen im achtzehnten Jahrhundert* (Hamburg: Meiner, 1987).

43. Cf. Joseph Goebbels, *Michael* 62:
"We people of today are expressionists. People who want to shape the outside world from within themselves.
The expressionist is building a new world within him. His secret and his power reside in his ardor. . . .
The soul of the expressionist: a new macrocosm. A world of its own.
Expressionist sense of the world is explosive. It is an autocratic sense of being oneself."

44. Compare Linda William's comments on similar dynamics in the classical horror film, "When the Woman Looks," in *Re-Vision: Essays in Feminist Film Criticism*, ed. Mary Ann Doane, Patricia Mellencamp, and Linda Williams (Frederick, MD: University Publications of America, 1984) 83–99.

45. Petro 33.

46. See note 34. It is interesting how with the coming of sound and the addition of a voice-over narrator to foreign-release versions of *The White Hell of Pitz Palü*, we find similar complaints about an extraneous and foreign element destroying the film's effect. Reviewers took issue with the traveloguish commentary of Graham McNamee. See George Blaisdell's review in *The International Photographer* 2.10 (November 1930): "The employment of McNamee as a lecturer on this marvelous subject provides partisans of silent pictures with the most potent arguments yet furnished them" (20). Even more disdainful is James Shelley Hamilton's notice in *Cinema* 1.8 (December 1930): "For certain stretches one may look. .and marvel, with no distraction, but always at the most engrossing points comes that voice, pepping the thing up in choicest MacNameese, applauding the heroic 'manoeuvers' of the rescuers, prodding on the enthusiasm like a Texas Guinan, till it reaches its climax of eloquence and blah . . ." (42).

47. Cf. Patricia Mellencamp's observations about the blindspot of *From Caligari to Hitler*, "Oedipus and the Robot in *Metropolis*," *Enclitic* 5.1 (Spring 1981): 25–6: "What is not in psychoanalysis' 'field of vision' as well as Kracauer's, except in absence or negative opposition, was female sexuality, the figure of woman, women's sex."

48. To quote Klaus Theweleit: "Powerful forces seem to be at work here." The ocean and mountain will, as the mother prophesies, never wed. In this regard, the film's ultimate denial of Diotima's fantasy resembles the virulently contrastive logic of the soldier male. "The defensive passages are consistently organized around the sharp contrast between summit and valley, height and depth, towering and streaming. Down below: wetness, motion, swallowing up. Up on the height: dryness, immobility, security." See *Male Fantasies. Volume 1: Women, Floods, Bodies, History*, trans. Stephen Conway et al. (Minneapolis: U of Minnesota P, 1987) 249.

49. *Das Echo vom Heiligen Berg* 43. Cf. Thomas Jacobs, "Der Bergfilm als Heimatfilm: Überlegungen zu einem Filmgenre," *Augen-Blick* 5 (1988): a rather banal plot line echoes the mother's wisdom, "the fateful impossibility that incompatible principles might ever unite" (24). In a close analysis which accords a decisive visual and narrative role to Diotima, Jacobs ultimately casts issues of gender aside. Sexual opposition does not figure in his conclusions about the film's critique of modernity and its links to blood and soil rhetoric.

50. In *Vossische Zeitung* 2 March 1931; reprinted in *Fanck—Trenker—Riefenstahl* E8.

51. A recent analysis of the film comes to a decidedly different conclusion, stressing how the exchanges between Hella and the meteorologist lack overt eroticism and parallel the chaste and "comradely" gender relations propagated by the pre-fascist "Bündische" youth movement. This reading, however, conveniently leaves the final sequence and its curious terms of closure unmentioned. See Beate Bechtold-Comforty et al., "Zwanziger Jahre und Nationalsozialismus: Vom Bergfilm zum Bauernmythos," in *Der deutsche Heimatfilm: Bildwelten und Weltbilder*, ed. Wolfgang Kaschuba (Tübingen: Tübinger Vereinigung für Volkskunde, 1989) 44.

52. For an extended analysis of this film, see my essay, "Fatal Attractions: Leni Riefenstahl's *The Blue Light*," *October* 48 (Spring 1989): 46–68.

53. See Zsuffa 202–26. Compare this to the director's autobiographical account in Leni Riefenstahl, *Memoiren* (Munich/Hamburg: Knaus, 1987) 137–52.

54. Cf. Kracauer's formulation in *From Caligari to Hitler* 259.

55. For descriptions of Riefenstahl's experiments with filters, time-lapse photography, and lighting, see Peggy Ann Wallace, "An Historical Study of the Career of Leni Riefenstahl from 1923 to 1933," diss., U of Southern California, 1975, 360ff.

56. *Metropolis* has given rise to much recent discussion centering around the relationship between women, nature, and machines in Weimar culture. See Mellencamp (note 47) and Andreas Huyssen, "The Vamp and the Machine: Fritz Lang's *Metropolis*," in *After the Great Divide: Modernism, Mass Culture, Postmodernism* (Bloomington: Indiana UP, 1986) 65–81; and Peter Wollen, "Cinema/Americanism/the Robot," *New Formations* 8 (Summer 1989): 7–34.

57. Mellencamp 33.

58. Cf. Theweleit, vol. 2: 416. See also Gisela von Wysocki's compelling treatment of the director, "Die Berge und die Patriarchen: Leni Riefenstahl," in *Die Fröste der Freiheit: Aufbruchsphantasien* (Frankfurt/Main: Syndikat, 1980) 70–85.

The Trouble with Hitler: Postwar German Aesthetics and the Legacy of Fascism

ERIC L. SANTNER

I

IN HIS catalog of the 1987 retrospective of work by Anselm Kiefer, Mark Rosenthal cites the German poet Friedrich Hölderlin as key to understanding Kiefer's formal and thematic preoccupations beginning with the series of staged tableaux composed in 1969 and published, some six years later, under the title *"Besetzungen"* [Occupations]. At issue, of course, is Kiefer's turn to what he has in large part become known for in the international art scene and market, namely an at times monomaniacal and disturbingly ambiguous exploration of German history and national and cultural identity.[1] Rosenthal refers in particular to Hölderlin's notion "that one must master what is innate in order to achieve great heights."[2]

The source of this notion, which found poetic expression in Hölderlin's own so-called *"vaterländische Umkehr"* or "patriotic turn" to intricately wrought hymns dealing with the spiritual destiny of Germany, and the West more generally, is a letter written in December 1801 to fellow poet Casimir Ulrich Böhlendorff just as he (Hölderlin) was preparing to leave his native Swabia to assume a post as private tutor in Bordeaux. In the letter, Hölderlin rejects any classicist identification of artistic virtue with the imitation of ancient models and formulates instead his own dialectical version of the *querelle des anciens et des modernes*, which does indeed include the notion that a people's innate or national traits require more rigorous attention and formal cultivation than what is foreign.

What is perhaps most important about this particular effort to overcome classicism is the association Hölderlin makes between poetics and funerary ritual, between modes of representation and patterns and procedures of mourning.[3] Commenting on the manuscript of a drama Böhlendorff had sent him, Hölderlin remarks:

> It seems to me that your good genius has inspired you to treat the drama in a more epic manner. It is, overall, an authentic modern tragedy. For this is the tragic in us: that, packed up in any container, we very quietly move away from the realm of the living, [and] not that—consumed in flames—we expiate the flames we could not tame.[4]

Reprinted from *New German Critique* 57 (1992): 5–24

What is at stake here is more than any obvious differences between burial in a coffin and cremation; the concern is rather with the efficacy of poetic speech and artistic creation more generally, in helping to negotiate, and ultimately navigate across, the boundary between the living and the dead.

In Hölderlin's view, one of the defining characteristics of "Hesperidean" or German modernity was precisely the fact that this elegiac efficacy was in question. In a word, Hölderlin was concerned, nearly two hundred years ago, with a certain German inability to mourn.[5] It comes as no surprise, then, that after his return from France the following year, Hölderlin immersed himself in the labor of translating and commenting on two of Sophocles' tragedies: *Oedipus Rex* and *Antigone*. No surprise, because translation was at a formal level itself an enactment of the transport and transference vis-à-vis the dead and the past that was Hölderlin's concern to reinvigorate; no surprise, because both plays address the catastrophic consequences of failing to settle symbolic debts of the past: of failing or refusing to mourn.

With regard to the question of mourning, *Antigone* is of course the far more interesting drama. And indeed, as George Steiner has admirably demonstrated, when mourning is experienced in its full cultural, political, and social dimensions, that is, as the labor in and through which a body politic reconstitutes and defines itself in the wake of traumatic upheaval, Antigone returns with predictable regularity.[6] I would like to address briefly one of Antigone's recent reappearances in the Federal Republic of Germany.[7] In doing so, I hope to sketch out some crucial features of the social and political context of cultural production in Germany during the last several decades and raise some questions concerning the transformed conditions of that production in the new, post-unification Germany.

II

Antigone's most recent and in some ways most disturbing return has occurred not on stage or in film but rather as the personification of the core rhetorical gesture and organizing principle of a collection of essays and aphorisms dealing with the fate of art in postwar Germany up to and beyond unification, published in 1990 by the German filmmaker and cultural critic Hans Jürgen Syberberg under the title *The Distress and Fortune of German Art After the Last War*.[8] Syberberg's obsessive ruminations continue lines of thought begun in earlier essays, most notably those grouped together under the title *Die freudlose Gesellschaft*.[9] The latter collection was published as a sort of cultural-critical postscript to the film that, in the late 1970s, established Syberberg's international reputation and notoriety, *Hitler, ein Film aus Deutschland*.

The "argument" at the core of that film and taken up in nearly everything Syberberg has done since, whether film, video or print, can be seen as an increasingly idiosyncratic appropriation and reworking of the well-known interpretation of postwar German culture offered by Alexander and Margarete Mitscherlich in the late 1960s in their famous book *The Inability to Mourn*.[10] Indeed, the moral, aesthetic, and intellectual challenge of Syberberg's work consists to a very large degree in the fact that he offers what appears to be a deeply reactionary version of the Mitscherlichs' thesis, a version that cannot, I believe, be simply brushed aside as so much perverse German nationalism or even neo-Nazism.[11]

In their study, the Mitscherlichs proposed that the psychic and political immobility of the postwar Federal Republic derived from a collective refusal or inability to settle accounts with the past, to come to terms with—to bring consciously and genuinely to a terminus—the enormous libidinal energies previously directed toward Hitler and the grandiose ideals of National Socialism. It was their contention that postwar Germans would never succeed in feeling any real empathy or mnemonic responsibility for the victims of Nazism until this more primitive psychic labor of de-cathexis had been achieved, the working through of what could be called the phantasmatic kernel of the "Third Reich." What most struck the Mitscherlichs was the absence of indications in the postwar population of what the psychoanalytically trained observer would have expected, namely a deep and widespread melancholia. Following Freud's theorization of mourning and melancholy, the Mitscherlichs identify the latter as the "normal" pathology that follows upon the shattering of narcissistic cathexes of the sort that so clearly sustained the fantasy of the *Volksgemeinschaft* in Nazi Germany.[12] This seemingly nonpathological condition of the German polity discovered by the Mitscherlichs in the 1960s could, I think, be profitably compared with Alfred Hitchcock's rigorously understated portrayal of blocked mourning in his film *The Trouble with Harry*.

The film follows various members of a New England village as, with remarkable good cheer and lack of concern, they deal with the various problems produced by the appearance of a dead body in their midst. As Slavoj Žižek has put it in his persuasive reading of the film:

> Far from diverting a peaceful, everyday situation into the *unheimlich*, far from functioning as the eruption of some traumatic entity that disturbs the tranquil flow of life, the "blot," Harry's body . . . functions as a minor, marginal problem, not really all that important, indeed, almost petty. The social life of the village goes on, people continue to exchange pleasantries, arrange to meet at the corpse, to pursue their ordinary interests.[13]

But just as the Mitscherlichs detected a disturbingly manic element in the grim efficiency with which postwar (West) German society set about clearing away the ruins and "normalizing" itself in the mold of a liberal democracy, the citizens of Hitchcock's New England hamlet clearly display the psychic costs of their own precarious equilibrium.

Žižek continues his reading of the film:

> Just like the obsessive personality described by Freud toward the end of his
> analysis of the "Rat Man," so the "official ego" of the characters in *The
> Trouble with Harry*, open, tolerant, conceals a network of rules and inhibi-
> tions that block all pleasure. The ironic detachment of the characters vis-à-vis
> Harry's body reveals an obsessional neutralization of an underlying traumatic
> complex.

The crux of this psycho-social blockage—the "trouble with Harry"—"consists in the fact that his body is present without being dead on the symbolic level." Žižek concludes his discussion of the film by noting the distance
traversed by western civilization with regard to funerary ritual and the
work of mourning:

> from Antigone's sublime features, radiant with beauty and inner calm, for
> whom the act is an unquestioned, accepted thing; through the hesitation
> and obsessive doubt of Hamlet who, of course, finally acts, but only after it is
> too late . . . to *The Trouble with Harry*, in which the entire affair is treated as
> some kind of quibble, a minor inconvenience, a welcome pretext for wider
> social contacts, but in which understatement nevertheless betrays the exis-
> tence of an utter inhibition, for which we would look in vain in either
> *Hamlet* or *Antigone*.[14]

What made Syberberg unique among German filmmakers in the 1970s,
what made him so difficult for his German audiences and so appealing, if
ambivalently and ambiguously so, to foreign audiences—and here the parallels with Kiefer are quite striking—is precisely the fact that he seemed to
be addressing more directly than any other postwar German artist what
might be called "the trouble with Hitler," that is, a certain inhibition
underlying aesthetic and political culture resulting from the failure to settle symbolic debts with National Socialism, to formally acknowledge and
bury the ideological phantasms that could be said to represent Germany's
symbolic "Polynices."[15] Furthermore, Syberberg's "dialogue" with the
ghosts of Nazism centered on the crucial role played by film, spectacle,
and cultural production in general in relaying and mediating libidinal
cathexes to the fantasy of the organic national community, the *Volksgemeinschaft*. In short, Syberberg's work, and the *Hitler* film above all,
seemed to translate into aesthetic practice not only the *Trauerarbeit*
called for by the Mitscherlichs but to offer as well a radical demonstration
and critique of that "aestheticization of politics" which Walter Benjamin
had identified as key to understanding the capacity of National Socialism
to mobilize the masses.[16]

As I have suggested earlier, in his most recent attempt to address these
issues, Syberberg tries to undo the historical trajectory leading from Greek
tragedy to the understatements of modern and postmodern popular cul-

ture—the trajectory from Athens to Hollywood—and to recuperate the sublime aesthetic stature of Antigone in the matter of elegiac discourse. In the course of this recuperation, however, Syberberg ends up recanting much of his own work, which was in its own way already "antigonistic," that is, dedicated to the task of burying the phantasmatic body of Polynices. By examining the terms of this recantation one gains access to the larger cultural and political stakes of Syberberg's enterprise.

Exactly halfway through his recent book, in a section entitled "Confessions: Beyond the Night," Syberberg announces in tortured prose typical for the text as a whole that his earlier work had been tainted by his eagerness to adapt to the dominant aesthetic theories and standards of the postwar period. These essays represent, in essence, Syberberg's attempt to disassociate himself from what he now perceives as a Frankfurt School-inspired, left-liberal consensus regarding standards of political correctness in artistic production in the postwar period. Anyone familiar with the terms of the debate on "pc" or political correctness at American universities will quickly recognize the historically specific contours of the German version of the debate. One might say that in Germany, pc stands not so much for political correctness in the American sense as for "proper coping" with the uniquely German legacy of Nazism and, above all, the "Final Solution."[17]

In Germany, the issue of *Vergangenheitsbewältigung* or "coming to terms with the past" has, furthermore, always been linked to the effort to define and identify with a notion of antifascism not only in the political sphere but in all realms of human existence: ethics, aesthetics, even intimate relations. One might wonder, of course, why any well-intentioned person would want to question this albeit utopian cultural project of cultivating antifascist behaviors.[18] But as any observer of the German cultural scene well knows, since the beginning of the end of state socialism in eastern Europe, and especially since the fall of the Berlin Wall, German intellectuals and artists have been doing little else than questioning this utopian project, agonizing over this very notion of antifascism insofar as it has figured as a sort of gold standard for moral, political, philosophical, and aesthetic value since 1945.

That the notion of antifascism as it functioned in the former GDR demands rethinking, I would imagine no longer presents great difficulties. Antifascism was the sign under which the GDR received and maintained its legitimacy and became something of a state-supporting myth foreclosing genuine possibilities of sustained moral and political reality testing. Perhaps most perversely, the practice of what might be called antifascist self-fashioning allowed the citizens of the GDR to avoid all too disturbing encounters with questions of individual complicity in the twelve years of German fascism.

As Christa Wolf put it in November 1989:

At a certain moment difficult to determine, the small group of antifascists who ruled the country transferred, for pragmatic reasons, their sense of victory to the entire population. The "victors of history" ceased to deal with their *real* past during the years of National Socialism: as the faithful, as the seduced, as fellow-travellers. They told their children little or nothing of their own childhood and youth. Their guilty conscience, persisting subconsciously, made it difficult for them to resist the Stalinist structures and patterns of thinking which for so long served as a test of "party discipline" and "loyalty" and which even today have not yet been radically and publicly abandoned.[19]

It was, of course, a debate about the East German writer Christa Wolf and her own idealizations of the "better Germany" that served as the occasion to extend this interrogation of what might be termed the mytheme of antifascism to the West German context. In one of his key essays on Wolf, Ulrich Greiner has argued that since 1945 both German literatures have been laboring under the strain of a specifically German mode of political correctness, that the aesthetic value of works of art has been determined according to their moral and political use-value as symbolic purgatives of past and immunizations against future fascism, understood not only as a politics but also as a state and structure of mind and imagination.[20]

In his contribution to this larger cultural debate, Syberberg offers several rather startling twists to the critique of what Greiner calls the *Gesinnungsästhetik* or "goodwill aesthetics" of the postwar era.[21] Whereas Greiner cites, as the crucial totemic figures embodying this aesthetic, the writers associated with the *Gruppe 47* and the ideal of a politically engaged literature—Böll, Grass, Lenz, Fried, Walser, Enzensberger, Weiss, Kipphardt, Andersch—Syberberg offers a rather different genealogy of the same aesthetic paradigm. In Syberberg's historicization of postwar aesthetics, the real totemic, or as he puts it, super-egoic figures of postwar culture all have Jewish names:[22]

The aesthetics of Adorno and Bloch to Benjamin, Marcuse and Kracauer determined . . . the cultural life of Germany after 1945. Untainted by Hitler, they became the spiritual patrons [*Gründungsväter*] of Germany's postwar history . . . What hounded . . . art in Germany after the last war was the curse of guilt which offered itself as a tool of intimidation by the left, in that leftists saw themselves as innocent and because Hitler persecuted the Jews—now in an unholy alliance of Jewish leftist aesthetics directed against the guilty, creating boredom and numbing all cultural life with lies, so that guilt could become a business, deadly for all fantasy life. . . . Whoever went with the Jews and the left had it made.[23]

In the continuation of his recantation of previous artistic efforts cited earlier, Syberberg explicitly takes leave of the cultural legacy of the Jewish émigrés:

> Didn't I too try to become the favorite son to the émigrés as the single authority which, undamaged by the guilt of the fathers, could interpret the world in spiritual terms . . . ; didn't I know that whoever finds recognition here has a chance for advancement . . . as in periods of Christian predominance in our culture, when zealousness was the basis of all culture, coupled with the anxiety of excommunication by the intellectual popes. (104)[24]

But Syberberg's genealogy of postwar aesthetics very quickly takes on much larger historical, not to say world-historical, dimensions. The émigré philosophers and aestheticians whose regime, Syberberg argues, utterly inhibited the production of authentic works of art in Germany after 1945, represent, through their unique syntheses of Marxism and psychoanalytic insight, the culmination of what Syberberg characterizes as the Jewish epoch of European culture:

> The Jewish interpretation of the world follows upon the Christian, just as the Christian one followed Roman and Greek culture. Thus the predominance of those analyses, images, definitions in art, science, sociology, literature, politics, information media. . . . Marx and Freud are the pillars marking the path from east to west. Neither are conceivable without Jewishness. Their systems are defined by it. The axis USA-Israel guarantees the external parameters. This shapes the way people feel, think, judge, act, and pass information. We live in the Jewish epoch of European cultural history, we who, at the pinnacle of technological power, live in apocalyptic expectancy of our last judgment. (79)

In Syberberg's view—in essence an anti-Semitic version of Nietzsche's anti-Socratic account of the decline of tragic drama presented in *The Birth of Tragedy*—the moral and aesthetic taboos and constraints that German artists accepted after the war as the price for the disaster are simply more radical manifestations of an ultimately Judaic inhibition and prohibition with regard to Apollonian pleasures in plastic representation and correlated Dionysian passions and intoxications.

Under the heading "The Curse," Syberberg identifies the two central taboos that in his view have inhibited the production of art in Germany after the war. The first is associated with Walter Benjamin and concerns the hypothesis that fascism depended on an aestheticization of politics. Citing the crucial role played by film in general and Leni Riefenstahl's films in particular, Syberberg remarks that Hitler

> made the masses themselves into . . . an object of his art, with the support of modern technology. By aesthetic I mean beautiful and, by implication, magical, in the sense of enchantment, myth, etc. Thus beauty succumbed to the taboo . . . since Hitler, according to universal consensus, stands for evil as such. The beautiful as the lie of evil succumbed to the absolute prohibition on beauty. (34)

The second taboo is associated with Theodor Adorno's much debated and misunderstood reflections on the impossibility of lyric poetry after Auschwitz. "This was equivalent," Syberberg says, "to an ancient prohibition of graven images, of poetic speech, of art as such. . . . Regardless of how it was meant or said, it had the effect of a general ban on poetry and even on emotion" (35–36). Syberberg's crucial point, however, is more radical still: through these taboos Germans were expropriated of the very aesthetic means and materials with which they might have been able to construct works of elegiac art and engage in an authentic labor of mourning; the so-called inability to mourn was, in this reading, imposed on the Germans who were prevented from libidinally cathecting the elegiac resources available to them in their own aesthetic tradition.

Continuing his characterization of the two taboos burdening aesthetic production in Germany after the war, Syberberg claims,

> With this defense against or repression of passionate enthusiasm, the old category of Dionysian intoxication also fell under the curse and therewith the origin of catharsis, the very purification which was ostensibly at stake. One can't help but wonder whether this purification was not determined to be highly undesirable. (35)

The kernel of Syberberg's remarkable and deeply disturbing reinterpretation of the Mitscherlichs' thesis might thus be put as follows: if only Germans could free themselves from the Jewish influence (via the Frankfurt School) on postwar German art, they could begin in earnest the work of mourning for the disaster they brought on in their grandiose efforts to eliminate the Jewish influence on German art and culture. One can see, now, how far Syberberg has come since his earlier work. In the *Hitler* film, the German cultural tradition, and above all the legacy of German Romanticism in literature, painting, music, and philosophy, was seen to have been polluted by the ways in which National Socialism appropriated that legacy, adapted it as a crucial support for the phantasmatic construction of the *Volksgemeinschaft*. In his latest revisitation of these matters composed in the "interregnum" of 1989–90, the pollution endangering the polity is traced not to any actual historical guilt staining the cultural tradition but rather to prohibitions imposed from the outside, by the law of the victors and their policies of moral, political, and cultural reeducation.[25]

This brings us back to the role of Antigone in Syberberg's new discourse of unification. As I see it, this discourse depends on a displacement of an ethical model of mourning—perceived now as repressively Oedipal and Jewish—by an aesthetic one, which Syberberg appears to associate with Antigone. Syberberg rejects, in other words, the ethical dimension of mourning, by which I mean the troping and chastening of desire, which of necessity proceeds in the name of a *law*, if only the minimal law of the survival of the intersubjective bond. Antigone now becomes, for Syberberg, the vehicle of a radically extra-moral and aestheticized conception of the work of mourning, a mourning subject to no law but those intrinsic to the work of art.[26] Syberberg sees the making taboo of any aspect of aesthetic experience, even those that formed the phantasmatic kernel of Nazism, as a kind of repressive Oedipalization imposed by a western and, ultimately, Jewish paternal agency. Syberberg now openly disavows this super-egoic injunction in the name of an Antigone whose unswerving attachment to Polynices becomes the emblem of his radical anti-Oedipalism. I see the most unsettling dimension of Syberberg's appropriation of Antigone as the reperiodization of modern German history constructed in these essays, a reperiodization occasionally at odds with his vision of a world-historical epoch of Jewish cultural domination.

The crucial gesture in this reperiodization is the displacement of 1933 by 1945 as the fundamental caesura of twentieth-century German history.[27] The "real cultural event at the end of the last war," Syberberg maintains, "was the triumph of vulgarity in art. . . . An aesthetic . . . of vulgarity realised itself, *standing in contrast to everything that had come before*" (29; my emphasis). A traditional kind of art, one produced in the context of a rigorously and ritually hierarchized rural society—no doubt the ultimate object of Syberberg's nostalgia for the phantasmatic Prussia of Kant and Kleist—is placed in opposition to the aesthetic imposed on Germany after 1945: "It is a question here of an art that found its demise after the re-education of 1945 as the saddest victim of the previous twelve years" (127).[28]

In an earlier passage on the classical ideal in art, Syberberg writes (in a convoluted syntax that can hardly be considered classical):

> Nature served as the standard . . . for the rural culture of Weimar and Prussia, for Hölderlin's odes to the Rhine and the Greece of his ideals [which] posited art as the *summum bonum* of the nature of earthly self-discipline, serving as the spiritual corrective of a fragile life. The goal . . . was a life for art, beauty as the highest freedom—until the collapse of 1945, which let the sons of this idealism fall, one after the other, on the battlefields of this century. (58)

One discovers the most glaring consequences of Syberberg's absolute fixation on 1945 as the crucial turning point in modern German history in those passages that array the perpetrators and the victims of National-Socialism on the same side of a world-historical ecological struggle, as allies in a sensibility that saw its demise only with the victory of the western powers over the people of the center of Europe. In one of many eco-fundamentalist passages on the degradation of rural landscapes and cultures, Syberberg describes with Heideggerian pathos the incursions of modernization into the Austrian community where he has, over the years, regularly spent his holidays. He writes of the survival of one dwelling, the home of a local judge, which still stands

> as it did . . . up to the time of Hofmannsthal, Schnitzler, Freud, Broch, and Bassermann, who all passed through this region, on the tracks of the emperor and the famous archduke, with Eichmann and Kaltenbrunner in their retinue. *Today*, the land has been placed at our disposal, a victim of the democratization of vacation in the tourist industry. (123; my emphasis)[29]

From Syberberg's onto-ecological perspective, the devastation to human life brought about by National Socialism is dwarfed to the point of near insignificance by the cultural, aesthetic, and environmental consequences of modernization, which in Syberberg's narrative takes on its most destructive characteristics only after 1945.

Even in the few passages where Syberberg explicitly addresses the Holocaust, the challenge and crisis that event represents for the *ethical* imagination is ultimately displaced by Syberberg's new national, ontological, and ecological priorities:

> The central themes of our time are the collapse of the German Reich under conditions of a rape presenting itself as liberation and re-education at the center of the continent and its consequences with the division of Germany and therewith of Europe and the disappearance of one of the central cultural nations, namely Prussia. Second, Auschwitz and the exodus of the European Jews to Israel and America. And third, the expulsion to the west of 15 million human beings from the eastern provinces of Germany. . . . In the meantime, an overarching theme of our endangerment and guilt . . . has emerged from . . . . Those named above, namely that of the exploitation of the world by man himself. (33)[30]

IV

One might ask, after this presentation of Syberberg's contribution to current debates on German cultural and national identity, why one should bother to take him as seriously as I have. Why not call these ruminations on aesthetics and politics what they in effect are: obscene. My answer would be that their interest lies precisely in their obscenity. The obscene dimension of Syberberg's reflections is perhaps most palpable in those passages where he would seem to assume a god's-eye perspective, looking down on the planet, melancholically taking stock of the desecration of the environment by man. The effect of reading these passages is similar to that of looking at a photograph, seemingly offering a neutral view of an object—a view of calm and equipoise, above the shortsighted, partisan strife of profane human affairs—and all of a sudden realizing that one is seeing the object from a thoroughgoingly interested, subjective, and even perverse perspective.[31] One realizes that the invitation to share the gaze of the photograph is an invitation to identify with someone's desire and fantasy. The force of Syberberg's work as an artist derives precisely from his programmatic insistence on the perverse perspective—the perspective stained by desire and fantasy—as a necessary condition of all aesthetic creation and reception.

If I have understood Syberberg correctly, the critical point behind his radical aestheticism is the speculative one that an ideological fantasy can never be dislodged, "deconstructed," by dint of good political or ethical intentions alone or even through critical insight into the cultural constructedness of ideological fantasies, but rather only through the support of another fantasy, another libidinal investment. There can be no immunity against fascist ideology, against the much-discussed fascination with fascism, without the material support of elements of fantasy. In other words, all *Ideologiekritik*—all antifascism—is of necessity "anaclitic" with respect to fantasy; it must, as it were, lean on the perverse materiality of fantasy if it is to be more than mere rote citation of politically correct positions.

Syberberg is at the same time horribly disappointing because, in a sense, he consistently allows himself to be blinded by his own best insights. Rather than seeing in fantasy a necessary support precisely for the ethical dimension of mourning, which as the Mitscherlichs indicated—and I think the Syberberg of the *Hitler* film understood—involves the difficult work of de-cathecting those ideological phantasms which in the Nazi period quite openly invited the violation of the intersubjective bond, he reproduces some of the most extreme gestures and positions of those very ideological constructions. The reason for this would seem to be that he is incapable of conceiving of fantasy except in deeply anti-Semitic terms. For Syberberg the aesthetic elaboration of fantasy will always be first and foremost an act of resistance against what is perceived as a repressive Judaic prohibition.

In conclusion I return, very briefly to Anselm Kiefer's series of staged photographs entitled "Occupations." The ambition behind these photographs, in which we see the artist performing the Hitler salute in a series of European landscapes, might best be characterized by noting the multiple layers of meaning in the title "Besetzungen," where the English translation gives only one meaning. *Besetzung* is, of course, the word used by Freud to signify a libidinal investment in some object, real or imaginary; English translations of Freud have, for better or worse, rendered it as cathexis, from the Greek for "holding fast" or "holding down." In German, *Besetzung* also signifies the cast of a play or film. One might thus understand Kiefer's series of photographs as a self-conscious performance of an aggressive ideological gesture—the Nazi fantasy of world occupation and domination—with the intention of dislodging the libidinal attachment to this very fantasy. By casting himself in the *role* of Nazi sympathizer and allowing himself to be thoroughly dwarfed by his surroundings in each photograph, Kiefer makes palpable—and somewhat ridiculous—the performative dimension of the ideological gesture in question, thus offering a breathing space where the work of decathexis might unfold.

Kiefer's series of staged tableaux thereby repeat the fundamental strategy of Brechtian "epic" theater. The logic of Kiefer's artistic development in the following years, his decision, as it were, to subject the photograph to all sorts of material transformations and manipulations, to cut it up and mix it with paint, lead, sand, straw, and other materials that, as with Beuys, can take on the the the quality of fetishes, emerges, I would like to suggest from the recognition that the success of the critical gesture intent on dislodging ideological investments cannot dispense with the support of fantasy and its multiple material embodiments. In a word, Kiefer comes much closer to understanding and putting into aesthetic practice what I take to be the crucial insight underlying Syberberg's otherwise reactionary pronouncements, namely that even the cultivation of antifascism may, in the end, have to depend on a healthy dose of perversity.[32]

Notes

*This essay was conceived as part of a volume to be published by The Walker Art Center, *Photography in Contemporary German Art: 1960 to the Present/Essays*, ed. by Gary Garrels.

1. Regarding Kiefer's position in the international art scene, see Andreas Huyssen "Anselm Kiefer: The Terror of History, the Temptation of Myth," *October* 48 (Spring 1989): 25–45.

2. Mark Rosenthal, *Anselm Kiefer* (Philadelphia: Prestel-Verlag, 1987) 17. In German cultural history after Nietzsche, Hölderlin has often had the value of a totemic figure under whose protection, often secured through violent misreadings of his work, a cultural or political enterprise is felt to gain authority.

3. For an excellent discussion of Hölderlin's letter to Böhlendorff, see Peter Szondi, "Überwindung des Klassizismus: Der Brief an Böhlendorff vom 4. Dezember 1801," *Schriften I* (Frankfurt/Main: Suhrkamp, 1978) 345–366. I have also profited from Aris Fioretos' paper on Hölderlin and tragedy, "Cesura: Hölderlin's *Antigonä*," MLA conference, 1991.

4. Thomas Pfau, trans. and ed., *Friedrich Hölderlin: Essays and Letters on Theory* (Albany: SUNY, 1988) 150.

5. One could argue that the key to Hölderlin's poetic procedures lies in his attempt to let the "modern" hollowing out of elegiac speech itself become the occasion and site for a renewal of elegiac potency. For more thorough discussions of the place of mourning in Hölderlin's life and work, see my introduction in *Friedrich Hölderlin: "Hyperion" and Selected Poems* (New York: Continuum, 1990); Rainer Nägele, *Text, Geschichte und Subjektivität* (Stuttgart: Metzler, 1985); Anselm Haverkamp, *Laub voll Trauer. Hölderlins späte Allegorie* (Munich: Wilhelm Fink, 1991). A remarkably lucid discussion of the conventions of elegiac poetry may be found in Peter Sacks, *The English Elegy: Studies in the Genre from Spenser to Yeats* (Baltimore: Johns Hopkins UP, 1985). Sacks points out that the

concern with the efficacy of elegiac speech does not begin with modernity, even if we locate its origins in the eighteenth century, but is rather nearly as old as the genre of elegy itself. He does note, however, that at particular historical moments the depletion of a culture's elegiac resources may reach crisis proportions. Thus, Sacks notes that toward the end of the sixteenth century:

> the question of "what should be said" in the face of suffering and death had become particularly vexing. Since supposedly immutable principles of divine, human, and natural order were increasingly suspected of being no more than man's figural impositions on an essentially intractable reality, the traditional means of consolation were robbed of their protective charm. (64)

It is, Sacks continues, above all in the revenge tragedies of the period—*Hamlet* stands out as the preeminent example—

> that one finds the most moving dramatization of the dilemmas that ensue when man's need for consolation or redress is obstructed by his loss of faith in the power of art's reply. With "art" we may here associate not only such fictions as those of pastoral elegy but also the no less artificial, and linguistic mediations of justice and the law. (64)

6. Steiner writes that:

> Antigone's constancy in the western poetic repertoire is literal. As is that of the Creon-Antigone confrontation and dialectic in their political, moral, legal, sociological ramifications. Named or implicit, the two figures and the mortal argument between them initiate, exemplify, and polarize primary elements in the discourse on man and society as it has been conducted in the West. . . . Since the fifth century BC, western sensibility has experienced decisive moments of its identity and history in reference to the Antigone legend and to the life in art and in argument of this legend.

(George Steiner, *Antigones: How the Antigone Legend Has Endured in Western Literature, Art, and Thought* [Oxford: Clarendon P, 1984] 108–9).

7. In his book, Steiner discusses several recurrences of "Antigone-fever" in postwar Germany. By far the most well-known and controversial of these "returns" was the Schlöndorff-Böll segment of the collaborative film *Deutschland in Herbst*, produced as a response to the political turmoil in the Federal Republic in the autumn of 1977:

> By far the subtlest collage of the antique and the contemporary, of Antigone-Ismene and the "woman question," is achieved in Heinrich Böll's script for *Deutschland im Herbst*. . . . The question is this: can Sophocles' *Antigone* be screened on television just when the "Red Faction" and the Baader-Meinhof gang have almost brought the country to its knees, at a time when acts of brutal terror are being carried out in the name of absolute justice? Imprisoned, almost literally buried alive in isolation cells, Ulrike Meinhof (Antigone?) finds means of commiting suicide. Andreas Baader (Haemon?) does so a year later. The state refuses to return their bodies to their families. Is Creon not justified in defending the survival of society against merciless killers? What *really* came to pass in Antigone's death cell?

(Steiner, 150–51).

8. Hans Jürgen Syberberg, *Vom Unglück und Glück der Kunst in Deutschland nach dem letzten Kriege* (Munich: Matthes and Seitz, 1990).

9. Hans Jürgen Syberberg, *Die freudlose Gesellschaft. Notizen aus den letzten Jahren* (Munich: Hanser, 1981).

10. Alexander and Margarete Mitscherlich, *The Inability to Mourn: Principles of Collective Behavior*, trans. Beverly Placzek (New York: Grove P, 1975).

11. Hellmuth Karasek's characterization of Syberberg as the eternal Hitler youth (*Spiegel* [36/1990]) is typical in this regard. For more differentiated reviews, see Alain Auffray, "Doing the Reich Thing," *Guardian* 14 December 1990 and Ian Buruma's excellent essay on Syberberg and Christa Wolf, "There's No Place Like Heimat," *The New York Review of Books* 20 December 1990.

12. See especially Mitscherlichs, 26:

> To millions of Germans the loss of the "Führer" (for all the oblivion that covered his downfall and the rapidity with which he was renounced) was not the loss of someone ordinary; identifications that had filled a central function in the lives of his followers were attached to his person. The loss of an object so highly cathected with libidinal energy . . . was indeed reason for melancholia. Through the catastrophe not only was the German ego-ideal robbed of the support of reality, but in addition the Führer himself was exposed by the victors as a criminal of truly monstrous proportions. With this sudden reversal of his qualities, the ego of every single German individual suffered a central devaluation and impoverishment. This creates at least the prerequisites for a melancholic reaction.

See also my efforts at a "postmodern" reformulation and application of the Mitscherlichs' thesis in Eric L. Santner, *Stranded Objects: Mourning, Memory, and Film in Postwar Germany* (Ithaca, N.Y.: Cornell UP) esp. 1–7.

13. Slavoj Žižek, *Looking Awry: An Introduction to Jacques Lacan Through Popular Culture* (Cambridge: MIT P, 1991) 26.

14. Žižek, 26–27. Perhaps one of the most interesting examples of the disorientation underlying life in the village is the utter inability of Arnie, the little boy who discovers Harry—who, we learn, is Arnie's step-father—to distinguish between past, present, and future verb tenses. It is as if the failure to settle the symbolic debt undoes the temporal dimension of syntax, producing a variety of what Jakobson has called a "contiguity disorder."

15. For detailed analyses of Syberberg's films with regard to the question of mourning, see, once more, Santner, *Stranded Objects*; Anton Kaes, *From Hitler to Heimat: the Return of History as Film* (Cambridge: Harvard UP, 1989); Thomas Elsaesser, "Myth as the Phantasmogoria of History: H. J. Syberberg, Cinema and Representation," *New German Critique* 24–25 (Fall/Winter 1981–82): 108–54; Timothy Corrigan, *New German Film: The Displaced Image* (Austin: U of Texas P, 1983); and finally Susan Sontag's seminal essay, "Syberberg's Hitler," *Under the Sign of Saturn* (New York: Vintage, 1981).

16. Philippe Lacoue-Labarthe and Jean-Luc Nancy explicitly make Syberberg's *Hitler* film the basis of their analysis of the "identificatory mechanism" and its various aesthetic supports, which they see as the core of Nazism. See "The Nazi Myth," trans. Brian Holmes, *Critical Inquiry* 16 (Winter 1990): 291–312.

17. It could be argued, of course, that the debates on political correctness in the United States have from the very start also been about "proper coping" with the past: the destruction of indigenous peoples and cultures in North America, slavery, the Vietnam War, the legacy of violence against women, and so on.

18. This project is by no means exclusively a German one. Foucault's preface to *Anti-Oedipus* suggests the comprehensiveness of the antifascist paradigm of culture, or at least of cultural critique:

> the major enemy, the strategic adversary is fascism. . . . And not only historical fascism, the fascism of Hitler and Mussolini—which was able to mobilize and use

the desire of the masses so effectively—but also the fascism in us all, in our heads and in our everyday behavior, the fascism that causes us to love power, to desire the very thing that dominates and exploits us. . . . How does one keep from being fascist . . . ? How do we rid our speech and our acts, or hearts and our pleasures, of fascism? How do we ferret out the fascism that is ingrained in our behavior?

Michel Foucault in Gilles Deleuze, Félix Guattari, *Anti-Oedipus: Capitalism and Schizophrenia* (Minneapolis: University of Minnesota Press, 1983) xiii.

19. Quoted in Christoph Klessmann, "Das Problem der doppelten 'Vergangenheits-bewältigung,'" *Die Neue Gesellschaft/Frankfurter Hefte* 12 (December 1991): 1101.

20. See Ulrich Greiner, "Die deutsche Gesinnungsästhetik," *Die Zeit* 9 November 1990. For the best discussion to date of the debate about Christa Wolf along with a number of other recent crisis moments in German literary and political culture, see Andreas Huyssen, "After the Wall: The Failure of German Intellectuals," *New German Critique* 52 (Winter 1991): 109–43. Huyssen's essay on Kiefer cited earlier already presents Kiefer as perhaps the most significant and provocative aesthetic challenge to the "liberal and social-democratic antifascist consensus" of the postwar era. See Huyssen, "Anselm Kiefer" 31.

21. I am using Huyssen's translation of an otherwise untranslatable word. See Huyssen, "After the Wall" 129.

22. One is reminded of the recent controversy over CCNY professor Leonard Jeffries's citation of "Jewish names" in his account of the sufferings of blacks in America.

23. Syberberg, *Vom Unglück und Glück der Kunst* 14. All subsequent references will be provided in the text.

24. Whether intentional or not, Syberberg's formulation, which I have translated as "favorite son," is strangely overdetermined. The German reads: "Suchte ich nicht auch mich Liebkind zu machen bei der Generation der Emigranten." By writing "Liebkind" for "Lieblingskind," Syberberg is, I suspect, saying, "didn't I play at being the good Jewish son to the émigrés."

25. Regarding the question of "pollution," we do well to recall Teiresias' plea to Creon regarding the dangers to the *polis* of failing to bury Polynices:

> There's a plague in Thebes, and its cause
> Is you, my lord. Our oracles, our holy shrines
> Have been polluted by dogs and birds
> Gorged on the flesh of Polynices
> Son of Oedipus; the gods refuse to hear us;
> The altar-fires reject our sacrifice;
> The birds of the air, drunk on human blood,
> Have no clear oracles to send us. Think hard
> My son. . . .
> Give way: yield to the dead. Where is the sense
> In killing a corpse twice over?

(Kenneth McLeish, trans., *Sophocles: Electra, Antigone, Philoctetes* [Cambridge: Cambridge UP, 1979] 92–93.)

Syberberg insists over and over again on a causal connection between the making taboo of elegiac resources—what he refers to as a *Klageverbot*, or prohibition of lamentation—and the exploitation and pollution of the environment in both parts of Germany.

26. In her essay "Heidegger on Hegel's *Antigone*: The Memory of Gender and the Forgetfulness of the Ethical Difference" (forthcoming, *Hegel and Heidegger*, ed. Rebecca Comay and John McCumber), Kathleen Wright argues that Heidegger's 1942 revision of his earlier interpretation of *Antigone* depends on a similar displacement of the ethical and

juridical dimensions of the tragedy by a more purely ontological and "poetic" understanding of the protagonist's situation.

27. I have argued elsewhere that such a reperiodization is an organizing principle of the vision of twentieth-century German history found in Edgar Reitz's film *Heimat*. See Santner, *Stranded Objects*, 57–102.

28. Though at first glance one might find certain similarities between Syberberg's call for a cultural and aesthetic renewal of national traditions and Karl Heinz Bohrer's critique of the left-liberal consensus in matters of aesthetics and national identity, Syberberg's compulsive references to the fantasy of an organic rural-aristocratic society—a sort of Prussian aristocratic version of Edgar Reitz's "Schabbach"—represents a return—with a vengeance—of the very provincialism Bohrer has identified as the real impediment to the formation of a German cultural identity in the postwar period. See Bohrer's glosses on "Provinzialismus" in *Merkur*, nos. 501, 504, 505, 507, 509, 514.

29. Speaking of the same landscape and the degradations it has suffered, Syberberg picks up this train of thought with an insensitivity that can only have been calculated as provocation:

> The old guests whom one likes to praise now, from Freud, the archaeologist of the soul, to Theodor Herzl, whose bicycle still stands in the folklore museum, before he set off for his promised land to lead his people to Israel, from Hofmannsthal to H. Broch to Gustav Mahler—they would all, as the local farmers say, "turn in their graves," if they saw what happened to their teachings and their land. (125)

The dialect expression Syberberg cites and that I have translated as "turn in their graves" reads in the original: "Truhn aussi reitn und wie der Blitz in den Schornstein einifahrn." A more literal translation might be: They'd jump like lightening out of their trunks [coffins?] *and up through the chimney.*

30. Syberberg's efforts to situate the Shoah within larger narrative concerns should sound familiar to anyone who followed the *Historikerstreit* of the mid-1980s. One thinks, for example, of Andreas Hillgruber's book, *Zweierlei Untergang: Die Zerschlagung des Deutschen Reiches und das Ende des europäischen Judentums* (Berlin: Siedler, 1986), which in many ways prepared the ground for Syberberg's more explicit "Antigonism." In his book, only a small part of which is dedicated to the "end" of European Jewry while the main body of the book deals with the "shattering" of the Reich, Hillgruber more or less programmatically sets out to restore his German audience's capacity to libidinally cathect and unproblematically identify with the defenders of Germany's eastern territories during the period of their collapse, even though these "valiant" efforts to hold back the anticipated reprisals of the Red Army allowed for the machinery of the death camps to continue unabated. Interestingly enough, Hillgruber characterizes the point of view of the soldiers defending the eastern territories as one determined by an ethics of responsibility (*verantwortungsethisch*) rather than one of conviction (*gesinnungsethisch*), which he associates with the members of the July 20th conspiracy against Hitler. The recent attack on *Gesinnungsästhetik* echoes, in a sense, this earlier critique of *Gesinnungsethisch*.

31. This effect has been lucidly analyzed by Slavoj Žižek in his commentary on a remarkable scene from Hitchcock's film *The Birds:*

> A fire caused by a cigarette butt dropped into some gasoline breaks out in the small town threatened by the birds. After a series of short and "dynamic" close-ups and medium shots that draw us immediately into the action, the camera pulls back and up and we are given an overall shot of the entire town taken from high above. In the first instant we read this overall shot as an "objective," "epic" panorama shot, separating us from the immediate drama going on down below

and enabling us to disengage ourselves from the action. This distancing at first produces a certain "pacifying" effect; it allows us to view the action from what might be called a "metalinguistic" distance. Then, suddenly, a bird enters the frame from the right, as if coming from behind the camera and thus from behind our own backs, and then three birds, and finally an entire flock. The same shot takes on a totally different aspect, it undergoes a radical *subjectivization:* the camera's elevated eye ceases to be that of a neutral, "objective" onlooker gazing down upon a panoramic landscape and suddenly becomes the subjective and threatening gaze of the birds as they zero in on their prey. (Žižek 96–97)

32. Here we might recall what Freud said about what he clearly thought was the paradigmatic perversion, namely fetishism. In the first of the *Drei Abhandlungen zur Sexualtheorie* (Frankfurt/Main: Fischer, 1988), Freud writes that psychological access to normal genital sexuality is mediated by an excessive libidinal investment in the love object and anything associated with it. "A certain degree of . . . fetishism is thus a regular component of normal love," (30). It would be productive, I think, to reconsider the problems inherent in Habermas's notion of *Verfassungspatriotismus* and "postconventional" or "posttraditional" identity in light of these psychoanalytic reflections on perversion. Habermas has said of Auschwitz that it

> can and should remind the Germans, no matter in what state territories they find themselves, of something else: that they cannot count on the continuities of their history. Because of that horrible break in continuity the Germans have given up the possibility of constituting their identity on something other than universalist principles of state citizenship, in the light of which national traditions can no longer remain unexamined, but can only be critically and self-critically appropriated. Post-traditional identity loses its substantial, its unproblematic character; it *exists* only in the method of the public, discursive battle around the interpretation of a constitutional patriotism made concrete under particular historical circumstances. (Jürgen Habermas, "Yet Again: German Identity—A Unified Nation of Angry DM-Burghers?" *New German Critique* 52 [Winter 1991]: 98)

It is interesting to note that Benjamin Buchloh has attacked Anselm Kiefer in light of Habermas's reflections on post-traditional identity. He writes, for example:

> Anselm Kiefer is only the most prominent of the German artists who have modeled themselves on concepts that Habermas has defined as "traditional identity." In the course of their restoration of these concepts, these artists have produced a type of work . . . that can best be identified as polit-kitsch. Its attraction seems not only to be its reconstitution of traditional identity for the generation of West Germans who wish to abandon the long and difficult process of reflection upon a post-traditional identity. The attraction of polit-kitsch also appears to be associated with the traditional identity, i.e., the claim to have privileged access to "seeing" and "representing" history. (Benjamin Buchloh, "A Note on Gerhard Richter's *October 18, 1977,*" *October* 48 [Spring 1989], 100)

What both Habermas and Buchloh fail to consider is that the often painful demands of assuming a post-traditional identity might require the material support of a "fetish," that is, residues of that "traditional" space of identity formation they both see in purely negative terms.

CONSTELLATION J
THE POST-AL PUBLIC SPHERE: POLITICS OF IDEOLOGY

This final constellation returns us to questions raised at the beginning of the "hour-glass" regarding the role and impact of the "German" on the global stage (Introduction and Constellation A ["German Cinema Studies"]). Via Katie Trumpener's liberal attention to a new Europe that is more ethnically diverse yet more nationalistic and xenophobic than before the Soviet break-up, questions of a post-national German subjectivity and a post-national German public sphere are foregrounded, echoing Constellation B's ("The Heimat *Debate") attention to the neonationalist notions of "homeland," "exile," and "repatriation" now reconstituted in the post-al disorderly context of German reunification and European Union. How does Trumpener's multicultural post-nationalism compare with Marc Silberman's appropriation of feminism for a post-Cold War look at the films of the former East Germany? How do both analyses' culturalist associations of class, gender, and nation lead them to disavow Mas'ud Zavarzadeh's political critique of these concepts vis-à-vis* Paris, Texas *(Constellation D ["The Euroamerican Question"])? Where is Stuart Liebman's reading of the Negt/Klugean public sphere located in this dialectic, and how does his valorization of a certain post-al montage effect in Kluge, as distinct from the intellectual montage of Eisenstein, recall the attendant idealism of Thomas Elsaesser's allegorical commodification of desire in Constellation D? Does Walter Benjamin's philosophical treatise on fascism intervene into the apparent divergences between and amongst these texts, pointing to the imminent dangers of their varied levels of post-al enthusiasm and/or millenarian trepidation over the prospect of a new global village? Or does its tendency toward mysticism merely reinscribe these post-al effects, as mutually inclusive aspects of global capitalist expansion, onto the ideological plane of German cultural studies? As the anthology draws to a close, we ask our readers to consider the significance of a radical disorderly German cinema studies and a radical stereoscopic German film theorist. What does it mean to maintain, as we do, that the current, post-al wave of German cinema studies anthologies forecloses the possibility of questions such as these by rearticulating and reifying occlusive tropes of the "national" or false binarisms of the "German"/non-"German"? How then does the political, materialist allegory made possible by radical disorderly theory mark an intervention into German cinema studies and, further, into the post-nationalist public sphere? At what cost will a reader decide to take up the challenge of such an intervention? Will she ask why the constellations of this anthology are included or arranged in particular ways, or won't she even register a difference? And if she opts for difference, will her work signal the advent of a radical* labor *or merely a return to entrepreneurial* work?

On the Road:
Labor, Ethnicity and the New "New German Cinema" in the Age of the Multinational

KATIE TRUMPENER

IN WEST GERMANY today, national self-understanding and cultural self-fashioning are marked by a number of striking contradictions which play themselves out in various kinds of cultural representation. In political culture, in consumer culture, in pop culture and in film culture, the new nationalism competes with a new internationalism; a generalised sense of post-modernity manifests itself as nostalgia for pre-modern society. An increasingly post-industrial culture longs at once for a work ethic it associates with industrialisation, and for a unified ethnos it associates with pre-industrial conditions of production. Thus in Uwe Schrader's 1988 film *Sierra Leone*, the main character, Fred, unemployed and culturally displaced, is haunted simultaneously by memories of his industrial work in the West German Ruhr area, and by nostalgic dreams of a pre-industrialised Africa. In summarising some of the important trends in contemporary political and cultural life, this essay will try to contextualise *Sierra Leone*'s persuasive vision of West Germany as a cross-over culture, a society caught in a painful process of change.

NATIONAL CULTURE AND THE CULTURE INDUSTRY

Beer and cola, you can get them anywhere in the world. Sometimes you think there is nothing else. (*Sierra Leone*)

Heimatsklänge, the Sounds of Home: as "European City of Culture 1988," the city of West Berlin sponsored a series of concerts last summer which featured the cross-over sounds of the so-called 'World Music'. A guitarist from Sierra Leone; a Rai singer hailing from Algeria, Morocco and Paris; dance music from the Croatian villages of Hungary; Tex-Mex and klezmer music (the accordion and brass music of Eastern Europe transformed by its new context in the ethnic ghettos of North America): this is travelling music, the rhythms of immigrants and emigrants. "Sounds of home?" The organisers explained: "It is a concentrate of steppes and beaches, distilled in the European metropolises. The music of the Moluccans in the

Reprinted from *Public Culture* 2.1 (1989): 20–29.

Amsterdam pedestrian malls, Turkish rhythms in the square in front of Cologne cathedral."[1]

Like Britain, France and Holland, where a history of imperialist expansion has come home to roost, West Germany is beginning to face a future as an increasingly multicultural and multiracial society, as the new and in most cases permanent home of a second generation of Southern European and Turkish guestworkers with their families, growing numbers of ethnically German 'resettlers' (*Aussiedler*) from Eastern Europe, and refugee groups from Asia, Africa and Latin America known officially as *Asylbewerber* (or, more pejoratively, as *Asylanten*), asylum seekers. The whole tenor and tendency of current immigration policies is in fact encapsulated in the euphemistic nomenclature used for different groups: the bureaucratic term *Asylbewerber* objectifies refugees, describing them solely in terms of their application process (rather than in terms of the suffering that caused them to leave their own countries), and implicitly disclaiming involvement or responsibility for its outcome. The term *Aussiedler*, on the other hand, evokes with sympathy the historical German colonisation and domination of the East: the *Aussiedler* are imaged as returning pioneers or colonists.

Despite official attempts to evoke sympathy for at least *some* immigrant groups, however, widespread fears that the numbers of immigrants to West Germany will lead to cultural 'alienation' (*Überfremdung*, literally 'becoming-overly-foreign') and economic hardship for Germans as well have, as elsewhere in Western Europe, led to a generalised hatred of 'foreigners', and given new strength to neofascist and white-supremacist groups. The *Horst Wessel Lied* (one of the main anthems of the Nazi Party in the 1930s) and newer songs calling for the gassing of Jews, Turks and *Asylanten* are openly sung at many meetings of the youth groups of the ruling Christian Democratic Party—to the embarrassment, it must be added, of the parent party. But local and national Christian Democrat governments themselves are doing little to alleviate the difficult situation of foreign nationals in the Federal Republic. The open racism of the rental market in most large cities has been aggravated by the attempts of city governments to prevent the formation of ethnic neighbourhoods by officially prohibiting Turks or other foreign nationals from moving into many inexpensive city districts. On the national level, the crackdown on the much-vilified 'economic refugees' and the more general attempt to discourage even genuine political refugees from seeking asylum in West Germany have resulted in a kind of punitive logic in the laws affecting the *Asylbewerber* already in the country—they now mandate a two-year wait for rulings on individual cases with severe restrictions, in the meantime, on the applicants' freedom of movement. The new foreigners' law (*Ausländergesetz*) proposed last summer would, if implemented as proposed, [Editors' note: it has been implemented] virtually prevent further immigration to West Germany (including dependents and other family members of foreigners already residing there), and would reduce still further the tenuous civil liberties of foreign nationals already in the country: as a 'preventive measure' they could be forbidden to leave their apartments during official state visits or international conferences, and might be subject to official relocation within the Federal Republic. To protect 'the self-esteem of the democratic state', furthermore, they could legally be deported if they "disparaged the Federal Republic or any of its national and federal institutions."

Such measures result not in the frictionless assimilation of a select group of particularly ingratiating immigrants, but rather in a growing number of illegal aliens, a growing black market for work and housing, an ethnic life in West Germany forced half underground. Conservatives justify their policies, however, with the reasoning that "Germany is not a traditional immigrants' land," that German cultural tradition consists in and depends on the self-enclosure and the self-sufficiency of the German people. To quote from the preamble to the proposed 'foreigners' law':

> The central issue is not an economic problem but a social one . . . the homogeneity of a society which is essentially determined by its membership in the German nation . . . Ideas which aim at a liberalisation of immigration for more foreigners meet with opposition in the German population. This attitude cannot be criticised as intolerant or "anti-foreign" . . . The preservation of a unique national character is the legitimate aim of every nation and state . . . For the Federal Republic, because of the unresolved national problem of the Germans, it is in addition a historical duty.[2]

As the left is quick to point out, of course, venerable historical traditions of German nationalism, insularity and intolerance towards minorities in fact caused Germany itself to produce large numbers of German emigrants fleeing political persecution from the nineteenth century onwards. In the 1930s, *Asylanten* from Hitler's Germany found refuge in countries including Turkey, China and Mexico. For the left, therefore, the historical duty of Germany is not the preservation, at all costs, of a 'national character', but rather a particular responsibility to offer political asylum to all who may need it. Immigration becomes not only a moral but a political question, informed always by the memory of emigration.[3] Thus the new rhetoric of Heimat and the renewed racism of the right and the far right are challenged, if not always matched, by a resurgence of internationalist and anti-racist movements on the left and far left. The range of interests and tactics is broad, from renewed discussions among liberals about bilingual and intercultural education; the formation of new socialist youth groups dedicated to anti-fascist and anti-racist activism within the schools; a huge protest conference accompanying the World Bank meetings in West Berlin last fall; all the way to the fire-bombings by the women's faction of the Red Cell, most recently of a West German clothing chain accused of exploiting labour conditions in South Korea, and a travel agency offering sex tours to Southeast Asia.

Somewhere in between these polarised political cultures of restriction and solidarity lies a new exoticist trend in mainstream consumer culture and cultural consumption. Growing numbers of West German tourists vacation in Turkey. African protest songs compete with American pop music on the West German charts. A decade after the arrival of McDonalds in Europe, a budding new restaurant culture has at least some West Germans eating Kurdish, Sudanese and Malaysian food. The quest for the unusual and the exotic has of course affected film culture as well: the 1988 Berlin Film Festival, for example, featured films from Mali and Estonia. West Germany is itself increasingly part of an international festival circuit. Before it had its West German premiere at Hof in the fall of 1987, Uwe Schrader's *Sierra Leone*, for instance, had already played at festivals in the United States, Canada, Italy and India.

Film as an import and an export, as immigrant and emigrant art: the movie theatre itself has become the site of 'intercultural education', meeting point of internationalist culture and international investments. This is noticeable already in the filmed advertisements which in West Germany precede and frame each commercial film screening, a national program of international ads which endlessly thematise the breaking down of borders, the creation of foreign markets for transnational junk food, a united world which sings of its love of M & Ms and Coca-Cola. Marketing as conquest: the M & Ms commercial seen in West German movie theatres last year sets out to conquer the youth market by appropriating subcultural style. Shot in slow motion, on grainy stock, it imitates the visual jaggedness of the underground, M & Ms as *The Last of England*. And a whole range of liquor commercials, set to calypso or salsa music, enact quite literally the bottling of the exotic, a concentrate of steppes, beaches and 'primitive' cultures (natives usually shown working or dancing) contained in every drink.

The cigarette commercials are even more direct in their depiction of conquest, the breaking down of national borders. The man from Camel explores and tames a thousand African jungles. In the commercial for West cigarettes, a rugged he-man on his way home from Mexico is turned back at the border by a group of Mexican border guards depicted as greasy, stupid and clearly corrupt. Our hero, however, is able to outwit them, sneaking his sports car across the line. From the land of the free, home of the brave, he looks back to give the startled guards the finger. The triumph of the West, ingenuity and daring vanquishing the forces of Southern despotism: the powerful mythology occludes the reality of American immigration policies. For in real life, of course, the true border is on the other side. It is not Mexican border guards who conspire to keep Americans in, but the American border patrol which functions with increasing effectiveness and ruthlessness to keep Mexicans and Central Americans out of the United States.

Parallel kinds of political projection, it can be argued, inform the recent wave of German feature films about Turkish life in Germany, despite the apparently liberal intentions of the filmmakers. Hark Bohm's *Yasmin*, following the pattern set by several other recent films,[4] uses the figure of the adolescent Turkish girl to explore the problems of integration and cultural conflict. As such films present it, the problem today is no longer the economic and political marginality of the Turks in Germany, the pervasive racism that still confronts them daily. Instead "the central issue" (to recycle the phrase used in the proposed foreigners' law) "is not an economic problem but a social one": the main source of conflict and tension appears to be the ethnic family and the Turkish community themselves, for their stubborn refusal to let go of their members, to let them become Westernised, German and free.

Thus Yasmin, born in Germany into a family of prospering Turkish storeowners, is a promising *Gymnasium* student who has the full support of her teachers for her plan to become a doctor. The film fails to make clear, of course, that this dream is virtually impossible, since like all other Turkish residents of Germany, Yasmin would have to apply to German universities as a foreign student, thus effectively put out of the running for the highly competitive admissions to study medicine.[5] Here, the trouble in the plot stems instead from the patriarchal structure of Islamic culture, embodied by the male heads of the family. Increasingly protective of the family honor, Yasmin's father and uncle remove the girl from school and, at the end of the film, kidnap her to be sent back against her will to a Turkey she does not see as home. Luckily, at the last possible minute, she is rescued by her German boyfriend and rides away with him on his motorcycle, having broken with her family forever. The triumph of the West: here it is not the Germans who agitate to send the Turks back to where they came from, or who create endless bureaucratic obstacles to the immigration of Turkish dependents. Instead it is the Turks themselves who threaten to send back their own Germanicised children, and concerned, caring bureaucrats who must take Turkish children away from their parents, for their own good. Under their superficial attempt at feminism, and their more earnest attempt at empathy, such 'immigrant films' hide a fundamental ethnocentrism. They create Turkish characters, and create audience identification with them, by conceiving of them as victimised *by* their Turkishness rather than *because* of it. Yasmin and her sisters just want to be like everyone else, German souls trapped in Turkish bodies, under their stifling headscarves.

The concurrent wave of 'emigrant films', self-referential 'art' films about exile and repatriation which self-consciously move beyond empathy and identification, short-circuit for different reasons. In Austrian director Axel Corti's *Welcome in Vienna*,[6] GDR-emigré Thomas Brasch's *The Passenger: Welcome in Berlin* (1988) and Wim Wenders' *Der Himmel über Berlin/Wings of Desire* (1988, his first film to be made in Germany again after several directed in Hollywood), émigrés return to Vienna or Berlin after years of exile, to make movies about the Third Reich, to work in theatres still filled with Nazi props, angels coming back to earth. Self-pitying, painful and sentimental by turn, these new Heimat movies blur over the problems of cultural continuity and political responsibility, posing them purely in aesthetic terms, to be lost somewhere amid the choice of narrative possibilities and career paths, in the alternation between black-and-white and colour,[7] in the graininess of the picture. The homecoming (*Heimkehrer*) film is here reborn as the M & Ms commercial, a kind of candy-coated underground.

The liberal press reviewed and championed Uwe Schrader's latest film as if it were one of these movies: a man comes back to Germany; a study of character, milieu and psychological alienation; an artisanal film shot with a hand-held camera. Segments of the leftist press, conversely, criticised the film severely for what they saw as its naturalism, its tendency to turn domestic misery into exotic spectacle for upper-class viewers. Both receptions miss the ambition and the scope of *Sierra Leone*, which in its understated way provides a concentrated summary of German life today: exoticism and homesickness, the rise of junk food and the renaissance of ethnic restaurants, the related perspectives of the immigrant and the emigrant. Perhaps most importantly, it presents the problem of culture as both an economic and a social one, tracing the distance and the similarities of German and *Gastarbeiter* perspectives, of ethnic identity and working-class experience.

Liberal critics were right, however, to see *Sierra Leone* as a new hope for the apparently moribund contemporary German cinema. Schrader's visual and narrative style, his minimalist realism, manages to avoid the slick international style that has increasingly characterised West German feature films, and to return to the documentarist social vision which has traditionally been the strength of postwar German cinema. With *Sierra Leone*, Uwe Schrader has created a road movie without the chic philosophising of a Wim Wenders, and a political movie that avoids the self-indulgent campiness of a Fassbinder on the one hand, the modernist distanciation and didacticism of a Kluge on the other. For all that, the film stands with *Yesterday Girl, The Fear of the Goalie at the Penalty Kick, Katzelmacher* (the crucial first feature films of the New German Cinéastes), marking both in subject matter and style an important and long-awaited renewal of the *Arbeiterfilm* (workers' film) of the 1970s, perhaps even of the New German Cinema itself.

INDUSTRIAL CULTURE IN A MULTINATIONAL FRAME

Once you've worked there [in the Ruhr steel mills], you can never forget it. . . . . It will follow you all the way to Africa. It's crazy. As long as you're away, you yearn to be back. Then when you're back again, you long to be there. There's a big world out there—here they don't even know it yet. (*Sierra Leone*)

When *Sierra Leone* opened in West Germany last year, the poster campaign for the film announced it as "A German Adventure," probably (mis-) leading some movie-goers to expect a feature-length version of the Western commercial or a domestic version of Werner Herzog's *Cobra Verde*. In Herzog's latest epic of imperialism, released at the same time, Klaus Kinski plays a maddened European slave trader, backed and attacked by a supporting cast of thousands of real (and partially naked) African tribesmen, against exotic African landscape shot on location. Schrader's film is considerably more mundane. We get a few glimpses of Sierra Leone only in the first three minutes of the film: a street where a brass band plays a jazzy hymn, a marketplace where locals and foreigners barter for handicrafts, a ferry landing. Fred, the central character who has spent the last three years working in Africa as a truck driver, is on his way home to West Germany, and the rest of the film laconically chronicles Fred's arrival and his non-arrival, his unsuccessful search for a home to come back to after three years away. The wife he deserted refuses to take him back, and he sees her in a discotheque dancing with an American GI. His old girlfriend still works the same job, at the American army mess— but she has long been living with someone else. Fred's old job at the smelting plant, with all the jobs like it, is in the process of being phased out altogether. "More and more machines, fewer and fewer people," as his old foreman puts it. "You're lucky you managed to get out when you did—things don't look so rosy any more."

But that is just Fred's problem: a lack of emotional separation from his old job, his old home. He had planned to come back in triumph; now it seems a mistake ever to have gone away. "Why did I work my butt off for three years in Africa, if I have to start over again here on the very bottom?" He is filled with a mixture of nostalgia, disappointment and anger that no one he comes back to can really understand; his distance, his longing, his success and his failure are equally threatening to those who are still just where he left them. Even his old pals from work are, finally, not really glad to see him. "You always thought you were better than us," one of them tells him. "No one can stand you. They've managed to repress how shitty everything is for them."

In fact, in the end there seems nothing left for Fred but to sign another work contract and return to Africa. When he arrives at the headquarters of his multinational, however, the secretary informs him that there has been a coup, a revolution in Sierra Leone, so they don't know if or when they will be hiring again. He should keep checking back with them every few days. In the driving around, the waiting around in motel rooms and bars, meanwhile, that fill up the last part of the film, he is joined by a fellow stray, a young woman who is similarly adrift. He soon becomes tired of both her haplessness and her hopeless dreams of self-improvement, and at the end of the film casually abandons her in a highway motel, along with his brokendown car and the last of the money he has saved. He walks outside to buy cigarettes, flags down a passing truck and rides away out of frame. The camera remains behind, fixed on the front of the motel, where we see the young woman looking around for Fred, not knowing that he is gone, that she is stranded while he travels on. Over the closing credits we hear the sound of African drums: an African song, a group of voices singing together.

The film presents a constantly changing landscape of *döner kebab* stands and highways that all look the same, a Germany composed of smokestacks, used-car lots, junk-food automats, army canteens, snack bars with ethnic food. No home to come back to, a home that has become somewhere else, and someone else's: Fred beats up the American GI who has literally taken his place in the arms of his wife. Yet only a few days later, Fred and his new girlfriend dance together at a Turkish wedding, clearly enjoying the sense of entering an unfamiliar world. Indeed the film suggests that both the current wave of racist violence against 'foreign' inhabitants, and the current fascination with 'ethnic' life are motivated by the same kind of envy. For Germans who feel increasingly isolated, deracinated, anxious about their cultural identity and their economic future, the ethnic minority groups seem enviably determined to resist full assimilation, and enviably confident—in the face of German hostility—of their own right to cultural difference. The mixture of envy and resentment, furthermore, that many German workers seem to feel towards their foreign counterparts and colleagues is intimately linked, Schrader suggests, to their perception that non-Germans lack work discipline. Since their sense of identity stems from their ethnic difference, minority workers are seen as less dependent for their sense of self-worth on their work as such; thus (according to this line of reasoning) the prospect of long-term unemployment does not call into question their very identity, the way it does for West German workers.

In a revealing sequence towards the end of the film, Fred talks about his experiences working in Africa. "There was no eight-hour day there": the work itself was satisfying in part because it could not, due to general economic conditions, be standardised or rationalised. "You have to improvise a lot, you don't just get every replacement part you need." At the same time, Fred's greatest pride is his success in establishing a European work discipline among 'his' Africans, 'the Blacks' who worked under him, and who previously, he claims, had spent much of the workday lying around under the trees, 'just like apes'. Rationalised and rationalising, workers like Fred would seem to play a pivotal if contradictory role in the consolidation and reproduction of the psychological and labour structures of international capitalism. Yet although Fred's role in Africa is in some ways an imperialist one, he recognises at the same time the inherent similarities between his own situation and that of the men who work for him; thus on his return to Germany, he grasps and sympathises—much more fully than his casually racist German pals are able to—with the situation of the guest-workers and the GIs.

The German truck driver in Sierra Leone; African workers and black GIs in the Ruhr; women from the Philippines and Thailand, arriving in Europe as *au pairs* or as mail-order brides, some sold into prostitution in Amsterdam and Hamburg: travelling from Africa to Germany, Schrader suggests the increasingly international scope of the guest worker syndrome in the import and export of labour to and from the Third World. The creation of a new international sub-proletariat—this contemporary slave trade is considerably less dramatic and less photogenic than the activities of Klaus Kinski as Cobra Verde. Post-socialist realism, industrial Heimatsfilm, anti-epic, *Sierra Leone* chronicles the death of national identity in the birth of the multinational, the dispersion of the 'union' and the loss of a teleological sense of time, as semi-skilled and long-term jobs give way to contract work, chronic unemployment, waiting and economic exile. New conditions of production make traditional working-class solidarity and activism a thing of the past: whether or not the workers unionise or strike, their work is being mechanised, then phased out forever. The breaking of the German working class as it outlives the kind of work it was created to sustain: the revolution here, significantly, takes place off-screen, far away in Sierra Leone, where it is little more than a temporary inconvenience to the international import-export business. "You know what it's like there," says the secretary calmly, between phone calls, "A putsch like that can be over right away . . . Then we just fly our people back in."

Trop tard, trop tôt: the Africa we saw in the first minutes of the movie (native prostitutes and peddlers speaking English to their German customers and French amongst themselves), an Africa of beer and cola (where a brass band plays Christian hymns with a jazz lilt), seems at once premodern and post-modern, indigenous and colonial culture inextricably mixed together. By the end of the film, though, the jarring juxtapositions and contradictions have resolved themselves into a single nostalgic mirage. Change is pain; Africa, as it is held in memory by a man now doubly exiled, has come to represent layer upon layer of loss: the creativity of improvisation, the satisfaction of hard work, the stability of an ethnic community, the power of unified political struggle. The music over the final credits throbs with cultural meanings. The drums of Africa, tribal drums, war drums, a native community, unvanquished, singing together harmoniously to the beat: *Heimatsklänge*, Sounds of Home.

Notes

An earlier version of this essay was presented at the 1988 German Studies Association Conference in Philadelphia. My thanks to Liz Corra and to Annette Deist, for specific ideas used here, for their company at the movies, and for their help over a period of many months in figuring out the logic of German political life.

1. The brochure and poster for the *Sounds of Home* concerts ("Urban Folk and Dance Music" sponsored in part by the "Jungle Fever" program of a government-run West Berlin radio station) sport as their logo a frog on a lilypad, sentimentally clutching his hand to his heart. The explanatory prose in the brochure contains a similarly uneasy mixture of sentiment and flippancy. "The European family of instruments invites you to dance, pressingly and unmistakably. No wonder that the accordion of Texan Flaco Jimenez finds its way back home this way. . . . Sounds of Home? Home is where you hang your fez, intone the singers of Three Mustaphas Three, whose passports are covered with stampings done the wrong way around. Sounds of Home? It's a musical banquet table, with guests of honour who have travelled from afar, a seven-week-long hubbub of voices and visiting without borders. Seven combinations that really cook . . . The meeting of the East and the West, of Folk Roots and World Music. . . . geo-cultural marriages. . ."

2. "Neues Ausländergesetz geplant: 'Bewahrung des eigenen nationalen Charakters,'" *Pass-port. Magazin für Ausländer und Deutsche*, No. 19 (Aug.–Sept. 1988), pp. 5–6.

3. See for instance the Amnesty International pamphlet of December, 1985, "Schutz für politisch Verfolgte. Verwirklicht das Grundrecht auf Asyl!" ("Protection for the Politically Persecuted. Put into Practice the Basic Constitutional Right to Political Asylum!"). It includes a short history of the notion of political asylum in West Germany ("The Federal Republic has a special responsibility for the politically persecuted because of its own history: countless people had to flee national socialism—to flee concentration camps, torture and murder. . .") and ends with a Brecht poem, "On the term 'Emigrant'," written during his exile in Denmark. (". . . But we did not emigrate, after choosing freely/picking another land. And we also did not/immigrate to a country, to stay there, if possible forever./ We fled rather. We were driven out, banished./ The land that takes us in will be no home, but an exile./ We sit here restlessly, as close to the borders as we can/ waiting for the day we can return, observing the smallest change/ on the other side, eagerly questioning every new arrival,/ forgetting nothing and giving nothing up/ and also forgiving nothing of what happened, forgiving nothing. . .")

4. The influence (and the success) of Tevfik Baser's *40 m² Deutschland* is clearly still being felt. *Aufbrüche/Breaking Away* (Medien Operative: Hartmut Horst and Eckart Lottmann, 1987) has a story line almost identical to that of *Yasmin*, save that it is less romantic, more ambivalent, more painfully "realistic." The adolescent protagonist of *Aufbrüche* has to find her own way; the attempts of her German boyfriend to "rescue" her are shown to be ineffectual, since he has little understanding of her culture or her situation. And where Yasmin seems fully integrated into her German peer group, the heroine of *Aufbrüche* struggles not only against her family but against the prejudices of some classmates and teachers. *Aufbrüche* also goes much further than *Yasmin* in identifying German culture as part of the problem rather than as the only solution, and in pointing out the near-universality of some forms of patriarchy, visible in Christian as well as in Muslim families. In one important scene, the German father of one of the heroine's friends discusses his decision to send away for a mail-order bride from Southeast Asia, clearly wishing for a wife who is humble, dependent and grateful.

A number of other recent films attempt a sympathetic reconstruction of the viewpoint of the asylum seeker and the immigrant. Two melancholy feature films, Rafael

Fuster-Pardo's *In der Wüste/In the Desert* (1986) and Jan Schütte's *Drachenfutter/Dragon Chow* (1987), emphasise both the financial and the emotional hardship suffered by many refugees in West Germany. Both films paint a grim picture of bureaucratic indifference and political hostility to the refugees' plight, but suggest at the same time (in their respective depictions of friendships between a Pakistani and a Chinese refugee who meet at their illegal workplace, and between a second-generation Turkish German and a Chilean exile who share a run-down apartment in West Berlin's poorest and most multi-ethnic neighbourhood) the growth of a multi-ethnic subculture or community in West Germany, a political solidarity among immigrants which cuts across national and racial lines. Several modest yet powerful documentaries, made by as well as about women (see especially Jeanine Meerapfel's *Die Kümmeltürkin Geht/Melek Leaves* [1985], and Gerlinde Bohm's *Heimkehr—von Berlin nach Lima/Coming Home—from Berlin to Lima* [1988]), use the question of repatriation to examine both the difficulties and the longings of foreign workers in Germany, and the problems they face in going home again. Conversely, Lea Rosh's ". . . *und dann haben wir uns verabschiedet": Buttenhausen 1933–65/". . . and then we said goodbye"* (1987) and Ed Cantu's autobiographical *Identy Kid* (1987) use two painfully ambivalent 'homecomings' to Germany from America to examine the legacy of anti-Semitism, fascism and the postwar occupation. Rosh's moving film (described at greater length in my "Reconstructing the New German Cinema: Social Visions and Critical Documentaries," forthcoming in *German Politics and Society* 18, Fall 1989), chronicles the visit of Jewish émigrés to their native village (which until the '20s had prided itself on its unusual degree of German and Jewish integration), while Cantu—raised in both Germany and the United States, and (as he learns in the course of the filming) the illegitimate son of a German mother and a father who was an American GI—uses his search for the traces of his mysterious father as a way to confront the question of his own conflicted sense of national identity; the title of course punningly refers to the Identy-Kits used by police artists to reconstruct the face of a perpetrator or a missing person from a few remembered features, using the kit's pre-given set of racial and feature markers.

5. This gap in the film's "realism" was pointed out by one adolescent reviewer in an otherwise favorable notice of the film which appeared in an anti-racist journal put out by a West Berlin high school collective. *Prometheus (Berliner Jugendzeitschrift)*, No. 6.

6. The film is part of Corti's "Where To and Back" trilogy (currently playing to critical acclaim in the United States), which examines the forced emigration of Austrian Jews to America and their eventual return to Europe with the American occupation forces. The trilogy, especially in its first part, draws heavily (and without acknowledgement) on the literature of and about exile by Anna Seghers, Brecht and other German Marxist writers (thus inducing a wearying kind of déjà vu effect in any viewer familiar with the writing of the period); throughout the trilogy, however, Corti's own depiction of Marxist émigrés (as distinct from other Jewish émigrés, who are treated with humor and a certain ironic sympathy) is consistently clichéd, reductive and openly hostile. At times, the dogmatism of the Marxist characters seems implicitly associated by Corti with fascist authoritarianism itself, even while their class-based analysis of the causes of fascism (which Corti presents in order to hold up to ridicule) in fact provides the trilogy's only persuasive and coherent explanation for what is happening in Central Europe.

7. Colour-coding: if black-and-white cinematography made an art-film comeback in the late '70s, with Woody Allen's *Manhattan* (a lyrical celebration of place, of rootedness, of intellectual *Heimat* in the modernist city of Gershwin and Tinguely), the alternation between black-and-white and colour, as it is used again and again in the art films of the late '80s, is meant to evoke a post-modern sense of geographical and historical displacement. Edgar Reitz's *Heimat*, Derek Jarman's *The Last of England* and Alan Rudolph's *The Moderns* (and even Rosa von Praunheim's *Anita. The Dance of Sin*) all, in very different ways, link the experience of modernity to expatriation or the sense of cultural dislocation. For an excellent discussion of the politics of *Heimat*, see the dossier in *New German Critique* 36 (Fall 1985), as well as Anton Kaes, *From Hitler to Heimat* (forthcoming, Harvard University Press).

Narrating Gender in the GDR: Hermann Zschoche's *Bürgschaft für ein Jahr* (1981)

MARC SILBERMAN

THE SECOND HALF of the sixties in the German Democratic Republic under the waning leadership of Walter Ulbricht was a period of restriction and censure aimed at preserving the image, if not the reality of a harmonious social configuration. In 1971, Erich Honecker's new team proposed an ideological framework for guiding modernization in East Germany that openly accounted for conflict potential within the society. A willingness slowly to accept détente with the West and economic reform was soon coupled with assurances to intellectuals and artists that the Party leadership trusted them and recognized their relative autonomy, both in the choice of subject matter and in formal questions.[1] Cinema production began to reflect these changes in cultural policy only after the Second Congress of the Film and Television Association in April 1972 (*Verband der Film- und Fernsehschaffenden der DDR*). In the two years between 1972 and 1974, the state-run DEFA studios produced and released a number of films whose innovative use of genre structures, heightened awareness of visual effect and controversial subject matter attracted new spectators and raised audience expectations. *Der Dritte* (The Third, Egon Günther, 1972), *Die Schlüssel* (The Keys, Egon Günther, 1973), *Die Legende von Paul und Paula* (The Legend of Paul and Paula, Heiner Carow, 1973), and *Leben mit Uwe* (Life with Uwe, Lothar Warneke, 1974), for example, address topical issues and moments of crisis in their protagonists' daily lives.[2] That all of these box office successes deal with partner relations points to a growing interest among the cinema audience in films reflecting personal rather than historical conflicts. The inclusion of dream sequences and even surrealistically inspired scenes—suggesting a curious mixture of Claude Lelouche and Ingmar Bergman as the major foreign influences rather than New German Cinema directors from the West, as might be expected—introduced an entirely new aspect of playfulness into the GDR cinema. Moreover, the emphatic focus on an individual's self-assertion against the norms and assumptions of a collective, be they fellow workers, friends, family or functionaries, parallels the commitment to a kind of documentary realism in establishing social context through details and gestures.

This combination of playfulness and serious questioning about limits to self-realization in the GDR context dominated artistic production in the sev-

Reprinted from *The Germanic Review* 66.1 (1991): 25–33.

enties. In the cinema, it brought forth a series of important "small" films, idiosyncratic contributions without strong narrative lines or traditional structure in the manner of the early French *nouvelle vague*. Konrad Wolf's *Der nackte Mann auf dem Sportplatz* (The Naked Man on the Playing Field, 1974), Lothar Warneke's *Die unverbesserliche Barbara* (Incorrigible Barbara, 1976) and Günter Reisch's *Anton der Zauberer* (Anton the Magician, 1977), for example, pursue individualists—an artist, a sports star, a nonconformist car mechanic—who attempt to carve out places for themselves in a society that is frequently shown as narrow-minded or provincial. Film critics and functionaries tended to be uncomfortable with these narratives because they lacked the usual partisan, optimistic message. Their uneasiness with new forms and with themes beyond the "big questions" often emerged through a critique of the way contradictions are supposedly worked out ineffectively.[3] The strategy behind these unresolved conflicts, however, asserted an open-endedness that projected the respective problem onto the spectator to judge and to draw conclusions. The quality and impact of DEFA films produced at the end of the decade—*Sabine Wulff* (Erwin Stranka, 1978), *Sieben Sommersprossen* (Seven Freckles, Hermann Zschoche, 1978), *Alle meine Mädchen* (All My Girls, Iris Gusner, 1979), *Solo Sunny* (Konrad Wolf, 1979), *Unser kurzes Leben* (Our Short Life, Lothar Warneke, 1980), *Die Stunde der Töchter* (The Hour of the Daughters, Erwin Stranka, 1980), to name just a few—reflected a deepening awareness of modern forms of alienation that had developed within a socialist, or at least postcapitalist, society. The fact that the protagonists in all of the above films are strong women bears witness to a critical sensibility for the complex relation between women and society as a paradigm for representing more generally the yearning for difference and otherness in a closed society like that in East Germany, where monotony and habit tended to dominate the everyday.

Hermann Zschoche's 1981 film *Bürgschaft für ein Jahr* is situated precisely at the point where the demands of a nonconforming woman disrupt social expectations. It opens up questions about how historically derived gender distinctions have continued to determine the way social structures are lived in a socialist society and what the cost of disciplining everyday life has entailed. In this respect, it builds on and extends a popular topos that literary and cinematic narratives had already firmly established.[4] The first GDR "woman's film" was Egon Günther's *Lots Weib* (Lot's Woman, 1965) in which a young woman demands a divorce from her husband when she comes to realize that a relationship without mutual love and respect is demeaning for both of them. The portrayal of a dramatic conflict in the private sphere as a vehicle for representing more generalized social problems was an innovation within the constraints of socialist realism as practiced in the GDR cinema. Many of the most popular DEFA films of the seventies went on to deal with a professional or married woman whose experience of some kind of private crisis leads to a confrontation with authorities or the guardians of propriety. Learning to articulate one's own wishes and desires in the face of resistance from all sides, no matter how inadequate the attempt, elicits from these "heroines" doubts and inhibitions that are then projected onto the spectator. Konrad Wolf's 1979 *Solo Sunny* was among the most influential of these films, the story of a young woman who pursues her dream of becoming a rock singer despite the professional and personal defeats she encounters. Produced by one of the few internationally acclaimed film makers in the GDR and someone identified with institutionalized power structures, the film's combination of excellent acting, good music and topical issues with a blunt insistence on the right to demand that society must also acknowledge an individual's self-interest seemed to signal an important ideological shift in popular entertainment films.

The focus on women who constantly experience their own vulnerability, who isolate themselves from others rather than trying to change them or themselves, is a radical reversal of the traditional positive hero in DEFA films. It also indicates an implicit revision of the orthodox Marxist view on the primacy of class oppression as the trigger of social transformations. In the most popular GDR films of the seventies, the many provocative women figures are concerned not with class issues but with the fundamental experience of sexual discrimination and gender conflict in their private lives, and this experience is portrayed as normal rather than extraordinary. Moreover, by calling attention to private problems in the realm of interpersonal relationships, it became possible for film makers to account for negativity and failure, aspects of the "human condition" which the revolutionary romanticism of socialist realism tended to exclude in its stress on the political struggles and triumphs in constructing "*der neue Mensch.*" As a result, an ideological and aesthetic space opened up for raising questions about society's responsibility toward the individual in contrast to the conventional position of seeking meaningful resolutions to narrative conflicts in the individual's integration into a harmonious utopia.

Trained in the GDR, Zschoche belongs to the second generation of directors who debuted in the sixties. After several prize-winning children's films, he gathered around himself a team with whom he has continued to work regularly, including cameraman Günter Jaeuthe and composer Günter Fischer. Many of his feature films address problems of young people, especially their love stories, and ironically treat everyday banalities of provincial life in the GDR.[5] *Bürgschaft für ein Jahr*, however, is aimed at a slightly older, more mature audience and focuses less on provincial attitudes than on the middle-brow values of the socially and economically secure. The protagonist, Nina Kern, is an extreme example of the kind of dramatic figure who challenges the comfortable conventions and presuppositions about human needs with which institutions rationalize their interventions in the name of social stability. A 27-year old woman, divorced from an alcoholic husband who beat her, and involved with a group of young drop-outs, she has, after many warnings from child welfare agencies, lost custody of her three young children owing to neglect. At a hearing called to finalize the children's institutionalization in state-run homes, Nina argues in front of the skeptical commissioner and social workers that she has finally seen the light and wants to change her ways. She begs for a last change to prove that she can become a responsible mother. One of the lay jurors assigned to the juvenile commission, Irmgard Behrend, is impressed by what appears to be Nina's honest remorse. She convinces her reluctant fellow juror, Peter Müller, to join her in taking on the personal responsibility of helping Nina to put her life in order so that she can "prove" herself and regain custody of the children.[6] With their assistance in reconnoitering the obstacles in the path to social reintegration and with the support of her lover, Nina settles down, and the commission once again allows her custody of the youngest daughter as a test of her resolve.

Nina's adjustment to the demands of a working mother is not without friction. During the day, she is preoccupied by a menial but strenuous job. At her daughter's nursery, she encounters the (female) director's disinterest and arrogance toward her daughter's special needs. The husband of a friend in her apartment building solicits sexual favors, using blackmail by threatening to denounce her to the juvenile welfare authorities. Moreover, Nina is not the easiest or most grateful person to help and she suffers relapses. During a party, she forgets her daughter, who runs away, and she sacrifices her reliable but boring lover for a passionate but short fling with another man. Finally, there are setbacks in Nina's efforts to learn housekeeping and budgetary restraint under the tutelage of her guarantors, moments that try their patience and throw the goal of their efforts into question. The film narrative ends on a sober and ambiguous note, neither celebrating the protagonist's small victories nor minimizing the personal price she pays in the process.

The first scene sets a number of crucial formal and contextual parameters for what is to come. In a languid, almost continuous take lasting several minutes, the camera pans and tracks around the anonymous meeting room in which Nina's case is being discussed, pausing to examine the different participants as they speak or react. The slow but rhythmical alternation between the camera's movement and its static watchfulness establishes a distant, observant relation between the spectator and what is seen. In effect, this relation reproduces at this point exactly the attitude shared by the various commissioners, consultants and juvenile authorities grouped around the table to deliberate the custody issue. The sequence begins *in medias res* as the Chair of the Juvenile Commission calls the meeting to order with a tired voice: "Dann wollen wir mal wieder. Der Fall Kern, ziemlich aussichtslos. Läuft wahrscheinlich auf Entzug des Erziehungs- rechts hinaus. Kindervernachlässigung, asozialer Lebenswandel, und- soweiter, undsoweiter." The setting, the camera work, and the direct sound suggest the tradition of the reportage film, drawing on its appeal to documentary authenticity in order to present "the Kern case" as just another of the daily proceedings, to be dealt with as quickly and as effort- lessly as possible.[7]

Yet, equally foregrounded in this discourse of authenticity is Nina Kern's presence as a dramatic character who will organize the narrative for the spectator. She enters the room, clearly upset and intimidated by the situation, seats herself at the table, and listens while an off-voice reads a biographical report sketching in (for the Commission and the spectator) the past history of her childhood, marriage and later asocial behavior. The camera remains fixed on Nina, pinning her down as it slowly zooms in closer and closer on the face whose features change as she remembers the events with shame, humiliation, or anger. Nina is mute. She swallows sev- eral times in embarrassed silence and once even starts to interrupt before catching herself and slumping back in her seat. The off-voice meanwhile is both the point of discursive origin, relating Nina's history for her, and inaccessible, spoken from a vantage point that is invisible and apparently omniscient. The disjuncture between the off-voice, invested with the authority to summarize this woman's life as an inadequate mother, and the image of the woman forced to listen to this voice, situates the narrative problematic from the outset within the context of female voicelessness in the regime of power relations and maternity.

When the (male) Chair of the commission allows Nina Kern to speak, she is inarticulate. Her (spoken) language is repetitious; her sentences are short; she hesitates frequently and can do little more than assert that she wants her children back. The Chair interrupts and symptomatically asks her to speak a bit louder. Nina lacks a voice in a society that identifies speech with paternalistic authority and mastery in their most general sens- es. In a later scene, shortly after the opening sequence, this point is made explicit when Nina half jokingly asks her live-in lover Werner about an ambiguous grammatical construction.[8] He responds by asking her what she wants to say, i.e., what she *means*, and Nina answers: "That I don't feel well." Her discomfort *in* language is one consequence of her rejection of the conventional female roles of wife, parent and (monogamous) sexual partner. Another consequence is the institutional diligence in containing and managing resistance against the coercion that imposing such a lan- guage entails. Nina does not articulate meaning in that language, and she is therefore excluded from the symbolic power and privilege associated with speech. Yet, as the narration will elaborate, her resistance and disruptions are potentially more valuable for negotiating the everyday than the stable order of power.

The hearing in the first long take ends after a brief dialogue between the Chair and Nina, and the second scene once again introduces the split between a disembodied male voice-off and her image. Low pans and crane shots of Nina descending the staircase in the administrative building, flanked by Werner and her neighbor and family friend Mrs. Braun, are coupled on the sound track with the Chair's voice-over reading the Commission's final report that recommends further study of the case. The intrusion of this administrative voice on the image of the sympathetic Nina animates the process of spectatorial identification that characterizes the rest of the narration. The spectator's imaginary activity is aligned with Nina's resistance to institutional interventions and against the accretion of disciplinary organization in everyday life in the name of normalcy and propriety. The Chair's voice provides a sound transition to the final scene of the introductory sequence when the camera cuts back to the conference room and the conditions of Nina's probation are ironed out. A black screen punctuates the end of the three introductory segments after which there follow the extended credits in black and white to the accompaniment of a rhythmically insistent but simple musical theme. The series of loosely connected episodes that comprise the narrative's main body present the everyday life of this working mother struggling to rehabilitate herself to the juvenile agency's satisfaction. Zschoche, a careful observer with a keen eye for details rather than for heroic or dramatic conflicts, fashions out of this laconic formal principle a space where ambiguity and ambivalence can elicit a skeptical attitude on the part of the viewer.

In *Bürgschaft für ein Jahr*, the narrative amplifies the structural oppositions established in the introduction in order to undermine a too easy legitimation of social authority, even in the socially sensitive area of child neglect. It should be pointed out that although the film does not dwell on the past history of Nina's child neglect, it in no way excuses it. Besides the details in the opening report, only one other scene refers to it, a dream montage triggered by Nina's guilt about this past.[9] Moreover, the report as well as Mrs. Braun's comments in a later scene suggest that Nina is acting out the trauma of inadequate mothering during her own childhood. The narrative, however, stresses the protagonist's will to revise the past. Like Irmgard Behrendt, the spectator is addressed in the opening sequence to identify with the protagonist's decision to regain her children because she has truly understood the importance of this family bond. Thus, it is no surprise that from the outset Nina's children want to return home. Her relationship to the youngest child, Mireille, the one most expansively pursued in the narrative, is open and trusting. Her son René is a mature, protective boy notwithstanding the accusation of negligent parenting, and although Jacqueline has serious adjustment problems, she too yearns to join her mother. The children whom the state is protecting, then, only reinforce the impression that their mother has something much more valuable to offer them than the security and order provided in juvenile institutions. The dilemma posed by the ambiguous ending asks to what extent individuals in this society can assert their will to change against the power of established social agencies and historically entrenched gender prejudices.

Within the dichotomy of male speech and female voicelessness, there is a whole series of behavioral characteristics associated with the lack of control and subjectivity developed around Nina's character. She frequently acts impulsively, for example. After the hearing, she learns that Behrendt and Müller will be "visiting" her apartment with a juvenile agency official, so she grabs a brush to paint the children's toy shelf. In her eagerness, however, she replaces the dolls and stuffed animals before the paint is dry, and they stick to the tacky finish. Similarly, she finds all sorts of creative tricks to freshen up the living room so that she can impress the "guests": spraying water from her mouth to hasten the ironing of wrinkled fabric, tacking curtains with taped-up hems to the sides of windows, smearing pieces of wood with black shoe polish so that they look like the coal briquets she had forgotten to buy for the heater. This kind of hectic behavior—conveyed with a humorous touch through very quick cutting and the stark strumming of the string bass—points to an appealing personality with a touch of naiveté and a lot of warmth. Later, when Nina is reunited with Mireille, her excitable character gains a further dimension of emotional spontaneity. She weeps on embracing her daughter; she acquiesces when Mireille insists on having sandwiches for lunch that do not conform to the nursery's rule; and she plays with Mireille on her roller skates although the passersby in the street look askance.

Nina's lack of voice, in other words, is recuperated through the portrayal of an internal vitality and dynamism. Although the actress Katrin Sass does not embody the typical alluring female in her dumpy and slightly dated clothes, the positive attributes of impulsiveness and spontaneity reflect conventional gender prejudices that place value on the woman as the repository of strong inner emotions. Nina protests the injustice to which her children are subject. She is angry when a female colleague feels she must have an abortion after her lover turns out to have deceived her about being married. She is insulted when Irmgard proposes that she give up a child for adoption. The narrative produces its momentum by positioning the spectator, on the one hand, to identify with these "human" responses as opposed to bureaucratic inflexibility and male egotism and, on the other, to anticipate her bonding within the family as a successful, nurturing mother that presupposes her ability to control such responses.

This ambivalence toward the power of female emotions as destabilizing source of revolt and guardian of humanizing unrest characterizes a fundamental contradiction in the narration.

Nina's emotional strength is clearly linked with qualities of interiority. Her femininity derives from a kind of subjective plenitude or wholeness related to her maternal role, but one that she must demonstrate to the authorities. This interiority makes her dependent on, yet sets her off against, male characters like her lover Werner and the lay juror Peter, who regulate and control the bounds of the acceptable. The lovers' diametrically opposed values are exposed when Nina wants to celebrate the news that Mireille will return home for Christmas by stopping in at a bar for a drink and a snack. Werner, forever the careful and responsible partner, argues that it is wasteful to buy restaurant food when they have something at home to eat.

> Nina: Willst du mir ernsthaft wegen einer lumpigen Mark den Abend versauen?
> Werner: Ich finde es unvernünftig [. . .]
> Nina: Ich will Buletten, jetzt. Und wenn du noch so weiter redest, dann schmeiße ich ungefähr das ganze Lokal. An so einem Tag.

Werner's simple equation of desire with the irrational might seem like an extreme formulation of male anxieties vis-à-vis female assertiveness, but an event that parallels this exchange puts it precisely into this perspective. Two men seated at the same table are impertinent enough simply to take her meatballs without a word while she is talking. The assertion of male desire, if this appetite can be so called, is not resisted by Werner but rather by Nina, who has the waitress kick them out. Werner's inability to respond to desire also influences his interaction with Mireille. The child's boredom with a jigsaw puzzle elicits from him, for example, the pithy moralism that "was man anfängt, muß man zu Ende führen."

Lack of imagination and reliance on ritualistic responses characterize Peter Müller as well. A family man himself, with housebound wife and young daughter, he is appalled and upset to discover the way in which the social agency with which he is cooperating intrudes on Nina's privacy. Yet he approaches life's more difficult challenges with the same attitude he does his professional responsibilities as a construction engineer. Problems are tasks to be mastered efficiently with principles, and he has no patience when Nina resists or fails to conform to his expectations of proper behavior. Thus, like the juvenile authorities, he applies what are no more than arbitrary rules meant to sustain the coherence and propriety of socially constructed norms at the expense of individual difference. Zschoche clearly shows the limitations of such middle-brow attitudes in a scene that pits the strength of Nina's intuition against Peter's rigidity. Excited by the prospect that the two older children will be returning home, she suddenly decides to rearrange all the furniture in her apartment with Peter's help. Against his advice she insists that they move the clothes cupboard to a small niche where it ends up fitting with a slight margin ("Spielraum" or, literally, a protected space to play). Then Peter decides the bed should be moved to the corner. Nina immediately recognizes that it is too large for the space, while he hops about with a tape measure, and after much pushing she is indeed right: "Spielraum vergessen, wah?" Peter's inability to accord that space of flexibility for play is a fundamental flaw in his principle of efficiency, and ultimately it leads him to abandon Nina mercilessly when, in a time of confusion and hurt, she gets drunk and insults him.

If the protagonist's childlike spontaneity places her in a much more favorable light than do the paternalistic stability and discipline of Werner and Peter, it is also the very source of the vulnerability that creates the obstacles to her reintegration. She is helpless, for example, when confronted by the authority of an institutional system. Irmgard has to argue for her and against the arrogant director of the nursery in order to readmit Mireille for daycare so that she can continue working. Later, Nina herself confronts the director because Mireille complains, only to discover that the school's compulsive orderliness and cleanliness allow no room for what she considers to be her child's rightful sense of privacy (the children are expected to use the toilets only at appointed times and in front of the other children). Faced with the intractability of this authority and the very real threat of losing the childcare, she retreats and even excuses herself, a hard-learned lesson in the strategies of self-denial necessary for living within the arbitrary rules of power. Nina also cannot plan. She has never learned to budget money and is threatened with having her television repossessed because of missed payments, so Irmgard instructs her in a simple system of accounting for each month's expenses. Yet, when Mireille fights with Peter's daughter over a doll carriage, Nina abandons the system and purchases the same expensive toy for her own child. Similarly, it is Irmgard who confronts Nina's former husband and threatens him with police reprisals if he does not pay his child support. Nina, quite to the contrary, made a practice of subsidizing her husband's drinking even after their divorce. In each case, Nina, who is intimidated by authority and overwhelmed by feelings of sympathy, has neither the emotional fortitude nor the verbal skills to defend herself.

The goal of "probation," then, is to domesticate the protagonist and to discipline her into the conventional gender role of the mother with all its attributes of dependency and self-denial.[10] The first sequence after the introduction symbolically sets this agenda. Nina unlocks her front door, enters the apartment, locks the door, goes directly to the window and lowers the key on a string to Mrs. Braun, who lives below and will unlock her door from outside the next morning. This routine, repeated two more times in the narration, is a form of voluntary entrapment, here implicitly an acquiescence to self-confinement in the home in the name of reestablishing the maternal function. To regain that status, Nina must learn to recognize boundaries. In fact, throughout the film she is constantly reminded about the limits of acceptable behavior. The opening sequence with its male voice-off already defined her earlier lifestyle as asocial, i.e., beyond the norm: alcohol, promiscuity, child neglect, disordered home. Because she revolted against domestic drudgery and asserted control over her sexuality, the juvenile authorities removed her children and placed them in state homes.

Nina conforms. She finds a job whose monotony is underscored by the way Zschoche returns briefly but repeatedly to images of her washing subway cars with the same tired gestures. She celebrates the Christmas holidays with a tree, puts her apartment in order, makes her purchases on a budget, avoids her former group of friends and stops drinking. Despite her efforts, she suffers the disapproving looks and remarks of those around her. The visit by the social worker, who must determine whether her home is in order before Mireille can return, is, for example, a humiliating experience both for Nina and for the two jurors who watch as the social worker goes through the cupboards, counts the bedsheets and examines the corners for dust. When Nina plays with Mireille, either the neighbors complain about the noise or strangers on the street make critical remarks about her "unseemly conduct." On an unannounced visit to the Müllers' apartment to seek help from Peter in resisting the sexual advances of Mrs. Braun's husband, she perceives how out of place she is in these surroundings. Peter's wife has nothing to say to her, and Nina realizes how remote her problems are from this island of familial repose when Mrs. Müller discretely removes the "good" ashtray from the coffee table so that Nina does not soil it with the cigarette she is nervously smoking.

Two separate episodes underscore the tentative nature of Nina's resolve to conform. Although she avoids the clique of social dropouts with whom she previously identified, they literally break in upon her one evening to dance and drink. Her protests quickly subside, and she joins them, only to realize later that Mireille has run away to escape the noise. One of the young men with whom she flirted at the party returns, and she quickly falls in love with him. Heiner, unlike Werner, is able to communicate well with the children and he shares Nina's desire for adventures. Unfortunately, Zschoche casts Nina in the most conventional role of the female lover who completely loses self-control to her passion. In a truly silly scene, she falls on her knees after a long kiss and begs Heiner to help her because she loves him so much. Notwithstanding the scene's excess, the situation does once again reveal how this film constructs femininity as the interiority that promises emotional intensity and plenitude (to men).

At the same time, however, this interiority is premised on dependency and loss of self, the foundation for the very power relations that aim to contain interiority in the name of stability and the maternal function. The consequences of the fundamental ambiguity of this femininity quickly come to haunt Nina. After leaving Mireille alone to go dancing with Heiner one evening, all of her efforts to conform come undone. Mireille awakens and, frightened at being alone, is perched to jump out the window. Werner discovers Mireille, waits for Nina to return and then realizes that he has been betrayed. The dramatic catastrophe is complete when Irmgard and Peter arrive the next morning at Mrs. Braun's bidding and discover a dishevelled Nina, drinking beer in bed, who can only express her contempt for everything they represent:

> Ihr habt darauf gewartet. Ja, ich trinke, weil es mir schmeckt. Ich war zwei Stunden tanzen. Jeden Abend zwei Bier vor dem Fernseher. Auf so ein Leben scheiß ich. [. . .] Ich bin nicht besoffen. Ich stink mich an. Manchmal bewundere ich euch. Immer so gleichmäßig und im Takt. Und manchmal, ihr kotzt mich an.

Although *Bürgschaft für ein Jahr* masks itself as a documentary case study, its plot more closely follows that of a classical drama with exposition (the introduction), complication (Mireille at home), crisis (the affair with Heiner), reversal (abandoned by Heiner) and resolution (protagonist's renunciation). Because Zschoche deemphasizes the drama's continuity, however, with his abrupt cutting and attention to small details, dramaturgical contrasts among characters rather than situations dominate the conflict. From this perspective, Nina confronts a series of characters who in various degrees are determined to change her. For all of the male characters, Nina represents a force that must be regulated in one way or another. The commissioner has the legal authority to judge and to discipline Nina in her role as mother. Peter Müller treats her as a "case," a systemic failure that can be rectified and function smoothly. The various men involved with Nina exploit her for their own ends: the former husband needs her money; the first lover Werner seeks the stability of a nuclear family through her; the second lover Heiner derives his sense of worth from her attention; the neighbor Mr. Braun preys on her for sex. Among the female characters, the social worker and the daycare director, like the other agents of institutional power, are contemptuous and condescending toward Nina. Mrs. Braun and Mrs. Müller provide contrastive roles as resigned wife and mother, the former compromised by a pandering husband and the latter at the service of her husband.

The sole mediating figure in this constellation is Irmgard Behrendt, a middle-aged, single woman and music teacher who neither judges nor uses Nina but rather takes an interest in her as an individual. She recognizes from the very first encounter something creative and valuable in this person.[11] Furthermore, she initiates the idea of probation and carries through the responsibility that will permit Nina to regain custody of her children. On the one hand, there is a clear suggestion that loneliness motivates Irmgard's activities, that she sublimates an emptiness in her own life by assuming the personal responsibility for Nina. On the other, several details point specifically to Irmgard as a practicing Christian with a commitment to social values, a fact that would not go unnoticed by the GDR audience. When she mentions "God" in an early dialogue with Peter, for instance, he immediately asks her if she belongs to a church, and a later sequence introduces her accompanying a pastor who sings a hymn at a seniors' home.[12] Whatever the reasons, Irmgard is the only character who empathizes with Nina and even admires her, providing the main vehicle for critical audience identification with the protagonist. In one episode, she agrees to babysit Mireille for an afternoon and must confront the harsh reality of childcare firsthand: the disinterest on the part of adults toward the child in a crowded public bus, the tiresome games the child plays to get what it wants, the energy necessary to supervise and occupy the child constantly. Irmgard realizes by observing Nina that her will power and vitality are admirable qualities to be nourished. Thus, it is no accident that following Nina's outburst the camera cuts to a scene in which a talented music pupil tells the disappointed Irmgard that on his father's advice, he has decided to pursue football rather than becoming a concert pianist because it promises easier success. And slightly later, Irmgard watches the way Nina coaxes the tired Mireille to walk home by pretending they are jumping over their shadows. In a brief moment of abandon, Irmgard too tries "jumping over her shadow," but quickly catches herself, looks around to see if anyone was watching, and continues on her way after straightening her hair.

The understated visual metaphor restates concisely the issue at stake in Zschoche's film: the need for society to learn to tolerate the emancipatory power of desire, even when it undermines that society's rules. Nina's voicelessness, her feminine interiority, is the counterpart to her ability to transgress boundaries. As she herself warns Irmgard in another context, this is a quality she shares with children: they too know no boundaries! In a sense, then, Nina's socialization as a mother recapitulates the process of growing up: learning to respect limits, to accept responsibility and to deny the self. The problem for Nina as well as for the textually inscribed spectator is to channel the imaginary power of transgression into a tolerable mode of existence, one that allows for or even sustains the contradiction between an individual's sensitivities and a society's tendency to preserve the system. By the end of the narrative, however, Nina has failed. Contrary to many of the seventies films featuring strong female protagonists, Zschoche's heroine surrenders, abandoning the dream of a family and resigning herself to isolation. When she and her children encounter Irmgard several months later in the penultimate sequence, Nina jokes to her that they are a "real family, only without a man." The import of defeat admits a serious betrayal, for she confides to Irmgard that she will keep only two of the children, giving up Jacqueline for adoption. Yet, when Jacqueline asks her mother in the brief last sequence whether she will be fetching them home soon, Nina assents with a slight nod, and the image freezes on a close-up of her sad, lifeless face. The narrative closure of the freeze frame confirms the irreducible disparity between desire and reality on Nina's part, while its suggestion of provisionality returns the spectator to the documentary fiction of the case study that continues beyond the moment frozen in time.

At the end of the film, Nina has lost the self-assurance that her claims to desire and independence are legitimate. Zschoche, however, constructs the narration in such a way that the spectator perceives this defeat and her betrayal of Jacqueline as a challenge aimed against a system of coherence that denies individual self-realization. The series of contrasts between the protagonist and her opposites substantiates the gulf separating the state's or society's investment in its power and the spectator's identification with the protagonist's vitality. By formulating the manifestations of this power as constructions, as arbitrary and reversible, Zschoche invites the spectator to imagine other possibilities beyond the provisional freeze frame. The state's paternalistic sovereignty, the hierarchy of public and private concerns, issues of socialization within the GDR become the object and the problem of the film's "imaginary." More specifically, the film locates the problem in the way social structures are lived on a daily basis in the GDR. The early integration of women into the labor force as well as extensive legal protection of women's equality have exacerbated contradictions between the rhetoric of the (nuclear) family and protectionist social policies for children.[13] Although *Bürgschaft für ein Jahr* is neither particularly innovative nor exciting in its technical craft, it does expose the complexity of these contradictions by thematizing female excess in a positive way and ironically playing on familiar images or situations in the GDR everyday.

This may account for the unenthusiastic response to the film on the part of some professional critics who cited the reductionism and caricature used for characterizing many of the secondary figures. Just as frequent was the concern with the valorization of a social outsider through the figure of Nina with her absolutist demands for self-realization.[14] Such criticism reflects a position with a longstanding tradition in socialist realism that directly relates a hero's positive traits to the moral impact on the spectator rather than focusing on the spectator's imaginary activity textually elicited through the film's narration. Beyond that, however, it is possible to trace in films produced by DEFA around this time a growing interest in socially marginal characters. Young dropouts or rock singers move in the small pockets of subcultural life; they live in run-down apartments and frequent the bar scene; their non-conformist demands on the system are presented as understandable and valid. Such a paradigm change in Marxist aesthetics from categories of typicality to a position that legitimates the social margin or periphery devalues reality as-it-is. *Bürgschaft für ein Jahr* contributes to the process of negotiating this change from an affirmative aesthetics of the acceptable to representations of difference by positing the present as the negative pole in a historical evolution aimed at the not-yet-achieved.[15]

An additional aspect of marginality, and one that throws a somewhat different light on its value in enunciating an imaginary position for the spectator, inflects the gender relations upon which this marginality builds. Nina is marginal not only because of her prior asocial behavior toward the children but also and primarily because she is a woman. Zschoche, like his other male colleagues at DEFA responsible for the remarkable series of "women's films," instrumentalizes the female protagonist as the site of discursive representation. He constructs a rigid binary opposition along the terms of silence and voice, interiority and exteriority, emotional excess and denial, indulgence and entrapment, spontaneity and stability, private and public, in which the female figure is identified exclusively with the first field. This offers the opportunity for presenting and analyzing contradiction, but it also erases the potentially more interesting hypothetical area between the opposing terms. Hence, the director does not fall into the practice of transforming his protagonist into an object of desire and visual pleasure for the male gaze in order to arrest her in a passive role. Instead, he thematizes the arbitrary, constructed nature of external authority as opposed to a more valuable psychic reality anchored within femininity. Zschoche, then, is still bound to a tradition of representation that posits the feminine beyond the realm of historically constructed and situated fictions. Yet, within this framework a protagonist like Nina Kern, even if burdened by traditional gender attributes, offers a position of female agency and perspectival knowledge that qualify manifestations of institutionalized power.

Notes

1. On the Eighth Party Conference in 1971 at which Erich Honecker took over the reins of the government, cf. Dietrich Staritz, *Geschichte der DDR 1949–1985* (Frankfurt/M.: Suhrkamp, 1985), pp. 198–203. Honecker's statement in December 1971 at a congress of cultural functionaries that there are "no taboos in the realm of art and literature" marked the first time in the history of GDR cultural policies that the Party relinquished its position as arbiter in ideological questions (cf. Honecker's speech in *Neues Deutschland*, December 18, 1971).

2. On the 1972 Film and Television Congress and its impact on film production, cf.

Hans Lohmann/Wolfgang Weiss, "Kinospielfilme der siebziger Jahre," in *Film- und Fernsehkunst der DDR. Traditionen, Beispiele, Tendenzen*, Hrsg. von der Hochschule für Film und Fernsehen der DDR (Berlin/GDR: Henschel 1979), pp. 365–421.

3. For example, in one retrospective discussion, two critics conclude: "Die Ablehnung des Fabelbaus, die Unterschätzung der Erkenntnisfunktion des künstlerischen Abbildes durch die Beschränkung auf das fotografische Abbild führten im dokumentarischen Spielfilm zu einer Vernachlässigung des Ideengehaltes sowie der Mittel zur künstlerischen Verallgemeinerung, was dem Zuschauer die Übertragung der Aussage erschwerte." Lohmann/Weiss, p. 372.

4. On the literary antecedents for female protagonists, cf. Patricia Herminghouse, "Wunschbild oder Porträt? Zur Darstellung der Frau im Roman der DDR," in *Literatur und Literaturtheorie in der DDR*, ed. Peter Uwe Hohendahl/Patricia Herminghouse (Frankfurt/M.: Suhrkamp, 1976), pp. 281–334. For a brief summary of "woman's films" produced in the GDR between 1971 and 1987, cf. Heinz Kersten, "The Role of Women in GDR Films since the Early 1980s," in *Studies in GDR Culture and Society* 8, ed. Margy Gerber et al. (Lanham/New York/London: University Press of America, 1988): 47–64. A more critical overview of the development of women's figures in the GDR cinema is presented by Sigrun D. Leonhard, "Testing the Borders: East German Film between Individualism and Social Commitment," in *Post New Wave Cinema in the Soviet Union and Eastern Europe*, ed. Daniel J. Goulding (Bloomington/Indianapolis: Indiana University Press, 1989), pp. 51–101, in particular the section "A Special Case: Rebellious Women," pp. 60–71.

5. For a valuable discussion of Zschoche's films prior to *Bürgschaft für ein Jahr*, cf. Christoph Prochnow, "Hermann Zschoche: Ironie und Sinnlichkeit," in *DEFA-Spielfilm-Regisseure*, ed. Rolf Richter (Berlin/GDR: Henschel, 1981), vol. 1, pp. 224–241. Further biographical and filmographical information can be found in the Zschoche article in *Cinegraph. Lexikon zum deutschsprachigen Film*, ed. Hans-Michael Bock (Munich: text + kritik, 1984). *Bürgschaft für ein Jahr* has not been released in the United States and is not currently available for viewing. Two earlier Zschoche films are, however, available from the Embassy of the GDR in Washington, D.C., *Sieben Sommersprossen* (1978) and *Glück im Hinterhaus* (1979).

6. Civil courts in the GDR include citizen representatives (Schöffen) who are elected as lay judges or jurors to participate in the proceedings. These jurors may, under certain circumstances, suggest a form of probation for the defendant in which they or other peers (often from the defendant's place of work) guarantee (bürgen) for the individual's improvement with conditions and responsibilities clearly spelled out. The "Bürgschaft" in the film's title refers to this type of guarantee and not to the kind of probation familiar in the American court system. On the GDR legal system, cf. *DDR-Handbuch*, ed. Hartmut Zimmerman, 2 vols. (Cologne: Verlag Wissenchaft und Politik, 1985³) under the entries "Strafensystem" and "Rechtswesen" (Part C), as well as G. Brunner, *Einführung in das Recht der DDR* (Munich: Beck, 1979²).

7. The scenario is based on Tina Schulze Gerlach's novel of the same title published in 1978, which was indeed drawn from a real case study. However, the novel's protagonist and narrative authority is not Nina Kern but the lay juror Irmgard Behrend. Cf. Gerlach, *Bürgschaft für ein Jahr* (Berlin: Union Verlag, 1978).

8. She cannot distinguish between the use of the accusative and dative case after the preposition "vor" with transitive and intransitive verbs.

9. The dream sequence reveals one way in which Nina's voicelessness is displaced, here into the role of the listener. Irmgard has noticed that the older daughter Jacqueline refuses to eat chocolate and asks Nina why. Obviously embarrassed by the question, she avoids an answer, but shortly thereafter a sound montage reveals the source of her discomfort. Threatening chords of rock music and the cacophony of adult voices are interspersed by a child's cries of "Mama, Mama." It is a flashback—consisting of dark, distorted images—to one of Nina's parties where, to quiet the child, a man pushes chocolate

into her mouth while Nina weakly protests. The only retrospective scene showing the protagonist's earlier negligence toward her children (albeit distorted through a dream), it places her in a helpless position of listening. Related to the role of Nina as a listener rather than a speaker is also the careful dramaturgy of noise in the film. Often the sound track is full of miscellaneous noise in scenes with Nina, particularly those set in her apartment: street noise of cars and trollies, calls of children in the apartment building courtyard or staircase, a church bell chiming, radio music, voices in the street, the bus or a bar, etc. The separation of sound from visible sources stresses once again Nina's lack of control, her exclusion from discursive authority posited in language. For a discussion of gender-specific issues of voice, sound and noise in the cinema, cf. Kaja Silverman, *The Acoustic Mirror. The Female Voice in Psychoanalysis and Cinema* (Bloomington/Indianapolis: Indiana University Press, 1988).

10. Reviews of the film tend to distort this process by describing it as positive experience toward social integration. The scriptwriter, Gabriele Kotte, however, confirmed the point I am making when she related how Zschoche and she went about transforming the novel into a filmscript: "Uns interessierte wie eine junge Frau, teils selbstverschuldet, teils unverschuldet, in eine Situation gerät, aus der sie unbedingt wieder herauskommen will. Und das heißt für sie, auf fast all das zu verzichten, was ihre Persönlichkeit ausmacht, nämlich dieses Leben von der Hand in den Mund und dieser Charakterzug, den einzelnen Tag wirklich auszuleben." Other comments from this discussion after a public showing of the film corroborate that at least some spectators also understood the film to be about institutional discipline in everyday life. Cf. the comments from a discussion at Kino International in Berlin/GDR, "Leben nach Regeln oder von der Hand in den Mund," *Sonntag* (November 1, 1981). For a complete list of GDR reviews of *Bürgschaft für ein Jahr*, cf. *Filmografischer Jahresbericht 1981* (Berlin: Henschel, 1984), pp. 287–288.

11. The film narrative adapts the conceit of the speaking name from the original novel. Nina's surname "Kern" means core or kernel and refers to that inner self or interiority which distinguishes her from all other characters in the film.

12. The popular medieval Christmas song "Es ist ein Ros entsprungen/Aus einer Wurzel zart" points once again to the motif of "the inner core" mentioned in footnote eleven and as such reinforces the relaion between Irmgard's religious and social values. The scene continues with the camera cutting and panning among the old people at the service and Irmgard at the piano who, after a brief pause at the end of the hymn, begins playing a catchy waltz for the seniors to dance. The editing makes clear that Irmgard, contrary to official state representatives, is a tolerant, flexible person who can recognize people's spiritual needs for community. Such scenes are relatively rare in topical DEFA films, where religion and religious persons rarely if ever play a positive role. In fact, not until 1988 did DEFA release a major feature film that thematizes church-state relations in the GDR in a serious manner (Lothar Warneke, *Einer trage des anderen Last . . . / Bear Ye One Another's Burdens*). Relations between the GDR government and the Protestant and Catholic Churches were strained until 1978, when Erich Honecker officially proclaimed the churches' right to contribute to the humanistic aims of the socialist society. 1981, the year in which Zschoche's film was released, saw the beginning of the Protestant Church's involvement in a controversial, non-State sanctioned peace movement that has increasingly attracted participation from citizens who do not or will not identify with the officially organized antiwar program. For further information on GDR church politics, cf. two West German publications: *Die evangelische Kirche in der DDR: Beiträge zu einer Bestandsaufnahme*, ed. Reinhard Henkys (Munich: Christian Kaiser, 1982), and Hellmuth Nitsche, *Zwischen Kreuz und Sowjetstern: Zeugnisse des Kirchenkampfes in der DDR (1945–1981)* (Aschaffenburg: Paul Pattloch, 1983).

13. On the history and status of women in the GDR, cf. *Zur gesellschaftlichen Stellung der Frau in der DDR* (Leipzig: Verlag für die Frau, 1978), and Gisela Helwig, *Frau und Familie. Bundesrepublik—DDR* (Cologne: Verlag Wissenschaft und Politik, 1987²).

14. Cf. for example, Fred Gehler's review "Bürgschaft für ein Jahr," *Sonntag* (October 11, 1981), Hans-Rainer Mihan's collective review of films with strong women figures outside

the mainstream, "Sabine, Sunny, Nina und der Zuschauer. Gedanken zum Gegenwartsfilm der DEFA (1)," in *Film und Fernsehen* 8 (1982): 9–12, and Carmen Blazejewski's longer discussion of the film, "Bürgschaft für ein Jahr," in *DEFA-Spielfilme am Beginn der 80er Jahre*, ed. Heinz Hofmann (*Podium und Werkstatt* 12) (Berlin/GDR: Verband der Film- und Fernsehschaffenden der DDR, 1982): 105–119. Zschoche's film went on to win prestigious prizes at several festivals in 1982: the Second GDR National Spielfilmfestival (best director, screenplay, sets, and costumes), the GDR Critics' Prize as the best contemporary DEFA film, and two prizes at the (West) Berlinale International Film Festival (the Silver Bear for Katrin Sass and the Catholic Film Bureau's Interfilm Prize).

15. Zschoche, in an article printed shortly after the film's release, is even more straightforward in pointing his finger at manifestations of petit-bourgeois or middle-brow conformity in the GDR as the precise object of the film's critique: "Man hat mich in einem Interview gefragt, ob ich diese Nina Kern als soziale Randfigur sehe, und ich habe geantwortet: 'Als solche Randfiguren sind nur Leute zu bezeichnen, die sich in einer heilen Welt, gesicherten Mitte der Gesellschaft wähnen. Vielleicht gibt es diese 'Mitte', nur sie reimt sich für mich auch auf mittelmäßig, lauwarm, 'Normalität' als farb- und charakterlose Durchschnittlichkeit . . .' Cf. Hermann Zschoche, "Was heißt hier Liebe," *Junge Welt* (Sept. 30, 1981).

Credits

Bürgschaft für ein Jahr (On Probation)

Released	1981, GDR
Producer	DEFA Studio für Spielfilm, Gruppe Berlin
Director	Hermann Zschoche
Screenplay	Gabriele Kotte, based on the novel by Tine Schulze-Gerlach
Cinematography	Günter Jaeuthe
Set decoration	Dieter Adam
Costumes	Anne Hoffmann
Makeup	Kurt Tauchmann/Christa Grewald
Music	Günther Fischer
Sound	Klaus Tolstorf
Editing	Monika Schindler
Cast	Katrin Sass (Nina Kern)
	Monika Lennartz (Irmgard Behrend)
	Jaecki Schwarz (Peter Müller)
	Jan Spitzer (Werner Horn, Nina's first lover)
	Christian Steyer (Heiner Menk, Nina's second lover)
	Heide Kipp (Mrs. Braun)
	Barbara Dittus (director of children's home)
	Ursula Werner (Mrs. Müller)
	Angelika Mann (Renate)
	Solveig Müller (social worker)
	Gabriele Methner (Fränzi)
	Dieter Montag (Kern, Nina's former husband)
	Heinz Behrens (Mr. Braun)
	Uwe Kockisch (Dieter)
	Werner Tietze (Chair of the Juvenile Commission)
	Peter Bause (director of children's home)
	Michaela Hotz (Mireille)
	Cornelia Förder (Jacqueline)
	Enrico Robert (René)
	Sebastian Reuter (music student)
Length	2545 m., 93 min.

Why Kluge?

STUART LIEBMAN

A T THE BEGINNING of the fifth section of Alexander Kluge's film *Artists under the Big Top: Perplexed* (1967), we see a troop of circus elephants rolling around in the mud, taking their morning bath. Their delightful play is cut short, however, by a gruesome story, "The Fire in the Elephant House in Chicago," announced and read in voice-over. As the elephants' horror and disbelief is recounted, shots from a familiar film—Eisenstein's *October*—appear on the screen, and a slow, scratchy recording of a tango is added to the sound track. The images are from several unrelated sections of the film: three shots of carefully composed rows of glassware in Kerenski's office; four of armed revolutionaries creeping down stairways in the Winter Palace; three almost abstract close-ups of the glittering chandeliers in the Tsarina's quarters; and finally, a low-angle shot of guns firing from a balcony, presumably from the "storming of the Winter Palace" section. Midway through the sequence, the music changes to a lilting violin melody and continues over a cut back to the elephants, which are now shown contentedly munching hay as they seem to sway in time to the rhythm. A female voice replaces that of the first narrator: "Freedom," she says, quoting one of the elephants, "means risking one's life, not because it means freedom from slavery, but because the essence of human freedom is defined by the reciprocal, negative relationship to another." A note in the published film script refers the reader to Hegel's *The Phenomenology of Mind.*[1]

This complex, overdetermined passage took shape during a period of looming crisis in the Federal Republic, in its film community, and in Kluge's cinematic career. Today, twenty years after the "events" leading up to 1968, the passage provides a kind of window onto these crises; then it served as an arena—perhaps, following Freud, one could call it a "playground"—in which the crises' multifaceted symptoms could be "worked through."[2] In its theme, structure, and purpose, which I would argue centrally involves a radical questioning of Eisenstein's cinema and its theoretical rationale, lie crucial clues to the nature of Kluge's aspirations and the strategies through which they are realized.[3] Why during the ferment of the *Tendenzwende* of the mid-'60s Kluge should have selected Eisenstein as a subject, and how Kluge's practice may be regarded as a species of critique,

Reprinted from *October* 46 (1988):5–22 by permission of the MIT Press, Cambridge, Massachusetts, Copyright 1988 for the Institute for Architecture & Urban Studies of the Massachusetts Institute of Technology.

will be the subject of this essay. I will return to it shortly. For now, it is enough to observe that this section of *Artists* is typical of Kluge's cinema: a montage (at best loosely tied to an episodic narrative) composed of images appropriated from other films (or paintings, or news photos, and so forth), set off by a title (here spoken, but more often written, as intertitles were in the silent film era), while the distinctive voice of a narrator (or perhaps, as here, more than one) speaks over strains of a forgotten piece of popular music or fragments from an opera, a text punctuated by some bit of aphoristic wisdom (lifted, as here, from a famous philosopher's treatise or, elsewhere, from the despairing cry of an anonymous charwoman). A range of possible implications hovers over the weave of images and sounds, but the point remains elusive, more felt than comprehended. Meanings proliferate and radiate out toward other sequences, producing, as the film's title itself acknowledges, as much perplexity as illumination. The films might be characterized as a string of digressions, woven into a picaresque plot—although the word *plot* implies causally related actions more emphatic than those normally encountered in Kluge's later work. In many of the films, the characters are allegorical ciphers, not "three-dimensional" figures; it is their (or rather Kluge's) projects, rather than any psychological motivation or causal logic, that provide the fragile, tentative links between incidents. In the most recent films, in fact, there are no central characters, no continuous narratives at all. The whole is a shifting and unstable assemblage of small, complexly interrelated units, each offering a different sort of attraction: a cinematic variety show, as it were.

This special issue of *October*, which serves as the catalogue of the retrospective exhibition of Kluge's films I organized for Anthology Film Archives and Goethe House, New York, has been prepared with the conviction that Kluge's "cinematic variety show"—tied as it is to a much larger project encompassing his fiction, social theory, film theory, television programs, and political action on various cultural fronts—constitutes a unique venture in the annals of postwar German culture. Kluge's is a radical *cinéma impur*, situated at the farthest possible remove from that conception of an autonomous, "pure" cinema which defines itself in opposition both to mass cultural film practices and to the terms and strategies of other modernist art forms developed since the 1920s.[4] The motives, themes, and *formal strategies* of Kluge's project raise questions in diverse areas of concern to us: about representation and gender, about history and memory, about theory in its relation to practice, about the ongoing vitality of modernism. Moreover, the work of Kluge is formulated—as one of his great precursors, Walter Benjamin, would have hoped—with an acute awareness of the most advanced "technical" means of production available as well as of the social circumstances in which production takes place in advanced industrial societies today.[5] The range of his concerns is visible both in the texts by Kluge published here and in the critical essays that follow.

Constructed in and through different disciplines, different discourses, these texts by Kluge are, we might say, "oriented toward the contemporary limits of the necessary," to borrow Foucault's reformulation of the aims of enlightenment.[6] Nevertheless, another overarching question or preoccupation, implied if not always directly stated, also animates Kluge's work, and it is one whose ongoing vitality the texts themselves—*pace* Foucault—demonstrate. Attentive (but critical) student of Marx and Adorno that he is, Kluge assumes the considerable burden of reflecting on the complex heritage of the Enlightenment, a period and a concept to which he often alludes in his writings and interviews. His work in all its forms reassesses the utopian promise immanent in reason's ambiguous legacy to the history of modernity as well as in the late eighteenth-century origins of both the Enlightenment and bourgeois capitalism in Germany. His (provisional) conclusion: enlightenment today depends on two crucial efforts. First, substantive reason must be reconstructed as a modality of sensory, imaginative experience; and second, a "public sphere" which could serve as a forum for individual imagination and unconstrained public debate must be created to respond to the contemporary threats of media concentration and the "industrialization of consciousness."[7] These are the larger goals toward which he works and the "red thread" woven through the themes and strategies of his artistic practice and his political initiatives. Although it was formulated in response to the specific historical and artistic conditions obtaining in West Germany, Kluge's project deserves our careful study, for our situation as intellectuals is different only in degree, not in kind, from that facing our counterparts in the Federal Republic. His efforts at resisting the seemingly relentless extension of private corporate control of our media should be of vital concern both to American filmmakers and to those attempting to understand the only apparently inchoate, uneasy pluralism that prevails today as "postmodernism."

Pessimism of the intelligence, optimism of the will.

—Antonio Gramsci

For those who came to maturity in Germany in the 1950s, the idea that the cinema might be a vehicle for artistic expression or social enlightenment would have seemed absurd. At the end of the war, the Allies, eager to reeducate their former foes, dismantled the centralized German film industry, while powerful American production and distribution companies, interested in securing a new market for their products, spurred them on. The Federal Republic's inadequate efforts during the '50s to stimulate the redevelopment of an indigenous film industry foundered again and again as a result of inadequate capitalization, ill-conceived subsidy statutes, and, by the end of the decade, the rapid diffusion of television into homes across Germany. A misguided policy of cultural insularity and economic autarky for the film industry, two dismal legacies of the Nazi period, dominated the thinking of German producers. The so-called *Heimat* film, sentimental and xenophobic depictions of bucolic regions of the country, became the most popular genre. Movie attendance dropped precipitously. The number of movie theaters began to plummet. The prospect of change seemed remote; by several accounts, more than half of all production personnel active in 1960 had been Nazi party members during the war.[8]

To those who were closely involved with the work of the reborn Frankfurt Institute for Social Research, the idea of an enlightened cinema would have seemed doubly absurd. In their great, dark work, *Dialectic of Enlightenment*, which had been published in 1947 but was only beginning to make its intellectual impact a decade later, Adorno and Horkheimer had, with certain interesting exceptions,[9] singled out the cinema as the chief vehicle of the "culture industry," the mass-media bulwark of a late capitalist social order whose devastations should have been readily apparent to all. The culture industry in general and the cinema in particular, "derisively fulfilling the Wagnerian dream of the *Gesamtkunstwerk*,"[10] purveyed—could only purvey—forms of entertainment urging accommodation to the claims of instrumental reason at the expense of a more substantive reason that had long been in retreat. The implicit challenge that autonomous art—the music of Beethoven, for example—once offered to the social irrationality produced by instrumental reason had grown increasingly weaker. Art, Adorno insisted, now had to withdraw, become difficult of access, wrap itself in a veil of technical and intellectual complexity, in order to preserve what limited degree of human freedom it embodied.[11]

This was the intellectual milieu in Frankfurt which the twenty-four-year-old lawyer Alexander Kluge entered when he arrived in 1956 for an internship with the noted educational reformer Hellmut Becker. Becker's contacts with the Frankfurt Institute, headed by Horkheimer and Adorno, were particularly strong,[12] and Kluge was quickly introduced into its inner circle. He soon became one of its legal advisors, handling, among other matters, the personal reparations cases of both Adorno and Horkheimer. Given their devastating indictment of the cinema in the "culture industry" chapter of *Dialectic of Enlightenment*, Kluge's decision, after moving to Munich three years later, to take up filmmaking might appear to be a gesture of defiance, especially since Kluge later ruefully remarked that he had received little support or encouragement for his creative work from Adorno.[13] Yet the character of what Kluge began to produce suggests that his film project was, in fact, a way of extending and testing isolated hints he discovered in *Dialectic of Enlightenment* which suggested to him the possibility of an alternative cinematic practice. As Miriam Hansen has observed, an attentive reading of *Dialectic of Enlightenment* "against the grain" and, perhaps even more importantly, of *Composing for the Films*, a text Adorno wrote with the composer and Brecht collaborator Hanns Eisler, would have yielded many ideas for a cinematic practice opposed to that of the culture industry.[14] "In some revue films, and especially in the grotesques and the funnies, the possibility of this negation does glimmer for a few moments," Adorno and Horkheimer remark. "The culture industry does retain a trace of something better in those features which bring it close to the circus, in the self-justifying and nonsensical skill of riders, acrobats and clowns."[15] These grudging and rather oblique asides to the main thrust of their theoretical argument, added to the more practical proposals in *Composing for the Films*, could suggest—to a reader like Kluge—new possibilities for cinematic construction.

The central premise of Adorno's critique of cinema is that the film image reproduces reality and affirms the existence of things as they are. The film image thereby congeals the meaning of depicted objects into univocal ciphers for experience. Synchronized sound and calculated doses of "irrational" musical effects reinforce the notion that the world is given and unchangeable and allows passive consumption to proceed smoothly. Conventionally used, then, film, according to this view, can only serve the larger, destructive cause of instrumental reason.

Editing, however, could potentially introduce the moment of negativity needed to block this instrumentalizing of the image. And sound could help to subvert the reification of meaning by explicitly working at cross purposes to the image track. Not surprisingly, the film theory of Eisenstein was a crucial foil for the articulation of Adorno and Eisler's views. Although the claims in his later writings concerning the synesthetic correspondence of sound and image were explicitly rejected, Eisenstein's more fundamental premise was accepted: editing individual shots together to produce conflictual effects countered the "reality effect" of the image. When extended to the domain of sound, the counterpoint between image, music, speech, and sound effects could serve as the basis for an alternative practice of cinema.[16] Amplified and refined by strategies proposed by Brecht—the use of quotations, shifts in the mode of representation, interruptions calculated to break routinized, passive responses, and so forth—montage could be used to produce a self-conscious construction, a kind of "writing" in images, music, and sounds which would be actively "read" by spectators. Such spectatorial engagement was essential if film was ever to constitute a *Kosmos*, an autonomous world of art not wholly isolated from social experience and potentially available to all.

The first films of Kluge—*The Eternity of Yesterday* (1960), *Teachers through Change* (1962–63), *Protocol of a Revolution* (1963)—are interesting to watch today for the way they bring together what have turned out to be persistent themes in his work with many of the ideas of Adorno and

Eisler about strategy and structure. Because they are rarely shown and discussed even in Germany, a brief description of them may be useful. *The Eternity of Yesterday* is a meditation on the recent Nazi past. Fragments of now-ruined monumental buildings and stadia constructed or imagined by the Nazis are conveyed in soberly composed shots (in a mixture of representational modes: still photos, sketches, drawings, building plans) and through camera movements freed of all narrative motivation. Suspended over the mute stones, part of the rubble of history, is a disjunctive sound collage—piano music in a chromatic idiom, snatches of martial music, citations from Auschwitz Commandant Höss's diaries and Hitler's speeches, and so forth. The "friction"—one of Kluge's favorite metaphors—generated by these fragments of reified discourses deployed in different formal parameters produces a shock to the spectator's memory and facilitates a more comprehensive grasp of the grim history they point to.[17]

Teachers through Change is a suite of four short portraits of teachers whose lives have been profoundly affected by historical events. Each laconic life story is told through a series of old photographs separated by titles. Some are progressive educators victimized by the Nazis; one is a vicious opportunist who benefited from the fascist takeover. Their lives are implicitly contrasted with those of ordinary, bureaucratized teachers today, whom we see in cinema-verité footage taken at a teachers convention, school meetings, and so on. The interruptions in the biographies figure the larger interruptions history makes in the lives of human beings (this is also a theme of a book of stories, *Lebensläufe* [*Curricula Vitae*], Kluge published in 1962). The dispersed narrative focus and the formal discontinuities resist the homogenizing narrative strategies of the culture industry and presage the method of "antagonistic realism" Kluge later formulates in discursive terms.[18]

Kluge is only credited with the script for *Protocol of a Revolution*, but the completed film is clearly consistent with his effort to develop strategies counter to those of mainstream culture industry discourse. *Protocol* is a simulated television documentary on a revolution in a South American country. The parody narrative clearly mocks culture industry conventions. Prefaced by and concluding with a distancing tracking shot into and away from a television set, the film mimics TV journalism's common practice by moving from apparently objective shots of crowds at rallies, tanks in action, and so forth, to interviews, "behind the scenes" accounts of torture and the dictator's private life, much of which is illustrated with an exaggerated pictorial verve and luridly recounted by a reporter's off-screen voice. Since the documentary shots are often staged (although "authentic" footage from actual documentaries is also used) and the fictionalized sections often depict actual events, the culture industry's rigid categories begin to blur. The dissolution of the boundaries between fiction and documentary, reality and fantasy, public and private, mass culture and high art would figure significantly in Kluge's creative and theoretical agenda.

With *Protocol of a Revolution*, Kluge had entered the territory of the narrative film, the principal product of the culture industry. This move and the work of preparing the script for *Yesterday Girl*, his first feature, impelled him to seek a more elaborate theoretical rationale for some of the things he had been doing in his short films. Thus, between the end of 1964 and the beginning of 1966, Kluge published two important articles, "Die Utopie Film" and "Wort und Film,"[19] and gave a number of interviews in which he discursively formulated his theoretical concerns for the first time. They warrant quotation at length. In "Die Utopie Film," Kluge writes,

> Film stands before a challenge, its material will always remain perceptions; montage allows us, however, to construct concepts. The smallest units of films, the parts called "shots," correspond to associations. In a film, the attempt by Joyce in *Finnegan's Wake* or by Hans G. Helms to decompose words into their associative components and recompose them anew, would not fail because of problems of comprehension; it [film] is in any case assigned the task of producing at every moment new units of meaning by the editing together of perceptions. . . . Film has methods similar to polyphony of organizing material relationships. Not only can it set movements of speech and image in opposition, film can also produce in the tense spaces between speech and image still another movement in the spectator's brain (not materialized in the film) which can furthermore stand in contrast to the film's movements, and so forth.

These remarks are amplified in an interview with Enno Patalas and Frieda Grafe shortly before the triumphant premiere of *Yesterday Girl* at Venice in September 1966.

> Very crudely put: the cuts, which are not contained in the film, are as important as the image. Adorno once said—mockingly—that the only thing that bothered him were the images. He meant that that which is always concretely perceptible, as long as it leaves no gaps in which fantasy can take root, kills rather than encourages fantasy. Film must provide a space for fantasy, yet despite this, must also convey something through the images. In silent films the titles always excited me. Since, from a literary point of view, the titles are mostly idiotic, hardly informative or well-placed, I asked myself why I like to look at them. I am glad to see them because at that moment my brain begins to work and has a moment to evolve independent fantasies. Then I am glad to see pictures again.[20]

Although differences in emphasis and rhetorical formulation appear in the effort to theorize his practical experience, Kluge accepts most of Adorno and Eisler's premises. His theory also pivots around the break in the flow of images, the cut between shots, or the cut to a title. The cut subverts the illusory plenitude of the individual image as well as the destructive logic implicit in narrative forms. Linear narratives, which according to Kluge embody the quantifying abstract logic of instrumental reason, must thus be abandoned, though narrative elements, punctuated by leaps and reversals of time and circumscribed by reflection-inducing montage sequences, could still be retained.[21] Most importantly (and most distinctively for Kluge's theory), editing opens a space in which "distracted" spectators can invest their imagination, or, as Kluge puts it, their "fantasy." "I believe this is the essential point: the film is composed in the head of the spectator; it is not a work of art that exists on the screen by itself. Film must work with the associations which, to the extent they can be estimated, to the extent they can be imagined, the author can arouse in the spectator."[22] Together, the "polyphonic" movements of the images, of the pictures with respect to sounds, and of the "film in the spectator's head"[23] produce a friction that explodes the meanings fixed by instrumental reason. Each shot becomes a volatile manifold, "a rich totality of many determinations and relations" which invite the spectator to experience the "*Sinnlichkeit des Zusammenhangs,*" the sensuous relationships among widely diverse things and experiences.[24] Although the metaphor is implicit in his earlier practice, Kluge now begins to liken his films to "construction sites" at which a variety of discourses intersect and clash, engendering what Barthes termed "the very plural of meaning."[25]

Its "irreducible plurality" of meanings allows the film text to offer a number of entry points to a wide audience. In this respect, film, with the variety of its structure and appeal, and the necessary participation of its spectators, functions as a paradigm of operations in a radically open and democratic public sphere. Because films require imaginative engagement and debate, they become training grounds for enlightenment as well as assembly points for the broadly based, spontaneous coalitions which are the ideal vehicle of progress toward it.[26]

It was the strong challenge to this utopian conception of the relationship between a conspicuously difficult art and politics, as well as changes in the immediate political environment surrounding film production, that brought about the crises of 1967 to which I referred earlier. The year 1966 had been an immensely gratifying one for Kluge. He had become the acknowledged leader of the movement then known as Young German Cinema. The Kuratorium Junger Deutscher Film, a development bank for younger filmmakers for which Kluge had been fighting since the declaration of the "Oberhausen Manifesto" in 1962,[27] was finally established in 1965, and its awards committee granted a 100,000 DM subsidy for Kluge's first feature project, which was to be based on "Anita G.," one of the stories from his *Lebensläufe.* The film that emerged, *Yesterday Girl,* was the first major German film since the war to receive a significant international prize: it won the "Silver Lion" at the Venice Film Festival.

By early 1967, however, problems began to emerge. At the Berlin Film Festival, Kluge and his long-time associate Edgar Reitz were charged with "elitism" by radical students. The experience caused a temporary break in their relationship, and Kluge withdrew to the sanctuary of the Ulm Institute for Film Construction.[28] In the next few months, it became increasingly apparent that the German federal government, unaccountably, wished to reverse its more enlightened film policies, which were only just beginning to produce results. In the Film Subsidies Bill passed later that year, the federal authorities did, in fact, again favor mainstream producers in the awarding of subsidies, reducing the amount of funding available to younger talent. Kluge found himself flanked on the Left by students whose conception of political films extended only to those thought to possess immediate political utility, and on the Right by a government that instinctively gravitated toward supporting the ailing and intellectually bankrupt representatives of the culture industry. Mysteriously, Germany seemed almost neurotically compelled to repeat the gross mistakes of its past cultural politics.

Artists under the Big Top is often described by critics as a disordered and despairing film, a product of Kluge's disorientation in the face of the full range of these historical events. There is little truth to this assessment, though the film was improvised without any preconceived plan or script.[29] In fact, *Artists under the Big Top* might be regarded as a kind of manifesto in which Kluge trenchantly, even defiantly, formulates his convictions. The difficulty of the plot is, in fact, a vital feature of his very conception of cinema. Leni Peickert, the allegorical heroine of the film, wishes to create a "reform circus" to exhibit animals "as they authentically are." This extravagant ambition is designed to topple the classic circus, which had always, since its birth during the French Revolution, celebrated the omnipotence of man. Leni's quest is presented as a gesture of both loyalty to and defiance of her dead father Manfred, a representative of the old circus, who dreamed of having elephants perform an aerial ballet at the very top of the big top. But despite her tireless efforts and a convenient surprise inheritance, Leni fails. This failure leads to an unmotivated, almost inexplicable decision to work in the mass media. She ends up studying television techniques (a denouement remarkably prophetic of the trajectory of Kluge's own career), the first uncertain step in a "long march through the institutions," toward the distant goal of becoming a secretary in the Foreign Office.

To summarize the plot in this way is to lend it a coherence and a linearity that the film itself refuses. Shots are informally, almost "amateurishly" composed, and nearly every standard connecting device (shot/reverse-shot construction, point-of-view cutting, cutting on motion, and so on) is eschewed by the editing.

Even more than *Yesterday Girl*, whose narrative line was also interrupted by digressions, but which still operated largely within the conventions of the 1960s international art cinema,[30] *Artists under the Big Top* contrives the breakdown of the standard language of cinema. *Artists'* highly self-conscious narration has an altogether different character than that of any of Kluge's earlier films. The fragile line of Leni Peickert's story is often erased by puzzling and at best tenuously related episodes—about her father and other now-dead circus artists, about a Frau Losemeyer, who flushes large sums of money down the toilet, about a Mr. Korti, a culture bureaucrat who eats a pig's ear, and so on. Interwoven with these episodes is a section using documentary footage of the 1939 Nazi "Day of German Art," short photographic montages of assorted circuses from the past, interviews with journalists and circus artistes, a visit to the last meeting of the "Gruppe 47," and the "Fire in the Elephant House in Chicago" sequence described earlier—to name some of the most memorable. Each is a self-contained unit which, like an act in a variety show—or a circus—defines its own space and is connected only obliquely to the others by associations that are not always apparent.

The film revolves around the themes of spectacle and domination, the products, according to the *Dialectic of Enlightenment*, of instrumental reason and the major threats to the dwindling legacy of rational enlightenment. The classic circus's fantasy of the domination of nature is only the most spectacular form of instrumental reason. Besides the circus, however, the film also models itself on a related format—the revue film—which, as I mentioned earlier, Horkheimer and Adorno had singled out as a potential source of resistance to the centralized narratives of the culture industry. Kluge uses the revue format to develop a counter-spectacle whose gaps and daring conceptual leaps open spaces in which imagination and substantive reason may be vitally engaged. A cinema based on these models offers no concessions to the demand for easy comprehensibility; instead, it demands an exertion of imagination by its spectators. Such a cinema also disavows any immediate political utility. No solutions are imposed; rather, questions are raised. The spectator must work through what is presented in sensory as well as rational terms, to make connections, discriminate differences, and establish new frameworks for speculation. Kluge's political commitment is most profoundly expressed in this call for imaginative engagement.[31]

The crucial point is this: in *Artists under the Big Top*, Kluge moves decisively toward a "cinema of ideas," or rather a "counter-cinema of ideas." We are now in a better position to understand why he inserts shots from *October* in his film, for Eisenstein—and his attempt to establish an "intellectual cinema"—must be seen as the great precursor of Kluge's cinema. Nevertheless, these quotations from *October* should not be read as an homage to an admired mentor, as quotations by Kluge's contemporaries in the French New Wave are read. The shots chosen for the "Fire in the Elephant House" sequence (and for two others in the film), their presentation, the resulting shifts in meaning, all suggest an unmistakable ambivalence, perhaps even an animus toward Eisenstein's work and theory.[32] If these quotations attest to Eisenstein's influence, it is the sort Harold Bloom describes: "a variety of melancholy or an anxiety-principle" which produces a significant swerve away from the achievement of a simultaneously feared and admired precursor.[33]

Even a cursory rereading of his texts and projects between 1924 and 1929, the gestation period for his first conceptualization of intellectual cinema,[34] makes it clear that Eisenstein approached his project from a perspective diametrically opposed to that of Kluge. From the first texts he wrote, Eisenstein wished to instrumentalize the image, to make it part of a spectacle delivering a precisely defined impact on spectators. "Theater is linked to cinema by a common (identical) material—the *audience*—and by a common purpose—*influencing this audience in the desired direction* through a series of calculated pressures on its psyche," he observed in "The Montage of Film Attractions."

> The method of agitation through spectacle consists in the creation of a new chain of conditioned reflexes by associating selected phenomena with the unconditioned reflexes they produce. . . . It is then possible to envisage in both theory and practice a construction, with no linking plot logic, which provokes a chain of the necessary unconditioned reflexes that are, at the editor's will, associated with (compared with) predetermined phenomena and by this means to create the chain of new conditioned reflexes that these phenomena constitute. This signifies a realization of the orientation towards thematic effect, i.e. a fulfillment of the agitational purpose.[35]

Later, he likened the "For God and Country" sequence in *October*, perhaps his most completely realized draft of intellectual cinema, to a process of logical deduction.

> In this case, . . . a chain of images attempted to achieve a purely intellectual resolution, resulting from a conflict between a preconception and a *gradual discrediting of it in purposeful steps.*
>
> Step by step, by a process of comparing each new image with the common denotation, power is accumulated behind a process that can be formally identified with logical deduction. . . .
>
> The conventional *descriptive* form for film leads to the formal possibility of a kind of filmic reasoning. While the conventional film directs the *emotions*, this suggests an opportunity to encourage and direct the whole *thought process*, as well.[36]

Elsewhere he compared the hold such sequences have over the audience to a lecturer's "steely embrace," in which "the breathing of the entire electrified audience suddenly becomes rhythmic."[37] Finally, Eisenstein celebrated cinema's ability "to penetrate the mind of the great masses with new ideas and new perceptions. Such a cinema alone will dominate, by its form, the summit of modern industrial technique."[38]

Intellectual cinema as a process of "logical deduction" for "great masses" whose minds are held in a "steely embrace" by an "industrial technique"—here, in astonishingly concise form, is a left-wing variant of the dialectic of enlightenment. Underlying its conception is a fantasy of audience control which differs little from similar fantasies entertained by the capitalist culture industry. For Kluge, however powerful the results of such a practice, it is clearly antithetical to any genuine process of enlightenment.[39] The task of a counter-cinema, therefore, is effectively to contest the authority—imagistic, narrative, political—of the original construction by undoing its logic, thereby redeeming the vibrant power of its fragments for the spectator.

Kluge's critique of the premises of Eisenstein's cinema begins by placing Eisenstein's striking, rigorously composed shots in the center of the screen and surrounding them with a black border. Reframed in this way, they lose their status as quasi-authentic documents of a momentous historical event. What is underscored is their identity *as pictures* that are being quoted, re-presented. Furthermore, as I noted at the beginning, the shots are taken from at least four unrelated sequences and shown out of their original order. Excerpted from their context, relations of cause and effect are severed, and the tension of Eisenstein's synthesizing logic is released. *October*'s epic, monological narrative of the Russian Revolution is simply halted and decomposed into so many autonomous, nonhierarchized "attractions"—the glassware, the glittering chandeliers, the columned rooms and staircases, the expressive slinking of the actors. As the "steely embrace" loosens, the spectator is enabled to admire the images for their physical beauty and to construct new configurations of meaning, new (hi)stories.

Such constructions are encouraged by the sound track. Many different kinds of sound, both music and voices, vie for attention. Like the grainy, slightly out-of-focus images, the two brief musical fragments are recorded from old, scratched records; music is eroded to sheer sound. Their age—the recordings probably date from the late '20s—engenders a nostalgia that is out of keeping with the depicted events. Yet, because these melodies seem to be contemporary with *October*'s creation, they suggest that the film is, like them, a charming antique.[40] Kluge also severely undercuts the voice-over narration's customary authority, and this helps to generate webs of meaning in which Eisenstein's imagery is caught. Each of the many narrating voices represents different characters and points of view. Several report the elephants' panic and despair at not having trusted the evidence of their senses when fire broke out; one speaks the part of the circus director, who falsely reassures them that there is no fire. Later in the sequence, the voice-over narration is splintered further as a group sings a Russian anti-Hitler song from World War II, another group expresses a profoundly ambivalent desire for revenge, while still others murmur that it is better to repress the painful memories. The allusions to Nazis and circus directors, elephants and Russian resistance fighters, victims and heros, revenge and repression, freedom and memory, allusions that will be amplified and further transformed during the rest of the film, here invoke new conceptual contexts through which Eisenstein's imagery can now circulate.

The spoken texts themselves thematize and reflexively legitimate the questioning and subversion of authority that runs through the sequence at all levels. Even the Marxist political perspective that authorizes the history *October* recounts is challenged. Eisenstein's emphatically clear political message that human liberation is essentially freedom from enslavement is dramatically undermined by Hegel's counter-claim, cited at the end of the passage, that freedom is an exercise in epistemological self-definition against unspecified others. The text should not be superficially read as condemning political action, or even revolutionary violence, as such; its crucial function is to put orthodox Leninist historiography into question and to provide a rationale for the act of self-definition Kluge includes as an essential moment of his critical project.

Leni Peickert wished to create a reform circus "worthy of a dead man." In order to do so, she had completely to reverse the conceptual terms of her father's enterprise. Similarly, Kluge's "reform" of the intellectual cinema of Eisenstein proceeds by "rewriting" his images as the basis for a more general critique of the premises underlying them. This process of rewriting may properly be considered allegorical. According to Craig Owens, "allegory occurs whenever one text is doubled by another . . . or read through another"[41]: this is precisely what Kluge's sequence does to Eisenstein's images. As in all allegories, the motivating impulse behind the "Fire in the Elephant House" sequence is a desire to redeem a distant past for the present. Kluge furthermore adopts the allegorist's method of appropriating fragments of the ruins he hopes to recover and piling them up in a synthetic, hybrid structure that "is the epitome of counter-narrative, for it arrests narrative in place, substituting a principle of syntagmatic disjunction for one of diegetic combination." His aim is not to restore the image's original significance, but to add another meaning to it, to expand its field of meaning. This surplus of meaning is fundamentally different from—and opposed to—a completion of meaning. Kluge's redoubled allegorical text begins, like all allegorical texts, in a state of perplexity, and remains until the end radically, bewilderingly incomplete—perplexing. A space is thus opened up for the film's spectators, whose efforts to decipher its meanings, fueled as much by resistance as by assent to what Kluge has constructed, will result in their own revisionary constructions, the "films in their heads." These "films" are the necessary next stage of an allegorical process that is the crucial vehicle of critique and enlightenment.

Notes

1. Alexander Kluge, *Die Artisten in der Zirkuskuppel: ratlos*, Munich, Piper, 1968, p. 15.

2. Sigmund Freud, "Further Recommendations in the Technique of Psychoanalysis: Recollection, Repetition and Working Through" (1914), in *Therapy and Technique*, ed. Philip Rieff, New York, Collier Books, 1963, pp. 157–166.

3. The insertion of four other shots from *October* develops this critique further. In these shots, the placement of a close-up image of an officer next to an image of a statue of Napoleon creates a false point-of-view structure. In the interview published in this issue, Kluge comments on this kind of manipulation: "If you speak of the influence of Eisenstein, you must look at what he did in *Strike*, in *October*. You remember in *Artisten in der Zirkuskuppel: ratlos* the quotation from *October*? I used the sequence with Bonaparte. I wanted to indicate that I hate Bonapartism in film, in all art. There are two characters in art. One character you could compare with a *dompteur* who forces animals to change their attitudes. The other would be the *jardinière*, the *agricultura*. The second type is my ideal." Kluge's terms are different from but entirely consistent with the reading I offer in this essay.

4. For an early and by no means isolated statement of these concerns, see Germaine Dulac, "Les Esthétiques. Les Entraves. La Cinégraphie Intégrale," *L'Art Cinématographique*, II (1927), trans. Stuart Liebman in *Framework*, 19 (1982), pp. 6–9. Although they explore and experiment with film form and technique, Kluge's films do not seek to articulate cinema's autonomy as an artistic medium, as do the films of orthodox modernists such as Paul Sharits, Malcolm LeGrice, or Wilhelm and Birgit Hein. The films of Kluge might be more usefully compared to Godard's *Two or Three Things I Know About Her* (1967), or Makaveyev's *Innocence Unprotected* (1968) and *WR: Mysteries of the Organism* (1971)—which bear a closer resemblance to his own.

5. I refer, of course, to Benjamin's positions in "The Author as Producer" (1934), trans. Anna Bostock, in *Understanding Brecht*, London, New Left Books, 1973, pp. 85–104.

6. Michel Foucault, "What is Enlightenment?," in *Foucault Reader*, ed. Paul Rabinow, New York, Pantheon, 1984, p. 43.

7. Kluge and Oskar Negt borrow the term from Jürgen Habermas's *Strukturwandel der öffentlichkeit*, Neuwied, Luchterhand, 1962, but they interpret it very differently. See translator's note to the selections from *The Public Sphere and Experience* presented in this issue. Also see Alexander Kluge, "Die Macht der Bewusstseinsindustrie und das Schicksal unserer öffentlichkeit. Zum Unterschied von machbar und gewalttätig," in *Industrialisierung des Bewusstseins*, Munich, Piper, 1985, pp. 51–129.

8. General background on this period is found in Thomas Elsaesser, "The Postwar German Cinema," in *Fassbinder*, second edition, ed. Tony Rayns, London, BFI, 1980, pp. 1–16; Eric Rentschler, *West German Film in the Course of Time*, Bedford Hills, New York, Redgrave, 1984, pp. 31–63, 101–108; James Franklin, *New German Cinema*, Boston, Twayne, 1983, pp. 21–34; and John Sandford, *The New German Cinema*, New York, DaCapo, 1980, pp. 9–16. See also Rainer Lewandowski, *Die Oberhausener*, Diekholzen, Verlag für Bühne und Film, 1982.

9. See, for example, their remarks about a number of popular minor forms such as chase films, farces, and cartoons in *Dialectic of Enlightenment*, trans. John Cumming, New York, Continuum, 1972, pp. 120ff. For an excellent short assessment of Adorno's views on cinema, see Miriam Hansen, "Introduction to Adorno's 'Transparencies on Film,'" *New German Critique*, 25–26 (Fall/Winter 1981–1982), pp. 186–198.

10. Horkheimer and Adorno, *Dialectic of Enlightenment*, p. 124.

11. Three representative Adorno texts available in English are: "Alienated Masterpiece: *Missa Solemnis,*" *Telos*, 28 (Summer 1976); *Prisms*, trans. Samuel and Shierry Weber, Cambridge, MIT Press, 1981, pp. 149ff; *Minima Moralia*, trans. E. F. N. Jephcott, London,

Verso, 1978, *passim*. For more about the *Dialectic of Enlightenment*'s analytic perspective on cinema, see Miriam Hansen, "Alexander Kluge: Crossings between Film, Literature, Critical Theory," in *Film und Literatur: Literarische Texte und der neue deutsche Film*, eds. Sigrid Bauschinger, Susan L. Cocalis and Henry A. Lea, Bern, Francke, 1984, pp. 169–196.

12. See, for example, the interviews Becker conducted with Adorno which were published as *Erziehung zur Mündigkeit*, ed. Gerd Kadelbach, Frankfurt, Suhrkamp, 1971.

13. See the interview with Kluge in this issue. Nevertheless, Adorno did introduce him to Fritz Lang, who had returned to Germany in 1958 to shoot what would be two of his last films, *The Indian Tomb* and *The Tiger of Eschnapur*. Lang permitted Kluge to observe him filming on the set, but the experience of watching the producer Artur Brauner dominate the legendary director was so painful to Kluge that he spent most of his time in the studio canteen writing the stories later published as *Lebensläufe*. For Kluge's account, see "Tribüne des Jungen Deutschen Films: Alexander Kluge," in *Filmkritik*, 117 (September 1966), pp. 490–491. Those seeking more biographical material on Kluge should consult Theodore Fiedler, "Alexander Kluge: Mediating History and Consciousness," in *New German Filmmakers*, ed. Klaus Phillips, New York, Ungar, 1984, pp. 195–229; see also Rainer Lewandowski, *Alexander Kluge*, Munich, C.H. Beck, 1980.

14. Hanns Eisler, *Composing for the Films*, New York, Oxford University Press, 1947, pp. 65–79 and 152–157. Because of his concerns about political persecution during the McCarthy period, Adorno only took credit for the book when a German edition was published shortly before his death in 1969. Indeed, in the preface to this reedition, Adorno claimed most of the credit for it. See Hansen's "Crossings," pp. 172–175, and "Introduction to Adorno," pp. 194ff.

15. Adorno and Horkheimer, *Dialectic of Enlightenment*, pp. 148–149, and *passim*. The passage from *Artists under the Big Top: Perplexed* with which I began, indeed the film's entire project, is profoundly indebted to remarks like this.

16. For a more comprehensive account of the book's argument, see Philip Rosen, "Adorno and Film Music: Theoretical Notes on *Composing for the Films*," *Yale French Studies*, 60 (1980), pp. 157–182. In fairness to Eisenstein, it must be pointed out that Adorno and Eisler base their critique on arguments presented in *The Film Sense* and overlook earlier statements, presumably available to them, that are quite close to their own position. In many respects, the earlier views of Eisenstein on sound anticipate theirs. For his most concise statement of these views, see "A Statement" (1928), trans. Jay Leyda, *Film Form*, New York, Meridian, 1957, pp. 257–259. Incidentally, in his later essay, "Transparencies on Film" (*New German Critique*, 24–25 [Winter 1981–1982], p. 201), Adorno argues that the images presented on screen have a structural affinity with the stream of associations in the human mind. This conception is, of course, very close to Eisenstein's second version of "intellectual cinema." See "A Course in Treatment" (1932), in *Film Form*, pp. 104–106.

17. Kluge derives the notion of friction (*Reibung*) from Clausewitz's writings on war. The notions of discontinuity, tension, and shock implicit in his practice are profoundly indebted to Benjamin, particularly to his "Theses on the Philosophy of History": "Materialistic historiography . . . is based on a constructive principle. Thinking involves not only the flow of thoughts, but their arrest as well. Where thinking suddenly stops in a configuration pregnant with tensions, it gives that configuration a shock, by which it crystallizes into a monad" (*Illuminations*, trans. Harry Zohn, New York, Schocken, 1969, pp. 253–264). Kluge's most far-reaching implementation of these ideas can be found in *Die Patriotin* (*The Female Patriot*).

18. Kluge developed the notion of "antagonistic realism" in his treatise "Zur realistischen Methode," in *Gelegenheitsarbeit einer Sklavin: Zur Realistischen Methode*, Frankfurt am Main, Suhrkamp, 1975, pp. 187–250, trans. James Terry Acuff, Jr., as *Toward a Realistic Method: Commentaries on the Notion of Antagonistic Realism*, Austin, Texas, University of Texas, unpublished Master's thesis, 1980. Kluge's fascination with the short

biography form is evident in his film portraits—*Proven Competence Portrayed, Fireman E. A. Winterstein, Frau Blackburn* . . . , *A Doctor from Halberstadt, A Woman of Means, Class of 1908*—as well as in the countless vignettes which appear in his features.

19. "Die Utopie Film," *Merkur*, 201, (December 1964), pp. 1135–1146; "Wort und Film," coauthored with Edgar Reitz and Wilfried Reinke, *Sprache im technischen Zeitalter*, 13 (January–March 1965), pp. 1015–1030. The latter essay has been translated for this issue.

20. "Tribune des Jungen Deutschen Films," in *Filmkritik*, September 1966, p. 490.

21. "Das Publikum soll zufrieden sein. Gespräch mit dem Regisseur Alexander Kluge bei den Dreharbeiten zu 'Abschied von gestern,'" *Die Welt*, March 19, 1966. For a more extended discussion of logic as supportive of the "mechanism of domination" [*Herrschaftsmechanismus*], see Ulrich Gregor, "Interview," in *Herzog/Kluge/Straub*, ed. Peter W. Jansen and Wolfram Schütte, Munich, Hanser, 1976, p.176 and *passim*.

22. Ibid., p. 489. Kluge adapts the notion of the "distracted viewer" from Benjamin. See "The Work of Art in the Age of Mechanical Reproduction," in *Illuminations*, pp. 239ff.

23. The idea that film mimes subjective experience is baldly asserted in "Die Utopie Film" ("Film is capable of miming the movement of human thought," p. 1144) and anticipates Adorno's position in "Filmtransparente." In *Gelegenheitsarbeit einer Sklavin*, Kluge writes: "One can look at it this way: for many tens of thousands of years a film has been playing in people's heads—a stream of associations, day dreams, experience, sensations, consciousness. The technical inventions of the cinema have merely added reproducible counterparts" (p. 208). In "Kluge, Cinema and the Public Sphere," Hansen observes the parallels with Bazin's views in "The Myth of Total Cinema" (1946). Kluge here also very closely approaches the rhetoric of Stan Brakhage in *Metaphors on Vision* (New York, Film Culture, 1963, n.p.). Brakhage consistently insists on the mimetic grounding of his films. The ambiguous oscillation between a constructivist and a mimetic rationale for the montage remains in Kluge's as well as Adorno's thinking.

24. Kluge borrows this formulation from Karl Marx, *Grundrisse*, trans. Martin Nicolaus, New York, Vintage, 1973, p. 100. Also see footnote 26.

25. Kluge, *Gelegenheitsarbeit*, p. 220. The passage from Barthes is worth quoting in full since it seems so aptly to describe Kluge's theory and practice. "The Text is plural. Which is not simply to say that it has several meanings, but that it accomplishes the very plural of meaning: an *irreducible* (and not merely an acceptable) plural. The Text is not a coexistence of meanings but a passage, a traversal; thus it answers not to an interpretation, even a liberal one, but to an explosion, a dissemination. The plural of the Text depends, that is, not on the ambiguity of its contents, but on what might be called the *stereographic plurality* of its weave of signifiers (etymologically, the text is a tissue, a woven fabric) . . . the citations which go to make up a text are anonymous, untraceable, and yet *already read*: they are quotations without quotation marks. . . . The metaphor of the text is that of the *network*; if the Text extends itself, it is a result of a combinatory systematic. . . . Hence, no vital 'respect' is due to the Text: it can be *broken* . . . ; it can be read without the guarantee of its father, the restitution of the inter-text paradoxically abolishing any legacy" (Roland Barthes, "From Work to Text," in *Image-Music-Text*, trans. Stephen Heath, New York, Hill & Wang, 1977, pp. 172–173). For Kluge's comments on the use of textual fragments, on works as part of a textual system, and on the idea of a "cinema of riddles" (*Rätselkino*), see the interview in this issue.

26. Marx is the theorist Kluge cites most often, but the political theorist whose practical interventions Kluge most admires is Rosa Luxemburg. A study of his use of their work as models for his films and film theory would be illuminating.

27. The Oberhausen Manifesto, signed by twenty-six filmmakers, cameramen, and actors, including Edgar Reitz and Kluge, was read on February 28, 1962, at the Oberhausen Short Film Festival. The manifesto proclaimed the complete collapse of the German film industry and the signatories' desire to create a new German feature film, free of industry conventions, commercial influences, and control by interest groups.

28. For more on the Ulm Institute, see the interview with Kluge in *October* 46 (1988).

29. The script, along with materials not included in the final version, was published after the fact in *Die Artisten in der Zirkuskuppel: ratlos*. Many of these segments were later used in the television production *The Indomitable Leni Peickert*. For background information on the film, see Rainer Lewandowski, *Die Filme von Alexander Kluge*, Hildesheim, Olms Presse, 1980, p. 119.

30. The best description of art-cinema's narrational strategies can be found in David Bordwell, *Narration in the Fiction Film*, Madison, University of Wisconsin Press, 1985, pp. 205–233. For a detailed reading of *Yesterday Girl*, see Miriam Hansen, "Space of History, Language of Time: Kluge's *Yesterday Girl* (1966)," in *German Film and Literature: Adaptations and Transformations*, ed. Eric Rentschler, New York, Methuen, 1985, pp. 193–216.

31. Though the course of Leni's career might seem to suggest that traditional modernist hopes for renewal through revolutionary formal and conceptual innovation are utopian at best and quixotic at worst, the film's formal complexity belies this suggestion. The final decision to attempt to reform the media from within may be interestingly compared to positions later taken by Hans Magnus Enzensberger in "Constituents of a Theory of the Media" [1971], trans. Stuart Hood in Enzensberger's *Critical Essays*, New York, Continuum, 1982, pp. 46–76. In his own cultural politics, however, Kluge has preferred to operate both inside and outside established governmental channels, temperamentally preferring the role of the critic.

32. It is unclear what Kluge knew of Eisenstein's theoretical writings at the time *Artists* was made. In some interviews, he implies that Eisenstein's montage theories were actively discussed at the Ulm Institute for Film Construction, while in others he claims not to have read any primary sources until 1973, when the controversy with the editors of *Frauen und Film* over his *Part-Time Work of a Female Slave* erupted. Concerning the discussions at Ulm, see Klaus Eder and Alexander Kluge, *Ulmer Dramaturgien*, Munich, Hanser, 1980, p. 38. Concerning Kluge's unfamiliarity with film theory, see the interview in this issue. For the controversy over *Part-Time Work*, see the interview in this issue, Kluge's *Toward a Realistic Method*, and articles by Kallweit, Sander, and Kemper listed in the bibliography.

33. Harold Bloom, *The Anxiety of Influence*, New York, Oxford University Press, 1973, pp. 7 and 14. Of the six "revisionary ratios" Bloom lists, two seem most appropriate: "*clinamen*, which is poetic misreading or misprision proper; . . . This appears as a corrective movement in his own poem, which implies that the precursor poem went accurately up to a certain point, but then should have swerved, precisely in the direction that the new poem moves," and "*kenosis*, which is a breaking-device similar to the defense mechanisms our psyches employ against repetition compulsions; *kenosis* then is a movement towards discontinuity with the precursor."

34. Eisenstein actually constructed two versions of his concept of intellectual cinema. The second version may roughly be dated 1928–1929, when Eisenstein began to read Joyce's *Ulysses* and conceived the project of miming the course of the thought process. This project is perhaps best described in "A Course in Treatment" (1932). I am, however, concerned here with the first version, which developed from the early "The Montage of Film Attractions" (1924) through "Perspectives" (1929) and "The Dialectic of Film Form" (1929). For an analysis of Eisenstein's ambitions, see Annette Michelson, "Reading Eisenstein Reading *Capital*," *October*, no. 2 (Summer 1976), pp. 27–38, and no. 3 (Spring 1977), pp. 82–89.

35. Sergei Eisenstein, "The Montage of Film Attractions," in *Eisenstein Writings 1922–34*, trans. and ed. Richard Taylor, Bloomington, Indiana University Press, 1988, pp. 39ff. Emphasis in original.

36. Eisenstein, "A Dialectic Approach to Film Form" [1929], trans. Jay Leyda, in *Film Form*, p. 62. Emphasis in original. Noël Carroll has convincingly analyzed this passage as a species of logical argument. See "For God and Country," *Artforum*, January 1973, pp. 56–60.

37. Eisenstein, "Perspectives," in *Film Essays and a Lecture*, trans. and ed. Jay Leyda, New York, Praeger, 1970, p. 43.

38. "Perspectives," p. 45. Incidentally, these phrases are taken from the German language version of the essay Eisenstein himself prepared for publication in *Der Querschnitt* (January 1930).

39. Miriam Hansen observes that Kluge would also reject the "representationalist and organicist implications of Eisenstein's theory. . . . Whatever relationship between author and spectator his films may project . . . Kluge would certainly not intend his audience to follow him as the 'creator' in the manner envisioned by Eisenstein" ("Crossings," p. 181). In fairness to Eisenstein, recent criticisms of his theory of representation in the image are almost always based on his later texts, and ignore alternative formulations in earlier writings. See, for example, Colin MacCabe, "Realism and the Cinema: Notes on Some Brechtian Theses," *Screen*, vol. 15, no. 2, pp. 7–27. Kluge figures the underlying similarity between Eisenstein and the culture industry when he films Leni Peickert watching fragments from three films: first, the machine gun slaughter from *October*, and finally, shots from a soft-porn film of the type stimulated by the 1967 Film Subsidies Bill. Wedged between the two are images from an unidentified *Autorenfilm*, the excluded third term in Germany's cinematic landscape.

40. For the best general description of Kluge's use of such music see Rudolf Hohlweg, "Musik für Film—Film für Musik," in Peter W. Jansen and Wolfram Schütte, eds., *Herzog/Kluge/Straub*, Munich, Hanser, 1976, pp. 45–68, 52 ff.

41. Craig Owens, "The Allegorical Impulse: Toward a Theory of Postmodernism," *October*, no. 12 (Spring 1980), pp. 67–86. The rest of this paragraph is indebted to his exegesis.

Theories of German Fascism:
On the Collection of Essays *War and Warrior* edited by Ernst Jünger

WALTER BENJAMIN

LÉON DAUDET, the son of Alphonse Daudet, who was himself an important writer and a leader of France's Royalist Party, once gave a report in his *Action Français* on the *Salon de l'Automobile* which concluded, in perhaps somewhat different words, with the question: "L'automobile c'est la guerre." This surprising association of ideas was based on the perception of an increase in technical artifacts, in power sources, and in tempo generally that the private sector can neither absorb completely nor utilize adequately but that nonetheless demand vindication. But vindication can only occur in antithesis to a harmonious balance, in war, and the destructive power of war provides clear evidence that social reality was not ready to make technology its own organ, and that technology was not strong enough to master the elemental forces of society. Without approaching the surface of the significance of the economic causes of war, one may say that the harshest, most disastrous aspects of imperialist war are in part the result of the gaping discrepancy between the gigantic power of technology and the minuscule moral illumination it affords. Indeed, according to its economic nature, bourgeois society cannot help but insulate everything technological as much as possible from the so-called spiritual, and it cannot help but resolutely exclude technology's right of co-determination in the social order. Any future war will also be a slave revolt of technology.

Today factors such as these determine all questions of war and one would hardly expect to have to remind the authors of the present volume of this, nor to remind them that these are questions of imperialist war. After all, they were themselves soldiers in the World War and, dispute what one may, they indisputably proceed from the experience of this war. It is therefore quite astonishing to find, and on the first page at that, the statement that "it is of secondary importance in which century, for which ideas, and with which weapons the fighting is done." What is most astonishing about this statement is that its author, Ernst Jünger, is thus adopting one of the principles of pacifism, and pacifism's clichéd ideal of peace have little to criticize each other for. Even the most questionable and most abstract of all its principles at that. Though for him and his friends it is not

Translation by Jerolf Wikoff. Reprinted, with permission, from *New German Critique* 17 (1979), 128–30.

so much some doctrinaire schema that lies behind this as it is a deep-rooted and—by all standards of male thought—a really rather depraved mysticism. But Jünger's mysticism of war and pacifism's clichéd ideal of peace have little to criticize each other for. Even the most consumptive pacifism has one thing over its epileptically frothing brother for the moment; a certain contact with reality, at least, some conception of the next war.

The authors like to speak—emphatically—of the "First World War." Yet how little their experience has come to grips with that war's realities—which they refer to in an alienated exaggeration as the "wordly-real"—is shown by the altogether thoughtless obtuseness with which they view the idea of future wars without any conception of them. These trailblazers of the *Wehrmacht* could almost give one the impression that the uniform represents their highest end, most desired by all their heartstrings, and that the circumstances under which one dons the uniform are of little importance by comparison. This attitude becomes more comprehensible when one realizes, in terms of the current level of European armaments, how anachronistic is their espoused ideology of war. These authors nowhere observe that the new warfare of technology and material [*Materialschlacht*] which appears to some of them as the highest revelation of existence, dispenses with all the wretched emblems of heroism that here and there have survived the World War. Gas warfare, in which the contributors to this book show conspicuously little interest, promises to give the war of the future a face which permanently displaces soldierly qualities by those of sports; all action will lose its military character and war will assume the countenance of recordsetting. The most prominent strategic characteristic of such warfare consists in its being waged exclusively and most radically as an offensive war. And we know that there is no adequate defense against gas attacks from the air. Even individual protective devices, gas masks, are of no use against mustard gas and Levisit. Now and then one hears of something "reassuring" such as the invention of a sensitive listening device that registers the whir of propellers at great distances. And a few months later a soundless airplane is invented. Gas warfare will rest upon annihilation records, and will involve an absurd degree of risk. Whether its outbreak will occur within the bounds of international law—after prior declarations of war—is questionable; but its end will no longer be concerned with such limitations. Since gas warfare obviously eliminates the distinction between civilian and military personnel, the most important basis of international law is removed. The last war has already shown that the total disorganization imperialist war entails, and the manner in which it is waged, threaten to make it an endless war.

More than a curiosity, it is symptomatic that something written in 1930 about "war and warriors" overlooks all this. It is symptomatic that the same boyish rapture that leads to a cult, to an apotheosis of war, is here heralded particularly by von Schramm and Günther. The most rabidly decadent origins of this new theory of war are emblazoned on their fore-heads: it is nothing other than an uninhibited translation of the principles of *l'art pour l'art* to war itself. But if, even on its home grounds, this theo-ry tends to become a mockery in the mouths of mediocre adepts, its out-look in this new phase of war is disgraceful. Who could imagine a veteran of the Marne or someone who fought at Verdun reading statements such as these: "We conducted the war on very impure principles. . . . Real fight-ing from man to man, from company to company, became rarer and rarer. . . . Certainly the front-line officers often made the war artless. . . . For though the inclusion of the masses, the lesser blood, the practical bour-geois mentality, in short the common man, especially in the officers' and non-commissioned officers' corps, the eternally aristocratic elements of the soldier's trade were increasingly destroyed." Falser notes could hardly be sounded, more inept thoughts could not be set down on paper, more tactless words could not be uttered. The authors' absolute failure here is the result—despite all the talk about the eternal and the primeval—of their unrefined, thoroughly journalistic haste to capitalize from the actual present without grasping the past. Yes, there have been cultic elements in war. They were known in theocratically constituted communities. As hare-brained as it would be to want to return these submerged elements to the zenith of war, it would be equally embarrassing for these warriors on their intellectual flight to learn how far a Jewish philosopher, Erich Unger,[1] has gone in the direction they missed. And it would be embarrassing for them to see to what extent his observations—made, if in part with questionable justice, on the basis of concrete data from Jewish history—would cause the bloody schemes conjured up here to evaporate into nothingness. But these authors are not capable of making anything clear, of calling things by their names. War: "eludes the usual economy exercised by the mind; there is something inhuman, boundless, gigantic in its Reason, something remi-niscent of a volcanic process, an elemental eruption . . . a colossal well of life directed by a painfully deep, cogently unified force, led to battlefields already mythic today, used up for tasks far exceeding the range of the cur-rently conceivable." Only an awkward lover is so loquacious. And indeed these authors are awkward in their embrace of thought, too. One has to bring them back to it repeatedly, and that is what we will do here.

And the point is this: War—the "eternal" war that they talk about so much here, as well as the most recent one—is said to be the highest mani-festation of the German nation. It should be clear that behind their "eter-nal" war lies the idea of cultic war, just as behind the most recent war lies that of technological war, and it should also be clear that these authors have had little success in perceiving these relationships. But there is some-thing rather special about this last war. It was not only one of material war-fare but also a war that was lost. And in that special sense it was the German war. To have waged war out of their innermost existence is something that other peoples could claim to have done. But to have lost a war out of their innermost existence, this they cannot claim. What is special about the present and latest stage in the controversy over the war, which has convulsed Germany since 1919, is the novel assertion that it is precisely this loss of the war that is characteristically German. One can call this the latest stage because these attempts to come to terms with the loss of the war show a clear pattern. These attempts began with an effort to pervert the German defeat into an inner victory by means of confessions of guilt which were hysterically elevated to the universally human. This political position, which supplied the manifestoes for the course of the decline of the West, faithfully reflected the German "revolution" made by the Expressionist avant-garde. Then came the attempt to forget the lost war. The bourgeoisie turned to snore on its other side—and what pillow could have been softer than the novel. The terrors endured in those years became the down filling in which every sleepyhead could easily leave his imprint. What finally distinguishes this latest effort from earlier ones in the process involved here is the tendency to take the loss of the war more seriously than the war itself. What does it mean to win or lose a war? How striking the double meaning is in both words! The first, manifest meaning, certainly refers to the outcome of the war, but the second meaning—which creates that peculiar hollow space, the sounding board in these words—refers to the totality of the war and suggest how the war's outcome also alters the enduring significance it holds for us. This meaning says, so to speak, the winner keeps the war in hand, it leaves the hands of the loser; it says, the winner conquers the war for himself, makes it his own property, the loser no longer possesses it and must live without it. And he must live not only without the war per se but without every one of its slightest ups and downs, every subtlest one of its chess moves, every one of its remotest actions. To win or lose a war reaches so deeply, if we follow the language, into the fabric of our existence that our whole lives become that much richer or poorer in symbols, images and sources. And since we have lost one of the greatest wars in world history, one which involved the whole material and spiritual substance of a people, one can assess the significance of this loss.

Certainly one cannot accuse those around Jünger of not having taken this into account. But how did they approach it, monstrous as it was? They have not stopped the battle yet. They continued to celebrate the cult of war when there was no longer any real enemy. They complied with the desires of the bourgeoisie, which longed for the decline of the West, the way a schoolboy longs for a inkblot in place of his wrong answer. They spread decline, preached decline wherever they went. Not even for a moment were they capable of holding up to view—instead of doggedly holding onto—what had been lost. They were always the first and the bitterest to oppose coming to one's senses. They ignored the great opportunity of the loser—which the Russians had taken advantage of—to shift the fight to another sphere until the moment had passed and the nations of Europe had sunk to being partners in trade agreements again. "The war is being *administered*, not *led* anymore," one of the authors complains. This was to be corrected by the German "post-war war" (*Nachkrieg*). This *Nachkrieg* was as much a protest against the war that had preceded it, as it was a protest against its civilian character. Above all, that despised rational element was to be eliminated from war. And to be sure this team bathed in the vapors rising out of the jowls of the Fenriswolf. But these vapors were no match for the [mustard] gases of the yellow-cross grenades. Such humbug about this arch-Germanic fate acquired a moldy luster when set against the stark background of military service in army barracks and impoverished families in civilian barracks. And without subjecting that false luster to materialist analysis, it was possible even then for a free, knowing, and truly dialectical spirit such as Florens Christian Rang[2]—whose biography better exemplifies the German than whole hordes of these desperate characters— to counter their sort with enduring statements: "The demonic belief in fate, that human virtue is superfluous—the dark night of defiance which burns up the victory of the forces of light in the universal conflagration of the gods . . . this apparant glory of the will in this belief in death in battle, without regard for life, flinging it down for an idea—this cloud-impregnated night that has hovered over us for millennia and which, instead of stars, gives us only stupefying and confusing thunderbolts to guide the way, after which the night only envelops us all the more in darkness: this horrible world view of world-death instead of world-life, whose horror is made lighter in the philosophy of German Idealism by the notion that behind the clouds there is after all a starry sky, this fundamental German spiritual tendency in its depth lacks will, does not mean what it says, is a crawling, cowardly, know-nothingness, a desire not to live but also a desire not to die either . . . For this is the German half-attitude towards life; indeed, to be able to throw it away when it doesn't cost anything, in the moment of intoxication, with those left behind cared for, and with this short-lived sacrifice surrounded by an eternal halo."

But in another statement in the same context, Rang's language may sound familiar to those around Jünger: "Two hundred officers, prepared to die, would have sufficed to suppress the revolution in Berlin—as in all other places; but not one was to be found. No doubt many of them would actually have liked to come to the rescue, but in reality—not actuality— nobody quite wanted to begin, to put himself forward as the leader, or to proceed individually. They preferred to have their epaulets ripped off in the streets." Obviously the man who wrote this knows from his very own experience the attitude and tradition of those who have come together here. And perhaps he continued to share their enmity to materialism until the moment that they created the language of material warfare.

If at the beginning of the war supplies of idealism were provided by order of the state, the longer the war lasted the more the troops had to depend on requisitions. Their heroism turned more and more gloomy, fatal and steelgray; glory and ideals beckoned from ever more remote and nebulous spheres; and those who saw themselves less as the troops of the World War than as the executors of the *Nachkrieg* more and more took up the stance of obstinate rigor. Every third word in their speeches is "stance." Who would deny that the soldier's position is one of stance? But language is the touchstone for each and every position taken, and not just, as is so often assumed, for that of the writer. But those who have conspired here do not pass the test. Jünger may echo the nobel dilettantes of the seventeenth century in saying that the German language is a primeval language, but he betrays what he means when he adds that as such it inspires an insurmountable distrust in civilization and in the cultivated world. Yet the world's distrust cannot equal that of his own countrymen when the war is presented to them as a "mighty revisor" that "feels the pulse" of the times, that forbids them "to do away with" "a tried and proven conclusion," and that calls on them to intensify their search for "ruins" "behind gleaming varnish." Far more shameful than these offenses, however, is the smooth style of these purportedly rough-hewn thoughts which could grace any newspaper editorial; and more distressing yet than the smooth style is the mediocre substance. "The dead," we are told, "went in their death from an imperfect reality to a perfect reality, from Germany in its temporal manifestation to the eternal Germany." This Germany "in its temporal manifestation" is of course notorious, but the eternal Germany would really be in a bad way if we had to depend on the testimony of those who so glibly invoke it. How cheaply they purchased their "solid feeling of immortality," their certainty that "the terrors of the last war have been frightfully exaggerated," and their symbolism of "blood boiling inwardly!" At best, they fought the war that they are celebrating here. However, we will not tolerate anyone who speaks of war, yet knows nothing but war. Radical in our own way, we will ask: Where do you come from? And what do you know of peace? Did you ever encounter peace in a child, a tree, an animal, the way you encountered a patrol in the field? And without waiting for you to answer, we can say No! It is not that you would then not be able to celebrate war, more passionately than now; but to celebrate it in the way you do would be impossible. How would Fortinbras have borne witness to war? One can deduce how he would have done it from Shakespeare's technique: Just as he reveals Romeo's love for Juliet in the fiery glow of its passion by presenting Romeo as in love from the outset, in love with Rosalinde, he would have had Fortinbras begin with a passionate eulogy of peace so enchanting and mellifluously sweet that, when at the end he raises his voice all the more passionately in favor of war, everyone would have wondered with a shudder: What are these powerful, nameless forces that compel this man, wholly filled with the bliss of peace, to commit himself body and soul to war?—But there is nothing of that here. These are professional freebooters speaking. Their horizon is fiery but very narrow.

What do they see in their flames? They see—here we can entrust ourselves to F.G. Jünger—a transformation: "lines of psychic decision cut across the war; transformations undergone by the war are paralleled by transformations undergone by those fighting it. These transformations become visible when one compares the vibrant, buoyant, enthusiastic faces of the soldiers of August 1914 with the fatally exhausted, haggard, implacably tensed faces of the 1918 veterans of machine warfare. Looming behind the all too sharply arched curve of this fight, their image appears, molded and moved by a forceful spiritual convulsion, by station after station along a path of suffering, battle after battle, each the hieroglyphic sign of a strenuously advancing work of destruction. Here we have the new type of soldier schooled in those hard, sober, bloody and incessant campaigns of attrition. This is a soldier characterized by the tenacious hardness of the born fighter, by a manifest sense of solitary responsibility, of psychic abandonment. In this struggle, which proceeded on increasingly deeper levels, he proved his own mettle. The path he pursued was narrow and dangerous, but it was a path leading into the future." Wherever precise formulations, genuine accents or solid reasoning are encountered in these pages, the reality portrayed is that of Ernst Jünger's "total mobilization" or Ernst von Salomon's "landscape of the front." A liberal journalist who recently tried to get at this new nationalism under the heading of "Heroism out of Boredom" fell, as one can see here, a bit short of the mark. This soldier type is a reality, a surviving witness to the World War, and it was actually this "landscape of the front," his true home, that was being defended in the *Nachkrieg*. This landscape demands further attention.

It should be said as bitterly as possible: in the face of this "landscape of total mobilization" the German feeling for nature has had an undreamed-of upsurge. The pioneers of peace, those sensuous settlers, were evacuated from these landscapes, and as far as anyone could see over the edge of the trench, the surroundings become a problem, every wire entanglement an antinomy, every barb a definition, every explosion a thesis; and by day the sky was the cosmic interior of the steel helmet and at night the moral law above. Etching the landscape with flaming banners and trenches, technology wanted to recreate the heroic features of German Idealism. It went astray. What is considered heroic were the features of Hippocrates, the features of death. Deeply imbued with its own depravity, technology gave shape to the apocalyptic face of nature and reduced nature to silence—even though this technology had the power to give nature its voice. Instead of using and illuminating the secrets of nature via a technology mediated by the human scheme of things, the new nationalists' metaphysical abstraction of war signifies nothing other than a mystical and unmediated application of technology to solve the mystery of an idealistically perceived nature. "Fate" and "hero" occupy these authors' minds like Gog and Magog, yet they devour not only human children but (new ideas) as well. Everything sober, unblemished, naive and humanistic ends up between the worn teeth of these Molochs who react with the belches of 42cm. mortars. Linking heroism with machine warfare is sometimes a bit hard on the authors. But this is by no means true to all of them, and there is nothing more revealing than the whining digressions exposing their disappointment in the "form of the war" and in the "senselessly mechanical machine war" of which these noble fellows "had evidently grown bored." Yet when one or another of them attempts to look things squarely in the eye, it become obvious how very much their concept of the heroic has surreptitiously changed; we can see how much the virtues of hardness, reserve and implacability they celebrate are in fact less those of the soldier than those of the proven class militant. What developed here, first in the guise of the World War volunteer and then in the mercenary of the *Nachkrieg*, is in fact the dependable fascist class warrior. And what these authors mean by nation is a ruling class supported by this caste, a ruling class—accountable to no one, and least of all to itself, enthroned on high—which bears the Sphinx-like countenance of the producer who very soon promises to be the sole consumer of his commodities. Sphinx-like in appearance, the fascists' nation thus takes its place as a new economic mystery of nature alongside the old. But this old mystery of nature, far from revealing itself to their technology, is exposing its most threatening feature. In the parallelogram of forces formed by these two—nature and nation—war is the diagonal.

It is understandable that the question of "governmental checks on war" arises in the best, most well-reasoned essay in this volume. For in this mystical theory of war, the state naturally plays more than a minor role. These checks should not for a moment be understood in a pacifist sense. Rather, what is demanded of the state is that its structure and its disposition adapt themselves to, and appear worthy of, the magical forces that the state itself must mobilize in the event of war. Otherwise it will not succeed in bending war to its purpose. It was this failure of the powers of state in the face of war that instigated the first independent thinking of the authors gathered here. Those military formations ambivalently hovering between comradely brotherhoods and regular government troops at the end of the war very soon solidified into independent, stateless mercenary hordes. And the captains of finance, the masters of the inflation to whom the state was beginning to seem a dubious guarantor of their property, knew the value of such hordes. They were available for hire at any time, like rice or turnips, by arrangement through private agencies or the *Reichswehr*.

Indeed, the present volume retains a resemblance to a slogan-filled recruiting brochure for a new type of mercenary, or rather *condottiere*. One of its authors candidly declares: "The courageous soldier of the Thirty Years' War sold himself life and limb, and that is still nobler than simply selling one's politics or one's talents." Of course, when he adds that the mercenary of Germany's *Nachkrieg* did not sell himself but gave himself away, then this is of a piece with the same author's comment on the comparatively high pay of these troops. This was pay which distinguished these warriors just as clearly as the technical necessities of their trade: as war engineers of the ruling class, they were the perfect complement to the managerial functionaries in their cutaways. God knows their designs on leadership should be taken seriously; their threat is not ludicrous. In the person of the pilot of a single airplane full of gas bombs such leadership embodies all the absolute power which, in peacetime, is distributed among thousands of office managers—power to cut off a citizen's light, air and life. This simple bomber-pilot in his lofty solitude, alone with himself and his God, has power-of-attorney for his seriously stricken superior, the state, and wherever he puts his signature no more grass will grow—and that is the "imperial" leader the authors have in mind.

Until Germany has broken through the entanglement of such Medusa-like beliefs that confront it in these essays, it cannot hope for a future. Perhaps the word loosened would be better than broken through, but this is not to say it should be done with kindly encouragement or with love, both of which are out of place here; nor should the way be smoothed for argumentation, for that wantonly persuasive rhetoric of debate. Instead, all the light that language and reason still afford should be focused upon that "primal experience" from whose barren gloom this mysticism crawls forth on its thousand unsightly conceptual feet. The war that this light exposes is as little the "eternal" one which these new Germans now worship as it is the "final" war that the pacifists carry on about. In reality that war is only this: The one, fearful, last chance to correct the incapacity of peoples to order their relationships to one another in accord with the relationship they posses to nature through their technology. If this corrective effort fails, millions of human bodies will indeed inevitably be chopped to pieces and chewed up by iron and gas. But even the habitues of the chthonic forces of terror, who carry their volumes of Klages in their packs, will not learn one-tenth of what nature promises its less idly curious, but more sober children, who possess in technology not a fetish of doom but a key to happiness. They will demonstrate this sobriety the moment they refuse to acknowledge the next war as an incisive magical turning point, and instead discover in it the image of everyday actuality. And they will demonstrate it when they use this discovery to transform this war into civil war and thereby perform that Marxist trick which alone is a match for this sinister runic humbug.

Notes

1 Erich Unger (1887–1952), member of the Oskar Goldberg circle of Kabbalistic studies and critic of empiricism from a magical and mystical viewpoint. (Ed.)

2 Florens Christian Rang, a close friend of Walter Benjamin's until his premature death in 1924. Rang incorporated Benjamin's ideal of an authentic and radical German spirit. (Ed.)

Index